D1718561

Prominent Families of New York

Anonymous

BIBLIOLIFE

PROMINENT FAMILIES

OF NEW YORK

BEING AN ACCOUNT IN BIOGRAPHICAL FORM OF INDIVIDUALS
AND FAMILIES DISTINGUISHED AS REPRESENTATIVES OF THE
SOCIAL, PROFESSIONAL AND CIVIC LIFE OF NEW YORK CITY

M-DCCC-XC-VII

THE HISTORICAL COMPANY

NEW YORK

NICOLL & ROY COMPANY
PRINTERS AND BINDERS
16 DEY STREET, NEW YORK

PREFACE

FOR several years the work incident to the production of this volume has engaged the services of a large staff of editors and contributors. The result of these labors is now laid before subscribers and the general public. Unique in conception and treatment, it constitutes one of the most original and most valuable contributions ever made to the social history of an American community. It arrays in a proper and dignified manner the important facts regarding the ancestry, personal careers and matrimonial alliances of those who, in each generation, have been accorded leading positions in the social, professional and business life of the metropolis. At the same time an additional interest attaches to the book from the fact, that while dealing primarily with New York City, its scope has not been limited to that locality alone. Owing to the wide distribution of the old New York families throughout the country and the constant absorption of representatives of other sections into this metropolitan community, the authentic and popular account here presented of the constituent elements of social New York, past and present, assumes a national importance. In the special field which it occupies, the volume is, to a considerable extent, a history of the entire country, since here in the metropolis have at all times assembled representatives of the historic families of the United States. Upon this particular point an exhibit is made in the following pages that will probably be surprising even to those who are most familiar with this side of New York's contemporaneous citizenship.

The records of the families of which the book treats have been arranged in a series of genealogical and biographical articles, relating to their lineal heads or most conspicuous representatives in the present generation. The adoption of this method of treatment has been fully justified by the results thus secured. The dry and unattractive manner in which genealogical facts have been hitherto almost universally presented, has been carefully avoided, and with the past thus linked to the present, the exhibition of lines of descent and the history of distinguished individual ancestors have acquired a more striking character than they might otherwise possess, and have been infused with an absorbing personal interest. Taken as a whole, the book constitutes an important page in the annals of this community and country.

From the beginning the editors have not lost sight of the fact that the fundamental plan of PROMINENT FAMILIES OF NEW YORK has contemplated an enduring and reliable historical record. With this end in view, the researches involved in the preparation and completion of the volume have been painstaking and thorough. They have included careful investigation of all accessible genealogical and historical records that bear upon the subject, and have also called for extensive labor in obtaining and collating a mass of heretofore unpublished data. In addition, a careful search has been conducted among genealogical records in Great Britain, France, Holland and other countries.

The comprehensiveness and accuracy of this work is in no small measure due to the interest which many individuals, whose names will be found in the sketches devoted to their families, have shown in its progress and to their keen appreciation of its important character. Members of families represented herein have placed at the service of the compilers valuable private and personal records. By this generous cooperation the stamp of authenticity has been placed upon the book and has aided in making it a permanent and reliable authority upon

7

CHARLES STEADMAN ABERCROMBIE

ONE of the oldest and most distinguished families of Scotland is that of Abercrombie, of which the Pennsylvania family of the name is a branch. In Burke's History of the Commoners of Great Britain and Ireland, the record of the family begins with Thomas Abercrombie, of the time of James II., of Scotland, who was one of the Lords of Session, or as it was then called, the Committee of Parliament. Humphrey de Abercrombie, who, about 1315, obtained a charter of lands from Robert Bruce, was the father of Alexander de Abercrombie, who acquired a half portion of the lands of Ardhuien. His son, Alexander de Abercrombie, of Pittmadden, was the father of the third Alexander de Abercrombie, who was living in 1454. In the next generation, the estate was inherited by James Abercrombie, who married Margaret Ogilvie, daughter of Sir James Ogilvie, of Findlater, and who is supposed to have fallen upon the field of Flodden. His son, George Abercrombie, had a son, James Abercrombie, who was living in 1527 and married Marjory Hay, daughter of William Hay, Earl of Errol.

Alexander Abercrombie, of Birkenbog, next of the line, married Elizabeth, daughter of Leslie, of Pitcaple. Their son, Alexander Abercrombie, of Birkenbog, succeeded his father, and married Margaret Leslie, daughter of William Leslie, of Balquan. The second son of this marriage was Alexander Abercrombie, of Fitterneir, whose son, Alexander Abercrombie, was the father of Francis Abercrombie, of Fitterneir, created by James VII., Lord Glassford, for life, and of Patrick Abercrombie, M. D., author of Martial Achievements of the Scottish Nation. The eldest son of Alexander Abercrombie and his wife, Margaret Leslie, was James Abercrombie, who was succeeded by his son, Alexander Abercrombie, of Birkenbog, Grand Falconer to Charles I.

The wife of this last Alexander Abercrombie was Elizabeth Bethune, daughter of Bethune of Balfour, by whom he had a daughter and three sons. The daughter married Robert Grant, of Dalvy. The eldest son and heir, Alexander Abercrombie, was created first baronet of Birkenbog, in 1636. General Sir Ralph Abercrombie, of the British Army, who commanded the army sent to drive the French from Egypt, and was slain after victory at Aboukir in 1801, descended from the second son of the first baronet. The present peerage of Baron Abercrombie was bestowed upon the family of Lord Ralph Abercrombie. John Abercrombie, of Glasshaugh, the second son of Alexander Abercrombie and Elizabeth Bethune, was the ancestor of the American branch of the family. His son, Thomas Abercrombie, of Dundee, married Agnes Aikman, and their son, James Abercrombie, of Dundee, who was born in 1693, was the father of James Abercrombie, an officer of the Royal Navy. The latter was the first of the name in America, coming to Philadelphia about 1750. He was lost at sea about 1759.

The Reverend James Abercrombie, D. D., son of James Abercrombie, of the Royal Navy, and grandfather of Mr. Charles Steadman Abercrombie, was born in Philadelphia in 1758 and died there in 1841. After graduating from the University of Pennsylvania in 1776, he studied theology. Being ordained to the Protestant Episcopal ministry, he was installed as one of the rectors of Christ and St. Peter's churches, Philadelphia, in 1793. He retired from the ministry in 1833. He was an able writer, principally upon religious subjects. Among his published works were Lectures upon the Catechism and several sermons. For nearly ten years he was principal of the Philadelphia Academy. His sons were James Abercrombie and Charles Steadman Abercrombie, M. D., of Roseland, Tenn. A son of the former, the Reverend James Abercrombie, D. D., died in 1889.

Mr. Charles Steadman Abercrombie, of New York, is the surviving son of James Abercrombie and grandson of the Reverend James Abercrombie, D. D., of Philadelphia. He was born in Baltimore, Md., and has long been a resident of New York. He married Nancy Osgood and his residence is in Madison Square, North. He is a member of the Metropolitan and the Field and Turf clubs. The arms of the Abercrombie family are: Argent, a fess engrailed, gules, between three boars' heads, couped, azure. The crest is a bee, volant, proper. Above the shield is the motto, *Vive ut vivas.* Under the shield is the motto, *Mens in arduis aequa.*

FRANKLIN ACKER

THE ancestors of the Acker family were of Dutch origin and came to this country early in the seventeenth century, settling in northern New Jersey. The name has been thoroughly identified with that section ever since, and various members of the family have obtained considerable prominence, while they have been always numbered among the stable and responsible citizens of the State and have contracted alliances with many other families of corresponding standing and noteworthy descent. In the present century, however, the branch to which attention is now directed became identified with the large commercial interests of New York, and attained prominence here.

David de Peyster Acker, father of Mr Franklin Acker, was born in Bergen County, N. J., in 1822. At an early age, he entered upon a business career in New York City, spent a number of years in subordinate employment, though constantly rising, and finally became, in 1857, a partner and head of the establishment in which he had originally served, and which, largely on account of his ability, energy and probity, became one of the most important of its kind, having connections and branches in various foreign countries. He was possessed of great executive ability and far-sighted enterprise, and secured and retained throughout his life the confidence and respect of all with whom he was brought in contact, either in business or socially.

Mr. Acker acquired great wealth in his years of devotion to business, and in the latter part of his life fully enjoyed the pleasures which well-earned leisure brought him. He was a frequenter of Saratoga Springs for many years, had a country seat at Fairlawn, near Paterson, N. J., where he spent every spring and autumn, and was a frequent visitor to Florida during the winter months. Political honors were offered him on several occasions, but public life failed to attract him and he refused even a nomination to Congress, though admirably fitted for such duties. He was a member of the Produce Exchange and the Chamber of Commerce, vice-president of the National Exchange Bank, a member of the Holland Society, and a member of St Thomas' Protestant Episcopal Church. Throughout his life he was notably, though unostentatiously, benevolent and considerate in his disposition. He was survived by his widow, who was Julia Whitney, and seven children.

Mr. Franklin Acker, son of the late David de Peyster Acker, was born in New York, February 16th, 1853. His early education was received in the local schools and he was then sent to an academy in Weston, Conn, and fitted for a commercial life. When he was seventeen years old, in 1870, he entered the employ of the business house his father had founded, and in 1888 was admitted to a partnership in the firm. He retired from active participation in business in 1892.

In 1884, Mr. Acker married Emma Brinckerhoff, daughter of former State Senator James J. Brinckerhoff, of New Jersey, one of a family that has been conspicuously identified with the business and public interests of the State of New Jersey, for several generations, and which is, like the Ackers, derived from notable Dutch ancestry, going back to the early days of the New Netherland, members of it having been, in many successive generations, people of social prominence in the city and State. Mr. and Mrs. Acker have two sons, David de Peyster and Irving Fairchild Acker. They live in West Seventy-seventh Street. Mr. Acker is now a director of the David D. Acker Company, of New York, and of the Fiberite Company, of Mechanicsville. He belongs to the Holland Society, and to the Colonial and Hardware clubs.

A brother of Mr Acker was the late Charles Livingston Acker, who was born in New York in 1846, and died in 1891. He was one of the junior partners of the firm that his father established, vice-president of the Hudson River Bank, treasurer of several other corporations, and a member of the Holland Society. His wife was Helena Brinckerhoff, sister of the wife of his brother, Mr. Franklin Acker, and he left a son, Charles Livingston Acker, Jr., and three daughters, Ella M., Louisa and Adele Acker.

CHARLES HENRY ADAMS

IN the eighth generation, Mr. Charles Henry Adams is descended from Henry Adams, of Braintree, the founder of the Adams family, that has borne so conspicuous a part in the public life of the United States. The pioneer came from England in 1634 and obtained a grant of land at Mt Wollaston, afterwards Braintree, and now Quincy, Mass. Henry Adams, second of the name, was born in England in 1614, and married, in 1643, Elizabeth Paine, daughter of Moses Paine. He was the first town clerk of Medfield, Mass., was a member of the Ancient and Honorable Artillery Company of Boston, in 1652, and a representative to the General Court, 1659-65 and 1674-75 He was a Lieutenant in the militia, and was killed by the Indians in 1676 during King Philip's War.

The line of descent from Henry Adams, of Braintree, is through Peter Adams; John Adams, who married Michal Bloyse, daughter of Richard and Michal (Jennison) Bloyse, of Watertown, Mass ; Isaac Adams; Joshua Adams, of Egremont, Mass. ; Dr Peter Charles Adams, and Dr. Henry Adams. The father of Mr. Charles Henry Adams, Dr. Henry Adams, was born in 1787, and died on the anniversary of his birth, at the age of seventy years He was a soldier in the War of 1812. His wife was Agnes Egberts, daughter of Anthony Egberts, a paymaster in the Revolutionary War, who married Evau Van der Zee. Dr. Peter Charles Adams, born in 1763, and the father of Dr Henry Adams, was sheriff of Greene County, N. Y., and a State Senator. His wife was Christina Van Bergen, daughter of Henry Van Bergen and Nellie Salisbury. The ancestor of Nellie Salisbury was Captain Sylvester Salisbury, who came to New Amsterdam from England in 1664, was in command of Fort Orange in the early history of that outpost, was sheriff of Rensselaerwyck in 1673 and, in association with Henry Van Bergen, obtained a patent of land in Greene County Henry Van Bergen was a grandson of Martin Gerrtisen Van Bergen, one of the early settlers of Albany. Through his mother, Mr. Charles Henry Adams is descended from the Egberts, one of whom married a granddaughter of Rip Van Dam, acting Colonial Governor of New York.

Mr Charles Henry Adams was born in Coxsackie, Greene County, N Y. He was educated at the Albany Academy, and studied law in the office of Cagger & Stevens, of Albany He applied himself to the practice of law until 1850, when he gave up professional life to engage in the woolen manufacturing business at Cohoes, N. Y. For a long time he was trustee and president of the Water Board of Cohoes, and was elected the first Mayor of the city after its incorporation. In 1851, he was an aide, with rank of Colonel, on the staff of Governor Hunt ; was elected to the State Assembly in 1857, and was a State Senator, 1872-73. He was a presidential elector in 1872, United States Commissioner to the Vienna Exposition in 1873, and a member of Congress in 1876. In 1859, he was elected a director of the Bank of Cohoes, and in 1869, became its president. In recent years, he has been a resident of New York City.

Mr. Adams has been twice married. His first wife, whom he married in 1853, was Elizabeth Platt, of Rhinebeck, and by her he had two children, Mary Egberts and William Platt Adams. In 1877, he married Judith Crittenden Coleman, whose grandfather was John Jordan Crittenden, 1787-1863, of Kentucky, a son of Major Crittenden, of the Continental Army, and a graduate of William and Mary's College in 1807. The children of Mr Adams by his second wife are, Agnes Ethel Crittenden and Judith Charles Berlina Adams. The city residence of Mr Adams is in East Sixty-seventh Street, his summer home being Mount Wollaston, East Hampton, Long Island He is a member of the Sons of the Revolution and of the St. Nicholas Society, as well as of the Metropolitan Club, the American Geographical Society and the Metropolitan Museum of Art, and is a director of the Maidstone Club, of East Hampton His eldest daughter, Mary Egberts Adams, became the wife of Robert Johnston, and has one son, Robert Johnston, Jr His only son, William Platt Adams, married Katherine Elseffer, of Red Hook, and has two children, Elizabeth Platt and Katherine Elseffer Adams.

EDWARD DEAN ADAMS

MR EDWARD D ADAMS comes of good old Puritan ancestors, his family being among the earliest settlers of New England and prominent in the affairs of the Massachusetts Bay Colony His father, Adoniram Judson Adams, is a well known citizen of Boston

Born in Boston, April 9, 1846, Mr. Edward D Adams was educated in the Chauncey Hall School, the noted private school for boys in Boston, and then went to Norwich Universty, at Norwich, Vt , where he was graduated as a Bachelor of Science in 1864 After spending two years in travel and study in Europe, he returned to Boston in 1866, and entered the office of a firm of bankers and brokers, where he remained three years as bookkeeper and cashier In 1870, he assisted in organizing the Boston banking firm of Richardson, Hill & Co., and was a partner in that house until 1878 He then removed to New York City and became a partner in the house of Winslow, Lanier & Co , a connection that he maintained until 1893

During his active business career as a banker, he took a prominent and influential part in many of the largest and most important financial transactions of the period. He is particularly conspicuous for his successful work in the reconstruction and reorganization of corporations. Some of his achievements in this line are part of the most brilliant pages of recent financial history.

In 1882-3, he organized the Northern Pacific Terminal Company, became its president, raised the capital for building the plant at Portland, Ore., and superintended the work of construction. In 1883, he organized the St Paul & Northern Pacific Railway Company, raised the capital for it, and became its vice-president. Two years later, he organized and constructed the New Jersey Junction Railroad Company, and leased it to the New York Central Railroad. In 1885, he planned and carried out the reorganization of the New York, West Shore & Buffalo Railroad, the New York, Ontario & Western Railroad, and the West Shore & Ontario Terminal Company. This was an exceedingly embarrassing and difficult undertaking, and the manner in which the work was carried out by Mr Adams evoked the admiration of financial circles and the approval of those most directly interested in the properties For this Mr Adams was personally and officially thanked by the Honorable Chauncey M Depew, and Messrs Drexel, Morgan & Co

The Central Railroad of New Jersey was saved from being thrown into the hands of a receiver in 1887 by the reorganization, conceived by and carried out under the direction of Mr. Adams, and in 18,0 he reorganized the American Cotton Oil Co , which was then severely embarrassed In 1888, he assisted in marketing the bond issue of the Philadelphia & Reading Railroad, and for this the special thanks of the board of directors of the road was voted him He became early interested in the problem of utilizing the power of Niagara Falls, and was elected president of the Cataract Construction Company. In this capacity he was successful in solving, not only the financial, but also the engineering difficulties, to which he specially addressed himself In 1893 the German bondholders of the Northern Pacific Railroad Company requested him to look after their interests, and he was chairman of the reorganization committee that straightened out the affairs of that company. Mr. Adams still retains connection with many of the corporations which he has organized or reconstructed. He is chairman of the board of directors of the Northern Pacific Railway Company, a director of the American Cotton Oil Company, president of the Cataract Construction Company, vice-president of the Central & Southern American Telegraph Company, a director of the West Shore Railroad, and a director of the Mercantile Trust Company, and numerous other companies.

Mr. Adams married Fannie A Gutterson, daughter of William E. Gutterson, of Boston, in 1872 He has two children, Ernest K. Adams, a graduate from Yale and Columbia Colleges, and Ruth Adams. He lives on Madison Avenue, and belongs to the Tuxedo, Metropolitan, Union League, Players, Riding, Grolier and other clubs, is a member of the New England Society, a fellow in perpetuity of the National Academy of Design, a patron of the American Museum of Natural History, a trustee of the Metropolitan Museum of Art, a fellow of the American Society of Civil Engineers, and a trustee of the gift fund of the American Fine Arts Society.

JOHN GIRAUD AGAR

SEVERAL families distinguished in the early history of the Southern States are among the ancestors of Mr. John Giraud Agar His father, William Agar, was a native of Ireland, belonging to one of the ancient families of County Carlow When young in years, William Agar came from his native land to this country and settled in New Orleans. Possessed of great natural ability, he soon took a foremost position in business in the Southern metropolis He married Theresa Price, of Louisville, Ky, descended from one of the early settlers of that State

Born in New Orleans, June 3d, 1856, Mr. John G Agar was a boy not yet in his teens when the Civil War was raging Instructed by private tutors, in 1869 he was sent to the preparatory school of the University of Georgetown, D C., to continue his studies, and in 1872 matriculated at the University, and was graduated in 1876 with the degree of B. A. Immediately he went abroad, and for two years studied in the Roman Catholic University of Kensington, London, devoting himself especially to biology and moral and mental science.

Returning to this country in 1878, he settled in New York and took a two years' course in Columbia College Law School, graduating in 1880 with the degree of LL. B. Admitted to practice at the bar of the State of New York, he soon won a leading position in his profession by the soundness of his legal attainments and by his eloquence as a public speaker. By birth, instinct and training a Democrat, and devoted to Democratic principles, his political affiliations have always been with that party, but he has stood for independence in political action and for honesty in the administration of public affairs In 1881, his prominence as a lawyer and his thorough independence in politics led President James A. Garfield to appoint him Assistant United States Attorney for the Southern District of New York. Official position had little attraction for him, however, and he resigned his office after a year of service and returned to private practice, as the senior member of the law firm of Agar, Ely & Fulton, which connection he still maintains.

The cause of reform in municipal administration early enlisted the support of Mr Agar, who has been one of the most energetic advocates of those measures leading to uprightness in the management of the city business that have characterized the political activity of New York during the last decade. One of the earliest and most prominent members of the People's Municipal League, he has contributed valuable service to the cause supported by that organization. He was also one of the first advocates of the State naval militia, and in 1891 Governor David B Hill commissioned him as a Lieutenant of the First Battalion of the Naval Reserve of Artillery of the State of New York and acting paymaster In the State campaign of 1891, he was chairman of the executive committee of the People's Municipal League, and it was largely due to his untiring efforts that the measure for the adoption of the Australian system of voting by blanket ballot was ultimately passed by the Legislature of the State. In October, 1896, he was appointed a commissioner of Public Schools by Mayor W L Strong; and as a member of the Reform majority of the Board ot Education, he was largely instrumental in procuring from the State Legislature adequate appropriations for the greatly needed increase in public school accommodations.

In 1888, Mr. Agar received the degree of M A., from the University of Georgetown, and the degree of Ph D from the same institution in 1889. His wife was Agnes Louise Macdonough, whom he married in 1892 at Washington, D. C. Mrs Agar's father was Joseph Macdonough, of San Francisco, one of the earliest American settlers in California Her mother was Catherine O'Brien, a sister of William S. O'Brien, of San Francisco, the noted financier. Mr. and Mrs Agar have two children, John Giraud, Jr., and William Macdonough Agar The residence of the family is in West Forty-eighth Street and they have a country place in Westchester County He is a member of the Metropolitan, Union, University, Lawyers', Reform, City, Players, Racquet, Catholic, Commonwealth, New York Yacht and Seawanhaka-Corinthian Yacht clubs, the Metropolitan Club of Washington, the Country Club of Westchester County, the Bar Association and the American Geographical Society.

MRS. CATHERINE BEEKMAN AITKEN

IN the year 1647, there came to New Amsterdam, in the same vessel with Governor and Captain General Petrus Stuyvesant, a young Hollander of position and wealth named Willhemus Beekman. His family were wealthy burgers, of Keulen, and he was born in 1623 at Hasselt, in Oberyssel. Being of higher social rank than most of the Colonists, and having the favor of the Governor, he at once became a man of mark, one of the first great matches in the history of New York being his marriage to Catherine De Boogh, the belle and heiress of the infant city. He became Schepen and Burgomeister of the town, and a large property owner, being in fact its richest inhabitant. Among other offices which he filled was that of Deputy Governor of the Dutch possessions on the Delaware River, which had been captured from the Swedes by Governor Stuyvesant in 1655. At all times during his career he showed a keen appreciation for valuable lands, and among his other estates, acquired by purchase or grant from the Dutch West India Company, was a large tract at Esopus. He partly resided on this estate, and was appointed Sheriff of the district, and in that capacity welcomed Governors Nicolls, Lovelace and Andros after the British occupation. He also purchased all the land around Rhinebeck, which place he named from the river on whose banks he was born, and built there a stone house which is still standing, the bricks of which its chimney is constructed having been imported from Holland. Notwithstanding his prominence, he was one of the leading Dutch citizens who were suspected of disloyalty by Governor Andros, and subjected to arrest by that official in 1675. In 1683 he, however, was named as Mayor of the city, and was for many years one of the aldermen, being throughout his career one of the most influential of the early Dutch inhabitants of the Province.

He bought Corlears Hook from Jacob Corlear soon after his arrival in the Colony, and in 1670 purchased of one Thomas Hall a large tract fronting on the East River and extending nearly across the island on a line with the present City Hall. Here he established his homestead, and it is recorded that his orchard was on the slopes where Beekman Street now descends, that thoroughfare, as well as William Street, taking their names from him. He died in 1707, at the ripe age of eighty-four, leaving a large family who have ever maintained the prominence which was given to the name by its founder.

His son, Colonel Gerardus Beekman, the eminent patriot, was a physician and surgeon. He married, in 1677, Magdalena Abeel, of Albany, and resided in Flatbush. In 1685, he was appointed Justice of Kings County. He was one of Leisler's Council. In 1687, he took the oath of allegiance. He became a member of the Colonial Assembly in 1698, and was afterwards Acting Governor. He was a large purchaser of lands on the Rantan and Millstone Rivers, in New Jersey, and was active in developing that section, dying in 1723.

Mrs. Aitken is directly descended from this branch of the family, being a daughter of the late Abraham Beekman and his wife, Elizabeth (Houghton) Beekman. The Houghtons are also a family of distinguished ancestry and connections, being related to many of the most celebrated names in Colonial history. The Beekman family twice intermarried with the Van Dyke family. Mrs. Aitken, in fact, can trace her descent back for three hundred years in no less than three direct lines to ancestors, all of whom were of prominence in the early records of the country, both in Colonial and Revolutionary times.

Among the other Revolutionary patriots included in the number was her great-great-grandfather, Rulof Van Dyke, member of the Provincial Congress of New York and of the Committee of Safety which governed the State during the Revolution, and who took an active and distinguished part in the public affairs of that period, being referred to in the accounts of those trying times as one of the most steadfast and energetic supporters of the American cause.

Mrs. Aitken is the widow of the late Honorable William B Aitken, who died in 1880. He was a lawyer and statesman. Her three children are Lydia A Aitken, Elizabeth (Aitken) Bull, wife of Charles Hudson Bull, and William B. Aitken, a lawyer of New York City.

LAWRENCE DADE ALEXANDER

VIRGINIA'S Colonial aristocracy is a factor which has exercised a powerful influence on the political history and material progress of the United States   It has been almost a predominant element in moulding the social side of the American character   Distinctions based on birth and ancestry were and are still cherished in the Old Dominion to a greater degree than any other State, and the descendants of its gentry, who sprang originally from families of social position and gentle blood in the mother country, are now found in every part of the land, and have preserved and upheld such traditions

Kentucky absorbed much of Virginia's best blood, and has in turn contributed its share to the social development of the country at large. During the first quarter of the present century, many representatives of the old families of tide-water Virginia migrated to the new region which extended from the Blue Ridge to the Mississippi   Among this number was Gerard Alexander, of Effingham, an estate in Prince William County, Va., who, with his wife, Elizabeth (Henry) Alexander, and his family went in 1823 to Breckenridge County, Ky., where he died in 1834. A granduncle of the gentleman whose name heads this sketch, General Edmund Brooke Alexander was an officer of reputation in the United States Army, and was distinguished in the Mexican War, in the operations against the Mormans in Utah, and in the war between the States

The father of Mr. Lawrence Dade Alexander was Junius B. Alexander, who as a youth accompanied his parents from Virginia to Kentucky. He engaged with success in the banking business at Louisville, St Louis, and later on in New York   The country seat he established here was Effingham, on Todt Hill, Staten Island, the name being taken from the ancestral Virginia estate, the property afterwards being inherited by his son, Frank D Alexander.   Another of the sons of Gerard Alexander was Colonel Thomas Ludwell Alexander, a prominent officer of the Mexican War, and who, under the administration of President Lincoln, became governor of the Soldiers' Home at Washington, D C. Junius B. Alexander married Lucy Fitzhugh Dade, a lady who also came of ancestors prominent in Virginian history, and was a native of that State.   Her maternal grandfather, General Lawrence Taliaferro Dade, was commanding officer of the State Militia, a member of the Legislature for Orange County, and an emigrant to Kentucky, where he died.   Her brother, Francis Cadwalader Dade, served with distinction throughout the Civil War and is now Chief Engineer on the retired list of the navy.

Mr Lawrence Dade Alexander was born of this parentage in Meade County, Ky., in 1843   He attended Washington University, St. Louis, and entered Jefferson College, Pennsylvania, where he took his degree. He entered his father's profession and followed him to New York City, becoming in 1869 a member of the New York Stock Exchange. He married Orline St. John, a daughter of the late Newton St. John, who for nearly a half a century was a prominent banker of Mobile, Ala.   Among her ancestors was General Bibb, the first Governor of the State of Alabama, and Colonel Charles Pope, of Delaware, who was prominent in the Revolution. Mrs. Alexander's brother, the late William Pope St. John, was president of a prominent national bank in this city, and was known for his contributions to economic science   The late Professor Samuel St. John, who for many years held the chair of chemistry in the College of Physicians and Surgeons, of New York, was also her cousin. Mr. and Mrs. Lawrence D. Alexander have four children, St John Alexander, Lawrence Dade Alexander, Jr., Orline Alexander, and Lucy Dade Alexander, the latter being now Mrs. E. A. W. Everitt

Mr. Alexander has a partiality for country life, characteristic of the race of Southern gentlefolk from which he is descended   He is a member of the University Club and the Southern Society. His inclinations are literary, and he has been an enthusiastic and judicious collector of books. In both respects, his tastes have a close connection with the sport of angling, in which he is an expert. He has been a contributor on this subject to The American Angler and to the work on American Sports issued by the Century Company.

ETHAN ALLEN

NEW JERSEY was debatable ground during the War of the Revolution, and some of the most important military movements of the Continental forces were within and across her borders   In particular, Monmouth County was not only the scene of a famous conflict—the battle of Freehold—but throughout the struggle between the Crown and the Colonies, its coast was subject to raids by the British land and sea forces.   The duty of patrolling its shores became one of the most imperative as well as most hazardous tasks of the time and was undertaken by some of its patriotic inhabitants.   Prominent among them was Captain Samuel Allen, a man of wealth and influence in the county, who from his own means raised and equipped a company of minute men for this purpose.   At their head, he took part in some of the most stirring events of the war, and rendered service of the highest value to the patriot cause   When British foes again threatened this part of the country, during the War of 1812, the son of this Revolutionary hero, Samuel Fleming Allen, performed a like duty on behalf of his State and country, and the State of New Jersey gave deserved recognition of the great value of his military services at that time by conferring upon him a State pension that ended only with his death, which occurred in 1882, at the ripe age of ninety-one.

Colonel Ethan Allen, son of Samuel Fleming Allen and grandson of Captain Samuel Allen of the Revolution, was born in Monmouth County, in the year 1832.   He was graduated from Brown University in 1860 with high rank, being orator of his class.   Adopting the profession of law, he thenceforth made New York City his residence, and entered upon an active and successful practice. At the outbreak of the Civil War, he was holding the important position of Deputy United States District Attorney for the Southern District of New York   His own desire was to enter the army, but Mr. Stanton, at that time Secretary of War, appreciated his services in his actual post so highly that he refused sanction to his proposed relinquishment of that position.   But he was enabled to devote himself to the military, as well as the civil, service of the Union, for Governor E D Morgan commissioned him a Colonel in the recruiting service, in which he rendered efficient aid to the Government in the war, recruiting for the army what was then known as the Blair Brigade, named after the veteran statesman, Francis P. Blair.

In 1861, Colonel Allen married Eliza Clagett, daughter of Darius and Providence Brice Clagett.   Mrs. Allen is a native of the District of Columbia, belonging to one of the most distinguished families in Maryland, or indeed in the country at large, and is a member of the Colonial Dames, of that State.   One of her remote ancestors was Augustine Heerman, who arrived in New Netherland in 1663 and afterwards removed to Maryland, where he became the Lord of Bohemian Manor in that Province and the founder of a noted family there   Among the other distinguished Maryland families with which she is connected by ties of blood and common descent are the Vanderhuydens, Brices, Frisbys, Dorseys and Pacas Tillmans, the name of Clagett having been for many generations famous in the same State   Her ancestry also includes such families in other States as those of Schuyler, Randolph and Jennings.

The Allen family residence is in West Fifty-second Street   Mr. Allen belongs to the Union League Club, and is also a member of the Sons of the American Revolution, the Brown University Alumni, and many political, charitable and social organizations.   He has traveled extensively in Europe, his tours covering all portions of the Continent, among his experiences being a visit to the North Cape of Norway and a sojourn in St. Petersburg and Moscow.   At the New York bar, he has won special distinction for his ability before a jury.   Out of the several hundred jury cases that he was engaged in during his twenty years or more of active practice, he rarely lost one   Among other celebrated cases in which he was retained as counsel was the famous contest growing out of the will of Commodore Cornelius Vanderbilt, his associate in this instance being former Attorney-General Jeremiah Black.   Mr Allen was chairman of the National Committee of 1872, which supported the cause of Horace Greeley for the Presidency of the United States.

ASA ALLING ALLING

INSTANCES are found in the early records where the name of the small and distinguished family to which this gentleman belongs is given as both Alling and Allen The former manner has been adhered to by the American bearers of the name descended from Roger Alling, the Puritan emigrant of 1637. Roger Alling was the son of James Alling, or Allen, of Kempston, Bedfordshire, England. Espousing Puritan opinions, he left England for Holland, and thence went to Massachusetts, removed to New Haven, Conn , and on June 4th, 1639, was a signer, in company with Davenport, Doolittle and others, of the historical New Haven Compact He became a man of mark in the community, was an officer of the church, Treasurer of the Colony and also a Judge, his name occurring repeatedly in the early history of New Haven, where he died, September 27th, 1674 Roger Alling married Mary Nash, daughter of Thomas Nash, one of the first settlers of New Haven, and left a family of seven children.

Members of the Alling family have always remained in New Haven and held distinguished positions there in the professions, in political life, and in connection with Yale College; John Alling, third son of Roger, having been one of the earlier treasurers of that institution and Judge of Probate 1711-17. Two grandsons of the original emigrant, however, removed before the year 1700 to New Jersey, where their descendants hold a distinguished place and have intermarried with the Hornblowers, Bradleys and other families of similar prominence in that State.

Samuel Alling, one of the pioneer Roger Alling's sons, was a proprietor of the New Haven Colony, and from him Mr Asa A Alling, of New York, is descended through his son, Caleb Alling The latter, born in 1694, married for his second wife Thankful Mix. His son, Asa Alling, the first of that name, was born in 1723, and married, in 1749, Ann Potter, of New Haven He removed to Nine Partners, now in Dutchess County, N Y , and thus founded the branch of the family known as the Hudson River Allings, which has since intermarried with the Knapps, Thompsons, Huntings and other leading families of that section. He had four sons, one of whom was the Reverend Abraham Alling, of Connecticut ; and another, Asa Alling, second of the name, who was born in 1751 and was known as Captain Alling from his service in the Revolutionary Army. He married Jemima Purdy, of Dutchess County, and had two sons and three daughters. One of the latter married Colonel Jordan, brother of Ambrose L Jordan, a leader of the New York bar in his day. Asa Alling, 1789-1864, third of the name, was a son of the second Asa Alling. He was a Judge in Dutchess County, N. Y , and married Cornelia Sackett in 1816. Their son, J. Sackett Alling, born in 1822, is the father of Mr. Asa A Alling J Sackett Alling became a leading merchant in New York In 1855, he married the present Mr. Alling's mother, whose maiden name was Anna E. Bertine, a descendant of Pierre Bertine, or Berton, a Huguenot of noble family, who, on the revocation of the Edict of Nantes, came to South Carolina and afterwards to Westchester County, N Y.

Born of this parentage, in New York City, May 4th, 1862, Mr. Asa A. Alling was educated at public and private schools and entered Cornell University, from which he was graduated Ph. B in 1883 He was ivy orator of his class and won the Woodford prize for oratory He then passed two years in the Law Department of Columbia College; and receiving the degree of LL B. in 1885, was called to the bar in the same year. He has since been engaged in active professional practice in this city, and is a member of the firm of Kenneson, Crain & Alling. Mr Alling has taken an active part in politics, being prominent in the councils of the Democratic party.

In 1894, Mr Alling married Louise Floyd Smith, a descendant of an old Long Island family and of distinguished Colonial and Revolutionary ancestry Mr. Alling is a member of the Metropolitan, University, Reform, Manhattan, Cornell University, Dutchess County and Democratic clubs, having been a governor of the latter He also belongs to the Bar Association, the West End Association, the New England Society, the New York Historical Society and the New York Genealogical and Biographical Society.

ELBERT ELLERY ANDERSON

L AWYER, soldier, political economist and publicist, Mr. E. Ellery Anderson has taken a prominent part in molding and directing opinion and action on the great public questions that have agitated the American people in the closing years of the nineteenth century. He is a thorough New Yorker, born in this city October 31st, 1833, and his scholastic temperament comes to him as an inheritance from his father, who was a distinguished educator and scientist.

Professor Henry J Anderson, M D , LL. D., the father, was born in 1799 He was graduated from Columbia College in 1818, and from the College of Physicians and Surgeons in 1823, two years later becoming Professor of Mathematics, Analytical Mechanics and Physical Astronomy in Columbia College For eighteen years he held that position, and then resigned on account of his wife's health and traveled in Europe. While abroad, he became identified with the Roman Catholic Church, and on his return to New York gave much time to the promotion of the interests of that ecclesiastical body. He was president of the Society of St. Vincent de Paul and was on the official boards of other church organizations. In 1851, he was elected a trustee of Columbia College, and in 1866 was made emeritus Professor of Mathematics and Astronomy When the American Scientific Expedition went to explore the level of the Dead Sea, Professor Anderson accompanied the party and conducted some interesting investigations. In 1875, he went to India to explore the Himalayas for ethnological and philosophical discoveries. While there, he was stricken with disease and died in October of that year

Mr. Anderson traveled in Europe in 1843 with his father, and returning to his studies was graduated from Harvard College in 1852. He was admitted to the bar in 1854 and has seduously applied himself to the practice of his profession ever since. He has had the management of many trust estates and has been engaged upon some very celebrated cases In 1868, he entered into partnership with Frederick H. Man, under the firm name of Anderson & Man. The partners have handled much litigation with railroads, and one of their most important cases was that in which they recovered some two million dollars interest due on bonds of the Missouri, Kansas & Texas Railroad. In 1862, Mr. Anderson went to the front as a Major in a regiment of New York volunteers and served until he was captured and returned home under a parole of Stonewall Jackson Although a strong Democrat, he joined in the movement against Tweed in 1871, and did good work in helping to overthrow the ring. As a Tammany man, he was for several years chairman of the Eleventh District, but in 1879, in company with Abram S. Hewitt, William C. Whitney, Edward Cooper and others, he withdrew from that organization and became one of the founders of the County Democracy, being for a long time chairman of the general committee

Although he has given considerable time to politics, he has never permitted his name to be used for any elective public office. He has, however, been a school trustee, and in 1896 was appointed a member of the Board of Education. He has also served on the Rapid Transit Commission, the Croton Aqueduct Commission and the Elevated Railroad Commission In 1887, President Cleveland appointed him on the commission to investigate the Union Pacific and Central Pacific railroads, and he prepared the majority report of the commission He was appointed one of the directors of the Union Pacific Railway Company on behalf of the Government, and in 1893 was appointed by the United States Court one of the receivers of that corporation.

It is as an advocate of tariff reform in recent years that Mr Anderson has made himself best known, and has exercised the widest and strongest influence. His services to the Democratic party on that issue in the Presidential campaign of 1892 were exceedingly valuable. He was president of the Reform Club and chairman of the Tariff Reform Committee, and wrote many papers and made many addresses. In the campaign of 1896, he was similarly active for the cause of sound money. Mr Anderson married Augusta Chauncey, and lives in West Thirty-eighth Street He is a member of the Metropolitan, Democratic, University, Reform, Whist and other clubs, and of the Bar Association.

HENRY BURRALL ANDERSON

OF ancient Scottish origin, that branch of the Anderson family of which Henry Hill Anderson, father of Mr Henry B Anderson, was the notable representative in New York for nearly fifty years, was long settled in the State of Maine The grandfather of Henry Hill Anderson was the Reverend Rufus Anderson, who was a graduate of Dartmouth College and a distinguished clergyman. His grandmother was a cousin of Chief Justice Theophilus Parsons, of Massachusetts Her grandfather was Ebenezer Parsons, of Gloucester, Mass , a trader with Indians, often a selectman and a deacon and ruling elder of the First Church His death occurred in 1763 The great-grandfather of Mrs Rufus Anderson was Jeffrey Parsons, who, near the close of the first half of the seventeenth century, sailed from England for the West Indies After remaining some time in Barbadoes, he came to Massachusetts, settling in Gloucester, on Cape Ann He had considerable means and was a successful merchant and also held town office His wife was Sarah Vinson, daughter of one of the first settlers of Gloucester.

The father of Henry Hill Anderson was the Reverend Dr Rufus Anderson, who was born in North Yarmouth, Me , in 1796, and died in 1880 After being graduated from Bowdoin College in 1818, he studied in the Andover Theological Seminary, being graduated therefrom in 1822 and ordained a minister two years after. He became the secretary of the American Board of Foreign Missions in 1832, holding that position for thirty-four years For two years following 1867, he was a lecturer on foreign missions in the Andover Seminary He traveled frequently upon business of the missionary society, visiting the Mediterranean in 1843, East India in 1854 and the Sandwich Islands in 1863 His numerous publications included many books, principally upon subjects relating to missionary work.

Henry Hill Anderson, who was born in Boston, November 9th, 1827, died in York Harbor, Me , in September, 1896 Prepared for college in Phillips Academy, Andover, he was graduated from Williams College in 1848, receiving the degree of M A in 1851 He studied law in New York and entered the office of Henry E Davies, then Counsel to the Corporation Entrusted with the defense of many important cases against the city, he was uniformly successful.

In 1852, he became a partner of the law firm of Willard, Sweeney & Anderson, a professional relationship that continued for five years, when, for domestic reasons, he retired and spent some time in foreign travel From 1859 to 1862, he was an assistant to Greene C. Bronson, Counsel to the Corporation, and afterwards, with Mason Young and Henry E Howland, established the firm which is now known as Anderson, Howland & Murray. He steadfastly refused proffers of public office that were frequently made to him, but in 1871, he was candidate for Judge of the Supreme Court, being defeated by Noah Davis He enjoyed a large and profitable private practice, had charge of many corporation interests and was frequently a referee For many years, he was a vestryman of the Calvary Protestant Episcopal Church, was one of the founders of the University Club and its first president, an office which he held for nine years His wife, Sarah B. Burrall, daughter of William P Burrall, of Hartford, survives him and lives in Gramercy Park, where the New York home of the family has always been.

Mr Henry Burrall Anderson, the eldest son of Henry Hill Anderson, was born in New York in 1863 Educated in Yale University, he was graduated therefrom in the class of 1885 and settled to the practice of law in New York, later becoming a member of the firm of which his father was the head. He married Marie W Larocque, daughter of Joseph Larocque, lives in East Fifty-seventh Street and spends the summer in Great Neck, Long Island He is a member of the University, New York and City clubs William Burrall Anderson, second son of the family, was graduated from Yale in 1886 and is also engaged in the practice of law He married Helen Tremain, and lives in Gramercy Park, being a member of the University, City, Lawyers' and other clubs The third son, Chandler P Anderson, was graduated from Yale in 1887, is also a lawyer and a member of the University and City clubs.

CONSTANT A ANDREWS

AMONG the many pioneer expeditions that came from England to the New World in the first half of the seventeenth century, that which sailed from London, in the ship Hector, was one of the most important as well as one of the most interesting. Under the leadership of John Davenport, Samuel Eaton, Theophilus Eaton and several other non-conformist clergymen, it was well equipped and its members were men and women of good standing in the communities from which they came. The company arrived in Boston, in June, 1637, and remained there for several months. Governor Winthrop endeavored to persuade these Colonists to take land in the Massachusetts Bay Colony and make their homes there, but they preferred to push further into the wilderness, and sent couriers to examine the land along the Connnecticut River and Long Island Sound. In 1638, the entire company sailed from Boston and settled the town of Quinnipiac, which they afterwards called New Haven. In this expedition, William Andrews was prominent, and during the early years of the settlement he was active in the administration of the affairs of the community. He was the ancestor of a family which has been notable in many ways in Connecticut and in New York His descendants have been successful business men, and have proved useful and patriotic citizens in public life

Loring Andrews, a descendant of the pioneer William Andrews, was during his lifetime one of the leading merchants of New York, and one of the prominent representatives of the great business interests in the district known as "the Swamp," where the leather trade of the country is centered. He was born in Windham, Greene County, N. Y., January 21st, 1799, and died in New York, January 22d, 1875 At fourteen years of age, he entered the service of a tanner, and, remaining there for eight years, learned the business thoroughly. He then traveled through the West for a couple of years and returned East to engage in business with his former employer, and finally became a partner. In 1829, he came to New York Beginning business with a small capital, before long he built up an extensive and successful trade. In 1832, he entered into partnership with William Wilson, Gideon Lee and Shepherd Knapp. The firm lost heavily in the panic of 1837, but Mr Andrews remained in business and made another fortune. In 1861, he organized the firm of Loring Andrews & Co., which in a few years became one of the most important in its line, controlling a large number of tanneries. He also owned much real estate in New York. He was a benefactor of the University of New York, giving one hundred thousand dollars for professorships in that institution, while he also contributed largely to philanthropic causes He was one of the first directors of the Mechanics' Bank, was the first president of the Shoe and Leather Bank, and first president of the Globe Life Insurance Company In 1839, he married Blandina B Hardenburgh, daughter of James B Hardenburgh, D D., and had seven children, William L., James B., Constant A., Loring, Walter S., Clarence and Isabelle Andrews.

Mr. Constant A. Andrews, the third son of Loring Andrews, was born in New York City, February 25th, 1844 He attended the Columbia College Grammar School and later went to Germany to complete his education. After the Civil War, he became a partner with his father, and subsequently was engaged with his brother, William L. Andrews, in the same business In a few years, he retired and passed some time in European travel

Upon returning from abroad, he organized the banking house of Constant A Andrews & Co, with which he has since been connected, and which has been noted for its conservative policy and its connection with legitimate investments Mr Andrews has other business associations, being president of the United States Savings Bank and a director of the Second Avenue Street Railroad Company and of other companies. He was an incorporator and the first treasurer of the Reform Club, and was for many years the treasurer of the New York City Mission and Tract Society, and of the Charity Organization Society, while he is also a supporter of the American Museum of Natural History and the Metropolitan Museum of Art He married Mrs. Blanche L Brewster, daughter of the Honorable S B H Vance, of New York, and lives in West Fifty-seventh Street.

RICHARD ALLARD ANTHONY

IN 1653, when the government of New Amsterdam was officially organized, five schepens were appointed to take charge of the city affairs, their names being Paulus Vander Grist, Maximilian Van Gheel, Allard Anthony, Peter Van Couwenhoven and William Beekman

Allard Anthony was a man of middle age, rich and influential, the consignee of a firm in Holland, with a store in the old church building erected by Wouter Van Twiller He owned a farm in the country, just above Wall Street, and had a city residence, one of the finest private buildings of its time, in Whitehall Street His son, Nicholas Anthony, was afterwards Sheriff of Ulster County, and his two daughters were among the most fashionable ladies of New Amsterdam The same year that he was schepen, Allard Anthony went to Holland as a special agent of the people of New Amsterdam, to present their affairs to the Amsterdam Chamber, and in 1664, he was elected Sheriff of the county, an office which he continued to hold under the administration of the English Governor, Colonel Richard Nicolls, and retained until 1673 The Anthony family is believed to have been originally of Spanish origin, as its coat of arms is the same as that of the old Spanish Antonio family, one member of which, a soldier of the Spanish Conquest, remained in Holland and established the Dutch family of Antoni.

Edward Anthony, the father of the subject of this sketch, was descended in the seventh generation from Allard Anthony, the Dutch pioneer His father was Jacob Anthony, for many years one of the principal tellers of the New York branch of the Bank of the United States, and cashier of the Bank of the State of New York Edward Anthony was born in New York, in 1819, was a civil engineer by profession, and died in 1888 He was graduated from Columbia College in 1838, and was in the engineer corps on the original Croton Aqueduct, and afterwards, with Professor James Renwick, was engaged in the survey of the northeastern boundary of the United States During this survey, he made some practical use of the new art of photography, and upon his return engaged in the business of manufacturing and supplying photographic materials In 1842, with his brother, Henry T Anthony, he organized the firm of E & H T Anthony & Co , which in 1877 was reorganized as a corporation, with Edward Anthony as president, a position that he retained until the time of his death

The mother of Richard A Anthony, whom his father married in 1848, was Margaretta R. Montgomery, a daughter of James Montgomery She was a direct descendant from the Count de Montgomerie, who accidentally killed a king of France in a tournament, in remembrance of which event, the arms of the Montgomery family display an arm holding a broken spear. The two daughters of Edward Anthony, Jane Kipp and Eleanor Anthony, married respectively Charles and Louis Solehiac

Mr. Richard Allard Anthony, the only son of Edward Anthony, was born in New York, May 24th, 1861. He attended Rutgers College for two years, but finished his collegiate course in Columbia College, being graduated from that institution in 1881 After completing his education, he entered the business house that his father had established When his uncle, H T. Anthony, died in 1884, he became secretary of the corporation, upon his father's death in 1888 was advanced to the position of vice-president, and in 1896 was elected president, which position he now holds He is a trustee of the United States Savings Bank, and for several years was a director of the Second Avenue Railroad. In 1895, Mr Anthony married Amelia Van Valkenburgh, a lady who, like himself, descends from an old New York Dutch family Mrs Anthony is the daughter of Lawrence H. Van Valkenburgh and his wife, Florence Vandewater Her paternal grandfather was John Lawrence Van Valkenburgh, of Albany, while on the maternal side her grandparents were Richard Vandewater, of Mobile, Ala., and his wife, Catherine H Vandewater. Mr Anthony belongs to the University, Storm King, and Richmond County Country clubs, and is a member of the Sons of the Revolution, the Holland Society, and the Columbia Alumni Association His residence is in New Brighton, Staten Island

DANIEL APPLETON

APPLETON is a familiar name in the annals of New England. The original members of the family came to America early in the seventeenth century, and took a prominent part in the work of developing the country and its institutions. Three of the great-grandfathers of Colonel Daniel Appleton fought in the Revolutionary War, and two of his grandfathers held commissions in the War of 1812. But it is in the more peaceful business and professional occupations that the Appletons have won their highest titles to fame, and in that direction they have achieved an international repute as one of the great publishing houses of this century. In that connection the name has been identified with New York for three generations.

Daniel Appleton, who founded the house of D. Appleton & Co., was born in Haverhill, Mass., December 10th, 1785. Early in life he was a dry goods merchant in his native town, then established himself in Boston, and in 1825 came to New York. In this city he began the business of book selling in connection with his dry goods store, from which it appears that the practice of dealing in dry goods and books in conjunction is not altogether a modern innovation. But Mr. Appleton soon gave up the dry goods branch of his establishment, and devoted himself entirely to importing and selling books, to which, in the course of time, he added the business of publishing. He published his first book, a religious work, in 1831. In 1838, he organized the firm of D. Appleton & Co., taking his son William H. into partnership, and, later on, three other sons, John A., Daniel Sidney and George, came into the firm. Daniel Appleton married Hannah Adams, daughter of John Adams, in 1813, and had five sons. Colonel Daniel Appleton, of the third generation that has been identified with the great publishing house, is a son of John Adams Appleton, who was born in 1817 and died in 1881. He was born in New York, February 24th, 1852, and received his early education in the public schools of New York, and at Carlsruhe, Germany, where he studied. On his return home from Germany he entered Harvard College, but did not remain to graduate, entering upon his duties as a clerk in the Appleton establishment in 1871. Since that time, he has been one of the most active members of the firm, and is at the head of its business department, having been a partner since 1879.

Colonel Appleton's inherited military tendencies early manifested themselves. When only fifteen years of age, he became a member of the famous Boston Cadet Corps, and drilled and camped with that organization for five years. After his return to New York to go into business, he was not long out of the ranks. In October, 1871, he enlisted as a private in Company F, Seventh Regiment, with which organization he has remained ever since. His military career has been notable, extending, as it has, over a period of more than a quarter of a century, and covering a wide and valuable experience, and important service to the State on many occasions. In April, 1873, he was promoted to be Corporal, and in November of the same year was advanced to the grade of Sergeant. He was made First Sergeant in March, 1875, and Second Lieutenant in May, 1876. In January, 1877, he was promoted to be Captain, and during the railroad riots of 1877, was on active duty with his company. Under his administration, Company F grew rapidly in membership, until it reached the maximum allowed by law, which figure has been maintained, while at the same time in military excellence it became one of the best companies of the regiment. When Colonel Emmons Clark retired from the Seventh in 1889, Captain Appleton was chosen by a unanimous vote of the regiment's officers to succeed him, and has seen much active service, particularly upon the occasion of the street railroad riots in Brooklyn.

Aside from his business and military life, Colonel Appleton has comparatively few interests. He is unmarried, and his regimental duties command most of his leisure time. He lives in West Seventy-second Street, and at the family country place, Rockhurst, Premium Point, New Rochelle. He is, however, a member of the Union, New York Athletic, New York Yacht, Aldine and Riding clubs and the Century Association. His mother, who was Serena P. Dale, survived her husband, and lives in New York and New Rochelle.

WILLIAM HENRY ARNOUX

AMONG the French soldiers who came to America with the forces sent to aid the Colonists in their struggle against the British Crown, was Jean B Arnoux, who was a native of Marseilles He was a Captain in the army of Count Rochambeau, who, family tradition says, was his cousin When the Revolutionary War came to an end, he decided to remain in this country, married one of his own countrywomen, and for a time made his home in Vergennes, Vt

Jean B Arnoux was the grandfather of Judge William H Arnoux Gabriel A Arnoux, his son, was born in Vergennes, Vt , in 1805, and died in New York in 1855 He was a successful merchant here from 1824 until his death, and a member of the Garde Lafayette, the French military organization of this city His wife was Ann Kennett, a descendant of Bishop Kennett, of England Her mother was a Whaley, a lineal descendant of General Edward Whaley, one of the regicide Judges who signed the death warrant of Charles I

Judge William Henry Arnoux was born in New York City, September 8th, 1831 He was educated here, and at an early age manifested a marked inclination for study He began to learn Latin at eight years of age and Greek at eleven, and when he was fifteen years old was fully prepared to enter Princeton College. His father, however, preferred that he should engage in business, and he accordingly entered a wholesale cloth house At the end of four years, his plans for the future were changed to accord more with his own wishes and his natural aptitude, and he was taken from business and afforded an opportunity to study law In four years, he passed the examination for admission to the bar, and in 1855 entered into partnership with Horace Holden, in whose office he had studied This firm continued for three years only, and for the following ten years, Mr Arnoux practiced his profession without an associate In 1868, he became a member of the firm of Wright, Merihew & Arnoux, and two years later organized the firm of Arnoux, Ritch & Woodford

In 1882, there being a vacancy on the bench of the Superior Court of the City and County of New York, caused by the resignation of Judge Spier, Governor Alonzo B Cornell appointed Mr Arnoux to fill the place The Judgeship was contested by Richard O Gorman, but the court to which the matter was submitted decided in favor of sustaining the Governor's action. Judge Arnoux served only for a short term as a Judge, but established a reputation for industry, legal learning and judicial ability that placed him in the front rank of his profession On the termination of his service on the bench, Judge Arnoux returned to his law firm and engaged in the active practice of his profession until the 1st of January, 1896, when he retired He has been especially noted for the exhaustive manner in which he investigated every case that he undertook. The results of one of his most remarkable professional studies of this character which was in connection with the elevated railroads, and involved research into the early Colonial history of the State, have been published as a valuable treatise upon the settlement of the Dutch Colonists in New Amsterdam Since his retirement from professional labors, he has been engaged in literary pursuits, principally of a scientific character

Judge Arnoux maintains a lively interest in public matters, is active in all movements for governmental reform and for the better administration of municipal affairs, and is connected with many benevolent and religious societies of the city. He was one of the founders of the Union League Club in the early days of the Civil War, and one of the originators of the Bar Association of the City of New York In 1889-90, he was president of the New York State Bar Association, and in 1890 chairman of the committee in charge of the celebration of the Centennial Anniversary of the establishment of the Supreme Court of the United States He is past vice-president-general of both the National and the State Society of the Sons of the American Revolution, and vice-president of the Society for the Prevention of Crime and of the Church Temperance Society He belongs to the Republican, Church and other clubs, and the New England Society He married Pauline Browne a descendant of Robert Hicks, the Quaker pilgrim of 1621

JOHN JACOB ASTOR

THE year 1783, which witnessed the British evacuation of the city, brought to New York the founder of one of its foremost families, in the person of the elder John Jacob Astor, a native of the town of Waldorf, in Germany. Only twenty years of age, and without capital or connections, he possessed education and ability besides a marked force of character which, by the beginning of the century, had made him a leader in business and a man of fortune. Then, as in the Colonial era, the fur trade was one of the chief fields for American enterprise, and divining the possibilities the Oregon territory afforded, he established at Astoria, Ore , the first permanent American settlement on the Pacific coast. During the War of 1812 he gave effectual aid to the government, and was the largest individual subscriber to the United States loans of that trying period. His acute judgment convinced him of New York's imperial destiny, and his large investments in property in the lines of the city's growth established a policy to which his descendants adhered, and to which the enormous proportions of their wealth are due. Public spirited and charitable in practical ways, John Jacob Astor's memory will always be preserved in New York by that noble foundation, the Astor Library, for the establishment of which he left on his death in 1848 the sum of four hundred thousand dollars. His own chief enjoyment was the society of literary friends, among whom were Fitz Green Hallock and Washington Irving.

John Jacob Astor, the elder, married Sarah, daughter of Adam Todd, of New York, a first cousin of Mrs. Henry Brevoort. Their son, William B. Astor, who succeeded to the family estate, married Margaret Armstrong, daughter of General John Armstrong, the soldier, statesman and author, who served in the Continental Army, taking part as Major in the battle of Saratoga, represented New York in the United States Senate, and became Minister to France, and Secretary of War during the War of 1812. His wife, the mother of Mrs. William B. Astor, was Alida Livingston, daughter of Judge Robert R. Livingston, and sister of the famous Chancellor Livingston.

The late William Astor, father of the present Mr. John Jacob Astor, was the son of William B. Astor and Margaret (Armstrong) Astor. He married Caroline Schermerhorn daughter of Abraham Schermerhorn and his wife Helen whose father, Henry White, married Ann Van Courtlandt. The Schermerhorn family descends from Jacob Janse Schermerhorn, who settled in New York in 1636, and on the side of a maternal ancestress from the famous Willhemus Beekman.

Mr. John Jacob Astor was born in 1864, at Ferncliff, on the Hudson River. He received his education at St. Paul's School, Concord, N H , and graduated from the scientific department of Harvard University in 1888 He traveled extensively both in this country and Europe, one of his remarkable experiences being the honor of a personal interview with the Sultan of Turkey. In 1891 he married Ava Willing, daughter of Edward Shippen Willing, of Philadelphia, and his wife, Alice Barton Willing The Willing family stands high in the Quaker City, descending from Charles Willing, who came to America in 1728, and was subsequently Mayor of Philadelphia in 1747 and again in 1754 His son, Thomas Willing, was also Mayor in 1753, a Judge of the Supreme Court of Pennsylvania from 1767 to 1777, and first president of the Bank of the United States, and has the distinction of having designed the present coat of arms of the United States. Mr. and Mrs John Jacob Astor have one son, William Vincent Astor.

On the death of his father, in 1892, Mr. Astor succeeded to the bulk of the family estate, and has since given his attention largely to the administration of his property. This, however, has not prevented him from taking an active interest in business and public affairs. He is a director in many financial and other corporations, and was an aide-de-camp with the rank of Colonel on the staff of Governor Levi P Morton. Society and sport have also not been neglected, both Mr and Mrs Astor being devoted to yachting, golf and other fashionable recreations. He owns the Nourmahal, one of the finest steam yachts in the country. A considerable part of each year is spent at his handsome Newport residence and his country place on the Hudson. Mr. Astor is a member of nearly all the foremost New York clubs, and of the Society of Colonial Wars.

JOHN W. AUCHINCLOSS

FOR upwards of a century, the Auchincloss family has been resident in New York, and during that time its members have closely identified themselves with the best interests of the city, social and commercial. Hugh Auchincloss, of Paisley, Scotland, came to the United States about the beginning of the century that is now drawing to a close. He had been a thrifty and enterprising merchant in his Scotch home, and after settling in New York, engaged, in 1803, in the business of importing dry goods. He was eminently successful, and before he died, in 1855, had accumulated a considerable fortune and built up a large and profitable business.

John Auchincloss, the eldest son of Hugh Auchincloss, is well remembered by the generation that is just passing off the scene. He was born in New York in 1810, and early in life entered his father's establishment and received a thorough mercantile training. Hugh Auchincloss, the younger son, was born in New York City in 1817. He also entered the paternal business house, becoming a partner with his father and elder brother. He was a member of Grace Protestant Episcopal Church and a director in several financial institutions, including the Merchants' National Bank and the Bleecker Street Savings Bank. His only daughter married Lewis P Child, of New Canaan, Conn., and he died at the home of his son-in-law, in 1890.

While on a visit to Quebec, Canada, John Auchincloss died there, June 26th, 1876. At that time, he was a director of the Merchants' Bank, a trustee of the Equitable Life Assurance Society, and actively connected with other fiduciary institutions. He was a member of the Fifth Avenue Presbyterian Church nearly all his life, and was a generous contributor to the religious and benevolent institutions that are supported by the charitably disposed people of the city. He left a family of six sons and two daughters, his wife, whose maiden name was Elizabeth Buck, being still alive at an advanced age. Her city home is in West Fifty-seventh Street, and she has a summer residence in Newport.

The firm founded by Hugh Auchincloss, the first of the name, which down to 1855 continued to do business under the title of Hugh Auchincloss & Son, held a high position in the mercantile community. In 1855, however, its style was changed to John & Hugh Auchincloss, and later on it became Auchincloss Brothers, which is its title to-day. For many years the business of Auchincloss Brothers has been continued by the third generation of the name in America, John W and Hugh D. Auchincloss, sons of John Auchincloss, who uphold the best traditions of the family establishment. The brothers were engaged in the dry goods commission business from 1880 to 1891, when they retired from that branch of commerce, and have since devoted themselves to managing and developing their manufacturing, railroad, mining and other properties.

Mr. John W. Auchincloss was born in New York, April 12th, 1853, and was educated in Yale College, graduating in 1873. He is a director of the Illinois Central Railroad Company and a trustee of the Mutual Life Insurance Company, the National Safe Deposit Company and other institutions. He married Joanna H. Russell, daughter of the late Charles H Russell, and lives in East Forty-eighth Street. His summer home is at Bar Harbor, Me. His clubs are the Metropolitan, Union League, University and New York Yacht, the Century Association and the New England and St. Andrew's societies.

Hugh D. Auchincloss, the younger son of John Auchincloss, was born in Newport, R. I., July 8th, 1858. He is a graduate from Yale College, in the class of 1879, and belongs to the Yale Alumni Association and the University Club. Among the other social organizations of which he is a member are the Metropolitan and New York Yacht clubs, the Century Association and the New England and St. Andrew's societies. The wife of Hugh D Auchincloss was Emma B Jennings, daughter of the late Oliver B Jennings. The New York home of the family is in West Forty-ninth Street and their summer residence is in Newport. Mr Auchincloss is a director in the Farmers' Loan & Trust Company, the Bank of the Manhattan Company, the Bowery Savings Bank and the Consolidated Gas Company.

SAMUEL PUTNAM AVERY

IN Normandy and in England, the Avery family was of high station and members of it were prominent in early records prior to the fifteenth century The Averys of this country belong to what is known as the Dedham branch of the family, and trace their descent from the Averys of the County of Somerset, England The arms of that family are: Gules a chevron between three besants, or Crest, two lions' jambs, or, supporting a besant Their estates were situated in the parish of Pill, now Pylle, Somersetshire

Robert Avery, the English ancestor of that branch of the family which is now under consideration, resided near Shepton Mallet, in the Hundred of Whitestone He had a son William and a grandson Robert, and his great-grandson, the son of Robert, was William Avery, of Dedham, Mass., who was one of the first of his name to come to the New England Colonies. William Avery migrated thither in 1650, with his wife and three children, from Barkham, Berkshire, in England After his settlement in this country, four more children were born to him He was a resident of Dedham for some fifteen years after the settlement of that place, was a large land owner, an officer of the militia, and a deputy to the General Court When the Massachusetts Colony gave to the town of Dedham a large tract of land at Deerfield on the Connecticut River, William Avery was one of the original proprietors of the grant, which comprised eight thousand acres In early life, he was a blacksmith, but became an educated man, was one of the earliest physicians in the Colony, a bookseller in Boston after 1680, and a patron of learning

The second son of William, was Robert Avery, who was born in England in 1649, and died in 1722 He married Elizabeth, daughter of Job Lane, of Malden, and when his widow died, in 1746, she left five children, thirty grandchildren, fifty-two great-grandchildren, and two great-great-grandchildren The Reverend John Avery, the son of Robert Avery, of the second American generation, was born in Dedham in 1684, graduated from Harvard in 1706 and was the pastor of the first church in Truro, Mass., from 1711 to the time of his death, in 1754 His wife, Ruth Little, was a daughter of the Reverend Ephraim Little, and a great-granddaughter of Richard Warren, who came over in the Mayflower. A son of the Reverend John Avery, was John Avery, 1711–1796, who became a merchant of Boston His son, John, born 1739, who graduated from Harvard in 1759, was one of the Sons of Liberty who had their meetings on Washington Street, Boston, under the famous Liberty tree He served for a number of years as Deputy Secretary of Massachusetts, and as Secretary for twenty-six years, and died in 1806 Another son, from whom the subject of this sketch descends, was the Reverend Ephraim Avery, born 1713, who graduated from Harvard in 1731, married, in 1738, Deborah Lothrop, and was the minister at Brooklyn, Conn., throughout his life and died there in 1754.

The Reverend Ephraim Avery, the second of the name and son of the above Reverend Ephraim and Deborah (Lothrop) Avery, was born at Brooklyn, Conn., in 1741, graduated at Yale in 1761, married Hannah Platt in 1762, taught school at Rye, N. Y., received the degree of Master of Arts from Kings College, New York, 1767, and died in 1776 John William Avery, eldest son of the Reverend Ephraim and Hannah (Platt) Avery, was born at Rye, N. Y., in 1767 He married Sarah Fairchild, of Stratford, Conn., in 1794, and died in 1799

Samuel Putnam Avery, second son of John William and Sarah (Fairchild) Avery, was born at Stratford, Conn., in 1797, and came to New York in early life He was a merchant on Catherine Street, but afterwards went into the hotel business and became proprietor of the East River Mansion House, where he died in 1832 He married, in 1821, Hannah Ann Parke, who survived him until 1888, a daughter of Captain Benjamin Parke, who was born in Charleston, R. I., 1766, and was in the shipping business in New York. He died 1807, and was buried in Trinity Church yard, where his tomb still stands His daughter, Hannah Ann, was a direct descendant from Richard Parke, of London, who came over in 1635, and settled at Cambridge, Mass; her grandfather was Captain Benjamin Parke, born at Westerly, R. I., 1735, who was at the reduction of Crown Point,

1756, and at the attack on Fort William Henry He took part in the Lexington alarm at the opening of the War of the Revolution, commanded a company of minute men and was mortally wounded at Bunker Hill

Mr Samuel Putnam Avery, the second of the name and the oldest child of the elder Samuel P and Hannah Ann (Parke) Avery, was born in New York, March 17th, 1822 In early life, he learned the art of copper-plate engraving and was first engaged with a bank note company. He, however, turned his attention to engraving on wood, being employed by various newspapers and publishers, and compiled several volumes of a humorous nature, also supplying the illustrations. In 1865, he added to his business, art publishing and dealing in works of art. Appointed commissioner of the American Art Department at the Universal Exhibition of 1867 in Paris, he decided on his return in the following year to abandon engraving and engaged in art enterprises on a large scale in Fifth Avenue. He became one of the most respected and successful dealers of the country, retiring from business in 1888.

For several years, Mr Avery filled the post of secretary of the art committee of the Union League Club, whose action led to the establishment of the Metropolitan Museum of Art, of which he became one of the founders and a trustee of continued standing. He is also a trustee of the New York Public Library, Astor, Lenox and Tilden Foundations; is president of the Grolier Club, vice-president of the Sculpture Society, honorary member of the Architectural League, and of the Typothetæ Society. Besides this, he is a member of the Century, Union League, Players, City, Tuxedo and other clubs, a member of the Civil Service Reform Association and of the Sons of the Revolution, a life member of the American Museum of Natural History, of the American Geographical, Historical and the Zoölogical Society, as well as of the National Academy of Design, the Chamber of Commerce, and other bodies. One of the collections of Oriental porcelains in the Metropolitan Museum of Art was formed by Mr Avery and was purchased by his friends and presented to the institution The Avery Architectural Library at Columbia College, now numbering about fifteen thousand volumes, was created and endowed by Mr and Mrs Avery in 1891 in memory of their deceased son, Henry Ogden Avery Mr. Avery has been a generous contributor to various artistic, literary and benevolent institutions of this city. His opinion in matters pertaining to the fine arts is regarded as authoritative.

Columbia College, in 1896, conferred upon him the degree of Master of Arts for his services to the cause of art and art culture in the United States The Century Magazine of December, 1896, contained an illustrated article on his art services and personal remembrances On his seventy-fifth birthday, March, 1897, a gold medal of artistic design, modeled by Professor Scharff, of Vienna, was presented to him by seventy-five leading citizens of New York, as a recognition of his various public services.

The wife of Mr Avery was Mary Ann Ogden, daughter of Henry Aaron and Katherine (Conklin) Ogden, of New York. Her name is associated with benevolent gifts Their oldest son is Samuel P Avery, Jr, who succeeded his father in business Another son, Henry Ogden Avery, was born in Brooklyn, 1852, and died in New York 1890. He was educated as an architect, studied seven years at the Ecole des Beaux Arts, Paris, lectured and wrote upon architectural subjects, and was a most promising and esteemed member of his chosen profession. The other children of Mr and Mrs Avery are Mary Henrietta Avery, who has been prominent in charitable works and is president of the Loan Relief Association, Fanny Falconer Avery, who married the Reverend M P Welcher, and Ellen Walters Avery, who died in 1893 and was a poetess of considerable talent. The books which she had collected were presented to the Teachers' College by her mother

The Honorable Benjamin Parke Avery, who as a mere youth emigrated to California in 1849, became a prominent editor and was appointed United States Minister to China, by President Grant, 1874, dying at Pekin, 1875, was the only brother of Mr Samuel P Avery, and Mary Rebecca Avery, who became the wife of the Reverend T De Witt Talmage, and died at Philadelphia in 1861, was his sister

28

SAMUEL D BABCOCK

JAMES BABCOCK, the founder of the family of his name in this country, was a native of Essex, and was born in 1580 He was one of the earliest and most steadfast Puritans, going to Leyden, Holland, and afterwards emigrating to America, with the band of Colonists who came to Plymouth in 1623, bringing with him his four children His second son, Captain John Babcock, became a prominent man in the Plymouth Colony and in Rhode Island. He lived in Newport and for some ten years dwelt among the Narragansett Indians. Afterwards he settled in Westerly, R. I, where he was a justice of the peace and town clerk and owned considerable land His son, Captain James Babcock, born in Westerly in 1650, who was the first male white child born in the Narragansett Colony, was also a man of wealth and influence, being the proprietor of a grant of two hundred acres of land. In 1687, he married Elizabeth Babbitt, the ancestress of the branch of the family now under consideration. She died in 1730, and afterwards, in 1731, he married Content Maxson, daughter of Jonathan Maxson, of a pioneer family of Westerly.

In the next two generations, members of this family became distinguished in public and professional life The Honorable Joshua Babcock, 1707–1783, the great-great-grandfather of Mr. Samuel D Babcock, was both a physician and jurist. He was graduated from Yale College in 1724, studied medicine in Boston, afterwards going to England to complete his education. He was a staunch patriot during the Revolutionary War, giving to the Continental cause valuable service, both in military and in civil life. He was Chief Justice of the Colony, several times a member and Speaker of the Rhode Island Assembly, and served his fellow-citizens in other positions of trust and responsibility. His first wife, the great-great-grandmother of Mr Samuel D. Babcock, was Hannah Stanton, of Pawtucket, R. I., who was descended from Thomas Stanton, one of the earliest settlers of the Providence Plantation and a famous Indian interpreter.

Colonel Henry Babcock, son of the Honorable Joshua Babcock, was born in Westerly, R I, in 1736, and was graduated from Yale College when sixteen years of age He began a brilliant military career before he had attained to his maturity. In the French and Indian War, he was Captain of a company of infantry. He was at the battle of Lake George, in 1755, captured Baron Dieskau, the French commander, and for his bravery was promoted to be Major At the age of twenty-one, he was a Colonel and the following year commanded the Rhode Island regiment in Abercrombie's expedition against Ticonderoga Afterward he spent a year in England, and when the War of the Revolution broke out was appointed Commander of the Continental forces of Rhode Island. After the war, he engaged in the practice of law. His wife was Mary Stanton, daughter of Robert Stanton, who came of the same family as his mother Colonel Babcock left two sons, Paul and Dudley Babcock. The younger son had one daughter, who married Phineas Stanton. The elder son left several male descendants, and it is through them only that the male line of Colonel Henry Babcock's family has been preserved.

Mr. Samuel D. Babcock, the prominent representative of this interesting family in the present generation, was born in Rhode Island and removed to New York at an early age. He has been connected with large business enterprises, particularly railroad corporations, having been president of, and otherwise active, in the management of several companies He lives in upper Fifth Avenue, and has a country seat at Riverdale-on-Hudson. His only son, Henry D. Babcock, was graduated from Columbia College in 1868, and married Anna M Woodward. Their children are Samuel D, Woodward and Alice W. Babcock He is a member of the firm of Hollister & Babcock, and belongs to the Metropolitan, Union League, University, Riding, Rockaway Hunt, Larchmont Yacht and New York Yacht clubs, and the Sons of the Revolution Mr. Samuel D. Babcock is a member of the Metropolitan, Union, Manhattan and New York Yacht clubs, the Downtown Association, the Country Club of Westchester County, the Century Association, the New England Society and the American Geographical Society, and is a supporter of the National Academy of Design, the Metropolitan Museum of Art and the American Museum of Natural History

JULES SEMON BACHE

A N intimate connection has always existed between the social world of New York and its great financial and business interests. The founders of the leading families of the city during the Colonial epoch and the early part of the present century were, almost without exception, successful and energetic men of business, actively engaged in trade, finance or in one of the learned professions. Mr Bache is personally an exemplar of the fact that this honorable tradition of the great commercial city is still in full force and effect. One of the most prominent men of affairs among the younger generations of society people, he is successful and popular in both relations

Mr Jules S Bache was born in this city on November 9, 1861. His father, Semon Bache, was an eminent and wealthy merchant, who was the founder of a house which took rank under his guidance as one of the largest importing establishments in the United States, if not in the world. The firm of Semon Bache & Co. has now been in successful existence for over half a century. Mr Bache's mother, the wife of Semon Bache, and born Elizabeth Von Praag, was a native of this city.

After an academic education at the Charlier Institute, New York, and at schools in Europe the subject of this sketch entered the banking profession, which he has pursued with the aid of inherited business ability and natural financial talent, being at present at the head of a large financial and banking firm bearing his own name, and is naturally a leading figure in Stock Exchange and banking circles. He has been intimately associated during his career with most of the prominent leaders of cotemporary finance and business, and has a wide circle of distinguished friends, not only in that connection, but socially as well. Mr. Bache has also taken an active and prominent part in a number of large and important financial transactions. Among other incidents of this character was the reorganization of the Distillers' and Cattle Feeders' Company, he having been one of the leaders in the movement to protect the shareholders of that corporation, and a member of the committee by which its involved affairs were adjusted and the company successfully reorganized as the American Spirits Manufacturing Company, in the board of directors of which Mr. Bache is a leading member and also holds the office of vice-president. Mr. Bache has also been intimately connected with several other prominent railroad and industrial corporations and has manifested the possession of financial talents of a high order.

In 1892 Mr. Bache was united in marriage to Florence R Sheftel, daughter of Adolph Sheftel, a retired merchant and capitalist long a resident of New York, and identified with the managements of some of the most prominent financial and charitable institutions of the city. Mr. and Mrs Bache have two daughters, Hazel Joy and Kathryn King Bache

The family residence is No. 13 East Sixty-fourth Street. Their country seat is Arsdale Manor, Wilson Park, Tarrytown-on-Hudson, an estate which includes on its grounds the spot on which Major Andre was arrested by the American soldiery and where the tragedy of his fate began. He also has a mountain place at Camp Winona, on Upper Saranac Lake, N. Y. Mr. Bache has traveled both in this country and in Europe and is a member of the New York Club, the Suburban Riding and Driving Club and the Liederkranz.

His own tastes and those of Mrs. Bache lean in the direction of art. Among the many paintings which he has brought together, are examples by Henner, Lesrel, Meyer Von Bremen, Schenck, Berne, Weiss and Schreger, the higher types of German art being particularly represented among his collection. It also includes a Napoleon by David, and with the other artistic treasures which he has gathered here and in Europe, is an interesting collection of miniatures of historical personages, particularly those of English and French beauties and celebrities of the preceding century, which ranks with the finest collections of a similar character in the country.

BRADY ELECTUS BACKUS, D.D.

WILLIAM BACKUS, from Norwich, England, was a settler at Saybrook, Conn., and a founder in 1659 of Norwich, in the same Colony. His son, also named William, born at Saybrook, in 1640, became a lieutenant, committeeman and deputy to the General Court 1680–93, and was an original patentee of Norwich and one of the company which, in 1678, obtained the grant of Windham, Conn. His wife, Elizabeth Pratt, was daughter of Lieutenant William Pratt, who came to Saybrook in 1633. The Pratt ancestry is traced to Sir William de Pratellis, a knight of Richard Cœur de Lion

The son of William Backus the second was John Backus, 1661–1744, who married Mary Bingham; and John Backus, Jr., their son, 1698–1769, moved, about 1737, to Woodbury, Conn. His wife was Sybil, daughter of the Reverend Samuel Whiting and his wife, Elizabeth Adams. Her father, the first minister of Windham, was the son of the Reverend John Whiting, a graduate of Harvard College in 1653, and Chaplain in King Philip's War, and her grandfather, Major William Whiting, who settled at Hartford in 1632, was Treasurer of Connecticut. Her mother, Elizabeth Adams, was a daughter of the Reverend William Adams and his wife, Alice Bradford, grand-daughter of Governor William Bradford, of Plymouth

Delucena Backus, great-grandfather of Brady E. Backus, was the son of John and Sybil Backus and was born at Woodbury, in 1744. He became a prominent member of the Masonic body, married Electa, daughter of Captain Abner Mallory, and died at Athens, N. Y., 1813. Lieutenant-Colonel Electus M. Backus, their son, born at Woodbury, in 1765, served in the Army of the Revolution when a lad, became a Captain in the United States Army, Major in 1808 and Lieutenant-Colonel the following year, and served also in the State Militia as Captain and Major. He commanded the American forces at Sackett's Harbor when it was attacked by the British, in 1813, and was slain defending it, being one of the officers whose deaths are commemorated by the monument there. He married Sabra, daughter of Nathan Judson, and one of his sons, Electus Backus, born in 1804, graduated at West Point in 1824, served in the Seminole and Mexican wars, was Colonel of the Sixth United States Infantry, and married Mary, daughter of General Hugh Brady, U. S. A. His elder brother, Augustus Backus, 1802–1866, was the Reverend Dr. Backus's father. He was in early life Professor of Music in the Emma Willard Seminary, at Troy, N. Y., and afterwards engaged in business in Grand Rapids, Mich.

Dr. Backus's maternal descent is also distinguished His mother was Martha Cordelia Mann, daughter of Judge Benning Mann, 1781–1863, of Hartford, Conn., whose wife was his cousin, Phœbe Mann, daughter of Andrew Mann, 1755–1846, a Captain in the Revolutionary Army Captain Mann's mother was Margaret Peters, daughter of John Peters, of Hebron, Conn, and a sister of the Reverend Dr. Samuel Peters, rector of St. Peter's Church, Hebron, Conn., and who was elected first Bishop of Vermont. The Peters family were descended from Sir John Peters, of Exeter, 1509, whose grandsons came to New England in 1634.

Born at Troy, in 1839, Dr. Brady Electus Backus was educated at Grand Rapids, Mich., was admitted to the bar and practiced law till 1866. He then entered Trinity College, being a member of the Ψ Τ fraternity, was graduated in 1870, and also from the General Theological Seminary, New York, in 1873, becoming in the latter year assistant minister of St. Peter's Church, New York, and in 1874 rector of Christ Church, Cooperstown, N. Y. Since 1876 he has been rector of the Church of the Holy Apostles, New York. In 1881, Nebraska College conferred on him the degree of D.D. He is a member of the New England Society, the Sons of the Revolution, the Society of Mayflower Descendants, the Society of Colonial Wars, the Society of the War of 1812 and the Washington Guards, and has been vice-president of the Trinity College Alumni of New York. In 1875, Dr. Backus married Annie Taylor, their surviving children being Cordelia M. Backus and Electus T. Backus His city residence is 360 West Twenty-eighth Street, and his country place is at Ridgefield, Conn

J. BAYARD BACKUS

THE Backus and Walworth families of New York have always occupied a prominent position in the social and political history of the State, while the name of Chester is one that occurs throughout the history of Connecticut. It is this Colonial and Revolutionary blood which is represented by the subject of these paragraphs. In addition, Mr Backus is one of the few Americans who can trace their descent to royalty on both the paternal and maternal sides in distinct and separate lines, as is displayed in full in Browning's work on Americans of Royal Descent, which volume sets forth in detail the right of the Backus family to such distinction.

Mr Backus was born at Schenectady, September 20th, 1853. His father, the Reverend Jonathan Trumbull Backus, D.D., LL.D., of Schenectady, N.Y., was one of the prominent Presbyterian divines of the United States. A graduate of Columbia College, he was famous for his piety, learning and eloquence. He was for many years a trustee of Union College, Schenectady, N.Y., and at the Assembly of the Presbyterian Church of America, held at Philadelphia, in 1870, occupied the distinguished position of moderator, it being the first General Assembly held after a permanent union between the Old and New School bodies of the Church had been agreed upon. That happy result was largely due to the personal influence of such men as Dr Backus. His wife, the mother of the gentleman we are considering, was Ann E Walworth, a daughter of the Honorable Reuben Hyde Walworth, of Saratoga Springs, the last of the Chancellors of the State of New York, and one of the most eminent lawyers who ever occupied that high office, and a jurist whose decisions are cited in every State of the Union.

The father of the Reverend Jonathan Trumbull Backus and paternal grandfather of the present Mr Backus of New York, was Eleazer Fitch Backus, who married Elizabeth Chester, a daughter of Colonel John Chester, a Revolutionary hero and a friend and trusted officer of General Washington, and a granddaughter of General Huntington. Colonel Chester, who was one of the wealthiest citizens of Connecticut, was an ardent patriot at the outbreak of the war against the mother country. He raised, and at his own expense equipped, a company of Connecticut troops, at the head of which he served throughout the Revolution. His command was noted for its discipline and efficiency. General Humphrey referred to it as the "Elite Corps of the (Continental) Army," and it was spoken of in Sweet's History in the following terms "Chester's company was by far the most accomplished body of men in the whole American Army." He was present at the Battle of Bunker Hill, and in Trumbull's historical painting of that famous engagement is depicted in a prominent position close to the dying General Warren, whom he supports in his arms. The genealogy of the Chester family has been delineated with unusual accuracy and completeness, several extended monographs on it having appeared in the various publications devoted to these subjects. Among the illustrious dignitaries who are found in Mr Backus's direct ancestral line were Governor William Bradford, of Plymouth, who stands to him in the relation of a seventh great-grandfather. Another is Governor John Haynes, Governor of both Massachusetts and Connecticut. A third was Governor Thomas Welles, of Colonial Connecticut, with many other worthies of the same type and age.

Mr Backus was graduated from Union College, and adopted the law as his profession. In 1877, he married Cornelia N Price, daughter of Joshua C Price, of Rockingham County, Va, a lady whose family is well known in Virginia and Maryland. Mr and Mrs Backus have one daughter, Elizabeth Chester Backus. Foreign travel has occupied a portion of Mr Backus's leisure. He was one of the original members of the University Athletic Club, is a member of the Society of Mayflower Descendants, the Society of Colonial Wars, the New England Society, the Metropolitan Museum of Art, and is a fellow of the American Geographical Society. He was one of the seven incorporators of the Society of Mayflower Descendants, is at present an active member of its Board of Assistants, and takes a warm interest in the organizations designed to nourish a love for the patriotic traditions of our country.

AUSTIN P. BALDWIN

ENGLISH blood mingled with that of the Dutch founders of New Netherland produced the race to which New York owes much of its preeminence in the country at large The same strain has also been dominant from the outset in the city's social organization Furthermore, each generation of this typical New York stock attracts to and reinforces itself with the best elements from every part of the land.

A striking and pertinent example of these interesting facts is furnished by the history of the Baldwin family. The name has long been familiar alike in the history of New York and that of Connecticut, many of its bearers having been prominent in Colonial, as well as in later days, in both political life and in professional and commercial pursuits The New York branch of the family was, at the beginning of the present century, well represented by Enos Baldwin, who married Mary Parker, a native of Cavendish, Vt. Their son, Austin Baldwin, the first of that name, born in Albany, N Y., became an eminent merchant in that city and a leader in politics. He was an adherent of the old Whig party and an associate of Henry Clay and the other leading men of the same political faith. He became a prominent figure in the higher councils of his party, frequently held office, was appointed to a position of national responsibility by President William Henry Harrison, and also served in the Assembly, becoming its Speaker.

In 1829, he married Julia Clarissa Huyck, daughter of Colonel John Van Heusen Huyck and his wife, Clara (Radcliffe) Huyck She was born at Rhinebeck, N Y , and descended on both sides from the oldest and most influential families of Colonial antecedents in the river counties of the State, her near relatives including such prominent names as Radcliffe, Van Ness, Dewitt, Van Hovenburg, Kip, Van Wagener, Van Heusen, Hogeboom and Schermerhorn. Her mother was a daughter of General William Radcliffe, an officer of the Revolutionary Army One of her brothers was Jacob Radcliffe, who became a Judge of the Supreme Court of New York, and was Mayor of the City of New York for two terms, in 1810-11 and again in 1815-18, and was one of the leading figures in the political life of his day in New York Another brother was Peter W. Radcliff, who was also a distinguished lawyer and active in politics, being a State Senator and Judge of the King's County Court. Few among the early settlers of this State held a more distinguished position or were more useful and patriotic citizens than the Radcliffs, descended from Joachim Radcliffe, one of the earliest settlers

Mr. Austin P. Baldwin is the son of Austin and Julia Clarissa (Huyck) Baldwin, and was born in New York in 1834. He was educated in Middletown, Conn., and entered business in early life, becoming an enterprising and successful merchant He married Alice Bradford, of Providence, R I , a member of a family whose lineage includes some of the most notable names in the Colonial and Revolutionary history of the New England States Mrs. Baldwin is a direct descendant of Governor William Bradford, one of the leaders of the Mayflower Pilgrims, Governor of the Plymouth Colony and the earliest historian of the Puritan settlement in America. Another of her ancestors in a direct line is Captain Miles Standish, 1584-1656, famous in New England tradition as the first commissioned military officer of the Colonists, and immortalized by the greatest of American poets. He was also the founder of Duxbury, Mass , and the magistrate of that town until his death The erection, in 1872, of the monument to the memory of Miles Standish, at Duxbury, was due to a movement in which Mrs Baldwin's father took an active part.

Mr Baldwin resides in West Thirty-second Street. His children are Standish Bradford, Austin Radcliffe, and Alice Maud Baldwin. His son, Austin R Baldwin, was graduated from Yale University in the class of 1886 Mr. Baldwin has traveled extensively, having made more than thirty visits to Europe In 1896, accompanied by his children, he made a trip to Japan. He is a member of the Union League Club, of the St Nicholas Society, and of the Downtown Association

GEORGE VAN NEST BALDWIN

E VEN before the Norman Conquest, the name of Baldwin occurs in English history. It was borne by several noble families of France and Normandy, while it was also the appellation of the ancient counts of Flanders In later times, there were several families of the landed gentry bearing the name in England and Normandy The American Baldwins trace their descent to Richard Baldwin, of Bucks County, England, one of a family which possessed estates in that locality The most eminent Baldwin of Bucks County was Sir John Baldwin, Chief Justice of England from 1536 until his death, in 1546. Richard Baldwin, of Donrigge, as the name appears in the records, was of the parish of Aston Clifton, Bucks County, where he died about 1552 His son Richard was born about 1530 and died in 1630 Three sons of this second Richard Baldwin, Nathaniel, Timothy and Joseph, came to this country early in the seventeenth century

Joseph Baldwin was born in Cholesbury, arrived in New England soon after 1620, and lived in Milford, Conn , where he is recorded among the first settlers in 1639 He remained in Milford nearly a quarter of a century, but about 1663 joined a company of pioneers, who pushed further west to the banks of the Connecticut River He settled in Hadley, Mass , and became a freeman of that place in 1666 He was married when he came to this country, and his second wife, whom he married here, was Isabel Northam, who died in 1676 Afterwards he married Elizabeth Hitchcock, who died in 1696, he having already died in 1684 In the second generation, Jonathan Baldwin, of Milford, 1649-1739, was a man of prominence His first wife, the ancestress of the subject of this sketch, was Hannah, daughter of John Ward His second wife was Thankful Strong, daughter of the famous Elder John Strong, of Northampton, Mass , who was the American founder of a family that became one of the largest and most influential in the annals of Colonial New England

John Baldwin, son of Jonathan Baldwin, was born in Milford in 1688, and removed to New Jersey with other families from Milford, who established a settlement called Connecticut Farms, in remembrance of their former home, there he died in 1773 In tne next generation, the ancestors of Mr George Van Nest Baldwin were Ezekiel Baldwin, 1719-1805, and his wife, Sarah Baldwin, who was his cousin, a daughter of Benjamin Baldwin Ezekiel Baldvrin was a soldier of the Revolutionary Army, serving in the New Jersey forces Jotham Baldwin, his son, was born in 1765 and died in 1854 His wife, Joanna Baldwin, was a cousin, being the daughter of Nathan Baldwin The Reverend Eli Baldwin, D D , their son and father of the gentleman referred to in this sketch, was born in 1791 and became an eminent divine of the Dutch Reformed Church His wife, Phœbe Van Nest, came of the old Dutch family of that name. Her grandfather, George Van Nest, served during the Revolutionary War as Captain in the First Battalion of the New Jersey Line After the war, he was a resident of Somerset County, N. J , and a large landowner Mr Baldwin's grandfather, Abraham Van Nest, was a wealthy New York merchant, and owned a country seat in Greenwich Village

Mr George Van Nest Baldwin was educated in private schools in New Brunswick, N. J., and was graduated from Rutgers College in 1856, and from the Law School of Columbia College in 1860, taking first honors there Admitted to practice in New York, he has since pursued his profession with distinction and success, and is a leading member of the bar. His attention has been largely given to the law of trusts, and in that branch of practice he is a recognized authority In late years his practice has been largely as consulting counsel and in the management of estates He has been a member of the Bar Association since its foundation, and is also a member of the Metropolitan and Union clubs and of the Century Association and the St. Nicholas Society He was one of the founders of the University Club, was its first vice-president, afterwards president, and for many years a member of its council He is also a trustee of the Society Library and belongs to many other literary and social organizations

MISS MARY E C BANCKER

T HE Bancker family has been prominently represented in New York history from the earliest Colonial days   Members of it have at all times been numbered among the leading citizens of the Metropolis and the State, and they have intermarried with such families as the de Peysters, Rutgers, Henrys and others   The family was of Dutch origin, and the coat of arms to which it is entitled and which are borne by its American representatives was given in 1448 to four brothers, Admirals in the Dutch Navy

Gerrit Bancker came from Holland about 1656   He was a native of Amsterdam, where he left a brother, Willem, who, according to the records, was living as late as 1700   Soon after arriving in New Amsterdam, Gerrit Bancker went to Beverwyck (Albany), where he engaged in business as a trader   He owned considerable real estate in various parts of that village, and was one of the fifteen proprietors of Schenectady.   His wife was Elizabeth Dircks, a daughter of Dirck Van Eps and Maritje Damens.   After his death, his widow removed to New York, where she died in 1693, being at that time the owner of houses and lands in Schenectady, Albany, Catskill and New York, besides a large amount of personal property

Evert Bancker, the second of the family name in this country, was the oldest son of Gerrit Bancker, and was born in 1665.   His sister, Anna, became the wife of Johannes de Peyster, Mayor of New York   Evert Bancker was a merchant of Albany, and was held in high esteem by his fellow colonists, who elected him to many important offices   He was Justice of the Peace in 1692 and Mayor of Albany 1695-6 and 1707-9   His wife was Elizabeth Abeel, daughter of Stoffer Janse Abeel   He died in 1734, his wife having departed only a few months previously.   The children of Evert and Elizabeth (Abeel) Bancker were Gerardus, Neeltje, Gerardus second, Elizabeth, Gerrit, Lansing, Christopher, Anna, Willem, Jannetje, Adrianus, Gerardus third, Anna second, Johannes, and Johannes second   Three of the sons of this family, Christopher, who was born in 1695, Adrianus and Gerardus, settled in New York, Christopher and his son Christopher, who was born in 1732, being the direct ancestors of Miss Mary E C Bancker   The Bancker homestead stood for many years on the site of the Bank of America in Wall Street   Evert Bancker, the great-grandfather of Miss Bancker, was one of the Committee of One Hundred appointed to govern the City of New York during the Revolution, 1779-1782.   In June, 1776, he and Comfort Sands constituted the committee to make statement to Congress of all the cargoes of vessels in port and of the amount of lead and powder in stock   Afterwards he was a member of the Assembly and Speaker of the House   Gerard Bancker was Treasurer of the State in 1789, and held that office until after 1798.   In 1784, Abraham B Bancker was elected clerk of the State Senate, to succeed Robert Benson, who had been the clerk through six preceding sessions   Abraham B Bancker was also one of the early Regents of the State University

The Banckers owned for many generations a large tract of land in the vicinity of Bancker, afterwards Madison Street, adjoining the Roosevelt property, from which Roosevelt Street received its name.   They were then among the largest land owners in the city   The men of the family were lawyers and merchants, and were often aldermen, when to be an alderman was regarded as one of the greatest civic honors that could be bestowed   In every generation they held seats in the Assembly and the Senate of the State Legislature

Miss Mary E C Bancker is the daughter of the late Josiah Hook Bancker and his wife, Mary Elizabeth Henry, daughter of Michael Henry, a famous New York merchant, born in New York City, in 1784   He was a merchant on Water Street, and afterwards proprietor of the New York Gallery at 100 Broadway, one of the first establishments devoted to the exhibition of paintings and fine arts in New York   The paternal grandfather of Miss Bancker was John Bancker, and her maternal great-grandfather was John Sinclair Henry, a merchant of the eighteenth century, Commissary General of United States Army from 1776 to close of the war, and one of the founders of the New York Stock Exchange.   Miss Bancker makes her home at Englewood, N J.

DAVID BANKS

DAVID BANKS, father of the subject of this sketch, was born in Newark, N J., in 1786 and died in New York in 1871. His early education was outlined with a view to his preparation for the legal profession, and when he was twenty years old he began the study of law in New York in the office of Charles Baldwin, whose partner he afterwards became. He was more thoroughly identified, however, with the business of publishing law books, than he was with active practice at the bar. In 1804, his attention was turned to the pressing need for more and better law books than were then procurable in this country. He formed a partnership with Stephen Gould, under the name of Banks & Gould, thus founding the publishing firm which has now been in existence for very nearly a century, and is the oldest law publishing house in the United States.

Apart from his business, Mr Banks was one of the popular and active men of his day. He took considerable interest in municipal affairs, and held the office of alderman and assistant alderman for nearly ten years, and during part of that time was president of the Board of Aldermen. During the latter years of his life, he was president of the East River Bank. His ancestors were of old Revolutionary stock. David Banks, his father, was a distinguished Revolutionary soldier who fought bravely throughout the entire struggle for independence and was a trusted soldier of General Washington, being one of the party which made that famous winter passage across the Delaware before the battle of Trenton. His uncle was the Right Honorable Sir Joseph Banks, for many years president of the Royal Society of England, and a companion of Captain James Cook on that explorer's first voyage around the world in 1768. He was an eminent patron of literary and philosophical writers, and personally engaged in many important researches in natural history in Newfoundland, Iceland and elsewhere. His expedition to Iceland in company with his friend, Dr. Solander, was one of the most important and fruitful scientific enterprises of the eighteenth century. Sir Joseph Banks was born in 1743, was created a Knight of the Bath in recognition of his services to the cause of science, and died in 1820.

During his long life, David Banks, Sr., was intimately associated with all the great political leaders of his day, numbering among his friends such men as ex-Governors Wright and Marcy, Chancellors Kent and Walworth, Judges Sanford and Samuel Jones, Chief Justice Nelson and President Martin Van Buren. He married early in life Harriet Breneck Lloyd, daughter of Paul B. Lloyd, of the old New York family of that name.

The present Mr. David Banks, his son, was born in New York, December 25th, 1827. He entered the publishing house of his father at an early age, and in time succeeded to the position of head of the establishment. He has been connected with many financial and social institutions, and is a vice-president of the East River National Bank, of which institution his father was the first president. By virtue of his ancestry, he is a member of the Sons of the Revolution and the Sons of Veterans of 1812, while he was the last Captain of the Old City Guard and is an honorary member of the Old Guard. He is also a member of the Society of Colonial Wars, and a commander of the Society of Foreign Wars. His club memberships include the Union, Manhattan, New York, Lawyers', St. Nicholas and City clubs. A devoted yachtsman, he owns the Water Witch and has been commodore of the Atlantic Yacht Club, belonging also to the New York Yacht Club and the Atalanta Boat Club. Naturally a patron of science and literature, he is a member of the American Geographical Society and the American Museum of Natural History, a member of the Council, and also a member of the building, library and law committees of the New York University. His residence is in West Fortieth Street.

The wife of Mr Banks was Lucetta G Plum, daughter of the late Elias Plum, of Troy Their daughter is Lucetta P Banks, and their son David Banks, Jr The latter is a graduate of Columbia University and is engaged in the law publishing business with his father. He is a member of the Calumet and Δ Φ clubs, the St. Nicholas Society, the Society of Colonial Wars and the Sons of the Revolution

THEODORE MELVIN BANTA

UNDER the title, A Frisian Family, Mr. Theodore M Banta has published an interesting account of the family of which he is a representative. The name of Banta is a very ancient one, and in Kemble's The Saxons in England, it is recorded as having been borne as early as 738 A D by a sub-king of Kent. Epke Jacobse Banta was the ancestor of the race in this country, the name of Epke being the Frisian equivalent of Egbert, while Jacobse signifies son of Jacob. This founder of the Banta family in the United States came from Harlingen, a seaport of the Province of Friesland, and arrived in New Netherland, in 1659, in the ship De Trouw, being accompanied by his wife and five sons. Settling near Flushing, Long Island, he removed to Bergen, N. J., ten years later, where, in 1679, he was one of the Judges of Oyer and Terminer.

In 1681 he purchased a large tract in Hackensack, N J, and with his sons was among the earliest settlers in that section. His son Hendrick was one of the deacons of the Dutch Reformed Church in Hackensack, when it was organized in 1616. Cornelius Epke Banta, probably the eldest son of Epke Jacobse, was born in Holland in 1652, his first wife being Jannetje, daughter of Jan De Pre and Jannetje De Ruine, who was baptized in New Amsterdam in 1662. He died in May, 1719.

Jacob Banta was the son of Cornelius Epke Banta by his second wife, Magdalena Demarest, and was born in 1702. His son, Cornelius Banta, who was born May 7th, 1730, and died in 1812, was a Chosen Freeholder for Hackensack township in 1800. By his second wife, Hendrickye Outwater, a daughter of Jacob Outwater, Cornelius Banta had several children, among them the grandfather of Mr. Theodore Melvin Banta, Jacob Banta, who lived in Winkleman, now Bogota, on the east side of the Hackensack river, opposite Hackensack, where he inherited a large amount of land from his father. In 1816 and in 1817, he was a member of the Assembly of the State of New Jersey from Bergen County, and in 1819 was elected Judge of the Court of Common Pleas. He died in 1844. His wife was Wintje, daughter of Jacob H. Zabriskie.

Albert Zabriskie Banta, the father of Mr. Theodore Melvin Banta, was born in Hackensack. He was a manufacturer in New York, and had a large establishment in Catherine Street, near East Broadway, in 1832. In 1837, he removed to Augusta, Ga, where he continued in business, and while there he held a commission as Lieutenant in the Georgia militia. Returning to New York, in 1841, he again engaged in business there until his death, in 1854. The wife of Albert Zabriskie Banta was Sarah Ann Sayre, of Essex County, N J. Her father, Calvin Sayre, was a descendant of Thomas Sayre, who came from Bedfordshire, England, in 1636 to Lynn, Mass, and was one of the founders of the town of Southampton, Long Island, in 1641. The mother of Sarah Ann Sayre was Mary Dickerson, a descendant of Philemon Dickerson, who was also one of the founders of Southold, Long Island, in 1641.

Mr. Theodore Melvin Banta was born in New York, November 23d, 1834. He entered the College of the City of New York at its first session, in 1849, and completed a two-years' course of study. For several years he was engaged as an accountant, and in 1858 took charge of the actuarial work of the New York Life Insurance Company, becoming, in 1863, cashier of that corporation. He belongs to the St Nicholas Society, the Huguenot Society, the New York Historical Society, the Society of Colonial Wars, the Order of the Founders and Patriots of America, the Long Island Historical Society, the Virginia Historical Society, the New York Genealogical and Biographical Society, the American Geographical Society and the Holland Society, of which he has been secretary since 1891. He also belongs to the Reform and Twilight clubs. He is a member of the Baptist Church, and has been president of the Baptist Social Union of Manhattan and treasurer of the Baptist Social Union of Brooklyn. In 1862, he married Cornelia Crane. Mr. and Mrs. Banta have had three children, of whom two daughters, May and Effie Banta, survive and are graduates of Wellesley College.

AMZI LORENZO BARBER

MORE than half a century ago, when the country was stirred to the depths on the slavery question, the trustees of the Lane Theological Seminary, in Cincinnati, O., interdicted the discussion of the subject in that institution. Several of the students, resenting this suppression of free thought and free speech, left the seminary, and journeyed across the State of Ohio to Oberlin College, where such privileges were not denied, and continued their studies there In this band of liberty-loving young men was Amzi Doolittle Barber, who graduated from Oberlin Theological Seminary in 1841, and became a Congregational clergyman, settled for many years in Saxton's River, Windham County, Vt. The great-grandfather of the Reverend Amzi D Barber was Thomas Barber, the elder of three brothers, who came from England before the Revolution. Thomas Barber settled in Vermont, and his descendants have been from that time prominent citizens of the Green Mountain State. Mr Amzi L Barber, son of the Reverend Amzi D. Barber, can trace his lineage to four nationalities. On his father's side, his ancestors were of Scotch and Irish blood, while his mother, who was born Nancy Irene Bailey, of Westmoreland, Oneida County, New York, belonged to a family of English and French origin.

Mr. Amzi Lorenzo Barber was born in Saxton's River, Vt, in June, 1843. His family moved to Ohio when he was a child, and he was educated in the schools and academies of several towns where his father occupied pastorates. He graduated from Oberlin College in 1867, and after a short postgraduate course in the theological department of that institution of learning, went to Washington in 1868, to take charge of the normal department of Howard University, under the direction of General O. O. Howard. Subsequently, he was in charge of the preparatory department, and also professor of natural philosophy in the same institution. He, however, finally turned his attention from letters to business. In 1872, he engaged in the real estate business in Washington; and while thus occupied, the subject of street improvement began to press upon his attention, and he made the construction of asphalt pavements, on a large scale, his occupation, incorporating in 1883 the Barber Asphalt Company He has also been a director of the Citizens' National Bank of Washington, and the Washington Loan & Trust Company.

Despite his business cares, Mr. Barber gives much time to yachting, a pleasure to which he is enthusiastically devoted. He has a steam yacht in commission at New York throughout the season, and makes many cruises in home waters In 1893–94, he made a yachting trip with his family to the Mediterranean and the East He is a member of the Royal Thames Yacht Club of London, and also of the New York, Seawanhaka-Corinthian and Larchmont Yacht clubs His other important clubs include the Metropolitan, the Engineers', the Church, and the Lawyers', for he is a member of the bar, although he has never practiced the profession. He is also a fellow of the American Society of Civil Engineers, a member of the Society of Arts, in London, a patron of the Metropolitan Museum of Art, and the American Museum of Natural History, and a member of the New England Society, the Ohio Society, and the American Geographical Society.

Mr. Barber built Belmont, a beautiful place in Washington; at one time he occupied the Cunard place on Staten Island, and now owns Ardsley Towers, a large country estate in Irvington, once the property of the late Cyrus W. Field. For many years his New York City residence was the Stuart mansion, at Fifth Avenue and Sixty-eighth street, recently sold to the Honorable William C. Whitney. In 1868, Mr. Barber married Celia M Bradley, of Geneva, O, who died in 1870 For his second wife he married Julia Louisa Langdon, daughter of J Le Droict Langdon, formerly of Belmont, N. Y., and a member of the Langdon family, conspicuous in the annals of New York City and State. Mr. and Mrs Barber have had five children, four of whom are living, Le Droict, Lorina, Bertha and Roland Langdon. His eldest son is a member of the New York Club. His eldest daughter, Lorina Langdon Barber, was married at Ardsley Towers, in June, 1897, to Samuel Todd Davis, of Washington.

HENRY ANTHONY BARCLAY

IN the early annals of New York, the name of Barclay is of constant recurrence, and the family's civic fame has been perpetuated in the naming of Barclay Street. Its representatives were of the eminent Scotch race known as de Berkeley, the ancestry of which is traced back to Edward I., King of England, and his Queen, Margaret, daughter of Philip III., of France. They were allied to the Earls of Kent and the Earls of Somerset, and were also descendants of King James of Scotland through the Gordons, Earls of Sutherland.

Colonel David Barclay, of Ury, born in 1610, was a son of David Barclay, laird of Mathers. He served in the Swedish Army as a Major and was commissioned Colonel by King Charles I He was Governor of Strathbogie, and a member of Parliament in 1654-58, but became a Quaker and was imprisoned for his belief. His wife was Catharine Gordon, daughter of Sir Robert Gordon, 1580-1656, of Gordonstown, the second son of the titular Earl of Sutherland, Alexander Gordon. The eldest son of this union was Robert Barclay, one of the proprietors of East New Jersey, and its Governor, an appointment which he held for life by the favor of Charles II. He never came to America, but governed through a deputy. His brother John, who removed to America, married Cornelia Van Schaick and became the ancestor of the New York Barclays. A sister of John Barclay married the son of Sir Evan Dhu Cameron, of Lochiel, and her daughters married the chiefs of such Scotch houses as Cameron of Dungallen, Campbell of Auchlyne, Macgregor of Bohawslie, Grant of Glenmoriston, McPherson of Cluny, and Cameron of Glendinning.

The eldest son of John Barclay was the Reverend Thomas Barclay, a man of great learning and influence in the City of Albany, where he was pastor of the Dutch Church. He married Anna Dorothea Drauyer, who was the daughter of Admiral Andries Drauyer, of the Dutch Navy, and granddaughter of Levinius Van Schaick. Their son, the Reverend Henry Barclay, was born in Albany and graduated from Yale College in 1734 He lived several years in the Mohawk Valley with the Indians, among whom he was a devoted Christian worker. In 1746, he became rector of Trinity Church, New York, and remained there until his death, in 1764. Shortly after coming to New York, he married Mary, the beautiful daughter of Anthony Rutgers. The eldest son of the Reverend Henry Barclay was Colonel Thomas Barclay, who was a Tory in the Revolution. His second son was Anthony Barclay, of Trains Meadow, Newtown, Long Island, who died in 1805, having married Anna Lent, daughter of Abraham Lent, and sister of Judge James Lent. The grandfather of Anna Lent was William Lawrence, of the celebrated New York family of that name. From this union came one son, Henry Barclay, who was born in 1794, married Sarah Moore, and lived until 1865.

Mr. Henry Anthony Barclay, the eldest son of Henry Barclay and Sarah Moore, and present head of this historic family, was born in Astoria, Long Island, December 4th, 1844, and was educated privately He married Clara Oldfield Wright, daughter of John Skinner Wright, of the firm of Wright, Maxwell & Co., and his wife, Isabella Mary Oldfield, daughter of Granville Oldfield. On the paternal side, Mrs Barclay's grandfather was the Honorable Robert Wright, who was the first Democratic Governor of Maryland, in 1806. Mr. and Mrs. Barclay have five children. Their sons, Henry Anthony, Jr., and Wright Barclay, are both members of Company K, of the Seventh Regiment. The three daughters of the family are Gertrude Oldfield, Mildred Moore and Clara Wright Barclay. Mr. Barclay's residence is in Madison Avenue, and he has a country house, Bonnie Brae, at Lenox, Mass. His clubs are the Union and Metropolitan.

The second son of Henry and Sarah (Moore) Barclay is James L. Barclay, who married Olivia Bell, only daughter of Isaac Bell, 1815-1897 She died in 1894 and he married Priscilla (Dixon) Sloan Mr Barclay's youngest brother, Sackett M Barclay, married his cousin, Cornelia Cockrane Barclay, and has five children, Harold, Robert Cockrane, Beatrice W., Ethel N. and Cornelia Barclay, his residence being in West Forty-sixth Street. Mr. Barclay's only sister, Fanny Barclay, married William Constable, of Constableville, N. Y

SAMUEL F. BARGER

OF Dutch origin, the name of Bergen, which was the family name of the American ancestor of Mr Samuel F Barger, signifies hill. It is common in the Netherlands, Germany and Ireland Hans Hansen Bergen, who was the first of the name in this country, was a resident of Holland in the early part of the seventeenth century When Wouter Van Twiller was sent to New Netherland as the second director-general of the Colony in 1633, he brought with him a large company of soldiers, officials and Colonists, and among them was Hans Hansen Bergen Six years after landing in New Amsterdam, this pioneer married Sarah Rapalje, daughter of Joris Jansen Rapalje The father of Sarah Rapalje was a Huguenot who came from Rochelle, France, in 1623, and settled in Fort Orange, Albany After a few years, he moved to Manhattan and thence to Wallabout, on Long Island In 1655, and several times thereafter, he was one of the magistrates of Brooklyn. His wife was Catalyntie Trico Sarah Rapalje became a historical personage from the fact that she was the first Christian female born in New Netherland When she was twenty-nine years of age her husband died and left her a widow with seven children She afterwards married Teunis Gysbert Bogaert, and was thus the ancestress of two of the greatest Dutch Colonial families of New Netherland

Jacob Hansen Bergen, son of the pioneer, was born in 1653 He took the oath of allegiance to the British Government in 1687, and was a constable in 1698 His wife was Elsje Frederiks, daughter of Frederik Lubbertsen and Tryntje Hendricks Their son, Frederick Jacobse Bergen, was the great-great-grandfather of Mr Samuel F Barger He was born in 1681 and died before 1762 In 1715, he was a private in the militia company of Brooklyn, in 1738, was a Lieutenant in the Richmond County militia, and late in life removed to Somerset County, N. J, where he died in 1762. His wife was Gerretye Vechte, daughter of Gerrit Vechte Henry Bergen, son of Hendrick Bergen and grandson of Frederick Jacobse Bergen, was born in 1757, lived on Staten Island and died in 1804 His wife, whom he married in 1783, was Polly, or Mary, Tyson. He changed his family name to Barger, and his descendants have since adhered to that usage Henry Barger, father of Mr Samuel F. Barger, was born in 1797 and died in 1867 He was engaged in mercantile life in New York, and was Colonel of a regiment of artillery in the Counties of Kings and Richmond His wife was Matilda Anna Frost.

Mr Samuel F Barger was born in New York, October 19th 1832. Educated in the Columbia College Grammar School and the University of the City of New York, he practiced law in the office of Aaron S. Pennington, of Paterson, N. J., being admitted to the bar of the State of New Jersey in 1854, and to the bar of the State of New York the following year Early in his professional career, he became a director of the New York Central Railroad Company When the New York Central and the Hudson River Companies were consolidated in 1869, he was retained as a director in the new corporation, and has since devoted himself, both in a business and in a professional way, to the interests of those railroads. He is a member of the executive committee, and chairman of the law committee of the New York Central & Hudson River Railroad Company, is officially connected with other companies of the Vanderbilt system, is a trustee of the Wagner Palace Car Company and of the Union Trust Company, and was for several years a director and member of the executive committee of the Western Union Telegraph Company He has served as a commissioner on the Board of Education of New York City, and was a Presidential elector on the Democratic ticket in 1876

In 1869, Mr Barger married Edna Jeanie Le Favor, of Medway, Mass, of distinguished ancestry, their children are Maud Anna, Edna Holbrook and Milton Sanford Barger His city residence is in Madison Avenue, and his summer home is Edna Villa, in Newport He is a member of the Metropolitan, Manhattan, Union, Knickerbocker, Tuxedo, New York Yacht, Riding and Racquet clubs, the St Nicholas Society, the Metropolitan Museum of Art, the New York Historical Society, the American Geographical Society and the Somerset Club of Boston

MRS. FORDYCE DWIGHT BARKER

MRS EMILY FRANKLIN (BABCOCK) BARKER is the widow of the late Fordyce Dwight Barker, who died in New York in December, 1893, and a daughter of Samuel D Babcock. The Babcock family were closely connected with the Colonial and Revolutionary history of Rhode Island. Mrs Barker's great-great-grandfather was the famous Colonel Henry Babcock, 1733-1800, who was a volunteer on the patriot side at the siege of Boston in 1775, and afterwards became Colonel of the Rhode Island militia, and Commandant of the Rhode Island Colony brigade of troops in the Continental service. Her great-great-great-grandfather was Major-General Joshua Babcock, who also at one time commanded the militia brigade of Rhode Island, was Chief Justice of the Colony, a member of the State Council of War during the Revolution, and several times a member and Speaker of the Rhode Island Assembly. The direct representative of this notable family removed from Stonington to New York, and it was in this city that Mrs. Barker was born and has since resided.

Her marriage with the late Fordyce D Barker took place in 1878. The latter inherited the blood of a number of prominent old New England families He was the son of Fordyce Barker and Elizabeth Lee Dwight.

Fordyce Barker, born in Winton, Me , bore a name which is widely known throughout that State, and which has been that of many men of prominence in its annals He was celebrated as one of the most skilful physicians in New York, being known throughout the United States and Europe as an eminent member of his profession in this country, and as a medical writer of the highest rank

Fordyce D. Barker was born at Norwich, Conn , in 1847, but in the second year of his age was taken to New York, where he resided during the rest of his life. On his father's side, he descended from a family of prominence in Maine and New Hampshire, his great-great-grandfather being Mayor Abiel Abbott, 1741-1809, who raised a body of troops in New Hampshire to reinforce the Continental Army at Ticonderoga. He was a member of the New Hampshire Provincial Congress in 1777, and as an ardent patriot, took a leading and influential part in organizing the Government of the State of New Hampshire, and completing the severance of the former Colony from Great Britain. Mr. Barker's mother, Elizabeth Lee Dwight, was born in Springfield, Mass , her family being one which has occupied many famous political and social position in Massachusetts for many generations, which supplied many famous clergymen, professors and lawyers, and which is connected by ties of blood and intermarriage with many of the illustrious names in the history of the State. Her great-great-grandmother was Mary Pitt, a favorite niece of the great Earl of Chatham. This lady was the mother of Benjamin Lee, of Taunton, England, who, while in the English Navy, was a fellow midshipman with the Duke of Clarence, afterwards King William the Fourth. Among other distinguished ancestors, Mr. Barker also numbered Nathaniel Gorham, one of the delegates from Massachusetts to the Convention, which in 1787 framed the Constitution of the United States, his signature being affixed to the document, in company with that of Rufus King, as representatives of Massachusetts.

Educated at private schools in New York and at Exeter, N H., followed by a course of study at Dresden, Germany, and at Versailles, France, Fordyce D Barker entered the banking profession in this city. After his marriage, he traveled abroad with his wife, and was an active participant in the social life of the city He was, in a moderate degree, a sportsman and a patron of hunting and the turf. At the time of his premature death, he was a member of the Union, Metropolitan, Riding and City Clubs, of the Rockaway Hunt and Coney Island Jockey Clubs, of the Sons of the Revolution and Seventh Regiment Veteran Association, and of Holland Lodge F.A M , and of many other social and benevolent organizations. Two children were born to Mrs Barker and her late husband, Elizabeth Crary Fordyce Barker and Lillian Lee Fordyce Barker. The family residence is at No. 36 West Fifty-first Street.

PETER TOWNSEND BARLOW

IN the early part of the seventeenth century the first Barlow emigrated to this country from England and settled in New England. Descendants of this pioneer have been prominent in the public affairs of that section and many of them have attained to high distinction in the councils of the nation. One of the most illustrious Americans who has borne the name was the Honorable Joel Barlow, who crowded into a long and busy life as much of variety, romance and usefulness as generally falls to the lot of a dozen ordinary men He is best recalled, perhaps, as the author of that remarkable effort in verse, The Columbiad. But he was more than a poet and author. He was a soldier of the Revolution, a Chaplain in the Continental Army, a practicing lawyer, a vigorous journalist, a bookseller, an agent for Western lands and a speculator. Sympathizing with the French Revolutionists, he became a leader in their councils and was made a citizen of the French Republic Some of the most brilliant political pamphlets of that interesting period were from his trenchant pen He served as the United States Consul to Algiers and also as United States Minister to France.

In the generation that is now passing away, Samuel L M. Barlow was a conspicuous figure in New York professional and social circles. He belonged to the Connecticut branch of the family, the same that nearly a century earlier had produced the Honorable Joel Barlow. His father was Dr Samuel Bancroft Barlow, a graduate from Yale College and a physician of high reputation. Dr Barlow practiced his profession in Connecticut for several years immediately following his graduation from Yale College, and then removed to New York. At one time he was president of the New York Homœopathic College.

Samuel L. M. Barlow was born in Granville, Hampden County, Mass., July 5th, 1826. When his father moved to New York City, he was a mere child. After completing his education, he engaged himself as office boy in a law office, where he earned a salary of one dollar a week. Within seven years from the time he started in this small way, he was manager of the firm at an annual salary of three thousand dollars, which was a large sum for those days During that period of seven years, he had attained the age of twenty-three, had studied law and been admitted to the bar. From that time on, his career was one of the most successful in the history of the New York bar. At the age of twenty-three, he settled a claim under the treaty with Mexico, for which he received a very large fee. A claim of two million dollars against the French Government for arms furnished by American manufacturers during the Franco-Prussian War was adjusted by him after about one hour's work, and for that he received twenty-five thousand dollars. He was employed by many railroad companies, and one of his greatest triumphs was in defeating Jay Gould for the control of the Erie Railroad, after which he was a director and the private counsel for that corporation In 1852, he became a member of the firm of Bowdoin, Larocque & Barlow, and afterwards, with Judges W. D Shipman and W G. Choate, organized the firm of Shipman, Barlow, Larocque & Choate. He controlled The New York World, 1864-69, was one of the founders of the Manhattan Club, a discriminating collector of pictures and bric-a-brac and the owner of one of the finest collections of Americana in this country. He died in Glen Cove, Long Island, July 10th, 1889.

Mr Peter Townsend Barlow, son of S. L. M. Barlow, was born in New York, June 21st, 1857 His mother was a daughter of Peter Townsend, after whom he was named. He was graduated from Harvard College in 1879 and studied law in the Law School of Columbia College and in the office of Shipman, Barlow, Larocque & Choate He lives at 55 East Twenty-first Street and his country residence is Tario, in New London, Conn. His club membership includes the Union, University, Harvard, New York Yacht and Racquet clubs and the ·Downtown Association He is also a patron of the Metropolitan Museum of Art. Mr. Barlow married, in 1886, Virginia Louise Matthews, daughter of Edward Matthews. Their children are Edward Matthews and Samuel L. M. Barlow.

JOHN SANFORD BARNES

GENERAL JAMES BARNES, the father of Mr John Sanford Barnes, lawyer and broker, was a distinguished civil engineer and soldier. Born about 1809, he was graduated from West Point in 1829, in the class with Robert E Lee, Joseph E Johnston and O M Mitchell During the seven years that he remained in the army, he was advanced to the rank of Lieutenant in the Fourth Artillery Resigning from the military service, he entered the engineering profession and was chief engineer and superintendent of the Western Railroad of Massachusetts from 1836 to 1848, and chief engineer of the Seaboard & Roanoke Railroad from 1848 to 1852 He was also engaged in the construction of the Rome & Watertown, the Sacketts Harbor & Ellisburg, the Buffalo, Corning & New York, the Terre Haute, Alton & St. Louis and the Potsdam & Watertown Railroads. During the Civil War, General Barnes performed distinguished service Going to the front as Colonel of the Eighteenth Massachusetts Volunteers, he was promoted in 1862 to be Brigadier-General of Volunteers, and took part in the battles of Fredericksburg, Chancellorsville and other contests of the Virginia campaign. At the battle of Gettysburg, he was severely wounded, while in command of the First Division of the Fifth Army Corps He was breveted Major-General of Volunteers in 1865, and mustered out of service the following year with health permanently impaired by wounds and exposure He died in Springfield, Mass., February 12th, 1869.

Mr John Sanford Barnes was born at West Point, May 12th, 1836, entered the Naval Academy at Annapolis, and was graduated in 1854. When the Civil War broke out, he was in the naval service of the United States and served throughout the struggle, being promoted from time to time until he attained the rank of Commander When the war was concluded, he resigned from the service, and prepared himself for professional life by studying law He was admitted to the bar, and practiced in Albany and New York City for a short time, and then became a partner in the banking firm of J S Kennedy & Co , where he was engaged for twelve years, withdrawing from that concern in 1879 After that, he devoted his attention to law business for several years, and then reengaged in banking

In 1862, Mr. Barnes married Susan Bainbridge Hayes, daughter of Captain Thomas Hayes, of the United States Navy. The grandfather of Mrs Barnes was the famous Commodore William Bainbridge, whose ancestors were settled in New Jersey soon after 1600 Sir Arthur Bainbridge, of Durham County, England, was the head of the family in the Old World, from which the New Jersey Bainbridges were descended. The father of Commodore Bainbridge was the sixth in descent from Sir Arthur Bainbridge Commodore Bainbridge is one of the most impressive figures in the naval history of the United States during the first quarter of a century of the republic. He was in the merchant marine at the age of fifteen, captain of a ship at nineteen, commander of a frigate in the wars with Algiers and Tripoli in the early years of the present century, and a prisoner in Tripoli for a year and a half. He was in command of the frigate Constitution in the engagement with and capture of the English frigate Java, and commanded the fleet composed of the Constitution, Essex and Hornet in the War of 1812 in some of the most brilliant episodes of that time. His portrait, painted by Chappel, by order of the City Government, hangs in the City Hall of New York The grandmother of Mrs Barnes was Susan Hyleger, whom Commodore Bainbridge married in 1798 at the Island of St Bartholomew Her grandfather was John Hyleger, of Holland, for many years Governor of St Eustatia

The children of Mr. and Mrs. Barnes are J Sanford Barnes, Jr , James Barnes and Edith S , Charlotte A and Cornelia R. Barnes. The city residence of the family is in East Forty-eighth Street, and the country home is in Lenox, Mass Mr Barnes is a member of the Union League, Metropolitan, Union, University, Knickerbocker, Whist, Riding and Westminster Kennel clubs, the Downtown Association and the New England and American Geographical Societies, and is a patron of the Metropolitan Museum of Art and the American Museum of Natural History.

JOHN CONNER BARRON, M.D.

WOODBRIDGE, N J, was settled in 1665, soon after the Duke of York's grant to Berkely and Carteret by families largely drawn from Connecticut, and was named after the Reverend John Woodbridge, the pastor and magistrate of its New England founders One of the names met most frequently in the early annals of this ancient town is that of Barron, a family of English origin, representatives of which came to the American colonies early in the seventeenth century

Elizeus Barron, it is shown by the records of the town, married Mary Andrews in 1705. John Barron built the church in 1714, and in 1774 Samuel Barron was chairman of the Freeholders of the county, while Ellis Barron was commissioned Captain in the First Middlesex Regiment in 1776 Of the same family were Captain Barron, Fleet Captain under Perry on the lakes ; Thomas Barron, a prominent financier in the early part of the century, and Director of the New Orleans branch of the Bank of the United States, as well as Commodore James Barron, one of the ablest officers in the infant Navy of the United States The attack on his vessel, the Chesapeake, by the British frigate Leopard, in 1807, was among the events which led to the War of 1812. The same occurrence also caused the feud between Barron and Commodore Stephen Decatur. The latter, though Commodore Barron's inferior in rank, was a member of the Naval Court which passed upon his conduct and which harshly sentenced him to suspension from the service. Decatur was particularly active in the matter, and this culminated in the famous duel in 1820, at Bladensburg, between the two officers, in which Decatur was slain. Commodore Barron's grandson, an officer of the United States Navy, adhered to the cause of the South in the Civil War, and was a Commodore in the Confederate States service

Mr John Conner Barron was born at Woodbridge, in 1837, of which town his direct ancestors were all natives. His great-grandfather, Samuel Barron, was a large land owner, and his grandfather, Joseph Barron, was prominent in the church at Woodbridge. Mr. Barron's father, John Barron, married a lady belonging to one of the oldest Revolutionary families on Staten Island, Mary Conner, daughter of Colonel Richard Conner and his wife, Mary Claussen. Colonel Conner was a member for Richmond County of the New York Provincial Congress of 1775, and took a prominent and patriotic part in the ensuing struggle

Educated at Burlington College, New Jersey, and at Yale (class of 1858), Dr Barron, who had entered the Medical Department of Yale College during his senior year, graduated in 1861 from the New York College of Physicians and Surgeons with the degree of M D In 1869 he married Harriet Mulford Williams, of Clinton, N. J , daughter of the Reverend Albert Williams, a direct descendant of Roger Williams, the founder of Rhode Island Mrs. Barron's great-grandfather was a lieutenant in the Second Regiment of the New Jersey Line during the Revolution, and served in all of Washington's campaigns. The issue of the Barron-Williams marriage are five children, Thomas, May, Carlile Norris, John Conner and Ellis Barron The family residence is Barron Court, a mansion and estate of fifty acres at Tarrytown-on-Hudson.

Foreign travel, society, literature and yachting have claimed Dr. Barron's attention rather than his profession. He has journeyed in Europe and the East, and is a member of the Union and Union League Clubs, a life member of the New York Historical Society, and a life Fellow of the New York Geographical Society. He was a box owner of the original Metropolitan Opera House. Belonging to the Jekyl Island, Currituck, and Narrows Island Shooting Clubs, he has been most active in the New York Yacht Club and the Seawanhaka Corinthian Yacht Club He sailed and owned the Wave, the match of which against the Scotch cutter Madge inaugurated international cutter racing, while he also built the Athlon, and owned the famous English cutter Clara. The arms of the Barron family, which Dr. Barron inherits and bears, are: A red shield with a gold chevron and three golden sheaves, the crest being an eagle and the motto *"Fortuna juvat Audaces "*

JOHN OLMSTED BARTHOLOMEW

ONE of the ancient families in England is that of Bartholomew. Its history is traced back to the early centuries, and before that there were branches existing in France. The American family is descended from that branch which was settled in Burford, England, whose arms, as they appear on tombs in the Bartholomew Chapel, are Argent, a chevron engrailed between three lions, rampant, sable. About the middle of the sixteenth century, three Bartholomews were living in Warborough, Oxfordshire. One of them, William Bartholomew, the immediate ancestor of the American Bartholomews, was born in Warborough in 1557 and died in 1634 He was a large wholesale dealer in silks and woolens, and accumulated a considerable property, so that he was a man of wealth for those days. His wife was Friswede Metcalf, daughter of William Metcalf, who was at one time Mayor of New Woodstock She died in 1647

The first Bartholomew to come to this country was William, the second son of William and Friswede Bartholomew. He was born in 1602, and received a good education in the grammar school of his native place His wife, whom he married before coming here, was Anna Lord, a sister of Robert Lord. He arrived in Boston in 1634, and immediately took a foremost position in the Colony, being admitted as a freeman of Boston the same year that he landed. A year later he went to live in Ipswich, and represented that town in the Great and General Court In 1637, he was called upon to serve upon a special grand jury in Boston. He was town clerk of Ipswich in 1639, a deputy in 1641, 1647 and 1650, and treasurer of the town in 1654. He died in 1680

In the second American generation, William Bartholomew, who was born in Ipswich in 1640, also took a leading part in the direction of affairs in the Colony. In 1663, he was in Medfield, and was living in Deerfield in 1678. Eleven years after he was an ensign in the New Roxbury, Conn., company of militia, and became Lieutenant of the company in 1691. He was a representative to the General Court from Woodstock in 1692, Woodstock being the new name of New Roxbury, of which place he was then a resident. He died in 1697. The wife of this William Bartholomew was Mary Johnson, daughter of Captain Isaac and Elizabeth (Porter) Johnson. Her grandfather was John Johnson, surveyor of the King's Army in America

In the succeeding four generations the ancestors of Mr John O. Bartholomew were Andrew Bartholomew, who was born in 1670, and died soon after 1752, and his wife, Hannah, daughter of Samuel Frisbie, of Branford; Joseph Bartholomew, who was born in Branford in 1712 and died in 1781, and his wife, Mary Sexton, of Wallingford; Ira Bartholomew, who was born in 1753 and died in 1828, and his wife, Caroline Shattuck; and Sherman Bartholomew, who was born in Wallingford in 1781 and died in 1814, and his wife, Sally Hackley Andrew Bartholomew was a prominent man in Branford. Joseph Bartholomew commanded all those who were subject to military duty in the town Ira Bartholomew was the first of his family to leave Connecticut, going to Cornwall, N. Y., then to Salisbury, and finally to Waterville, where he died. Sherman Bartholomew was a physician in Brownsville, Jefferson County, N Y. In the War of 1812, he was a surgeon in the Federal Army, and falling sick at Sackett's Harbor, died there He was the grandfather of the subject of this sketch Dr Erasmus Darwin Bartholomew, the father of Mr John Olmsted Bartholomew, was the son of Dr. Sherman Bartholomew He was born in Waterville, N Y, in 1804, studied medicine and had an extensive practice in the western part of the State His wife, whom he married in 1826, was Mary Seline Brewster, a descendant of the Pilgrim elder, William Brewster Dr Bartholomew died in 1836, and his widow survived him for forty-four years, dying in 1880

Mr. John Olmsted Bartholomew, the eldest son of Dr. Erasmus Darwin Bartholomew, was born in Denmark, Lewis County, N Y, February 10th, 1827. He came to New York early in life, and has since been a resident of this city, first being engaged in the British importing business, and later as a member of a banking firm in Wall Street. He is a member of the Metropolitan and Union clubs

EDMUND LINCOLN BAYLIES

IN the middle name of Mr Edmund Lincoln Baylies the connection of his ancestors with one of the most famous soldiers of the Revolutionary War and a participation in some of the most glorious events of that patriotic struggle are commemorated. His great-grandfather, Hodijah Baylies, of Massachusetts, was an officer in the Continental Army, serving from the beginning to the close of the war. He was a member of the staff of General Benjamin Lincoln, and fought at the siege of Charleston and again at the capitulation of Yorktown, where his commander was deputed by Washington to receive the sword of Lord Cornwallis.

General Lincoln's family was of English extraction and his ancestors were among the earliest settlers of New England From one of its branches President Abraham Lincoln descended, while another branch produced Levi Lincoln, 1749–1820, one of the leading Revolutionary patriots and lawyers of Massachusetts, and his equally famous son, Governor Levi Lincoln, 1782–1868, who was foremost among the statesmen of the early part of this century. General Benjamin Lincoln was born in Hingham, Mass , in 1733 ; was a member of the Colonial Assembly, and as Colonel of the militia was active in organizing troops at the outbreak of the Revolution, and in the siege of Boston; he became a Major-General in 1776 and served throughout the war, being wounded at Bemis Heights, in the Saratoga campaign, while acting as second in command under General Gates. He was in command of the Southern Department and became Secretary of War under the Confederation from 1781 to 1784 ; suppressed the famous Shay's Rebellion in Massachusetts; was Lieutenant-Governor of the State in 1787, and held many offices of prominence, including that of Commissioner to various Indian tribes. Before his death, in 1810, his daughter Elizabeth became the wife of Colonel Baylies, soon after the end of the Revolutionary War In 1782, Colonel Baylies was selected by Washington as aide-de-camp. After the war he occupied various civil positions of prominence, including that of Collector of the Port of Dighton, Mass. In 1810, he became Judge of Probate for Bristol County, Mass , which office he occupied till 1834

His son, Edmund Baylies, was born in Hingham, Mass., in 1787, and married Elizabeth Payson, of Charlestown, Mass Their son, Edmund Lincoln Baylies, Sr., was born in Boston, Mass , in 1829, and married Nathalie E Ray, of the notable New York family of that name, which has given a number of distinguished men to the city and State.

Mr. Edmund Lincoln Baylies, their son, thus combines in his ancestry families of the highest consideration in both this State and New England. He was born in New York in 1857 and graduated A. B. from Harvard University in the class of 1879, receiving the degree of LL. B. from the same institution in 1882, his legal training being supplemented by a course in Columbia College in this city. He has pursued the practice of law with energy and success, being a member of the firm of Carter & Ledyard.

By his marriage in 1887, Mr. Baylies became connected with one of the very foremost of the old families of New York, if not of the country at large. His wife was Louisa Van Rensselaer, a direct descendant of the original patroon of Rensselaerwyck. The founder of the Colony, it is well known, was Kiliaen Van Rensselaer, a rich merchant of Amsterdam, who, in 1630, obtained from the Dutch West India Company, lords of New Netherland, and from the States General, the grant of an enormous tract of land composing nearly all of the present counties of Albany and Rensselaer. This was erected into a manor with feudal rights and remained as such under the rule of the successive patroons down to the Revolution, when the manorial privileges were abolished The original Kiliaen Van Rensselaer never visited his transatlantic estates, but his sons came here and from them descended a numerous family connection. Taking an active interest in society, Mr Baylies was one of the Patriarchs and, among other clubs, belongs to the University, City and Knickerbocker. His residence is in West Thirty-sixth Street.

GERARD BEEKMAN

AMONG the honored family names of this country none has stood higher than that of Beekman. It is also one of the oldest, the founder of the American branch of the family having made his advent on these shores in 1647. Its representatives in both the Netherlands and Germany had gained distinction in war and peace as far back as the thirteenth century. In those countries, they were of titled rank, and ancient records show that the heads of the family were often sent upon embassies, or were called upon as representatives of the State to entertain dignitaries from other countries

A characteristic which has been transmitted to the American bearers of the Beekman name is a religious temperament and courage in the assertion of their convictions For two hundred and fifty years these traits have appeared in the successive generations of the New York Beekman family In the various professional occupations, bearers of the name have stood in the forefront, while they have consistently evinced a philanthropic spirit and as citizens have shown a patriotic devotion that has won public acknowledgment Socially they have been true to the obligations of their origin, and have become allied by marriage with the leading families of the Middle and New England States

Wilhelmus Beekman came to New Amsterdam in the year mentioned above, with Director General Peter Stuyvesant, as treasurer of the Dutch West India Company He also became Vice-Governor of the Dutch Colony upon the South or Delaware River, and afterwards filled many offices, including those of Vice-Governor at Esopus, now Kingston, alderman of New York and Deputy Governor In some of these or other equally honorable offices, his sons and grandsons also served with public approval Soon after his arrival he married an heiress and in the course of time increased his possessions by obtaining large grants of land from the Dutch Government He resided for many years near the East River, at the intersection of Pearl and Beekman Streets As the city extended, he removed to the northward, to what was termed "the Hook." His great grandsons went even further north on the island. James, one of them, purchased in 1762 a country place near Turtle Bay, at the present Fiftieth Street, and two of his brothers settled half a mile beyond that point The Beekmans have always been large landholders in New York, and it is of interest to note their preference for a water view in connection with the estates upon which they established their homes

Of the numerous descendants of Wilhelmus Beekman, none observed the injunction contained in his last will and testament, to remember that "A good name is more to be desired than great riches," more than James William Beekman the elder, father of the gentleman whose name heads this article He was the son of Gerard Beekman and descended, in the sixth generation, from the family's founder His aim in life was to do good, devoting time and means to the acquisition of such knowledge as would benefit his fellow men Much of the intelligent labor of his life was given to hospitals and their improvement, and the result of his investigations were embodied from time to time in reports and addresses for general circulation His last illness, in 1877, was caused by too close attention to such duties as a governor of the New York Hospital. He was long an eminent member of the bar, and married Abian Steele Milledolar

His two sons, Mr Gerard Beekman and Mr James William Beekman, have continued the work which interested their father The former is, like his father, a graduate of Columbia College, and has been for some years one of its trustees The latter graduated from Columbia Law School, and was admitted to the bar in 1871, but devotes much attention to charitable institutions, being a trustee of the New York Hospital and officially identified with other similar organizations. Both brothers are connected with the principal social clubs and patriotic societies Mr. James William Beekman, among other distinctions, was made a Knight of the Order of Orange Nassau, by the Queen Regent of the Netherlands, in recognition of his services to the officers of the Dutch man-of-war Van Speijk during the Columbian Naval Review in 1893.

MILO MERRICK BELDING

THE Belding family is old as well as influential. The first of the name to come to this country was William Belding, who settled in Wethersfield, Conn, about 1640. His descendants scattered throughout the Connecticut River Valley, and many of them found their way northward into the State of Massachusetts. That branch of the family from which the present Mr Belding is descended was settled in the Berkshire hills of Massachusetts long before the Revolution. Mr Belding's great-grandfather was Samuel Belding, and his grandfather, John Belding, was a Revolutionary soldier. His father, Hiram Belding, of Ashfield, Mass, was a prosperous farmer and country merchant, and also taught school. On his farm was built the first house erected in Ashfield, the old homestead being still preserved.

Mr Milo Merrick Belding was born in Ashfield, April 3d, 1833. He was educated in the village school, and then attended the Shelburne Falls Academy in the winter and worked on the farm in the summer. When he was only seventeen years of age, he began to devote himself to business, and after a time went into the employ of a firm in Pittsfield, Mass, where he remained until 1858. Then he started independently, and in a few years became one of the prosperous young merchants of Western Massachusetts. His father and two brothers had removed to Michigan in 1858, and Mr Belding commenced sending them invoices of silk. From this small beginning began the business which in five years culminated in the establishment of a house in Chicago, and two years later a branch in New York City. In 1866, the firm started a silk mill in Rockville, Conn, and in 1874 built a larger mill in Northampton, Mass. Later on, their growing business led to the establishment of another mill in Belding, Mich, a village which they founded. They now own five mills in different parts of the country, and have offices in New York, Boston, St. Louis, Cincinnati, Philadelphia, Chicago, St. Paul, San Francisco and Baltimore, employing in the manufacture and sale of their goods over three thousand people. The village of Belding, Mich., covers nine hundred acres of land, and is now a town of over five thousand inhabitants. It has ten mills, several other manufacturing establishments, and all the accessories of a prosperous community. It is a monument to the enterprise and public spirit of the family which established it, and from which it takes its name.

Mr Belding is actively interested in other enterprises besides that with which his name has become most prominently connected. He is the president of the Livonia Salt and Mining Company, of Livonia, and president of the St Lawrence Marble Company, which owns extensive quarries in Gouverneur, N. Y. Some years ago, he became interested in mining and lumber, and is now a large owner of mining and timber interests in North Carolina and Tennessee, industries which, under his direction, have developed into large and profitable proportions. He also has large ranch properties in Montana. In financial enterprises, he has also taken an active part, being one of the organizers and the first president of the Commonwealth Fire Insurance Company, and president of the American Union Life Insurance Company.

In 1858, Mr Belding married Emily C Leonard, daughter of William Leonard, of Ashfield, Mass, a descendant from Noadiah Leonard, of Sunderland, Mass, who was a Captain in the Revolutionary Army, and fought at Bunker Hill. The mother of Mrs Belding was Almira A. Day, who came of an old Colonial family of New England. Mr. and Mrs. Belding live in West Seventy-second Street, near Central Park. They have one son, Milo M. Belding, Jr, who married Anne Kirk, daughter of Daniel Kirk, of Belfast, Ireland, and is in business with his father. Mr. Belding belongs to the Chamber of Commerce, the Sons of the Revolution, the American Geographical Society, the Order of the Founders and Patriots of America, and the Silk Association. His clubs are the Colonial and Merchants' Central. Milo M. Belding, Jr, is a member of the Chamber of Commerce, and belongs to the Union League, New York Athletic, Montauk, Marine and Field, and Merchants' Central clubs. The country residence of the family is at the ancestral home, in Ashfield, Mass.

ROBERT LENOX BELKNAP

BORN in New York, July 23d, 1848, Mr Belknap was a representative of several of the oldest American families. He was directly descended from Abraham Belknap, who died in 1643, one of the earliest settlers of Salem, Mass, and from Joseph Belknap, 1630-1712, one of the founders of the old South Church in Boston. Joseph Belknap's grandson, Samuel Belknap, 1707-1771, of Woburn, Mass., sold his Massachusetts estate in 1751, and removed to Newburg, N. Y., where he purchased nearly the whole of a tract called the Baird patent. Abel Belknap, 1739-1804, son of Samuel, was a member of the County Committee during the Revolutionary War. His son, Aaron Belknap, 1789-1847, was a distinguished lawyer, and married his cousin, a daughter of Samuel Belknap, Captain of the Massachusetts provincial troops, and afterwards a member of the State Legislature.

Their son, Aaron Betts Belknap, 1816-1880, was, like his father, a lawyer of high distinction. He was also a leader in the Presbyterian Church, and was connected with many public and charitable institutions—among them the Princeton Theological Seminary, the Lenox Library, the Presbyterian Hospital, the Port Society and others. He married Jennet Lenox Maitland, daughter of Robert Maitland, 1768-1848, and his wife, Elizabeth Sproat Lenox. The Maitlands come of ancient Scotch lineage, tracing their descent to Sir Robert Maitland of Thirlstane, Knight, who died in 1434. The Lenoxes, also of old and honorable Scotch origin, are another of New York's foremost families, one of its representatives being the founder of the Lenox Library, now merged in the New York Public Library, Astor, Lenox and Tilden Foundations.

Mr. Robert Lenox Belknap, their son, was educated at Columbia College, receiving the degrees of A B in 1869 and of A M. in 1872 Entering upon a business career, he speedily displayed marked abilities in the conduct of large enterprises. His first achievement was his active share in the completion of the Northern Pacific Railroad, of which he was treasurer from 1879 to 1888. He contributed largely to the opening up of the great Northwest by the prominent part he took in the development of the lake ports at the head of Lake Superior. The National Guard movement owed much to Mr. Belknap's disinterested efforts. Entering the Seventh Regiment, in 1866, after being president of his company for several years, he became Lieutenant-Colonel and Chief-of-Staff of the First Brigade. After four more years' service he resigned his active commission, receiving the brevet rank of Colonel. In 1875, having been detailed as Acting Assistant Inspector-General, he made many of the inspections and reports which inaugurated the reforms that have made a new era in National Guard affairs. Mr. Belknap also devoted much time to charitable, philanthropic and educational work. For twelve years he served as treasurer of the Presbyterian Hospital He was a trustee of the Princeton Theological Seminary, a member of the Church Extension Committee of the Presbytery of New York, and treasurer of the Lying-in Hospital

He was one of the founders of the Phi Beta Kappa Chapter at Columbia College, and was for two years president of the Psi Upsilon Club. He was also a member of the Union, Union League, University, Down Town, New York Yacht and Seawanhaka Yacht Clubs of New York, besides the Minnesota Club of St Paul, the Kitchi Gammi Club of Duluth, and the Superior Club of Superior ; a member and manager of the New York Society of the Sons of the Revolution, and a hereditary member of the Society of Cincinnati, and of the Society of the Colonial Wars.

Mr. Belknap married, in 1870, Mary Phœnix Remsen, daughter of Henry Rutgers Remsen and his wife, Elizabeth Waldron Phœnix, both of whom represented old New York families He died March 13th, 1896, at his residence in New York city. His widow and six children survived him. On January 25th, 1897, his eldest son, Robert Lenox Belknap, Jr., died The remaining children are Waldron Phœnix, Mary Remsen, Jennet Maitland, who is the wife of Robert McAllister Lloyd, Elizabeth and Maitland Belknap.

ISAAC BELL

REPRESENTATIVES of the Bell family were among the first settlers of this country in the early part of the seventeenth century. Isaac Bell, the progenitor of the New York branch, came to America from Edinburgh in 1640, and settled in Connecticut. He purchased a tract of land eight miles square from the Indians, and soon became a prosperous and influential man One of his descendants was James Bell, the great-grandfather of the subject of this sketch James Bell, who was born in 1709, owned property near Stamford, Conn By his wife, Sarah, he had five sons. James, born in 1734; Isaac, 1736, Jacob, 1738 ; Jesse, 1746, and Jared, 1755 His son, Isaac Bell, 1736-1809, the ancestor of the New York Bells, married Hannah Holley, and their daughter, Hannah Bell, married Fitch Rogers, son of Samuel Rogers, of Norwalk, Conn The second wife of Isaac Bell, the second of the name, was Susannah Smith, who died in 1807, and who was a daughter of Ephraim Smith, of Stamford. Adhering to the Royal cause at the time of the Revolution, Isaac Bell and his wife, like other Loyalists, suffered many losses, their property being confiscated and much of it destroyed He owned several mills in Stamford and was also a large shipping merchant in New York. Leaving his possessions in Connecticut, he came within the British lines in New York, and, in 1783, took his family to St John, New Brunswick, where they remained for several years He was annually elected Chamberlain of the city, as long as he remained in that Province

The children of Isaac and Susannah (Smith) Bell were James Bell, who died in Frederickton, New Brunswick, Henry Bell, 1765-1773, who was accidentally killed in New York, and was buried in Trinity Churchyard; Isaac Bell, who was born in 1768, and Catharine Bell, who was born in 1770 and married Nehemiah Rogers, a brother of Fitch Rogers

Isaac Bell, third of the name and father of the subject of this sketch, was born in Stamford, Conn , being the third son of Isaac and Susannah (Smith) Bell His boyhood was spent in New York during the British occupation of the city He married, in 1810, Mary Ellis, daughter of John Ellis, 1754-1812, and Marie Faugeres, 1767-1846 The father of Mary Ellis was a native of Yorkshire, England, and came to this country in 1783 Her mother was a daughter of Dr Lewis Faugeres and Evana, or Eve, Remsen, of New Lots, Long Island Dr. Faugères was born in Limoges, France, in 1731, and was the son of Francis Faugeres, a surgeon in the French Navy He was brought to New York in 1756, a prisoner of war, and remained permanently in this country thereafter. His mother was Magdalen Bertrand, of a noble French family. His wife, Eve Remsen, was a daughter of Jacob Remsen, a merchant of Brooklyn, by his wife, Maria Voorhies, of Gravesend. Her grandparents were Rem Remsen, 1652-1742, of New Lots and Flatbush, and Marratie Janse Van Der Bilt, of Flatbush, who was a daughter of Jan Aertsen Van Der Bilt, the ancestor of the Vanderbilt family.

The sons of Isaac and Mary (Ellis) Bell were John Ellis, who died in 1837; James Henry, Isaac, Mary Ellis and Edward R Bell. James Henry Bell, who died in 1851 in Philadelphia, before he had attained the age of forty, was an accomplished civil engineer, and before he reached his majority, was chief engineer of five railroads The only daughter of the family, Mary Ellis Bell, married Henry Farnum, of Philadelphia The youngest son, Edward R Bell, was educated as a civil engineer, and in 1836 was engaged on a survey for the first railroad in Ohio In 1837-38, he was in Michigan, and was afterwards employed upon the boundary survey between the United States and Great Britain under the Ashburton treaty. He now resides in New York and has two sons, Gordon Knox and Bertrand Faugères Bell.

Isaac Bell, the third son of Isaac and Mary (Ellis) Bell, and the fourth to bear that name in America, was the head of this historic family for more than half a century and passed away, ripe in years and rich in the affection of his fellow citizens, on September 30th, 1897 Mr Bell was born August 4th, 1815, in New York Receiving a business training in early life, he went South in 1836 and engaged in the cotton trade His interest in public affairs began while he was living in Mobile, Ala He was on the staff of the Governor of Alabama, with the rank of Captain, and was elected a member of the Alabama Legislature In 1856, he returned to New York, and during the rest of his life made his home here. His wealth, his business training and his public spirit made him one of the prominent citizens of the metropolis, and for thirty-five years he devoted a large portion of his time to municipal affairs. He was a Democrat and a member of Tammany Hall, and his first public service was as a member of the Board of Supervisors Afterwards he became one of the ten governors of the Almshouse, a position he held until that municipal department was succeeded by the Department of Charities and Corrections, of which he was one of the first commissioners, and the president of the board from 1860 to 1873 He was also a member of the Board of Education and Commissioner of Immigration Largely by his efforts the Normal College was established, and for many years he was chairman of its executive committee. He was the founder of the Bellevue Medical College, and for thirty years president of its board of trustees It was due to him that the schoolship under control of the Department of Charities and Corrections and the Department of Education was put into service

In 1863, with Paul S. Forbes and Leonard Jerome, Mr Bell organized the Riot Relief Fund for the police of the city, and for many years was its financial manager Nominations for Mayor and Member of Congress were frequently offered to him, but were invariably declined. During the Civil War, he was one of the most devoted supporters of the Union cause. He was associated with William M. Evarts, Alexander T. Stewart, John Jacob Astor, William E Dodge, Hamilton Fish and others in the organization of the Union Defense Committee of the State of New York, and became its vice-chairman and one of its most untiring officials He was the owner of the steamships Arago and Fulton, which were used as transports during the war, and afterwards were included in the fleet of the New York & Havre Steam Packet Company, of which he was president The Old Dominion Steamship Company was organized by him in 1866, and he was vice-president of that corporation for twenty-two years and a prominent director of the Farmers' Loan & Trust Company, while he was also actively interested in other financial institutions

In the social world, Mr. Bell was not less conspicuous than in public affairs At the time of his death he was the third oldest member of the Union Club, was one of the founders of the Manhattan Club, a member of other leading social organizations and of the Metropolitan Museum of Art and American Museum of Natural History His wife, whom he married in 1844, was Adelaide Mott, daughter of the famous surgeon, the elder Dr. Valentine Mott Mrs Bell, who survives her husband, is descended from Adam Mott, of Hempstead, Long Island, the American pioneer of the name. She was educated in France, where she enjoyed the intimate acquaintance of members of the Orleans family. Four children were born to Mr. and Mrs. Bell The eldest son was the Honorable Isaac Bell, who was born in New York in 1846 He had a short and successful business career, being principally engaged in the cotton trade in the years following the close of the Civil War In 1878, he married Jeanette Bennett, daughter of James Gorden Bennett, founder of The New York Herald In 1885, President Grover Cleveland appointed him United States Minister to the Netherlands, and in that position he acquitted himself with dignity and honor to his country In 1888, he was a delegate to the National Democratic Convention in St Louis When he died, in 1889, he left three children, one son and two daughters His son inherited the family name of Isaac. The second son of Isaac and Adelaide (Mott) Bell is Louis V Bell, a leading member of the New York Stock Exchange, who belongs to the Metropolitan, Union, Meadow Brook Hunt, Manhattan, Riding and Seawanhaka Yacht clubs The third son of this family is the Honorable Edward Bell, who is a member of the Stock Exchange. He married Helen A Wilmerding, daughter of Henry A Wilmerding; lives in Lexington Avenue, and has a country residence in Southampton, Long Island He has been a member of the Board of Park Commissioners and also a member of the Board of Education and succeeded his father as custodian of the Riot Relief Fund His clubs include the Metropolitan, Union, Manhattan, Democratic and Shinnecock Golf and the Downtown Association The only daughter of Mr. and Mrs Isaac Bell was Olivia Bell, who married James L Barclay and died in 1894.

PERRY BELMONT

FOR more than fifty years, the late August Belmont was a conspicuous figure in the political and financial history of our country and in its social development. In the present generation, his sons inherit his force of character, and exhibit the same traits that made him famous The family name has thus become distinctly American, though August Belmont was born, in 1816, at Alzey, in the Rhenish Palatinate, where, for several centuries, his ancestors were people of wealth, and where, at the present day, representatives of the name occupy the same position His grandfather, A. J. Belmont, and his father, Simon Belmont, were landed proprietors, and his uncle, Joseph Florian Belmont, was a man of great influence. The latter's daughter, Anna, became the wife of the German statesman, Louis Bamberger.

Educated at first with a view to the law, August Belmont was at an early age placed in the banking house of the Rothschilds, in Frankfort, and was for a time in their Naples establishment. In 1837, he came to New York as representative of the Rothschilds, and founded the banking firm which, bearing his name, has now had an honorable history for sixty years. For the rest of his life, Mr. Belmont was a power in the American financial world, but nothing was more conspicuous in his character than his conservatism and his avoidance of speculative ventures.

He became an American citizen soon after arriving in New York, and thenceforward no native of the United States exhibited more patriotic devotion to its interests. In this he set an example to other prominent men of his day, who were inclined to hold aloof from participation in politics Mr. Belmont, however, considered it a duty he owed to his adopted land, and became prominent in the Democratic party. The only public office he accepted was the post of Minister to the Netherlands, which he held under President Pierce. He effected important negotiations between the United States and Holland, and received the special thanks of the Department of State. From 1860 to 1872, he was chairman of the Democratic National Committee. While the Civil War was in progress, he supported the Government effectively, and visited Europe on confidential financial missions, receiving the thanks of President Lincoln for his services and advice. In another direction, August Belmont left a strong impression of his personality. Coming from the capitals of Europe and familiar with their social life, his example was most beneficial in New York, and his tastes for the letters, for art and for music, as well as for country life and gentlemanly sports, were an important part of the influence he always exerted. His love for outdoor recreation revealed to Americans the necessity of such relaxation. He was one of the first patrons of the turf in America, his interest in it being as an amusement only, and was for twenty years the president of the American Jockey Club. He married the beautiful daughter of Commodore Matthew C Perry, U. S. N , and dying in 1890, left three sons, Perry Belmont, August Belmont, Jr , and Oliver H P. Belmont, and a daughter, Frederika, who is Mrs. Samuel S. Howland.

On their mother's side, Mr. Belmont's children are descended from Edmund Perry, a Quaker, who came from Devonshire, England, to Sandwich, Mass. In 1676, he was fined for a "railing" written against the magistrate of Plymouth, and retired to Rhode Island. Christopher Raymond Perry, 1761-1818, the fifth in descent from Edmund, was born at Newport, R. I., and was an officer of the Continental Navy. His wife was Sarah Alexander, a native of Newry, County Down, Ireland, whom he met while a prisoner of war at that place. The five sons of Captain Perry all distinguished themselves in the navy of the United States. One daughter, Sarah Wallace Perry, married Captain George W. Rogers, U S N., and another, Jane Tweedy Perry, became the wife of Dr. William Butler, of the navy, and was the mother of Senator Matthew C. Butler, of South Carolina. Commodore Oliver Hazard Perry, 1785-1819, one of the sons of Captain Perry, lives in American History through his victory on Lake Erie in 1813.

Matthew Calbraith Perry, a younger brother, was born in Newport in 1794, and served in the navy during the War of 1812 under his brother. From 1833 to 1843, he was commandant at the Brooklyn Navy yard and devoted himself so assiduously to the study of his profession that he earned the title of "Chief Educator in the United States Navy" He also advocated the adoption of steam power for men of war, and from 1838 to 1840 commanded the first steam vessel in our navy—the Fulton II. Attaining the rank of Commodore, he commanded various squadrons and took part in the naval operations of the Mexican War. He was at the head of the American expedition to Japan, and negotiated the famous treaty of March 21st, 1854, which opened that empire to civilization. He died at New York in 1858, his services being commemorated by a statue in Touro Park, Newport, a bust at Albany, and other memorials His wife, Mrs. Belmont's mother, was Miss Slidell, a sister of the Honorable John Slidell, Senator from Louisiana prior to the war. He, with his fellow Confederate Commissioner to England, Mr. Mason, were the central figures in the Trent affair in 1861. Through the relationship with the Slidell family, General Ronald McKensie, U. S A., was a cousin to the Messrs. Belmont.

In the eldest sons of August Belmont are found all the strong traits of character of the Belmonts and Perrys, determination, energy, patriotism, a keen sense of right and wrong, and fearlessness in their convictions. The Honorable Perry Belmont, the eldest son, was born in New York, December 26th, 1851, and graduated at Harvard in 1872, taking special honors in history and political economy He then studied civil law in the University of Berlin, and, graduating from the law school of Columbia College in 1876, entered into a law partnership with Dudley Vinton and George Frelinghuysen. Mr. Belmont has been professionally engaged in important litigation before the higher courts, and, in 1880, argued, in the Supreme Court of the United States, the constitutional points in the well-known Pensacola Telegraph case, the decision of which was in favor of his clients. He is not a member of the firm of August Belmont & Co. Sharing his father's belief as to the duty of a citizen, Mr. Belmont has taken an active part in public life and lent his efforts toward the success of Democratic principles. He was elected to Congress in 1880 from the First New York District, and was re-elected three times, serving during four successive terms. He had a brilliant career in Congress and won a national reputation, opposing nefarious legislation and supporting all measures for the benefit of the people. He was a zealous advocate of tariff reform and was also prominent in constructive legislation, securing the passage of useful measures. During his last four years in Congress, he was head of the House Committee on Foreign Affairs, one of the most important chairmanships. He was a forcible debator, and is also a public speaker of ability, while he has been a prominent figure in the conventions of his party. In 1882, the delegates of his own district pressed his name for the Democratic nomination for Governor of New York, an honor which he declined In 1888, President Cleveland appointed Mr. Belmont Minister to Spain.

Among the incidents of his public life he received the Cross of Commander of the Legion of Honor from the French Government for his efforts to secure the co-operation of the United States in the last Paris International Exhibition, at a critical moment, when the monarchical governments of Europe had officially declined anything more than commercial co-operation, withholding official recognition on account of the political aspect of that exhibition, held to celebrate the triumph of the revolution of 1789, and the establishment of the French republican form of government.

August Belmont, second of the name and the second son of the family, was born in 1854, and graduated at Harvard in 1874. He was trained in business under his father's eye and in the latter's banking office, succeeding to the senior partnership in the establishment on the death of August Belmont, Sr. He has shown great ability as a financier and has carried out many large monetary transactions. He was prominently identified with the syndicate of 1895, which subscribed for a large issue of Government bonds and thus assured the ability of the Government to continue specie payments. In 1881, he married Bessie Hamilton Morgan, and has three sons, August, Jr., Raymond and Morgan. He displays a fondness for the turf as a recreation for his leisure hours, and has done much for its welfare, his position in this connection resembling that which his father occupied He is chairman of the Jockey Club and was appointed chairman of the State Racing Commission by Governor Morton

GEORGE HOFFMAN BEND

O N the maternal side, this gentleman's ancestors belong to the famous New York Ludlow family. He is a descendant in the seventh generation of Gabriel Ludlow, the first of that family in America, and beyond that point his lineage can be traced in clear and distinct form to some of the oldest families of nobility and landed gentry in Great Britain On one side the family line goes back to Edward I of England, in 1272, and his second wife, Margaret, daughter of Philip III of France In the tenth generation from Edward I , Edith, the daughter of Lord Windsor, married George Ludlow, of Hill Deverhill, Wiltshire. George Ludlow was the fourth in direct descent from William Ludlow, and his son, Sir Edmund Ludlow, was the grandfather of Major-General Edmund Ludlow, of the Parliamentary Army, and one of the judges of the court which tried and condemned Charles I , and by his second wife, was the grandfather of Gabriel Ludlow, the first of the name, who was the father of Gabriel Ludlow, the American immigrant. The grandfather of the second Gabriel Ludlow was Thomas Ludlow a cousin of General Ludlow.

Gabriel Ludlow, who established the family name in this country, was born at Castle Carey, England, in 1663 Coming to New York in 1694, he became one of the most successful merchants in the young metropolis of the New World, and was a man of high standing in the community In 1697, he married Sarah Haumer, daughter of the Reverend Dr Joseph Haumer, and had a family of thirteen children, six of whom were sons William Ludlow, the fourth son of Gabriel Ludlow, married Mary Duncan, daughter of Captain George Duncan, and had a family of twelve children. James Ludlow, the tenth child, was born in 1750 and married, in 1781, Elizabeth Harrison, daughter of Peter and Elizabeth (Pelham) Harrison He was graduated from Columbia College in 1768, and his second daughter, Frances Mary, married Philip Thomas, son of Philip Thomas, of Rockland, Cecil County, Va., and his wife, Sarah Margaret Weems, daughter of William Weems, of Weems Forest, Calvert County. The Thomas family of Virginia also had a remarkable Old World ancestry. Philip Thomas, of Rockland, was a descendant of John, the fourth Baron Mowbray, and his wife, Lady Elizabeth Seagrave, great-granddaughter of Edward I of England, and a great-great-grandson of John, third Baron Mowbray, and Lady Joan Plantagenet, daughter of Henry, third Earl of Lancaster, a grandson of Henry III of England

On the paternal side, Mr George Hoffman Bend has a distinguished American ancestry. His grandfather was the Reverend Doctor Joseph G Bend, rector of St. Paul s Episcopal Church, Baltimore, who married a granddaughter of Mary Boudinot, sister of Elias Boudinot This latter name was established in America by Elle Boudinot, a French Huguenot refugee. His descendant, Elias Boudinot, was a Revolutionary patriot and was president of the Continental Congress from 1779 to 1783 His only daughter married William Bradford, Attorney-General in President Washington s second cabinet

William Bradford Bend, the son of the Reverend Dr Bend, was the father of Mr George Hoffman Bend He married Catherine Ann Thomas, daughter of Philip and Frances Mary (Ludlow) Thomas Besides Mr George H Bend, the children of this alliance were : William Bradford Bend, second of the name, who married Isabella Innes, their children being Isabella Hadden, who married George Edward Wood, Harold Pelham, Meredith and Mary Aspinwall Bend; Catherine Ann Bend, who married James K Whitaker, their daughter being Marion Ludlow Whitaker, and Elizabeth Pelham Bend, who married Henry Asher Robbins, her children being Henry Pelham Robbins and Maud Robbins, who married Harry Whitney McVicker

Mr George Hoffman Bend is the second son of William B and Catherine Ann (Thomas) Bend He has long been an active member of the New York Stock Exchange and is prominent in both business and society. He married Elizabeth A Townsend, their children being two daughters, Amy and Beatrice Bend The family residence is in West Fifty-fourth Street Mr Bend is a member of the Union, Metropolitan, Union League, New York City Riding, Players, and New York Yacht clubs, and of the American Geographical Society

CHARLES LINNEAUS BENEDICT

A MONG the prominent early settlers of Connecticut and Long Island was Thomas Benedict, from Nottinghamshire, England, who died in Norwalk, in 1685. Of his children, John Benedict, who was born in Southold, Long Island, was the ancestor of that branch of the family of which the Honorable Charles Linneaus Benedict is the prominent representative in this generation Removing to Norwalk, John Benedict was a freeman of that place in 1670, a selectman, a deacon and a representative to the General Assembly. His wife was Phœbe Gregory, daughter of John and Sarah Gregory and a descendant of Henry Gregory, of Springfield, Mass. His son, James Benedict, 1685-1767, with several associates, purchased from the Indians the land whereon the town of Ridgefield, Conn., was established in 1708. He was an ensign and Captain in the train band, a justice of the peace, and several times a representative to the General Court. His wife was Sarah Hyatt, daughter of Thomas and Mary Hyatt.

Peter Benedict, of the third American generation and great-great-grandfather of Mr. Charles L. Benedict, was born in Ridgefield in 1714, was educated in Yale College and afterwards entered the Colonial Army. His death occurred in 1787. His second wife, the great-great-grandmother of the subject of this sketch, was Agnes H Tyler, daughter of John Tyler, of Branford, Conn. His son, the Reverend Abner Benedict, 1740-1818, was next in line of descent of this branch of the family, graduated from Yale College in 1769, was ordained to the Congregational ministry and settled over the church in Middlefield, Conn. During the War of the Revolution, he was engaged in the patriot cause, taking part in the battles of White Plains, Harlem and elsewhere. After the war, he was settled in New Lebanon, North Salem and North Stamford, Conn , and Roxbury, N. Y His wife, whom he married in 1771, was Lois Northrop, daughter of Dr. Northrop, of New Milford, Conn His son, the Reverend Joel Tyler Benedict, 1772-1833, studied law and was admitted to the bar in Fairfield County in 1794, but afterwards entered the ministry as a Presbyterian clergyman. In his later years, he was connected with the American Tract Society of Philadelphia. His wife was Currance Wheeler, daughter of Adin Wheeler, of Southbury, Conn.

The father of Mr Charles L. Benedict was George Wyllys Benedict. He was born in North Stamford, Conn , in 1796, and died in Burlington, Vt., September 24th, 1871 Graduated from Williams College, he became the principal of the academy in Westfield, Mass , then was a tutor in his alma mater, principal of the Newburgh Academy in Newburgh, N. Y, and a professor in the University of Vermont. He was also secretary and treasurer of the University board of trustees, and was the proprietor and editor of The Burlington Free Press. Twice he was elected a member of the Vermont State Senate. The degree of LL. D. was conferred upon him by the University of Vermont. His first wife, the mother of Mr. Charles L. Benedict, was Eliza Dewey, daughter of Stephen and Elizabeth (Owen) Dewey, of Sheffield, Mass

The Honorable Charles Linneaus Benedict was born in Newburgh-on-the-Hudson, in 1824. He was educated in the University of Vermont, being graduated from that institution in 1844. Taking up the study of law in the office of his uncle, Erastus C. Benedict, of New York, he was admitted to the bar and entered upon practice as a partner of his uncle. In 1865, President Abraham Lincoln established the United States Court of the Eastern District of New York and appointed Mr. Benedict to be Judge thereof. His career as a Judge was long and brilliant and he was recognized as one of the ablest, most independent and upright members of the judiciary. He resigned his position, June 19th, 1897, having occupied it for thirty-two years. The first wife of Judge Benedict, whom he married in 1856, and who died in 1858, was Rosalie Benedict, daughter of Abner Benedict. By her he had one son, George Abner Benedict His second wife was Sarah Cromwell, daughter of Dr William Seaman, of New York, and widow of Henry B Cromwell, of New York. His city residence is in Fifth Avenue and his country home is Far View, Dongan Hills, Staten Island Judge Benedict is a member of the Century Association, the New England Society and the Hamilton Club of Brooklyn

ELIAS CORNELIUS BENEDICT

DETAILED reference is made in another page of this volume to the origin of the Benedict family, of New England and New York, and to the circumstances connected with the emigration of its founder, Thomas Benedict, or Bennydick, as it was sometimes written in his own day, who arrived at Boston in 1638. As related therein, he finally settled in Norwalk, Conn., where he was a town official and a legislator. One of his sons, James Benedict, settled in Danbury, Conn., and had a son who was the first white child born in that place.

Descendants of this and of the other sons of Thomas Benedict were pioneers in the settlement of the different parts of the present State of New York, and during the Revolution members of the family were prominent and active patriots both in the army and in civil offices of honorable character. In each successive generation of the Benedict family, the bearers of the name have been distinguished by industry, intelligence and success in practical matters, while among their number have been some who have attained eminence in public and professional life or in the higher ranks of business. In fact, while the family is not as extensive as many of those which trace their descent from Puritan worthies of the early New England type, it has produced an unusually large number of men of the highest character and corresponding standing and influence in the community, while some of its members, notably the subject of this article, have, by their energy and attention to business affairs, contributed much to the material development of the country.

Mr. Elias Cornelius Benedict is one of the leading representatives of the family in this generation. He is the son of the Reverend Henry Benedict and his wife, Mary Betts Lockwood, and was born January 24th, 1834, in the town of Somers, Westchester County, N. Y., where his father was pastor of a church. He was educated in schools at Westport, Conn., and Buffalo, N. Y., part of his early youth having been spent in the latter city. When fifteen years of age, he entered upon business life as a clerk in the Wall Street office of Corning & Co. In 1857, when twenty-three years old, he succeeded to their business, organizing the banking firm of Benedict & Co., of which he has ever since been at the head. In 1871, Roswell P. Flower, who at a later date was Governor of New York, joined the firm which took the name of Benedict, Flower & Co., this partnership continuing for about four years. The firm has made a specialty of investment securities and in recent years has been largely interested in gas securities. Mr. Benedict is also connected with many financial institutions. The Gold Exchange Bank, which grew out of the gold speculation of the war time, was founded by him and his brother, and he has been prominent in the management of railroad and financial enterprises of great magnitude. He is a Democrat, but has never taken any active part in politics, although political preferment has often been tendered to him. He is an intimate friend of ex-President Cleveland.

In 1859, Mr. Benedict married Sarah C. Hart, daughter of Lucius Hart, of New York. They have four children. Frederic Hart Benedict, the only son, married first Jennie Flagler, daughter of Henry M Flagler, of New York, and after her death married Virginie Coudert, daughter of Frederic R. Coudert. Martha Benedict, the eldest daughter, married Ramsay Turnbull and lives in Bernardsville, N. J. The two unmarried daughters are Helen Ripley and Louise Adele Benedict.

The family residence is 10 West Fifty-first Street and Mr. Benedict owns an estate at Indian Harbor, Greenwich, Conn., once the site of the famous Americus Club. Yachting engages much of his leisure time. He owns the steam yacht Oneida, belongs to the New York, American, Seawanhaka-Corinthian and other yacht clubs and is also a member of the Manhattan, Players and City clubs and the New England Society. He is also a trustee of the New York Homeopathic Medical College and Hospital, and a director of the New York Ophthalmic Hospital, having served as its treasurer for over twenty-five years.

HENRY HARPER BENEDICT

A S far back as the beginning of the sixteenth century, William Benedict is mentioned in the records of Nottinghamshire, England, as a man of substance and member of a family that for several generations had been resident in the same county. Thomas Benedict, the great-grandson of William Benedict, who was born in Nottinghamshire in 1617, came to America when he was twenty-one years of age and was the founder of the family in this country. At first he lived on Long Island and was one of the founders and a deacon of the first Presbyterian Church of Jamaica, held several important local offices and was a delegate to Governor Nicolls' convention which was called to make laws for the inhabitants of Long island. For five years, from 1670 to 1675, he was a member of the Assembly of the Province of New York. Removing afterwards to the Connecticut Colony, he died in Norwalk in 1690.

James Benedict, a son of Thomas Benedict, the pioneer, was one of the company that settled the City of Danbury, Conn., where his son, James, was born in 1685, being the first male child born in that place. John Benedict, a grandson of James Benedict, Sr., was prominent in the administration of public affairs, being a Captain in the militia and for many years a member of the Legislature. After the Revolution, James Benedict, the son of John Benedict, removed to New York State, where he settled originally in Ballston, and finally in 1793 in Auburn. One of the first settlers of Herkimer County, N. Y., in 1790, when that section was far upon the frontier, was Elias Benedict, the son of James Benedict, of Auburn. He owned a farm in the wilderness and built one of the first houses ever erected in that part of the country. There his son, Micaiah, the father of Mr. Henry Harper Benedict, was born in 1801. Micaiah Benedict was an energetic, enterprising man of the most approved frontier stamp and made his own way in the world. Throughout most of his life an ardent Jackson Democrat, he became a Republican in the period just before the Civil War, casting his last Democratic vote for Franklin Pierce in the Presidential campaign of 1852. He was a member of the Order of Free Masons, and for several years Deputy Grand Master in New York State. His death occurred in 1881.

Mr. Henry Harper Benedict was born in German Flats, Herkimer County, N. Y., October 9th, 1844. He was educated in the Little Falls Academy, the Fairfield Seminary, and the Marshall Institute in Easton, and then took a regular course in Hamilton College, from which institution he was graduated in 1869. During a portion of the time that he was in college, he was also engaged as professor of Latin and higher mathematics in Fairfield Seminary. He was a member of the Δ K E fraternity.

After he had completed his college course, he entered the establishment of E. Remington & Sons, at Ilion, N. Y., in a confidential position. Within a short time, he became one of the directors of Remington & Sons, and the treasurer of the Remington Sewing Machine Company. In 1882, he became a member of the firm of Wyckoff, Seamans & Benedict, and removed to New York. He is now the president of the corporation of the same name, having the foreign interests of the company under his care.

While living in Ilion, N. Y., Mr Benedict assisted in organizing the first Presbyterian Church of that place, and of which he was an elder, trustee and treasurer. He was also president of the Herkimer County Bible Society and for many years president of the Ilion Literary Association Since his removal to New York, he has made his home on the Heights, in Brooklyn. He has intimate social relations in New York City, however, and is a member of the Fifth Avenue Presbyterian Church. He belongs to the Hamilton Club, the Riding and Driving Club, and the Long Island Historical Society of Brooklyn, and to the Grolier, Δ K E, Republican and Union League clubs of New York. He is a trustee of Hamilton College and of the Brooklyn Institute of Arts and Sciences In 1867, he married Maria Nellis, a daughter of Henry G. Nellis and granddaughter of General George H. Nellis, of Fort Plain, N. Y. Mr. and Mrs. Benedict have one daughter, Helen Elizabeth Benedict.

LE GRAND LOCKWOOD BENEDICT

THE family name of Benedict is of very ancient origin. It is derived from the Latin Benedictus, or Blessed, and in different forms is common in all languages. First it was undoubtedly applied as a designation of ecclesiastics, but after a time it became secularized and adopted as the family name of those who had no special connection with the church. The ancestors of the American Benedicts are believed to have been originally Huguenots. Thomas Benedict, of Nottinghamshire, was living there in the seventeenth century, but his progenitors had removed from France, first to Germany, then to Holland, and finally to England in successive generations He was an only son and bore a name that had been confined to only sons in the family for more than a hundred years About the middle of the sixteenth century, to escape the oppressions of King Charles and Archbishop Laud, he exiled himself to this country Upon the vessel in which he came to New England, in 1638, was Mary Brigdum, daughter of a widow, who had been his father's second wife.

Thomas Benedict and Mary Brigdum were married soon after they arrived in this country, and resided for some time in the Massachusetts Bay Colony. Afterwards they removed to Long Island, where they lived at Huntington, Southold and Jamaica, and finally at Norwalk, Conn. Thomas Benedict was a freeholder of Jamaica in 1663 and a magistrate the same year, a commissioner of Huntington in 1662, a Lieutenant in 1663, town clerk of Norwalk, Conn., in 1665, and the following year was reappointed to that position, which he retained until 1674. He was a representative to the General Assembly in 1670 and 1675. John Benedict, son of Thomas Benedict, was a freeman of Norwalk, Conn., in 1680, selectman in 1689, 1692-4, and 1699, and representative to the General Assembly in 1722 and 1725. In the third generation, John Benedict was a selectman in 1705 and 1715, a Sergeant of the troops in 1711 and held other local offices. Nathaniel Benedict, son of the second John Benedict, was a selectman in 1755-1778, a Lieutenant of the militia in 1762 and a representative to the General Assembly the same year. The second Nathaniel Benedict, who was born in 1744 and died in 1833, was a justice of the peace, a surveyor and a grand juror. Seth Williston Benedict, grandson of the second Nathaniel Benedict and the descendant in the seventh generation from Thomas Benedict, the pioneer, was the grandfather of the present Mr. Benedict. He was born in 1803 and became one of the leading newspaper owners and editors of the early part of the present century. Originally he was proprietor of The Norwalk (Conn.) Gazette. He removed to New York in 1833, and became proprietor and publisher of The New York Evangelist, a business relation that he maintained until 1837. In the latter year, he became publisher of The Emancipator and was also connected with other literary enterprises. In 1848, he commenced the publication of The New York Independent, but gave up his connection with that periodical in 1853 He was prominent in the religious life of the metropolis in the first half of the century, being a trustee and elder of the Thirteenth Street Presbyterian Church, and for many years a trustee and deacon of the Broadway Tabernacle. He died in 1869.

James Hoyt Benedict, son of Seth Williston Benedict, was born in 1830, in Norfolk, Conn , and throughout the active years of his life was one of the leading bankers in New York City. His first wife, who was the mother of Mr. Le Grand Lockwood Benedict, was Mary Elizabeth Andrews, daughter of Samuel Andrews The children of James Hoyt Benedict were Alida Andrews, Le Grand Lockwood, James Henry, Charles Williston, Howard Robinson and Elliot S Benedict

Mr. Le Grand Lockwood Benedict was born in New York City August 24th, 1855, and is a graduate of the Rensselaer Polytechnic Institute, Troy, N Y In 1881, Mr. Benedict married Sarah Collier Blaine and has two children, Le Grand Lockwood, Jr., and Margaret Dewitt Benedict. Mr. Benedict's residence is at Cedarhurst, Long Island, and he is a member of the Union and Rockaway Hunt clubs

FREDERICK HENRY BETTS

FOR seven generations, members of the Betts family have been prominent in Connecticut and New York, and by marriage have been connected with many other leading families of the Connecticut and Massachusetts Colonies   The lineage of Mr. Frederick Henry Betts goes back to distinguished ancestry   Thomas Betts, the head of the family in England, was the owner, in 1386, of Hastings and Whitefoots Hall manors, Norfolk.   One of his descendants, Thomas Betts, born in England in 1618, emigrated to America in 1639 and was among the original founders of Guilford, Conn , and an early settler in Norwalk   Made a freeman of Norwalk in 1664, with fourteen others he received a grant of land in Wilton   He died in 1688. Daniel Betts, son of Thomas Betts, was born in 1657.   He was a large land owner and lived to be over one hundred years old   His grandson, Samuel C Betts, 1732-1823, was one of the first settlers of Berkshire County, Mass   He was a member of the Ninth Regiment of Foot in the Revolution.   Uriah Betts, the great-grandson of Sergeant Daniel Betts, born in Norwalk in 1761, died in Newburgh, N Y , in 1843   With his five brothers, he went into the Continental Army and served throughout the war

The father of Mr. Frederick Henry Betts was Frederick J Betts, son of Uriah Betts.   He was prominent in the military and civil life of New York half a century and more ago   Born in Richmond, Mass , in 1803, he was graduated from Williams College in 1821, became District Attorney of Orange County, N, Y , in 1824, and later on Master in Chancery   In 1826, he was Quartermaster of the Second Brigade of Cavalry and on the staff of Governor George Clinton   From 1827 to 1841, he was clerk of the United States District and Circuit Courts in New York, and 1868–69, Judge of the Hastings Court, Campbell County, Va

A review of the female ancestry of Mr. Betts brings up a long line of personages distinguished in the first two centuries of the country   His mother, whom his father married in 1833, was Mary Ward Scoville, who was descended on her father's side directly from John Scovil, one of the original proprietors of Waterbury, Conn , and on her mother's side from John Eliot, the famous apostle to the Indians, and Andrew Ward, who was a Colonel in the Colonial wars   She was also descended from George Wyllys, one of the first settlers in Hartford, Conn , and the second Governor of the Colony   Mr Betts' grandmother was a daughter of the Honorable Nathan Rossiter, of Richmond, Mass , and a descendant in the third generation from the Honorable Josiah Rossiter, Assistant-Governor of Connecticut   His great-grandmother was a descendant from Captain John Taylor, of Northampton, Mass , and a generation further back the female head of the house was Sarah Comstock, granddaughter of Christopher Comstock, representative to the General Assembly of Connecticut, 1686–90.

Mr Frederick Henry Betts was born in Newburgh, N. Y., March 8th, 1843   He was graduated from Yale College in 1864, and studied law in the law department of Columbia College, graduating therefrom with the degree of LL B in 1866   Yale gave him the degree of A M in 1867.   He entered at once upon the practice of law and established a large practice   In 1872–73, he was counsel for the Insurance Department of the State of New York, and was lecturer on patent law in Yale College, 1873-84   In 1879, he published the Policy of Patent Laws, and he is recognized as one of the leading patent lawyers of the United States. Deeply interested in public affairs and a Republican in politics, he was a member of the Republican County Committee, 1884-85, a member of the Citizens' Committee of Seventy in 1882, a member of the Citizens' Committee of One Hundred in 1883, vice-president of the City Reform Club, vice-president of the Republican Club in 1885 and a member of the People's Municipal League in 1890-91   He belongs to the University, Century, Grolier, Riding and other clubs.   He married, in 1867, Louise, daughter of John F Holbrook; they have three children, Louis Frederick H Betts, Yale 1891; M Eliot Betts, who married Russell H Hoadley, Jr. , and Wyllys Rossiter Betts, Yale 1898   In 1875, he founded the Betts prize in the law department of Yale College.

JOHN BIGELOW

JOURNALIST, historian, statesman and diplomat, the Honorable John Bigelow comes of one of the oldest New England families. John Bigelow, the ancestor of the Bigelows of America, was an Englishman who settled in Watertown, Mass., before 1642 His son Joshua, 1655-1745, was a soldier in King Philip's War, where he was wounded. For his valiant services he received a grant of land in Westminster, Mass, and became one of the first citizens of that place. His grandson John, 1681-1770, went in early life to Hartford, Conn, and thence to Colchester, Conn, where he was a prominent man, being ensign and Lieutenant in the militia. In subsequent generations, the descendants of the first John Bigelow were prominent in Colchester, Marlborough and Glastonbury, Conn., and in Malden, N. Y The father of the Honorable John Bigelow was Asa Bigelow, of Malden, who was born in Marlborough, Conn., in 1779 and died in Malden, in 1850. He was of the sixth generation in descent from John Bigelow, of Watertown, Mass.

The Honorable John Bigelow was born in Malden, N. Y, November 25th, 1817, and was graduated from Union College in the class of 1835. Admitted to the bar in 1839, he engaged in active practice for several years, but becoming interested in journalism was editor of The Plebeian and The Democratic Review. From 1845 to 1848, he was an inspector of the State prison at Sing Sing In 1849, he began an active journalistic career that lasted for several years Becoming associated with William Cullen Bryant as joint owner of The Evening Post, he was managing editor of that journal until 1861. With the accession of Abraham Lincoln to the Presidency his most conspicuous public service began. In 1861, he was appointed to the United States Consulate in Paris, and after the death of Minister Dayton, in 1865, was advanced to the position of United States Minister to the Court of France, which position he retained until 1867. Returning home at the expiration of his term of service he was elected Secretary of State of New York in 1868.

During the last twenty-five years, Mr. Bigelow has been principally engaged in literary work. In 1886, he inspected the Panama Canal for the New York Chamber of Commerce and made a valuable report of that undertaking as a result of his investigations. The same year he received the honorary degree of LL. D from Racine College, Wisconsin, and was made an honorary member of the Chamber of Commerce. His first book, Jamaica in 1850; the Effects of Sixteen Years of Freedom on a Slave Colony, the result of several trips made to the West Indies, was published in 1850 In 1856, he published A Life of Fremont and, in Paris, in 1863, Les Etats Unis d'Amerique. While in Paris he discovered original manuscripts of Benjamin Franklin which he edited in an Autobiography of Franklin published in 1868, and the following year he published Some Recollections of the late Antoine Pierre Berryer. His other literary productions include The Wit and Wisdom of the Haytiens, Molines the Quietist, Life of William Cullen Bryant, Some Recollections of Edouard Laboulaye, the Complete Works of Benjamin Franklin, and France and Hereditary Monarchy.

Mr. Bigelow has come again into special public prominence during the last few years through his connection with the estate of Samuel J. Tilden When Mr. Tilden died, in 1886, he made Mr. Bigelow one of his executors and his authorized biographer, and a two-volume edition of the writings and speeches of Mr. Tilden has been one of the results of this trust. He is president of the Tilden Trust, that has the management of Mr. Tilden's bequest for a free public library in New York, and is president of the board of trustees of the New York Public Library.

Mr Bigelow has a city residence in Gramercy Park and a country home at Highland Falls. He belongs to the Century Association and other clubs, is a member of the New England Society and a patron of the Metropolitan Museum of Art, and connected with other literary and social organizations In 1850, he married Jane Tunis Poultney, of Baltimore, Md. His eldest son is Captain John Bigelow, U S A., and another son is Poultney Bigelow, the traveler and author. His daughter, Grace Bigelow, has also done some excellent literary work.

ARTHUR F. BISSELL, M. D.

ON the female side of his house Dr. Arthur F. Bissell traces his ancestry back to the Wolcott family, famous in the early annals of New England. The Wolcotts were aristocratic English folk, and Henry Wolcott, who came to America in 1630, was one of the first settlers in Windsor, Conn. Among his numerous descendants within two centuries were eleven Governors of States, thirty judges and many lawyers and clergymen of prominence In Connecticut, Governors Roger, Oliver and Oliver Wolcott, Jr., and Governors Matthew and Roger Griswold, were most distinguished in the family in the last century. Branches of the family have since become established in other parts of the United States, and the bearers of the name have in many instances displayed an hereditary talent for public life, as well as for professional, literary and business pursuits.

The Wolcott ladies were celebrated for their beauty, and none more so than Jerusha, grand-daughter of Governor Roger Wolcott, who married Epaphras Bissell and became the mother of a family that has given many able men and women to professional and business life both in the States of Connecticut, New York and elsewhere. Dr Arthur F Bissell is the grandson of Epaphras and Jerusha (Wolcott) Bissell. His father, Edward Bissell, the second child of Epaphras Bissell, was born in 1797. He married Jane Loring Reed, and became a leading merchant and manufacturer in the western part of New York State He built and operated mills in Lockport, and conducted other important business interests In 1833, he moved to Toledo, O., was one of the founders of that city and very largely instrumental in its development. The Erie and Kalamazoo Railroad, from Toledo to Kalamazoo, was constructed by him in the face of much opposition, and this was the beginning of the railroad operations in that section which resulted in making Toledo the commercial centre that it is to-day Edward Bissell died in 1861 A condensed history of Toledo, published in 1869, says : "Whatever Toledo may become in the future, she will always owe her first start in life to Edward Bissell, a gentleman of high education and refinement, of great foresight and sagacity."

The Bissells, paternal ancestors of the gentleman whose descent is traced in this page, were French Huguenots. The arms of the family, as described by Burke, are : gules, on a bend or ; three escallops, sable, crest a demi-eagle, with wings displayed, sable ; charged on the neck with an escallop shell or. Motto, *In Recto Decus* Leaving France after the massacre of St. Bartholomew, members of the family went to England. John Bissell emigrated to America, coming to Plymouth, Mass, in 1628 He afterwards removed to Connecticut, and was among the first founders of the settlement of Windsor, a community that stands preëminent in the annals of New England as the home from which have sprung so many families of great distinction in public service, and in professional and commercial life. Epaphras Bissell's father was a Captain in the Revolutionary war, and the fourth in descent from the original John Bissell, through his second son, Thomas.

Dr. Arthur F. Bissell, son of Edward Bissell, is of the seventh generation from John Bissell of Windsor. Born in Geneseo, N. Y., June, 1826, he studied medicine in the College of Physicians and Surgeons of New York City, from which institution he was graduated in 1848. Until 1863, he practiced medicine in Toledo, O., where he built up a large practice Since that date he has been actively engaged in manufacturing business in New York City. In 1851, he married Anna E., daughter of Judge Nehemiah Browne, of Rye, N. Y, a descendant of Thomas Browne, of Rye, England, who was a descendant of Sir Anthony Browne, Standard Bearer of all England in the reign of Henry VII., and who married Lady Lucy Neville, fourth daughter of Sir John Neville, Marquis of Montague. In 1664, Thomas and Haekaliah Browne, with their friend, Peter Disbrow, removed to Rye, Westchester County, N Y, where they became its largest land owners, naming the town from Rye, in the County of Sussex, England, which had been their former home in the mother country.

PELHAM ST. GEORGE BISSELL

ONE of the first individuals to divine the vast stores of wealth that were hidden for centuries in the petroleum fields of Pennsylvania was George H. Bissell, college professor, journalist and scientist. He was a descendant in direct line from John Bissell, the American pioneer, who was one of the first settlers of the town of Windsor, Conn. A member of a noble and ancient Huguenot family, John Bissell came from England to the Plymouth Colony in 1628. His numerous descendants have been conspicuous in business and in public life in Connecticut and elsewhere in every generation since his time. One of them, Isaac Bissell, the father of George H. Bissell and a Revolutionary soldier, born in Connecticut, was noted as a fur trader in Mackinaw and Detroit.

The mother of George H. Bissell was Nancy Wemple, daughter of Captain John Wemple, of Revolutionary fame, and herself the owner of an estate on the Mohawk River, near Johnstown, N. Y. Captain John Wemple commanded the Tryon Company of Militia in 1775. His father, who died in Schenectady in 1749, was one of the patentees of that place, and his grandfather, Myndert Wemple, a justice of the peace, who was killed in the massacre of the Mohawk Valley in 1690, married Diewie, daughter of Evert Janse Wendel, a member of another noted Dutch family of Western New York. Jan Barentse Wemple, the first of the name in this country, was the ancestor of George H. Bissell in the fifth generation. Born in Doit, Lower Netherlands, in 1620, he came to America in 1640 and settled in Esopus, now Kingston. He moved to Albany about 1643, and was one of the fifteen original settlers of Schenectady. In the old records, he is set down as the owner of the bouwery in Lubberdes Land, now Troy. He died in 1663, and his widow, Maritie Myndertse Wemple, who spent the remaining years of her life with her son Myndert in Schenectady, perished in the massacre of 1690, when the Indians destroyed that little settlement and nearly all its inhabitants.

George H. Bissell, who was born in Hanover, N. H., in 1821, died in New York in 1884. He was graduated from Dartmouth College in 1845, and became a professor of Greek and Latin in the University of Norwich, Vt. Subsequently he was the Washington correspondent of The Richmond Times, traveled extensively throughout the West Indies, was a journalist in New Orleans, and principal of the High School and superintendent of the schools in the same city. The observation of traces of coal oil in specimens of rock from Pennsylvania that had been submitted to him for examination at Dartmouth, led him to look carefully into that subject. He became convinced of the existence of reservoirs of oil underground where these specimens had come from, and coming to New York in 1853, he organized, the following year, the Pennsylvania Rock Oil Company, the first petroleum company ever started in the United States. In association with J. G. Eveleth, he leased land in Titusville, Pa., and began operations. The first venture was not a success, however, and in 1855 the company was reorganized, although it was not until 1859 that rich veins of oil were struck. Mr. Bissell, with his partners, reaped handsome financial returns from their enterprise, and in a few years he retired from business and settled in New York City, spending the remaining years of his life in caring for his real estate interests. He always retained his early affection for Dartmouth College, and presented to that institution its handsome gymnasium.

Mr. Pelham St. George Bissell, son of George H. Bissell and his wife, Ophie Louise Griffin, was born in New York, December 5th, 1858. Educated in the Columbia Grammar School and in Columbia College, he graduated from the latter institution in the class of 1880. He succeeded his father in the care of the family property, and is also interested in the manufacture of paper, being the organizer and a large owner of the Adirondacks Pulp Company. He married Helen Alsop French, daughter of Colonel Thomas J. French, lives in West Thirty-ninth Street, and has one son, Pelham St. George Bissell, Jr. He is a member of the Columbia College Alumni Association, the New York Athletic Club and the New York Historical Society.

GEORGE DACRE BLEYTHING, M D.

ON the one hand Dr Bleything's descent is traced to a family of Welsh gentry, possessing aristocratic connections, which at an early date in the history of this country became identified with its social and material progress, and on the other it is connected with the struggle for independence through a family which took a patriotic part in the conflict His great-grandfather was William Bleything, of Wrexham, in the County of Denbigh, Wales, a landed gentleman of ancient descent, the family coat of arms being still borne by its American branch. He married Ellen Duckworth, of the same county, and their second son, Joseph Duckworth Bleything, grandfather of the subject of this article, became a prominent manufacturer, possessing large mills for the manufacture of paper at Manchester, Eng ; Whippany, Morris County, N J , Paterson, in the same State, and Westchester, N Y. His largest interests were in this country, and it was in his establishment at Whippany that paper was first manufactured by machinery in the United States The wife of Joseph Duckworth Bleything was an English lady of high connections, Mary Hughes, daughter of Captain John Hughes of the Royal Navy, and his wife, Mabel Beresford Hope, whose family, it is needless to say, has for many generations occupied a place in the British peerage and taken a conspicuous place in the history of the mother country, many of its representatives being noted in annals of the British Army and Navy or in Parliamentary and administrative affairs. Members of it have intermarried with a large number of the families of nobility and gentry in the United Kingdom and it continues to the present day one of the most representative names of its class in England

Edmund Langstreth Bleything, Dr Bleything's father, was the son of Joseph Duckworth Bleything and his wife, Mary Hughes, and married Mary Ward Tuttle, of Morris County, N J , her family having taken part in the Revolutionary War on the patriotic side. The Burn, at Whippany, near Morristown, now Dr. Bleything's country residence, occupies the site of the old Colonial mansion in which the American and French officers of Washington were often hospitably entertained by his mother's family when the Continental headquarters was established at Morristown The estate was a Colonial giant, and was inherited by its present possessor through his mother, whose family was noted in the early history of Morris County, being among the earliest people of social distinction in that section of the present State. The original papers relating to their grant are still in the possession of the family.

Dr George Dacre Bleything was born in Morris County, October 18th, 1842 He was educated under a private tutor at Trenton, N J , and entering Columbia College, graduated from the medical department with the degree of M.D , and has since practiced his profession in this city. His marriage connected him with one of the most prominent families in New England ; Mrs. Bleything, who was a native of Savannah, Ga , having been born Maria Howard Bulfinch. Her father was the Reverend S G. Bulfinch, of Boston, and her mother Maria Howard, of Savannah, Ga , daughter of Samuel Howard, who was the first in this country, after Robert Fulton, to construct steamboats Her maternal grandfather, it should also be noted, figured in the Boston Tea Party On the paternal side, Mrs. Bleything's grandfather was the famous Charles Bulfinch, the leading American architect of the period succeeding the Revolution, whose work is still admired in the venerable State House at Boston, and who designed the west wing of the Capitol at Washington, D C. Her grandmother was Susan (Apthorpe) Bulfinch, and the family is still represented in Boston society, its members possessing many valuable and interesting relics, including family portraits by Sir Joshua Reynolds, Lely, Coply, Smibert, Sir Benjamin West and Angelica Kaufman

Dr. Bleything's town residence is No 1008 Madison Avenue, and, as already indicated, his country place is the old seat of his maternal ancestors in Morris County, N. J , which has come down to him as the representative of its original Colonial grantees and which is one of the historical places of that vicinity

CORNELIUS NEWTON BLISS

SEVERAL branches of the Bliss family have been prominent in New York during the last two generations or more. They are derived from different sons of Thomas Bliss, the American pioneer, who came from Devonshire, England, to America about 1635, lived in Braintree, Mass., and Hartford, Conn., and died about 1640. The Honorable Cornelius Newton Bliss is descended from Jonathan Bliss, of Rehoboth, Mass., who was born in England about 1625, the son of Thomas Bliss, the pioneer. Jonathan Bliss was a freeman of Plymouth in 1655 and a freeman of Rehoboth in 1658, being one of the first settlers of that place. His wife, whom he married in 1648, was Miriam Harmon. He died in 1687. His son, Jonathan Bliss, of Rehoboth, who was born in 1666, married, in 1691, Miriam Carpenter, daughter of William and Miriam (Searls) Carpenter. Their son, Lieutenant Ephraim Bliss, who was born in 1699, married, in 1723, Rachel Carpenter. Captain Jonathan Bliss, of Rehoboth, 1739-1800, married, in 1759, Lydia Wheeler. Their son, Asahel Bliss, who was born in 1771, was a deacon of the Congregational Church of Rehoboth for fifty years. His wife, whom he married in 1794, was Deborah Martin, daughter of Edward Martin. He died in 1855 and his wife survived him three years, dying in 1858. Asahel N. Bliss, 1808-1833, son of Deacon Asahel and Deborah (Martin) Bliss, was the father of the Honorable Cornelius N. Bliss. He was a prominent merchant of Fall River, Mass. His wife, whom he married in 1831, was Irene B. Luther.

The Honorable Cornelius N. Bliss was born in Fall River, January 26th, 1833. His father died while he was still an infant, and his mother, after some years of widowhood, married Edward S. Keep, of Fall River. Mr. and Mrs. Keep removed to New Orleans in 1840, but the son was left with friends to attend school until he had attained the age of fourteen. Then he joined his mother in New Orleans and completed his education in the high school in that city. When he was through with his books, he entered the counting-room of his step-father, and after remaining there for a year, left New Orleans for Boston and went into the dry goods and jobbing house of James M. Bebee & Co. In 1866, the firm was dissolved, and Mr. Bliss became a member of the firm of John S. & Eben Wright & Co., one of Boston's largest commission houses. But after the Civil War, Boston began to lose its great dry goods trade, that had been centered in that city for a quarter of a century or more, and that now was gradually shifting to New York, and shortly Mr. Bliss removed to the metropolis and established a branch of the Boston house. Important branches were established afterwards in Philadelphia and Chicago, and the concern has become one of the largest and most influential in its trade in the country. In the course of time, the firm name was changed to Wright, Bliss & Fabyan, and later to Bliss, Fabyan & Co., as it now stands.

Politically Mr. Bliss is a Republican, and his activity in the party organization has given him a national reputation. He has been particularly prominent in the interest that he has taken in municipal affairs and is a recognized leader in every movement for honest government. The Republican nomination for Governor of the State was suggested to him in 1885, but he resolutely declined the honor, and again in 1891 he refused to be a candidate for the same office. In 1892, and in 1896, in important Presidential campaigns, he was treasurer of the Republican National Committee. In 1897 he became a member of the Cabinet of President McKinley, taking the portfolio of the Interior Department.

For several years he was a vice-president of the Union League Club, and one of the most active and honored members of that influential organization. He has been chairman of the executive committee and vice-president of the Chamber of Commerce; vice-president of the Fourth National Bank; president of the New England Society; a governor and treasurer of the New York Hospital, and is at the head of many social and benevolent organizations. He married, in 1859, Elizabeth Plumer, daughter of the Honorable Avery Plumer, of Boston, and has two children living, a son, Cornelius Bliss, Jr., and a daughter. His residence is in Madison Avenue.

GEORGE BLISS

ONE of the foremost lawyers of his time, and also noted for his public spirit and devotion to the cause of religion, Colonel George Bliss had a line of distinguished New England ancestry. His remote progenitor was William Bliss, of Belstone, Devonshire, a wealthy landowner who, as a Puritan, was subjected to persecution in the time of Archbishop Laud and suffered the loss of his estate. His sons sought refuge in the New World and one of them, Thomas Bliss, 1580-1640, founded the branch of the family to which Colonel Bliss belonged. Thomas Bliss lived in Braintree, Mass., and Hartford, Conn., his son being Samuel Bliss, 1624-1720, of Springfield, Mass, who married Mary Leonard. Next in line of descent were Ebenezer Bliss, 1683-1717, who married Mary Gaylord, and Jedediah Bliss, whose wife was Rachel Sheldon. The Honorable Moses Bliss, 1736-1814, was their son. He was graduated from Yale College in 1755, studied theology and preached for a short time, but finally abandoned the church for the bar, becoming a very successful lawyer and a Judge in Hampshire County, Mass. He was a strong patriot in the Revolution. His wife was Abigail Metcalf, daughter of William and Abigail (Edwards) Metcalf Their son, the Honorable George Bliss, of Springfield, was born in 1764, graduated from Yale in 1785 and in 1823 was made an LL D. by Harvard. He also was a very distinguished lawyer, a member of the Massachusetts Legislature, Senate and Executive Council, and a delegate to the famous Hartford convention His wife was Hannah Clarke, daughter of Dr. John Clarke, of Lebanon, Conn. The Honorable George Bliss, second of the name, was born in Springfield in 1793 and was graduated from Yale in 1812. In the war with England, he served as aide, with rank of Colonel, on the staff of General Jacob Bliss. He was several times in the Massachusetts Legislature, being Speaker of the House in 1853, president of the Senate in 1855, a member of the Council and a Presidential elector. He was one of the founders of the Boston & Albany Railroad and president of the company, 1836-42, and also president of several other roads His wife, Mary Shepard Dwight, was the daughter of Jonathan and Sarah Dwight.

Colonel George Bliss, of New York, was born of this parentage in Springfield, May 3d, 1830. He graduated from Harvard in 1851, studied law and made New York City his home. In 1859, he was private secretary to Governor Edwin D. Morgan, and was on the Governor's staff with rank of Colonel, was Captain in the Fourth Heavy Artillery, and raised several regiments of colored troops for the Civil War.

The services of Colonel Bliss to the community and to his own profession have been notable. During 1872-77, he was United States District Attorney, and was one of the commission to revise and condense the laws relating to New York City As an author, he is known throughout the whole United States for his great work, Bliss' Annotated Code of Civil Procedure of the State of New York. Early in his legal career, he issued a standard treatise on The Law of Life Insurance. He was an active member of the Republican party and a leader in its councils in this city and State.

During the administration of President Arthur, the property of the American Catholic College in Rome was threatened with confiscation by the Italian authorities, though belonging to American citizens Colonel Bliss actively interested himself in the matter and secured the intervention of the United States, the protest of our Minister at Rome, W. W. Astor, being effectual to stop the spoliation In 1895, His Holiness, Pope Leo XIII., in recognition of this and other services of Colonel Bliss to the Church, made him a Knight Commander of the Order of St. Gregory.

In 1858, Colonel Bliss married Catharine Van Rensselaer Dwight, daughter of Frances Dwight, of Albany She died in 1884 In 1887, he contracted a second alliance with Anais Casey, daughter of Henry H Casey, of New York. Three children were born to them, of whom Ruth Alice Bliss and George Bliss, Jr, survive Colonel Bliss died September 2d, 1897. The family residence is in West Thirty-ninth Street, and Colonel Bliss' clubs embraced the Union League and Catholic, and he belonged also to the New England Society.

JAMES ORVILLE BLOSS

A MONG the early settlers of Watertown, Mass., were Edmund Bloys, or Bloss, Robert Jennison and James Cutler   From these pioneers, as well as from other early Colonists of New England, Mr. James Orville Bloss is descended.   Edmund Bloss, the first American ancestor of the family, was admitted a freeman of Watertown in 1639, and was one of the leading men of that place.   He was a native of England and came of an old Suffolk family. His first wife, Mary, died in 1675, and he afterwards married Ruth Parsons, daughter of Hugh Parsons.   He died in 1681, having been born in 1587.   Ruth Parsons was a niece of Joseph Parsons, who, with his brother Hugh, was settled in Springfield before 1636.   The brothers came originally from Devonshire, England.

Richard Bloss, of the second American generation, was born in England in 1623 and took the oath of fidelity in Watertown in 1652.   He died in 1665   His wife, whom he married in 1658, was Micael Jennison, daughter of Robert Jennison, who was a freeman of Watertown in 1645 and owned many acres of land there.   Robert Jennison came to this country with his brother, William Jennison, as a follower of Governor John Winthrop.   William Jennison became prominent in early Colonial affairs, was a freeman of Watertown in 1630, frequently a selectman of the town, a representative to the General Court and Captain of the train band.   The New England families now bearing the name are all descended from Robert Jennison.

Richard Bloss, grandson of Edmund Bloss, the pioneer, was born in 1659 and removed from Watertown to Killingly, Conn., in middle life, being a freeman of that place in 1690.   He married, in 1688, Ann Cutler, daughter of James and Lydia (Wright) Cutler, of Cambridge Farms, now part of the town of Lexington, Mass.   Her father was born in 1635 and died in 1685   He was a farmer and a soldier in the War with King Philip's Indians.   His wife, whom he married in 1665, was the widow of Samuel Wright and daughter of John Moore, of Sudbury.   The paternal grandfather of Ann Cutler was James Cutler, who was born in England in 1606 and settled in Watertown in 1634, being one of the original grantees of that place.   Tradition says that his wife, Anna, was a sister of the wife of Captain John Grout.   About 1651, he removed from Watertown to Cambridge Farms.

James Bloss, 1702-1790, of Killingly, Conn., was the great-great-grandfather of Mr. James Orville Bloss.   The great-grandparents of Mr. Bloss were James Bloss, of Hebron, Conn., who was born in Killingly and died in New Rochelle, N. Y., in 1776, and his wife, Elizabeth Clough, 1733-1803, daughter of Jonathan and Mary Clough.   James Bloss was a soldier in the Revolutionary War and his son, Joseph Bloss, grandfather of the subject of this sketch, was also a Revolutionary soldier, being in the detachment of troops that was on duty at the execution of Major Andre. Joseph Bloss was born in Thompson, Conn , in 1759 and died in 1838   His wife was Amy Kennedy, who was born in Milton, Mass , in 1768, daughter of Andrew Kennedy, 1729-1788, and Amy Wentworth, 1732-1802.   The father of Mr. Bloss was James Orville Bloss, Sr , of Rochester, N. Y., who was born in Alford, Mass , in 1805 and died in Rochester in 1869.   His wife was Eliza Ann Lockwood, 1810-1880, daughter of Roswell Lockwood, 1783-1863, and Thalia Oviatt, 1787-1873.

Mr James Orville Bloss was born in Rochester, N. Y., September 30th, 1847.   Early in life, he determined to devote himself to business pursuits, and with that end in view secured a thorough business training.   When he arrived of age, having settled in New York, he became a cotton merchant and has followed that business with success.   In 1892, he was elected president of the New York Cotton Exchange and reelected to that honorable position in the following year.   He is also a member of the Chamber of Commerce and a director of the Third National Bank.   Although actively engaged in business for many years, he has found time and opportunity for extensive travel abroad.   He is unmarried and resides in East Forty-seventh Stret.   His clubs are the Metropolitan and the Union League.

CARL F. W. BODECKER, D.D.S.

CARL F. W. BODECKER, D.D.S., M.D.S., is of German birth. His parents, Henry Bodecker and Doris Bodecker, born Lohmann, were residents of Celle, Hanover, where Dr. Bodecker was born July 6, 1846. He was educated in the schools of his native city. He began the study of dentistry in Germany, in 1866, he went to London, Eng., where he was engaged in the practice of his profession till 1869, when he came to this country. He graduated from the New York College of Dentistry in 1871, receiving the first prize awarded by the faculty

One of the most successful and most popular members of the dental profession in this city, he has made his personal impression on dental science, and is a member of many societies connected with his profession, both in the United States and in Europe In 1878, when the Dental Society of the State of New York desired that the practitioners whose interests it concerned should be represented in the book entitled The Public Service of the State of New York, Dr. Bodecker was one of four gentlemen honored by being selected to have their portraits as representative dentists appear in the volume. When the International Medical Congress, made up of delegates from all parts of the world, assembled in Washington, in 1887, Dr. Bodecker was Chairman of the Dental Clinic. Again, in 1893, he presided over the Clinic of the International Dental Congress, that met at Chicago during the World's Fair, and has held a distinguished position in other scientific gatherings connected with his chosen profession and its interests in various directions.

Aside from his private practice, Dr. Bodecker has occupied many important positions in connection with dental institutions. He was a professor of Dental Histology and Embryology in the New York College of Dentistry, and occupied the same chair in the University of Buffalo. Many dental societies have honored him with election as an honorary member ; in this country, the New Jersey State Dental Society, the New Jersey Central Dental Society, and the California State Odontological Society. He is also an honorary member of the American Dental Society of Europe, Der Central Verein Deutscher Zahnarzte, and the Svenska Tandlakave Sallskapt. Dr. Bodecker has written much upon the subject of dentistry, contributing many valuable papers to dental periodicals, and publishing several pamphlets. He is also the author of The Anatomy and Pathology of the Teeth, a work that has been accepted by the profession as an authoritative treatise, and which has been quoted with high commendation by the leading authorities upon dentistry, both here and abroad, as one of the most advanced works of its kind of the present age.

In 1874, Dr. Bodecker was married to Wilhelmina Himbeck, who came from a German family distinguished in the annals of the State Her grandfather was the Count Von Himbeck, and her father was in the direct line of inheritance to the title, which is an ancient one, descending from a line of eminent ancestors He married Doris Konig, who did not belong to the nobility, and for that reason forfeited his right to the title, which passed to collateral heirs. Dr. and Mrs. Bodecker have two sons. Charles F. Bodecker is a minor. Dr. Henry W. C. Bodecker is a practicing dentist, who has taken his degrees of B S. and D D S , and is associated with his father in the practice of his profession and gives promise of sustaining the paternal reputation for original scientific investigation.

Dr. Bodecker resides at 60 East Fifty-eighth Street, and has a country residence at Centre Moriches, L. I. He is interested in gentlemanly outdoor life, but especially in yachting and riding. He is not much of a club man, finding recreation from his professional life only in the German Liederkranz. He has traveled extensively throughout Europe, and has had entrance to the most aristocratic society. He has been presented at court in the Old World. At home he is a generous entertainer and has had, from time to time, as his guests, many distinguished foreign visitors.

JOHN BOGART

FOR centuries the name of Bogart has been borne by many Hollanders of distinction Sometimes it has been spelled Bogart, and again Bogert, and different branches of the family have at times used the prefixes, van den or van der. A Bogart was Minister of Remonstrants in the sixteenth century. Another was Recorder General of the Dutch Provinces in the seventeenth century, and his portrait appears in one of Rembrandt's famous paintings. William Jans Boogaert was a kirk-meister in Amsterdam in 1590, Jan Willem Boogaert was a commissioner in the same city in 1611, and Johan Bogaert was a deputy sheriff. Some members of the family Latinized the name, and thus, in this country, we have Everhardus Bogardus, who was one of the earliest Dutch clergymen in New Amsterdam Several pioneers of the name settled in New Jersey, and on the Hudson, and one influential branch went to Beverwyck, now Albany.

Teunis (Anthony) Bogaert was the Dutch ancestor in the old country of that branch of the family which settled in Beverwyck. He was a resident of Schoenderwoert, a small village near Leerdam, in the southern part of Holland His son, Cornelis Bogaert, of Schoenderwoert, was the father of Cornelis Bogaert, who was buried in Albany in 1665. The second Cornelis Bogaert came from Holland in 1640 to Rensselaerwyck, where he held land under the Patroon Van Rensselaer in 1641. He also owned land in Beverwyck. His descendants married and intermarried with the leading Dutch families of Albany and vicinity. His son, Jacob, who died in 1725, married Jannetje, daughter of Pieter Quackenbush, and his grandson, Isaac, who died in 1770, married Hendricke, daughter of Hendrick Jants Oothout. His great-grandson, Hendrick I., who was born in 1729 and died 1821, married Barbara, daughter of Johannes Marselis.

During the Revolutionary War, Hendrick I Bogart was Assistant Deputy Quartermaster-General under Colonel Morgan Lewis, and a member of the Committee of Safety, was appointed by Congress Commissioner of Stores and Provisions in 1775, and by General Washington Inspector of Revenues of the Port of Albany in 1791. He was an alderman in 1767 and city surveyor.

Johannes Bogart, who was the son of Hendrick I. Bogart, was born in 1761, married Christiana, daughter of Captain John Vought, of Duanesburgh, and died in 1853, aged ninety-two. At the time of his death he was the oldest mariner of the Hudson River, having commanded a vessel in 1776, and was an intimate friend of General Phillip Schuyler, of the old Patroon Stephen Van Rennselear and of other leading men of that period. He was the father of John Henry Bogart, who, born in Albany in 1809 and educated in the Albany Academy, was a prominent merchant of Albany and New York, and who married Eliza Hermans, daughter of John Hermans, of Albany.

Mr John Bogart, civil engineer, was the oldest son of John Henry Bogart and his wife Eliza. He was born in Albany, February 8th, 1826. His early education was secured in the Albany Academy, and he then attended Rutgers College, in New Brunswick, N J., graduating therefrom in 1853. Immediately after completing his education he entered upon the practical work of civil engineering. His first employment was in the location and construction of several railroads and upon the enlargement of the Erie Canal. For a short time he was an instructor in the Albany Academy, and was then engaged upon the original construction of Central Park. During the Civil War he was in the Engineer Service of the Union Army, stationed most of the time at Fortress Monroe In the years immediately following the war he was engaged largely upon public parks, his work being principally in laying out Prospect Park, Brooklyn, the West Chicago Parks, the State Capitol Grounds of Nashville, Tenn., and the Albany Park, the construction of which he designed and supervised. He was engineer-in-chief of the Brooklyn Park Commission, chief engineer of the Department of Public Parks of New York, and director and secretary of the American Society of Civil Engineers. He is a member of the Century Association, the University, $\Delta\Phi$, Lawyers' and Engineers' clubs, the Essex Club of Newark and the Essex County Country Club, the Holland Society and the St Nicholas Society His wife was Emma Clara Jeffries, daughter of Professor William J Jeffries, of Westchester, Pa.

FRANK STUART BOND

WILLIAM BOND, who was baptized in St James Church, Bury St Edmonds, September 8th, 1625, the ancestor of Mr Frank S Bond's family in this country, came from England in 1630, with Deacon Ephraim Child, whose wife was his father's sister. They settled in Watertown, Mass., of which town he became a prominent citizen. He was of the Council of Safety in 1689, and speaker of the General Court of Massachusetts Bay in 1691. He was also the first speaker elected under the new Royal Charter, that united the Colonies of Plymouth and Massachusetts Bay into one Colony in 1692, which office he held in 1695, when he died. He married, February 7th, 1649, Sarah, the daughter of Nathaniel Biscoe, an original settler of Watertown. William Bond was the third son of Thomas Bond, of Bury St. Edmonds, Suffolk, England, and grandson of Jonas Bond of the same place.

A son of William Bond was Colonel Jonas Bond, of Watertown, 1664-1727, who was Lieutenant-Colonel in the expedition to Canada under Sir William Phipps, in 1690, and was a representative of Watertown to the General Court. The great-great-grandson of Colonel Jonas Bond was the Reverend Dr. Alvan Bond, a distinguished Congregational minister of Massachusetts and Connecticut. He was born in 1793, graduated from Brown University in 1815, and from Andover Theological Seminary in 1818. He was pastor of the Congregational Church in Sturbridge, Mass., from 1819 to 1831, and Professor of Sacred Literature in Bangor Theological Seminary from 1831 to 1835. In 1835 he went to Norwich, Conn., as pastor of the Second Congregational Church, and remained there until he died, in 1876. His first wife, the mother of Major Frank S. Bond, was Sarah Richardson. She was the daughter of Ezra Richardson, of Medway, Mass., and granddaughter of Captain Joseph Lovell, of the Massachusetts Militia, in the Revolutionary War A recent volume, entitled Alvan Bond, Life and Ancestry, 1896, contains sketches of forty-two early settlers, ancestors of Mr. Frank S. Bond

Born in Sturbridge, Mass , in 1830, the seventh in descent from William Bond, Mr. Frank S. Bond began his business career before he was twenty years of age. In 1849 he entered the office of the Norwich & Worcester Railroad Company ; removed to Cincinnati in 1850, and became secretary of the Cincinnati, Hamilton & Dayton Railroad Company ; came to New York in 1857, and until 1861 was an officer of other roads

When the Civil War broke out, Mr. Bond gave up his business and went into the service of his country. In 1862, he was commissioned First Lieutenant in the Tenth Regiment of Connecticut Volunteers, and assigned as aide-de-camp to Brigadier-General Daniel Tyler, then serving in General Pope's command in the Department of Mississippi, and who took an active part in the operations that led to the capture of Corinth. After that he served as Captain and aide-de-camp on the staff of Major General W. S. Rosecrans, at Stone River, Murfreesboro, Tullahoma, Chattanooga, Chickamauga and in other engagements. After the death of Lieutenant-Colonel Garaseche, Chief of Staff to General Rosecrans at the Battle of Stone River, Captain Bond was appointed by the President, Major and aide-de-camp, and assigned as senior aide-de-camp on staff of Major-General Rosecrans.

At the end of the war, Major Bond again entered the railroad service and became vice-president of the Missouri, Kansas & Texas Railroad, 1868-73 ; vice-president of the Texas & Pacific, 1873-81 ; president of the Philadelphia & Reading, 1881-82 ; president of the five associated roads, the Cincinnati, New Orleans & Texas Pacific , the Alabama Great Southern ; New Orleans & Northeastern ; Vicksburg & Meridian, and Vicksburg, Shreveport & Pacific, 1884-86. Since 1886 he has been first vice-president of the Chicago, Milwaukee & St. Paul Railway Company, with headquarters in New York City He belongs to the Sons of the American Revolution (Connecticut Society) ; the Military Order of the Loyal Legion of the United States ; the Metropolitan, Century, Union League, and Union clubs, the New England Society, the New York Historical Society, the American Geographical Society, and is a life member of the National Academy of Design, the American Fine Arts Society, and the New York Zoological Society.

ROBERT BONNER

SPRUNG from sturdy Scotch-Irish stock, this eminent citizen of New York was born in Ramelton, Ireland, in 1824 Several members of his maternal grandfather's family had emigrated to this country early in the present century, one of his uncles being a landowner near Hartford, Conn Crossing the ocean in 1839, Mr Robert Bonner came to this uncle and began life as an apprentice in the composing room of The Hartford Courant Here he was thoroughly grounded, not only in the details of the printing trade, but in those of publishing and in editorial work In 1844, he came to New York and formed a connection with The New York Evening Mirror, then conducted by Nathaniel Parker Willis He also became the New York correspondent of The Hartford Courant, and acted in the same capacity for newspapers in Washington, Boston and Albany In 1850, when he had been six years in New York, he undertook the publication of The Merchants' Ledger, an insignificant commercial paper In a short time, he became its owner, and gradually abandoning the commercial features in favor of fiction, he changed its name in 1855 to The New York Ledger, a publication which revolutionized the business of weekly periodicals in this country Mr Bonner's remarkable success was due to the combination of features which he originated and employed in this connection He made the tone of the paper healthy and pure, his advertising was conducted upon a phenomenal scale, and he engaged a notable array of writers, including such eminent names in American literature as Fanny Fern, John G Saxe, N P Willis, Edward Everett, Henry Ward Beecher and Horace Greeley Mr. Bonner continued in active business and editorial charge of his paper until 1887, when he permanently retired from journalism and was succeeded by his sons

For many years Mr. Bonner has been identified with the development of the American trotting horse His interest in driving was originally due to his physician, who advised him to thus obtain exercise and healthful recreation He has never been interested in the turf, and is unalterably opposed to betting and gambling, nor have any of the horses he owns ever been entered on the race track Peerless, Rarus, Dexter, Maud S and Sunol, the most celebrated trotting horses in the world, have been inmates of Mr. Bonner's stable, being used simply for his own pleasure His liberality has raised the value of horses throughout the country, and his example has done much to cultivate the taste of Americans for highly-bred horses His stock farm, near Tarrytown, N Y , is one of the most famous establishments of its kind in the world Religious and educational objects have been largely benefited by Mr Bonner's generosity He contributed a considerable amount toward the building of the Fifth Avenue Presbyterian Church and has made numerous gifts to Princeton University, contributing half the expense of its new gymnasium. In Mount Auburn Cemetery, Boston, a beautiful marble monument which he erected marks the last resting place of the authoress, Fanny Fern Mr Bonner has been president of the Scotch-Irish Society of America from its foundation to the present time, and is a member of the Metropolitan Museum of Art His city residence is in West Fifty-sixth Street.

Since 1887, the three sons of Mr Bonner have conducted the journal which he established The eldest, Andrew Allen Bonner, married Jeanette Fitch, daughter of George B. Fitch, of Lawrenceburg, Ind. He inherits his father's tastes for horses, and owns, among others, the celebrated Alcantara and King Rene, Jr.

Robert Edwin Bonner, the second son, born in New York in 1854, graduated from Princeton University in 1876 In 1880, he married Kate Helena Griffith, daughter of Edward Griffith, of this city They have four children, Griffith, Hampton, Kenneth and Kate d'Anterroches Bonner. He is a member of the Metropolitan, University, Princeton, Press and Fulton clubs and the Princeton Alumni Association, and takes an active part in social life.

Frederick Bonner, the youngest of the family, is also a graduate of Princeton University. He married Marie Louise Clifford, daughter of Robert H Clifford He is a connoisseur of art and a writer of marked ability.

ROBERT ELMER BOORAEM

WILLIAM JACOBSE van BOERUM, who came to the New Netherland in 1649, sprang from a family that ranks among the nobility of the Low Country The name was changed in spelling several times by its American bearers and was finally transformed to Booraem early in the eighteenth century It is derived from the town of Burum or Boerum, near Dokkum, in the Dutch province of Friesland Its first representative in this country was a magistrate at Flatbush, L I, in 1657, 1662 and 1663, and represented the same place in a convention held by the Dutch government of the Province in February in 1664, as recorded in The Early Settlers of Kings County, by Tunis Bergen. Among his descendants was the patriot Simon Boerum, whom death alone deprived of the honor of signing the Declaration of Independence.

About 1718 the family established their seat at New Brunswick, and it is in this line that Mr Robert Elmer Booraem traces his descent New Brunswick was noted in early days for its cultivated society and at the era of the Revolution the great leaders were entertained there when passing between New York and Philadelphia Representing, as he does, one of the most ancient Dutch names in New York's history, he is also related to such New York, New Jersey and New England families as Rutgers, Brinckerhof, Morrell, Van Vechten, de Mott, de Genereux, Van Horne, Rolfe, Gale, Van Wagenen, Potter, Petit, as well as Van Vorst, Vacher and Elmer Hendrick Booraem, his grandfather, mentioned in The Old Merchants of New York, was noted for the elegance of his manners. He was Colonel of one of the New York City militia regiments The business place of the large importing house of which he was the head was in Pearl Street, near Wall, and in 1815 his residence was at No 16 Dey Street About 1826 he removed to No 24 Warren Street, and when, some years later, he built a house at No 481 Broadway, he was thought to have moved out of town He was warden of Christ Church when it was in Anthony Street, and was a trustee and incorporator of the Marble Cemetery, where the family vault is situated The wife of Hendrick Booraem was Hannah Radley Morrell, of the old New York family of that name.

His son, Henry A. Booraem, and the father of Mr. Robert Elmer Booraem, was born in Dey Street, New York, September 3d, 1815. He entered his father's business house and later on became prominent in the importing trade as a partner in the firm of L & B Curtis and Company. He retired some thirty years ago, and died, at his residence in Jersey City in 1889 Respected in both business and social life as a man of the highest character, he was a member of the Board of Trade and of the Committee of One Hundred in Jersey City.

Cornelia (Van Vorst) Booraem, his wife, was a daughter of John Van Vorst. Cornelius Van Vorst, from whom she was descended in the seventh generation, came over in June, 1636, as Commander and Superintendent of Pauw's Colony of Pavonia, now in part Jersey City. His son, Ide Van Vorst, is mentioned by the historians of the New Netherland as the first white male child born and married within its limits The same authorities also make many references to him, as for instance when he saluted Governor Wouter Van Twiller and when he entertained the latter, Domine Bogardus, Captain de Vries and other dignitaries representing church and State with princely hospitality from his cellar newly filled with the wine of Bordeaux. His family was of importance, one of his relatives being John Van Vorst, a Professor at the University of Leyden.

The large landed possessions acquired by Cornelius Van Vorst included the tract which became Van Vorst Township, fronting on the Hudson River, Hudson County, N J, and which later was united with Jersey City. A large part of this estate continued in the possession of his descendants through all the succeeding eight generations, and Mr Robert E. Booraem owns a portion of this ancestral property. The members of the family presented the Jersey City municipality with the land for Van Vorst Square, and Grace Church, Van Vorst, in that city, was organized by the efforts of Mr Booraem's father, the late Henry A Booraem, and owed much to the generosity and support of his mother-in-law, Sarah (Vacher) Van Vorst, and others of her family.

Mr Booraem's maternal grandmother was born Sarah Vacher, and was the daughter of the

Revolutionary hero and famous New York surgeon, Dr. John Francis Vacher The latter was born in 1751 at Soliers, a small town near Toulon, France He received his medical degree in 1769 from the College de Chirugie of Montpelier, in Lower Languedoc Coming to New York City at the outbreak of the Revolution, he was made surgeon to the Fourth New York Regiment. His services among the starving troops at Valley Forge were particularly memorable. At the close of the war, under Act of Congress of October 21st, 1780, he was discharged after serving his adopted country faithfully in its time of need, and he was among the group of officers who originated the Society of the Cincinnati. Resuming the practice of his profession in New York City, he numbered among his patients members of leading families. His residence was in Fulton, then called Fair Street, and his country home at Bottle Hill, now Madison, N. J.

On his father's side, Mr. Booraem also descends from an eminent New England family whose lineage is of the most ancient description, his own second name, Elmer, commemorating this connection. Aylmer, or Elmer, was an officer of State in the reign of Edward the Confessor, and his large estates in Essex are mentioned in Domesday Book John Aylmer was tutor to the unfortunate Lady Jane Gray, and afterwards Lord Bishop of London under Elizabeth. His son was Sir Robert Aylmer, and his grandson, Edward Aylmer, came to America in 1632, settled in Cambridge, Mass., became one of the original proprietors of Hartford, Conn, and was slain in King Philip's War The name was transformed in spelling to Elmer. One of its representatives was the Reverend Jonathan Elmer, who graduated in Yale in 1747, and subsequently became identified with the town of Elizabeth, N. J., and was the editor of the first newspaper there.

Born at Jersey City, March 28th, 1856, Mr. Robert Elmer Booraem was educated at schools in Germany and at the Anthon Grammar School in New York. He then entered the School of Mines of Columbia College, and after graduation took a post-graduate course for the degree of Doctor of Philosophy, and in 1878 was given the degree of Engineer of Mines. Soon after he took up active work as assayer at the great mining camp at Leadville, Col, and finally became manager of the well-known Evening Star Mine. He afterwards successfully assumed a similar post with the Morning Star Mining Company, and had charge of the Farwell Gold Mine at Independence, Col., and after eight years in Colorado, became the executive head of the Blue Bird Mining Company, of Montana, which under his administration produced several millions for its owners. He also acquired a number of silver mines at Aspen, Col. Mr. Booraem confesses to a fascination for the mining country, and after twelve years there returned to the East with regret. He is Director and Consulting Engineer of the properties with which he was identified, and though now making his home in New York at 2 East Fifteenth Street, takes frequent trips to the West in connection with his mining and other interests, the latter including real estate in Salt Lake City and a large ranch on Salina River, Kan.

His immediate family includes four brothers living and two sisters, one of whom, Frances D. Booraem, is a member of the Colonial Dames, admitted through thirteen distinct lines of descent. She is also Treasurer of the Daughters of the Cincinnati, and is the first Directoress of the Home for Aged Women in Jersey City, an institution founded by one of her family His other sister, Josephine, is Mrs. Augustus Zabriskie, her husband being the youngest son of the late Chancellor Zabriskie of New Jersey.

Mr. Booraem owns a number of old family portraits and paintings of the Dutch School. He has musical tastes and is a member of a number of social organizations, including the Calumet, American Yacht and Badminton clubs, also of the Society of Colonial Wars, the Sons of the Revolution, the St. Nicholas Society and the American Institute of Mining Engineers. He is active in the Alumni of the School of Mines, Columbia College, and in 1894 was appointed a member of the Alumni of the School in connection with the removal of Columbia University to Morningside Heights, and Class Treasurer of the Alumni Memorial Hall Fund.

The arms of van Booraem are:—Gold, a Moor's head with silver head band accompanied by three green clover leaves, two above, one below, surmounted by a knight's helmet with necklace. The family is now represented in the nobility of the Netherlands

MRS. J. A. BOSTWICK

EARLY in the seventeenth century, the name of Bostwick appeared among the English founders of the New England Colonies. The family, while not large, was, however, scattered during the succeeding generations, until its representatives are found in many portions of the country. The late Jabez Abel Bostwick belonged to the branch of his family which became established in Delaware County, N. Y., where he was born in the town of Delhi, September 23rd, 1830 His parents removed to Ohio when he was quite young, and there he received his education and at an early age engaged in the business pursuits in which he was to be so successful. Beginning life with little beyond his education and natural ability, his progress was rapid and steady. He resided for a time in several Western cities, including Cleveland, O., Lexington, Ky., and Cincinnati, O. He was engaged both in banking and in mercantile business, and was noted for his comprehensive grasp of the largest and most involved affairs, and naturally became at a comparatively early age possessed of considerable means. Although personally retiring and extremely modest by nature, he took a natural position of leadership in the situations in which he was placed by the mere force of talent, and by the unceasing industry which throughout his life was one of his marked characteristics.

New York City, however, presented, as it always does, a wider field for one of Mr. Bostwick's capacity and energy in affairs, and in 1866 he removed here and founded a cotton brokerage firm under the title of Bostwick & Tilford, his partner being John H. Tilford, the son of one of the gentlemen with whom, in Lexington, Ky., his own first business experiences had been obtained. At that time, the discovery of mineral oil and its utilization for so many different purposes had only begun Mr. Bostwick was one of the first in the country to appreciate the possibilities in that connection as a source of both individual and national wealth and a leading and useful industry. He entered into the business, in all its branches of production and manufacture, with characteristic energy and success and attained a commanding influence in the trade, so that when the great combination of such interests was formed which is now known as the Standard Oil Company, he was one of its leading members and took charge of its finances with the position of treasurer. Other large and varied interests also engaged his attention. He was prominent in railroad affairs and was at one time president of the New York & New England Railroad Company, and the largest owner of the Housatonic Railroad, while he was interested in innumerable enterprises of various kinds, many of them tending to increase the commercial and manufacturing importance of New York. He was a member of the New York Stock Exchange, and of the Cotton Exchange and many other prominent commercial bodies.

Although typically American in his devotion to the vast business interests of which he was the creator, Mr. Bostwick enjoyed the social side of life and was a member of the Union League, Manhattan, New York Yacht, Riding and other clubs, and was throughout his entire career noted for his generous and unostentatious gifts for charitable and philanthropic causes. Southern educational institutions were in particular the beneficiaries of his liberality, among them being the Wake Forest College, in North Carolina, and Richmond College, Virginia. He built and endowed the Emanuel Baptist Church, in Suffolk Street, New York, while he was a liberal supporter of many charitable objects His death occurred in August, 1892.

Mr. Bostwick married, in New York City, in 1866, Helen C. Ford, daughter of Smith R. Ford, a retired merchant. The family of Mr. and Mrs. Bostwick consisted of three children, Albert Bostwick and two daughters, the eldest of whom is the widow of the late Francis Lee Morrell, of this city, the younger being Mrs. Carstairs, wife of Captain Albert Carstairs, of the Royal Irish Rifles. Both Mrs Morrell and Mrs. Carstairs before marriage were prominent figures in the hunting field and the social coterie devoted to such sports in Westchester County. The Bostwick town house, which Mrs. Bostwick occupies in upper Fifth Avenue, is one of the handsomest in that residential portion of New York.

FREDERICK GILBERT BOURNE

OF English origin, the immediate ancestors of Mr. Frederick Gilbert Bourne were residents of Massachusetts and Maine. His paternal grandparents were Benjamin Bourne and Mary Hatch. His father was the Reverend George Washington Bourne, who was born in 1813 and married Harriet Gilbert in Portland, Me, in 1843, his death occurring in 1872. The Reverend George W. Bourne was the last of his immediate race, most of his family in his generation having died young. Mrs. Bourne was born in 1817 and, surviving her husband, is now a resident of New York. Her father was an importer of iron and steel. He was born in Brookfield, Mass., in 1775 and for many years was engaged in shipping, in Portland.

Mr. Frederick Gilbert Bourne was born in Boston, Mass., in 1851. He was educated in the public schools of New York, and early in life entered upon a business career, his first position being with the Atlantic Submarine Wrecking Company, in 1865. Later he became secretary to Edward Clark, and upon his death, in 1882, Mr. Bourne was made manager of the Clark estate. In 1885, he was elected secretary of The Singer Manufacturing Company, and in a few years was advanced to the presidency of that corporation, which position he now holds. Mr. Bourne is a member of the Chamber of Commerce, and a director in the Bank of the Manhattan Company, Knickerbocker Trust Company, Central Railroad of New Jersey and Long Island Railroad Company. A sister of Mr. Bourne is Clara (Bourne) Whitman, of Groton, Conn., widow of John Loring Whitman, who was a son of the Reverend Alphonso Loring Whitman, of Norwich, Conn., of one of the oldest Colonial families of New England. Another sister, May Louise, married Charles A. Miller, of New York. Mr. Bourne's only brother is William Theodore Bourne, of California

Mr. Bourne married, February 9th, 1875, Emma Keeler, who belongs to an old New York family. The father of Mrs. Bourne was James Rufus Keeler and her mother was Mary Louisa Davidson, daughter of J. E. Davidson, of Scotland. Her father was born in 1818, the youngest son of William and Deborah (Lounsbury) Keeler, of Norwalk and Stamford, Conn. William Keeler, 1782-1822, married, in 1804, Deborah Lounsbury, 1784-1849, daughter of Amos and Elizabeth (Lockwood) Lounsbury; he was the eldest son of Isaac Keeler, of Norwalk, 1759-1814, whose wife was Deborah Whitney, 1758-1838, daughter of David and Elizabeth (Hyatt) Whitney. David Whitney, 1721-1816, was a master mariner of Norwalk, and tradition says that he was a soldier in the Revolutionary War. His wife, 1718-1798, was a daughter of Ebenezer and Elizabeth Hyatt, of Norwalk. He was the third son of Joseph and Hannah (Hoyt) Whitney.

Joseph Whitney, 1678-1741, was the second son of John and Elizabeth (Smith) Whitney. He married, in 1704, Hannah Hoyt, daughter of Zerubbabel Hoyt, of Norwalk, whose father, Walter Hoyt, was born about 1618, was in Windsor in 1640 and an early settler of Norwalk, in 1653. The father of Walter Hoyt was Simon Hoyte, who, born in England about 1595, came to Salem, Mass, in 1628, was in Charlestown the following year and afterwards lived in Dorchester and Scituate, Mass., and Windsor, Fairfield and Stamford, Conn., in which latter place he died in 1657 John Whitney, the father of Joseph Whitney, was a son of Henry Whitney, the American pioneer, and his mother was a daughter of Richard Smith. Henry Whitney was a native of England, where he was born about 1620. He was settled on Long Island prior to 1649, being a citizen of Southold, Huntington and Jamaica, and afterwards of Norwalk, Conn.

The city residence of Mr. and Mrs. Bourne is at the corner of Seventy-second Street and Central Park, West. Their country place is Indian Neck Hall, in Oakdale, Long Island. Their surviving children are Arthur Keeler, May Miller, Marion, Alfred Severin, Florence, George Galt, Marjorie, Kenneth and Howard Bourne. Frederick Gilbert, Jr., Louise and Helen Bourne, are deceased Mr Bourne belongs to the New York, Larchmont, Atlantic and Seawanhaka-Corinthian Yacht clubs, and the Racquet, South Side Sportsmen's and Lawyers' clubs. Mrs. Bourne's sisters are Mrs Frederick E. Ballard and Mrs. Harry Cowdrey, of this city Her only brother, James Waterbury Keeler, and her eldest sister, Mis Harry M. Dodge, are deceased.

GEORGE SULLIVAN BOWDOIN

A S the name indicates, the family of which Mr George Sullivan Bowdoin is the prominent representative in New York in the present generation, is of French origin Its American ancestor was Pierre Baudouin, a Huguenot, who first emigrated to Ireland, thence to Portland, Me, in 1678, and finally came to Boston in 1690 The grandson of Pierre Baudouin was Governor James Bowdoin, of Massachusetts, one of the famous pre-Revolutionary statesmen, who was also renowned as a lover and patron of learning. The University of Edinburgh gave him the degree of LL D., and he was one of the founders and first president of the American Academy of Arts and Sciences The son of Governor Bowdoin, James Bowdoin, was not less eminent. He studied at Oxford and was graduated from Harvard in 1771, was Minister to Spain in 1804, founded Bowdoin College, and was noted for his philanthropy

After the formation of the Federal Government, when New York City became a political, business and social centre, two of the conspicuous figures of this last decade and a half of the century were Sir John Temple and his wife, Lady Temple, who was a daughter of Governor James Bowdoin Lady Elizabeth Temple, according to the writers of the day, was "very distinguished looking and agreeable and one of the popular ladies in New York She received guests every Tuesday evening and gave dinners, noted for their costliness, nearly every week to twenty or more guests" Mr. George S Bowdoin is a direct descendant of Sir John and Lady Elizabeth Temple in the fourth generation Sir John Temple, 1730-1798, was Lieutenant-Governor of New Hampshire, 1768-74, surveyor-general of the Northern District of America, 1761-77, and the first Consul-General of Great Britain to the United States, 1786-98 He was the son of Captain Robert Temple, of Charlestown, Mass., and Mehitable Nelson, who was the daughter of John Nelson, a member of the Committee of Safety in Boston, by his wife Elizabeth Tailer, daughter of William Tailer. John Nelson was a grandson of Sir John Temple, of Biddleson, who died in 1632, and a great-grandson of Sir Thomas Temple, of Stowe, who died in 1637, by his wife, Esther Sandys, daughter of Miles Sandys, of Latimers, Bucks. Sir Thomas Temple, 1542-1603, was the son of John and Susan (Spencer) Temple and descended in the eighth generation from Richard de Temple and Lady Agnes Stanley, daughter of Sir Ralph Stanley; and in the ninth generation from Nicholas de Temple and his wife, Lady Margery Corbet, daughter of Sir Robert Corbet Thence the line of lineage runs back seven generations to Edwyn, Earl of Leicester and Coventry, the first of the family to assume the name of Temple. Edwyn Temple was descended from Algar, King of the East Saxons, who was the son of Leofric, King of Leicester, and his wife, Lady Godiva.

The great-grandmother of Mr Bowdoin was Elizabeth Temple, the third child of Sir John and Lady Temple. She married, in 1786, Thomas Lindall Winthrop, of Massachusetts, who was born in New London in 1760, graduated from Harvard College in 1780, and died in Boston in 1841 In his early life he was an active Federalist, but became a Republican in 1812. He was a State Senator, Lieutenant-Governor of Massachusetts, 1826-32, a Presidential elector, and president of the Massachusetts Agricultural Society, the Massachusetts Historical Society and the American Antiquarian Society He was the great-grandson of Governor John Winthrop, of Connecticut, who was born in Groton Manor, England, in 1606, and died in Boston in 1676. Educated in Trinity College, Dublin, he came to this country in 1631 and settled in Ipswich, Mass, being one of the first assistants of Massachusetts In 1646, he settled the plantation of Pequot, now New London, Conn, and was Governor of Connecticut from 1646 until his death He was twice married, his first wife being his cousin, Martha Fones, and his second wife Elizabeth Reade, daughter of Edmund Reade, of Wickford, Essex. The father of John Winthrop was John Winthrop, the celebrated first Governor of Massachusetts The mother of Governor John Winthrop, of Connecticut, was Mary Forth, daughter of John Forth, of Essex, England, and his grandparents were Adam Winthrop and Anne Browne, of Groton, Suffolk, England The grandmother of Mr. Bowdoin was Sarah Winthrop, 1788-1864, the eldest daughter of Thomas Lindall Winthrop and Elizabeth Temple. She was a sister of the Honorable Robert C Winthrop, of Boston. The grandfather of Mr. Bowdoin was George Sullivan, 1783-1866 He was the son of James Sullivan, 1744-1808, who married for his first wife, Hetty Odiorne, daughter of William Odiorne, and for his second wife Martha Langdon, sister of Governor John Langdon, of New Hampshire. James Sullivan was king's attorney in 1770, a member of the Provincial Congress in 1774, Judge of the Supreme Court in 1776, delegate to Congress, 1784-85, a member of the Massachusetts Legislature, of the Governor's Council in 1787, Attorney-General, 1790-1807, and Governor of Massachusetts, 1807-08. He was descended, through the O Sullivan-Bease family of Ireland, from Louis VII, of France. His father was Master Sullivan, born in the County Kerry, Ireland, in 1690, who came to this country in 1723 and settled in Berwick, Me. The father of Master Sullivan was Major Philip O'Sullivan, of Ardea, County Kerry, son of Owen O'Sullivan, who was descended from Daniel O'Sullivan, Lord of Bearehaven, and Joan McCarthy, daughter of Dermod McCarthy, of Killoween.

The father of Mr Bowdoin was George R J. Sullivan. Graduating from West Point, he took the name of Bowdoin, the family name of his great-grandmother, Lady Temple. He married Frances Hamilton, granddaughter of Alexander Hamilton and his wife, Elizabeth Schuyler, daughter of General Philip Schuyler, and thus Mr. George Sullivan Bowdoin traces his lineage to the Hamiltons, Schuylers, Van Rensselaers, Morrises, and other great families of New York, as well as to the notable New England families that have already been referred to The father of Frances Hamilton and the grandfather of Mr. Bowdoin was James Alexander Hamilton, 1788-1878. He was graduated from Columbia College in 1805, and during the War of 1812 was Brigade Major and Inspector of the New York State Militia After the war, he engaged in the practice of law. During the first administration of President Andrew Jackson, he was Secretary of State, and in 1829 became United States District Attorney for the Southern District of New York. He received the degree of LL. D from Hamilton College and published a volume of reminiscences of his distinguished father. His wife was Mary Morris, daughter of Gouverneur Morris.

Mr George Sullivan Bowdoin was born in New York. He received his education in private schools and in the scientific department of Harvard College, where he studied for three years Early manifesting a predilection for business, he entered the counting house of Aymar & Co, the great New York merchants, in South Street. He became a member of the firm of Morton, Bliss & Co, of New York, and of Morton, Rose & Co., of London, in 1871, and remained associated with them for thirteen years. He then connected himself with the banking house of Drexel, Morgan & Co., and its successor, J. P. Morgan & Co., in which he is a partner, taking a prominent and active part in the business.

He has been largely interested in railroad enterprises, having been actively concerned in the financial affairs of the West Shore, the Philadelphia & Reading and many other railroad corporations Other business enterprises have sought his services in their directorates, and he has had official connection with the New York Life Insurance & Trust Company, the Mutual Life Insurance Company, the Guarantee Trust Company, the Commercial Union Fire Insurance Company, of London, the Bank for Savings, and is a governor of the New York Hospital.

Interested in art, literature and science, Mr. Bowdoin is a member of the Century Association, the Metropolitan Museum of Art, and the American Museum of Natural History, and is a member of the Chamber of Commerce, the Metropolitan, Union, Union League, Knickerbocker, Tuxedo, Players, Manhattan and other clubs, belongs to the New England Society, the Sons of the American Revolution, and is treasurer of the Huguenot Society of America. Mr. Bowdoin married Julia Irving Grinnell, daughter of Moses H. Grinnell, the celebrated New York merchant, who on her mother's side is a great-niece of Washington Irving. They have one daughter, Edith Grinnell Bowdoin, their married daughter, Fanny Hamilton Bowdoin, having died at the age of twenty-eight. Their son, Temple Bowdoin, is a graduate of Columbia University in the class of 1885, and is engaged in the banking business in his father's firm He married Helen Parish Kingsford Mr. Bowdoin's New York residence is 39 Park Avenue and his country seat is at New Hamburgh-on-Hudson.

JOHN MYER BOWERS

FOR several generations, the Bowers family, of whom this gentleman is the representative at this day, has been identified with Cooperstown, N. Y. Of English origin, the ancestors of its American branch came to Massachusetts early in the history of the Colony. Henry Bowers, of Somerset, Mass, who was a brother of Colonel Jerathmeel Bowers, descended from the earliest settlers in that section of the country. His son was Henry Bowers, 1747–1800, of Brighton, Mass., who married Mary Myer, of New York, a daughter of John Ray Myer and his wife, Ann Crommelin, daughter of Charles Crommelin. Mary (Myer) Bowers was the great-granddaughter of Adolph Myer, the American pioneer of that name. He came from Ulsen, in the parish of Bentheim, in Westphalia, and settled in Harlem in 1661. In 1671, he married Maria, daughter of Johannes Verveelen. He became the owner of a large estate, was assistant alderman in 1693, and died in 1711. His son was Hendrick Myer, who was born in Holland in 1673, but removed to New York, married Wintie Ray, daughter of John Ray, and died in 1753. John Ray Myer, son of Hendrick Myer and Wintie Ray, was born in 1719, and became a wealthy merchant. After the death of his first wife, Ann Crommelin, he married Helena (Rutgers) Scott, widow of the Honorable John Morin Scott.

John Myer Bowers, 1772–1846, first of the name, was the son of Henry and Mary (Myer) Bowers. He settled at Cooperstown, N. Y., and built the homestead there which for more than a century has been in the possession of the family. He married Margaret M. S. Wilson, 1776–1872, a daughter of Robert Wilson, 1751–1779, of Landsdowne, N. J., and his wife, Martha Stewart, 1757–1852, whose father, Colonel Charles Stewart, of Landsdowne, came from Gortlee, County Donegal, Ireland, and was the founder of the prominent Stewart family of New York.

Mr. John M. Bowers was born in Cooperstown, N. Y., November 27th, 1849. He received his education in private schools in Cooperstown and studied law in New York, where he was admitted to practice in 1871 and has long been one of the leading members of the bar. Interested in public affairs, he has been prominent in the councils of the Democratic party. Mr. Bowers married Susan Dandridge, a native of Ohio. Her great-great-grandfather was Governor Alexander Spotswood, who was born in Tangiers in 1676 and served with distinction under the Duke of Marlborough, being wounded at the battle of Blenheim. He came to this country as Governor of Virginia, holding that office from 1710 until 1723. He brought with him a concession of the right of habeas corpus, which up to that time had been denied the Virginians During his official career, he was active in resisting the encroachments of the French upon the Colony and in suppressing piracy. He also rebuilt the College of William and Mary, and was a pioneer in iron manufacturing in America. Governor Spotswood was a son of Robert Spotswood, who died in 1688, and a grandson of Sir Robert Spotswood, who was appointed by Charles I. Lord President of the College of Justice and Secretary for Scotland. He was descended from Robert Spottiswoode, of the barony of Spottiswoode, parish of Gordon, County of Berwick, Scotland. Tradition says that the family was descended from the house of Gordon. His wife, whom he married in 1724, was Ann Butler, daughter of Richard Bryan, of Westminster Governor Spotswood died in Maryland in 1740. His daughter, Dorothea, married Captain Nathaniel West Dandridge, of the British Navy, son of Captain William Dandridge of Elson Green. Captain Dandridge and his wife, Dorothea, were the ancestors of Mrs. Susan (Dandridge) Bowers. Mr. and Mrs Bowers have five children, Spotswood Dandridge, Henry Myer, William Crain, Mary Stewart and Martha Dandridge Bowers. The city residence of the family is in West Twenty-first Street, and their country home is the old family mansion in Cooperstown.

Mr. Bowers belongs to the Union, Metropolitan, Manhattan, Riding and Whist clubs, the Bar Association, the Downtown Association, the Sons of the Revolution, the Society of Colonial Wars and the American Geographical Society. A brother of Mr. Bowers was Henry C. Bowers, who died in Cooperstown in 1896.

JAMES LAWRENCE BREESE

O NE of the old tombstones in Trinity Churchyard bears this quaint epitaph :

"SIDNEY BREESE, JUNE 8, 1767
MADE BY HIMSELF
HA ! SIDNEY, SIDNEY,
LYST THOU HERE ?
I HERE LYE,
TILL TIME HAS FLOWN,
TO ITS EXTREMITY "

Thus Sidney Breese, the old time merchant, proverbial for his honesty as well as for his wit, commemorated himself. He was a native of Shrewsbury, England, born in 1709. Having been a warm partisan of Charles the Pretender, on the failure of the movement in behalf of that Prince, he entered the British Navy as a purser. After a few years he gave up his commission and came to New York and settled, being at one time master of the port here, as well as being a man of note in a commercial and social sense.

A son of Sidney Breese was Samuel Breese, 1737-1802, Colonel in the Continental Army and a Judge of the State of New Jersey Judge Breese's first wife was Rebecca Finley, grand-daughter of the Reverend Dr. Samuel Finley, president of Princeton College, and one of his grand-sons—son of his eldest daughter, Elizabeth Ann, who married the Reverend Jedediah Morse, the celebrated divine and geographer—was Professor Samuel Finley Breese Morse, inventor of the electric telegraph system.

Mr James Lawrence Breese is a great-grandson of Judge Breese. His grandfather, Arthur Breese, of Utica, N. Y., 1770-1825, was a graduate of Yale College and a lawyer, who married Elizabeth Anderson, of Scotch-French descent, granddaughter of the Reverend James Anderson, first pastor of the Wall Street Presbyterian Church, in 1718 Several sons of Arthur Breese became distinguished in National affairs. Rear Admiral Samuel Livingston Breese, 1794-1870, was a brave officer of the United States Navy. He was a midshipman in 1810, an officer on the ship Cumberland in the battle of Lake Champlain, in service in the wars with Tripoli and with Mexico, Commandant of the Norfolk Navy Yard, 1853-5, in command of the Mediterranean Squadron, 1856-8, and Commandant of the Brooklyn Navy Yard, 1859-61 He married Rose Lee, daughter of Colonel Thomas Lee, of Baltimore, Md. Another son was Judge Sidney Breese, of Illinois, 1800-1878, a graduate from Union College in 1818, Assistant Secretary of the State of Illinois, State Attorney in 1827, Lieutenant Colonel in the Black Hawk War, Circuit Judge 1835, Supreme Court Justice 1841, United States Senator 1843-9, Speaker of the Illinois House of Representatives 1850, Chief Justice of the Circuit Court 1855, Justice of the Supreme Court 1857, and Chief Justice of the Supreme Court 1873-1878 Lieutenant James Buchanan Breese of the United States Marine Corps, who married Josephine Ormsbury, daughter of Edward M. Yard, late Commander in the United States Navy, was another member of this family.

J Salisbury Breese, born in Utica, N Y., in 1812, was a son of Arthur Breese. He died in 1865 His wife was Augusta Eloise Lawrence, descended from John Lawrence, who came to Plymouth Plantation on the ship Planter in 1635, and also from Johannes Lowesen Bogert, who came from Haarlem, Holland, in 1671, and bought the Harlem Flats in New Netherlands

Mr. James Lawrence Breese, the son of J Salisbury Breese, was born in New York City, December 21, 1854 He graduated as a civil engineer from the Rensselaer Polytechnic Institute, of Troy, N. Y , in 1875, and afterwards studied architecture. Recently he has made photography his special pursuit, and is recognized as one of the leading artistic amateur photographers in the world, having received numerous medals from exhibitions in this country and abroad He has a handsome studio in New York City, a cottage at Tuxedo Park, is prominent in society, and belongs to the Union and Racquet Clubs, the Players, and other social organizations.

CALVIN S BRICE

THE Brice family is of old and honorable extraction in Scotland The first representatives of the name to come to the New World settled in Maryland, in the early part of the seventeenth century. They were a branch of the Bruces, of Airth, Scotland, who spelled their name Bryce, as is also the case with the members of another great northern house, Bruce, of Kinnaird. Edward Brice or Bryce, through whom the American Brices trace their descent to their Scottish progenitors, was a Presbyterian minister in Ireland, and is called Bryce in Scottish and Brice in the Irish records. He was the second son of Sir Alexander Bruce, of Airth, by Janet, his wife, the daughter of Alexander, fifth Lord Livingston, who died about 1553.

The father of Mr. Calvin S Brice was the Reverend William K. Brice, a Presbyterian clergyman of prominence in the church, who moved from Maryland to Ohio in 1812 His wife was Elizabeth Stewart, of Carrollton, Md , a descendant of the famous Scottish house of Stuart She has been described as "a woman of good mind, eminent for the graces and charms of her personal character" Mr Calvin S Brice, their son, was born in Denmark, O , September 17th, 1845. He had all the advantages of the best instruction in his boyhood, his education being supervised by his father, until he entered Miami University in 1858.

His patriotism led him to abandon college life at the opening of the Civil War in April, 1861, and he enlisted first in a company of three months' troops, and again in 1862 in the Eighty-sixth Regiment of Ohio Infantry After serving in the Virginia campaign, he returned to college and was graduated in 1863, but went to the front again as Captain of an infantry company and was advanced to the rank of Lieutenant-Colonel

When his military career ended, Colonel Brice entered the Law School of the University of Michigan, at Ann Arbor, and in the spring of 1866 was admitted to the bar. For ten or fifteen years he was actively engaged in the practice of his profession in Lima, O., as junior member of the firm of Irvine & Brice He devoted himself largely to corporation law, and that naturally led to his becoming interested in the subject of railroad transportation, which, with politics, has mainly engrossed his mature powers His first railroad experience was in the legal department of the Lake Erie & Louisville Railroad, a line of which, under the title of Lake Erie & Western, he is now president. He conceived and built the New York, Chicago & St. Louis Railroad, better known as the "Nickle Plate" road, which is now part of the Vanderbilt system, and has been a director, or officer, in many railroads and other corporations, a considerable part of his attention having been devoted to the development of the South

Colonel Brice has been as successful and eminent in politics as in business For many years he has been one of the leaders of the Democratic party. In 1876, he was on the Tilden Electoral ticket, and in 1884 was again an Elector when Mr Cleveland was elected. His State sent him as a delegate-at-large to the Democratic National Convention in 1888, and he was made a member of the National Committee. As chairman of the latter body he directed the Democratic National Campaign in that year. In 1890, he was elected United States Senator from Ohio, and served the full term of six years. In 1892, he was again delegate-at-large from Ohio to the Democratic National Convention and chairman of the Ohio delegation, and was re-elected a member of the Democratic National Committee Colonel Brice was married in 1870 to Catherine Olivia Meily, and has a family of three sons and two daughters.

While Colonel Brice is, and has always been, a citizen of Ohio, retaining a residence at Lima, in that State, his large and varied business interests oblige him to spend a considerable portion of his time in New York. The New York residence of the Brice family is at No 693 Fifth Avenue, and they also have an establishment in Newport At both places Mr and Mrs Brice entertain upon a large scale, and have become important factors in social life Mr Brice belongs to the Ohio Society, the Manhattan, Lawyers', Riding, and other clubs, and is a member of the American Geographical Society. Among his other cultured tastes is the collection of rare books.

CHARLES ASTOR BRISTED

THREE noted American families unite in the person of Mr Charles Astor Bristed, the Dwights and the Sedgwicks, of Massachusetts, and the Astors, of New York. The paternal grandfather of Mr Bristed was the Reverend John Bristed, who was born in Dorsetshire, England, in 1778, and died in Bristol, R. I., in 1855. Graduated from Winchester College, England, he studied medicine and law, and, coming to the United States in 1806, practiced law in New York. Subsequently he studied theology, and in 1828 was ordained to the Protestant Episcopal ministry. Until 1843, he was rector of the Church of St Michael, Bristol, R I, succeeding the Reverend Dr. Griswold. He conducted The Monthly Magazine in 1807 His wife, whom he married in 1819, was Magdalen (Astor) Bentzen, daughter of the first John Jacob Astor and his wife, Sarah Todd, and widow of Governor Bentzen, of the Island of Santa Cruz

Charles Astor Bristed, first of the name and father of the subject of this article, was the son of the Reverend John Bristed, born in New York in 1820 and died in Washington, D C, in 1874 Graduated from Yale College in 1839, he studied in Trinity College, Cambridge, England, for five years, and upon graduating, in 1845, he studied for and was about to obtain a fellowship at Cambridge, but finally determined to return to his own country, making his home in New York and Lenox, Mass He wrote much for newspapers and magazines, generally over the nom-de-guerre of Carl Benson, and published a number of books, among which were Letters to Horace Mann, The Upper Ten Thousand, Five Years in an English University, The Interference Theory of Government, and Pieces of a Broken-Down Critic. He was one of the trustees of the Astor Library from the foundation of that institution. His first wife was Laura Whetten Brevoort, daughter of Henry Brevoort, the only child of this marriage being J. J Astor Bristed, who died in 1880. His second wife, the mother of Mr Charles Astor Bristed, was Grace Ashburner Sedgwick, daughter of Charles Sedgwick, of Lenox, Mass, a son of the Honorable Theodore Sedgwick, Member of Congress, United States Senator and Judge of the Supreme Court of Massachusetts

The great-grandfather of Mrs. Bristed was Deacon Benjamin Sedgwick, 1716-1757, and she was descended in the seventh generation from Major-General Robert Sedgwick, who came to America in 1636 and was one of the most distinguished men of his time in Massachusetts Through her mother, Elizabeth Buckminster Dwight, Mrs Bristed was descended from John Dwight, who came to this country in 1634 and settled in Watertown, and afterwards in Dedham, Mass. The great-great-grandfather of Elizabeth B Dwight was Captain Timothy Dwight, 1629-1717, who was ten years town clerk of Dedham and twenty-five years selectman and representative to the General Court The descent to Mrs Bristed was through the third wife of Captain Timothy Dwight, who was Anna Flint, the daughter of the Reverend Henry Flint by his wife, Margery Hoar. The son of Captain Timothy Dwight was Captain Henry Dwight, 1676-1732, who married Lydia Hawley, daughter of Captain Joseph Hawley, of Northampton. His son, Colonel Josiah Dwight, born in 1715, was graduated from Yale College in 1736, and was a Lieutenant Colonel and Judge and father of the Honorable Josiah Dwight, Jr, of Stockbridge, State Treasurer of Massachusetts The latter, by his second wife, Rhoda Edwards, daughter of Timothy Edwards and Rhoda Ogden, a daughter of Robert Ogden, of New Jersey, became the father of Elizabeth Buckminster Dwight, wife of Charles Sedgwick. After the death of her husband, Mrs. Bristed resided abroad, principally in Rome, and died in Paris in 1897.

Mr Charles Astor Bristed was born in New York in 1869 He was educated at Stonyhurst, and afterwards was matriculated at Trinity College, Cambridge, England, and was graduated in 1893 He studied law, and has been engaged in the practice of that profession. In 1894, Mr. Bristed married Mary Rosa Donnelly, daughter of Edward C. Donnelly, of Grove Mount, Manhattanville. They have two children, Mary Symphorosa and Katharine Elizabeth Grace Bristed Mr Bristed s residence is in Lenox, Mass, and he is a member of the Knickerbocker and Catholic clubs of this city.

FREDERIC BRONSON

MEMBERS of the Bronson family were early settled in the Connecticut Colony, being especially numerous and influential in Hartford, Farmington and Waterbury. On the old records of Hartford, the name is usually spelled Brownson, while the Farmington records have it as Brunson. But whatever the spelling, all these pioneers came from the same parent stock. From Richard Bronson and John Bronson most of the Bronsons, of Connecticut, and their descendants in New York have been derived. John Bronson is believed to have been a member of the company that settled Hartford under the Reverend Thomas Hooker in 1636. The following year he was engaged in the famous battle with the Pequot Indians, and in 1641 removed to Farmington. In 1651, he was a deputy to the General Court, in 1652, a constable, and in 1669 was made a freeman. Isaac Bronson, son of John Bronson, the pioneer, was one of the first settlers of the town of Waterbury. He was active in church affairs, a Corporal and Sergeant of the train band in 1689 and 1695, a deputy to the General Court in 1697 and 1701, and frequently held other public offices, such as town surveyor and school committeeman.

In the four succeeding generations, the head of this interesting Colonial family was an Isaac Bronson. In the third generation, Captain Isaac Bronson married Mary Brockart, and their son, Isaac Bronson, who was born at Breackneck, now Middlebury, Conn., in 1760, became a distinguished physician, soldier and financier. His father was frequently a member of the General Assembly of Connecticut. The son studied medicine, and, although at the time of the Revolution he had not attained to his majority, he entered the Continental Army as junior surgeon. In 1779, he was in the Second Regiment of Light Dragoons of the Connecticut Line, serving under the immediate command of General Washington. After the war, he went abroad to travel, visiting all parts of Europe and India. Returning to the United States in 1789, he settled in Philadelphia, where he lived for several years, afterwards removing to New York and engaging in the banking business. Subsequently he established a banking house in Bridgeport, Conn. He died at his summer residence, Greenfield Hill, Conn., in 1839.

Isaac Bronson married, about 1789, Anna Olcott, daughter of Thomas Olcott, of Stratford, Conn., of one of the oldest Colonial families of that State. He had a large family of children, of whom several attained to prominence. His daughter Maria married Colonel James B. Murray, of New York. His daughter Caroline married Dr. Marinus Coillet. His son, Oliver Bronson, married Joanna Donaldson. Another son, Arthur Bronson, who was born in New York, married Anna Eliza Bailey, daughter of General Theodorus Bailey. A third son, Frederick Bronson, who was born in 1802, in New York, married Charlotte Brinckerhoff, of the well-known Dutch family of that name, that has been prominent in New York and New Jersey.

Mr. Frederic Bronson, the representative of this family in the present generation, was born in New York, educated in Columbia College, and graduated therefrom with the degree of B. A. in the class of 1871. Pursuing his studies further in the Law School of Columbia, he was in due course admitted to the bar, and has been a lawyer in active practice for more than twenty years. He married Sarah Gracie King, daughter of Archibald Gracie King, and has one daughter. The history of the King and the Gracie families, to both of which Mrs. Bronson belongs, has been fully set forth on other pages in this volume. Mrs Bronson includes in her ancestry such distinguished personages as Rufus King, James Gore King, Mary Alsop and Archibald Gracie.

The home of Mr. and Mrs. Bronson is in Madison Avenue, and their country seat is at Greenfield Hill, Southport, Conn., the ancestral home of the Bronsons. Mr. Bronson belongs to the Metropolitan, Knickerbocker, Union, Racquet, Riding, City, New York Yacht, Coaching and Δ Φ clubs, the Country Club of Westchester County, the Downtown Association and the Columbia College Alumni Association. He is a famous whip, and has long been a leading spirit in the Coaching Club. For several years he was vice-president of the club, and in 1897 was elected to the presidency, succeeding Colonel William Jay in that position.

JOHN CROSBY BROWN

A LEXANDER BROWN, the head of a family that has made a marked impression upon the business and financial interests of this country during the present century, was a native of Ireland, born in Ballymena, County Antrim, November 17th, 1764 He was a linen merchant, a man of good family, business enterprise, strict integrity, and some means. He came to this country in 1798, and going to Baltimore, started a linen store, dealing in goods that he imported principally from Ireland. As his business grew, he turned his attention to financial affairs and established a bank. He died in Baltimore in 1834. Four sons of Alexander Brown, all of them born in Ballymena, became associated with their father under the firm name of Alexander Brown & Sons Each of them attained to distinction in business and finance The eldest, William Brown, returned to England in 1809 and established a branch house there, now the celebrated banking firm of Brown, Shipley & Co. The second son, George Brown, remained in Baltimore and became the head of the house there. The third son, John A. Brown, went to Philadelphia, and was the representative of the firm in that city.

The youngest of the four sons, James Brown, born in 1791, came to New York in 1825 and started the house known as Brown Brothers & Co. He became one of the representative bankers of New York, and was for fifty years a member of the Chamber of Commerce. In the panic of 1837, the English branch of the firm of which Mr. Brown was the representative was able to secure a loan of ten million dollars from the Bank of England to carry them over the crisis and the loan was repaid within six months This achievement put the firm at once in the front ranks in the financial world, a position that it has maintained ever since.

James Brown was deeply interested in religious, educational and philanthropic enterprises. For thirty years he was president of the Society for Improving the Condition of the Poor, and among his benefactions was a gift of three hundred thousand dollars to the Union Theological Seminary. At the time of his death, in 1877, he was, with two exceptions, the oldest living member of the Chamber of Commerce, his membership covering more than half a century Mr. Brown was twice married. His first wife was Louisa Benedict, daughter of the Reverend Joel Benedict, of Plainfield, Conn. Two sons, James and William Brown, and three daughters were born of this union One daughter became the wife of Alexander Brown, of Richmond Hill, England The second daughter is the widow of the late Howard Potter, the well-known banker of New York and London. The third daughter married James Couper Lord. For his second wife, Mr Brown married Eliza Maria Coe, an accomplished and devoted Christian woman, who was the daughter of the Reverend Dr. Jonas Coe, of Troy.

Mr John Crosby Brown was the second of the three sons of James Brown by his second wife Born in New York, May 22d, 1838, he was graduated from Columbia College with the degree of B A. and has since received the degree of M A. During his entire business career, he has been connected with the banking house of Brown Brothers & Co in New York, of which he is now the head A gentleman of culture, deeply interested in art and literature, he has been a member of the Board of Education, a trustee of Columbia College, a trustee of the Metropolitan Museum of Art, vice-president of the board of trustees of the Union Theological Seminary, and a director in the Presbyterian Hospital. His clubs include the Metropolitan, City, University, Union, and Riding, the Century Association, the Downtown Association, and the Columbia College Alumni Association He married, in 1864, Mary E. Adams, daughter of the Reverend Dr William Adams, pastor of the Madison Square Presbyterian Church, and president of the Union Theological Seminary Mr. and Mrs Brown have two daughters and two sons Their eldest son, James Crosby Brown, is a graduate from Yale in the class of 1894. The youngest son, Thatcher M Brown, is a graduate from Yale in the class of 1897 The city residence of the family is in East Thirty-seventh Street and their country seat is Brighthurst, in Orange, N J

JUSTUS LAWRENCE BULKLEY

IN the reign of King John of England, in the twelfth century, Robert Bulkeley, Baron, was Lord of the Manor of Bulkeley in the County Palatine, of Chester   He was a nobleman of high standing and his descendants were allied in marriage to many of the first families of Great Britain.   In the ninth generation from Robert Bulkeley came the Reverend Edward Bulkeley, who was the father of the Reverend Peter Bulkeley, the American emigrant, one of the most famous clergymen of New England in the first years of the Massachusetts Colony.   The Reverend Peter Bulkeley was born in Woodhill, Bedfordshire, England, in 1583, was educated in St. John's College, Cambridge, and became a fellow there.   Subsequently he took orders and succeeded to the living of his father in Odell, holding that place for twenty-one years.   His independence brought him under the ban of Archbishop Laud, and he was removed from his living for non-conformity

With others of his faith, clergymen and laymen, the Reverend Mr. Bulkeley turned to the New World for freedom, and coming to this country in 1634, settled first in Cambridge, Mass , and afterwards was one of the founders of Concord.   He was the first pastor of the Concord Church and held that pulpit until the time of his death, in 1659.   The descendants of the Reverend Mr. Bulkeley, in both the male and the female line, have been especially famous in New England as clergymen.   He wrote several books, among them The Gospel Covenant; or, The Covenant of Grace Opened   His first wife was Jane Allen, daughter of Thomas Allen, of Goldington, England His second wife was Grace Chetwood.   Mr. Justus Lawrence Bulkeley is a lineal descendant in the eighth generation from the Reverend Peter Bulkeley.

In the second generation the Reverend Gershom Bulkeley was born in 1636 and, studying in Harvard College, was graduated in 1655.   Called to be the second minister of the church in New London, Conn., in 1661, he remained there for six years and then in 1667 removed to Wethersfield. In 1675, he was surgeon of the Connecticut Colonial troops   His death occurred in 1713.   His wife was Sarah Chauncy, daughter of President Charles Chauncy, of Harvard College, and through her his descendants trace their lineage to another great Colonial family and back to the nobility and royalty of England and France, the wife of the Reverend Charles Chauncy being Catharine Eyre, daughter of Robert Eyre and Ann Still, granddaughter of the Right Reverend John Still and Lady Jane Horner, and descended in the thirteenth generation, through the Spekes, Berkeleys and Staffords, from Edward I , King of England

In the subsequent generations, the ancestors of Mr. Justus L. Bulkley were Edward Bulkeley, who was born in 1673 in Wethersfield and died there in 1748, and his wife, Dorothy Prescott, daughter of Jonathan Prescott, of Concord; Peter Bulkeley, who was born in 1712 and died in 1776, and his wife, Abigail Curtis, who was born in 1741 and died in 1762; Joseph Bulkeley, who was born in 1742, and his wife, Mary Williams, daughter of Moses Williams; Edmund Bulkeley, who was born in 1787, and his wife, Nancy Robins; and Joseph Edmund Bulkley, who was born in 1812, and his wife, Mary (Lawrence) Bicknell, daughter of John Lawrence, of Newtown, Long Island   Peter Bulkeley, the great-great-grandfather of Mr. Justus Lawrence Bulkley, was a justice of the peace for Hartford County, Conn., in 1775.   His son, Joseph Bulkeley, was a merchant of Rocky Hill, Conn , a justice of the peace and a member of the State Legislature.   Joseph Edmund Bulkley, the father of Mr. Bulkley of the present day, came to New York at an early age, and entering upon mercantile life, soon became one of the leading leather merchants of the metropolis in the last generation   His wife was of the famous Lawrence family of Long Island.

Mr. Justus Lawrence Bulkley was born in New York in 1840, and has been engaged in the leather importing business during his entire mercantile career.   In 1871, he married Laura E Caldwell and has three children, Josephine, Helen C and Joseph F Bulkley.   His son is a student in Yale University in the class of 1899.   The city residence of the family is in upper Madison Avenue and their summer home is Homestead, in Rocky Hill, Conn.   Mr. Bulkley is a member of the Metropolitan and Riding clubs.

WILLIAM LANMAN BULL

ON both his father's and his mother's side, Mr William Lanman Bull is descended from several of the oldest and most distinguished families of New England. He can count among his ancestors the Bulls, the Lanmans, the Trumbulls, the Boylstons, the Coits and others who were prominent in the Colonial and Revolutionary periods. His remote paternal ancestor was Henry Bull, a native of South Wales, who came to America in 1635. After a short residence in the Massachusetts Bay Colony, he went to Rhode Island, being numbered among the followers of Roger Williams. With seventeen associates, he purchased land in 1638 and joined in the settlement of Newport, becoming at once one of the leading men in the new Colony. He held many positions of trust, and was a commissioner of Newport in 1655, a commissioner of Providence in 1657, and Governor of Rhode Island in 1685-6, and 1689-90. Governor Henry Bull was born in 1610 and died in 1693. His first wife was named Elizabeth, his second wife, whom he married in 1676, was Esther Allen, and his third wife, whom he married in 1677, was Ann Clayton. Many of his descendants were prominent in the early history of Rhode Island. Henry Bull, his grandson, 1687-1774, was Attorney-General of the Colony in 1727.

The father of Mr. William Lanman Bull was Frederic Bull, a prominent business man of New York and a descendant in direct line from Governor Henry Bull. He died at his country seat in Montclair, N. J., in 1871. Mr Bull's mother was Mary Huntington Lanman, who married Frederic Bull in 1829, and died in 1880. Her family was of English origin. The arms of the branch founded in this country by Peter Lanman, and to which Mrs Frederic Bull belonged are a shield azure, three garbs or. Motto, *Fortuna favet audace.*

James Lanman, a native of London, came to America about 1700 and settled in Boston. In 1714, he married Joanna, daughter of Dr. Thomas Boylston, of Roxbury, of one of the oldest Colonial families of Massachusetts. James Lanman moved with his wife to Plymouth, and his descendants have lived in that part of Massachusetts ever since. Peter Lanman, son of James Lanman, 1725-1804, married Sarah Spaulding Coit, daughter of Colonel Samuel Coit, of Preston, Mass, in 1764. His son was Peter Lanman, of Norwich, Conn., 1771-1854, the father of Mary Huntington (Lanman) Bull. The maternal great-great-grandfather of the subject of this article was a conspicuous figure in the Revolutionary period, his grandmother, the wife of Peter Lanman, Jr, of Norwich, Conn., having been a daughter of David Trumbull, whose father was Jonathan Trumbull, Governor of Connecticut from 1769 until 1783, through the whole period of the American Revolution, a trusted supporter and confidential adviser of General Washington. Governor Trumbull's wife was Faith Robinson, a direct descendant of John Alden and Priscilla Mullins.

Mr William Lanman Bull is the seventh child and the youngest son of his father's family. He was born in New York City, August 23, 1844. After a preparatory education, he completed his studies in the College of the City of New York. Then he began his business career by entering the banking house of Edward Sweet & Co, Mr. Sweet, the senior partner of this firm, having married a sister of Mr Bull. In 1867 he became a partner in the firm, a relation that he has maintained uninterruptedly down to the present time, a period of thirty years. Outside of his banking business, Mr Bull has been otherwise prominent in business and in social life. Twice he has been President of the New York Stock Exchange, and his important railroad connections have included membership in the directorates of the Northern Pacific, the East Tennessee, Virginia & Georgia, the New York, Susquehanna & Western and the Atchison, Topeka & Santa Fe Railroads, and he is now President of the St Joseph & Grand Island Railroad Company,

In 1870, Mr Bull married Tasie M. Worthington, daughter of Henry R. Worthington. His children are Frederic Henry Worthington, and William Lanman Bull, Jr. The family residence is at 805 Fifth Avenue. Mr Bull is a member of the Metropolitan, Century, University, Grolier, Union, Riding, Players, Church, and Mendelssohn Glee clubs, and belongs to the New England Society, the Sons of the American Revolution, and the Society of Mayflower descendants.

JAMES ABERCROMBIE BURDEN

AMONG the most talented inventors and successful business men of his generation in the United States, was Henry Burden One of his great-grandparents was of Feddal-Perth-shire and he was born in Dumblane, Scotland, April 20th, 1791. Displaying the bent of his genius at an early age, he took a course of engineering in Edinburgh, and came to the United States in 1819, settling in Albany, where he began the manufacture of agricultural implements He was phenomenally successful and his inventions and improvements in labor-saving devices in many ways revolutionized the industry of the country Among his inventions were improved agricultural implements, machines for making wrought-iron spikes, a machine for making horse shoes, and a suspension over-shot water wheel, sixty feet in diameter, of the design of bicycles of the present day

Mr Burden was one of the organizers of the Hudson River Steamboat Company The Hendrick Hudson, which in its time was one of the finest and fastest steamboats on the river, was built according to his models, and attained a speed of twenty miles an hour Another boat that he designed was called the Helen, it had two cigar-shaped hulls and on the trial trip in December, 1833, made eighteen miles an hour. Mr Burden made a study of nautical architecture, and it is one of the curious and interesting things in his career that, in 1846, he anticipated nearly all that has been accomplished in fast ocean travel during the last decade or more It was in that year he issued a prospectus of what he called Burden's Atlantic Steam Ferry Company, with himself as managing director, inviting subscriptions to the stock In this prospectus he said, "All experience in steam navigation shows that increase in size and power has been invariably attended with increase of speed, economy and comfort," and proceeding from those premises, he affirmed his confidence of being able "to establish boats of power, dimension and strength sufficient to make the passage from Liverpool to New York in eight days certain." He planned to build the first vessel six hundred feet long The company was never organized, however, and it required more than half a century for the commercial world to come to a full appreciation of his ideas

Mr. James Abercrombie Burden is the eldest son of Henry Burden He was born in Troy, N. Y., January 6th, 1833. Educated under the direction of private tutors, he also studied in the Yale Scientific School and the Rensselaer Polytechnic Institute, and then gained practical experience in manufacturing by an apprenticeship in his father's establishment in Troy. Ultimately he became president of the Burden Iron Company, of Troy, and in 1883 was president of the Hudson River Ore and Iron Company He inherited mechanical ability and inventive genius, and has taken out eighteen important patents in connection with the iron manufacturing industry

Mr Burden married Mary Irvin, daughter of Richard Irvin, the banker of New York His city residence is at 908 Fifth Avenue. Mr. and Mrs Burden have four sons, James A , Jr , Richard Irvin, Williams Proudfit and Arthur Scott Burden Mr. Burden is a member of the Civil Engineers, Mechanical Engineers and the American Institute of Mining Engineers He was president of the Society of New York Farmers, and belongs to the Metropolitan, Union, Union League and Riding clubs, and several scientific societies in Great Britain He was the first president of the Engineers' Club Although prominent socially, he has never taken an active part in public affairs, but has been three times a Presidential elector on the Republican State ticket James A Burden, Jr , graduated from Harvard University in the class of 1893 He married Florence Adele, daughter of William D Sloane ; is a member of the University and Knickerbocker clubs and the Sons of the Revolution. His country place is Messina, Barrytown-on-Hudson, N. Y.

Mr I Townsend Burden, the younger son of Henry Burden, married Evelyn Byrd Moale, of the Baltimore family of that name, her sister, Judith E Moale, is the widow of Robert Livingston Cutting, second of the name Mr and Mrs. Burden live in East Twenty-sixth Street, Madison Square, and their summer residence is Fairlawn, in Bellevue Avenue, Newport. They have four children, William A M and I Townsend Burden, Jr , and Evelyn B and Gwendolyn Burden.

HENRY LAWRENCE BURNETT

ONE of the most famous representatives of the ancestors of Burnett name was Gilbert Burnett, 1643-1715, Bishop of Salisbury, who was the son of a lawyer of an ancient family of the County of Aberdeen, Scotland, and who, after the Restoration, was appointed one of the Lords of Session, with the title of Lord Crimond. Gilbert Burnett studied at Marischal College, Aberdeen, and at Oxford and Cambridge, becoming a clergyman of the Church of England, and was a prominent figure in the political struggles which led to the English revolution of 1688. When William III. ascended the throne of England, Burnet was advanced to the See of Salisbury, and retained that position until his death, in 1715. His wife, Mary Scott, was a lady of considerable fortune. William Burnett, son of the Bishop, who was born at The Hague, Holland, in 1688, and died in Boston, Mass , in 1729, was intimately connected with the American Colonial governments He was bred to the law in England, and in 1720 was appointed by George I. Governor of New York and New Jersey, and afterwards of Massachusetts, in 1728. His administration in the Province of New York was successful, and he did much to strengthen the Colony against the French, establishing the first English fort at Oswego. He was the ancestor of many of the Burnett family in this country.

Thomas Burnett, the direct ancestor of the branch of the family to which General Henry Lawrence Burnett belongs, came to this country from England, and settled first in Lynn, Mass., afterward becoming a resident of Southampton, Long Island. Early in the seventeenth century, bearers of the name established themselves in New Jersey. William Burnett, of the New Jersey branch, was graduated from Princeton College in 1749, became one of the leading physicians of Newark, was an ardent patriot, a friend of Washington, and sacrificed his fortune in support of the cause. After the close of the Revolutionary War, he removed to Northern Ohio His first wife was Mary Camp, daughter of Nathaniel Camp. His second wife was Gertrude Van Cortlandt, widow of Colonel Phillip Van Cortlandt, of Newark, and daughter of Nicholas Gouverneur The grandfather of General Burnett was Samuel Burnett, who also went to Ohio in the first Westward movement immediately after the close of the Revolution, and was the father of Henry Burnett. The latter married Nancy Jones, who was a member of a Virginia family.

General Henry Lawrence Burnett, their son, was born in Youngstown, O., December 26th, 1838. He attended school in the Chester Academy, where President James A Garfield was also a student. In 1859, he was graduated from the Ohio State and National Law School, and admitted to the bar. Two years after, at the beginning of the Civil War, he entered the army, becoming Captain in the Second Ohio Cavalry. His regiment saw service in Missouri and Arkansas, and he was advanced in rank until he became Brigadier-General. In 1863, General Ambrose E. Burnside appointed him Judge-Advocate of the Department of Ohio, his jurisdiction being extended later to include the Northern Department. In association with Judge Advocate-General Holt and the Honorable John A. Bingham, he was engaged in the prosecution of the assassins of President Abraham Lincoln. In 1865, General Burnett resigned from the army and engaged in the practice of law in Cincinnati. Removing to New York in 1872, he was for a time associate attorney and counsel for the New York & Erie Railroad, but later engaged in general practice, being first associated with Benjamin H. Bristow, William Peet, and William S Opdyke, and afterwards with Edward B. Whitney. He has been connected with some of the most important litigation in the New York and United States Courts since he made New York his home.

By his marriage with Agnes Suffern Tailer, General Burnett became allied to another family that has been distinguished in the social life of New York for several generations, his wife being a daughter of Edward N and Agnes (Suffern) Tailer. General and Mrs Burnett live in East Twelfth Street. Their summer home is Oak Spring Farm, Stoneboro, Pa. General Burnett belongs to the Metropolitan, Union and Republican clubs, the Ohio Society, of which he is president, and the Century Association, the Bar Association, and the Military Order of the Loyal Legion.

MIDDLETON SHOOLBRED BURRILL

ACCORDING to the History of Lynn, Mass, "The Burrill family was formerly called the royal family of Lynn, in view of the many famous persons connected with it." Its founder in this country was George Burrill, who came from Seven Oaks, England, in 1630. He was among the large landowners of Lynn, having some two hundred acres of land, and was one of its most influential citizens. Both he and his wife, Mary, died in 1653. His son, Lieutenant John Burrill, was a representative in the General Court and married Lois Ivory, in 1656. In the third American generation came the Honorable Ebenezer Burrill, 1678-1761, son of Lieutenant John Burrill and ancestor in the sixth generation of Mr. Middleton Shoolbred Burrill. Ebenezer Burrill married Martha Farrington and settled in Swampscott. He was for many years a representative to the Massachusetts General Court and for nine years a member of the Governor's Council. His son, Ebenezer Burrill, Jr, who was born in 1702, was for seventeen years town clerk and a representative for twelve years. The wife of the second Ebenezer Burrill was a daughter of the famous General Mansfield. Their son was John Ebenezer Burrill, of Rhode Island and New York, who became a successful merchant. During the Revolution, he was an officer in the Continental Army. His son, the grandfather of the subject of this sketch, was Ebenezer Burrill.

In collateral lines, the present Mr. Burrill has had many distinguished relatives. Sarah Burrill, daughter of Lieutenant John Burrill and Lois Ivory, married John Pickering, of Salem, and became the grandmother of the celebrated Senator and Cabinet Minister, Timothy Pickering Samuel Burrill, son of the second Ebenezer Burrill, was a representative to the General Court of Massachusetts during the War of the Revolution and a member of the Constitutional Convention. John Burrill, brother of the first Ebenezer Burrill, was a member of the Massachusetts General Court for twenty-two years and Speaker of that body for ten years James Burrill, son of the second Ebenezer Burrill, was one of the leading citizens of Providence, R. I., in the closing years of the last century, and his son was the Honorable James Burrill, Chief Justice of the Supreme Court of Rhode Island and United States Senator from that State. The town of Burrillville, R. I., was established by him. He was a graduate from Brown University.

The father of Mr. Middleton Shoolbred Burrill was John Ebenezer Burrill, who was born in Charleston, S. C., in 1822, and died in Lenox, Mass., in 1893. Prepared for college in private schools, he entered Columbia and was graduated with high honors in 1839. Taking up the study of law, he was admitted to practice in 1842, and for more than half a century was one of the most successful as well as ablest members of the New York bar A staunch Democrat, he maintained a deep interest in public affairs, but had little inclination for political life When he was a young man, he served for a short time as assistant district attorney of the city and was a member of the Constitutional Convention in 1867, but he was not otherwise conspicuous in public affairs. He was one of the founders and an officer of the Bar Association of the City of New York. In 1853, he married Louise M. Vermilye, daughter of William M. Vermilye, the well-known New York banker, who belonged to an old New York Huguenot family, dating back to the early Colonial period Johannes Vermilye, her ancestor, was one of the leading citizens of New Amsterdam in the early years of this settlement, holding office in both church and municipality.

Mr. Middleton Shoolbred Burrill was born in New York, October 16th, 1858. He was prepared for college in a private school and under the direction of a tutor, and then entering Harvard University, was graduated in 1879. He studied law in the Law School of Columbia University and in the office of a leading law firm, and was admitted to practice in 1881. Since 1884, he has been a member of the firm of Burrill, Zabriskie & Burrill, of which his father was the head. In 1885, he married Emilie Neilson, daughter of William Hude and Caroline (Kane) Neilson. His city residence is 104 East Thirty-fifth Street, his country home being at Cedarhurst, Long Island. He belongs to the Union, Knickerbocker and Rockaway Hunt clubs, the Sons of the Revolution, the Bar Association and the Downtown Association

GEORGE HENRY BUTLER, M. D.

A NCESTORS of Dr George Henry Butler were among the early pioneers of New England. Thomas Butler, who settled in Kittery, Me , before 1695, was one of the ancient English house of Ormonde, and being a man of high character and superior intellectual attainments, took a leading part in the affairs of that part of the Massachusetts Colony for more than a quarter of a century He was an accomplished scholar and one year taught Latin gratuitously in the schools, when it happened that the services of no other teacher "who had the Latin tongue" could be procured At the same time, he was a selectman and a surveyor of public lands, frequently a moderator of the town meeting, and was elected more than thirty-five times to hold various other offices in the gift of his fellow townsmen.

Thomas Butler, son of the first Thomas Butler, was also prominent in the affairs of the township He was born in Berwick, Me., in 1698, and in the old records is described as a "gentleman " In 1725, he was a constable, and for many years a surveyor of lands His brother, Moses Butler, held a commission as Captain in the Colonial Army and took part in the capture of Louisburg in 1745 He held many town offices, and in 1749 was representative to the General Court at Boston, the Maine plantation being at that time part of the Massachusetts Colony. Dr. George Henry Butler is a descendant in the fifth generation from the second Thomas Butler, of Berwick The family has been prominent in the section where it was founded in 1695, and in many branches of it there have been those who have attained to distinction in Maine, Massachusetts and elsewhere Moses Butler, great-grandfather of Dr. Butler, was an officer in the Continental Army during the war for independence, and saw service about Machais and Frenchman's Bay, Me His brother, Thomas Butler, was a Lieutenant in the Continental Line In contemporaneous times, the Reverend Dr John Butler, a Free Baptist clergyman, was the author of many books and at one time editor of the newspaper organ of the Baptist Church in New England Another editor in the family was the Honorable J E Butler, and the Honorable Moses Butler was an eminent jurist and three times Mayor of the City of Portland, Me

Both the father and the grandfather, as well as other ancestors of Dr George H Butler, were natives and residents of Berwick, Me , and there he was born May 31st, 1841 He was educated in the High School of Great Falls, N H , Bowdoin College and the University of Pennsylvania, and finished his professional studies in the Bellevue Hospital Medical College He has been a practicing physician and surgeon, principally in New York, for more than thirty years, but has found time to travel extensively throughout Europe During the Civil War, for nearly five years, he was Passed Assistant Surgeon in the United States Navy In club land he is known as a member of the Union League Club, and is also a member of the Sons of the Revolution, the Loyal Legion, the New England Society, and the New York Genealogical and Biographical Society

The wife of Dr Butler, to whom he was married in 1872, was Henrietta Louisa Lawrence, of the celebrated Lawrence family of Long Island, from which have come so many distinguished men and women Mrs Butler is seventh in descent from Thomas Lawrence, founder of the family in this country, who came to Long Island in the latter part of the seventeenth century. Her great-grandfather was Jonathan Lawrence, the wealthy merchant, 1737-1812, who was a Major in General Woodhull s Brigade of Long Island troops in 1777, a member of the Provincial Congress 1775-76, and a State Senator in 1777 Her grandfather was the Honorable Samuel Lawrence, 1773-1837, member of the State Assembly, Member of Congress and a Presidential elector in 1816; and her granduncle was the Honorable William T Lawrence, Captain of Artillery in the War of 1812, County Judge in 1838 and Member of Congress, 1847-49

Dr and Mrs Butler live in Fifth Avenue. Their country residence is the Lawrence homestead, in Odessa, N Y. The Butler arms are Or , a chief indented azure The crest shows, out of a ducal coronet or , a plume of five ostrich feathers, argent, therefrom a falcon rising, argent The Lawrence arms are A cross, regular gules Crest, a demi-turbot argent

PRESCOTT HALL BUTLER

JUSTIN BUTLER, of New Haven, and his wife, Lucy Davis, were the great-grandparents of Mr. Prescott Hall Butler, whose grandparents were Henry Butler and Rebecca Green Several sons of Henry Butler and Rebecca Green have occupied commanding positions in professional life in New York City. The eldest son, George B Butler, who was born in New Haven in 1809 and died in New York in 1886, is still remembered as one of the proprietors of The New York Journal of Commerce, and secretary and attorney of the Hudson River Railroad Company His son, George Butler, is the distinguished artist, one of the foremost American painters of this generation.

A brother of George B Butler was Charles E. Butler, who was born in Richmond, Va , in 1818, and began the study of law in 1836 in the office of the late Jonathan Prescott Hall. When he was twenty-four years old, in association with William M Evarts, he founded the law firm of Butler & Evarts, now Evarts, Choate & Beaman Retiring from professional work in 1879, he spent most of his time, after that, upon his estate in Stockbridge, Mass His first wife was Louisa Clinch, sister of Cornelia Clinch, who became the wife of Alexander T Stewart, the great merchant prince Mrs Butler died in 1852 She was the mother of six children, Prescott Hall, Maxwell Evarts, Rosalie, Helen C , Virginia and Lilian, who is Mrs John Swan. Rosalie Butler died in 1897 The maternal grandmother of Mr Prescott Hall Butler, Rebecca Green, who married Henry Butler in 1807, was born in New Haven in 1788, the daughter of Samuel Green, 1744-1799, and his wife, Abigail Buell, who was born in Killingworth, Conn , in 1749 and died in Richmond, Va , in 1819 Abigail Buell was descended in the fourth generation from William Buell, the American pioneer of the family William Buell, or Bewelle, or Beville, was born in Chesterton, Huntingdonshire, England, about 1610 Emigrating to America as early as 1630, he settled first in Dorchester, Mass., and then in 1635 joined the first company that went westward to found the town of Windsor. He died in Windsor in 1681. His son, Samuel Buell, was born in Windsor in 1641 and after 1664 lived in Killingworth, where he died in 1720 In the old records he is especially set down as a "gentleman," was an extensive landowner and was honored by his fellow citizens by election to many positions of trust and responsibility.

By his marriage, in 1662, to Deborah Griswold, 1646-1719, Samuel Buell allied himself to another of the great Colonial families of Connecticut His wife was a daughter of Edward Griswold, of Windsor, brother of Governor Matthew Griswold The Griswold family is descended from Humphrey Griswold, of Greet, Lord of the Manor Their ancestors came originally from Cambridgeshire, where they were established as early as 1135 The grandparents of Abigail Buell, and the ancestors in the sixth generation of Mr. Prescott Hall Butler, were Benjamin Buell, of Killingworth, 1686-1725, and Hannah Hutchinson, of Hebron, whom he married in 1710. Her parents were John Buell, who was born in Killingworth in 1717 and died in 1752, and Abigail Chatfield, daughter of John Chatfield

Mr Prescott Hall Butler was born in Richmond County, N. Y , March 8th, 1848, and educated in Harvard College, being graduated from that institution in the class of 1869 He is engaged in the practice of law in New York, is a member of the law firm of Evarts, Choate & Beaman, and belongs to the Bar Association. In 1874, he married Cornelia Stewart Smith, daughter of J Lawrence Smith and Sarah Clinch and a descendant from Jacob Clinch, the father of Mrs. A T Stewart, Mrs Butler being a grandniece of Mrs Stewart Mr and Mrs Butler live in Park Avenue Their summer home is Bytharbour, St James, Long Island They have one daughter, Susan L. Butler, and two sons, Lawrence and C Stewart Butler, who are students in Harvard University. Mr. Butler belongs to the Century Association, the University, Racquet, Riding, Harvard, Players. Metropolitan, Adirondack League, Seawanhaka-Corinthian Yacht, New York Yacht, Larchmont Yacht and Jekyl Island clubs, and the Downtown Association, and is a patron of the American Museum of Natural History.

DANIEL BUTTERFIELD

JOHN BUTTERFIELD, the American ancestor of the family of which General Butterfield is a prominent representative in the present generation, came from England and settled in Virginia, but some of his descendants removed from Virginia to New England. The paternal grandfather of General Butterfield was Daniel Butterfield, and his maternal grandfather was Gamaliel Olmstead, a Connecticut soldier of the War of the Revolution. His father was John Butterfield, a substantial business man of Oneida, N. Y., his mother being Malvina H Olmstead.

General Daniel Butterfield was born in Oneida County, N Y , October 31, 1831. He received a liberal education in local schools, was graduated from Union College in 1849, and has since received the degree of LL D. Completing his collegiate course, he came to New York, where he engaged in business until the Civil War began. He entered the National Guard of New York in 1850 and became Major and Lieutenant-Colonel of the Seventy-First and Colonel of the Twelfth Regiment. Holding the latter rank when the Civil War opened, he at once offered his command to President Lincoln, and went to Washington at the head of his regiment, April, 1861. In July, 1861, he led the advance into Virginia over the Long Bridge, and subsequently joined General Patterson on the Upper Potomac, where he was immediately placed in command of a brigade and actively engaged in service, overstaying the three months time of his enlistment and receiving commendatory orders therefor. When, as part of the plan for carrying on the war, the regular army was enlarged, Colonel Butterfield was made Lieutenant-Colonel of the Twelfth Regulars and was commissioned Brigadier-General of Volunteers. His next service was under General Fitz John Porter in the Peninsula Campaign, and he was engaged in the battles of Mechanicsville, Gaines' Mill and Malvern Hill and other engagements. At Gaines' Mill he was wounded, and, while still suffering from his wounds, commanded a detachment of troops sent to the south side of the James River to cover the retreat of McClellan's Army. During the entire campaign of August and September, 1862, under Generals Pope and McClellan, he was constantly at the front and took part in all the battles.

In 1862, General Butterfield was commissioned Major-General of Volunteers. The following year he was made Colonel of the Fifth Infantry Regiment in the regular army. At the battle of Fredericksburg he was in command of the Fifth Army Corps During the summer of 1863, he was Chief of Staff of the Army of the Potomac, then commanded by General Hooker. At the battle of Gettysburg, where he was Chief of Staff of the Army of the Potomac, under General Meade, he was wounded. Later in the same year, he was detailed to reinforce the Army of the Cumberland, and was Chief of Staff to General Hooker at Lookout Mountain, and in all the famous engagements around Chattanooga. In the celebrated Atlanta Campaign of one hundred days, which ended in the capture of Georgia's capital, General Butterfield commanded a division of the Twentieth Corps, and for gallant and meritorious conduct was brevetted Brigadier-General and Major-General in the regular army. After the close of the war, General Butterfield was assigned to superintend the recruiting service of the army. In 1869, he resigned from the army, and the same year President Grant appointed him Assistant United States Treasurer in New York. Retiring from that position, he became interested in the banking business and is now connected with many large corporations

In 1886, General Butterfield married Mrs. Julia L. James, of New York, a daughter of Captain Safford, who commanded privateers in the War of 1812. The ceremony was performed at St Margaret's, Westminster, England, the Bishop of Bedford and Canon Farrar officiating. He lives in Fifth Avenue, his country residence being Cragside, Cold Spring, N. Y. He is a member of the Union, Military and Σ Φ clubs and belongs to the Sons of the Revolution, the Loyal Legion and the Union College Alumni Association. In 1891, he was president of the Society of the Army of the Potomac He has the special distinction of holding the United States Medal of Honor for notable bravery upon the field of battle, at the action of Gaines' Mill

JOHN LAMBERT CADWALADER

A MONG the distinguished citizens of Philadelphia in the early Colonial days, none was more highly esteemed than John Cadwalader, who came from England soon after William Penn's organization of the Colony of Pennsylvania. He was a freeman of Philadelphia in 1705, a member of the Common Council, 1718-33, and a member of the Provincial Assembly from 1729 to the time of his death, in 1734. His wife, whom he married in 1699, was Martha Jones, daughter of Dr Edward Jones and maternal granddaughter of Dr Thomas Wynne, of Philadelphia. John Cadwalader could trace his descent through a notable line of ancestry. His family was Welsh and his mother, Ellen Evans, who was the daughter of Owen ap Evan, and granddaughter of Evan ap Robert ap Lewis, of Rhiwlas and Vron Goch, married Cadwalader Thomas ap Hugh, of Kiltalgarth, Llanvawo, Merionetshire, Wales. Evan ap Robert ap Lewis was in the twenty-fifth generation from Rhodri Mawr, King of all Wales, who died in 876.

The second child and the oldest son of John Cadwalader, the pioneer, was Dr Thomas Cadwalader, of Philadelphia, a member of the Provincial Council of Pennsylvania in 1755 and a medical director in the Continental Army during the War of the Revolution. His wife was Hannah Lambert, daughter of Thomas Lambert, and his eldest son was General John Cadwalader, of Philadelphia, 1742-1786. General John Cadwalader married a daughter of Edward Lloyd, of Nye House, Talbot County, Md., and among his descendants were Dr John C A Dumas, Captain George A McCall, U. S A, General Samuel Ringgold, U S A., Major Samuel Ringgold, U. S A, and Rear Admiral Cadwalader Ringgold, U. S N.

Colonel Lambert Cadwalader, the second son and third child of Dr. Thomas Cadwalader, was born in Trenton, N J, in 1743. He was Colonel of a New Jersey regiment at the outbreak of the Revolution, was taken a prisoner by the British at the capture of Fort Washington in 1776, and being released on parole retired to his estate. From 1784 to 1787, he represented New Jersey in the Continental Congress, was a member of the Constitutional Convention and a Member of Congress from New Jersey, 1789-95. He died at his homestead, Greenwood, near Trenton, N J, in 1823. He married Mary McCall, daughter of Archibald McCall, of Philadelphia, in 1793.

Among other distinguished members of this notable family have been Major-General George Cadwalader, who served in the Mexican and the Civil wars, John Cadwalader, 1742-1786, who was a Brigadier-General in command of the Pennsylvania military forces during the War of the Revolution; Captain Samuel Dickinson, of the United States Army, who is descended from Dr Thomas C Cadwalader through his daughter, Mary; Judge J Meredith Read, Chief Justice of Pennsylvania, and his son, John Meredith Read, Jr, United States Consul to Paris and United States Minister to Greece, who were respectively son and grandson of John Read, whose father, George Read, signed the Declaration of Independence, and of Martha Meredith Read, the daughter of General Samuel Meredith, the first Treasurer of the United States, and his wife, Margaret Cadwalader, who was the seventh child of Dr. Thomas C Cadwalader.

Mr. John L Cadwalader is the grandson of Colonel Lambert Cadwalader His father was Major-General Thomas Cadwalader, who was born in 1795 and died in 1873. His mother was Maria C Gouverneur, daughter of Nicholas Gouverneur, of New York, and his wife, Hester Kortright, who was a daughter of Lawrence Kortright Mr Cadwalader was born November 17th, 1836 He was graduated from Princeton College, educated for the law and entered upon the practice of his profession in New York. In 1874, he was Assistant Secretary of State of the United States His club membership includes the Metropolitan, Union, Knickerbocker, Century, University, Riding, Lawyers', Commonwealth, New York Yacht and Seawanhaka-Corinthian Yacht He belongs also to the Tuxedo colony, is a member of the Bar Association, the Sons of the Revolution and the Downtown Association, and a patron of the American Museum of Natural History.

JOHN CALDWELL CALHOUN

A N Irish Presbyterian, James Calhoun, came from Donegal, Ireland, in 1733, and founded the Calhoun family in the United States He first settled in Pennsylvania, subsequently removed to Kanawha, Va , and in 1756 went to South Carolina, where he established a settlement in the district of Abbeville Patrick Calhoun, son of the pioneer, married Martha Caldwell, daughter of a Presbyterian emigrant from Ireland Their third son was the Honorable John C Calhoun of South Carolina, the great champion of the South in national politics Born in 1782, he was graduated with honors from Yale College in 1804 and studied law in the Litchfield Law School He began the practice of law in Abbeville and soon became actively engaged in politics In 1807, he was in the State Legislature and, in 1811, became a Member of Congress, where he was one of the prominent advocates of the war with England For seven years after 1817, he was Secretary of War under President Monroe, in 1825 he became Vice-President of the United States, and in 1829 was reëlected upon the ticket with President Jackson. After his term expired, he was a Member of the United States Senate until his death, in 1850 Calhoun never advocated slavery or nullification for their own sakes He was ardently in favor of preserving the Union, as is shown in his biography by Von Holst He believed in the sovereignty of the States, and hence slavery was assailed ; it being a question for the States alone to decide, he incidentally defended that institution to protect the rights of the States in the Union It was the same with nullification He held it to be one of the reserved rights of the States under the Constitution, and that the exercise of it by the States did not necessarily dissolve the Union, but would strengthen it by preserving the autonomy of the States He supported the annexation of Texas and championed the cause of peace when the war with England was threatened by the Oregon dispute His wife was his cousin, Florida Calhoun, daughter of the Honorable John Ewing Calhoun, United States Senator from South Carolina.

The father of Colonel John Caldwell Calhoun, Andrew Pickens Calhoun, was the eldest son of South Carolina's great statesman His mother, Margaret N Calhoun, was a remarkable woman and a famuos belle, related to Chief Justice John Marshall Andrew Pickens Calhoun owned an extensive plantation near Demopolis, Ala , and was a large cotton planter.

Colonel Calhoun has many distinguished ancestors His maternal great-grandfather, William Green, was a soldier with Washington at Valley Forge, when only fifteen years old, and was with General Morgan at Cowpens in 1781 His maternal grandfather was General Duff Green, son of William Green. Duff Green was born in Kentucky about 1780 and died in Georgia in 1875 Admitted to the bar in 1801, he was for several years publisher of a newspaper in Baltimore, entitled The Merchant, and from 1825 to 1829 edited a Washington newspaper in opposition to President John Quincy Adams During the first term of President Jackson, he conducted The United States Telegram in Washington, in support of the administration, but in 1830 cast his lot with Calhoun upon the nullification question, and in 1836 supported South Carolina's great son for the presidency General Duff Green's wife was Ann Willis, a daughter of Colonel Henry Willis and Mildred Washington, cousin of George Washington The maternal grandmother of Colonel Calhoun was Lucretia Edwards, daughter of the Honorable Ninian Edwards, 1775-1833, the distinguished jurist who was Chief Justice of Kentucky in 1808, Governor of the Territory of Illinois in 1809, and the first elected Governor of that commonwealth, in 1826

Mr. John Caldwell Calhoun was born upon his father's plantation in Alabama, July 9th, 1843 When he was eleven years old, his parents returned to South Carolina, and settled at Fort Hill, upon the old homestead of his illustrious grandfather He entered the State University of South Carolina in 1859 When the Civil War opened, he enlisted in the company of cadets which was organized among the students of the University, and went with his command to Charleston, where he was present at the bombardment of Fort Sumter After the hostilities had fully opened, his company joined the army in Virginia and was attached to General Wade Hampton's Legion, and although he was not yet eighteen years old, he was elected Color-Sergeant of the Legion Cavalry. Having served upwards of a year, he was honorably discharged from the army on account of his extreme youth. Upon returning to his home in South Carolina, he was again influenced by the war spirit, organized a cavalry troop of one hundred and sixty men, of which he was placed in command, and with which he hastened back to the army in Virginia, and joined the Fourth South Carolina Cavalry, Donovan's Brigade of General M. C Butler's Division. At that time he was said to be the youngest Captain in the Confederate service At the battle of Trevellyn Station, he especially distinguished himself in a gallant charge against the brigade of General Custer.

After the close of the war, Colonel Calhoun returned to the family homestead in South Carolina and entered energetically upon the task of recreating his fallen fortunes and reviving the prosperity of the section of the country in which he resided. He took the position at that date that the conditions which caused the war had been settled by the arbitrament of the sword, and urged upon the people of his section to devote themselves to the restoration of prosperity and the reestablishment of their fortunes. His father was dead and the support of his mother, sister and three younger brothers devolved upon him. He soon became the second largest cotton planter in the South, and also engaged in other business enterprises of considerable importance One of his plans contemplated the establishment and development of extensive plantations in the Yazoo Valley of Mississippi. Disposing of his interests in this successful enterprise, he then carried out a similar undertaking upon a larger scale in Arkansas, where he was president of the Calhoun Land Company and the Florence Land Company, and president of the Levee Commission of Arkansas He was the first to organize the emigration movement of negroes from various parts of the South to the Mississippi Valley, colonizing more than five thousand freedmen in that section. In 1883, he was a delegate from Arkansas to the Cotton Exposition in Louisville, and again a delegate to the Cotton Exposition in New Orleans the following year. In 1884, he was vice-president of the convention in Washington which petitioned Congress for the improvement of the Mississippi River and its tributaries.

Removing to New York some fifteen years ago, Colonel Calhoun soon became prominent in Wall Street circles and has been connected with many important railroad enterprises. His first conspicuous operation was the consolidation of the Southern Railway systems into the Richmond Terminal Company, and he had an active part in the operations connected with the control of the Central Railroad of Georgia, becoming a director and afterwards vice-president of that company under its new management, and chairman of the Finance Committee. He was elected to the directorate of the Richmond & West Point Terminal Company, and has been officially connected with many other railroads, chiefly in the Southern States

In December, 1870, Colonel Calhoun married Linnie Adams, only daughter of David Adams, of Lexington, Ky., and grandniece of the Honorable Richard M Johnson, former Vice-President of the United States. Colonel and Mrs. Calhoun have four children, James Edward, David Adams, Julia Johnson and John Caldwell Calhoun The eldest son, James Edwards Calhoun, who was born in 1878, is now being prepared for admission to Yale College. The city residence of the family is in West End Avenue, and their country places are in Chicot County, Ark., and at Abbeville, S. C. Colonel Calhoun belongs to the Manhattan, Lawyers', Reform and Democratic clubs, and the Sons of the American Revolution, of which he is senior member of the board of managers. He was appointed special ambassador of the Sons of the American Revolution, to invite the President and Ministry of the French Republic and the descendants of Lafayette, Rochambeau and DeGrasse and the representatives of art, science and literature to attend the banquet given by the society on February 6th, 1897, in celebration of the one hundred and nineteenth anniversary of the signing of the treaty between France and America. In recognition of his services, the society, in October, 1897, made him an honorary life member and acknowledged his services, and the high esteem in which it held him, by formal resolutions, which were engrossed and presented to him He is also a member of the Southern Society and the Gate City Club, of Atlanta, Ga. He has long been one of the most active supporters of the Southern Society, of which he was president in 1889, and it was mainly through his efforts that the society was incorporated and acquired a permanent home

SIR RODERICK WILLIAM CAMERON

CLAN CAMERON has from immemorial times been one of the great races of the Scottish Highlands A tradition exists that it descends from a younger son of the Danish royal family who assisted King Fergus II in regaining the Scotch throne in the fifth century. The more conservative historians of the family, however, consider, in view of all the evidence, direct or otherwise, that it is more probable that the Camerons sprang from the original inhabitants of the district of Lochaber, where their homes and possessions were found at the earliest times. There is, however, some ground for the theory that originally the Camerons and the Clan Chattan sprang from the same source, though the division, if there was one, took place in times so far remote that little or no importance was attached by either Clan to the alleged circumstance Originally known in the Gaelic nomenclature of the Highlands as the Clan Maclaufhaig, or Servants of the Prophet, they were divided, as far back as any records on the subject extend, into several distinct septs or divisions, a circumstance not uncommon among the larger Scottish Clans   The most conspicuous of them were the Camerons of Lochiel, whose lairds became the Captains of the Clan Cameron, and were for many centuries famous in the history of the Highlands and of that of Scotland, the various chiefs, among whom was the noted Sir Ewen Dhu Cameron, taking prominent part in all the Jacobite risings   The prominence which the Lochiel branch of the Camerons has assumed with reference to the entire Clan has also been increased by the number of romantic incidents connected with the careers of some of its chiefs.   Passing as their names and achievements have done into history and romance, they have in common acceptation become the representatives of an entire race of which they and their immediate followings were but a part .Another branch of the ruling family of Cameron chiefs, however, one which is asserted by good authorities to be an elder one, was the Cameron of Glenevis, to whose family and followers the appellation of Clan Soirlie was applied, and which was not less prolific in Highland warriors and statesmen.   As far as the records are to be found, the Glenevis Camerons had lands in Lochaber, and from the circumstance that they were often at feud with the Lochiel Camerons, it has been asserted that they were originally of another Clan   The chief of Glenevis at the time of the Jacobite rebellion of 1745 was imprisoned in Edinburgh Castle, and his wife, a lady of the Cameron family of Lochiel, was cruelly persecuted by the English, about which a number of romantic traditions are still current in the Highlands, the silver plate which she preserved from the marauders being still preserved by the family.   There was an offshoot of the Glenevis branch, which was known as the Camerons of Speyside, and from the same source came also the Camerons of Dawnie, both of them being families of importance in the Highlands

Sir Roderick William Cameron, of New York, is a descendant of the Lairds of Glenevis, his ancestor being Donald Cameron, a cadet of that family, who received the lands of Morsheirlich, from one of the chiefs of Lochiel, with whom it would seem that he was on friendly terms, but he was ousted from them by the successor, who thus manifested the traditional hostility of the Lochiel Camerons for those of the Glenevis family.   He then removed to Glenmoriston, Inverness-shire, where his descendants were people of property and note in that section   One of them, Alexander Cameron, born at Glenmoriston, in 1729, married, about 1760, Margaret Macdonell, of the same place, and came to the Province of New York, from which he removed to Canada about 1776, being one of the United Empire Loyalists, who have been a most important element in the development of the Canadian Provinces and the present Dominion   Alexander Cameron established himself in Williamstown, County of Glengarry, Canada, where he died in 1825   He was succeeded by his son, Duncan Cameron, born in Glenmoriston, Scotland, 1764, who became one of the founders of the Northwest Fur Company, of Canada, and passed a number of years in the far West, where he commanded Fort Garry, on the site of the City of Winnipeg   In 1818, he went to Great Britain, was presented at court and visited the Highlands, where he made the acquaintance of the lady, Margaret

94

Macleod, daughter of Captain William Macleod, of Hammer, who in 1820 became his wife, having accompanied her brother, Dr. Roderick Macleod, to Canada Duncan Cameron represented the County of Glengarry in the Parliament of Upper Canada from 1820 to 1824, and resided on an estate which was called Glenevis House, after the home of his ancestors, in Scotland. He died in 1848, aged eighty-four years

Of his two sons, the eldest died in infancy The second, Roderick William, was born July 25th, 1825. He was educated at local academies and at Kingston, Canada, and in his early youth hunted throughout the Canadian Northwest. He entered business life at an early age, and in 1852 came to the City of New York with the intention of going to Australia on a mercantile enterprise Instead, however, of going permanently to Australia, he established a line of ships between that part of the world and New York, and thus laid the foundation of a commercial establishment of great importance to New York and to this country, and of which he remains the head. Successful from the outset, he not only sent many emigrants to Australia, but built up an export trade in American products there, which has been of much benefit to this country. Up to 1870, he did business alone, but in that year William A. Street was admitted and the style of the house was changed to R W. Cameron & Co., the establishment having branches at Sydney, New South Wales, and London.

Despite his long residence in America and his interest in social and public affairs, Sir Roderick Cameron has always retained his allegiance to the British crown, and in 1883 his services in the development of Australia were recognized, the honor of knighthood being conferred on him by the Queen. He, however, earnestly supported the Union cause during the Civil War here and organized the Seventy-Ninth New York Regiment. In 1876, he was the honorary commissioner of Australia to the Philadelphia International Exposition, and served in the same capacity at Paris in 1878 In 1880 and 1881, the Dominion of Canada made him honorary commissioner to the Exposition at Sydney and Melbourne. His report on these expositions was an exhaustive document, valuable for its treatment of interesting statistical and commercial matters, and was published as a blue book by the Dominion Government In early life, he married Miss Cummings, of Quebec, who died in 1859 Some years after he contracted a second matrimonial alliance, with Anne Fleming Leavenworth, daughter of Nathan Leavenworth, of New York, whose wife, Alice Johnston, was the daughter of a Scottish gentleman who settled in New York in the last century. The Leavenworth family is descended from a noted Puritan divine in early New England days. Mrs. Cameron died in 1879. The children of this marriage are Margaret S. E., Duncan Ewen Charles, Roderick McLeod, Catherine N., Anne Fleming, who in 1895 married Belmont Tiffany, son of the late George Tiffany, and Isabella Dorothea Cameron.

In many public and social capacities, Sir Roderick Cameron has shown his sympathy for the country of his residence He is a member of the leading New York clubs, including the Metropolitan, Knickerbocker and New York, and the Downtown Association. In London, he belongs to the Junior Carleton, Turf, Hurlingham, Beefsteak and Wellington clubs, and is a member of various artistic and scientific bodies, including the American Geographical Society and the Metropolitan Museum of Art He has been a member of the Highland Society of London since 1856, and spent some time in a prolonged visit to the Highland home of his ancestors. He long maintained an active interest in the turf and imported into this country Leamington, sire of Iroquois, the only American winner of the Epsom Derby. The city residence of Sir Roderick Cameron is 185 Madison Avenue, and he has a country house, Clifton Berley, on Staten Island, as well as a summer retreat at Tadousac, at the mouth of the Sagenany River, in Quebec, the latter place being formerly the property of the Earl of Dufferin, when Governor of Canada Duncan E C Cameron, his elder son, is a member of the Knickerbocker Club, of New York, and the Bachelors and Junior Carleton, in London. His younger son, Roderick McL. Cameron, is a member of the Union, Knickerbocker and Racquet clubs, of New York, and of the Junior Carleton Club, in London.

HUGH NESBITT CAMP

PROMINENT among the New York merchants and men of affairs of the last generation was Hugh Nesbitt Camp His parents were Isaac Brookfield Camp and Jeanette Ely, who were members of families that have been settled in New Jersey for many generations, and that have been distinguished from time to time in public affairs. His maternal grandfather was Calvin Ely, who lived in the town of Livingston, N. J., a small place about ten miles from Newark Mr. Camp's parents were residents of New York, but he was born in the house of his grandfather in Livingston, October 14th, 1827. Brought to his parents' New York home a month later, he lived in New York from that time on throughout his long life. Educated in schools here, he began to work when he was fourteen years of age, finding employment in subordinate positions until 1843, when he entered the counting house of James A Edgar, with which firm, and with the firm of Booth & Edgar, its successors as commission merchants, he remained for many years, gaining a large experience and becoming a successful man of business.

In 1854, Mr. Camp became interested in sugar refining. At that time, he organized a firm under the name of Camp, Brunsen & Sherry, and with a small capital, advanced by gentlemen who believed in his ability and integrity, established a plant in Bristol, R I Within a year the new firm was so successful that it was able to discharge its obligations in full, and thenceforward continued a profitable business. The relations of the partners continued undisturbed for fourteen years, when the firm was dissolved. Mr. Camp bought out the interests of his associates and formed a new partnership under the name of Hugh N Camp & Co, with George Robertson and William McKay Chapman as partners. The over-stimulation in business brought about by the commercial inflation of the war period and the intense competition that ensued, proved disastrous to the firm, which, in 1870, was forced to relinquish business.

After his affairs were readjusted, Mr. Camp, however, went into the real estate business as a broker and auctioneer and met with instantaneous and gratifying success. In a few years he became a large real estate investor on his own account, and was particularly interested in real property in the Twenty-third and Twenty-fourth wards of the city, north of the Harlem He was also heavily engaged in lead mining in Missouri and in the cement business in Pennsylvania. In 1880, Mayor Franklin Edson appointed him one of a committee of seven to investigate and report upon the necessity of an additional water supply for the city, and in that position he rendered important service to the municipality.

During his lifetime, he was a trustee of the National Life Insurance Company, a director of the Mechanics' National Bank, the Continental Trust Company, the Twenty-third Ward Bank, the Title Guarantee and Trust Company, of which he was vice-president ; a trustee of the Clinton Hall Association, of which he was secretary for thirty years , and a trustee of the Skin and Cancer Hospital and the House of Rest for Consumptives. He was secretary and treasurer of the St. Joseph Lead Company, the Doe Run Lead Company, and the Mississippi River and Bonne-Terre Railroad Mr. Camp died September 20th, 1895. For many years he was a member of the Chamber of Commerce, belonged to the Century, Union League, Grolier and other clubs, and was a patron of the Metropolitan Museum of Art and the American Museum of Natural History.

In 1854, Mr Camp married Elizabeth Dorothea McKesson, daughter of John McKesson. There were eight children of this alliance, six of whom survived their father. Edward B. Camp is a broker, residing in New Jersey. Maria Lefferts Camp became the wife of Perry P Williams. John McKesson Camp is a broker. Frederick Edgar Camp is a merchant and treasurer of several of the corporations in which his father had interests. The present Hugh Nesbitt Camp is the youngest son and was associated with his father in the management of the real estate business for a number of years. He resides at Morris Heights, in the old homestead, Fairlawn, which was built by his father in 1863 He belongs to the Union League and Seventh Regiment Veteran clubs, having been a member of the Seventh Regiment for several years

HENRY WHITE CANNON

ONE of the facts which explains New York's preeminence as the real centre of the Western Hemisphere is its capacity to attract and incorporate in its citizenship the ablest and most prominent men that all other sections of the country develop. Mr. Cannon, though his career commenced in the West, is of a New England and New York family His grandfather, Benjamin Persis Cannon, a native of Hebron, Tolland County, Conn, was born in 1776, while his wife was born at Fairfield, in the same State, in 1799 Removing to New York in 1810, Benjamin P. Cannon settled in Tompkins, the name of which was changed to Cannonsville in his honor He was noted as a sagacious business man and had a deserved reputation for integrity His son, George Bliss Cannon, the father of the subject of this article, was born in Cannonsville, N. Y., in 1820. In 1849, he removed to Delhi and was prominent in both business and politics, being a close personal friend of Horace Greeley. He made New York City his residence in his later years and died in 1890, survived by his widow, who was Ann Eliza White, daughter of Elijah and Marietta White, of Franklin, N. Y., where she was born in 1825. On his mother's side Mr Cannon descends from Peregrine White, who was born on the Mayflower as she lay in Cape Cod Harbor in 1620, and was the first European child to see the light in New England His maternal grandmother, Marietta Jennings, was a descendant of William Jennings, of Suffolk, England, and his maternal great-grandfather was a soldier of the Revolution, who died, while a prisoner of war, in the old Sugar House of New York.

Mr. Henry W Cannon was born in Delhi, Delaware County, in 1850. He was educated in private schools, and before attaining his majority became an official of a bank. He soon removed to the West and entered the banking business in St. Paul. When barely twenty-one years of age, he successfully organized a National Bank in Stillwater, Minn, and became its president. Recognized as one of the foremost bankers of the Northwest, Mr. Cannon was appointed in 1884, by President Arthur, Comptroller of the Currency of the United States as the successor to the late Honorable John Jay Knox. He had no sooner taken office than the panic of 1884 swept over the country His practical experience was of the greatest benefit at this crisis, not the smallest of his services being to avert contemplated interference by Congress with the efforts of the banks, and particularly those of New York, to allay the panic. President Cleveland, in 1885, requested Mr. Cannon to continue as Comptroller, but he resigned in 1886.

Making New York his home from that time, Mr. Cannon became vice-president of the National Bank of the Republic, but soon after accepted the post of president of the Chase National Bank, which, under his management, has become one of the foremost financial institutions of the city. He has been a leader in the Clearing House Association, being chairman of the Clearing House committee, and is one of the men to whom the financial interests of New York instinctively turn, in moments of difficulty, for counsel and assistance. Positions of a public character have continued to seek Mr. Cannon since he became a New Yorker. He was appointed by Mayor Grant as a member of the Aqueduct Commission, and in 1892 was one of the American representatives to the International Monetary Conference held at Brussels, Belgium.

In 1879, Mr Cannon married Jennie O. Curtis, daughter of Gould J Curtis, a prominent member of the Minnesota bar and a native of Madison County, N Y At the outbreak of the Civil War, Mr. Curtis raised a company, which he commanded, in the Fifth Minnesota Volunteer Infantry, and died in the service in 1862. Mr. and Mrs. Cannon have two sons, George C Cannon, born in 1882, and Henry White Cannon, Jr., born in 1887. Mr. Cannon's only brother, James G Cannon, is also a prominent banker in New York, being vice-president of the Fourth National Bank Mr Cannon resides in Madison Avenue and is a member of many of the city's prominent social organizations, including the Metropolitan and Union League clubs, the Century Association, the Sons of the Revolution, the New England Society, the Metropolitan Museum of Art and numerous political, patriotic and benevolent institutions

HENRY T CAREY

MARRIAGES between members of distinguished New York families and representatives of European aristocracy have been of frequent occurrence both in the past and in recent times Instances in which such alliances have been followed by the residence of the contracting parties in this country, and the founding of a new American house of patrician standing, are, however, somewhat rare The name of Carey is one of these few exceptional cases in New York s social history. The original seat of its possessors was in the County of Surrey, England, where several landed families of Careys, or Carews, have been established for centuries, one of which, the Carews of Beddington, have held a baronetcy since 1715 In England the Carey family is connected by ties of descent and marriage with a large number of other families of prominence in the peerage or among the landed gentry of the oldest type throughout the kingdom

Samuel Carey, the grandfather of Mr Henry T Carey, held an estate in Surrey His son, Samuel Thomas Carey, having changed his residence to the United States, became an adopted citizen of New York, through his marriage with Marion de Peyster, daughter of George de Peyster Mr. Henry T. Carey was born of this alliance in 1845 The de Peysters are one of the oldest families in the State or City of New York In every generation since the original Dutch settlement, it has produced men of prominence in public and social life, while the marriages of its members has allied it with nearly all the families of real distinction, in either the Colonial or post-Revolutionary history of the metiopolis The race is of Huguenot origin and noble descent, and its progenitor in America, Jan or Johannes de Peyster, came hither from Holland in the early days of the settlement, his marriage in 1649 with Cornelia Lubberts being one of the first recorded in the annals of the New Netherland His descendants included a succession of individuals distinguished in Colonial and Revolutionary times Perhaps the most prominent of them was Colonel Abraham de Peyster, his son, Mayor of the city, Chief Justice and acting Governor of the Province, though in every generation this typical New York family has possessed representatives who have been prominent in the affairs of the city and State, or who have been conspicuous in social life

Colonel de Peyster owned the land extending along the north side of the present Wall Street, and presented to the city the ground on which the old City Hall was erected, the same site being afterwards used for the Federal Hall in which President Washington was inaugurated, and which has been succeeded by the present Sub-Treasury Building The numerous descendants of the de Peysters, direct or through female lines, have always been an important element in the city's social organization, and frequent mention of its various branches and relationships will be found throughout this volume. There are indeed few of the older families of the city who do not prize a relationship to the race in question

On his paternal side, Mr. Carey is also connected with a family of the highest position in New York. His cousin John Carey married Alida Astor, a daughter of William B. Astor, and was the founder of a branch of the name which includes a number of the prominent members of the highest circles of metropolitan society.

Mr Henry T. Carey is engaged in the banking profession, having been a member of the New York Stock Exchange since 1868 He resides at No 41 West Forty-sixth Street, and among other clubs belongs to the Metropolitan, Union League, Tuxedo and South Side.

Of the other children of Samuel and Marion (de Peyster) Carey, Samuel Carey, second of the name and brother of Mr Henry T Carey, is a merchant in New York He married Laura Silliman Taylor. Another brother, George Carey, who was also in the banking business, died some years ago He married Clara Foster, and left two children, a son, Frederick Foster Carey, who married A. Madeleine Lewis, and a daughter. Marion de Peyster Carey, who is now the wife of William B Dinsmore, Jr , of this city.

GEORGE W CARLETON

A LONG line of distinguished ancestry is the family inheritance of Mr. George W. Carleton, who bears an old and honored name   The family dates from the time of the Norman Conquest in 1066.   The name was originally a title of nobility, and its first bearer was a Carleton-Baldwin de Carleton, of Carleton Hall, near Penrith, Cumberland County, England

In the sixth generation from Baldwin de Carleton came Adam de Carleton, head of the Cumberland family, from whom was descended Sir Guy Carleton, Commander-in-Chief of the British Army in the American Colonies during the Revolutionary War   In later time came John Carleton, of Sutton and Walton-upon-Thames, the ancestor in the sixth generation of the American pioneer of the family.   His grandson, John Carleton, of Walton-upon-Thames and Baldwin Brightwell, married Joyce, daughter and coheir of John Welbeck, of Oxonheath, Kent, and his wife, Margaret Culpepper, whose sister, Joyce Culpepper, was mother of Queen Catharine   Edward Carleton, Lord of the Manor of East Cloud-on-Surrey, a son of this union, married Mary, daughter of George Bigley, of Cobham, Surrey, and became the father of Erasmus Carleton, merchant of London and father of Edward Carleton, the American pioneer.

Edward Carleton, of London, came to this country in 1639 and settled in the town of Rowley, Mass   There he was a freeman in 1643, and for several years a member of the General Court   He returned to England before 1656, but his children remained in the New World Lieutenant John Carleton, of Haverhill, Mass , who was born in England about 1630, settled in Haverhill, Mass , about 1661, and died there in 1668.   His wife was Hannah Jewett, daughter of Joseph Jewett ; Joseph Carleton, of Newbury, Mass , their second son, was born in 1662, and married Abigail, daughter of Christopher Osgood, of Andover, Mass.   In the next generation, Jeremiah Carleton, of Lyndeborough, N. H., born in 1715, married Eunice Taylor, of Nottingham.   Jeremiah Trent Carleton, born in 1743, was a soldier in General Wolfe's army, was wounded at the capture of Louisburg, and marched in defense of Ticonderoga

Several of Mr. Carleton's ancestors performed distinguished service during the War of the Revolution.   Moses Carleton, of Boxford, Mass., his paternal great-grandfather, was a private in a Lexington Alarm Company of the Massachusetts minute men, Noadiah Leonard, of Sunderland, Mass., his maternal great-grandfather, being Captain of the same company   Noadiah Carleton was at the battle of Bunker Hill, participated in the siege of Boston, and also acted as a member of the Committee of Safety.   Henry Hodge, of Wiscassett, Me., then Massachusetts, another great-grandfather, was a private in the Massachusetts militia   The parents of Mr. Carleton were Cyrus Carleton, of Alma, Me., and Maria Leonard Arms, of Deerfield, Mass.   His paternal grandparents were Joseph Carleton, of Newton, N H , and Margaret Hodge, who was born in Wiscassett, Me.   The parents of his mother were Eliakim Arms, Jr , who was born in Deerfield, Mass , and Tabitha Leonard, of Sunderland, Mass.

Mr George W Carleton was born in New York, January 16th, 1832, was educated in Dr Hawk's Classical Seminary, Flushing, Long Island, and has been a resident of this city during his business life, having been one of the leading American book publishers in the last generation   He retired from business in 1886   Mr. Carleton married Elizabeth H. Baldwin, daughter of Moses G. Baldwin and Elizabeth Bolles, of Newark, N J   They have two daughters, Ida B and Louise Carleton.   The residence of the family is in West Thirty-seventh Street   Mr Carleton belongs to the Union League and Lotus clubs, and the Sons of the Revolution, and is a patron of the Metropolitan Museum of Art and a director of the Equitable Life Assurance Society.   His brother, Cyrus Carleton, is engaged in machinery manufacturing, in Providence, R. I.   The arms of the Carleton family are those borne by the Carletons of Lincoln and Oxfordshire, England: Argent, on a bend sable, three mascles of the field.   The crest shows. Out of a ducal coronet or , a unicorn's head sable, the horn twisted on the first and second.   The motto. *Non ad perniciem,* may be rendered in English, injury to none.

ANDREW CARNEGIE

IN 1848, the family of a respectable Scotch artisan emigrated from Dumferline, in what was once termed the Kingdom of Fife, and settled in Pittsburg, Pa. William Carnegie, its head, had been a master weaver employing the labor of others, but was forced to emigrate by the introduction of steam power and of the factory system. He was a man of intelligence, a radical in politics and had attained reputation as a public speaker. His wife possessed in a remarkable degree that union of a strong character and resolute will with a fine temperament that is found in the best representatives of the Scottish race. These traits she transmitted to the eldest of her two sons, Andrew, who, at the time of the family migration, was eleven years old, having been born in Dumferline, November 25th, 1837.

In Dumferline, young Andrew Carnegie had attended a private school, but in Pittsburg it was necessary for him to contribute his childish efforts toward the support of the family. This he commenced to do at twelve years of age, first as a boy in factories, running a steam engine and acting as clerk for one employer. When two years older he obtained the place of messenger in a telegraph office. This opened a new world to the ambitious lad, who improved his opportunities and soon became an expert telegraph operator, the death of his father throwing on him the duty of supporting his mother with his small salary. Attracting the attention of Thomas A. Scott, who was then superintendent of the Pennsylvania Railroad's Western division, he became secretary to that gentleman. He remained in the railroad service thirteen years, and finally assumed the place of superintendent on Mr Scott's promotion to the company's vice-presidency. The latter, when Assistant Secretary of War during the Civil War, called Mr Carnegie to Washington and put him in charge of the Government's military railroads and telegraphs. While with Mr. Scott, he made his initial step toward becoming a capitalist, and was instrumental in introducing the first sleeping cars on the Pennsylvania Railroad.

Appreciating the fact that iron bridges must supersede those of wood, he left the railroad service and organized the Keystone Bridge works, in Pittsburg, the nucleus around which he developed the largest group of iron and steel manufacturing establishments in the world. Comprising as they now do the Homestead, Edgar Thomson, Duquesne and Union Mills and allied establishments in and around Pittsburg, they represent an enormous aggregate of capital and of employees, while they also constitute the most perfect example of modern invention applied to such purposes.

As success has crowned Mr Carnegie's enterprises, he has left the details of his business to associates and has given a large share of his attention to travel, to literature and to eminently practical efforts to benefit and elevate others. Of his many gifts, it is only possible to speak of the magnificent library, concert hall and gallery he presented to Pittsburg or the free library given by him to Allegheny City, or the aid he extended to the Edinburgh library and that in his native town of Dumferline. The Carnegie Music Hall, in New York, is only one of the benefits he has conferred on the metropolis since he made this city his residence.

In 1879, Mr Carnegie published Around the World, a record of his travels. An American Four-in-Hand in Britain was made public in 1884, and in 1886 appeared his best known book, Triumphant Democracy, which has been translated into many foreign languages. This work, which is the most graphic illustration of the progress of the United States ever written, was issued in 1893 in a revised form based on the Government Census of 1890, and has had a wide circulation in both Europe and America. He has also written many noteworthy articles in reviews. Mr Carnegie married Miss Whitfield, daughter of John Whitfield, of New York, in 1887. They have one child, an infant daughter. During a part of each year, Mr. and Mrs. Carnegie reside on his Scotch estate, Cluny Castle, in the Highlands of his native country, for which he maintains an attachment second only to that he feels for the great Republic of which he is such an eminent and useful citizen.

GOUVERNEUR MORRIS CARNOCHAN

GALLOWAY, the ancestral home of the Carnochan family, in Scotland, borders upon Ayrshire, the land of the poet Burns, who was a friend of William Carnochan, great-uncle of Mr Gouverneur Morris Carnochan Early in the present century, William Carnochan, with his two brothers, Richard and John, came to America. William became a planter in Georgia; Richard settled in Charleston, S C , John went to the Island of Nassau, where he married Harriet Frances Putnam, daughter of Henry Putnam and Frances Frazer, whose father, Major James Frazer, was an officer of the British Army Subsequently, John Carnochan came to Georgia, where he was a large landed proprietor His wife was the great-granddaughter of Henry Putnam, of Salem, who was killed at the battle of Lexington, and a grandniece of General Putnam

Dr. John Murray Carnochan, their son, became a famous surgeon He was born in Savannah, Ga , July 4th, 1817, and died in New York, October 28th, 1887. When a boy, he was taken to Edinburgh, where he was educated in the High School and the University. Returning to the United States at the age of seventeen, he entered the office of Dr. Valentine Mott and took his degree of M. D from the College of Physicians and Surgeons in New York. Devoting himself with ardor to the study of anatomy, he acquired special distinction in that branch of his profession, and gave lectures to private classes. In 1841, he again visited Europe, where he passed several years in attendance upon the clinical lectures of the principal hospitals of Paris, London and Edinburgh, under such men as Liston, Brodie, Roux and others Returning home in 1847, he practiced in New York and soon had an established position among American surgeons In 1851, he was appointed surgeon and subsequently surgeon-in-chief of the State Emigrant Hospital, which position he held for over a quarter of a century

His services to the cause of science were no less conspicuous than those he rendered to humanity Many of his operations were of the most original and brilliant character, and established him as one of the foremost surgeons of the day. For twelve years he was professor of the principles and operations of surgery in the New York Medical College, and for two years was Health Officer of New York. He published numerous papers in medical journals, and was the author of important books upon surgical practice, and of several volumes of lectures. His professional activity continued almost to the day of his death. In September, 1887, a month before he died, he attended the International Medical Congress at Washington and read two papers.

Dr. Carnochan married Estelle Morris, a daughter of Brevet Major-General William Walton Morris, U. S A., a distinguished officer, who came of a long line of soldiers. The father of General Morris was Lieutenant William Walton Morrris, of the Second Artillery, Continental Line, aide-de-camp to General Anthony Wayne in the Revolution. His grandfather was General Lewis Morris, signer of the Declaration of Independence, and his great-grandfather was the Honorable Lewis Morris, Lord of the Manor of Morrisania. His great-great-grandparents were Lewis Morris and Isabella Graham, daughter of the Honorable James Graham.

Mr Gouverneur Morris Carnochan, the youngest and only surviving son of Dr John Murray Carnochan, was born in New York. He was educated at Harvard University and was matriculated at the École de Medicine in Paris, his father intending him for the medical profession. After completing his studies at Harvard, he followed his own inclination and entered the banking business, being now a member of the New York Stock Exchange. He lives in Fifth Avenue and at Riverdale-on-the-Hudson. His club membership includes the Calumet, Military, New York Athletic, Δ Φ, the Country Club of Westchester County and the Society of Colonial Wars. He is a member of the Seventh Regiment, being inspector of rifle practice, with the rank of First Lieutenant In 1888, he married Matilda Grosvenor Goodridge, daughter of the late Frederic Goodridge, and has had three sons, two of whom are still living. His youngest son, Gouverneur Morris Carnochan, Jr., is in the fifth generation of Gouverneurs, bearing the name of their relative and eminent statesman, Gouverneur Morris, the first United States Minister to France.

HERBERT SANFORD CARPENTER

WESTERN New York was peopled largely by New Englanders, but, though that strain is the dominant one, it has been transformed by the local environments When this section in question was thrown open to civilization, after the close of the Revolution, its fertile plains and valleys proved especially attractive to the inhabitants of the Eastern States, who found there that ease of life that was denied in the rugged localities in which the Puritans at first established themselves The consequence has been a modification of the New England character, which, under such circumstances, became changed into something softer, while preserving all of its original energy and activity, both mental and physical, and has been an element of importance in the development of the entire country

Mr Carpenter, on both the paternal and maternal sides, represents this happy modification of the pure New England type of Americans His grandfather, Asaph H. Carpenter, and his grandmother, Elmira Clark Carpenter, were of families which established themselves early in the present century in Western New York, and which have furnished many distinguished individuals to professional and other pursuits His father, the famous artist, Francis B. Carpenter, however, illustrates the tendencies to which we have referred in the preceding sentences, and is a striking instance of this modification of the New England race.

Francis B Carpenter was born at Homer, N Y., and adopted art as his profession, making portrait-painting his specialty, a branch of the profession in which it is safe to say he has for years past been one of the foremost exponents in this country. Few artists of his day have enjoyed sittings from so many of the most celebrated men of the times; a list of his works would indeed include a long line of our leading statesmen, generals, and other celebrities. Among his most renowned productions is the Signing of the Emancipation Proclamation, which now hangs in the Capitol of the United States, at Washington, and for which he made original studies of President Lincoln and his Cabinet. Another work which attracted great attention had for its subject Arbitration, commemorating the signing, in 1871, of the Treaty of Washington, by which the Alabama claims were settled, and cause for international difficulties between England and the United States was obviated. This painting was presented to Queen Victoria, and holds a place of honor among the historical works of art belonging to the British Crown. Mr. Carpenter, Sr , enjoyed the confidence and regard of President Lincoln to an unusual degree, and has embodied his experiences in a volume—Six Months at the White House; or, The Inner Life of President Lincoln—which is one of the most valuable and authentic records of the character and conversation of the nation's martyred dead. His wife, Augusta (Prentice) Carpenter, was a native of Ithaca, N Y , a member of a family of prominence in that portion of the State, descended from a line of Revolutionary ancestors, some of its members also taking high positions in public life in other parts of the United States, among them being statesmen, lawyers and editors of national reputation.

Mr Herbert Sanford Carpenter was born in Brooklyn, in 1862, and was educated in this city, and has adopted the profession of banking In 1890, he became a member of the firm of Charles Head & Co., and in 1895 retired from that firm and became a member of the firm of Thomas L Manson, Jr., & Co., in the same line of business. In 1883, he married Cora Anderson, of Louisville, Ky., a lady belonging to one of the oldest families of that city Mrs. Carpenter's father was distinguished during the war between the States by his adherence to the cause of the Union, though among his immediate relatives were some who adopted a contrary course and lent their efforts in support of the South. Mr. and Mrs. Carpenter, while old New Yorkers, now live at Flushing, L. I. They have one daughter, Cora Carpenter

Mr Carpenter naturally inherits artistic tastes, and is the owner of a number of carefully selected pictures, while in sport he is a devoted bicyclist and golf player. He is a member of the Oakland Golf Club, New York Athletic Club, and the Colonial Club of New York.

ROYAL PHELPS CARROLL

I N ancient Ireland, one of the most powerful families was that of Carroll, descended from the Kings of Munster and the Lords of the Barony of Ely in Leicester. Such was the ancestry of the first Charles Carroll, founder of the representative Maryland family of his name. He came to America in 1688 and settled in Annapolis, being the agent for Lord Baltimore's Maryland estates; he also obtained large grants of land for himself His son, Charles, was born in 1702 and married Elizabeth Brooke. Their son was the famous Charles Carroll, of Carrollton, 1745-1832. His territorial designation was taken from his estate in Frederick County, Md. He was educated in France and London, and, returning, married Mary Darnell in 1768. He warmly espoused the patriot cause in the Revolution, was a signer of the Declaration of Independence, and at the time of his death was the last survivor of the signers. He filled many important offices, including the United States Senatorship for Maryland He was the foremost Catholic layman in America and his cousin, the Reverend Dr. John Carroll, 1735-1815, was the first Archbishop of Baltimore and primate of the Roman Catholic Church in the United States. The only son of Charles Carroll, of Carrollton, was Charles Carroll, who married Harriet Chew, daughter of Chief Justice Benjamin Chew, of Pennsylvania. The four Caton sisters, granddaughters of Charles Carroll, of Carrollton, were famous beauties. Three of them married English noblemen, the oldest becoming the wife of the Marquis of Wellesley, and sister-in-law of the Duke of Wellington

The Honorable John Lee Carroll is the great-grandson of the patriot, Charles Carroll. He studied law and resided in New York for some years, was a State Senator of Maryland in 1867 and 1871 and was elected Governor of Maryland in 1875. Governor Carroll's wife was Miss Phelps, daughter of Royal Phelps, the famous New York merchant and banker.

The Phelps family was of Welsh origin, the name being abbreviated from Phyllyppes, an ancient Staffordshire cognomen. Their name is mentioned in Rymers Foedera. Sir Edward Phelps was Master of the Rolls and Speaker of the Commons in the time of Queen Elizabeth. George and William Phelps, of Devonshire, came to America in 1630 and settled first in Dorchester, Mass., and, in 1635, formed part of the company that founded Connecticut. George Phelps lived in Windsor, Conn., but in 1668 joined in the settlement of Westfield, Mass. His son, Captain Isaac Phelps, and his grandson, Lieutenant John Phelps, took active part in the wars with the Indians. A son of Lieutenant Phelps, the Honorable John Phelps, 1734-1802, graduated from Yale in 1759 and became a leading lawyer and prominent public man in Western Massachusetts The Reverend Royal Phelps, his youngest son, was a respected Congregational minister in the western part of New York State Mr. Carroll is also descended from Colonel John Spofford, of Tinmouth, Vt., an officer in the Revolutionary Army. His great-grandmother was the daughter of Colonel Spofford and sister of Horatio Gates Spofford, the author.

The grandfather of Mr. Carroll, Royal Phelps, 1809-1884, began a commercial life in New York City when he was only fifteen years old, and spent some fifteen years in the West Indies and in Venezuela. In 1840 he established a business house for himself, and the rest of his active career was devoted to the West Indian and South American trade. He married a lady of Spanish family in 1831, and his only daughter became the wife of Governor John Lee Carroll

Mr. Royal Phelps Carroll, their son, fifth in descent from Charles Carroll, of Carrollton, was born in New York, October 29th, 1862. He attended schools in France and England and was graduated from Harvard University in the class of 1885. In 1891, he married Marion Langdon, daughter of Eugene and Harriet (Lowndes) Langdon, and has one daughter, Marion Dorothea Carroll. Mr. Carroll has residences in New York and Newport, and is a member of the Union, Knickerbocker, Racquet and other clubs He is a skillful and enthusiastic yachtsman, and owns the Navahoe, which, in 1894, he sailed in the principal European regattas, beating the Prince of Wales' Britannia in the race for the Brenton Reef Cup Mr Carroll flies the pennants of the Seawanhaka-Corinthian, Larchmont and Eastern Yacht clubs.

COLIN SMITH CARTER, D. D. S.

MR COLIN SMITH CARTER was born in Middletown, Conn., April 13th, 1857. His ancestry is mainly English and Welsh, a single line extending into France His earliest American ancestor was Elder William Brewster, of the Mayflower, from whom he is ninth in lineal descent He is also descended from Thomas Gardner, overseer of the first emigrants that landed at Cape Ann (now Gloucester), Mass., in 1624. Others of his ancestors were of the distinguished companies that came to that Colony with Governor Winthrop, in 1630, and to New Haven, with Governor Eaton, in 1637. Of his English ancestors, he is ninth in descent from Thomas Morton, who was graduated from Cambridge, became Bishop of Chester 1615, Litchfield 1618, Durham 1632, and whose daughter Ann married first David Yale, and second Governor Eaton, of the New Haven Colony. A daughter of David and Ann (Morton) Yale married Governor Edward Hopkins, of the Connecticut Colony, their son, Thomas, married Mary, daughter of Captain Nathaniel Turner, they being the parents of Elihu Yale, after whom Yale University was named, and also the great-grandparents of Ann Yale, who, May 8th, 1733, married William Carter, the great-great-grandfather of the subject of this sketch. Dr Carter is also seventh in descent from Thomas Roberts, the last Colonial Governor of New Hampshire, and eighth in descent from Governor Thomas Prince, of the Plymouth Colony. One of his ancestors owned Breed's Hill, on which the Battle of Bunker Hill was fought, others were among the courageous protectors of the regicides, while more than a score served in the Pequot and King Philip's wars, and in the General Courts of the Colonies of Plymouth, Mass, Connecticut, New Haven and New Hampshire. Three of them were among the thirteen members of the convention which met in 1639 to frame for the Colony of Connecticut a written constitution, the first ever adopted by any people, and the leading features of which have since been incorporated in both the Federal and most of our State constitutions He is a great-grandson of Sergeant William Taylor, who enlisted in the Lexington alarm, from Simsbury, Conn., when only seventeen years of age, was at Bunker Hill, Monmouth and Stony Point, served until the close of the war and was awarded a pension He is also fourth and fifth in descent respectively from Private Joseph Gaylord and Captain Nathaniel Bunnell, likewise Connecticut soldiers of the Revolution. His grandfather Carter held the offices of assessor, collector and postmaster, and his father, Walter S. Carter, is a well-known New York lawyer, noted as an art collector and for his interest in hereditary-patriotic societies His maternal grandfather was the late John Cotton Smith, of New Hartford, Conn , a leading manufacturer, whose wife, Ellen (Fox) Smith, was descended from one of the best-known families in the central portion of the State

Dr. Carter was educated in the public schools, at the Wilbraham Academy, and the Polytechnic Institute, Brooklyn. He entered the Dental Department of the University of Pennsylvania, in 1881, and was graduated with the degree of Doctor of Dental Surgery two years later. Upon his graduation he was appointed Assistant Demonstrator of Operative Dentistry, which position he filled until the following year, when he commenced practice in New York, in which he has achieved distinguished success.

In 1892, Dr Carter married Rose Esterbrook, daughter of the late Richard and Antoinette (Rose) Esterbrook, of Bridgehampton, L. I The latter was a daughter of Judge Rose, who was of an ancient Long Island family, a graduate of Yale, and noted as the author of a valuable and learned commentary on constitutional law.

Dr. Carter is a member of the Union League, Republican and American Yacht clubs, the New England Society, Sons of the Revolution, Sons of the American Revolution, Society of Mayflower Descendants, Founders and Patriots of America, America's Founders and Defenders, and other patriotic, political and social organizations In religion he is a Methodist, being a member of St Paul's Church, in this city.

JAMES C. CARTER

AMONG the Puritan clergy whose influence was so marked in the early history of Massachusetts was the Reverend Thomas Carter, who came of an excellent English family in Hertfordshire, and received his education at St. John's College, Cambridge, taking his degrees there in 1629 and 1633. The date of his birth was 1610, and he was a young man of only twenty-five years when he joined the movement of the Puritans to the Massachusetts Bay Colony, coming over in 1635 on the ship Planter, with the Reverend Thomas Hooker and others who attained prominence in the Colony at that time. He resided at first in Dedham and afterwards in Watertown. He was ordained a minister of the gospel in 1642, and his first pastorate, which he entered upon in November of that year, was over the church in Woburn, Mass. There he remained for some forty years, until his death, in 1684. His wife, Mary, survived him less than three years, dying in Woburn in 1687.

Several of the children of the Reverend Thomas Carter became clergymen. One of them, the Reverend Samuel Carter, who was graduated at Harvard College, in 1660, bought land in the town of Lancaster, Worcester County, in the central part of Massachusetts. From him have descended numerous families, which have been located for generations in Lancaster, Leominster and other towns in that section. To one of these families the subject of this article belongs, his father and mother being Solomon and Elizabeth (White) Carter.

Mr. James C. Carter was born in Lancaster, Mass., October 14th, 1827. He received his preparatory education at the Derby Academy, Hingham, Mass., and entering Harvard College, at the age of eighteen, was graduated from that institution in the class of 1850. During his college course, he took a high rank and won prizes for essays and for a dissertation in Latin. After completing his studies, he came to New York and was for a year in the office of Kent & Davies, the senior partner of which was Judge William Kent, son of Chancellor Kent, and the junior the well-known Judge Henry E. Davies. Then he entered the law department of Harvard and was graduated therefrom with the degree of LL. B in 1853. Returning to New York in 1853, he went into the office of Davies & Scudder, where he remained for a year, when that firm was dissolved and was succeeded by the firm of Scudder & Carter, in which Mr. Carter was the junior partner. On the death of Henry J Scudder the present firm of Carter & Ledyard was formed, of which Mr. Carter is the senior member.

For more than forty years, Mr. Carter has been one of the foremost advocates at the bar in New York City. He has been identified with scores of leading cases in this city and State, as well as before the Supreme Court of the United States. One of his most notable professional engagements was as counsel for the United States before the Tribunal of Arbitration at Paris in 1893 in connection with the Alaska Seal Controversy, and another was as one of the counsel who argued in favor of the constitutionality of the Income Tax Law before the United States Supreme Court in 1894. He was counsel and a close friend of the Honorable Samuel J Tilden during the greater part of that eminent statesman's life, and defended his will against the legal attacks that were made upon it by Mr. Tilden's heirs.

Mr Carter has written much for publication, principally upon legal subjects, and has made many public addresses. His works include The Attempted Codification of the Common Law, The Province of the Written and the Unwritten Law, an address before the Virginia State Bar Association in 1882; and The Ideal and the Actual in the Law, an address delivered before the American Bar Association, in 1890. In 1885, he received the degree of LL. D. from Harvard University. He was for years president of the Harvard Law Association, and is now president of the Bar Association of the City of New York. He is a member of the Metropolitan, Harvard, City, Century, Union League, University and A Δ Φ clubs, the Downtown Association, the New England Society, the National Academy of Design, and other public bodies. His city residence is 277 Lexington Avenue

HAMILTON WILKES CARY

IN England, the family of Cary is old as well as illustrious In 1198, Adam de Kari was Lord of Karey, in Somersetshire Red Castle, an Irish estate in the County of Donegal, and also White Castle were granted to him His arms were Argent on a bend sable, three roses of the first Crest, a swan argent William Cary, of Bristol, Somersetshire, was born in 1500, and during the reign of King Henry VIII , in 1532, was sheriff of the City of Bristol and Mayor in 1546 He left two sons, one of whom, Richard, born in Bristol in 1525, succeeded him and died in 1570 William Cary, 1550-1632, the son of Richard Cary, also succeeded to the family estate He was sheriff of Bristol in 1599 and Mayor in 1611 His son, James Cary, who was born in Bristol in 1600, was the American ancestor of the family

James Cary emigrated from England in one of the first companies that came to Massachusetts He was in Charlestown, Mass , in 1639, was town clerk and held other offices. He died in 1681 His wife, whom he married in England, was Eleanor Hawkins In the second American generation, Jonathan Cary, of Charlestown, 1647-1738, was a deacon of the church of Charlestown, and married in 1675 Hannah Windsor In the next two generations came Samuel Cary, 1683-1741, and his wife, Mary Foster, daughter of Richard Foster, and Captain Samuel Cary, 1713-1769, and his wife, Margaret Graves, daughter of the Honorable Thomas Graves. Captain Samuel Cary commanded a ship in the London trade and married his wife there in 1741. The great-grandfather of Mr Hamilton Wilkes Cary was their son, Samuel Cary, 1742-1812, who was born in Charlestown, Mass When a young man, he went abroad and was successfully engaged in mercantile life in the West Indies in 1762-72 In the latter year, he returned to his native place and married a daughter of the Reverend Ellis Gray Taking his bride with him, he returned to the Island of Grenada in the West Indies, where he had large business interests, and remained there for several years thereafter, eventually, however, returning to Massachusetts, living in the old family mansion in Chelsea, where he died

His son, William Ferdinand Cary, was born in Chelsea, Mass , in 1795 In 1815, he came to New York and established himself in business Here he remained for more than fifty years and became a successful merchant In old age, he returned to Boston in 1876 and lived there the rest of his life His wife was Nancy Cushing Perkins, a daughter of Thomas Handasyd Perkins, one of Boston's famous merchants Her grandfather was also a Boston merchant and her paternal grandmother was Elizabeth Peck, one of the founders and earnest supporters of the Boston Female Asylum and of other philanthropic institutions. Her mother, whom her father married in 1778, was Sarah Elliot, daughter of Simon Elliot, of a well-known Boston family, whose ancestry goes back to the foundation of the Colony.

Thomas Handasyd Perkins, the great-grandfather of Mr Hamilton Wilkes Cary, was born in Boston in 1764 and died in Brookline, Mass , in 1854 His brother was at the head of a mercantile house in the Island of San Domingo, and thither he went in 1785 to engage in business. A few years after, he returned to Boston, and from 1789 onward made several mercantile voyages to the East Afterwards he formed a partnership with his brother James, but having accumulated a fortune retired from business in 1822 In 1805, he was a member of the Massachusetts Senate and for eighteen years thereafter was in either the upper or lower branch of the Legislature and was Lieutenant-Colonel in the militia He gave a house and grounds in Boston for a Blind Asylum, was a large contributor to the Boston Atheneum and was active in the erection of the Bunker Hill Monument

William F Cary, son of William Ferdinand and Nancy Cushing (Perkins) Cary, was born in New York in 1832 He lived at Irvington-on-the Hudson, and in 1860 married Lena Haight, who survives him, residing in Park Avenue. Mr Hamilton Wilkes Cary is their son and was born in New York in 1862 He is a member of the Metropolitan, Union and Knickerbocker clubs His only sister is Catharine Caroline Cary

CHARLES FREDERICK CHANDLER

ONE of the distinguished American scientists of this generation, Professor Charles Frederick Chandler, Ph. D., M. D., LL. D., has for over thirty years been prominent in the social, scientific and literary life of New York His parents were Charles Chandler, of Petersham, Mass., and Sarah Whitney, of Boston. He is descended from William and Annis Chandler, who settled in Roxbury, Mass, in 1637. Three of his ancestors bore the name of John Chandler, and filled, in succession, the positions of Judge in Worcester County, Mass., and Colonel in the Colonial Army One of them married Hannah Gardiner, of Gardiner's Island. Professor Chandler's paternal grandmother was Dollie Greene, a descendant of Thomas Greene, of Stone Castle, Old Warwick, R. I.

Mr. Charles Frederick Chandler was born in Lancaster, Mass, December 6th, 1836, and was educated in the Lawrence Scientific School of Harvard College and the Universities of Göttingen and Berlin. In 1856, he received the degree of Ph. D from the University of Göttingen. For eight years he was instructor and lecturer on chemistry, mineralogy and geology in Union College, and in 1864, in association with Professor Thomas Egleston and General Francis Vinton, he founded the School of Mines of Columbia College, becoming dean of the Faculty and professor of chemistry and lecturer on geology. For thirty-three years he was at the head of this school, resigning the position of dean in 1897, in order to devote himself to his work in chemistry and allied branches In 1872, he became connected with the New York College of Physicians and Surgeons, and on the death of Professor St. John, who held the chair of chemistry and medical jurisprudence, succeeded to the vacancy. He was one of the founders of the American Chemical Society and has been the vice-president and president of that association. With his brother, Professor Chandler, of Lehigh University, he founded The American Chemist, and in recent years has edited The Photographic Bulletin For nearly thirty years, he has been professor of chemistry in the New York College of Pharmacy. His connection with the New York Board of Health began in 1866. In 1873, he was appointed president of the Board, and in 1877 reappointed for a full term of six years

In 1873, the University of New York conferred upon him the degree of M D, and the same year he received the degree of LL D from Union College. He is a member of the National Academy of Sciences, the Sociedad Humboldt of Mexico, the American Association for the Advancement of Science, the American Philosophical Society, the New York Academy of Science, chairman of the American Section of the English Society of Chemical Industry, and a life member of the London, Berlin, Paris and American Chemical Societies. He lives at 51 East Fifty-fourth Street and has a summer home, The Cherries, in West Hampton, Long Island. His clubs include the Metropolitan, University and Grolier, and the Century Association. He is also a member of the New England Society and the New York Farmers' Club. He was for many years a member of the Union League and the Tuxedo clubs.

In 1861, Professor Chandler married Anna Maria Craig, of Schenectady, N. Y., a daughter of James R. Craig and Margaret Walton. She was a descendant, on her father's side, of Anneke Jans, and on her mother's side, of William Hyde, of Hartford, Conn, 1636, Elisha Sill, of Lyme, Conn, 1730; Thomas Russell Gold, of Goshen, Conn, and General Robert Sedgwick, who came from London to Charlestown, Mass., in 1636. The only child of Professor Chandler is Margaret Chandler, wife of Charles Ernest Pellew, adjunct professor of chemistry in Columbia University Mr. Pellew comes of a distinguished English family His father was Henry Edward Pellew, of Katonah Wood, Westchester County, N. Y. His mother was a granddaughter of the celebrated Chief Justice John Jay and daughter of Judge William Jay. His grandparents were the Reverend George Pellew, D D, dean of Norwich, and Frances Addington, daughter of Henry Addington, Viscount Sidmouth and Prime Minister of England. The great-grandfather of Charles E Pellew was Admiral Edward Pellew, Viscount Exmouth, 1757-1833, who married Sarah Frowde, daughter of James Frowde, of Wiltshire. Mr. and Mrs. Pellew have one child, Anna Craig Pellew.

WINTHROP CHANLER

CIVIC distinction attaches to the family name of Mr. Winthrop Chanler. His great-grandfather was Dr Isaac Chanler, a prominent physician in Charleston, S. C, surgeon in the Continental Army in the Revolution, and first president of the Medical Society of South Carolina. A son of Dr. Chanler was the Reverend John White Chanler, a prominent clergyman of the Protestant Episcopal Church, who married Elizabeth Sheriffe Winthrop, a descendant of Governor John Winthrop The Honorable John Winthrop Chanler, their only son and father of Mr Winthrop Chanler, was born in New York in 1826 Graduated from Columbia College, he became one of the leading lawyers of his day, and active and influential in public affairs For many years he was a prominent member of the Tammany Hall organization. Elected a member of the Assembly in 1857, he declined a renomination, but was elected a member of the Thirty-eighth Congress in 1862, and was returned to the National House in 1864 and 1866 Failing health led to his retirement in 1875, and he died at his country residence in Rhinebeck, in 1877. His wife was Margaret Astor Ward, only daughter of Samuel Ward, Jr.

Mr. Winthrop Chanler is descended from two of the most distinguished soldiers of the Colonial and Revolutionary period. His great-great-grandfather was General John Armstrong, of the Revolutionary War and the War of 1812, son of General John Armstrong, of the French War and the War of the Revolution. The elder John Armstrong, 1720-1795, was a native of Ireland, came to America in 1745 and founded Carlisle, Pa., in 1750 As a Colonel of Pennsylvania troops, he took part in the expedition against the Indians in 1756, where he was brilliantly successful, and received a medal from the Provincial authorities, and was in the advance upon Fort Duquesne. In 1776, he became Brigadier-General in the Continental Army and saw service at Fort Moultrie, Charleston, Brandywine and Germantown. After the war, he was a member of Congress in 1787

The second General John Armstrong, 1758-1843, graduated from Princeton College in 1775, and enlisted in the Continental Army. He served on the staff of General Hugh Mercer, and afterwards on that of General Horatio Gates at Saratoga, and in 1780 was Adjutant-General of the Southern Army. After the war, he was Secretary of State and Adjutant-General of Pennsylvania for several years. Removing to New York, he became a member of Congress in 1787, was a United States Senator in 1800 and United States Minister to France and Spain in 1804-1810. In the War of 1812 he was a Brigadier-General, and in 1813 was Secretary of War in the Cabinet of President James Madison, resigning in 1814 His wife was Alida Livingston, daughter of Judge Robert R. Livingston and a sister of Chancellor Livingston. Margaret Armstrong, daughter of General John Armstrong, became the wife of William B Astor, and her eldest daughter, Emily Astor, born in 1819, was the mother of Margaret Astor (Ward) Chanler Through the Astor connection, Mr. Chanler is descended from Adam Todd, whose granddaughter, Sarah Todd, was the wife of the first John Jacob Astor.

Through his grandfather, Samuel Ward, Mr. Chanler is descended from another Colonial family. John Ward was an officer in Cromwell's Army, and came to America after the accession of Charles II His son, Thomas Ward, was treasurer of the Rhode Island Colony; his grandson, Richard Ward, was its secretary and Governor of Rhode Island in 1740; and his great-grandson, Samuel Ward, was also Governor of Rhode Island, in 1762-63 and 1765-67, and a member of the Continental Congress in 1774. His great-great-grandson, Lieutenant-Colonel Samuel Ward, married a daughter of Governor William Greene, of Rhode Island; their son, Henry Ward, was the father of Samuel Ward, and grandfather of Samuel Ward, Jr , who married Emily Astor.

Mr Winthrop Chanler is the second son of the Honorable John Winthrop Chanler. He was born in New York and married Margaret Terry, daughter of John Terry He belongs to the Tuxedo, Knickerbocker, Union, Racquet and City clubs of New York, and the Metropolitan Club of Washington. He makes his home in Tuxedo Park.

ALFRED CLARK CHAPIN

DEACON SAMUEL CHAPIN, of Springfield, Mass., from whom have descended many men prominent in professional and public life in the United States during the last two hundred and fifty years, was the ancestor of the Honorable Alfred Clark Chapin The latter's grandparents were Atlas Chapin and his wife, Mary, and his father was Ephraim A Chapin. Through his mother, Josephine Clark, Mr. Chapin is also descended from another great Colonial family of New England, his mother's ancestor being Lieutenant William Clark, who came from England in 1630, and settled in Northampton, Mass, in 1657.

Mr. Chapin was born in South Hadley, Mass., March 8th, 1848. When an infant, he was taken to Springfield by his parents, who, in 1852, removed to Keene, N H , and when he was fourteen years old to Rutland, Vt His early education was secured in Keene and Rutland, and in 1865 he entered Williams College, being graduated from that institution in the class of 1869, with the degree of A B Afterwards he attended the Harvard Law School, receiving his degree of LL B. in 1871, and then came to New York. For a year he continued his studies and in 1872 was admitted to the bar of New York State. He has since been engaged in the active practice of his profession in New York and Brooklyn. Making his residence in Brooklyn soon after he had entered upon professional life, he became interested in public affairs, and took an active and intelligent part in politics in that city An adherent of the Democratic party, he was elected the first president of the Young Men's Democratic Club of Brooklyn in 1880, and was at once recognized as a leader of the younger element of his party. In 1881, he was elected Assemblyman from the Eleventh District of Kings County.

His career in the Assembly was especially distinguished by an unswerving opposition to corrupt legislation of all kinds, and he soon became a leader there. Home rule for the city of Brooklyn and a constitutional amendment restricting the debt-making power of cities were measures that were advanced and advocated by him, and that brought him forward into special public prominence throughout the State. He also secured the passage of the Chapin Primary Law, which was the first step toward securing the purity of primary elections. He was also chairman of a special committee to investigate receiverships of insolvent insurance companies In 1882, he was reëlected to the Assembly by a greatly increased majority, and upon taking his seat the following year was chosen Speaker. In that position, he was again successful in meeting the highest expectations of his supporters, by his integrity and devotion to public interests. The State Convention of his party in 1883 nominated him for State Comptroller and he was elected to that office Reëlected for a second term, his administration was characterized by honesty of purpose, fearlessness and admirable business judgment By his influence, a bill was passed by which a large amount of delinquent taxes due by corporations to the State were recovered. Upon the expiration of his second term of service as State Comptroller, Mr. Chapin received the Democratic nomination for Mayor of Brooklyn and was elected In 1889, he was reëlected by the largest majority ever given for a Mayor of the city up to that time His administration of the municipal affairs was eminently successful, and under his direction the city prospered in every way. He gave especial attention to street improvements, to the cause of education and to the enlargement of the police force, and inaugurated the erection of the Brooklyn Memorial Arch to the memory of the soldiers killed in the Civil War Further political honors were bestowed upon him after the expiration of his Mayoralty term, and he was elected a Member of the National House of Representatives. He also served as a member of the Board of Railroad Commissioners of New York.

Mr. Chapin married Grace Stebbins in 1884 Mrs. Chapin was the daughter of Russell and Alice (Schieffelin) Stebbins The children of this marriage are two daughters, Grace and Beatrice Chapin Mr. Chapin is now a resident of New York, his home being in East Fifty-sixth Street, near Fifth Avenue His country place is at Pointe-à-Pic, Province of Quebec, Canada His clubs are the Metropolitan and the Union.

WILLIAM VIALL CHAPIN

SPRINGFIELD, Mass, originally Agawam, was settled in 1636 by a band of stout-hearted Puritans, who traversed the wilderness between the coast and the fertile valley of the Connecticut under the leadership of William Pynchon and Samuel Chapin. The latter, in fact, was the practical founder of the town, and attained a deservedly high place among the early worthies of the Bay Colony, all of which is fittingly commemorated by the statue of him that has in later days been erected at Springfield He became also the progenitor of a family which from that time forth has been notable in various parts of New England, and which, besides furnishing a Colonial Governor, has been fertile in distinguished clergymen, scholars, and men of note in all stations of life

Mr. William Viall Chapin comes of the Rhode Island branch of the family, Royal Chapin, his paternal grandfather, having been its Governor, and his father being General Walter B Chapin. His mother, who was born Ann Frances Low Viall, was also a member of a distinguished family Her ancestor was William Viall, a French refugee, who, about 1790, settled at Seekonk, now a suburb of Providence, and whose descendants have been prominent in the State, and have intermarried with its foremost families of the original Puritan stock One of his great-granddaughters is the wife of General Elisha Dyer, the present Governor of Rhode Island, and whose father, Elisha Dyer, Sr, also occupied the same position in 1857 Mr Chapin's maternal grandmother was born Eliza Bowen, a daughter of Ezra Bowen, another Governor of Rhode Island, and a man famous in its political and social annals

Born at Providence, R I, January 1st, 1855, and educated at the famous St Paul's School, Concord, N H, Mr Chapin entered Trinity College, Hartford, Conn, from which he graduated with the degree of B A, that of A M being conferred upon him in due course In his college years he became a member of the Φ B K He made New York his residence after graduation, and elected to follow a business career, joining the New York Stock Exchange in 1880, with which body he remained connected for the ten succeeding years

By his marriage, which occurred in 1890 Mr Chapin became allied with a prominent New York family, notable in a historical sense not only in Colonial and Revolutionary days, but in the later history of the country as well His wife was Mary Worth White, daughter of Loomis L White, of the city, a banker and prominent member of the New York Stock Exchange Mrs Chapin is a direct descendant of Peregrine White, who was one of the band of Pilgrim Fathers who came to Plymouth in the Mayflower Her great-great-grandfather was the first Chancellor of the University of the State of New York, and also a State Senator. Her great-granduncle, Lebeas Loomis, was private secretary to General Washington, his portrait and that of his wife being in Mrs Chapin's possession. Her mother, born Emma Worth, belonged to an old New York and New England family, and a great-uncle on the maternal side was Major-General William Worth, of the United States Army, who was a prominent figure in the war with Mexico, his monument opposite Madison Square in this city having been erected by the municipality as a tribute to this distinguished son of New York He took part in all the engagements of the Mexican War, commanding a division of the American Army under Generals Taylor and Winfield Scott The City of Fort Worth, Tex, and Lake Worth, Fla, were named after him

Among other social organizations, Mr Chapin is a member of the Knickerbocker Club, of New York, and of the Hope Club, the leading one of his native city, Providence, R. I. His town residence is No. 5 East Sixty-sixth Street, and his country place is Dunworth, at Pomfret, Conn, while he has a winter residence, Dunworth Lodge, at St Augustine, Fla. The Chapin arms, as well as the family name, are of French origin The shield is parti-colored, blue and gold, bearing three dragons' heads The crest is a naked sword piercing a cavalier's hat Motto. *Tiens a la foy avant le Roy*

ELIHU CHAUNCEY

THE Chauncey family is of ancient renown in England. Its progenitors were among those who came from Normandy with William the Conqueror, and through the alliances of their ancestors with members of noble and royal families the American Chaunceys can trace their descent to the most aristocratic races of England and Europe   In the United States, the lineage goes back to the Reverend Charles Chauncey, the Puritan clergyman, a graduate from Trinity College, Cambridge, who came to the Massachusetts Bay Colony among the first emigrants   He was the second president of Harvard College   The line of descent in the following generation is through the Reverend Nathaniel Chauncey, 1639-1685, of Hatfield, Mass , son of the Reverend Charles Chauncey, and in the next generation through the Reverend Nathaniel Chauncey, 1681-1756, of Durham, Conn , and his wife, Abigail Sarah Judson, daughter of Captain James Judson, of Stratford

In the fourth American generation came Elihu Chauncey, the son of the Reverend Nathaniel Chauncey, of Durham   Elihu Chauncey was born in 1710 and died in 1791   He was a representative of the town of Durham in the Legislature continuously for thirty-nine successive terms, except when in the army.   During the French and Indian War, he was a Colonel of one of the Connecticut regiments and was engaged in active service on the northern frontier.   He displayed great ability as a military officer and was a valued adviser in the councils of the officers of the regular army   He was also Chief Justice of the County Court, was a large landed proprietor, and in the latter years of his life had important mercantile interests in Boston, where he established a store and carried on a general trading business between Connecticut and the Massachusetts capital.   His wife was Mary Griswold, daughter of Samuel Griswold, of Killingworth, Conn

The grandfather of Mr Elihu Chauncey was Charles Chauncey, LL D., of New Haven, 1747-1823   He was King's Attorney in 1776 and Judge of the Superior Court in 1789   Resigning from the bench in 1793, he retired from public life   He was a graduate from Yale College and received the degree of LL D from Middlebury College, Vermont, in 1811   The wife of Charles Chauncey was Abigail Darling, 1746-1818, daughter of Thomas and Abigail Darling, of New Haven   The eldest daughter of the family, Sarah Chauncey, born in 1780, married William W. Woolsey, the eminent merchant of New York and treasurer of the American Bible Society   She was his second wife, his first wife having been Elizabeth Dwight, sister of President Dwight of Yale College and mother of President Woolsey, of Yale.   A son of Charles Chauncey and his wife, Abigail Darling, was Charles Chauncey, LL D , 1777-1849, a graduate from Yale College in the class of 1792 and an eminent lawyer of Philadelphia   He was for several years a member of the Common Council of Philadelphia and a delegate to the Constitutional Convention in 1827-28   Another son, Elihu Chauncey, one of the leading citizens of Philadelphia, was president of the Reading Railroad, editor of The North American Gazette, and prominent in connection with the Bank of the United States and the Bank of Pennsylvania   Nathaniel Chauncey, another son, was born in 1789, and was the father of Mr. Elihu Chauncey.   He was graduated from Yale College in 1806 and became a member of the Philadelphia bar.   His wife, whom he married in 1836, was Elizabeth Sewall Salisbury, daughter of Samuel and Nancy Salisbury, of Boston.

Mr Elihu Chauncey was born in Philadelphia, August 17th, 1840, and was educated in Harvard College, receiving the degrees of A B and A. M   Settling in New York, he married in 1871 Mary Jane Potter, daughter of the Right Reverend Horatio Potter, Bishop of New York.   The residence of the family is in East Twenty-second Street   Mr Chauncey is a member of the University, Groher and Harvard clubs, the Century Association, the Society of Colonial Wars, the New York Historical Society and the American Geographical Society, and is a patron of the Metropolitan Museum of Art   Mr and Mrs. Chauncey have one daughter, Nathalie Elisabeth Chauncey

ROBERT A CHESEBROUGH

PROMINENT among New Yorkers of the Colonial period were the Maxwells The family was of Scottish descent, from the earldoms of Nithsdale and barons of Herries, and one of its members, General Maxwell, did valiant service for the Colonies in the Revolution. William Maxwell was vice-president of the Bank of New York, the first financial institution established in the State His son, James Homer Maxwell, was an intimate friend of Washington, and married Catharine Van Zandt, daughter of Jacobus Van Zandt, who was a surgeon in Washington s army at Trenton and Valley Forge and a member of the first Provincial Congress that met in New York, May 23d, 1775 Miss Van Zandt was a very beautiful woman and a leading belle of the city She opened the first inauguration ball as the partner of President Washington. The grandson of James Homer Maxwell was William H Maxwell, who, at the time of his death, in 1856, was the titular earl of Nithsdale. A granddaughter was daughter of Richard M Woodhull, grandniece of General Woodhull, of the Continental Army, who met his death in the battle of Long Island, and mother of Mr Robert A Chesebrough

On his father's side, Mr Chesebrough is descended from Robert Chesebrough, founder and president of the Fulton Bank. His father was Henry A Chesebrough, an old-time dry goods merchant of New York. The ancestor of the family, William Chesebrough, accompanied Governor John Winthrop from Cowes, in March, 1630, and settled in Boston. He was one of the leading citizens of the community, and in 1634 was High Sheriff. In 1651, he settled upon a grant of land made to him by the General Court of Connecticut and built a homestead. The City of Stonington now stands upon the grant that he then occupied. In this new commonwealth, William Chesebrough was the first Commissioner or magistrate, and in 1664 was chosen as the first representative to the General Court in Hartford Robert Chesebrough, the grandfather of the subject of this sketch, was the fifth son of Nathaniel Chesebrough, who was the grandson of this William Chesebrough.

Mr Robert A Chesebrough was born in London, England, January 9th, 1837. He was educated abroad, applying himself specially to the study of chemistry, and then traveled two years in Europe. Returning to New York City in 1858, he established himself as a manufacturer of petroleum and coal oil products, and in 1870 discovered and patented the product known as vaseline. In 1876, he organized the Chesebrough Manufacturing Company, which now has branches in all the principal cities of Europe. He was one of the prime movers in the proposition to establish the New York Real Estate Exchange and was the second vice-president and one of the building committee of the Consolidated Exchange He is a member of the Union League, Riding, Manhattan and other clubs and societies and is also interested in many charitable organizations. In 1890, he was president of the Downtown Republican Club His literary taste has been shown in occasional public addresses and in a volume entitled A Reverie and Other Poems Mr Chesebrough maintains a deep interest in public affairs, although he has never aspired to public office Frequently urged to accept nominations by the Republican party, to which he belongs, he yielded on one occasion and made the campaign for Congress in the Twelfth District, but was not successful, although he largely reduced the normal Democratic majority in the district.

In the Senate House in Kingston, N. Y , among the Revolutionary relics there preserved, are two large oil paintings of the father and mother of William Maxwell These portraits hung in the old Maxwell mansion in Wall Street during the British occupation of the city, and they still show the holes made by the bayonet thrusts of the British soldiers. The portraits were presented to the Senate House by Mr Chesebrough Among other interesting heirlooms of the family are the Bibles of the Maxwells and the Van Zandts In 1864, Mr Chesebrough married Margaret McCredy, sister of the wife of Frederic R Coudert Mrs Chesebrough died in 1887, leaving three sons and one daughter, Robert M , William H , Frederick W. and Marion M. Chesebrough. The residence of the family is in East Forty-fifth Street.

BEVERLY CHEW

FIRST of his name to appear in America was John Chew, a cadet member of the family of Chew, of Chewton, Somersetshire, England, He came to Virginia in the ship Charitie before 1620, and his wife Sarah followed two years after. In 1623, he was a member of the Virginia House of Assembly, afterwards a Burgess, and was in the Assembly until 1642. He had five sons, Samuel, Joseph and three others Samuel Chew, the eldest son, went to Maryland before 1655, and took up land in Herring Bay, Calvert County. His grandson, Dr Samuel Chew, was a well-known physician and jurist of a later time. Judge Benjamin Chew, 1722-1810, the son of Dr Samuel Chew, was one of the most famous Judges of his generation.

Mr Beverly Chew is a descendant in the seventh generation from John Chew, the pioneer His line of descent is from Joseph Chew, the second son of John Chew Joseph Chew died in Maryland in 1716 His second wife was a Miss Larkin, of Annapolis, and his son, Larkin Chew, who settled in Virginia in the latter part of the seventeenth century, married Hannah Roy, daughter of John Roy, of Port Royal, Va John Chew, son of Larkin Chew, married Margaret Beverly, daughter of Colonel Robert Beverly.

Colonel Robert Beverly, who was born in 1675 and died in 1716, was a prominent man in the Colonial affairs of Virginia He was a son of Major Robert Beverly, who was clerk of the Virginia Council for many years, and succeeded his father in that position in 1697 He was best known as one of the earliest American historians His History of the Present State of Virginia, an exhaustive work, was published in London in 1705, and reprinted in 1722 The second John Chew, son of John Chew and Margaret Beverly, was a Colonel in the Revolutionary War, and married Anna Fox, daughter of Thomas Fox. He died in 1799 and his wife survived until 1820. Beverly Chew, their son and the grandfather of Mr Beverly Chew, of New York, was born in 1773 Soon after he became of age, he removed to New Orleans from Virginia, and from 1817 to 1829 was Collector of the Port in that city He became a prominent business man, and was president of the Branch Bank of the United States, and Russian Vice-Consul.

The wife of Beverly Chew, the elder, whom he married in 1810, was Maria Theodora Duer, daughter of Colonel William Duer, of New York, and granddaughter of Major-General Lord Sterling, of the Revolutionary Army She died in 1831 Lord Sterling was one of the most prominent and faithful patriots of the Revolutionary War. He was the son of the famous New York Colonial lawyer, James Alexander, and through his mother a descendant of the de Peysters He owned estates in New York and New Jersey, and his county seat, near Morristown, was one of the handsomest in the colonies The mother of Maria Theodora Duer was Lady Catherine Alexander, the youngest of the two daughters of Lord Sterling, the elder being the wife of Robert Watts Alexander La Fayette Chew, son of Beverly and Maria Theodora (Duer) Chew, married in 1849 Sarah Augustus Prouty, daughter of Phinehas Prouty, of Geneva, N Y. His children were · Beverly, Harriet Hillhouse, who was born in 1852 and married in 1874, Ernest Cleveland Coxe, son of the Right Reverend A Cleveland Coxe, Bishop of Western New York; Phinehas Prouty, who was born in 1854; Thomas Hillhouse, born in 1856; Alexander Duer, born in 1858, Kate Adelaide; Theodora Augusta, and Lillian Chew The second daughter died in 1874.

Mr Beverly Chew, the eldest son, was born in Geneva, N Y, March 5th, 1850. He was educated at the Peekskill Military Academy, and at Hobart College, from which he was graduated in 1869 He has been engaged in financial pursuits in New York during most of his lifetime, and at the present time is secretary of the Metropolitan Trust Company. A man of pronounced literary tastes, he is a member of the Century, University, Players and Grolier clubs, having been president of the latter for four years, and is also a member of the Σ Φ and Church clubs. In 1872, he married Clarissa Taintor Pierson, daughter of the Reverend Job Pierson, of Ionia, Mich Mrs Chew died May 30th, 1889. Mr Chew's brother, Alexander Duer Chew, is also a resident of New York, and a member of the Players, St. Nicholas and other clubs.

DANIEL BREWER CHILDS

WHEN the ship Arabella came to Massachusetts in 1630, it brought several members of the Child family, who were natives of Suffolk, England. One of these, Deacon Ephraim Child, the personal friend of Governor John Winthrop, settled in Watertown, where he was a freeman in 1631, and in after years a representative, selectman and town clerk, as well as one of the wealthiest men in the community. Benjamin Child, his nephew, was also in this company and settled in Watertown, but removed to Roxbury and died in 1678. His son, Ephraim Child, a soldier, was killed in 1675 by the Indians at Northfield during King Philip's War The wife of Benjamin Child was Mary Bowen and their son, Benjamin Child, 1656-1724, was baptized by the Apostle Eliot. He married in 1683 Grace Morris, daughter of Lieutenant Edward Morris, a proprietor of Woodstock, Conn.

In the next generation, Ephraim Child, 1683-1759, was born in Roxbury, but removed to New Roxbury, afterwards Woodstock, Conn., and in 1735 erected the Child mansion, still preserved there. He married Priscilla Harris, 1684-1780. Their son, Ephraim Child, Jr., 1711-1775, was an ensign in 1750 and married Mary Lyon. His son, Captain Increase Child, 1740-1810, served seven years, from 1755 onward, under Israel Putnam in the French war. When the Revolution began he raised a company in Dutchess County, N. Y., and served under Generals Schuyler and Gates in the Saratoga Campaign. He married Olive Pease, 1738-1822, one of their sons being Judge Salmon Child, of the Saratoga County Court, and another, Dr. Ephraim Child, 1773-1830, the grandfather of Mr. Daniel Brewer Childs Dr Child was a distinguished physician, residing in Stillwater, Saratoga County, and was a founder of the medical society of that county. He was also a Surgeon in the War of 1812. He married Mary Woodworth, 1781-1843, daughter of Captain Ephraim and Anna (Moore) Woodworth and cousin of Judge Ambrose Spencer

Noadiah Moody Childs, father of Mr. Daniel Brewer Childs, was born in Stillwater in 1806, and died in 1896 During part of his life he was a civil engineer, associated with his brother, Colonel Orville W. Childs, formerly State engineer, and was engaged on many important works, particularly in connection with the New York canal system In 1841, he became a manufacturer of salt, and was president of the Syracuse Salt Company. He was frequently honored by public office His first wife was Martha Brewer, daughter of Simeon and Eunice (Macy) Brewer, of Providence, R. I, and a descendant from Governor John Carver, of the Mayflower. His second wife was Sarah Elizabeth Dawes, daughter of Dr Ebenezer Dawes

Mr. Daniel Brewer Childs was born in Syracuse, N. Y., May 5th, 1843. On the maternal side he is descended from Daniel Brewer, who settled in Roxbury, Mass., in 1632, and from the Reverend Daniel Brewer, D. D, pastor of the first church in Springfield, Mass., for forty years, who died in 1733, and whose wife, Catharine Chauncy, was a granddaughter of the Reverend Charles Chauncy, the second president of Harvard College, whose lineage has been traced elsewhere in this volume to Alfred the Great and Charlemagne Mr. Childs studied at Oberlin College, and spent a year at Yale, graduating therefrom in 1863. He then entered the Albany Law University and graduated in 1864 Being admitted to the bar, he entered the office of Charles Andrews, of Syracuse, now Chief Justice of the Court of Appeals, and in 1867 came to New York and engaged in practice for over twenty-five years in the firm of Childs & Hull. He has devoted himself principally to civil and commercial branches of law, to practice in bankruptcy and real estate cases, and to the charge of large trust estates

Mr Childs married Kathryn B Cass, daughter of Dr. Jonathan and Mary (Peet) Cass. Dr. Cass was a Surgeon in the United States Army, 1861-65, was chief of staff of the Alexandria Hospital, served throughout the Civil War, and died in New York in 1886. The residence of Mr. and Mrs. Childs is in East Seventy-seventh Street, near Fifth Avenue, and their summer home is in Great Barrington, Mass. Mr Childs was an early member of the University and Lawyers' clubs, having been one of the founders of the former

JOSEPH HODGES CHOATE

JOHN CHOATE, the ancestor of the Choate family in this country, settled at Chebacca, Ipswich, now Essex, Mass According to the court files at Salem, he was about forty years old in 1664 His descendants for several generations continued to live upon the ancestral estate, and ever since they have been one of the most noted and influential families of that part of the Old Bay State. Many of them have achieved distinction in various fields of activity, but more especially in the legal and other learned professions Rufus Choate, the great lawyer and United States Senator for Massachusetts, was a direct descendant from John Choate in the fifth generation. Of this distinguished family came Mr Joseph Hodges Choate, who takes rank as one of the leaders of the New York bar, and who was born in Salem, Mass , January 24th, 1832. He was in early boyhood prepared for Harvard College, which he entered when he was sixteen years of age and from which he was graduated in 1852, in a class which included many men subsequently of high distinction Fixing upon law for his life pursuit, he entered the Dane Law School of Harvard, whence he was graduated in 1854 A year later he was admitted to practice at the bar of the Commonwealth of Massachusetts In 1856, he came to New York and was admitted to practice in the courts of this city, and promptly advanced to the front rank as one of the most brilliant young advocates of that time

During the four decades that Mr Choate has practiced at the New York bar he has borne a leading part and has achieved fame for his learning and for his forensic ability, second to no other lawyer in this country. He has been engaged in many of the most famous cases that have been before the courts of the State or the National tribunals. One of his most notable causes was that of General Fitz-John Porter. The latter had been deprived of his military rank by sentence of a court martial on a charge of disobedience of orders at the second battle of Bull Run After sixteen years a board of inquiry was appointed by the President to review the action of the court martial, and the injustice of its decision being demonstrated, Mr Choate's client, General Porter, was at last reinstated in his commission and rank in the army. To review all the litigation in which Mr Choate has been engaged would be to write a history of the New York bar of the present era. Excelling as an advocate before a jury, he is also a constitutional lawyer of the first rank, and has been engaged in many of the most important causes of that class that have been argued before the Supreme Court of the United States. His successful argument against the constitutionality of the income tax law before the latter tribunal in 1896, will be regarded as one of the greatest victories ever won by an American lawyer

Politically Mr Choate is a Republican and one of the conspicuously active members of his party He has never held public office, although frequently mentioned for political honors He takes a prominent part in National, State and municipal affairs and exercises a wide and strong influence upon public matters generally He was one of the original Committee of Seventy which was organized to overthrow the Tweed ring, and in conjunction with his friend and associate, Charles O Conor, contributed very substantially to the success that was achieved in that movement for reform In 1894, he was president of the Constitutional Convention that formulated the new constitution for the State of New York.

As an orator, Mr Choate has a widespread reputation, and whether at the bar, upon the political platform or at dinners or other social gatherings, he has few recognized rivals He married Caroline D Sterling, of Salem, Mass , the children of this union being Mabel Choate and Joseph Hodges Choate, Jr , an undergraduate at Harvard Mr Choate is a member of many clubs of the city, among them the Metropolitan, the Century, the Union League, the University, the New York Athletic and the Harvard He has been president of the Union League Club and also of the New England Society of New York His brother, the Honorable William G Choate, has also been prominent at the New York bar, and was Judge of the United States Court He married Mary Lyman Atwater.

BENJAMIN SILLIMAN CHURCH

EXCEPTIONAL interest attaches to the career of John Barker Church, ancestor of the subject of this sketch   Born in 1739, of a family of wealth and influence, at Great Yarmouth, England, his liberal opinions caused him to take active service on behalf of the Colonies   He became Commissary General to the French forces, and being one of the few American officers who understood French, was the means of communication between Washington and Rochambeau. In 1777, he married Angelica, daughter of General Philip Schuyler, and became a brother-in-law to Alexander Hamilton. His wife accompanied him throughout the war, and in 1778, their son, Philip Church, was born, and as an infant, with his mother, was at General Schuyler's house when the attempt was made to capture the General by the British, the child receiving a wound, the scar of which remained for life.

At the end of the war the family returned to England, and in 1788, John B Church was elected member of Parliament for Wendover   Down House, his London residence, was noted for its hospitality and for the gatherings of notabilities, including Fox, Pitt, Burke, Lord Grenville and even the Prince of Wales, afterward George IV. Mr Church also aided Talleyrand and other emigrés, and in his house the plan of releasing Lafayette from Olmutz was matured and by his aid carried into effect In 1797, John B. Church returned to New York and was considered one of the richest men of the country, but as an underwriter suffered heavy losses from the French spoliations. He was prominent in the first efforts to supply New York with water, and was president of the company In 1799, he fought a duel with Aaron Burr, at Weehawken, in which neither party was injured The pistols used in the fatal encounter in 1804 between Hamilton and Burr belonged to Church, and are still in the possession of the family.

Philip Church, his son, had graduated with credit at Eton College and begun the study of law at the Temple, in London. He returned to America, entered the office of Nathaniel Pendleton, and was admitted to the bar in 1804. In 1801, he was second to Philip Hamilton in the duel with Eckhard, in which young Hamilton fell fatally wounded While pursuing his legal studies, Philip Church, then nineteen years old, was appointed in 1798 a Captain in the Provincial Army, formed in anticipation of war with France, and became aide and private secretary to Alexander Hamilton. Bearing despatches to General Washington, he won the latter's esteem, and letters from Washington, inviting him to Mount Vernon, are among the most treasured heirlooms of the family. In 1799, Captain Church visited Canandaigua, N Y, to attend the foreclosure of a tract of one hundred thousand acres in Ontario, now Allegheny County, belonging to Robert Morris, on which his father owned a mortgage. He bid the property in and finally abandoned the law to make the development of this domain his labor. The site selected for a village is now the town of Angelica, named after his mother, and two miles from it he chose two thousand acres of land for his own residence, calling it Belvidere. Here he erected a wooden house, afterwards replaced by a mansion long famous as the only stone house in Western New York In 1805, he brought to Belvidere his bride, Anna Matilda, daughter of General Walter Stewart, the Revolutionary hero. Her mother was the famous beauty, Deborah McClanaghan, daughter of Blair McClanaghan, a wealthy Philadelphian, whose residence was the Chew House at Germantown At their marriage in 1781, Washington presented them with his own miniature, now a treasured family possession, and also a cabinet containing one hundred volumes of poetry, which is owned by Colonel Benjamin S. Church. Captain Church visited England in 1812 to import fine live stock While abroad, he was entertained by the Duke of Bedford and other noblemen, and given a public banquet at Great Yarmouth Returning to America, he continued his efforts to improve his estate and devoted great attention to plans of internal improvement The only office he ever accepted was that of Judge of the County Court, which he filled from 1807 to 1821. He zealously aided the construction of the canal system. At an early date, Judge Church advocated railroads, and ere his death, in 1861, he had witnessed the completion of the Erie Railroad

John B Church, Judge Church's eldest son, graduated at Yale in 1829 and was admitted to the bar He never practiced and resided chiefly at Belvidere He interested himself in public enterprises, notably the early plans for rapid transit in New York City. He married a daughter of Professor Benjamin Silliman, Sr., of Yale, and his son traces his maternal ancestry to John Robinson, one of the Mayflower Pilgrims, to John and Priscilla Alden, to Governor Jonathan Trumbull and to General Gold Silliman. Mr Benjamin Silliman Church, their son, was born at Belvidere, April 17, 1836. When a child, he was sent to be educated by his grandfather, Professor Silliman, at New Haven, and attended the famous Russell School there. He entered the Chandler Engineering Department of Dartmouth College, graduating in 1856. He was then engaged as engineer on the surveys of Central Park, of the Croton River and of the new Central Park reservoir, and in 1860 became principal assistant on the Croton aqueduct. At the outbreak of the Civil War, Mr. Church went to the front as Captain of Engineers in the Twelfth Regiment In 1863, he again entered the service as Captain of Engineers on General Yates's staff, and after the war was Colonel of Engineers on the staff of Generals Shaler and Louis Fitzgerald. Colonel Church s professional life has been identified with New York s water supply. His studies convinced him that the city was outgrowing the existing facilities, and in 1875 he prepared the plans for conserving the entire Croton watershed. In 1883, the new Aqueduct Commission was constituted, and Colonel Church made Chief Engineer. His plans for the work, one of the great achievements of modern engineering, were accepted, including the tunnel thirty miles long through solid rock and under the Harlem River, and were carried to completion on the exact lines he had designated. In 1889, he retired from the aqueduct, but that great work remains a testimonial of his services to the metropolis Since the year mentioned, he has practiced his profession as engineer chiefly in its hydraulic and mining branches

In 1875, Colonel Church married Mary Van Wyck, daughter of Abraham Van Wyck, whose grandfather was the Revolutionary patriot, Theodore Van Wyck, member of the Committee of Safety Mrs. Church is related to a large number of old New York Dutch families, among her ancestors being Pieterse Schuyler, Robert Livingston, Abraham de Peyster, Pierre Van Cortlandt, Cornelis Mellyn, the patroon of Staten Island, David Prevoost, Wilhelmus Beekman and other founders of the New Netherland. She is also great-granddaughter of Samuel Howell, of Pennsylvania, member of the Revolutionary Committee of Safety, and also descends from Peter Stretch, who served in the Philadelphia City Council from 1708 to 1746, and from his son, Thomas Stretch, who in 1732, on the formation of the famous Philadelphia Colony of Schuylkill, better known as the Fish House (now the oldest social organization in the world), was elected its Governor and held the office till his death, in 1765 Peter Stretch, his son, was in 1776 and 1778 chosen by Congress to sign the Continental bills of credit Mrs. Church's maternal ancestry connects her with prominent Southern families Her mother was Elizabeth Searcy Cantrell, daughter of Stephen Cantrell, of Davidson County, Tenn., and niece of Judge Granville Searcy. Stephen Cantrell, Sr., received a large tract of land near Nashville for distinguished services in the Indian wars of North Carolina, and was one of the early settlers of Tennessee. Stephen Cantrell, Jr., in 1806, married a famous beauty, Juliet Wendell, niece of George Michael Deadrick, an opulent citizen of Nashville, the courtship and marriage taking place in the stately Deadrick mansion, near Nashville, still in possession of the family. Mrs. Church is also related to the Polk, Frentress and other leading Southern families.

Mrs. Church was a founder of the original Society of Colonial Dames and of the New York Society of that order, being vice-president of the latter. She is also vice-regent of the Mary Washington Colonial Chapter of the Daughters of the American Revolution Colonel and Mrs Church reside at No. 36 West Twelfth Street They have one daughter, Angelica Schuyler Church. Colonel Church belongs to the Manhattan, Union League, and Engineers and Century clubs, the New York Historical Society, and the Loyal Legion.

JOHN CLAFLIN

FOR more than a century and a half, the Claflin family in Massachusetts has contributed to the welfare of that Commonwealth The original Claflins, of Scotch descent, were among the pioneers who settled the town of Hopkinton early in the eighteenth century Their descendants for many generations owned land in Hopkinton, Sherburne, Sudbury and other towns in the central and eastern portions of the old Bay State. Ebenezer Claflin, the ancestor of Mr John Claflin, removed from Hopkinton to Milford some time previous to the Revolutionary period. His wife, whom he married in 1739, was Hannah Smith. His son, John Claflin, of Milford, who was born in 1750, married, in 1770, Mary Sheffield, daughter of Isaac Sheffield John Claflin, Jr , 1775–1848, was the son of John and Mary Claflin. He was a justice of the peace for thirty years, and a Major of artillery, a substantial citizen, who was frequently honored with public office at the hands of his fellow citizens. His wife was Lydia Mellen, daughter of Henry Mellen.

Horace B Claflin, son of John Claflin, of Milford, was born December 18th, 1811, received a good education and in 1832, with his brother and his brother-in-law, entered upon mercantile life in his native town. In a year or more, the young men were able to open a branch store in Worcester, that soon became the largest and most prosperous store in New England outside of Boston Mr. Claflin had long been intent upon coming to New York, and in 1843, selling out his interest in the Worcester establishment, he started the firm of Bulkley & Claflin, to engage in the wholesale dry goods business in the metropolis This firm was succeeded by Claflin, Miller & Co., and soon took a position in the front rank In 1864, the firm name became H. B Claflin & Co , and Mr Claflin continued in active control until his death in 1885. He made a large fortune and was one of the most generous men of his time.

The wife of Horace B. Claflin was Agnes Sanger She was the daughter of Calvin Sanger, 1768–1835, by his wife Anna Phipps, daughter of Jedediah Phipps, who was a great-grandnephew of Sir William Phipps, and whose wife was Sarah Learned, daughter of Captain Edward Learned and Sarah Leland Calvin Sanger was one of the leading citizens of Sherburne, Mass. He was a lawyer, Captain and Colonel of cavalry, a representative to the Massachusetts General Court for thirty years, town clerk for twenty-five years, a State Senator and a magistrate from 1806 until the time of his death He was the son of Captain Samuel Sanger, 1725–1822; grandson of Richard Sanger, 1706–1786, a successful merchant of Sherburne and Boston, and a member of the Committee of Safety in 1776. Richard Sanger was a grandson of Richard Sanger, the pioneer, who came to this country in 1638, settled in Watertown and was a soldier in King Philip's War.

Mr John Claflin, who succeeded his father as the head of the Claflin house, was born in Brooklyn, July 24th, 1850. The New England idea was adhered to in his education, and he was taught in the public schools and in the College of the City of New York, from which institution he graduated with honors in 1869. The following twelve months he traveled in Europe and the Orient and in September, 1870, entered the Claflin establishment Three years later, he became a junior partner, and upon his father's death became the head of the concern. In 1890, he formed the corporation of The H B Claflin Company, of which he is president.

Mr. Claflin is a member of the Metropolitan Club, but club and social life has little charm for him. He takes his recreation from business in travel and exploration, and has made long and often dangerous journeys in the United States, Mexico, South America, Europe and Asia. Few men, save professional explorers, have penetrated further into the wild places of the world, in desert lands and among savages. He married Elizabeth Stewart His winter residence is in East Sixty-ninth Street, but the greater part of the year he spends in Kingsbridge, now the Twenty-fourth Ward of the city, where his father many years ago purchased a large estate.

JOHN HERBERT CLAIBORNE, JR., M.D.

O
N the male side, the Claiborne family of Virginia commences with Bardolph, 1086, Lord of Ravensworth, the common ancestor of several noble North Country families This Bardolph was brother to Alan Fargeant, who led the Breton auxiliaries at the Battle of Hastings. The name of Cleburne was first worn by Alan Fitz Hirvey *dictus* Cleburne, a grandson of Bardolph, who received as his portion a moiety of the manor of Cleburne, in the County of Westmoreland. On the "spindle" side, the lineage goes back to Malcom II, of Scotland, and to the Earls of Northumberland and Dunbar, and the Lords of Seton.

Edmond Cliborne, Lord of the manors of Cliburne and Killerby, married in 1576 Grace Bellingham, daughter of Sir Alan Bellingham. Their son, Captain William Claiborne, seventeenth in line of descent from Bardolph, was born in 1587, and came to Virginia in 1621. He was secretary, treasurer and surveyor-general of the Colony, and distinguished himself by his contention with Lord Baltimore for the possession of Kent Island He resided at Romancock, King William County, and died in 1676 His wife, whom he married in England, was Jane Buller. Their son, Lieutenant-Colonel Thomas Claiborne, of Romancock, 1647–1683, was slain in battle with the Indians. His wife was a member of the Danbridge family. The next in line was Captain Thomas Claiborne, of Sweet Hall, King William County, 1680–1732, who married three times and had twenty-seven children. By his wife Anna Fox he had Colonel Augustine Claiborne, 1721–1787, of Windsor, whose wife was Mary Herbert, daughter of Buller Herbert, of Puddledock, Prince George County. The Herberts were an aristocratic Virginia family, and Mary Herbert inherited a large fortune from her uncle John Herbert, whose tombstone, with the Herbert arms, has been transported from Puddledock and set in the wall of the Blandford Church, at Petersburg. Their seventh child, John Herbert Claiborne, born 1763, was the great-grandfather of the gentleman now referred to He was one of the volunteers who formed a troop of horse and rode with "Light Horse" Harry Lee in the Revolution. His wife was a daughter of Roger Gregory, of Chesterfield, and their son, the Reverend John Gregory Claiborne, became a prominent clergyman in Virginia, and married Mary E. Weldon, of Weldon, N C.

A son of this marriage is Dr. John Herbert Claiborne, of Petersburg, Va., father of Dr. Claiborne, of New York The former holds a high professional rank in his native State, and before the Civil War took an interest in public affairs, being a member of the State Senate in 1858. He was Surgeon and Major of the Twelfth Virginia Regiment in the war. Dr. Claiborne married twice, his first wife being Sarah Joseph Alston, of Halifax, N. C., and his second, Annie Leslie Watson, by whom he has a son and a daughter.

Mr. John Herbert Claiborne, Jr., M D, is the eldest son of his father's first marriage He was born in Louisburg, N. C., 1861; was educated at Petersburg, and was graduated in belles lettres at the University of Virginia in 1881. In 1883, he received his degree of M D at the same institution, and visiting Europe during the ensuing two years, pursued his studies in the Universities of Halle and Berlin, and at the clinics of Paris and London. Since 1886, he has practiced in his specialties of eye and ear diseases in New York. He now holds the position of instructor in ophthalmology in Columbia University. He has made many contributions to the medical literature of the times, and is the author of several standard works relating to his special field of practice. He is a member of many leading professional bodies.

For five years he served as a National Guardsman in the New York Militia. He was a private in Troop A, N. G. N. Y., and afterwards held a warrant as Sergeant in Troop 1, when Troop A was converted into a squadron He is a member of the Southern Society, and of the University, Calumet, Fencers and Military clubs. His residence is No. 39 West Thirty-sixth Street The Claiborne arms are quarterly first and fourth, argent three chevronels interlaced in base sable, a chief of the last. Second and third, argent a cross engrailed vert. Crest, a demi-wolf proper, rampant, regardant. Motto, *Lofe clibbor na sceame*

JOHN MITCHELL CLARK

ABOUT 1635, some of the principal inhabitants of Ipswich, Mass., becoming dissatisfied with church affairs in that town, petitioned the General Court of the Colony for permission to remove and establish themselves elsewhere. The Reverend Mr. Parker, a learned minister, who had been associated with the Reverend Mr. Ward, of Ipswich, headed the little band of Colonists who removed and settled the town of Newbury, Mass. Nathaniel Clark, the ancestor of Mr. John Mitchell Clark, was one of these settlers of Newbury and a strong supporter of the Reverend Mr. Parker in the religious controversies that distracted that town from 1665 to 1669. In 1667, he was town constable; in 1678, served on the jury; was a selectman, 1682–88, and frequently held other town offices. In 1684, he was appointed naval officer of the ports of Newbury and Salisbury, and the following year was an ensign in Captain Daniel Pierce's Company, of Rowley. His death occurred in 1690. The wife of Nathaniel Clark, whom he married in 1663, was Elizabeth Somerby, daughter of Henry and Judith Somerby, of Exeter, N. H. Henry Somerby was the second son of Richard Somerby, of Little Bytham, Lincolnshire, England. Judith Somerby was a daughter of Edmund Greenleaf, who was of Huguenot origin and one of the most prominent settlers of Newbury. He came from Ipswich, in Suffolk, England, in 1638, and belonged to a French family, the name of which was originally Feuillevert, afterwards anglicized into Greenleaf.

In the second American generation, Henry Clark, who was born in Newbury in 1673, removed to Greenland, N. H., and died there in 1749. His wife was Elizabeth Greenleaf, daughter of Captain Stephen and Elizabeth (Gerrish) Greenleaf. Captain Greenleaf was a prominent citizen of Massachusetts and a representative to the General Court. His father, Captain Stephen Greenleaf, was the second son of Captain Edmund Greenleaf. His mother, Elizabeth Coffin, was a daughter of Tristram and Dionis (Stevens) Coffin, of Brixton, near Plymouth, England. His great-grandparents were Peter and Joan (Thember) Coffin and Robert Stevens, of Brixton. Enoch Clark, 1709–1759, son of Henry Clark, was a selectman of Greenland, N. H., 1744–50–53, a moderator in 1756 and auditor in 1748 and 1755–57. His son, Enoch Clark, 1735–1774, was town clerk, selectman, auditor and moderator, and otherwise engaged in the town's service.

Both the father and the grandfather of Mr. John Mitchell Clark were men of prominence. His grandfather, Captain Thomas March Clark, 1771–1850, of Newburyport, Mass., was graduated from Phillips Exeter Academy in 1786. During the War of 1812 he was engaged in the defense of Newburyport against the British, and was one of the committee to receive President James Monroe in 1817 and General Lafayette in 1824. His wife, whom he married in 1811, was Rebecca Wheelwright, 1782–1863, of Newbury. She was descended from the Reverend John Wheelwright, who was born in 1594, the son of Robert Wheelwright, of Saleby, Lincolnshire, England, a graduate of Sydney College, Cambridge, Vicar at Billsby, Lincolnshire and a settler of Salisbury, Mass.

The Reverend Thomas March Clark, father of Mr. John Mitchell Clark, was born in Newburyport, in 1812, and graduated from Yale College in 1831. He was one of the most eminent clergymen in the country in the middle of the present century. First rector of Grace Church in Boston in 1836, he afterwards occupied the pulpit of St. Andrew's Church in Philadelphia, and of Grace Church in Providence, and was elected to the Bishopric of Rhode Island in 1854. He received the degree of D. D. from Union College and Brown University, and LL. D. from the University of Cambridge. His wife was Caroline, daughter of Benjamin Howard, of Boston.

Mr. John Mitchell Clark was born in Boston, Mass., July 23d, 1847. He was educated at Brown University and received the degree of Ph. D. in 1865. Entering upon commercial life, he was engaged in the iron business with Naylor & Co., in Boston. For many years past he has been in the iron business in New York, where he is at the head of the house of Naylor & Co. His principal clubs include the Metropolitan, Tuxedo, Union, and he belongs to the Downtown Association and the Brown University Alumni Association, and is a patron of the Metropolitan Museum of Art.

RICHARD HENRY CLARKE

IT is the glory of Maryland that religious toleration was the guiding principle in its establishment as a Colony. Among the cavalier pilgrims who aided in carrying out the broad views of Lord Baltimore was Robert Clarke, who came to Maryland in 1636, was a Privy Councilor and Surveyor-General of the Province, and a member of the Assembly of 1649, in which he took part in passing the act for establishing religious liberty in the Colony.

Dr. Richard Henry Clarke, of New York, descends in a direct line from Robert Clarke, his grandfather being Captain William Clarke, an officer of the Maryland line during the American Revolution, who fought at Long Island and Trenton, at Staten Island, Monmouth, Brandywine, and endured the privations of Valley Forge. Dr. Clarke's father, Walter Clarke, was born in St Mary's County, Md, and married Rachel Boone, of Prince George's County, whose brother, an uncle of Dr Clarke's, Captain John Boone, was also an officer of the Revolution. Mr. Richard Henry Clarke was born at Washington, D. C., in 1827. He was educated at Georgetown University, which has added to his degree of A B. those of Master of Arts and Doctor of Laws in recognition of his professional and literary eminence. He also holds the degree of LL D conferred by St. John's College, Fordham, N. Y, while Notre Dame University, Indiana, has awarded him a golden cross in recognition of his literary works. Dr. Clarke was called to the bar in Washington City, and engaged in active practice in that city till 1864, and since then in this city. He was associated with the celebrated Charles O'Connor in some of his prominent cases, and was retained with Mr. O'Connor in the defence of Jefferson Davis. Literary labors have occupied his attention in recent years in addition to his practice of the law. Dr Clarke is regarded as a foremost lay writer on Catholic Church history. He is the author of The Lives of American Catholic Bishops, The History of the Catholic Church in the United States, and Old and New Lights on Columbus. He received a letter from Pope Pius IX accepting and commending his Lives of the Bishops. He is the editor of The History of the Bench and Bar of New York, the associate editors being several Judges of the Supreme Court of the State of New York.

In 1858, Dr. Clarke married Ada Semmes, of Georgetown, daughter of Raphael Semmes and Matilda Jenkins Semmes. The Semmes family also furnished several officers to the Revolutionary Army, while Mrs. Clarke's first cousin, Raphael Semmes, was the famous Confederate Admiral, who commanded the Sumter and the Alabama of the Confederate Navy. The issue of this marriage are Maude, a Dominican Sister of the Perpetual Adoration; Walter Semmes, a journalist; Mary Ada, Mary Agnes, wife of the Honorable Thomas C. T. Crain, lately Chamberlain of New York; Clara Agnes, wife of Captain Henry P Birmingham, Surgeon U. S A ; Richard Henry, Jr, of the New York bar, and Anna Cora Angela Clarke.

Dr. Clarke possesses a notable collection of engravings and prints particularly rich in those relating to Columbus, a large library, and a number of examples and copies of paintings by old masters. He has entertained many distinguished clerical and lay guests, including Cardinals McCloskey and Gibbons, Cardinal Vaughn, now Primate of England, Archbishop Corrigan, Admiral de Couverville, and the Society of the Sons of the American Revolution. Active and eminent in all church and charitable works, Dr Clarke has been President of the Alumni of Georgetown University, and of the New York Catholic Protectory, and a delegate to the American Convention of Charities and Correction, to the American Catholic Lay Congress and the Catholic Summer School. The cause of reformed politics has his earnest support; he is an earnest advocate of Civil Service reform, and he is also a member and officer of the Society of Sons of the American Revolution. He was selected to write the history of the Catholic Church in New York City in General James Grant Wilson's Memorial History of the City of New York, and has lately issued a paper on the aid rendered by France to America in the War of Independence, which is regarded as a most thorough monograph on that subject

JOHN VAN BOSKERCK CLARKSON

IN 1688, Matthew Clarkson was Secretary of the Province of New York, by appointment of William and Mary, and held that office for thirteen years. He was the son of the Reverend Daniel Clarkson, an English clergyman, who was born at Bradford, Eng, in 1622. His mother was Elizabeth, daughter of Sir Henry Holcroft, whose wife was the daughter of Francis, Lord Aungier, who descended from the sovereigns of England   He married, January 19th, 1692, Catherine, daughter of Goosen Gerriste Van Schaick, of Albany, connected with the Van Courtlandts, the Verplancks, the Barclays and the Schuylers   The oldest son of Matthew Clarkson, David Clarkson, 1694-1751, was at one time a merchant in London, but returned and settled in New York, was a member of the Assembly, 1739-1751, and an uncompromising patriot.   A grandson of the original Clarkson was Gerardus Clarkson, one of the most distinguished physicians of Philadelphia, one of his great-grandsons was Matthew Clarkson, who served with distinction throughout the Revolutionary War; and among his other descendants were Matthew Clarkson, Mayor of Philadelphia and a Member of Congress; the Reverend Doctor Howard Crosby, Chancellor of the University of New York, and Bishop Robert Harper Clarkson, of Nebraska.

A son of Doctor Gerardus Clarkson was William Clarkson, a physician of Philadelphia, and in after years a Presbyterian minister, who had pastorates at Bridgeton, N. J ; Schenectady, N. Y , Savannah, Ga., and St. John's Island, S C   He married Catharine, daughter of William Floyd, 1734-1821   William Floyd was the son of Nicoll Floyd, and grandson of Richard Floyd, of Brookhaven, the ancestor of the Floyd and Floyd-Jones families in this country. He was an enthusiastic patriot during the Revolution, and served the Colonial cause well.   He was a delegate from New York to the Philadelphia Congress in 1774, a member of every Continental Congress from 1775 to 1782 inclusive, a signer of the Declaration of Independence, State Senator of New York, 1777-1788, Presidential elector and Major-General of the militia.

Samuel Floyd Clarkson, a son of William and Catharine Clarkson, and a lawyer of New York City, married Amelia A., daughter of William A. Baker, a New York merchant.   Colonel Floyd Clarkson was the son of Samuel Floyd Clarkson.   He was educated at private schools in New York City, and then engaged in the hardware business, in which he continued until the beginning of the Civil War   When President Lincoln called for troops in April, 1861, Floyd Clarkson was a private in the Seventh Regiment, and was in the famous march to Washington. In November, 1861, he became Major of the Sixth New York Cavalry, and served in the Peninsula and North Carolina campaigns, and was breveted Lieutenant-Colonel

Upon returning from the war, Colonel Clarkson entered business, first as cashier in a commission house, and then successively as secretary of the Equitable Savings Bank, secretary and agent for Woodbury G. Langdon, and finally as a real estate agent for himself.   He was trustee of the Union Dime Savings Bank, president of the Riverside Bank, a prominent Free Mason in Kane Lodge, a member of the Dutch Reformed Church, Chancellor of the New York Commandery of the Military Order of the Loyal Legion, Commander of the New York Department of the Grand Army of the Republic, a member of the St. Nicholas Society, and vice-president of the Sons of the Revolution   In March, 1857, he married Harriet A Van Boskerck, daughter of John Van Boskerck, a retired merchant of Holland descent.   Ten children were born of this union, and five sons and two daughters grew to maturity   Colonel Clarkson died January 2d, 1894.

Mr John Van Boskerck Clarkson is the eldest surviving son of Colonel Floyd Clarkson. He is a prominent real estate operator, going into that business with his father in 1884, under the firm name of Floyd Clarkson & Son, which still remains unchanged.   He lives in the family residence at 48 East Sixty-sixth Street, occupied by his father for many years   He is a member of the St. Nicholas Club and the Sons of the Revolution, Society of Colonial Wars, Military Order of Loyal Legion, Metropolitan Museum of Art, and a Director of the Riverside Bank.

HENRY CLEWS

BANKER and man of public affairs, Mr. Henry Clews has long held a preeminent position in the metropolis. For forty years he has been prominent in Wall Street, and during that entire time has also taken an active part in national and municipal affairs. Mr. Clews was born in Staffordshire, England, where his family ranks as one of the oldest and most substantial in that part of the country. His father was a man of high social and business standing, engaged in prosperous manufacturing enterprises, largely in connection with the American market. He prepared his son for admission to Cambridge University, with the intention of having him enter the ministry of the Established Church.

Having occasion to visit the United States on a business trip, the senior Mr. Clews brought with him his son, who was then only fifteen years of age. Something in the bustling commercial life of the country caught the fancy of the boy, and he persuaded his father to allow a change in his plans and to permit him to enter upon a business, rather than a professional career. Remaining in New York, a position in the importing house of Wilson G. Hunt & Co. was secured for him, and since that time he has been wholly identified with the city of his adoption. He continued in the importing business for several years, but having an ambition to become a banker, in 1857, was admitted to membership in the Wall Street firm of Stout, Clews & Mason. From the outset he was successful in his new field of labor, and in the years since then has attained to a foremost place among financiers, and was prominent in all the patriotic work that engaged the attention of the community at that time. About 1861, he became a junior partner in the firm of Livermore, Clews & Co. His firm received its first impetus during the Civil War, through the loyalty of Mr. Clews to the National Government and his confidence in the ultimate triumph of the Union cause. Secretary of Treasury Chase appointed his firm fiscal agents for the sale of the five-twenty Government loan, and this trust was carried out with a success that called out the commendation of Mr. Chase for the patriotism and energy shown in the handling of the business. Mr. Clews was also foremost during the Civil War in organizing many of the large mass meetings that were held to stimulate patriotism and encourage the Government in Washington. In 1877, the firm of Henry Clews & Co., of which he is still actively at the head, was organized by him.

As a public-spirited citizen of the metropolis, Mr. Clews has taken a deep interest in politics, but has always declined political preferment. He was an original member of the famous Committee of Seventy, and untiring in the work of that organization in overthrowing the Tweed Ring. He was offered the office of City Chamberlain as a bribe to withdraw his opposition; of course, the proposal was spurned. Other tenders of political positions have come to him at different times in his career. Twice the Secretaryship of the Treasury was offered to him, and twice the Republican nomination for Mayor of New York, and President Grant also desired to nominate him for the office of the Collector of the Port of New York in 1873.

For many years, Mr. Clews was treasurer of the American Geographical Society, and also of the Society for the Prevention of Cruelty to Animals, when Henry Bergh was its president. He has been connected with other city institutions and has given generous support to many humanitarian enterprises. He was one of the founders of the Union League Club, and is also a member of the Union and other leading clubs. His interest in art subjects is shown by the fine gallery of paintings that he owns, and he is one of the thirty-five stockholders and owners of the Metropolitan Opera House. He is the author of Twenty-eight Years in Wall Street, a book that reviews the financial history of New York's great money centre during one of its most interesting periods. In 1847, he married Lucy Madison Worthington, of Kentucky, who comes of an old and aristocratic Southern family, being a grand-niece of President James Madison. His city residence is in West Thirty-fourth Street, and his summer home is The Rocks, in Newport. He has one son, Henry Clews, Jr., and one daughter, Elsie Clews.

CHARLES WILLIAM CLINTON

PARTICULAR interest attaches to the present representatives of names which in Colonial New York or in the early history of the State were borne by the great families. Among them none occupied a higher position than the Clintons, who are an English family of ancient origin, and represented in England now by the Duke of Newcastle. The family was established in America by Charles Clinton, 1690-1773, who was born in the County of Longford, Ireland, a descendant of Henry, the second Earl of Lincoln, and a man of property and influence. In 1731, he purchased a large tract of land at Little Britain, Ulster County, and became the most prominent man in that section. During the French and Indian war, he served as Lieutenant in Bradstreet s expedition of 1756 against Fort Frontenac, and was also Judge of the County Court. He was a relative of Admiral George Clinton, the Royal Governor of the Province from 1743 to 1753, and of the latter's son, Sir Henry Clinton.

This relationship did not prevent the New York Clintons from warmly espousing the patriotic side in the struggle, and two of Charles Clinton's sons became leaders in the American cause. One of them, General George Clinton, 1739-1812, was a delegate to the Continental Congress of 1775 and voted for the Declaration of Independence, but did not sign it, having been recalled to New York to assume a military command. In 1776, he was made a Brigadier-General by Congress, and in 1777 was elected Governor of New York under the first State Constitution. He held this post by five successive elections till 1795. He was again elected Governor of New York in 1801, and became Vice-President of the United States in 1805, in the second administration of Jefferson, being re-elected in 1808 with Madison.

His elder brother, General James Clinton, was born in 1736, distinguished himself in the French and Indian war, became a Colonel in the Army of the Revolution, and as such took part in General Montgomery's expedition against Quebec. Appointed Brigadier-General in 1776, he served under Putnam on the Hudson, defended Fort Clinton when it was stormed by the British in 1777, and after a gallant resistance escaped severely wounded. He was present at the siege and capitulation of Yorktown, was subsequently a member of the State Convention of 1788, which ratified the Federal Constitution, and a State Senator, dying in 1812.

His wife was Mary, daughter of Egbert DeWitt, the most famous of his family being his son, DeWitt Clinton, 1769-1828, whose political career as Senator, Mayor of New York, Lieutenant-Governor, 1811-1813, and finally Governor, 1817-1822, and 1824-1828, are part of the history of the State and the county, while his advocacy and success in carrying through the completion of that great work, the Erie Canal, opened in 1825, was the groundwork of New York's financial and commercial supremacy. Charles Clinton a brother of DeWitt Clinton, was Mr Charles William Clinton's grandfather. His son, Alexander Clinton, was a physician of ability and reputation, and married Adeline Arden Hamilton, daughter of Alexander James Hamilton, an officer of the British Army and a representative of a distinguished Scottish family.

Mr Charles William Clinton is the offspring of this alliance. He was born in New York, received an academical education and studied architecture under the late Richard Upjohn. Mr Clinton has been for many years engaged in the practice of his profession, in which he has attained the foremost rank. Among the many creations with which he has adorned this city, such edifices as the Mutual Life Insurance Building and the Seventh Regiment Armory may be specially mentioned. He was one of the vice-presidents of the New York Chapter of the American Institute of Architects, which office he held for seven years. He served in the Seventh Regiment, volunteering three times when it was called into active service during the Civil War. Besides the various associations connected with his profession, such as the Institute of Architects and the Architectural League, Mr Clinton also belongs to the Chamber of Commerce and several literary, artistic and social clubs, among which are included the Century Association, the Tuxedo Club and the Municipal Art Society

JOHN COCHRAN

WHEN General Lafayette lay dangerously ill with a fever for many weeks in the Ver Planck mansion in Fishkill, in the autumn of 1778, he was closely attended by Dr John Cochran, of Washington's army, of whom he became very fond, and to whom he was accustomed to apply the endearing soubriquet, "the Good Doctor Bones." Dr Cochran rendered noble service to the Patriot cause. He was a native of Pennsylvania, born in 1730. His father was a farmer, who had emigrated to the Colonies from the North of Ireland. He received a careful education and finished his medical studies in season to take part in the French and Indian War of 1755, serving as a surgeon's mate and winning a reputation as a skillful practitioner. In 1776, he volunteered his services to the Patriots and was appointed Physician and Surgeon General by Washington. Congress made him Director General of Hospitals in 1781. When peace was declared, he made his home in New York City, and at one time held the office of Commissioner of Loans for the State, by appointment from Washington. Early in life, he married Gertrude, sister of his intimate friend, General Philip Schuyler, and lived in New Brunswick, N J, where he practiced his profession and was at one time president of the Medical Society of that State. Mrs. Cochran was the great-granddaughter of John Schuyler, who led an expedition to Canada against the French and the Indians in 1690, and who was the youngest son of Philip Pieterse Schuyler, the American ancestor of the family, and his wife, Margaret Van Schlichtenhorst.

The son of Dr John Cochran was Walter L. Cochran, who married Cornelia Smith, daughter of Judge Peter Smith, of Peterboro, N. Y. The ancestors of Judge Smith came from Holland, and he was a large land owner in Western New York, reputed at one time to be in possession of nearly one million acres He was also a partner with John Jacob Astor in the fur business, and his son, Gerritt Smith, was the famous philanthropist and anti-slavery advocate and staunch friend of John Brown. Mrs. Cochran's mother was Elizabeth Livingston, oldest daughter of Colonel James Livingston, of the Army of the Revolution, who drove the British sloop Vulture from the North River, thus bringing about the capture of Major André and the preservation of West Point from falling into the hands of the enemy. This James Livingston was the descendant of Robert, the nephew of Robert, the first Lord of the Manor, and the first American Livingston, and of his wife, Margaretta Schuyler, daughter of Colonel Peter (Queder) Schuyler, having been a son of John, the youngest son of Robert, the nephew, and of his wife, Catherine Ten Broeck.

General John Cochran can thus trace his ancestry from the great families of the Colonial and Revolutionary period. The son of Walter L. Cochran, he was born in Palatine, Montgomery County, N. Y, August 27th, 1813. Graduated from Hamilton College in 1831, he was admitted to the bar three years later, removed to New York in 1846, and began a career that for more than a quarter of a century kept him actively engaged in the public service. In 1853, he was appointed United States Surveyor for the Port of New York, and from 1857 to 1861 was a Member of Congress. In 1864, he was made a Vice-Presidential candidate on the ticket with John C. Fremont, but withdrew before the election came on. Upon the breaking out of the Civil War, he recruited and took command of a regiment and served until 1863, when he resigned on account of disabilities. He was the first man to advise arming the slaves in the Civil War, urging that military measure in a speech in November, 1861.

In civil life, since the war, he has borne a conspicuous part, having been Attorney-General of the State of New York, 1863-65, president of the Common Council of New York City in 1872, and a police justice in 1889. He was a delegate to the National Liberal Republican Convention in 1872, and declined the Ministry to Uruguay and Paraguay in 1869 He is a member of the Society of the Cincinnati, in which he is the president of the New York Society, a member of the Loyal Legion, the Sons of the Revolution, the Tammany Society and other social, political and military organizations. He lives in East Sixty-second Street, and his summer home is in Brookside, Morris County, N. J

DAVID VESEY SMITH CODDINGTON

LINCOLNSHIRE was the English home of William Coddington, who was born in 1601, came to this country in 1630 and settled in Salem, afterwards removing to Boston He was a magistrate of Massachusetts, and owned valuable land Sympathizing with the sectaries whom the Colonial authorities persecuted, he defended Ann Hutchinson and Mary Dyer, but was unable to save the latter, and, arousing bitter opposition, he withdrew to Rhode Island, where he was a Judge, and in 1640 Governor. When the Providence Plantations were incorporated, in 1647, he became assistant president, and succeeded to the presidency in 1648. In 1674-75 and 1678 he was elected Governor of the Colony. He built the first brick house in Boston.

John Coddington, a gentleman of wealth for his day, married Margaret Edgar and removed to New Jersey. His son, James Coddington, 1754-1816, was in the Revolutionary Army He commanded the body guard Washington gave to Lafayette at the Brandywine and was wounded there He married Experience (Inslee) Randolph, widow of Captain Nathaniel Randolph Their son, Jonathan I Coddington, 1784-1856, was born at Woodbridge, N J., and was a prominent merchant in New York He also had a notable political career, and was the friend of Presidents Jackson and Van Buren. In 1827, he was a member of the Assembly, and in 1836 was appointed postmaster at New York, then one of the most lucrative Federal offices He held the place under Presidents Jackson, Van Buren and Harrison. The latter informed him that, though a political opponent, he would not be disturbed, and after General Harrison's death, Tyler's representative asked him to renew his bond While debating whether to do so or not, he learned that John Lorimer Graham had been appointed in his place. He was a Presidential elector in 1844, and in the same year was the Democratic candidate for Mayor He declined the Gubernatorial nomination of the Republican party in 1856 on account of failing health At one time he served on the staff of Governor Tompkins. He married Matilda Palmer, daughter of William Palmer

The three sons of Jonathan I. and Matilda (Palmer) Coddington were David Vesey Smith, Gilbert Smith and Clifford Coddington, the first and last now deceased. Clifford Coddington entered the Civil War as Lieutenant in the Fifty-First New York Regiment. He took part in Burnside's North Carolina expedition, and in his first battle was mentioned for conspicuous gallantry. At Antietam, he showed great courage under fire, and was wounded. He subsequently was aide to Major-General Potter, and after the siege of Knoxville was retired for disability. Later, he became Colonel of the Twenty-First Regiment, N G S N Y. David Vesey Smith Coddington was a distinguished lawyer and orator Vice-President Dallas once said of him : "There is a young man whom I consider one of the great men of the country He should be here in the Senate "

Gilbert Smith Coddington was born in New York in 1835, and was educated here and in Geneva, Switzerland He has traveled much, and spent twenty-five years in Europe. During the Civil War, he supported the Government with energy, and recruited many men at his own expense. In 1862, he was Captain of the Twentieth New York Battery. In 1880, Mr. Coddington married Amelia N Stilwell, daughter of the Honorable Silas M. Stilwell, 1800-1881, an eminent lawyer of New York. Her great-uncle was the Revolutionary General Garret Stilwell. Early in life, her father was a member of the Tennessee Legislature and of the Virginia House of Burgesses. After 1828, he resided in New York and was a member of the Assembly, acting Mayor, United States Marshall and author of the Stilwell Act and the United States Banking law. Mrs Coddington is descended from John Cook, the regicide, who came to America, changed his name to Stilwell and was the ancestor of many prominent families.

Mr. Coddington is a member of the Metropolitan, Reform and St. Nicholas clubs, the New York Historical Society, New York Genealogical and Biographical Society and American Geographical Society, also of various clubs in Europe

CULLEN VAN RENSSELAER COGSWELL

AFTER a long and tempestuous passage across the Atlantic in 1635, the ship Angel Gabriel ended its voyage by dashing upon the rock-bound coast of Maine during a terrible storm. Most of the passengers were washed ashore and escaped with their lives, among them being John Cogswell and his wife, the American ancestors of the family to which Mr Cullen Van Rensselaer Cogswell belongs. John Cogswell was the son of Edward and Alice Cogswell, of Westbury Leigh, Wiltshire, England, where he was born in 1592. His wife was Elizabeth Thompson, daughter of the Reverend William and Phyllis Thompson. He was a manufacturer and owned several large mills Belonging to an English family, at the head of which, in 1447, was Lord Humphrey Cogswell, to whom a coat of arms was granted, he was forty-three years of age when he came to this country and was summarily tossed ashore upon the rocks of Maine. He settled in Ipswich, Mass, of which place he was a freeman in 1636

In the second American generation was William Cogswell, who was born in England in 1619 and accompanied his parents to this country He was a resident of Ipswich, where he was a surveyor of the public ways and active in church and town affairs. His wife was Susannah Hawkes, daughter of Adam Hawkes and Anne Hutchinson. His death occurred in 1700. His son, Jonathan Cogswell, who was born in 1661 and died in 1717, was a merchant, justice of the peace and Captain of the train band. He married, in 1686, Elizabeth Wainwright, daughter of Francis Wainwright, who came from Chelmsford, England, and was a soldier in the Pequot War. Jonathan Cogswell, second of the name, grandson of William Cogswell, was born in Ipswich in 1687 and died in 1752. He was a justice of the peace in 1733 His second wife, the ancestress of Mr. Cullen Van Rensselaer Cogswell, was Elizabeth Wade, daughter of Jonathan Wade

In the fifth generation, Nathaniel Cogswell, great-grandfather of Mr. Cullen Van Rensselaer Cogswell, was born in Ipswich in 1739 and died in 1822. His life covered the period of the Revolutionary War, and he was prominent in the events of that time, being a member of the Committee of Correspondence in 1775 and a member of the Committee of Safety in 1776. He was educated as a physician, but did not practice, preferring to devote himself to agriculture. He was twice married, his second wife, Lois Searle, daughter of William and Jane Searle, being the mother of the Reverend Jonathan Cogswell, grandfather of Mr. Cullen Van Rensselaer Cogswell.

The Reverend Jonathan Cogswell was born in 1782 in Rowley, Mass Graduated from Harvard College in 1806, he was a tutor in Bowdoin College for two years and was then graduated from the Andover Theological Seminary in 1810, and ordained the same year, being settled over the Congregational Church in Saco, Me. There he remained until 1828, when he removed to New York, being subsequently settled in Berlin, Conn., and holding the chair of ecclesiastical history, and also that of church history in the Theological Institute of Connecticut, in East Windsor Hill. The University of the City of New York conferred upon him the degree of S T. D. He was a member of many religious societies and founded a scholarship in Rutgers College. His death occurred in 1864 His second wife, Jane Eudora Kirkpatrick, was a daughter of Andrew Kirkpatrick, chief justice of New Jersey, and granddaughter of Colonel John Bayard, of Maryland. Andrew Kirkpatrick Cogswell, father of Mr. Cullen Van Rensselaer Cogswell, was born in 1839 in East Windsor, Conn., and married, in 1867, Mary Van Rensselaer, daughter of General J. Cullen Van Rensselaer, of Cazenovia, N. Y. He served for some years, before his death, as a Judge in the New Jersey Supreme Court.

Mr. Cullen Van Rensselaer Cogswell was born in New Brunswick, N. J, September 5th. 1869. He was educated in St Paul's School, Concord, N H. He married, in 1896, A Eugenie Nickerson, of Riverdale, Dedham, Mass, daughter of Albert W. Nickerson, formerly president of the Atchison, Topeka & Santa Fé Railroad Company. His residence is in Fifth Avenue. He is a member of the Union, City and Seventh Regiment Veteran clubs, the Sons of the Revolution and the Society of Colonial Wars.

HENRY RUTGERS REMSEN COLES

THE ancestral record of Mr Henry Rutgers Remsen Coles is a long list of names of those who for three centuries were prominent in the affairs of the Colonies, the States and New York City In his name he carries remembrance of three families that have been distinguished in the business, social and political life of the metropolis of the new world, and the history of whose activities fill many pages in local annals of New York and New England. Mr. Coles's father was Isaac Underhill Coles, a descendant from Captain John Underhill, and his mother was Catherine S Remsen, daughter of Henry and Elizabeth Waldron (Phœnix) Remsen. His grandfather was Edward Coles, whose wife was Hester Bussing Moulton

Captain John Underhill, whose name Mr Coles's father bore, was an Englishman who had fought in the Low Countries and who came to America with Governor John Winthrop. He was one of the most valiant and able soldiers in the early wars of the Massachusetts Bay Colony with the Indians, and after removing to New Netherland, in 1644, was equally successful in helping to protect this settlement from the hostile Indians Other ancestors of Mr Coles who were engaged in the Colonial wars that raged upon the borders of New Netherland were Captain John Seamen, Major Richard Smith, Captain Ebenezer Moulton, Captain Harman Rutgers, Henry Rutgers, William Hallett and Captain William Hallett Mr Coles is also able to trace his pedigree back to Johannes de Peyster, that courtly Huguenot of a noble French family who came from Holland about 1650 to New Amsterdam Another ancestor of the same early period was Matthais Nicolls, 1621–1687, who came to New Netherland in 1664 with Colonel Richard Nicolls, the Governor appointed by the Duke of York to take charge of the Colony in behalf of the English Matthais Nicolls was the first secretary of the Province under Governor Nicolls, a member of the council under Governor Lovelace, Mayor of the city in 1671, Speaker of the first Colonial Assembly of New York in 1683, and the first Judge of the Court of Oyer and Terminer

In the War of the Revolution, ancestors of Mr Coles were not less patriotic and active Among them were Captain Henry Remsen, member of the Committee of One Hundred in 1775, Lieutenant-Colonel Stephen Moulton, and Daniel Phœnix, who lives in the memory of New Yorkers as one of the leading business men of his day, and as the City Treasurer or Chamberlain in 1789 and many years following, and came of a noble English family

The wife of Mr Coles, whom he married in 1896 at Geneva, Switzerland, was Margaret Miller Davidson, born in Yokohama, Japan, September 24th, 1873 They have a son, H R R. Coles, Jr., born May 28th, 1897 Mrs Coles, too, comes of a distinguished ancestry, being a descendant from a famous old Scotch family, the Davidsons of Dingwall, Scotland, who are now represented at the head of the family by Duncan Davidson, chief of the clan. Her grandfather was a physician of Plattsburg, N Y ; her grandmother was a writer of verse, and the Davidson sisters, the celebrated American poetesses of the early part of this century, were her aunts. Lucretia Maria Davidson, who died in 1825, at the age of seventeen, and Margaret Miller Davidson, who died in 1838, at the age of fifteen, were the precocious literary geniuses of their time Mrs Coles is descended from Captain John Underhill, Major Thomas Jones, Captain Ephenetus Platt and others who were prominent in the Colonial Wars, and many of her ancestors were patriots in the War for Independence

Mr Coles was born in Tarrytown, N Y , July 15th, 1873 He was educated in private schools, has traveled abroad and now lives in Englewood, N. J Interested in historical and genealogical subjects, he is a compiler and publisher of genealogies His membership in social organizations includes the Union and the New York Athletic clubs; he is a life member of the Sons of the American Revolution and the Society of Colonial Wars, belongs to the New York Historical Society, the Geographical and Biographical Society, the Underhill Society of America, and is a member of Squadron A, New York State National Guard

WALTER HENRY COLES

FOR three hundred years the Coles family has been settled on the northern shores of Long Island, and its members have been connected by marriage with all the other old-time families of that section and of New York. Robert Coles, who was the first of the race to come to America, lived in Suffolk, England. He was a friend of John Winthrop, of whose expedition to New England he was a member, settling in Roxbury, or Ipswich, Mass., in 1630. Being a relative of Roger Williams, he sympathized with that eminent divine in his controversies with the Plymouth and Massachusetts Bay Colonies and went with him to Providence, R. I., dying there in 1654 His son, Nathaniel Coles, came to Long Island, was one of the first settlers of the town of Oyster Bay, a merchant and many years justice of the peace. He died in 1707

The grandson of Nathaniel Coles, also named Nathaniel, succeeded to the family estates at Dosoris and Oyster Bay. He was a prominent man in the community, active in good works and public-spirited. An enthusiastic patriot, at the time of the Revolution, when hostilities between America and England were ended, in 1783, he celebrated the occasion by inviting the entire population of his town to feast upon a whole roasted ox. General Nathaniel Coles, 1763-1824, the son of this Nathaniel Coles, was a land owner, an extensive mill proprietor owning several large mills, and one of the most celebrated breeders of fine horses in his generation. His most extensive mill property was at West Island. The grandfather of Walter H Coles was Butler Coles, son of General Nathaniel Coles. He was born in 1797 at Dosoris and died in 1840. He, too, was one of the large mill owners in the neighborhood of New York in the first half of the present century, and also served on the military staff of General Floyd.

In every generation, the wives of this family have come from the best Colonial stock. The first Nathaniel Coles married Martha Jackson, descended from Robert Whitehead, one of the first settlers of Hempstead, a large real estate proprietor, and owner of Dosoris. His son, Nathaniel, married a member of the Townsend family, granddaughter of Henry and Anne (Coles) Townsend and of Nicholas Wright, one of the founders of Oyster Bay. Other women of the family were descendants of William Butler, who was early settled in Oyster Bay, and of John Townsend, Benjamin Birdsall and Nathan Birdsall. The wife of the third Nathaniel Coles was Hannah Butler, daughter of John and Martha Butler, and the wife of General Nathaniel Coles was Elizabeth Townsend, daughter of James and Freelove Townsend. The grandmother of Walter H. Coles was a descendant of Francis Weeks, one of the first Colonists of Hempstead and Oyster Bay, and of the Reverend Francis Doughty, of Flushing.

Edwin Sands Coles, the father of the subject of this sketch, was born at Dosoris in 1828, and died in 1896. Throughout his entire life, he was identified with financial affairs in New York, being a stock broker, and prominent in many positions of financial responsibility. For more than thirty years he was secretary of the Stock Exchange Building Company. He was a member of the St. Nicholas Society by virtue of his ancestry and belonged to the American Geographical Society and other organizations. The wife of Edwin Sands Coles is still living. She was Sarah Townsend, daughter of Dr. Charles De Kay Townsend and his wife, Maria Fonda, of Albany. She is a descendant of Henry and Anne (Coles) Townsend, and also of Captain Thomas de Kay, of the United States Navy, and his wife, Christianna Duncan, who was a granddaughter of the noted Anneke Jans, whose estate on Manhattan Island three centuries ago, which passed under the control of Trinity Church Corporation, still continues to be a cause of speculation and an object of popular interest

Mr. Walter Henry Coles, the second child and the only son of Edwin S. Coles, was born in Albany, N. Y., June 29th, 1865. His sisters are Sarah Townsend Coles and Julia Weekes Coles. He lives in West Fifty-ninth Street, with his mother and sisters. Their country home is in Northwood, Oyster Bay, Long Island, the ancestral estate of the family

JAMES BOORMAN COLGATE

NORWICH, England, furnishes the earliest records of the Colgate family, there being a Colgate Ward of the town, a Colgate Street, and an old church, St George Colgate, dating from the eleventh century there Later on the family was established near Sevenoaks, in Kent In the middle of the last century, John Colgate, one of its members, was one of the few Englishmen who expressed sympathy with the American Colonists His son Robert held similar views, and favored the liberal ideas of some of the leaders of the French Revolution to such an extent, that he was marked for prosecution. He was, however, a friend of the famous William Pitt, who advised him to leave England for America, where his views would be tolerated, and this he did, coming to Baltimore in May, 1795

Residing for a time in Maryland, and then for a few years in New York City, Robert Colgate moved to Delaware County, N Y William Colgate, his eldest son, came with his father to America, and in 1806 established a mercantile firm in New York, where he died in 1857 He married an English lady, Mary Gilbert, and had nine children, of whom four sons, Robert, James B , Samuel and Joseph, and two daughters survived him He was one of the incorporators of Madison University, Hamilton, N. Y , which, under its present name of Colgate University, is one of the chief educational institutions of the Baptist churches.

Mr James B Colgate was born in New York, March 4th, 1818 He was educated in Connecticut and in this city, and preferring business to a collegiate course, served seven years as a clerk, four of them in the office of his relative, James Boorman, of the firm of Boorman, Johnson & Co Mr Boorman was the projector of the Hudson River Railroad Ill-health necessitated a visit to Europe, in 1841, and on Mr Colgate's return he engaged in the wholesale dry goods trade. In 1852, he entered into the stock business with the late John B Trevor, founding the firm of Trevor & Colgate, and a bullion department being added five years afterwards, the concern became the largest dealers in stocks and the precious metals in this country, their transactions, especially in the time of the war, being enormous. Soon after the death of Mr. Trevor, in 1890, Mr. Colgate associated his son, James Colby Colgate, in the partnership, still maintaining the firm name of James B Colgate & Co. During the war, Mr. Colgate was for several years president of the New York Gold Exchange, and he has long been vice-president of the Bank of the State of New York He has made finance his lifelong study, and has been one of the most influential advocates of the remonetization of silver, having written much of great value on the subject and on the currency problem. Throughout the Civil War, Mr. Colgate manifested his loyalty to the Union cause in many ways

Mr Colgate's first wife, Ellen Hoyt, of Utica, lived only two years after their marriage, and left one son, William Hoyt Colgate In 1851, Mr Colgate married his present wife, Susan F Colby, daughter of Governor Anthony Colby, of New Hampshire. They have two children, James Colby Colgate and Mary Colgate

Religion and education have been the chosen objects of Mr. Colgate's attention He is a member of the Baptist denomination, and has given munificent aid to various church works Rochester University, the Columbia University, Washington; Colby Academy, New London, N H , and Rochester Theological Seminary are among the recipients of his bounty, and for Madison, now Colgate, University he has always shown a strong attachment. Becoming a trustee in 1861, he has been president of the board since 1864, while the sum of his gifts to the institution has been some $1,250,000 He also founded and endowed Colgate Academy

Mr. Colgate throughout life has been noted for decision of character and the courage with which he upholds his convictions. He is a member of the Chamber of Commerce, the Stock Exchange, the New England Society, many benevolent, artistic and scientific bodies; and a patron of both the Metropolitan Museum of Art and the American Museum of Natural History He is interested in floriculture, and the greenhouses at his Yonkers residence are famous.

JAMES MANSELL CONSTABLE

A NATIVE of England, the gentleman to whom this article is devoted has been for more than half a century a citizen of New York and has attained high rank, not only in the commercial world with which he has been identified, but as one of the public-spirited business men of the metropolis in the present period. He was born in the County of Surrey in 1812. His first definite knowledge of the United States was gained when, as a very young man, he made a journey for pleasure to this country with one of the older members of his family. Attracted by the opportunities for successful business life, and by other advantages for a capable and enterprising youth which seemed to open before him in the United States, he formed a determination to establish himself here, and accordingly returned to New York in 1840 to make it his residence. He was not without some influential acquaintance in the New World. One of his friends was Aaron Arnold, who was then a member of the firm of Arnold, Hearn & Co., of this city, and with him he soon became interested in business. Two years after he had arrived in New York, he entered into a partnership with Aaron Arnold under the firm name of A. Arnold & Co. Subsequently the name of the establishment was changed to Arnold, Constable & Co., Mr. Constable being now at the head of the house, all his early associates in the business having passed away. The style of the firm has, however, remained unchanged for nearly forty-five years, while in the face of all the vicissitudes of that period, it has been uniformly successful and stable in its operations, holding its place in the foremost rank of business establishments of its character, and having a reputation that extends far beyond the limits of New York.

In 1844, Mr. Constable married Henrietta Arnold, the only daughter of Aaron Arnold. Mrs. Constable's father was a native of the Isle of Wight, having been born there in 1794. In 1825, looking to the New World for opportunities in business of a more advantageous nature than were then afforded by his native land, he came to this country with his wife and daughter. Settling first in Philadelphia, he remained there only a short time and removed to New York, where he established himself, in 1827, in the dry goods business under the name of Arnold & Hearn, the junior partner of the establishment being his nephew, George A Hearn, Sr. This was the beginning of the house now known as Arnold, Constable & Co. The death of Aaron Arnold occurred in 1876, after he had attained to the ripe age of eighty-two.

Richard Arnold, the only son of Aaron Arnold, was born in New York in 1825 and died here in 1886. He was identified throughout his life with the business house which his father had established, being a partner in the concern from 1853 until the time of his death. His first wife was Pauline Bicar, daughter of Noel J Bicar; his second wife being Georgiana E Bolmer, daughter of M. S. Bolmer. He left four children, only one of whom at present survives. Mrs. James M. Constable died in 1884. Her husband and children have since built as a memorial to her a handsome Protestant Episcopal Church at Mamaroneck, N. Y.

Mr. Constable is a member of the Reform Club, belongs to the American Geographical Society and is a patron of the Metropolitan Museum of Art, the American Museum of Natural History and the National Academy of Design. The children of Mr and Mrs Constable are a son and two daughters. The only son of the family, Frederick A. Constable, lives in East Eighty-third Street, near Fifth Avenue. He is a member of the New York Yacht, Larchmont Yacht, American Yacht and Riding clubs. The eldest daughter, Harriet M. Constable, married Hicks Arnold, who is a member of the firm of Arnold, Constable & Co. Hicks Arnold is a cousin of the late Richard Arnold and nephew of Aaron Arnold. He was born in England and, coming to this country, went into business with the house of which he is now a partner. He is a director of the Bank of the Metropolis and has other important business connections with corporations of a financial character. Amy H Constable, the youngest child of Mr. and Mrs James M. Constable, married Edwin H Weatherbee, an account of whose family appears in another part of this volume. The city residence of Mr Constable is at 240 Madison Avenue, and his country home is in Mamaroneck, N. Y.

SAMUEL VICTOR CONSTANT

EXHIBITING a deep interest in the patriotic societies that have come into existence during the last few years, Mr. Samuel Victor Constant bases his connection with these associations on many lines of descent from distinguished ancestors. He traces his descent to John Tuttle, who came to this country, in the ship Planter, in 1635. He was a native of St Albans, England, and settled at Ipswich, Mass. He represented his town in 1644 in the General Assembly. At the same date, he became a member of the Ancient and Honorable Artillery Company. After a time he returned to England, but his sons remained in America. Another of Mr. Constant's ancestors was Nicholas Noyes. He belonged to Choulderton, England, and came over on the ship Mary and John in 1634, with his brother, the Reverend James Noyes. Mr Constant's descent is traced from both of these brothers. Nicholas Noyes became Representative in 1660, 1679 and 1680. Another ancestor was Lieutenant James Smith, born at Newbury, Mass., 1645, who served in the expedition against Quebec under Sir William Phipps. Another ancestor was Lieutenant Tristram Coffin, Deputy Governor of Massachusetts Bay in 1695, 1700-2, Mr. Constant can also trace his descent from a large number of individuals distinguished in the early history of New England, including the Reverend Michael Wigglesworth, the celebrated divine, author of The Day of Doom, who was the grandfather of Lydia Tappan, great-great-grandmother of the subject of this sketch. Among them are also Sergeant Abraham Adams, of Newbury; Daniel Pierce, of Newbury, Captain and Representative 1632-3, a member of the Council of Safety in 1689, Colonel of Essex Regiment and Representative in 1692; and Major Charles Frost, 1632-1679, Representative in 1658-60-61, a member of the Provincial Council of New Hampshire in 1681, and prominent in the early Indian wars. Besides whom may be mentioned Richard Smith, who was captured by the British during the Revolutionary War, and confined on the Jersey prison ship, as well as Jedediah Tuttle, a soldier in the Continental Army.

Samuel S. Constant, the father of Mr. Constant, was a prominent manufacturer of this city. Mr. Samuel Victor Constant was born in New York City. He was educated at the Charlier Institute, at Professor Anthon's Grammar School and by private tutors, graduating from Columbia College in 1880, and from its law school in 1882. Admitted to the bar in the latter year, he has since been in active practice.

He has given much attention to literature and scientific investigation, and is a member of the American Oriental Society, and of the Royal Asiatic Society of Great Britain, the American Academy of Sciences, and the Mercantile Marine Service Association of Great Britain, incorporated under special act of Parliament to conserve the interests of the British mercantile marine, and is also solicitor of the association in the United States. He is a member of the American Historical Association, the New York Historical Society, the New York Genealogical and Biographical Society, and the Virginia Historical Society. He enjoys the distinction of having first proposed the organization of a society composed of the descendants of those who participated in the Colonial Wars, from the time of the Pequod War of 1639 down to the beginning of the Revolution As a result of this suggestion, he, with others, founded the Society of Colonial Wars, which has now a large membership.

In 1876, he joined the First Company, Seventh Regiment, and also belongs to the Seventh Regiment Veteran Association. He is one of the board of directors of the Young Men's Christian Association and a member of its International Committee. Mr. Constant is thoroughly American in his ideas and belongs to the Sons of the Revolution, is school inspector of the Thirteenth District, is a member of the Ψ Τ Club, St David's Society, the Ancient and Honorable Artillery Company, the New York State Society of the Founders and Patriots of America, and is also a member of the Founders and Defenders of America. He has also retained an active interest in Columbia College, and is a member of its building committee.

EDMUND COGSWELL CONVERSE

RECORDS of the Converse family extend back to Roger de Coigneries of France, and afterwards of Durham, England. In the third generation, the head of the family was Roger de Coniers In the sixth generation came Sir Humphrey Conyers, of Sockburn England, and thence the line is through eleven generations of the Conyers, of Sockburn, Hornby and Wakerly to Edward Convers, the first American emigrant, who was born in Wakerly, Northamptonshire, in 1590, and arrived in Salem, Mass , in 1630. Soon after he settled in Charlestown, where he was a selectman, 1635-40 He established the first ferry between Charlestown and Boston, paying to the city forty pounds a year for the franchise He was one of the seven first settlers of the town of Woburn in 1642, and was its first selectman, and a deputy to the General Court in 1660 He built the first house in Woburn, and died there in 1663 Lieutenant James Converse, son of Deacon Edward Convers, was born in 1620, and died in Woburn in 1715. He was a Sergeant in 1658, ensign in 1672, and Lieutenant in 1688, serving in King Philip's War From 1679 to 1689, he was a deputy to the General Court His first wife was Anna Long, daughter of Robert Long Major James Converse, 1645-1706, their son, commanded the troops at the defense of Storer's Garrison, 1691-92, and was promoted to be Major, and placed in charge of the military forces of Massachusetts He was deputy to the General Court, 1679-92, and Speaker of the House of Representatives in 1699 and in 1702-03 In 1668, he married Hannah Carter, 1650-1691

In the ensuing three generations, the ancestors of Mr. Edmund Cogswell Converse were John Converse, of Woburn, 1673-1708, and his wife, Abigail Sawyer, daughter of Joshua Sawyer, Joshua Converse, of Woburn and Litchfield, N. H., 1704-1744, and his wife, Rachael Blanchard, daughter of Joseph and Abiah (Hassel) Blanchard, and Joseph Converse, of Litchfield and Chesterfield, N H , 1739-1828, and his wife, Elizabeth Davis Joshua Converse was a selectman of Litchfield in 1741, and a representative to the General Court the same year His son, Joseph Converse, who lived in Bedford, Mass., at the beginning of the Revolution, was a member of the Lexington alarm company in 1775

The Reverend James Converse, son of Joseph Converse, and grandfather of Mr. Edmund Cogswell Converse, was born in Bedford, Mass , in 1772, and died in Wethersfield, Vt., in 1839 He was graduated from Harvard College in 1799, and ordained a minister of the Church of Christ in Wethersfield, Vt , in 1802 He was a member of the Vermont Legislature in 1819, and was elected State Chaplain His first wife, Mehitable Cogswell, was a daughter of William and Abigail Cogswell, of Marlborough, Mass. She was a descendant in the sixth generation of John Cogswell, of Wiltshire, England, who settled in Ipswich, Mass , in 1635 Their son, William Cogswell, married Susanna Hawkes, their grandson, Jonathan Cogswell, married Elizabeth Wainwright; their great-grandson, Francis Cogswell, married Elizabeth Rogers, daughter of the Reverend John Rogers, and was the grandfather of Mehitable (Cogswell) Converse. James Cogswell Converse, father of Mr Edmund Cogswell Converse, was born in 1807, and died in 1891 He received an academic education, and engaged in business in Vermont and afterwards in Boston. He was one of the founders of the Boston Board of Trade, of which he was president In 1869, he became president of the National Tube Works of McKeesport, Pa He married Sarah Ann Peabody.

Mr Edmund Cogswell Converse was born in Boston, November 7th, 1849. He was educated in the Boston Latin School, entered into active business, and has been connected for twenty-five years with the National Tube Works Company, of which he is president and general manager He has made New York his residence for a number of years. In 1879, he married Jessie Macdonough Green, who is related to the Macdonough and Van Nyce family, of Long Island They have three children, Antoinette Macdonough, Edmund Cogswell, and Katherine Peabody Converse. The winter residence of the family is 8 East Sixty-seventh Street. Mr Converse belongs to the Metropolitan, Union League, Lawyers', New York Athletic and other clubs, and to the Society of Colonial Wars, and the Sons of the American Revolution.

HENRY HARVEY COOK

OF Norman origin, the Cook family was settled in Leeds, England, before the middle of the twelfth century. A hundred years later one branch of it was well established in Ireland   Edward Cook, who was born in 1450, and was Mayor of Doncaster, Yorkshire, England, in 1504, was the ancestor of the English family as it exists to-day   In the sixth generation from Edward Cook, George Cook, the head of the family, was made a baronet in 1661, and in the next generation, Sir George Cook, who succeeded to the estate and title of his uncle as third baronet, married Catherine Copley, daughter of Sir Godfrey Copley, of a family which descends from William the Conqueror, and which through collateral lines is represented in the peerage of the mother country.

Captain Thomas Cook, of Earle's Colne, Essex County, who founded the family fortunes in America, was born in England in 1603, and came across the Atlantic in 1635, when he was thirty-two years of age.   Settling first in Boston, he afterwards removed to Taunton, Mass , in 1637, becoming one of the original proprietors of that place.   Subsequently he was a founder of Portsmouth, R. I , and lived there the rest of his life, being at one time deputy to the General Assembly of Rhode Island   John Cook, the second son of Captain Thomas Cook, was born in England in 1631.   In 1665, he married a sister of Matthew Borden, who was the first white person born in the Colony of Rhode Island. He had a family of four sons and thirteen daughters, and died in 1691.

The second son of John Cook was Joseph Cook, who was born in 1662, and was a deputy to the General Assembly of Rhode Island in 1704   Constant Cook, grandson of Joseph Cook, was born in 1724 and died in 1800.   He lived in Portsmouth and Newport, but before the War of the Revolution removed to Springfield, N. Y.   He was the head of the New York branch of the family   His wife was Isabel Duell, daughter of Joseph Duell, of Dartmouth, Mass.   The grandson of Constant Cook and the father of the subject of this sketch, was Judge Constant Cook, lawyer, banker and contractor of Warren, N. Y.   He was born in Warren in 1797.   In early life he was a farmer, and also owned and managed several passenger and mail routes in that section of the State   In 1843, he removed to Bath, N. Y., and took a contract for building part of the Erie Railroad. Subsequently he built the Buffalo, New York & Corning road, and as a contractor in other enterprises accumulated a fortune.   He established a private banking house in Bath, which afterwards became the First National Bank   He was a generous man, and gave abundantly to the support of religious and educational institutions.   In 1840, he was made a county Judge of the community in which he lived.

Mr. Henry Harvey Cook, the oldest surviving son of Judge Constant Cook, was one of a family of eight children.   He was born in Cohocton, Steuben County, N. Y., May 13th, 1822. Educated at first in local schools, he then attended an academy in Canandaigua, after which he was for two years in business houses in Auburn and Bath.   From 1844 to 1854 he was engaged in mercantile pursuits in Bath, and was highly successful.   For a few years he was connected with the Bank of Bath, serving first as cashier and then as president.   In 1875, he removed to New York City.   Becoming interested in railroad enterprises, he has been active in the management of some of the largest railroads of the country, having been a director of the Union Pacific, the New York, Lake Erie & Western and the Buffalo, New York & Erie companies   He is also a director of the American Surety Company, the State Trust Company, and the National Bank of North America, in this city

Mr Cook married Mary McCay, daughter of William W. McCay, of Bath, N. Y.   Their children are, Mrs. Clinton D McDougal, Mrs. M Rumsey Miller, Mrs C. F. Gansen and Mrs. C de Heredia   Mr Cook is a member of the Metropolitan and Union League clubs, is a patron of the Metropolitan Museum of Art, and belongs to the New York Historical and the New York Geographical societies.

EDWARD COOPER

NO New Yorker is more gratefully remembered by his fellow-citizens for his manifold good deeds, or held in higher esteem for his integrity, than Peter Cooper, the distinguished philanthropist, who was the father of the Honorable Edward Cooper His ancestors were citizens of New York from about the middle of the seventeenth century. On his father's side, his mother was the daughter of John Campbell, who was a successful business man and by his industry and business ability accumulated a considerable fortune before the Revolutionary period. He was an unflinching patriot in the stirring times that preceded the Revolution, and when the war finally broke out, he entered the Continental Army and served as Deputy-Quartermaster. His patriotism impelled him not only to give his services, but also to devote his means generously to the cause of the struggling Colonies, and he was a large contributor to the Continental treasury, sacrificing the greater part of his ample fortune to the needs of his country After the war, he was an alderman of New York The father and the grandfather of Peter Cooper were of English origin Both served in the Continental Army and the former held a commission as Lieutenant.

When peace had been declared between Great Britain and the United States, Lieutenant Cooper resumed his business, which was that of hatter, and resided in a house near Coenties Slip There his son, Peter Cooper, was born, February 12th, 1791. The school education of Peter Cooper was limited Most of his time he was employed in assisting his father in business. He learned the carriage making trade as an apprentice, but upon coming of age began the manufacture of machines for shearing cloth, and in a few years succeeded in laying the foundations for the great fortune that he subsequently acquired He was engaged in other business enterprises until 1828, when he established the Canton Iron Works in Baltimore, Md, where he built, from his own designs, the first locomotive engine constructed on this continent. After that, he built other iron factories, rolling mills and blast-furnaces in Pennsylvania, New York and New Jersey Mr Cooper established the famous Cooper Union and liberally endowed it both during his life time and by his will, and the institution has ever since been the special care of the Cooper family. He was an earnest student of political economy, and in 1876 was a candidate of the National Independent Party for the Presidency of the United States. He died April 4th, 1883.

Six children were born to Peter Cooper and his wife, Sarah Bedel, whom he married in 1813 Two only survived Sarah A. is the wife of Abram S Hewitt. The son, Mr Edward Cooper, was born in New York, October 26th, 1824 He was educated in the public schools and in Columbia College. After a short time spent in traveling in Europe, he returned to associate himself with his father in business He organized the firm of Cooper, Hewitt & Co, with his college classmate and friend, Abram S Hewitt, and in the course of time the new concern succeeded to the vast interests of the Peter Cooper iron business As an iron master and a practical and scientific metallurgical engineer, he stands at the head of his profession

Politically, Mr Cooper is a Democrat and has taken a prominent part in the councils of the party locally and nationally. About his first appearance in public affairs was as a member of the Committee of Seventy, through whose efforts the Tweed ring was overthrown, and there his labors were energetic and capable. He was a delegate to the Democratic National Convention in Charleston in 1860, and since then has been a delegate to nearly all the National Conventions of his party He was Mayor of New York, 1879–81, and has been mentioned for the Democratic nomination for Governor of the State. He has been identified with many corporations, including the United States Trust Company As one of the trustees of the Cooper Union, he has been active in fostering and developing the institution that his father founded Mr Cooper resides at 12 Washington Square, North, and is a member of many social and benevolent organizations His club membership includes the Union, Metropolitan, University and Knickerbocker clubs and the Century Association

AUSTIN CORBIN

THE Corbin family is of sturdy New England stock New Hampshire was the residence and birthplace of the ancestors of the subject of this article for many generations, and in that State the family has always been well known and of high standing. The present Mr. Corbin's grandfather on his father's side was one of the substantial landowners of the Granite State, and for several years sat in the Senate of New Hampshire.

The father of Mr. Austin Corbin brought the family name into high prominence in the business world during the last generation The senior Austin Corbin, financier and railroad manager, was a native of Newport, N. H , where he was born July 11th, 1827. His father's circumstances afforded him every opportunity for a liberal education, and he was sent to an academy and to Harvard College, graduating finally from the Harvard Law School. Having been admitted to the bar, he practiced law for two years or more in New Hampshire, his partner at that time being Ralph Metcalf, who afterwards became Governor of the State

In 1851, Mr. Corbin went West, and, taking up his residence in Davenport, Ia., soon met with an even greater degree of success in his profession than he had achieved in New Hampshire. Gradually he became interested in the banking business, and established a private bank in Davenport, an institution that weathered the financial storms of 1857 and was reorganized in 1863 as the First National Bank of Davenport, being the first banking establishment in the United States to begin business under the Federal Banking Law that had then just been passed.

In 1865, Mr Corbin removed to New York and devoted himself especially to banking and negotiating mortgage loans on farms in Iowa and other Western States, a business that was then beginning to attract considerable attention in financial circles. In 1873, he established the Corbin Banking Company, of which he was the head He undertook the reorganization of the Indiana, Bloomington & Western Railroad, and in 1880 became receiver of the Long Island Railroad, being made president of the corporation a year later.

His success in reorganizing the Long Island road and in developing the attractions of the summer resorts on Long Island in the interest of increased travel over the road are so well known that they need not be dwelt upon here. He was also prominently identified with the reorganization of the Philadelphia & Reading Railroad Company, of which he was first a receiver and afterwards president. He was also president of the New York & New England, and the Elmira, Cortlandt & Northern Railroad, of the Manhattan Beach Company, and the New York & Rockaway Beach Railway, and a director of the American Exchange National Bank, the Western Union Telegraph Company, the Nassau Fire Insurance Company, and the Mercantile Trust Company. He was a member of the Manhattan, Players, Lawyers', Seawanhaka-Corinthian Yacht, Meadowbrook Hunt and Southside Sportsmen's clubs, and the New England Society of New York, and of the Somerset Club in Boston.

The mother of Austin Corbin, Jr., whom his father married in 1853, was Hannah M. Wheeler, daughter of Simeon Wheeler, a prominent citizen of Newport, N. H. Isabella, a daughter of this union, married George S Edgell, and another daughter, Anna, was married in 1896 to Hallet Alsop Borrowe, son of the late Samuel Borrowe Mary, the eldest daughter, married Rene Cherennot Champollion, grandson of Jean Francois Champollion, one of the first and most distinguished of French Egyptologists Both M Champollion and his wife are dead, her death occurring in Paris, in 1892. Their only son, Andre, the sole male descendant of the illustrious Champollion family, is being educated in America Mr. Austin Corbin, Sr., died in 1896, as the result of an accident, being thrown from his carriage at his country estate in Newport, N H

Mr. Austin Corbin, Jr , who succeeds to his father's name and to the care of the family estate, was born in Brooklyn, N. Y., in 1873. He graduated at Harvard in the class of 1896, and is a member of the Somerset Club, of Boston His residence is at 763 Fifth Avenue.

JOHN CORNELL

THOMAS CORNELL, who came to Boston in 1636 from Essex, England, was born in 1595, of a family which is numbered among the nobility and gentry of England, the name being originally Cornewall. The founder of the American branch of the family and ancestor of the subject of this article probably accompanied the celebrated Ann Hutchinson when she and her followers left Massachusetts in 1640. In 1646, he received a grant of about 160 acres from the local authorities at Portsmouth, R. I., which is still in the possession of the family. Later in the same year, he was in the New Netherland and received from Director General Kieft a grant of 700 acres on the East River, in Westchester County, which is still known as Cornell's Neck. Driven from this place by the Indians, he returned to Portsmouth, R I., where he died in 1655, and was interred in the family burial ground upon the Cornell homestead, which has ever since been used for that purpose by the family. The Cornell's Neck tract passed to the Willett family through Sarah Cornell, daughter of Thomas, who married Thomas Willett.

Before leaving England, Thomas Cornell had married Rebecca Briggs and had five sons and four daughters. It is to Richard, the second son, that the Reverend Mr. Cornell traces his ancestry. Richard Cornell became the grantee of Rockaway, Long Island, and had a numerous family, his second son, William, 1670–1743, being the father of John Cornell, who married Abigail Whitehead. Their son, Whitehead Cornell, married Margaret Sebring and was father of John Cornell, of Brooklyn, 1753–1820, whose wife was Sarah Cortilyou, of New Utrecht. The Cortilyou property was acquired from the Najak Indians by Jacques Cortilyou, a learned Huguenot refugee, who was both a physician and sworn land surveyor to the Dutch Colony.

The family connection is a large one, and its representatives were found throughout the New England and Middle Colonies, whence branches have now reached all parts of the United States, the family name being in some instances changed or modified. Among its noteworthy members in early days were, John Cornell, a son of Richard, of Rockaway, who in 1741 was Colonel of the Queens County Militia. Ezekiel Cornell, a Rhode Island Revolutionary patriot, was Lieutenant-Colonel of Hitchcock's Regiment, became Deputy Adjutant-General of the Continental Army in 1776, and afterwards commanded a brigade of State troops In 1780–83 he was delegate to Congress In the last generation the name was rendered famous by the munificence of Ezra Cornell, who founded Cornell University at Ithaca, N Y

Isaac Russell Cornell, the father of the subject of this article, was the son of John and Sarah Cortilyou Cornell. He was born in Brooklyn in 1805 and married Elizabeth Mary Duyckinck, of New Brunswick, N. J., their son, Mr. John Cornell, being born in New York in 1839. He was educated at the Churchill School at Sing Sing, and was graduated at Princeton College in 1859 with the degree of B. A., receiving that of M. A. three years later. Adopting the clerical profession, he studied theology at the General Theological Seminary and was ordained to the ministry of the Protestant Episcopal Church in 1863. In 1878 Mr. Cornell married Margaret Kathrine Osterberg, of Stockholm, Sweden.

A large portion of Mr. Cornell's life has been spent in foreign travel and residence For nearly eighteen years he was Rector of the American Episcopal Church at Nice, France He has visited all the chief cities and countries of Europe, and also traveled through the Holy Land and the Levant. Since his return to America, a few years since, Mr. Cornell has not taken a parish and has resided in the main at Washington, D. C.

Mr. Cornell owns the homestead of his first American ancestor, at Portsmouth, R I , as well as the family burial ground, the whole comprising eighty acres of the original one hundred and sixty. The original Colonial house, parts of which dated back over two hundred years, was burned in 1889, but he has restored it upon the old foundation and substantially upon the old plan. The Cornell arms, borne by the family both in England and America and as given in Bolton's History of Westchester County, are: five castles in a cross, sable. Motto, *Deus Noster Salus*.

JOHN M CORNELL

FIRST of the Cornell name to appear in the New World was Thomas Cornell, a son of Richard Cornell, of London Arriving in the Massachusetts Bay Colony in 1636, he removed to Rhode Island after a year or two, and thence to New Netherland, settling in Flushing, Long Island, where, in 1643, he received a grant of land from Governor Kieft He also acquired real estate on the main land, afterwards called Cornell's Neck, now known as Willet's Neck or Point From Thomas Cornell have come many distinguished descendants Ezra Cornell, the founder of Cornell University, Alonzo B Cornell, former Governor of the State of New York, Thomas Cornell, of Rondout, one of the first steamboat men of the Hudson River and a Member of Congress, ex-President Theodore Woolsey of Yale College, and Colonel Marinus Willett, the eminent Revolutionary patriot, and other noted Americans, are among those who have pointed to him as their common ancestor

The eldest son of Thomas Cornell was Richard Cornell, one of the most influential citizens of Flushing during the latter years of the Dutch regime He was a deputy to the convention called by Governor Richard Nicolls in 1665, and under the English rule held the office of justice of the peace He acquired considerable land by purchase from the Indians and other owners, and much of this property has remained in the hands of the family down to the present generation Richard Cornell left five sons, and his grandson, Thomas Cornell, became one of the wealthiest and most influential residents of Long Island, serving continuously, save for one term, as a member of the Colonial Assembly, from 1739 until his death, in 1764 Three of the grandsons of Thomas Cornell remained loyal to the mother country in Revolutionary times, and two of them were Captains in the British Army, removing to Nova Scotia, with other royalists, at the close of the war The third brother of this family was Whitehead Cornell, grandfather of the celebrated iron merchants who, in the last generation, made the name famous the world over Whitehead Cornell held himself neutral during the Revolution, and afterwards was several times elected to the General Assembly of the State He married Abigail Hicks, a descendant of John Hicks, one of the first settlers in Flushing

Six of the grandchildren of Whitehead Cornell, children of his son Thomas, were boys, and born mechanics, and all of them were possessed of remarkable mechanical ability One of the youngest, John B Cornell, born in Far Rockaway in 1821, entered the iron business in 1836 with a firm of which his elder brother was the head, and which was the pioneer in its line in the United States. In 1847, he founded a new firm, and in 1848, when the elder brother died, the business that he had built up fell largely to the younger members of the family. The business prospered and soon became one of the largest and most important of its kind in this country Mr Cornell, who died in 1887, had completed fifty years of active business and accumulated a fortune, and was one of the most public-spirited and benevolent men of his generation He was a member of the Methodist Episcopal Church, a staunch abolitionist and a devoted temperance man Much of his time and much of his wealth was given to educational, religious and philanthropic enterprises He was a working member of the boards of trustees of many of the benevolent and other societies of the Methodist Church, president for fourteen years of the New York City Church Extension and Missionary Society, president of the board of trustees of the Drew Theological Seminary, and a member of the board of trustees of several of the leading charitable institutions of New York

Mr John M Cornell, who succeeded his father at the head of the concern that still retains the name of J B & J M Cornell, is the eldest of a family of seven He was born in New York, August 27th, 1846 After his education in Mount Washington Collegiate Institute, he entered his father's establishment to learn the business It was not long before he was taken into the concern as a partner of which he is now the sole owner He married, in 1873, Sarah Keen, lives in East Thirty-Seventh Street, and has a summer residence in Seabright, N J

CHARLES HENRY COSTER

SINCE the latter part of the last century, the name of Coster has been prominent in both the business and the social world of New York. Its first representatives were two brothers, Henry A. and John Gerard Coster, natives of the City of Harlem, in the Netherlands, who came hither about the end of the last century. John G. Coster, the younger brother, had been educated as a physician, and had served in the Dutch Navy, but after the independence of America had been secured, and New York became the seat of 'an active and increasing commerce, he joined his brother in founding a mercantile house which in time became, under their guidance, one of the most important in the city. Having connections with their native Holland, their business was at first mainly in the products of that country; but as their operations extended, they became the owners of numerous vessels and traded with the East and West Indies, and exported American commodities to Europe. At the same time that the brothers Coster were conspicuous for their success and enterprise, they were noted for their integrity and personal standing at a period when the merchants of New York were the most influential class in the community, and both were directors in many of the financial corporations of that date.

John Gerard Coster, the grandfather of Mr. Charles Henry Coster, among other positions of prominence, was a director of the Manhattan Company's Bank in 1813, and in 1826, on the death of Henry Remsen, became president of that institution, holding the office until 1830. He was also a director for many years of the Phœnix Insurance Company, and was a generous friend to various philanthropic institutions. He died in 1846, having resided from about 1833 in a house which he built on Broadway, north of Canal Street, and which was considered in its day one of the finest residences in New York. His brother, Henry A. Coster, lived in Chambers Street.

The wife of John Gerard Coster was Catharine Margaret Holsmann, and their sons were John H., Gerard H., Daniel J. and George Washington Coster, all of whom married representatives of prominent New York families. John H. Coster, the eldest son, married a daughter of Daniel Boardman. The wife of Gerard H. Coster was a daughter of Nathaniel Prime, the famous banker. Daniel Coster became a member of the firm of Hone & Coster and married a daughter of Oliver de Lancey, and George Washington Coster, the youngest son, married Elizabeth, a daughter of the eminent New York merchant, Daniel Oakey.

Mr. Charles Henry Coster, a prominent representative of his family in the present day and a son of George W. Coster, was born at Newport, R. I., July 24th, 1852. He was educated in private schools and began business life in 1867, in the counting room of the firm of Aymar & Co., importing merchants. In 1872, the business of that house was taken over by Fabbri & Chauncey, which was one of the largest firms engaged in the shipping and South American trade, and remained with them until the latter part of 1883. In the following year, Mr. Coster became a partner in the banking house of Drexel, Morgan & Co., and is now a member of its successor, J. P. Morgan & Co. He is also a partner of Drexel & Co., of Philadelphia, and Morgan, Harjes & Co., of Paris, France. He has taken a conspicuous part in the large transactions with which the name of these establishments is identified, more particularly in connection with railroad corporations. Mr. Coster is a director of many large organizations of this nature and takes an active part in their management.

In June, 1886, Mr. Coster married Emily Pell, daughter of Clarence and Anne (Claiborne) Pell. She is a descendant of Thomas Pell, proprietor of Pelham Manor, Westchester County, and of General Ferdinand L. Claiborne, of Mississippi, and of William Claiborne, 1587-1676, Secretary of Virginia. Mr. and Mrs. Coster have three daughters, Emily, Helen and Maud Coster, and one son, Charles Henry Coster, Jr. Their residence is 27 West Nineteenth Street, while they spend the greater part of the year at their Tuxedo home. He is a member of the Metropolitan, City, Racquet, Reform, St. Nicholas, New York Yacht and Tuxedo clubs, and a life member of the Academy of Sciences.

FREDERIC RENE COUDERT

NO soldier more faithful than Charles Coudert fought in the battalions of the first Napoleon. He was a young man, born in Bordeaux in 1795, and came of a good and ancient family. He received his baptism of fire before he was out of his teens, and when barely eighteen years of age, was wounded in the famous three days' battle before Leipsic. As an officer in tne Guard of Honor attached to the Imperial Guard, he was in the front of every fiercely-fought contest, took part in the battles of Montereau and Montmirial, and served actively in the desperate engagements that were fought prior to the entry of the allies into Paris. The overthrow of Napoleon did not weaken his enthusiasm for the Napoleonic dynasty, and after the Bourbon restoration he entered with energy and devotion into all the plans of the Bonapartists to make the Duke of Reichstadt the Emperor of France, as Napoleon II. As the world knows, these plans did not succeed, and, with others of his associates, the loyal young soldier was apprehended, tried and condemned to be executed as a traitor to the ruling House of France. Before sentence could be executed, he escaped to England. Two years later he returned to France in disguise, was detected and put under arrest, but again escaped and sailed for the United States in 1824.

His devotion to the fortunes of the Bonapartes brought Charles Coudert two medals, one of the Legion of Honor and the other that of St. Helena, that in fulfilment of the request of the dying Napoleon I, Louis Napoleon awarded to every surviving officer and soldier of the First Empire. Mr. Coudert, thus exiled from his native land, settled in New York and began life here by establishing a private school. He became one of the leading and influential members of the little colony of French exiles in New York. He was a man of much culture and refinement, and an unswerving Bonapartist to the day of his death, entertaining Louis and Joseph Bonaparte at his home during their visit to the United States.

Mr. Frederic Rene Coudert, son of Charles Coudert, was born in New York in 1832. His early education was secured in his father's school, and at the age of fourteen he entered Columbia College, being graduated in 1850 with high honors. He engaged in newspaper work and teaching for a short time, meantime entering upon the study of law, and in 1853 was admitted to the bar. Soon after, with his brothers Louis and Charles Coudert, Jr., he organized the firm of Coudert Brothers, which became one of the most successful legal firms in the city. He has built up a large practice and has been the legal representative of nearly all the great governments of Europe in this country. For his services, he has received the decoration of the Legion of Honor from the French Government and similar distinction from the Italian Government. He has achieved renown as an orator and has delivered addresses on many public occasions, such as the Columbia College Centennial in 1887, the reception of the Bartholdi Statue of Liberty and the dedication of the Lafayette and Bolivar statues.

A Democrat, with independent proclivities, Mr. Coudert was a supporter of Samuel J Tilden in 1876, and was a member of the Democratic Committee appointed to go to New Orleans and watch the electoral count in that year. A strong supporter of Cleveland, he made many speeches for the Democratic ticket in the campaign of 1892. He has steadfastly refused all offers of political preferment, and has even declined a nomination for the Supreme Court of the United States. He represented the United States before the international tribunal that considered the Bering Sea question, and also served as a member of the commission appointed by President Cleveland to investigate the Venezuelan boundary question. He is a member of many leading clubs and has been president of the Manhattan Club. He married Elizabeth McCredy and lives in West Fifty-eighth Street, having a summer home, Robinvale, in Metuchen, N. J. His son, Frederic R Coudert, Jr, was graduated from Columbia University in 1890 and married Alice T. Wilmerding, daughter of the late Ferdinand Wilmerding and granddaughter of the Honorable Benjamin F. Tracy. His daughter, Renee M Coudert, is unmarried. His brother, Charles Coudert, died in July, 1897, leaving a widow, Marie M. Coudert, six daughters and one son

JOHN ELLIOT COWDIN

ORIGINALLY from Scotland, the family to which Mr. John Elliot Cowdin belongs has for many generations been conspicuous in the annals of New England. Its members have been particularly identified with business interests and public affairs in Massachusetts. Captain Thomas Cowdin, the great-grandfather of Mr. John E. Cowdin, was a resident of Fitchburg, Mass., in the early part of the last century. He was prominent in the Massachusetts militia, and gave valiant service to the patriot cause in the American Revolution. He was frequently elected to office by his townspeople, and was several times a member of the General Court. His son, Angier Cowdin, was a large landowner in Vermont, and a man of influence. Several sons of Angier Cowdin attained to pre-eminence in public life. General Robert Cowdin was one of the bravest and most distinguished officers in the Union Army during the Civil War. The Honorable John Cowdin took a leading part in public affairs in Massachusetts in the last generation, being several times a member of the House of Representatives of that State.

Elliot Christopher Cowdin, another son of Angier Cowdin, was a noted importing merchant of Boston and New York. Born in Jamaica, Vt., in 1819, he died in New York in 1880. His early years were spent in Boston, where, before he had attained to his majority, he entered upon business life. In 1853, he came to New York and established the firm of Elliot C. Cowdin & Co., engaged in the importation of silks and silk ribbons. Eminently successful in his new undertaking, despite occasional reverses, he was able to retire from active business in 1877. During the latter years of his life, Mr. Cowdin spent much of his time in foreign lands. He crossed the Atlantic more than eighty times, and was in Paris at the time of the Franco-Prussian War.

Mr. Cowdin was notable no less for his intellectual than for his purely business activity, and also for his labors in many enterprises of a public character. He was one of the active members of the Mercantile Library Association, of Boston, in early life, being its president in 1843. He was also a member and an officer of the New York Chamber of Commerce, and instrumental in founding the New England Society of New York, of which he was the second president. He was a vice-president of the Union League Club, a valued member of the Century Association, and belonged to many other leading clubs and social organizations of the metropolis. In 1867, he was United States Commissioner to the Exposition in Paris. In 1876, he was elected a member of the State Assembly. He was often called upon to preside at public gatherings, and upon many of these occasions made addresses which were of a notable character. Several of his papers, speeches and addresses upon public questions of the day have been printed. The wife of Mr. Cowdin, whom he married in 1853, was Sarah Katharine Waldron, daughter of Samuel Wallis Waldron, of Boston. Mr. Cowdin died in New York in 1880, leaving six children, Katharine W., John Elliot, Martha W., Winthrop, Alice and Elliot C. Cowdin. Katharine W. Cowdin became the wife of Gaspar Griswold. Martha W. Cowdin married Robert Bacon and Alice Cowdin married Hamilton L. Hoppin.

Mr. John Elliot Cowdin, the eldest son of the family, was born in Boston in 1858. Educated in Harvard University, he was graduated from that institution in 1879, and has since been engaged in mercantile life. He married Gertrude Cheever, daughter of John H. Cheever, and lives in Gramercy Park, having a summer residence in Far Rockaway, Long Island. His children are Elliot C., Ethel and John Cheever Cowdin. He is a member of the Union, Harvard, University, Racquet, Rockaway Hunt and Players clubs. Winthrop Cowdin, the second son, was graduated from Harvard University in the class of 1885, and married Lena T. Potter. He lives in West Eleventh Street, and has a summer home, Newcastle House, in Mt. Kisco, N. Y. He belongs to the Union and University clubs. The youngest son, Elliot Channing Cowdin, was graduated from Harvard University in the class of 1896, and is a member of the Union and Racquet clubs. He lives with his widowed mother in West Twenty-first Street, and spends the summer upon the family estate, Maplehurst Farms, at Newcastle, Mt. Kisco, N. Y.

WILMOT TOWNSEND COX

FOR two and a half centuries the Cox family has been identified with Long Island. James Cock, as the name was spelled for several generations, came to Setauket, Long Island, before 1659 and within three years settled in Oyster Bay. He acquired land from the Indians at Killingworth, now Matinecock, where he died in 1698. Part of his estate is still held by bearers of his name. Members of this pioneer family have married with many other prominent families of Long Island and the State at large.

Among Mr Cox's distinguished ancestors is Henry Wisner, signer of the Declaration of Independence, member of the State Assembly for Orange County and of the Constitutional Convention in 1788, State Senator, 1777-82, and one of the first Board of Regents of the University of New York, in 1784. On both paternal and maternal lines, Mr. Cox descends from John Townsend, one of the early settlers of Long Island, and traces back through three distinct lines to Lieutenant Robert Feke, who in 1631 assisted in organizing the first military force of Massachusetts, fought in the Indian Wars and in 1634-39 represented Watertown in the General Court, and whose wife, Elizabeth, was a niece of Governor Winthrop. Other Colonial worthies whose blood he inherits are Robert Coles, who came to Massachusetts with John Winthrop and followed Roger Williams to Rhode Island, and Nathaniel Coles, Judge of Queens County in 1689. A direct ancestor, Daniel Cock, of Matinecock, was Captain of the militia of Oyster Bay, Long Island, in the Revolution.

Daniel Townsend Cox, 1800-1891, grandfather of Mr. Wilmot Townsend Cox, married Hannah Wilmot Coles, daughter of General Nathaniel Coles. Their son, Townsend Cox, formerly of Dosoris, now of Mill Neck, Oyster Bay, was born in Matinecock in 1828, and throughout his life has been identified with leading business interests in New York. He was a prominent member of the Stock Exchange from 1865 to 1885 and president of the Gold Exchange in 1869. From 1874 to 1882, he was a Commissioner of Charities and Correction of New York City, and from 1885 to 1892, president of the State Forest Commission. He was a founder and president of the Mendelssohn Glee Club and a governor of the Manhattan Club. He married Anne Helme Townsend, daughter of Walter Wilmot Townsend, and Anne Helme, a descendant of Christopher Helme, who settled in Warwick, R. I., in 1650. The children of this marriage are Wilmot Townsend, Charlotte Townsend, Townsend, Irving and Daniel Cox.

Mr Wilmot Townsend Cox, the eldest son, was born in New York in 1857, educated in St. Paul's School, Concord, N. H., and graduated from Harvard in 1879 and from the Columbia College Law School in 1881. He commenced the practice of his profession in the Corporation Counsel's Office of New York, and is now a member of the law firm of Scudder, Tappan, Seaman & Cox.

In December, 1896, Mr Cox married Maria Duane Bleecker Miller, daughter of the late John Bleecker Miller, and his wife, Cornelia Jones. Mrs. Cox is one of the five incorporators of the Colonial Dames of New York, and is descended on both paternal and maternal lines from families renowned in the Colonial, Revolutionary and later history of this State. Among her ancestors are Jan Jansen Bleecker, Mayor of Albany in 1700, Rutger Bleecker, Mayor of Albany 1726-29, Major Abraham Staats; Abraham Ver Planck; John Miller, one of the patentees of East Hampton in 1640, Major Thomas Jones, who came to America in 1692, having fought for King James in the battle of the Boyne and at Limerick; Samuel Jones, Recorder of New York during the Revolution, James Duane, member of the Continental Congress of 1774, first Judge of the United States District Court in New York and first Mayor of New York after the Revolution; Rip Van Dam, member of the council and Lieutenant-Governor of the Province in 1731-32, and the famous Robert Livingston, founder of a great New York family and first Lord of Livingston Manor. Among her more immediate ancestors is Judge Morris S. Miller, one of the founders of the City of Utica, N. Y., and Judge of Oneida County in 1810-24. Through a joint descent from Lieutenant Robert Feke and John Townsend, first of the names, Mr and Mrs Cox are related to each other. Mr. Cox's city residence is 58 West Ninth Street

FREDERIC CROMWELL

S EVERAL families in this country trace their descent to the same stock as that from which Oliver Cromwell, the Protector, came, and which is believed to have been originally of Welsh extraction, as the name itself would perhaps indicate. Colonel John Cromwell, Oliver's cousin, and like him a cadet of the great house of the Cromwells, of Hinchinbrook, was the ancestor of the American Cromwells John Cromwell, son of Colonel John Cromwell, came to New York about 1686 and took up his abode at Long Neck, Westchester County, on the shore of Long Island Sound, afterwards called Cromwell's Point From him has descended a branch of the family that has been particularly identified with New York City and Westchester County for upwards of two hundred years

David Cromwell, who traced his lineage direct to John Cromwell, of Cromwell's Neck, was a business man of New York City some sixty years ago When he retired from business, he established his home in the Village of Cornwall-on-Hudson, was one of its most respected residents, and died there in 1857 His wife, the mother of Mr Frederic Cromwell, was Rebecca Bowman, who was descended from John Bowman, an English emigrant to the Colonies in 1661 Henry Bowman, son of John Bowman, joined the Society of Friends in 1667, and his descendants for many generations thereafter held to the faith of their fathers and were steadfast in their adherence to the tenets of that religious body.

Mr. Frederic Cromwell was born at Cornwall-on-Hudson, February 16th, 1843 After receiving his early education in preparatory schools, he entered Harvard College and took his degree of A B there in 1863 He then applied himself to the study of law, in which he was engaged for a year, and followed that by a year of travel in Europe When he returned to America, he established a cloth importing firm, but remained in that business only three years

He then became a resident of Brooklyn, and turned his attention to the problems of gas manufacturing and supply, which at that date were still treated in an elementary way In 1870, he was one of the founders and president of the People s Gas Light Company, of Brooklyn He was also interested in the gas companies of Baltimore, Md. In 1871, Mr Cromwell removed to St Louis, Mo , where he resided four years, and constructed the works and organized the business of the Laclede Gas Light Company, of that city Then followed another year of travel in Europe, after which he returned to Brooklyn and associated himself with Colonel William H Husted, his brother-in-law, in the purchase of a controlling interest in one of the local street railway companies In 1880, he was elected a trustee of the Mutual Life Insurance Company of New York, and in 1884 became its treasurer, an office he now holds. He has been connected with other corporations as a director, including the New York Guarantee & Indemnity Company, the National Union Bank, the Brooklyn Trust Company, the Bank of New Amsterdam and the New York & East River Gas Company

Interested in public affairs, Mr Cromwell was one of the original members of the Civil Service Reform Association, of Brooklyn, and was elected its first president He was also a member of the first civil service commission of that city, and did intelligent and effective work in elevating the standard of the civil service in the municipality He has been president of the Brooklyn Art Association and vice-president of the Philharmonic Society. In 1868, Mr Cromwell married Esther Whitmore Husted, daughter of Seymour L Husted and Mary J Kendall The father of Mrs Cromwell was a well-known business man and street railroad president of Brooklyn Mr and Mrs. Cromwell have three daughters, Mary R , Gladys H , and Dorothea H. Cromwell, and one son, Seymour Le Grand Cromwell, who is a graduate from Harvard, in the class of 1892, and a member of the University, Racquet and Metropolitan clubs. The city residence of the family is in West Fifty-sixth Street, and their country home is Ellis Court, Bernardsville, N J Mr Cromwell belongs to the Century, Metropolitan, University and Harvard clubs and the Downtown Association, as well as to the Hamilton Club, of Brooklyn

OLIVER EATON CROMWELL

IN the genealogy of the Cromwell family are found some of the most illustrious names in English history Thomas Cromwell, the Cromwell of Shakespeare, Earl of Essex, friend of Cardinal Wolsey and Vicar General of Henry VIII , beheaded in 1540, was of this family He was the uncle of Sir Richard Cromwell, who was knighted by Henry VII., and whose son, Sir Henry Cromwell, of Hinchinbrook, surnamed the Golden Knight, was the grandfather of the Lord Protector, Oliver Cromwell Sir Henry's wife, Elizabeth Stewart, was a relation of the royal family of Stuart.

Sir Oliver Cromwell, of Hinchinbrook, eldest son of Sir Henry and uncle of the Great Protector, had several children, of whom Colonel John Cromwell was the second son. Although in general a supporter of his distinguished cousin, the Protector, Colonel Cromwell was opposed to the execution of King Charles Noble, the historian of the Cromwell family, says that by his wife, Abigail, he had children, one of whom, it is now fully understood, was John Cromwell, who emigrated from Holland to the New Netherland in the latter part of the seventeenth century and went to Long Neck, Westchester County, afterwards called Cromwell's Neck From the two sons of this John Cromwell, John and James, have descended the Cromwells of New York, who, during the Revolution, were active in the patriot cause.

The grandfather of Mr. Oliver E. Cromwell was John Cromwell, of New York, who married Elizabeth Thorn, of Glen Cove, Long Island. He was a merchant, but abandoned business when the War of 1812 began and entered the army as Lieutenant of Artillery, commanded a company at Plattsburg, and was brevetted and mentioned in general orders for bravery. After the war he retired and lived in Glen Cove until his death in 1824. Charles T. Cromwell, the father of Mr. Oliver E. Cromwell, was a prominent lawyer of New York more than fifty years ago. He was born in this city in 1808. While a student at Union College, from which he graduated in 1829, he was one of the founders of the Σ Φ Society. After studying law he traveled in Europe, and, returning home, attained a large practice. He had a summer residence on Manursing Island, in Long Island Sound, off Portchester, one of the handsomest country homes of his time. Mr Oliver E Cromwell traces his lineage to the English Cromwells through a maternal line as well as through his father. His mother was Henrietta Amelia Brooks, daughter of Benjamin Brooks, of Bridgeport, Conn., and descended from the celebrated Colonel William Jones, who was born in England in 1624 and came to New Haven in 1660. The mother of Colonel Jones was Catherine Henrietta, sister of the Protector, Oliver Cromwell, cousin of John Hampden and Edward Whalley, the regicide, and aunt by marriage to William Goffe, the regicide, and General Ireton. The father of Colonel William Jones was her second husband. Colonel Jones, who was Deputy Governor of the New Haven and Connecticut Colonies from 1683 to 1698, married Hannah Eaton, daughter of Theophilus Eaton, the first Governor of the New Haven Colony. The honorable Anson Jones, President of the Republic of Texas, 1844-6, was a descendant of Colonel Jones.

The representative of this historic and distinguished family in the present generation is Mr. Oliver Eaton Cromwell, who is a broker in New York and occupies the ancient family mansion on Manursing Island. He was born in New York, October 6th, 1848 Graduating from Columbia College with the degree of M E., he has since been engaged in active business He was a County Commissioner of Bernalillo County, Territory of New Mexico, in 1891. He is a member of the Union, Metropolitan and Δ Φ clubs and the St. Nicholas Society, and also belongs to the New York, American and Seawanhaka-Corinthian Yacht clubs.

The wife of Mr. Cromwell, whom he married in 1890, was Lucretia B. Roberts, daughter of James H Roberts, of Chicago Their children are Henrietta Louise, Oliver Eaton and James Roberts Cromwell. The Cromwell arms are: sable, a lion rampant, argent, with a crest showing a demi-lion rampant, argent, in his dexter gamb a gem ring, or

ERNEST HOWARD CROSBY

ORIGINALLY of Massachusetts, the early Crosbys were active in public affairs in that Colony Joseph Crosby, of Braintree, was a Judge, and his son, Ebenezer, 1753-88, was a graduate from Harvard College in 1777, a surgeon in Washington's Life Guard, and a professor in Columbia College. William Bedlow Crosby, son of Ebenezer Crosby, was born in New York City in 1786 His mother was Catherine Bedlow, daughter of William Bedlow, and a favorite niece of Colonel Henry Rutgers, one of the most public-spirited New Yorkers of his day Colonel Rutgers donated land ·for churches and other public institutions, and gave the site for the first free school of the city, erected in 1809 He was a member of the first Assembly of the State. William Bedlow Crosby was the heir of Colonel Rutgers. His property included nearly all of the Seventh Ward, and before the Astors became real estate investors, he was one of the largest owners of real estate in the United States. He spent his life in caring for his property and in benevolent work, and is still remembered for his philanthropy.

The Reverend Howard Crosby, the father of Mr Ernest H Crosby, was the son of William B. Crosby, and was born in New York City February 27th, 1826 Graduated from the University of the City of New York at eighteen years of age, he entered upon educational work, and at the age of twenty-five was professor of Greek in his alma mater. In 1852, he was elected president of the Young Men's Christian Association, and in 1859 became professor of Greek in Rutgers College, New Brunswick, N J. While holding the latter place, he studied theology and was ordained pastor of the first Presbyterian Church of New Brunswick. In 1863, he resigned his pastorate and professorship to become the pastor of the Fourth Avenue Presbyterian Church, of New York City, and for nearly thirty years was one of the most prominent figures in the religious, educational and reform movements of the metropolis. From 1870 to 1881, he was chancellor of the University of the City of New York He was a member of the American Committee for the Revision of the Bible, and later one of the commissioners appointed to revise the New Testament. In 1873, he was moderator of the General Assembly of the Presbyterian Church, and in 1877, a delegate to the Pan-Presbyterian Council at Edinburgh.

The activity of the Reverend Dr. Crosby in reform and benevolent enterprises kept him much before the public. In 1877, he was one of the founders of the Society for the Prevention of Crime, and was its first president. He was a strong advocate of the license system for restricting the liquor traffic in the interests of temperance, and in 1888 was a member of the State Committee to revise the liquor laws. His literary work was abundant and learned, and included commentaries on several books of the Bible, a volume of lectures, Lands of the Moslem, the Œdipus Tyrannus of Sophocles, with notes, a Life of Jesus, Social Hints, and numerous review articles, tracts and pamphlets. He received the degree of D. D from Harvard in 1859 and the degree of LL. D. from Columbia in 1871.

In addition to the illustrious ancestors already noted, Mr. Ernest Howard Crosby has descent from William Floyd, signer of the Declaration of Independence, who was his great-grandfather His uncle was William Henry Crosby, professor of Latin and Greek in Rutgers College, vice-president of the New York Bible Society, and long engaged in literary pursuits. His cousin is Colonel John Schuyler Crosby, soldier of the Civil War and on the frontier, United States Consul to Florence, Governor of Montana and First Assistant Postmaster-General.

Mr. Crosby devotes much time to philanthropic and reform work, following in the footsteps of his distinguished father. He is a lawyer, served in the New York Legislature, 1886-89, and was appointed by President Benjamin Harrison Judge of the International Court in Alexandria, Egypt, in 1889. That position he resigned in 1894, and he then returned to the United States Mr. Crosby married Fanny Kendall Schieffelin, daughter of the late Henry Maunsell Schieffelin, of New York. The city residence of Mr. and Mrs. Crosby is in Fifth Avenue, and their country place is Grassmere, in Rhinebeck-on-Hudson.

JOHN SCHUYLER CROSBY

DESCENDED on his mother's side from the Schuylers, a family which came from Holland in 1645, having extensive grants of land in what is now Albany, Rensselaer and Schenectady counties, where their influence with the Indians of the Six Nations, and the leading part they took in the French and Indian Wars, as well as in the Revolution, made them prominent in the early history of America, on his father's side Colonel Crosby's family were among the earliest of New England settlers. His great-grandfather, Ebenezer Crosby, was surgeon of Washington's Life Guards. His son, William Bedloe Crosby, the New York philanthropist, married Harriet Clarkson, granddaughter of William Floyd, a signer of the Declaration of Independence Clarkson Floyd Crosby, Colonel Crosby's father, their son, served in both branches of the Legislature, and married Angelica Schuyler, daughter of Colonel John Schuyler and Maria Miller.

Colonel John Schuyler Crosby was born September 19th, 1839, at Quedar Knoll, near Albany, N. Y., the country seat of five generations of Schuylers, and was educated at the University of the City of New York. At the outbreak of the Civil War, he received the commission of Second Lieutenant in the First Artillery. He was in the Army of the Potomac under McClellan, served on the staffs of Banks, Canby and Sheridan, and was brevetted four times for distinguished gallantry, being wounded once. His services in carrying despatches through the enemy's country to Admiral Farragut, secured special mention by President Lincoln. After the War he was Adjutant-General under Sheridan and Custer, and he resigned in 1871.

In 1863, he married Harriet Van Rensselaer at the old Van Rensselaer Manor House, near Albany, Mrs. Crosby being the youngest daughter of General Stephen Van Rensselear, the last patroon of Rensselaerwyck, and a great-granddaughter of General Philip Schuyler and Alexander Hamilton. Colonel and Mrs Crosby have two children, a son, Stephen Van Rensselaer Crosby, a Harvard graduate, an all-around athlete and well-known football player, who married Henrietta Grew, of Boston, and a daughter, Angelica Schuyler Crosby.

Since Colonel Crosby left the army, he has occupied several important positions in civil life, among them, Governor of Montana, Assistant Postmaster-General in the administration of President Arthur, Consul at Florence and School Commissioner of New York City For some years Colonel Crosby's residence has been divided between New York and Washington, and cruising all over the world. The Metropolitan, Union, Knickerbocker, Tuxedo, St Nicholas in New York, and the Metropolitan and Country clubs in Washington, are a few of his many clubs. His travels have been more than usually varied. In 1859, he crossed South America from Valparaiso to Montevideo Colonel Crosby has been presented at the courts of St. James, Constantinople and Rome. King Victor Emmanuel gave him the order of the Crown of Italy, with rank of Chevalier.

Among the patriotic American orders of which he is a member are the Loyal Legion, the Grand Army and Sons of the Revolution. He was an originator of polo playing in America and an early member of the famous Westchester Club. As Governor of Montana, he was interested in protecting the Yellowstone Park from trespassers and preserving the large game of the Northwest, and took part in hunting trips with Generals Sheridan and Custer, and President Arthur. Prominent in yachting, and one of the oldest members of the New York Yacht Club, he was an actor in one of the saddest events in the history of American sport The official letter of June 30th, 1877, in which Secretary John Sherman transmitted to Colonel Crosby a gold medal of the first class for life saving, recounts the disaster to Commodore William A. Garner's yacht Mohawk, which foundered off Staten Island on July 20th, 1876 Colonel Crosby was a guest aboard, and after rescuing Edith May he returned to the cabin of the sinking yacht and attempted to rescue Mrs Garner and Miss Hunter, who with Commodore Garner and several others were drowned. He escaped when the vessel was under water Secretary Sherman said : "In sending you this medal, the highest recognition of your conduct the Government can give, it is felt that no words can add distinction to the splendid gallantry which the token seeks to commemorate and honor."

STEPHEN VAN RENSSELAER CRUGER

INVESTIGATION has shown that the name of Cruger probably originated as Cruciger or Cross-bearer, and that the ancestors of the family were settled in Germany, Holland, Denmark and England. Sir Philip de Cruciger, from whom the English branches trace descent, accompanied Richard I on his crusade. In England the name was long connected with the City of Bristol, many of the family holding important offices there from the time of Henry VIII.

John Cruger came to America in 1700 and was an alderman of New York from 1712 to 1733, becoming Mayor in 1739, and holding that office until his death, in 1744. In 1703, he married Maria Cuyler, 1678-1724, daughter of Major Hendrick Cuyler, of Albany. Henry Cruger, 1707-1780, their second son, was a member of the Assembly from 1745 to 1759, and subsequently a member of the Council of the Province. He went to England in 1775 and died there His brother, John Cruger, second of that name, 1710-1791, was Mayor of New York from 1756 to 1765, and from his pen came the Declaration of Rights and Grievances of the Stamp Act Congress in 1765. He also organized and was first president of the New York Chamber of Commerce.

Henry Cruger married first, Hannah Slauter and second, Elizabeth Harris, of Jamaica, West Indies. One of his sons by his second wife was Henry Cruger, 1739-1827, second of the name, who was educated in Kings College, New York, and in 1757 engaged in business in Bristol, England, being Mayor of that city in 1781. In 1774, he was chosen to represent Bristol in the British Parliament, as a colleague of Edmund Burke, and was again elected in 1784 About 1790, he returned to his native city, and in 1792 was a member of the New York Senate. He married three times and has numerous descendants. Nicholas Cruger, 1743-1800, the fourth son of Henry and Elizabeth (Harris) Cruger, was the great-grandfather of the subject of this article. Born in New York, he was a merchant here and in St Croix, West Indies His estate in New York, known as Rose Hill, then in the suburbs, is now in the centre of the city. He was the patron of Alexander Hamilton, who served in his counting house and came to New York at his instance, and he was also a friend of Washington. In 1772, he married Anna de Nully, 1747-1784, daughter of Bertram Pierre de Nully, of St Croix, and his wife, Catharine Heyliger, daughter of General Pierre Heyliger, Governor of the Danish West Indies. Bertram Pierre Cruger, 1774-1854, the eldest son of this marriage, was born in St Croix and married Catharine Church, daughter of John B. Church, of New York, and his wife, Angelica Schuyler, daughter of General Philip Schuyler.

John Church Cruger, 1807-1879, the eldest surviving son of Bertram Pierre and Catharine (Church) Cruger, was the father of Colonel Stephen Van Rensselaer Cruger. His residence was Cruger's Island, in the Hudson River, and he married first, Frances A. Jones and second Euphemia White Van Rensselaer, daughter of General Stephen Van Rensselaer, the last patroon of Rensselaer-wyck. The only child of John Church Cruger's first marriage was Eugene Cruger, 1832-1867, who married Jane Marie Jauncey, and had three sons, William Jauncey, Eugene G. and James Pendleton Cruger.

Colonel Stephen Van Rensselaer Cruger is the eldest child and only son of John Church and Euphemia White (Van Rensselaer) Cruger. He was born in New York, May 9th, 1844, and was educated here and in Europe. At the beginning of the Civil War, he entered the army as First Lieutenant of the One Hundred and Fiftieth New York Volunteers. He took part in the Gettysburg and Atlanta campaigns, was severely wounded at the battle of Resaca, and retired from the army with the brevets of Major and Lieutenant-Colonel. After the war, he was for several years Colonel of the Twelfth Regiment, N. G. S. N. Y. Colonel Cruger has been engaged in the real estate business and is connected as a director or officer with many large corporations. He is the senior warden of the Trinity Church Corporation and a trustee of the New York Public Library. He married Julie Grinnell Storrow. His residence is in East Thirty-fifth Street, and his country place in Bayville, Long Island. He is a member of the Metropolitan, Tuxedo, Knickerbocker, Union League, Union and other clubs.

MRS. GEORGE WILLIAM CURTIS

HENRY CURTIS was the Puritan ancestor of the family of which the late George William Curtis was the best known modern representative. The original emigrant of the name arrived in Massachusetts in 1635 and settled in Watertown, removing later to Sudbury He married Mary Guy, daughter of Nicholas Guy, who came from Upton Gray, near Southampton, England Their son, Ephraim Curtis, who was born in Sudbury, in 1642, was one of the first settlers of Worcester, Mass, and for gallantry in an Indian fight in 1675 was made Lieutenant of the militia of that town John Curtis, one of his descendants, born in Worcester in 1707, was a Captain in the French and Indian War, and George Curtis, the father of the late George William Curtis, was a great-grandson of Captain John Curtis George Curtis was born in Worcester, Mass, in 1796, and became a prominent business man in Providence, R. I. In 1839, he removed to New York, and was president of the Continental Bank. He married Mary Elizabeth Burrill, daughter of James Burrill, Chief Justice of Rhode Island and a United States Senator for that State

George William Curtis, the second son of this marriage, was born in Providence, R. I, February 24th, 1824 He was educated at schools in Massachusetts, removed with his family to New York, and spent a year in mercantile life In 1842, he joined the Brook Farm Association in West Roxbury, Mass In 1846, he went to Europe, studied in the University of Berlin and traveled in the East In 1850, he returned home and published his first book, Nile Notes of a Howadji He joined the staff of The New York Tribune and published other works. From 1853 to 1857, he was the editor of Putnam's Magazine, and after the latter date was connected with Harper's Monthly Magazine and originated the famous Editor's Easy Chair in that periodical, which he contributed to it from 1858 until his death; from 1861 onward he was political editor of Harper's Weekly. During some years, Mr. Curtis also appeared in public as a lecturer He took an active and brilliant part in politics and was a delegate to many Republican National Conventions from 1860 to 1884. He frequently refused public offices, including the English and German Missions offered him by President Hayes, but accepted that of a Regent of the University of New York in 1864. In 1871, he was appointed, by President Grant, a member of the Civil Service Commission, and became chairman of that body, with which civil service reform originated, a cause to which he gave his unfaltering support. He died in August, 1892, having exercised a greater influence upon American public opinion than any man of letters of this period.

Mrs. George William Curtis, who was born Anna Shaw, married her distinguished husband in 1857 She is the daughter of Francis George Shaw and his wife, Sarah Blake Sturgis Her grandparents were Robert Gould Shaw, who married Susan Parkman, and, on the maternal side, Nathan Russell Sturgis, whose wife was Elizabeth Parkman In the two preceding generations, her paternal ancestors were Francis Shaw, a merchant of Boston, who, in 1770, with Robert Gould, founded the town of Gouldsboro, Me, and his son, Francis Shaw. Robert Gould Shaw, 1776-1853, was born in Gouldsboro and was a merchant in Boston after 1789. His eldest son, Francis George Shaw, 1809-1882, was a student in Harvard in 1825, but entered business life before he graduated, and retired in 1841. After 1855, he resided on Staten Island, was distinguished by his philanthropy and published translations of a number of French works. The only son of Francis G. Shaw was Colonel Robert Gould Shaw, who was killed in the Civil War while leading the Fifty-Second Massachusetts Regiment at Fort Wagner, S C He married Anna Haggerty, daughter of Ogden Haggerty, of New York. The other daughters of Francis G. Shaw are Susannah, who married Robert B. Minturn, Jr, Josephine (Shaw) Lowell, widow of General Charles Russell Lowell, and Ellen, widow of General Francis C Barlow

The children of Mr and Mrs Curtis are Elizabeth Burrill Curtis and Frank George Curtis, M D, a practicing physician in Newton, Mass., who married Ruth W. Davison. Mrs. Curtis resides in Bard Avenue, New Brighton, Staten Island, and has a country place in Ashfield, Mass.

E. HOLBROOK CUSHMAN

ONE of the energetic promoters of the exodus of the Pilgrims from Holland to America in the seventeenth century was Robert Cushman, who was born in Kent, England, about 1580 With John Carver, he was active in bringing about the emigration of the Pilgrims to Holland, whom he afterwards joined at Leyden, and was one of the first to engage in negotiations with the English authorities for the transfer of his coreligionists to the New World In 1617, he went to London with Carver to arrange with the Virginia Company for such a settlement in that part of the New World. The plans came to naught, however, because the King would not grant that liberty of conscience demanded by the proposed Colonists In 1619, Robert Cushman and Elder Brewster renewed the negotiations, this time with success, and Cushman and Carver arranged the details for the voyage

Robert Cushman was the business man of the enterprise. He chartered the Mayflower, was assistant governor of the company, and when the Mayflower sailed remained behind in England to take charge of the financial interests of the Pilgrims In 1621, he visited Plymouth, but returned again to England, where he died in 1625 Thomas Cushman, the only son of Robert Cushman, was born in England in 1608, and died in Plymouth, Mass , in 1692, in the eighty-fourth year of his age. He married Mary, daughter of Isaac Allerton, was a close friend of Governor William Bradford, and ruling elder of the church on the death of Elder Brewster in 1649 His wife died in 1699 at the age of ninety-nine years, one of the last surviving members of the Mayflower company. A monument to the memory of Robert Cushman, his son Thomas and other early members of this pioneer family was erected several years ago, on Burial Hill, in Plymouth, by their descendants

Thomas Cushman and his wife, Mary, were the American ancestors of the Cushmans in this country who trace their family line to the pre-Revolutionary period One of the descendants was a pioneer settler of Otsego County, N Y His fifth son, Don Alonzo Cushman, was born in Covington, Ky , October 1st, 1792, and died in New York City, May 1st, 1875 Brought up on his father's place, and educated in the local school, in 1805 he entered business in Cooperstown, N Y After several years he came to New York, where in 1810 he secured a position in a store Five years after he became senior partner of the firm of Cushman & Falconer, which afterward became D. A Cushman & Co , and so remained until Mr. Cushman's retirement, in 1855.

Early in life, Don A Cushman became interested in real estate investments in New York City, and was a pioneer in the development of Chelsea Village as an urban residential district He acquired considerable property there, built many houses, established his own dwelling-place on Ninth Avenue opposite the Episcopal Theological Seminary, and was more instrumental than any other single individual in making that section of the city one of the fashionable residential localities of half a century ago In 1815, Mr Cushman married Matilda C. S Ritter, daughter of Peter Ritter, of New York. He had a family of thirteen children. Of his daughters, Mary Matilda Falconer became the wife of Philip F. Pistor, Catharine Ritter married N B Smith, of New Orleans; Caroline E married James Talman Waters, and Angelica B. married George Wilcoxson, of Nyack. Three daughters died while young.

Mr. E Holbrook Cushman, son of Don Alonzo Cushman, was born in New York in 1832. He has retired from business and is principally engaged in caring for the large real estate holdings of the family. He lives in West Twenty-second Street and is a member of the New York Athletic and the Mendelssohn Glee clubs Archibald Falconer Cushman, his brother, is a Columbia College graduate, a practicing lawyer, and a member of the Columbia Alumni Association and the Church Club Another brother, William F Cushman, is also a graduate of Columbia College, and engaged in the practice of medicine James Stewart Cushman, who was the fifth of the six sons of the family, died in 1894 He was a well-known stock broker and one of the original members of the Gold Exchange.

WILLIAM BAYARD CUTTING

SEVERAL generations of the Cutting family have been eminent citizens of New York. Their ancestor, the Reverend Leonard Cutting, who was of English birth, took orders in the Church of England and, coming to America, had parishes at New Brunswick, N J, Hempstead and Oyster Bay, Long Island, and in 1765 was a tutor and professor in Kings, afterwards Columbia College. In 1766, he established a school at Hempstead, which became a noted institution. His wife was a daughter of John Pintard, an alderman of New York in 1738, and a representative of a family of Huguenot descent which had settled at New Rochelle.

William Cutting, their only son, graduated from Columbia College in 1793 and became an eminently successful lawyer, being associated in practice with F. R. Tillou. He was Sheriff of New York County in 1807-08. He was also closely identified with his brother-in-law, Robert Fulton, in successful experiments in steam navigation, and secured the franchise for a term of years of the ferry between New York and Brooklyn at the foot of the present Fulton Street. He died in 1820. Gertrude Livingston, his wife, whose sister married Robert Fulton, was the daughter of Walter Livingston and Cornelia Schuyler, daughter of Peter Schuyler, and a niece of Chancellor Livingston. Walter Livingston was the son of Robert Livingston, of Livingston Manor, the head of that notable family, and was a member of the Assembly and its Speaker, a Regent of the University, County Judge and a trustee of Columbia College. His father was the eldest son of Philip Livingston, who, in turn, was the eldest son of the first Robert Livingston.

The descendants of William and Gertrude (Livingston) Cutting have been prominent professionally and socially in New York and have intermarried with many other distinguished families. Fulton Cutting, their fifth son, was the father of Mr. William Bayard Cutting. Fulton Cutting's wife was Justine Bayard, daughter of Robert and Elizabeth (McEvers) Bayard. Her paternal grandfather, William Bayard, who married Eliza Cornell, was of a race which had occupied a conspicuous position in New York since the days of the Dutch settlement, while her maternal grandfather, James McEvers, whose wife was Ruth Hunter, bore the name of a family also of great social importance

Mr William Bayard Cutting, born in New York January 12th, 1850, is a conspicuous representative of his family in this generation He is a graduate of Columbia College and also took the degree of LL. B. in the law school of that institution While engaged in the practice of the legal profession, he has devoted considerable time to the cause of reform in the city's administration, taking a leading part in movements to that end. He has also been a Civil Service Commissioner of New York City. He resides in Fifth Avenue, with a country place, Westbrook, Oakdale, Long Island He is a member of the Metropolitan, Union, University, Century, Church, Δ Φ and Riding clubs, and the Downtown Association. He married Olivia Murray, daughter of Bronson Murray and his wife, Anne E. Peyton, her grandparents being James B. Murray and Maria Bronson His children are William Bayard, Jr., Justine Bayard, Bronson Murray and Olivia Cutting.

Among other sons of William Cutting, the Honorable Francis Brockholst Cutting attained particular prominence in the last generation, being a lawyer of high reputation and a Member of Congress 1853-55. He died in 1870, his sons being Heyward Cutting, who died in 1876, General William Cutting, who died in 1897, and Brockholst Cutting, who died before his father. The sons of Brockholst Cutting were William Cutting, Jr., who resides in Madison Avenue, and Francis Brockholst Cutting, second of the name, who died in 1896. Another brother of Fulton Cutting, was Robert Livingston Cutting, an eminent banker and socially distinguished, who married Juliana De Wolfe, daughter of James De Wolfe, of Bristol, R I. His sons were Robert Livingston Cutting, second of the name, who married Judith E. Moale, and left two sons, James De Wolfe Cutting and Robert Livingston Cutting, the third of that name, and Walter Cutting, who married Madeline C. Pomeroy and has three children, Walter Livingston, Juliana and Madeline Cutting

THOMAS DE WITT CUYLER

NO American family has a more honorable record than that derived from Hendrick Cuyler, who was born in Amsterdam, Holland, in 1637, came to Beverwyck, near Albany, in 1664, with his wife, Annetje Schepmoes, and was Major of cavalry in the French War His eldest son, Johannes Cuyler, married Elsje, daughter of Dirk Wessels Ten Broeck, in 1684 The second son, Abraham Cuyler, married Caatje Bleecker, of New York, and had numerous descendants Maria, the eldest daughter of Hendrick Cuyler, married John Cruger, Mayor of New York. Rachel Cuyler, the next daughter, married Myndert Schuyler, and from them many of the Schuylers and de Peysters are descended Johannes Cuyler was the ancestor of the branch of the family now under consideration He was a merchant and Mayor of Albany He had twelve children, who were the ancestors of families living in New York, Pennsylvania, Maryland, Virginia and Georgia. Cornelius Cuyler, his eldest son, married Cathalyra Schuyler, and their son, born in 1740, was a loyalist in the Revolution, removed to England and was made a baronet.

One of the prominent representatives of the family in the last generation was the Reverend Dr Cornelius C. Cuyler, who was born in Albany in 1783 and died in 1850 Graduated from Union College in 1806, he studied theology, and in 1809 became pastor of the Reformed Dutch Church in Poughkeepsie, and occupied that pulpit for more than twenty-five years. He then became pastor of the Second Presbyterian Church of Philadelphia, and remained in that charge until his death. He received the degree of D. D. from Union College in 1838

Theodore Cuyler, the only son of the Reverend Cornelius C Cuyler, was for many years a distinguished member of the bar of Philadelphia. He married the eldest daughter of the Reverend Thomas De Witt, for forty years pastor of the Collegiate Dutch Church of New York Thomas De Witt Cuyler, the eldest son of Theodore Cuyler, is a graduate from Yale College and a member of the Philadelphia bar. He is, however, well known in New York and has many interests here, both business and social. He is a director of the Equitable Life Assurance Society and of several railroad and other corporations, and is a member of the Lawyers', University and other clubs, the Holland Society and the Society of the Cincinnati Mr Cuyler married Frances Lewis Their country place is Edgewood, Haverford, Pa Cornelius Cuyler Cuyler, second son of Theodore Cuyler, was graduated from Princeton University in 1879 He entered the banking profession, and is now head of the firm of Cuyler, Morgan & Co, of this city He is a member of the Union, Princeton, City, University, Manhattan, Calumet and University Athletic clubs, and also belongs to the Holland Society and the Downtown Association

The Georgia and Virginia branch of the family descends from Henry and Katherine (Cruger) Cuyler, of New York, whose son, Captain Teleman Cruger Cuyler, removed to Savannah, Ga., in 1768 He married Jeanne de la Touche and died in 1772 One of his daughters married Captain George Bunner, the ancestor of Henry Cuyler Bunner, the author The eldest son, Captain Henry Cuyler, was killed at the siege of Savannah The third son, Jeremiah La Touche Cuyler, was the first Federal Judge in Georgia His eldest son, Richard Randolph Cuyler, was president of the Central Railroad of Georgia. Another son, Dr John M. Cuyler, 1810-1884, was Surgeon and Brevet Brigadier-General, United States Army, and married Mary Wayne Their son, James M Cuyler, married Alice Holden; the only child of this marriage, Caroline Campbell Cuyler, married Sir Philip Egerton, Baronet, of England. The youngest daughter of Judge Jeremiah La T Cuyler, Estelle Cuyler, married Captain Henry Hunter Smith, their son being Teleman Cuyler Smith, a lawyer of Atlanta, Ga

The Reverend Theodore Ledyard Cuyler, son of B. Ledyard Cuyler, has added to the distinction of the family Born in Aurora, N Y, in 1822, he was graduated from the Princeton Theological Seminary in 1846, and was ordained to the Presbyterian ministry in 1848 His early pastorates were in Trenton, N J, and New York, and since 1860 he has been minister of the Lafayette Avenue Presbyterian Church in Brooklyn.

ERIC B. DAHLGREN

JOHAN ADOLF DAHLGREN, 1744-1797, the great-grandfather of the present generation of the American bearers of his name, was an eminent Swedish scientist and physician A graduate of the University of Upsala, his scientific writings were honored at that seat of learning, and he also held professional positions in the service of his native country His son, Bernhard Ullrik Dahlgren, born in 1784, was also a graduate of Upsala Espousing liberal opinions, he became involved in a republican movement in 1804, and was obliged to flee from Sweden After a time, the Swedish government took him once more into favor, and he became its consul at Oporto, Portugal, and afterwards at Philadelphia, where he was a merchant, and where he died in 1824 He married an American lady, Martha Rowan, daughter of James Rowan, who during the Revolution served with General Lacy's Brigade of the Pennsylvania Line

Their famous son, Admiral John Adolf Dahlgren, U S N , was born in Philadelphia in 1809 Entering the navy as a midshipman in 1826, his subsequent life was part of the country's history He created the ordnance department of the navy, and by his scientific labors fairly revolutionized the prevalent ideas of ordnance, while his active service in the defense of Washington, at the beginning of the Civil War, in the South Atlantic blockade squadron, and in the naval operations against Charleston, S C , made his part in the conflict successful and conspicuous He was one of the five Admirals created by special Act of Congress with the thanks of the nation He died in Washington, while commandant of the Navy Yard there Admiral Dahlgren wrote a number of scientific works relating to gunnery and ordnance. He married Madeline Vinton, only daughter of the Honorable Samuel Finley Vinton, of Ohio, a distinguished lawyer and statesman, who was a Member of Congress for twenty-two years, and was author of the Act of 1849, which established the Department of the Interior. Vinton County and the town of Vinton, O , were both named after him His wife was Romaine Madeline Bureau, whose father, the son of a Revolutionary soldier, emigrated to Ohio in 1792, and was one of its early State Senators Mrs Madeline (Vinton) Dahlgren survives her husband, and is well known in the literary world. She has written a Memoir of Admiral Dahlgren and other works

Several of Admiral Dahlgren's sons were conspicuous in the public service The eldest son, Colonel Ulric Dahlgren, 1842-64, had a heroic career in the army during the Civil War, and was killed while engaged in a cavalry raid designed to liberate Federal prisoners confined in Richmond In 1872, a memoir of his life was published by his father Another son, Captain Charles Dahlgren, served with distinction in the navy under Admiral Porter and under his father Lieutenant Paul Dahlgren served in the army, and afterwards was United States Consul-General at Rome, where he died in 1874 He married Annie Rutherford Morgan, who survives him, their daughter being Romola Dahlgren.

Eric B Dahlgren is the fourth and eldest surviving son of Admiral John Adolf and Madeline (Vinton) Dahlgren He was born in Washington, D C , September 15th, 1866, and was graduated from Harvard College with the degree of A B in 1889 He married Lucy Drexel, daughter of the late Joseph W Drexel, of this city, a member of the banking firm of Drexel, Morgan & Co Her mother, Lucy (Wharton) Drexel, is a lineal descendant of the Revolutionary patriot and first Governor of Pennsylvania, Thomas Wharton

John Vinton Dahlgren, the youngest son of Admiral Dahlgren was born in Valparaiso, Chili, April 22d, 1868 He was graduated from the University of Georgetown, D C , in 1889, and from the law school of the same institution in 1891 In 1892, he was admitted to the bar, and, removing to New York, entered the law office of Lord, Day & Lord In 1895-96, he was attorney to the Building Department of this city, and compiled the Dahlgren Building Law Manual He married Elizabeth Drexel, sister of the wife of his brother, Eric B Dahlgren His residence is in West Fifty-sixth Street, and he is a member of the Catholic, Republican and New York Athletic clubs, and of many literary and historical associations.

CHARLES P. DALY

AS far back as Irish history extends, the O'Dalys, of County Galway, are mentioned, and have given to their country scholars, soldiers, legislators and others prominent in the public eye Ex-Chief Justice Daly, of our own Court of Common Pleas, descends from this ancient race, his father having come from the North of Ireland in the earlier part of this century and settled in New York.

Judge Daly was born in this city October 31st, 1816. He received a sound education in a private school, with the object of fitting him for one of the learned professions. Among his schoolmates were the late Cardinal-Archbishop of New York McCloskey and the eminent advocate, James T Brady. The death of his father, while he was still a lad, clouded his prospects; but filled with a determination to make his own way, he went to Savannah, Ga., and found occupation as a clerk Dissatisfied with his occupation, he went to sea as a sailor before the mast In this rude employment, he visited many distant parts of the world, but from his seafaring life he gained the love of geographical research, which was to play a part in his subsequent life second only to his professional career Forsaking the sea after an experience of three years, he returned to New York and apprenticed himself in a mechanical trade

His intellectual qualities now, however, asserted themselves. He devoted his spare hours to study, and joined a debating society, in which he soon distinguished himself by his ability and eloquence. One of his fellow members was William Soule, a lawyer, who, struck with the young mechanic's ability, advised him to study law, and offered him the means for a course at Union College. He, however, not only declined this, but on the death of his master, which released him from all obligation, voluntarily remained and worked for his employer's widow till his indentures had expired. Hardships were disregarded in his intense application to his studies, and such was his progress that in 1839 Chief Justice Nelson relaxed all rules in his behalf on the score of his fitness and admitted him to the bar. He then formed a professional partnership with Mr. McElrath, who was afterwards associated with Horace Greeley in founding The Tribune. He subsequently formed other partnerships, and soon came into notice at the bar for the soundness of his legal attainments. In 1843, he served in the Legislature of the State and refused a nomination, equivalent to an election, to Congress, preferring his profession to politics. In 1844, however, promotion came in the form of an appointment to the bench of the Court of Common Pleas of New York City by Governor Bouck That position he held for forty-two years, till 1885, when he retired under the age provision of the State Constitution. When Judge Daly assumed his office it was appointive. When, however, the Constitution of 1846 made it elective, he was promptly elected to succeed himself, and was four times reelected, being chosen in 1858 as Chief Justice of the Court to succeed Judge Ingraham. In 1871, when the end of one of his terms was expiring, the so-called Tweed Ring, having no favor for a magistrate of Judge Daly's integrity, were determined to defeat his renomination. The overthrow of the ring prior to the election, however, checked this plan, and Judge Daly received evidence of the approval of his fellow citizens in the form of a nomination from all political parties, so that the votes at the election were cast unanimously for him.

During his judicial career, Judge Daly sat in many important cases. One of the most noted incidents was when he presided at the trial of the Astor Place rioters, in 1849 On this occasion, he gave ample evidence of his firmness and impartiality as a judge, defining the law of riots so that, while the result was the conviction of the guilty persons, he fixed the legal principles involved for all time in New York On leaving the bench, in 1885, Chief Justice Daly received the exceptional honor, on December 30th of that year, of a general meeting of the bar, presided over by ex-President Arthur and attended by the leaders of the legal profession, at which resolutions expressing profound respect and admiration for the retiring judge were feelingly adopted. On the evening of the same day, Judge Daly was offered a further tribute in the form of a complimentary dinner at Delmonico's, given by all the judges of the courts of New York City and county. Since that time, he has retained full interest in the profession to which he devoted his early life, and which in his judicial capacity he did so much to dignify

Judge Daly's services to the public were not, however, confined to his duties on the bench A Democrat always, he nevertheless gave his unswerving support to the Union in the Civil War, and was frequently consulted during the struggle by President Lincoln, Secretary William H. Seward, Chief Justice Chase, and the other leaders of the national cause Upon the expression of Judge Daly's opinion, that, although the seizure of Mason and Slidell would be justified by the English interpretation of the law, it was contrary to the law of nations and the decisions of our own Supreme Court, Secretary Seward unwillingly consented to surrender them, though previously strongly opposed to doing so; by which a war with England was averted In 1867, Judge Daly was a member of the State Constitutional Convention

Outside of his profession, Judge Daly has won fame as a man of letters and scientist. In 1851, he visited Europe and made the intimate acquaintance, among other famous men, of Lord Brougham, Freiherr Von Bunsen and Baron Von Humboldt In his published correspondence, Humboldt writes to Bunsen: "Few men have left upon me such an impression of high intelligence on subjects of universal interest, and in the judgment of apparently opposite directions of character among the nations that inhabit the ever-narrowing Atlantic basin Add to this, what is very uncommon in an American, and still more uncommon in the practical life of a greatly occupied magistrate, that this man of high character and intellect is not wanting in a lively interest for the fine arts, and even for poetry. I have led him from conversations on slavery, Mormonism and Canadian feudalism to the question so important to me—whether anything can be expected from the elegant literature of a nation of which the noblest productions have their root in a foreign country?" He was one of the earliest members of the American Geographical Society, and has been its president for thirty-four years, making it one of the most useful scientific institutions of the metropolis The annual addresses he has delivered before the society have taken rank among the most valuable contributions to geographical literature Foreign men of science have paid him many tributes, and he is an honorary member of the Geographical Societies of England, Germany, Russia, Holland, Spain, Sweden, Brazil and Portugal, and a member of the National Geographical Society of Washington, and the Geographical Club of Philadelphia. In 1860, Columbia College conferred upon him the degree of LL. D, in recognition of his professional and literary services.

Judge Daly is a lover of books, and has collected one of the choicest private libraries in New York He has written much, among his published works being an Historical Sketch of the Tribunals of New York, 1625–1846, The Nature, Extent and History of the Surrogate's Court of the State of New York, Comparisons Between Ancient and Modern Banking Systems, and a History of the Settlement of the Jews in North America, besides addresses, essays and articles upon many subjects, legal, scientific and literary, including poetry and the drama, upon both of which he is an authority.

While an honored member of many leading social organizations, there is no notable literary, artistic or scientific body in the metropolis with which he is not connected He is a life member of the National Academy of Design, of the New York Historical Society, and of a number of Historical Societies throughout the United States Besides that, he is an honorary member of the Metropolitan Museum of Art and of the Mercantile Library Association, a member of the American Museum of Natural History, as well as of the American Philosophical Society For many years he was president of the Friendly Sons of St. Patrick, and is a member of the Century, Union, Authors', City and Players clubs.

In 1856, Judge Daly married Maria Lydig, a lady belonging to an old and eminent New York family. His residence in Clinton Place is noted for its cultured hospitality, and there Judge Daly is rounding out the evening of a laborious, useful, successful and happy life

JOSEPH F. DALY

ONE of the most conspicuous New Yorkers of Southern birth is the Honorable Joseph F. Daly, of the Supreme Court, and Presiding Judge of the Appellate Term   Judge Daly is a New Yorker by education and life-long association.   Born in Plymouth, N C., in 1840, his family removed to New York before he was nine years old.   Here he received his schooling , began the study of law in the office of S. W. & R. B Roosevelt ; in May, 1862, was admitted to the bar, and in 1865, upon the dissolution of the firm, succeeded to their business, entering at once upon an extensive general practice, and quickly took high rank as one of the most promising young attorneys of that time

One of the first things to bring him notably to the attention of the public was the part which he took in the citizens' movement against municipal corruption during the years between 1864 and 1870   He was one of the most active counsel of the reform movement, and gave valuable legal assistance in the work of securing better government for the city, under the leadership of Peter Cooper and such eminent lawyers as Charles O'Conor, Benjamin D. Silliman, Alexander Hamilton, Jr., Benjamin W Bonney, Charles Tracy, James R Whiting, William Curtis Noyes, and others. His duties embraced the prosecution of charges of official malfeasance before the Governor, making arguments upon the tax levies and reform bills before legislative committees, and the bringing of injunction suits to prevent the misappropriation of public funds

Judge Daly was elected first to the Court of Common Pleas in May, 1870, when he was twenty-nine years of age, and in 1884 he was re-elected, he and his associate, Judge Larremore, being the only candidates elected on their ticket.   Judge Daly's popularity was attested by the fact that he led the list of nine candidates in the field.   He is now serving his second term, to which he was chosen by votes from all political parties, and which expires in 1898.   He was chosen by his associates in 1890 to be Chief Justice, and was the last Chief Judge of the Court of Common Pleas, which was abolished by the Constitution of 1896, the judges being transferred to the Supreme Court   He has long been recognized as one of the ablest lawyers in the city or in New York State, and is one of the most upright members of the judiciary that the bench of this city has ever known, being noted for his high judicial attainment and his profound legal knowledge.

Outside of his professional life, Judge Daly is deeply interested in art, literature and science. He is a man of high culture, thoroughly well informed in general literature, and especially interested in the drama   He was one of the founders of the Players Club, with Edwin Booth, Lawrence Barrett and his brother, Augustin Daly, the eminent dramatist and manager, who has done probably more than any man in the annals of the American stage to uphold the dignity of the profession and bring the theatre up to the highest standard of literary and dramatic excellence. Justice Daly belongs to the Metropolitan, Manhattan, Democratic, Players and Catholic clubs (of the latter he is president for the fourth term), the Bar Association, the Southern Society, the Dunlap Society, the New York Law Institute, the Geographical Society, and the Board of St. Vincent's Hospital, and has been for many years a manager of the Roman Catholic Orphan Asylum.   He received the degree of LL D in 1883, from St. John's College.   His city residence is 19 East Sixty-second Street

Justice Daly is the son of Captain Denis Daly, who was born in Limerick, about 1797, and who, after serving as purser's clerk in the British Navy, resigned and came to America, where he built and sailed his own vessels, finally settling in Plymouth, N C, in 1838, as wharfinger and merchant.   He married, in 1834, Elizabeth Therese Duffey, born in Montego Bay, Jamaica, W. I , in 1812, the daughter of Lieutenant John Duffey, of the One Hundred and First Regiment, and of Margaret Moriarty, of Tralee, Ireland.   Justice Daly married, in 1873, Emma Robinson Barker, step-daughter of the late Judge Hamilton W Robinson, by whom he has two sons, Edward Hamilton and Wilfrid Augustin, and a daughter, Elizabeth Theresa.   His wife dying in 1886, he married, in 1890, Mary Louise, daughter of Edgar M. Smith, of this city.

CHARLES ANDERSON DANA

MANY distinguished men in the United States have borne the name of the family whose first American representative was Richard Dana, who came from France to Boston about 1640 From him have descended the Danas of Massachusetts and other parts of the country, who have been famed in law, statesmanship and literature, or men of mark in other pursuits Among them the names of Chief-Justice Francis Dana, of Massachusetts, and Richard Henry Dana, father and son, lawyers and authors, will naturally suggest themselves

One branch of the family settled in Pennsylvania, Anderson Dana, who came to the Wyoming Valley in 1772, being a grandson of Jacob, who was a son of the original Richard Dana of Massachusetts He was a volunteer aide to Colonel Zebulon Butler when the settlement was attacked by the Indians, and perished in the Wyoming Valley massacre One of the great-grandsons of Anderson Dana was General Edmund L Dana, of Pennsylvania

The late Charles Anderson Dana was a great-grandson of Anderson Dana, the first of the name, being the son of Anderson Dana and his wife, Ann Dennison, and the grandson of Daniel and Dollie (Kibbee) Dana. He was born in Hinsdale, N H , August 8th, 1819 His father, Anderson Dana, was a merchant in Hinsdale, but was not successful, and his son, when a boy of only ten years of age, went to Buffalo, where he was employed in his uncle's business house for several years, but in 1839 began a college course in Harvard Failing eyesight compelled him to leave college after two years study, but later in life Harvard conferred on him the degree of A M In 1842, he joined the Brook Farm community, where he was associated with Nathaniel Hawthorne, George Ripley, John S Dwight, Minott Pratt and others For several years he had been writing for The Harbinger, a Brook Farm periodical, and at the age of twenty-seven began to work regularly on The Boston Chronotype, where he earned his first money in the newspaper profession

In 1847, Mr Dana came to New York and joined the staff of The Tribune, and in 1848 spent eight months in Europe as a correspondent of The Tribune, Chronotype, Commercial Advertiser and other papers Returning in 1849, he became managing editor of The Tribune and held that place for fifteen years Differences with Horace Greeley regarding its attitude on the Civil War led him to leave The Tribune in 1862 Secretary Stanton then employed him in the War Department and finally appointed him Assistant Secretary of War He held the position until hostilities were over, and while in office rendered invaluable service to the Union cause, spending much of his time at the front in confidential and perilous missions After the war he was engaged for a short period on The Chicago Tribune, but in 1867 came to New York and in partnership with several friends bought The Sun. From that time until his death in October, 1897, the history of The Sun was Mr Dana's, and he was regarded as the dean of American journalists

His country residence on Dosoris Island, near Glen Cove, Long Island, is a magnificent garden and he was an authority upon horticulture He was also an art connoisseur, and his city house, 25 East Sixtieth Street, contains a large and valuable art collection, while he was also an authority on pictures and an expert upon the subject of porcelains

Despite the exactions of daily newspaper work, Mr Dana found time for extensive travels abroad as well as to cultivate literature He was a remarkable linguist, having command of nearly all modern and ancient languages. He compiled The Household Book of Poetry, Fifty Perfect Poems, and other anthologies, wrote a Life of General Grant in collaboration with General James H Wilson, and with George Ripley planned and edited The New American Cyclopedia He was a member of the Sons of the American Revolution and the New England Society, and a supporter of the Metropolitan Museum of Art In 1846, Mr. Dana married Eunice McDaniel, of Maryland, who survives him They had three daughters, Ruth, who married William H Draper, M D , Eunice, who married Dr John W Brannan, and Zoe, who married Walter M Underhill Their only son, Paul Dana, born in 1852, married Mary Duncan He was at one time president of the Board of Park Commissioners of New York, and has succeeded his father as editor of The Sun.

RICHARD STARR DANA

ICHARD DANA was the progenitor of a family that has been illustrious in many walks of life in this country during the last two centuries and a half. He left his native country, England, in 1640, and coming to America, settled in Cambridge, Mass. He was a man of education and means, and his Cambridge property is still in the family. The third son of Richard Dana was Benjamin Dana, the great-grandfather of the Reverend Samuel Dana, of Marblehead, Mass., who was the grandfather of Mr. Richard Starr Dana. The great-grandfather of Mr. Dana was Joseph Dana, who was born in Pomfret, Conn., in 1742, and died in Ipswich, Mass., in 1827. Graduated from Yale College in 1760, he studied theology, and in 1765 was ordained minister of the South Congregational Church of Ipswich, retaining that pulpit during the greater part of his life. His son, the Reverend Samuel Dana, followed in the footsteps of his father, and became one of the most eminent clergymen of Eastern Massachusetts.

The Reverend Samuel Dana had many distinguished descendants. His eldest son was Richard Perkins Dana, the father of Mr. Richard Starr Dana. Another son was Israel Thorndike Dana, who was born in Marblehead, Mass., in 1827, and graduated from the Medical School of Harvard College in 1850, with the degree of M. D. He was one of the founders of the Portland School of Medical Instruction and of the Maine General Hospital. He was also professor of materia medica and professor of the theory and practice of medicine in the Medical School of Maine. The Reverend Samuel Dana, of Groton, Mass., was another distinguished member of this family. Born in Cambridge, Mass., in 1739, he was graduated from Harvard College in 1755, and in 1761 settled as a minister over the church in Groton. Afterwards he turned his attention to the study of law, and was admitted to the bar. Removing to Amherst, N. H., he was Judge of Probate for Hillsborough County, in 1789, and in 1793 was elected a member of the State Senate. James Freeman Dana, grandson of the Reverend Samuel Dana, of Marblehead, was born in 1793 and died in 1827. Graduated from Harvard College in 1813, he was assistant professor of chemistry in that institution, the first professor of chemistry and mineralogy in Dartmouth College, in 1820, and professor of chemistry in the College of Physicians and Surgeons in New York in 1825. Samuel Luther Dana, brother of James Freeman Dana, was born in 1795, graduated from Harvard College in 1813, and became a famous chemist. During the War of 1812, he was an officer in the artillery service, and after the war was graduated from the Harvard Medical School in 1818.

Richard Perkins Dana, the father of Mr. Richard Starr Dana, was born in 1810 and died in 1894. A collegiate career was planned for him, but before he had completed his studies for college, he relinquished that purpose and entered the counting house of his uncle, Israel Thorndike, in Boston. While thus engaged, he made several voyages as supercargo of vessels, owned by his uncle, visiting different parts of the world. The literary tastes inherent in his family early manifested themselves, and he wrote valuable accounts of the places that he visited. During part of his lifetime he resided in China, principally in Canton and Hong Kong, being connected with business houses in those places. After his retirement from active business in the East, he settled in New York. For sixteen years he was a director of the New York Juvenile Asylum, and was one of the governors of the Woman's Hospital. His wife was Juliette H. Starr, of the old Connecticut family of that name. His son, William Starr Dana, now deceased, was a Commander in the United States Navy, and served with much distinction. His only daughter became the wife of General Egbert L. Viele.

Mr. Richard Starr Dana is the eldest son of Richard Perkins Dana. He was born in New York in 1836. Educated in Columbia College, he was graduated from that institution in the class of 1857. On leaving college, he entered the banking and commission house of Russell & Co., China, merchants, becoming a partner in that firm in 1863. He married Florine Turner. He is a member of the Union Club, the Sons of the Revolution, the Society of Colonial Wars and the Colonial Society of the Acorn. He has two sons, Richard T. and David T. Dana.

GEORGE TRIMBLE DAVIDSON

THE clan McDavid, originally a part of the clan Chattan, derives its name from the marriage of a daughter of the Lord of the Isles with the second son of David I, King of Scotland When the Scottish crown fell into abeyance, upon the death of Margaret of Norway, the representative of the Davidson family was one of the nine nobles of royal blood who competed for the throne. From his family came Malcolm Davidson, whose son Nicholas emigrated to Lynn, England, and established another branch there.

In 1639, Mathew Craddock, the royal Governor of Massachusetts Bay, selected Nicholas Davidson to come to this country as his personal representative He landed, in 1639, at Charlestown, Mass, where he took up his residence, and at the time of his death possessed one of the largest estates in the Colony, inventoried at the sum of £1,869

His descendant, Mr. George Trimble Davidson, is a son of Colonel Mathias Oliver Davidson a distinguished civil engineer, who served upon the construction of the Croton aqueduct, and subsequently opened the coal regions of Western Maryland. In 1856, he took charge of the construction of the railroads in the island of Cuba; in 1865-70, built the New Haven & Derby Railroad, and in 1870-2 laid out the series of avenues which cross the upper portion of the City of New York. Colonel Davidson had relations with foreign governments, and the Emperor Maximilian of Mexico, where he was employed professionally upon important works, tendered him the title of Marquis, which, however, he did not assume. Mr. George Trimble Davidson's grandfather, Dr Oliver Davidson, of Plattsburg, N Y, was a descendant in the fifth generation of Nicholas Davidson, of Charlestown Dr Davidson married Margaret Miller, a daughter of Dr Mathias Burnett Miller, of Utica, and a sister of Judge Morris S Miller, Mrs. John Schuyler, of Albany, and Mrs Charles Dudley Their children, besides Mathias Oliver, were Lucretia Maria and Margaret Miller Davidson, whose precocious poetic genius astonished the literary world half a century ago, and Lieutenant Levi P Davidson, a graduate of West Point. Dr Oliver Davidson, after the death of his wife, who possessed great literary distinction, purchased the Sir William Johnson place in Amsterdam, N. Y, where he resided until his death, in 1847. Mr. Davidson's mother is also of distinguished descent She is a daughter of the late Captain Mathew Miles Standish, of Plattsburg, and Catharine Phœbe Miller, who was a first cousin of Mr Davidson's paternal grandmother, Mrs Oliver Davidson Her father, Captain Mathew Miles Standish, who served during the War of 1812 in the battle of Plattsburg, was the direct descendant in line of primogeniture of Captain Miles Standish. Her second husband, also deceased, was Colonel James Woodruff Romayn, of Detroit

The paternal arms to which Mr Davidson is entitled are : on a field azure three pheons argent, on a fess or., a stag attired with ten tines, couchant proper, crest, a falcon's head couped. Motto, *Viget et cinere virtus*. The Standish arms are on a field azure, three standishes argent; crest, a cock proper Motto, *Constant en tout* Mr George Trimble Davidson was born in Fordham, N Y, October 21st, 1863. He was educated in St. Paul s School, Concord, N H, and graduated from the Columbia Law School, being admitted to the bar at the head of his class in January, 1885. He is engaged in the practice of law and is a member of the Manhattan Club. He occupies a high social position, having been a frequent guest at prominent social functions, and active in the management of the important social affairs. In 1893, he was one of the organizers of the Committee of One Hundred, which received the foreign guests of the city at the Columbian celebration He has entertained the Infanta Eulalia, Don Antonio of Spain, Prince Roland Bonaparte, the Duc de Lerme, the Duc de Veragua, the Grand Duke Alexander of Russia, Prince Charles de Hatzfeldt-Wildenberg, the Duke of Marlborough, the Duc de Tamames, and other royal and noble foreigners

Mr Davidson owns a collection of paintings, including canvases that formerly belonged to Joseph Bonaparte. He has written considerably in prose and verse

WILLIAM GILBERT DAVIES

FOR more than a century and a half the Davies family has been established in this country. In Britain, its lineage is traced to Robert Davies, of Gwysany Castle, high sheriff of Flintshire, who was descended from Cymric Efell, Lord of Eylwys Eyle, in the thirteenth century The American ancestor, John Davies, 1680-1758, of Kinton, Hertfordshire, came to this country in 1735, settled in Litchfield, Conn., and married Catherine Spencer He is especially remembered as one of the founders and benefactors of St Michael's Church, Litchfield, a tablet in that church preserving his memory His son, John Davies, Jr , married Elizabeth Brown, and had, with other children, Thomas Davies, 1737-1766, who graduated from Yale College, was ordained a clergyman in England, and returned to America as a missionary of the Society for Propagating the Gospel in Foreign Parts.

The third John Davies, 1735-1799, eldest son of John Davies, Jr , married Eunice Hotchkiss and was the father of Thomas John Davies, 1767-1845, who removed to St. Lawrence County, N. Y., in 1800, and was Sheriff and county Judge The Honorable Henry E Davies, 1805-1881, was the son of Thomas John Davies Admitted to the bar in 1826, he removed to New York, and was long prominent in public life. In 1840, he was an alderman, in 1850 Corporation Counsel, in 1856 a Justice of the Supreme Court, in 1860 a Judge, and afterwards Chief Justice of the Court of Appeals In 1855, he married Rebecca Waldo Tappan, daughter of John Tappan, a Boston merchant, whose brothers, Arthur and Lewis Tappan, were prominent in the abolition movement. Her grandfathers, Benjamin Tappan and John Foote, were both Revolutionary soldiers. The Tappan family is descended from Abraham Tappan, who came to America in 1630. She was also descended from John Hull, the Master of the Mint and Treasurer of Massachusetts, who coined the pine tree shillings Through his mother, the present Mr Davies traces his descent to the Quincys, Salisburys, Wendells, and other great New England families, and to the famous Anneke Jans.

Mr. William Gilbert Davies was born in New York, March 21st, 1842, graduated from Trinity College in 1860, also studied at the University of Leipzig, Germany, and was admitted to the New York bar in 1863 During the Civil War, he was a member of the Twenty-Second New York Regiment. A considerable part of his professional life has been spent as counsel to one of the large insurance corporations. His practice now is mainly as chamber counsel. He is a member of the American, State and City Bar associations, and the Law Institute, and is a lecturer on the law of life insurance in the University of the City of New York. In 1870, Mr. Davies married Lucie C Rice, daughter of the Honorable Alexander H Rice, who was Mayor of Boston, a Member of Congress, and for three terms Governor of Massachusetts. Mr. Davies lives in East Forty-fifth Street He is an active member of the New York and Virginia Historical societies, and the New York Genealogical and Biographical Society. He also belongs to the Union, University, Lawyers', Manhattan, Tuxedo, Grolier and St. Nicholas clubs, the Century Association, the Liederkranz, the Φ B K Alumni Association, the Sons of the Revolution, and the Society of Colonial Wars.

Julien Tappan Davies, younger son of the Honorable Henry E. Davies, was born in New York, September 25th, 1845, was educated at Mt Washington Collegiate Institute and at the Walnut Hill School, Geneva, N Y , and was graduated from Columbia College in 1866, and from the Columbia Law School in 1868 He has made corporation law his specialty. Early in his career, he became a trustee and one of the counsel of the Mutual Life Insurance Company, and in 1884 succeeded David Dudley Field as general counsel of the Manhattan Railway Company. He is the senior member of the law firm of Davies, Stone & Auerbach. In 1869, he married Alice Martin, daughter of Henry Martin, of Albany, N Y They have three children, Ethel, Cornelia S and Frederick Martin Davies. The city residence of the family is in West Ninth Street, and their summer home, Pinecroft, in Newport Mr. Davies belongs to the Metropolitan, Union League, University, Lawyers', City, Players, Church, Republican and New York Yacht clubs, the Society of Colonial Wars and the St. Nicholas Society, and is vice-president of the St. David's Society.

FELLOWES DAVIS

A N old Tudor mansion, the manor house at Twickenham, England, now in ruins, was the original seat of the Davis family, which was transplanted to the New World by William Davis, 1617-1683 He settled in Roxbury, Mass , in 1638, being among the first of the band of Puritan gentlemen and yeomen who escaped from the persecutions of Charles I and Archbishop Laud and sought an asylum in New England, where they could find religious freedom. This pioneer's grandson, Colonel Aaron Davis, was a member of the Massachusetts Provincial Congress, Colonel of the Militia, a prominent local and State official, an active patriot during the Revolution, and a leading citizen of Massachusetts in that period. His two sons, Captain Aaron Davis, Jr , and Moses Davis, were also active patriots, the latter serving as a minute man at Lexington and Concord, and the former as an officer of State troops. His house was destroyed by orders of Washington, as being in range of the American artillery trained on Boston at the siege of that city The two branches of the family were, however, united when William Davis, Jr., grandson of Moses Davis, espoused Maria Davis, granddaughter of Aaron Davis, Jr., the issue of this marriage being Mr Fellowes Davis, who thus represents both lines of descent from Colonel Aaron Davis

Mr Davis's ancestry also includes some of the most famous names in the early history of the country. The wife of Moses Davis, Mr Davis's great-grandmother, was Hannah Pierpont, daughter of Ebenezer Pierpont, a descendant of the "Founder of Massachusetts," John Winthrop, and of his colleague and successor as Governor of the Colony, Thomas Dudley.

Second to Winthrop alone in his services, Dudley, who was of the blood of the Earl of Leicester, was one of the high born and bred Puritan gentlemen who formed the natural leaders of the Massachusetts settlement In youth he had been a soldier on the Protestant side in France, and when, in 1630, he migrated to New England, held an important office under the Earl of Lincoln, one of the political supporters of the Puritan cause He was four times Governor and several times Deputy Governor of Massachusetts, and, at sixty-eight years of age, was the commander of the troops of the Colony He was noted even among the Puritans for his piety and the austerity of his life, while his devotion to the interests of New England knew no bounds One of his sons, Joseph Dudley, was also a statesman and administrator in the early Colonial period, and rendered effective service to both Crown and Colonists. After acting as president of the Council of Massachusetts and Chief Justice of New York, he was appointed by Queen Anne Governor of his native Province, which office he held for seventeen years

Thomas Dudley's son, the Reverend Samuel Dudley, married Mary Winthrop, and their daughter, Ann, marrying Edward Hilton, was the grandmother of Ann Hilton, wife of Ebenezer Pierpont Mr. Davis, indeed, can claim descent in two lines from Governor Dudley, whose daughter, Mary, married John Woodbridge, and was the ancestor of Sarah Smith, wife of his grandfather, William Davis, Sr

Mr. Davis married, in 1871, Marie Antoinette Baker, of Boston Mrs Davis is also directly descended from Governor Dudley, and from many pioneers of distinction, her ancestor, Robert Baker, having come over with the Endicott fleet and was granted a tract of land by the Crown, in Salem, Mass., 1637 Jonathan Baker served in the French and Indian War with distinction, and Benjamin Baker and Jesse Davidson, both great-grandfathers of Mrs Davis, served in the Revolution, the former at Bunker Hill The issue of this marriage are four children, Fellowes Davis, Jr , Marie Antoinette Davis, Pierpont Davis and Dudley Davis. The family residence is 57 West Forty-eighth Street. Mr. Davis is one of the board of managers of the Society of the Sons of the Revolution, a member of the Council of the Military Order of Foreign Wars, the Society of Colonial Wars, the Historical Society, and of the Union Club The arms of the Davis family, of which one of the earliest examples is still found carved in the stone work of the old manor home at Twickenham, England, consist of a red shield bearing a gold griffin rampant, the crest being a barred helmet surrounded by a rampant griffin, and the motto is *Deo Duce Ferro Comitante*

CHARLES EVERETT DAVISON

THE branch of the Davison family which is represented in New York City in the present generation by Mr Charles Everett Davison, is of English extraction. That gentleman's descent is from ancestors who, from their first appearance in America, showed a patriotic devotion to it His grandfather, Peter I. Davison, and his wife, a Miss Garrett, were both born in England, but came to this country soon after the Revolution, settling in Chenango County, N Y. Peter I. Davison became a man of wealth and prominence in that section of the State, and warmly espoused the cause of his adopted country in the War of 1812 against Great Britain, in which conflict he served in the United States Army with the rank of Captain. His son, John Garrett Davison, was born at Sherburne, Chenango County, N. Y, and married Sarah Amelia Stanton, of Little Britain, Orange County, N Y, a lady belonging to a family of Irish origin with New England connections, which has produced many distinguished ministers and lawyers, as well as men prominent in other pursuits, both in its early and more recent generations. Her grandfather was at one time Mayor of Dublin, Ireland. She was also a cousin of Secretary Stanton, President Lincoln's great Secretary of War

Mr Charles Everett Davison, their son, was born in New York in 1857, and received his education here and at Heidelberg University, Germany, where he passed some years. Mr. Davison then took up his legal studies in this city. His professional preceptor was Vine Wright Kingsley, of the New York bar, one of the old Kingsley family and an eminent lawyer as well as a distinguished litterateur. Mr. Davison also followed the law course of the University of the City of New York, graduating in 1878, and in the same year was admitted to the bar of this city and has been an active and successful practitioner from that time to the present day. He has made a special study of medical jurisprudence, in which difficult branch of the law he is regarded as an expert, and is one of the founders and active supporters of the Medico-Legal Society, one of the leading bodies of its class, not only in New York but in the world at large. He has been associated as counsel in some of the most remarkable trials in the annals of the city, the special professional studies to which he has in a large measure devoted his attention, rendering him an authority upon such subjects and causing him to be called in consultation in different causes involving questions of medical jurisprudence.

In 1885, Mr Davison married Mary Eva Travers, of New York. Mrs. Davison's father was James P. Travers, a native of New Orleans, La , having been born there in 1824. Removing to New York in 1844, he engaged in mercantile business in the metropolis, founding a large export trade, his offices being in a large building in Beekman Street, which he erected for his own use. Mr Travers enjoyed the distinction of having first introduced blotting paper into general use throughout the United States. Mr. Travers was twice offered, but declined, a nomination for Member of Congress for the second district of Long Island.

Though essentially of scholarly and literary tastes and devoted to his professional pursuits, Mr. Davison has taken a prominent part in society, and is not without interest, though not of an active nature, in yachting and other leading sports. He has, as already referred to, resided and traveled abroad, and is, as the result of his journeyings, unusually well acquainted with foreign countries and affairs, and at his residence, 13 Charles Street, in the old Ninth Ward, possesses a collection of choice paintings of American and European artists. He has taken a patriotic interest in national and local politics, and in 1891 was a candidate for the nomination to the State Senate for the first district, the opposing candidate being S D Townsend. The result was an exciting struggle in the convention, which lasted from ten o'clock in the morning to a late hour in the evening, though it eventually ended in the nomination of Mr. Townsend, who was finally elected by the constituency.

Mr. Davison, in addition to his town residence, has two country seats, one at Manhanset, Long Island, and another at Monroe, Orange County, N. Y.

CLARENCE SHEPARD DAY

ROBERT DAY, who emigrated from England to this country in 1634, was the first American ancestor of Mr Clarence Shepard Day, He was a native of England, where he was born about 1604, and came from Ipswich, with his wife Mary, on the ship Elizabeth When he landed in Massachusetts, he settled in Newtown, now Cambridge, becoming a freeman in 1635 When the Reverend Thomas Hooker headed the company which moved to Connecticut and founded Hartford, Robert Day and his family went with them His first wife having died, he married, second, Editha Stebbins, of Hartford, and died there in 1648

In subsequent generations, the ancestors of Mr. Clarence Shepard Day were Thomas Day, who in 1659 married Sarah Cooper, daughter of Lieutenant Thomas Cooper, and died in 1711, his wife dying in 1726; John Day, of West Springfield, Mass., who was born in 1673 and died in 1752, and his wife, Mary Smith, of Hadley, whom he married in 1697 and who died in 1742; Colonel Benjamin Day, of West Springfield, who was born in 1710, and his wife, Eunice Morgan, whom he married in 1742 and who died in 1765; Benjamin Day, who was born in 1747, graduated from Yale College in 1768 and died in 1794, and his wife, Sarah Dwight, of Springfield, who was married in 1772 and died in 1785; and Henry Day, who was born in 1773 and died in 1811, and his wife, Mary Ely, who was born in 1774, married in 1794 and died in 1859.

The father of Mr. Clarence Shepard Day was Benjamin Henry Day, son of Henry and Mary (Ely) Day He was born in West Springfield in 1810, and for many years was engaged in the publishing business in New York. He is best remembered in connection with The New York Sun, which he founded in 1833 and which he subsequently sold, in 1837, to his brother-in-law, Moses Y. Beach He afterwards established the paper known as The Brother Jonathan, which he edited and published for twenty years, and then, relinquishing active professional pursuits, lived in retirement and died in 1889. The mother of Mr. Clarence Shepard Day, whom Benjamin Henry Day married in 1831, was Eveline Shepard, who was born in Amsterdam, N. Y , in 1806, daughter of Mather Shepard and Harriet Day.

Through his grandmother, Mary Ely, Mr. Clarence S. Day is descended from another notable Colonial family His first American ancestor in that line was Nathaniel Ely, of Ipswich, England, who came to Massachusetts in 1634 and afterwards took part in the settlement of Hartford and Norwalk, Conn , finally establishing his family in Springfield, Mass. Mary Ely was a descendant in the sixth generation from Nathaniel Ely, the pioneer Her father was William Ely, of West Springfield, 1743-1825, her mother being Drusilla Brewster, 1745-1828, daughter of William Brewster, of Windham, Conn , who was a direct descendant of William Brewster, of Plymouth. Her grandmother was Mercy Bliss, daughter of Samuel Bliss, of the Bliss family of Springfield, and her great-grandmother was Mary Edwards, daughter of Deacon John Edwards, of the same family as the famous Jonathan Edwards. Her great-great-grandmother, Mary Day, was a daughter of Robert Day, the pioneer, and thus through two lines of descent, on both sides, the subject of this article traces his lineage to Robert Day.

Mr. Clarence Shepard Day was born in New York, August 9th, 1844 Prepared for college in the public schools, he then studied in the College of the City of New York During the Civil War, he served, in 1862, with the Seventh Regiment. For thirty years past, he has been occupied with financial affairs and is one of the best known bankers and stock brokers in Wall Street He is a member of the Metropolitan, Union League, Lawyers' and Riding clubs and belongs to the New England Society and the Chamber of Commerce In 1873, he married Lavinia Elizabeth Stockwell, who, through her mother, is descended from the Parmly family of New York. They have four children: Clarence S Day, Jr , who graduated from Yale in 1896; George Parmly Day, who also graduated from Yale in 1897; Julian Day, now a Yale undergraduate, and Harold C. Day The city residence of the family is in Madison Avenue, and they have a country home, Upland Farm, in Harrison, Westchester County, N Y.

GEORGE LORD DAY

ACCORDING to tradition, the Day family was originally settled in Wales, and it is said that the name was derived from the Dee, a small river in the principality. In the course of time, its representatives moved into England, some of them becoming people of importance in the eastern counties and London. By the early records of the Massachusetts Bay and Plymouth Colonies, it appears that during the first quarter of a century of the New England settlement eight persons of the name came hither as Colonists.

Robert Day, of Cambridge, who arrived in America in 1634, was the ancestor of the branch of the family to which attention is now directed. He was born in Ipswich, England, in 1604, and when he came to this country brought with him his wife, Mary. Settling first in Newtown, now Cambridge, he was a freeman of that place in 1635, and in 1639 removed to Hartford, in the company led by the Reverend Thomas Hooker. His second wife, whom he married after settling in Hartford, was Editha Stebbins, sister of Deacon Edward Stebbins, of Hartford. Robert Day died in 1648. In the next five generations the ancestors of Mr. George Lord Day were . John Day, of Hartford, and his wife, Sarah Maynard , John Day, the second of the name, 1696-1752, of Colchester, Conn , and his wife, Grace Spencer, of Hartford, Abraham Day, 1712-1792, of Colchester, and his wife, Irene Foote, Ezra Day, 1743-1823, of South Hadley, Mass , and his wife, Hannah Kendall , and Pliny Day, 1782-1846, of West Springfield, Mass , and his wife, Deborah Butts Many members of this old New England family were soldiers of the patriot army during the War of the Revolution.

Henry Day, the father of the subject of this sketch, was one of the most distinguished lawyers of New York in the last generation. He was born in South Hadley, Mass , in 1820, being a son of Pliny Day and Deborah Butts. His brother, the Reverend Pliny Day, was a prominent clergyman of western Massachusetts. Henry Day attended school in Derry, Conn , and then entered Yale College, graduating from that institution in 1845. For some time he was engaged in teaching at Fairfield, Conn , and then attended the law school at Harvard College, coming to New York after his graduation therefrom, and entering upon the practice of law. In 1849, he became a partner in the legal firm of Lord, Day & Lord, of which the distinguished Daniel Lord was the senior member. It was not long before Henry Day became one of the most eminent lawyers in New York and a prominent figure in the social life of the metropolis. Interested in the organization of the Equitable Life Assurance Society, he became attorney and a director of that institution, and was also a director of the Consolidated Gas Company, the Mercantile Trust Company, and the Lawyers' Title & Guarantee Company. The legal affairs of many large estates were entrusted to him, including those of Professor Samuel F B Morse, Edward Morgan and the Astors. A member of the Presbyterian Church, he was a director of the Union Theological Seminary, and gave much labor to the cause of philanthropy. He was the author of The Lawyer Abroad, and From the Pyrenees to the Pillars of Hercules. The Hill, in Morristown, N J , was long his country residence. At the time of his death, in 1893, he was the sole survivor of the original members of Lord, Day & Lord, with which he had been connected for nearly forty-five years. The wife of Henry Day was Phebe Lucretia Lord, daughter of Daniel Lord.

Mr. George Lord Day, son of Henry Day and Phebe Lord, was born in New York City. Educated at Princeton College and graduating with the Latin salutatory address, he studied law and became a member of the law firm with which his father and maternal grandfather had been connected. After a severe accident in the hunting field with the Meadow Brook hounds, in 1894, he retired from active professional life. His wife, whom he married in England, in 1896, was Adele Mittant. Mr Day is a member of the Manhattan, Lawyers', University, Racquet, Princeton, Union, New York Athletic, Meadow Brook Hunt, and New York Yacht clubs, the Bar Association and the Downtown Association.

GEORGE B DE FOREST

A MONG the Huguenot refugees who established themselves on the free and hospitable soil of the New Netherland was Isaac De Forest, a native of Northeastern France. He was one of the earliest settlers of the Colony, and, dying in 1674, left ten children, who have perpetuated his name in modern New York, where it has ever been regarded as representative in the highest degree of the founders of our city.

Lockwood De Forest, a descendant in the second or third generation of Isaac De Forest, the progenitor of the family, was born in 1775, and became one of the leading merchants of the city in the period succeeding the Revolutionary War In 1824, he was a member of the committee composed of the most prominent men of New York, appointed to convey to De Witt Clinton the condemnation of the people of the metropolis of his removal from the position of Canal Commissioner by his political opponents Lockwood De Forest was the father of five sons, among whom were William W De Forest and George B De Forest (the elder), both distinguished business men and eminent citizens of New York. William W. De Forest is remembered as one of the South Street merchants engaged in the South American trade.

His brother, George B. De Forest, Sr., 1806-1865, was identified with the West India trade, and possessed remarkable ability and enterprise, as well as a noteworthy degree of public spirit. The merchants of old New York were a distinguished body of men, and in their galaxy no names were higher than those of the present Mr. De Forest's father and uncle.

Mr. George B. De Forest is the son of the late George B. De Forest, Sr., and his wife, Margaret E. De Forest, and was born in this city in 1848. In 1882, Mr. De Forest married Anita, daughter of Louis S Hargous. The latter played a distinguished part in the war between the United States and Mexico, having been United States Consul at the City of Mexico prior to the outbreak of hostilities. His local knowledge was of great assistance to the leaders of the American forces which invaded and conquered Mexico, and he served throughout the war on the staff of General Worth, becoming after the peace a prominent banker in the City of Mexico. Mr. and Mrs De Forest have one son, Louis S. H De Forest, born in 1884, and named after his maternal grandfather.

A leading figure in New York society, Mr. De Forest is connected with the more prominent clubs, including the Metropolitan, Union, Union League, Knickerbocker, Century, Players, Racquet, Grolier, Westchester Country and Fencers He is also a member of the Seventh Regiment Veterans and of the Sons of the American Revolution; Mrs De Forest being a member of the Daughters of the Revolution. Though not an active sportsman, Mr. De Forest, as may be noticed from some of his club affiliations, takes a decided interest in such pursuits, and is a member of the New York Yacht Club, while he is a patron of all the fashionable amusements both in this city and Newport.

It is as a judicious patron of art and literature that Mr. De Forest finds his chief pleasure. His collection of rare books, particularly upon art subjects, is famous among American and European bibliophiles. It is particularly rich in the products of the French printers and binders of the period of Louis XV. and the Regency, and also in books with original drawings and water color illustrations His knowledge and taste in all that relates to these subjects is well known, and his treasures bear the stamp of a discriminating personal selection. To these fascinating pursuits he has devoted not merely a lavish though judicious expenditure, but has made them the object of a lifelong study. In fact, the reputation of Mr. De Forest as a connoisseur of art is so well established that he ranks among the foremost authorities on such subjects in the United States

The De Forest residence is 14 East Fiftieth Street, but Mr. and Mrs De Forest usually reside during the greater part of each season at Newport, being numbered among the most conspicuous members of the colony which makes the city in question a social centre.

MATURIN LIVINGSTON DELAFIELD

JOHN DELAFIELD, who was born in 1748, and came to this country in 1783, was the eighth of his family to bear the name of John, and was the representative of a landed family in Bucks and Oxfordshire, England. He became one of the most successful merchants of New York, retiring from business in 1798, and was President of the United Insurance Company, and a director of the New York branch of the Bank of the United States He died in 1824 His residence, on the Long Island shore of the East River, opposite Blackwell's Island, was one of the finest mansions around New York In 1784, he married Ann Hallett, who survived till 1839. She was the daughter of Joseph and Elizabeth (Hazard) Hallett, and a granddaughter of Nathaniel and Elizabeth (Drummond) Hazard Her father was one of the first Sons of Liberty in New York, a member of the Committee of Safety, and of the three first New York Provincial Congresses

Of the thirteen children of John and Ann (Hallett) Delafield, seven sons and four daughters survived. The eldest son, John Delafield, 1786–1853, was president of the Phenix Bank, and of the New York State Agricultural Society. He married, first, his cousin Mary, only child of John Roberts, of Whitchurch, Bucks, England, and second, Harriet Wadsworth, daughter of Colonel Benjamin Tallmadge, and had issue by both marriages Henry and William, twin sons of John and Ann (Hallett) Delafield, were born in 1792. William died unmarried in 1853 Henry married Mary, daughter of Judge Monson, and died in 1875 He had one child, a daughter, who died young Doctor Edward Delafield, 1794–1875, was a president of the College of Physicians and Surgeons He married, first, Elinor E , daughter of Thomas Elwyn Langdon, and granddaughter of Governor Langdon, President of Congress, and second, Julia, daughter of Colonel Nicoll Floyd, and granddaughter of General William Floyd, of Mastic, Long Island, and left issue by this marriage. General Richard Delafield, 1798–1873, became a Brigadier-General and Chief of Engineers, United States Army He married, first, Helen, daughter of Andrew Summers, and, second, Harriet Baldwin, daughter of General E M Covington, by whom he left children Rufus King Delafield, 1802–1874, was a merchant, and married Eliza, daughter of William Bard, by whom he had children The only daughter of John Delafield who married, was Susan Maria, 1805–1861, the wife of Henry Parish, and had no children

Major Joseph Delafield, 1790–1875, the second son of John Delafield, was born in New York, graduated from Yale in 1808, and was admitted to the bar in 1811 In 1812, he entered the United States Army as Captain, and became Major of the Forty-sixth Infantry After the War, he resigned, and in 1821–28 was agent for the Government in fixing the northern boundary of the United States under the Treaty of Ghent He was president of the New York Lyceum of Natural History from 1827 to 1866 In 1833, Major Delafield married Julia Livingston, 1801–1882, daughter of Judge Maturin Livingston, of Staatsburgh, and his wife, Margaret Lewis, daughter of General Morgan Lewis, and granddaughter of Francis Lewis, signer of the Declaration of Independence

Mr Maturin Livingston Delafield, the second son of Major Delafield, was born in New York in 1836 He graduated from Columbia College in 1856, and received his degree of A. M in 1860 In 1868, he married Mary Coleman Livingston, daughter of Eugene Augustus and Harriet (Coleman) Livingston, their children being five sons and three daughters. The family residence is in Fifth Avenue, and Mr Delafield has a country-seat, Fieldston, Riverdale-on-Hudson. He is a member of the Metropolitan and Union clubs and the American Museum of Natural History, and is a Fellow of the American Geographical Society

Lewis Livingston Delafield, 1834–1883, Major Delafield's eldest son, graduated from Columbia in 1855, and was a member of the bar He married Emily Prime, daughter of Frederick Prime and his wife, Lydia, daughter of Dr Robert Hare, of Philadelphia, and had three sons and a daughter The only sister of Mr Delafield is Julia Livingston Delafield

RICHARD DELAFIELD

T HE Counts De la Feld, whose castle still stands near Colmar, Alsace, were the ancestors of the Delafield family in England and America. Hubertus De la Feld accompanied William the Conqueror to England in 1066, received grants of land and had descendants who were numbered among the landed nobles in the reign of subsequent British sovereigns. John Delafield, who lived in the time of Henry III., married Elizabeth Fitzwarine, daughter of the Lord Warden of the North, and from him in direct line descended Sir Thomas Delafield (*tempore* Henry VI), of Ailesbury, in England, and the Baronies of Fieldstone and Culdnuffe in Ireland Ninth in descent from Sir Thomas Delafield, as set forth in Burke's Genealogical and Heraldic Dictionary, was John Delafield, who was born in 1647 and entered the service of the Emperor of Germany. He fought against the Turks under the famous Prince Eugene of Savoy, and in 1697 was created a Count of the Holy Roman Empire for his distinguished gallantry at the victory of Zenta. This dignity is inherited by all his male descendants, and there is no American family of prominence possessing more distinct rights to a title of nobility than that of Delafield. The arms of the family are a black shield with a gold cross-patonce on the breast of the Imperial eagle of Germany. Their crest is a dove, proper, holding an olive branch in its beak. Mottoes, *Insignæ Fortunæ Paria and Fest*, signifying steadfastness and loyalty.

The great-great-grandson of John, Count Delafield, also named John Delafield, came to the United States and married Anne, daughter of Joseph Hallett, of Hallett's Point, N. Y. He died in 1824, having been one of the most eminent citizens of New York in the early part of the present century. One of his seven sons was Rufus King Delafield, who married Eliza Bard, a daughter of William Bard and his wife, Katherine Cruger, a member of the old and distinguished New York family of that name A prominent representative of the Bard family was Dr Bard, the noted physician of the latter part of the last century, who attended President Washington in a professional capacity when the seat of the Federal Government was in New York Mr Richard Delafield is the son of this marriage, and was born in 1853, at the country residence of his father, at New Brighton, Staten Island, his mother's family being also residents and large land owners on Staten Island. In 1880, Mr Delafield married Clara (Foster) Carey, of New York, whose great-uncle was the celebrated Philip Hone, Mayor of New York in 1826, and a leader in the city's society at that time, his name being coupled prominently with the leading institutions of the city of that period. Dr Elisha Kent Kane, the famous Arctic explorer, was also a connection of Mrs. Delafield's family

Educated at the famous school of Dr. Charles Anthon, in New York, Mr. Delafield evinced from the outset remarkable talent as a man of affairs, and at an early age became an active and successful merchant He is now the senior partner of the firm of Delafield & Co , of New York, Chicago and San Francisco, which house he founded. He is vice-president of the National Park Bank, a vestryman of Trinity Church and ex-president of the New York Mercantile Exchange. He has avoided political life, but has been active in forwarding the interests of the city, serving as president of the New York Commission for the World's Columbian Exposition, representing in that body the First District of New York, and as a member of the Committee of One Hundred which had charge of the New York Columbian Quadro-Centennial

Mr. Delafield has traveled extensively, both in Europe and this country. He is decidedly musical in his tastes, and has taken a prominent part in leading organizations to further that art, his connection with such bodies having included the presidency of the Staten Island Philharmonic Society, and the secretaryship of the New York Symphony Society. He is a member of the Sons of the Revolution and of the Merchants', Union League and New York Athletic clubs Among the charitable organizations to which he has devoted his time and energy, are the Sea Side Home of Long Island, of which he is president, and the Varick Street Hospital, being a member of the executive committee of that institution.

EDWARD FLOYD DE LANCEY

IT has been well said that "no American had greater influence in the Colonies than James de Lancey." He came from an ancient family of France, springing from Guy de Lancey Ecuyer, Vicomte De Laval et de Nouvion, who, in 1432, held of the Prince-Bishop of the Duchy of Laon the fiefs of Laval and of Nouvion. The Seigneur Jacques (James) de Lancey, second son of Charles, the fifth Vicomte de Laval, became a Huguenot, and his grandson, Etienne (Stephen) de Lancey, was forced to flee from persecution after the revocation of the Edict of Nantes in 1685. Escaping to London, he became an English subject, and then came to New York. He amassed a fortune as a merchant, and became influential in Colonial affairs, serving as a representative in the Provincial Assembly for twenty-six years, 1702-08, 1710-15 and 1725-37 He married, in 1700, Anne Van Cortlandt, second daughter of Stephanus Van Cortlandt, of the Manor of Cortlandt.

James de Lancey, the eldest son of Etienne (Stephen), was born in 1703, educated in New York and in the University of Cambridge, England, and studied law in the Inner Temple, London. He was a councilor of the Province in 1729 and Judge of the Supreme Court in 1731. In 1730, he was the head of the commission which framed the charter of the City of New York. In 1733, he was commissioned Chief Justice of New York, and filled the office until his death, in 1760. In 1747, he was appointed Lieutenant-Governor, and served during the rest of his life. On the tragic death of Sir Danvers Osborne, in 1753, he succeeded as Governor-in-Chief, serving until Sir Charles Hardy arrived, in 1755 On Governor Hardy's resignation, June 3d, 1757, he again succeeded as Governor-in-Chief, and remained such until his death, a little over three years later. The wife of Governor de Lancey was Anne Heathcote, eldest daughter of Colonel Caleb Heathcote, of West-chester County, Lord of the Manor of Scarsdale, Judge of its Court of Common Pleas, and Mayor of New York

John Peter de Lancey, a younger son of Governor de Lancey, born in 1753, was educated in England, and was a Captain in the regular British Army. After the Revolution, he returned to America and settled upon the Heathcote estate, which he inherited from his mother. In 1785, he married Elizabeth Floyd, daughter of Colonel Richard Floyd, of Long Island. William Heathcote de Lancey, 1797-1865, who became the first Bishop of Western New York, was their youngest and only surviving child. Graduated from Yale College in 1817, Bishop de Lancey was connected with Trinity Church and Grace Church of New York and St. Peter's Church, Philadelphia; was provost of the University of Pennsylvania, 1828-33, and Bishop of Western New York, 1839-65.

Mr. Edward Floyd de Lancey, born October 23d, 1821, at Mamaroneck, N. Y., the present representative of this historic family, is the eldest son of Bishop de Lancey. His mother was Frances Munro, second daughter of Peter Jay Munro. Her paternal grandfather was the Reverend Dr. Henry Munro, the last English rector of St. Peter's Church in Albany, and her paternal grandmother was a daughter of Peter Jay, a descendant of the Van Cortlandts of Yonkers, and the only sister of Chief Justice John Jay, while her maternal grandmother was Eve Van Cortlandt White also a Van Cortlandt of Yonkers. Mr. de Lancey was educated at Geneva, now Hobart, College and the Harvard Law School. He is a lawyer, and belongs to the Bar Association, the St. Nicholas Church and other clubs, and is a member of the American Geographical Society and chairman of the executive committee of the New York Historical Society He is the owner of the old Heathcote estate, Heathcote Hill, Mamaroneck. His wife was Josephine Matilda, eldest daughter of William S de Zeng, of Geneva, N Y., son of Baron Frederick A. de Zeng, Captain in a Saxon regiment in the British service, who married and remained in New York after the Revolution. He has one son living, Edward Etienne de Lancey, one of the engineers on the Croton Aqueduct. The arms of the de Lancey family are: Azure, a tilting lance, proper, point upward with a pennon argent, bearing a cross gules, fringed and floating to the right, debruised of a fess, or. Crest, a sinister arm in armor embowed, the hand grasping a tilting lance, pennon floating, both proper. Motto: *Certum voto pete finem.*

HENRY CHAMPION DEMING

JOHN DEMING, one of the first settlers of Wethersfield, Conn., who often represented that town in the General Court between 1649 and 1661, was the first American ancestor of this family His son was David Deming, and his grandson was the Reverend David Deming, who graduated from Harvard College in 1700, was minister of Medway, Mass, and Middletown, Conn, and married Martha Brigham, of Boston. His son, David Deming, 1709-1781, lived in Lyme, Conn, and married in 1740, Mehitable Champion, 1720-1817, of East Haddam, Conn. Jonathan Deming, their son, entered the Continental Army in 1777, served throughout the war and died in 1788 In 1767, he married, in Colchester, Conn, Alice Skinner, 1747-1824, daughter of the Reverend Thomas and Mary (Thompson) Skinner Their son, David Deming, 1781-1827, the fourth of that name, was engaged in business in Colchester and represented his town in the Connecticut Assembly from 1811 to 1823. In 1819, he was Brigadier-General of the State Artillery He married his cousin, Abigail Champion, 1787-1835.

The Honorable Henry Champion Deming, son of General David and Abigail (Champion) Deming, was the father of Mr Henry Champion Deming, of New York He was born in Colchester in 1815, and died in Hartford in 1872. He was graduated from Yale College in the class of 1836, studied law in the Harvard Law School, graduating in 1839, and came to New York to practice. Literature, however, engaged his attention, and in association with Park Benjamin he started The New World Removing to Hartford in 1847, he practiced law and took an active interest in politics In 1849 and in 1859, he was a member of the Connecticut Assembly, and a State Senator in 1851. He was Mayor of Hartford from 1854 to 1858, and again in 1860 In the Civil War, he became Colonel of the Twelfth Connecticut Volunteers and accompanied the expedition to New Orleans Upon the surrender of that city, he was appointed Provisional Mayor. In 1863, he resigned from the army and, returning to Hartford, was three times elected a Member of Congress, for three successive terms. In 1868, he wrote a life of General Grant, and many of his addresses were published. He married Sarah Clerc, daughter of Laurent and Eliza C (Boardman) Clerc. Laurent Clerc was the founder of deaf mute instruction in America In 1816, he was invited and came from Paris to be the head of the first institution for the instruction of the deaf and dumb in this country.

On the female side, Mr. Henry C. Deming is descended in two lines from Henry Champion, who settled at Saybrook as early as 1647, and was one of the first proprietors of the town of Lyme. His grandson, Lieutenant Henry Champion, born in 1695, married Mehitable Rowley One of their daughters was Mehitable Champion, who in 1740 married David Deming, of Lyme. Colonel Henry Champion, son of Lieutenant Henry Champion, born in 1723, was a distinguished soldier of the Revolutionary War and Commissary-General of the Eastern Department of the Continental Army His son, General Henry Champion, born in 1751, in Westchester, Conn., also had a brilliant military career. He was in the Continental service from the battle of Lexington until the close of the war. He fought at Bunker Hill, was Adjutant of the Twenty-Second Connecticut Regiment at Long Island, and Adjutant-Major of the First Battalion of the Light Brigade. In civil life, he was frequently a deputy to the General Court of Connecticut, and otherwise prominent in public affairs. His daughter, Abigail Champion, married General David Deming, grandfather of the present Mr. Deming.

Mr. Henry C Deming was born in Hartford, Conn, in 1850, and was graduated from Yale College in 1872. For several years he was secretary and is now vice-president of the Mercantile Trust Company. He lives in East Twenty-seventh Street and is a member of the University, Union, Lawyers', Manhattan and Players clubs. His brother, Charles Clerc Deming, is a lawyer and a member of the Union, University and Racquet clubs Another brother, Laurent Clerc Deming, graduated from Yale College in 1883, is secretary of the Atchison, Topeka & Santa Fé Railway Company and a member of the University and other clubs.

CHAUNCEY MITCHELL DEPEW

BORN in Peekskill, N. Y., April 23d, 1834, on an estate which his paternal ancestor purchased from the Indians over two hundred years ago, this eminent citizen of New York is of Huguenot descent The family name, which occurs in the form of both Depew and De Puy, has been identified with the Province and State of New York since its first representatives settled in the town of New Rochelle, Westchester County Isaac Depew, father of the Honorable Chauncey Mitchell Depew, was a respected citizen of Peekskill, and married Martha Mitchell, daughter of Chauncey R Mitchell, a distinguished and eloquent lawyer Her mother, Ann Johnston, was a daughter of Judge Robert Johnston, who was Senator and Judge of Putnam County, N Y, for many years, and a large land owner On the maternal side, Mr Depew also descends from one of the most prominent New England Revolutionary families, his mother having been a granddaughter of the Reverend Josiah Sherman, brother of Roger Sherman, the signer of the Declaration of Independence. The Reverend Josiah Sherman was Chaplain of the Seventh Connecticut Regiment of the Continental Line, and three of his brothers were also in the Patriot Army

Entering Yale College, Chauncey Mitchell Depew graduated in 1856 His alma mater in 1887 conferred upon him the degree of LL D, and he has ever been prominent in promoting the interests of Yale Immediately after graduation, he began the study of law with the Honorable William Nelson, in his native town, in 1858 He was an adherent of the Republican party, and early became noted as an effective political speaker Taking an active part in the Lincoln presidential campaign of 1860, he was elected to the New York State Legislature in 1861, reelected in 1862, and in 1863 successfully headed the Republican State ticket as candidate for Secretary of State He subsequently declined the post of Minister to Japan, to which he was appointed by President Johnson, and was an unwilling candidate for the Lieutenant-Governorship in 1872 Though prominent in the councils of his party, he has accepted no public office in late years Indeed, in 1884, he declined a unanimous tender of the United States Senatorship by the Republican party in the Legislature, and also the position of Secretary of State of the United States, which was offered by President Benjamin Harrison At the Republican National Convention of 1888 he received the unanimous support of the New York delegation for the Presidential nomination, and a flattering vote

Political ambition in Mr Depew's case has been subordinated to his business responsibilities. In 1866, his friendship for Commodore Cornelius Vanderbilt and his son, William H Vanderbilt, led to his becoming attorney for the New York & Harlem Railroad, and when Commodore Vanderbilt, in 1869, acquired control of the New York Central and consolidated it with the Hudson River Railroad, he was elected a director In 1875, he became general counsel for all the Vanderbilt railroad companies In 1882, when William H Vanderbilt retired from the presidency, Mr Depew became second vice-president of the New York Central, and in 1885, on the death of James H Rutter, succeeded to the presidency, an office which he still holds, being at the same time president, vice-president, or a director, of all the railroads and other companies of the Vanderbilt system In 1871, Mr Depew married Elise Hegeman, of New York, who died in 1893 One son, Chauncey M Depew, Jr, was the result of this union.

As a public speaker Mr Depew's reputation is established He has been the orator on many public occasions, including the celebration of Washington's inauguration as the first President, the dedication of Bartholdi's Statue of Liberty, the centennial of the formation of the Government of the State of New York, and the opening of the World's Fair at Chicago He was seven times president of the Union League Club, ten times of the Yale Alumni, twice of the St. Nicholas Society, and seven times of the Sons of the American Revolution, in which, as befits his Revolutionary lineage, he is deeply interested, while he is also prominent in the Holland Society and the Huguenot Society of America

FREDERIC JAMES de PEYSTER

DESCENDED through the eldest surviving male representatives in successive generations, Mr. Frederic James de Peyster is now at the head of that historic New York family whose name he bears. He is in the seventh generation from Johannes de Peyster, the founder of the family in New York, a gentleman of noble blood, who was distinguished among the original Colonists of New Netherland by his wealth and business ability. His ancestors fled from France to Holland, in the sixteenth century; he was born in the latter country, and came to New Amsterdam about 1645. Among other positions that he held was that of schepen in 1677, alderman, 1666-69, and burgomaster in 1675.

Colonel Abraham de Peyster, 1698-1728, son of Johannes de Peyster, was a native of New Amsterdam, and one of its most public-spirited citizens, being a councilor, an alderman, Judge of the Supreme Court, Mayor of the city in 1691, Acting Governor in 1701, and treasurer in 1706. He was a strong advocate of public improvements, and among other benefactions presented to the city the plot of ground on which the old City Hall was built in Wall Street. He married a cousin, Catherine de Peyster. Abraham de Peyster, Jr., 1696-1767, the eldest son in his father's family, was a figure of prominence in Colonial affairs, being provincial treasurer from 1721 until the time of his death, a period of over forty-five years. His wife, whom he married in 1722, was Margaret Van Cortlandt, daughter of Jacobus Van Cortlandt and Eve Philipse. He had eleven children. James de Peyster, his eldest son, who was born in 1726, married, in 1748, Sarah Reade, daughter of the Honorable Joseph Reade, one of the king's councilors The line of descent through the third Abraham de Peyster, eldest son of James and Sarah de Peyster, failed through the successive death of all the male members of his family without male issue. His brother, James de Peyster, left no children, The youngest son, Frederic de Peyster, married for his first wife, Helen Hake, daughter of Samuel Hake. After her death in 1801, he married Ann Beekman, only daughter of Gerard G. Beekman, and granddaughter of Lieutenant-Governor Pierre Van Cortlandt.

Captain James Ferguson de Peyster, eldest son of Frederic de Peyster and Helen Hake, became the head of the family. Frederic de Peyster, Jr., who was the first president of the New York Historical Society, and father of General John Watts de Peyster, was his brother. He entered the United States Army in 1814, at the age of twenty-one, being commissioned as First Lieutenant of the Forty-Second Infantry, and was shortly promoted to be Captain In later years he was active in civil life in New York, being particularly identified with educational matters, as a member of the Board of Education, and as trustee of the College of the City of New York.

Mr. Frederic J. de Peyster, son of Captain James F. de Peyster, and Frances Goodhue Ashton, was born in New York, February 5th, 1859, and was graduated from the College of the City of New York in 1860, and from the Columbia College Law School two years later. He has practiced his profession with success, most of his time, however, being fully occupied with the care of his family property. But he is more generally known from his connection with educational, charitable, and other public institutions. He is president of the Holland Society, a governor of the Society of Colonial Wars, president of the New York Dispensary, and of the St. Nicholas and Orpheus Societies, and chairman of the New York Society Library. He belongs to the University, St Nicholas, City and Century clubs

In 1871, Mr de Peyster married Augusta McEvers Morris, daughter of William H. Morris, of Morrisania. The paternal grandfather of Mrs. de Peyster was James Morris, who married Helen Van Cortlandt, daughter of Augustus Van Cortlandt and Helen Barclay; he was the fourth son of Lewis Morris, one of the signers of the Declaration of Independence, by his wife, Mary Walton, daughter of Jacob Walton and Maria Beekman Mr. and Mrs de Peyster have three daughters, Helen Van Cortlandt, F G and M A. de Peyster, and one son, Frederic Ashton de Peyster. The residence of the family is in East Forty-second Street, near Fifth Avenue, and their country home is at Lake Placid, N Y.

JOHN WATTS DE PEYSTER

SIXTH in descent from Johannes de Peyster, the ancestor of one of the most distinguished families that are recorded in the annals of New York, was Frederick de Peyster, Jr., father of General John Watts de Peyster. The line of descent from Johannes de Peyster to Frederick de Peyster, Jr., was through Abraham de Peyster, first of the name, 1657-1728, Abraham de Peyster, second, and his wife, Catharine, Abraham de Peyster, third, 1696-1767, and his wife, Margaret Van Cortlandt, James de Peyster and his wife, Sarah Reade, and Frederick de Peyster, Sr. The youngest son of James de Peyster, Frederick de Peyster, Sr, was, with his elder brothers, the third Abraham de Peyster and James de Peyster, prominent in military affairs Each was Captain of a company in the King's Regiment before they had scarcely attained their majority

Frederick de Peyster, Jr, was born in New York in 1796 and died at the family homestead, Rose Hill, Dutchess County, N Y, in 1872 Although the youngest son, he became the most distinguished member of his father's family. Graduated from Columbia College, he was active in public and private life, and was called upon by his fellow citizens to fill many positions of trust and responsibility He is especially remembered as the first president of the New York Historical Society. In 1820, he married Mary Justina Watts, daughter of the Honorable John Watts

The founder of the Watts family in New York was Robert Watts, a Scotch gentleman of birth, whose family owned the estate of Rosehill, near Edinburgh. He came hither towards the close of the seventeenth century, was a member of the Council, married Mary, a daughter of William Nicholls and Anna Van Rensselaer, and was the father of the Honorable John Watts, Sr., also a Councilor of the Province and President of the King's Council, who married Ann de Lancey. John Watts, Jr, called The Recorder, to distinguish him from his father, the Councilor, was born in 1749 and died in 1836, having been the last Recorder of the city under the royal authority. He married Jane, daughter of Peter de Lancey and Elizabeth Colden. His special claim to remembrance is firmly established by the foundation of the Leake and Watts Asylum, to which he bequeathed a large portion of his wealth.

General John Watts de Peyster was born in New York in 1821, and married Estelle, daughter of John Swift Livingston Possessed of wealth, he adopted no active profession, but has devoted his life to literature and to the interests of his native city and State. Military life had great attraction for him, and in 1845 he was commissioned a Colonel of the National Guard, becoming Brigadier-General in 1851, and in 1855 Adjutant-General of the State. In 1866, the brevet rank of Major-General was conferred on him by concurrent action of the State Legislature, for services to the State and United States prior to and during the Civil War. He has taken an active part in various municipal reforms, particularly the organization of the police force on its present basis and the establishment of a paid fire department. His literary activity also has been noteworthy, embracing frequent contributions to periodicals, as well as a number of historical and other works, among which may be mentioned The Life of Torstenson, 1855, The Dutch at the North Pole, 1857, and The Personal and Military History of General Philip Kearny, 1869, the latter being his cousin.

The permanent residence of General de Peyster is Rose Hill, at Tivoli-on-Hudson For fifty years he has been a prominent figure in metropolitan literary, social and philanthropic circles. He is a member of the Century Association, the Military Order of the Loyal Legion, the St Nicholas Society, the Holland Society, and other leading organizations of the city. Three sons of General de Peyster were in the Union Army during the Civil War, and two of them lost their lives. His eldest son, John Watts de Peyster, Jr., was a Major, and was breveted Colonel for distinguished services at Chancellorsville. Frederic de Peyster, Jr, was breveted Colonel for gallantry at the first battle of Bull Run. The third son, Johnston L de Peyster, hoisted the first American flag 'over the capitol in Richmond, Va., in 1865 and received the brevet of Lieutenant-Colonel and Colonel in recognition of his bravery He married Annie Toler and now lives in New York.

MRS. NICHOLAS de PEYSTER

UPON preceding pages of this volume the history of Johannes de Peyster, who came to New Amsterdam in the early part of the seventeenth century and founded a family that has been one of the most distinguished in the annals of New York City and State, in Colonial, Revolutionary and contemporaneous times, has been fully reviewed   His name and that of his son and grandson, Abraham de Peyster and Abraham de Peyster, Jr., will be always conspicuously identified with the commencement of New York's civic life.   The descendants of this Huguenot gentleman have had a large part in public affairs and in every generation have conspicuously adorned public and private life.   In their several branches they have been connected in marriage with all the great Colonial families of New York, and those who bear the name to-day trace their lineage to the Van Cortlandts, Livingstons, Reades, Beekmans, Schuylers and others famous in the early history of New Netherland and New York.

Nicholas de Peyster, the husband of the lady whose family is under consideration in this article, was one of the leading representatives of this historic house in the present generation.   He was a native of New York, where he spent most of his life and where he died February 17th, 1889. His father was George de Peyster and his mother Lydia Jackson, of Long Island, his grandfather being Nicholas de Peyster and his grandmother Marion de Kay.   He received a thorough education under private tutors, and inherited large means from the estates of his father and grandfather.   He was among the pioneers to California in 1849 and was very successful there.   After returning to the East he lived the life of a gentleman of leisure and cultivated tastes, being thoroughly identified with the social and material interests of the metropolis and spending much time in foreign travel He was a member of the St Nicholas, American Yacht and New York clubs and the Century Association.

Before her marriage, in 1871, Mrs. Nicholas de Peyster was Marianna Moore, daughter of William Stewart Moore, of New York.   She was a relative of Clement C Moore, the celebrated scholar and professor of Hebrew in the New York Theological Seminary for more than forty years, and who gave to the seminary the land upon which its buildings stand.   He was a son of Bishop Benjamin Moore, compiled the earliest Hebrew and Greek lexicons published in America, and is known wherever the English language is spoken as the author of that popular household poem beginning, "'Twas the night before Christmas."

Mrs. de Peyster is also descended from Governor Thomas Dongan, who came to New York in 1682, under appointment of King James II, and gave to the city its famous charter of 1686, ever since known as the Dongan Charter, which, after the lapse of two hundred years, has continued to influence the destinies of the city.   Governor Dongan was the youngest son of Sir John Dongan, an Irish Baronet, and nephew to Richard Talbot, Earl of Tyrconnel.   He was created Earl of Limerick by George I.

Mrs. de Peyster still lives in West Fifteenth Street, in the family mansion that was occupied for sixty years by her maternal grandparents   The house is one of the old-time residences of the city, and contains one of the finest collections of rare antiques and paintings in New York.   Among the pictures in Mrs. de Peyster's possession are, a Reubens, a Vanderlyn, a Sir David Wilkie and many other masterpieces, including the Hemicycle at Rome.   Mrs de Peyster has traveled much in Europe and has been entertained by members of the nobility in Great Britain and on the Continent. At her home in this city she has received many distinguished guests.   She also has a summer home on the ocean front at Long Branch.   The only son of Mr. and Mrs. de Peyster is William Moore Dongan de Peyster, who has already achieved reputation by his interest in sports   He rides to hounds, and his hunters are among the noted horses of their class in the vicinity of New York. Mr de Peyster performed a notably heroic deed a few years ago in stopping a runaway team at Long Branch, thereby saving the lives of two ladies.   He is a life member of the New York Historical Society, and a patron of the American Museum of Natural History

HENRY DEXTER

CHIEF JUSTICE of Ireland in 1307, Richard de Exeter was doubtless the ancestor of the Dexter family. His immediate descendants resided for many generations in County Meath, the family name in the course of time being changed to its present form of spelling. Richard Dexter, born in 1606, fled from Ireland, his native land, before the great Irish Rebellion and massacre in the time of the English Commonwealth and sought refuge in New England. He was admitted a freeman of Boston, Mass., and resided in both Malden and Charlestown, dying at the latter town in 1680. John Dexter, his only son of whom there is any record, was born in Ireland in 1639 and died in Malden in 1677. Richard Dexter, of Lynn and Malden, Mass., was born in Malden in 1676 and died there in 1747. He was the second son of John Dexter and married, in 1697, Sarah Bucknam, daughter of Joses and Judith (Worth) Bucknam. Land purchased by Richard Dexter in 1663 in Malden has remained continuously in the hands of his descendants down to the present time. Richard Dexter, of the next generation, 1714-1773, married, in 1741, Rebecca, daughter of David and Sarah (Pope) Peabody, of a Massachusetts family that has been preeminently distinguished in subsequent generations both in the United States and Europe, and which, through the marriages of its members with other noteworthy families, is constantly referred to in these pages.

David Dexter, son of the third Richard Dexter, was born in Malden in 1745 and died in Boston in 1821. He was at different times a resident of Haverhill and Woburn, Mass., and Pembroke, Hampstead and Atkinson, N. H. His wife was Lydia Marsh, daughter of Jonathan and Elizabeth (Merrill) Marsh, and a descendant of the oldest families of Haverhill and Newbury. Dr. Aaron Dexter, of Boston, professor in Harvard College, 1783-1829, was a younger brother of David Dexter. Jonathan Marsh Dexter, of Billerica and West Cambridge, Mass., and New York, who was born in Haverhill, Mass., March 24th, 1775, and died in New York March 26th, 1861, was the eldest son of David Dexter and the father of Mr. Henry Dexter. His wife, whom he married in 1808, was Elizabeth Balch, daughter of Joseph and Abigail (Audebert) Balch. Joseph Balch's mother was of the distinguished Cushing family, famous in the annals of Massachusetts, and her maternal grandmother was a Palfrey, belonging to another notable New England race which has produced many men and women of distinction.

Mr. Henry Dexter was born in West Cambridge, Mass., March 14th, 1813. He was educated in the public schools of his native city and began his business career at an early age, being employed in several publishing houses in Boston and Cambridge. When he was twenty-three years of age, he removed to New York City and was for some time engaged in the hardware business with the Whittemores, the famous inventors of cotton card-making machines. His experience with publishing firms had fixed his mind upon that line of activity and he became convinced of the great possibilities in the wholesale trade in books, newspapers and periodicals. An elder brother had already been engaged in this business for some time in a small way. In 1842, Mr. Dexter joined his brother and in a short time conceived the original plans of the American News Company, which, however, he was not able to realize fully until 1864, when the company was organized with Mr. Dexter as its first president, a position which he still holds, while under his charge the concern has attained a marked success.

In 1853, Mr. Dexter married Lucretia Marquand Perry, daughter of Orrando Perry, of Easton, Conn.; he has one daughter and one son. His son, Orrando Perry Dexter, who was born in 1854, was graduated from Oxford University, England, in 1878, taking the degree of A. M. in 1881, and subsequently pursuing a law course in this city at the Columbia College Law School, was graduated in 1880 with the degree of LL. B. He is a practicing lawyer and has written much, principally on genealogical and mathematical subjects. The Dexter family owns a large tract of land in the Adirondacks, where their summer residence is situated. The city residence of Mr. Dexter is in West Fifty-sixth Street.

LOUIS PALMA DI CESNOLA

AS early as 1094, the noble family of Palma di Monte San Giuliano, which originally came from Spain, resided in Sicily. The Counts of Palma di Cesnola, of Rivarolo in Piedmont, are an offshoot of this ancient race. Pietro Palma, a Captain in the Army of Manfred, King of Sicily, was sent in 1260 on a diplomatic mission to Piedmont. His royal master was slain at the battle of Benevento in 1263, and he remained in Piedmont, and in 1262 was invested with feudal rights over the town of Rivarossa. The family of Palma removed in the fifteenth century from Salassa to Rivarolo, near Turin, where its representatives still live and are the proprietors of palaces and estates. Four generations ago the family divided into two branches, the Counts Palma di Cesnola, and a junior branch, the Counts Palma di Borgofranco.

General Louis Palma di Cesnola was born at the house of his ancestors in Rivarolo, Piedmont, June 29th, 1832, and was the son of Count Victor Maurice Palma di Cesnola and his wife, Countess Eugenia Ricca di Castelvecchio, his grandparents being Count Emmanuele and Countess Irene Grassotti. Being destined for the priesthood, he was educated at Ivrea and the University of Turin, but when the war of 1848 broke out his patriotic ardor carried him into the Sardinian Army as a volunteer. He at once displayed soldierly qualities, and for bravery at the battle of Novara was promoted, in 1849, to the rank of Lieutenant, being at the time the youngest commissioned officer in the Sardinian service. After the war, he entered the military academy at Cherasco, graduating in 1851. He served thereafter for several years in the army as aide-de-camp of General Ansaldi, and was in the Sardinian contingent sent to the Crimean War.

In 1860, he came to New York and in the following year was commissioned a Major and then Lieutenant-Colonel of the Eleventh New York Volunteer Cavalry ("Scott's Nine Hundred"), and in 1862, was appointed Colonel of the Fourth New York Cavalry. In 1863, he was wounded and taken prisoner at Aldie, Va., and was for nine months confined in Libby Prison, Richmond, but was exchanged. His bravery and efficiency as a cavalry officer were frequently recognized officially, and among other incidents of a like character, General Judson Kilpatrick, in 1863, in personally complimenting him on his conduct in the field after several brilliant cavalry charges, presented him with his own sword. During the Shenandoah Valley campaign, under General Sheridan, he was at the head of Devin's Brigade, seeing service which was not interrupted till the term of service of his regiment expired, at the end of 1864, and early in 1865, President Lincoln conferred on him the rank of Brevet Brigadier-General.

General di Cesnola had married, on the 11th of June, 1861, Mary Isabel Jennings Reid, daughter of Captain Samuel C. Reid, of New York, and in due time became an American citizen. In 1865, having been appointed United States Consul to Cyprus, he became interested in archæological investigations. Armed with a firman from the Sultan, he instituted researches, identifying the remains of the ancient cities of Idalium, Salamis, Citium and Golgos, at the latter of which he uncovered the ruins of the Temple of Venus, and discovered hundreds of statues and other objects. In 1873, he returned to America, bringing a collection of many thousand objects, comprising statuary, bronzes, vases, gems and coins, the whole of which was acquired for the newly established Metropolitan Museum of Art, in New York. Going back to Cyprus, though hampered by the hostility of Turkish officials, General di Cesnola continued his researches, identified other cities, and, in 1875, explored the ruins of Paphos, Amathus and Curium, where he discovered further treasures, which were added to the collection at the Metropolitan Museum, raising it to forty thousand objects and making it an unrivaled presentation of ancient Cypriote civilization. In 1877, the United States Consulate to the island was abolished, and General di Cesnola occupied himself with the preparation of his great work, Cyprus, its Ancient Cities, Tombs and Temples, published in 1878. Universities and learned societies throughout the world recognized the value of his labors, and among other distinctions, both Columbia and Princeton Universities conferred upon him the degree of LL. D., while he was elected an honorary member of the Royal Society of London, of the Royal Academy of Sciences of Turin, and of many similar bodies. Victor Emmanuel, King of Italy, and the King of Bavaria, bestowed knightly orders and decorations on him, and King Humbert, of Italy, caused a gold medal to be struck in honor of his labors.

In 1878, having arranged the Cypriote collection at the Metropolitan Museum, the General was elected a trustee and secretary of the institution, and in 1879, he was also made its director. In this position during nearly twenty years General di Cesnola's executive ability, learning and artistic taste have been of incalculable service to the museum, the city and the cause of art and archæology.

Madame di Cesnola, whose marriage to the General, in 1861, has already been referred to, is of a parentage illustrious in our country's history. She was the second daughter of Captain Reid, the hero of the naval battle of Fayal. Her grandfather was Lieutenant John Reid, of the British Navy, a lineal descendant of Henry Reid, Earl of Orkney. While in command of a British expedition against New London, Conn., in 1778, Lieutenant Reid was captured by the Americans, and after a lengthy detention as a prisoner of war, resigned his commission, remained in this country, and in 1781, married Rebecca Chester, daughter of Colonel John Chester, of Norwich, Conn. The Chesters were descended from the ancient Earls of Chester. Sir Robert Chester, who was knighted by James I, in 1603, had a son, Captain Samuel Chester, who, in 1662, emigrated to Connecticut and settled in New London. His grandson, John Chester, served at Lexington and Bunker Hill, and was an officer in the Army of the Revolution.

Samuel Chester Reid was born at Norwich, Conn., in 1783. At eleven years of age he went to sea, and afterwards entered the United States Navy as a midshipman, and on the outbreak of the War of 1812, took command of the American privateer brig, General Armstrong, of New York, which he made one of the efficient vessels of its class. So great was the exasperation of the British Navy against the General Armstrong, that, finding her in the harbor of Fayal, in September, 1814, a British squadron endeavored to cut the Armstrong out. Captain Reid's crew was ninety men. Under his leadership they fought with superhuman valor, and the British only gained the deck to retire repulsed after one of the most desperate conflicts in naval history. Captain Reid then scuttled and abandoned his vessel rather than allow her to be captured, and on his return to New York, he was received with the distinction his heroism merited, among other marks of honor being the presentation by the city of a silver service, and a gold sword, in company with General Scott and General P. B. Porter. For some years afterwards he was an officer in the navy, but retiring, became Warden of the Port of New York. He organized the present pilot system, established a marine telegraph between Sandy Hook and New York City, and founded the Marine Society. Another of his notable services was the designing, in 1818, of the national flag in its present form, so as to symbolize the motto of the United States, "E Pluribus Unum." Stripes and stars were then being added to it, on the admission of each new State, and the flag had become unwieldy in form. Captain Reid proposed that in future the stripes should be reduced to thirteen, commemorative of the original States, and the stars formed into one great star, Government flags to have stars in parallel lines. This design was adopted by an Act of Congress to Establish the Flag of the United States, approved 31st March, 1818. The first flag of this design was made by the wife of Captain Reid, and was first raised over the capitol at Washington, on the 13th of April, 1818. Captain Reid died in 1861, after a useful and honored life. His wife was Mary, daughter of Captain Nathan Jennings, of Wilmington, Conn., who fought at Lexington, at the battle of Trenton, and other engagements of the Revolution.

General and Madame di Cesnola have two daughters, Eugenie Gabrielle and Louise Irene di Cesnola. The family residence is 109 East Fifty-seventh Street. The General's country seat, La Favorita, is an estate of seventy-six acres, in the village of New Castle, Westchester County, N. Y. The arms of Palma di Cesnola are : a palm tree, proper, crest, a count's coronet, supported by a lion and a crowned eagle, proper. Motto : *Oppressa Resurgit.*

175

HORACE EDWARD DICKINSON

THE Dickinsons are descended from an old English county family of Yorkshire. Through one of his ancestors in the sixteenth century, Mr Horace E. Dickinson can trace his lineage direct to King Edward III., of England. The line of descent from this royal ancestor is through Joan of Beaufort, daughter of King Edward's son, John, of Gaunt, Duke of Lancaster. Joan of Beaufort married Ralph Nevill, the first Earl of Westmoreland, and her great-grandson, Richard Nevill, second Lord Latimer, had a daughter, Elizabeth Nevill. The husband of Elizabeth Nevill was Sir Christopher Danby, High Sheriff of Yorkshire, in 1545, and great-grandson of Sir Richard Danby, of Farnley, who was Chief Justice of the Court of Common Pleas, 1460–72 Elizabeth Danby, the daughter of Sir Christopher Danby and his wife, Elizabeth, married John Dickinson, of Leeds, one of the leading woolen merchants and cloth manufacturers of his day, and an alderman of the city from 1525 until the time of his death, in 1554. John Dickinson and his wife, Elizabeth, were the ancestors of Mr. Horace E. Dickinson.

John Dickinson was in the ninth generation from the first of the family name in England, Johnne Dykonson, who was a freeholder of Kingston-upon-Hull, East Riding, of Yorkshire, in the reigns of Henry III. and Edward I and II His wife was Margaret, daughter of Sir Thomas Lambert, of Pinchbeck, Lincolnshire, and of the Well Close, in Hull, an estate that came into her possession after her father's death Well Close was originally an old Saxon monastery, dating from the time of St. Cuthbert and the Danes, and took its name from an old well in the close to whose waters peculiar curative powers were ascribed. Hugh Dykensonne, of Hull, a grandson of Johnne Dykonson, was a prominent merchant of that city, and one of the original Governors of the Guild of the Holy Trinity, now called Trinity House. His son, Anthoyne Dickensonne, of Hull, was a merchant and master-builder. He made some extensive repairs to York Minster, in 1385, and also erected the Priory and Hospital of St. Michael, founded by his father-in-law, Sir William de la Pole, who was First Gentleman of the Bed Chamber to Edward III , second Baron of the Exchequer, Collector of the Ports of Boston and Hull, 1338–56, and first Mayor of Hull from 1332–35, and again from 1338–56.

The grandson of Anthoyne Dickensonne was Thomas Dickinson, of Hull, who was the first to spell his name as it is now most commonly used. He was an alderman in 1443, and Mayor in 1444. He married his kinswoman, Margaret Lambert, daughter of Sir Thomas Lambert, of Oulton, County Durham, standard bearer to Richard II. The mother of Margaret Lambert was Joan Umfravill, daughter of Sir Thomas Umfravill, of Harbottle Castle, Northumberland County, and sister of Sir Robert Umfravill, Knight of the Garter and Lord High Admiral of England.

Hugh Dickinson, of Hull, the son of Mayor Thomas Dickinson, and the seventh in descent from the first of the family name, sold the family homestead, Well Close, on the Humber, and bought Kenson Manor, on the Aire, near Leeds. His son, William Dickinson, of Kenson Manor, married Isabel Langton, of Ecclesfield, daughter of John Langton, of Ecclesfield, High Sheriff of Yorkshire in 1509, and his grandson was the John Dickinson who, in the sixteenth century, became the husband of a descendant from King Edward III To this John Dickinson was granted the coat of arms to which the family has since been entitled · Azure, a fesse ermine between two lions passant, or.; crest, a demi-lion rampant, per pale ermine and azure. Motto · *Esse Quam Videri*

William Dickinson, the son of John Dickinson and Elizabeth Danby, removed to the parish of Bradley, South Staffordshire, where his father erected for him a substantial mansion, the lower story of stone and the upper stories of timber This he named Bradley Hall, and it has remained standing and in good preservation down to this generation, as one of the most substantial and picturesque of the old English manor houses. Thomas Dickinson, the grandson of William Dickinson, was connected with the Portsmouth Navy Yard from 1567 to 1587, and settled in Cambridge in 1587, where he married Judith Carey, daughter of William Carey, of Bristol

Three grandsons of Thomas Dickinson, sons of William Dickinson, barrister at law, of Cambridge, came to America in the seventeenth century. The second son, John Dickinson, arrived in Boston, in 1630, and went to live, first at Barnstable, Mass., then at Salisbury, Mass., and finally at Oyster Bay, Long Island. He was a sea captain and became a Quaker. The third son, Thomas Dickinson, also came to Boston, in 1630, and settled at New Haven, in 1643, and Fairfield, Conn., in 1645, dying in the latter place in 1658.

Nathaniel Dickinson, the elder of these three brothers, and from whom the subject of this sketch is descended, was born in Ely, Cambridgeshire, England, in 1600, the fourteenth in descent from the original Johanne Dykonson, of the thirteenth century. Educated at Cambridge, he became a non-conformist and joined the Cambridge Company that was formed in August, 1629, by Winthrop, Dudley and Saltonstall, and sailed from Southampton for Massachusetts in March of the next year. He first settled at Watertown, Mass., where he remained for five years, and then removed to Wethersfield, Conn. In 1637, he was a freeman of that town, recorder or town clerk, 1640–59, and a representative to the General Court and selectmen, 1646–56. With the Reverend Mr. Russell, he was appointed to lay out the town of Hadley, Mass., to which place he removed in 1659. There he was town clerk in 1660, rate maker, 1661–76; selectman, 1660 and 1666; member of the Hampshire Troop of Horse, 1663; one of the committee to build the meeting house in 1661, and school director, 1669–76. He was the progenitor of all the New England Dickinsons.

The seventh son of Nathaniel Dickinson, the American pioneer, himself named Nathaniel Dickinson, lived in Wethersfield, Conn., and Hadley and Hatfield, Mass., being a selectman and surveyor of the latter town. He died in 1710. His grandson, John Dickinson, 1707-1799, was a Colonel and Revolutionary soldier, a Captain in the French-Indian Wars, and, in the War for Independence, Lieutenant-Colonel of the Second Hampshire Regiment of Militia.

General Lemuel Dickinson, son of Lieutenant-Colonel John Dickinson, was also a soldier of the Revolution. He was born in Hatfield, Mass., in 1753. In the Revolutionary War he was a private, in Captain Joseph Raymond's company, that formed a part of Colonel Hyde's Regiment of Massachusetts Militia. Afterwards he was commissioned Captain, and then a Colonel, in the Massachusetts Militia, and during Shays Rebellion was Brigadier General of the troops. His wife, whom he married in 1770, was Molly Little, who was a descendant of Richard Warren, who came over in the Mayflower. Richard Warren was a descendant in the direct male line from William, first Earl de Warrenre, who married Gundred, daughter of William the Conqueror. Molly Little was also a descendant of three Colonial Governors, John Haynes, of Massachusetts and Connecticut, Thomas Dudley, of Massachusetts, and George Wyllys, of Connecticut. General Dickinson died in 1835. His eldest son, Horace Dickinson, was born in Hatfield, Mass., in 1780. Horace Dickinson removed to Canada, when he was about thirty years of age, and became a prosperous merchant in Montreal, establishing a line of mail and passenger steamers and coaches from Montreal to Kingston. He married Amelia, daughter of Abijah Bigelow, of Waltham, Mass., who was a minute man at Lexington, fought at Bunker Hill, and in the Revolutionary War.

Mr. Horace Edward Dickinson, the grandson of Horace Dickinson, of Montreal, Canada, is in the twenty-first generation of descent from Johanne Dykonson, of England, and in the seventh generation of descent from Nathaniel Dickinson, who came to America in 1630. He was born in New York City, in 1858, and is now engaged in the dry goods importing business. He lives at 85 East Sixty-fifth Street, and belongs to the New York Athletic and Knickerbocker Riding clubs, and is a member of the Sons of the Revolution.

In 1887, Mr. Dickinson married Nellie R. Poulet, daughter of Alexis Poulet and Rebecca Acton. Through her mother, Mrs. Dickinson is a lineal descendant of Captain Richard Acton, of the English Navy, the third son of Sir Edward Acton, Baronet of Aldenham Hall, County Salop. He fought under Admiral Blake against the Dutch in 1650-60, and came to Maryland with Governor Charles Calvert, about 1665, settling at Calverton, in Anne Arundel County, where he died.

JOHN FORREST DILLON

BORN in Northampton, Montgomery County, N Y., December 25th, 1831, John Forrest Dillon was only seven years of age when his parents removed to Davenport, Ia., which at that time was a village far upon the frontier There the family lived for many years, and there the future Judge Dillon was brought up and made his home for forty years. In early life, he had an inclination to the study of medicine, and applied himself to that pursuit for about three years Eventually, however, he determined to become a lawyer, but when he was about twenty years of age, the death of his father led him to go into business life, in which he was engaged until 1852. During this time, however, he continued his legal studies, and in 1852 was admitted to the bar, becoming a partner in the firm of Cook & Dillon, which was afterwards Cook, Dillon & Lindley.

The same year that he began to practice, he was elected State prosecuting attorney for Scott County, Ia. In 1858, he was elected Judge of the Seventh Judicial District of Iowa, and from that time on his judicial career was uninterrupted for about twenty years He served two terms as incumbent of the judicial office to which he was first elected, and six years as a Judge of the Supreme Court of Iowa. Reëlected to that position in 1869, he resigned to accept an appointment as United States Circuit Judge for the Eighth Judicial Circuit, which embraced the States of Minnesota, Iowa, Nebraska, Missouri, Kansas, Arkansas and Colorado. As a Judge he had a reputation throughout the country for his uprightness, for the fullness of his legal knowledge and for the breadth, originality and soundness of his opinions.

In 1879, Judge Dillon was offered the position of professor of real estate and equity jurisprudence in the Law School of Columbia College. That position he accepted and removed to New York in September, 1879, returning to private practice in conjunction with his duties in the law school. He became general counsel for the Union Pacific Railroad Company and formed a law partnership with General Wager Swayne, which continued for several years. He is now the senior member of the firm of Dillon & Hubbard, is counsel for the Union Pacific Railroad, and also general counsel in New York for the Missouri Pacific Railway system and other railroad corporations.

Judge Dillon is recognized as one of the greatest corporation lawyers of the United States, and also has a high reputation as an author of legal works. During his career in Iowa, he established and edited The Central Law Journal, the only law periodical published in the Mississippi Valley at that time. He also edited and published The Digest of Iowa Reports and a five-volume edition of United States Circuit Court Reports. He is the author of Dillon on Municipal Corporations, a work which has passed through many editions and has been characterized as a legal classic. It is constantly cited as an authority by the courts, not only in the United States, but in all English-speaking countries Another of his works is The Laws and Jurisprudence of England and America, which was originally a series of lectures delivered at the Yale Law School. He has also published many occasional addresses and lectures on legal subjects. In 1875, Judge Dillon made a tour of Europe and attended the third annual conference of the Association for the Reform and Codification of the Law of Nations, which met at The Hague, and of which he was a member. He made a second tour of Europe in 1883, and the following year was elected a member of L'Institut de Droit International. In 1896, he was a member of the commission appointed to draw up the charter for the Greater New York.

In 1853, Judge Dillon married a daughter of the Honorable Hiram Price, of Davenport, Ia., and has had a family of two sons and two daughters. His elder son, Hiram Price Dillon, was graduated from the Law School of the University of Iowa, and is now a practicing lawyer in Kansas The other son, John M. Dillon, is also a lawyer, and a graduate from the Columbia Law School. He married Lucy Downing. Judge Dillon is a member of the Bar Association of the City of New York and of the Union League, Lawyers' and University clubs, and is a patron of the Metropolitan Museum of Art He resides at his country home, Knowlcroft, in Far Hills, N. J.

WILLIAM B DINSMORE

IN Ireland and Scotland, the names of Dunsmore, Dinsmuir and Dinsmore are frequently found, the different forms all pertaining to different branches of the same family. In Ireland, many Dinsmoors have been located from time immemorial in the vicinity of Ballymoney, County Antrim. They are probably descended from John Dinsmoor, who emigrated from Scotland to Ulster. Laird Dinsmoor, the progenitor of the family and the earliest known ancestor, was a Scotchman, who was born about 1600. John Dinsmore, the son of Laird Dinsmoor, who was born in Scotland about 1650, left the paternal home and removed to the Province of Ulster.

John Dinsmore, who was born in Ballywattick, Ballymoney, County Antrim, Ireland, as early as 1671, was the son of John Dinsmore and grandson of Laird Dinsmoor. He was the progenitor of nearly all the Dinsmoors or Dinsmores who have been distinguished in the history of New England. Coming to America about 1723, he was early taken prisoner by the Indians, but finally settled in the Scotch Colony of Londonderry, N. H. Afterwards he made his home in what is now Windham, Vt., where he prospered as a farmer and died in 1741. Robert Dinsmore, son of the American pioneer, came to New Hampshire in 1730 with his wife, Margaret Orr, whom he had married in Ireland. He became prominent in town affairs and held many public offices. He died in 1751 and his wife died the following year. From Robert Dinsmore and his wife, Margaret Orr, have come many distinguished descendants. One of his grandsons was Colonel Silas Dinsmore, who was born in Windham, N. H., in 1766 and died in Kentucky in 1847. Another distinguished descendant was Governor Samuel Dinsmore, who was born in 1766, graduated from Dartmouth College, was a member of the National House of Representatives and Governor of the State of New Hampshire. His son, Samuel Dinsmore, was also Governor of New Hampshire. Among other distinguished descendants from Robert Dinsmore, have been the Honorable Leonard Allison Morrison, member of the House and Senate of the New Hampshire Legislature, and the Reverend C. M. Dinsmore, the Methodist clergyman.

A prominent representative of the family in the last generation, and in the eighth generation of descent from Laird Dinsmoor, was William B. Dinsmore, well known in the business world from his long-time connection with the Adams Express Company. He was born in Boston in 1810 and spent his boyhood days upon a farm in New Hampshire. Returning to Boston when still a young man, Mr. Dinsmore became associated with Alvin Adams, who was then starting an express line between Boston and New York. Mr. Dinsmore came to New York in 1842 to take charge of the business here, while Mr. Adams was its manager in Boston. His success here from the outset was decided, and soon afterwards he became associated with John Hoey, who in the course of time became his partner. To Mr. Dinsmore and Mr. Hoey, after Alvin Adams, was entirely due the phenomenal success of the Adams Express Company. Upon the death of Alvin Adams, Mr. Dinsmore became president of the company. He was a director in the American Exchange Bank, the Pennsylvania Railroad and other corporations. He owned one of the largest herds of Alderney cattle in the United States, and made his home principally at Staatsburgh, N. Y. His wife was Augusta M. Snow, of Brewster, Mass., and when he died, in 1888, he left two sons, William B. and Clarence Gray Dinsmore.

Mr. William B. Dinsmore, second of the name, was born in New York in 1844 and is secretary of the express company with which his father was so long identified. He married, in 1866, Helen F. Adams, daughter of Alvin Adams, his father's business associate. The home of the family is in East Forty-seventh Street. Mr. and Mrs. Dinsmore have two daughters, Helen Gray, who married R. P. Huntington, and Madeleine I. Dinsmore. Their only son, William B. Dinsmore, Jr., graduated from Harvard University in the class of 1893 and married Marion de Peyster Carey. The senior Mr. Dinsmore is a member of the Union League, New York Athletic, Racquet and New York Yacht clubs. His brother, Clarence Gray Dinsmore, married Kate Jerome and is a member of the Metropolitan and Tuxedo clubs and prominent in social life.

CHARLES HEALY DITSON

NO name is better known in the annals of music in the United States than that of Ditson. Oliver Ditson, who was the first of the family so prominently identified with it, was a native of Boston, where he was born in 1811. His family belonged to the old North End, which a century ago and less was the aristocratic section of the city. Opposite to the home of his boyhood, was the residence of Paul Revere, of Revolutionary renown. The father of Oliver Ditson was a ship owner, and both his parents were of Scottish descent. Oliver Ditson attended school in Boston until prepared for a business life. At an early age, he entered the book store of Colonel Samuel H Parker, and within a few years was a partner with his employer, under the firm name of Parker & Ditson. His musical tastes had already manifested themselves, and before he was out of his teens he was organist and choir leader in the Bulfinch Street Baptist Church, and had organized and led the Malibran Glee Club. In 1840, he bought out his partner and became the sole proprietor of the establishment, entering upon a business that soon brought him both fame and fortune.

Soon after acquiring possession of this business, he gave up bookselling entirely, and began to publish music, an employment for which his natural musical tastes, combined with a keen business sagacity, eminently qualified him. From that time on, he became exclusively a music publisher, and before many years had elapsed the house he had established was one of the foremost concerns in the world in that particular line. He absorbed several other music publishing houses and concentrated the entire business in Boston, investing a large amount of capital in so doing. In 1867, Mr Ditson opened a branch house in New York City, under the direction of his son, with the firm name of Charles H. Ditson & Co. The Philadelphia house of J. E. Ditson & Co, with another son at its head, was established in 1875, the Chicago branch, known as Lyon & Healy, became the largest of its kind in the Northwest, and there was another branch in Boston, known as John C. Haynes & Co. For twenty-one years, Oliver Ditson was president of the Continental National Bank of Boston, and a trustee of the Franklin Savings Bank and of the Boston Safe Deposit Company.

Apart from his services to music in his business, Mr. Ditson was one of the most active and generous supporters of all musical enterprises. He sent talented young people to Europe for study, promoted many orchestral and musical societies and saved the first Peace Jubilee in Boston from failure by subscribing some twenty-five thousand dollars to carry through the enterprise at a time when its discouraged promoters were about to abandon it.

Mr Charles Healy Ditson, who has been at the head of the New York branch of the Ditson publishing house for thirty years, is the eldest son of Oliver Ditson and was born in Boston, Mass, August 11th, 1845, receiving his education in that city. His mother, whom his father married in 1840, was Catharine Delano, of Kingston, Mass, daughter of Benjamin Delano, who was a direct descendant of William Bradford, the second Governor of the Plymouth Colony. Mr Ditson has one elder sister, the widow of Colonel Burr Porter. He had two brothers, James Edward Ditson, who died in 1881, and Frank Oliver Ditson, who died in 1885. For twelve years, Mr. Charles H Ditson was secretary and treasurer of the Music Publishers' Association of the United States. He is now treasurer of the Oliver Ditson Co., of Boston, of Charles H. Ditson & Co., of New York, and of the Oliver Ditson Society for the Relief of Needy Musicians, and is also a trustee of his late father's estate.

In 1890, Mr. Ditson married Alice Maud Tappin, daughter of John Tappin and his wife, Jane Lindsley, and a granddaughter of the Reverend Henry Tappin, all of Mrs. Ditson's ancestors being of English stock. Mr Ditson's city residence is at 17 East Thirty-eighth Street, and he has a country home, the Boulders, in Jackson, N. H. He belongs to the Players Club, and is a member of the New England Society of this city and the Algonquin Club of Boston.

MORGAN DIX, D.D.

THE Dix family were English Puritans, Anthony Dix being a resident of Plymouth, Mass., in 1623, while Edward Dix was a freeman of Watertown, Mass., in 1635, and Ralph Dix was one of the early settlers of Ipswich, Mass. His grandson, Jonathan, born in Reading, Mass., removed to Contocook, afterwards Boscawen, N. H, and was the father of Timothy Dix, a Lieutenant in the Revolution and postmaster at Boscawen under President Jefferson. Timothy Dix, Jr, was a member of the State Legislature, 1801-4 In the War of 1812, he held a commission in the regular army and at the time of his death, in 1813, was Lieutenant-Colonel of the Fourteenth Infantry. His wife was Abigail Wilkins, of Amherst, N. H., whose father was a Captain in the Revolution and perished during Montgomery's expedition against Quebec.

General John A. Dix, son of Timothy and Abigail Dix, was born in Boscawen, N. H., in 1798 He was entered in the college of the Sulpicians, in Montreal, but upon the opening of the War of 1812 was appointed a cadet in the United States Army. In 1813, when he lacked four months of being fifteen years old, he received a commission as ensign and was assigned to the Fourteenth Infantry, stationed at Sackett's Harbor, under command of his father, being the youngest officer in the service. In 1814, he became a Third Lieutenant and was assigned to the artillery, and during the war rendered valuable service to his country In 1816, he became First Lieutenant, in 1819 was aide-de-camp to Major-General Jacob Brown, Commander-in-Chief of the army, while in 1825 he was Captain of the Third Artillery. After thirteen years of military service, he resigned from the army, married, and was admitted to the bar in 1828. Politics, however, engaged his attention, and in 1831 he was appointed Adjutant-General of the State; in 1833 he became Secretary of the State of New York, and in 1842 he was elected to the Legislature. In 1845, he was elected United States Senator to fill the vacancy caused by the resignation of Silas Wright, who had been chosen Governor, and served four years in that position. He was Assistant Treasurer of the United States in New York City in 1853 and Postmaster of New York in 1859.

When the Civil War was impending, he was made Secretary of the Treasury in the cabinet of President Buchanan ; and when the war actually began, promptly offered his services to President Lincoln, and was successively appointed Brigadier-General and Major-General of Volunteers, and afterwards elevated to the same rank in the regular army His services were energetic and valuable. In 1863, he was made military commander of the Department of the East, a post which he held until the close of the war, and was in command at New York during the draft riots. In 1866, he was appointed Naval Officer at New York, and in that same year United States Minister to France, a position which he resigned after two years. In 1872, he was elected Governor of the State as a Republican, but was defeated for the same office in 1874. He was a man of great culture, and was the author of several works of travel.

General Dix married Catherine, niece and adopted daughter of John J. Morgan, Member of Congress from New York, Miss Morgan's father, who was the brother of Mr. Morgan's wife, Catherine Warne, being a nephew of Colonel Marinus Willett The eldest son of General and Mrs. Dix, the Reverend Dr. Morgan Dix, was born in New York City, November 1st, 1827. He was graduated from Columbia College, in 1848, and from the General Theological Seminary in 1852. Three years later, he was appointed assistant minister in Trinity parish, and in 1862 he became rector, a position that he has held ever since. He has been indefatigable in his work for Trinity and is one of the leading divines of the church in this country. He has published many books on religious subjects and a memoir of his father In 1874, Dr Dix married Emily Woolsey Soutter, eldest daughter of General William Soutter and his wife, Agnes G (Knox) Soutter. He is a member of the Grolier Club, and the Sons of the Revolution, and is president and commandant of the Society of the War of 1812.

GRENVILLE M DODGE

TWO brothers named Dodge emigrated from England in the early part of the seventeenth century and settled in Essex County, Mass. One of their descendants was Captain Solomon Dodge, of Rowley, Mass., grandfather of the subject of this sketch. Sylvanus Dodge, the son of Captain Solomon Dodge, born in Rowley, in 1800, died in 1872, and in 1827 married Julia F. Philips, of New Rowley, now Georgetown, Mass., a lady belonging to a family celebrated in the annals of Massachusetts and who, throughout a long life, exhibited remarkable force of character In 1834, Sylvanus Dodge was appointed postmaster of South Danvers, Mass, and held that office for ten years, when he went West He was an old school Democrat, but later in life changed his politics and became active in the organization of the Republican party. He was among the pioneers who developed the Territory of Nebraska, and was for many years Register of the United States Land Office in the district in which he resided

Major-General Grenville M Dodge is the second son of Sylvanus Dodge and his wife, Julia Philips Dodge. He was born in Danvers, Mass., April 12th, 1831. In 1847, he entered the Military University of Norwich, Vt., from which institution he was graduated in 1851 as a civil engineer. He then went West, taking up his residence in Illinois, where he engaged as an assistant engineer in the construction of the Chicago & Rock Island and other railroad lines in Illinois and Iowa. For some time he was a resident of Iowa City, and finally of Council Bluffs, Ia.

When the Civil War broke out, General Dodge was Captain of the Council Bluffs Guards which enlisted for service at the front. The Governor of Iowa appointed him an aide on his staff, with the rank of Lieutenant-Colonel, and he organized the Fourth Iowa Infantry and the Dodge Battery, which was attached to the same command. In July, 1861, he joined, with his regiment, the army of General Fremont at St Louis. In January, 1862, he was assigned to the command of a brigade, leading the advance in the movement on Springfield, Mo., and in the capture of that city, and took part in the engagements at Sugar Creek and Blackburn's Mills. At the battle of Pea Ridge, he was conspicuous for bravery, and in recognition of his gallant services was made Brigadier-General of Volunteers. He superintended the rebuilding of the Mobile & Ohio Railroad, was promoted to the command of the Central Division of Mississippi, defeated the Confederates in several important battles, captured General Faulkner and his forces near Island No. 10, and was assigned to command the Second Division, Army of the Tennessee. In 1863, he defeated the Confederate forces under General Forest and commanded the Sixteenth Army Corps in all the great battles of General Sherman's Atlanta campaign, the brunt of the Battle of Atlanta, July 22d, 1864, in which General McPherson was killed, falling on his command. A few days later General Dodge was severely wounded and was prevented from taking part in the March to the Sea In June, 1864, he was commissioned Major-General of Volunteers, and took command of the Department of Missouri. In 1865, he commanded the United States forces in Kansas and the Territories. Returning to civil life, he assumed the position of chief engineer in charge of the construction of the Union Pacific Railroad. In 1866, he was elected a member of the Thirty-Ninth Congress from the Fifth District of Iowa. For the last thirty years, he has been engaged in great railroad enterprises. He was a director of the Union Pacific Railroad Company, and has been identified with the building and operation of many railroads in the West and Southwest, including the Texas & Pacific, the Missouri, Kansas & Texas, the International & Great Northern, the Fort Worth & Denver City, and other lines.

General Dodge is a member of the Union League and the United Service clubs, belongs to the New England Society, and is a member of the Metropolitan Museum of Art He is president of the Society of the Army of the Tennessee and chairman of the committee charged with the erection of a statue of his friend and commander, General William T Sherman In May, 1897, he was chief marshal of the procession in New York City at the dedication of the Grant Mausoleum in Riverside Park.

WILLIAM EARL DODGE

WILLIAM DODGE, who settled at Salem, Mass., in the year 1629, was the progenitor of a race representatives of which are now found in many portions of the United States A branch of the family established itself in Connecticut, from which the four generations of eminent merchants and philanthropists who have made the name of Dodge famous in New York's annals derive their origin.

The first of this line was David Low Dodge, who was born in Connecticut in 1774 He was a highly educated man, and was in his early years head of a private school at Norwich, Conn., which he made famous by the introduction of novel educational methods. He married a daughter of the Reverend Aaron Cleveland, the grandfather of ex-President Grover Cleveland Entering business life, David Low Dodge established himself in Hartford, Conn., in 1802, but in 1805 came to New York City as partner of the firm of Higginsons & Dodge, which became the largest wholesale dry goods house of its day, having establishments at Boston, New York and Baltimore; but owing to the loss of many vessels, their business was broken up by the embargo. The latter, however, stimulated the growth of domestic manufacturers, and Mr. Dodge was a pioneer in the field. Returning to Norwich, Conn., he built a large cotton mill, one of the first in New England, but later on he returned to New York and established the firm of Ludlow & Dodge. Retiring from business in 1827, his life till his death in 1852 was mainly devoted to religious and literary labors. He was an elder of the Wall Street Presbyterian Church, and with Robert Lenox had charge of building its new structure He was among the founders of the American Tract and Bible societies, and was the first president of the American Peace Society. Among his works on religious and social subjects was a volume, War Inconsistent with the Religion of Jesus Christ, which was reprinted in England and translated into several European languages. His brother-in-law was the famous preacher, the Reverend Samuel Hanson Cox, D. D , whose son, the late Right Reverend Arthur Cleveland Cox, was Bishop of Western New York.

The Honorable William Earl Dodge, Sr., his son, was born at Hartford in 1805, and was educated at Norwich and at Mendham, N. J., under his uncle, the Reverend Dr. Cox. His earliest business experience was as a clerk in the mill at Norwich; but from his youth he was identified with New York, and in 1827 established the house of Huntington & Dodge here. He married a daughter of Anson Green Phelps, of the firm of Phelps & Peck, which Mr Phelps had founded, and which was the largest establishment in the metal trade in the United States. In 1833, William E. Dodge entered this house, the style of which was changed to Phelps, Dodge & Co., which it has since retained. His interests were, however, as varied as they were extensive. He developed large lumber properties both in Canada and the South; he was among the first directors of the Erie Railroad, of the Central Railroad of New Jersey, of the Delaware, Lackawanna & Western Railroad, being one of the founders of the latter, while he was also president of the Houston & Texas Central Railroad. His enterprise and probity were rewarded not only by material success, but by the recognition of his fellow merchants. He joined the Chamber of Commerce in 1855, became its vice-president in 1863, and was elected president of the organization from 1867 till his voluntary retirement, in 1875.

Prior to the outbreak of the Civil War, he labored to secure an honorable settlement of sectional differences. He was a member of the Peace Congress in 1861, but when the war began gave an unswerving support to the Union In 1864, he was elected a Member of Congress from the Eighth District of New York, and distinguished himself by his opposition to unsound financial measures, but declined a renomination. In 1872, he was a member of the Electoral College of this State, and, among many other public services, was a member of a commission which investigated the condition of the Indians.

The fame of William Earl Dodge, Sr , rests, however, upon a better basis than that of a successful career and public honors. Strong religious and humanitarian views came to him by inheritance, were confirmed throughout his life, and became the guiding principles of his existence. He was ever active in religious work, but his charities knew no limits of creed or section, and the title of the "Christian Merchant," by which he was known, was fully deserved by the tenor of his life. He gave his efforts freely to the cause of religion, temperance and benevolence, and among other positions was president of the Evangelical Alliance and the National Temperance Society and similar bodies. He gave aid to the furtherance of education among the freedmen of the South after the war, and it should be noted that after the struggle for the Union had been crowned with success, he was one of the first to inculcate conciliation and harmony among all sections. His death, in 1883, called forth earnest expressions of appreciation of his character and services from public, mercantile, religious and benevolent bodies, and the erection in 1885, under the auspices of the Chamber of Commerce, of his statue, at Broadway and Thirty-fourth Street, was a fitting tribute to one of the most eminent citizens of the metropolis

His son, Mr. William Earl Dodge, Jr, was born in New York City in 1832. He entered mercantile life in his youth, and in 1864 became a partner in Phelps, Dodge & Co, of which he is now the senior member. He is also president of the Ansonia Brass Company and other corporations at Ansonia, Conn, a town founded by and named after his grandfather, Anson G. Phelps During the Civil War, he was one of the Commissioners of the State of New York to supervise the condition of its troops in the field. His commission was among the first signed by President Lincoln, and at the conclusion of his services he received the thanks of the State in a joint resolution of the Legislature He was also an officer of the Loyal Publication Society, an advisory director of the Woman's Central Association of Relief, out of which the United States Sanitary Commission grew, and was one of the founders of the Union League Club.

Mr Dodge followed the example of his father in his devotion to religious and charitable work. He was long the president of the Young Men's Christian Association, which, under his administration, erected its building at Twenty-third Street and Fourth Avenue, the first in the country devoted to the special use of an Association He succeeded his father as president of the Evangelical Alliance, was vice-president of the American Sunday School Union, and chairman of the National Arbitration Committee. Among other services to the metropolis, he is a trustee of the Slater fund, a member of the executive committee of the Metropolitan Museum of Art, the Museum of Natural History, and the New York Botanic Garden Mr Dodge has also filled the post of vice-president of the New England Society, and is a member of the Metropolitan, Union League, Century, City, Reform, Riding, Presbyterian, Country, and other clubs, and of the American Geographical Society and a large number of other social, scientific and benevolent bodies. His town residence is in Madison Avenue, and his country place is Greyston, Riverdale-on-Hudson. In 1854, Mr Dodge married Sarah Tappen Hoadley, daughter of the late David Hoadley, president of the Panama Railroad Company.

The other sons of William E. Dodge, Sr, are Anson Phelps Dodge, Norman W Dodge and George E Dodge, who are all identified with the business interests and social life of the city; the Reverend D Stuart Dodge, D D, founder of the Syrian Protestant College at Beirut, Syria, to which his father was a liberal benefactor; Brigadier General Charles Cleveland Dodge, a prominent cavalry officer during the Civil War and Major of the New York Mounted Rifles; and the late Arthur Murray Dodge.

Cleveland Hoadley Dodge, the son of Mr. William Earl Dodge, Jr., was born in New York City in 1860 He is a member of the firm of Phelps, Dodge & Co, a trustee of the Farmers' Loan and Trust Company, and a director of the National City Bank and other corporations, while he has been actively interested in a number of local charities, and is president of the Young Men's Christian Association, in succession to his father He married Grace Parish.

Grace Hoadley Dodge, daughter of Mr. W E Dodge, Jr, has distinguished herself by her practical work on behalf of her sex She founded the Working Girls' clubs of New York City, and originated the Teachers' College, now affiliated with Columbia University. She was also the first woman appointed a member of the New York Board of Education.

WILLIAM GAYER DOMINICK

THE Huguenot emigration brought to New York, in 1742, George Dominique, who was born at La Rochelle, France, in 1739. George and his brother, François Dominique, became merchants in Cherry Street, New York. George was a Captain in the Second New York Militia in 1775, and a vestryman in Trinity Church, 1787–1792, Dominick Street being named for him. In 1761, he married Elizabeth Blanchard, who was also of Huguenot parents, though born in Amsterdam, Holland. Their son, James William Dominick, a merchant of eminence, was one of the founders and president of the Eastern Dispensary, a trustee of the American Tract Society, one of the executive committee of the Bible Society, and a director of the Tradesman's Bank. He married Phœbe Cock, daughter of Major James Cock, Adjutant in the Patriot army at the Battle of White Plains, and Commissary under Washington throughout the entire war Major André was a prisoner in Major Cock's house. The night before his execution, he kissed Phœbe Cock, then an infant, and said, "Oh! happy childhood ; we know thy peace but once , would that I were as innocent as thou."

Among the lineal descendants of James William Dominick, first in the male line, are Marinus Willet Dominick, a son of his second wife, Margaret Eliza Delavan, and five grandsons : Henry Blanchard Dominick and the late Alexander, sons of James W Dominick, second, and the sons of the late W F. Dominick, George Francis Bayard and the late Mr William Gayer Dominick.

William Francis Dominick, the latter's father, was the son of James William Dominick and Phœbe Cock, and though born in New York, went to Chicago in 1844, and was one of the early merchants there, retiring from business and returning to New York in 1855. He married, in 1844, Lydia Gardner Wells, a descendant of Governor Wells, of Connecticut , of Robert Day, whose name appears on the Founders' Monument at Hartford, and of Richard Gardner, of Nantucket. Their eldest son, Mr. William Gayer Dominick, was born in Chicago, in 1845, and died suddenly August 31st, 1895. He was educated at Churchill's Academy, Sing Sing, and in 1863 entered the banking business in Wall Street. In 1869, he joined the Stock Exchange, and formed, with Watson B. Dickerman, the firm of Dominick & Dickerman, to which his brother, Bayard, was admitted

Mr. Dominick served seventeen years in the Seventh Regiment, ten years as First Lieutenant, and at the time of his death was Captain of the Ninth Company of the Veteran Association, and a Governor of the Seventh Regiment Veteran Club. He was a member and one of the board of managers of the Sons of the Revolution, a manager of the New York Huguenot Society, and one of the advisory board of the Young Women's Christian Association, a member of the Society of Colonial Wars, of the War of 1812, the Aztec Society, and the Historical Society Among other prominent organizations, he belonged to the Union League, City and Riding clubs, and the Narrows Island Shooting Club, of Currituck, N C A life membership of the Metropolitan Museum of Art was conferred on him in 1892, when he joined his brothers in presenting the picture by Schraeder, Queen Elizabeth Signing the Death Warrant of Mary Stuart.

In 1874, Mr. Dominick married Anne De Witt Marshall, daughter of Henry P. Marshall and his wife, Cornelia Elizabeth Conrad. The Marshall family descends from Edward Marshall, who settled in Virginia in 1624, died in New York 1704, and is buried in Trinity churchyard Mrs Dominick's great-grandfather, the Reverend John Rutgers Marshall, was one of the ten clergymen who elected Samuel Seabury, the first Bishop of the Protestant Episcopal Church in the United States. Another ancestor was Colonel Charles DeWitt, the Revolutionary patriot, and among her early ancestors are Hermanus Rutgers, Parson Thomas Hooker, the Reverend Everardus Bogardus and Anneke Jans. Mr and Mrs. Dominick's four children are William Francis (now at Yale, class of 1898), Elsie, Alice and Anne Marshall Dominick. Mr Dominick was a member of St. Thomas's Church, Fifty-third Street and Fifth Avenue, where a beautiful altar rail has been placed, "To the Glory of God and in blessed memory of him whose gentle, manly, Christian character made him beloved by all who came in contact with him." The Dominick coat of arms was granted in 1720.

ROBERT OGDEN DOREMUS

THOMAS CORNELIUS DOREMUS, father of the subject of this article, was a New York merchant in the early part of the present century. In 1821, he married Sarah Platt Haines, the daughter of Elias Haines, her mother being a daughter of Robert Ogden, a lawyer who belonged to a famous New Jersey Colonial family. Through life, Sarah Platt (Haines) Doremus was noted for the active part she took in many noble charities. In 1842, she was prominent in founding the institution for discharged female prisoners, now the Isaac T. Hopper Home, and was its first president. Dr. J. Marion Sims, who founded the Woman's Hospital in the State of New York in 1855, left it on record, that he could make no headway with the project until he applied to Mrs. Doremus, "who touched it and it lived." She was the first president of the Woman's Hospital, holding that office at her death in 1877.

The son of Thomas Cornelius and Sarah Platt (Haines) Doremus is Professor Robert Ogden Doremus. He was born in this city, entered Columbia College in 1838, and graduated from the University of New York in 1842. He was the first private pupil of the celebrated Professor John W Draper, and in 1843 became his first assistant. He held that position for some years, and assisted in many of Professor Draper's famous researches. In 1847, he went to Europe and continued his studies of chemistry in Paris. Returning to New York in 1848, he established, with Dr. Charles T Harris, an analytical laboratory, and in 1849 was elected professor of chemistry in the New York College of Pharmacy. Meantime, he continued the study of medicine with Dr. Abraham L. Cox, receiving the degree of M. D from the University of the City of New York in 1850. At a later date, the University conferred on him the degree of LL. D. He was one of the founders of the New York Medical College, and at his own expense equipped for it the first chemical laboratory attached to a medical college in the United States. He organized a similar analytical laboratory in the Long Island Hospital Medical College in 1859

The investigations of Professor Doremus in toxicology effected a revolution in medical jurisprudence He has been an expert in that field, and has also made many important chemical and scientific discoveries He is distinguished as a lecturer, and has frequently appeared in that capacity in aid of charitable causes. At the unveiling of Humboldt's monument in Central Park, he delivered the English oration. He was one of the editors of the Standard Dictionary of the English language, having charge of the chemical definitions. He has been president of the New York Philharmonic Society and the Medico-Legal Society, is a fellow of the Academy of Sciences of New York and the American Geographical Society, was one of the first members of the Union League Club and belongs to the St. Nicholas Society.

Professor Doremus married Estelle E Skidmore, daughter of Captain Hubbard Skidmore, and a descendant of the famous Captain John Underhill, of the Colonial period Mrs. Doremus was, for several years, regent of the New York Chapter of the Daughters of the American Revolution and is now one of the honorary vice-presidents of the National Society of that organization. The children of this marriage are: Charles Avery, Thomas Cornelius, Robert Ogden, Fordyce Barker, Estelle Emma, Austin Flint, Clarence Seward and Arthur Lispenard Doremus. The eldest son, Charles Avery Doremus, born in 1851, graduated in 1870 from the College of the City of New York, and studied at Leipsic and Heidelberg, taking the degree of A. M and Ph. D. at the latter university From 1877 to 1882, he was professor of chemistry in the Medical Department of the University of Buffalo, and received the honorary degree of M D. He was afterwards adjunct professor of chemistry in Bellevue Hospital Medical College, and assistant professor in the College of the City of New York, and represented the United States Government at the International Congress of Applied Chemistry at Paris in 1896. He has devoted much of his attention to original research, and is an expert authority upon chemistry in connection with patent and other litigation. In 1880, he married Elizabeth Johnson Ward, of Newport, Ky., their surviving child being Katherine Ward Doremus.

ORLANDO PORTER DORMAN

TWO famous Colonial families of New England are represented in the person of Mr. Orlando Porter Dorman. His first paternal American ancestor was Thomas Dorman, a native of England, who came to Boston when a young man and was a freeman of Ipswich in 1636, afterwards becoming one of the founders of the town of Boxford, Mass. The father of Mr. Dorman was Orlin C. Dorman, a lineal descendant from Thomas Dorman. He was a prominent citizen of Connecticut, held many important positions in connection with the Legislature of that Commonwealth, and was also an active member of the militia. The paternal grandfather of Mr. Dorman was Amos Dorman, who was a citizen of considerable prominence and a large real estate owner in Ellington, Conn.

The mother of Mr. Dorman was Juliana Doane, of Tolland, Conn. Through her, his ancestry goes back to Normandy in the tenth century. One branch of the family went from Normandy to Germany, where they were made barons and exercised the rights of nobility for many generations. They were at one time deprived of their titles, which, however, were restored upon the accession of another dynasty to the throne. John Doane, the pioneer American ancestor of Mr. Dorman's mother, was one of the famous Puritans of Plymouth. He came to the Plymouth Colony in the ship Charity in 1621, and, in 1632, was chosen an assistant, being a member of the first body of that character of which there is any record, and was associated with William Bradford, Miles Standish, John Howland, John Alden, Stephen Hopkins and William Gilson. A resident of Eastham after 1644, and one of the first seven proprietors of that town, he was an assistant, 1649-50, and a deputy in 1659, and frequently in later years. When he went to Eastham, he was forty-nine years of age and he died in 1707 at the age of one hundred and ten. His property in Eastham consisted of some two hundred acres of land, and the boundaries he marked with stone posts cut with his initials, which have remained standing to this day. The descendants of John Doane have been numerous in the eastern part of Massachusetts and in Connecticut in every generation since their ancestor established the family there.

Mr. Orlando P. Dorman was born in Ellington, Conn., February 3d, 1828. Receiving an academic education, he entered upon business life when he was nineteen years old, going into a dry goods store in Hartford There he obtained a thorough business training, and after five years came to New York, where he was associated with the late William H. Lee as a partner in the firm of Lee, Case & Co. and William H Lee & Co, having charge of the foreign business of the house. After he had retired from that business, he organized the Gilbert Manufacturing Company, which was incorporated in 1881, and of which he has since been the president. He is recognized as one of the foremost American manufacturers in the particular line of trade to which he has devoted himself.

Although he takes a deep interest in public affairs and is a thoroughly patriotic American, Mr. Dorman has never engaged in public life He has, however, devoted much of his time and a generous share of his wealth to the cause of charity and education. He has been specially interested in educating young men for the ministry, several members of that profession having been enabled to secure their theological training through his beneficence. Senior warden of the Church of the Heavenly Rest, and also of the Church of the Holy Spirit, he has been active in the field of Christian work, and has been especially interested in the particular charities that are promoted by those two church organizations. The wife of Mr. Dorman, whom he married in 1850, was Delia Anna Taylor, of Hartford. The city home of Mr. and Mrs. Dorman is at Seventy-sixth Street and West End Avenue. They also have a country seat, Auvergne, at Riverdale-on-Hudson. They have had two children, a son and a daughter. The son, Harry H, graduated from St Paul's School, in Garden City, Long Island, at the age of seventeen and is now in business with his father. He married, in 1893, Florence Page, of New York Mr. Dorman's daughter, Anna Belle, married, in 1894, Franklin H Smith, Jr, of New York.

WILLIAM PROCTOR DOUGLAS

A NCESTORS of Mr. William Proctor Douglas were of the great Scottish family of that name, of high rank and imperishable renown. That branch of the family to which Mr. Douglas belongs has been settled in this country for a hundred years. Its members were large land owners in Scotland, but disposed of their possessions there and emigrated to this country in the early years of the present century. George Douglas, the father of Mr William Proctor Douglas, was born in Scotland in 1792. Coming to the United States early in life, he was one of the leading merchants of his generation. The house of George Douglas & Co., which he founded, did an East India commission business not excelled in extent and importance by any of their rivals in the city, and had an enviable commercial renown even in Europe.

George Douglas was an intense Democrat, and his firm was one of the few business establishments in New York that sided with President Andrew Jackson in the warfare of that executive against the United States Bank. In the Presidential campaign of 1844, he was a Democratic elector at large for the ticket headed by James K. Polk. He was a staunch temperance man throughout his life and carried his temperance principles so far that he refused to receive consignments of brandy and wine sent to his firm, which was the first establishment in the city to take such action.

The Douglas city residence was at 55 Broadway, in a house built by Mr. Douglas when lower Broadway and Battery place were the fashionable residence localities of the city. After that he lived in Park Place, and then in West Fourteenth Street. Later in life, he bought the famous Van Zandt estate, at what is now called Douglaston, Long Island, and thenceforth made that his family residence. This place, on the east side of Flushing Bay, was formerly part of the Weekes farm Wynant Van Zandt, the New York merchant and alderman, 1789-1804, bought the land in 1813 and built there the residence, which is still standing and which has been for nearly three quarters of a century the home of the Douglas family The wife of George Douglas was a daughter of Dr Maxwell, a celebrated physician of Scotland. Dr. Maxwell died in Scotland, and after his death his wife and three daughters came to the United States and made their home in New York. The daughters were handsome women of distinguished character. One of them married James Scott Aspinwall and another became the wife of a member of the Rogers family of Long Island.

Mr. William Proctor Douglas was born in New York in 1842, and was educated in Edinburgh, Scotland. He inherited from his father the estate at Douglaston, Little Neck Bay, comprising nearly three hundred acres, where he has made his home His only business pursuit has been in caring for the estate and the corporate investments which his father left to the family. He is a large stockholder in several of the leading banks of New York. Mr. Douglas' interests in gentlemanly sports have made him famous the world over. He has been particularly known for his untiring efforts in promotion of yachting and for his activity in measures for the defense of the America Cup against its British challengers One of the first yachts that sailed in defense of the America Cup, the Sappho, which defeated the Livonia, in 1871, was owned by him. In later years, he was part owner of the Priscilla, built for a cup defender. He is a member of the New York Yacht, New York Athletic, Racquet, Carteret Gun, Seawanhaka-Corinthian Yacht, Douglaston Yacht, Westminster Kennel, Rockaway Hunt, Meadow Brook Hunt and Coaching clubs, the Country Club of Westchester County and other organizations of similar character. He is also a member of the Metropolitan, Tuxedo and Union clubs. The Metropolitan Museum of Art and the New York Academy of Design have him enrolled among their patrons. He is also a member of several European clubs, among them the Austrian Yacht Club.

In 1879, Mr. Douglas married Adelaide L. Townsend, daughter of Effingham Townsend, of the old Long Island family of that name Two children have been born of this alliance, Edith Sybil and James Gordon Douglas The city residence of the Douglas family is in West Fifty-seventh Street, near Fifth Avenue.

ANDREW ELLICOTT DOUGLASS

IN the latter part of the seventeenth century, members of one branch of the Douglass family were settled in Bergen County, N. J. They were of Scotch origin, descended from the great Scottish family whose name they bore. David Douglass, the ancestor of Mr Andrew Ellicott Douglass, was a resident of Hanover Neck, where he was born about 1715 and died about 1765 His second wife, whom he married in 1755, was Esther Reed. Deacon Nathaniel Douglass, his son, was the grandfather of the subject of this sketch. Born in Hanover Neck in 1760, part of his lifetime he was a resident of Pompton, N. J, and for many years was a member of the firm of Vanderpoel & Douglass, leather manufacturers, of Newark. In 1813, he removed to Caldwell, N. J., and resided there the rest of his life, dying in 1824. His wife was Sarah, daughter of David Bates. She was born in 1762 and died in 1816.

Major David Bates Douglass, son of Nathaniel Douglass and father of Mr. Andrew Ellicott Douglass, was born in Pompton, N. J., in 1790 and died in 1849. He was graduated from Yale College in 1813 and received the degree of M. A. in 1816. Commissioned a Second Lieutenant of Engineers in the United States Army in 1813, he was first ordered to West Point, and during the Niagara campaign of 1814 saw service at the front, being promoted to be First Lieutenant, and then Brevet Captain the same year. In 1819, he was made Captain of Engineers. In January, 1815, he was appointed assistant professor of natural philosophy at West Point, and the same year was detailed to examine and report upon the defenses of Narragansett Bay, New London Harbor, Saybrook and New Haven. In 1817, he made a study of the eastern entrance of Long Island Sound, with a view to its fortification, and in 1819 was United States Astronomical Surveyor In 1820, he joined the North West Expedition as civil and military engineer and astronomer, and the same year succeeded his father-in-law, Andrew Ellicott, as professor of mathematics at West Point, becoming professor of engineering in the same institution three years after. Resigning from the Government service in 1831, Major Douglas became professor of natural philosophy and afterwards professor of architecture and engineering in New York University; from 1840 to 1844 was president of Kenyon College, and was professor of mathematics in Geneva College 1848-49. Yale College gave him the degree of LL. D. in 1841. He died in October, 1849. He married Ann Eliza Ellicott, daughter of Andrew Ellicott, the distinguished surveyor and mathematician. In 1786, Andrew Ellicott was a member of the American Philosophical Society, and made the surveys of the City of Washington as it now stands. During the latter years of his life, he was professor of mathematics at West Point, where he died in 1820

Mr Andrew Ellicott Douglass was born at West Point, November 18th, 1819. He was educated in private schools and graduated from Kenyon College in 1838 After a successful business career of thirty-seven years, he retired and has since devoted himself to the study of American archæology, traveling extensively and making many original explorations, especially along the Southern coast of the United States. He is a member of the leading scientific associations in this country and in Europe, belongs to the Century Association and the Church Club, and is the author of many essays, principally on archæological subjects. His collections relating to American archæology are among the most valuable in their particular line that have ever been made.

In 1847, Mr Douglass married Sarah Cortelyou Cornell, daughter of George Lecky Cornell and his wife, Isabella Woodbridge Sheldon, daughter of Charles Sheldon, of Hartford, Conn. Mr. and Mrs. Douglass have but one child, a daughter, Isabel Douglass, who in 1876 married Charles Boyd Curtis, of New York, well known as an author on art matters. They have four children, Ellicott Douglass, Charles Boyd, Isabel Woodbridge and Ronald Eliot Curtis. Mrs. Curtis is corresponding secretary of the Society of Colonial Dames of the State of New York, and president of the Woman's Auxiliary for Domestic Missions of the Diocese of New York. The Douglass and Curtis family residence in New York is in East Fifty-fourth Street, and their country home is Locustwood, on Milton Point, in Rye, Westchester County.

WILLIAM DOWD

GUILFORD is one of the Connecticut towns that were founded by Colonists from England who came to America under the leadership of a Puritan clergyman. In this case, the pastor was the Reverend Henry Whitfield, who arrived with his flock in 1639. He remained in Guilford for some years, but finally returned to England and died there in 1650 Among the number who accompanied him to the New World was Henry Dowd, who died in Guilford in 1668 and left several children, the most noteworthy of whom was Thomas Dowd, of East Guilford Born in England, Thomas Dowd came to this country with his father as a member of the Whitfield Colony. He rose to be a man of mark in the Colony, and died in 1713 In the next generation, Thomas Dowd, second of the name, was born at East Guilford in 1684, and died in 1711 He was a resident of Killingworth, now Madison, Conn, and lived and died in the old homestead, which was standing until a few years ago The wife of the second Thomas Dowd was Silence Evarts, who belonged to the family from which the Honorable William M. Evarts is descended.

Joseph Dowd, grandson of the second Thomas Dowd, was born in Killingworth in 1744 and died there in 1809. He married, in 1768, Mary Blatchley, whose ancestors were among the Mayflower Pilgrims in 1620. Joseph and Mary (Blatchley) Dowd were the grandparents of Mr. William Dowd The father of Mr. Dowd was Joseph Dowd, who was born in Madison, Conn., in 1773, and died in Stafford, N. Y., in 1854 He was a landowner and merchant and the owner of several ships trading with the West Indies. His third wife, whom he married in 1820, and who was the mother of Mr William Dowd, was Polly Dutton, daughter of Deacon Joseph Dutton and his wife, Priscilla Stuart, of Royalston, Vt Priscilla Stuart was born in Scotland and was a daughter of Sir Elkanah Stuart, who was disowned by his family for marrying a lady of French Huguenot parentage

Mr. William Dowd was born in Batavia, N Y., August 30th, 1824 Receiving a common school education, he went into business when he was twenty years of age and came to New York. His first situation was with the firm of Lyman Cook & Co. In two years he became a junior member of the concern under the firm name of Cook, Dowd & Baker, afterwards changed to Dowd, Baker & Whitman, when he became head of the house. In 1874, Mr. Dowd became president of the Bank of North America, retaining that position until his final retirement from all business cares, a few years ago In 1878, he was chairman of the Clearing House Association and was reëlected the following year. For twenty-one years he was chairman of the finance committee of the Importers' & Traders' Insurance Company. He was president of the Hannibal & St. Joseph Railroad from 1877 to 1883, and was connected with other important enterprises.

Actively interested in municipal affairs, Mr Dowd was appointed a member of the Board of Education, and held that position for ten years He was for four years chairman of the committee on finance of the board and several years chairman of the committee on colored schools He was also chairman of the executive committee of the trustees of the College of the City of New York. In 1880, he was the Republican candidate for Mayor of New York and, from 1883 to 1888, was a member of the Aqueduct Commission.

In 1851, Mr Dowd married Maria Eliza Merrill, who was born in Clinton, Conn., in 1824 and is of Puritan descent. They have had five children. The eldest son is William B. Dowd. Colonel Heman Dowd, the second son, is a graduate of West Point, commanded the Eighth Regiment, N G S N. Y., and is assistant cashier of the National Bank of North America. He married Miss Loveland Joseph Dowd, the third son, is a merchant, engaged in the woolen business in this city The youngest son is George M Dowd, and the only daughter of the family is Mary E. Dowd Mr Dowd is a member of the Union League Club and the New England Society, being treasurer of the latter, and a patron of the American Museum of Natural History and the Metropolitan Museum of Art

MRS. JOSEPH W. DREXEL

BEFORE her marriage, Mrs. Joseph W. Drexel was Lucy Wharton. She comes of distinguished Pennsylvania lineage, being the daughter of Thomas Lloyd Wharton, of Philadelphia, 1799-1869, and his wife, Sarah Ann Smith, daughter of Richard Rodman Smith. Her grandfather was Kearny Wharton, of Philadelphia, 1765-1848, a president of the Common Council of Philadelphia and one of the most influential citizens of the Quaker City, his wife was Maria Saltar, daughter of John and Elizabeth (Gordon) Saltar

The great-grandfather of Mrs. Drexel was Thomas Wharton, Jr., 1735-1778. He was president of the Supreme Executive Council of Pennsylvania in 1777 and was otherwise conspicuous in public life. Thomas Wharton, Jr., was the grandson of Thomas Wharton, who was the son of Richard Wharton, of Westmorelandshire, England, and came to this country in the latter part of the seventeenth century The elder Thomas Wharton belonged to the Society of Friends and was a member of the Council of the City of Philadelphia. His wife was Rachel Thomas, a native of Wales His death occurred in Philadelphia in 1718 and his widow survived him for twenty-nine years, dying in 1747. The great-grandmother of Mrs. Drexel, whom Thomas Wharton, Jr., married in 1762, was Susannah Lloyd, daughter of Thomas Lloyd, of Philadelphia, who died in 1754, and his wife, Susannah (Kearny) Owen, daughter of Philip Kearny, of Philadelphia, and widow of Dr. Edward Owen. Thomas Lloyd was the son of Thomas Lloyd and a grandson of Thomas Lloyd, the first Deputy Governor of Pennsylvania and president of the Provincial Council, 1684-88 and 1690-93. The mother of Susannah Kearny was Rebecca Britton, daughter of Lionel Britton. Through the Lloyd branch of her ancestry, Mrs. Drexel goes back in fourteen generations from the first Thomas Lloyd to Edward I., King of England, by his first wife, the Princess Eleanor, daughter of Ferdinand, King of Castile. Among her royal ancestors from King Edward are the Princess Joan d'Arce; Gilbert de Clare, a descendant of King Alfred, the Great; Lady Eleanor Holland, a descendant of Henry I, King of France, and his wife, Anne of Russia; Sir John de Grey, Earl of Tankerville, a descendant of King Henry III., of England, and Lady Antigone Plantagenet, a descendant of King Henry IV., of England.

Joseph W. Drexel, who married Lucy Wharton in 1865, was one of the noted American bankers of the last generation. He was born in Philadelphia in 1831. His father, Francis M. Drexel, was a native of Austria and an accomplished artist, who practiced his profession in Philadelphia until 1840, when he entered the banking business, taking into partnership, eventually, his three sons. After being connected with his father's banking institution for several years, Joseph W. Drexel went to Chicago and established himself in business there. Upon his father's death, he returned to Philadelphia and in 1871, in association with Junius S Morgan, established the banking house of Drexel, Morgan & Co. in New York. He was also the head of the house of Drexel, Harjes & Co., of Paris, and had a large interest in The Philadelphia Public Ledger.

After 1876, Mr. Drexel lived in retirement from active business until his death, in 1888. Greatly interested in artistic and musical affairs, he was one of the most active supporters of the Metropolitan Museum of Art, president of the Philharmonic Society and director of the Metropolitan Opera House, and a trustee of the Bartholdi Statue Fund. He made many generous contributions of paintings and other interesting art objects to the Metropolitan Museum of Art, and bequeathed his valuable musical library to the Lenox Library.

Mrs. Drexel has four daughters. Her eldest daughter, Katharine Drexel, married Dr Charles Bingham Penrose, of Philadelphia. Lucy Drexel is the wife of Eric B. Dahlgren, son of Admiral Dahlgren Elizabeth Drexel is the wife of John Vinton Dahlgren, also a son of Admiral Dahlgren. The youngest daughter is Josephine Wharton Drexel Mrs. Drexel lives in Madison Avenue and is interested in art and book collecting She owns one of the most valuable collections of rare books and manuscripts in the United States. Her summer residence is Penn Rhyn, a family place, on the Delaware River, Bucks County, Pa.

ARTHUR DUANE

ONE of the prominent lawyers of Philadelphia in the first years of the present century, who also held a high position in national politics, was the Honorable William John Duane. He was born in 1780 in Ireland, where his father, who was an American, was then living. He learned the printer's trade, but studied law and became a leader of the Philadelphia bar Among his clients was the famous merchant and philanthropist, Stephen Girard, whose confidential friend and adviser he became. He drew the will by which Mr. Girard bequeathed the bulk of his fortune to found the college for orphan youths which bears his name. This instrument was fiercely assailed in the courts but was never broken, and Mr. Duane was one of the first trustees of the college Entering into public life, he was several times a member of the Legislature of Pennsylvania President Andrew Jackson invited him into his Cabinet as Secretary of the Treasury, but in 1833 deprived him of his portfolio because he refused to carry out the wishes of the President in the famous controversy with the United States Bank Mr Duane was an author of repute, publishing several books, among them The Law of Nations Investigated.

The father of the Honorable William John Duane was William Duane, 1760-1835, who was prominent in politics and journalism in the early days of our National Government Early in life, he left the United States and went to Ireland, where he became a printer and editor. In 1784, he went to India and was proprietor of a newspaper there, from which he realized a fortune. Falling, however, into disfavor with the East India Company's officials, his property was confiscated and he was summarily sent back to England. He established The General Advertiser, in London, which was afterwards merged in The London Times, and in 1795 returned to the United States, becoming editor of The Philadelphia Aurora, the organ of the Republican or Anti-Federalist party President Jefferson appointed him Lieutenant-Colonel in 1805, and he was an Adjutant-General in the War of 1812 In 1822, he went to South America, as a representative of the creditors of Columbia and other newly established republics there. He was the author of many valuable books, among them, A Visit to Columbia, and The Mississippi Question. He also compiled and edited several important works of reference, among them, A Military Dictionary, The American Military Library, and An Epitome of the Arts and Sciences.

Mr. Arthur Duane is the grandson of the Honorable William John Duane, and great-grandson of William Duane. Through the female side of his house, he also comes of distinguished ancestors His grandfather married Deborah Bache, granddaughter of Benjamin Franklin. The Bache family trace their ancestry to the French province of Normandy. The name was originally de la Beche, as it appears in the English records, the immediate ancestors of the American branch residing in Yorkshire. Theophylact Bache, whose name is frequently mentioned in this volume, came to this country in 1751 and was one of the most prominent New York merchants of the Revolutionary period Richard Bache, the youngest brother of Theophylact Bache, emigrated to America before 1760 and settling in Philadelphia became a wealthy and influential merchant. He married in 1767 Sarah Franklin, the only daughter of Benjamin Franklin, Mr Duane's grandmother being one of the three daughters of this marriage.

The father of Mr Duane was the Reverend Richard Bache Duane, a distinguished divine of the Protestant Episcopal Church and for many years rector of St. John's Church in Providence, R I He married Margaret A. Tams, daughter of William Tams, of London, England, but who was long a resident of Philadelphia. Mr. Tams was a famous shot, cricketer and horseman. Mr. Duane's maternal grandmother was Anne Hennessey, who was born in London, England, was celebrated for her beauty and was prominent in Philadelphia society.

Mr. Arthur Duane was born in Honesdale, Pa., May 8th, 1859. His city residence is in West Fifty-ninth Street, his country place being Cool Gales, Sharon, Conn. He married in 1886 Julia Drake, of Binghamton, N Y., and has one child, Virginia Richards Duane He is a member of the Calumet Club and also of the Country Club of Westchester County.

JAMES GORE KING DUER

IN the Duers of to-day are united several great Colonial families, their ancestors including Duers, de Peysters, Livingstons, Beverlys, Alexanders and others   Colonel William Duer, the first American of the name, was born in Devonshire, England, in 1747, son of John Duer, a wealthy planter of Antigua, and of Frances Frye, daughter of General Frederick Frye, of the British West India service.   Educated at Eton, he went to India as an aide-de-camp to Lord Clive in 1762, and came to New York in 1768.   He was Colonel of the militia, member of the New York Provincial Congress, delegate to the Continental Congress in 1777, delegate to the first Constitutional Convention of New York and Assistant Secretary of the Treasury.   He married Lady Catherine Alexander, daughter of the famous William Alexander, Lord Stirling.

The Alexander family was of ancient descent in Scotland, its lineage going back to King Robert II.   It was established in America by James Alexander, who came here in 1716 and married a granddaughter of Johannes de Peyster.   His only son, William Alexander, Lord Stirling, married Sarah Livingston, daughter of Philip Livingston, the second Lord of Livingston Manor.   He was a Major-General in the Revolution and died in 1783.

The elder son of William Duer and Catherine Alexander was William Alexander Duer, 1780-1858, president of Columbia College, 1829-42, whose son, William Denning Duer, 1812-1891, married Caroline King, daughter of James Gore King, the New York merchant, son of Rufus King, the statesman.   Their children were Edward Alexander, James Gore King, Rufus King, William Alexander, Denning, Sarah Gracie and Amy Duer.   Edward Alexander Duer married Anna Vanderpool, daughter of John Van Buren and granddaughter of President Martin Van Buren   James Gore King Duer is engaged in the banking business.   In 1864, he married Elizabeth Wilson Meads, daughter of Orlando Meads, of Albany.   He has three daughters, Caroline King, Eleanor Theodora, the wife of Joseph Larocque, Jr., and Alice Duer.   Rufus King Duer, now deceased, was an officer in the United States Navy.   William Alexander Duer, the fourth son, graduated from Columbia in 1869 and is a member of the New York bar. He married Ellin Travers, daughter of William R. Travers and granddaughter of Reverdy Johnson, and lives in West Twenty-first Street.   He has one child, Katharine Alexander Duer.   He belongs to the Union, Manhattan, Knickerbocker, Lawyers', City and Riding clubs   Denning Duer is a graduate from Columbia College, married Louise Suydam, daughter of Henry Lispenard Suydam, and lives in New Haven, Conn.   He has one daughter, Caroline Suydam Duer.

Another branch of this family is descended from John Duer, 1782-1858, second son of Colonel William Duer and Catherine Alexander.   He was a delegate to the State Constitutional Convention in 1821 and Associate Judge of the Superior Court, being Chief Justice after 1857.   His wife was Anna Bunner.   William Duer, his son, was born in New York in 1805.   Graduated from Columbia College in 1824, he practiced law in Oswego, N. Y., and New Orleans.   He was a member of the Assembly from Oswego in 1840, District Attorney, 1845-47, a Member of Congress, 1847-51, and United States Consul to Chili.   His wife was his cousin, Lucy Chew, her mother being Maria Theodora Duer, daughter of Colonel William Duer.   Her father was Beverly Chew, of New Orleans, Collector of the Port, 1817-29, president of the branch Bank of the United States and Vice-Consul of Russia.

John Duer, eldest son of William and Lucy (Chew) Duer, born in New York, graduated from Columbia in 1859, and is a lawyer.   In 1871, he married Sara, daughter of Henry Du Pont, of Wilmington, Del   He lives in West Eighty-sixth Street, and his widowed mother lives with him.   He has two brothers and three sisters, Beverly Chew Duer, a member of the Union Club, who married Sophie Lawrence Pool, and has one child, Beverly Duer; Alexander, Maria Theodora, Anna Cuyler, and Katharine Alexander Duer, who married C Vincent Smith.   He is a member of the Metropolitan, Knickerbocker and City clubs, the Bar Association, the Downtown Association, the Columbia College Alumni Association and the St. Nicholas Society.

CORNELIUS ROOSEVELT DUFFIE, D. D.

THE name of the Duffie family was formerly MacDuffie, and more anciently MacDhubhi, or MacPhee   The ancestor of the New York branch was Duncan Duffie, born in Edinburgh, in 1733   His father, John Duffie, was lost at sea, while on his way to America, in 1741   His mother was Catherine Carmichael, of a Huguenot family   Duncan Duffie married Mary Thompson, whose mother was Hannah Cannon   He was a commissary, with the rank of Major, during the Revolution, and died soon after the war   Elbridge Gerry, the signer of the Declaration of Independence, married Mrs   Duncan Duffie's sister

John Duffie, 1763–1808, the son of Duncan Duffie, was the grandfather of Dr. Cornelius Roosevelt Duffie.   In early life he was engaged in business with his brother-in-law, Cornelius C Roosevelt, and was trustee of the Gold Street Baptist Church   The grandmother of Dr. Duffie was Maria Roosevelt, daughter of Cornelius and Margaret (Herring) Roosevelt   Cornelius Roosevelt was born in 1731, the son of Johannes Roosevelt, alderman in New York, from 1717 to 1733   The parents of Johannes Roosevelt were Nicholas Roosevelt, and his wife, Heyltje Jans, and his grandfather, Claes Martenson Van Roosevelt, came from Holland, in 1654. The maternal grandmother of the Reverend Dr   Duffie descended from Peter Herring and Margaret Cozine, the first couple married in the new Dutch Church, in 1662   Her grandparents were Peter Herring and Margaret Bogart.   Her father was Elbert Herring, born in 1706, and her mother, Catherine Lent, a descendant of Abraham Ruyken Van Lent

The father of the Reverend Dr Duffie was the Reverend Cornelius Roosevelt Duffie, 1789–1827, an Episcopalian clergyman, who graduated from Columbia College, in 1809   He studied law with his mother's cousin, the Honorable Samuel Jones, afterwards Chancellor of the State.   For a time he was in business, and, from 1817 to 1823, was a vestryman of Trinity Church   Early in life he was ensign and Lieutenant in the New York Militia   In 1821, he began the study of theology, became a deacon in 1823, the following year was ordained a priest, and founded and was the first rector of St Thomas' Church.   His wife was Helena Bleecker, daughter of James Bleecker, a merchant of New York, whose wife was a daughter of the famous Theophylact Bache.   Her American ancestor was Jan Jansen Bleecker

The Reverend Cornelius Roosevelt Duffie was born in New York, in 1821.   He graduated from Columbia College, in 1841, and from the General Theological Seminary, in 1845, being ordained deacon by Bishop Brownell, the same year.   In 1846, he became connected with Trinity Church, New York, and in 1848, was the founder and first rector of the Church of St. John the Baptist, now, by consolidation, the Church of the Epiphany, of which he is rector emeritus.   In 1849, he was ordained a priest, and became chaplain of Columbia College, in 1857, of which he is now chaplain emeritus, and trustee of the General Theological Seminary, in 1865   His degree of D. D. was conferred by the University of the City of New York.

The first wife of the Reverend Dr Duffie was Sarah Brush Clark, daughter of Joel and Mary (Brush) Clark   Joel Clark was a son of Timothy Clark and Patience Osborn.   Timothy Clark was a nephew of Abraham Clark, member of the Continental Congress from New Jersey, and a signer of the Declaration of Independence.   Sarah Brush (Clark) Duffie died in 1880 Dr Duffie subsequently married Lillian A. Pelton, daughter of John Pelton, who was connected with the Honorable Samuel Jones Tilden.   Dr. and Mrs. Duffie live at 263 Lexington Avenue ; their country seat is at Litchfield, Conn.   The Doctor's children are · Cornelius Roosevelt Duffie, Jr , who married Edith Normanton Langdon, Archibald Bleecker Duffie, who married Antoinette Lerocque Roe, and Jane Antoinette Duffie, the wife of Edward Hamilton Cahill

Nearly one hundred local names in and around New York are derived from Dr Duffie's ancestors and connections.   Through the Bleeckers, Barclays and Gordons, Dr Duffie can trace his descent to six generations of the Earls of Sutherland, and over twenty generations of Kings of England, Scotland and France, a Queen of Castile, and an Empress of Germany.

WILLIAM WEST DURANT

F AMILY tradition and public records connect the Durants of Massachusetts with those of Virginia. According to these authorities, George Durant, who was born in Malden, Mass , in 1661, was a son or nephew of William Durand, or Durant, who was sent by the Boston church in 1644, as ruling elder of the Puritan Congregation in Nansemond County, Va , and also nephew or cousin of George Durant, the first English settler of North Carolina It is believed that William Durant was a son of Richard Durant, who was twice Mayor of Bodmin, in Cornwall, England, and who died there in 1632.

George Durant, of Malden, removed to Middletown, Conn., in 1663 After 1683, he was a resident of Lyme, where he died in 1687. Edward Durant, his son, was born in 1652, settled in Boston previous to 1686, and in 1691 became the owner of the Lamb Inn, in Washington Street His first wife and the mother of his children was Anne Hall Edward Durant, second of the name, 1695-1740, lived in Winter Street, Boston, in a house adjoining that of Judge Sewall In Newton, he built a house that is still standing on Nonantum Hill. He left an estate appraised at nearly twelve thousand pounds, being one of the wealthiest men in the Massachusetts Colony His wife was Judith Waldo, 1692-1785, daughter of Cornelius and Faith (Peck–Jackson) Waldo.

In the fourth generation was another Edward Durant, 1715-1782, the eldest child of Edward Durant, of Newton. Graduated from Harvard College in 1735, he received the degree of M A in 1738 and was one of the leading citizens of Newton From 1763 to 1775, he was moderator of twenty-six town meetings, in 1774 was chairman of the Committee of Correspondence, and in 1774 and 1775 was a representative to the Provincial Congresses His wife was Anne Jackson, daughter of Captain John Jackson Thomas Durant, 1746-1831, son of Edward and Anne Durant, of Newton and Middlefield, Mass , was engaged in the Lexington-Concord fight in 1775 and served in the Continental Line His wife, whom he married in 1775, was Elizabeth Clark, daughter of William Clark, who, although almost sixty years old, took part in the Lexington-Concord fight. Elizabeth Clark, 1752-1853, was descended from Thomas Clark, who came to Plymouth, Mass., on the first voyage of the Mayflower and, returning to England, came back on the ship Ann in 1623 His name appears in the allotment of lands of the Plymouth Colony in 1624. He died in 1697, and one of the oldest gravestones on Burial Hill stands to his memory.

Thomas Durant, second of the name, 1791-1866, married, in 1815, Sybil Wright, 1788-1866, daughter of Nathan and Mary Wright. He was the son of Thomas Durant and Elizabeth Clark and the grandfather of William West Durant His son, Thomas Clark Durant, was born in Lee, Mass., in 1820, was graduated from the Albany Medical College at the age of twenty-one, and engaged in the practice of his profession Later he gave up professional for business pursuits, becoming a partner of the firm of Durant, Lathrop & Co, of Albany, which had a large business with European ports In 1848, he turned his attention to railroads in the Great West, and was prominent in organizing and developing the Michigan Southern, the Chicago & Rock Island and the Mississippi & Missouri railroads It was due to his enterprise that the Union Pacific Railroad was carried through to completion He was, from 1861 to the time of the driving of the last spike, the vice-president and general manager of this great transcontinental railroad and acting president most of the time, during the absence of its actual president, General John A Dix, American Minister to France After this work was accomplished, he continued the construction of the Adirondack Railroad, of which he was president He married, in 1847, Heloise Hannah Timbrel, of England When he died, in North Creek, N Y , in 1885, he left a widow, a daughter and one son.

Mr William West Durant, the only son of Dr Thomas C Durant, was born in Brooklyn, N Y , November 23d, 1850 He has been principally interested in railroad enterprises and real estate in the Adirondacks. He is a member of the Metropolitan Club and his special interest in yachting has led him to confine his further club membership to the New York, Seawanhaka-Corinthian, Larchmont, Eastern and other yacht clubs.

HIRAM DURYEA

WHILE descending primarily from French ancestors, the Duryea family in this country is essentially of Dutch origin. Joost (George) Durie, the ancestor of the family in the New Netherland, was a French Huguenot, who, after the revocation of the Edict of Nantes, sought a refuge at Manheim, of the Rhenish palatinate. In 1660, he married Magdalena LeFevre, and soon after that came to this country. As early as 1675, he was a resident of Long Island and lived, for various periods, in New Utrecht, Bushwick and Brooklyn, his death occuring in Bushwick, in 1727.

Abraham Durije, the son of Joost Durije, 1685–1753, the originator of the name here, married Elizabeth, daughter of Theodoris and Aertje (Bogart) Polhemius, he the son of the Reverend Johannes Polhemius, and she the daughter of Teunis Gysbertsen Bogarts. Daniel Durije, the son of Abraham Durije, married a descendant of Laurens Cornelisen Koeck, who came over to the New Netherland in 1661, and Gabriel Durije, his grandson, married Femetije (or Phœbe) Hoogland, daughter of Cornelius and Sarah (Woertman) Hoogland. Cornelius Hoogland was a descendant of Dirck Jansen Hoogland, who came from Naerseveen, Utrecht, in 1657 ; and Sarah Woertman was descended from Dirck Jansen Woertman, who came from Amsterdam, in 1647.

Gabriel Durije was the great-grandfather of General Hiram Duryea, whose grandfather, Cornelius Duryea, was born in 1776. Beginning at that period, the family name was generally spelled in its present form of Duryea. The grandmother of General Duryea was Jemima Van Nostrand, daughter of John and Hannah (Bedell) Van Nostrand. She was descended from Hans Hansen Van Nostrand, who came from Noorstrand, Holstein, in 1739, and also from Robert or Daniel Beedle or Beadell, one of the early settlers of Hempstead, Long Island.

The father of General Duryea was Hendrick Vanderbilt Duryea, who was born in Syosset, Long Island, in 1799, and died in 1891. The General's mother was Elizabeth Wright, who was born in 1801, was married to Hendrick V. Duryea in 1819, and died in 1881. She was the daughter of Zebulon and Catharine Wright, of Glen Cove, Long Island. Zebulon Wright was the fifth in descent from Peter Wright, who came, with his brothers, Anthony and Nicholas, from the County of Norfolk, England, to the Massachusetts Bay Colony in 1635. Peter Wright moved to Long Island in 1653, and was one of the first settlers of Oyster Bay. His sons married daughters of the old established families in that section.

On the female side of his house, as well as through the paternal line, General Duryea can trace his descent to most distinguished Colonial ancestry. His grandmother, wife of Zebulon Wright, was Catharine Gritman, descended, on the maternal side, from Edward and Faith Dotey, who came over on the Mayflower, and his great-great-grandmother was Clemence Feke, daughter of Robert Feke, a descendant of Robert Feke, who came over to Massachusetts with Governor John Winthrop, and a descendant of William Ludlam, who came from Matlock, England, in 1655. A generation further back, the wife of Gideon Wright, son of Peter Wright, the pioneer, was Elizabeth Townsend, daughter of John Townsend, one of the early settlers of Oyster Bay, and of his wife, Elizabeth Montgomerie, a cousin of the Colonial Governor Dongan, of New York.

General Hiram Duryea was born at Manhasset, Long Island, April 12th, 1834. He received a good education in public and private schools, and, at the age of twenty-one, became a partner with his father in the starch manufacturing business. He was vice-president and president of the Glen Cove Starch Manufacturing Company for many years, and afterwards became president of the National Starch Company, which succeeded the Glen Cove Company.

The military career of General Duryea was very creditable. In 1855, Governor Myron Clark commissioned him First Lieutenant of Artillery in the Forty-eighth Regiment of the State Militia, a commission which he held for several years. At the beginning of the Civil War, he promptly tendered his services to the State, and on April 25th, 1861, was commissioned Captain in the Fifth New York Infantry (Duryee Zouaves), and on August 15th, 1861, was commissioned Major in the same regiment, and on September 3d, Lieutenant-Colonel. After the siege of Yorktown he commanded the regiment in the Peninsula and Maryland campaigns. In the Seven Days' Battles, and in the operations before Richmond, his regiment was specially mentioned for its gallantry and efficient services, being one of the most famous New York commands in the war, and he was several times commended, in official reports, for distinguished service. He was appointed Colonel of the same regiment October 29th, 1862, and on May 26th, 1866, was commissioned by the President of the United States, Brevet Brigadier-General of Volunteers "for distinguished conduct at the Battle of Gaines Mills, Va." He retired from the service December, 1862, in consequence of permanent injuries received in the field.

General Duryea was married, in 1868, to Laura D. Burnell, daughter of Leander Burnell and Anna Noble (Dewey) Burnell. His children are, Harry H., Chester B., Anna E., and Millicent S. Duryea. The General is a member of the Veteran Association of the regiment which he commanded during the war, of the Society of the Fifth Army Corps, of the United Service Club, and of the Military Order of the Loyal Legion.

According to the old records, the Durie family originated in the Province of Burgundy, France. The history, traditions and genealogies of the race were published in Nice, France, some years ago, and reference is made therein to some of its members having been born in the Town of Marcigny. The family was prominent, representatives of it having been distinguished as judges, advocates and men of letters, and divines.

Originally spelled Durie, the name sometimes appeared as Duryer, and in a very remote period as Du Ryer. The spelling Duryea, or Duryee, is, of course, a more modern variation of the same patronymic. The arms of the family, according to Burke, are Azure, a chevron between three crescents, argent.

Andre Duryer, or Du Ryer, who was born in Marcigny, in Burgundy, lived in the first half of the seventeenth century, and was a Gentleman of the King's Bed Chamber, the French diplomatic agent at Constantinople, and the Consul for France at Alexandria, in Egypt. He lived many years in the East, was one of the most accomplished Oriental scholars of his time, and published a translation of The Gulistan of Saadi in 1634, and one of the Koran in 1647. Pierre Duryer, born in Paris, 1605, was a French dramatist and man of letters, and a competitor of the celebrated Corneille when the latter was admitted to the French Academy in 1646. Charles Henri Durier, who was born in Paris in 1830, was chief in the Bureau of the Minister of Justice and a Chevalier of the Legion of Honor.

English records show that members of the family emigrated to Scotland about the year 1500. Among the most eminent members of the Scottish branch of the family have been Andrew Durie, who died in 1558, and who was Bishop of Galloway and Abbot of Melrose, George Durie, 1496–1561, Abbot of Melrose ; Sir Alexander Gibson, Lord Durie, a Scottish judge, who died in 1644 ; John Durie, a Scottish Jesuit, who died in 1587 ; John Durie, 1537–1600, a Presbyterian minister of prominence, and Robert Durie, 1555–1616, also a minister of the same denomination. Sir Robert Bruce, of Clackmore, who had the honor of knighthood conferred upon him by King James VI., of Scotland, married for his second wife, Helen, daughter of Robert Durie, by whom he had one daughter, who became the wife of Alexander Shaw, of Sautrie. Andrew Boswell, seventh son of Sir John Boswell, of Balmuto, had a daughter, Janet, who became the wife of her cousin, John Durie, of Grange. Andrew, the fourth Earl of Rothes, married for his third wife, Janet, daughter of David Durie, of Durie. The mother of this Janet Durie was Catharine Ramsey, the daughter of George, Lord Ramsey of Dalhousie, and his wife, Margaret, the only child and heiress of Sir George Douglass, of Melinhill.

Members of the various branches of the Scotch family of Durie have, it is seen, allied themselves in marriage to some of the most prominent noble families of that kingdom. The identification of this branch of the family with that of the French line, is complete and unmistakable through the records of ancient chronicles and documents and the blazons of heraldry.

ELISHA DYER

FROM England to Boston, before 1629, came Edward, George and Tabitha Dyre, two brothers and their sister The son of one brother and the daughter of the other, who accompanied their parents, afterwards married and became the ancestors of the Dyer family in New England William Dyre, or Dyer—the name is variously spelled in the old records— was a freeman of Boston in 1635 He was one of the company of seventeen persons who, in 1638, purchased from the Narragansett Indians the territory that afterwards became the Colony of Rhode Island At the first general court of elections held at Newport, in 1640, he was chosen secretary of the Colony. Seven years later, he was a recorder of the General Assembly, and in the contest between the New Englanders and the Dutch, of New Amsterdam, was in command of a privateer Mary Dyer, wife of William Dyer, was one of the religious martyrs of New England. She became a follower of Ann Hutchinson, and was among those who were ordered to depart from Massachusetts in 1659 Subsequently returning to that Colony, she was imprisoned as a Quaker and sentenced to death Through the interposition of her family she was reprieved, but upon returning in opposition to a second decree of expulsion, was again taken into custody and executed upon Boston Common

John Dyer, a grandson of William and Mary Dyer, married Freelove Williams, a great-granddaughter of Roger Williams Their son, Anthony Dyer, was the father of Elisha Dyer, who married Frances Jones, a daughter of Esther Jones and a great-granddaughter of Mary Vernon, daughter of Gabriel Vernon, of an ancient Huguenot family from La Rochelle, France The Honorable Elisha Dyer, son of Elisha and Frances (Jones) Dyer, was born in Providence, R I , in 1811, and graduated from Brown University in 1829 Entering upon mercantile life, he became his father's partner in 1831, and after the latter's death was the owner of the Dyerville Manufacturing Company For nearly half a century he was one of the most prominent men in Rhode Island In 1840, and for five successive terms, he was Adjutant-General of Rhode Island. In 1857, he was elected Governor of the State, and was reelected in 1858, but declined to accept the second term

General Elisha Dyer, son of the Honorable Elisha Dyer, was born in Providence in 1839. He studied in Brown University and at the University of Geissen, in Germany, and graduated from the latter in 1860 with the degree of Ph D During the Civil War, he served in the Rhode Island Light Artillery as Lieutenant, and was wounded and promoted to be Major In 1863, Governor James Y Smith appointed him on his military staff with the rank of Colonel, and after the war he commanded the artillery of the State of Rhode Island His public career began in 1877, when he was elected to the State Senate, and in 1881 he was a member of the General Assembly In 1896, he was elected Governor of the State, and was inaugurated in 1897, forty years after his father's assumption of that office In 1861, General Dyer married Nancy Anthony Viall, daughter of William and Mary B (Anthony) Viall They have three sons, Elisha Dyer, Jr., George Rathbone Dyer and Hezekiah Anthony Dyer

Mr Elisha Dyer, Jr , was born in Providence, R I , in 1862 He was educated in St Paul's School, Concord, N H , and was graduated from Brown University He studied law, and was admitted to the bar, but coming to New York engaged in the banking business, and for some years has been secretary and treasurer of the Brooklyn Elevated Railroad Company. In 1891, Mr Dyer married Sidney (Turner) Swan, of Newport, R. I. Mrs Dyer's family has been prominent in Baltimore, Md She is a descendant of the Turners of Virginia and the Pattersons of Maryland, her grandfather having been a brother of Madame Jerome Bonaparte Mr and Mrs Dyer's residence is in West Thirty-second Street, and their Newport home is Wayside, in Bellevue Avenue. He is a member of the Knickerbocker Club His brother, George Rathbone Dyer, a graduate of Brown University, is engaged in business in New York, and is a Captain in the Twelfth Regiment, N. G. S N Y

HENRY EARLE

FOR nearly five hundred years previous to the beginning of the migration from England to this country, members of the Earle family were inhabitants of the territory included in the adjoining counties of Dorset, Somerset and Devon. The family is of ancient origin, dating to Saxon ancestry prior to the Roman Conquest Sir Walter Earle, of Charborough, was one of the first patriots of the English Revolution of 1649. Ralph Earle, 1606-1678, the American progenitor of the family, was contemporary with and probably a kinsman of Sir Walter Earle. He came to this country in 1638 or before. In the records of the City of Newport, he appears in a list arranged in October, 1638, as "A catalogue of such persons who, by the general consent of the company, were admitted to the inhabitants of the island, now called Aqueednec, having submitted themselves to the government that is or shall be established according to the word of God therein." In 1655, he was a juryman and again in 1669, and was also Captain of the troop of horse. By his wife, Joan Savage, he had two sons and three daughters

A son of Ralph Earle and the ancestor of the branch of the family to which Mr. Henry Earle belongs, was William Earle, who died in 1715. He was a freeman of Portsmouth, R. I., in 1658, and afterwards removed to Dartmouth, Mass., where he was living in 1670. He was a deputy from Portsmouth to the General Assembly in Providence in 1704, and again to the General Assembly in Newport in 1706 His wife was Mary Walker, daughter of John and Katherine Walker. His son, Thomas Earle, lived in Portsmouth and Swansea, and died in Warwick, R I., in 1727. The wife of Thomas Earle was Mary Taber, daughter of Philip and Mary Taber, of Dartmouth, Mass Oliver Earle, of the next generation, was a native of Swansea. For several years he lived in New York, where he was engaged in the East India trade. His wife was Rebecca Sherman, of Portsmouth, daughter of Samuel and Martha (Trip) Sherman.

In the succeeding generations from Oliver Earle to Mr. Henry Earle, came Caleb Earle, of Swansea, 1729-1812; Weston Earle, of Swansea, 1750-1838; Caleb Earle, of Providence, 1771-1851, and Henry Earle, of Providence, 1815-1854 The first Caleb Earle married Sarah Buffington, daughter of Benjamin and Isabel Buffington, and she was the ancestress in the fifth generation of Mr. Henry Earle. After the death of his first wife, he married Hannah Chace, daughter of Daniel and Mary Chace. Weston Earle, 1750-1838, son of Caleb Earle, married Hepzibeth Terry for his first wife, and their son, Caleb Earle, second of the name, the grandfather of Mr. Henry Earle, was a prominent citizen of Providence and served for one term as Lieutenant-Governor of the State of Rhode Island. His wife was Amey Arnold, daughter of Nehemiah and Alice Arnold, of Foster, R. I The father of Mr Henry Earle was Henry Earle, a son of Lieutenant-Governor Caleb Earle, his mother being Mary T. Pitman, daughter of Judge John and Rhoda (Talbot) Pitman, of Providence The children of Henry and Mary T. (Pitman) Earle were: Mary T., who died in infancy; Henry, William P., and Joseph Pitman Earle.

Mr. Henry Earle, the eldest son of Henry and Mary T. (Pitman) Earle, was born in Providence, R. I., November 20th, 1843. He is engaged in mercantile business in New York and lives in Brooklyn. He married, in 1874, Alice Morse, daughter of Edwin and Abby M (Clary) Morse, of Worcester, Mass., and has had four children, Alice Clary, Mary Pitman, Alexander Morse, and Henry Earle, his youngest child, who died in 1892. He belongs to the Downtown Association, the Marine and Field, Crescent Athletic, Barnard and Twentieth Century clubs, and is secretary of the Brooklyn Club

The youngest brother of Mr. Earle, Joseph P. Earle, born in Providence in 1847, was graduated from Brown University in the class of 1871, and for many years has been engaged in business in New York He is a member of the Tuxedo, Union League, Union, University, New York Yacht, Seawanhaka-Corinthian Yacht, Atlantic Yacht and other clubs, belongs to the Downtown Association and the Geographical Society, and is a patron of the Metropolitan Museum of Art and a member of the Chamber of Commerce. He lives in East Twenty-sixth Street

DORMAN BRIDGEMAN EATON

A MONG the passengers on the ship Elizabeth and Ann, that sailed from London to the Massachusetts Bay Colony in 1635, were John Eaton, his wife Abigail and two children. They settled in Watertown, Mass , and the head of the family was a freeman in 1636. Subsequently he removed to Dedham, where he died in 1658. He was the ancestor of a family that is known in the history of New England as the Dedham Eatons, and which includes many representatives who have been distinguished in business and professional life His son, John Eaton, who was born in 1636 and died in 1694, had by his wife Alice seven sons and one daughter, and of these sons, Thomas Eaton, who was born in 1675 and died in 1748, having married Lydia Gay in 1697, removed to Connecticut and was a man of much influence in Woodstock David Eaton, 1706–1777, son of Thomas and Lydia (Gay) Eaton, was three times married First to Dinah Davis; second to Bethia Tiffany, and third, to Patience Kendall. His son, David Eaton, removed to Hanover, N. H , and was a prominent citizen there, being an elder in the Presbyterian church in 1775 and a soldier in one of the Hanover companies of militia in the general alarm of 1777. He was the great-grandfather of the Honorable Dorman Bridgeman Eaton. Some of his descendants removed to Vermont and became the heads of families of prominence in that State. His grandson was the Honorable Nathaniel Eaton, who married Ruth Bridgeman, who was also of the best Vermont stock, coming from one of the old families of Caledonia County, in that State.

The Honorable Dorman Bridgeman Eaton, the son of Nathaniel Eaton and Ruth Bridgeman, was born in Hardwick, Vt., in 1823. He was graduated from the University of Vermont in 1848 and from the Law School of Harvard College in 1850. Admitted to the New York bar in 1851, he was early associated with Judge William Kent, whom he assisted in editing the Commentaries of the illustrious Chancellor James Kent. He has practiced with success at the bar and is the author of several legal works, and of many articles and addresses on similar subjects. Mr Eaton has been one of the conspicuous leaders in the political reform movement, that has characterised the closing years of the century, in the United States. His life has been spent in New York, but his labors in the cause of civil service reform have given him an international reputation, while he is also an authority on municipal administration. An early member of the Union League Club, he was for many years chairman of its committee on political reform, and he drafted the laws under which the salaried fire department and the metropolitan Board of Health were created In 1867, he drew up the sanitary code for New York and the act organizing the police courts of the city.

He has made the reform of the civil service virtually his life work. In this cause, he was a pioneer and has been the most uncompromising opponent that the spoils system has ever been called upon to face In 1870, he went to Europe and spent three years studying the civil service systems of England and the Continental countries. The value of his work was acknowledged by President Grant, who made him a member of the first National Civil Service Commission, his predecessor being the late George William Curtis. In 1877, he again visited Europe, the result of his investigations this time being a volume upon the Civil Service of Great Britain, which was published by authority of Congress and by Harper & Brothers. He drafted the act passed in 1883 organizing the United States Civil Service Commission, and was the first commissioner appointed thereto by President Arthur. In 1874, he drafted a code for the Government of the District of Columbia, at the request of the joint committee of both Houses of Congress.

Mr. Eaton has written much for the magazines and other periodicals, principally upon subjects relating to municipal and national government, among his most important essays having been The Independent Movement in New York, 1880, Term and Tenure of Office, and Secret Sessions of the United States Senate. He married Annie S Foster and resides in East Twenty-ninth Street. He is a member of the Century Association, the Union League and Reform clubs, the leading legal societies, including the Bar Association, and the various organizations for municipal and civil service reform.

DAVID S. EGLESTON

EXETER, Devonshire, was the home of Bagot Egleston, who was born in 1590 and came to America in 1630. He married, while in England, Mary Talcott, of Braintree, in Essex. In 1631, he was a freeman of Dorchester and a man of influence. Afterwards he removed to Windsor, Conn, and died in 1674. His eldest son, John Egleston, married Hester Williams, sister of Morgan Williams, and was prominent in the Pequot War. Joseph Egleston, 1700–1774, of Windsor, Conn, and Sheffield, Mass, married, in 1730, Abigail Ashley, and thus became allied with many prominent New England families. Indeed, the Eglestons, Pattersons, Ashleys and Hydes frequently intermarried during the Colonial period. Seth Egleston, 1731-1772, the son of Joseph, was born in Westfield, Mass., and died in Sheffield. In 1754, he married Rachel Church, 1736-1825.

Major Azariah Egleston, paternal grandfather of the gentleman whose name appears at the head of this sketch, was the son of Seth and Rachel (Church) Egleston. He was one of the prominent men of western Masssachusetts in the last quarter of the eighteenth century and the early years of the present century. He was born in Sheffield, Mass., in 1757 and died in Lenox in 1822. He was an active promoter of the famous Berkshire Convention, and it was very largely owing to his energetic work that the Solemn League and Covenant was adopted by that body. When the Revolution began, he, with his three brothers, enlisted in Captain Noble's Company. He was engaged in the battle of Bunker Hill, made the Canadian Campaign and fought at the battle of the Cedars and for his gallant conduct there was promoted to be ensign in 1777 He participated in the battles of Trenton and Princeton and endured the trials of Valley Forge with the army in the winter of 1777–78. He was a Lieutenant in the Massachusetts line in 1780. In 1786 he was aide-de-camp to Major-General Paterson, with the rank of Major and was active in the suppression of Shay's Rebellion, He was subsequently on the staff of Major-General Astley. He was a valued friend of Generals Lafayette and Kosciusko, and enjoyed confidential relations with General Washington. After the war, he was one of the founders of the Society of the Cincinnati and of the Massachusetts branch of that order. He held the position of justice of the peace of Berkshire County for nearly thirty years, was a representative to the General Court of Massachusetts, 1796-99, a State Senator, 1807-09 and Associate Judge of the Court of Sessions in 1808.

Thomas Jefferson Egleston, father of the gentleman whose name heads this article, was the son of Major Azariah Egleston. He was born in Lenox in 1800, and for more than twenty-five years was a prominent merchant in New York, where he died in 1861. In 1828, he married Sarah Jesup Stebbins, who was born in 1809. The children of this alliance were Thomas Stebbins Egleston, who was born in 1829 and died in 1831; David S. Egleston, born in 1830 ; Thomas Egleston, born in 1832; Theophilus S Egleston, born in 1835 and died in 1838; Sarah Elizabeth, born in 1837; William Couch, born in 1839; George Washington Egleston, born in 1843; and Henry Paris Egleston, born in 1848 and died in 1886.

Mr. David S. Egleston is the eldest surviving child of the family Early in life, he engaged in business as a merchant in New York. He married Fannie Hawley and resides in East Thirty-fifth Street, near Fifth Avenue. Mr. Egleston is a member of the Metropolitan, Union, and New York Yacht clubs, the Century Association, the Downtown Association, the National Academy of Design and the New England Society.

Professor Thomas Egleston, the second son, is a graduate of Yale College and of the School of Mines at Paris, France, and became a distinguished professor in Columbia College He is an officer of the Legion of Honor of France. He married Miss McVickar and lives in Washington Square He is a member of the Century Association and the Grolier Club. William Couch Egleston, the third surviving son of Thomas J. Egleston, is a graduate of Yale College, a member of the Metropolitan and Union clubs and a patron of the National Academy of Design. He resides in West Fifty-sixth Street.

GEORGE WILLIAM ELY

IN the first two American generations of the Ely family were Nathaniel Ely and his wife, Martha, and Samuel Ely and his wife, Mary Day, daughter of Robert Day and Editha Stebbins Nathaniel Ely, who was born in England in 1605, came to Massachusetts in 1634 and was one of the first settlers of the town of Hartford His son, Samuel Ely, was a large property owner in Hartford, where he died in 1692 In the third American generation, Samuel Ely, second of the name, grandson of the pioneer, was the ancestor in the sixth generation of Mr George William Ely. He was born in Springfield, Mass., in 1668, and died in West Springfield, in 1732. One of the earlier settlers of the town of Springfield, he was prominent in the local affairs of that community, being a selectman in 1702, 1716 and 1719. He was clerk of the town of West Springfield for nineteen years, beginning with 1702. He was twice married His first wife was Martha Bliss, daughter of Samuel and Mary (Leonard) Bliss. She was born in Longmeadow, Mass , in 1674, and died in West Springfield in 1702, and was a member of the famous Bliss family, that has been prominent and influential in Western Massachusetts since the earliest Colonial days. His second wife, whom he married in 1704 and who died in 1766, was Sarah Bodurtha, daughter of Joseph and Lydia Bodurtha.

The third Samuel Ely was born in Springfield, in 1701, and died in West Springfield in 1758. He married, in 1722, Abigail Warriner, daughter of Samuel and Abigail (Day) Warriner Abigail Warriner was descended on both sides from several of the oldest Colonial families of Western Massachusetts She was born in 1703 and died in 1762. Thomas Ely, son of the second Samuel Ely, was born in West Springfield in 1725 and died in 1790 His wife, whom he married in 1756 and who died in 1807, was Sarah Merrick, daughter of Joseph and Mary (Leonard) Merrick. Their son, Captain Darius Ely, was born in West Springfield in 1761 and was among the early pioneers to the Western Reserve. He settled in Ravenna, Portage County, O., where he died in 1844. His wife was Margaret Ashley, daughter of Joseph Ashley, of West Springfield. She was born in 1765, married in 1786, and died in Ravenna in 1838. Joseph Merrick Ely, son of Darius and Margaret (Ashley) Ely, was born in West Springfield in 1802. Entering Yale College, he was graduated from that institution in 1829, and became one of the prominent educators of his generation, being principal of a classical school in New York for more than twenty-five years The latter part of his life was spent in Pennsylvania, and he died in Athens, Bradford County, in that State, in 1873. His wife, whom he married in 1834, was Juliette Marie Camp, daughter of William and Abigail (Whittlesey) Camp.

Mr. George William Ely, the son of Joseph M. Ely, was born in New York, January 6th, 1840. After a thorough education, principally in private schools, he entered upon business life and has been for many years one of the prominent stock brokers of Wall Street. He has a seat in the Stock Exchange and is a member of the New York, Lawyers', Barnard and Whist clubs. Early in life, he joined the Seventh Regiment, and in 1862 went to the front as Captain, being the youngest Captain that the Seventh Regiment ever had. In 1864, Mr Ely married, in Seymour, Conn , Frances Almira Wheeler, daughter of Henry and Nancy (Hotchkiss) Wheeler. For many years the residence of the family was in Brooklyn, but is now in West Eighty-eighth Street, near Central Park

Mr. and Mrs. Ely have three children Their elder son, Henry Bidwell Ely, who was born in New York in 1866, graduated from Columbia College in the class of 1888, is a lawyer, and one of the trustees of the William Astor estate He belongs to the University, New York Athletic, Church and Λ Δ Φ clubs and to the Columbia College Alumni Association. He married Lillian E Kissam and lives in West Twenty-sixth Street. The second son, Leonard W. Ely, who was born in Brooklyn in 1868, is a graduate from Columbia College and a practicing physician. He belongs to the New York Athletic Club and the Columbia College Alumni Association. The youngest child of the family is Agnes Merrick Ely.

THOMAS ADDIS EMMET, M. D.

THE Emmets, who have been prominent in New York for three-quarters of a century, come from the stock made famous by the Irish patriot, Robert Emmet, who was executed in Dublin in 1803, and whose name has been from that time a rallying cry of Irish liberty. The father of Robert Emmet was a prominent physician in Dublin. His eldest son, Thomas Addis Emmet, who was the first of the family to come to this country, was born in Cork, April 24th, 1764. He was graduated from Trinity College, Dublin, and from Edinburgh University in 1784, studied law in the Temple and was admitted to the Dublin bar in 1791. Becoming a leader of the United Irishmen, he was apprehended by the British authorities and confined in Kilmainham Jail, Dublin, and in Fort George, Scotland, for nearly four years, being liberated and exiled from his native land after the Treaty of Amiens. In 1804, he came to the United States.

In this country the talented advocate and Irish patriot soon rose to a position of prominence as a leader of the New York bar, and in 1812 became Attorney-General of the State. He died suddenly in 1827, while conducting a case in the United States Circuit Court, and was buried in the Marble Cemetery in Second Street, near Second Avenue. A monument to his memory stands in St. Paul's churchyard, in Broadway. Close by, in the same cemetery, is another shaft to the memory of Dr William J. McNevin, the personal friend and revolutionary associate of Emmet, in collaboration with whom he wrote Pieces of Irish History. Several sons of Thomas Addis Emmet were prominent in New York during the first half of the present century. Robert Emmet, 1792-1873, was a lawyer and a leader in the contemplated Irish insurrection of 1848. Another son, Thomas Addis Emmet, 1798-1863, was a lawyer and Master in Chancery A grandson, Thomas Addis Emmet, 1818-1880, was a civil engineer, for a long time connected with the aqueduct department of the City of New York.

The second son of Thomas Addis Emmet was Dr John Patten Emmet, who was born in Dublin in 1797 and died in New York in 1842 He was at West Point for three years, and studied medicine for four years under Dr. William J. McNevin. Graduating with the degree of M. D. from the New York College of Physicians and Surgeons, he practiced in Charleston, S C., 1822-24, and was then for many years professor of chemistry and natural history in the University of Virginia. He published many papers, principally upon chemistry, and was a sculptor of considerable skill.

Dr. Thomas Addis Emmet, the present representative of the name, is the son of Dr. John Patten Emmet, and was born in Virginia, May 29th, 1828. He studied in the institution with which his father was connected, and then, graduating in medicine from the Jefferson Medical College of Philadelphia in 1850, began the practice of his profession in New York In 1855, he became assistant surgeon to the Woman's Hospital, and in 1862 was promoted to be surgeon-in-chief, which position he held for ten years and then became one of the board of surgeons, and has remained as a visiting surgeon until the present time. He has written many papers upon medical subjects, and is the author of several publications in book form, among them, The Treatment and Removal of Fibroids, and The Principles and Practice of Gynecology, the latter being a standard work, published in the United States, England, Germany and France.

Dr. Emmet married Kate Duncan and has several children, his son, Dr J Duncan Emmet, being one of the assistant surgeons of the Woman's Hospital. The other children are Mrs Charles N. Harris, Kathleen Emmet, Thomas Addis Emmet, Jr., and Robert Emmet, who, in 1897, married Louise, daughter of James A. Garland, of this city Belonging to the chief medical societies of this country, Dr. Emmet has been elected an honorary member of many prominent bodies of that character in Europe In 1897, Notre Dame University, of La Porte, Ind., awarded him the Laetare Medal, which is annually bestowed upon the most distinguished American Roman Catholic and which is regarded as one of the highest honors that can be paid in this country to lay members of that church.

AMOS RICHARDS ENO

UNDOUBTEDLY of Huguenot origin, the Eno family emigrated to England from France, where the name was Hennot, or Henno, and also existed in other forms of spelling. For a long time the family was established in Colchester, Essex County, England, where its members were people of high standing and influence. In this country the name has been variously spelled, Enno, Eno, Enos, Enoe, Eanos. The Rhode Island branch of the family has always used the name with a final s, the Delaware Enos are descended from the Rhode Island family. James Enno, the first American ancestor of that branch of the family to which the subject of this sketch belongs, was a native of London. He studied medicine and surgery in the institution in which the celebrated Sir Astley Cooper and others were afterwards apprentices, and, coming to this country in the early part of the seventeenth century, settled in Windsor, Conn., in 1648, where he married Anna Bidwell, daughter of Richard Bidwell. She died in 1657, and he married for his second wife Elizabeth Holcombe, widow. For his third wife, he married Hester Egleston, who was born Williams, the first white child in Hartford.

In the second generation, James Eno, son of the pioneer, was a soldier in the Indian Wars and fought in the famous Swamp Fight against the King Philip Indians. He married Abigail Bissell, daughter of Samuel and Elizabeth (Holcombe) Bissell, and died in 1714. The son of the second James Eno was David Eno, of Simsbury, Conn., 1702-1745. David Eno was a soldier in the French-Indian War, and died while taking part in the Cape Breton campaign. He married Mary Gillet, daughter of Nathan Gillet, and descended in the third generation from Nathan Gillet, who came from England to Connecticut in 1634. Jonathan Eno, of Simsbury, son of David Eno, was the grandfather of Mr. Amos Richards Eno. He died in 1813. His wife was Mary Hart, daughter of Elijah and Abigail (Goodrich) Hart, of Berlin, Conn., and a descendant from Stephen Hart, who came to Cambridge, Mass., in 1630. She was born in 1744 and died in 1834. Salmon Eno, 1779-1842, father of Mr. Amos Richards Eno, was a man of prominence in Simsbury, and a member of the Connecticut Legislature in 1834. He had a family of six children; Emmeline, who married Ozias B. Bassett; Aaron Richards; Salmon Chester; Mary, who married Milton Humphrey; Jane, who married, first, Horatio Lewis, and second, Paris Barber; and Amos Richards.

Mr. Amos Richards Eno, present head of this family, was born in Simsbury in 1810. When he was a young man about twenty-one years of age, he came to New York and, in partnership with his cousin, John J Phelps, opened a dry goods store. The new firm was soon one of the leading wholesale houses in the city. Mr. Eno continued in this business for nearly twenty years, when the firm was dissolved. Meantime he had become largely interested in real estate in New York, and thenceforth devoted himself to those interests. Through his real estate transactions, he accumulated a handsome fortune, and has long been rated as one of the most substantial real estate owners in New York. He has been a director of the Second National Bank, and a member of the Reform Club and the New England Society, and has been connected with many other leading financial institutions and social organizations. Mr. Eno married Lucy Jane Phelps, daughter of the Honorable Elisha and Lucy (Smith) Phelps, of Simsbury. Mr. Phelps was a member of the National House of Representatives from Connecticut and Speaker of the House in 1821 and 1829.

Amos F Eno is the eldest son of Mr. Amos R. Eno. He was born in New York and has been chiefly engaged throughout his business life in real estate transactions. He is a member of the Manhattan and Union League clubs, the Century Association, the Downtown Association, the New England Society and the American Geographical Society, and is a patron of the American Museum of Natural History.

Other children of Mr. Eno are: Mary J., Anna Maria, Henry Clay, Antoinette, John Chester, and William Phelps Eno. Henry Clay Eno was graduated from Yale College in 1860, received the degree of A. M. in 1863, and the degree of M. D. from Columbia College in 1864, and has resided for some years in Saugatuck, Conn.

JOHN ERVING

ONE of the most distinguished families of New York and New England is that to which Mr. John Erving belongs. He is descended from General William Shirley, Colonial Governor of Massachusetts Bay, and from the Langdons, who in early Colonial and Revolutionary times were prominent in the affairs of New Hampshire and have been related in marriage to the Astors, Kanes, Van Rensselaers and other great families of New York. The remote ancestors of Mr. Erving were King Henry I., of France, and his wife, Anne of Russia, daughter of the Grand Duke Jaroslaus, of Russia. The line of lineage is through Prince Hugh, the Great, son of King Henry and his wife, Lady Adela, who was descended from Edward, King of England, Robert de Beaumont, Earl of Leicester and Mellent, and his successors, the Barons and Baronesses of Dudley, down to Edmund Sutton de Dudley, in the sixteenth century, who married Lady Maud, daughter of the eighth Lord of Clifford, and was the father of Thomas Dudley, the great-grandfather of Thomas Dudley, the American immigrant.

Thomas Dudley was born in Cannon's Ashby about 1576. At the siege of Amiens, he commanded a company of Northamptonshire men. He was steward to the Earl of Lincoln until 1630, when he came to America with Governor John Winthrop. Before leaving England, he was chosen Assistant and Deputy-Governor of the Massachusetts Colony, was elected Governor in 1634, and for three times thereafter, and in 1644, was Commander-in-Chief of the Colonial forces. He died in Roxbury, Mass., in 1653. The Reverend Samuel Dudley, son of Thomas Dudley, was born in England about 1606, and came to this country with his father. He was a deputy to the General Court of Massachusetts for several years. By his first wife, Mary Winthrop, daughter of Governor John Winthrop, whom he married in 1632, he had a daughter, Elizabeth, who married Judge Kinsley Hall, of Exeter, N. H. The granddaughter of Judge Kinsley Hall and his wife, Elizabeth Dudley, was Mary Hall, who married John Langdon, of Portsmouth, N. H., and became the mother of Governor John Langdon.

Governor Langdon was one of the most distinguished members of a family that stood high in public councils and wielded great influence in New Hampshire in the last century. He was born in 1740 and died in 1819, was a delegate to the General Congress in 1775, a Judge of the Court of Common Pleas in 1776, Speaker of the House of Representatives of New Hampshire, 1776-82 and 1804-05, delegate to the Continental Congress in 1783, a State Senator in 1784, Governor of the State, 1785-88 and 1805-11, and United States Senator for twelve years after 1789. A brother of Governor John Langdon was Judge Woodbury Langdon, delegate to the Continental Congress in 1779 and Judge of the Superior Court, 1762-91. Caroline Langdon, daughter of Judge Woodbury Langdon, married Dr. William Eustis, who was Governor of the State of Massachusetts, 1823-25. Walter Langdon, son of Judge Woodbury Langdon, married Dorothea Astor, daughter of John Jacob Astor, and became the head of a family that has been prominent in New York business and social life for several generations. Governor Langdon was the grandfather of Mr. Erving. His wife, whom he married in 1777, was Elizabeth Sherburn. His eldest daughter, Catharine C. Langdon, married Benjamin Woolsey Rogers, and his second daughter, Eleanor E. Langdon, became the wife of Dr. Edmund Delafield. The father of Mr. Erving was Colonel John Erving, U. S. A., who died in 1862. His mother was Emily S. Elwyn Langdon, the fourth child of Governor Langdon.

Mr. John Erving was born in 1833 and was graduated from Harvard College in 1853. He has been in the active practice of his profession as a lawyer in New York for more than forty years. He married Cornelia Van Rensselaer, daughter of William and Sarah (Rogers) Van Rensselaer, of Albany, N. Y. His sons are J. Langdon Erving and William Van Rensselaer Erving, and he has several daughters. His city residence is in West Twenty-second Street, and he has a country home at Manursing Island, Rye, N. Y. He is a member of the Union League, Harvard and City clubs and the Bar Association.

WILLIAM MAXWELL EVARTS

LIKE many of New York's most eminent citizens, Mr. William M. Evarts is of New England descent. His father, Jeremiah Evarts, was born at Sunderland, Vt., in 1781, was graduated from Yale College in 1802, and in 1804 married Mrs. Mehitabel Barnes, daughter of Roger Sherman, 1721–1793, one of the signers of the Declaration of Independence, and a member of the committee which drafted it. Jeremiah Evarts practiced law at New Haven for some years, but becoming interested in religious work, he removed in 1810 to Charlestown, Mass., and till his death, in 1831, was identified with the cause of foreign missions. He was editor of The Panoplist, and of its successor, The Missionary Herald. In 1812, he became treasurer of the American Board of Foreign Missions, and in 1821 was made its corresponding secretary, a position he retained till his death. The Honorable William Maxwell Evarts, his son, was born at Charlestown, Mass., February 6th, 1818. He received his education at the Boston Latin School, and entering Yale College graduated in 1837. He then taught school, attended the Harvard Law School, and finally entered the law office of Daniel Lord, the celebrated lawyer in this city. Admitted to the bar in 1841, he formed a partnership from which the law firm of Evarts, Choate & Beaman originated.

Mr Evarts' legal and political career were to a large extent interwoven, owing to the fact that he was universally recognized by the profession and the public as one of the ablest constitutional and international lawyers this country ever possessed In 1860, he was chairman of the New York delegation to the Republican National Convention at Chicago, supporting William H Seward. For some years afterwards he was mainly occupied with causes before the Supreme Court, but in 1863 went to England, for the Government, on a confidential mission.

In 1868, he came prominently before the country for his defense of Andrew Johnson in the impeachment proceedings. At their conclusion, he was appointed by President Johnson Attorney-General of the United States, which office he held for the remainder of that administration. In 1871, President Grant appointed him the leading counsel for the United States (his associates being the late Chief Justice Waite and Caleb Cushing) to present this country's case before the international tribunal at Geneva, under the treaty of Washington The result, an award of fifteen million dollars, paid by England to the United States, for depredations on our commerce committed by the Alabama and other Confederate cruisers fitted out in England during the Civil War, was largely due to Mr. Evarts' diplomatic skill and the knowledge of international law displayed in his presentation of the case. In 1875–76, Mr Evarts was senior counsel in the defense of the Reverend Henry Ward Beecher. In the early months of 1877, he appeared as the leading counsel for the Republicans before the Electoral Commission President Hayes then appointed Mr Evarts Secretary of State, which office he filled with honor to himself and the country. In 1881, he was appointed by President Garfield a delegate to the International Monetary Conference at Paris, and in 1885 one of his few personal ambitions was fulfilled by an election as United States Senator for this State. At the conclusion of his Senatorial term he gradually retired from public life.

Few lawyers of such eminence have ever been so popular with their professional associates as Mr. Evarts He was the first president of the New York Bar Association, which office he held for ten years, and he has long been a member of the Union, Union League, Century and other clubs, of the New England Society and of many social and literary bodies. His reputation as an orator is also deservedly high. The public occasions on which he appeared in this rôle include a eulogy of Chief Justice Chase at Dartmouth College in 1875, the Centennial oration at Philadelphia in 1876, and that at Newburgh in 1893, as well as addresses at the unveiling of the Seward and Webster statues in New York, and of Bartholdi's Statue of Liberty.

Mr Evarts married Helen Minerva Wardner, daughter of Allen Wardner, of Windsor, Vt Their surviving children are Allen Wardner Evarts, Mrs. Charles C Beaman, Mary Evarts, Mrs Charles H Tweed, Mrs Edward C Perkins, Sherman Evarts, the Reverend Prescott Evarts, Mrs Charles D. Scudder, and Maxwell Evarts.

CHARLES STEBBINS FAIRCHILD

FOR two generations, in the person of father and son, the Fairchilds have exercised a potent influence in the business and political life of the Empire State   The father, Sidney T Fairchild, eldest son of John and Flavia Fairchild, was born in Norwich, N Y, November 15th, 1808 His parents removed to Cazenovia when he was a mere child, and he attended the seminary in that place, going afterwards to Hamilton College and then to Union College, being graduated from the latter institution in 1829   After studying law in Cazenovia, he was admitted to the bar in 1831, and removed to Utica, where he began the practice of his profession   His marriage in 1834 to Helen Childs, daughter of Perry G Childs, of Cazenovia, brought him back to that place to reside, and there, in 1835, he became a member of the law firm of Stebbins & Fairchild   Corporation law was his specialty, and he soon became one of the leading members of the bar in that section of the State   He was made attorney of the Syracuse & Utica Railroad, which afterwards became a part of the New York Central system, and from 1858 until his death, in 1889, was the general attorney of the New York Central Railroad.

An accomplished gentleman and lawyer, Sidney T Fairchild made a great reputation, and was very successful in his professional career   Outside of his legal practice, he had important business interests   He was a director and the secretary and treasurer of the third Great Western Turnpike Railroad Company, a director of the Madison County Bank, president of the Cazenovia & Canastota Railroad, and a trustee of the Union Trust Company of New York   He was a Democrat of deep convictions and active in the party councils.   Although a leader in conventions and in shaping the party policy in the State, he never accepted public office, although such honors were many times tendered him   He was the valued adviser and esteemed friend of such great Democrats as Horatio Seymour, Dean Richmond, John T Hoffman, Samuel J. Tilden, Lucius Robinson and Grover Cleveland

The Honorable Charles Stebbins Fairchild was born in Cazenovia, N Y, April 30th, 1842 Prepared for college in the Cazenovia Seminary, he was graduated from Harvard College in 1863 and from the Law School of Harvard in 1865.   He studied law in Albany, was admitted to the bar in 1866, and a few years later became a member of the firm of Hand, Hall & Swartz.   In 1874, Attorney-General Daniel Pratt appointed him Deputy Attorney-General of the State, and in the following year he was nominated for the position of Attorney-General on the Democratic ticket, and elected by a substantial majority   After a term of two years as Attorney-General, he spent two years in travel and study in Europe, and then settled to the practice of law in New York City.

In 1885, Mr. Fairchild entered upon a larger career of public usefulness, when President Grover Cleveland appointed him Assistant Secretary of the United States Treasury.   When Secretary Daniel Manning broke down in health under the strain of the labors of the Treasury Department, Mr. Fairchild became Acting Secretary, and upon the resignation of Mr. Manning in 1887, was advanced to the position of Secretary, remaining a member of the Cabinet until the close of President Cleveland's first administration in 1889.

Since 1889, Mr Fairchild has been the president of the New York Security & Trust Company.   He is one of the leaders of the anti-machine Democrats of the State, and as such took an active and influential part in the campaign for the nomination and election of Grover Cleveland to the presidency in 1892, and in the municipal reform movement that resulted in the overthrow of Tammany Hall in 1894   In 1897, he was prominent in the Citizens' Union political movement, and was a candidate of that party for Comptroller in the first Greater New York municipal campaign. He belongs to many of the leading clubs, including the Metropolitan, University, Century and Reform   He married, in 1871, Helen Lincklean, daughter of Ledyard and Helen Clarissa (Seymour) Lincklean, of Cazenovia, N Y   The city residence of Mr and Mrs Fairchild is in Clinton Place, and they have a country home, Lorenzo, at Cazenovia

WILLIAM HENRY FALCONER

PIERRE FAUCONIER, a Huguenot of Tours, came to England with his wife, Magdalene Pasquereau, and was naturalized in London in 1685. In 1702, he migrated to New York and became a merchant here, being also high in favor with the two Colonial Governors, Lords Bellamont and Cornbury In 1705, he was made Collector of Customs and Receiver-General of the Province, and obtained large grants of land, among them being a patent to a tract within the town of Rye, and it was in Westchester County that the family he founded became permanently established; the name of Fauconier after the first generation being changed to its English equivalent, Falconer

His second son, John Falconer, of East Chester, who was born in 1747 and married Elizabeth Purdy, had a distinguished Revolutionary record. He is named among the officers of the Revolutionary Army in the military archives of the State of New York. At the outbreak of the revolt from Great Britain, he raised a company of troops in Westchester and fought as Captain and aide-de-camp to General Washington at the battle of Chatterton Hill, near White Plains In a subsequent engagement, he was captured by the British, and was for a long time confined on the Jersey prison ship When the French allies moved from Rhode Island to the South, prior to the Yorktown campaign, the Duc de Lauzan, second in command to Rochambeau, made the Falconer mansion, on Broadway, White Plains, his headquarters, the circumstances connected with this event being described in an article in The Magazine of American History The entertainment of the French commander and his officers was for years remembered in that vicinity After the war, General Falconer, as he was called, was one of the most influential citizens of Westchester County, and was elected for eighteen consecutive terms supervisor of the town of White Plains.

The present representative of this family in New York society, Mr William Henry Falconer, is a great-grandson of the Revolutionary hero He was born in this city in 1830, and is the son of David Falconer, of New York, a grandson of Rodger Falconer, of White Plains Mr Falconer was educated at Canandaigua Academy, New York, and was for many years identified with large real estate operations, but has withdrawn from all active cares concerning the details of his extensive property in the city, and has devoted himself to a life of cultured leisure and travel

Mr. Falconer married Margaret Culbertson McLean, of Fayetteville, Pa, a lady whose family were old settlers in the Cumberland Valley, and prominent in the Revolution The Culbertsons, from whom Mrs Falconer is descended, through her mother, were also highly distinguished among the pioneers of Western Pennsylvania, and took an active part in the historical events which occurred in that region before and subsequent to the Revolution Their family history and genealogy constitutes a record of great interest They have three children, Bruce McLean Falconer, Elizabeth DeHass Falconer and Sarah Louise Falconer, none of whom are as yet married

Mr. Falconer is a member of the Union League, and a life member of the St Nicholas Society. His travels have been of an extensive character, embracing all portions of the United States, from Mexico to Alaska, as well as several visits to Europe. In the year 1890, his entire family accompanied him in a journey around the world. China, Japan, India, the Nile, the Orient, and the Continent of Europe were visited in turn; this tour, which occupied three years, terminating in 1892, being replete with interest of every kind During their journey, Mr and Mrs Falconer and their family, who were specially accredited by the late Mr Blaine (then Secretary of State) to the representatives of the United States at foreign courts, were presented to Queen Victoria, the Princesses Louise and Beatrice, His Holiness Pope Leo XIII, the Empress of Japan, the King of Greece, the Sultan of Turkey, and the Khedive of Egypt.

No small portion of Mr. Falconer's attention has been given to hospitals and benevolent institutions, which he has served as trustee and in other capacities He is also the owner of a collection of fine paintings, his tastes and preferences in that direction being for the work of American artists

GUSTAVUS FARLEY

THE first Farley in New England was Michael, who came from England to Ipswich, Mass., with his two sons about 1675. The object of his coming was to attend to some of the American interests of Sir Richard Saltonstall. Mesheck Farley, of Ipswich, Mass., the son of Michael Farley, the pioneer, was born in England about 1662, and came to this country with his father and his brother Michael. He married here Sarah Burnham, daughter of Lieutenant Thomas Burnham, of Ipswich, and died in 1696. Lieutenant Thomas Burnham was a member of the expeditions against the Pequot Indians under Endicott in 1636, and Stoughton in 1637.

A grandson of Michael Farley, the American founder of the family, was General Michael Farley, of Ipswich, who was born there in 1719 and died in 1789. For many years he was a representative to the General Court of the Massachusetts Colony, and was a member of the Provincial Congress, 1766-79. In 1774, he was chosen a councilor, but his election was negatived by General Gage, who had placed him under the ban with such other eminent patriots as Bowdoin, Winthrop and Adams. At one time, he was a Major-General of the militia, succeeding General Warren, and also a member of the executive council of the Governor of Massachusetts. He married, in 1745, Elizabeth Choate, of the notable Essex family of that name. The epitaph upon his tomb, in North Cemetery, at Ipswich, Mass., refers to him "the Honorable Michael Farley, Esq., Major-General of the militia and Sheriff of the County of Essex, who died June 20th, 1789, Æt. 70. With a mind open, honest and generous, with a heart alive to humanity and compassion, he served for many years in various stations, public, private and honorable, his neighbors and his country, with such integrity, zeal and diligence as merited an extensive approbation and rendered his death justly regretted." The epitaph of his wife refers to her as "Mrs. Elizabeth Farley, consort of the late General Farley."

Robert Farley, who was born in Ipswich in 1760, the son of General Michael Farley, died in the place of his birth in 1823. Although he was only fifteen years of age when the Revolution began, he enlisted in the following year and served throughout the war. Part of the time he was confined in the English prison ship Jersey, in New York harbor. After the war he maintained his interest in military matters and became Major in the militia. In civil life, he was High Sheriff of Essex County, and at one time Collector of Internal Revenue. The wife of Robert Farley, whom he married in 1786, was Susannah Kendall, descended from Francis Kendall, who came to this country from England before 1640, when a young man under twenty years of age, and was one of the earliest settlers in the town of Woburn, Mass.

Mr. Gustavus Farley is the grandson of Robert Farley and his wife, Susannah Kendall. His father was Gustavus Farley, of Cambridge, Mass., who was born in Ipswich in 1814 and died at Cambridge in 1897, and who married Amelia Frederika Neuman, of Ipswich, a native of Gottenburg, Sweden. The subject of this sketch was born in Chelsea, Mass., July 4th, 1844. He was educated in private schools, and soon after he was seventeen years of age went to England. After several years abroad, he returned to his home, and in 1864 went to Hong Kong, China. He spent two years in China and then resided in Japan, where he was in business for seventeen years. Returning to the United States in 1883, he has since been in mercantile life in New York City. The wife of Mr. Farley was Katharine Sedgwick Cheney, daughter of Frank Cheney, of South Manchester, Conn. The father of Mrs. Farley belongs to the celebrated Cheney family, which has been so prominent in the development of silk manufacturing in the United States. Distinguished members of the family have been Charles Cheney, the father of Colonel Frank W. Cheney, now the head of the firm of Cheney Brothers, Ward Cheney; Seth Wells Cheney, the artist; John Cheney, the engraver, and Ednah D. Cheney, the authoress and wife of Seth Wells Cheney.

Mr. and Mrs. Farley live at 42 East Twenty-fifth Street. They have one son, Frank Cheney Farley, born at Yokohama, Japan, in 1880. Mr. Farley is a member of the Union, Century and New York Yacht clubs, the Downtown Association, and the Sons of the Revolution.

PERCIVAL FARQUHAR

THE family to which Mr. Percival Farquhar belongs is of mingled Scotch, English and German ancestry. His great-great-great-grandfather, William Farquhar, came from Scotland in the closing years of the seventeenth century, on account of religious causes, and brought with him a company of his coreligionists, settling in Frederick County, Md. The earlier ancestors of the family were chiefs of the Scottish clan Farquhar.

On the maternal side, Mr Farquhar descends from Robert Brook, of the House of War- wick, who was born in London, in 1602, and who in 1635 married Mary Baker Mainwaring, daughter of Roger Mainwaring, Dean of Worcester. In 1650, Robert Brook, with his wife, ten children and twenty-eight servants, came to this country and settled in Charles County, Md. He became commandant of the county and president of the Council of Maryland His descendants spread throughout that Colony, some of them settling in Montgomery County, where they married into the Farquhar family.

The great-grandfather of Mr Percival Farquhar, Amos Farquhar, removed to Pennsylvania, in 1812, and became a cotton manufacturer This business not proving successful, after the close of the War of 1812, he returned to Maryland, where he had charge of a seminary at Fair Hill. Arthur B Farquhar, grandson of Amos Farquhar, and the father of the present Mr. Farquhar, was born in Montgomery County, Md., in 1838 He was instructed at a private school for boys at Alexandria, Va, and his talent for mechanics showing itself early, his education was completed in the line of a thorough practical mechanical instruction. He then went to York, Pa, engaged in the manufacture of agricultural implements, and finally established the A B Farquhar Company of that place Arthur B Farquhar has been a student of political economy, finance and the tariff throughout his life, and has written many essays and pamphlets on finance, and a book entitled, Economic and Industrial Delusions He has held many responsible public positions, especially in connection with the World's Columbian Exposition, of which he was a commissioner, and president of the National Organization of Executive Commissioners He married Elizabeth N. Jessop, daughter of Edward Jessop, of Baltimore, president of the Short Mountain and Tunnelton Coal Companies, and head of the firm of Jessop & Fulton.

Mr. Percival Farquhar, son of A. B. Farquhar, was born in York, Pa, and educated at the York Collegiate Institute, and at Yale College, from which he graduated with the degree of Ph B., in 1884. After a course of study at the Columbia Law School, he was admitted to the bar in 1886. For one year, 1887, he was president of the Columbus and Hocking Valley Coal and Iron Company. Since then he has been engaged in the practice of law, is connected with important business enterprises and is active in politics. In 1889, he was defeated in a campaign for the Assembly in the Third New York City District, but the following year was elected by a majority of two thousand, reëlected in 1891, and again in 1892 He was one of the leading members of the Assembly, and established a reputation for knowledge of public affairs Especially interested in the electoral franchise, he introduced and had charge of much important legislation relating to that subject, including the New York City Inspection Bill, the Personal Registration Bill, the Ballot Reform Amendments, the Codification of Laws relating to the Ballot, the Revisions of the Penal Code, and various measures affecting the National Guard.

Mr. Farquhar has been actively interested in the militia. He joined the Seventh Regi- ment in 1887, and in 1888 accepted a commission in the Second Battery of Artillery, where he was promoted to be Second Lieutenant and then First Lieutenant He is one of the board of managers of the A B Farquhar Company, of York, Pa, a member of the firm of A B. Farquhar & Co, of New York, and vice-president of the New York and Staten Island Land Company. He is a member of many clubs and social organizations ; among them, the Southern Society and the United Service, Manhattan, Reform, Calumet, Lawyers', Seventh Regiment Veteran, Democratic, Tuxedo, Riding and University Athletic clubs.

SIGOURNEY WEBSTER FAY

FOR two centuries, the members of the Fay family have been among the most prominent citizens of a cluster of towns near the central part of the State of Massachusetts. They have held town offices, have been members of the State Legislature, leading merchants, and otherwise active and influential in their several communities.

John Fay was the American progenitor of this interesting family. His parents belonged in London, and he was left an orphan at an early age. In 1656, when he was only eight years old, he was a passenger on board the ship Speedwell, which sailed from Gravesend with a company of Colonists for Boston. Arriving there, he was taken to Sudbury, where he was brought up. In 1669, he was in Marlborough, a town adjoining Sudbury, and already had several children. When King Philip's war broke out, he served in a military company, and after a time went with the other settlers to Watertown for greater safety. He returned to Marlborough when quiet was restored by the death of Philip and the subjugation of his tribe, and remained there until his death, in 1690.

A great-grandson of John Fay was Josiah Fay, who was born in Westboro, Mass., in 1732, and fought at Bunker Hill, being a member of the Westboro company which marched to Boston as soon as the news of the battle at Lexington and Concord had been heard. During the ensuing years of war, he was a member of the First Continental Infantry. In the same company with Josiah Fay was Elisha Forbes, of the same town, and the two remained comrades-at-arms throughout the long struggle for independence. Both these patriots were ancestors of Mr. Sigourney W. Fay, the New York merchant, one being his great-grandfather in the paternal and the other his great-grandfather in the maternal line, a son of Josiah Fay marrying a daughter of Elisha Forbes.

Mr. Sigourney Webster Fay was born in Boston, Mass., February 6th, 1836. His father Nahum Fay, was a well-known merchant fifty years ago. The son was graduated with honors from that rival of the famous Boston Latin School, the English High School. Fixing upon a business career for his future, he started as a clerk in the great dry goods store of Lawrence Stone & Co., of Boston, and then gained a further knowledge of the special line of business that he had selected to follow by a term of service in the Middlesex Mills, of Lowell, Mass., one of the leading manufactories of its class.

In 1860, when he was only twenty-four years of age, he concluded to start out for himself, and helped to organize and to establish in New York the great commission house of Stone, Bliss, Fay & Allen. For nearly a decade this was one of the largest commission houses in the woolen goods trade in New York City. At one time, it was the selling agent of fifteen of the largest and most important factories in New England. In 1864, the firm was reorganized into Perry, Wendell, Fay & Co., and in 1878 it became Wendell, Fay & Co.

Mr. Fay has other important business and social connections. He is a member of the Chamber of Commerce, has been a director of the Hanover National Bank since 1876, and is one of the governors of the House of Refuge. He belongs to the Union League Club, as one of its veteran members, having been among the first to join the club was organized, in February, 1863. For several years he was secretary of the club, his first elevation to that position being when he was only twenty-seven years old. His other clubs include the Metropolitan, Players, City, and Merchants, and he is a member of the New England Society, and, by virtue of his patriotic ancestry, one of the Sons of the American Revolution. In 1860, he married Delia A., daughter of Emery B. Fay, of Boston, and for twenty-five years he has resided at 35 West Fiftieth Street. He possesses very pronounced literary tastes and talent, and is an acute dramatic critic, being a close student of the drama past and present. He has lectured frequently and successfully on literary subjects, and among other works has written an able analytical essay on Charles Lamb.

GEORGE RICHMOND FEARING

SEVERAL branches of the Fearing family, members of which have been prominent in the social world and in business life in Newport and New York during the last hundred years or more, trace their descent to a common ancestor, who came to this country about 1638 John Fearing, this pioneer, was a native of England, and one of the company of Colonists that came on the ship Diligent and landed in Hingham, Mass After arriving here, he rapidly came to the front as an energetic man of affairs, and became prominent in the town of Hingham, where he settled In 1648, and again in 1661 and 1663, he was elected a selectman, was a constable in 1650, a freeman in 1652 and the clerk of writs in 1657 His death occurred in 1665.

After John Fearing, there were four generations in which the head of the family was an Israel Fearing Israel Fearing, 1644-1693, of the first generation from the pioneer, lived in Hingham, and married Elizabeth Wilde His son Israel, 1682-1754, married Martha Gibbs His grandson Israel, 1723-1753, married Hannah Swift. The fourth Israel Fearing, 1747-1826, was a Brigadier-General of the Massachusetts militia and a soldier of the Revolution. By his wife, Lucy Bourne, General Fearing became the great-grandfather of George R. Fearing and Daniel B. Fearing, of Newport, and also of Charles F Fearing and William H Fearing, of New York. The grand-parents of both these branches of the family were William Fearing, 1771-1845, a shipping merchant of Massachusetts, and his wife, Elizabeth Nye

Daniel Butler Fearing, son of William Fearing, was born in 1804 and became one of the most prosperous and influential merchants in New York. His wife was Harriet Richmond, of Providence, R I Mr Fearing died in 1870, and his widow passed away a year later. Henry Seymour Fearing, his son, lived in Newport, where he owned a fine estate, inherited from his father His death occurred in 1886 His wife, whom he married in 1857, was Serena Mason Jones, daughter of George and Serena (Mason) Jones Daniel Butler Fearing, son of Henry Seymour Fearing, inherited his father's estate in Newport and makes his residence in that city He was graduated from Harvard College in 1882, and in 1887 married Henrietta I Strong, daughter of James H and Georgiana (Berryman) Strong, of New York He belongs to many of the leading clubs and other organizations in the metropolis, his club membership including the Metropolitan, Union, Knickerbocker, Manhattan, Calumet, Players and Grolier, and the Somerset and Tavern clubs of Boston

Colonel George R Fearing is a brother of the late Henry Seymour Fearing He was born in New York and was graduated from Columbia College in 1860 He has a home in Fifth Avenue, but spends most of his time in Newport He is a member of the Metropolitan, Union, Knickerbocker and other clubs. He has one son, George R. Fearing, Jr, who was graduated from Harvard University in the class of 1893, and married, in 1897, Hester Cochrane, daughter of Alexander Cochrane, of Boston

Charles Nye Fearing, another son of William Fearing, was born in 1812, was graduated from Brown University, and during his business life was in the commission dry goods trade in New York His wife, whom he married in 1839, was Mary Swan, daughter of Benjamin L and Mary S Swan William H Fearing, the second son of Charles Nye Fearing, was born in New York and has been engaged in the importing business. He married Gertrude Lea, daughter of Joseph Lea, of Philadelphia. His residence is in East Forty-third Street, and his clubs include the Metropolitan, Tuxedo and Union, and he is a member of the American Geographical Society. He has three sons, Joseph Lea, William Henry, Jr, and Frederick Charles Fearing The elder surviving son of Charles Nye Fearing is Charles F. Fearing, who was born in New York and was graduated from Harvard College in 1863 He engaged in business as a stock broker, but has spent much of his time in foreign travel He is a member of the Metropolitan, Union, Harvard and South Side Sportsmen's clubs, and of the Sons of the American Revolution Edward Swan Fearing, the brother of William H and Charles F. Fearing, died in 1881

CORTLANDT DE PEYSTER FIELD

THE distinguished family to which Mr. Cortlandt de Peyster Field belongs has spread widely all over the United States, and has given many useful and eminent men to society, business and public life. The first of the name in this country was Robert Field, of Flushing, a descendant from Hubertus de la Field, who came to England with William the Conqueror. Hazard Field, the grandfather of the subject of this sketch, was named after his mother's family, the Hazards, who were descended from Thomas Hazard, of Lyme Regis, Dorsetershire, who came to New England in 1636. His grandmother was of the Burling family, of Flushing, and his great-great-grandmother was Hannah Bowne, of the ancient Long Island Quaker family of that name. Hazard Field, the eldest child of a group of sixteen brothers and sisters, and the fifth in descent from the original Robert Field, of Flushing, was born in 1764, and died in 1845

Benjamin Hazard Field, the eldest son of Hazard Field by a second wife, and the father of Mr Cortlandt de Peyster Field, was a distinguished New York merchant and philanthropist. He was born in the village of Yorktown, Westchester County, May 2d, 1814, and died in New York City, March 17th, 1893. After a substantial education in the public schools and academies, he came to New York and entered the office of Hickson W. Field, who was a leading merchant in the trade with China, as well as in the wholesale drug trade, three-quarters of a century ago In 1832, he became a member of the firm and when, in 1838, his uncle retired, he succeeded to the business. During the next twenty-five years, he was one of the most active and public-spirited citizens of the metropolis In 1865, he retired from business

As a philanthropist, perhaps, Benjamin H Field was known to the whole community He was actively interested in nearly every important undertaking for the public good in his generation. He was a trustee of the New York Dispensary, of the New York Institution for the Instruction of the Deaf and Dumb, the Sheltering Arms, the Children's Fold and the Roosevelt Hospital. A director of the House for Incurables, he was president of that corporation from its organization, in 1866, and in connection therewith erected an Episcopal Church, at his own expense, upon the grounds of the home. It is said that he spent an extremely large amount for those times in the cause of education, religion and charity In the commercial world, he held high rank, even after his retirement He was a life member of the Chamber of Commerce, a director of the Atlantic Mutual Insurance Company, the Old Fulton Bank and the Greenwood Cemetery Company, and vice-president of the Bank for Savings. A life member of the St. Nicholas Society, he was at one time its president, was a life member of the New York Historical Society, being for twenty years its treasurer, and in 1885 its president, and in 1859, he became a life member of the American Geographical Society. Deeply interested in art, he was a trustee of the American Museum of Natural History and was chiefly instrumental in securing the erection of the Farragut and the Halleck statues.

The mother of Mr. Cortlandt de Peyster Field was Catherine M. Van Cortlandt de Peyster, daughter of the senior Frederic de Peyster. Through her, Mr Field is connected with the Livingston, Beekman, Van Rensselaer, Van Cortlandt and other great New York families Mr Field was born in New York City, December 28th, 1839 Graduated from Columbia College in 1859, with the degree of B A , and that of M A being afterwards conferred upon him, he went into his father's office and in 1865, succeeded to the business, which has since been conducted under the firm name of Cortlandt de Peyster Field & Co He is a devoted member of the Protestant Episcopal Church and generous to educational and benevolent enterprises. When in town, he lives in East Twenty-sixth Street, but makes his residence in the ancestral house in Yorktown, N Y Mr Field's wife, whom he married in 1865, was Virginia Hamersley, daughter of John Hamersley, of one of the oldest and wealthiest families of New York and Virginia, representatives of the name having been prominent in the Colonies from an early date

NICHOLAS FISH

THE English family of Fish is said to be a branch of the old Saxon family of Fyche, which in the tables of German nobility dates from a remote period. At what time the family removed to England is not definitely known, but it was settled there in the early centuries after the Conquest. The ancestor who first appears in English historical annals was Simon Fish, who was a lawyer in London and died about 1531. Early in the seventeenth century, three members of the family, Nathaniel, John and Jonathan, came to New England, settled in Lynn, Mass., and then in Sandwich, on Cape Cod. Jonathan Fish, the progenitor of the branch of the family that has been distinguished in public life in New York, was the youngest of the three brothers. Born in England in 1610, he removed from Sandwich to Newtown, Long Island, of which place he was one of the first settlers in 1659. For several years he was a magistrate, and died in 1663. In the second generation of this Long Island family, Nathan Fish, son of Jonathan, was born in Sandwich, Mass., in 1650, removed to Newtown in 1659 with his father, and died there in 1734. His son, Jonathan, 1680–1723, was for fifteen years town clerk of Newtown. His grandson, Samuel, of Newtown, 1704–1767, married Agnes Berrien, and his great-grandson, Jonathan, 1728–1779, married Elizabeth Sackett and was a merchant of New York.

Colonel Nicholas Fish, 1758–1833, son of Jonathan Fish and Elizabeth Sackett, was one of the foremost representatives of the patriotism which the leaders of social New York exhibited in the trying times of the Revolution. Born in 1758, he had just left Princeton College to take up the study of law, when the war against Great Britain began. As an aide-de-camp to Brigadier-General John Morin Scott, he served at the battle of Long Island and in the operations around New York, and afterwards participated in the battle of Saratoga and commanded a corps of light infantry at Monmouth. At the siege of Yorktown he was a Lieutenant-Colonel, commanding a portion of the New York line. After the war, he was equally distinguished in civil life, both in society and business pursuits. President Washington appointed him Supervisor of the Revenue, which at that time was one of the highest positions in the Treasury Department, and he also became Adjutant-General of the State of New York. In 1797, he was treasurer of the New York Society of the Cincinnati. His death occurred in 1833. The wife of Colonel Fish was Elizabeth Stuyvesant, great-great-granddaughter of Governor Peter Stuyvesant. Through her mother, Margaret Livingston, she descended from Robert Livingston, the first Lord of Livingston Manor.

The Honorable Hamilton Fish, son of Colonel Nicholas Fish and his wife, Elizabeth Stuyvesant, was a man whose eminent public services and high personal character placed him in the front rank of the last generation of Americans. Born in New York in 1808, and graduated from Columbia College in 1827, he took an active part in political life, was prominent in the Whig party of those days, served in the State Assembly, and in 1843 was elected to Congress. In 1847, he was chosen Lieutenant-Governor, and was then elected Governor, serving from 1849 to 1851, in which latter year he was made United States Senator from New York. In 1869, President U. S. Grant appointed him Secretary of State of the United States, and in this great office he served for the entire eight years of President Grant's two terms. While in that position he carried through the Treaty of Washington in 1871, which led to the settlement of the Alabama Claims through the Geneva arbitration of 1872. His death occurred in 1893.

In 1836, Mr. Fish married Julia Kean, daughter of Peter Kean, of Ursino, N. J. His children were Sarah Morris Fish, who married Sidney Webster, Elizabeth Stuyvesant Fish, who married Frederick S. G. d'Hauteville, Julia Kean Fish, who married Colonel S. N. Benjamin, U. S. A.; Susan Leroy Fish, who married William E. Rogers, and Nicholas, Hamilton, Jr., Stuyvesant, and Edith Livingston Fish.

Mr. Nicholas Fish, the eldest son of Hamilton Fish, was born in New York, February 19th, 1846. He was graduated from Columbia College in 1867 and from the Dane Law School, of Harvard, in 1869. In 1871, he was second secretary of the United States Legation in Berlin, becoming first secretary in 1874. From 1877 to 1881, he was charge d'affaires to the Swiss Confederation and United States Minister to Belgium, 1882–86. Since 1887, he has been engaged in the banking business in New York and prominent in financial affairs. He married Clémence S Bryce and has two children, Elizabeth S Clare and Hamilton Fish, Jr. His town house is in Irving Place and his country residence is Wahnfried, in Tuxedo. Mr Fish belongs to the Metropolitan, Tuxedo, University, Players, Lawyers', University Athletic, St Anthony and Riding clubs, and is also a member of the Century Association, the Society of the Cincinnati, the St Nicholas Society and the New York Historical Society.

The second son of Hamilton Fish, statesman and diplomat, is the Honorable Hamilton Fish of this generation, who worthily bears his father's name. He was born in Albany, April 27th, 1849, and in 1869 was graduated from Columbia College. During the ensuing two years he was private secretary to his father, who was then Secretary of State in Washington. In 1873, he graduated from the Law School of Columbia College. He was aide-de-camp on the staff of Governor John A Dix, 1873–74, and in 1874, and for several terms thereafter, was returned to the Assembly of the State of New York for Putnam County. Since that time he has been one of the leaders in the Republican party of the State, having been Speaker of the Assembly, and for many years chairman of the Republican county committee of Putnam County. In 1884, he was a delegate to the National Republican Convention, and has received other honors at the hands of his political associates. He married, in 1880, Emily M Mann, daughter of the late Honorable Francis N Mann, of Troy, N. Y., and has two children. His residence is Rocklawn, in Garrisons, N. Y. He is a member of the Union, Metropolitan, Union League and other clubs, and of the Bar Association.

Stuyvesant Fish, the youngest son of the senior Hamilton Fish, was born in New York, June 24th, 1851, and graduated from Columbia College in the class of 1871. He entered the service of the Illinois Central Railroad in a responsible position the same year that he was graduated from college, and from 1872 to 1876 was engaged with the banking house of Morton, Bliss & Co. Since 1877, he has devoted himself entirely to railroad affairs. In that year, he was elected a director of the Illinois Central Railroad, became the secretary of the Chicago, St Louis & New Orleans Railroad the same year, and was elected vice-president of the latter road in 1882. Made vice-president of the Illinois Central in 1883, he was advanced to the presidency in 1887 and holds that position at the present time. He is also connected with other railroads and is a director in the National Park Bank, the New York Life Insurance & Trust Company and the Mutual Life Insurance Company.

In 1876, Mr. Fish married Marion G Anthon, daughter of William Henry Anthon. The father of Mrs Fish, one of the prominent lawyers of the New York bar in the last generation, was born in New York in 1827 and died in 1875. In 1851, he was a member of the New York Assembly, and during the Civil War served as Judge-Advocate-General on the staff of Governor Edwin D Morgan. He was the son of John Anthon, the distinguished lawyer and jurist, and grandson of Dr George C Anthon. His grandfather was a native of Germany, who entered the British Army and attained to the rank of Surgeon-General, serving from the commencement of the French War, until after the close of the Revolutionary War, when, in 1784, he resigned from the army and settled in New York. John Anthon, grandfather of Mrs Fish, was born in Detroit in 1784, and died in New York in 1863. Graduated from Columbia College in 1801, he studied law, was one of the founders of the New York Law Institute, of which he was president, and was the author of many valuable legal treatises and law reports. The establishment of the Supreme Court of New York City was largely due to his efforts. During the War of 1812, he commanded a company of militia and served in defense of the city.

The city residence of Mr and Mrs Stuyvesant Fish is in Gramercy Park, and they have a summer home in Newport. They have one daughter and two sons, Marion, Stuyvesant, Jr, and Sidney Webster Fish. In his club membership, Mr Fish includes the Metropolitan, Union, Riding, Players and St Anthony, the Downtown Association, the St Nicholas Society and the Southern Society.

HALEY FISKE

IN the reign of King Edward IV. of England, Lord Symond Fiske, grandson of Daniel, Lord of the Manor of Stadhaugh, Parish of Laxfield, County Suffolk, died in 1464 and left a son William Fiske, who married Joan Lynne, of Norfolk, and died before 1504. William Fiske and Joan Lynne were the English ancestors of the family to which Mr. Haley Fiske belongs. The line of descent from this William Fiske to the first American ancestor of the family is through Symond Fiske, of Laxfield; his son, Symond Fiske, who died in 1505; his grandson, Robert Fiske, who died in 1551; his great-grandson, William Fiske, who was born in 1566; and his great-great-grandson, John Fiske, who was born in St. James, where he died in 1633, and who married Anne Lantersee, daughter of Robert Lantersee

William Fiske, son of John and Anne (Lantersee) Fiske, was born in England about 1613 and came to this country in 1637, settling in Salem, Mass , of which place he was a freeman in 1642 His wife was Bridget Muskett, of Pelham, England, whom he married after coming to this country. Removing to Wenham, Mass , he was the first town clerk there, 1643-50, and a representative to the General Court, 1647-52 His death occurred in 1654. William Fiske, of the second American generation, 1643-1728, was a representative to the General Court in 1701, and for several terms thereafter, was a moderator, in 1702-03-12-13-14, and a Lieutenant of the militia. His wife was Sarah Kilham, daughter of Austin Kilham, who emigrated from Kilham, Yorkshire, England, and was one of the first settlers of Wenham In the next four generations, the line of descent is through Samuel Fiske, of Wenham and Rehoboth, and his wife, Elizabeth Browne ; Josiah Fiske, of Cumberland, R. I., 1702-1773, and his wife, Sarah Bishop; John Fiske, of Cumberland, 1729-1789, and his wife, Mary Bartlett; and Ensign Squire Fiske, 1756-1804, Colonel of a Rhode Island regiment in the War of the Revolution, and his wife, Amey Lapham, daughter of Abner Lapham.

Judge Haley Fiske, 1793-1877, grandfather of Mr. Haley Fiske, was the son of Ensign Squire and Amey (Lapham) Fiske. In the War of 1812, he raised a company of troops of which he was Lieutenant He was a civil engineer and had charge of the building of the lower locks of the Delaware & Raritan Canal. For more than thirty-five years, he was a justice of the peace and was a close friend of Henry Clay. He married, in 1815, Judith Qureau, who was born in 1801 and died in 1865. The father of Mr Haley Fiske was William Henry Fiske, who was born in Yonkers, N. Y , in 1818 and died in 1892 He was an accomplished civil engineer, and in the period immediately following the Civil War was connected with the street department of the City of New York. His wife, whom he married in New York in 1840, was Sarah Ann Blakeney, who was born in 1818 and died in 1884.

Mr Haley Fiske was born in New Brunswick, N J., March 18th, 1852. Educated in Rutgers College, he was graduated in the class of 1871 and studied law in the office of Arnoux, Ritch & Woodford, becoming a partner in that firm He had a successful career at the bar, being engaged in some of the most important cases of the present generation, his last appearance as an attorney being in the Fayerweather will contest. In 1891, he gave up his legal pursuits to take the position of vice-president of the Metropolitan Life Insurance Company, and has since been engaged in that business. Other interests have commanded his attention and he has been a director in various corporations, including the Metropolitan Trust Company and the National Shoe and Leather Bank. He is treasurer of the Church of St Mary, the Virgin.

The first wife of Mr Fiske, whom he married in 1878, was Mary Garrettina Mulford, who died in 1886 His second wife was Marione Cowles Cushman His children are Helen Fiske, who was born in 1884; Archibald Falconer Cushman Fiske, who was born in 1888, and Marione Virginia Fiske, born in 1896. Mr. and Mrs. Fiske live in Riverside Drive, at the corner of Seventy-sixth Street He is a member of the Players, Grolier, City, Church and Δ Φ clubs and the Bar Association.

LOUIS FITZGERALD

B ORN in New York, May 31st, 1838, General Louis Fitzgerald has been thoroughly identified with the metropolis during a long and active public and business career, and has been especially distinguished for his brilliant military service to the State and the country. After receiving a thorough education in public and private schools, he engaged in business and promptly identified himself with the militia In 1857, he became a member of New York's famous Seventh Regiment, and since then his military service has been unbroken down to the present time, a period of forty years.

When the Seventh Regiment was summoned, in 1861, to march to the front in defense of the City of Washington from the invading Confederate forces, Private Fitzgerald was among those who went at the country's call. After the temporary term of service for which the regiment had been summoned had expired, he entered the Union Army as a volunteer, being commissioned First Lieutenant in the Eleventh New York Infantry Participating in the first battle of Bull Run, he displayed special gallantry on the field and won his commission as Captain. After the disbandment of that regiment he became First Lieutenant in the Fortieth New York Infantry, and was again promoted to be Captain for gallant services at the battle of Fair Oaks. During the Peninsular Campaign, he served as Provost Marshal and aide-de-camp on the staff of Major-General Philip Kearny. For his bravery in this campaign, he won the honor of wearing the Kearny Cross, being one of the few officers entitled to that distinction. Subsequently he was aide-de-camp to Major-General D. B Birney, commanding the Third Corps, and was afterwards attached to the staff of Major-General J. G. Foster, commanding the Eighteenth Corps. In 1864, he was advanced to rank of Major and subsequently Lieutenant-Colonel of the First Mississippi Regiment. When peace had been declared, he retired from the army, bearing wounds received at Bull Run, Williamsburg and Fair Oaks.

Returning to New York, his bravery and brilliant service upon the field of battle was further rewarded by a commission as brevet Lieutenant-Colonel in the National Guard of the State of New York His love for his old regiment brought him into the ranks again and he rejoined the Seventh, being appointed Regimental Adjutant. In 1875, he became Lieutenant-Colonel of the Seventh and held that position for the next seven years. His reputation as a tactitian and disciplinarian had in these years brought him into notice as one of the most earnest and efficient officers of the State National Guard, and in 1882 he was commissioned Brigadier-General of the First Brigade of the State of New York, comprising the Seventh, Eighth, Ninth, Twelfth, Twenty-Second, Sixty-Ninth and Seventy-First Regiments, the First and Second Batteries of Artillery, and Squadron A of Cavalry. During the fifteen years that he has been at the head of the brigade, his command has developed in effectiveness, until it stands second to no other militia organization in the country and compares favorably with regular troops

In the business world, General Fitzgerald has been interested in large and important financial affairs. For many years he has been president of the Mercantile Trust Company. He is one of the leading financiers of Wall Street and has taken an active part in the reorganization of the affairs of some of the most important railroad corporations of the country. In 1872, General Fitzgerald married Gelyna, youngest daughter of William S. Ver Planck, and granddaughter of Gulian C. Ver Planck They have four children: Geraldine, who in 1896 married Ernest R Adee, son of the late George T. Adee, Louis, Jr, Adelaide and Eleanor, who are unmarried. The residence of the family is in Lexington Avenue and they have summer homes at Seabright, N. J., and at Garrison-on-the-Hudson. General Fitzgerald is a member of the Union, University, Metropolitan, United Service, Lawyers', Princeton and Westminster Kennel clubs, the Military Order of the Loyal Legion, the Society of Colonial Wars and the American Geographical Society, and is a patron of the Metropolitan Museum of Art

CHARLES RANLETT FLINT

THOMAS FLINT, who came from Wales in 1642 and settled in that part of Salem, Mass., now known as South Danvers, was the ancestor of Mr. Charles R. Flint The latter's father was Benjamin Flint, who married Sarah Tobey, and during his earlier career was a shipowner in Thomaston, Me In 1858, he removed to New York and became prominent in commercial life, residing in Brooklyn. Mr. Charles Ranlett Flint, son of Benjamin Flint, was born in Thomaston, January 24th, 1850. He was educated in his native place, in Topsham, Me., and in Brooklyn, and graduated from the Brooklyn Polytechnic Institute, being president of his class and later of the Alumni Association.

Entering business life, Mr. Flint became a partner in Gilchrist, Flint & Co. in 1871, and in 1872 was one of the founders and partners of W. R. Grace & Co. In 1874, he traveled in South America and afterwards paid a second visit to Brazil. In 1878, he organized the Export Lumber Company, Limited, and in 1885 became a partner with his father and his brother, Wallace B Flint, in the firm of Flint & Co Later on, he brought about a consolidation of exporting interests under the title of Flint, Eddy & Co., the houses of which he is the head being in the front rank of American exporters and merchants of the present day. In 1892, Mr. Flint originated the United States Rubber Company and is its treasurer.

In a public capacity, Mr Flint has been Consul of Chili in New York and Acting Chargé d'Affaires of that country to the United States, Consul of Nicaragua and Consul General of Costa Rica In 1889-90, he was a delegate to the Conference of American Republics in Washington and, owing to his knowledge of South American affairs, was an important factor in that gathering Secretary of State Blaine, in a letter to Mr Flint, said: " Your services are so valuable, that we need you every hour Though your large business interests demand your attention just now, it must be patriotism first and business afterwards " Mr. Flint proposed the organization of the Bureau of American Republics, to carry out the vote of the conference for uniform statistics and the extension of trade between the Americas. Later on, Mr Flint was confidential agent of the United States in negotiating a reciprocity treaty with Brazil, which became the basis for treaties with other South American States and Spain At the time of threatened trouble between this country and Chili, through his efforts the mediation of Brazil was offered. When an attempt was made to reëstablish the monarchy in Brazil, Minister Mendonça, representing President Piexoto, empowered Mr. Flint to procure vessels and munitions of war in the United States for the constitutional government, and through his energy Ericsson's Destroyer, and the two fast yachts, Feiseen and Javelin, converted into torpedo boats, and the steamships, El Cid and Britannia, changed to armed cruisers under the names of the Nictheroy and America, were placed at the service of the Republic of Brazil.

Mr Flint is connected with many financial institutions, being a director of the National Bank of the Republic, the State Trust Company, the Knickerbocker Trust Company and the Produce Exchange Bank. He has also been identified with other corporate interests and is one of the council of the New York University. In spite of his many business cares, he maintains an active interest in outdoor recreations and habitually spends one day each week with either rod or gun He has hunted in Canada, the Rocky Mountains and South America, and has killed nearly every variety of big game found in the two Western Continents He is also a prominent yachtsman and was owner of the Gracie, which probably won more prizes than any yacht in the United States He was a member of the syndicate which built and raced the Vigilant in the contests for the America cup against the Valkyrie. He is a member of the Union, Riding, Metropolitan and South Side Sportsmen's clubs, the New York, Seawanhaka-Corinthian, and Larchmont Yacht clubs, the New England Society and the Century Association.

In 1883, Mr. Flint married E. Kate Simmons, daughter of Joseph F Simmons, of Troy, N Y. Mrs Flint possesses marked musical ability She has devoted the receipts of her musical compositions to charity, and with one of them endowed a bed in St Luke's Hospital.

ROSWELL PETTIBONE FLOWER

T HE progenitor of the Flower family in America was Lamrock Flower, who was born in Ireland in 1660, and coming to America in 1685 settled in Hartford, Conn. He had a son, Lamrock, whose son Elijah removed to New Hartford, and married Abigail Seymour. George Flower, son of Elijah Flower, was born in New Hartford in 1760, became one of the early settlers of Oakhill, Greene County, N. Y., and married Roxaline Crowe, of New Hartford, who was of French descent, her ancestors having emigrated from Alsace. They had a family of ten children, one of whom, Nathan M Flower, born in 1796, married Mary Ann, daughter of Thomas Boyle, the builder of the first water-works in New York City. Nathan M. Flower went into business, in Springfield, N. Y , and afterwards in a settlement on Indian River, in Jefferson County, which became the village of Theresa. He was a Justice of the Peace there for fourteen years.

Mr. Roswell Pettibone Flower, the sixth of the nine children of Nathan M. and Mary Ann Flower, was born August 7th, 1835. His father died when he was only eight years of age, but he secured a good education, became a teacher, engaged in business, and finally became assistant postmaster of Watertown, the county seat of Jefferson County. A few years later he established himself as a jeweler and was very successful Meantime, he kept up an extended course of reading in law and political history, and as a result was well fitted for the responsibilities which devolved upon him later.

In 1859, he married Sarah M. Woodruff, daughter of Norris M Woodruff, of New Hartford, Conn. Mrs Flower's elder sister was the wife of Henry Keep, the New York capitalist. Mr. Keep died in 1869, leaving a large estate, with the request that his brother-in-law assume its management. Accordingly, Mr. Flower removed to New York City and at once entered upon the career that has brought him wealth and renown The Keep estate was so prudently administered that it quadrupled in value and Mr Flower soon attained to prominence in the financial world. He organized the brokerage and banking firm of Benedict, Flower & Co., afterwards R. P. Flower & Co., which, in 1890, became Flower & Co. and in which he is now a special partner.

Mr Flower has for many years been an important factor in New York State and national politics. He is a lifelong Democrat, of the school of Silas Wright, whose teachings he imbibed in youth. His first conspicuous appearance in public life was in 1881, when he defeated William Waldorf Astor for election to Congress from the Eleventh New York District In 1882, he was urged to take the Democratic nomination for Governor of the State, but declined in favor of Grover Cleveland. The history of the country was changed by this decision. The offer of a second nomination for Congress was also declined, and in 1885, when nominated for Lieutenant-Governor, he refused the honor. In 1888, he was a delegate-at-large to the Democratic National Convention; in the same year was elected a member of the Fifty-first Congress, and in 1892 was the successful Democratic candidate for Governor of the State. He has frequently been mentioned for the Presidency of the United States, and in 1892 his friends made an active campaign in his behalf for the Democratic nomination.

Mr. and Mrs Flower live in Fifth Avenue They are noted for their charities, and for many years have set aside one-tenth of their income for benevolence. The St Thomas House, an establishment for work among the poor of this city, was built by Mr. Flower, and he erected the Presbyterian Church in Theresa, N. Y., as a memorial to his parents. He also built the Flower Surgical Hospital in New York City, opened in 1890. In his charities Mr. Flower has the generous coöperation of his brother, Anson R. Flower Together they built Trinity Episcopal Church, at Watertown, N Y , and presented it to the parish Mr and Mrs. Flower have had three children, one daughter, Helen, and one son, Henry K , are deceased The surviving daughter, Emma G Flower, married John B Taylor, of Watertown, N Y Anson R. Flower married Ida Babcock and lives in Madison Avenue. He is a member of the Metropolitan, Manhattan, Riding, Lawyers' and Democratic clubs.

WILLIAM CHAUNCEY FLOYD-JONES

IN 1654, there came from England to Long Island a band of Colonists, headed by Richard Woodhull, who became patentees of a large plantation at Setauket Prominent among them was Richard Floyd, a native of Brecknockshire, Wales, and the progenitor of the Floyd family in this country He was a man of intelligence and vigor, acquired large estates, and was early chosen Judge of Suffolk County, and Colonel of the militia, which positions he held until his death, in 1690 The eldest son of Richard Floyd, also named Richard, 1661–1737, inherited his father's property, and was for many years Judge of the Court of Common Pleas and Colonel of the militia of Suffolk County. In 1686, he married Margaret, oldest daughter of Colonel Matthias Nicoll, secretary of the Duke of York's commissioners, and the first secretary of the Province of New York.

Richard Floyd, the third of the name, 1703–1771, was also a Judge and Colonel of the militia, and a man of eminence in the community. The fourth Richard Floyd, 1736–1791, like his ancestors, held the offices of Judge and Colonel, which by that time had come almost to be considered appendages of the family. He settled upon the estate at Mastic, and was noted as a gentleman of the old school. His house was always open for entertainment, and it was said of him that "no man ever went from his house either hungry or thirsty." In the Revolution he espoused the royalist cause, and, by the act of attainder, his estate was forfeited and sold, in 1784, his brother being the purchaser He then removed to St. John, N. B.

The wife of Richard Floyd, the fourth, whom he married in 1758, was Arabella, daughter of Judge David Jones, of Fort Neck, and a sister of Judge Thomas Jones, a Justice of the Supreme Court of the State of New York. Judge Thomas Jones died without issue, and, in accordance with the terms of the will of his father, the estate at Fort Neck reverted to the male issue of the daughter, Arabella, upon condition that they should add his name to their own. Consequently, David Richard, the only son of Richard and Arabella Floyd, became David Richard Floyd-Jones, and this change of name was confirmed by act of the Legislature, in 1788 Since that time, the senior branch of the family has borne the double patronymic, while the junior branches only have retained the name Floyd.

David Richard Floyd-Jones, 1764–1826, married a daughter of Henry Onderdonk, in 1785, and settled upon the estate at Fort Neck He had two sisters, one of whom, Elizabeth, married John Peter DeLancey, son of Lieutenant-Governor DeLancey, and was the mother of Bishop William H. DeLancey, of Western New York, and of a daughter, Susan, who became the wife of James Fenimore Cooper. The sons of David Richard Floyd-Jones were Brigadier-General Thomas Floyd-Jones, 1788–1851, who succeeded to the estate, and at whose death the entail came to an end ; and Major-General Henry Floyd-Jones, 1792–1862, who was a member of the Assembly in 1829, State Senator and member of the Court of Errors from the district comprising Kings, Queens, New York and Richmond counties 1836–40. David Richard Floyd-Jones was the eldest son of Thomas Floyd-Jones, and was conspicuous in public affairs throughout his life He made a worthy place for himself in the legal profession, but his activity was largely in politics He was a member of the Assembly for New York State, in 1841, 1842, 1843 and 1857, a State Senator 1844–7, inclusive, a member of the Constitutional Convention of 1846, Secretary of State, 1860–1, and Lieutenant-Governor, 1863–4 The other two sons of Brigadier-General Thomas Floyd-Jones were William Floyd-Jones, of Massapequa, a merchant of New York, and Elbert Floyd-Jones, also for several terms in the Assembly.

Mr. William Chauncey Floyd-Jones, one of the sons of the late William Floyd-Jones, is a representative in the present generation of this distinguished family He is a member of the New York Stock Exchange, and his residence is on the ancestral estate at Massapequa, Long Island. He is a member of the Union, the Racquet, the Westminster Kennel and the Country clubs

GEORGE WINTHROP FOLSOM

BORN in Kennebunk, Me., in 1802, the Honorable George Folsom, the father of Mr George Winthrop Folsom, was a distinguished lawyer, statesman and man of letters in the last generation Graduated from Harvard College in 1822, he studied law in Saco, Me., and practiced there and in Framingham and Worcester, Mass, for many years. He removed to New York in 1837 and became prominent in all the intellectual activities of the metropolis in that period, and died in Rome, Italy, in 1869. While living in Worcester, George Folsom was interested in historical research and was chairman of the American Antiquarian Society. In later years, he was president of the American Ethnological Society, and upon taking up his residence in New York, became one of the active members of the New York Historical Society. In 1844, he was elected a member of the State Senate, and in 1850 President Zachary Taylor appointed him Chargé d'Affaires at The Hague, a position he held for four years. Among his published works were Sketches of Saco and Biddeford, Dutch Annals of New York, Letters and Dispatches of Cortez, Political Condition of Mexico, and an Address on the Discovery of Maine

George Folsom came from a family that traces its descent from old-time English ancestors. In the first half of the fourteenth century, there was a John Folsom, Prior of the Carmelite monastery in Norwich and *præses provincialis* of all England He was a D. D. of Cambridge University and died in the great plague of 1348. Richard Folsom, his brother, was much in evidence in the Court of John XXII., of Rome, 1316-1334. The first member of the family in this country was John Foulsham, of Hingham, England, descended from Roger Foulsham, of Necton, Norfolk County, who died about 1534 He was born in 1615, and arrived in this country in 1638, with his wife, Mary Gilman, who was the daughter of Edward and Mary (Clark) Gilman Settling first in Hingham, Mass., he went to Exeter N. H., in 1650, being a selectman there in 1659, dying in 1681.

The descendants of John Foulsham in direct line to the subject of this sketch were Peter Folsom, 1649-1717, and his wife, Susannah Cousins, or Coffin, of Wells, Me ; Peter Folsom, 1682-1718, and his wife, Catharine, daughter of John Gilman and granddaughter of Edward Gilman; James Folsom, 1711-1748, and his wife, Elizabeth, daughter of Captain Jonathan King ; James Folsom, 1737-1824, and his wife, Elizabeth Webster, daughter of Thomas Webster ; and Thomas Folsom, of Kennebunk and Portland, Me., born 1769, and his wife, Edna Ela. Peter Folsom, 1649, was a Lieutenant in the militia. His son Peter, 1682, was a man of talent and of great influence in the community in which he lived and successful in business, accumulating considerable wealth. Thomas Folsom, who was born in 1769, and lived in Kennebunk and Portland, was the father of the Honorable George Folsom.

Mr. George Winthrop Folsom was born in New York and received a collegiate education. His mother, whom George Folsom married in 1839, was Margaret Cornelia Winthrop, daughter of Benjamin Winthrop Through her, he is descended in direct line from Governor John Winthrop, of Massachusetts; Governor John Winthrop, of Connecticut, Major Waite Still Winthrop, Governor Thomas Dudley, of Massachusetts; Governor Joseph Dudley, of Massachusetts, and Governor Peter Stuyvesant, of New Amsterdam. Mr. Folsom has had a city residence in East Seventeenth Street, but has been principally identified with Lenox, Mass. He is a member of the Century, University and St. Anthony clubs and the American Geographical Society, and is a patron of the Metropolitan Museum of Art. The wife of Mr. Folsom, whom he married in 1867, was Frances Elizabeth Hastings Fuller, of Cambridge, Mass, daughter of William Henry Fuller and granddaughter of Timothy Fuller. He had two sisters, Margaret Winthrop and Helen Stuyvesant Folsom. The latter was a member of the Sisterhood of St. John the Baptist, and founded the corporation known as the St John Baptist Foundation, which carries on various charitable works, among others the mission church and schools of the Holy Cross in Avenue C, a school for girls in East Seventeenth Street and St. Hilda's Home on Long Island, all of which are under the care of the Sisters of St. John the Baptist. Helen Stuyvesant Folsom died in 1882.

THEODORE FRELINGHUYSEN

FOR nearly two hundred years, the Frelinghuysen family has been conspicuous in the clerical and professional life of this country, and more than three centuries ago, in Holland, men of the name were leaders in religious thought The ancestor of the American branch, the Reverend Theodorus Jacobus Frelinghuysen, was born in West Friesland in 1691, and was ordained to the ministry in the Reformed Dutch Church in his native land at the age of twenty-six He was selected to establish a mission in the new settlement on the Raritan River, in New Jersey, and came to this country in 1720. He was an energetic, devoted man and has been called One of the greatest divines of the American church." When he died, in 1747, he left five sons, all of whom were ministers, and two daughters who married ministers. His second son, the Reverend John Frelinghuysen, 1727-1754, succeeded to much of his father's work

The only son of the Reverend John Frelinghuysen was General Frederick Frelinghuysen, who was born in 1753, graduated from Princeton in 1770, and was admitted to the bar in 1774 He was a member of the Provincial Congress of New Jersey in 1775-76, and of the Continental Congresses in 1778, 1782 and 1783 At the Battle of Trenton, he was Captain of a company of Artillery, and a tradition exists that a shot from his pistol killed Colonel Rahl, the Hessian commander He became a Colonel before the war ended, and in 1794 was Major-General of the New Jersey Militia. After the Revolution, he held several public positions, and in 1793 was United States Senator from New Jersey, but resigned his seat in 1796 on account of family bereavements. John, the eldest son of General Frederick Frelinghuysen, 1776-1833, held a Brigadier-General's commission in the War of 1812, and his second son, Theodore, 1787-1861, was an eminent lawyer, Attorney-General of the State of New Jersey, United States Senator, 1829-35, Mayor of the City of Newark, 1836-38, Chancellor of the University of New York, president of Rutgers College, 1850-61, and Whig candidate for the Vice-Presidency of the United States on the ticket with Henry Clay in 1844

The Honorable Frederick Frelinghuysen, son of Frederick Frelinghuysen and grandson of General Frederick Frelinghuysen, has also been distinguished in public life Born in 1817, he was adopted and brought up by his uncle Theodore, his father having died when he was an infant He was graduated from Rutgers College in 1836 and was admitted to the bar three years later He advanced rapidly in his profession, and in time succeeded to the practice of his uncle, becoming one of the leading members of the New Jersey bar He was city attorney of Newark, N J., and for ten years counsel for the New Jersey Central Railroad and the Morris Canal Company, and Attorney-General of the State in 1861-66. Appointed to the United States Senate to fill a vacancy in 1866, he was elected to the seat in 1867 and reëlected in 1871. During his last term of service, he was a conspicuous figure in the national councils, and in 1877 was a member of the Electoral Commission appointed to settle the disputed Presidential contest of 1876. In 1881, he became a member of President Arthur's cabinet, succeeding James G. Blaine, as Secretary of State. The wife of Frederick Frelinghuysen was Matilda Griswold, daughter of George Griswold, a descendant of the Griswold family, of Connecticut, and one of New York's great merchants of the early part of the century

Mr. Theodore Frelinghuysen is the son of the Honorable Frederick Frelinghuysen and Matilda Griswold He was born in 1860, and is engaged in active business. He married Alice Coats, daughter of James Coats. Their residence is in West Fifteenth Street His clubs are the Knickerbocker, Union, Metropolitan, Merchants', and the Country Club of Westchester County The other children of Frederick Frelinghuysen are · George Griswold Frelinghuysen, who married Sarah L Ballantine, lives in West Forty-third Street, near Fifth Avenue, and has a country place, Whippany Farm, in Morristown, N J ; Frederick Frelinghuysen, of Newark, N. J.; Matilda C., who married Henry Winthrop Gray ; Sarah Helen, who married the Honorable John Davis, and Lucy Frelinghuysen.

AMOS TUCK FRENCH

EDWARD FRENCH was born in England and settled first in Ipswich, Mass., in the year 1636, and afterwards became one of the original settlers of Salisbury, Mass. He was a prominent member of the community, one of the prudential men in 1646, and paid the third heaviest tax in the town for many years. Daniel French, of Salisbury, 1708–1783, was the fourth in descent from Edward French. Daniel French, of Chester, N. H., the grandson of Daniel French, of Salisbury, was the grandfather of Francis Ormond French, so prominent in the financial circles of New York City. He was born in 1769 and died in 1840; he was a lawyer and for several terms was Attorney-General of the State of New Hampshire. His wife was Mercy Brown, sister of the Reverend Francis Brown, president of Dartmouth College. He was also the grandfather of Daniel Chester French, the sculptor.

The son of Daniel French was Benjamin B. French, 1800–1870. He was born in Chester, N. H., practiced law for some ten years, and served in the New Hampshire Legislature. In 1833, he entered the clerk's office of the House of Representatives at Washington, and was clerk of the House from 1845 to 1847. President Lincoln appointed him Commissioner of Public Buildings in Washington in 1861, a position that he retained until 1865. He was associated with Professor S. F. B. Morse and Postmaster-General Amos Kendall, in the first efforts to establish the telegraph, and was president of the Magnetic Telegraph Company, organized to construct a line between Washington and New York. The wife of Benjamin B. French, whom he married in 1825, was Elizabeth Smith Richardson, a daughter of Chief Justice William Merchant Richardson, of New Hampshire. Her family was connected with the early history of Charlestown, Mass. One of its members took part in the celebrated Tea Party in Boston Harbor in 1772, and another was a Captain in the Continental Army.

Francis Ormond French, their son, was born in Chester, N. H., in 1837. He was fitted for college at Phillips Exeter Academy, entered the sophomore class of Harvard College in 1854, and was graduated in 1857. At that time, he evinced decided literary tastes, being secretary of the Hasty Pudding Club, and class poet and a favorite pupil of Professor James Russell Lowell. He graduated from Harvard Law School in 1859, and, entering the office of Thomas Nelson, in New York City, was admitted to the New York bar in 1860 and went to Exeter, N. H., to practice. In 1862, the appointment of Deputy Naval Officer of the Port of Boston was offered him under his father-in-law, the Honorable Amos Tuck, who was Naval Officer. In 1863, he was promoted to be Deputy Collector. In 1865, he resigned from the Government employ and entered the banking firm of Samuel A. Way & Co., Boston, and subsequently founded the banking house of Foote & French. In 1870, he returned to New York City and became a partner in the firm of Jay Cooke & Co., and was the representative of the London firm of Jay Cooke, McCullough & Co., remaining with them until 1873. In 1874, he was one of the capitalists who acquired control of the First National Bank of New York City, and became connected with its management. His most notable work in the financial field was in relation to the funding of United States loans. From 1888 until his death, in 1893, he was president of the Manhattan Trust Company. He was president of the Harvard Club of New York City for two years, and a trustee of Phillips Exeter Academy. He married Ellen Tuck, daughter of the Honorable Amos Tuck, of Exeter, N. H., Member of Congress, 1847–53, and Naval Officer of the Port of Boston, 1861–5.

Mr. Amos Tuck French, the only son of Francis Ormond French, is prominent in the business and social life of the metropolis. Having graduated from Harvard College, Mr. French entered upon a financial career in New York City. He was secretary of the Manhattan Trust Company under the presidency of his father, and is now vice-president of that institution. He is a member of the Tuxedo colony, and belongs to the Metropolitan, Union, Racquet, Knickerbocker, Harvard and New York Yacht clubs.

FREDERIC GALLATIN

THE rival of Alexander Hamilton in renown as a financier and statesman, Albert Gallatin followed him in public service by some years and now, for nearly half a century, has slept his last sleep beside his predecessor in Trinity churchyard.   Gallatin, like Hamilton, was foreign born, but cast his lot with this country before he had reached his maturity.   He was born in Geneva, Switzerland, in 1761, a descendant of an ancient patrician family that for many generations had been prominent in Swiss history   His father, Jean Gallatin, died when he was only two years old and he lost his mother, Sophie Albertine Rolaz du Rosey, before he was ten years of age. He was baptized Abraham Alphonzo Albert, and after being graduated from the University of Geneva with high rank in 1779, he ran away and came to this country to escape the importunities of members of his family who wished him to enter the army and engage in the Hessian service of Frederick of Hesse Cassel

Arriving in Boston in 1780, Gallatin was successively soldier, teacher, and instructor in Harvard College   Then he went to Pennsylvania, bought real estate, engaged in business, and about 1790 entered upon his political career by going to the Legislature.   He was in Congress in 1795 as a follower of Madison, and was the recognized leader of his party.   Secretary of the Treasury, 1801–13, one of the Commissioners to arrange the Treaty of Ghent, United States Minister to France in 1815, Envoy Extraordinary to Great Britain in 1826, and otherwise prominent in public service, he filled out a long life of activity and usefulness.   After his retirement to private life, he was president of the National Bank of New York, 1831–39, one of the founders of the New York University in 1830, the first president of the American Ethnological Society in 1842, and from 1843 to the time of his death, in 1849, president of the New York Historical Society.

A grandson of Albert Gallatin, Mr Frederic Gallatin is descended through his grandmother from James Nicholson, of the United States Navy.   James Nicholson was born in Chesterfield, Md., in 1727, and came of ancestors who had settled in that locality a century before.   His father had a grant of what was called Nicholson's Manor, and was in the official employ of the British Government.   James Nicholson went into the navy at the outbreak of the Revolution, commanded the Defense in 1775, was made ranking Captain by resolution of Congress in 1776, became Commander-in-Chief of the Navy in 1777, commanded the frigate Trumbull in the battle with the Wyatt in 1780, and in 1781 was taken prisoner and held until the close of the war.   Returning to civil life, he settled in New York and remained a resident of this city until his death, in 1804   His daughter married Albert Gallatin.

The father of Mr. Frederic Gallatin was Albert R. Gallatin, the second son of Albert Gallatin. He was liberally educated and was graduated from Princeton College.   Although he was admitted to the bar in Pennsylvania, he practiced only a short time and then removed to New York and engaged in financial pursuits.   At one time, he was in business with John Jacob Astor and his ventures were generally profitable, so that he was able to accumulate a considerable fortune.   He was the companion of his father a great part of the time, and in consequence was thrown into association with people of public note.   He went abroad with his father several times, to France in 1816, to Great Britain in 1826 and upon other occasions   On these trips, he made the acquaintance of many eminent Europeans and became the personal friend of the Duke of Wellington and of many of the leaders in the French Revolution   He lived until 1890, a connecting link between this generation and the deeds and the men of the infant days of the Republic

Mr Frederic Gallatin is a University man and a lawyer.   He married Amy G. Gerry, and occupies a residence in upper Fifth Avenue, near Central Park.   He belongs to the Metropolitan, Century and other clubs, and his interest in scientific matters is indicated by his membership in the American Geographical Society.   He is an enthusiastic yachtsman and devotes considerable time to that sport, being a member of the New York, Seawanhaka, Larchmont and Atlantic Yacht clubs.

THOMAS GALLAUDET, D. D.

OF French origin, the first American ancestors of the Gallaudet family were among the Huguenots who participated in the famous migration to America in the early part of the eighteenth century. Pierre Elisee Gallaudet, a physician, first appeared in New York. He was born in Moze (Mauze) pays d'aunis, near Rochelle. His father was Joshua Gallaudet and his mother was Margaret Prioleau, daughter of Elisha Prioleau, minister of Niort, 1639–50. Dr Gallaudet came to New Rochelle, N. Y., as early as 1711. His son Thomas, the great grandfather of the subject of this sketch, was born about 1724, and lived until 1772. His wife was Catharine Edgar, who was born in 1725 and died in 1774. They had a family of six children. Their second son, Peter Wallace Gallaudet, was born in 1756, in New York, and died in Washington, D. C., in 1843. His wife, whom he married in 1787, was Jane, or Janet, Hopkins, daughter of Captain Thomas and Alice (Howard) Hopkins She was descended in the sixth generation from John Hopkins, of Hartford, Conn., who came over in 1634.

The Reverend Thomas Hopkins Gallaudet was born in Philadelphia in 1787, and died in Hartford in 1851 Graduated from Yale College in 1805, with the degree of A. B., he received the degree of A. M. in 1808 For two years, 1808–10, he was a tutor in Yale College, and then studied in the Theological Seminary in Andover, being licensed to preach as a Congregational minister in 1814. The greater portion of his lifetime was spent in philanthropic work. In 1816, he was the founder and incorporator of the Connecticut Asylum for Deaf and Dumb, the first school of the kind in the United States, and he devoted many years and much energy to the care of the unfortunate insane. In 1815, he visited London, Edinburgh and Paris. He was the author of Bible Stories for the Young, Child's Book of the Soul, and Youth's Book of Natural Theology. His wife was Sophia Fowler, of Guilford, Conn., one of his earliest deaf-mute pupils.

The Reverend Thomas Gallaudet, the son of Thomas H. Gallaudet, was born in Hartford, Conn., in 1822. For more than half a century he has been prominently connected with institutions for the instruction of deaf mutes and improving their material and spiritual condition In this field of labor, he has been one of the most active and most useful workers in the world, and has acquired an international reputation For fifteen years, 1843–58, he was an instructor in the New York Institution for the Instruction of the Deaf and Dumb. Meantime, having been ordained in the Protestant Episcopal Church, he founded, in 1852, St. Ann's Church for deaf mutes and their hearing friends. Since 1869 he has been pastor of the Sisterhood of the Good Shepherd, and was for three years Chaplain of the Midnight Missions. Since 1872, he has been general manager of the Church Mission to Deaf Mutes. He has traveled extensively in the interest of the cause to which he has devoted his life, visiting Europe several times In 1885, he founded the Gallaudet Home for Deaf Mutes on a farm near the Hudson River, between Hamburgh and Poughkeepsie Trinity College made him a D. D. in 1862, and he belongs to the Trinity College Alumni Association.

In 1845, Dr. Gallaudet married Elizabeth Budd, daughter of Dr. and Mrs. B. W. Budd. The family home is in West Thirteenth Street Dr. and Mrs. Gallaudet have five daughters, Virginia B, Elizabeth F and Edith Gallaudet, Mrs. A. D. Shaw and Mrs. R. M. Sherman. Their son, Dr. Benjamin Gallaudet, is a well-known surgeon, demonstrator of anatomy in the College of Physicians and Surgeons of New York. A brother of the Reverend Dr. Thomas Gallaudet is Peter Wallace Gallaudet, a broker, who lives in West Forty-eighth Street, is a member of the New York Club and the New England Society, and was at one time treasurer of the Huguenot Society. Another brother is Dr. Edward Miner Gallaudet, president of Gallaudet College for the Deaf, in Washington, D C. This college was founded in 1864, at the suggestion of its president, who has been at the head of the institution, of which the college is a part, for more than forty years. The college received its name in honor of Dr. Thomas H. Gallaudet, as the founder of deaf-mute education in America.

HUGH RICHARDSON GARDEN.

DISTINGUISHED Southern Colonial families unite in the person of this gentleman. The father of Mr Garden was born Alester Garden Gibbes, who, at the request of an uncle, Major Alexander Garden, changed his name to Alester Garden He was a descendant of Stephen Gibbes, 1594, of Edmonstone Court, England. The latter's son, Robert Gibbes, was appointed about 1648 a member of the Council at the Barbadoes, where his son, Robert, was born. The second Robert Gibbes became Chief Justice of South Carolina, and his son was John Gibbes, who married Mary Woodward, of St. James' Parish, South Carolina The next in line of Mr. Garden's ancestors, Robert Gibbes, third of the name, married Sarah Reeves, of Johns Island, S. C , and their son, Wilmot S. Gibbes, 1781-1852, married Anna Frances de Saussure, the last named couple being the parents of Alester Garden Gibbes. Thomas S Gibbes, whose descendants have held a high position in New York, was a brother of Wilmot S Gibbes.

The Garden family descended from George Garden, 1555, Laird of Banchory. His great-grandson, the Reverend Alexander Garden, 1685-1756, came to this country, and was head of the Church of England in the Carolinas. His son, Dr. Alexander Garden, 1730-1791, a physician in Charleston, adhered to the Royal cause in the Revolution, and returned to England in 1783. Major Alexander Garden, 1757-1829, his son, married Mary Ann Gibbes, daughter of the third Robert Gibbes. He was educated at the University of Edinburgh, and, returning to Charleston, espoused the patriotic side in the Revolution, being a Lieutenant in Lee's Legion, and aide-de-camp to General Nathaniel Greene. He was vice-president of the South Carolina Society of the Cincinnati after the war.

On his grandmother's side, Mr. Garden descends from Henri de Saussure, a Huguenot of ancient family, who came from Lorraine to South Carolina about 1700 His son, Daniel de Saussure, of Beaufort, S. C., married Mary McPherson, and was a Revolutionary patriot. He was a member of the Provincial Congress, served at the siege of Charleston in 1780, and was captured and imprisoned by the British. After the war, he was a State Senator until 1791, and was president of the Senate. His son, the Honorable Henry William de Saussure, 1763-1837, the great-grandfather of Mr. Garden, fought as a boy in the defense of Charleston, and was made prisoner. Afterwards he studied law in Philadelphia, and became a member of the South Carolina Constitutional Convention in 1789; was a member of the Legislature and Chancellor of the State from 1808 to 1837. He was also director of the United States Mint in 1794, and coined the first gold eagles

Mr. Garden's maternal grandfather was William G. Richardson, son of Captain William Richardson, 1740-1793, and Anna (Poinsette) Richardson. Captain Richardson was a grandson of William Richardson, 1680, Jamestown, Va., and owned Bloomhill, in the hills of Santee, S C. He was a member of the Provincial Congress, a Captain in the Continental Army, and a supporter of General Marion. Emma C. Buford, wife of William G. Richardson, was a granddaughter of Colonel William Buford, of Virginia, of the Continental Army, whose name was derived from a younger son of the Duke of Beaufort.

Mr. Hugh R. Garden was born in Sumter, S C , July 9th, 1840, and graduated with honors at the South Carolina College in 1860. He entered the Confederate Army, served at Fort Sumter and Manassas, and raised and equipped the Palmetto Battery, of which he was Captain He commanded the artillery of General Lee's rear guard at Appomattox. After the war, he studied law in the University of Virginia, was admitted to the bar and practiced in the South until his removal to New York in 1883. He has devoted himself largely to corporation law, while he acquired international reputation by his part in the settlement of the Virginia debt. Mr. Garden has been president of the Southern Society of New York In 1892, the University of the South conferred the degree of D. C. L. upon him. In 1868, Mr Garden married Lucy Gordon Robertson, daughter of the Honorable William J. Robertson, formerly a Judge of the Virginia Court of Appeals, and granddaughter of General William F. Gordon, the friend of Jefferson, Madison and Monroe.

JOHN LYON GARDINER

L ION GARDINER, the founder of one of the foremost of New York's manorial families, was an English officer who had seen service in the low countries under Lord de Vere and became Engineer and Master of Works to the Prince of Orange in his campaigns He crossed the Atlantic in 1635 and landing at Boston was entrusted by Winthrop with the building of the fortifications which defended that city until after the Revolution. He commanded the garrison of Saybrooke, Conn , during the Pequot War, but in 1639 removed with his wife, Mary Willemsen Deurcant, to that beautiful island at the extremity of Long Island which bears his name. His daughter Elizabeth was the first child of English parentage born in New York. Lion Gardiner, it is recorded, purchased his island from Wyandanck, the Sachem of the Long Island Indians His possession was also known as the Isle of Wight, and his title was confirmed by the Earl of Sterling, who made claim to eastern Long Island, and was also subsequently ratified by the Dutch authorities Gardiner's Island was erected into a lordship and manor in 1667, with all the customary feudal privileges Lion Gardiner died in Easthampton in 1665, and his tomb there is marked by a recumbent effigy in armour, erected in 1886 as a monument by his descendants

His successor was his son David, the first European child born in Connecticut, who became the second Lord of Gardiner's Island, and whose son John was the third Lord of the Manor Gardiner's Island had in the meantime been the scene of romantic events The famous pirate, Captain Kidd, landed there and buried some of his treasures The island was plundered by Spanish pirates, but the Gardiner family clung to their manor, the estate being entailed

David Gardiner, 1691-1751, was the fourth of the Lords, his successor being John, the fifth in the line David Gardiner, the sixth Lord, died in 1774, just as the Revolution began. His eldest son, John Lyon Gardiner, 1770-1816, was a minor, in the charge of guardians, and the island was in a prosperous condition. It was ravaged repeatedly by the British forces, who left marks of their occupation which are still to be discovered in the stately manor house which the sixth Lord had completed the year of his death John Lyon Gardiner, the seventh of the Lords of Gardiner's Island, restored the prosperity of his dominion and, though the Revolution had obliterated his manorial rights, was, during his life, known to his neighbors by the same title as his ancestors In 1803, he married Sarah Griswold, daughter of John Griswold, of Lyme, Conn., and granddaughter of Governor Matthew Griswold. The island was again visited by a British fleet during the War of 1812, but escaped without serious damage

David Johnson Gardiner, eldest son of John Lyon Gardiner, became the eighth Lord, being the last to receive the estate under the entail Dying unmarried and intestate, it was inherited by his brother, John Griswold Gardiner, the ninth Lord He also died unmarried, and his heir was his brother, Samuel Buell Gardiner, tenth Lord of the manor. He married Mary Thompson, their children being David Johnson Gardiner, Colonel John Lyon Gardiner and three others The manor was bequeathed to David Johnson Gardiner, but being unwilling to assume the care of such a large estate, he disposed of his rights to his brother, Colonel John Lyon Gardiner, the present and twelfth Lord of this ancient manor The history of Gardiner's Island probably presents the only instance in America where an estate has descended for two hundred and sixty years, or since 1639, according to the law of primogeniture.

Colonel John Lyon Gardiner married Elizabeth Coralie Livingston-Jones, a descendant of the Jones family, of Long Island, and also of the Livingstons, of New York. Their children are: Coralie Livingston Gardiner, who married Alexander Coxe, an English gentleman whose estate is near Sevenoaks, Kent; Adele Griswold Gardiner, Lion Gardiner, the future thirteenth Lord of the manor, who will be of age in 1899, and who is now a student at St. Paul's School, Concord, N. H ; John Gardiner and Winthrop Gardiner Mrs Gardiner was a founder and the first vice-president of the original Society of Colonial Dames of America. The family residence is at Gardiner's Island and the town house is 674 Madison Avenue

DUDLEY GREGORY GAUTIER

A FRENCH Huguenot, who came to this country after the revocation of the Edict of Nantes, was the progenitor of the Gautier family in New York and New Jersey. He was descended from an ancient family, formerly of St. Blanchard, in Languedoc. Originally the family was of noble extraction, and attained eminence during the religious wars of France. Jacques Gautier, its first American representative, had two sons, Daniel and Francois, and several daughters.

Daniel Gautier came to this country with his father, and was married in the Dutch Church in New York, in 1716, to Maria Bogaert. In the early dissensions in the Huguenot Church, caused by the claims of rival ministers, Daniel Gautier sided with the De Lancey party, and, when Governor Burnet decided adversely to that faction, left that church to attend the Dutch Church, though his children became members of the Church of England, in Trinity parish, with which their descendants have since been connected. Andrew Gautier, son of Daniel Gautier, was born in 1720. For his first wife he married Elizabeth Crossfield, a lady of English birth, and sister of Stephen Crossfield, one of the proprietors of the Totten and Crossfield land patents. His second wife, whom he married in 1774, was Margaret Hastier, daughter of Jean and Elizabeth (Perdrian) Hastier. Andrew Gautier became a large property owner, an assistant alderman, 1765-77, and an alderman, 1768-73. During the Revolution, his sympathies were with the mother country. It is related of him that, in 1749, when fire threatened to destroy Trinity Church, he climbed the steeple of the church at great personal risk and extinguished the flames. For this the parish presented him with a silver bowl, appropriately inscribed, which is still preserved in the family.

Andrew Gautier, second of the name, was born in 1755 and educated in King's College, now Columbia University His first wife, whom he married in 1772, and who became the ancestress of that branch of the family now referred to, was Mary Brown, daughter of Captain Thomas Brown, 1717-1782, and Mary Ten Eyck, of Bergen County, N J Captain Brown, who was of mingled English and Dutch parentage, followed the sea in his youth, and during the French wars was captain of a privateer. He owned the ferry across the Hackensack River, and acquired large estate in Bergen County. During the Revolution, he espoused the patriot cause, in 1775 was a member of the Committee of Correspondence for Bergen County, and occupied many positions of prominence. His second wife, the mother of Mary Brown, was Mary Ten Eyck, daughter of Samuel and Mary (Gurney) Ten Eyck

Thomas Gautier, 1774-1802, the great-grandfather of Mr Dudley G. Gautier, was a prominent lawyer in New Jersey and New York. His wife was Elizabeth Leavy, daughter of John and Elizabeth (Dickson) Leavy Thomas Brown Gautier, their son, was born in 1797, graduated from the College of Physicians and Surgeons of New York in 1823, and received the degree of M. D. from Rutgers College in 1831. He was an eminent physician of Hudson County, N. J. His first wife belonged to one of the most distinguished New Jersey families. She was Elizabeth Hornblower, daughter of Josiah and Anna (Merselis) Hornblower. Josiah Hornblower Gautier, their son, was born in 1818, and graduated from the University of New York and from its medical department in 1844 He engaged in the practice of medicine in Jersey City, but finally engaged in business, and in time became the principal partner in the firm of J. H. Gautier & Co., manufacturers of plumbago crucibles. His wife was Mary Louisa Gregory, daughter of the Honorable Dudley S. and Ann Maria Gregory. They had a family of seven children: Dudley Gregory, Thomas Brown, Maria Louisa, Josiah Hornblower, Anna Elizabeth, Charles Edward and Clara Sutton Gautier

Mr. Dudley Gregory Gautier was born in Jersey City, February 2d, 1847, and received his education in Germany. He is engaged in the steel business, being head of the firm of D G Gautier & Co , and resides in Hempstead, Long Island. He is a member of the Union Club, the Meadow Brook Hunt Club and the Downtown Association

JAMES W. GERARD

AMONG the distinguished families that were compelled to flee from France by the persecutions of the reign of Louis XVI, were the Gerards. They went to Scotland, and there William Gerard was born His parents were Robert and Elizabeth Gerard, who, in 1774, resided at Mill of Carnousie, near Banff He was for a time a resident of Gibraltar, but previous to 1780 came to this country and engaged in business The year after his arrival here he married Christina Glass, of a Sutherlandshire family. Her father was John Glass, of Tain, and her mother was a Monroe, from Ross-shire, a grandniece of Sir Thomas Hector Monroe, Governor of the East Indies, and a favorite niece of Dr Alexander Monroe, one of the founders of the University of Edinburgh. A brother of Miss Glass, Alexander S Glass, was a well-known New York merchant of the early part of the nineteenth century Their mother came to this country, a widow with a family of young children, just before the Revolution, and afterwards married Alexander McLean, a Surgeon in the British Army. Her son was Dr. Hugh Monroe McLean, an eminent physician in New York City in the early part of this century. His home on Beekman Street and afterwards in Warren Street, where he lived with his two maiden half-sisters, was one of the social centres of the city.

William and Christina Gerard had seven children Ann married Andrew Hosie and was the mother of Mrs. Schuyler Livingston Christina married Dr. Jeremiah Fisher, a Surgeon in the United States Army in the War of 1812 James W. Gerard, born in 1794, was the youngest of the three sons, and was graduated from Columbia College in 1811. In 1812, he joined the "Iron Greys," a company organized for home defense. After the war, he entered the law office of George Griffin, who was then one of the giants of the New York bar, and in 1816 he took the degree of M. A. from Columbia, at the same time being admitted to the practice of his profession, in which he gained great distinction. He was by instinct a philanthropist, and it was mainly owing to his efforts that the first House of Refuge was established in this city in 1825. A uniformed police force of this city was also first advocated by him. He died in 1874, and during the latter part of his career devoted himself to the cause of public education, holding the offices of school trustee and inspector, and was assiduous in his attention to the public schools.

Early in life he married Eliza, daughter of the Honorable Increase and Elizabeth Sumner, of Boston, of the renowned New England family of that name, originally from Bicester, Oxfordshire, descended from William Sumner, a freeman of Dorchester, Mass, prior to 1637. The father of Eliza (Sumner) Gerard was Chief Justice of the Supreme Court and Governor of Massachusetts, and her brother, General William H Sumner, was aide-de-camp to Governor Strong of Massachusetts during the War of 1812

Mr. James W Gerard, the second of the name, was born in New York City. He was graduated from Columbia College with the honors of valedictorian in 1843, and the same institution conferred the degree of LL. D. upon him in 1892. He followed his father in the legal profession and won an excellent reputation in the specialty to which he devoted himself, real estate and property, and became a recognized authority upon those subjects and was also an able advocate in the courts. He has devoted a great deal of his time to the schools of his native city, and was one of the Commissioners of Education and a State Senator in 1876-7 He is an author of repute, having written much on historical and legal subjects, and also in a lighter vein. The Peace of Utrecht is his most important historical work. He is also the author of Titles to Real Estate in the State of New York, a standard book of the legal profession He married, in 1866, Jenny Angel, daughter of the Honorable B. F. Angel, formerly United States Minister to Sweden He is a member of the Players, the Tuxedo, the St. Nicholas and Union clubs Mrs. Gerard is a vice-president of the Society of Colonial Dames, being a descendant of Elder Brewster, who came over in the Mayflower.

ELBRIDGE T. GERRY

ELBRIDGE GERRY, the grandfather of the present representative of the family, was a prominent patriot of the Revolutionary period and a statesman of eminence in the earlier annals of the United States Government A native of the town of Marblehead, Mass., where he was born in 1744, and a graduate of Harvard in 1762, he became a leader in the movement which resulted in separating the Colonies from Great Britain He was one of the Massachusetts delegates to the Continental Congress, and affixed his signature to the Declaration of Independence His prominence continued throughout the struggle, and he again represented Massachusetts in the Convention of 1787, which framed the Constitution of the United States. At the same time he opposed the ratification of that instrument, and became one of the anti-Federal leaders, and then a founder of the party out of which the existing Democratic party in the United States was evolved Massachusetts, however, chose him as one of its representatives to the first United States Congress, which met in New York in 1789, and he remained a member of that body until 1793 In 1797, he was one of the three envoys of this country sent to Paris to treat with the French Directory, and was elected Governor of Massachusetts in 1810, and again in 1811, while in 1812 he was elected Vice-President of the United States on the same ticket with President Madison He did not complete his term of office, but died in Washington in 1814. Slight and small in stature, Elbridge Gerry was noted even among the gentlemen of those days for his attractive personality and urbane manners; and the political rivalries in which his life was passed never conflicted with the personal friendship of his leading contemporaries. His wife was Miss Thompson, who was one of the leaders of New York's social life in the early days of Washington's first administration.

Thomas R Gerry, his son, became an officer in the United States Navy, and in 1835 married Hannah Goelet, of the old New York family of that name, a sister of Peter and Robert Goelet Mrs Gerry's husband died in 1845. She survived him for fifty years, dying, in 1895, in the old Goelet mansion at Nineteenth Street and Broadway. There were two children of this union, Mr Elbridge T. Gerry and a daughter, who became the wife of Frederic Gallatin, grandson of Albert Gallatin.

Mr. Elbridge T Gerry was born in New York, in 1837, and graduated from Columbia College in 1857. He adopted the profession of law, and soon became an active and successful practitioner His law library is considered one of the finest private collections of the kind in the country. He has not taken an ambitious part in politics, and his principal efforts in public affairs have been in the field of philanthropy. He was associated with Henry Bergh in the early growth of the American Society for the Prevention of Cruelty to Animals, and was for many years its counsel. He is now its first vice-president and chairman of its executive committee

In 1867, he served as a member of the State Constitutional Convention He was appointed in 1892, by the Mayor of New York, chairman of the special commission of inquiry which investigated the public care of the insane. He is a governor of the New York Hospital, and was chairman of the New York State Commission on Capital Punishment In 1875, he was a founder of the Society for the Prevention of Cruelty to Children, and became its president in 1879, a post in which he still continues.

From early youth, he has been an enthusiastic yachtsman, making himself practically acquainted with the details of the sport. The steam yacht Electra, of which he is owner, master and pilot, was built for him in 1884, and from 1886 to 1893, he was Commodore of the New York Yacht Club He is a member of the Metropolitan, Knickerbocker, and other clubs of New York, and the Fort Orange Club, of Albany Since 1882, he has been president of the X Ψ fraternity. Commodore Gerry married Louisa M Livingston, daughter of the late Robert J. Livingston, of New York, and has two sons and two daughters. His town house is at the corner of Sixty-first Street and Fifth Avenue. He also has a summer home in Newport.

ROBERT GOELET

L IKE many of the families which have assumed the lead in all phases of life in New York, the Goelets are of Huguenot descent. Their ancestors lived in La Rochelle, and during one of the persecutions to which the members of their faith were exposed, during the seventeenth century, escaped to Holland, the records of the Dutch City showing their presence in Amsterdam in 1621. Francis Goelet, the youngest son of the family, came to the New Netherland in 1676, bringing with him his son, Jacobus, a lad about ten years of age. Returning to Holland on business, Francis Goelet was presumably lost at sea, the ship which carried him never having been heard from, and the orphan lad, Jacobus, was brought up by Frederick Phillipse, the famous merchant of New York's early history. He married Jannetje Coessar, who was also a member of a Huguenot family, and at his death, in 1731, left a family of six children. His third son was John Goelet, who, in 1718, married Jannetje Cannon, daughter of Jean, or Jan, Cannon, a merchant of New York, who was also of French Protestant ancestry. John Goelet died in 1753, and was the father of several children.

Peter Goelet, the fourth son of John, was born in 1727, and became an eminent and opulent merchant in New York. His place of business was in Hanover Square, being designated according to the custom of that time by the sign of the Golden Key. He was at first in partnership with Peter T. Curtenius, but from 1763 onward carried on business by himself, his name appearing frequently in the public journals and official records of the city as a man of prominence in mercantile life. In 1755, he married Elizabeth Ratse, daughter of a wealthy merchant who had his residence in lower Broadway near the Bowling Green, which locality was then the abode of the leading men of the community.

Peter P. Goelet, son of Peter Goelet, was born in 1764 and died in 1828. He inherited considerable real estate and other property, and throughout his life steadily added to his possessions. In 1799, he married Almy Buchanan, daughter of Thomas Buchanan, one of the leading merchants of the Revolutionary period and a member of the Committee of One Hundred, which took charge of the city in 1775. The Buchanan mansion was in Wall Street, and in it the marriage of his daughter to Peter P. Goelet was celebrated. They had four children, Peter, Jean B., Hannah and Robert. Their daughter, Hannah, married Captain Thomas R. Gerry, U. S. N., son of Elbridge Gerry, the signer of the Declaration of Independence, Governor of Massachusetts and Vice-President of the United States. Her son is Elbridge T. Gerry, ex-Commodore of the New York Yacht Club.

Peter and Robert Goelet were closely associated throughout their lives. Peter Goelet was born in 1800 and died in 1879. He was unmarried and resided in the house at the corner of Broadway and Nineteenth Street, which until its removal, a short time since, was one of the landmarks of Broadway. He was retiring in his habits, but was charitable and contributed generously to aid the sick and wounded soldiers of the Civil War. His brother, Robert Goelet, was born in 1809 and died in 1879, two months before Peter Goelet's decease. He married Sarah Ogden, daughter of Jonathan Ogden, of the famous family of that name which has been conspicuous in New York and New Jersey for fully two centuries, and was the father of Mr Robert Goelet and of the late Ogden Goelet. The brothers, Peter and Robert Goelet, continued the policy which had been pursued by their father of investing in real estate, upon the lines of the city's growth and improvement, and in this manner became the owners of one of the largest and most valuable estates in New York. They were also numbered among the founders of that famous New York financial institution, the Chemical Bank.

Mr. Robert Goelet, of the present generation, was born at his father's house, 5 State Street, fronting the Battery, September 29th, 1841. He graduated from Columbia College in 1860, was admitted to the bar, but has devoted his attention to the care of the large estate left by his father and uncle. He has been distinguished, not only by remarkable discernment and foresight in the conduct of affairs, but for the policy he has pursued of improving his properties in a manner which would beautify the city In this connection, Mr Goelet has not only displayed a notable degree of civic pride in the municipality with which his family has been so long identified, but has given a useful lesson to other large real estate owners in New York of the advantage of taking into consideration such features apart from any mere question of revenue. He is a director in some of the largest financial institutions of the country, including the Chemical National Bank, and, while declining public office, takes an active interest in national and city affairs His tastes are intellectual, and he has been the guiding influence in administering the extensive estates which he and his younger brother, the late Ogden Goelet, inherited In 1879, Mr Goelet married Henrietta Louise, daughter of George Henry Warren, Sr., a distinguished lawyer of this city They have two children, Robert Walton Goelet and Beatrice Goelet Mr Goelet's city residence is 591 Fifth Avenue, and he also has country places at Newport, R I, and Tuxedo, N Y He is a member of the Bar Association and of the Holland and St Nicholas societies, while among the many clubs to which he belongs the Union, Metropolitan, Knickerbocker, Racquet, New York Yacht and Players of this city may be mentioned, as well as the Metropolitan of Washington and the Philadelphia Club He is also a member of the Royal Clyde Yacht Club and the Royal Northern Yacht Club, of Glasgow, Scotland, and is the owner of the steam yacht Nahma, which was designed by George L Watson and built at Thompson's works on the Clyde, and completed in 1897. This vessel is three hundred and six feet over all in length, and is equipped for lengthy cruises, its machinery and other features making it a representative modern yacht of the highest type.

The late Ogden Goelet, the younger son of Robert and Sarah (Ogden) Goelet, was also born at the family residence, 5 State Street, in this city, on June 11th, 1846, and died August 27th, 1897, on board his yacht, the Mayflower, at Cowes, Isle of Wight, England He devoted himself in youth to the business interests connected with the family property In 1877, he married Mary R. Wilson, eldest daughter of Richard T Wilson, of this city Their family consisted of two children, a son, Robert Goelet, and a daughter, Mary Goelet The family residence is on Fifth Avenue, at the corner of Forty-ninth Street, and they also have a country home at Newport. Ogden Goelet was a member of the Union, Metropolitan and other leading clubs, and a member of prominent scientific, artistic and patriotic societies. He was, however, during his life most prominently identified with yachting He was long a member of the New York Yacht Club and other institutions in this country for the promotion of the sport, and owned at one time the fine schooner yacht Norseman. In 1882, he gave to the club the Goelet Cups, which are annually contested for by sloops and schooners respectively, the possession of which are considered the chief prizes of the American yachting world

For some years before his death, the late Ogden Goelet spent most of his time abroad, pursuing his favorite sport He chartered the steam yacht White Ladye, in which he cruised in English waters and in the Mediterranean, and was a member of the Royal Yacht Squadron, and of the principal Continental clubs connected with the sport He also, while abroad, gave a number of handsome cups and prizes to be raced for at the important regattas, one of which was won in the Mediterranean by the famous cutter Britannia, belonging to the Prince of Wales. In 1896, he commissioned the noted designer, George L. Watson, to build for him a steam yacht representing the most advanced ideas that had yet been applied to the construction of such craft. This was the Mayflower, which was built on the Clyde at the works of the Messrs Thompson, the builders of the New York, Paris and other celebrated ocean steamers. The Mayflower, which was launched in November, 1896, is of eighteen hundred tons and three hundred and twenty-one feet over all in length, with nine water-tight compartments Many novel ideas were included in the machinery, fittings and adornment of the yacht, which was in fact a luxurious floating home for its owner. In it he contemplated some extended cruises, and among the other features, making it suitable for voyages to distant and little visited portions of the world, are the six rapid fire guns on the bridge deck Mr. Goelet made the Mayflower his home from her completion until his lamented death, in August, 1897.

BRENT GOOD

THE English surnames Goode and Good seem to have been derived through various transformations from the Anglo-Saxon Goda, a name which frequently occurs in early English
history. In the Domesday Book, which records the ownership of the lands of
England, after the occupation of the country by William the Conqueror, between thirty and
forty Godes and Godas appear as holding possessions in various parts of England under the
new monarchy. It was toward the end of the fourteenth century that the name first assumed
the form of Goode or Good. In 1398, Richard Gode was rector of Busham, St. Andrew, in
Norfolk, and afterwards rector of St Mary's, at Peak Hall, Norfolk. Early in the fifteenth century,
Richard Goode was a rector in Norfolk County, and in 1500 one of the same name was a tenant
of Trinity corporation of Windsor. William Good was a Jesuit priest and missionary to
Ireland, Sweden and Poland in the sixteenth century. Representatives of the name were widely
distributed throughout Lincolnshire, Dorsetshire, Somersetshire, Cornwall and elsewhere, though
families bearing it were most numerous in the western part of England.

Brent Good, the elder of that name, was of the Somersetshire branch of the family, and
established himself in this country in the early part of the present century. He was a descendant from the Goods of Hutton Court, Weston Super Mare, Somersetshire. His ancestors had
long held that manor, which came into their possession through a marriage with the heiress
of the Brent family. Certain representatives of the Brents, it may be remarked, came to this
country and settled in Virginia about a century and a half ago. There they intermarried with
the descendants of another branch of the Good family, representative of the Cornwall Goodes,
who had also established themselves in Virginia at an early date in its history. Brent Good, the
first of the name when he came to this country, settled in Troy, N. Y., where he died in 1837.
He left a son, Brent Good, second of the name in America, who died in Buffalo in 1839, and upon
his death the English estate, to which the American members of the family were heirs, was
disposed of.

One of the sons of the second Brent Good is Mr Brent Good, of New York, who has
been distinguished in the commercial life of the metropolis in this generation. He was born
in Rochester, N Y, in 1837. When he was two years old his family removed to Canada and
settled upon a property at the Bay of Quinte, in upper Canada, where he was brought up and
received his education. When old enough to enter upon a business career, he began his
experience in a drug establishment at Belleville, Ont. In 1856, when nineteen years of age,
he came to New York and entered the employ of Demas Barnes & Co

Mr. Good became a partner in 1863, but retired from the firm in 1869, to become the
senior partner of an importing house, Good, Roof & Co, which he established, remaining
in that business for more than fifteen years. Since 1879, however, he has been interested in
the manufacture of medicinal articles and organized the Carter Medicine Company, of which he
is the president. He has been connected with other business enterprises, having served as
president of several corporations and as director of the Franklin National Bank, of which, in
1890, he was one of the founders. He is also the owner of the Lyceum Theatre, in this city,
and president of the Tutt Manufacturing Company.

Mr Good married a daughter of Henry I Hoyt, of Norwalk, Conn. She was of a
family that has been long noted in Connecticut and New York, and died in 1894. In 1896,
he married Frances Colfax Colwell, of Brooklyn, a member of a Virginia family which removed
from that State at the time of the Civil War. Mr Good's surviving children are Henry Hoyt and
Kate Hamilton Good. He is interested in yachting and is a member of the New York Yacht
Club, and also belongs to the New York Athletic, Lotos, Manhattan, Hardware and Wa-Wa-Yonda
clubs, and to the St. James Club, of Montreal. He lives at 130 West Fifty-seventh Street and
has a country residence at Monmouth Beach, N. J

FREDERIC GOODRIDGE

THE American ancestor of the Goodridge family was William Goodridge, who came from England and settled in Watertown, Mass, in 1636, being a freeman of that place in 1642 From him Mr. Frederic Goodridge was descended in the seventh generation Benjamin Goodridge, son of the pioneer, was born in Watertown in 1642 He was a man of consequence in the town of Newbury, where he grew up He was killed in 1692 by the Indians Samuel Goodridge, son of Benjamin Goodridge, was born in Newbury in 1682, and afterwards moved to Boxford, where he became prominent His wife was Hannah Frazer, daughter of Colin and Anna (Stewart) Frazer, of Newbury. John Goodridge, in the fourth generation from the pioneer of the family, was born in Boxford in 1729, and lived in that place until he was twenty-eight years of age. He married in 1751, Abigail Hall, daughter of Ambrose and Joanna (Dodge) Hall, and in 1757 removed with his wife to Marblehead, going to Keene, N. H, in 1773, and to Grafton, Vt, in 1783 He died in 1815, and she died in 1821. John Goodridge was the great-grandfather of Mr Frederic Goodridge, and his wife, a daughter of Ambrose Hall, was a granddaughter of Joseph Hall, of Newbury, great-granddaughter of Thomas Hall, of Newbury, and great-great-grand-daughter of Thomas Hall, who emigrated to New England and settled in Newbury in 1637. One generation further back, she was descended from Thomas Hall, of the parish of Walton-at-Stone, Hertfordshire, England, and his wife, Joan Kirby.

The grandfather of Mr Goodridge was Moses Goodridge, who was born in Marblehead, Mass, in 1764, and was afterwards a resident of Grafton, Vt. He died in Michigan in 1838. His wife was Abiah, daughter of Samuel and Huldah (Heaton) Wadsworth, of Keene, N H. Mr. Goodridge's father was Samuel Wadsworth Goodridge, who was one of the great merchants in the East India trade in the last generation. He was born in Grafton, Vt, in 1793, and entered upon mercantile life in Rockingham, Vt, being a partner in a business house there. In 1819, he removed to Saxton's River, Vt, and in time became one of the most extensive wool buyers in that State. In 1834, he disposed of his business there, and removing to Hartford, Conn., engaged in the East India and China trade, afterwards establishing himself in the shipping and East India trade in New York, becoming one of the foremost merchants in that line in his generation. He died in 1868. His wife, Lydia Read, whom he married in 1819, was a daughter of the Reverend Peter Read, of Ludlow, Vt, the first representative to the Vermont Legislature from that town. She was born in 1798 and died in 1843.

Mr Frederic Goodridge was born in Hartford, Conn, January 11th, 1836. He was long a leading merchant of New York, being engaged for many years in the business of importing from China and the East Indies, in which he accumulated a large fortune. During the latter years of his life, he was retired from active business. He was a graduate from Trinity College, a member of the Manhattan Club, the Century Association, the Liederkranz, the American Geographical Society and the Trinity College Alumni Association, and a patron of the American Museum of Natural History His death occurred in 1897.

In 1864, Mr. Goodridge married Charlotte Matilda Grosvenor, daughter of Jasper and Matilda A Grosvenor, her father being a prominent merchant of New York in the last generation Mrs. Goodridge has a town house, at 250 Fifth Avenue, and a country residence, Springhurst, at River-dale-on-Hudson Her receptions and musicals have been distinguishing features of every New York social season for many years

Mr. and Mrs Goodridge had five children. The eldest son, Jasper Grosvenor Goodridge, who was born in 1866, died an infant The eldest daughter, Matilda Grosvenor Goodridge, is the wife of Gouverneur Morris Carnochan. The second daughter, Charlotte Grosvenor Goodridge, married George Edward Wyeth The youngest daughter is Caroline L Goodridge. The youngest child is Frederic Grosvenor Goodridge, who was born in 1873, and is a student in Harvard University.

CLIFFORD CODDINGTON GOODWIN

ON his father's side, Mr. Clifford Coddington Goodwin is descended from Ozias, brother of William Goodwin, who arrived in Boston from England in 1632, removed to Newtown, now Cambridge, Mass , the same year, and became one of the ruling elders of that place and a representative to the General Court in 1634. William and Ozias Goodwin accompanied the colony that removed to Hartford, Conn , in 1635, and were prominent men in that community They were directly descended from the Goodwins of East Anglia, whose names appear in the records of Norwich, England, as early as 1238 They were sturdy, independent Pilgrims, intolerant of oppression, and among the most substantial and most useful citizens of the New World. Samuel Goodwin, 1682-1712, great-grandson of Ozias Goodwin, was the ancestor of that branch of the family to which Mr. Clifford Coddington Goodwin belongs. The wife of Samuel Goodwin was Mary Steele, daughter of Lieutenant James and Sarah (Barnard) Steele, of Hartford. Their son, Samuel Goodwin, 1710-1776, was a resident of Hartford, where he was collector in 1737-45-47, grand juror in 1743 and ensign of the military company in 1749. His second wife, the ancestress of the subject of this sketch, was Laodamia Merrill, daughter of Moses and Mary Merrill, of Hartford.

The great-grandfather of Mr. Clifford Coddington Goodwin was George Goodwin, who was born in Hartford, in 1757. He entered the office of Thomas Green, founder of The Connecticut Courant, and in 1777 was admitted to a partnership in the business, being for the rest of his life identified with that newspaper, with which he had been connected almost from its foundation He retired in 1825, after more than sixty years of devotion to business, and his sons succeeded him. The wife of George Goodwin, whom he married in 1779, was Mary Edwards, daughter of Richard and Mary (Butler) Edwards, of Hartford. She died in 1828 and he lived until 1844. The grandfather of Mr Goodwin was Oliver Goodwin, who was born in Hartford, in 1784. During the War of 1812 he was an ensign in Captain Samuel Waugh's company and was also prominent in the administration of public affairs in Litchfield, where he lived, being frequently honored with public office He died in 1855. His wife, whom he married in 1818, was Clarissa Leavitt, daughter of David and Lucy (Clark) Leavitt, of Bethlehem, Conn. The father of Mr. Goodwin is Edward Clark Goodwin, who was born in Litchfield, Conn., in 1825, and is still living in the old Goodwin mansion, in Fifth Avenue

The mother of Mr Goodwin was Matilda Eleanor Coddington, daughter of Jonathan Inslee Coddington. Mrs. Goodwin's father was born in Woodbridge, N J., in 1784 and died in New York in 1856. He was a member of the Assembly from New York City in 1827, Presidential elector in 1844 and Postmaster of New York, 1836-42 His grandfather was John Coddington, of Woodbridge, N. J , who died there about 1758 ; his father was James Coddington, 1754-1816, of Woodbridge, a Revolutionary soldier who married Experience Inslee, daughter of Jonathan and Grace (Moore) Inslee. Several brothers of Mrs. Goodwin have been distinguished in public life. Colonel Clifford Coddington, after whom the subject of this sketch was named, was born in New York in 1841 and died in 1892 He was a lawyer and broker, a member of the Seventh Regiment and a soldier in the Civil War Another brother was David Smith Coddington, 1823-1865, an orator and frequently a member of the Assembly from New York City. A third brother is Gilbert Smith Coddington, of New York, to whom reference is made in another part of this volume

Mr Clifford Coddington Goodwin was born in New York, December 3d, 1860, and educated at the Columbia University Washington, D C He resides in Fifth Avenue, in the same block where three generations of his family have been born and lived. His summer residence, the country home of the family, is Edgewater, in Barrytown-on-Hudson. He belongs to the St. Nicholas and New York clubs. His brother, Edward Leavitt Goodwin, was born in 1859 and died in 1878. Another brother, Henry Leavitt Goodwin, was born in 1862 and married, in 1889, Mary Bowditch Osborne.

JAMES JUNIUS GOODWIN

IN the burying ground connected with the First Church of Hartford, Conn, stands a monument erected to the early settlers of that place. Inscribed thereon are the names of William and Ozias Goodwin, two brothers who were of the company that, in 1635, led by the Reverend Thomas Hooker, left Newtown, now Cambridge, Mass., and went to Connecticut to found a new Colony. Ozias Goodwin was the first American ancestor of Mr. James Junius Goodwin. He was born in England about 1596 and died in Hartford in 1683. His wife was Mary Woodward, of Braintree, England. The line of descent from Ozias Goodwin to the subject of this sketch is through the son, Nathaniel, 1637-1713; the grandson, Ozias, 1689-1776, who was a deacon of the First Church of Hartford, and married Martha Williamson, daughter of Captain Caleb Williamson; the great-grandson, Jonathan Goodwin, 1734-1811, the great-great-grandson, James Goodwin, 1777-1844, and the great-great-great-grandson, James Goodwin, 1803-1878, who was the father of Mr. James J. Goodwin.

The wife of Jonathan Goodwin, great-grandfather of Mr. James J. Goodwin, was Eunice Olcott, of Hartford, daughter of Joseph Olcott. She was descended from Thomas Olcott, who was one of the first settlers of Hartford with William and Ozias Goodwin. The grandmother of Mr. Goodwin was Eunice Roberts, daughter of Lemuel Roberts, who was a Captain in one of the Connecticut regiments during the War of the Revolution. Her remote American ancestor was John Roberts, who assisted in founding the town of Simsbury, Conn., in 1688. James Goodwin, of Hartford, Mr. J. J. Goodwin's father, was born in that city in 1803 and died in 1878. He was well known in the business world, having been president of the Connecticut Mutual Life Insurance Company for more than thirty years. His wife, whom he married in 1832, was Lucy Morgan, daughter of Joseph Morgan. She was descended from Captain Miles Morgan, one of the first settlers of Springfield, Mass, an associate of Colonel William Pynchon and Deacon Samuel Chapin and the ancestor of many distinguished men and women.

One of the sons of James Goodwin was the Reverend Francis Goodwin, of Hartford, who was born in 1839, was ordained a priest in the Protestant Episcopal Church in 1863, and was the rector of Trinity Church, in Hartford, from 1865 to 1871. He had charge of various parishes from 1872 to 1877, and after 1877 was a trustee and president of the Watkinson Farm School. He was also on the boards of street, park and school commissioners of Hartford, and for many years a trustee of the Berkeley Divinity School and Trinity College. His wife was Mary Alsop Jackson, daughter of Captain Charles H. Jackson, of the United States Navy, and a lineal descendant of Deacon John Jackson, of Newtown, Mass., 1639.

Mr. James Junius Goodwin was born in Hartford, Conn. Educated in private schools and the Hartford High School, he spent two years traveling in Europe after 1857. Upon his return to the United States in 1859, he removed to New York and, in 1861, became associated with his cousin, J Pierpont Morgan, in the foreign banking business. He continued this relation for ten years, when he retired, in 1871. In 1873, he married Josephine Sarah Lippincott. Mrs. Goodwin is of Quaker parentage. Her father was Joshua B Lippincott, the Philadelphia publisher, 1813-1886, who for fifty years after 1836 was at the head of the great publishing house which he founded. He was a man of high culture and thorough literary attainments, a patron of the Philadelphia Academy of Fine Arts and a trustee of the University of Pennsylvania.

The city residence of Mr. and Mrs. Goodwin is in West Thirty-fourth Street and they have a country home in Hartford, Conn. Their children are Walter L., James L. and Philip L Goodwin. Walter L. Goodwin graduated from Yale University in the class of 1897. Mr Goodwin is a member of the Metropolitan, City, Union, Century and Riding clubs, the American Geographical Society, the Society of Colonial Wars of New York and Connecticut, the Sons of the Revolution and the Sons of the American Revolution, and is a patron of the Metropolitan Museum of Art and the National Academy of Design.

GEORGE JAY GOULD

THE history of the Gould family, which has been so prominent in the financial affairs of the metropolis and of the country for two generations, goes back to the earliest Colonial period. Originally derived from good old English stock, the lineage of those of the present day can be traced, through several lines, to ancestors who were prominent and active in the formative period of the new Republic, in Colonial times and in the American Revolution.

Major Nathan Gould, the ancestor of the subject of this article, was a native of St. Edmondsbury, England. Coming to Fairfield, Conn., about 1645, with Governor John Winthrop, he became a leading man in the community, and with Winthrop, Samuel Wyllys, General Mason, John Talcott and others, joined in the petition to Charles II. for a charter of the Colony; his name being on the venerable instrument that was granted to Connecticut. He was an assistant to the Governor, an office that corresponded to our State Senators, in 1657, and for every year thereafter, except one, to 1662. In 1670, he was rated as the richest man in the community where he lived, and when he died, in 1694, he was spoken of in the town register of Fairfield as "the worshipful Major Nathan Gould, Esq" Nathan Gould, Jr, son of Major Nathan Gould, was town clerk of Fairfield, Deputy Governor in 1706 and Chief Justice of the Supreme Court of the Colony of Connecticut. His wife was Hannah Talcott, daughter of John Talcott, the secretary of the Colony, and he had seven sons.

Samuel Gould, grandson of the pioneer, died in Fairfield in 1723, at the age of seventy-seven, and Colonel Abraham Gould, his son, was an officer in the Revolution and was killed in battle at Ridgefield, in 1777. Two brothers of Colonel Abraham Gould, Daniel Gould and Abel Gould, were also Revolutionary soldiers.

Jay Gould, who brought the family name into prominence in the last generation by his ability and success as a financier and railroad manager, was the great-grandson of Colonel Abraham Gould. The wife of Colonel Abraham Gould was Elizabeth Burr, a descendant of John Burr, who came to America in 1630, with Governor Winthrop, and was one of the eight founders of Springfield, Mass. Their son, Captain Abraham Gould, settled in Roxbury, N. Y., 1780, and his son, John Burr Gould, was the first male white child born in that town, and became the father of the late Jay Gould. His wife was Mary More, granddaughter of John More, a Scotchman who came from Ayrshire in 1772.

Jay Gould was born in Roxbury May 27th, 1836. Educated in the public schools, in local academies and at Albany, he entered upon a business career early in life, learned surveying and map making, mapped several counties and townships in New York, Ohio, and Michigan, surveyed several railroads, wrote a history of Delaware County, which was published in 1856, founded the town of Gouldsboro in Eastern Pennsylvania and built large tanneries there, laying the foundation for the great fortune that he afterwards accumulated. Shortly before the Civil War broke out, Jay Gould became interested in railroad enterprises His first step in this direction was when he obtained control of The Rutland & Washington Railroad Company, becoming president, treasurer and superintendent of the road. He also became interested in the Cleveland & Pittsburg Railroad and other lines in various parts of the country. He then became a member of the stock brokerage firm of Smith, Gould & Martin, of New York City, and from that time on his life was a history of the greatest railroad and financial enterprises that this country has ever seen His connection with the Erie, the Union Pacific, the Texas & Pacific, the Wabash and the Missouri Pacific Railroads, the Atlantic & Pacific and the Western Union Telegraph Companies and the Manhattan Elevated Railroad, of New York, is too well known to be dwelt upon here He died in 1892. Several years ago, his children built the handsome Dutch Reformed Church at Roxbury, N. Y, as a memorial to him. Mr. George Jay Gould is the eldest son of Jay Gould. His mother was Helen Day Miller, daughter of Daniel S Miller, a prominent wholesale merchant of New York, a descendant of an old English family, settled at Easthampton, Long Island, in the early Colonial days

Mr Gould is a native of New York, having been born in 1864 He was educated in private schools and under tutors, and when still a comparatively young man became the associate and assistant of his father in the latter's vast railroad and business enterprises He was soon placed in highly responsible positions of an executive character, being at first an assistant to the president of the Missouri Pacific Railway Company, and from time to time assumed other places of importance, relieving his father of much of the burden which the active charge of such great interests involved He traveled abroad to a limited extent and visited nearly all portions of the United States, giving special attention to the sections of our country traversed by the railroad lines with which he was officially connected, and making close study of their capabilities. The ability and capacity which he developed in his business pursuits were recognized in the terms of the will of Jay Gould, who, in bequeathing to his eldest son an additional share of his estate, placed this particular mark of approbation upon the ground of his devotion to such cares and the talent which he had shown for his duties

On the death of his father, Mr. George J. Gould became, with his brothers and sisters, an executor of the paternal estate, and at the same time naturally took the place for which his training had fitted him as the head of the various corporations with which the family interests were identified At the present time, Mr Gould is president of the Missouri Pacific Railway, of the Texas Pacific Railway, and the Manhattan Elevated Railway, and is a director and member of the executive committee of the Western Union Telegraph Company. He is also an officer or director of many other corporations He married Edith Kingdon, of Brooklyn, and has five children ; three sons, Kingdon, Jay, and George J. Gould, Jr., and two daughters, Marjorie G and Helen Vivien

Mr Gould is interested in yachting and belongs to the New York, American, Larchmont and Atlantic Yacht clubs He owns the handsome steam yacht Atalanta, which his father built He also purchased the celebrated America cup defender, Vigilant, which he sailed in a series of international races in European waters in the season of 1894, defeating the Prince of Wales' yacht, Brittania, in one race. Mr Gould is also a member of the Lawyers', New York Athletic, New York and Jekyl Island clubs, and the American Geographical Society, and is a patron of the Metropolitan Museum of Art. His city residence is in Fifth Avenue, at the corner of Sixty-seventh Street, and he has a country home at Lakewood, N J.

Edwin Gould, brother of the subject of this article and the second son of Jay Gould, was born in 1866 He entered Columbia College and was a member of the class of 1888 He has since been a liberal friend of his alma mater, to which he has made several noteworthy gifts, including a splendid boat house He showed a decided interest in military matters, becoming a member of Troop A of the National Guard, and was subsequently appointed Inspector of Rifle Practice to the Seventy-first Regiment, with the rank of Captain. He married a daughter of Dr George F Shrady and resides at Irvington, N Y. Edwin Gould also devotes his attention to the management of his large corporate and financial interests, and is the vice-president of the St Louis Southwestern Railway and a director of the Missouri Pacific Railway, Western Union Telegraph Company and other corporations

Howard Gould, the third son of the family, is unmarried and has taken a prominent position as a yachtsman He has raced his yacht, the Niagara, in British waters for several seasons, meeting the most prominent boats of its class on the other side The youngest brother, Frank J. Gould, is still under age

Helen Miller Gould, the eldest sister of George J Gould, is noted for her interest in and devotion to church and benevolent work. She resides in the Gould family place, Lyndhurst, at Irvington-on-the-Hudson The younger sister of the family, Anna Gould, was married in 1895 to Count Paul Marie Ernest Boniface de Castellane, a French nobleman of ancient lineage, and since her marriage has made her home in Paris

WILLIAM RUSSELL GRACE

R AYMOND LE GROS, a Norman baron who took part in the occupation of Ireland by the Plantagenet kings, obtained extensive possessions in Kilkenny and the adjoining counties. His descendants added to the family's power and influence, their name being modified to its present form, Grace, but when English oppression involved the Norman-Irish as well as the Celtic inhabitants, the lands of the Graces were confiscated, and they were forced to retire to Connaught. In a later generation, the head of the family, who was great-grandfather of the gentleman now referred to, returned to the South of Ireland and attempted to regain possession of his ancestral estates, and, though unsuccessful in this, his children attained substantial prosperity.

James Grace, father of the Honorable William R. Grace, inherited a fortune, but lost a large part of it and almost sacrificed his life in efforts to free Venezuela from Spain. His wife was Ellen Mary Russell, a member of a family which has been distinguished in Ireland for several centuries. The Honorable William Russell Grace, the eldest of their four sons, was born in Riverstown, County Cork, Ireland, May 10th, 1832. An ambitious and spirited lad, at fourteen years of age he ran away from school and worked his passage to New York on a sailing vessel. Remaining two years, he then returned home, but in 1850 again left Ireland and entered the employ of Bryce & Co., of Callao, Peru. Becoming a partner two years later, the name was changed to Bryce, Grace & Co. and the firm did a large mercantile business at the ports of Peru and Chili. A few years later, it became Grace Brothers & Co., Mr. Grace's brother, Michael P. Grace, entering it as a partner.

In 1865, Mr. Grace, after close application to business for nearly twenty years, came to New York intending to retire. His health returning, he remained in business, and in 1894 the corporation of W. R. Grace & Co. was organized, with Mr. Grace as president. It has branches in London, San Francisco, Peru and Chili, and occupies a preëminent position in the business world of three continents. He has been a director of the Lincoln National Bank, and the Lincoln Safe Deposit Company, and a trustee of the New York Life Insurance Company, the Terminal Warehouse Company and the Brooklyn Warehouse and Storage Company, and is identified with other corporations. As a Democrat he has taken a conspicuous part in the politics of New York, being a leader in local matters and influential in the councils of his party in the State. In 1880, he was nominated by the combined Democracy for Mayor of New York City and was elected to that office, despite strong opposition, based principally on religious grounds. His administration of municipal affairs was, however, distinguished by impartiality, and when, in 1884, he was again nominated for the Mayoralty, he was reëlected by the support of citizens of all classes.

In September, 1859, Mr. Grace married Lillias Gilchrist, daughter of George W. Gilchrist, of St. George, Me. He has five children: Alice, widow of W. E. Holloway, of San Francisco; Joseph P., Lillias J., Louisa and William R. Grace, Jr. Mr. and Mrs. Grace live at 31 East Seventy-ninth Street. He is a member of the Manhattan, Metropolitan, Lawyers', Reform, Catholic, Country and other clubs, and is a trustee of St. Patrick's Cathedral. His donations to benevolent causes and institutions have been munificent In 1879, he was one of the largest contributors to the relief of the famine in Ireland. In 1897, he took steps to establish a large institution in New York City for the manual instruction of girls. Its founder's hope is that it will accomplish much practical good; it will be entirely supported by Mr. Grace and members of his family, and will be known as the Grace Institute.

Mr. Grace has three brothers, all of whom are distinguished for their ability and business achievements John W. Grace established the branch house in San Francisco, but now lives in New York and takes an active part in the management of the entire business Michael P. Grace founded the firm in London and is largely interested in many prominent financial corporations. The youngest brother, Morgan S. Grace, who went to New Zealand as an army surgeon, has been prominent in politics there, becoming a member of Parliament, and is now a life member of the upper House of the Colony.

MALCOLM GRAHAM

BORN in Edinburgh, in 1694, John Graham, the great-great-grandfather of Mr Malcolm Graham, came of the family of which the dukes of Montrose are the heads He was educated at the University of Glasgow and became a physician In the early part of the eighteenth century, he came to Exeter, N H , and turning from medicine to theology, was the first pastor of the church in Stafford, Conn , in 1723 In 1732, he was called to the church in Southbury, Conn , where he remained for over forty years and was especially active in the great New England revival of 1740 He died in Woodbury, Conn., in 1774 His wife was Abigail Chauncey, daughter of the Reverend Doctor Nathaniel Chauncey Andrew Graham, their son, became a physician He was a Revolutionary patriot and a member of the Committee of Safety At the battle of Danbury, he acted as regimental surgeon and at the battle of White Plains he was taken prisoner and not released until the surrender of Cornwallis For many years he represented the town of Woodbury in the General Court of Connecticut He married, in 1753, Martha Curtiss and died in 1785 His son, John Andrew Graham, 1764-1841, was born in Southbury, Conn , was admitted to the Connecticut bar in 1785, and removed to Rutland, Vt , where he became prominent in his profession. He visited Europe several times, and in 1796 received the degree of LL D from the University of Aberdeen After 1805, he was a resident of New York and became a well-known lawyer His second wife, the grandmother of Mr Malcolm Graham, was Margaret Lorimer, daughter of James Lorimer, of London

Colonel John Lorimer Graham, father of Mr Malcolm Graham, was born in London in 1797 and died in Flushing, N Y , in 1876. He studied law in the celebrated school of Judge Tapping Reeve at Litchfield, Conn , and afterwards with John Anthon, of New York, being admitted to the New York bar in 1821 and becoming a member of the law firm of Graham, Sanford & Noyes He entered the military service of the State in 1817, and in 1819 became a member of Governor De Witt Clinton's staff, with the rank of Colonel. In 1834, he was regent of the State University, from 1840 to 1844 Postmaster of New York, and after 1861 an officer in the Treasury Department at Washington He was a member of the Historical, New England, St George's and St Andrew's societies, and a life director in the American Bible Society A member of the council of the University of the City of New York, he founded a free scholarship in that institution His wife was the youngest daughter of Isaac Clason and he left four sons, James, Clinton, Augustus and Malcolm Graham, and one daughter, Emily Graham

Mr Malcolm Graham, the youngest son of Colonel John L. Graham, was born in New Jersey, July 27th, 1832 In 1854, he formed, with Marcellus Hartley, the firm of Hartley & Graham, of which he is still a member. He lives in West Seventeenth Street and has a summer home, Cedarcroft, at Seabright, N J. He married, in early life, Annie Douglas, daughter of George Douglas, of New York. She died in 1873, and in 1876 he married Amelia M Wilson, daughter of J B Wilson, of New York. Mr Graham is a member of the Metropolitan, Union League, Union, Lawyers', New York Yacht, and Riding clubs, the Century Association, the Saint Andrew's Society, the Sons of the Revolution, the Metropolitan Museum of Art, the National Academy of Design, the American Museum of Natural History, and the Chamber of Commerce He has two sons, Malcolm, Jr , and Robert D Graham, and one daughter, Mary Douglas Graham Malcolm Graham, Jr , graduated from Princeton University in 1890, married Maud L Brightman and lives in New Brighton, Staten Island He is a member of the University, Lawyers', Δ Φ and New York Yacht clubs, the Saint Andrew's Society, and the Chamber of Commerce Robert D Graham married, in 1896, Edith Sands, daughter of Philip J. Sands

The arms of the Graham family are Quarterly ; first and fourth, or , on a chief sable, three escallops of the field for Graham , second and third, argent, three rose gules, barbed and seeded, proper for Montrose. The crest is an eagle, wings hovering, or , perched upon a heron lying upon its back, proper, beaked and membered, gules Motto, *Ne oubliez*

FREDERIC DENT GRANT

IT has been noticed as a curious and interesting fact that the four great Generals of the American Civil War were descended respectively from the four representative peoples of the British Isles, Grant from the Scotch, Sherman from the Saxons, Sheridan from the Irish and Thomas from the Welsh   The Grant family has been sturdily American in all its branches for nearly three centuries   The first of the name who came from Scotland were two brothers, the eldest of whom, Matthew Grant, arrived in Massachusetts in May, 1630, on the ship Mary and John.

Matthew Grant was only twenty-nine years old when he emigrated   In 1635, he was in the company which settled the town of Windsor, Conn., and there he lived until his death, in 1681, being one of the leading citizens of the place, clerk of the town and surveyor of land.   His wife died in 1644, and a few years after he married a Mrs. Rockwell, who had several children by her first marriage, and others by her second husband.   General Ulysses S Grant in his memoir relates that by intermarriages two or three generations later he was descended from Matthew Grant and from both his wives.   In the French and Indian War, in 1756, Noah Grant and his younger brother, Solomon, held commissions in the English Army and were killed in the field.   Noah Grant, in the fifth generation from Matthew Grant, was the great-grandfather of General Ulysses S. Grant   His son, also named Noah, General Grant's grandfather, was born in 1748 and died about 1821, having served in the Continental Army throughout the War of the Revolution, participating in the battle of Bunker Hill, and being present at Yorktown.   After the war, he removed to Westmoreland County, Pa., and being a widower, there married again, and in 1799 moved still further West to Ohio

The eldest son of Captain Noah Grant by his second wife was Jesse R. Grant, who was born in 1794 and died in 1873   He was brought up in the family of Judge Tod, father of Governor Tod, of Ohio, but on coming of age learned the trade of tanning.   He became an energetic business man, fairly prosperous, and married, in 1821, Hannah Simpson, a young lady of Scotch descent, who came of a family that had lived in Montgomery County, Pa., for several generations   General Ulysses S. Grant, soldier and eighteenth President of the United States, eldest son of Jesse R and Hannah (Simpson) Grant, was born in 1822 and died in 1885.   There is no call now to dwell upon his notable career.   The record of his student days at West Point, his service in the old army of the United States, in the Mexican War and in California, his incomparable service to his country in the Civil War, the civic honors that were showered upon him alike in his native land and in foreign countries during the journey around the world which he took after his presidential term expired, has become a familiar household story to the present generation.

Colonel Frederic Dent Grant, the eldest son of General Grant, is in the ninth generation from Matthew Grant.   His mother was Julia T. Dent, of St. Louis, whom General Grant married in 1848   Colonel Grant was born in St. Louis, May 30th, 1850, and was with his father during most of the Civil War, being present at five battles before he was thirteen years old.   He was graduated from West Point in 1871, and served on the frontier in active military duty until 1881, part of the time as aide-de-camp to General Sheridan, with the rank of Lieutenant-Colonel.   He retired from the army in 1881 to enter business, and in 1892 was appointed United States Minister to Austria.   In 1894, he became a member of the Board of Police Commissioners of New York City, and resigned that position in 1897.   Naturally, he is a strong Republican, and is a member of the Republican and Union League clubs.

The wife of Colonel Grant was Ida Honore, of Chicago, and descended from an old-time aristocratic French family of Kentucky   A sister of Mrs. Grant is Mrs. Potter Palmer, of Chicago and Newport.   Colonel and Mrs Grant have two children, Ulysses S. Grant, third, and Julia Grant.   The family residence is in East Sixty-second Street, and they spend the summer in Newport.

JOHN ALEXANDER CLINTON GRAY

IN the year 1795, Alexander Gray, the grandfather of the subject of this sketch, came from the North of Ireland to the United States and died in Philadelphia soon after his arrival, leaving a widow and a son, John Gray, who died in 1816, and who was the father of Mr. John Alexander Clinton Gray, of New York   The widow of Alexander Gray was Mary Little Gray, a lady of the Clinton family, illustrious in the Revolutionary annals of New York, and after her husband's death she became the second wife of her deceased husband's cousin, General James Clinton, the Revolutionary soldier.   By his first wife, Mary De Witt, General James Clinton was the father of one of the most famous men of this State, De Witt Clinton, Governor of New York and creator of the Erie Canal.

The Clinton family in Ireland and America came from the same race as the Earls of Lincoln in England.   William Clinton, who established the Irish branch, was an officer in the army of Charles I , and after the overthrow of the royal cause and the execution of the King, took refuge in Ireland.   His son, James Clinton, married Elizabeth Smith, whose father had been a Captain in the Parliamentary Army during the Civil War, and it was their son, Charles Clinton, 1690-1773, who came to New York in 1729, and established the settlement of Little Britain in Ulster, now Orange County.   His most celebrated sons were General James Clinton, the stepfather of John Gray, and the Honorable George Clinton, 1739-1812, who was one of the most prominent and active Revolutionary patriots during the agitation which preceded the rupture with the mother country, and a member of the Continental Congress.   He afterwards became the first Governor of the State of New York and later Vice-President of the United States.

Mr. John Alexander Clinton Gray was born in 1815, in the Clinton mansion, at Little Britain, Orange County, N. Y., and has since his boyhood been a resident of New York City.   He entered business life at an early age, retiring in 1852.   Since that time, he has been interested in various railroad enterprises, but much of his time has been passed in Europe and devoted to travel   When the original Central Park Commission was formed Mr. Gray was its vice-president.   In 1837, he married Susan M. Zabriskie, daughter of George Zabriskie, a prominent citizen of New York, an alderman of the city and a member of the State Assembly.   Mrs Gray was a descendant in the sixth generation of Albrecht Zaborowsky, a native of Poland, who came from Prussia to New Amsterdam in 1662, and took up his residence in New Jersey, purchasing lands at Paramus.   His son, Jan, married Margaretta Duryea, and his grandson, Joost, married Annetje Terhune, daughter of John Terhune, while his descendants have been since prominent both in New Jersey and New York and have become allied with the oldest families in both States.   Mr. Gray is a member of the Union League Club.

The two elder sons of Mr and Mrs. Gray have been distinguished clergymen and scholars. The Reverend George Zabriskie Gray was for nearly twenty years dean of the Protestant Episcopal Divinity School at Cambridge, Mass., and the Reverend Albert Zabriskie Gray was graduated from the General Theological Seminary, New York, in 1864, served as a chaplain in the field during the Civil War, held several pastorates and was warden of Racine College in 1882.   In 1889, he received the degree of Doctor of Divinity from Columbia College.

The Honorable John Clinton Gray, the youngest son of Mr. and Mrs Gray, has earned the highest honors of the legal profession in New York.   Graduating from the University of New York, he took the degree of LL. B at Harvard Law School and also studied law at the University of Berlin   Engaging in the practice of his profession in this city, he was a member of the law firm of Gray & Davenport   In 1888, Governor Hill appointed him to fill the vacancy in the Court of Appeals, caused by the death of Judge Charles A. Rapallo, and at the election held that year he was chosen for the full term of fourteen years.   Judge Gray is a member of the Bar Association, and of the Metropolitan, Manhattan, Century and Union League clubs, and of the National Academy of Design and the Metropolitan Museum of Art

FRANCIS VINTON GREENE

DISTINGUISHED Colonial lineage is the proud heritage of the family to which Colonel Francis Vinton Greene belongs and which has held high rank in business and in social life in the State of Rhode Island. The first of the family to come to this country was John Greene, an English surgeon, who arrived with Roger Williams on the ship Hampton in 1635 His ancestors for several generations were gentlemen and landed proprietors in Dorsetshire. He settled first in Salem, Mass., and then went with Roger Williams to found the Colony of Providence in 1636. He was a leading man of the Colony, one of the twelve whom Williams recorded as his "loving friends and neighbors," and was on the organization committee of ten. His son was one of the ten assistants to the Governor under the charter of 1663, and his immediate descendants were Governors, Deputy Governors, Secretaries of the Colony and delegates to the General Assembly. One of his most distinguished descendants was General Nathaniel Greene, the Revolutionary patriot, Washington's trusted friend, the famous Quartermaster-General of the Continental Army, and the brilliantly successful commander of the Army of the South who compelled the British forces to abandon South Carolina.

Colonel Francis Vinton Greene was born in Providence, R. I., June 25th, 1850, a direct descendant from the pioneer, John Greene, and collaterally related to General Nathaniel Greene. He was graduated from West Point in 1870, at the head of a class of fifty-eight cadets. Assigned first to the artillery service, he was transferred in 1872 to the Corps of Engineers. For four years he was detailed for service with the joint commission that had in charge the survey of the boundary line between the United States and the British possessions from the Lake of the Woods to the Rocky Mountains, being assistant astronomer and surveyor.

During the year of 1876, he was in the office of the Secretary of War in Washington, and in 1877 was detailed as military attaché to the United States Legation at St Petersburg, his special duty being to make a study of the military operations during the war between Russia and Turkey He accompanied the Russian Army throughout its celebrated campaign, and returned to the United States in January, 1879. The same year he was assigned to duty as assistant to the Engineering Commissioner in Washington, D. C, and had charge of the engineering work upon the streets, roads and bridges in the District of Columbia. After six years of this service, he was sent in July, 1885, to the Military Academy at West Point, as instructor of practical military engineering. In January, 1886, he resigned from the army and became vice-president of the Barber Asphalt Paving Company. Soon after, he was advanced to be president of the same corporation and now holds that position.

Colonel Greene's interest in military affairs followed him into civil life, and in 1889 he joined the National Guard of the State of New York, being commissioned as Major and Engineer of the First Brigade. In February, 1892, he was elected Colonel of the Seventy-First Regiment and has held that position since. He has contributed much to military literature. His official report upon the Turko-Russian War was published in two volumes by the United States Government in 1879, under the title of The Russian Army and its Campaigns in Turkey, 1877-78. In military circles this is recognized as the one authoritative work upon the particular subject with which it deals Colonel Greene is also the author of an entertaining and popular book on Army Life in Russia, of a volume entitled The Mississippi, which treats of the campaigns of the Civil War, and of a biography of Nathaniel Greene, which appeared in the Great Commander Series. He has written much for magazines, reviews and other periodicals, chiefly upon military, historical and allied subjects.

The residence of Colonel Greene is in East Thirtieth Street, and he has a country home in Jamestown, R. I. He married Belle Chevallie He belongs to the Century, University, Union League, Metropolitan, Lawyers', and New York Yacht clubs and to the Metropolitan Club of Washington. From the Czar of Russia he received the decorations of St. Vladimir and St. Anne and the campaign medal, and from the Prince of Roumania the Star of Roumania and the Roumania Cross.

RICHARD HENRY GREENE

WILLIAM GREENE, who married Desire Bacon, daughter of John Bacon and Mary Hawes, is believed to have descended from James Greene, who came to Massachusetts in 1634. Mary Hawes was the granddaughter of Edmund Hawes and of Captain John Gorham, who was mortally wounded in King Philip's War, and whose wife was Desire Howland, daughter of John Howland and Elizabeth Tilley, both of whom came in the Mayflower. Desire Bacon was a great-granddaughter of the Reverend John Mayo, whose daughter, Hannah Mayo, married Nathaniel Bacon and was the mother of John Bacon

Captain James Green, son of William and Desire Greene, and ancestor of Mr. Richard H. Greene, of New York, was born September 17th, 1728, and was Captain of the Second Connecticut Horse in the Revolution. He was with Washington's army in 1766 and with Gates at Saratoga. Ruth Marshall, his wife, was a daughter of John Marshall and Elizabeth Winslow, a descendant of Kenelm Winslow, who came on the second trip of the Mayflower, in 1629, and was a brother of Governor Edward Winslow, the Mayflower Pilgrim John Marshall's grandfather, Captain Samuel Marshall, commanded the Windsor Company in King Philip's War and was killed in the great Swamp fight in 1675. His mother, Mary Drake, was a granddaughter of Henry Wolcott, 1578-1655, and through her Mr. Greene can trace his descent back to remote ages, having collected the names of two thousand ancestors Mr. Greene's grandfather, Captain Richard Green, of East Haddam, Conn, served in the War of 1812, and married Sarah, daughter of William Webb. The latter's father, William Webb, fought at the battle of Long Island in Colonel Josiah Smith's regiment. He married Elizabeth Hudson, daughter of Richard and Keturah (Goldsmith) Hudson. The Webbs, Hudsons and Goldsmiths were early settlers on Long Island. William Webb Green, Mr Greene's father, was born in 1807, was a merchant in New York and Captain in the Tenth Regiment, National Guard. In Brooklyn, prior to 1856, he was an alderman and Judge

Mrs. William W Green was Sarah A , daughter of Colonel William Whetten Todd, born in 1781, and who, in early life, was associated in business with his uncle, the first John Jacob Astor He married Maria Caroline Duffie; from 1798 to 1848 he was engaged in the business founded by his father-in-law, John Duffie, and the latter's brother-in-law, Cornelius C. Roosevelt. He was Lieutenant-Colonel of the Fifty-First Regiment, New York Militia, and a sachem of Tammany. His father, Captain Adam Todd, was at Kingston when that place was burned during the Revolution, and was confined in the Provost Prison, New York. He married Margaret Dodge, daughter of Jeremiah Dodge and Margaret Vanderbilt, great-great-granddaughter of Aert Vanderbilt and Jan Vandervliet. Captain Adam Todd was a brother of Sarah Todd, the wife of the first John Jacob Astor and son of Adam Todd, who came to New York 'n kilt and plaid. Mr. Greene's maternal grandmother, through her grandparents, Cornelius Roosevelt and Margaret Herring, descended from the earliest Dutch settlers; among them, Claes Martense Van Roosevelt, Barent Kunst, Cornelius Barentse Slegt, Olfert de Metzelaer, Jan Cloppers, Peter Haering, Louen Bogaert and Jan de Conseille.

Mr. Richard Henry Greene was born January 12th, 1839, and graduated from Yale in 1862, and from the Law School of Columbia College He engaged in the practice of law as a member of the firm of Roosevelt & Greene, and later, as counsel, was drawn into the management and presidency of local street railway corporations, and retired from active practice in 1886. In 1867, Mr. Greene married Mary Gertrude Munson, daughter of Captain Edwin Beach and Amelia C. (Sperry) Munson, of New Haven, a descendant of Thomas Munson, a settler of New Haven, Conn. Mrs. Greene also descends from the same Mayflower Pilgrims as her husband They have a son, Marshall Winslow Greene, and a daughter, Edna M Greene. Their residence is 235 Central Park West Mr Greene belongs to the Sons of the Revolution, Society of Colonial Wars, Society of American Wars, Society of the War of 1812, Seventh Regiment War Veterans, New York Historical Society, New York Genealogical and Biographical Society, and the Yale Club.

JOHN GREENOUGH

FROM the earliest days of Boston's history the Greenough family and their kindred have held prominent places in that city Mr. John Greenough, of New York, belongs to the seventh generation in line of descent from Captain William Greenough, who was born in England in 1639, and came, with his uncle, to Boston in 1642 Captain Greenough was a shipmaster, and established a shipyard, which is prominently indicated upon the earliest map of Boston now extant. His title of Captain, however, came from his military service. He commanded one of the eight train bands of the town of Boston, and was called out in King Philip's War in 1676, rendering important service He was also Ensign of the Ancient and Honorable Artillery in 1691. He married Ruth Swift in 1660, and died in Boston in 1693, his tomb with its inscription being still seen in one of the ancient burial grounds of Boston.

His son, John Greenough, born in Boston in 1672, married Elizabeth Gross in 1693 and died in 1732; and their son, Thomas Greenough, who was born in 1710 and died in 1785, married Sarah Stoddard in 1750. During the Revolution, Deacon Thomas Greenough was a member of the Committee of Correspondence. His wife was also a member of a Boston family of standing, being a daughter of Simeon Stoddard and a granddaughter of Anthony Stoddard. The latter was constable of Boston in 1642, which, at that time, was an office of considerable importance. Simeon Stoddard also played quite an important part in the local history of his day, having been one of the three substantial citizens of Boston selected by King James II to act under a power of attorney in the matter of certain royal grants David Stoddard Greenough, 1752-1826, the next in the direct line of descent, married, in 1784, Ann Doane. After the War of Independence, he moved to Jamaica Plain, then a suburb of Boston. The house in which he lived is still occupied by members of the family, and is one of the few surviving historic landmarks of that period. It was built in 1760 by Commodore Loring, then chief of the British forces in Massachusetts, and during the siege of Boston was occupied by General Greene as his headquarters. His son, David Stoddard Greenough, second of that name, born in 1787, married Maria Foster Doane, daughter of Elisha Doane, of Cohasset, Mass , in 1813, and died in 1830. He was a graduate of Harvard College in the class of 1805. Becoming interested in military matters, he was for a long period Colonel of the Boston Cadets. That organization acts as the body guard of the Governor of Massachusetts and has always been, as it still is, one of the most select military bodies in the entire country.

David Stoddard Greenough, 1814-1877, the third of that name and father of Mr. John Greenough, was the eldest son of the second David Stoddard Greenough. He, like his father, graduated at Harvard, in the class of 1833, and also held the rank of Colonel of the historic Corps of Cadets. His wife, the present Mr. Greenough's mother, belonged to a Boston family of prominence. She was Anna A Parkman and was a granddaughter of Samuel Parkman, who, in the early portion of the present century, was one of the most eminent merchants of Boston. She was closely related to the Shaw, Sturgis, Russell and other leading families of Boston In fact, on both sides of the present Mr. Greenough's relationships are found the names of many who have achieved more than local reputation in professional life, in literature and in art. The late Francis Parkman, the historian, was Mr. Greenough's cousin, as likewise was Horatio Greenough, whose statue of Washington which adorns the national capitol was the first work of an American sculptor to gain international recognition.

Mr. John Greenough was born in 1846, graduated from Harvard in 1865, and was the first member of his family to leave Boston. He engaged in business in New York early in life, and is now a member of the banking firm of Poor & Greenough. In 1879, Mr. Greenough married Carolina H. Storey, daughter of John M Storey, of this city. His residence is 31 West Thirty-fifth Street, and his summer home is in Tuxedo. Mr. Greenough is a member of the University, Harvard and Tuxedo clubs, as well as the Sons of the American Revolution and other patriotic and public societies.

ISAAC JOHN GREENWOOD

AMONG the earlier immigrants to the Massachusetts Bay Colony was Nathaniel Greenwood, who was born in Norwich, England, in 1631 and died in Boston in 1684 He was a shipbuilder at the North End, Boston, in 1654, a water bailiff in 1670, and a selectman. His wife was Mary Allen, daughter of Samuel Allen, of Braintree Nathaniel Greenwood was of a family that had been long established in Norwich. His father, Miles Greenwood, was a citizen of Norwich in 1627, and the eldest son of Miles Greenwood, of the parish of St Peter's-in-Mancroft, who married, in 1599, Anne Scath, of Barnham-Broome, County Norfolk. The family was a branch of the Yorkshire Greenwoods, who trace their descent to Guiomar, or Wyomarus, de Grenewode, of Greenwood Lee, Achator to the household of the Empress Maud, whose son was Henry II of England. The arms of the Norwich Greenwoods, as borne by Miles Greenwood on his ring, are, argent, a fess sable, between three spur-rowels in chief, and three ducks in base, all sable. Crest, a spur-rowel between two duck-wings sable Motto, *Ut Prosim.*

In the second American generation, Samuel Greenwood, son of Nathaniel Greenwood, also a shipbuilder and selectman, married Elizabeth, daughter of Robert Bronsdon, of Boston, and died in 1721. His son, Isaac Greenwood, born in 1702, graduated from Harvard College in 1721, studied divinity, and, perfecting himself in mathematics with Dr. Desaguliers, in London, became the first Hollisian professor of mathematics and natural philosophy in Harvard College in 1727. His wife, Sarah, daughter of Dr. John Clarke, was a niece and namesake of the Reverend Doctor Cotton Mather's last wife.

Isaac Greenwood, son of Professor Isaac Greenwood, was born in Cambridge in 1730 and died in 1803. He was one of the expert makers of mathematical instruments in his generation, his services being called into requisition by Dr Benjamin Franklin. His wife, Mary I'ans, was a sister-in-law of Colonel Thomas Walker, of Montreal, remembered for his endeavors to arouse the Canadians to join us in our struggle for independence. His son, Dr. John Greenwood, born in Boston in 1760, became a famous physician in New York City. A devoted patriot, he joined the provincial army of Boston in 1775, but after the battle of Trenton, left the land service, and, sailing on various privateers, attained the rank of Captain, and was four times a prisoner of war. At the end of the hostilities, he settled in New York City, where he lived until his death, in 1819. His son, Dr. Isaac John Greenwood, M. D., D. D. S, born in 1795, was a member of the Governor's Guard during the War of 1812. He succeeded to his father's practice, retired in 1839, and died in 1865 By his first wife, Sarah Vanderhoof Bogert, daughter of John Gilbert and Jane (Earl) Bogert, he had three daughters His second wife, whom he married in 1832, was Mary McKay, daughter of John and Elizabeth (Riddell) McKay, of New York, and was mother of two sons, Isaac John and Langdon Greenwood

Mr. Isaac John Greenwood, son of Dr. Isaac John Greenwood, was born in New York, November 15th, 1833 Graduated from Columbia College in 1853, he received the degree of A. M in 1857 He studied chemistry with Professor Robert Ogden Doremus and attended lectures in the New York Medical College, 1856-61. Having been one of the original members in 1859, Mr. Greenwood was an incorporator and first vice-president of the American Numismatic and Archæological Society in 1864. He is also a corresponding member of the New England Historical and Genealogical Society and of the Buffalo Historical Society, and a member of the New York Historical, the New York Genealogical and Biographical, the American Geographical and Statistical, and the Long Island Historical Societies, the Dunlap Society, and the Prince Society of Boston; also of the Metropolitan Museum of Art, the American Museum of Natural History, and the New York Botanical Garden and Zoölogical Societies. He is also a member of the Sons of the Revolution and of the Grand Consistory of the Collegiate Dutch Church. His wife, Mary Agnes Rudd, daughter of Joseph and Eliza E (Barnes) Rudd, whom he married in 1866, died in October, 1890. He lives at 271 West End Avenue, and is a member of the Colonial Club.

FRANCIS BUTLER GRIFFIN

O F Welsh origin, the Griffins and Griffings of the present generation trace their descent from the Griffiths and Gruffids, great families in the history of the principality. The last Prince of Wales, Llewellyn ap Griffiths, is the progenitor of the different branches In the United States, there have been two notable Colonial families bearing the name One descends from Cyrus Griffing, of Virginia, and the other from Jasper Griffing, who was born in Wales about 1648, and came to New England when a child. He resided in Essex, Mass , in 1670. He married in Massachusetts, and with his wife, Hannah, moved to Southold, Long Island, in 1675. His descendants in Long Island, Connecticut and New York have been numerous.

In the second American generation, Jasper Griffin, second of the name, born about 1675, married Ruth Peck, daughter of Joseph and Sarah Peck, of Lyme, Conn. Lemuel Griffin, son of the second Jasper Griffin, was born about 1704, and married Phœbe Comstock. George Griffin, son of Lemuel Griffin and great-grandfather of Mr. Francis Butler Griffin, was born in 1734, and married Eve Dorr, daughter of Edmund Dorr The father of Eve Dorr was born in Roxbury, Mass , in 1692, settled in Lyme, Conn , and died in 1734. He was the sixth son of Edward Dorr and Elizabeth Hawley. His father emigrated from the West of England, where he was born in 1648, and settled in Boston in 1670, becoming the progenitor of the Dorr family in New England The mother of Eve Dorr was Mary Griswold, a daughter of Matthew Griswold and his wife, Phœbe Hyde, who was a daughter of Samuel and Jane (Lee) Hyde, of Norwich, Conn. Matthew Griswold was one of the founders of Lyme, Conn., in 1666. He was a son of Matthew Griswold, who was descended from Sir Matthew Griswold, of Malvern Hall, England, and came to this country in 1639, and settled in Windsor, Conn. He married Anna Wolcott, daughter of Henry Wolcott, son and heir of John Wolcott, of Golden Manor, England. Henry Wolcott came to America in 1630, was one of the founders of Windsor in 1636, and was annually elected to the General Court of Connecticut until the time of his death. George Griffin and his wife, Eve Dorr, have had many distinguished descendants, among whom was the Reverend Edward Dorr Griffin, D D.

The grandfather of Mr. Francis Butler Griffin was George Griffin, 1728-1860, second of the name. He was graduated from Yale College in 1797 and became a lawyer Removing to Wilkesbarre, Pa., he remained there until 1806, when he returned to New York and became one of the distinguished members of the bar In 1801, he married Lydia Butler, of Wilkesbarre, who was the daughter of Colonel Zebulon Butler, of that city, and his wife, Phœbe Haight, of Fishkill, N. Y. Colonel Butler was a distinguished officer of the Revolutionary War. He was in command of the American forces at the time of the massacre in the Wyoming Valley, and after the treason of Benedict Arnold was assigned to duty at West Point by special order of General Washington. On the paternal side, his ancestry was traced from the family of the Earls of Ormond.

George Griffin, the third of the name and the father of Mr. Francis Butler Griffin, attended Williams College and settled in Catskill, N. Y., of which place he became a prominent citizen. His third wife, the mother of the subject of this sketch, was Elizabeth Frances Benson, daughter of Abraham Benson, of Fairfield, Conn. The children of George Griffin by this marriage were Francis Butler, Lydia Butler, Sophy Day, George and Caroline Griffin.

Mr. Francis Butler Griffin was born in New York, November 8th, 1852, and has been engaged in the hardware business for the last twenty-five years He is a director of the National Shoe and Leather Bank He married Anne M. Earle, daughter of the late John H. Earle, their residence being in East Forty-first Street. Mr. Griffin is a member of the City and Presbyterian clubs, and he also belongs to the Sons of the Revolution, the Society of Colonial Wars and the Metropolitan Museum of Art. He is one of the managers of the Presbyterian Hospital, is on the executive committee of the board of that institution, and is treasurer and one of the managers of the New York Infant Asylum.

IRVING GRINNELL

MATTHEW GRINNELL, a member of a Huguenot family in France, came to America with two brothers in 1632. Settling in Rhode Island, he was a resident of Newport, in 1638, and died in 1643. His will shows that he was a man of comfortable means and of high standing in the Colony. Matthew Grinnell, the son of the pioneer, was a freeman in Portsmouth, R I , in 1655, a constable of the town and frequently a moderator of the town meetings He died at Portsmouth in 1705.

A descendant from these pioneers was Cornelius Grinnell, whose wife was Sylvia Howland, a descendant of John Howland of the Mayflower in 1620 Cornelius Grinnell was a successful shipping merchant in New Bedford, Mass. Three sons of Cornelius Grinnell attained prominence in mercantile pursuits in New York and were among the most public spirited citizens of their day. The eldest brother, Joseph Grinnell, came to New York in 1815 and established the firm of Fish & Grinnell. His brothers, Henry and Moses Hicks, became partners in 1825 and soon after Joseph retired. Henry Grinnell, 1800-1874, was identified with the business interests of New York for half a century In 1850, he organized the Arctic expedition to search for Sir John Franklin, and in 1853, with George Peabody, organized the second expedition for the same purpose.

Moses Hicks Grinnell, father of Mr Irving Grinnell, was the third of those great merchants and one of six brothers He was born in New Bedford, Mass., March 23d, 1803, and died in New York, November 24th, 1877. His early education was secured in the New Bedford Academy, and he had his first business experience in his father's counting room. For a short time he was a clerk for a New Bedford firm engaged in importing Russian goods, but soon engaged in business on his own account, and before he had attained his majority went on a voyage to Brazil and France as supercargo of a vessel. In 1825, he came to New York City with his brothers, and in 1828, after Joseph Grinnell had retired, he organized, with his brother Henry, the firm of Grinnell & Minturn, of which Robert B. Minturn was junior partner This concern soon came to be one of the most prosperous in its class of business. It probably built more ships, prior to 1860, than any other mercantile house in this country. The partners were the owners of about fifty vessels engaged in the South American and foreign trade, and in the packet service to England They established the Blue and White Swallow-Tail Line to Liverpool, and the Red and White Swallow-Tail Line to London.

Mr. Grinnell was one of the leading citizens of the metropolis and prominent in all public enterprises In 1838, he was president of the Phœnix Bank, and early in his career was elected a member of the Chamber of Commerce, of which he was the eighteenth president, succeeding Robert Lenox in that position, which he occupied for five years. In his youth he was a Democrat and a member of Tammany Hall, and in 1838 was elected a Member of Congress as a Whig, but in 1856 he was a Presidential elector-at-large on the Fremont ticket From 1860 to 1865 he was a Commissioner of Charities and Correction. In 1869, President Grant appointed him Collector of the Port of New York. During the Civil War, he was a member of the Union Defense Committee, and was a generous contributor in support of the Union cause. He was one of the original members of the Union League Club.

Mr Irving Grinnell, the second child of Moses H. Grinnell, was born in New York, August 9th, 1839. His mother, whom his father married in 1836, was Julia Irving, a niece of Washington Irving, and descended from William Ervine, a companion-in-arms of Robert Bruce. His sister, Julia Irving Grinnell, married George S Bowdoin, and another sister, Fanny Leslie Grinnell, married Thomas F. Cushing, of Boston Mr. Grinnell was educated in Columbia College. He married, April 28th, 1863, Joanna Dorr Howland, daughter of Gardiner G and Louisa (Meredith) Howland, and descended from John Howland, of the Mayflower Mr. and Mrs. Grinnell live at New Hamburgh-on-Hudson He belongs to the New York Yacht and Hudson River Ice Yacht clubs, and for several years has been treasurer of the Church Temperance Society.

WILLIAM MORTON GRINNELL

MATTHEW GRINNELL, who was a freeman of Newport in 1638, was the American ancestor of a notable family. The Honorable George Grinnell, of Greenfield, Mass., who was born in 1786 and died in 1877, was in the seventh generation of descent from Matthew Grinnell. He was graduated from Dartmouth College in 1808, and became one of the most prominent public men in Western Massachusetts, being a member of the Massachusetts Senate and of the National House of Representatives, and a Judge in Franklin County, Mass., 1849-53. Judge Grinnell's wife, Eliza Seymour Perkins, descended from the Pitkins, a leading family in early Connecticut. William Pitkin, its founder, was born near London, England, in 1635. He was a lawyer of high attainments and in excellent standing when he came to this country and settled, about 1659, in Hartford, Conn., where he held many public offices. William Pitkin, in the second generation, born in Hartford, in 1664, was a Judge, and was otherwise prominent in Colonial affairs. In the third generation, William Pitkin, born in Hartford, in 1694, was a Colonel of militia, Chief Justice of the Colony, Lieutenant-Governor 1754-66, and Governor 1766-69, and one of the most useful public men of the pre-Revolutionary period. Mrs. Grinnell was also descended from Thomas Clap, one of the early presidents of Yale College, and included other Colonial New England families among her ancestors.

The Honorable William F Grinnell, father of Mr William Morton Grinnell, was the son of Judge Grinnell, and was born in 1831. For several years he was actively engaged in mercantile pursuits, and at one time was a partner in business with the Honorable Levi P. Morton. In 1877, he was appointed, by President Hayes, Consul of the United States in St. Etienne, France He held that office during five successive administrations, and was afterward United States Consul in Manchester, England, being acknowledged to be one of the most accomplished consular officials in the service. In 1856, he married Mary Morton, daughter of the Reverend Daniel D Morton, of Vermont, and his wife, Lucretia Parsons, daughter of the Reverend Justin and Electa (Frary) Parsons Daniel D Morton, 1788-1852, the son of Levi Morton, of Middleboro, and a Revolutionary soldier, was minister of the Congregational Church in Shoreham, Vt., 1814-31, and afterward occupied several pulpits in Vermont, Massachusetts and New Hampshire. The Honorable Levi Parsons Morton is Mrs. Grinnell's brother, and an uncle of the subject of this sketch.

Through his mother, Mr Grinnell is descended from George Morton, the first of that name in America, who was born about 1585 in Austerfield, Yorkshire, England. He was a member of the ancient Morton family, whose arms were: Quarterly gules and ermine, in the dexter chief and sinister base, each a goat's head, erased, argent, attired or. Crest, a goat's head argent attired or. George Morton was one of the Pilgrims who settled in Leyden, Holland, where he married in 1612 After serving as London agent for the Pilgrims in 1620, he came to this country in 1623, but returned some years later and died in England. The ancestors of Mrs. Grinnell included George Morton, of Plymouth, deputy to the General Court.

Mr. William Morton Grinnell was born in New York, in 1857. He entered Harvard College, but on account of ill health left college before taking a degree, and went abroad. Returning to America, he was graduated from the Law School of Columbia College, was admitted to the bar, and practiced his profession in this city. For several years he resided in Paris as counsel to the American legation there. In 1890, the French Government conferred on him the decoration of Chevalier of the Legion of Honor. In 1892, he was appointed Third Assistant Secretary of State by President Harrison, and held that position until the coming in of the Cleveland administration. Since 1894, he has been a partner in the banking firm of Morton, Bliss & Co. He has two sisters, Mary Lucretia, wife of Edward H. Landon, and Ethel Morton Grinnell His brother, Richard B. Grinnell, is a member of the New York bar. Mr. Grinnell, who is unmarried lives in East Sixty-sixth Street. He is a member of the Metropolitan, University, Harvard and Lawyers' clubs, and of the Metropolitan Club of Washington.

CLEMENT ACTON GRISCOM, JR.

AN exceptionally large number of names distinguished in the histories of Pennsylvania and New Jersey are found in Mr Griscom's ancestry The family which he represents has been identified with those States and with the City of Philadelphia for over two centuries It was in the Quaker City that Mr. Griscom was born, June 20th, 1868, his parents being Clement A Griscom and his wife Frances Canby Biddle Griscom   His grandparents were Dr. John D Griscom and Margaret Acton, daughter of Clement Acton, of Salem, N. J., while his maternal grandfather was William C Biddle   On his father's side, Mr. Griscom descends from one of the earliest settlers of Pennsylvania, Andrew Griscom, who accompanied William Penn to the New World in 1682, and who was prominent in the early history of the Province, having been a member of the first grand jury that was impaneled there   Another of Mr. Griscom's ancestors was Thomas Lloyd, Deputy-Governor of Pennsylvania from 1691 to 1693, and who also held the offices of Provincial Councilor, Master of the Rolls and Keeper of the Great Seal   Samuel Preston, son-in-law of Thomas Lloyd, who also appears in the Griscom ancestry, was a member of the Provincial Council and of the Pennsylvania Assembly, and in 1711 was Mayor of the City of Philadelphia.   Samuel Carpenter, Deputy-Governor of Pennsylvania, 1694–1698, Member of the Governor's Council, Treasurer of the Province and Member of the Pennsylvania Assembly, is still another distinguished ancestor of the subject of this article

The maternal line in this instance represents, however, names and families fully as distinguished and interesting   Mr Griscom's mother is a direct descendant of William Biddle, the founder of the Philadelphia Biddle family, who settled in New Jersey early in the history of that Province, was a member of the Governor's Council in 1682, and held other important offices. An ancestor of this connection was Owen Biddle, a member of the Provincial Council held in Philadelphia in 1775, and who took an active and patriotic part in the Revolution   From his mother, Mr Griscom, moreover, can claim a long line of good New Jersey and Pennsylvania names, such as Thomas Olive, Deputy-Governor of New Jersey, Member and Speaker of the Council, and Member of the Assembly, Isaac and Thomas Marriott, Elisha Bassett, Ebenezer Miller, Henry Wood, William Bates, Thomas Thackara, Daniel Leeds, and others, all of whom filled Colonial offices in New Jersey, together with Robert Owen and Joseph Kirkbride, both members of the Pennsylvania Assembly in the last century

Clement A Griscom, Sr., the father of the subject of the article, is one of the leading citizens of Philadelphia, and has been active and successful in restoring the prestige of the United States upon the ocean, and in regaining our country's share of the world's carrying trade.   Born in Philadelphia, in 1841, and educated there, Mr. Griscom was from early life connected with the Philadelphia shipping house of Peter Wright & Sons, in which he soon became a partner, and was a founder of the International Navigation Company, the corporation owning the American and Red Star line of ocean steamers, of which company he is now president   He is a director of the Pennsylvania Railroad Company and of many financial institutions.   He was a delegate and influential member of the International Maritime Conference at Washington, and since its foundation has been president of the Society of Naval Architects and Marine Engineers. He is a member of many clubs in Philadelphia, New York and London, and enjoys honorary membership in numerous scientific bodies both here and in Europe

His eldest son, Mr Clement A Griscom, Jr., was educated at the University of Pennsylvania, taking the degree of Ph B.   He has made New York his home for some years, being manager of the International Navigation Company in this city   He resides at 303 West Eighty-fourth Street, and has a country home at Flushing, Long Island   In 1889, Mr. Griscom married Genevieve Ludlow, daughter of Colonel William Ludlow, of the Engineer Corps, U. S. N   Mr. Griscom is a member of the Metropolitan and Lawyers' clubs of New York and of the University Club of Philadelphia.

CHESTER GRISWOLD

THE Connecticut Griswolds, from which family Mr. Chester Griswold is descended, were of English root, an ancient family established in Warwickshire prior to the year 1400 They had a long and honorable pedigree and were entitled to a coat of arms Argent, a fess, gules between greyhounds, courant, sable John Griswold, who, about the middle of the fourteenth century, came to Kenilworth and married the daughter and heiress of Henry Hughford, of Huddersley Hale, was the first of the name to come into historical prominence King Henry VI, in 1436, granted the estate, Solihule, to Thomas Griswold, and from his descendant, Richard Griswold, of the reign of Henry VIII, have sprung the other branches The family was one of local distinction, and held many local offices.

Edward and Nathan Griswold, who came to America from Kenilworth, England, in 1639, were men of education and property They were members of the Reverend Ephraim Huit's party, that settled in Windsor, Conn. Matthew Griswold became the father of a family that has given many eminent men to public service, Governors, Senators, judges, clergymen and educators Edward Griswold, the ancestor in direct line of the subject of this sketch, was born in England, about 1607, and died in 1691 He built the old fort in Springfield, was a deputy to the General Court from Windsor, 1656-63, and after his removal to Killingworth, now Clinton, Conn, a place that he founded, in 1667, was magistrate and deputy there continually up to the time of his death He was always an active and influential member of the Legislature, and since that time there has rarely been an Assembly of the State of Connecticut in which some of his descendants, and those of his brother, Matthew, have not been members

Simon Griswold, in the fourth generation from Edward Griswold, was born in Bolton, Conn, in 1753, and died at Nassau, N Y, in 1793 When he was just of age the War of the Revolution began, and he enlisted, serving about Boston, and on Long Island and with Washington, in New Jersey The son of Simon Griswold was Chester Griswold, of Nassau, N. Y., who was born in Bolton, Conn, in 1781, and died in 1860 He was active in public affairs throughout his long life, holding many town and State official positions, and being a member of the New York Legislature, 1823-31.

The son of Chester Griswold was the Honorable John A Griswold, for more than twenty-five years one of the most prominent citizens of Troy, N Y He was born in Nassau, November 11th, 1818, and for a time lived in the family of General John E Wool, who was his uncle Early in life he became interested in the Rensselaer Iron Company, eventually became the principal owner of the concern, and, with his associates, introduced the Bessemer steel process into this country. In 1861, in connection with C. F. Bushnell and John E. Winslow, he built Ericsson's monitor, and also aided in building seven others of the monitor class, including the monitor Dictator He was Mayor of the City of Troy, in 1850, aided in raising three regiments of infantry in the Civil War, as well as the Black Horse Cavalry and the Twenty-first New York or Griswold's Light Cavalry, was a Representative to Congress, 1863-9, Republican candidate for Governor in 1868, and trustee of Rensselaer Polytechnic Institute, 1860-72.

Mr Chester Griswold, the son of the Honorable John A Griswold, was born in Troy, N. Y., September 10th, 1844 He is a steel manufacturer, and president of the Crown Point Iron Company, and vice-president of various manufacturing organizations He is prominent in the social life of the metropolis, being a member of the Tuxedo, South Side Sportsman's and Riding clubs, and other exclusive social organizations He also belongs to the Metropolitan, Union, Racquet, New York Yacht, and other clubs, the Sons of the Revolution and the Downtown Association, and is a patron of the American Museum of Natural History Mrs Griswold is a daughter of Le Grand B. Cannon, and is descended from the old-time Connecticut family of that name

EGBERT GUERNSEY, M. D.

A MONG the two hundred Puritans who went from Boston in 1638 to found New Haven, was John Guernsey, a native of the Island of Guernsey. He was the ancestor in direct line through six generations of Dr. Egbert Guernsey. John Guernsey became prominent in the Colony and was one of the party that protected the regicides, Goff and Whalley.

The descendants of John Guernsey were numerous in Connecticut, and in the struggle for independence, thirteen of the family were in the Continental Army. His great-grandson, John, who was born in Woodbury, Conn., in 1709, removed to Amenia, Dutchess County, N. Y., and Noah Guernsey, his son, was the grandfather of Dr. Egbert Guernsey; his wife, whom he married in 1770, being a Hollister, a direct descendant from William Clinton, the first Earl of Huntington, A. D. 1350, whose descendant during the reign of Henry VIII. was created Earl of Lincoln, a title subsequently merged into that of the Dukes of Newcastle   The mother of Dr. Guernsey was Amanda Crosby, daughter of William Crosby, of the same family as Enoch Crosby, the famous spy of the Revolution.

Dr. Guernsey's parents were long-time residents of Litchfield, Conn., and there he was born, July 3d, 1823. He was educated at Phillips Academy, Andover, Mass., and the scientific department of Yale College. He studied medicine under Dr. Valentine Mott, and in 1846 was graduated from the medical department of the University of New York. For a short time he was an editor of The Evening Mirror. Associated with N. P. Willis and George P Morris, and with George Bennett and Aaron Smith, he established The Brooklyn Times, of which he was editor for two years. He, however, continued the practice of his profession without interruption and was city physician of Brooklyn   He also wrote a school history of the United States which became an accepted text-book   Ill health compelled his temporary retirement, but in 1850 Dr. Guernsey returned to his profession in New York City and in a few years attained an exceedingly large practice.

In addition to his private practice, Dr Guernsey has been prominent in many ways. For six years he was professor of materia medica and of theory and practice in the New York Homœopathic Medical College, and he was one of the founders and the first president of the Western Dispensary and the Good Samaritan Hospital, and a member of the medical staff of the Hahnemann Hospital   In 1877, he was largely instrumental in having the Inebriate Asylum on Ward's Island converted into a general hospital under the Department of Charities and Corrections and placed in the hands of the Homœopathic School of Practice   Since that time, he has been the president of the medical faculty of the institution   He was also one of the originators of the State Insane Asylum at Middletown, N Y , and was many years a trustee and vice-president   In medical literature, also, Dr Guernsey is prominent. In 1852, he was one of the editors of Jahr's Manual, and in 1872 he founded The New York Medical Times, of which he has always been the senior editor. In 1855, he published Domestic Practice, which has passed through many editions and been republished in Europe in four languages. He has also been a frequent contributor to medical journals and is an active member of many societies.

The wife of Dr Guernsey, whom he married in 1848, was Sarah Lefferts Schenck, whose maternal ancestors were the Huguenot Merseroles, of Picardy, and on the paternal side the Lefferts and Schencks   The latter family descended from Edgar de Schencken, who in 798 was seneschal to Charlemagne. From him came the Baron, Schenck Van Mydeck, of Gelderland, the ancestors of Johannes Schenck, who came from Holland in 1683, and from whom Mrs Guernsey is descended in the sixth generation   Dr. Guernsey is a member of the Union League Club, of which he was one of the founders   He also belongs to the Sons of the American Revolution, the National Academy of Design and the New England Society, and resides at 180 Central Park South. He has had two children, a daughter, Florence Guernsey, who is still living, and a son, Dr. Egbert Guernsey, Jr , of Florida, who died July 25th, 1893

ERNEST RUDOLPH GUNTHER

STUDENTS of American genealogy are acquainted with the fact that many of the families prominent in the social, professional and business world in this country are descended from ancestors belonging to the class of nobles in the various countries of Europe. The Napoleonic wars, which convulsed Germany at the close of the last century and the first decades of the present one, brought to the United States a number of representatives of noble families whose estates had been confiscated in the course of the violent changes that marked the period in question, or who for various political reasons found it prudent to leave their native country for other lands. Among them was Christian G. Von Günther, who came to New York in 1815, became a successful and respected citizen of this country, and was the grandfather of the gentleman of whom this sketch treats.

The Von Günthers were originally a noble family of Germany, with a long ancestry extending back for many generations. Many representatives of the race remained in their native country, while others had distinguished themselves in the service of various monarchs and foreign powers. An uncle of Christian Von Günther, who made Holland his adopted country, became a prominent officer in the Dutch Navy. The principal German branch of the family was established in the Kingdom of Saxony, where they were high in the favor of the electors and kings of that country. They possessed a castle, paintings of which are among the heirlooms now in the possession of the American representatives of their name. The father of Christian Von Günther was a physician and a man of the highest scientific attainments, and was surgeon to the King of Saxony. His son entertained liberal opinions and followed the example of his royal master in giving support to the cause of the Emperor Napoleon and of France, during the trying times that preceded the downfall of the Empire. For this the King of Saxony, when Napoleon was overthrown, was punished by the allied Powers assembled at the Congress of Vienna. One-half of his dominions, comprising some of the richest portions of the kingdom, were taken from him and annexed to Prussia. Von Günther, who was among the supporters of the French cause and liberal opinions, thereupon came to America, taking with him the emblazoned coats of arms of his family and portraits of some of its members, including those of himself and brother, and of the uncle (the Dutch naval officer already mentioned) and his wife, these last two being in the court costume of the period.

Once in the New World, Von Günther became imbued with democratic sentiments, identifying himself thoroughly with this country and its institutions and discarded the aristocratic prefix Von of his name, the American branch of the Von Gunther family having since adhered to the name of Gunther. He entered business life with energy and success and attained a high position in the commercial world in New York, which city he had from his arrival in the United States selected for his abode. His son, the late William Henry Gunther, followed in his footsteps and pursued an energetic and successful business career, having the respect and confidence of the community in which his modest and useful life was passed.

Mr. Ernest Rudolph Gunther is the son of the late William Henry Gunther, and the grandson of Christian Gunther. He was born in this city in 1862, in Gunther Row, a block of handsome residences built by his father at Fourteenth Street and Second Avenue, then the fashionable part of New York. After a course of study in private schools in New York and on the Hudson, he received his final education abroad. Mr. Gunther has been a prominent patron of art, and these tastes are gratified by the possession of a number of examples of paintings by the foremost artists of Europe, prominent among which is The Communicants, by F. Estran, of Vienna. He takes great interest in horses, and his brake and four are well known in the park. Mr. Gunther is a member of the City, Country and Union League clubs. He is also well known for his entertainments, to which his artistic and musical tastes give a marked character.

ABRAM EVAN GWYNNE

JOHN CLAYPOOLE, who was a member of Cromwell's House of Peers, and whose eldest son married Elizabeth, daughter of Cromwell, was of royal descent. He came from an old Welsh family, and among his ancestors in direct line were Sir Robert Winfield, William de Bohun, Earl of Northampton, Henry de Bohun, the first Earl of Hereford and Essex, and his successors in that peerage for four generations; Edward I., King of England, William the Conqueror, St David, King of Scotland, Henry II., Emperor of Germany, Edmund Ironsides, King of the Anglo-Saxons, A. D. 989; Baldwin, Count of Flanders, Hugh Capet, King of France, A D. 940, and other sovereigns of England and France. He was ninth in descent from Princess Elizabeth, daughter of Edward I. of England, and her husband, Humphrey de Bohun, the fourth Earl of Hereford and Essex, who were married in 1306.

James Claypoole, a son of John Claypoole, came to this country in 1683 on the ship Concord, landing in Philadelphia. He became a merchant and was treasurer of the Free Society of Traders of the Province of Pennsylvania. His son and his grandson in succession were eminent in that Colony and each held the office of Sheriff of Philadelphia County, while his great-grandson was Captain Abraham Claypoole, of Philadelphia, 1756-1827, an officer in the Continental Army and one of the original members of the Pennsylvania Society of the Order of the Cincinnati. Among the descendants of Captain Claypoole by his first wife, Elizabeth P. Falconer, are the Rockhill and Biddle families, of Philadelphia and Baltimore, and the Claypoole and Carson families, of Cincinnati and Columbus, O.

Captain Claypoole married, for his second wife, Elizabeth Steele, in 1795, and his second child, Alice Ann Claypoole, became the wife of Major David Gwynne, of Cincinnati. Major Gwynne was a First Lieutenant in the United States Army in 1812, a Captain in 1813, a Major in 1814 and a Major and Paymaster in 1816 He resigned from the army in 1830 and died at his country seat, near Louisville, Ky., August 21st, 1831 The eldest son of Major David Gwynne was Abraham Evan Gwynne, of Cincinnati, a lawyer and a partner of the famous Judge Storer of that city. He married Cettie Moore Flagg, daughter of Henry Collins Flagg, who was Mayor of New Haven, Conn , 1836-41, and his third child was Alice Claypoole Gwynne, who is well known to New Yorkers of this generation as the wife of Cornelius Vanderbilt, the present head of the Vanderbilt family

Mr. Abram Evan Gwynne, of New York, is the fourth child and second son of Abraham Evan Gwynne His birthplace was Cincinnati, O , where he was born November 22d, 1847. His early education was received at Starr's Military Academy, Yonkers, N. Y., and at the famous Phillips Academy, Andover, Mass. He then entered Columbia College, New York, and was graduated from that institution in the class of 1870 Immediately after completing his college course, Mr. Gwynne began his active career by entering a banking office in Wall Street He remained there for several years, but in 1876 accepted a responsible position on the staff of the New York Post Office, under Postmaster Thomas L. James. This place he gave up two years later to enter the service of the Canada Southern Railway Company, one of the roads of the Vanderbilt system, in its executive offices in this city. Mr. Gwynne's experience in the railway business lasted only two years and he returned to Wall Street and the banking business, and a short time afterwards, with his brother, David Eli Gwynne, joined the Stock Exchange firm of Chauncey & Gwynne Brothers. This association lasted ten years, and when it was dissolved the Messrs. Gwynne formed a firm of the same character, under the title of Gwynne Brothers, Abram Evan Gwynne being the junior partner in this establishment.

Mr Gwynne is an amateur painter of talent, having inherited a taste and aptitude for art from his celebrated ancestor, Washington Allston, who was half-brother of his grandfather on his mother's side. He is also a frequent contributor to the newspaper and magazine literature of the day.

JOHN HALL, D. D.

FEW clergymen, whether foreign or native born, have played a more important part in the religious life of New York than the Reverend Dr. John Hall, pastor of the Fifth Avenue Presbyterian Church. As a pulpit orator he is preëminent, while his activity in the cause of education has been notable. The ancestors of Dr. Hall were Scotch Presbyterians, who emigrated from Scotland to Ireland two centuries ago and were active in the settlement of the Province of Ulster. The Reverend Dr. John Hall was born in 1829, in the County of Armagh, Ireland, on the place occupied by his ancestors for six generations, and which is still held by the family. His father was an elder of the Presbyterian Church and the family held a good social position. Being the eldest son, Dr. Hall received the Christian name of his grandfather, John Hall. Receiving a classical preparatory education in private schools, he entered Belfast College before he was thirteen years old. During his college course, he gained reputation by his scholarly attainments, winning the prize for excellence in the Hebrew language. After graduating, he studied for the Presbyterian ministry, and in 1849, when twenty years of age, received his license to preach from the Presbytery of Belfast. He then accepted a call to a missionary station in the west of Ireland. After a few years, he was called to the First Church of Armagh, where he was installed in 1852. For six years he held that pulpit, and then, in 1858, he became the junior pastor of St Mary's Abbey, now Rutland Square, Dublin. There he rapidly attained to prominence, and also became identified with educational affairs, receiving a royal appointment as Commissioner of Education.

In 1867, Dr. Hall was a delegate from the Irish General Assemby to the Assemblies of the Presbyterian Churches of the United States. His reputation had preceded him to this country, and his presence here attracted further attention from both clergy and laymen. Called to the pulpit of the Fifth Avenue Presbyterian Church, he accepted and was installed in November, 1867. For thirty years he has occupied that pulpit, and has brought the church to a foremost position. Its gifts to the missionary and benevolent work of the Presbyterian denomination have been of a notable character.

In literary and educational work, Dr. Hall has also achieved fame. His contributions to the religious press have been abundant, and he is frequently a speaker on public occasions. Among his published works are Family Prayers for Four Weeks, Papers for Home Reading, Familiar Talks to Boys, Questions of the Day, God's Word through Preaching, and Light upon the Path. From 1882 until the appointment of Dr MacCracken, he was Chancellor of the University of the City of New York, succeeding the Reverend Dr. Howard Crosby.

In 1852, after his settlement in the City of Armagh, Dr. Hall married Emily (Bolton) Irwin, the daughter of Richard Bolton, who long occupied Monkstown Castle, County Dublin. Her first husband was John Irwin, a gentleman of County Roscommon, who died in early life. Her son by her first marriage, William Irwin, is a well-known lawyer of this city. Dr. Hall was a missionary in County Roscommon, where he met Mrs. Irwin, who was doing much voluntary work for the poor during and after the famine. Dr. and Mrs. Hall have had four sons and a daughter. The eldest son, Robert W. Hall, graduated from Princeton in 1873 and is a professor in New York University. The second son, Bolton Hall, graduated from Princeton in 1875. He married Susie Hurlbut Scott, daughter of William H. Scott, and lives in East Forty-sixth Street. He is a member of the City and Reform clubs and has taken an active part in reform movements, gaining distinction as a platform orator, and a writer on social questions. The third son, a prominent surgeon, died recently, and the youngest is a Presbyterian minister, and has rendered good service in Omaha and Chicago. He married the daughter of the great botanist, Professor Bartling, of Göttingen, Germany. The only daughter, Emily Hall, married William E Wheelock. Dr. Hall's residence is in upper Fifth Avenue and his vacations, as a rule, are passed in his native Ireland.

FREDERIC ROBERT HALSEY

B
ORN in Hertfordshire, England, in 1592, Thomas Halsey was the progenitor of the American family that bears his name. He came to this country before 1637, being a resident of Lynn, Mass , in that year. He was one of the founders of Southampton, Long Island, in 1640, where he was considered one of the most respected citizens. He was a delegate to the Connecticut General Court in 1664, was named in the patent of confirmation in 1676, was also named in Governor Dongan's patent in 1686, and took an active part in all the town affairs and in the controversies between the Dutch and the English. His first wife, Phœbe, who was murdered by the Pequot Indians in 1649, was the ancestress of that branch of the Halsey family which is here under consideration. His second wife was Ann Johnes, widow of Edward Johnes.

Descendants of Thomas Halsey distributed themselves throughout various parts of the South and West, and many of them were prominent in the settlement of Oneida and Otsego Counties, and other portions of New York State which were then a wilderness In Tioga County is a village called Halsey Valley, in Tompkins County is Halseyville, in far-off Oregon there is a village named Halsey, while, nearer at home, Halsey Street in Brooklyn still preserves the memory of the family. Many of the Halseys took part in the early French and Indian wars, and their names are recorded in the Colonial records of New York. They served in the Revolution, notably at Fort Ticonderoga, and in the Wars of 1812 and 1848. In the Civil War, several of them won high rank in defense of the cause of the Union.

Daniel Halsey, of the second American generation, 1630-1682, the third son of Thomas Halsey, was the ancestor in direct line of Mr. Frederic Robert Halsey. His son, Daniel Halsey, 1669-1734, married Amy Larison, daughter of John Larison. His grandson, Silas Halsey, 1718-1786, married Susanna Howell, and was chairman of the Committee of Safety of Southampton, Long Island, on the breaking out of the Revolution Dr Silas Halsey, second, 1743-1832, and his second wife, Hannah (Jones) Howell, whom he married in 1780, were the great-grandparents of Frederic Robert Halsey. Silas Halsey studied medicine in New Jersey and practiced his profession in Southampton until 1776. His uncompromising patriotism brought him particularly under the ban of the British authorities in New York, and he was forced to remove to Connecticut, where he remained for three years. After the war, he returned to his former home and was Sheriff of Suffolk County in 1787 by appointment of Governor Clinton. In 1793, he removed to Ovid, N Y. For several years he was supervisor and a member of the Assembly, in 1801, a delegate to the Constitutional Convention; in 1804, a member of the National House of Representatives, and in 1807, a State Senator. His son, Nicoll Halsey, 1782-1865, grandfather of Mr. Frederic R Halsey, married, in 1806, Euphemia McDowell, daughter of Robert and Margaret McDowell, of Kingston, Pa He was a member of the State Assembly of New York in 1824, and a Member of Congress, 1833-35 The parents of Mr Frederic R. Halsey were Robert Halsey, who was born in 1809 and died in 1896, and his wife, Sarah Stewart.

Mr. Frederic Robert Halsey, in the eighth generation of the American Halseys, was born in 1847, in Ithaca, N. Y. He was graduated from Harvard College in the class of 1868 and from the Columbia College Law School in 1870, and engaged in the practice of his profession in New York Interested in public affairs and in the militia, he was appointed, in 1893, Paymaster-General on the staff of Governor Roswell P. Flower, with the rank of Brigadier-General. He is the author of a book treating of the engraved works of Raphael Morghen. He married, in 1872, Emma Gertrude Keep, only child of Henry Keep. His city residence is 22 West Fifty-third Street, and his country residence, is Egeria, Tuxedo Park. Mr. and Mrs Halsey have no children He is a member of the Union, University, Tuxedo, Manhattan, Racquet, New York Athletic, Harvard and Westminster Kennel clubs, and is a patron of the American Museum of Natural History and the Metropolitan Museum of Art He also belongs to the Gun Club of Philadelphia, the Olympic Club of Long Island and the St. James Club of Paris.

JAMES HOOKER HAMERSLEY

IN 1716, William Hamersley, an officer in the British Navy, a descendant of Sir Hugh Hamersley, Lord Mayor of London, 1627, was stationed at New York and married into the old Dutch family of Van Brugh He became a resident of the city, a vestryman of Trinity, and is buried in its historic graveyard. Hamersley Street, changed in later times to West Houston, was named after him He was furthermore the founder of a family which has lived in New York for five generations, which has always been identified with its interests, and which has been distinguished by high character, social position and noteworthy alliances.

In the fourth generation in direct descent from Mr. William Hamersley is James Hooker Hamersley. He was born in New York, 1844, being the son of the late John William Hamersley, also born in New York, and of his wife, Catharine Livingston Hooker, born at Poughkeepsie, N. Y The paternal grandparents were Lewis Carré Hamersley, of New York, who married Elizabeth Finney, born in Accomac County, Va.; while on the maternal side were the Honorable James Hooker, born at Windsor, Conn., and his wife, Helen Sarah Reade, born at Red Hook, properly Reade Hoeck, Dutchess County, N. Y.

Mr. Hamersley's family is thus connected with some of the most eminent names in early Colonial history. It may be mentioned that he is fifth in descent from Judge Thomas Gordon, of the Council of the Province of East Jersey, Deputy-Secretary and Attorney-General, 1692, Receiver-General and Treasurer, 1710-19, and one of the Lords Proprietors; sixth in descent from Robert Livingston, Speaker of the New York Assembly, 1718-25, and founder of Livingston Manor; seventh in descent from Filyp Pieterse Van Schuyler, Captain of New York Provincial forces, 1667, and eighth in descent from Brant Arentse Van Schlichtenhorst, Governor of the Colony of Rensselaerwyck, 1648, and commandant of the fort and garrison at Rensselaerstein, who led his forces against Governor Stuyvesant, of New Amsterdam, and was in the main successful. Through his mother's family, Mr Hamersley is also connected with the Van Cortlandts, de Peysters and Stuyvesants, while among his other ancestors is Henry Beekman, the patentee from Queen Anne of a large amount of land in Dutchess County, N. Y., a portion of which has never left the hands of his descendants, and is owned by Mr. Hamersley.

Mr. Hamersley graduated with honors from Columbia College in 1865, and took the degree of LL.B. at the Law School of the same institution two years later He practiced the legal profession successfully for some years, but finally retired to devote himself to the duties of cotrustee of the large estate left by his father In April, 1888, he was married to Margaret Willing Chisolm, born at College Point, Long Island, daughter of William E Chisolm and his wife, Mary A. Rogers, daughter of John Rogers. The Chisolms are of a prominent South Carolina family, the Rogers being large owners of real estate in New York. The sister of John Rogers married William C. Rhinelander. Mrs. Hamersley is also a great niece of William Augustus Muhlenburg, who founded St. Luke's Hospital, and is a direct descendant of Frederick Augustus Muhlenburg, first Speaker of the United States House of Representatives. Mr. and Mrs. Hamersley's two children are Catharine Livingston Hamersley and Louis Gordon Hamersley.

He is an extensive traveler, including some twenty voyages across the Atlantic, a participator in the pleasures of society, member of a number of clubs, including the Metropolitan, University and City clubs and St. Nicholas Society, president of the Knickerbocker Bowling Club, member of the New York Geographical Society, the Society of Colonial Wars, etc. The engrossing occupations incident to the care of his family property have not prevented Mr. Hamersley from taking an active interest in politics. Literature is, however, the favorite pursuit of his leisure, and he writes occasional articles on the live topics of the day, such as law, religion, and politics and history. Mr. Hamersley is a graceful poet, his verse appearing in various periodicals and collections of poems, though they have not yet been brought together in one volume.

WILLIAM GASTON HAMILTON

EVERY schoolboy knows the story of the career of Alexander Hamilton. Born of parents in moderate circumstances, on the Antilles island of Nevis, through the kindness of friends he studied in Kings (Columbia) College, was a soldier in the Continental Army, and on the staff of Washington with the rank of Lieutenant-Colonel, was Secretary of the Treasury in Washington's first Cabinet, one of the ablest jurists and statesmen of the early period of the United States, and among the greatest men that have been called upon to serve the Republic. His death in a duel with Aaron Burr in 1804 has always added a melancholy interest to the story of his life, and was a striking and impressive end to a brilliant and picturesque career.

The descendants of Alexander Hamilton have been conspicuous in military and civil life. His eldest son, Philip, was killed in a duel before he had attained his majority, on the same spot where his father fell three years later. His second son, Alexander, was a soldier in the War of 1812, and another son, James Alexander, also served in the War of 1812, was a lawyer and United States District Attorney. William Stevens Hamilton was a Colonel of Volunteers in the Black Hawk War, and the youngest son, Philip, was a lawyer in New York, and at one time an Assistant District Attorney.

The fourth son of this interesting and notable family, Colonel John Church Hamilton, was the father of Mr. William Gaston Hamilton. Born in Philadelphia, in 1792, he was graduated from Columbia College in 1809, and was admitted to the bar. When war with Great Britain was declared in 1812, he offered his services and was commissioned a Lieutenant. Later he was an aide on the staff of General Harrison, with the rank of Lieutenant-Colonel. The greater part of his life was given to literary pursuits. His important literary work related to the life and career of his distinguished father. In 1834-40, he edited and published the Memoirs of Alexander Hamilton; in 1851, his Works of Alexander Hamilton appeared in two volumes, and in 1850-58 he published, in seven volumes, A History of the Republic as Traced in the Writings of Alexander Hamilton.

Mr. William Gaston Hamilton, the fourth son of Colonel John Church Hamilton, was born in New York in 1832. Through his grandmother, Elizabeth Schuyler, sister of General Philip Schuyler, he is descended from another noted Colonial family. His mother was Maria Eliza Van den Heuvel, daughter of Baron John Corneilus Van den Heuvel, once Governor of Dutch Guiana, and a resident of New York. The brothers of Mr. Hamilton are Alexander Hamilton, of Tarrytown, General Schuyler Hamilton and Judge Charles A. Hamilton, of the Supreme Court of Wisconsin. His sister Elizabeth married, first, Major-General Henry W. Halleck, and, second, Major-General George W. Cullum.

Mr. Hamilton is a civil and mechanical engineer, and has been connected with many important business enterprises, having been president and engineer of the Jersey City Locomotive Works, vice-president of the Ramapo Wheel and Foundry Company, president of the Hamilton Steeled Wheel Company, Consulting Mechanical Engineer to the Pennsylvania Railroad, and vice-president and director of the Mexican & Central and the South American Telegraph Companies. He is a vice-president of the New York Association for Improving the Condition of the Poor, vice-president of the Demilt Dispensary, a manager of the New York Cancer Hospital, the Woman's Hospital, and the New York Blind Asylum, and chairman of the Mayor's advisory committee on public baths. In his clubs he includes the Century, Metropolitan, Tuxedo and Church, and he is a member of the American Society of Civil Engineers, the Sons of the Revolution, the American Geographical Society, and the St. Nicholas Society, and a patron of the Academy of Design and the American Museum of Natural History. He married Charlotte (Jeffrey) Pierson. His city residence is at 105 East Twenty-first Street, and he has a country home in Ramapo, N. Y. His son, William Pierson Hamilton, married Juliet P. Morgan, daughter of J. Pierpont Morgan. His daughters are Helen M. and Marie V. Hamilton.

WILLIAM ALEXANDER HAMMOND, M. D.

THE Hammonds of Maryland inherit the blood of Rollo, the first Duke of Normandy. Among the principal followers of William the Conqueror, and of his son, William Rufus, were Robert Fitz Hammon, Earl of Corbeille, and his brother Hammon, Viscount of Thonars, from the last of whom the Hammonds of Acrise are directly descended, as well as the Hammonds of Kent and various other parts of England John Hammond, who came to Maryland in the reign of Charles I., was a cadet of that noble house. He was an earnest royalist, though other representatives of his name had espoused the Parliamentary side, and in 1654-1655 played an energetic part in opposing the Puritan faction in Maryland His son, the Honorable John Hammond, was Major-General of the Province, a member of its Council and Judge in Admiralty. He died in 1705, and was buried at the family estate in Anne Arundel County, where the inscription on his tomb is still legible after nearly two hundred years and where his descendants continued to reside. His great-grandson, Philip, married Nancy Joyce, noted for her beauty, one of their children being Dr. John W. Hammond. The latter married Sarah Pinkney, of Annapolis, daughter of Jonathan Pinkney, and niece of the famous statesman, William Pinkney, United States Senator, Minister to England, and Attorney-General of the United States

Dr. William Alexander Hammond, who was born at Annapolis in 1828, was the second son of this marriage, but by the death of his elder brother, the Reverend J. Pinkney Hammond, D. D, he became the head of the family. Educated at St John's College, Annapolis, and receiving his medical degree from the University of the City of New York, he was appointed in 1849 First Lieutenant and Assistant Surgeon in the army. After about ten years' service, he resigned to accept the position of Professor of Anatomy and Physiology in the University of Maryland, at Baltimore. On the beginning of the Civil War, he returned to the army and was soon afterwards made Surgeon-General with the rank of Brigadier-General. He was removed from his office about the end of the war, but was reinstated in 1879, after full inquiry, and is now Surgeon-General and Brigadier-General on the retired list of the army.

Dr. Hammond's first wife was Helen, daughter of Michael Nisbet, of Philadelphia, his second alliance being with Esther Dyer, daughter of John F. Chapin, of Providence, a lady related to prominent New England families and a descendant of Baron de Bernon, the Huguenot settler in Rhode Island. The two surviving children of Dr. Hammond are Clara, who married the Marquis Lanza di Brolo, cousin of Cardinal Rampolla, and Graeme Monroe Hammond, M D, who married Louisa Elsworth, a descendant of Oliver Elsworth The Marquise Lanza has inherited her father's literary talent.

After residing in New York for twenty years, Dr. Hammond returned to Washington in 1888, his house, Belcourt, Columbia Heights, being the finest reproduction of a French château in America. Identified socially as well as professionally with New York, he has long figured in its most exclusive circles and still retains his membership in the Manhattan Club. His Washington clubs include the Metropolitan, Army and Navy, Country and Chevy Chase. Though not an active sportsman, he was a member of both the New York Yacht and American Jockey clubs.

Dr. Hammond's professional career has placed him in the front rank of modern scientists. It is possible to speak only briefly of his honors, which include professorships in the leading medical schools of the country and membership in the foremost scientific bodies of the United States and Europe. He is the author of many professional works which have been translated and reproduced in Europe, and is a frequent contributor to both scientific and popular periodicals. He has also found relaxation and fame as a writer in a lighter vein, being the author of five successful novels and many short stories His son, Dr. Graeme Monroe Hammond, succeeded his father as professor in the New York Post-Graduate Medical School and Hospital, and is the author of many articles and monographs upon medical subjects

WAINWRIGHT HARDIE

S HORTLY after the close of the Revolutionary War, two young men of good family, John and James Hardie, natives of Aberdeen, Scotland, came to America. James Hardie was a scholar and writer, at one time a professor in Columbia College, and the author of several standard works, among them a history of the State of New York. John Hardie settled at Sharon, Conn., and married Elene Bogardus, a direct descendant of the famous Anneke Jans by her second husband, Domine Everardus Bogardus (her first husband having been a member of the princely house of Orange), the exceedingly prominent place which she occupies in the ancestry of many New York families of distinction being well known, while her gifts to Trinity Church, it is needless to say, created the prosperity of that corporation.

Allen Wardwell Hardie, the son of John and Elene Bogardus Hardie, was born at Sharon, in 1799, and died in 1849. He was prominent in politics and business in New York City and State, and operated largely in lands, having offices both in Albany and New York. He was an old-fashioned Democrat, possessed great influence in the Hudson River counties, and was the intimate associate of the prominent statesmen of his time, including President Van Buren, the Honorable Gulian Ver Planck, and others of similar eminence. He was also Captain in the Ninth Regiment, New York State Artillery Militia, his commission, signed by De Witt Clinton, Governor of the State of New York, being preserved among the family papers. His correspondence with various prominent statesmen of the time was also very extensive, and was conducted on a footing which indicates not only confidence and intimacy, personal and political, but also shows the respect which men of that standing entertained for him.

His wife, Caroline Cock Hardie, 1800-1876, born in New York, belonged to a well-known Quaker family of Long Island, the Cocks, of Oyster Bay. She was present at the reception given by the Society of New York to the Marquis de Lafayette on September 10th, 1826, her card of invitation being also preserved among the family archives, with other interesting mementoes of the early social life of the city, in which Mrs. Hardie was prominent. The family residence was then in Cortlandt Street.

Mr. Wainwright Hardie is a son of this marriage. He was born in this city, and was baptized at old St. Anne's Church, Fishkill-on-Hudson, where the family at that time had a country seat. He was named after the famous Bishop Wainwright, then rector of old Grace Church, Broadway and Rector Street, of which his parents were attendants and pew holders.

His education was received principally at St. John's School, Varick Street, over which Doctor Wainwright, then rector of St. John's Chapel, presided as founder and patron. His business career commenced with the Commercial Mutual Marine Insurance Company, at the time of its organization, and after many years' service in various positions, latterly as the company's vice-president, he retired for rest and recreation, and made an extended tour in Europe. Mr. Hardie is unmarried; he resides at 8 East Twelfth Street, and devotes himself to business and to the affairs of charitable organizations.

Members of the families of Mr. Hardie's mother and grandmother fought in the Revolutionary War and in the War of 1812. In the war between the States, a distinguished representative was furnished in the person of a brother of the subject of this article, General James Allen Hardie, U. S. A. The latter, born in New York in 1823, entered the United States Military Academy at West Point, and was a classmate of General Ulysses S. Grant. General Hardie served throughout the Civil War with distinction, and enjoyed the confidence and friendship of Generals Grant and Sherman, and was the intimate friend of Lincoln and Stanton. His military record is set forth in full in the annals of the War Department. After the close of the war, he was appointed Assistant Inspector-General of the United States Army, and died in 1876. His son is Captain Francis Hunter Hardie, of the Third Cavalry, United States Army, who, like his father, is a graduate of the United States Military Academy, at West Point.

ORLANDO METCALF HARPER

JOHN HUMFREY, who was born in Dorchester, England, about 1600, died in his native place, in 1661. For fifteen or twenty years he was notably identified with the first English enterprises that resulted in the settlement of New England. Educated as a lawyer, he became renowned in his profession, and was a man of considerable wealth, for those times In 1628, he was one of a company of six individuals of similar views to his own, who were the original purchasers of the territory that subsequently became the Massachusetts Bay Colony, and was the first treasurer of the Plymouth Colony

At the second meeting of the Massachusetts Bay Company, John Humfrey was chosen Deputy-Governor, and came to New England in the discharge of the duties of his position. On his voyage to the New World he was accompanied by his wife, Lady Susan Clinton, daughter of Thomas Clinton, third Earl of Lincoln, and Lady Elizabeth, his wife. Six children of Governor Humfrey came with their parents He settled in Swampscott, Mass, and was chosen the first Major-General of the Colony With several of his associates he laid out the town of Ipswich, in 1636 He returned to England, in 1641, but several of his children remained in the New World, and from them have come many illustrious descendants.

Mr Orlando Metcalf Harper is the descendant in the ninth generation on his mother's side from Governor John Humfrey The great-grandfather of Mr Harper was Arunah Metcalf, a man of distinction in public affairs, in the central part of the State of New York, in the early years of this century. During most of his life he resided in Otsego County. In 1810, he was elected to represent the Otsego County district as a Democrat in the Twelfth United States Congress, and was returned to the State Assembly, in 1814-16, and 1828.

Mr Orlando Metcalf Harper was born in Pittsburg, Pa, September 17th, 1846 His father, John Harper, was president of the Bank of Pittsburg, and identified with other large financial institutions and public enterprises. He was especially interested in the cause of philanthropy, and gave considerable attention to the object of caring for the insane, and improving their condition He was a descendant of a good English family, of considerable antiquity and prominence His son, the present Mr. Harper, was primarily educated in the academic schools of his native city, and then went to Yale College Before he had completed his collegiate course, an injury to his eyes compelled him to forego further study, but Yale University has since conferred upon him the honorary degree of M A.

Returning to Pittsburg in 1867, he engaged in the cotton manufacturing business there, in which he was eminently successful for nearly twenty years He was president of the Eagle Cotton Mills Company, director of the Bank of Pittsburg, and of the Pittsburg and Alleghany Suspension Bridge Company, president of the Eagle Mills, at Madison, Ind, and for a time vice-president of the Association of Southern and Western Cotton Manufacturers. He was also editorially connected with one of the daily newspapers in the city of Pittsburg.

In 1886, Mr Harper removed to New York City and established the cotton dry goods commission business, in which he is still engaged He is a member of the New York Cotton Exchange, of the Chamber of Commerce, the Pennsylvania Historical Society, the New York Historical Society, the New York Geographical Society, the New England Society and the Yale Alumni Association His club memberships include the Union League, the Merchants', and the Riding clubs He is a member of the Sons of the American Revolution and of the Metropolitan Museum of Art His business connections, outside of his commission house, include the Merchants' Reliance Company, of which he is president

In November, 1877, Mr Harper married Kathleen Theodora Ludlow, daughter of John Livingston Ludlow, and granddaughter of the Reverend Dr John Ludlow, an eminent Dutch Reformed clergyman, and a member of one of the oldest and most distinguished Colonial families of New York

SAMUEL CARMAN HARRIOT

HERIOT'S Hospital, one of the historical monuments of the ancient city of Edinburgh, was founded in 1628 under a bequest by George Heriot, the friend and courtier of King James I of England and VI. of Scotland, and a figure of prominence in the times when England and Scotland were united under one crown by the accession of the monarch in question to the throne of the former country In the capacity of a man of business, as well as a courtier, Heriot accumulated great wealth for those days.

The Scottish philanthropist figures as one of the characters in Sir Walter Scott's Fortunes of Nigel. His own romance connected him with the Primroses of Rosebery, the family of which the former Prime Minister of England, the Earl of Rosebery, is the representative. George Heriot's wife, Alison Primrose, daughter of James Primrose, clerk of the privy council, having died before her twenty-first year, it was in memory of her that his large fortune was mainly devoted, on his death, to the foundation of the hospital for the education of the children of citizens of Edinburgh, which bears his name, and which to the present day is regarded as one of the chief charitable and educational institutions of the city to which his noble benefaction was dedicated nearly three hundred years ago All visitors to the historic capitol of the Scottish Kingdom have, without doubt, heard of this fact

Mr. Samuel Carman Harriot bears the same arms as the famous George Heriot, and is descended from a brother of the latter; members of the family having aided in the establishment of the Colony of West Jersey, where they attained wealth and prominence. His grandfather, Samuel Harriot, of New Jersey, married Abigail Carman, and was the father of Samuel Carman Harriot, born at Woodbridge, N. J

The elder Samuel C Harriot inherited an ample fortune and estate from his father, and was not engaged in active business pursuits, but accepted the presidency of the Greenwich Fire Insurance Company of New York, a post which he filled for over thirty-one years, being an influential and esteemed citizen His wife, the mother of the gentleman to whom this refers, was Martha Crozier Dawes, daughter of Charles Dawes, of Philadelphia, and Deborah Williams Elliott, of Darby, Pa, her grandfather, Rumford Dawes, having been a famous shipping merchant of Philadelphia, and an elder of the Friends or Quaker Society. On her mother's side, Mrs. Harriot is descended from the Earls of Guys, her great-grandmother, Elizabeth Guy, who married John Elliott, having also been a niece of William Penn, the famous founder of the State of Pennsylvania

Mr. Harriot was born of this ancestry in the City of New York, in 1863 He was educated under private tutors here and pursued a course of study at Paris Care of his large real estate interests has filled the place of professional employment He is still unmarried, and resides with his mother and sister, Florence Harriot, at 454 West Twenty-third Street, the house in which he was born, a residence containing many paintings by celebrated artists, statuary, mosaics and other works of art collected by members of the family in Europe, as well as a carefully selected library Mr. Harriot's own tastes are literary, artistic and musical He has spent no inconsiderable portion of his life in travel, and has visited nearly every part of Europe, including some countries and districts to which ordinary tourists rarely penetrate. He has been presented to many representatives of royalty, and numbers among his friends numerous members of the nobility. While in England, during the Queen's Jubilee year, 1887, he was present at the ball given in London in honor of the late Crown Prince Rudolph, of Austro-Hungary, at which the latter, with the Prince of Wales and other representatives of royalty, were the prominent guests He is a member of the City Club, and is also a member of the St Andrew's Society and the New York Society of the Sons of the Revolution, in both of which organizations he takes an active interest as befits the descent from Colonial and Revolutionary ancestors which he represents

MARCELLUS HARTLEY

IN the collateral line of Mr. Marcellus Hartley's ancestry, a notable name is that of David Hartley, the English diplomat, who was born in 1729, and died in 1813, and was prominently identified with the early history of the American Republic. He was educated at Oxford, and became a member of Parliament for Kingston-upon-Hull. His name appears conspicuously in the history of our country from the fact that he was the British Plenipotentiary appointed to arrange for terms of peace with John Jay, Benjamin Franklin and Charles Laurens, the American commissioners in Paris after the War of the Revolution

The father of David Hartley was David Hartley, the elder, founder of the English Association of Psychologists, author of Observations on Man, published in 1749, and whose life was that of a benevolent and studious physician, principally in London and Bath. The father of Dr. Hartley was the Reverend David Hartley, vicar of Armley, in Yorkshire, an eminent clergyman, whose family, of great antiquity, was descended from the Hartleys of Chorton.

Another son, Dr. David Hartley, was James Hartley, of Boughton, England, where he was born in 1736, and died in 1776. He was a business man, chiefly engaged in manufacturing, and was noted for his piety and intellectual vigor. Robert Hartley, son of James Hartley, was a native of Boughton, where he was born in 1736, and succeeded to his father's business as a manufacturer During the latter part of his life, he lived at Cockermouth, England, where he died in 1803. His wife, whom he married in 1754, was Martha Smithson, daughter of Isaac Smithson, a son of Sir Hugh Smithson, baronet, head of a family whose name is identified with the United States through the Smithsonian Institution, which was endowed by one of its members in a latter generation.

Isaac Hartley, the son of Robert Hartley and his wife, Martha, was born in Cockermouth, England, in 1766, and was the first of his family to remove to the United States. He married Isabella, daughter of Joseph Johnson, of Embleton, England. He settled in Perth, N. Y., and died in 1851. His wife died in Schenectady, in 1806. Robert Milham Hartley, son of Isaac Hartley, was born in Cockermouth, England, in 1796, and died in New York in 1881 He was educated in Fairfield Academy, New York, and became one of the distinguished philanthropists of the metropolis in the first half of the present century. In 1829, he was one of the founders of the New York City Temperance Society, of which he was the secretary for nine years. He was also active in founding the New York Association for Improving the Condition of the Poor in 1844. The Workingmen's Home, the Demilt Dispensary, the Juvenile Asylum, the New York Society for the Relief of the Ruptured and Crippled, and the Presbyterian Hospital were other benevolent undertakings fostered by him The wife of Robert Milham Hartley, whom he married in 1824, was Catharine Munson, daughter of Reuben Munson. Her father, a New York merchant, was an alderman, 1813-23, and a member of the Assembly, 1820-22.

Mr. Marcellus Hartley, the elder son of Robert Milham and Catharine (Munson) Hartley, is a prominent New York merchant and financier, a member of the Union League, Lawyers', Riding and Presbyterian clubs, and the New England Society, and a patron of the Metropolitan Museum of Art He married Frances Chester White, daughter of Dr. S. Pomroy White, and lives in Madison Avenue.

Joseph Wilfrid Hartley, another son of Robert M. Hartley, was born in New York, and early in life began a business career. For more than thirty years he was a shipping merchant, but later became interested in electrical science, an occupation that engages his attention at the present time. He married, in 1854, Florinda Morton, daughter of Henry Grant and Florinda (Berga) Morton. Mrs. Hartley's father was a native of East Windsor, Conn., a descendant of one of the early settlers of that Colony. Mrs. Hartley died in 1871. The city residence of Mr. Hartley is at 34 Gramercy Park, where he lives with his two daughters, Florinda Morton and Isabel S. Hartley

LEWIS CRUGER HASELL

THE bearings which constitute the coat of arms of the Hasell family, of England and America, comprise a gold shield with a blue band, on which are three silver crescents, between three hazel nuts, proper. The crest is a silver squirrel feeding on a hazel nut proper, encircled with hazel branches, and the motto is *Labor omnia vincit*. These arms and crest were granted shortly after the English Herald's College became an incorporated body, during the reign of Richard III At that time and since "every gentleman entitled to bear coat armor was noble, whether titled or not, though this fact has been forgotten in recent times, and the term nobility appropriated exclusively to the peerage."

An account of this ancient family (whose name is pronounced Hazel), which was first established in Cambridgeshire, England, and a description of their coat of arms is given in Sir Bernard Burke's Genealogical and Heraldic Dictionary, commencing with John Hasell, who was buried in Bottisham Church in 1572. From him was descended Sir Edward Hasell, who was knighted by William III., and who settled in Cumberland, having purchased in 1665 the estate of Dalemain, Parish of Dacre, which property is still in the possession of kinsmen of the American branch of the family, and who entertain a cordial family correspondence with the latter The Reverend Thomas Hasell was the first of John Hasell's descendants who came to America and settled in South Carolina, in 1705. He was a graduate of Cambridge University, was ordained deacon in 1705, and priest in 1709, by Bishop Compton, of London. He was the first Episcopalian minister of the Parish of St. Thomas and St. Dennis, South Carolina. An account of his long and eminent services is given in Dalchos's History of the Church in South Carolina. Among his descendants was Bishop Gadsden, of South Carolina The Reverend Thomas Hasell died in 1744, leaving, by his wife, Elizabeth Ashby, whom he married in 1714, eight children One of them was Andrew Hasell, 1729-1763, who married Sarah Wigfall in 1751, and was the father of Andrew Hasell, the second of that name. The latter, 1755-1789, married in 1778 Mary, daughter of General Job Milner, of the British Army, whose wife, Mary, was the daughter of Jacob Bond and his wife, Susan Maybank

George Paddon Bond Hasell, M. D., was the son of Andrew Hasell the second, and was born in South Carolina, in 1781. He graduated at the University of Edinburgh and became an eminent physician in his native State, where he died in 1818. While abroad he married, in 1802, Penelope, daughter of Bentley Gordon Bentley, of Chipping Norton, England, and his wife, Penelope Bentley, who was descended from Edward Bentley, who resided at Little Kingston, Warwickshire, in 1595. Bentley Gordon Bentley's father was Alexander Gordon, whose name was changed by act of Parliament to Alexander Gordon Bentley, in order that he might inherit the Bentley estates.

Bentley Hasell, son of the preceding, was born on Sullivan's Island, S C , in 1807, graduated at Yale and from the Litchfield (Conn.) Law School in 1827. In 1828 he married Catherine de Nully Cruger, daughter of Nicholas Cruger and his wife, Ann Trezevant. Ann Trezevant first married Daniel Heyward, of South Carolina, by whom she had Elizabeth, who married General James Hamilton, Governor of South Carolina Ann Trezevant was the granddaughter of Theodore Trezevant, the leader of the Huguenot Forty Families, who, on the revocation of the Edict of Nantes, fled from France, in 1685, and settled in South Carolina He brought with him wealth, acquired several plantations, and gave financial assistance to his less fortunate compatriots. He was deputed by the Huguenot families to correspond with the English Government as to the rights and privileges which should be accorded them, which task he executed to the satisfaction of both the Colonists and the Government

The Cruger family, famous both in New York and in South Carolina, descends from John Cruger, who came to New York prior to 1700, married Maria Cuyler, daughter of Major Hendrick Cuyler, of Albany, and his wife, Annetje Schepmoes John Cruger was appointed

Mayor of New York in 1739, and remained in office till his death, in 1744 His son, John, was also Mayor of New York, from 1756 to 1765 inclusive, was the Speaker of the first Colonial Assembly, and founder and first president of the New York Chamber of Commerce His nephew, Henry Cruger, was Mayor of Bristol, England, and was the colleague of Edmund Burke as a member of the English Parliament for the same constituency. His other nephew, Nicholas Cruger, the first of that name (and the grandfather of Catherine de Nully Cruger-Hasell), was born in New York in 1743, and died at Santa Cruz, West Indies. He owned the beautiful Rose Hill estate, which is now in the heart of New York City He was the friend of Washington and the patron of Alexander Hamilton, who obtained his first mercantile clerkship in Mr. Cruger's counting house at Santa Cruz, and came to New York under his auspices. Nicholas Cruger's first wife was Ann de Nully, daughter of Bertram Pierre de Nully and his wife, Catherine Heyliger, daughter of General Pierre Heyliger, Chamberlain to Christian V., of Denmark, and Governor-General of the Danish West Indies. Bertram Pierre de Nully was the son of Count Bertram de Nully, a planter of Martinique.

Bentley Hasell died in 1836, and his wife, Catherine de Nully Cruger, died in 1870. They are buried in the family vault in St. Mark's churchyard in this city, jointly built by their uncle, William Bard, and Ferdinand Sands They left two sons, Bentley Douglas Hasell, C E., and Lewis Cruger Hasell, M. D., who died in 1889 at his country residence, near Georgetown, S C. Bentley Douglas Hasell was born in Charleston, S. C , February 27th, 1829, and in 1852 married Hannah, daughter of Judge Jesse Morgan and his wife, Jane Cisna, who died in 1875. After leaving Trinity College, in 1848, he adopted the profession of a civil engineer, and has been engaged on many important public works, among which were the United States dry dock at the Brooklyn Navy Yard, New York; the Erie Railroad, Michigan Southern, Northern Indiana Railroad, and Quincy & Toledo Railroad. He was chief engineer and general manager of the New Orleans, Jackson & Great Northern Railroad, now the Southern division of Illinois Central Railroad; held the same position on the Memphis & Ohio Railroad, now a part of the Louisville & Nashville system, and was president of the Charleston & Savannah Railroad. He has for some years past been in business in New York, as head of the firm of B. D Hasell & Co., and is president of a company bearing his name, controlling a perfected automatic railroad block signal system Mr. Hasell was for seventeen years a member of the Union Club, and is a life member of the New York Genealogical and Biographical Society, and a member of the American Society of Civil Engineers and of the Downtown Association. He published, in 1892, for private distribution among his relatives, a chart of the Cruger family in America descended from John Cruger. In 1896, he also published a chart of the Rhinelander family in America, descended from Philip Jacob Rhinelander, who came to this country in 1686, and founded the notable New York family of that name.

Mr Lewis Cruger Hasell, born in 1858, is the only surviving child of Bentley Douglas Hasell and his wife, Hannah Morgan. Mr. Hasell is a merchant in this city, where he resides, having also a country residence at Greenwich, on the Sound, and is a member of the Calumet Club. In 1884, he married Mary Mason Jones, daughter of Mason Renshaw Jones and his first wife, Lydia Haight. Mrs. Hasell is a granddaughter of Isaac Jones, president of the Chemical Bank of New York, and his wife, Mary Mason, daughter of John Mason, founder of the Chemical Bank Frances A Jones, sister of Isaac Jones, married John Church Cruger, the father of Colonel Stephen Van Rensselaer Cruger Mr. Lewis Cruger Hasell and his wife, Mary Mason Jones, have three children, Mason Cruger, Alice and Mary Mason Hasell, who are the eighth generation of their name in this country.

To recount the alliances of the Hasells, Trezevants, Crugers, de Nullys, Heyligers and Bentleys would be to enumerate a majority of prominent family names in South Carolina, Virginia and New York, as well as the oldest families in England, France and Denmark, the entire subject being of great interest to the genealogist and student of the Colonial and later history of our country.

CHARLES WALDO HASKINS

BORN in Brooklyn, January 11th, 1852, Mr Charles Waldo Haskins has been socially prominent in New York and is actively identified with several patriotic bodies of the highest standing, while he has achieved success and reputation in a difficult profession His parents were Waldo Emerson Haskins and his wife, Amelia Rowan Cammeyer. After graduating from the Brooklyn Polytechnic Institute, Mr. Haskins entered the accounting department of F Butterfield & Company, of New York, where he spent five years and then traveled abroad for two years, after which he became connected with the brokerage firm of W. E Haskins. For three years he was engaged upon the accounts of the North River Construction Company, which built the West Shore Railway, and then began practice as an expert accountant, in which profession he has taken a leading place He was also secretary of the Manhattan Trust Company, of New York, for some time, but his principal work was one which has given him national reputation. This was nothing less than the reorganization of the Government's system of accounts, which had never been altered since the Treasury and the other departments were established To this task Mr. Haskins was called by a joint commission of Congress, and, in association with his present partner, E W Sells, performed it in such a radical, yet judicious, manner that the public business has been simplified and expedited to a marked extent The methods he suggested have all been adopted, and, after thorough experience, have won the approbation of the executive and accounting officials of the Government and the warm thanks of the commission in charge of the matter. Mr Haskins is president of the board of examiners, appointed by the regents of the University of New York to pass on the qualifications of applicants for certificates as Certified Public Accountants, and is president of the New York Society of Certified Public Accountants. He is also comptroller of the Central of Georgia Railway Company, and is officially connected with other corporations, besides holding important fiduciary positions

Mr Haskins inherits the characteristics as well as the blood of a notable New England ancestry His paternal line in America begins with Robert Haskins, a resident of Boston early in the eighteenth century "Honest John Haskins," his son, born in 1729, became an eminent citizen of Boston, famed for his probity and sterling qualities, and was Captain in the old Boston Regiment, his commission dating from 1772 He was also one of the first Sons of Liberty, and was active on the patriotic side in the agitation that led to the Revolution John Haskins' wife, Hannah Upham, came of prominent Puritan families She was descended from John Upham, who came to Massachusetts in 1635, while among her other ancestors were Captain John Waite, of Malden; Rose Dunster, sister of the first president of Harvard; Thomas Oakes, cousin of Dr. Oakes, the fourth president of the same college, and John Howland, the famous Mayflower Pilgrim Robert Haskins, son of John and Hannah (Upham) Haskins, married Rebecca Emerson, daughter of the Reverend William Emerson, who died while chaplain of the Patriot army at Ticonderoga in 1776 Ruth Haskins, Roberts sister, married the second Reverend William Emerson and was the mother of Ralph Waldo Emerson, the great New England poet and philosopher The grandparents of the present Mr Haskins were Thomas Haskins, son of Robert, and Mary (Soren) Haskins, Waldo Emerson Haskins having been the child of the latter couple.

In 1884, Mr Charles Waldo Haskins married Henrietta Havemeyer, daughter of Albert Havemeyer, the youngest brother of William F Havemeyer, Mayor of New York, 1848–49 and 1873-74 The issue of this marriage is two daughters, Ruth and Noeline. The family reside in West Fourteenth Street Mr. Haskins is a member of the Manhattan, Riding and Westchester County clubs in New York, the Metropolitan Club in Washington, and the Piedmont Club of Atlanta, Ga. He is, as already referred to, actively identified with patriotic societies, being a member of the Society of Mayflower Descendants and treasurer general of the National Society Sons of the American Revolution, 1892-97, while he was secretary of the Empire State Society of that organization, 1893-94, and has done much to advance its interests

CHARLES HAYNES HASWELL

B ORN in New York City in 1809, and identified with the naval service of the United States, as well as with some of the most remarkable feats of American engineering science in the present century, the parents and ancestors of the subject of this article were, nevertheless, natives of the Island of Barbadoes. The families from which he descends were on both sides numbered among the royalist gentry who, after the overthrow of Charles I. and the loss of their cause at the battle of Worcester, migrated to Barbadoes and other West India islands, where they became wealthy and prominent. Mr. Charles Haynes Haswell is the son of Charles Haswell and his wife, Dorothea Haynes, the latter being the daughter of Richard Haynes and Anna Elcock. One of Mr. Haswell's uncles, the Honorable Robert Haynes, was Speaker of the House of Assembly of Barbadoes and Lieutenant-General of the royal forces of the island, while another uncle, Henry Haynes, was a Post Captain of the British Royal Navy, and at his death was at the head of the list of Captains in that service. The Haynes coat of arms, borne by the representatives of the family both in England and the Western hemisphere, is: Quarterly, first and fourth, argent, three crescents, paly, wavy gules and azure, and second and third gules, two billets, argent, and the crest of Haswell is the head of the talbot, or hunting dog, erased, azure, collared, ermine. The crest of the Haynes is a stork, with wings displayed, proper, bearing a serpent in its beak.

Mr. Haswell received a classical education at academies in Jamaica, Long Island, and the City of New York, and in 1828, after a complete early training, began his career as a civil and marine engineer. In 1836, he entered the United States Navy as Chief Engineer, and in 1845 was commissioned Engineer in Chief. While in the service, he bore a most useful share in the first steps that led to the evolution of the modern war ship, designed and superintended the construction of a number of the earlier steam vessels of the navy, and in the line of duty, while on active service at sea, visited not only Europe, but Africa and South America. Leaving the navy in 1851, after fifteen years passed in the service of the Government, he has since been engaged in the succesful practice of his profession, being regarded as one of its foremost members, filling, among other important public and private duties, those of the engineer of the Board of Health and trustee of the Brooklyn Bridge. He was a member of the Common Council of the City of New York in 1854-56, and its president in 1857. In 1862, he accompanied Major-General Burnside on his expedition to North Carolina as Chief Engineer of the Naval Service, and was present at the bombardment and capture of Roanoke Island and other operations of that campaign. He is the author of several important professional works, his Engineers' Pocket Book having more than a national reputation, and is a member of many scientific bodies, including the American Society of Civil Engineers, the Naval Architects and Marine Engineers, and the Institutions of Civil Engineering and Naval Architecture of Great Britain, and others of similar character and prominence. Among the many flattering testimonials to his services, he received, in 1853, a diamond ring from the Emperor Nicholas of Russia. It is impossible to mention the numerous inventions and improvements he originated, beyond noting that he designed and directed the construction of the first steam launch in 1837, and in 1847 he first applied zinc to prevent oxidization in marine boilers and in the holds of iron vessels.

In 1829, Mr. Haswell married Ann Elizabeth Burns, of New York, their children being Sarah Haynes, Edmund Haynes, Frances Roe, Gouverneur Kemble, Charles Haynes and Lillie Bulwer Haswell. Mr. Haswell resides at 324 West Seventy-eighth Street, New York, and possesses, in addition to a collection of statuary and paintings, a large and valuable library.

Leading an active life, full of grave responsibilities and labor, he has found pleasure in society and yachting, and is a member of the Union and Engineers' clubs, as well as of the American Yacht Club. His interest in yachting has been active, and for many years he acted as chairman of the Regatta Committee of the New York Yacht Club.

HENRY OSBORNE HAVEMEYER

NEARLY a century ago, the two brothers, William and Frederick Havemeyer, established themselves in New York and founded families that have since been extremely prominent in many directions. The younger of these brothers, Frederick C. Havemeyer, was the ancestor of that branch of the family to which Mr. Henry O. Havemeyer and the late Theodore A Havemeyer belong. The elder, William Havemeyer, as will be seen from the ensuing page, was the father of Mayor William Frederick Havemeyer and his line.

Frederick C. Havemeyer, grandfather of Mr Henry O Havemeyer, was the junior member of the firm of W. & F. C Havemeyer, which engaged in sugar refining in New York in 1807. His son, Frederick Christian Havemeyer, the father of Mr. Henry O. Havemeyer, was born in 1807 in New York After spending two years in Columbia College, he entered the paternal establishment in Vandam Street as an apprentice, and gained a thorough knowledge of sugar manufacturing. In 1828, he became associated with his cousin, William F. Havemeyer, under the firm name of W. F. & F. C. Havemeyer, and continued in business for fourteen years. After the death of his father, he had the management of the large estate left by the latter, and also traveled extensively in the United States and in Europe. In 1855, he returned to business, establishing the firm of Havemeyer, Townsend & Co., which afterwards became Havemeyer & Elder, one of the largest sugar refining houses in the world. During the time that he was out of business, he applied himself to literary pursuits as well as to travel. His favorite study was the Latin language and literature. For many years he was president of the school board of Westchester County, where he had his residence. In 1831, he married Sarah Osborne Townsend, daughter of Christopher Townsend, one of his business associates. Ten children were born of this union. The sons were Charles, Theodore A., George W , Henry O , Thomas J., Warren H., and Frederick C. Havemeyer Mary O Havemeyer, the eldest daughter, became the wife of J. Lawrence Elder; Kate B. Havemeyer married Louis J. Belloni, and Sarah Louise Havemeyer married Frederick Wendell Jackson.

Mr. Henry O Havemeyer, the fourth son of his father's family, was born in New York, October 18th, 1847 Educated in private schools, he entered the firm of which his father was head, and in 1869 was admitted to partnership. He soon became the manager of the firm, whose members, besides his father, were Theodore A , Thomas J. and Henry O Havemeyer, J Lawrence Elder and Charles H. Senff The development of the business of which he is now at the head makes one of the most interesting pages in the industrial and commercial history of the country It was mainly through his initiative that the American Sugar Refining Company, in which were merged nearly all the great refineries of the United States, was organized in 1891 and has become one of the greatest corporations in the country.

In 1883, Mr. Havemeyer married Louisine Waldron Elder, daughter of George W Elder, who was also well known from his connection with the sugar business. Mr and Mrs Havemeyer have three children, Adeline, Horace and Electra Havemeyer. The city residence of the family is at the corner of Sixty-sixth street and Fifth Avenue Mr Havemeyer also has a home in Greenwich, Conn., one of the finest country seats on the Long Island Sound, situated on a ridge overlooking the water and the surrounding country. Mr. Havemeyer is interested in the breeding of cattle and high grade stock, and has at his place a notable herd of cattle and fine specimens of horses and Southdown sheep. A large public school building, which he erected and presented to the town of Greenwich at a cost of two hundred and fifty thousand dollars, is a proof of his active interest in public education. He is a member of the Grolier and Riding clubs and a patron of the Metropolitan Museum of Art The best known of his brothers was the late Theodore A. Havemeyer, who married Emilie de Loosey, daughter of Charles F de Loosey. His sons are Theodore A., who married Katherine Aymar Sands, and Henry O Havemeyer, Jr. He was for many years consul-general of Austria-Hungary in New York, and was active in business, but also was prominent in society and sport and was largely instrumental in making golf popular in this country.

WILLIAM FREDERICK HAVEMEYER

IN Germany, the history of the Havemeyer family can be traced back for more than three hundred years. Herman Havemeyer, who lived in Bueckeburg, Germany, before 1600, was the ancestor of William Havemeyer, who came to this country and founded an American family that for three generations has been eminently distinguished in mercantile and civic life. When only fifteen years of age, William Havemeyer left his German home and went to London There he learned the art of sugar refining, and in 1799 he came to the United States. In less than ten years he began business on his own account, taking as a partner his younger brother, Frederick C. Havemeyer. The two brothers were, respectively, the American ancestors of the two branches of the Havemeyer family of New York. William Havemeyer was the ancestor of the branch of the family of which Mr. William Frederick Havemeyer is the representative. Frederick C. Havemeyer was the ancestor of the branch to which Henry O. Havemeyer belongs.

The eldest son of William Havemeyer was William Frederick Havemeyer, who was born in New York in 1804, and graduated from Columbia College in 1823 In 1828, with his cousin, Frederick Christian Havemeyer, he established the firm of W. F. & F. C. Havemeyer. He was also interested in other business enterprises, being elected president of the Bank of North America in 1851 and president of the New York Savings Bank in 1857. He was vice-president of the Pennsylvania Coal Company and of the Long Island Railroad, and a director in other corporations.

It was in public life, however, that William Frederick Havemeyer became best known. As early as 1844, he took an active part in politics, becoming a delegate to the Democratic general committee of New York City. In the same year, he was a Presidential elector for the successful Polk and Dallas ticket In 1845, he was elected Mayor of the city, and after serving one year declined a renomination. The subject of emigration had for many years engaged his attention, and when the law creating the Board of Emigration Commissioners of this State was passed in 1847, he became its first president. In 1848, he was elected Mayor of the city for the second time, and again in 1859, he was nominated for the same office, but on this occasion was defeated by Fernando Wood. He maintained his active interest in municipal affairs, and during the Civil War was one of the most devoted supporters of the national government When the transactions of the so-called Tweed-ring were exposed in 1870, he again exhibited his unswerving devotion to the public interests and to the welfare of the city, and as vice-president and afterwards president of the Committee of Seventy rendered untiring and efficient service to the reform movement. For the fourth time, in 1871, he was nominated for Mayor and elected for the third time. He died suddenly in November, 1874, while in his office at the City Hall.

William Frederick Havemeyer married in 1828, at Craigville, N. Y., Sarah Agnes Craig, daughter of Hector Craig, who was a member of the National House of Representatives, 1823-25, and was afterwards reëlected in 1829, subsequently serving a term as Surveyor of the Port of New York The children of this marriage were six sons and two daughters. Sarah C Havemeyer, who became the wife of Hector Armstrong, and Laura A. Havemeyer, who married Isaac W Maclay, were the daughters. The sons were John, Henry, Hector Craig, James, Charles and William F Havemeyer, Jr.

Mr William F. Havemeyer, of the present generation, was born in New York, and after receiving his education, engaged in the sugar business, becoming vice-president of the Havemeyer Sugar Refining Company, of which his brother, Hector Craig Havemeyer, was president He lives in East Fifty-seventh Street, near Fifth Avenue. The clubs of which he is a member include among others the Metropolitan, Grolier and City, the Century Association and the Downtown Association.

GEORGE GRISWOLD HAVEN

B ELONGING to an old family that had long been established in the West of England, Richard Haven came from his native land to Massachusetts in 1645. One or more brothers came with him, and from them are descended all the Havens of this country who trace their lineage to Colonial ancestry. John Haven, 1656-1705, a son of Richard Haven, was an important man in Lynn, Mass, frequently serving on committees of the town, while he was a selectman several times and a representative to the General Court in 1701 and again in 1702. In the next generation, Joseph Haven, 1698-1776, was as prominent in public affairs as his father. In 1732, he was a surveyor, was elected a selectmen the following year, and was a justice of the peace from 1756 until the time of his death. His wife was his cousin, Mehitable Haven, daughter of Moses Haven. She died in 1780.

Samuel Haven, 1727-1803, son of Joseph Haven, was the great-grandfather of Mr. George Griswold Haven. His first wife was Mehitable Appleton, daughter of the Reverend Dr Appleton, of Cambridge He was graduated from Harvard College in 1749, entered the ministry, was ordained over the South Church in Portsmouth, N. H, in 1752, and occupied that pulpit for fifty-one years, retiring in 1803 on account of advanced years He received the degree of D D from the University of Edinburgh in 1772, and Dartmouth College conferred the same honor upon him in 1773. The grandfather of Mr George Griswold Haven was John Haven, who was born in Portsmouth, N. H, and became one of the leading merchants of that city. His wife, whom he married in 1791, was Ann Woodward, of a prominent Colonial family of New Hampshire Joseph Woodward Haven, son of John Haven, was born in 1803 and was also engaged in mercantile pursuits. His wife, whom he married in 1833, was Cornelia Griswold.

Mr. George Griswold Haven, son of Joseph Woodward Haven, was born in Portsmouth, N. H., in 1837, and was graduated from Columbia College in 1857 The greater part of his lifetime has been spent in New York, engaged in the banking business. He was for a long time at the head of the firm of George G Haven & Co., in Wall Street. After his retirement from active business, the firm became Hollister & Babcock, in which Mr Haven and Samuel D Babcock are special partners. For a third of a century Mr Haven has held a conspicuous place in financial affairs, being a director in several banks, trust companies and other institutions. He is vice-president of the National Union Bank and a trustee of the Mutual Life Insurance Company. In the social world, he has also been prominent. He was active in forming the organization which resulted in the building of the Metropolitan Opera House, was president of the corporation which carried that work to completion, and has given effective support to the various operatic enterprises associated with the Metropolitan Opera House Several times the nomination for Mayor of the city has been tendered to him, but he has resolutely refrained from entering into the field of politics. He has, however, served on committees that have worked in the interests of healthy municipal government, and has been a member of the Board of Park Commissioners

Mr. Haven married Emma Martin, daughter of Isaac P. Martin She died in 1872, and in 1880 he married Fannie (Arnot) Palmer, widow of Richard Suydam Palmer Their home is in East Thirty-ninth Street and their country residence in Lenox, Mass. Mr Haven belongs to the Tuxedo colony, and is a member of the Metropolitan, Knickerbocker, Union, Manhattan, Union League, Whist, Coaching and Players clubs, the New England Society, the Downtown Association, the Columbia College Alumni Association, and the American Museum of Natural History. His children are Joseph Woodward, George Griswold, Jr, and Marian A Haven

Joseph Woodward Haven, the eldest son, married Lorriette Cram. He belongs to the Metropolitan, Knickerbocker and Grolier clubs. George Griswold Haven, Jr, graduated from Yale in 1887, and is a banker. He married Elizabeth Shaw Ingersoll. He lives in East Forty-fourth Street, and has a country home in Ridgefield, Conn He is a member of the Metropolitan, Union, Knickerbocker and University clubs, and the Yale Alumni Association

HENRY EUGENE HAWLEY

THE Hawleys came over from Normandy to England with William the Conqueror in 1066. Their name appears on the roll of Battle Abbey, among the leaders of the victorious Norman Army, as Hauley. In the course of time, several branches of the family were established in different parts of England and attained to prominence. One branch, in Somersetshire, had for their arms: Emerald, a saltire, engrailed, pean. Crest, an Indian goat's head, holding a three-leaved sprig of holly, proper. Motto, *Survez Moi* The chief seat of this branch of the family is Buckland House, in the County of Somerset. The arms of the Derbyshire Hawleys are: Vert, a saltire, engrailed, argent. Crest, a dexter arm in armor, proper, granished or., holding in the hand a spear, point downwards, proper. Motto, *Suivez Moi.* The American family is entitled to these arms, also to the crest, a winged thunderbolt.

Thomas Hawley, the first of the name in this country, came to Roxbury, Mass., early in the seventeenth century. He married Dorothy Harbottle, and during King Philip's War, was killed by the Indians in 1676 at the famous Sudbury fight. Captain Joseph Hawley, the representative of the family line in the next generation, graduated from Harvard College in 1674, was a freeman of Northampton, Mass., in 1678, Lieutenant of the provincial troops in 1687, and afterwards Captain, justice of the peace and representative to the General Court of the Colony. His wife was Lydia Marshall, daughter of Captain Samuel Marshall, of Windsor, Conn. The great-great-grandfather of the subject of this sketch was the Reverend Thomas Hawley, who was the son of Captain Joseph Hawley, and whose wife was Abigail Gold, daughter of Colonel Nathan Gold, of Fairfield, Conn. His great-grandparents were Captain Thomas Hawley, 1723-1765, and Elizabeth Gold, 1725-1807, of Fairfield, Conn., and his grandparents were Elisha Hawley, 1759-1850, of Ridgefield, Conn., a Revolutionary soldier, and Charity Judson, 1760-1860, daughter of Daniel Judson.

The father of Mr. Henry E. Hawley was Irad Hawley, who was born in 1793, and was a prominent New York merchant, a member of the firm of Holmes, Hawley & Co, in 1812, and a Captain in the War of 1812-14. After 1839, he became interested in railroad and coal enterprises, being a director in the Boston & Providence Railroad, the Chicago & Rock Island Railroad, chairman of the financial committee of the Delaware & Hudson Canal Company, and president of the Pennsylvania Coal Company. He married, in 1819, Sarah Holmes, daughter of Eldad and Lucy (Lockwood) Holmes, and had eight children. He died in Rome, Italy, in 1865.

Mr. Henry Eugene Hawley, the youngest son of Irad Hawley, was born in New York in 1838. Graduated from Yale University in 1860, he became a partner in the firm of Carter, Hawley & Co. in 1864 In the course of some years, he became the head of the house in question, which has an extensive business throughout the United States, in South America, the East Indies, Europe, China and Japan, being correspondent of the Netherland Trading Society of Holland, and the Surinam Bank of Paramaribo, Dutch Guiana. For twenty years, he has been a member of the Chamber of Commerce of the State of New York, and is a director in several prominent corporations. He has devoted much time to philanthropic causes, having long been a trustee of the Children's Aid Society and of the Five Points House of Industry.

In 1862, Mr. Hawley married Jane Elizabeth Lockwood, daughter of William S. and Catharine (Hawley) Lockwood, of Norwalk, Conn. Mr. and Mrs. Hawley lived in West Thirty-third Street for twenty-five years. Their present residence is Ashton-Croft, Ridgefield, Conn. The old homestead, in Ridgefield, has been in possession of the family since 1713, when, in the settlement of the town, the land was apportioned to the Reverend Thomas Hawley, the first minister there. Mr and Mrs Hawley have had four children, Sarah, Henrietta Eugenie, Edith Judson and Elizabeth, who died in 1865 Edith Judson is the wife of Coleman G. Williams, and Sarah is the wife of Dr. T. Halstead Myers. Mr. Hawley belongs to the Union League, Century, University and Riding clubs, the Downtown Association and the Yale Alumni Association, and is a patron of the American Museum of Natural History.

BRACE HAYDEN

AN ancient family of knightly rank is the description given in the English genealogies of the Heydons of Hayden, in Norfolk, from whom the American Haydens are believed to descend Their original seat was Baconsthorp Hall, Norfolk, but in the thirteenth century John de Heydon, one of the scions of the Norfolk house and a Judge under Edward I., established a branch of the family in Devonshire, where his descendant, John Heydon, also an eminent lawyer in the reign of King Henry VIII , became possessed of the Cadhay Hall estate, Ottery St. Mary's, Devonshire, where, before 1650, he built a stately Tudor mansion, still standing, though many generations ago it passed out of the hands of its original possessors

Three Haydens, William, John and James, came to Massachusetts in the first emigration They are thought to have been brothers belonging to the west country branch of the English family. William Hayden arrived in Dorchester, Mass , in 1630, but removed to Hartford and in 1640 to Windsor, Conn , subsequently going to Kenilworth, now Clinton, Conn , where he died in 1669. In the Pequot War, in 1637, he served under Captain Mason and saved that famous officer's life from the Indians. His sword is now in the Connecticut Historical Society's collection. He received an allotment of land at Windsor, the locality being now called Haydens, where, in 1885, upon the old home property, a gathering of his descendants dedicated a memorial inscription, cut in a natural boulder. His first wife's name has not been preserved. Her death is, however, recorded in 1655, and he afterwards married Margaret, the widow of William Wilcoxson, of Stratford. His son was Daniel Hayden, 1640–1672, whose wife, Hannah Wilcoxson, was the first English child born in Connecticut

The succeeding three generations of ancestors of Mr. Brace Hayden were Samuel Hayden, 1677–1742, who married Anna Holcomb; Deacon Nathaniel Hayden, 1709–1803, whose wife was Naomi Gaylord, a descendant of William Gaylord, one of the first settlers of Windsor, and Levi Hayden, 1747–1821, who served in a cavalry regiment in the Revolutionary Army, and, after the war, held various offices and represented his town in the Legislature He married Margaret Strong, daughter of Lieutenant Return and Sarah (Warham) Strong, and a descendant of the famous Elder John Strong, of Northampton.

Their son, Hezekiah Hayden, 1777–1823, was the grandfather of Mr. Brace Hayden. He married, in 1801, his cousin, Hannah Hayden, like himself a native of Haydens, Conn. As a young man, he went to sea and made several voyages to Europe, but early in the present century removed to Otsego, N. Y., finally settling in Springfield, in that county. He engaged in manufacturing and was among the first to establish woolen mills in this State, having made himself a master of the art, then a new one in the United States; he also owned extensive saw mills and other properties in that section of New York. Albert Hayden, his second son, was born in Springfield, in 1807, and early in life engaged successfully in business in Buffalo, N. Y. In 1849, however, the California excitement led him to attempt the perilous overland journey to the new land of gold. He started as the leader of a party of twelve, but died in June, 1849, near Fort Laramie, of an illness contracted during the expedition. In 1831, he married, at Black Rock, N. Y., Sevilla Brace and had a family of eight children

Mr. Brace Hayden, the eldest son and third child of this marriage, was born in Buffalo, N Y., August 10th, 1836, and was educated in that city. He removed to New York City, where for forty years he has been in active commercial life. For a long period, he has been connected with a leading hardware and metal establishment of San Francisco, Cal., being vice-president of the corporation In 1870, he married Kate Quinan, who died in 1871, and in 1880 he contracted a second marriage, with Abbey Jewell Crane His children are Kitty Quinan, Florence, Sevilla and Curtis Crane Hayden Mr. Hayden's residence is in Seventy-ninth Street, near Madison Avenue, and he is a member of the Republican, Church, Hardware and New York Athletic clubs, the American Geographical Society, and a patron of the Metropolitan Museum of Art.

JOHN GERARD HECKSCHER

O NE of the most eminent and respected merchants of New York in the first half of the century was Charles Augustus Heckscher. He came to this country from his native Germany in 1830, and through his remarkable business talent achieved a high position in the commercial world. For some years he was Consul of the Duchy of Mecklenburg in this city, and became senior partner of the house of Heckscher & Coster, one of the foremost mercantile concerns of its day. As his wealth increased, he extended the field of his enterprises and was one of the first to appreciate the value of the Pennsylvania anthracite fields, acquiring valuable coal mines in that State. He was thus conspicuously identified with the development of the anthracite industry and in addition had many other important financial and business interests. He was the father of the gentleman whose name heads this article.

The wife of Charles Augustus Heckscher, the present Mr. Heckscher's mother, was Georgina Louisa Coster, daughter of John Gerard Coster and his wife, Catharine Margaret Holsmann. Mrs. Charles A. Heckscher was a woman of great beauty, was prominent in society and well known for her charities. John Gerard Coster, a native of Harlem, Holland, came to New York about 1790, and was for many years one of the most distinguished merchants of the city and president of the Bank of the Manhattan Company.

Mr. John Gerard Heckscher, who was named after his maternal grandfather, is the prominent representative of his family in this generation. He was born in New York in 1837. During the Civil War, he served for two years under General McClellan as First Lieutenant in the Twelfth United States Infantry. He engaged in active business early in life, but has given the greater share of his attention to society, and particularly to the higher forms of sport. He was the friend and intimate associate of Messrs. Belmont, Jerome, Travers and the other gentlemen who established racing in America on a firm foundation. Mr. Heckscher was also one of the founders of the Coney Island Jockey Club, and was one of the organizers of the National Horse Show Association, laboring actively and efficiently as an officer and director of the latter to give it popularity and success. The institution has fully justified Mr. Heckscher's views concerning the influence of the horse show it conducts, and has benefited the breeding of the highest type of horses in this country, while it has been the example for the horse shows now so frequent and popular in all parts of the Union. Mr. Heckscher still maintains his official connection with the organization which owes so much to his efforts and counsels. He is a member of the Jockey Club as well as of the New York Yacht Club, the South Side Sportsmen's Club, and the Metropolitan, Union, Racquet and Army and Navy clubs, while he also belongs to the Military Order of the Loyal Legion.

In 1862, Mr. Heckscher married Cornelia Lawrence Whitney, a descendant of Henry Whitney, who settled at Norwalk, Conn., and died in 1673. His great-great-grandson was Stephen Whitney, the famous New York merchant three-quarters of a century ago. His son, Henry Whitney, born in New Haven in 1812 and graduated from Yale in 1830, was Mrs. Heckscher's father. Her mother was Hannah Eugenia Lawrence, daughter of the Honorable Isaac Lawrence and his wife, Anna Beach, daughter of the Reverend Abraham Beach, of Trinity Church. Mrs. Heckscher died some years ago. In 1892, Mr. Heckscher contracted a second marriage, with Mary Travers, eldest daughter of the late William Riggin Travers. The career of William R. Travers and the national reputation he possessed as a financier, sportsman and wit are fully set forth on another page.

Of Mr. Heckscher's four daughters by his first wife, two survive. The elder, Georgiana Louisa, is the wife of the Honorable George Brinton McClellan, son of General George Brinton McClellan, U. S. A., the illustrious soldier of the Civil War, whose wife was the daughter of General Randolph B. Marcy, U. S. A. Mr. Heckscher's younger daughter, Emeline Dora, is the wife of Egerton Leigh Winthrop, Jr., of New York, whose family and ancestry are described in a separate article in this volume.

ALONZO BARTON HEPBURN

PETER HEPBURN, a native of Scotland, who came to this country in the early part of the eighteenth century, was the earliest American ancestor of that branch of the Hepburn family to which the above-named gentleman belongs. The wife of Peter Hepburn, whom he married after coming to this country, was Sarah Hubbell, of Newton, Conn. He was a resident of Stratford, Conn, and died there in 1742. Four sons and one daughter, Joseph, Peter, Sarah and George Hepburn, comprised the family of Peter Hepburn and his wife.

Joseph Hepburn, the eldest son, was born in 1729 and was the great-grandfather of Mr Alonzo Barton Hepburn. His wife, whom he married in 1751, was Eunice Barton, of Stratford, daughter of Judson Barton and Eunice Lewis. She was born in 1732. Eight children were born to Joseph Hepburn and his wife, Joseph, Silas, Lewis, Patrick, George, Eunice, Sarah and Ann Hepburn. The eldest son, Joseph, was born before 1756, married Hannah Lobdell and settled in Hotchkisstown, Conn., now Westville. He was the father of Zina E. Hepburn, who, born in 1798, died in 1874, having married Beulah Gray, who was born in 1807, in St. Lawrence County, N. Y.

Mr. Alonzo Barton Hepburn was the son of Zina E Hepburn and his wife, Beulah Gray. He was born in Colton, N. Y., in 1846. His early education was secured in the local schools, but afterwards he attended the St. Lawrence Academy of Potsdam, N. Y, and the Valley Seminary in Fulton, N. Y., in which institution he was prepared for college. He entered Middlebury College, Vermont, graduating in the class of 1871. After this, he became professor of mathematics in the St Lawrence Academy and was principal of the Ogdensburg Educational Institute in 1870. Having meantime applied himself to the study of law, he was admitted to the bar and entered upon practice in his native town of Colton. He also took an active part in public affairs in that section of the State and was elected a school commissioner of St. Lawrence County. That position he resigned in 1875 to take a seat in the New York Assembly and there, for five successive years, he represented his district, holding during that time a high position as an able and conscientious member of that body.

In 1880, Mr. Hepburn was appointed, by Governor Alonzo B Cornell, superintendent of the Banking Department of the State of New York, in which position he rapidly achieved reputation as a conservative and skilful official and an expert upon matters of banking and finance. In 1883, he was appointed receiver of the Continental Life Insurance Company, of New York, and successfully wound up the affairs of that corporation. In 1889, his reputation as a financier led to his being chosen for a responsible and important place under the Treasury Department, and he was appointed National Bank Examiner for New York and Brooklyn. While holding that position, in 1890, he was instrumental in exposing the maladministration of the Sixth National Bank, of this city. In 1892, President Benjamin Harrison promoted him to be Comptroller of the Currency of the United States, a position that he retained until the change of national administration, by the election of President Grover Gleveland, brought about his retirement in the following year.

After resigning his office in Washington, Mr. Hepburn became president of the Third National Bank of this city, and has since then resided here. On the merging of that institution with the National City Bank, in 1897, he assumed the vice-presidency of the latter, which, through this consolidation, became the largest bank on this continent.

In 1873, Mr Hepburn married Harriet A. Fisher, of St. Albans, Vt., who died in 1881. Later he married Emily L Eaton, of Montpelier, Vt. By his first wife he has one surviving child, Charles Fisher Hepburn, born in 1878. The children of his second marriage are two daughters, Beulah Eaton Hepburn, born in 1890, and Cordelia I. Hepburn, born in 1894. Mr. Hepburn's residence is in West Fifty-seventh Street. He is a member of the Metropolitan, Union League and Δ K E clubs, and of other social and scientific organizations

JACOB HOBART HERRICK

IN olden times, the name of Hireck, Hericke and Herrick was prominent in England, and in other parts of Great Britain. The name and the family is of ancient origin, and naturally recalls the Norse name of Eric, and that some members of the family were descended from the Norsemen does not admit of doubt. The first English ancestor of whom there is definite historic record was Eyryk, of Great Stretton and Houghton, Leicester County, in the time of Henry III, 1216-72, a lineal descendant of Eric the Forrester In the eighth generation from Eyryk of Great Stretton, was Sir William Herrick, of Leicester, London and Beau Manor, 1557-1652, a member of ' Parliament, 1601-30, and a knight in 1605 His wife was Joan May, daughter of Richard May, of London, and Mary Hilderson, of Devonshire

Sir William Herrick was the father of Henry Herrick, who was born in 1604 and came to America, first to Virginia and afterwards to Massachusetts Most of the representatives of the family were devoted to the cause of church and King, but Henry Herrick, the ancestor of the New England branch, seems to have been an exception to this rule, and was a Puritan Coming to this country in the early years of the seventeenth century, he finally settled on Cape Ann, on the banks of the Bass River, near what is now the town of Beverly. He was a close friend of the Reverend Thomas Higginson, the dissenting minister of Leicester, and was among the thirty who founded the first church in Salem and Beverly. His wife was Editha Laskin, daughter of Hugh Laskin, of Salem.

Ephraim Herrick, son of Henry Herrick, the pioneer, was born in 1638 and died in 1693 He lived in Beverly, Mass, having settled on a farm given to him by his father, on Birch Plain, as it was called. In 1668, he was a freeman of Bass River, and from time to time held various public offices. In 1661, he married Mary Cross, of Salem Samuel Herrick, the son of Ephraim and Mary Herrick, was born in 1675 in Beverly, but early in life removed to Connecticut, settling in the town of Preston, there becoming the head of the large and important Connecticut branch of the family His wife, whom he married in Massachusetts in 1698, before he removed to Connecticut, was Mehitable Woodworth, of Beverly

Animated by the pioneer spirit that possessed the early settlers of New England, and that was continually moving them to seek new homes further and further away from the coast towns, where they were first settled, Stephen Herrick, son of Samuel Herrick, of Connecticut, moved to Dutchess County, N Y, and established there the family from which is descended the gentleman whose name appears at the head of this sketch. Stephen Herrick was born in 1705, in Preston, Conn, and was married in 1726 to Phœbe Guild The great-grandfather of Mr Jacob Hobart Herrick was Joseph Herrick, of Amenia, Dutchess County, N Y, son of Stephen Herrick He was born in 1735 and his wife was Elizabeth Burton, of Preston. Their son was Josiah Herrick, of Dutchess County, who married Margaret Hicks, of the ancient Hicks family of Long Island. The parents of Mr Herrick were Jacob Burton Herrick, who was born in 1800, and Julia Ann Lyon, who was born in 1804 and married in 1825 He removed to New York before middle life, and was in business here until the time of his death, in 1864

Mr Jacob Hobart Herrick was born in New York in 1833, and has been a leading merchant in the grain trade. In 1884, he was president of the New York Produce Exchange He is a trustee of the Mutual Life Insurance Company, and is connected officially with several other corporations. He has achieved distinction as a graceful and forcible public speaker. His wife, whom he married in 1859, was Maria Amelia McKesson, daughter of John McKesson. Mr. and Mrs Herrick have had five children, Caroline McKesson, Henry Hobart, Florence, Isabel May and Ethel Hull Herrick Florence Herrick is the wife of Clarence H. Wildes, and Isabel May Herrick married H Montague Vickers The city residence of the family is in West Sixty-eighth Street and they have a summer home at Monmouth Beach, N J Mr Herrick is a member of the Union League and Whist clubs and of the Century Association

ABRAM S. HEWITT

ON his mother's side, Mr. Abram S Hewitt is descended from the Garniers, an old Huguenot family As early as the close of the seventeenth century, Garniers were settled in New York City Francis Garnier, who came over with Peter (Pierre) Jay, who fled from France after the revocation of the Edict of Nantes, was the head of that branch of the family from which Mr. Hewitt is descended He settled in Rockland County, and in the course of time the name of the family was locally changed to Gurnee Mr. Hewitt's father was an eminent civil engineer and machinist, who came to America in 1790. He assisted in putting up the first steam engine works, and in building the first steam engine ever made wholly in the United States. A destructive fire in his machine shops brought on financial reverses after he had enjoyed a long and successful business career, and he retired to private life on the ancestral farm that belonged to his wife, in Haverstraw.

The Honorable Abram S. Hewitt was born, July 31st, 1822, in the old homestead, in Haverstraw, and in 1842 was graduated from Columbia College at the head of his class. He became a member of the faculty of his alma mater, an acting professor of mathematics, and in 1845 visited Europe. He was admitted to the bar, but close application to his college and subsequent law studies, and to his duties as a teacher and professor, had impaired his eyesight, and he was forced to forego a legal career. Turning his attention to business occupations, he became associated with Peter Cooper, soon becoming junior partner in the firm of Cooper & Hewitt, with Edward Cooper, who had been his classmate in college. The firm succeeded to the business of the elder Mr Cooper, and developed it into one of the largest and most successful iron establishments of its kind in the country As a man of business, an executive, and a manufacturer, Mr. Hewitt has achieved remarkable success, and he is recognized as one of the world's great authorities upon all kinds of iron and steel work.

In 1862, Mr. Hewitt went to England, and brought home with him the most recent improvements in the manufacture of gun barrel iron, and later on was the first to introduce into the country the Martins-Siemens, or open-hearth, process for the manufacture of steel. In 1867, he was commissioned by President Grant to visit the Paris Exposition and report on the iron and steel exhibits there, and his report was of such a thorough character that it was translated into nearly all European languages For more than a quarter of a century he has taken an active part in public affairs. He has been prominent in the councils of the Democratic party, and was a Member of Congress from New York City, 1874-86, with the exception of one term, was elected Mayor of New York in 1886, and was chairman of the Democratic National Committee in 1876. On social, financial and industrial questions, Mr. Hewitt is a recognized authority, and is a frequent writer and public speaker upon such subjects. It was principally due to his advocacy of the plan that the United States Geological Survey was created by Congress. His address on A Century of Mining and Metallurgy in the United States, delivered upon his retirement from the presidency of the American Institute of Mining Engineers in 1876, was recognized as an important historical monograph.

Columbia College gave Mr. Hewitt the degree of LL. D. in 1887, and he was elected president of the Alumni Association in 1883. The industrial and educational benefactions of Peter Cooper, that are centred in the well-known Cooper Union, have been practically managed by him as the active member and secretary of the board of trustees for nearly forty years Mr. Hewitt married, in 1855, Sarah A. Cooper, daughter of Peter Cooper, and with his family lives in Lexington Avenue, near Gramercy Park. His sons are Peter Cooper Hewitt, who married Miss Work; Abram S. Hewitt, Jr., and Erskine Hewitt, Princeton, 1891. His daughters are Sarah Cooper and Eleanor G Hewitt The leading clubs of the city count him on their membership rolls, among them being the Metropolitan, Century, City, Church, Union, Engineers', Tuxedo, Players, Riding and South Side Sportsmen's.

CHARLES BETTS HILLHOUSE

FREEHALL, one of the large estates of Ireland, was the birthplace of the Reverend James Hillhouse, the second son of its owner, and the first representative of the name in America, to which he came in 1720   The property had long been, and is still in the family, but passed into the female line, owing to the part its American branch took in the Revolutionary War in this country.   The family was of great local prominence in its native seat, an uncle of the Reverend James Hillhouse being Captain James Hillhouse, mentioned in Macauley's history for bravery at the siege of Londonderry, and afterwards its Mayor

The Reverend James Hillhouse, who was Mr. Charles Betts Hillhouse's American ancestor, settled in Connecticut and married a great-granddaughter of the famous Captain John Mason, "The Indian Killer."   William Hillhouse, their son, was prominent in Connecticut during the Revolution.   He was a member of the Continental Congress, which first met at Philadelphia, in September, 1774, and paved the way for the Declaration of Independence, became a Major of Cavalry in the Army of the Revolution, and represented his town in one hundred and six semi-annual State Legislatures.   Sarah Griswold, his wife, was a daughter of John Griswold, of Lyme, Conn., and a sister of Governor Matthew Griswold, of Connecticut.   Her grandfather, Matthew Griswold, was Deputy Governor of the Colony.   Their son, Thomas Hillhouse, moved to Albany, and married Ann Van Schaick Ten Broeck, whose father, John Cornelius Ten Broeck, great-grandfather of Mr. Charles Betts Hillhouse, was a prominent Revolutionary patriot.   He was a Major in the Continental Army, and was present at Valley Forge, Brandywine and the siege and surrender of Yorktown   His regiment, the First New York, formed part of Lafayette's division, and he was among the officers who originated the Order of the Cincinnati.

Mr. Charles Betts Hillhouse possesses other ancestors representing eminent names of our early Colonial history.   He is a direct descendant of Colonel Olaf Stevensen Van Courtlandt, the last burgomaster of New Amsterdam under the Dutch rule; from Kiliaen Van Rensselaer, the first patroon of Rensselaerwyck; from Jeremias Van Rensselaer, Speaker of the Colonial Assembly of 1664; from Johannes Cuyler, Mayor of Albany ; from Henry Wolcott, the royal charterer, and from Major Dirk Wessels Ten Broeck, Mayor of Albany in 1696.

William Hillhouse, son of Thomas, married Frances J. Betts, daughter of Judge Samuel Rossiter Betts, who for forty years was Judge of the United States Court at New York, and of his wife, Caroline Dewey, of Massachusetts.   Charles Betts Hillhouse, the son of William and Frances (Betts) Hillhouse, and the subject of this article, was born November 25th, 1856, and graduated from Yale College in the class of 1878

In 1888, Mr Hillhouse married Georgiana Delprat Remsen, daughter of Robert G. Remsen and his wife, Margaret Delprat.   Robert G Remsen, the father of Mrs. Hillhouse, was a conspicuous figure in the social life of New York in the last generation, and was one of the three gentlemen who organized the famous Patriarchs   He died in January, 1896.   Mrs Hillhouse also traces an ancestry to Revolutionary and Dutch families.   Her paternal grandfather was Henry Remsen, private secretary to President Jefferson, his father being Hendrick Remsen, known in the American Revolution as Patriot Remsen.   Through her paternal grandmother, Elizabeth de Peyster, she is descended from the Honorable Johannes de Peyster, burgomaster, of New Amsterdam, in 1674, as well as from Johannes de Peyster, Mayor of the city, in 1698.   Another ancestor of Mrs. Hillhouse was Jans Joris de Rapelye, who came to America in 1623, his grandfather, Gaspard Colet de Rapelye, having been an officer of Francis I. and Henry II.   Among other families from which she descends are the Banckers, Rutgers and Roosevelts.   Her maternal great-grandfather was the Reverend Daniel Delprat, court chaplain of Louis Bonaparte, King of Holland, and who later on had charge of the education of William III. when Prince of Orange   Through her maternal grandmother, Elizabeth Steuart, of Baltimore, she is descended from the Steuart family, famous in the history of Scotland.

THOMAS HILLHOUSE

JOHN HILLHOUSE, of Freehall, County Londonderry, was the father of the Reverend James Hillhouse, *circa* 1688–1740, ancestor of the Hillhouse family of Connecticut and New York, of which the late General Thomas Hillhouse was a representative. The preceding page, relating to another branch, gives an account of the first three generations in America, and of their relationship to prominent Colonial families of Connecticut and New York.

The late General Thomas Hillhouse was the eldest son and second child of Thomas Hillhouse and Ann Van Schaick Ten Broeck, his wife. His father was born at Montville, New London County, Conn., but removed to New York early in the present century, and made his home at Walnut Grove, an estate at Watervliet, near Troy, which once formed part of the Van Rensselaer Manor. General Hillhouse was born at Walnut Grove, March 10th, 1816. He was preparing for college at Chase's Academy, Chatham, N. Y., but the death of his father obliged him to assume the care of the estate and the position of head of the family. In 1851, he moved to Geneva, N. Y., where he resided until he came to New York.

Much of his leisure was devoted to the study of political and military science, and becoming deeply interested in the vital questions of the day, he was an opponent of slavery and a supporter of Fremont in 1856 He was elected State Senator in 1859, and in 1861 was called by Governor Morgan to assume the duties of Adjutant-General, which position he held for two years. In this post, he transformed a virtually civil place into an arm of the Government, organizing two hundred thousand men for service in the Union Army, and was appointed by President Lincoln Assistant Adjutant-General of Volunteers. In 1865–66, he was Comptroller of the State, and rendered important service in the foundation of Cornell University. In 1870, President Grant appointed General Hillhouse Assistant Treasurer of the United States in New York, which position he held until 1882, throughout the administrations of Grant and Hayes. In 1882, he founded the Metropolitan Trust Company, of New York, and was its president until his death, in July, 1897.

In 1844, General Hillhouse married Harriet Prouty, daughter of Phinehas Prouty, a lineal descendant of Richard Prouty, of Scituate, Mass., 1667. Her mother, Margaret Matilda Van Vranken, daughter of the Reverend Nicholas Van Vranken, was a descendant of the most eminent families of Colonial Rhode Island, among her ancestors being Richard and Thomas Arnold, Thomas Angell, the companion of Roger Williams, Captain Samuel Comstock, John Wickes, a royal charterer, Samuel Gorton, Randal Holden, and the Reverend Chad Brown. The children of General Hillhouse were Margaret Prouty Hillhouse, Thomas Griswold Hillhouse, who married Julia, daughter of the Honorable John C. Ten Eyck, United States Senator from New Jersey; Phinehas Prouty Hillhouse, who married his fourth cousin, Caroline Matilda, daughter of the Reverend Maunsell Van Rensselaer, D. D.; Harriet Augusta Hillhouse, who married Walter Wood Adams, Anna Hillhouse, who died young, and Adelaide Hillhouse.

In the voluminous correspondence which General Hillhouse left are included letters of some of the most distinguished men in public life for the last fifty years, the portion relating to the Civil War and financial affairs having a peculiar value He wrote the Report on National Difficulties presented to the New York Legislature on the eve of the Rebellion, which had a decisive effect on the position taken by the Empire State in the Civil War; and another pamphlet written by him entitled, A Defense of the Conscription Act, had great influence upon public opinion. He also wrote other pamphlets and reports of importance, as well as occasional articles for the press. General Hillhouse was one of the earliest members of the Union League Club, and was also a member of the Grolier Club. He belonged to the New England Society, the New York Historical Society, the American Museum of Natural History, and the Metropolitan Museum of Art. For many years he was a manager of the House of the Holy Comforter, served as president of the Hahnemann Hospital, and was connected with various benevolent institutions. The motto on the coat-of-arms borne by the Reverend James Hillhouse is *Time Deum*

THOMAS HITCHCOCK

ON the ship Susan and Ellen, in 1635, came Matthias Hitchcock from London to America. Landing in Boston, he settled in Watertown, Mass. In 1639, he removed to New Haven, of which place he was one of the original founders This pioneer belonged to an old English family, one branch of which had been established in Wiltshire from the time of William the Conqueror. Anciently there were two families. The arms of one were ⋅ Argent, on a cross, azure, five fleurs de lis, or , in the dexter chief quarter, a'lion rampant, gules, ' crest, a castle, gules, on the tower a lion's head erased, in the mouth a round buckle ; motto, *Esse quod opto.* The arms of the other branch were: Gules, a chevron, argent, between three alligators; crest, an alligator. Luke Hitchcock, brother of Matthias, was a freeman of New Haven in 1644. He married a sister of William Gibbens, one of the original settlers of Hartford, who came in 1636. He was a large landowner in Wethersfield, Conn , and established very friendly relations with the Indians. His eldest son, John, married a daughter of the famous Deacon Samuel Chapin, of Springfield, Mass , and became the progenitor of a family that has been prominent and influential in the western part of the State of Massachusetts for several generations.

Eliakim Hitchcock, son of Matthias Hitchcock, married, in 1666, Sarah Merrick, daughter of Thomas Merrick, of Springfield, Mass., who came from Wales in 1630, settled first in Roxbury, Mass., and removed to Springfield in 1636, one of the company of pioneers who pushed through the wilderness to make new homes for themselves on the banks of the Connecticut. The great-great-grandfather of Mr Thomas Hitchcock was Joseph Hitchcock, youngest son of Eliakim Hitchcock He was born in 1686 and died in 1758, was a large landowner in Norwalk, Conn , a vestryman of the church and generally prominent in public affairs. His second son, John, was born in Norwalk, in 1726, and bought land in Greenwich of John Coscob, the Indian who gave his name to that part of the town, an appellation that has been retained in local annals to this day.

Thomas Hitchcock, the grandson of Eliakim Hitchcock, was born in Greenwich, in 1757, and died in 1813. He was a patriot of the Revolutionary period and served as a soldier in the war, being a Lieutenant in the company of Captain Nehemiah Mead. In 1784, he married Clemence Reynolds, daughter of William Reynolds. William Reynolds Hitchcock, son of Thomas Hitchcock and father of the subject of this sketch, was the sixth child in his father's family. He was born in Greenwich in 1794 and died in New York in 1857. His wife was Elithea Lockwood

Mr Thomas Hitchcock was born in New York, December 1st, 1831. He was educated in private schools and was graduated from the University of the City of New York in 1849 Then he studied law in the law department of Harvard College and was graduated in 1851. Until 1864, he was engaged in the practice of law, but since that time has devoted himself to journalistic and literary pursuits. In 1868, he joined the editorial staff of The New York Sun, and his work upon that newspaper has been principally on book reviews and philosophical and religious topics His regular Monday morning financial letter, under the signature of Matthew Marshall, who, by the way, was chief clerk of the Bank of England fifty years ago, has become one of the many valuable features of The Sun, and is regarded by the commercial and financial world generally as one of the most important periodical contributions to the financial literature of the day.

Mr. Hitchcock resides in East Twenty-ninth Street, and is a member of the Century Association and the National Academy of Design. His son, Center Hitchcock, is a prominent figure in social circles and a member of the Metropolitan, Union, Knickerbocker and other clubs. Another son, Francis R. Hitchcock, is a graduate from Columbia College, is a steward of the Jockey Club, for many years has been master of the Meadow Brook Hunt, and belongs to the Union, Knickerbocker and other clubs. His third son, Thomas Hitchcock, Jr , married, in 1891, Louise Eustis, only daughter of the late George Eustis, of New Orleans, and granddaughter of the late W. W. Corcoran, the famous banker of Washington; he lives in Westbury, Long Island, and is a member of the Meadow Brook Hunt, Metropolitan, Knickerbocker, Union and other clubs.

GEORGE HOADLY

IN the Revolutionary War, Timothy Hoadley, of Northford, Conn., a representative of a family which settled in New England at the beginning of the colonization, was Captain in the Second Regiment, Connecticut Militia, and as such was repeatedly in active service during the contest   After the peace, he was prominent in civil life, being twenty-six times a member of the Connecticut Legislature   He married Rebecca Linley, and their son, George Hoadly, was the father of the Honorable George Hoadly, of New York.

George Hoadly, the elder, was born in Northfield in 1781, graduated from Yale College in 1801, and was a tutor there from 1803 to 1806.   He pursued his professional studies with Judge Nathaniel Chauncey and practiced law for some years in New Haven, Conn.   For one term he was Mayor of the city, and also became president of the Eagle Bank of New Haven.   In 1830, however, after the failure of the bank, he removed to Cleveland, O , of which city he also became Mayor, and in which he died in 1857.   He was a man of great learning and marked public spirit, and wherever he lived was a leading citizen

Through his mother, who was Mary Anne Woolsey, widow of Jared Scarborough, the present George Hoadly traces his descent from one of the oldest pioneer families of Long Island. His first American maternal ancestor was George Woolsey, a resident of Yarmouth, England, in 1610, who afterwards went to Holland and finally came to New York with the Dutch immigrants in 1623, settling in New Amsterdam as a clerk in the employ of Isaac Allerton, of Mayflower fame, afterwards removing to Jamaica, Long Island.   His son, George Woolsey, had two sons, the Reverend Benjamin Woolsey, the younger, being the ancestor of that branch of the family to which attention is now directed

The Reverend Benjamin Woolsey, the great-grandfather of Mary Anne (Woolsey) Hoadly, was born in Jamaica, Long Island, and graduated from Yale College in 1707   In 1720, he succeeded the Reverend Joshua Hobart in the pastorate of the First Congregational Church at Southold, Long Island.   His son, Benjamin Woolsey, Jr., who was born in 1720, was graduated from Yale in 1744, and resided at Dosoris, Long Island, where he died in 1771.   He was, by his second wife, the father of Major Benjamin Woolsey, who was an officer in the Queen's Rangers during the Revolution, of William Walton Woolsey, born in 1766, and George Muirson Woolsey, and of Elizabeth (Woolsey) Dunlap, wife of the renowned artist, author and stage manager, William Dunlap.   Both William W. and George M Woolsey were prominent figures among the leading merchants of New York in the closing years of the last century, and the first quarter of the present one.   William W. Woolsey was in the hardware trade, and was a partner of Moses Rogers, of Stamford, who married his elder half-sister ; while George M. Woolsey engaged in business as a sugar refiner, and made a large fortune.   When William Walton Woolsey died, in 1839, he was president of the Boston & Providence Railroad Company, and at an earlier date of the New York Merchants' Exchange.

The wives of these members of the Woolsey family came from ancestors not less eminent than those of their husbands.   The Reverend Benjamin Woolsey married Abigail Taylor, daughter of John Taylor, of Oyster Bay, Long Island, and Mary Whitehead, his wife.   The Taylors and the Whiteheads were among the first families to settle in that part of the New York Colony Through his wife, the Reverend Benjamin acquired a great landed estate on Long Island, to which he gave the name of Dosoris, by which the property is still known, the title being formed from the two Latin words, *dos uxoris*, and was applied to the property because it was his wife's dowry. Benjamin Woolsey, Jr , married for his second wife, who was the grandmother of Mary Anne (Woolsey) Hoadly, Anne Muirson, daughter of Dr. George Muirson, and granddaughter of William Smith, of Tangier, Chief Justice and a member of the Council of the Colony of New York The wife of William Walton Woolsey, and the mother of Mary Anne (Woolsey) Hoadly, was Elizabeth Dwight, daughter of Major Timothy Dwight, of Northampton, Mass., and his wife,

Mary Edwards. Mary (Edwards) Dwight was one of the daughters of the celebrated New England divine, Jonathan Edwards, and was a sister of the mother of Lieutenant-Colonel Aaron Burr. Timothy Dwight, the first president of that name of Yale College, was the eldest son of Mary (Edwards) Dwight, and thus uncle of Mary Anne Woolsey. Major Dwight was a gallant soldier of the Colonial forces during the French and Indian wars, and died in an unsuccessful effort to colonize Mississippi, then owned by the English, at Natchez, just before the Revolution.

George Hoadly and his wife had several children. Their second child, Elizabeth Dwight Hoadly, was born in 1822 and married the Honorable Joshua Hall Bates, son of Dr. George Bates, of Boston, Mass. Joshua Hall Bates graduated from West Point in 1837, is a lawyer, was a member of the Ohio State Senate in 1864, and 1877, a Lieutenant in the United States Army during the Florida War, and a Brigadier-General of Ohio Volunteers in 1861. The eldest daughter of George Hoadly, Sr., Mary Anne Hoadly, was born in 1820, and married Dr. Thomas Fuller Pomeroy, son of Dr. Theodore Pomeroy, of Utica, N Y. Dr. Thomas F. Pomeroy was a graduate of Union College in 1835, and afterwards a physician in Detroit, Mich. His wife died in 1862 and he died in 1896 A noteworthy fact connected with Governor Hoadly's family is that among his ancestors and relatives, including those on the maternal side, there have been three presidents and nine professors of American colleges. The late President Woolsey, of Yale College, was the youngest son of William Walton Woolsey, and brother of Mary Anne (Woolsey) Hoadly.

The Honorable George Hoadly, of New York City, is his father's only son, and was born July 31st, 1826. He was educated at the Western Reserve College, from which institution he was graduated in 1844 Afterwards he studied at the Harvard College Law School His own alma mater gave him the degree of Doctor of Laws, and the same distinction was conferred on him by Yale in 1885 and by Dartmouth College in 1887. In 1847, he was admitted to the bar, beginning the practice of his profession in Cincinnati, O., as a junior partner of the Honorable Salmon P. Chase, afterwards the famous Secretary of the Treasury in President Lincoln's Cabinet and Chief Justice of the Supreme Court of the United States, and who was Governor Hoadly's lifelong friend. In 1851, he was elected Judge of the Superior Court of Cincinnati, and was City Solicitor in 1855. In 1859, he was again returned to the bench of the Second Superior Court, holding his seat there for nearly seven years, when he resigned to engage once more in private practice. From 1864 onward, he was for twenty years a professor of law in the Cincinnati Law School. In 1873-74, he was a member of the Constitutional Convention of the State of Ohio, and in 1883 was elected Governor of the State, and served a term in that high office. In 1887, he moved to New York City, where he has since been a member of a leading law firm.

The wife of the Honorable George Hoadly was Mary Burnet Perry, daughter of Samuel Perry, one of the pioneers of Cincinnati and of Ohio, and his wife, Mary Burnet Thew, of Rockland Lake, then known as Thew's Pond, in Rockland County, N. Y. Her father, Abraham Thew, was a lawyer in New York, who lost his health in one of the epidemics which afflicted the city early in the century, and, retiring to his ancestral home, at Rockland, soon died, leaving two daughters, afterwards known by their married names as Mrs Samuel Perry and Mrs. Nathaniel Wright, the latter being the wife of a very distinguished lawyer of Cincinnati. The two orphan girls were taken by their uncle, Judge Jacob Burnet, on a visit to Ohio in 1815, where both married ; Mrs Samuel Perry, the elder, dying at the advanced age of eighty-seven in 1881.

Mr. Hoadly's family consists of his son George, a graduate of Harvard, Class of 1879; Laura, the widow of Theodore Woolsey Scarborough; and Edward, who graduated from the Rensselaer Polytechnic Institute in 1889. George Hoadly, Jr., who is a lawyer at Cincinnati, O., married Genevieve Groesbeck, daughter of the late Colonel John Groesbeck, Thirty-Ninth Ohio Volunteer Infantry, and has two children, George, the fourth of this name, and Genevieve Olivia Laura (Hoadly) Scarborough has a daughter, Mary Hoadly Scarborough, born in 1891

Governor George Hoadly is a member of the Bar Association, the Ohio Society and the American Geographical Society, as well as of the Manhattan, Metropolitan, Century, Lawyers' and Reform clubs, while he is also a patron of the Metropolitan Museum of Art.

CORNELIUS NEVIUS HOAGLAND, M D

ON his father's side, Dr Cornelius Nevius Hoagland is descended from Christoffel Hooglandt, a native of Holland, born in 1634 Coming from Haarlem to New Amsterdam in early youth, he engaged in business, united with the Dutch Church in 1661, was an alderman in 1669 and a Lieutenant of the militia He married Catharine Cregier, daughter of Captain Martin Cregier, who was one of the prominent citizens in New Amsterdam, Captain of the military company and often in command of expeditions into the interior In 1653, he was one of the first burgomasters of New Amsterdam, his associate being Arent Van Hattan

In the second generation, Christopher Hooglandt, 1669-1748, was a resident of Long Island and afterwards of New Jersey. His second wife, the ancestress of the branch of the family to which Dr. Cornelius N Hoagland belongs, was Helena Middagh, daughter of John and Adriana Middagh. His son, Christopher, 1699-1777, married Catalyntie Schenck His grandson, Christopher, 1727-1805, who changed the spelling of his family name to Hoagland, was a prominent citizen of Somerset County, N. J., where he was a justice of the peace in 1776, an elder in the church and a member of the New Jersey Legislature in 1778. The wife of Christopher Hoagland, whom he married in 1752, was Sarah Voorhis

Isaac Hoagland, son of Christopher and Sarah Hoagland, was the grandfather of Dr Cornelius Nevius Hoagland. He was born in Somerset County, N J, in 1771. He entered Rutgers College, but he left that institution and went to Princeton, where he was graduated He then settled in Sussex County, and having studied medicine, received an appointment as surgeon's mate in the United States Army Ordered to service in the garrison in East Florida, he died there two years after. His wife, whom he married while a student in Rutgers College in 1792, was Margaretta Machett. Andrew Hoagland, the father of Dr Hoagland, was born in New Jersey in 1795 and died in 1872. He went West in 1834 and settled in Miami County, O. In the latter years of his life he lived in Troy, the county seat of Miami County, where he died in 1872 In 1828, he married Jane Hoagland, daughter of Cornelius and Katharine Hoagland. She was descended in the sixth generation from Dirck Jansen Hoagland, who came from Holland in 1657. Her family was not related to that of her husband, although it bore the same name.

Dr Cornelius Nevius Hoagland was born in Somerset County, N. J, in the family homestead, November 23d, 1828. Taken to Ohio with his parents, he attended school in West Charleston until 1845, and graduated from the medical department of the Western Reserve University, Cleveland, in 1852. Engaging in the practice of medicine in Miami County, he also became interested in politics, and was elected auditor of the county in 1854 and in 1856 When the Civil War began, he enlisted in the Eleventh Ohio Infantry, becoming First Lieutenant in that regiment In October, 1861, he was appointed surgeon of the Seventy-First Ohio, and served until the close of the war, principally in the campaigns in Tennessee, Georgia, Alabama and Texas, being actively engaged in many great battles in connection with the duties of his position, serving on brigade and division staffs, and frequently having charge of important field hospitals

After the war, he returned to Ohio to the practice of his profession, but in 1868 removed to New York and engaged in mercantile pursuits, which have since occupied his attention. He is a director of the People's Trust Company and the Dime Savings Bank, and connected with other corporations In 1887, he founded and amply endowed the Hoagland Laboratory, which is devoted to original medical research. The wife of Dr. Hoagland was Eliza E Morris, daughter of Judge David H Morris, of Ohio His children are Cora, wife of George P. Tangeman; Elizabeth, wife of Charles O Gates, and Ella Hoagland The family residence is in Brooklyn Dr Hoagland is a member of the Hamilton, Union League and Brooklyn clubs of Brooklyn, the Downtown Club, Ohio Society, and Military Order of the Loyal Legion He is a fellow of the Royal Microscopical Society of London, and of the American Geographical Society of New York, and a member of the New York Genealogical and Biographical Society and the Long Island Historical Society.

ROBERT HOE

A TWO-FOLD interest attaches to the name which heads this article It recalls a family which has supported the fame of this country throughout the world for invention and workmanship in a most important branch of mechanics. Furthermore, the gentleman of whom we speak is personally recognized as one of the foremost American patrons of art and letters, and as having made his taste and knowledge of inestimable value to this city.

Robert Hoe, first of the name, was born in Leicestershire, England, in 1784 He was an expert mechanician, and, coming to New York, in 1803, engaged in the business of making printing presses , his establishment, which, from that day to the present, has been conducted under the style of R Hoe & Co., being in Maiden Lane and later in Gold Street. Its founder took out some of the first patents for improvements in printing presses, and at his works steam was first employed as a motive power in New York. He made the earliest presses of the cylinder type constructed in the United States, which, though based upon European models, represented a great improvement over the originals. Retiring from business, in 1832, he died at his country seat, in Westchester, in the following year, leaving his sons, Richard M. and Robert Hoe, as his successors

Robert Hoe, second of the name, was a noted patron of the fine arts, was distinguished by his discriminating liberality to young artists, and was one of the founders of the National Academy of Design. He died in 1884, he and his brother being succeeded in business by his son, the present Mr. Robert Hoe, who was born in this city, in 1839.

Mr. Hoe is the head of the firm of R. Hoe & Co., which, as it exists to-day, is largely his creation, and which he has brought to the height of reputation it now enjoys. The works in Grand Street embrace now the largest manufacturing plant of its kind in or around New York. Employing at least one thousand six hundred skilled mechanics, the works support some ten thousand of the city's population. It is the only large manufacturing establishment conducted by individual owners, that remains in the city. Other concerns of similar magnitude have either been absorbed in some of the numerous combinations of industrial capital, or have been removed from New York on account of the taxation and the restrictive laws that prevail here. Many inducements have been offered to Mr Hoe to remove his plant elsewhere. He has, however, uniformly rejected all such offers, and in a true spirit of local pride, keeps his establishment in the city of his own birth, and where it also grew up. Some seven years ago, Mr. Hoe inaugurated a branch of R Hoe & Co., in London, which is unique of its kind in England, and supplies the principal printing offices of that country, and its Colonies.

Inheriting in a full degree the mechanical and business talents of his family, Mr. Hoe has thus continued and improved upon its record for success. He is, however, a student and connoisseur, quite as much as a man of affairs, and in the former connection has a more than national reputation. He was one of the founders of the Metropolitan Museum of Art, and an earnest laborer for its success. One of New York's valued literary institutions, the Grolier Club, sprang from his suggestion, and, as its president, he has contributed effectively to incite interest in the arts pertaining to the production of books, which are the objects of its attention. Mr. Hoe is an indefatigable collector of books and works of art, and his magnificent private library is universally admitted to be the most remarkable and valuable in America, while he has written, at times, upon the subjects that engross his attention.

Mr. Hoe married Olivia P. James, daughter of Daniel James, of New York and Liverpool, England Their children are: Carolyn, now Mrs. Leon Marie; Olivia, now Mrs. Henry Lewis Slade; Laura, the wife of Ernest Trow Carter; Ellen James, Ruth L., Robert, Jr , and A. I. Hoe

The family residence is 11 East Thirty-sixth Street, and Mr. Hoe's country seat is at Lake Waccabuc, N. Y His clubs, in addition to the Grolier, are the Century, Union League, Players, Engineers' and Fencers'

EUGENE AUGUSTUS HOFFMAN, D.D.

HIMSELF a foremost representative of the culture, refinement and Christian activity of the metropolis in the present generation, the Very Reverend Eugene Augustus Hoffman, D.D., LL. D., D.C. L , comes of old Knickerbocker stock The family, for two centuries and a half, has been prominent in New York, Kingston and Red Hook, and much of the land originally patented by its founders still remains in the possession of their descendants in Ulster and Dutchess counties. Those of this generation can trace their lineage with the Ver Plancks, Beekmans, Bensons and other leading families of New York State The American founder of the family was Martinus Hoffman, who was born in Sweden about 1640, and was a ritmaster in the army of Augustus Adolphus, of Sweden. He came to this country about 1660, and settled in New Amsterdam. Then he removed to Albany and became a large land owner, but finally settled in Ulster County, where he founded the village that was named after him, Hoffmantown

Nicholas Hoffman, son of Martinus Hoffman, lived in Kingston and married Jannitie Crispell, daughter of Antoine Crispell, a Huguenot and one of the patentees of New Paltz Their son, Martinus Hoffman, 1706-1772, settled in Red Hook and was a man of much wealth and local importance, being a justice of the peace and Colonel of a militia regiment; his wife was Trintie Benson, daughter of Robert and Cornelia (Roose) Benson. The son of Martinus and Trintie Hoffman was Harmanus Hoffman, who married Catherine Ver Planck, daughter of Samuel and Effie (Beekman) Ver Planck, and became the father of Samuel Ver Planck Hoffman, the grandfather of the Reverend Eugene A. Hoffman.

Samuel Ver Planck Hoffman, 1802-1880, was a lawyer early in life, but in 1828 established a dry goods house, in which he remained until his retirement, in 1842 He was a director in several insurance companies and other corporations, a member of the Union League Club, a trustee of the General Theological Seminary, a vestryman of Trinity Church, and a generous supporter of philanthropic enterprises. By his marriage with Glorvina Rossell Storm, daughter of Garrit Storm, the New York wholesale merchant, he had two sons, the Reverend Dr. Eugene A Hoffman and the Reverend Dr. Charles F. Hoffman.

Dean Eugene A. Hoffman was born in New York, March 21st, 1829, and educated in the Columbia Grammar School and Rutgers College, from which he was graduated when only eighteen years of age. His studies were further continued in Harvard, and from that University he has the degrees of B. A. and M A Graduated from the General Theological Seminary in 1851, he was ordained a deacon by Bishop Doane, of New Jersey, the same year and entered at once upon parochial work in Christ Church, Elizabeth, N. J. He continued actively in the ministry for twenty-eight years, holding rectorships in Burlington, N. J , Brooklyn and Philadelphia

In 1879, he was elected to the office of dean of the General Theological Seminary, and his administration has covered the period of the greatest prosperity that that famous institution has ever enjoyed. His management of the seminary has revealed him as a man of executive ability, deep religious fervor and broad sympathies. He has improved and added to the buildings of the seminary, which is now one of the chief educational and architectural ornaments of the city. Over a million dollars have been added to the funds of the institution, chiefly by the munificence of Dean Hoffman and members of his family He married, in 1852, Mary C Elmendorf, daughter of Peter Z. Elmendorf, of New Brunswick, N. J. His residence is in Chelsea Square and he belongs to the Century, City, Riding, South Side Sportsmen's, St. Nicholas and Jekyl Island clubs, and the St. Nicholas Society. His son, Samuel Ver Planck Hoffman, was graduated from Columbia College and married Louisa M Smith. His only brother, the Reverend Charles F Hoffman, married Eleanor F. Vail. Their son, Charles Frederick Hoffman, Jr , was graduated from Columbia College in 1878, and their daughter, Eleanor L. Hoffman, married William MacNeill Rodewald Dean Hoffman is interested in many humanitarian institutions, is a member of many church boards and is connected with numerous literary and scientific societies.

ROBERT JOSEPH HOGUET

THE ancestors of Mr. Robert Joseph Hoguet belonged in France originally The name was attached to one of the most ancient Catholic families in that country, where for many generations it was substantial and influential. The great-grandfather of the subject of this sketch, Joseph Hoguet, was the first of the name to leave his native land. In the latter part of the eighteenth century, he went to Ireland, and there established himself in business The son of this French exile was Robert Joseph Hoguet, who was a leading merchant of Dublin. He married Eleanor Pontet, a compatriot, also descended from an eminent French Catholic family of the old régime and herself a native of France

Henry Louis Hoguet, the sixth child of Robert Joseph Hoguet and his wife, Eleanor, was brought up under the instruction of private tutors until he was thirteen years of age, having been born in 1816 He was then sent to France to complete his education, and in 1829, was entered as a pupil in the Massin Institute, an appendage to the ancient Charlemagne College in Paris There he prosecuted his studies for the ensuing four years, completing his course in the autumn of 1833 In April of the year following his graduation from Charlemagne College, although he had not yet completed his eighteenth year, he became possessed of an ambition to seek his fortunes in the New World. Accordingly he sailed for New York, whither several of his brothers had already preceded him The firm of Hoguet & Son had been established several years previous to this time and was already doing a flourishing business in Maiden Lane The house had been founded by his father, who had sent over his second son, Anthony Hoguet, to manage the business. Henry L Hoguet, upon arriving in New York, took a place in his father's firm, where he remained for several years and then, in 1838, went into the employ of William Kobbe.

In 1846, Mr. Hoguet determined to engage in business for himself and assisted in founding the firm of Chesterman & Hoguet, of which he was the junior partner After three years, this partnership was dissolved, and the firm of Wilmerding, Hoguet & Humbert succeeded to the business Subsequently, the firm name became Wilmerding, Hoguet & Co The establishment was moved from William Street, where it had existed from its earliest days, to a location in Broadway, and became one of the leading business houses of the metropolis. Mr. Hoguet was also for many years president of the Emigrants' Savings Bank

A devoted member of the Roman Catholic Church, Mr Hoguet was long prominent in the lay councils of that denomination For many years he was a trustee of the old St. Patrick's Cathedral in Mott Street, when that church was the leading ecclesiastical institution of the Roman Catholics in New York. He was also one of the managers of the Roman Catholic Orphan Asylum, a trustee of the St. Vincent de Paul's Church, treasurer of St Vincent de Paul's Orphan Asylum, and one of the founders of the New York Catholic Protectory, being for many years president of the latter institution His valuable and unselfish services in the cause of religion and charity commanded the attention and the approval of the church authorities, and, in 1880, Pope Leo XIII. created him a Chevalier of the Order of St Gregory, and conferred upon him the cross and diploma of that order, an exceptional honor to be bestowed upon a lay member of the church. Mr Hoguet was twice married His first wife, whom he married in 1838, was Miss Atkinson, granddaughter of Captain John O'Connor. She died in 1869 His second wife, whom he married in 1872, was a French lady, a native of Paris; she survived her husband

Mr. Robert Joseph Hoguet, the only son of Henry L Hoguet and his first wife, was born in August, 1839, and succeeded his father in the business of Wilmerding, Hoguet & Co, with which he has been connected from his early manhood He married Marie Noel, a lady of French descent, and lives in the old family residence, at the corner of the Boulevard and West One Hundred and Forty-first Street, overlooking the Hudson River. He belongs to the Catholic and Merchants' clubs, and has followed in the footsteps of his father as a generous supporter of religious and benevolent institutions

HENRY HUTCHINSON HOLLISTER

LIEUTENANT JOHN HOLLISTER, who was born in England in 1612 and emigrated to this country in 1642, was one of the influential men in the early days of the Connecticut Colony He married Joanna Treat, daughter of the Honorable Richard Treat, Sr., and became the ancestor of the Hollister family, representatives of which have been prominent in Connecticut and New York. His son, John Hollister, who was born in Wethersfield, Conn, about 1644, was the ancestor of the branch now under consideration. He was one of the principal men of Glastonbury, to which place he moved from Wethersfield, and where he died in 1711. His wife, Sarah Goodrich, came from another leading Colonial family. She was a daughter of William Goodrich and Sarah Marvin, her maternal grandfather being Matthew Marvin, who came from London in 1635, and was an original proprietor of Hartford and one of the grantees of Norwalk, in which he settled in 1653

The successive representatives of the family line from John Hollister down to Mr. Henry H. Hollister, of New York, were Thomas Hollister, 1672-1741; Gideon Hollister, 1699-1785; Nathaniel Hollister, 1731-1810; Gideon Hollister, 1776-1864, and Edwin M. Hollister, 1800-1870 Thomas Hollister resided in Glastonbury, where he was a deacon in the church. His wife was Dorothy Hills, 1677-1741, daughter of Joseph Hills, of Glastonbury, a son of William Hills, who came to America in 1632, settled in Roxbury and afterwards moved to Connecticut His first wife was Phyllis Lyman, daughter of Richard Lyman, and his second wife was the widow Mary Steele, daughter of Andrew Warner, of Hadley. Gideon Hollister, son of Thomas Hollister, was a Lieutenant in the Militia in 1736. He married, in 1723, Rachel Talcott, 1706-1790, daughter of Nathaniel Talcott, of Glastonbury The wife of Nathaniel Hollister in the next generation was Mehitable Mattison, 1739-1824. Gideon Hollister, the son of Nathaniel Hollister, and the grandfather of Mr Henry H. Hollister, removed to Andover, Conn., where he was engaged in business as a paper manufacturer. His wife was Mary Olmstead, of East Hartford, who died in 1827. Their son, Edwin M Hollister, removed early in life to Hartford, where he was engaged for many years as a dry goods merchant. Afterwards he resided in Windsor and became a prosperous paper manufacturer. His wife was Gratia Taylor Buell, who was born in 1801, her father being Major John H Buell, who was an energetic patriot, served in the Revolutionary Army, and was an original member of the Society of the Cincinnati.

Mr. Henry Hutchinson Hollister, the youngest son of Edwin M and Gratia (Buell) Hollister, was born in Brattleboro, Vt., in 1842. His early years were spent in Vermont, but when young he removed to New York and entered upon a successful business career For many years he has been a banker and broker, and is connected with many financial enterprises. In 1871, he married Sarah Louise Howell, daughter of William A. Howell and Lucetta B. Gould, of Newark, N. J. His second wife was Anne Willard Stephenson, daughter of J. H. Stephenson, of Boston; her grandfathers being Benjamin Stephenson, of Scituate, Mass., and Aaron Willard, of Boston. The children of Mr. Hollister by his first wife were Louise Howell, Henry Hutchinson, Jr, Louise and Buell Hollister. Henry H. Hollister, Jr., is an undergraduate at Yale University. The residence of the family is in West Forty-ninth Street Mr. Hollister is a member of the Metropolitan, Union, New York, Riding, Whist and South Side Sportsmen's clubs, and belongs to the New England Society, the Sons of the Revolution and the Society of the Cincinnati

The brothers and sisters of Mr. Hollister, children of Edwin M. and Gratia (Buell) Hollister, were Edward Hubbell Hollister, born 1826, who married Emily H. Phelps and died in 1868; Sarah Buell Hollister, who married the Honorable Broughton D Harris, of Vermont; George Hollister, born in 1832, who married Phœbe Conkling; Mary Louise Hollister, born in 1834, who married Walter A Pease, Helen Mercia Hollister, born in 1836, who married Effingham Maynard, and John Buell Hollister, born in 1838, who married Ellie Crane.

CHARLES RUSSELL HONE

ONE of the most distinguished Mayors that New York City ever had, and one of the most courtly gentlemen of the metropolis in the last generation, was the Honorable Philip Hone. His son, Robert S. Hone, was the father of Mr. Charles Russell Hone   Robert S. Hone was prominent in business affairs, being for many years president of the Republic Fire Insurance Company, vice-president of the New York Institution for the Blind, and a director and trustee of many other charitable and philanthropic institutions of the city.   The wife of Robert S. Hone was Eliza Rodman Russell, of Providence, in which city she was born in 1819.   Mr and Mrs Hone had four children.   Mary Schermerhorn Hone married Horace W. Fuller, son of Dudley B. Fuller, and had two children, Dudley and Arthur Fuller.   The other children were Anna Russell Hone, Charles Russell Hone and Robert Hone.

Through his mother, Mr. Charles Russell Hone is descended from several of the most distinguished families of Rhode Island.   Eliza Rodman Russell was a daughter of Charles Handy Russell by his first wife, Ann Rodman, whom he married in 1818.   The father of Ann Rodman was Captain William Rodman, of Newport and Providence, who married Ann Olney, niece of Colonel Jeremiah Olney, of Revolutionary fame.   Captain William Rodman was descended from Dr. Thomas Rodman, the first American ancestor of the family, who was born in 1639 and died in 1727   The line of descent was through Samuel Rodman, who was born in 1703 and died in 1749; William Rodman, who married Lydia Gardner about 1757; Captain William Rodman, second, who was born in 1758 and became the father of Ann Rodman   One of the daughters of Captain William Rodman, Elizabeth Rodman, married John Rogers, of Providence, and another daughter, Mary Rodman, married Stephen Hopkins, of Providence, son of Stephen Hopkins, one of the signers of the Declaration of Independence.

The maternal grandfather of Mr. Charles Russell Hone was Charles Handy Russell, one of the most distinguished merchants and business men of Newport and New York in the last generation, and prominently identified with many financial institutions of New York, and with the public service and literary and social enterprises.   Mr. Russell traced his descent on the maternal side back through several generations to Samuel Handy, a native of England, and an early settler of the Maryland Colony in the first part of the eighteenth century   The grandmother of Mr. Russell was Ann Brown, descended from Chad Brown, one of the first settlers of Newport, who was born in 1671, and died in 1731, and whose wife was Elizabeth Cranston, daughter of Governor John Cranston.   Her father was Captain John Brown, of Newport, a grandson of Chad Brown.   Members of the Brown family were especially distinguished in the early generations in Rhode Island.   John Brown, the eldest son of Chad Brown, married Jane Lucas, daughter of Augustus and Bathsheba Lucas, of Newport, and descended from the Reverend Joseph Eliot, of Guilford, Conn., son of John Eliot, the Indian Apostle, whose wife was Sarah Brenton, daughter of Governor William Brenton.   Ann Brown, who married Charles Handy, was the eighth daughter of this Captain John Brown.   All her descendants are, therefore, descendants of Governor William Brenton, the Reverend John Eliot, Governor John Cranston and of Governor Jeremiah Clark.

On the Russell side of the house, the ancestry of Mr. Charles Russell Hone goes back to John Russell, who came to Charlestown, Mass., before 1640, and among his antecedents along this line are: the Reverend John Russell, Jr , one of the first Baptist ministers of Boston, and Major Thomas Russell, an aide-de-camp to Brigadier-General John Stark, during the War of the Revolution, and afterwards at the head of the great East India importing house of Russell & Co.

Mr. Charles Russell Hone was born in New York, May 8th, 1849, was educated in New York and New Haven, and has been engaged in the banking business   His wife, whom he married in 1876, was Josephine Hoey, and they have two sons, Charles R. Hone, Jr , and Harold Hone   The residence of the family is at Westbury Station, Long Island   Mr Hone is a member of the Union, Knickerbocker, Country and Meadow Brook Hunt clubs, and of the New England Society.

GEORGE BEVAN HOPE, M. D.

PRIOR to the Revolution, representatives of the Hope family came from Scotland to the American Colonies The name is one of great antiquity, as well as of historical prominence in the annals of the Scottish Kingdom, and has been represented, not only in the nobility of the country, but in the professions and in the highest ranks of Great Britain's commerce Among the first baronetcies of Scotland was that represented in this age by Sir John D Hope, whose hereditary title dates back to 1628 In 1703, another of the branches of the family was invested with the Earldom of Hopetown, and a century later the then bearer of the dignity received the English baronage of the same title. By their intermarriage with the highest nobility and gentry of the United Kingdom, the Hopes have become allied with many families of the first distinction, one instance of which is afforded by the well-known Beresford-Hope family, which for some generations has been prominent in the social and political life of the mother country. Closely connected were the famous Hopes of Amsterdam, Holland, merchants and bankers, who, during the last century and the earlier part of the present one, were among the most powerful financiers of the world To this portion of the family belonged the traveler and philosopher, Thomas Hope, 1770-1831, the author of Anastasius, and other works, who was also famous for his munificence in the cause of art The branch to which Dr. George Bevan Hope, of New York, belongs, established itself in Pennsylvania about 1760 Both his grandfather, Richard Hope, and his father, Matthew Boyd Hope, were natives of that State, the latter adopting the ministry and becoming a member of the faculty of Princeton College, in which institution he was a professor for many years, and the author of numerous educational and other works His wife was Agnes C Bevan, of Philadelphia, a daughter of Matthew L. Bevan, one of the most noted citizens of that city in the early part of the century

The Bevan family descended from English Quakers, who came to Pennsylvania in the early days of the Province Matthew L Bevan was a merchant of the highest standing in the East India trade As was the custom of those days, he owned his own ships and personally made several voyages to China He took a prominent and active part in benevolent and religious work in Philadelphia, and was one of the foremost laymen of the Presbyterian Church in America In politics, also, he was an influential factor and a friend and adviser of the foremost men of his time His intimacy with Henry Clay was especially close, and, accompanied by his daughters, he made the long and then wearying journey across the mountains from Philadelphia to Kentucky, for the purpose of visiting the statesman at his home at Ashland Without having held public office, Matthew L Bevan rendered many important services to his State and country. The most notable of these was the winding up of the Bank of the United States on the expiration of its charter in 1835 At a critical juncture, President Jackson selected him as the associate of Albert Gallatin in that task, which, owing largely to his financial knowledge and the confidence reposed in him by the business community, was accomplished with complete success

Dr. George Bevan Hope accordingly takes his middle name from his maternal ancestry. He was born at Princeton, N J , in 1847, and graduated from the college in the class of 1869 Adopting the medical profession, he pursued his studies in this city at Bellevue Medical College, graduating in 1876, followed by a residence abroad of several years, during which he took a post-graduate course at the famous medical schools of Vienna and Paris In his profession, Dr Hope has devoted himself to a specialty—the throat—upon which he is one of the foremost authorities, and holds professorships in the Post-Graduate Medical School in this city, as well as in the medical faculty at the University of Vermont, at Burlington His published writings have been confined to professional subjects, and have appeared in the leading medical periodicals of the country

Dr Hope has a wide circle of personal friends in New York society He is unmarried, and is a member of the Union League Club, his residence being at 34 West Fifty-first Street

WILLIAM BUTLER HORNBLOWER

JOSIAH HORNBLOWER, an eminent English civil engineer, was born in 1729 At the request of Colonel John Schuyler, he came to the United States in 1753, and settled near Belleville, N J , where he erected the first stationary engine known in this country. He managed the copper mines of Belleville for several years and served as a Captain in the French and Indian wars In the Revolution, he was an uncompromising patriot and was Speaker of the Lower House of the New Jersey Legislature in 1780 His activity in devising and promoting important measures to advance the interests of the patriot cause excited the special ire of the British, who unsuccessfully tried to kidnap him In 1781, he was elected to the upper branch of the Legislature, where he remained until 1784, when he was selected to represent the Colony in the Continental Congress In 1790, he was appointed Judge of the Court of Common Pleas in Essex County, N. J , and continued on the bench for many years

The son of Josiah Hornblower was Joseph C. Hornblower, 1777-1864, who was admitted to the bar in 1803 He was a Presidential elector in 1820, and voted for James Monroe, was elected Chief Justice of the State of New Jersey in 1832, and reëlected in 1839, was a member of the Constitutional Convention in 1844; was appointed Professor of Law in Princeton College in 1847; was a vice-president of the First National Republican Convention, in 1856; was president of the Electoral College of New Jersey in 1860, voting for Lincoln and Hamlin, was one of the original members of the American Bible Society and president of the New Jersey Historical Society The Reverend William Henry Hornblower, 1820-1883, son of Judge Hornblower, was a prominent Presbyterian divine. He was educated in Princeton College, was engaged in missionary work for five years, was pastor of the First Presbyterian Church in Paterson, N J , for twenty-seven years, and a professor in the Theological Seminary in Allegheny, Pa , for twelve years. He married Matilda Butler, of Suffield, Conn , whose ancestry runs back to the Puritans Of this union came two sons and one daughter

Mr. William Butler Hornblower, the second son, was born in 1851 He was prepared for college in the collegiate school of Professor George P Quackenbos, matriculating at Princeton in 1867, at the age of sixteen, and being graduated four years later For two years he devoted himself to literary studies, but in 1873 entered Columbia Law School and was graduated in 1875. Entering upon the practice of law, he connected himself with the firm of Carter & Eaton, of New York, retaining that professional association until 1888, when he founded the firm of Hornblower & Byrne, which subsequently became Hornblower, Byrne & Taylor. Since 1880, Mr Hornblower has been counsel for the New York Life Insurance Company. He has been very successful in bankruptcy cases, of which, at one time, he made a specialty. In the famous Grant & Ward case, he was counsel for the receiver. He was also successful in several important tontine insurance cases that he tried for the New York Life Insurance Company. For several years past he has had a large practice in the United States Courts, and among other important cases there he appeared in the Virginia bond controversy, and the railroad bond litigation of the City of New Orleans.

A Democrat of independent proclivities, he has exercised a considerable influence in contemporaneous political movements in the State of New York. He has been frequently mentioned for public office, and in 1893 was nominated by President Cleveland to be a Justice of the Supreme Court of the United States His fitness for the place was generally conceded, but his independence in politics had placed him in opposition to some of the leaders of his party, and the Senate refused to confirm the nomination In 1882, Mr Hornblower married Susan C. Sandford, of New Haven, Conn , who was descended from several of the old Puritan families of New England Mrs. Hornblower died in 1886, leaving three children He married, in 1894, Emily (Sandford) Nelson, widow of Lieutenant Colonel A D Nelson, of the United States Army, and a sister of his first wife He lives in upper Madison Avenue, and his summer home is Penrhyn, Southampton, Long Island He belongs to the Metropolitan and other leading clubs and social organizations

HARRY LAWRENCE HORTON

BARNABAS HORTON, the first American ancestor of the family to which Mr. Harry Lawrence Horton belongs, came of an ancient English family. Robert De Horton appears in the old records as the master of the Manor of Horton in the thirteenth century Other members of the family also had a manor house in Great Horton William Horton, of Frith House, Barksland, who was descended from Robert De Horton, married Elizabeth Hanson, daughter of Thomas Hanson, of Toothill. His son, Joseph Horton, who was born about 1578 and settled in Mousley, Leicestershire, was the father of Barnabas Horton

Tradition says that Barnabas Horton came to this country in the ship Swallow, that was commanded by one of his relatives, Captain Jeremy Horton. He was born in 1600, and emigrated to the New World in 1633 or soon after, landing in Massachusetts. Before 1640, he removed to New Haven, Conn., and afterwards formed one of the company that crossed to the eastern end of Long Island, and settled the town of Southold, being one of the patentees of that place. He was a constable in 1656 and 1659, a deputy to the General Court of the Connecticut Colony, 1654-64, a freeman of the Colony in 1662, and a magistrate of the town of Southold from 1664 until the time of his death, in 1680. Joseph Horton, son of Barnabas Horton, who was born in England, came to this country with his parents when an infant. Brought up in the town of Southold, he removed to Rye, Westchester County, N. Y., in 1664, was a freeman of the Connecticut Colony in 1662, a selectman of Rye in 1671, a justice of the peace in 1678, and a Lieutenant and then Captain of the militia. His wife was Jane Budd, daughter of John Budd, one of the thirteen original settlers of Southold.

In successive generations from Joseph Horton, the ancestors of Mr. Harry Lawrence Horton were: David Horton, who was born in Rye in 1664, and his wife, Esther King; John Horton, who was born in White Plains in 1696, and his wife, Elizabeth Lee, Richard Horton, who was born in White Plains and married Jemima Wright; Elijah Horton, who was born in Peekskill in 1739 and died in Bradford County, Pa., in 1821, and his wife, Jemima Currie; Elijah M Horton, who was born in Peekskill in 1768 and died in Sheshequin, Pa, in 1835, and his wife, Abigail Bullard; and William Bullard Horton, who was born in Sheshequin, in 1807, and died in 1867, and his wife, Melinda Blackman, daughter of Colonel Franklin Blackman and Sybil Beardsley

Mr. Harry Lawrence Horton was born in Sheshequin, Bradford County, Pa., January 17th, 1832. Having received a sound education in the schools of his native place, he entered upon mercantile life in Horn Brook, Pa., at the age of seventeen. After that, he traveled extensively throughout the West, and then settled in Milwaukee, Wis, and engaged in the produce commission business in 1856 For nine years he remained in Milwaukee, and was a successful man of affairs. Then coming to New York in 1865, he established the banking house of H. L Horton & Co., of which he has been the senior member for more than thirty years. He has spent considerable time abroad in the business interests of his house, and has also traveled extensively for pleasure. He is a member of the New York Stock Exchange and the Produce Exchange, as well as of the Chicago Board of Trade and other similar business organizations.

Mr Horton married Sarah S Patten, of New York, and has two daughters, Blanche and Grace Horton The city residence of the family is in West Fifty-seventh Street, and they have a summer home at Monmouth Beach, N. J. For many years, Mr. Horton resided at New Brighton, Staten Island, and was president of the Board of Trustees of that town for three years One of the most enterprising and most public-spirited citizens of New Brighton, he was chiefly instrumental in promoting the Staten Island Water Supply Company and the Rapid Transit Company. He contributes generously in support of charity, and is an intelligent patron of art and literature. He is a member of the Manhattan, Union League, Lawyers', New York Athletic and Riding clubs

ALFRED CORNELIUS HOWLAND

ON another page will be found the full and detailed account of the ancestry of the Howland family, descended from John Howland, the Mayflower Pilgrim, and Elizabeth Tilley, his wife. The branch to which attention is now directed is represented in New York not only by Judge Henry E Howland, but by his younger brother, the distinguished artist whose name heads the present article. The father of these gentlemen, Aaron Prentiss Howland, was a respected citizen of Walpole, N. H., and an architect. In connection with his profession he was also a builder, and both designed and built many of the principal churches and other edifices of the large towns of New Hampshire and Vermont He was also prominent in local affairs, and in addition to his own distinguished descent was connected by marriage with families of prominence.

Mr. Alfred Cornelius Howland is the younger son of Aaron Prentiss and Huldah (Burke) Howland, his birth having taken place in 1838 at Walpole, N. H. His artistic talent was displayed at an early age, and after preliminary study in this country, he became a pupil at the Academy of Dusseldorf, Germany, under Professor Andreas Müller, and afterwards in the private studio of Professor Flamm, followed by a course of several years under the celebrated artist, Emil Lambinet, at Paris. He first exhibited in the Academy of Design in 1865, and was elected an Associate of the National Academy in 1876, and a member of that body in 1882. Mr. Howland is also a member of the Century and Salmagundi clubs, and of the Artist Fund Society, of the National Academy of Design, and of other leading professional bodies of New York. Many of his pictures are included in the collections of the most noted lovers of art, among whom may be named Governor George Peabody Wetmore, the late George I. Seney, Chauncey M. Depew, the Honorable William M. Evarts, Charles C. Beaman, William H. Fuller and Thomas B. Clarke. His large picture of the historic Yale Fence was presented by Mr. Depew to Yale College, and is now one of the chief features of the new gymnasium. The Fourth of July Parade, belonging to Mr. Fuller, was exhibited at the World's Fair in Chicago. Mr Howland has also exhibited in Paris and Munich. The Layton Art Gallery, at Milwaukee, contains his genre picture, entitled Driving a Bargain

By his marriage, which took place in 1871, Mr. Howland became connected with a New York family of old descent and high position, his bride being Clara Ward, daughter of the late Oliver Delancey Ward, a distinguished merchant of this city, and a descendant of the Delancey family so famous in the early history of the Province of New York, his own name recalling the celebrated Chief Justice Oliver Delancey, in many respects the most eminent man in the entire Colonial history of the Province of New York Andrew Ward, the founder of Mrs Howland's family in America, belonged to an ancient race settled at Goilston and Homesfield, Suffolk, England, and was descended from William de la Ward, who flourished in 1154-89. He came to Massachusetts in 1630, accompanied the first settlers to Connecticut, was elected a magistrate in 1636, and became a resident of Fairfield in 1649.

His grandson, Edmund Ward, removed to Eastchester, N. Y., and was a member of the Colonial Assembly in the early part of the eighteenth century. Mrs. Howland's grandfather, named like her father, Oliver Delancey Ward, owned Ward's Island, in the East River, where he had his summer residence until the island was purchased by the city. The Ward homestead still defies age and weather, and is used as the residence of the chaplain of the island, which forms part of the municipal charities On the side of her mother, Emily Potter Ward, Mrs. Howland is also a descendant of Edward Winslow, who came to Plymouth in the Mayflower, and among her other collateral ancestors were Governor John Winthrop and John Hancock. Mr. and Mrs Alfred C. Howland's children are Winthrop Prentiss Howland, born in 1873, and Alice Ward Howland, born 1878. Mr. Howland's studio is at 318 West Fifty-seventh Street, New York, and he also has one in his summer house, The Rooftree, at Williamstown, Mass., where he passes a considerable portion of each year.

GARDINER GREENE HOWLAND

THE first American ancestor of the Howland family was the celebrated Puritan leader, John Howland, who came from England on the Mayflower and settled in Plymouth. He was early a freeman of Plymouth, an assessor in 1633, and a selectman in 1666 For six years, between 1652 and 1666, he was a deputy to the General Court, and was also a member of the Governor's Council His wife was Elizabeth Tilley. He died in 1673. Joseph Howland, son of the pioneer, was also a man of importance in Plymouth, where he was Lieutenant of the militia in 1679. His wife was Elizabeth'Southworth, daughter of Thomas and Elizabeth (Reynor) Southworth. In the two following generations the ancestors of that branch of the family which is here under consideration were Nathaniel Howland and his son Nathaniel. The elder Nathaniel, 1671-1746, had for his first wife Martha Cole, daughter of James Cole, and for his second wife Abigail Churchill, daughter of Eleazer and Mary Churchill. The second Nathaniel was the son of the first wife, and was born in Plymouth in 1705 and died in 1766. His second wife, whom he married in 1739, and who was the mother of Joseph Howland, next in the line of descent, was Abigail Burt, daughter of the Reverend John Burt, who was killed at Bristol, R I, by the British in 1775

Joseph Howland, the grandfather of Mr. Gardiner Greene Howland, was born in Boston in 1749, became one of the great merchants in the West India trade and died in 1836. Settling in Norwich, Conn , he engaged in business and, about the beginning of the century, removed to New York, the firm of Joseph Howland & Son becoming one of the largest shipowners of that time. In 1808-31 he was president of the Highland Turnpike Company, afterwards merged in the Hudson River Railroad Company. His wife was Lydia Bill, daughter of Ephraim Bill, of Norwich, Conn.

Gardiner Greene Howland, the father of Mr. Gardiner Greene Howland, was one of the great merchants of New York in the last generation. He was born in 1787 and soon after he had become of age, was intrusted with the management of many of his father's business affairs. Afterwards, with a younger brother as a partner, the firm of G. G. & S Howland became one of the most successful importing houses in New York in the first quarter of the present century. He was a director of the Old Bank of New York and was connected with insurance and other financial institutions. One of the greatest enterprises of his life was the construction of the Hudson River Railroad, in which company he was for a long time a director. Mr. Howland was twice married, first to Louisa Edgar, daughter of William Edgar, and second to Louisa Meredith, daughter of Jonathan Meredith, of Baltimore By his first wife he had five children, William Edgar, Annabella Edgar, Abbie Woolsey, Robert Shaw and Maria Louisa Howland. By his second wife he had six children, Rebecca Brien, who married James Roosevelt; Meredith, who married Adelaide Torrence; Gardiner Greene, Joanna Dorr, who! married Irving Grinnell, Emma Meredith, and Samuel Shaw Howland.

Mr. Gardiner Greene Howland, the second son of his father's second wife, was born in New York in 1834. For many years he has been the general manager of The New York Herald. His wife, whom he married in 1856 and who died in 1897, was Mary Grafton Dulany, and he has four children, Gardiner Greene, Jr , Dulany, Meredith and Maud Howland, who married, in 1889, Percy R. Pyne, son of Percy R. Pyne and Albertina Taylor. The city residence of the family is in East Thirty-fifth Street, and they also have a home in the old Bennett mansion, on Washington Heights. Mr. Howland is a member of the Metropolitan, Union, Lawyers', Racquet and New York Yacht clubs.

Samuel Shaw Howland, the youngest son, was born in New York, August 28th, 1849. He married Frederika Belmont, daughter of August Belmont, Sr. The city residence of Mr. and Mrs. Howland is in West Eighteenth Street. Their country home is Belwood, Mt Morris, N. Y., and they also spend much time in Washington, D. C , where Mr. Howland has important professional and social connections Mr Howland is a member of the Metropolitan and Union clubs of New York, the Philadelphia Club of Philadelphia and the Metropolitan Club of Washington.

HENRY ELIAS HOWLAND

A MONG the Pilgrims on the Mayflower who signed the compact that served as a constitution for the first political community in North America, was John Howland, who became the ancestor of a family of worth and substantial qualities. He shared the rigors of the landing and first winter of the Plymouth settlement, was a leader of the Colony's military and exploring expeditions and furnished a touch of romance to its history, since his marriage was one of the first the Pilgrims celebrated in their New England home, his wife being Elizabeth Tilley, who had also been a passenger on the Mayflower. He lived to a ripe old age and was the last survivor of the entire number of those who came over to the New World on that remarkable voyage. John and Elizabeth Howland, the Pilgrim couple, had a large family, and their descendants, both of the same name and through females, are numerous. One of their great-grandchildren was the Reverend John Howland, who graduated at Harvard College in 1741 and became a distinguished preacher. For nearly sixty years he occupied the pulpit of the Congregational Church in the town of Carver, Mass. Branches of the family were established in New Hampshire and New York at an early date, and the old-time merchants of this city, G. G. Howland and Samuel S. Howland, derived their descent from the same source.

Judge Henry E. Howland comes of the New Hampshire branch of this notable family. His father, Aaron Prentiss Howland, was a direct descendant in the sixth generation from John Howland, the Pilgrim of the Mayflower, and was a grandson of the Reverend John Howland above referred to. His mother, whose maiden name was Huldah Burke, came also of a distinguished family of that section of the country. She was a near relative of the eminent New Hampshire politician and Congressman, Edmund Burke, who, among other offices, was Commissioner of Patents under the administrations of Presidents Pierce and Buchanan.

Mr. Henry E. Howland, the elder son of this marriage, having been born at Walpole, N H., in 1835, was educated at the Kimball Union Academy in Meriden, N. H., entered Yale College and was graduated in the class of 1854. He then took a course in the Harvard College Law School and in 1857 received the degree of LL B. He was admitted to practice in 1857 and made New York his home, and has since then practiced here, except for a period in 1873, when Governor John A Dix appointed him to the bench of the Marine Court to fill an unexpired term. He served in the Twenty-Second Regiment of the National Guard of the State for seven years, and he was a Captain in that command while it was mustered in the United States service in 1862 and 1863. Judge Howland has been active in the Republican party and was an alderman of the city in 1875 and 1876. In 1880, he was appointed by Mayor Cooper, president of the Municipal Department of Taxes. In 1884, he was his party's candidate for Judge of the Court of Common Pleas, and received a similar nomination in 1887 for the bench of the Supreme Court. Judge Howland has been for some years a member of the Corporation of Yale University. He is president of the Society for the Relief of the Destitute Blind, and also president of the Board of the Manhattan State Hospital of this city.

In 1865, he married Louise Miller, daughter of Jonathan and Sarah R. Miller, and granddaughter of Edmund Blunt, the famous mathematician and author of Blunt's Coast Pilot. Six children were born to them, Mary M, Charles P, Katharine E., John, Julia Bryant and Frances L., of whom three survive, none, however, are married.

As a speaker, either in court, at political meetings, or on social occasions, Judge Howland has a widespread reputation. He is governor-general of the National Society of Mayflower Descendants and governor of the New York Society, president of the Jekyl Island Club, secretary of the Century Association, president of the Meadow Club of Southampton, and one of the council of the University Club. His other club affiliations include membership in the Metropolitan, Union League, Players, Republican and Shinnecock Hills Golf clubs, as well as the Bar Association. His city residence is 14 West Ninth Street, and his country home is at Southampton, Long Island.

ALFRED MILLER HOYT

REPRESENTATIVES of the Old New England family of Hoyt have been prominent in New York for the last four generations All of them have come from the same parent stock, though their lines of descent in most instances separated several generations ago. The subject of this sketch is descended from the first Simon Hoyte, who came to Massachusetts from England in 1628 and afterwards was one of the first settlers in Connecticut, being a resident of Windsor, Fairfield, Stamford and other towns His son, Walter Hoyt, the ancestor of the branch of the family now under consideration, was one of the first settlers of Norwalk, a selectman of the town, deputy to the General Court, and Sergeant of the militia. The line of descent thence is through Deacon Zerubbabel Hoyt, 1650–1727 ; Joseph Hoyt, 1676-1708; and James Hoyt, 1708-1774, who married Hannah Goold

Colonel Jesse Hoyt, the son of James Hoyt and his wife, Hannah, was the grandfather of Mr. Alfred M. Hoyt He was born in Norwalk, Conn, in 1744 and lived in Norwalk, Oyster Bay and Huntington, Long Island, and Weymouth and Annapolis, Nova Scotia, dying in Annapolis in 1822 He was a prosperous landowner and Colonel of the militia. In 1764, he married Mary Raymond. James Moody Hoyt, the son of Colonel Jesse Hoyt, was born in Weymouth, Nova Scotia, in 1789 When about seventeen years of age, he came to New York, where he was engaged in business During the latter part of his life, he made his home in Norwalk, Conn, and there his death occurred in 1854. In 1814, he married Mary Nesbitt, daughter of Dr Samuel Nesbitt, a native of Scotland She survived him until 1867

Mr. Alfred M. Hoyt, their son, was born in New York in 1828. He was educated at private schools, entered college and graduated with honors, and afterwards studied law In 1854, he became a member of the firm of Jesse Hoyt & Co, in partnership with his brothers, Jesse and Samuel N. Hoyt, and Henry W Smith, the firm succeeding to the business interests of his father. Samuel N Hoyt soon retired from business, but Mr. Alfred M Hoyt and his brother Jesse continued together until 1881. The two brothers were largely interested in the development of the great Northwest, where they owned extensive tracts of timber land Mr Hoyt was also interested in grain elevators in Chicago, Milwaukee and other cities of the Northwest, as well as in several railroads and other important properties In conjunction with his brothers and other associates, he was one of the builders and owners of the Flint & Pere Marquette Railroad, the Winona & St Peter Railroad, now part of the Chicago & Northwestern system, and the Milwaukee & Northern Railroad, of which he was the president. Of late years he has been engaged in banking

In 1858, Mr. Hoyt married Rose E Reese. The city residence of the family is in upper Fifth Avenue, and their summer home is at Montauk, Long Island Mr. and Mrs Hoyt have three sons, Henry R , Alfred William and John Sherman, and three daughters, Florence Cecilia, now Mrs. W. K Otis, Mary E , deceased, and Rosina Sherman Hoyt Mr Hoyt belongs to the Metropolitan, Union League, Grolier and Riding clubs, the Century Association, the American Geographical Society, and is a patron of the Metropolitan Museum of Art, the National Academy of Design and the American Museum of Natural History He is a trustee of the Bank for Savings, a director of the Merchants National Exchange Bank, the Continental Trust Company, and other corporations His eldest son, Henry R Hoyt, graduated from Harvard College in 1882, studied law in Columbia Law School and was a student in the office of Elihu Root. Soon after he was admitted to the bar, he formed a partnership with Ex-Chief Justice Charles P Daly and Alexander T Mason, under the firm name of Daly, Hoyt & Mason. The second son, Alfred William Hoyt, was graduated from Harvard College in 1885 and is engaged in the banking business with his father, he is a member of the Metropolitan, Calumet, Union, Seawanhaka-Corinthian Yacht, University and Harvard clubs and the Century Association Mr. Hoyt's third son, John Sherman Hoyt, was graduated from Columbia College School of Mines, and is a civil engineer.

COLGATE HOYT

IN the first and second American generations, the ancestors of Mr. Colgate Hoyt were Simon Hoyte, who came to Massachusetts in 1628 and settled in Windsor, Conn., in 1639, and his son, Walter Hoyt, 1618-1698, one of the first settlers of Norwalk. John Hoyt, who stands at the head of that branch of the family to which Mr Colgate Hoyt belongs, was a son of Walter Hoyt and was born in Windsor in 1644. He was one of the original settlers of Danbury in 1685, and died in that place in 1711. His wife was Mary Lindall. His son, John Hoyt, 1669-1746, married Hannah Drake, daughter of John Drake, of Simsbury, Conn., and their son, Drake Hoyt, of Danbury, 1717-1805, married Hannah Knapp. In the next generation came Noah Hoyt, 1741-1810, who represented Danbury in the Legislature and was otherwise a leader in town affairs He was three times married; first to Abigail Curtis, then to Sarah Comstock and lastly to Ellen Purdy His son, David P. Hoyt, who was born in 1778 and died in 1828, removed from Danbury to Utica, N Y, and was a successful merchant in the hide and leather business. He was a member of the New York Assembly in 1820 He married Mary Barnum, daughter of Gabriel Barnum, in 1802

James Madison Hoyt, father of Mr. Colgate Hoyt, was the son of David P. Hoyt. He was born in Utica in 1815 and was graduated from Hamilton College in 1834 Studying law, he removed to Cleveland, O., and engaged in practice there for nearly twenty years, after which he became interested in the real estate business. For twenty-six years he was superintendent of the Sunday School of the First Baptist Church in Cleveland, in 1854 was licensed to preach, for many years was president of the Ohio Baptist State Convention and, 1866-70, was president of the American Baptist Home Missionary Society. His eldest son was the distinguished Reverend Dr. Wayland Hoyt, who was born in Cleveland in 1838, graduated from Brown University in 1860 and was for many years pastor of the Strong Place Church, in Brooklyn

Mr. Colgate Hoyt was born in Cleveland, O., March 2d, 1849 He was educated in the public schools of Cleveland and then was sent to the celebrated Phillips Academy in Andover, Mass., to prepare for college. Ill health compelled him to forego his plans of study, and he returned to Cleveland to enter upon a business career He went into his father's law office and finally into the real estate business, and in 1881 removed to New York, becoming a member of the banking and bullion firm of J. B. Colgate & Co. In 1882, he was appointed by President Arthur one of the Government directors of the Union Pacific Railroad Company, and during his entire term of service was chairman of the board. He became a trustee of the Wisconsin Central Railroad in 1884, his co-trustees being Charles L Colby and Edwin H. Abbott, and through their labors that road was rehabilitated and the Chicago & Northern Pacific terminal in Chicago developed. He was also a director of the Union Pacific Railroad.

Mr. Hoyt was a director of the Oregon Railway & Navigation Company, the Northern Pacific Railroad and the Oregon & Transcontinental Company, and in 1890 reorganized the latter company under the name of the North American Company. His master hand was also seen in work for the Northern Pacific Railroad Company, to meet the urgent needs of which he formed the Northwest Equipment Company and raised $3,000,000. In 1889, he was called to undertake the reorganization of the Missouri, Kansas & Texas Railroad, in which work he was associated with Frederic P Olcott, president of the Central Trust Company. He has been connected with many important business enterprises aside from railroads, among them the Spanish-American Iron Company, a corporation that he organized to develop the Lola iron mines in Cuba In 1888, he organized the American Steel Barge Company, that built the first whaleback steamship

In 1873, Mr Hoyt married Lida W. Sherman, daughter of Judge Charles T. Sherman and niece of General W. T. Sherman. He has a family of four children. He is a popular clubman, among his clubs being the Metropolitan, Union League, Lawyers', Riding, Seawanhaka-Corinthian Yacht, and the Ohio Society. He is a trustee of Brown University. He lives in Park Avenue and his country home is Eastover Farm, Oyster Bay, Long Island.

GROSVENOR SILLIMAN HUBBARD

JOHN HUBBARD, the ancestor of the family from which this gentleman descends, came over to the Massachusetts Bay Colony from England and settled in Boston before 1670 He was a soldier in King Philip s War in 1675–6. About 1686 he left Massachusetts and went to Connecticut, being one of the proprietors and founders of New Roxbury, afterwards Pomfret. His son, John Hubbard, 1689–1731, and his grandson, Benjamin, who was born in 1714, lived for a time in Newport, R I, the latter's wife being Susannah Cady His great-grandson, Benjamin, who was born in 1741, lived in Smithfield, R. I, and Pomfret, Conn, and died in 1790. He was Major in the militia and married Chloe Comstock Stephen Hubbard, 1776-1853, the son of Major Benjamin Hubbard and the grandfather of the subject of this sketch, married, in 1803, Zeruiah Grosvenor, daughter of Oliver and Zeruiah (Payson) Grosvenor

The father of Mr Grosvenor Silliman Hubbard is Professor Oliver Payson Hubbard, who was born in Pomfret, Conn, in 1809 After studying at Hamilton College, he graduated from Yale College in 1828, where he acted for a time as assistant to the elder Professor Benjamin Silliman In 1836, he became professor of chemistry, mineralogy and geology at Dartmouth College, where he remained for thirty years. In 1883, he was made Professor Emeritus and still maintains that connection He served two terms as a member of the New Hampshire State Legislature. South Carolina Medical College gave him the degree of M D in 1837, and in 1861 he received the degree of LL D from Hamilton College. In 1844 he was one of the founders and one of the secretaries of the American Association of Geologists and Naturalists, and at different times was recording secretary, vice-president and president of the New York Academy of Sciences, and was connected with various other prominent scientific bodies and associations

The mother of Mr. Grosvenor Silliman Hubbard was Faith Wadsworth Silliman, who was born in New Haven in 1812 and died in New York in 1887 She was the daughter of the elder Professor Benjamin Silliman and his wife, Harriet Trumbull, both Mayflower descendants Through her father she was descended from Judge Ebenezer Silliman, of Connecticut, 1707-75 Judge Silliman graduated at Yale in 1727 and was a deputy and Speaker to the General Assembly, a member of the House of Assistants, and a Major in the militia and Judge of the Superior Court, 1743-66 His son was Gold Selleck Silliman, of Fairfield, Conn, 1732-1790, Yale College, 1752 He was attorney of Fairfield County under the Crown, a Colonel of Cavalry at the outbreak of the Revolution, became Brigadier-General in the Continental Army, and in 1779 was captured by the British, who sent a special body of troops to his home to secure him and held him on parole until he was exchanged for Judge Jones, the well-known Long Island Tory. Professor Benjamin Silliman, his son, 1779-1864, Yale College, 1796, was well called by Edward Everett "the Nestor of American science " For more than sixty years he was connected with Yale College, and also identified with some of the most important scientific investigations and results of the last generation. Professor Silliman's wife, the grandmother of the subject of this sketch, was Harriet Trumbull, daughter of the second Jonathan Trumbull, 1740-1809, and granddaughter of the first Jonathan Trumbull, a graduate of Harvard, and the great Connecticut patriot of the Revolutionary period The second Jonathan Trumbull was a Harvard graduate, an aide-de-camp to General Washington in 1780, and after the war was a member of Congress, Speaker of the House of Representatives, Second Congress, United States Senator in 1795, and Governor of Connecticut from 1798 until the time of his death. His brother was the well-known painter, John Trumbull

Mr Grosvenor Silliman Hubbard was born in Hanover, N H, October 10th, 1842 He was educated at Dartmouth College, Yale, and Columbia College Law Schools, and has practiced his profession in New York for many years He is a member of the Metropolitan, Lawyers', University and New York Yacht clubs, the Bar Association, Dartmouth Alumni Association, New England Society and the Sons of the Revolution His city residence is in West Fifty-fifth Street.

THOMAS H HUBBARD

THE sixteenth Governor of the State of Maine, elected in 1849, and again in 1850, was Dr John Hubbard His ancestors were pioneers of the State of New Hampshire, and those from whom he was immediately descended moved into the Colony of Maine, and helped to establish the village of Redfield His father was a medical practitioner, Dr John Hubbard, and his mother was Olive Wilson The father owned large property and was a man of prominence, serving at one time as a representative in the General Court of Massachusetts when Maine was part of Massachusetts. Dr John Hubbard, Junior, graduated from Dartmouth College in 1816, and was subsequently made an M D by the University of Pennsylvania, and became eminent as a physician and surgeon In 1843, he was elected to the State Senate of Maine, and six years later became Governor of that State He gave much attention to the cause of education, and it was during his administration that the Maine Liquor Law was first enacted. In 1857 and 1858, Dr. Hubbard was a special agent of the United States Treasury Department to inspect Custom Houses. In 1859, President Buchanan appointed him a commissioner, under the reciprocity treaty between the United States and England, to settle the fisheries disputes Dr Hubbard married, in 1825, Sarah H. Barrett, of Dresden, Me., a granddaughter of Oliver Barrett, one of the minute men at Lexington, who was killed at the second battle of Stillwater during the Saratoga campaign of the Revolutionary War

General Thomas H. Hubbard, the son of Dr John and Sarah H. Hubbard, was born in Hallowell, Me , December 20th, 1838, and graduated from Bowdoin College in 1857 Taking up the study of law, he was admitted to practice in the courts of the State of Maine in 1860 The following year, he took a further course of study in the Law School of Albany, N Y , and in May, 1861, was admitted to practice in New York With the opening of the Civil War, Mr Hubbard returned to his native State and joined the Twenty-Fifth Maine Regiment, with the commission of First Lieutenant and Adjutant He served with the regiment during the year for which it had been mustered in, and part of the time was Assistant Adjutant-General of the brigade to which he was attached. When his term of service had expired, he recruited for the Thirtieth Maine Volunteer Infantry, of which he was made Lieutenant-Colonel The regiment took part in the Red River expedition, and was present at the battles of Sabine Cross Roads, Pleasant Hill, Monett's Bluff and other engagements, and was employed in the engineering work of that campaign In 1864, Lieutenant-Colonel Hubbard was commissioned Colonel of his regiment, and his command was transferred to the Army of the Potomac. In Virginia, he took part in the Shenandoah Valley campaign of 1864-65, being at times in command of his brigade He saw further service in 1865 in Georgia, and the same year received the brevet rank of Brigadier-General in recognition of his faithful service and gallantry.

After the termination of his military service, General Hubbard returned to New York City and resumed the practice of law For a short time he was associated with the late Charles A. Rapallo, afterwards a judge of the Court of Appeals. In 1867, he entered the law firm of Barney, Butler & Parsons, which some years later was succeeded by the firm of Butler, Stillman & Hubbard. For many years General Hubbard has been chiefly engaged in railroad management, and is a vice-president of the Southern Pacific Company, president of the Houston & Texas Central and Mexican International Railroad companies and of several corporations allied to the Southern Pacific Company, and is also a director of the Wabash Railroad Company.

In 1868, General Hubbard married Sibyl A Fahnestock, of Harrisburg, Pa. Three children of this marriage survive The family reside at 16 West Fifty-eighth Street. General Hubbard is a member of the Metropolitan, Union League, City, Lawyers', Riding and Republican clubs, the Downtown Association and the New England Society, as well as of the Bar Association and the New York State Bar Association. His other affiliations include membership in the Military Order of the Loyal Legion, the Metropolitan Museum of Art and the American Museum of Natural History.

CHARLES BULKLEY HUBBELL

ACCORDING to well-supported tradition, the Hubbell family is descended from a Danish nobleman, Harold Hubbell, who came to England with King Canute in 1016 and received estates in Northumberland, with the fortress of Haroldstone. He died in 1035; two of his sons fell at the battle of Hastings, and the third, Hugo Hubbell, driven from the North County, settled on the estates of Hunsborg and Horstone, in Rutlandshire. The family lost its estates in the wars of York and Lancaster, and Andrew Hubbell subsequently became a merchant of Plymouth, where he died in 1515. Richard Hubbell, 1627–1699, his descendant, came to New England about 1645. In 1647, he took the oath at New Haven, settled at Guilford, Conn., in 1663, was a freeman of Fairfield in 1669, and a man of substance, his estate being appraised at eight hundred and sixteen pounds. His wife was a daughter of John Meigs, who came to America about 1640 with his father, Vincent Meigs, of Dorsetshire. John Meigs lived in East Guilford, Conn., and was a freeman of that place in 1657.

In the second generation, Mr. Charles Bulkley Hubbell's ancestor, Richard Hubbell, 1654–1738, of Stratfield, held many public offices and married Rebecca Morehouse. The silver communion service now used by the Congregational Church, at Fairfield, Conn., was his gift. His elder brother, John Hubbell, was a Lieutenant in the expedition against the Indians after the Schenectady massacre. The great-great-grandfather of the present Mr. Hubbell was Captain Eleazar Hubbell, 1700-1770, of Stratfield and New Fairfield, his wife, Abigail Burr, being of the same family as Aaron Burr. Next in line of descent were Eleazar Hubbell, 1749–1810, of Jericho, Vt., and his wife, Anna Noble. The family was engaged in the West India trade and Eleazer Hubbell and his brother during the Revolution captured a British brig off the town of Newfield, using one of their own vessels. The present Mr. Hubbell's grandparents were Major Lyman Hubbell, 1768–1859, of Williamstown, Mass., and his wife, Louisa Rossiter, daughter of Nathan and Hannah (Tuttle) Rossiter.

Dr. Charles Lyman Hubbell, 1827-1890, son of Lyman and Louisa (Rossiter) Hubbell, was a well-known physician of Troy, N. Y. In 1852, he married Julia E. Bulkley, daughter of Gershom Taintor Bulkley, of Williamstown, Mass. The Bulkley family descends from the Reverend Peter Bulkley, a graduate of St. John's College, Cambridge, the first minister of Concord, Mass., who contributed one-sixth of the volumes that comprised the original library of Harvard College. Gershom Bulkley graduated in one of the first classes at Harvard, married the daughter of Charles Chauncy, its second president, and gave to the college the ground on which Gore Hall now stands. He was the first Surgeon-General of Connecticut.

Mr. Charles Bulkley Hubbell, the eldest son of Dr. Charles Lyman Hubbell, was born in Williamstown, Mass., July 20th, 1853. He was educated at Williams College, from which institution he was graduated in the class of 1874. At college he was a noted athlete, being a member of the University crew, and was the first student of Williams College to win honors in intercollegiate athletic sports. After completing a course of study at law, he was admitted to practice, and has since been an active and prominent member of the bar in New York. His wife, Emily Allen Chandler, was a daughter of the Honorable William A. Chandler, of Connecticut, and is a direct descendant of Gurdon Saltonstall, an early Governor of Connecticut. Mr Hubbell's marriage took place in 1879. Their family consists of three daughters. The country home of the family is at Brookside Farm, Williamstown, Mass., a place that was owned by Captain Absalom Blair, one of Mr. Hubbell's ancestors, in 1764.

Mr. Hubbell has long taken a great interest in educational matters, has been for several years a member of the Board of Education of New York and is now its president. He has served as a trustee of Williams College, and is at present the president of its Alumni Association in New York. He is a member of the New England Society, the Bar Association, the Sons of the Revolution, the Society of Colonial Wars and the University Club.

298

CHARLES I. HUDSON

A LTHOUGH one of the successful men of affairs in New York of the present day, Mr. Hudson's immediate ancestry was identified with the learned professions and the world of letters His paternal grandfather was a clergyman in Bradford, England, and his father, Isaac N. Hudson, who was born in England and came to this country in 1830, entered the ranks of American journalism, becoming one of the best known newspaper writers and managers of the period preceding the Civil War. He was connected with leading papers in various parts of the country, including California, whither he went soon after the gold discoveries and the great development of the Pacific Coast. His wife, to whom he was married in 1851, was a New York lady of established family, Cornelia A. Bogert Haight, daughter of John Edward Haight, a well-known New York merchant of that period.

Mr. Charles I. Hudson was their eldest son, and was born in this city August 20th, 1852. He received his early education at schools in this city, but, determining to follow a business career, he went into Wall Street while still a mere lad and began his active life as a junior employee of S. M. Mills & Co., at that time one of the most prominent brokerage houses in the city. The period at which Mr. Hudson thus made his début was one of more active and excited speculation than the country had ever seen before or since. The years succeeding the Civil War produced also some of the largest speculators that ever appeared in Wall Street, and the record of those days is one of gigantic operations, which attracted the attention of the entire country. Mr. Hudson from the outset manifested an aptitude for the profession he had chosen, and not only was his advancement rapid, but he made the acquaintance and secured the friendship of a number of the most prominent financiers and speculative operators. Having also been prudent and successful in his personal affairs, he purchased a seat in the New York Stock Exchange in 1874 and entered the brokerage business on his own account. In 1876, Mr. Hudson established the firm of C. I. Hudson & Co ; his partner at the outset being Henry N. Smith, a gentleman of great prominence in Wall Street, and who at one time was the partner of the famous Jay Gould. While Mr. Hudson has been its head throughout, the composition of the partnership has undergone several changes, but the same style has been retained. The present partners are Mr. Hudson and A. H. DeForrest, also a member of the Exchange.

Mr. Hudson has taken an active place not only in banking and brokerage fields, but in the management of the Stock Exchange. As a candidate on an independent ticket, he was in 1891 chosen one of the governors of that institution for a term of four years and was again elected in 1896. He is noted for his original and far-sighted ideas in business, an instance of which is afforded by the part he took in introducing the securities of large industrial corporations upon the Stock Exchange and making them features of the Wall Street market. Appreciating the possibilities such organizations held forth to the members of the Exchange as vehicles for investment and speculation, he was personally instrumental in having the shares of some of the first companies of this kind admitted to regular quotation and made such securities a specialty with his firm, which for this reason, as well as for the generally wise policy of its head, acquired an enormous business.

Outside of Wall Street, Mr. Hudson has few interests. In 1888, he was an organizer of the Fourteenth Street Bank and one of its directors for some years. His clubs include the Manhattan, Colonial, Democratic, New York Athletic, Riding, Larchmont Yacht and American Jersey Cattle clubs. His country home is The Ledges, a handsome place among the Thousand Islands of the St. Lawrence, and he was one of the organizers and a director of the Thousand Island Club and is a member of the St Lawrence River Association.

In 1876, Mr. Hudson married Sarah E Kierstede, of Scranton, Pa., a lady descended from New York Dutch families, the famous Anneke Jans being among her ancestors. Mr. and Mrs. Hudson have four children, Percy Kierstede, Hendrick, Hans Kierstede and Charles Alan Hudson.

GEORGE HUNTINGTON HULL

IN the early records of the New England Colonies appeared the names of the five brothers of the Hull family, John, George, Richard, Joseph and Robert, natives of Derbyshire, England, who, with their descendants, early attained prominence in the Colonies   Richard Hull, who resided in Dorchester, Mass., in 1634, was the founder of that branch of the family to which the subject of this sketch belongs.   Moving to New Haven, in 1639, he became a representative to the General Court of Connecticut, and died in 1662.   Dr. John Hull, his son, was born in New Haven in 1640.   He resided in Stratford, 1661-68, was one of the original twelve settlers of Pawgassett, now Derby, and afterwards resided in Wallingford, where he died.   He was a selectman, 1677-80-83-87, a member of the General Assembly, and received a grant of seven hundred acres of land in Wallingford for his services as surgeon in King Philip's War.   Dr Benjamin Hull, his son, 1672-1771, was a prominent physician in Wallingford.   His son, Dr John Hull, was born in Wallingford in 1702 and married Sarah Ives in 1727   Dr Zephaniah Hull, their son, 1728-1760, married Hannah Doolittle in 1749.   He practiced medicine in Bethlehem, where he attained to a great influence.   Dr Titus Hull, their son, was born at Bethlehem in 1751.   He married, second, Olive (Lewis) Parmelee in 1778.   He was a surgeon in the War of the Revolution and moved to New York State in 1807   The Reverend Leverett Hull, son of the last named, was born in Bethlehem, Conn., in 1796, graduated from Hamilton College in 1824, and from Auburn Theological Seminary.   He spent his life in the ministry in New York State and in Ohio, whither he moved in 1844, dying there in 1852.   He married, in 1830, for his second wife, Sarah Lord, of Rome, N Y.

Mr. George Huntington Hull, son of the Reverend Leverett Hull and Sarah Lord, was born in Dansville, N Y , in 1840, and was taken to Ohio with his parents in 1844   He was educated in Oakfield and Alexandria, N. Y., and then went into mercantile life in Cincinnati.   At the beginning of the Civil War, he was a member of the Cincinnati Zouaves, the first company to leave for the war on President Lincoln's call for troops, and afterwards was in the United States Quartermaster's office in Cincinnati.   Returning to civil life, he joined a mercantile firm in Cincinnati.   In 1871, he established an iron business in Louisville, Ky , and in 1890, removing to New York, founded the American Pig Iron Storage Warrant Company, and has since been its president.

In 1877, Mr. Hull married Lucia Eugene Houston, of Louisville, Ky , daughter of Judge Russell and Grizelda (Polk) Houston.   On both sides, Mrs. Hull is descended from families of importance in the Southern States.   On the paternal side, her grandparents were David and Hannah (Regan) Houston.   Her maternal grandfather, Dr. William Julius Polk, whose wife was Mary L Long, belonged to a race which sprang from noble ancestors in Europe and has been of prominence in the United States.   The name of Polk, originally spelt Pollock, is traced to Fulbert, the Saxon, *Tempore* Malcom III , of Scotland, who held the great feudal barony of Pollok in Renfrewshire.   From him came a long line of Barons de Pollok   A branch of this family was established in the North of Ireland, by Sir Robert de Pollok, one of whose descendants, Robert Bruce Pollok, with his wife, Magdalen Tasker, and six sons and two daughters, came to Somerset County, Md., about 1680.   John Pollock, or Polk, son of Robert Pollok, married Joanna Knox, and their son, William Polk, removed to North Carolina and married, first, Priscilla Roberts.   One of William Polk's sons, Ezekiel Polk, was the grandfather of James Knox Polk, President of the United States.   Mrs. Hull's ancestor was another son of William Polk.   General Thomas Polk, who was prominent in the Mecklenburg Declaration, was with Washington at Brandywine and Valley Forge, and married Susan Spratt.   Colonel William Polk, his son, was also in the Revolutionary Army and married, first, Grizelda Gilchrist, by whom he was the father of Dr. William Julius Polk, who was Mrs. Hull's grandfather.

Mr and Mrs Hull make their residence in Tuxedo Park.   He is a member of the Union League, Lawyers' and Tuxedo clubs, the Sons of the Revolution, the Sons of the American Revolution, the Society of Colonial Wars and is a patron of the Metropolitan Museum of Art

RICHARD HOWLAND HUNT

ANCESTORS of this gentleman figured prominently in the public affairs of the country, while his immediate family have been identified with the contemporary development of art in the United States. Mr Hunt s father was one of the foremost architects of America, and his uncle had a leading place among distinguished American painters John Hunt, the founder of this interesting American family, came from England and settled in Connecticut, where he married a daughter of John Webster, the fifth Governor of that Colony. His son, Jonathan Hunt, from whom the branch of the family to which this refers is descended, was born in 1637, and moved from Connecticut to Northampton, Mass , in 1670 He was a freeman in 1662, a deacon of the church and a representative to the General Court. The son of Jonathan Hunt and his wife, Clemence (Hosmer) Hunt, was Jonathan Hunt, of Northampton, 1665-1738, who married Martha Williams, daughter of Samuel and Theoda (Park) Williams, and his grandson was Samuel Hunt, 1703-1770, who married Ann Ellsworth, daughter of John and Esther Ellsworth, of Windsor, Conn.

In the third generation after Jonathan Hunt, of Northampton, came the Honorable Jonathan Hunt, of Vermont, the great-grandfather of Mr. Richard Howland Hunt Jonathan Hunt was born in 1738, and early in life removed to Vermont, where he became prominent in public affairs. In 1780, he was a member of a committee appointed to consider plans for the union of New York and Vermont, was one of the claimants to lands in Vermont which had been ceded to New York, was sheriff of Windham County, an associate censor in 1786 to revise the State Constitution, and afterwards Lieutenant-Governor, dying in 1823. Jonathan Hunt, son of Lieutenant-Governor Hunt, was born in 1787. He graduated from Dartmouth College in 1807, became a prominent lawyer, was a representative to the State Legislature at an early age and a Member of Congress, 1827-32, dying at Washington during his term of office. His wife was Jane Marie Leavitt Their sons were Richard M. Hunt, the architect, and William M. Hunt, the painter

Richard Morris Hunt, father of Mr. Richard Howland Hunt, was born at Brattleboro, Vt , in 1828, and died in Newport, R. I , in 1895 Graduating from the Boston High School in 1843, he went to Europe the same year and studied architecture in Geneva, Paris and elsewhere. In 1855, he returned to the United States, where he soon took rank as one of the greatest architects of his generation, attaining an international reputation. Among his many notable works are, the Lenox Library Building, the Presbyterian Hospital, The New York Tribune Building, the William K. Vanderbilt, Ogden Mills, Elbridge T. Gerry, John Jacob Astor and Henry G. Marquand houses in New York; the Cornelius Vanderbilt, Ogden Goelet and O. H. P Belmont residences in Newport; the Vanderbilt place at Biltmore, N C., the Marquand chapel at Princeton College; the Divinity School Building at Yale College, and the Vanderbilt mausoleum on Staten Island.

He received many professional honors from all parts of the world, and a public memorial to him is soon to be erected in Central Park, New York. He was awarded the Queen's Gold Medal by the Royal Institute of British Architects in 1893; in 1894, was elected an associate member of the Academie des Beaux Arts; was an honorary member of the Central Society of French Architects, the Architects' Society of Vienna, the Royal Institute of British Architects, the Academy of St Luke in Rome, and received the Cross of the Legion of Honor, of France. His wife, Catharine Howland, survives her distinguished husband and resides at 178 Madison Avenue.

Mr. Richard Howland Hunt is their son, and was born at Paris, France, in 1862. He was educated at the Institute of Technology, and, finishing his studies at the École des Beaux Arts at Paris, with a view to following his father's profession, has gained individual distinction as an architect. In 1885, Mr. Hunt married Pearl Carley, daughter of Francis D. Carley, of this city, and his wife, who was Grace Chess. Mr. and Mrs Hunt have three children, Richard Carley, Frank Carley and Jonathan Hunt Mr Hunt belongs to the American Institute of Architects and the Architectural League and other professional bodies, and is a member of the Players and Racquet clubs and the Century Association

COLLIS POTTER HUNTINGTON

S TARTING upon the voyage to New England in 1633, Simon Huntington, who was born in Norwich, England, died on the way and was buried at sea His widow, whose maiden name was Margaret Barnet, landed in Boston with her three sons, Christopher, Simon and Samuel, and settled in Roxbury, afterwards removing to Windsor, Conn , where she married again, and with which town some of the Huntington family were long identified Simon Huntington, the second son of this family, was born in England in 1629, and grew to manhood in this country. One of the first settlers of the town of Norwich, he was a deacon of the church, 1660-96, a representative to the General Court in 1674 and 1685, and died there in 1706. By his wife, Sarah Clark, who was the daughter of Joseph Clark, of Windsor, he left a large family.

Simon Huntington was the great-great-great-grandfather of Mr. Collis Potter Huntington. His son, Samuel, who was born in Norwich in 1665, died in 1717. Removing to Lebanon in 1700, he was a large landholder, a Lieutenant of the militia and held many public offices He married, in 1686, Mary Clark, daughter of William Clark, of Wethersfield. Their son, John, who was born in 1706 and married Mehitable Metcalf, was the great-grandfather of Mr. C. P Huntington, whose grandparents were Joseph Huntington, 1739-1820, and Rachel Preston. The father of Mr. Huntington was William Huntington, who was born in 1784, married Elizabeth Vincent and lived in Walcottville, where he was a manufacturer

One of the most distinguished members of this historic family was the Honorable Samuel Huntington, who represented Connecticut in the Continental Congress and signed the Declaration of Independence, being afterwards Chief Justice and Governor of the State The family also furnished many Revolutionary soldiers. Major-General Jabez Huntington, 1719-1786, graduated from Yale College in 1741, was frequently a member of the Legislature, a Speaker of the House and member of the Governor's Council. His son, Ebenezer Huntington, 1754-1834, graduated from Yale College in the class of 1771 and was a Lieutenant-Colonel, Major and Adjutant-General during the War of the Revolution, General of the State Militia in 1792, and a member of the National House of Representatives in 1810 and in 1817

Mr. Collis Potter Huntington illustrates in his career the qualities inherent in the strong New England race of which he is a descendant. In his case, the ability and energy characteristic of the family were directed into the new channels opened by the country's material expansion, his fame resting upon his success in the conception and execution of enterprises that rank among the greatest public works of the century. Mr. Huntington was born in Harwinton, Litchfield County, Conn., October 22d, 1821. After receiving a substantial education, he went into business at an early age, and in 1849 joined the exodus to the Pacific coast, where he established himself in business, becoming one of the most influential merchants of California. In association with Mark Hopkins, Leland Stanford and Charles Crocker, he constructed the Central Pacific Railroad, and has maintained a dominant influence in the subsequent railroad operations which led to the building of the Southern Pacific system, and to the concentration of the great railroad properties of that section of the country under the corporate title of the Southern Pacific Company. He is president of the Southern Pacific Company, and also of the Pacific Mail Steamship Company.

Since 1880, he has made New York his permanent home. His residence, at the corner of Fifth Avenue and Fifty-seventh Street, is distinguished for both its architectural features and the character of its interior decorations He also possesses a summer home at Throgg's Neck, on Long Island Sound, a feature of which is the extensive green-houses Mr Huntington's devotion to his business interests is proverbial and his capacity for work is remarkable His tastes, apart from his absorbing occupations, are entirely domestic, but he is a member of the Union League Club and a patron of the Metropolitan Museum of Art, the American Museum of Natural History and the American Geographical Society. His town residence contains a choice collection of paintings, and he is also a discriminating collector of books.

DANIEL HUNTINGTON

BOTH the paternal and maternal ancestry of Mr. Daniel Huntington is traced back to Simon Huntington, 1629-1706, of Norwich, Conn., one of the three brothers whose father, Simon Huntington, died at sea in 1633 while on the way to New England. In successive generations from the second Simon Huntington, the ancestors of Mr. Daniel Huntington were: Daniel, 1676-1741, and his wife, Rachel Wolcott, Benjamin, 1736-1800, and his wife, Anne Huntington; and Benjamin, 1777-1850, and his wife, Faith Trumbull Huntington, daughter of General Jedediah Huntington. The first Benjamin Huntington graduated from Yale College in 1761. He was a member of the Connecticut Committee of Safety from 1775 to 1778, and of the Continental Congress from 1780 to 1784 and in 1787-88. In 1789, he was a member of the first Congress under the Constitution, a State Senator from 1781 to 1799, Judge of the Connecticut Superior Court from 1793 to 1799, and was also chosen the first Mayor of Norwich, Conn., when it became a city, in 1784 The second Benjamin Huntington was a well-known broker in New York.

Mr. Huntington's mother also traced her ancestry through another line to Simon Huntington She was sixth in descent from Simon Huntington, of Norwich, Conn., her ancestor being Simon Huntington, 1659-1736, a brother of Daniel, the ancestor of her husband. This Simon Huntington married Lydia Gager, daughter of John Gager, whose grandfather came to America in 1630. Their son was Joshua Huntington, 1698-1745, and their grandson, General Jabez Huntington, 1719-1786, was a member of the Connecticut General Assembly, Major-General of the militia and member of the Committee of Safety. His first wife, the grandmother of Faith Trumbull Huntington, was Elizabeth Backus, daughter of Samuel and Elizabeth (Tracy) Backus. Jedediah Huntington, 1743-1818, son of General Huntington, graduated from Harvard College in 1763. He was active in the War of the Revolution, attaining the rank of Brigadier-General and brevet Major-General in the Continental Army He was afterwards Treasurer of Connecticut, delegate to the State Convention which adopted the Federal constitution, and collector of the port of New London His second wife, Ann Moore, daughter of Thomas Moore, of New York, was the mother of Faith Trumbull Huntington. Several sons of Benjamin and Faith Trumbull Huntington became distinguished men. The Reverend Dr. Gurdon Huntington, 1818-1875, was an eminent clergyman of the Protestant Episcopal Church. Another son, the Reverend Jedediah Vincent Huntington, 1815-1862, entered the ministry of the Protestant Episcopal Church in 1841, but afterwards became a Roman Catholic.

Mr. Daniel Huntington, a son of Benjamin Huntington and his wife, Faith Trumbull Huntington, was born in New York, October 14th, 1816. After a course at Hamilton College, in 1835, he began the study of art in the studio of Professor Samuel F. B. Morse, then president of the National Academy of Design. He produced several paintings, which were successful as works of art and decided his future career. In 1839, he went to Europe, resided several years in Rome, perfecting himself in his chosen profession. Upon his return to New York, he made portraits and genre work his specialties, and soon attained a prominent position among American painters. He has painted portraits of many of the most famous American public men of his day, and few of our painters have exhibited greater versatility of talent or broader and purer artistic sympathies. In 1840, Mr. Huntington was elected a member of the National Academy of Design, of which institution he was president from 1862 to 1869, and from 1877 to 1892.

In 1842, Mr. Huntington married Harriet S. Richards, second daughter of Charles and Sarah (Henshaw) Richards. Mrs Huntington's direct ancestors were Lieutenant John Richards, 1666, and Captain Guy Richards, 1722, of New London, while she also descends through maternal lines from Elder William Brewster and John Alden, of the Mayflower. Mr. and Mrs Huntington had one son, Charles Richards Huntington, of this city, who married Mary Irving, daughter of Edgar Irving. Mr. Huntington lives in East Twentieth Street He is a member of the Century Association, the A Δ Φ club, and the American Geographical Society, and is a trustee of the Metropolitan Museum of Art.

WILLIAM REED HUNTINGTON, D. D.

GRACE CHURCH is distinctly the parish of the older New York families, and is, therefore, one of the most important charges of the Episcopal Church, not only in New York, but in the whole country For more than fourteen years it has been under the charge of Dr Huntington, who, though now completely identified with New York, is a New Englander by birth and early associations, and is a descendant of a race that holds a high place in the annals of Massachusetts and Connecticut, and which has furnished many members of prominence in various walks of modern American life The ancestors of this remarkable family were among the early Puritan emigrants to Massachusetts, but left the Bay Colony with the first settlers of Connecticut, since which time the latter Colony and Commonwealth has never been without distinguished representatives of the name

William Reed Huntington, D D , who was born at Lowell, Mass., in 1838, is the son of Elisha Huntington, M D , and his wife, Hannah Hinckley, the latter being a daughter of Joseph and Deborah Hinckley, of Marblehead The Huntington family in New England springs from Christopher and Simon Huntington, two brothers who arrived in Boston in 1633, and whose father, Simon, died during the voyage from England to the New World The two took part in the founding of the town of Norwich, Conn , in 1660 The brothers had numerous descendants in both Connecticut and Massachusetts, some of whom took active parts in the Colonial struggles with the French and their savage allies, as well as in the Revolutionary War, while among them were numbered many ministers of the gospel, Dr. Huntington himself being the grandson of the Reverend Ashahel Huntington, of Topsfield, Mass., who married Alethea Lord, of Abington, Conn Their son, Elisha Huntington, was born in Topsfield in 1796, graduated at Dartmouth College in 1815, and at the Medical School of Yale in 1825 He established himself at Lowell, of which city he was Mayor for eight terms, and in 1855 was elected Lieutenant-Governor of the Commonwealth of Massachusetts A leader in the medical profession, he served as president of the Massachusetts Medical Society, and delivered many addresses before it and other bodies, while, as already noted, he took an active part in political life

His son, Dr William Reed Huntington, passed his youth in Lowell, and entered Harvard College, from which he was graduated in 1859 He was the poet of his class, and in 1870 was again honored by his alma mater as the Φ B K poet for that year The degree of Doctor of Divinity was conferred on him in 1873 by Columbia College, and by Princeton University at its sesqui-centennial in 1896 He has also been given the degree of D C L by the University of the South He entered the Protestant Episcopal ministry in 1861, was at first attached to Emmanuel Church, Boston, and became the rector of All Saints, Worcester, in 1862 From this post he was called to Grace Church, New York, in 1883 To describe Dr Huntington's labors in this distinguished but trying charge would be but to rehearse the progress of the church during the past fourteen years Possessing not only lofty and convincing eloquence as a pulpit orator, Dr Huntington has exercised a marked personal influence among both clergy and laity His literary activity has been considerable, his published writings including, among other books, The Church Idea, Conditional Immortality, Causes of the Soul, The Peace of the Church, and A Short History of the Book of Common Prayer, and many papers on ecclesiastical and literary subjects

In 1863, Dr Huntington married Theresa, youngest daughter of Dr Edward Reynolds, of Boston, a granddaughter of John Phillips, the first Mayor of Boston, and niece of the orator and philanthropist, Wendell Phillips The children of this marriage are Francis Cleaveland Huntington, a lawyer of this city, and three daughters, Margaret Wendell, Theresa, wife of Royal Robbins, of Boston, and Mary Hinckley, wife of William G Thompson, a lawyer of Boston Dr Huntington is a member of the Century, University and Harvard clubs, and resides with his family in the beautiful rectory of Grace Church, now the only dwelling left in Broadway south of Union Square

AUGUSTUS S. HUTCHINS

NEARLY half a century has elapsed since the family name which this gentleman bears became prominent in law and politics in New York. Both his paternal and maternal ancestry is derived from illustrious and patriotic Connecticut families. His father, Waldo Hutchins, was born in Brooklyn, Conn., in 1823, and was descended from the Puritan founders of that commonwealth. Graduated from Amherst College, he was admitted to the bar and beginning the practice of his profession in New York, was thereafter identified with this city. Becoming an active supporter of the Democratic party, Mr. Hutchins was a member of the State Assembly in 1852, and in 1867 was elected to the Constitutional Convention. In 1878, he was chosen a Member of Congress from the Westchester County District, his residence being in Kingsbridge, and was reëlected for two succeeding terms. For many years he was a Park Commissioner, and in many ways active in municipal councils.

The maternal grandfather of Mr. Augustus S. Hutchins was Governor William Walcott Ellsworth, of Connecticut. Governor Ellsworth was born in Windsor, Conn., in 1791, and died in Hartford, in 1868. Graduated from Yale College in 1810, he studied law in Litchfield and Hartford and was admitted to the bar in 1813, beginning practice in Hartford. In the same year, he married Emily Webster, eldest daughter of Noah Webster, the great lexicographer, who was descended from John Webster, one of the founders of Hartford and an early Governor of Connecticut ; and on his mother's side from William Bradford, the second Governor of the Plymouth Colony. While a student in Yale College, Noah Webster volunteered and served in the Continental Army in the Saratoga Campaign. In 1817, William Walcott Ellsworth became a partner with his brother-in-law, Judge Williams, and from 1827 until the time of his death, a period of forty-one years, was a professor of law in Trinity College. From 1829 to 1834, he was a Whig Member of Congress. In 1838, he was chosen Governor of Connecticut and was reëlected for three successive terms. In 1847, he became Judge of the Superior Court of Connecticut, and remained on the bench until he was seventy years of age. His twin brother, Henry L. Ellsworth, was Commissioner of Patents from 1836 to 1848

The great-grandfather of Mr. Hutchins was Chief Justice Oliver Ellsworth, 1745-1807, who studied in Yale College, but was graduated from Princeton in 1766 He was admitted to the bar in Hartford, in 1771, and was State's Attorney in 1775, being in the following year a representative from Windsor, in the General Assembly. He was a delegate to the Continental Congress in 1777, a member of the Governor's Council 1780-84, Judge of the Connecticut Superior Court 1784-87, and in 1787 a member of the Federal Convention at Philadelphia He was one of the Senators for Connecticut in the first United States Congress, and a devoted supporter of Washington's administration. In 1796, he was appointed, by Washington, Chief Justice of the United States Supreme Court, and in 1799 went abroad as one of the Envoys Extraordinary of the United States to negotiate a treaty with France. Upon his return from Europe in 1800, he resigned from the bench, but in 1807 was appointed Chief Justice of Connecticut.

Mr. Augustus S. Hutchins is the eldest son of Waldo Hutchins, and was born in New York in 1856. Educated in Amherst College, he was graduated from that institution in the class of 1879 and supplemented his collegiate course by a study of law, after which he entered upon the practice of his profession in New York. The Hutchins family having a very large interest in the Second Avenue Railroad Company, Mr. Hutchins has for many years been the counsel for that company, has been the legal representative of other corporations, and is also vice-president of the Metropolitan Savings Bank. He is unmarried and resides in the old family homestead in Kingsbridge. He is a member of the Manhattan Club, the Bar Association and the New England Society His brother, Waldo J. Hutchins, is a graduate from Yale College, and a lawyer ; another brother, William E Hutchins, was formerly president of the North River Fire Insurance Company.

EDWIN FRANCIS HYDE

NORWICH, Conn, was settled in 1660, by a company of proprietors, principally from Saybrook and New London, and included the founders of several families of distinction. Among them was William Hyde, the ancestor of the Hyde family, who came to America with the Reverend Thomas Hooker, and lived successively in Newton, Mass, Hartford, Saybrook and Norwich, where he died, in 1681 His daughter, Hester, and her husband, John Post, accompanied him to Norwich, as well as his son, Samuel, who was born at Hartford, in 1637, and died in 1677 Samuel's son, John Hyde, of Norwich, 1667-1727, married his second cousin, Experience Abel, daughter of Caleb Abel, and their son, Captain James Hyde, 1707-1793, also married a cousin, Sarah Marshall, daughter of Abijah and Abial (Cuff) Marshall.

Captain James Hyde, of Norwich, 1752-1809, the son of the first James Hyde, was an officer in the Continental Army, throughout the Revolutionary War. In civil life, he was a man of considerable prominence and attained more than local distinction His wife, whom he married in 1774, was Martha Nevins Lathrop, who was born in Norwich, in 1756, her father and mother, Nevins and Mary Lathrop, being prominent residents of that place in the early part of the eighteenth century Her grandfather, Lieutenant-Colonel Simon Lathrop, commanded a Connecticut regiment at the siege of Louisburg, and was in charge of that fortress after its capture Their son, the grandfather of Mr Edwin Francis Hyde, was Erastus Hyde, who was born in Norwich, in 1775. He lived in Norwich until after he had arrived at full age, and then, soon after 1800, removed to Middlebury, Vt Subsequently, he lived at Mystic and Groton, Conn His wife, whom he married in 1797, was Fanny Bell, born in 1775, the daughter of Captain Joseph Bell, of Stonington, Conn Edwin Hyde, son of Erastus Hyde, was born at Groton, Conn, in 1812 Early in life he came to New York and entered upon business life, becoming in time one of the most prosperous merchants of the city. His wife was Elizabeth Alvina Mead, whom he married in 1833 She was born in Belleville, N J, and was the daughter of Ralph Mead, a prominent merchant of New York The firm of Ralph Mead & Co was one of the most substantial of its kind in the city ; in its successive forms it occupied the same location in Coenties Slip for over seventy years

Edwin Hyde and his wife, Elizabeth Alvina, had a family of nine sons. Augustus Lord Hyde, the eldest, was born in 1835 , the second son, Ralph Mead Hyde, was born in 1837, and died in 1839 , the third, also named Ralph Mead, was born in 1839 , Edwin Francis Hyde was born in 1842 , Frederick Erastus Hyde was born in 1844 , Clarence Melville Hyde was born in 1846 , Edmund Janes Hyde was born in 1848, and died in 1849 , Herbert Mortimer Hyde was born in 1850 , and Samuel Mead Hyde was born in 1853 Several of this family have been prominent in New York Augustus L Hyde, the eldest son, married Miss St John, lives in East Eighteenth Street, and has one son and one daughter Ralph Mead Hyde is a member of the New England Society and the Union League Club. Frederick Erastus Hyde is a well-known physician, residing in West Fifty-third Street, and is a member of the Metropolitan Club Clarence Melville Hyde is a graduate of Columbia College, a lawyer and a member of the Metropolitan Club, and married a Miss Babbitt

Mr Edwin Francis Hyde, the third surviving son of this interesting family, has been prominent in financial circles He is now vice-president of the Central Trust Company, of New York He married Marie E. Brown, daughter of Albert N Brown, and lives at 835 Fifth Avenue He is a member of the Bar Association, the Century Association, the Downtown Association, the American Geographical Society, and the New England Society, the Metropolitan, City, Lawyers', Union League, Riding and Presbyterian clubs, and is a patron of the Metropolitan Museum of Art He is interested in the progress of orchestral music, and has been for ten years president of the Philharmonic Society of New York He is a member of many benevolent and scientific societies, and is an elder and trustee of the Fifth Avenue Presbyterian Church.

HENRY BALDWIN HYDE

SEVERAL families bearing the name of Hyde have been settled in this country since the Colonial period, and can trace their origin to undoubted English ancestry. It is not certain, however, that they have all had a common progenitor, at least so far as researches in modern historical times have revealed. Among the first Hydes to come to this country was Samuel Hyde, who was settled in Newtown (Cambridge), Mass., in 1640. About the same time, his brother Jonathan arrived. Humphrey Hyde came to Fairfield, Conn., in 1665. John Hyde immigrated in 1750, and went to Richmond, Va., where many of his descendants have been people of importance. William Hyde, the ancestor of the subject of this sketch, undoubtedly belonged to the same family as Samuel and Jonathan Hyde, who were in Massachusetts in 1640. He came of a worthy English family, and in England was among the followers of the Reverend Thomas Hooker, immigrating to this country as one of the band of Colonists which that eminent divine brought over in 1633. First he settled in Newtown, Mass., where he lived for a few years. But when the Reverend Mr. Hooker organized that famous migration that resulted in the settlement of the Hartford Colony in 1636, William Hyde accompanied him.

In Hartford, William Hyde took up a considerable section of land, and became one of the leading men of the new settlement. He prospered in worldly affairs, and had much to do with the management of the Colony. Upon the monument in the old cemetery of Hartford, Conn., his name appears among those of the original settlers. The land which he owned remained in the possession of his descendants for several generations. When the town of Saybrook was established, he removed to that place, and afterwards was one of the pioneers engaged in the first settlement of the town of Norwich. Samuel Hyde, son of William Hyde, the pioneer, was born in Hartford, about 1637. He removed to Norwich in 1660, where he was engaged in farming, and where he died in 1677. His wife, whom he married in 1659, was Jane Lee, of East Saybrook, daughter of Thomas Lee.

The son of Samuel Hyde and his wife, Jane Lee, was Thomas Hyde, who was born in Norwich in 1673, the fourth son in his father's family, was a farmer, and died in 1755. Mary Backus, his wife, was a daughter of Stephen Backus and Sarah Gardner, who belonged to the first company of settlers in Norwich. In the next generation, Abner Hyde, who was born in Norwich in 1706, the third son of Thomas Hyde, married Jerusha Huntington, daughter of Captain James Huntington and his wife, Priscilla Miller. Jerusha Huntington was a granddaughter of the pioneers, Deacon Simon Huntington and Sarah Clark, of Norwich. Abner Hyde and his wife settled at West Farms, Norwich, Conn., where she died in 1733. His second wife, the ancestress of the subject of this sketch, was Mehitable Smith, second daughter of Captain Obadiah Smith and Martha Abel. The paternal grandfather of Mehitable Smith was Edward Smith, of New London. Her mother was the second daughter of Joshua Abel, one of the first settlers of Norwich.

Asa Hyde, the great-grandfather of Mr. Henry Baldwin Hyde, was born in Norwich in 1742, and died in 1812. His wife was Lucy Rowland. Mr. Hyde's grandfather was Wilkes Hyde, of Catskill, N. Y., where he died in 1856, and his grandmother was Sarah Hazen, daughter of Jacob Hazen, of Franklin, Conn.; his father was Henry Hazen Hyde, born in Catskill, N. Y. in 1805, and his mother was Lucy Baldwin Beach, who was born in 1807, and died in 1846, daughter of the Reverend James Beach and Hannah C. Baldwin, of Winsted, Conn.

Mr. Henry Baldwin Hyde, the second son in his father's family, was born February 5th, 1844. He has been connected with the insurance business during the greater part of his life, and is now president of the Equitable Life Assurance Society. He married Anna Fitch, lives in East Fortieth Street, and has a son, James Hazen Hyde, who is a student in Harvard University. He belongs to the Union, Union League, Lawyers', South Side Sportsmen's, Riding and Westminster Kennel clubs, and the American Geographical Society, and is a patron of the Metropolitan Museum of Art.

J. E. HINDON HYDE

ONE of the band of Colonists brought over to America by the Reverend Thomas Hooker, William Hyde, the ancestor of Mr. J. E. Hindon Hyde, is first recorded in Hartford, Conn., in 1636. For a short time before going to Hartford he lived in Boston and vicinity, and subsequently settled in Norwich, in which place he died in 1681. He was one of the original proprietors of Norwich in 1660 and frequently a selectman of that town. Samuel Hyde, of Norwich, son of William Hyde, was born in Hartford about 1637 and died in Norwich about 1677, having gone to that place with his father. He was a prosperous man and married Jane Lee, daughter of Thomas Lee, of Lynn, England, who sailed from England in 1641, but died on the voyage, his widow and children settling in Saybrook. John Hyde, of Norwich, who was born in 1667 and died in 1727, succeeded to the estate of his father, Samuel. He married, in 1698, his second cousin, Experience Abel, daughter of Caleb and Margaret (Post) Abel.

In the next generation, James Hyde, of Norwich, was born in 1707 and became the great-great-grandfather of Mr. J. E. Hindon Hyde. He was a leading shipmaster and one of the influential men in Norwich, where he lived throughout his life. In 1743, he married his third cousin, Sarah Marshall, daughter of Abijah Marshall. He died in 1793, preceded by his wife in 1773, leaving a family of six children. Both he and his wife are buried in the old cemetery in Norwich. Ebenezer Hyde, in the following generation, was born in Norwich in 1748 and died there in 1816. His first wife, whom he married in 1752, and who became the great-grandmother of the present Mr. Hyde, was Chloe Ellsworth, daughter of Daniel and Mary Ellsworth, of Ellington, Conn. He married, second, in 1747, Phœbe Huntington, daughter of Peter Huntington, and third, in 1799, Elizabeth Peck. By his first wife he had two sons, the youngest of whom, John Ellsworth Hyde, was born in Norwich in 1781 and became one of the leading importers and wholesale merchants in New York City during the first half of the present century. His wife was Maria Little, daughter of Jonathan Little, of Lebanon, Conn., who was his third cousin. He died in New York in 1844.

The father of Mr. J. E. Hindon Hyde was John James Hyde, son of John E. Hyde. He was born in New York in 1818 and died in St. Servan, France, in 1889. He succeeded to his father's business as importer and was one of the foremost merchants in his line of business about the middle of the present century. He married Maria L. Card, daughter of William Card. Her father was a wealty grain merchant, and at one time owned one of the largest fleets of vessels that plied upon the Hudson River. When John J. Hyde died, he left two sons and two daughters.

The elder son of this family, Mr. J. E. Hindon Hyde, was born in New York, April 13th, 1856, and was graduated from Columbia College in 1876, and from the Columbia Law School, with the degree of LL. B., in 1878. He lives in West Eleventh Street and is a member of the Metropolitan Club. In 1889, he married Ellen Elizabeth Hulings Williams, daughter of Goodwin G. Williams, of Baltimore, a member of one of the oldest families on the eastern shore of Virginia. The first ancestors of this historic Williams family were settled in Virginia in the earliest Colonial period. Mr. and Mrs. Hyde have one daughter, Helen Elizabeth Williams Hyde, and one son, John James Hindon Hyde.

The younger son of John James Hyde is William H. Hyde. He was born in New York in 1858. He married Mary Boyd Potter, daughter of the Right Reverend Henry Codman Potter, Bishop of New York. Mr. and Mrs. Hyde have a daughter, Sylvia Hyde. The sisters of Mr Hyde are C. Emily Hyde and Eva M. (Hyde) Chase, wife of Leslie Chase. His widowed mother and her unmarried daughter live in Waverly Place when in New York, but in late years they have spent considerable time at their European residence in St. Servan, France.

GEORGE LANDON INGRAHAM

ONE of the most eminent and most wealthy merchants of New York, in the closing years of the eighteenth century, was Daniel Phœnix, whose name is also conspicuous on the roll of those who served the city in an official capacity. He was the first City Treasurer and Chamberlain, being appointed to office in 1789, and held the position for twenty years. Daniel Phœnix was the son of Alexander Phœnix, who was born in 1726. His great-grandfather was Alexander Phœnix, who came to New York in 1640, and who was a younger son of Sir John Fenwick, head of a distinguished Northumbrian family.

Daniel Phœnix was born about 1737 and died in 1812. He was twice married; first to Elizabeth Treadwell and afterwards to Elizabeth Platt, and had a large family of children. The Reverend Alexander Phœnix, 1777-1863, who graduated from Columbia College in 1794, became pastor of the Congregational Church at Chicopee, Mass., and died in New York, was the only one of the sons who left male descendants. Rebecca Phœnix, one of the daughters of Daniel Phœnix, married Eliphalet Williams, of Northampton, Mass., and another daughter, Jennette Phœnix, married Richard Riker, the famous District Attorney and Recorder, of New York. The remaining daughter, Elizabeth Phœnix, married Nathaniel Ingraham, and was the mother of Judge Daniel P. Ingraham, and the grandmother of the subject of this sketch.

The Honorable Daniel Phœnix Ingraham, who was named after his maternal grandfather, was born in New York, April 22d, 1800, and died December 12th, 1881. He was educated in a private school in Morristown, N. J., and at the age of thirteen entered Columbia College, from which institution he was graduated in 1817. He then began the study of law in the office of his uncle, the Honorable Richard Riker, Recorder of New York City. Admitted to practice in due course, he was for many years one of the best known lawyers in the city. For a time, he was interested in politics and in 1835 was an assistant alderman from the Twelfth Ward, being elected an alderman the following year, and again in 1837. In 1838, Governor Marcy appointed him a Judge of the Court of Common Pleas, to fill a vacancy on the bench, and in the election of 1843, he was elected to that place for a full term.

Ten years later, he was chosen Chief Justice of the Court, which position he held until 1858. In 1857, he was elected to succeed Judge Mitchell, as a Justice of the Supreme Court, and was reëlected in 1865. In 1870, upon the reorganization of the Judiciary under the State Constitution, adopted in 1869, Governor John T. Hoffman appointed him Presiding Justice of the Supreme Court for the First Department, and while holding that position many important cases came before him. For many years Judge Ingraham belonged to the New York Historical Society and the American Geographical Society. He was a member of the Reformed Dutch Church for fifty years and one of the elders of the Collegiate Dutch Society of New York. He married Mary Landon, daughter of George Landon, of Guilford, Conn.

The Honorable George Landon Ingraham is the second son of Judge Daniel Phœnix Ingraham. He is a native of New York, born August 1st, 1847. In 1869, he was graduated from the Columbia College Law School, and admitted to practice in the same year. After successfully pursuing his profession before the courts of New York for some years, he was, in 1882, elected a Judge of the Superior Court of this city. In 1887, he was designated by the Governor to sit in the Supreme Court, and upon the death of Judge Brady of that court, in 1891, was appointed to the vacancy. In the following November, Judge Ingraham was nominated and elected a Justice of the Supreme Court, which position he now holds. When the Appellate Division of the Supreme Court was organized, in 1895, he was designated by Governor Morton as one of the justices of that court in the First Department. Judge Ingraham married Miss Lent, and has one son, Phœnix Ingraham. He is a member of the Metropolitan, Manhattan, New York Yacht and New York Athletic clubs. Arthur Ingraham, the youngest son of the late Judge Daniel P. Ingraham and brother of Judge George L. Ingraham, was graduated from Columbia College in 1870.

HUGH MARTIN INMAN

SOUTHERN interests and the Southern element are naturally of the greatest importance in New York Mr Inman's father, the late John Hamilton Inman, was a New Yorker by adoption for over twenty-five years, and was identified in every way with this city Throughout the whole country he was known as having taken an exceptionally prominent part in inaugurating and shaping the marvelous advance which Southern commerce and industry have displayed in the past two quarters of a century

Born in Jefferson County, Tenn , in 1844, the outbreak of the war between the States found John H Inman a youth of seventeen. Prior to this, he had already shown his business ability, and his first employment was as a clerk in a bank, of which one of his uncles was president, in a Georgia town, becoming assistant cashier. The great convulsion interrupted his financial education and career, and he entered the army of the Confederate States, the next four years of his life being spent in military service in the First Regiment of Tennessee Cavalry, which terminated only with the disbandment of the Southern forces Under these circumstances, and without capital save his ability and force of character, he came to New York in the autumn of 1865, almost at the conclusion of the hostilities between the States, and began a commercial career of uninterrupted success He chose the cotton business as his field, making his start at the foot of the ladder of commercial life Mr Inman's early struggles were, however, not of long duration. He was soon in independent circumstances, and before many years he had established the firm of which he was the head till his death, in 1896, and which became the leading house of its kind and, financially, one of the strongest in New York.

Success of this kind has not been uncommon in the metropolis Each generation of New York merchants can show similar instances The exceptional and striking feature in the late John H Inman's life is in the fact that he was one of the very first to appreciate the possibilities which the mineral wealth and other undeveloped resources of his native section afforded, and that his efforts were successfully employed in bringing to it the capital which has diversified Southern industries and developed its latent powers. As a necessary incident to this, he was closely identified with Southern railroad and other industrial interests, but in all directions his influence was potent in shaping the destiny of the New South

While not a politician in the ordinary sense, John H Inman took an active and beneficial interest in public affairs, and was the trusted adviser of many of the leading public men, both in New York and throughout the various Southern States He consistently refused many tenders of public office, but accepted a position on the Rapid Transit Commission, which laborious post he filled with marked wisdom and ability from the time the commission was first established to the date of his lamented death His tastes were eminently domestic and he joined only two clubs, the Manhattan and Metropolitan The handsome family residence at 874 Fifth Avenue, one of the most costly and finished in all its features in the entire Lenox Hill district, was completed under his personal supervision only a short time before his decease. He was deeply interested in many forms of religious and philanthropic work, and was unostentatious and eminently practical in his many benefactions of a private character He was almost from the time he first resided in New York a member of the Fifth Avenue Presbyterian Church, of which Dr John Hall is pastor In 1870, the late Mr Inman married Margaret McKinney Coffin, of Tennessee. Their children were six in number. Hugh Martin Inman, John Hamilton Inman, Jr., Frederick Clark Inman and Charles Chade Inman, and Lucy and Nannie Coffin Inman.

Mr Hugh Martin Inman, the eldest son and now the head of the family, graduated at the Sheffield Scientific School of Yale University in the class of 1896 The death of his father called him at an early age to the responsibilities and cares which the vast interests of such an estate involve, and to this task he devotes his energies. Mr. Inman is a member of the Metropolitan and St Anthony clubs.

JOHN BUSTEED IRELAND

THE family of Ireland traces its descent to Sir John de Ireland, one of the followers of William the Conqueror, at the battle of Hastings. In the course of time his descendants became established in the southern part of Ireland, William Ireland, having married, about 1630, Margaret Decourcy, only sister of Almericus Decourcy, Earl of Kinsdale. John Ireland, born at Dundannon, Black Rock, County Cork, came to America and, marrying Judith Lawrence, of Newtown, Long Island, became the father of John Lawrence Ireland, of New York.

John L. Ireland, after graduating from Columbia College, married Mary Floyd, born at Mastic, Suffolk County, N. Y., a granddaughter of General William Floyd, one of the most famous New York Revolutionary patriots, and for a few years subsequently resided in Steuben County, N. Y., on an estate inherited from the family of his mother, and there Mr. John B. Ireland was born. His early days were, however, spent in New York, his father having returned to this city, where he was for many years a prominent figure in society. Mr. Ireland graduated from the University of the City of New York, and was admitted to the bar, but has not for many years engaged in the active practice of his profession.

In addition to direct descent from a race distinguished in the history of the British Islands, Mr. Ireland descends on the maternal side, from both his mother and grandmother, from ancestors of the highest consequence in the Colonial history of New York, and conspicuous in the foundation of the State. His great-grandfather, Mayor Jonathan Lawrence, was a member of the Provincial Congress of 1775-87, and took an active and patriotic part in the proceedings which attached New York to the cause of the other Colonies. After the Revolution, he was a member of the first Senate of the State of New York, representing Long Island in that body. Another great-grandfather of the subject of this sketch was General William Floyd, an active patriot of the Revolutionary period, a member of the Continental Congress from 1774 to 1783, and a signer of the Declaration of Independence.

In 1863, Mr. John B. Ireland married Adelia Duane Pell, born in the City of New York, the daughter of Robert Livingston Pell. Mrs. Ireland's family is also of Revolutionary extraction. Her great-great-grandfather was the celebrated Robert Livingston, the last lord of the manor of Livingston, a leading patriot in the revolt against England. One of her great-grandfathers was Colonel Robert Troup, who was conspicuous in the battles of Long Island, Stillwater and Saratoga, and who, after the war, was a leader of the New York bar. On the paternal side, her great-grandfather was Judge James Duane, a member of the Provincial Congress from 1774 to 1784, a member of the New York Senate, Mayor of New York, 1784-1789, and the first Judge of the United States District Court in New York. The Robert Livingston Pell place, a large estate at Esopus, belongs to Mrs. Ireland, who inherited it from her father. There are seven children of this union, John Decourcy, Robert Livingston, Marie Louisa, Augustus Floyd, Adelia Avena, Laura Duane and James Duane Ireland.

Among the historical and artistic treasures in Mr. Ireland's possession are a portrait of Lafayette, presented by its subject to Miss Duane, daughter of Judge James Duane, and a portrait of Alexander Hamilton, also a gift to Colonel Troup, who was Hamilton's college companion and friend. The town residence of the Ireland family is 15 East Forty-seventh Street, and, in addition to the Pell estate at Esopus, Mr. Ireland owns two handsome residences on Long Island, one Rosedale, at Brookhaven, built by his father, the late John L. Ireland, which includes three hundred acres of ground, and another small place of fifty acres at West Islip. Mr. Ireland's club is the conservative Union. He is also a member of the Sons of the Revolution and St. Nicholas Society, and of the Church Club of New York. As a young man, he remained abroad six years, explored every country of Europe and the Levant, and extended his journey to India, in which country he spent two years, returning to Europe by way of the Cape of Good Hope. The journal of this tour was published in 1860, under the title of Wall Street to Cashmere.

ADRIAN ISELIN

ISAAC Iselin, father of Mr. Adrian Iselin, was a prominent and successful merchant of New York in the early part of the present century For a time he was engaged in business by himself, but after the War of 1812 was associated with Henry C de Rham, under the firm name of de Rham, Iselin & Moore While on a visit to Europe, in 1837, he was accidentally drowned, near Geneva. His wife was the youngest daughter of the junior partner of the well-known mercantile house of Rossier & Roulet.

Mr. Adrian Iselin, who was born in New York, is one of the sons that survived Isaac Iselin and his wife. For many years during his early business career he was engaged in importing with his brother, William Iselin, being one of the most successful merchants of New York in the middle of the century. After retiring from the importing trade, he established the banking house of Adrian Iselin & Co, but has been entirely out of active business since 1883 In 1845, he married Eleanora O'Donnell, daughter of Columbus O'Donnell, of Baltimore. Her father was at the head of one of the foremost families of that city, and was a leading financier of Maryland, being connected with the Baltimore & Ohio Railroad and other important corporations. Mr. and Mrs. Iselin celebrated their golden wedding in December, 1895. Mrs. Iselin's death occurred November 27th, 1897.

Adrian Iselin, Jr., the eldest son of Mr. and Mrs. Iselin, married Miss Caylus. He is at the head of the banking house of Adrian Iselin & Co., and is a member of the Metropolitan, Union, Knickerbocker, Riding and New York Yacht clubs and the Century Association. His residence is in East Twenty-sixth Street. William E. Iselin, the second son, was graduated from Columbia College in 1869, married Alice Rogers Jones and is engaged in the wholesale dry goods business. He lives in upper Fifth Avenue and at Quaker Ridge Farm, New Rochelle, and is a member of the Metropolitan, Tuxedo, Union, Knickerbocker, Rockaway Hunt, New York Yacht, Riding and other clubs Columbus O'Donnell Iselin, the third son, is associated in the banking business with his brother He married Edith Jones and lives in West Fifty-second Street. He is a member of the Metropolitan, Union, Knickerbocker, New York Yacht and Riding clubs and other social organizations. C. Oliver Iselin, the youngest son, is the noted yachtsman, who has been especially before the public of late years as one of the owners of the Vigilant and the Defender He graduated from Columbia College in the class of 1877, and is a member of the Union, Tuxedo, Knickerbocker, Reform, Riding, New York Yacht and Larchmont Yacht clubs. He has been twice married. His first wife was a daughter of William Garner, who was drowned on the yacht Mohawk in New York Harbor, in 1876. His present wife was Hope Goddard, daughter of Colonel William Goddard, of Providence, R. I. His home is All View, in New Rochelle.

The eldest daughter of the family is Eleanora, wife of Colonel Delancey A Kane. The other daughters, Georgie and Emilie Iselin, are unmarried. The town house of the family is in Madison Square, and they also have a home, Soucie, in New Rochelle. Mr. Iselin has given much, in time and money, to the development of New Rochelle. With his wife he built and permanently endowed the Church of St. Gabriel, in that place, and by her will Mrs Iselin left a large bequest to the church They also gave to the parish a handsome building for a school and furnished it complete, so that it is now one of the best equipped educational institutions of its kind in the country Mr Iselin established the present system of water-works in New Rochelle, and has been in other ways a benefactor of the town He belongs to the Tuxedo, Metropolitan, Union, Union League, Knickerbocker, Racquet, City, Riding, Reform, Seawanhaka-Corinthian Yacht, New York Yacht and New York Athletic clubs, the Country Club of Westchester County, the Downtown Association, the Century Association and the National Academy of Design, and is a patron of the Metropolitan Museum of Art and the American Museum of Natural History. He has a box at the Metropolitan Opera House, having been long treasurer and director of the corporation owning the opera house, and was one of the patrons of the Patriarchs' Ball during the existence of that social organization. For many years he was the Consul of the Swiss Republic in New York.

WILLIAM BRADLEY ISHAM

ONLY two branches of the Isham family exist in this country, one of which was established in New England and the other in Virginia The ancestor of the New England branch, that to which the New York Ishams belong, was John Isham, of Barnstable, Mass., who was a native of England. He came from the Old World to the transatlantic Colonies in the latter part of the seventeenth century from Northamptonshire and made his abode for the greater part of his life, in the Cape District, as it has always been called, in Massachusetts. He died at Barnstable in 1713. His wife, whom he married in 1670, was Jane Parker, the daughter of Robert Parker, of Barnstable. She was born in 1664 and died seven years after the decease of her husband. The second son of John Isham was Isaac Isham, of Barnstable, who was born in 1682 and died in 1771, having married, in 1716, Thankful Lumbert, daughter of Thomas Lumbert, Jr

In the next generation of the family in America, John Isham, second of the name, the son of Isaac Isham, was born in Barnstable, 1721, and became a resident of Colchester, Conn., where he married, in 1751, Dorothy Foote, daughter of Ephraim Foote, of Colchester. During the French and Indian Wars, he was Captain of a company of Colonial militia and was also engaged in the disastrous expedition sent from New England against the French possessions in the West Indies. His son, Samuel Isham, was born in 1752 and died in 1827, and was the father of Charles Isham, of Malden, Ulster County, N. Y., who was born at Farmington, Hartford, Conn , August 20th, 1784, and died in 1856. Charles Isham married, in 1814, Flora Bradley, daughter of Judge William Bradley, of Hartford, Conn

Mr. William Bradley Isham, second son of Charles and Flora (Bradley) Isham, was born in Malden, N Y., in 1827. He has been a resident of New York for many years and has been engaged in the banking business. He is vice-president of the Bank of the Metropolis, in this city, and is president of the Bond and Mortgage Guarantee Company. In 1852, Mr. Isham married Julia Burhans, daughter of Colonel Benjamin Peck Burhans, of Warrensburg, N. Y. The city residence of the family is in East Sixty-first Street, near Fifth Avenue, and their country home is on Kingsbridge Road, Washington Heights. Mr. Isham is a member of the Metropolitan and Riding clubs, the Downtown Association, the New England Society and the National Academy of Design, and is a patron of the American Museum of Natural History.

Mr Isham has three sons. The eldest, Charles Isham, was born in 1853, and was graduated from Harvard University in 1876 with the degree of B A. He married Mary Lincoln, daughter of the Honorable Robert T. Lincoln, of Chicago, and granddaughter of President Abraham Lincoln. His city residence is in East Sixty-sixth Street. He is a member of the Century Association, the Bar Association, the Harvard and University clubs, the American Geographical Society and the Sons of the Revolution. Samuel Isham, the second son, born in 1855, was graduated from Yale College in 1875 and is a well-known artist. He is a member of the Century Association, the Metropolitan, University, Riding and Players clubs, the New England Society, the Yale Alumni Association and the Architectural League. William Burhans Isham, the third son, was born in 1857 and graduated from Princeton College in 1879. He is engaged in business with his father. His clubs are the Metropolitan and University, and he also belongs to the Downtown Association.

Charles H. Isham, the younger son of Charles and Flora (Bradley) Isham, was born in 1829 and is engaged in mercantile pursuits. He married, in 1861, Joanna Muller, daughter of Adrian H. Muller, of this city, and has two sons, Charles Bradley and F. De Forrest Isham, and an only daughter, Joanna M. Isham. He lives in East Thirty-seventh Street and belongs to the Union League Club and the New England Society and is a patron of the Metropolitan Museum of Art. The only daughter of Charles and Flora (Bradley) Isham and sister of the gentlemen referred to in this article, is Flora E. Isham, who is unmarried.

BRAYTON IVES

A MONG the pioneers of New England in the seventeenth century, were members of the Ives family that was of ancient renown in the old country. The first of the name who appeared on this side of the Atlantic was William Ives, who landed in Massachusetts and settled in Boston, where he remained for several years. He joined in that famous exodus from the Massachusetts Colony to Connecticut, and helped to found the city of New Haven From him have sprung members of the family who in many generations have been distinguished Three of his descendants, Levi, Eli and Charles L. Ives, father, son and grandson, all of whom were resident in New Haven, were eminent physicians, and connected with the medical department of Yale College. Combined, their professional lives covered nearly a century and a half The Reverend Dr Levi S Ives, Bishop of the Protestant Episcopal Church, and afterwards a Roman Catholic theologian and educator, came of the same stock, and so also did Lieutenant-Commander Thomas B Ives, of the United States Navy, who bore an active and useful part in naval operations during the Civil War.

Born in Farmington, Conn., in 1840, General Brayton Ives, who is the conspicuous representative of his family in the present generation, was graduated from Yale College in the class of 1861 The piping times of war called him to action immediately after the completion of his college career, and he quickly changed the cloister for the camp. Entering the army as Adjutant of the Fifth Connecticut Infantry, he went to the front at once, and served with distinction to the end of the war. In 1861, he was commissioned a Captain, and the next year served as Assistant Adjutant-General, with the rank of Captain, on the staff of General O S. Terry. In 1864, he became a Major in the First Connecticut Cavalry, and was successively promoted to be Lieutenant-Colonel and Colonel in the same regiment. During that time he served under Generals Custer and Sheridan. When the war closed he held the rank of Brevet Brigadier-General at the age of twenty-four, being one of the youngest officers in the service with that high rank.

Coming to New York after the war, General Ives entered Wall Street, and in 1867 became a stock broker He has long been recognized as one of the leading financiers of the metropolis in this generation. One of the prime promoters of the movement that led to the establishment of the Stock Exchange, he was vice-president of that organization, 1876-77, president, 1878-79, and a member of the Governing Committee for thirteen years After being twenty-two years in Wall Street, he retired in 1889, and the following year took the presidency of the Western National Bank, a position that he held several years. As a student of finance, he is an accepted authority, and especially has an expert knowledge of railroad finance. For many years he was president of the Northern Pacific Railroad Company, and has been a director in the Mercantile Trust Company, the United States Guarantee Company, and the New York Stock Exchange Building Company He is also chairman of the Westinghouse Electric and Manufacturing Company.

In private life General Ives is known as a patron of art and literature. He is a discriminating collector of books, pictures and bric-à-brac, and has written a great deal upon art and allied subjects His collection of pictures which he sold a few years ago was one of the finest and most carefully selected in the city. A collection of Japanese swords that he made, and that is now in the Metropolitan Museum of Art, is regarded as one of the best of the half a dozen similar collections of importance in this country.

In 1867, General Ives married Eleanor A. Bissell, daughter of the Reverend B. S Bissell, of Norwalk, Conn, thus connecting himself with one of the pioneer families of that State. His son, Sherwood Bissell Ives, was graduated from Yale University in 1893, and is a physician. He also has three unmarried daughters, Winifred, Eunice and Frances H. Ives. The city home of the family is in East Thirty-fourth Street, and their summer residence in Seabright, N. J. General Ives is a member of the New England Society, the American Geographical Society, the Century Association, and the Military Order of the Loyal Legion, and belongs to the Metropolitan, Union League, Grolier, Players, Riding, University and New York Yacht clubs.

JOSEPH COOKE JACKSON

FEW Americans can claim more illustrious ancestry than General Joseph C. Jackson. Many citizens of New York, New Jersey and Connecticut, conspicuous in public service for nearly three hundred years, including the Wolcotts, Huntingtons and Pitkins, of Connecticut, are his lineal ancestors. On his father's side, General Jackson traces descent from Colonel Philip Pieterse Schuyler, magistrate of Albany, in 1656, from Colonel John Brinckerhoff, of Revolutionary fame, whose house, at Fishkill, was General Washington's headquarters, and from the Reverend Benjamin Van der Linde. The Jacksons are an ancient English family. The Honorable John P. Jackson, of New Jersey, the father of General Jackson, graduated with first honors from Princeton College, studied law at Litchfield, Conn., and practiced in New Jersey. He was instrumental in organizing the New Jersey Railroad and Transportation, and the Jersey City Ferry companies, and was Speaker of the State Legislature.

General Jackson's mother was Elizabeth Wolcott, daughter of the Honorable Frederick Wolcott, of Litchfield, Conn. The progenitor of the Wolcott family in America, Henry Wolcott, born in 1578, left Tolland, Somersetshire, England, in 1628. Among his numerous descendants were Roger Wolcott, Colonial Governor of Connecticut; Major-General and Governor Oliver Wolcott; Governor Oliver Wolcott, second, Secretary of the Treasury in Washington's and John Adams' administrations, and Judge Frederick Wolcott, son of Oliver Wolcott, signer of the Declaration of Independence, Major-General of the Connecticut Militia, and Governor. It was to Governor Wolcott's house, in Litchfield, that the famous leaden statue of King George III., torn from its pedestal in Bowling Green, New York, was taken, and there moulded into bullets, by his son, Frederick, and others. Major-General Jabez Huntington, Commander-in-Chief of the Connecticut Militia, at the capture of Louisburg, in 1758 was a maternal great-grandfather of General Jackson.

General Joseph Cooke Jackson was born in Newark, N. J., August 5th, 1835. He attended Colonel Kingsley's Military School, at West Point, graduated from Phillips Academy, Andover, Mass., in 1853; from Yale College, in 1857; from the New York University Law School, in 1858, and from Harvard Law School, in 1860, receiving the degree of LL B. from both New York and Harvard Universities. At the outbreak of the Civil War, he was Second Lieutenant in the First New Jersey Volunteers, and became aide to General Philip Kearny, was on the staff of Major-General W. B Franklin, and subsequently was made Captain and aide-de-camp of United States Volunteers, for gallant conduct during the Seven Days' battles before Richmond. In 1862, he was commissioned Lieutenant-Colonel of the Twenty-Sixth New Jersey Volunteers, and was brevetted Colonel "for gallant and meritorious conduct at the battle of Fredericksburg, Va.," and Brigadier-General for a like reason in 1865. He was United States Commissioner of Naval Credits, in 1864, but resumed the practice of law, in New York, and, in 1870 and 1871, was Assistant United States District Attorney.

In 1864, he married Katharine Perkins Day, daughter of the Honorable Calvin Day, of Hartford, Conn., a man of distinguished character, and a direct descendant of Robert Day, who came to America in 1634 Mrs. Jackson's mother was Catherine Seymour, also of Hartford, Conn., daughter of Charles Seymour, and granddaughter of Captain Charles Seymour, of the Revolution. Among her ancestors are Governor William Bradford, Governor John Haynes, Governor George Wyllys, Governor Thomas Dudley, Governor John Webster, Governor William Pitkin, Judge William Pitkin, his father, and the Honorable William Pitkin, his grandfather, first Treasurer of the Colony of Connecticut; the Reverend John Wareham, William Whiting, Treasurer of the Colony, and President Thomas Clap, of Yale College. She is also a descendant of Mabel Harlakenden, wife of Governor John Haynes. The children of General Jackson are Joseph C. Jackson, Jr., John Day Jackson, both graduates of Yale; Katharine Seymour Jackson, and Elizabeth Huntington Wolcott Jackson. The family residence is 138 East Thirty-fourth Street.

D. WILLIS JAMES

ANIEL JAMES, the father of Mr. D. Willis James, was a leading merchant of New York and Liverpool, England, for more than fifty years. He began life with the present century, having been born in 1801. His first mercantile experience was with the metal house of Phelps & Peck, and he became a partner in the celebrated firm of Phelps, Dodge & Co , which succeeded Phelps & Peck About 1831, he went to Europe and lived there for the remainder of his life as a member of Phelps, James & Co., who were the English partners of the New York house. Throughout his long career, he was recognized as a business man of the highest type, public-spirited and deeply interested in philanthropic causes He died at Beaconsfield, near Liverpool, England, in 1876, and left five children Three sons have made their homes in England, and his daughter, Olivia P. James, became the wife of Robert Hoe

On his mother's side, Mr James is descended from a family of position in New York, and also from distinguished Colonial ancestors in Connecticut. His mother was Elizabeth Woodbridge Phelps, daughter of Anson Greene Phelps, senior member of Phelps, Dodge & Co , and one of New York's famous philanthropists in the last generation Her mother, Olivia Eggleston, was a daughter of Elihu and Elizabeth (Olcott) Eggleston, of Middletown, Conn., a descendant of the Olcott and Eggleston families, which were established in the Connecticut Colony in its earliest period. The Phelps family goes back to George Phelps, of Tewksbury, England, who was born about 1605 and came to New England in 1630, being at first a resident of Dorchester, Mass , and then of Windsor, Conn., at its settlement in 1635. His second wife, the ancestress of that branch of the family to which Mr James belongs, was Frances Dewey. The subsequent generations down to Anson Greene Phelps were John Phelps, 1651-1741, and his wife, Sarah Buckland, Thomas Phelps, 1687-1750, and his wife, Hannah Phelps; Thomas Phelps, 1711-1777, and his wife, Margaret Watson, daughter of John and Sarah (Steele) Watson, and Thomas Phelps, 1741-1789, and his wife, Dorothy Lamb Woodbridge, daughter of Haynes and Elizabeth (Griswold) Woodbridge, who were the parents of Anson Greene Phelps.

The second Thomas Phelps served in the Continental Army. His wife, Dorothy Lamb Woodbridge, was descended from the Woodbridge, Griswold, Haynes and Wyllys families. Her father was the son of the Reverend Timothy Woodbridge, of Hartford, who married Mabel Wyllys, daughter of the Honorable Samuel Wyllys, secretary of Connecticut, and a granddaughter of Governor John Haynes. The Reverend Timothy Woodbridge was the son of the Reverend John Woodbridge, of Newbury, Mass., and of his wife, Mercy Dudley, daughter of Governor Thomas Dudley, of Massachusetts. Elizabeth Griswold, the wife of Haynes Woodbridge and grandmother of Anson Greene Phelps, was a daughter of Samuel Griswold, 1684-1777, a representative to the General Assembly in 1732 and a son of Thomas Griswold, 1658-1727, and Hester Drake, who was a granddaughter of the Honorable Henry Wolcott. Thomas Griswold was the son of George Griswold, 1633-1704, and a grandson of Edward Griswold, who came from Kenilworth, Warwickshire, in 1639, settled in Windsor and was associated with his brother, Governor Matthew Griswold

Mr. D. Willis James was born in Liverpool, England, April 15, 1832, and has been connected with the business house with which his father was identified. His wife was Ellen S. Curtiss The city residence of the family is at Park Avenue, corner of Thirty-ninth Street, and their country home is Onunda, Madison, N. J. Mr. James belongs to the Metropolitan, City, Riding, Reform, A Δ Φ and Morris County Golf clubs, the Century Association, the Downtown Association and the American Geographical Society, and is a patron of the Metropolitan Museum of Art, National Academy of Design and American Museum of Natural History. Mr and Mrs. James have one son, Arthur Curtiss James, who married Harriet Eddy Parsons, and lives in Park Avenue He is a graduate of Amherst College, class of 1889, and a member of the Metropolitan, University, City, Riding, A Δ Φ, Morristown, Morris County Golf, New York Yacht and Seawanhaka-Corinthian Yacht clubs and the Downtown Association.

THOMAS LEMUEL JAMES

ORIGINALLY of Welsh extraction, the family of which General Thomas L James is the representative, has been long established in America. Mr. James was born in Utica, N. Y., March 29th, 1831. He attended school in that city and then entered the printing office of Wesley Bailey, the veteran abolitionist editor. The year before he became of age, he went into business as part proprietor of The Madison County Journal, a Whig newspaper in Hamilton, N. Y. He was active and prominent in politics, and when the Republican party was formed gave his adherence to it and supported John C. Fremont for the presidency in 1856. For two years, 1856–58, he was connected with the administration of the State canals.

In 1861, Mr. James was appointed to a post under the Collector of the Port of New York and removed to this city, with which he has since been identified He was soon promoted, and when Thomas Murphy became Collector, was made Deputy Collector. In March, 1873, President Grant appointed him Postmaster of New York, and four years later President Hayes tendered him the position of Collector of the Port, and afterwards that of Postmaster General, but he declined both offices. In March, 1881, President Garfield made him Postmaster General, and when President Arthur succeeded to the presidency, Mr. James was retained in that position, but soon resigned the office and returned to private life, after twenty years of arduous and successful public service. During his incumbency of the office of Postmaster General, he introduced many reforms in the management of the post-office department, reducing the annual deficiency and making the department self-sustaining. He was particularly active in unearthing and correcting abuses that had long existed in the service, more particularly the Star Route frauds, and raised the whole department to a higher plane of efficiency than it had ever before attained. Since his retirement to private life, Mr James has been president of the Lincoln National Bank, a position that he assumed in January, 1882. He is also president of the Lincoln State Deposit Company, and is connected with other large corporations.

Mr. James married, in 1852, Emily I. Freeburn, who is descended from Ethan Allen, the famous American Revolutionary General, and is also a descendant of that branch of the Lamb family of which Charles Lamb, the essayist, was a member. One of Mr. James' daughters, Ellen M. James, married Henry G. Pearson, for many years Postmaster of New York. Another daughter, Harriet Weed James, is unmarried. Mr. James is a member of the Union League and many other clubs. His residence is in Highwood, N. J. Hamilton College conferred upon him the degree of A. M. in 1862, and Madison University gave him the degree of LL. D. in 1882. St John's College, of Fordham, N. Y., and the College of St. Francis Xavier have also conferred upon him the degree of LL. D.

Colonel Charles F. James, the son of the Honorable Thomas L. James, was born in Hamilton, N. Y., July 12th, 1856, and has displayed an hereditary talent for public affairs and finance. He entered the College of the City of New York in 1873, but completed his education in Madison, now Colgate University, Hamilton, N. Y., graduating from that institution in 1876, and subsequently receiving the degree of A M. and Ph. D. Attending the law department of Columbia College, he received his degree of LL. B. in 1879, was called to the bar and was appointed counsel to the New York State Commissioners of Emigration. Subsequently he was Assistant United States District Attorney for the Southern District of New York under General Stewart L. Woodford, and then Assistant Corporation Counsel for the city under Judges Andrews and Lacombe. Latterly he has been engaged in private practice, his most recent professional association being as a member of the firm of Dittenhoefer, Gerber & James. In 1893, he organized the Franklin National Bank, and as vice-president and cashier managed the affairs of that institution In 1897, he became president, succeeding the Honorable Ellis H. Roberts, who was appointed Treasurer of the United States. He is president of the St. David's Society, and is a member of the Union League Club, the Φ Γ Δ fraternity, the New York Athletic Club and the American Geographical Society.

JOSEPH EDWARD JANVRIN, M. D.

FOR many centuries the family of Janvrin held possessions in the Island of Jersey, its ancestry being traced back to the Crusades The first of the name in America was Captain John (Jean) Janvrin, who was a ship owner of St Helier, Jersey. He came on one of his own vessels to Portsmouth, N H, and married, in 1706, Elizabeth Knight, daughter of John Knight, an officer in the Indian wars Captain Janvrin died in 1718 His eldest son, John, was graduated from Harvard College in 1728 His son, William Janvrin, grandfather of the subject of this article, married Abigail Adams, daughter of Dr. Joseph Adams, of Portsmouth

Dr Adams, a graduate of Harvard in 1745, was a son of the Reverend Joseph Adams, who also graduated from Harvard in 1710 and removed from Braintree, Mass, in 1715, to Newington, where he became minister and married the widow of Captain Janvrin in 1720 His pastorate lasted sixty-eight years, till his death in 1783 He was a great-grandson of Henry Adams, of Braintree, who descended from the Ap Adams family of Wales Dr Joseph Adams was a cousin of both President John Adams and Samuel Adams. Through the Bass and Adams family marriages, Dr. Janvrin is descended from John Alden He is also descended from Governors Thomas Dudley and Simon Bradstreet, of the Massachusetts Bay Colony, and from Major Ezekiel Gilman, of Exeter, who was prominent at the capture of Louisburg in 1745 Joseph Adams Janvrin, son of William and Abigail Adams Janvrin and father of Dr Janvrin, was a landowner at Exeter, N H, and held many public positions His wife was Lydia Ann Colcord, daughter of George Colcord, and a descendant of Edward Colcord, a founder of Exeter in 1638

Mr Joseph Edward Janvrin was born at Exeter, January 13th, 1839, graduated at Phillips Exeter Academy in 1857 and began the study of medicine with Dr William Gilman Perry in his native town In 1861, he temporarily abandoned it and entered the Second New Hampshire Infantry, serving as Assistant Surgeon in the campaigns of the Army of the Potomac under Generals Burnside and Hooker. In December, 1862, he was transferred to the Fifteenth New Hampshire Regiment, with which he served in the Department of the Gulf under General Banks, becoming Acting Surgeon of his command, and was mustered out in 1863 Resuming his studies, he entered the medical department of Dartmouth College and became a pupil of Professor E. R. Peaslee, graduating in 1864 from the College of Physicians and Surgeons in this city.

For a short time he was assistant surgeon in the Emory Hospital, Washington, D C, but in 1865 returned to New York and became associated with Dr Peaslee, and has held notable professional offices and appointments, being president of the New York County Medical Association, and has been professionally connected with the Demilt Dispensary, the Woman's Hospital, New York Skin and Cancer Hospital, Orphans' Home and the Asylum of the Protestant Episcopal Church. He is ex-president of the New York Obstetrical Society and is a member of many national and international medical bodies. Dr Janvrin has also written a large number of papers on professional topics, many of which have commanded international attention.

In 1881, Dr Janvrin married Laura L La Wall, daughter of the late Cyrus La Wall, of Easton, Pa Mrs Janvrin's grandfather was an officer in the Revolution, as were two ancestors on her mother's side, Colonel Robert Scott, of Pennsylvania, and John Schureman, of New Jersey Dr and Mrs Janvrin have two children, Edmund Randolph Peaslee Janvrin and Marguerite La Wall Janvrin Their residence is 191 Madison Avenue. Dr. Janvrin is a member of the Union League Club, the Society of Colonial Wars, the Loyal Legion and the Grand Army of the Republic.

The Janvrin arms are· Azure, a chevron argent between two bezants or in chief and a fleur-de-lys of the second in base, surmounted by an escutcheon quarterly, first; the arms as above, the chevron charged with a crescent gules, second, argent, three escallops gules, third, gules a mullet argent, on a chief of the second an arm erect couped at elbow, vested azure, cuffed argent, hand gules, fourth; argent on a chief sable three griffins' heads erased argent. Crest, a griffin's head couped between the wings or Motto, *Labor ipse voluptas*

JOHN CLARKSON JAY, M. D.

WHEN Chief Justice John Jay went abroad in 1794 to negotiate "Jay's Treaty," he was accompanied by his eldest son, Peter Augustus Jay, as his private secretary The son was born in Elizabethtown, N. J, January 24th, 1776, and graduated from Columbia College in 1794. His ancestry and connections are given in the sketch pertaining to Colonel William Jay, who is descended from a younger branch. The main line of the family is transmitted from Augustus Jay and Chief Justice John Jay through Peter Augustus Jay, who became a lawyer and achieved high rank at the New York bar In 1816, he was a member of the Assembly, held the office of Recorder of New York City in 1819, and was a member of the Constitutional Convention in 1827. Columbia College selected him as a trustee in 1812-17, and again in 1823-43, and part of the time he was chairman of the board. The New York Historical Society made him its president for three years, 1840-43. Harvard College gave him the degree of LL D in 1831, and Columbia conferred the same honor in 1835. He was a man of great learning and an accomplished jurist When in the Assembly he had the honor, with his brother William, of introducing the first bill for the abolishment of slavery in New York. His wife, Mary Rutherfurd Clarkson, who married Peter A. Jay in 1807, was a daughter of General Matthew Clarkson, 1759-1825, the patriot of the Revolution, and a great-granddaughter of the first Matthew Clarkson, who was secretary of the Province for thirteen years. She was also a granddaughter of Abraham de Peyster.

The father of the present Doctor Jay was the first Doctor John Clarkson Jay, the eldest of their family of eight children. Born in 1808 and graduated from Columbia College in 1827 and the College of Physicians and Surgeons in 1831, he was a successful practitioner and an accomplished scientist. He devoted much time to the study of conchology and became an expert on that subject, writing many essays and several books upon it. His valuable collection was purchased after his death by Catherine L Wolfe and presented to the American Museum of Natural History, where it is kept intact as the Jay collection. Doctor Jay was one of the founders of the Lyceum of Natural History, afterwards the National Academy of Science, and was its treasurer from 1836 to 1843. He was also one of the founders of the New York Yacht Club, of which he was the first secretary. His wife was Laura Prime, daughter of Nathaniel Prime, the famous New York merchant, descended from Mark Prime, who came from England to Massachusetts about 1638

Dr. John Clarkson Jay of the present generation was their youngest son He was educated at the Dudley Collegiate Institute, Northampton, Mass., Charlier's French school in New York, the Columbia College Grammar School, Columbia College and the College of Physicians and Surgeons, graduating from the latter in 1865 During the Civil War, he served in the Seventy-First Regiment, New York State Militia, and was also Acting-Assistant Surgeon at the United States Army hospitals in Washington and New Orleans After the war he studied in Vienna and Prague, and, returning, began the practice of his profession in New York. From 1869 to 1871, he was attending physician to the New York Dispensary, from 1880 to 1892, was attending physician to the out-patient department of the New York Hospital, was one of the founders of the New York Free Dispensary for sick children, and since 1892 has been an examiner of lunacy in the State of New York.

Doctor Jay is a member of the Medical Society of the City and that of the County of New York, the Physicians' Mutual Aid Association, the City Club, the Century Association, the Union League Club and the Sons of the Revolution. He has translated several important medical works from the French and German.

The wife of Doctor Jay, whom he married in 1872, was Harriette Arnold Vinton, daughter of Major-General David H Vinton, U S. A. The residence of Doctor and Mrs. Jay is at 54 West Forty-seventh Street. They have two children, Edith Van Cortlandt Jay and John Clarkson Jay, Jr., who is a student at St. Paul's School, Concord, N. H.

WILLIAM JAY

PIERRE JAY, a wealthy Protestant merchant of La Rochelle, France, was the ancestor of a family which, for two hundred years, has been the accepted representative of the Huguenots in America, and which has furnished men of the highest eminence to their adopted country. At the time of the revocation of the Edict of Nantes, in 1685, Pierre Jay and his family escaped to England. One of his sons, Augustus Jay, born in 1665, was absent on a voyage to the African Coast, and returned to France in ignorance of the blow which had fallen on his coreligionists. He, however, made his way to New York in the same year and established himself there. His wealth, education and personal presence made Augustus Jay a man of mark, and his position was further raised by his marriage, in 1697, to Anne Maria Bayard, daughter of Balthazer Bayard and his wife, Maria Lockermans, a grandniece of Governor Stuyvesant. He died in New York in 1751. His son Peter, born in 1704, bought in 1745 a large estate near Rye, in Westchester County, and married Mary Van Cortlandt, daughter of Jacobus Van Cortlandt and Eve Philipse, the family thus from the very commencement allying itself with the most prominent representatives of social importance and culture in the city.

The eighth child of this marriage was the celebrated John Jay. Born in 1745, he was graduated at Kings (now Columbia) College in 1764, and was called to the bar in 1768. In 1774, he married Sarah Livingston, daughter of Governor William Livingston, of New Jersey. In the struggle with the mother country, he took part from the first, being a delegate to the Continental Congress of 1774 and that of 1775. While a member of the latter, he was elected to the New York Provincial Congress and drafted the first constitution of the State. In 1778, he was president of Congress, in 1780 became Minister to Spain, and in 1782 was one of the Commissioners who negotiated the peace between the United States and Great Britain. He coöperated with Hamilton and Madison in the authorship of The Federalist, and on the adoption of the Constitution, in 1789, was appointed the first Chief Justice of the United States in 1794. While still Chief Justice, he was Envoy to England, and completed his political career by service as Governor of New York from 1798 to 1801, resigning the Chief Justiceship to become Governor. The remainder of his life, till his death, in 1829, was passed at the mansion he had built, Bedford House, Katonah, N. Y., an estate inherited from his Van Cortlandt ancestors. This house is still inhabited by his descendants and belongs to Colonel William Jay.

Judge William Jay, his second son, 1789-1858, was a graduate of Yale in 1807 and became a prominent jurist and philanthropist. He was a judge of Westchester County from 1818 to 1835, was one of the earliest and most active opponents of slavery, and by his writings contributed greatly to making that question one of public conscience. He married Augusta, daughter of John McVicker, whose family had long been prominent in the metropolis.

The late Honorable John Jay, the only son of this alliance, was born in 1817, and followed his father's example in his hostility to slavery, and his advocacy of philanthropic causes. He was United States Minister to Austria from 1869 to 1875, and took an active part in promoting reform of the civil service. He married Eleanor Kingsland Field, daughter of Hickson W. Field, and died in 1894, his career having been one of devotion to duty as a citizen and Christian.

Colonel William Jay, his only son, was born in 1841, entered the United States Army, served throughout the Rebellion, being on the staff of General George B. Meade, the Commander of the Army of the Potomac, and attained the rank of Lieutenant-Colonel by brevet. Resigning from the army, he was called to the bar and is in active practice in New York. Colonel Jay married Lucy Oelrichs, daughter of Henry Oelrichs, a leading New York merchant. He is a vestryman of Trinity Church, a position which he is the fifth in line of his family to occupy, his ancestor, Augustus Jay, having been one of the early members of the vestry. One prominent sport owes much of its prestige in New York to Colonel Jay's efforts. He was one of the first members of the Coaching Club and was its president from 1876 to 1896.

FREDERICK BEACH JENNINGS

FROM Joshua Jennings, the American pioneer, have sprung many families, which have been prominent and influential in the State of Connecticut, where their common ancestor originally settled, and in other parts of the United States. Joshua Jennings was born in England about 1620 and came to this country when he was nearly twenty-five years of age Settling first in Hartford, he afterwards removed to Fairfield, where he died in 1674. In each of the five successive generations from Joshua Jennings to Mr. Frederick Beach Jennings came an Isaac Jennings. The Isaac Jennings of the second American generation was born in 1663 and died in 1746. The next Isaac Jennings was born in 1692, and the third Isaac Jennings, 1743-1819, was a prosperous farmer and manufacturer of Fairfield During the War of the Revolution, he served as a Lieutenant. His wife was Abigail Gould, 1754-1795, daughter of Colonel Abraham Gould, of Fairfield, and descended from Major Nathan Gould or Gold, one of the early settlers of Connecticut

Isaac Jennings, the grandfather of Mr. Frederick Beach Jennings, was born in Fairfield in 1788, was a resident of Derby, Conn., and afterwards of Oberlin, O, where he died in 1874. Educated as a physician, he received the degree of M. D. and engaged in practice at Derby He was best known as a writer upon medical and allied subjects, especially regarding hygiene. His published works included Medical Reform, The Philosophy of Human Life, The Tree of Life and Orthopathy. The wife of Dr Isaac Jennings was Anne Beach, daughter of Eliakim Beach, of Trumbull, Conn.

The Reverend Isaac Jennings, son of Dr Isaac Jennings, was the father of Mr. Frederick Beach Jennings. He was born in Fairfield in 1816, but removed to Derby with his parents in 1822. Graduated from Yale College in 1837, he taught school in Washington, Conn., and then had charge of the Hopkins Grammar School in New Haven for one year While teaching in New Haven he studied theology and afterwards attended the Theological Seminary at Andover, Mass., from which institution he was graduated in 1842. Settled at first over the Second Congregational Church of Akron, O., in 1843, he became pastor of the First Church in Stamford, Conn, in 1847, and pastor of the First Church of Christ in Bennington, Vt., in 1853 He traveled in Europe in 1859 and wrote much for publication, his principal work being a book entitled Memorials of a Century His wife, whom he married in Mansfield, O, in 1847, was Sophia Day, daughter of Matthias Day

Mr. Frederick Beach Jennings was born in Bennington, Vt, in 1853 Prepared for college in the local academy, he went to Williams College, from which institution he was graduated in 1872 and of which he subsequently became a trustee. Taking up the study of law in the Dane Law School of Harvard University, he was graduated therefrom with the degree of LL. B. in 1874, and the following year was graduated from the Law School of New York University with the same degree, taking at his graduation first prize for the best essay. The same year he was admitted to practice and established the firm of Jennings & Russell, and is now a member of the firm of Stetson, Tracy, Jennings & Russell. He is the counsel of the Erie Railroad Company, as well as of various other railroads and corporations. He is also interested in business enterprises and is an officer and member of the board of directors of various corporations, including several railroad companies, a bank and other financial and business organizations

In 1880, Mr. Jennings married Laura Hall Park, daughter of the Honorable Trenor W. Park, of North Bennington, Vt., and granddaughter of former Governor Hiland Hall, of Vermont. Mr. and Mrs. Jennings have four children, Percy Hall, Elizabeth, Frederic B., Jr., and Edward Phelps Jennings. The city residence of the family is at 86 Park Avenue, and their summer home is Fairview, North Bennington, Vt Mr. Jennings is a member of the University, Metropolitan, Union League, Δ K E, New York Athletic, University Athletic, Racquet and City clubs, the Century Association, the Country Club of Westchester County, the Downtown Association, the Williams College Alumni Association, the New England Society and the Metropolitan Museum of Art. He is also a member and one of the executive committee of the Bar Association

WALTER JENNINGS

JOSHUA JENNINGS, who emigrated to this country from England, about 1645, and settled in Hartford, Isaac Jennings, of Hartford, Isaac Jennings, of Fairfield, and Lieutenant Isaac Jennings, of Fairfield, were the ancestors in the first four American generations of the Jennings family. In the fifth generation, Captain Abraham Gould Jennings, the grandfather of Mr. Walter Jennings, was born in Fairfield, in 1781. Early in life he went to sea, and finally had command of large ships sailing between New York and Europe, being thus engaged until after the War of 1812. Subsequently he was in the trade with China, and after 1835, owned, among other mercantile interests, a large share in a line of vessels sailing between New York and Charleston, S. C

The mother of Abraham Gould Jennings, whom his father, Isaac Jennings, married in 1770, was Abigail Gould, the daughter of Colonel Abraham Gould, who was killed by the British at the Battle of Ridgefield, in 1777 The Gould, or Gold, family descended from Nathan Gold, who came from St. Edmundsbury, England, to Fairfield, Conn., in 1675 He was educated and wealthy, and took a prominent position in the Colony, being one of the petitioners for the charter of Connecticut, in 1674, and an assistant and member of the Governor's Council, in 1657–94. His son, Nathan Gould, Jr., was town clerk of Fairfield, in 1684–1706, town clerk and Deputy-Governor, 1706–24, and Chief Justice of the Supreme Court, in 1712. His wife was a daughter of Lieutenant-Governor John Talcott, of Connecticut, and his grandson, Colonel Abraham Gould, was the fifth son of Samuel Gould. The wife of Colonel Abraham Gould and mother of Abigail (Gould) Jennings was Elizabeth Burr, daughter of Captain John Burr. The wife of Captain Abraham Gould Jennings whom he married in Fairfield, in 1807, was Anna Burr. She was the daughter of Peter Burr, one of the largest landholders in Fairfield. The first American ancestor of Anna (Burr) Jennings was Jehu Burr, 1600–1672, one of the early settlers of Fairfield, in 1644. He came to this country with Governor John Winthrop, in 1630, settling first in Roxbury, Mass, but in 1636, was one of the founders of Agawam, now Springfield, Mass After taking up his residence in Connecticut, he was a representative to the General Court, from the town of Fairfield.

Oliver Burr Jennings, the father of Mr. Walter Jennings, was the son of Captain Abraham (Gould) Jennings and his wife, Anna Burr. He was born in Fairfield, in 1825, received an academic education, and began business life in Bridgeport, Conn He remained there for several years, and came to New York City, in 1843. In 1849, he was among the pioneers who went to California, and there entered into mercantile business, becoming senior member of the firm of Jennings & Brewster. In 1865, he returned to New York and was associated with the Messrs. Rockefeller and others in the petroleum business, being one of the directors of the Standard Oil Company His summer home was an estate in his native town, Fairfield, Conn. His wife was Esther Judson Goodsell, daughter of David Judson Goodsell, of Tiffin, O. When he died, in 1893, he left five children . Annie Burr, Walter, Helen Goodsell, the wife of Dr. Walter B James ; Emma Brewster, who married Hugh D Auchincloss, and Oliver Gould Jennings. Mrs. Oliver B. Jennings and her eldest daughter reside in the old family home in Park Avenue

Mr. Walter Jennings, the eldest son of Oliver Burr Jennings, was born in San Francisco, in 1858 Prepared for college at Hopkins Grammar School, New Haven, Conn., he was graduated from Yale University in the class of 1880, and from Columbia College Law School, in 1882, being admitted to the bar in the same year. He has since been mainly occupied with the care of the family property, although he is also actively identified with the Standard Oil Company. In 1891, Mr. Jennings married Jean Pollock Brown, and they have one son, Oliver Burr Jennings. Mr. Jennings belongs to the Metropolitan, University, University Athletic, New York Yacht, and St. Andrews Golf clubs, the Country Club, of Westchester County, the Downtown Association, the Yale Alumni Association, and the New England Society. His home is in East Forty-first Street, near Fifth Avenue, and his country residence is at Cold Spring Harbor, Long Island.

WILLIAM TRAVERS JEROME

THE name of Jerome, as well as the family which bears it, is of French origin, but it was for many centuries established in the Isle of Wight, England Many wills and conveyances bearing the signatures of its members who resided in that part of England are preserved in the public records of the County of Hampshire, and in the archives of the Bishopric of Winchester, among them being a will dated 1503, which was executed by one Henricus Jerome de Wallop. Representatives of the name were also found among the early settlers of the New England Colonies. The grandfather of Mr. William Travers Jerome was Isaac Jerome, who was born at Stockbridge, Mass. He removed to New York State early in the present century, becoming a prominent and influential citizen of the central portion of the State. He married Aurora Murray, born at Ballston, N. Y., who was a member of a family possessing a distinguished Revolutionary record. Her father, Reuben Murray, was a Lieutenant in the New York State service during the contest, while another ancestor, Major Lebbens Ball, served throughout the Revolutionary War in one of the regiments of the Massachusetts Line in the Continental service He was a descendant of Francis Ball, who came to New England in the infancy of the Colonies and settled at Springfield, Mass., in 1644.

Lawrence Roscoe Jerome, father of Mr. William Travers Jerome, was born of this parentage at Pompey, N. Y. Becoming a successful man of business at an early age, he made New York City his home some time prior to the beginning of the Civil War, and was for many years one of the foremost figures in both the financial and social circles of the metropolis. He pursued the profession of a banker and broker with talent and success, and was long identified with Wall Street affairs, and interested in some of the largest enterprises of his day. Possessing exceptional personal qualities and geniality of character, he was one.of the natural leaders of a group of famous club men and wits whose reputation has never been equaled in New York. The name borne by his son, the subject of this article, commemorates the warm personal and business friendship which existed between Lawrence R Jerome and the celebrated William Riggin Travers, the noted financier, sportsman and man of the world. Lawrence R. Jerome was also a prominent patron of sport, and was associated with his equally well-known brother, the late Leonard Jerome, with William R. Travers, the elder August Belmont, and others of similar prominence in the creation of Jerome Park, and in the formation of the American Jockey Club, the organization which first gave character and standing to the American turf, and attracted the interest and support of the wealth and fashion of New York to the sport. He took a leading part in yachting and other higher forms of amusements, and ranked as a power in the most select club circles. The daughter of his brother Leonard, Jennie Jerome, married the late Lord Randolph Churchill, the English statesman, who was brother of the late and uncle of the present Duke of Marlborough. Lady Randolph Churchill has been one of the most prominent American women who married Englishmen of rank. Lawrence R. Jerome married Katharine Hall, of Palmyra, N. Y.

Mr. William Travers Jerome was born in New York City in 1859. He was educated at schools in this city, and at Loney, Switzerland, and was graduated with degree of A. M. from Amherst College. He then entered the Law School of Columbia College, and was graduated LL. B. from that institution in 1884 He was admitted to the bar of New York, and has since pursued the practice of his profession with success. For three years Mr. Jerome served as Assistant District Attorney of New York County, and was engaged, both officially and as an advocate, in many of the most famous trials which have occupied the courts in recent years. His political and legal ability made him a prominent actor in the proceedings by which the corruption of the city departments was exposed in 1894, and soon afterwards he was elected to the bench of one of the city's tribunals. In 1888, Mr. Jerome married Lavinia Howe, of Elizabeth, N. J They have one son, William Travers Jerome, Jr. Mr. Jerome is a member of the Union, City and Nineteenth Century clubs.

JAMES RILEY JESUP

B ROOM HALL, near Sheffield, England, was the seat of the family to which Edward Jesup, the pioneer of the American branch, belonged. He was one of the founders of Stamford, Conn., but moved to Westchester County, N. Y. Among the records at Albany is an Indian deed for a tract of land purchased by Edward Jesup and another in 1664. Edward Jesup, his son, 1663-1732, was born at West Farms, N Y., but became a freeman of Fairfield, Conn, and about 1720 moved to Stamford. He married Elizabeth Hyde, daughter of John and Elizabeth (Harvey) Hyde. The third Edward Jesup, 1697-1750, born at Fairfield, was a Captain of militia and married Sarah Blackback. Ebenezer Jesup, 1739-1812, their son, graduated from Yale in 1760, became a physician, and was a surgeon in the Revolutionary Army. By his first wife, Eleanor Andrews, he was the father of Ebenezer Jesup, second of the name, 1767-1851. The latter was a merchant in Saugatuck, Conn., and from 1832 to 1837 was president of the Bridgeport Bank. He was also a director of the Fairfield County Bank in Norwalk, and a Major in the Revolution. In 1790, he married Sarah Wright, daughter of Obadiah Wright and Sarah Adams, of Norwalk. The father of Obadiah Wright was Dennis Wright, who was one of the first settlers of Oyster Bay, Long Island.

William Henry Jesup, grandfather of Mr James R Jesup, was the son of the second Ebenezer Jesup. He was born in Saugatuck, now Westport, Conn., in 1791. Educated in Lebanon, now Goshen, New London County, at an early age he became associated with his father in business. Removing to New York before he had reached middle age, he successfully engaged in business in Wall Street His first wife was Charity Burr Sherwood, daughter of the Honorable Samuel B Sherwood, of Saugatuck, Conn. She was born in 1794 and died in 1816. His second wife, the grandmother of Mr James R. Jessup, was Mary Hannah Riley, whom he married in 1818. She was the daughter of Appleton Riley and Mary Griswold, of Goshen, Conn. Her father was the son of John Riley and Lucy Case. The wife of the Honorable Horatio Seymour, United States Senator from Vermont in 1821, was a cousin of Appleton Riley.

John Riley, ancestor of Mary H. Riley, came to Connecticut in 1645; his descendant and namesake, John Riley, father of Appleton Riley, was a wealthy land owner in New Jersey During the War of the Revolution, several of the family were in command of privateers which were fitted out at Connecticut ports The mother of Mary Hannah (Riley) Jesup was a member of the celebrated Griswold family and directly descended from Edward Griswold, who came with his brother, Matthew Griswold, from England in 1639 and settled in Windsor, Conn ; the line of descent from Edward Griswold to Mary (Griswold) Riley was through George Griswold, who was born in England, and settled in Windsor, Conn ; George Griswold, born in 1671; Zaccheus Griswold, who was born in 1705 and married, for his second wife, his cousin, Mary Griswold, daughter of Frances Griswold and Giles Griswold, who married Mary Stanley in 1762.

James Riley Jesup, Sr , the father of the subject of this sketch and the son of William Henry Jesup and Mary Hannah Riley, was born in Saugatuck, Conn., in 1819 Prepared for college in the academy at Wilton, he entered Yale College and was graduated from that institution with the degree of A B. in 1840. Beginning the study of law in the office of the Honorable Eliphalet Swift, of Westport, he was admitted to the bar in Fairfield County in 1843. Soon after he moved to New York, where he made his home for the rest of his life and became a leading member of the bar. In 1848, he married Mary Black, daughter of William and Phoebe C. (Heyer) Black

Mr. James Riley Jesup, Jr , the eldest child in his father's family, was born in Brooklyn in 1849 He has been occupied in financial affairs throughout his business career, has been for many years senior member of the firm of Jesup & Lamont, stock brokers, and is a member of the New York Stock Exchange. In 1877, he married Mary E. Lamont, daughter of Charles A. Lamont, of New York. His city residence is at 555 Fifth Avenue, and he is a member of the Tuxedo Club. He is also a patron of the Metropolitan Museum of Art and the American Museum of Natural History.

MORRIS KETCHUM JESUP

W ESTERN Connecticut was the residence of the successive generations of the Jesup family from Edward Jesup, the emigrant of the seventeenth century, down to the last generation. On the preceding page of this volume the family line is traced from Edward to Ebenezer Jesup, of Fairfield, 1767-1851, the second of that name, who was the grandfather of the eminent banker and citizen of New York, referred to in this article.

Charles Jesup, 1796-1837, son of Ebenezer and Sarah (Wright) Jesup, was the father of Mr. Morris K. Jesup. He was born in Saugatuck, Conn., and after graduating from Yale College in 1814, traveled in Europe and engaged successfully in business, while he was also deeply interested in religious matters. In 1821, he married Abigail Sherwood, daughter of the Honorable Samuel B. Sherwood, 1767-1833, a leading lawyer of Fairfield County, Conn , and a Member of Congress in the session of 1817-1819. His father was the Reverend Samuel Sherwood and his grandfather, who was also named Samuel Sherwood, married Jane Burr, sister of the Reverend Aaron Burr, the first president of Princeton College.

Mr. Morris Ketchum Jesup was born at Westport, Conn., June 21st, 1830. In 1842, his widowed mother removed with her family of children to New York, and her son, Morris K., entered the office of Rogers, Ketchum & Grosvenor, of the Paterson Locomotive Works, where he received his preparatory business training. In 1852, he formed the firm of Clark & Jesup, and in 1856 founded the banking house of M K. Jesup & Co. The latter firm has been in continuous and successful existence from that time to the present day, although its name has been varied. It became successively Jesup, Paton & Co , and John Paton & Co , and more recently was changed to Cuyler, Morgan & Co , Mr. Jesup being a special partner. During his business career, Mr. Jesup has been a director of many large corporations, and through his connections abroad, has done much to secure the investment of European capital in the United States. During the Civil War he warmly supported the Union cause and was treasurer of the Christian Commission. Since 1863, he has been a member of the Chamber of Commerce, and is now its first vice-president.

Much of Mr. Jesup's attention has been devoted to religion and charity. He was a founder of the Young Men's Christian Association, was its president in 1872 and is at the present time one of its trustees. He is president of the New York Mission and Tract Society, of the American Sunday School Union and the Five Points House of Industry, vice-president of the Society for the Prevention of Cruelty to Animals and of the Institute for the Instruction of the Deaf and Dumb, treasurer of the Slater Fund for the education of freedmen and a trustee of the Half Orphan Asylum. He presented Jesup Hall to the Union Theological Seminary.

Education and science have also been objects of Mr. Jesup's labors, which have been recognized by Yale and Williams Colleges, both of these institutions having conferred the degree of M. A. upon him. He is a trustee of the American Geographical Society, and in 1881 was elected president of the American Museum of Natural History, having been one of its founders To it he presented the superb Jesup collection illustrating the woods of the United States, while he took a leading part in securing the enactment of laws in this State for the preservation of its forests, having through his efforts enlisted the support of the Chamber of Commerce in the movement. Mr. Jesup is a member of the Metropolitan, Century, University, New York Yacht and other leading clubs, the Sons of the Revolution and the New England Society.

In 1851, Mr. Jesup married Maria Van Antwerp De Witt, daughter of the Reverend Thomas De Witt, the distinguished minister of the Collegiate Dutch Church and a member of one of the oldest Colonial families. Mrs. Jesup, like her husband, takes a warm interest in religious and philanthropic work. Their city residence is in Madison Avenue and their country home, Belvoir Terrace, Lenox, Mass.

HUGH JUDGE JEWETT

NEAR Glenville, Md , is an estate known as Lansdowne with a venerable stone homestead which for several generations has been in the possession of the Jewett family. The bearers of that name are descended from Joseph Jewett, who, belonging to a good family in the West Riding of Yorkshire, came to America in 1639 and was one of the first settlers of Rowley, Mass. In 1650, and the ten succeeding years, he represented that town in the General Court of the Massachusetts Bay Colony.

One branch of the family became established in Maryland over a hundred years ago, and to it the subject of this article belongs. His father, John Jewett, of Glenville, Md., married Susanna Judge, daughter of Hugh Judge, of Philadelphia. She belonged to an old Quaker family and was herself distinguished as a preacher in the Society of Friends Several of the sons of this marriage became men of great prominence. The eldest son, the Honorable Thomas L Jewett, was a leading lawyer and Judge in Ohio, and became president of the Pittsburg, Cincinnati & St. Louis Railroad and vice-president of the Pennsylvania Railroad Company. His brother, Isaac W. Jewett, was a prominent business man in Baltimore, Md , and president of the Potomac Fire Insurance Company A third brother, the Honorable Joshua H. Jewett, settled in Kentucky, and was a Member of Congress for several terms immediately before the Civil War.

The Honorable Hugh Judge Jewett is another of these remarkable brothers. Born in Glenville, Md , July 1st, 1817, he studied law and was admitted to the bar in 1838. Removing to Ohio, he practiced for ten years in St. Clairsville and then established himself in Zanesville. He attained high political distinction in Ohio, being elected to the State Senate in 1853 and was appointed United States District Attorney by President Pierce. In 1861 and 1863, he was nominated for Governor and was a candidate for the United States Senatorship. In 1872, he was elected Member of Congress for the Columbus, Ohio, district.

About 1852, he became interested in the financial and railroad affairs to which much of his life has been devoted. In that year he became president of the Muskingum branch of the Ohio State Bank and later was the founder of and partner in a banking firm in Zanesville. Made a director of the Ohio Central Railroad in 1853, he became its president in 1857. In 1868, he was elected president of the Pittsburg, Cincinnati & St. Louis, the Little Miami and the Columbus & Xenia railroads, and was interested in the construction of the Kansas Pacific and other Western lines In 1874, he removed to New York City, and became president of the Erie Railway, was appointed its receiver in 1875, and when the property was reorganized as the New York, Lake Erie & Western Railroad was president of that company until 1884 He was also a director of the Western Union Telegraph Company and other large corporations Since 1884, he has practically retired from active business and spends much of his time at Glenville, Hartford County, Md., on his ancestral estate. In early life, he married Sarah J. Ellis, daughter of Judge Ellis, of St Clairsville, two sons of this marriage, John Ellis and George Monypenny Jewett, living to maturity. In 1853, he married, for his second wife, Sarah Elizabeth Guthrie She was the daughter of Julius Chappell Guthrie and descended from the Colonial Governor, Thomas Welles, from the Reverend Abraham Pierson, first president of Yale College, and from the Bradley, Buckingham, Hawley, Huntington and Sturgis families. Mr Jewett is a member of the Union, Metropolitan and City clubs

Mr Jewett's only son by his second marriage is William Kennon Jewett. His two daughters are Helen Pamelia and Sarah Guthrie Jewett. William Kennon Jewett was graduated from Williams College in 1879. In October, 1881, he married Patty Kyle Stuart, daughter of George Hay Stuart, of Philadelphia, a prominent merchant and philanthropist in that city. Among her ancestors are the Dennison, Stanton and Spaulding families of New England William Kennon Jewett resides at New Brighton, Staten Island, and is president of the Staten Island Cricket and Baseball Club. He belongs to the Ohio Society, the University, University Athletic and Σ Φ clubs, and the Williams College Alumni Association.

EDWARD RODOLPH JOHNES

UNTIL the year 1891, there stood in the town of Southampton, Long Island, an historic dwelling built in 1650 by Edward Johnes, one of the first settlers of that place, the house having been occupied continuously by his descendants up to 1835. The family from which he sprang was established in the counties of Berks, Salop and Somerset, as well as in London, Sir Francis Johnes, who was Lord Mayor of that city in 1620, being of the Johnes of Claverly, Salop. The coat of arms borne by the American branch of the family is that confirmed by the Heralds College in 1610, and is a golden lion passant, between three gold crosses, formee fitchee, on a blue shield, with a gold chief, the crest being a golden lion rampant, supporting a blue anchor with gold flukes, and the motto, *Vince Malum Bono.* Edward Johnes sailed to America with Winthrop, in 1629, and settled in Charlestown, Mass. He was an office-holder and land owner in Charlestown, and is described in the early town records with the prefix "Mr.", which in those days implied social importance. In 1640, he married Annie, daughter of George Griggs, who in 1635 came from Landen, Bucks County, in the Hopewell; in 1644 he sold his land in Charlestown and removed to Southampton, where he built the old home and died in 1659.

The Reverend Timothy Johnes, D. D., grandson of the pioneer, was the son of Samuel Johnes, of Southampton, who entertained Governor Lovelace in 1669 when he made a tour through Long Island. Timothy Johnes was born in 1717 and graduated from Yale College, which in 1782 conferred upon him the degree of D. D. He became minister of the Presbyterian Church in Morristown, N. J. He died in 1794, leaving by his second wife, Kesiah Ludlow Johnes, a son, William Johnes, 1755–1836, who was a Captain in the Continental Army, fought at the battle of Springfield, and married Charlotte Pierson, a descendant of the Reverend Abram Pierson, who landed at Boston in 1639. Charles Alexander Johnes, son of William Johnes, was born in 1796 and became a merchant in New York and Newburgh, and Mayor of the latter place. He married Sarah Middlebrook Pettit, a descendant of a Huguenot family which migrated to Long Island in 1683. Their son, William Pierson Johnes, married Anna Louisa Gold, of Whitesboro, N. Y., whose grandfather, Thomas R. Gold, was distinguished in State politics and as a Member of Congress for twenty years, being also the agent of the United States for the Six Nations. He was the legal adviser, in America, of Louis Philippe.

Mr. Edward Rodolph Johnes, the son of this marriage, was born in Whitesboro, N. Y., in 1852. His father dying in 1853, his mother married the Reverend J. S. Shipman, D. D., rector of Christ Church, New York City, and his early days were spent in Mobile, Ala., and Lexington, Ky. He entered Yale College, being graduated in 1873, and was a member of the Skull and Bones Society and the class poet. After a year spent in foreign travel, he entered the Columbia Law School, and was called to the bar in 1876. Mr Johnes married Winifred Wallace Tinker, of Erie, Pa., a lady of literary taste and ability. Both Mr. and Mrs. Johnes have written many poems, stories and essays which have appeared in the leading periodicals. They have two children, Edward Gold and Raymond Middlebrook Johnes.

Among Mr. Johnes' artistic treasures are many old family portraits and two pictures presented to his great-grandfather, Thomas R. Gold, by Louis Philippe. He has, in addition, a choice collection of paintings, and is a connoisseur of art. During his travels abroad, he enjoyed the distinction of being presented at three foreign courts, those of France, Greece and Egypt. A short time since, the Government of Venezuela decorated him with the Order of the Liberator Bolivar, of the grade bestowed on foreign ambassadors. This honor was in recognition of his services to that Republic through a pamphlet, in which he pointed out the applicability of the Monroe Doctrine to the boundary dispute between Venezuela and Great Britain, and which was published some years in advance of the enunciation of similar views by President Cleveland and Secretary of State Olney. Mr Johnes is a member of the University, St Nicholas, Colonial and other clubs.

BRADISH JOHNSON

FOR three generations the family represented by the gentleman whom we are now considering has held a prominent position in both New York and Louisiana. William M Johnson, grandfather of Mr Bradish Johnson, was a native of Nova Scotia, who came to the United States at an early age and became an eminent merchant and manufacturer in this city, being respected for his wealth, influence and high personal integrity. In addition to his possessions here, he acquired large property and commercial interests in the South, owning several plantations near New Orleans, La

He married Sarah Rice, a member of the leading Boston family of that name. Their son, Bradish Johnson, Sr, was born, in 1811, at Woodlawn Plantation, a beautiful place on the Mississippi River some distance below the City of New Orleans, and which was renowned as one of the finest places of its kind in the State, or, indeed, in the entire Southwestern section of the United States. Bradish Johnson, Sr, was for many years a prominent figure in the business and social worlds, both in New York and New Orleans, spending portions of each year in either city. At the outbreak of the Civil War he was residing on his plantation in Louisiana, and in the early days of the great struggle, considerably before President Lincoln had issued the proclamation of emancipation, he voluntarily freed his many slaves

It is also related of him that when the United States fleet engaged in the capture of New Orleans came up the Mississippi to where his plantation was, he at once raised the national flag and kept it flying as long as the war lasted. His New York residence was the dignified mansion at Twenty-first Street and Fifth Avenue long occupied as a club house by the Lotos Club prior to its removal up-town. He retired from active business cares of all kinds some years before his death, which occurred in 1892, at Bayshore, Long Island

His wife, born Louisa A. Lawrence, was a member of the distinguished and ancient New York family of that name, which has been identified with the Province and State from the earliest days of its settlement. She was a granddaughter of Jonathan Lawrence, one of the most active supporters of the patriotic cause in New York during the American Revolution He was not only a member of the New York Provincial Congress in 1775-7, but became Major of the Queens County Militia in 1775, Lieutenant-Colonel of the New York State forces in 1780, and Captain of Sappers and Miners in 1792 Through his mother, the subject of this article is thus connected by blood or intermarriage with many of the most prominent and respected old New York and Long Island families, while his Lawrence ancestry also extends back to European progenitors who were numbered among the nobility and gentry of England

Mr Bradish Johnson is the son of the late Bradish Johnson, Sr, and his wife, Louisa (Lawrence) Johnson, and was born in New York in 1851 He was educated in Europe, which he has revisited on several occasions, making extended journeys in all its various countries Mr. Johnson has not adopted any profession, but finds ample scope for his ability in the care and management of the large property interests left by his father in this and other portions of the United States, his duties in this connection indeed occupying the major portion of his attention In 1877, he married Aimee Elizabeth Gaillard, of this city Mr and Mrs Johnson have two sons, Bradish Gaillard Johnson and Aymar Johnson, and a daughter, Aimee Gaillard Johnson. Their town residence is 102 Fifth Avenue, with a country seat at East Islip, Long Island, and they have also passed a considerable portion of their time in travel, not only in Europe, but in the United States as well.

Mr. Johnson has taken an active, though not a conspicuous, part in social and club life in the city of his birth. He was a member of the Patriarchs, and belongs to the Union and Metropolitan clubs, and to the South Side Club of Long Island He is a member of the St Nicholas Society and of the Sons of the American Revolution, being very active in the latter patriotic body, of which he is a trustee

EASTMAN JOHNSON

ONE of the foremost American genre and portrait painters in this generation, Mr. Eastman Johnson, was born, in 1824, in Lovell, near Fryeburg, Me. His father, Philip C. Johnson, was for many years Secretary of State of Maine. In 1845, he removed to Washington to accept a place in the navy department and held that position until his death. His first wife was Mary Kimball Chandler and his second wife, Mrs Mary (Washington) James, a sister of Richard Washington and among the nearest of kin of the surviving relatives of George Washington

As a young man, Mr. Eastman Johnson began the practice of his profession by the execution of portraits in black and white in Maine. While residing with his parents in Washington, he drew portraits of Daniel Webster, John Quincy Adams and other statesmen of that period and also of Mrs. Dolly Madison, Mrs. Alexander Hamilton and other ladies. From 1846 to 1849 he was in Boston, where he made portraits of Emerson, Longfellow, Hawthorne, Sumner and other celebrities. Going abroad in 1849, he entered the Royal Academy of Dusseldorf, then studied with Leutze and afterwards spent four years at The Hague. Then he sent home his first important pictures, The Savoyard, The Card Players and others. He finished his European experience in Paris and then returned home in 1856, residing in Washington in the winter, but passing the summers of two years among the Northwestern Indians, of whom he made many important studies. After establishing himself in New York he painted pictures of American life, and his Old Kentucky Home, in 1858, fully established his reputation. In recent years, he has devoted himself almost entirely to portraiture. Among his most important works have been portraits of President Grover Cleveland, President Chester A. Arthur, President Benjamin Harrison, the Reverend Dr. James McCosh and the Honorable William M. Evarts. Some of his most important genre works have been The Old Stage Coach, Milton Dictating to his Daughters, and The Wandering Fiddler.

The wife of Mr. Johnson, whom he married in 1869, was Elizabeth Williams Buckley. Her father was Phineas Henry Buckley, born in 1800, and her mother Phœbe McCoun, daughter of Townsend and Sarah McCoun, of Troy, N. Y The grandfather of Mrs. Johnson was Thomas Buckley, who was born in Bristol, R. I, in 1771, and, removing to New York, engaged in mercantile life, being president of the Bank of North America and connected with many charitable institutions. His wife, whom he married in 1793, was Anna Lawrence, daughter of John L and Ann (Burling) Lawrence, among whose ancestors were the wife of Sir George Carteret, who in Colonial times was Governor of Virginia, and Judge Lawrence, of Bay Side, Long Island, who married, in Revolutionary times, the sister of the Earl of Effingham.

The Buckleys in America came from the Buckleys of Lancashire, England. The earliest ancestor was John de Buckley, whose son, Geoffrey Buckley, was slain at the battle of Eversham in 1265. The Buckleys of New York had their direct origin from Phineas Buckley, a cadet of the Lancashire family and a native of London. He was a trader to the West Indies and the North American Provinces, and came to Philadelphia in 1713, where he married Sarah Hugg, daughter of Elias Hugg, of Gloucester County, N. J. William Buckley, son of Phineas Buckley, was born in Philadelphia in 1715, was educated there, made several voyages to the West Indies and then in 1741, having married Ruth Leach, daughter of Thomas and Sarah Leach, of Newport, settled there in mercantile business and died in 1759. Phineas Buckley, son of William Buckley, and great-grandfather of Mrs. Johnson, was born in Bristol, R. I., in 1742 and died in 1826. He was a prominent member of the Society of Friends. His second wife, the mother of his son, Thomas, Mrs Johnson's grandfather, was Mary Shipley, daughter of Thomas and Mary Shipley, of Brandywine, N. J.

Mr. and Mrs. Johnson live in West Fifty-fifth Street. They have one daughter, Ethel Eastman Johnson, who married Alfred Ronald Conkling. They belong to the Tuxedo colony Mr. Johnson is a member of the Union League, Century and Players clubs, is a patron of the Metropolitan Museum of Art and has been a member of the National Academy of Design since 1860

SHIPLEY JONES

PATERNAL ancestors of Mr Shipley Jones were prominent in the foundation and early government of the Province of Pennsylvania, while the lines of his descent in England are from illustrious personages. His grandfather was Isaac C Jones, of Philadelphia, and his father Samuel Tonkin Jones, of the same city. Isaac C Jones married Hannah Firth, daughter of Ezra Firth, of Salem County, N J Her mother was Elizabeth Carpenter, daughter of Judge Preston Carpenter and granddaughter of Samuel Carpenter, Jr, of Philadelphia Her great-grandmother was Hannah Preston, daughter of Samuel Preston, Mayor of Philadelphia in 1711 and Treasurer of Pennsylvania, 1714-43, and whose mother was Rachel Lloyd, daughter of Thomas Lloyd, the companion of Penn in the foundation of the Colony in 1683, and Deputy Governor, descended in the twenty-fifth generation from Alfred the Great, Edward the elder, King of England, and Henry I, of France, as well as from the Barons de Wake, the Princess Joan Plantagenet, "Fair Maid of Kent," and the Earls of Kent.

On the maternal side, Mr Jones' American ancestors include the Thomas family, of Maryland, and the Ludlows of New York His mother, the wife of Samuel Tonkin Jones, was Martha Mary Thomas, daughter of Philip Thomas, of Maryland, 1783-1848, whose wife, Frances Mary Ludlow, was the daughter of James Ludlow, of New York, and his wife, Elizabeth Harrison, of Newport, R I. Samuel Thomas, of Anne Arundel County, Md, 1655-1743, was eighteenth in descent from Llewelen, the Great Prince of North Wales, who died in 1240, and whose second wife was the Lady Joan Plantagenet, daughter of King John In succeeding generations the line is traced through the Lords of Gower and Barons Mowbray Samuel Thomas married Mary Hutchins, and their son, Philip Thomas, 1694-1763, married for his second wife, in 1724, Ann Chew, the daughter of Samuel and Mary Chew. Their grandson, Philip Thomas, of Rockland, Crest County, Md, married Sarah Margaret Weems, daughter of William and Catharine (Crumpton) Weems, of Weems Forest, great-grandparents of Mr Shipley Jones.

The Ludlow family, from which Mr Jones descends through his maternal grandmother, Frances Mary (Ludlow) Thomas, was founded in America by Gabriel Ludlow, who came to New York in the seventeenth century. He married Sarah Hanmer, in 1697, and had a number of sons, all of whom married daughters of prominent citizens of that day His tenth child, James Ludlow, born in New York, and graduated from Kings College, now Columbia University, was the great-grandfather of Mr Jones. Elizabeth Harrison, wife of James Ludlow and mother of Frances Mary (Ludlow) Thomas, was the daughter of Peter Harrison, collector of the port of New Haven, whose wife, Elizabeth Pelham, was the great-granddaughter of Benedict Arnold, the first Governor of Rhode Island.

Samuel Tonkin Jones, Mr Shipley Jones' father, married first, Sarah Margaret Thomas, and second, her younger sister, Martha Mary Thomas. Another sister, Catharine Ann Thomas, married William B Bend, of New York, and a fourth sister was Elizabeth Frances Thomas. Ludlow Thomas, a brother, married Mary S. Thompson and another brother, Philip Thomas, married Anna Ellen Raymond.

Mr Shipley Jones was the third child of his father's second marriage He was born in New York, and was graduated from Columbia College, in 1869, with the degree of A B, receiving later the degree of A M. He is a stock broker by profession, and his home is The Cedars, New Brighton, Staten Island He is a member of the Metropolitan club, and of the Society of Colonial Wars and other organizations. Of Mr Jones' immediate relatives, his half sister, the only child of his father's first marriage, is Frances Mary Jones, who married the late Richard M. Pell, and after his death became the wife of Louis T Hoyt. His eldest sister, Sarah Margaret Jones, married Henry Beadel, and has two children, Henry Ludlow and Gerald Woodward Beadel. His younger sister, Elizabeth Ludlow Jones, married John Dash Van Buren, and has two sons, John Dash, Jr, and Maurice Pelham Van Buren

CHARLES CONOVER KALBFLEISCH

NOTWITHSTANDING their comparatively small number, the original Holland settlers of New York have left a remarkably distinct impression on the course of American history and on the character of the American people. Valuable as this element has been, it received no reinforcement from the mother country from the date of the English occupation of the New Netherland, and but few instances can be cited of further additions to the population of the United States from the same source. Mr. Kalbfleisch's family furnishes one of the few exceptions, and supplies in the record of its founder an example of the force of character, patriotism and other qualities which are so noticeable in Americans of Dutch blood, and which have been so influential in shaping the destinies of the metropolis.

The late Martin Kalbfleisch, the grandfather of Mr. Charles C Kalbfleisch, was born at Flushing, in the Netherland province of Zeeland, in 1804, and received a thorough education in his native place. In after life, he was distinguished for a knowledge of languages, for a wide acquaintance with literature and for a devotion, whether in private or public station, to the cause of education. In 1822, he sailed to the Dutch East Indies on an American ship, and through this association imbibed a desire to make the United States his home. This he put into execution in 1826, when he came to New York, where, after a few years, his integrity, energy and ability enabled him to found a manufactory of chemicals in Harlem. Some years afterwards, he removed his business to Connecticut, but in 1842 located his works at Greenpoint, Long Island. His manufacturing interests soon became one of the most important concerns of the kind in the country, and some years afterwards he relinquished their care to his sons and retired from business, partly to enjoy his well-earned fortune, but more especially to devote his time to the public service. His interest in this connection began in Brooklyn Soon after he established his works at Greenpoint, he secured for that district, partly at his own expense, its first free school facilities. In 1851, he was Supervisor of Bushwick, Kings County, afterwards part of the City of Brooklyn. In 1853, he was president of the commission which arranged the consolidation of the old town of Williamsburgh with the City of Brooklyn, and in 1854 was Democratic candidate for the Mayoralty of the consolidated city, but was defeated at the polls by a narrow majority. From 1855 to 1861, he was a member of the Board of Aldermen of Brooklyn, and was three times president of the board; in the last above mentioned year he was elected Mayor, his service in that office being followed in 1862 by a term as Representative in Congress, and in 1867 by a second election as Mayor of Brooklyn. In addition to his various public positions, Martin Kalbfleisch was prominent among the founders, and as a director of many of the largest and most successful banks, trust companies and insurance corporations of his adopted city, was universally regarded as a leader of the business world, and in the performance of every duty earned and retained the entire respect and confidence of the community.

By his marriage with Elizabeth Harvey, a lady of English birth, Martin Kalbfleisch had several sons, who were prominent in business and social life in New York and Brooklyn One of them was Charles Henry Kalbfleisch, the father of the subject of this article. He became a member of the firm of Martin Kalbfleisch's Sons, the house founded by his father. He married Josephine Conover, of New York, and had a son, Mr Charles Conover Kalbfleisch, and a daughter, Josephine, who, in 1895, married John Howard Adams, of this city.

Mr. Charles Conover Kalbfleisch was born in this city July 30th, 1868. He graduated from Columbia University in the class of 1891, receiving, in the following year, the degree of A M, and was graduated from the law school of the same institution in 1893, being admitted to the bar in the same year, and has since then been engaged in the practice of his profession. In October, 1897, Mr Kalbfleisch married, at Babylon, Long Island, his cousin, Maud Kalbfleisch, daughter of Franklin H. Kalbfleisch. Mr. Kalbfleisch is a member of the Bar Association, the Columbia College Alumni Association, The Players and The Grolier Club

DELANCEY ASTOR KANE

U P to the time, under Queen Elizabeth and her successors, when the native families were deprived of their lands, what is now County Londonderry and part of County Antrim, Ireland, were known as the O'Kanes country and were held by the ancient noble family of that name. From this possession the Kane family, distinguished in American records, derives its origin. Their ancestry is traced from Evanne O'Kane, whose son, Bernard, married Martha O'Hara, daughter of Captain O'Hara and granddaughter of O'Neil, of Shane's Castle, County Antrim. Their eldest son, John O'Kane, born in 1734, came to this country in 1752.

John O'Kane, in America, dropped the prefix from his name and was known as Kane. At the time of the Revolution, he resided on his estate, Sharyvogne, Dutchess County, N. Y., and being a Royalist, was included in the confiscation directed against supporters of that cause Losing all his property, he returned to England with his brother, Captain Kane, who had served in the Royalist forces during the Revolution His wife was Sybil Kent, daughter of the Reverend Elisha Kent, who was a graduate of Yale in 1729, filled several pulpits in Putnam County, N. Y., and elsewhere, and died in 1776. His wife, Abigail Morse, was daughter of the Reverend Joseph Morse, of Derby, Conn., 1679-1732, who graduated at Harvard in 1699 and was one of the first five to receive an honorary degree from Yale He was descended from John Moss, one of the founders of New Haven and a representative in the early Connecticut Legislature The wife of the Reverend Joseph Moss was Abigail Russell, daughter of the Reverend Samuel Russell, of Hadley, Mass., and a descendant of John Russell, who came to Massachusetts in 1636, and who, for sixteen years, sheltered the regicides Goffe and Whalley in his house at Hadley.

The children of John and Sybil (Kent) Kane were six in number. Their eldest son, John Kane, was a famous New York merchant, and his sons were J. Grenville Kane, long the secretary of the Union Club, and Pierre G. Kane, who married Edith Brevoort. The second son, Elisha Kane, married Alida, daughter of General Robert Van Rensselaer, and the third son, Oliver, grandfather of Colonel Delancey Astor Kane, married Eliza Clark, daughter of John Green Clark, of Providence, R. I. Of the daughters of John and Sybil Kane, Abigail married Dr John Prescott Lawrence, Adeline married Jeremiah Van Rensselaer and Sarah married Thomas Morris, son of Robert Morris, the Revolutionary financier. Among the descendants of the family's different branches have been many men of distinction, including Judge John K. Kane of the United States District Court in Pennsylvania, Dr. Elisha Kent Kane, the Arctic explorer, and General Thomas Lawrence Kane, Commander of the Pennsylvania Bucktail Brigade in the Civil War.

Oliver Kane and his wife Eliza (Clark) Kane were the parents of Delancey Kane, of Newport, R. I. The latter married Louisa Langdon, daughter of Walter Langdon and his wife, Dorothea Astor, daughter of John Jacob Astor, the first of that name in America. Walter Langdon's father, John Langdon, was Governor of New Hampshire and United States Senator.

Colonel Delancey Astor Kane is the son of Delancey Kane, of Newport, and his wife, Louisa Langdon, and was born at Newport, R. I, in 1844. He was graduated from the United States Military Academy, West Point, in 1868, and was a Lieutenant, First Cavalry, United States Army, from 1868 to 1870. He studied at Trinity College, Cambridge, England, and graduated in 1873 from the Law Department of Columbia College, New York In 1872, Colonel Kane married Eleanora Iselin, daughter of Adrian Iselin, of this city, their only child being Delancey Iselin Kane. Colonel Kane's city residence is 7 West Thirty-fifth Street, and he has a country place at New Rochelle, N. Y. He is a member of the Union, Metropolitan, Knickerbocker, Country, Coaching, New York Yacht and Larchmont Yacht clubs.

The brothers of Colonel Kane are S Nicholson Kane, John Innes Kane, who married Annie C Schermerhorn, and Woodbury Kane. Another brother, Walter Langdon Kane, married Mary Rotch Hunter, of Newport, where he died in 1896 His sisters are Louise Langdon and Sybil Kent Kane and Emily A , wife of Augustus Jay.

JOHN KEAN

URING the Revolutionary period, John Kean, the great-grandfather of the above gentleman, was a leading patriot of South Carolina, where he was born about 1756. He was an officer in the Revolutionary Army, and being taken prisoner, was confined on a prison ship in Charleston harbor. After the war, he was a Member of Congress from South Carolina from 1785 to 1787, and although he represented a Southern constituency, voted against the extension of slavery into the Northwestern territory. Removing to Philadelphia, he became cashier of the Bank of the United States. In 1786, he married Susan Livingston, 1759-1831, daughter of Peter Van Brugh Livingston, 1710-1793, the son of Philip Livingston, second Lord of Livingston Manor. The wife of Peter Van Brugh Livingston was Mary Alexander, daughter of James Alexander, Surveyor-General of East Jersey, member of the King's Council and Attorney-General of New York, whose wife, Maria (Spratt) Provoost, was the daughter of John Spratt and Marie de Peyster, and widow of Samuel Provoost.

Peter Philip James Kean, the son of John Kean and his wife, Susan Livingston, was the grandfather of the present Mr. John Kean. He was born in 1788, was Major of the New Jersey militia, and died in 1828. He married Sarah Morris, daughter of General Jacob Morris, who was born in Morrisania in 1755, served during the Revolution as aide-de-camp to General Charles Lee, and died at his estate, Butternuts, Otsego County, N. Y., in 1844. General Morris was the son of Lewis Morris, signer of the Declaration of Independence, and a grandson of Lewis Morris, 1671-1746, Chief Justice of New York and New Jersey, and Governor of New Jersey in 1736. The founder of the family in this country was Richard Morris, who received the royal grant of Morrisania, Westchester County, N. Y. One of the daughters of Peter Philip James and Sarah (Morris) Kean, and an aunt of the present Mr. John Kean, was Julia Kean, who married Hamilton Fish, of New York, Governor, Senator and Secretary of State of the United States.

John Kean, second of the name, and father of Mr. John Kean of the present generation, was born in 1814. He resided on the family estate, Ursino, Elizabeth, N. J., and was president of the Elizabethtown Gas Company, and vice-president of the Central Railroad Company, of New Jersey. He married Lucy Halsted, daughter of Caleb Halsted, a well-known New York merchant. Mrs. Kean survived her husband, and resides in East Fifty-sixth Street and at Ursino. The eldest son of this marriage, Peter Philip Kean, died young, in 1849, and the eldest daughter, Caroline Morris, who married George Lockhart Rives, of New York, died in 1887. The surviving children of the family are Susan Livingston, John, Julian Halsted, Lucy Halsted, Hamilton Fish, Elizabeth d'Hauteville and Alexander Livingston Kean.

Mr. John Kean, the eldest surviving son, was born at Ursino, N. J., in 1852. He was graduated from Yale College in 1876, and has been engaged in the banking business and connected with financial affairs in this city, being now vice-president of the Manhattan Trust Company. Mr. Kean resides at Ursino, and is a member of the Metropolitan, University and Essex County Country clubs, the Downtown Association and the Metropolitan Club, of Washington. Julian Halsted Kean, the second son, was born in 1854, was graduated from Yale in 1876, and is a member of the New York bar. He belongs to the Metropolitan, University, Players and Riding clubs, and the Downtown Association. Hamilton Fish Kean, the third son, was born in 1862, and in 1888 married Katharine Taylor Winthrop. He has two children, John and Robert Winthrop Kean. He resides in Park Avenue, and is a member of the Union, Knickerbocker, Metropolitan, St Anthony and other clubs. Alexander Livingston Kean, the youngest son, was born in 1866. He is a member of the Metropolitan and other clubs. The eldest surviving daughter of the family, Christine Kean, married W. Emlen Roosevelt. The other daughters are unmarried.

The arms of the Kean family are: Argent, a chevron sable, between two doves, sable. The crest is a griffin's head proper, couped, with an olive branch in its beak. Motto: *Mea Gloria Fides*

EDWARD KELLY

ONE of the direct ancestors of Mr Edward Kelly was a member of the Irish Parliament in 1585, and the family is one of the most ancient and honorable in Ireland The grandfather of Mr. Kelly was Thomas Boye O'Kelly, of Mullaghmore. During the reign of Queen Elizabeth the Mullaghmore branch of the family was deprived of much of its property. As a consequence, the head of the house moved to the North of Ireland and purchased an estate, still in the hands of his descendants. The ancestors of the O'Kellys for many generations were buried in the Abbey of Killconnel, which they founded in the fourteenth century, the first abbot having been Hugh O'Kelly, of Mullaghmore. In 1798, the grandfather of Mr. Edward Kelly took part in the political troubles which occasioned much disturbance in Ireland at that period and changed his name from O'Kelly to Kelly.

The late Eugene Kelly was born in County Tyrone, in 1806, and at the age of twenty-four came to the United States. When he landed in New York he had a small capital, and became a clerk in the mercantile house of Donnelly Bros After a few years, he removed to Maysville, Ky., and went into business, but later on established himself in St Louis. When the California excitement began, he saw the opportunity and went to San Francisco in the latter part of 1849, opening a mercantile establishment there in partnership with Joseph A. Donohoe, Daniel T. Murphy and Adam Grant. After ten years of prosperous business, the firm dissolved, and Mr. Kelly took part in founding the Pacific Coast banking house of Donohoe, Ralston & Co., in San Francisco, and the firm of Eugene Kelly & Co., in New York. For nearly thirty-five years this business was continued, until, in 1894, Eugene Kelly retired and the house was dissolved He was a factor in railroad business and banking for a third of a century He founded the Southern Bank of the State of Georgia and contributed largely to the rebuilding of the town hall of Charleston, S. C , after the war He was a director in the National Park Bank, the Bank of New York, the Equitable Life Assurance Society, the Emigrant Industrial Savings Bank, and the Title Guarantee and Trust Company, while he was also connected with many other corporations of the greatest importance in the financial and railroad world.

He held an important position in the social life of the metropolis A generous supporter of charity and education, he was one of the original life members of the National Academy of Design, for thirteen years a member of the Board of Education, a patron of the American Museum of Natural History and the Metropolitan Museum of Art, and a member of the Chamber of Commerce. In 1884, he was Elector-at-Large and chairman of the Electoral College of the State. In the Roman Catholic Church, of which he was a member, he was a prominent layman, being one of the founders of the Catholic University of America, and a director until his death. He was also a trustee of Seton Hall College and a member of the committees which had oversight of the construction of St Patrick's Cathedral, the Washington Memorial Arch and the Bartholdi Statue of Liberty erected in New York harbor.

The first wife of Eugene Kelly was a Miss Donnelly, who died in 1848. His daughter, Eugenia, by his marriage, became the wife of James A G. Beales, of New York In 1857, he married Margaret Hughes, niece of Archbishop John Hughes, and four sons by this marriage survived him—Eugene, Edward, Thomas Hughes and Robert J Kelly

Mr. Edward Kelly, the son of Eugene Kelly, was born in New York in 1863, and was educated at Stonyhurst College, Lancashire, England. He was engaged in the banking business with the firm of Eugene Kelly & Co , from 1881, and was a partner from 1885 till its dissolution in 1894 He is a patron of the Metropolitan Museum of Art, is a life member of the American Geographical Society, and also a member of various social clubs, and of the sheriff's jury, succeeding his father in that position. In 1882, Mr Kelly married Helen Mitchell Pearsall, of the old Long Island family of that name. He has had three children Helen Margaret Angela, born in 1884; Eugene Edward, who was born in 1890 and died in 1893, and Eugenia, born in 1895.

JOHN STEWART KENNEDY

NEW YORK owes much to its adopted citizens of Scottish birth. In the early history of the city many of its most enterprising settlers came from Scotland, and contributed by their energy and thrift to the commercial and industrial growth of the metropolis After the close of the Revolutionary War, young men of the same nationality took a conspicuous part in the commercial activities of New York in that period Since that time, also, others from the land of the thistle have followed in the footsteps of those who preceded them in earlier times.

Mr. John Stewart Kennedy is a conspicuous representative of that large and influential class of business men, and of patriotic citizens, who, of Scottish birth, have made this city the field of their activities and the scene of their successes. Mr Kennedy was born near Glasgow, Scotland, on the banks of the River Clyde, in 1830. His father was John Kennedy and his mother Isabella Stewart. His family on both the paternal and maternal side were of good old Presbyterian stock. He was the sixth of a family of nine children, and received his elementary education in the Glasgow public schools. Early imbued with the importance of self-reliance and industry as indispensable factors of success in life, he began his business career in a shipping office in Glasgow, when he was thirteen years of age. After an apprenticeship of four years, he entered the office of an iron and coal company, where he remained for three years longer. During all this time he applied himself closely to his books and acquired a substantial education.

In 1850, Mr. Kennedy made his first visit to this country, traveling in Canada and the United States, in the interests of a firm engaged extensively in the iron trade. Establishing his head-quarters in New York, he remained in America about two years and then returned to England and took charge of the Glasgow house of the firm with which he was connected. Four years later, he came back to New York and for the next ten years was a partner in the firm of M. K. Jesup & Co., of New York, and Jesup, Kennedy & Co., of Chicago. In 1867, he retired temporarily from business, and spent a year in Europe in travel and recreation. The following year he returned to New York and established the firm of J. S. Kennedy & Co., which he conducted with uninterrupted prosperity until 1883, when he permanently retired, leaving the business to be carried on by his partners under the name of J. Kennedy Tod & Co. In addition to his business as merchant and banker, Mr. Kennedy was engaged in important railroad enterprises, serving as president, vice-president, director, receiver or trustee of many large corporations. Among other financial institutions and railroad companies, in which he has been a director, are: The National Bank of Commerce, the Manhattan Company's Bank, the Central Trust Company, the New York, Chicago & St. Louis Railroad Company, the Pittsburg, Fort Wayne & Chicago Railroad Company, and the New Brunswick Railroad Company

Few citizens of New York have manifested a deeper public interset in the benevolent institutions of the city than Mr. Kennedy, or have been more open-handed in their benefactions. He is president of the Presbyterian Hospital, the Lenox Library and the board of trustees of the American Bible House of Constantinople, vice-president of the New York Historical Society, trustee of the Metropolitan Museum of Art, the New York Society for the Ruptured and Crippled, the Fifth Avenue Presbyterian Church and the Theological Seminary of Princeton, N. J., and manager of the Board of Home Missions of the Presbyterian Church in the United States. The United Charities Building, at the corner of Twenty-second Street and Fourth Avenue, was built by him at his own expense, for the headquarters of the charity organizations of New York.

Mr. Kennedy married Emma Baker, daughter of Cornelius Baker. He lives in West Fifty-seventh Street, and his summer home is Kenarden Lodge, in Bar Harbor, Me. He is a member of the Metropolitan, Union League, Century, South Side Sportsmen's, Reform, Grolier, City, New York Yacht and Riding clubs, the Downtown Association, the American Geographical Society and the Mendelssohn Glee Club, and is a patron of the Metropolitan Museum of Art, the National Academy of Design and the American Museum of Natural History.

WILLIAM KENT

THOMAS KENT was probably a brother of Richard Kent, of Old Newberry, Mass, who came to America in the Mary and John from Gloucester, England, in 1638 Thomas was a resident of Gloucester, Mass, in 1644, and became the ancestor of an American family remarkable for the eminent professional men it has produced His eldest son, Samuel Kent, was the father of John Kent, who settled in Suffield, Conn, about 1680, where he married Abigail Dudley, a daughter of William Dudley, of Saybrook, and had a family of nine children The Reverend Elisha Kent, 1704-1776, the youngest son of John Kent, was graduated from Yale College in 1729 He became a minister of the Presbyterian Church of Newtown, Conn, but about 1740 moved to Dutchess County, now Putnam County, N Y, and was minister of a church there He has had many illustrious descendants, among them Dr Elisha Kent Kane, the Arctic explorer, Chancellor James Kent and the present generations of Kanes, well known in New York

The wife of Reverend Elisha Kent was a daughter of Reverend Joseph Moss, of Derby, and their son, Moss Kent, 1733-1794, graduated from Yale College in 1752, and was admitted to the bar in Dutchess County in 1755 About the time of the Revolutionary War, he removed to Green Farms and afterwards to Lansingburgh, N Y, where he was a justice and surrogate He had two sons, the younger, Moss Kent, Jr, State Senator and Member of Congress, dying unmarried. The eldest son of Moss Kent was the famous James Kent, Chancellor of the State of New York, the great-grandfather of Mr. William Kent He was born in 1763, and spent his childhood, from 1768 to 1772, with his grandfather, Dr Uriah Rogers, of Norwalk, Conn He was elected to the New York Legislature in 1790, 1792 and 1796 Previous to 1798, he was Professor of Law in Columbia College In 1796, Governor John Jay appointed him a Master-in-Chancery, in 1797, he was a Recorder of the City of New York, in 1798, a Justice of the Supreme Court of the State, and in 1804, its Chief Justice. He became Chancellor in 1814, and held that office until 1823. During his judicial career, he resided in Albany, but returning to New York, again became Professor in Columbia College and engaged in private practice For many years he was president of the New York Historical Society. He was the author of Kent's Commentaries on American Law, a work found in the library of every American lawyer

Judge William Kent, son of Chancellor Kent, was born in Albany, in 1802 Graduated from Union College, he became a lawyer in New York, a Judge of the Circuit Court, 1841-45, and a Professor in Harvard College Law School, 1846-47. He returned to practice in New York in 1847, dying in Fishkill in 1861 The son of Judge William Kent was James Kent, who was born in 1830, studied law in his father's office, was admitted to the bar in 1851 and resided throughout his life in Fishkill-on-the-Hudson.

His son, Mr. William Kent, is descended on the maternal side from several early Connecticut and New York families. His great-great-grandfather, Moss Kent, married Hannah Rogers, a daughter of Dr. Uriah Rogers, of Connecticut. The wife of Chancellor Kent was Elizabeth Bailey, daughter of Colonel John Bailey, of Poughkeepsie, N Y., and his wife, Altie Van Wyck, daughter of Theodore Van Wyck Their son was the Honorable Theodorus Bailey, Member of Congress, 1793-1797 and 1799-1803, United States Senator in 1803 and Postmaster of New York. The grandmother of Mr Kent, wife of Judge William Kent, was Helen Riggs, daughter of Caleb S. Riggs and granddaughter of Colonel William Burnet of the Continental Army

Mr William Kent was born in Fishkill-on-the-Hudson, March 19th, 1858 After graduating from Columbia College, he studied law and entered upon the practice of his profession in New York He married, in 1881, Emily Lorillard, daughter of Pierre Lorillard The children of Mr and Mrs. Kent are William, Jr, Emily Lorillard, Peter Lorillard and Richard Kent The residence of the family is at Tuxedo Park Mr Kent is a member of the Bar Association, the Columbia College Alumni Association, the New York State Bar Association and the Union, Country and New York Yacht clubs

JOSEPH FREDERIC KERNOCHAN

MORE than twenty-five years ago, Joseph Kernochan was a famous merchant in New York. He was of Scottish birth, a member of a good family, and came to this country in the latter part of the eighteenth century. Soon after 1800, he was a clerk in the store of Thomas Powell, in Newburgh, N Y. One of his fellow-clerks was Henry Parrish, a nephew of Thomas Powell, and the intimacy that sprang up between the two young man ultimately resulted in the establishment of one of the great dry goods houses of New York City in the early part of the present century. In 1833, only fourteen years after he had come to New York, Mr. Kernochan was able to retire with one of the largest fortunes of that day to his credit. He was a public-spirited man, interested in municipal affairs, and concerned in the highest social, literary and educational interests of the city. He was president of the Fulton Bank, and connected with other corporations, and was one of the earliest members of the Friendly Sons of St. Patrick. He married Margaret Seymour She was a niece of Thomas Powell, and a cousin of her husband's subsequent partners, Henry and Daniel Parrish.

Mr. Joseph Frederic Kernochan is the son of Joseph and Margaret (Seymour) Kernochan. Born in New York, he was graduated from Yale College, in 1863, and from the Law School of Columbia College, in 1865. He has been engaged in the practice of law. His wife, whom he married in 1869, was Mary Stuart Whitney, a daughter of William Whitney and Mary Stuart McVickar. The father of Mrs. Kernochan was born in 1816, and died in 1862. His wife was a daughter of James and Eweretta (Constable) McVickar, of Constableville, N. Y. James McVickar was a brother of the Reverend John McVickar, who was a professor in Columbia College for fifty-one years and a son of John McVickar and Abigail Moore, of Newtown, Long Island Abigail Moore was a daughter of John Moore, granddaughter of Benjamin and Anna (Sackett) Moore, great-granddaughter of Samuel and Mary (Read) Moore, and the great-great-granddaughter of the Reverend John Moore, the first minister of Newtown. The father of Mrs. Kernochan was a son of the famous New York merchant, Stephen Whitney, and his wife, Harriet Suydam, daughter of Hendrick and Phœbe (Skidmore) Suydam, of Hallet's Cove, N Y. Stephen Whitney was in the fifth generation of descent from Henry Whitney, one of the first settlers in Connecticut and Long Island. Mr. and Mrs Kernochan have a town house in Madison Square, and their summer home is at the Highlands of Navesink, N J. They have three children, Eweretta, Mary S. W. and Frederic Kernochan. Mr. Kernochan is a member of the Tuxedo, University, City and Yale clubs, the Bar Association and the Downtown Association

James P. Kernochan, another son of Joseph Kernochan, was born in New York, in October, 1831 Inheriting wealth from his father, he never actively engaged in business, but devoted his time to the management of his own property and the John Rutgers Marshall, the Lorillard, the Gasquet and the Spencer estates. Besides his town house, at 384 Fifth Avenue, he owned a beautiful country place at Ochre Point, Newport, and large tracts of real estate in New York. He was a member of the Union, Metropolitan, Knickerbocker, New York Yacht, Riding, and Meadow Brook Hunt clubs, and was a member of St. James' Protestant Episcopal Church. He died as a result of an accident, March, 1897 His wife, who survived him, was Catherine Lorillard, daughter of Peter Lorillard. Her mother was Catherine A. Griswold, daughter of Nathaniel L. Griswold, of the great china importing house of W. L. & George Griswold. Her grandfather was Peter A. Lorillard, who was born in 1763 and died in 1843, and her grandmother was Maria Dorothea Schultz. Her great-grandparents were Peter Lorillard and his wife, Catherine Moore, sister of Blazius Moore James Lorillard Kernochan, son of James P. Kernochan, married Eloise Stevenson, has a country home, The Meadows, in Hempstead, Long Island, and a summer residence in Newport He is a member of the Knickerbocker, Metropolitan, New York Yacht, Riding and Meadow Brook Hunt clubs, and of the American Geographical Society. His sister, Catherine Lorillard, is the wife of Herbert C. Pell

HENRY SCANLAN KERR

ON the paternal side, Mr. Henry S Kerr is descended from an English family. His grandfather was George Kerr, a native of England, who came to this country in the early part of the present century He settled in the West, and there his descendants have attained distinction in professional and public life, and have been eminently successful in business pursuits. William H Kerr, son of George Kerr and father of the gentleman whose family is here under consideration, was for many years Prosecuting Attorney of Ohio On his mother's side, Mr Kerr is descended from one of the old families of Ireland. His mother was Harriet Scanlan, daughter of Stephen Scanlan, of Ireland, and his wife, Mary Hardy. Stephen Scanlan and his wife were for a long time residents of Canada. A sister of Harriet Scanlan is the wife of Charles T. Wing, of New York Stephen Scanlan was a member of the family to which Tyrone Powei, the celebrated Irish comedian and dramatist, belonged He was a cousin of Tyrone Power and second cousin of the present Sir William Tyrone Power, member of Parliament, who was the eldest son of Tyrone Power, the actor. His maternal ancestors were of an old family of Waterford.

Mr. Kerr is a native of Cincinnati, O , having been born in that city, September 4th, 1865 His early education was secured in the Chickering Institute, of Cincinnati He then completed a course of study in the Montgomery Bell Academy, in Nashville, Tenn., and was graduated from that institution with first honors and as valedictorian of his class. Coming to New York, he engaged in business pursuits, entering the office of his uncle, Charles T. Wing, in Wall Street. There he remained from 1885 until 1892 In the last-mentioned year, he joined in organizing the firm of Redmond, Kerr & Co , of Wall Street, of which he is now one of the active partners Interested in military affairs, he enlisted in Squadron A of the National Guard of the State of New York soon after coming to this city, and served six years. During that time, he had practical military experience with his command in the Buffalo and the Brooklyn railroad riots and on other occasions He attained to the rank of First Sergeant and received his honorable discharge in 1894.

On October 16th, 1895, Mr. Kerr married Olive Grace, daughter of John W. Grace, of New York. The father of Mrs. Kerr is a member of the firm of W. R. Grace & Co., South American importers and shipping merchants. He is the brother of former Mayor William R Grace, being the second son of his father's family, and was the founder of the San Francisco branch of the Grace mercantile house. He belongs to one of the ancient and honorable families of Ireland. His father, James Grace, of Queens County, Ireland, was born in 1794 and lived at Sheffield House, where John W. Grace was born, in 1836. The wife of James Grace, whom he married in 1827, was Ellen Mary Russell, daughter of Michael Russell, of Ninagh, County Tipperary. The Russell family is one of the well-known Protestant families of Ireland. James Grace died at Farranville House in 1869. He was the son of John Grace and Alice Horenden, John Grace being the great-grandson of Michael Grace, of Gracefield, 1682–1760, and Mary Galwey, daughter of John Galwey, of Lota House, County Cork The Grace family was originally of Norman extraction, and in the early centuries its members were large landholders in Queens County. Being devoted Catholics, they lost their possessions when Ireland was subjugated by the English, but they have still remained residents of the country with which their ancestors and themselves have been so conspicuously identified

Mr. and Mrs. Kerr have one son, Henry Grace Kerr, who was born August 15th, 1896. Their residence is in East Seventy-fifth Street, at the corner of Madison Avenue, but they spend the summer months at their country place in Great Neck, Long Island Mr Kerr is a member of several of the leading clubs, including the Union League, Union and Racquet Gentlemanly sports engage his attention to some extent, and he is a member of the New York Yacht Club and the Country Club of Westchester County. For several years he has been a member of the Chamber of Commerce, and as a loyal son of Ohio is a member of the Ohio Society.

ALEXANDER PHŒNIX KETCHUM

O N both sides of the house, Colonel Alexander Phœnix Ketchum and his brother, Edgar Ketchum, trace their ancestry from illustrious New York families. Their paternal grandparents were John Jauncey Ketchum and Susanna Jauncey, who were nearly related, having descended from Guleyn Vigne, one of the first settlers of New Amsterdam, who came to this country in the first decades of the seventeenth century. The son of Guleyn Vigne was Jean Vigne, the first male child born in New Amsterdam of European parents. The date of his birth has been set down as 1614, and his father owned a farm near Wall Street, then a suburb of the town of New Amsterdam, which property the son inherited. Jean Vigne also owned a large windmill, was a brewer as well as a farmer, and was one of the great burghers of the city and held several times the honorable position of a schepen. His three sisters were wedded by representatives of prominent Dutch families of that period. Maria married Abraham Verplank, ancestor of the famous New York family of that name which has had many notable representatives in the history of the State. Christiana became the wife of Dirk Volckersten, and Rachel was the second wife of Cornelis Van Tienhoven.

It is from Cornelis Van Tienhoven and his wife Rachel that the Ketchums are descended, Sarah Van Tienhoven, their daughter, becoming the wife of John Jauncey, the father of John Jauncey Ketchum. Cornelis Van Tienhoven was an important member of the settlement of New Amsterdam. He was secretary under Governor William Kieft, and was retained in that position under Governor Peter Stuyvesant; was one of the first surveyors of the village, appointed in 1647; was sent by Stuyvesant as one of his representatives to The Hague in 1648, and was appointed to the office of sheriff in 1650. The mother of Colonel Ketchum was Elizabeth Phœnix, daughter of the Reverend Alexander Phœnix and Patty Ingraham. Alexander Phœnix was the eldest surviving son of Daniel Phœnix. To those who have studied the early social and political history of New York City, the name of Daniel Phœnix is sufficiently familiar, for he held many conspicuous and honorable positions. He was born about 1737, and as merchant and city officer played an active part in the commercial and public life of the city during and after the Revolutionary period. He was a man of wealth, for those days, and his reputation for financial ability and probity was such among his fellow citizens that he was selected by them to be their first city treasurer and their first city chamberlain when the municipality assumed its present form. For twenty years he held those posts and discharged their duties in a manner that commanded the admiration and the approval of the entire community. He was also a leading member of the Chamber of Commerce, and when General Washington entered the city, on November 26th, 1783, after the evacuation by the British troops, Mr. Phœnix headed the delegation that welcomed the Commander-in-Chief of the American forces. He died in 1812 and left several children, one of whom was the mother of Judge Daniel P. Ingraham, while another was the wife of the famous Richard Riker, the Recorder of New York City. The Reverend Alexander Phœnix was born in 1777 and graduated from Columbia College in 1794. He was pastor of the Congregational Church of Chicopee for many years and died in New York City, in 1863.

Edgar Ketchum, Sr., who married Elizabeth Phœnix, was born in 1811. He was a lawyer and a man of public affairs, at one time public administrator, for twelve years United States Loan Commissioner, Collector of Internal Revenue during President Lincoln's administration, and Register in Bankruptcy from 1867 to the time of his death, in 1882. Much of his time was devoted to educational and benevolent undertakings, and he was prominently identified with the administration of the public school system in the city, of which he was a great benefactor. During many years, he was president of the board of managers of the House of Refuge on Randall's Island. The Harlem Presbyterian Church, the Pilgrim Congregational Church in Harlem, the American Missionary Society, the Harlem Library and the Hampton Institute, for the education and training of colored youth, were also objects of his intelligent and benevolent attention. Mr. Ketchum had four sons and one daughter. The daughter of his family, Susan Ketchum, married the Reverend S. Bourne.

Colonel Alexander Phœnix Ketchum, the eldest son of Edgar Ketchum, was born in New Haven, Conn , May 11th, 1839 He was educated in the public schools, and graduated from the College of the City of New York with the degree of B A. in 1858. In 1861, he received the degree of M. A , from his alma mater, and the same year was graduated from the Albany Law School with the degree of LL B When Fort Sumter was fired upon, he answered the call for troops, and was assigned to a place on the staff of General Rufus Saxton, Military Governor of South Carolina. Subsequently transferred to the staff of General O O. Howard, he served until 1867, when he resigned from the army. In 1869, President Grant appointed him an assessor of internal revenue, from which position he was promoted to be collector of internal revenue, and in 1874 was appointed general appraiser in the customs department of the port of New York. During the administration of President Chester A. Arthur, in 1883, he again entered the service of the National Government and was made chief appraiser at New York, a position that he held for several years

Colonel Ketchum left the public service to devote himself to the practice of law. He was admitted to the bar in 1860, and is now one of the leading lawyers of the metropolis. Interested in religious and educational matters, he was one of the promoters of the New York Collegiate Institute, and has been an active worker in the Young Men's Christian Association. He is a member of the Republican Club of New York, and of the Harlem Republican Club, the Military Order of the Loyal Legion, and the Bar Association of New York , was president of the Presbyterian Social Union, and has been for several years president of the City College Club. His membership in other social organizations includes the Larchmont Yacht, Atlantic Yacht, New York Yacht, Quill and A Δ Φ clubs, the New England Society, and the American Museum of Natural History. He is also a member of the Board of Education of New York, having been originally appointed a commissioner by Mayor William L Strong, to fill an unexpired term in that body, and was afterwards reappointed for the full term of three years. His residence is in Mount Morris Park West.

Edgar Ketchum, the second son of Edgar Ketchum, Sr., was born in New York, July 15th, 1840, and graduated from the College of the City of New York in 1860. He studied law in his father's office and afterwards in the Columbia College Law School, from which he was graduated, in 1862, with the degree of LL. B , and was admitted to the bar. The degree of A M. was conferred upon him by his alma mater in 1863 But the practice of law was set aside by the call to battle, and he went to the front as an officer of the Regular Army, having previously served in the ranks of New York's celebrated Seventh Regiment. Appointed by the President an officer in the Signal Corps, he served in the Army of the James before Richmond, and took a conspicuous part in the second Fort Fisher expedition, and the capture of Fort Anderson and Wilmington, N. C His gallant conduct twice brought him promotion, and in that campaign he served on the staff of Generals A. H. Terry, C. J Paine, John M. Schofield and Jacob D. Cox. At the close of the Civil War, he formed the decision of leaving the army and was honorably discharged from the service with the rank of Captain.

Returning to civil life, he began the practice of law, to which he has devoted himself ever since. He renewed his connection with the Seventh Regiment, but was soon afterwards appointed Chief Engineer, with the rank of Major, in the First Brigade, First Division, New York National Guard. Resigning that position after three years of service, he gave up military life. He is still, however, connected with many social and military organizations, being a member of the Military Order of the Loyal Legion, the War Veterans of the Seventh Regiment, Post Lafayette, G. A. R., the Society of the Army of the Potomac, and the Veteran Signal Corps Association. He married Angelica S. Anderson, daughter of Smith W. Anderson, and granddaughter of James Anderson, in 1870, and has two children, one son and one daughter. He lives in the northern part of the city, in a house that stands upon part of the Anderson ancestral estate.

EDWARD KING

H ISTORY has awarded to Rufus King one of the highest places among American statesmen and patriots of the period which succeeded the Revolution. Born at Scarborough, Me , in 1755, the son of a merchant, Richard King, he graduated at Harvard in 1777, and in the following year served as aide to General Glover in an expedition to Rhode Island In 1784-86, he was a delegate from Massachusetts to the Congress of the Confederation, and had the honor of proposing the immediate prohibition of slavery in the Northwest territory He acted on the commission which settled the boundary between Massachusetts and New York, and in 1787 was one of the Massachusetts delegation to the convention which framed the Constitution of the United States. In 1786, he married Mary, daughter of the patriotic New York merchant, John Alsop, who had been a member of the first Continental Congress in 1774-76, of the New York Provincial Congresses of 1775-76, and the Committee of Safety in 1775. Removing to New York in 1788, Rufus King, who was already one of the champions of Federalism, found his adopted State no less ready than Massachusetts had been to bestow its honors on him. In 1789, it elected him, with General Schuyler, as its first United States Senators, and in 1796 he became Minister to England, where he remained till 1803 After ten years passed in private life, he was, in 1813, a second time elected a Senator by the State of New York, and was again chosen in 1819. When in the Senate, he combated slavery and opposed the Missouri Compromise. Appointed Minister to England once more, in 1825, he was forced by failing health to resign the position and returned to New York to die in 1827, after devoting fifty years of honorable and successful service to his country, leaving a name second to none among the patriots of that portion of our history as a nation.

His sons were John Alsop King, Governor of New York in 1857; Charles King, president of Columbia College, and James Gore King, the famous banker. The latter, Mr Edward King's father, was born in New York in 1791, and died in 1853. He was educated in Europe, and in 1813 married Sarah Rogers Gracie, daughter of Archibald Gracie. Between 1818 and 1824, he resided in Liverpool, engaged in the American trade, but returned to New York to become a partner in the banking house of Prime, Ward & King. He was a Member of Congress in 1849, and was president of the Chamber of Commerce, while his services to the mercantile community are too numerous for rehearsal. One instance, however, must be mentioned. After the panic of 1837 and the suspension of specie payments, he went to London, and by his influence and ability induced the Bank of England to advance five million dollars in gold to his firm, which was the basis for the resumption of specie payments throughout the United States.

Mr. Edward King is the son of James Gore King and his wife, Sarah Rogers Gracie, and was born at the family country seat, Highwood, Weehawken, N J , in 1833 He graduated from Harvard, and has been president of the Harvard Club of New York Mr King engaged in banking, and served as president of the New York Stock Exchange. In 1873, he was called to the presidency of the Union Trust Company, at a time when that institution's affairs were in a critical state. Under Mr. King's management, its position was soon restored and its present prosperity attained He has taken no active part in public life, but has lent his influence in aid of the Government, giving assistance as well as expert counsel to the secretaries of the United States Treasury on occasions of difficulty with the national finances.

Mr King is president of the St Nicholas Society, and is a member of the Century Association, the Harvard and University clubs, the Metropolitan Museum of Art and the National Academy of Design. He is also a member and treasurer of the board of trustees of the New York Public Library, Astor-Lenox-Tilden Foundations, and a governor of the New York Hospital. His residence in town is 1 University Place, and he has a country seat at Grymes Hill, Staten Island. He married, in early life, Isabella Ramsey Cochrane, niece of Dean Ramsey, of Edinburgh, and some years after her death contracted a second marriage with Elizabeth Fisher, of Philadelphia.

ISAAC LEWIS KIP

IN the earliest annals of New Netherland, the name of Kip holds an honorable and distinguished place. Even before the first permanent settlements of the Hollanders were made on the shores of the Hudson, members of this notable old Dutch family took an active part in the work of exploration. Hendrick Kype was among the associates who, in 1594, dispatched an expedition from Holland for the purpose of discovering a northeast passage from Europe to the Indies, and on the failure of this attempt sent Hendrick Hudson upon his fruitful voyage to America in 1609. It will be remembered that the purpose of Hudson's exploration was to open up a sea route to the Pacific, and that his first impressions of our noble bay and the great river beyond were that they answered the object of his search. Disappointed in this respect, the accounts which Hudson brought back, however, led to the resolution of the Dutch West India Company to colonize New Netherland. In this, as in earlier efforts, Hendrick Kype took part, and in 1635 came to the infant settlement of New Amsterdam. He shortly, however, returned to the old country.

The De Kype family, from whom have come the Kips who have held high position in New York, formerly lived near Alençon, Bretagne, France. Ruloff Kype, grandson of Ruloff De Kype, who fell in battle in 1562, settled in Amsterdam, and Hendrick Kype, the American pioneer, was his son, born in 1576. Hendrick Kype had three sons, who remained in this country, Hendrick, Jacob and Isaac. Hendrick married a daughter of Nacasius de Sille. Jacob Kip is referred to on the following page of this volume as the ancestor of another branch of this historic family. From Isaac Kype, or Kip as the name finally became, is derived the branch of the family that has been represented in New York's social and business affairs in the present generation by the gentleman who is the subject of this sketch.

Isaac Kype ranked among the larger land owners in the beginnings of our city's history. He obtained a grant of a large tract, which included the site of the present City Hall Park, and the first name of the Nassau Street of to-day was Kip Street, in his honor. His son, Jacobus Kip, was born here in 1666 and also became the possessor of large estates. In conjunction with his brother Henry, he purchased from the Indians a large tract on the east side of the Hudson, comprehending within its limits the present village of Rhinebeck. Isaac Kip, son of Jacobus Kip, was born in New York in 1696, and married Cornelia Lewis, daughter of Leonard Lewis, a leading merchant and alderman of the city from 1696 to 1700. Their son, Leonard Kip, was the father of Isaac Lewis Kip, who, born in 1767, was a lawyer of eminence in the period succeeding the Revolution. He became the professional partner of Judge Brockholst Livingston, but was afterwards appointed to an office in the Court of Chancery of the State, holding that position under Chancellors Livingston, Lansing and Kent.

The wife of Isaac Lewis Kip, first of the name, was Sarah Smith, daughter of Colonel Smith, of Powles Hook. Their son, Leonard W. Kip, also became a lawyer of high rank in his profession. He was noted as an authority upon real estate titles in New York, but at the same time gave much attention to the cause of philanthropy and education, taking a prominent place in bodies devoted to those purposes. The University of the City of New York was among the institutions which were benefited by his unselfish labors, and for a number of years he was a member of its board of council.

Dr. Isaac Lewis Kip, son of Leonard W. Kip, was born in New York. He received his early education here and was graduated from the University of the City of New York, his academical training being followed by a course of study in, and a medical degree from, the medical department of the same institution. Dr Kip, however, engaged in the active practice of his profession for a few years only, but was for some time connected in a professional capacity with the Mutual Life Insurance Company. He married Cornelia Brady, daughter of the Honorable William V. Brady, who was Mayor of New York in 1847. Their two children are Adelaide, who married Philip Rhinelander, and William V. B. Kip. The residence of Dr. Kip is in Fifth Avenue.

LAWRENCE KIP

THE remote ancestor of the New York family, now under consideration, was Ruloff de Kuype, a French knight. From him descended Hendrick Hendrickzen Kip, who arrived at New Amsterdam prior to 1643. He was one of the foremost men of the Colony in character, as well as in birth, and in 1645 stoutly refused to do honor to the tyrannical Governor Kieft, but became a member of Governor Stuyvesant's Council of nine men, in 1647, and schepen of the infant town in 1656. His three sons, of whom Jacob Kip was the eldest, were included in the census taken under the orders of Stuyvesant, as among the twenty burghers or greater citizens of the place. In 1654, Jacob Kip married Maria de la Montague, daughter of Dr. Johannes de la Montague, and in 1655 built a house, famous in the annals of New York as the original of the historic Kip mansion, on the farm fronting on the East River, at or about the present Thirty-fifth Street, and which has given the name of Kip's Bay to that part of the city. Over the door was carved in stone the family arms—a gold chevron, between two sealed griffins, on a blue shield, the crest being a demi-griffin, holding a cross and the motto *Nulla Vestigia*.

Colonel Lawrence Kip descends in direct line from the New Amsterdam Patrician, his paternal grandfather being Leonard Kip, 1774-1846, and who married Maria Ingraham, 1784-1876, daughter of Duncan Ingraham, of Philadelphia. Colonel Kip's father, the Right Reverend William Ingraham Kip, D D, was one of the offspring of this marriage, and was born in New York in 1811, graduated at Yale in 1831, and, after studying law, devoted himself to the ministry. He was ordained Deacon in 1835, and in 1838 became Rector of St. Paul's, Albany, and in 1853 was consecrated Bishop of California. He married Maria Elizabeth Lawrence, daughter of Isaac Lawrence, 1768-1841, and his wife, Cornelia Beach, this alliance making him a relative of the many leading families with which the Lawrences are connected. Bishop Kip was one of the most eminent clergymen in the United States, and a man of great executive ability.

The family connection, to which Colonel Kip belongs, includes on both sides relatives distinguished in all stations in life. Bishop Burgess, of Maine, was an uncle of the subject of this article, and the celebrated Noah Webster was a great uncle, while a maternal cousin was Commodore Ingraham, of the United States Navy, the hero of the Koszta incident in 1853, and afterwards an Admiral in the Confederate service. Another uncle was the Honorable William Beach Lawrence, Governor of Rhode Island.

Born in Morristown, N. J, Mr. Lawrence Kip was educated at the Churchill Military School, Sing Sing, and in 1853 was appointed from California as a cadet at West Point, receiving the commission of Second Lieutenant of Artillery in 1857. He served through the Civil War on General Sheridan's staff, becoming Captain in 1866, and received brevets of Major and Lieutenant-Colonel in 1865 for gallantry at Five Forks, but resigned in 1867. In 1864, Colonel Kip married Eva Lorillard, daughter of Peter Lorillard and Catherine Griswold Lorillard. The issue of this marriage have been two children, Edith Kip McCreery and Lorillard Kip, the latter of whom died in June, 1896.

Colonel Kip, while active in society and as a sportsman, inherits literary tastes and ability. His father, Bishop Kip, was famous as a theological writer, and some years ago published an interesting record of California, Early Days of My Episcopate. His relative, Bishop Burgess, and an uncle, Leonard Kip, of Albany, were also authors, and he has published an account of his own military experiences, under the title of Army Life on the Pacific. Colonel Kip has also been deeply interested in every effort to raise the character of the American turf, is president of the Coney Island Jockey Club, and identified with other organizations of like character, and has owned many road and track horses. He was one of the Patriarchs, his clubs being the Metropolitan, Union, Tuxedo, Suburban and Riding and Driving. Colonel Kip is also prominent among the supporters of the National Horse Show Association, of which he is vice-president, and has won many prizes with his own horses.

GUSTAV EDWARD KISSEL

A GRAND-UNCLE of the gentleman referred to in this article was one of the most prominent civic magistrates of Frankfort-on-the-Main a century ago When Frankfort ranked as one of the free cities of Germany and held an important place in the politics and history of the country as a free community, he was burgomaster and one of its leading citizens, being a representative and descendant of an ancient burgher family, which had been well known for several centuries, not only in the city of Frankfort, but throughout the Palatinate of the Rhine and the surrounding districts

The father of Mr. Gustav E Kissel, Gustav Hermann Kissel, was one of the leading merchants of New York in the first half of this century He was born in Frankfort, Germany, May 11th, 1810, came here in early life and attained wealth and social and business prominence, dying on Staten Island, July 23d, 1876, at his country seat in the village of New Brighton, where the name of a street now commemorates the residence of the family in the place At the time of his death, Mr Kissel had been a citizen of New York for forty years. He was one of the early abolitionists, becoming an advocate of that cause immediately after arriving in this country, and was intimately associated with its leading upholders During the Civil War, he was an enthusiastic supporter of the Union cause, taking part in all the movements instituted by the leading citizens of the metropolis to that end, and in many ways rendered efficient service to the national Government, sometimes at great personal as well as pecuniary sacrifice to himself When, in 1863, the draft rioters were in possession of the city, he opened his house to persecuted negroes and gave them refuge till the disturbance was quelled and order restored in the city, and was in all ways a patriotic citizen.

The mother of Mr Gustav E Kissel was Charlotte Anne Stimson, daughter of Dr Jeremy Stimson, one of the most distinguished physicians of the City of Boston half a century ago. She was married to Mr. Kissel soon after his arrival in this country. Of the children of this marriage, Eleanora married Dr F. P. Kinnicutt, a leading physician of New York, Godfrey married a daughter of Dexter Bradford, of Boston, and Rudolph Hermann married a daughter of G T Morgan Mr Gustav Edward Kissel, the second child and the oldest son of Gustav Hermann and Charlotte Anne (Stimson) Kissel, was born in New York, September 30th, 1854. His early education was secured at the celebrated private schools of Dr. Charlier and J H Morse, of New York After his preparatory instruction was completed, he was sent abroad for further study He first, for some time, attended the academy at Lausanne, Switzerland, and then matriculated at the University of Heidelberg, in Germany, where he remained for three years. Returning to this country, he entered upon the business pursuits which have now engaged his attention for nearly twenty years Finance and banking possessed unusual attractions for him, and shortly before he was twenty-five years of age, in 1879, he entered Wall Street in the firm of Kessler & Co , the New York branch of an international banking house which had been in existence in Europe for many years, and which possesses extensive connections in Germany and Switzerland. As partner of this establishment, Mr Kissel has been constantly engaged in business operations of the largest character and has personally gained a position among the most respected and prominent representatives of his profession He has also contributed efficiently to making investments in American corporations and other securities popular in Europe

In 1884, Mr Kissel married Caroline Thorn, daughter of William K Thorn Mr and Mrs. Kissel live at 15 West Sixteenth Street, and also have a country house at Morristown, N. J , where they spend a portion of each year They have four children, William Thorn, Dorothea, Louise Baring and Jeannette Kissel. In his club memberships Mr. Kissel includes the Union, Knickerbocker, Century, Racquet, Morristown, Reform and City He is a member of the Downtown Association, of the Chamber of Commerce, and a trustee of the American Geographical Society and the American Museum of Natural History.

GOUVERNEUR KORTRIGHT

FOR two centuries the Kortrights and the Gouverneurs have ranked among the leading families of New York. They have intermarried with each other, and with the Ver Plancks, Tillotsons, Lawrences, Livingstons and other great Colonial families. Kortryk, a Flemish town on the river Lys, gave its name to the family. The ancestors of the Kortrights were Protestants, of Flanders. In the religious troubles that vexed that country three hundred years ago, Sebastian, or Bastiaen, Van Kortryk went to Leerdam to escape persecution, and settled there. His two sons, Jan and Michiel, came to New Amsterdam in 1663. They first settled upon Governor Stuyvesant's bowery, but afterwards removed to Harlem. From them have descended all the Kortright or Courtright families of New York and New Jersey.

Cornelis Jansen Kortright, the ancestor of Mr Gouverneur Kortright, was born in Beest, Gelderland, in 1645. He came to this country with his father, Jan Bastiaensen, in 1663. His wife, whom he married in 1665, was Metje Elyessen, daughter of Bastiaen Elyessen. He was a member of the troop of horse, and died in 1689, leaving four children, Johannes, Laurens, Aefie and Annettie. His eldest son, Johannes Cornelissen Kortright, who was born in 1673 and died in 1711, married Wyntje Dyckman, and their son, Nicholas Kortright, who married Elizabeth Van Huyse, daughter of Eide Van Huyse, was a constable and collector of the town of Harlem.

Lawrence Cornelisen Kortright, the second son of Cornelis Jansen Kortright, was the ancestor of that branch of the family which Mr Gouverneur Kortright represents. He was born in 1681, and was a constable of Harlem in 1708. His wife, whom he married in 1703, was Helena Benson, daughter of Captain John Benson, who was of an old New York family. The oldest son of this union, born in 1704, was Cornelius Kortright, who married, in 1730, Hester Cannon, daughter of John Cannon, another New York merchant, who was an assistant alderman, 1738-40, and whose death occurred in 1762. Cornelius Kortright died in 1743, as the result of an accident, and his widow survived until 1784. Three sons and three daughters were of this family. The youngest son, Cornelius Kortright, married a Miss Hendricks, a wealthy lady of the Island of Santa Cruz. Maria Kortright married John W. Hanson. Helena Kortright married Abraham Brasher, and Elizabeth Kortright married William R. Van Cortlandt.

Lawrence Kortright, eldest son of Cornelius and Hester (Cannon) Kortright, was a noted merchant of New York a hundred years ago, being associated with Luke Van Ranst and Isaac Sears. He was a large owner in several privateers in the French War, and one of the original incorporators of the Chamber of Commerce in 1770. The town of Kortright, N. Y., where he had purchased large tracts of land intending to found a manor, was named for him. His death occurred in 1794. His wife was Hannah Aspinwall. One of his daughters married James Monroe, afterwards President of the United States, and another became the wife of Nicholas Gouverneur, of the great commission house of Gouverneur, Kortright & Co, after whom Gouverneur Street and Gouverneur Lane were named. The only son of Lawrence Kortright was Captain John Kortright, whose wife was Catherine Seaman, who, after the death of her first husband, became the second wife of Judge Henry Brockholst Livingston. Captain John Kortright was a member of the St George's Society in 1789. His children were John L, Edmund, Robert and Gouverneur; Eliza M., who married Nicholas Cruger, and Hester Mary, who married Billop B Seaman. Edmund Kortright married Miss Shaw. Robert Kortright became a physician. Gouverneur Kortright married Miss Allaire, of a Winchester, Va., family.

Mr Gouverneur Kortright, head of this historic family in the present generation, lives in East Fifty-sixth Street. He married Therese White, descended from Peregrine White, who was born on the Mayflower in the harbor of Plymouth in 1620. Mr Kortright belongs to the Metropolitan, Racquet and Knickerbocker clubs, and his interest in gentlemanly sports is indicated by his membership in the New York and Larchmont Yacht clubs. His summer residence is The Moorings, in Newport. He has one daughter, Alice Gouverneur Kortright.

345

PERCIVAL KÜHNE

NEAR the City of Magdeburg, Germany, is an estate which for hundreds of years has been the property of Mr. Kühne's ancestors The latter's grandfather, John Frederick Kühne, was born there in 1792. In 1814, he joined the German Army and fought at the battle of Waterloo, where he was severely wounded. He was decorated and rewarded for bravery, and died in Magdeburg in 1855. His musical ability was of the highest order, and he followed music—not as a profession—but from love of art Richard Wagner, who in early life pursued his musical studies in Magdeburg, became one of Herr Kühne's intimate friends, and the violin owned and used by Wagner at that time is still among the possessions of the Kühne family.

The late Frederick Kühne, his son, born at Magdeburg in 1824, was for over thirty years a leading representative of the Germans in this city, where he arrived in 1851 He was a trained financier and established the banking house of Knauth, Nachod & Kühne, in which, till his death in Paris, France, in 1890, he maintained an active and leading interest. By reason of his wide connection with the social and business world, and his ability and exceptional energy, he gave the firm that high standing in international and domestic finance which it still retains. Prior to the foundation of the German Empire, he represented, for over sixteen years, fifteen of the separate German States as their Consul-General in New York, and was decorated by the various princes in recognition of his services, in several instances conferring upon him the rank of Chevalier. He enjoyed the confidence of many illustrious personages, and was honored by audiences with the Emperor William I. and the Emperor Frederick, and was frequently entertained by the Grand Duke of Saxe-Weimar, with whom he maintained a warm friendship. He was prominent in many of our financial institutions, being among the founders of the German-American and Lincoln National banks, while he was for twenty years vice-president of the Citizens' Savings Bank Becoming an American citizen, he took a patriotic and prominent share both in municipal and national politics. He was several times offered the nomination for Mayor, and was an elector at the election of Grant, and again at the election of Hayes, while he was warmly interested in educational questions, and at the time of his death was a school commissioner and a governor of the city institutions at Randall's Island. He was an original member of the Union League, and belonged to many social organizations. His wife, the mother of the present Mr. Kühne, was Ellen Josephine Miller, born in New York in 1833.

Mr. Percival Kühne, their son, was born in New York, April 6th, 1861. He attended the University of the City of New York, and then continued his studies in Germany. Upon his return, he entered the paternal banking house, in which, on his father's death, he succeeded to the place held by his father, both in New York and in Leipzig, Germany. He is a member of the Chamber of Commerce, and has taken an active part in several large financial institutions, among others, being one of the organizers and a trustee of the Colonial Trust Company. He is a veteran of the Seventh Regiment, a member of Holland Lodge, No. 8, F A M., and belongs to the Metropolitan, Union League, City and Military clubs, to the Metropolitan Museum of Art, the New York Botanical Garden, and many other organizations.

In 1893, Mr. Kühne married Lillian Middleton Kerr, granddaughter of John Kerr, the founder and first president of the Broadway & Seventh Avenue Railroad Company. Mrs. Kühne is also a granddaughter of Addison Smith, whose mother was Margaret Worthington, a lineal descendant of Nicholas Worthington, who took the oath of allegiance in 1678. The Worthington family is traced back in Burke's Landed Gentry to Henry III.

Mr. Kühne's visits to Europe have naturally been frequent and he has received many social attentions Mr and Mrs. Kühne were the only American guests present at the wedding of Princess Helen of Orleans to the Duke D'Aosta, in July, 1895, at Kingston, near London. Besides the Orleans family, all the English royal family except the Queen were present on this interesting occasion.

EDWARD R. LADEW

L ITTLE difficulty exists in tracing the family which this gentleman represents to a Huguenot origin. In fact, the name itself suggests an ancestry of that character For a number of generations, the ancestors of Mr. Edward R Ladew resided in the town of Mount Pleasant, Ulster County, N. Y., the locality taking from them the name of Ladew's Corners, by which it was known from an early date in the present century It was there that Abraham D. Ladew, grandfather of the subject of this article, lived and was successfully engaged in business, having an interest in leather manufactories at various points in that section.

His son, Harvey Smith Ladew, was born at Ladew's Corners in 1826. He attended the local schools and at an early age acquired a thorough knowledge of the art of tanning in his father's establishment. In 1866, he came to New York to represent the family enterprise in the metropolitan market He also became a member of the firm of Hoyt Brothers, and when the name of that establishment was changed to J B. Hoyt & Co, was one of the principals. In 1884, he became associated with Daniel S. Fayerweather, under the style of Fayerweather & Ladew, which attained the position of the most important firm in the "Swamp" district of New York, and which controlled a large portion of the leather product of the entire United States, and had important interests in all parts of the country. Daniel S Fayerweather is remembered by the bequest of his great wealth to a large number of colleges and institutions of learning. His partner, Harvey Smith Ladew, was a merchant of the old school and wielded great influence in mercantile circles until his death in 1888. He married, in 1849, Rebecca, daughter of Reuben Krom, and had two sons, Edward H and Joseph Harvey Ladew, and a daughter, Louise, who married John Townsend Williams. They have two sons, Harvey Ladew and John Townsend Williams, Jr

Mr. Edward R. Ladew, the eldest son of Harvey Smith Ladew, was born in New York City, February 18th, 1855. He was educated at the Charlier Institute and the Anthon Grammar School in this city. He then entered business life and acquired a practical knowledge of the mechanical processes of the industry with which his family was identified. After a time he became a member of the firm of J. B Hoyt & Co, and later of Fayerweather & Ladew, taking the position of acting manager of the latter. Since his father's death, in 1888, he had been in partnership with his brother. He was active in the foundation of the United States Leather Company, one of the largest and most important business enterprises in the United States, and was elected vice-president of that corporation. He is also connected with, and is a director in, a number of business, financial and fiduciary companies.

In 1886, Mr. Ladew married Louise B Wall, daughter of Charles Wall, one of whose ancestors was William Wall, the last Mayor of Williamsburgh, prior to its consolidation with Brooklyn. Their children are: Harvey S. and Elsie Wall Ladew. Mr. Ladew is a noted sportsman, has shot large game in many countries and is greatly interested in yachting, being a member of the New York, Larchmont, American, Atlantic and Hempstead Harbor Yacht clubs, and is owner of the steam yacht Orienta His social clubs include the Union League, Fulton, Hide and Leather, and the Liederkranz Society. The family residence is in East Sixty-seventh Street, near Central Park. Their country seat is Elsinore, Hempstead Harbor, Long Island, which was once owned by William E. Burton, the famous actor and manager. The place now comprises, among other features, a remarkable collection of blooded live stock of all kinds, including horses, dogs of several breeds, sheep and high grade poultry. Mrs. Ladew gives this portion of the establishment her personal supervision. Many prizes and awards have been taken at horse shows, fairs and exhibitions by the owners of Elsinore, which is regarded as one of the most perfectly appointed places of the kind in the vicinity of New York The house also contains a large number of trophies of the chase from various parts of the world, nearly all the specimens having been shot by Mr. Ladew or his friends, as well as a remarkable collection of weapons of all countries and ages, to the gathering of which their owner has devoted much time and attention.

DANIEL SCOTT LAMONT

SPRUNG from Scotch ancestry, whose lineage has been traced back to the year 1250, the
Honorable Daniel Scott Lamont has achieved success in political life and in financial affairs
His ancestors came to this country in the early part of the present century and took up
their residence in Delaware County, N Y His paternal grandparents were Daniel and Margaret
Lamont, and those on the maternal side, Andrew and Helen J Scott. His father and mother,
John B Lamont and Elizabeth Scott, after their marriage, removed from Delaware County to Cort-
land County, N Y. John B Lamont, who died quite recently, was a merchant at McGrawville,
N Y His son, Mr Daniel S. Lamont, was born in the town of Cortlandville, Cortland County,
N Y., February 9th, 1851 He was taught in the local schools and at the New York Central
Academy in McGrawville, and in 1868 entered Union College, in the class of 1872

He did not, however, complete his course, but after pursuing it for two years, left college to
accept an appointment as a deputy clerk of the New York Assembly and subsequently became
Chief Clerk of the State Department when the Honorable John Bigelow was Secretary of State
He became active in the Democratic party of the State during the years of the Honorable Samuel J
Tilden's governorship, and had the confidence of that gentleman to such an extent that during the
interesting years from 1874 to 1882, he was actively connected with the affairs of his party
From the State Department he retired to take up editorial work on the staff of The Albany Argus,
then controlled by Daniel Manning, of which paper he became one of the owners While in that
position, he came into relations with the Honorable Grover Cleveland, who was then Governor
of the State, and who offered Mr Lamont a position as Military Secretary on his staff with the
rank of Colonel. Shortly after, Mr. Lamont became Grover Cleveland's private secretary, holding
that position as long as the latter retained the Governorship of New York

When Grover Cleveland was elected President of the United States, in 1884, Mr. Lamont
went to Washington with him as his private secretary. In the larger field of national affairs, he
displayed the same qualities that had brought him into prominence at Albany, and won a national
reputation as one of the ablest private secretaries of the Executive who had ever entered the White
House. When the first administration of President Cleveland was at an end, Mr Lamont became
associated with the Honorable William C. Whitney and other capitalists in the management of the Metropolitan Traction Company and other corporations in this city. In 1892, he
contributed much by his labors to the reëlection of Grover Cleveland to the Presidency and to the
success of the Democratic party in the general election of that year. In the formation of the new
Cabinet, in 1893, Mr. Lamont was named Secretary of War, and held that portfolio throughout
President Cleveland's second term of office. He was in that office eminently successful in the
administration of the business of the War Department.

Since the close of President Cleveland's last term, in 1897, Mr Lamont has remained in
private life. He has, however, been mentioned for the Governorship of the State of New York,
for the mayoralty of the city, and for a seat in the United States Senate But to the present, he
devotes his attention to business affairs. In the summer of 1897, he was elected to the vice-
presidency of the Northern Pacific Railway Company and is president of the Northern Pacific
Express Company He is also a director in the Syracuse, Binghamton & New York Railroad Company, the Monongah Railway Company, the National Union Bank and the American Surety
Company For some years past, his home has been in New York, save when residing in Washington on account of his public duties He lives at 26 West Fifty-third Street He married
Juliet Kinney, daughter of Orson A Kinney, of McGrawville, Cortland County, N. Y., their
family consisting of four young daughters.

Mr. Lamont is a member of the Metropolitan, Colonial, Lotos, Lawyers' and Democratic
clubs, and the Union Alumni Association, and is a patron of the Metropolitan Museum of Art
Union College conferred upon him the degree of A M., in 1886.

FRANCIS G LANDON

FORTUNE and position in the social world of New York have never been any bar to the performance on the part of their possessors of useful and energetic service to the city and to the community at large. The gentleman to whom this article is devoted is an exemplar of the facts just referred to. The possessor of an honored family name, identified with the leading religious and benevolent interests of the metropolis, as well as with its most important business and financial organizations, and enjoying an extensive connection among the best social elements of the metropolis, joined to cultivated tastes and to sufficient means to gratify them at will, he has devoted his time and attention to the performance of duties of an exacting character in connection with an organization which has made itself a matter of pride to the city of his birth, and which, in addition to this, is a real bulwark of the entire community under the reign of law and liberty.

Mr. Landon's father, the late Charles Griswold Landon, was a descendant of English ancestors, whose settlement in the town of Southold, Long Island, dates back to 1640. In the course of time, some of its representatives became allied with old and notable Connecticut families, and took up their residence in that State. Charles Griswold Landon was born at Guilford, Conn., in 1818. He engaged in business in New Haven, but in 1842 came to New York, and was, for some years, a partner in the firm of S B Chittenden and its successor, George Bliss & Co., becoming finally head of the wholesale house of Charles G Landon & Co. He was long identified with Grace Church Parish, of which he was the senior warden for many years, and was noted for his devotion to religious and benevolent work. He was a trustee of St. Luke's Hospital, and among other positions of prominence which he held in the business and financial world was that of a director in the Equitable Life Assurance Society, the Greenwich Savings Bank, the Central Trust Company and the Bank of America. He married, in 1849, Susan H. Gordon, daughter of Charles Gordon, of Virginia, and a descendant of the Hunt, Hunters and other distinguished families of the Old Dominion. She died in 1885. The children of this marriage were Henry H , Edward H., and Francis G. Landon ; Annie, the wife of L. Townsend Howes, and Mary G , wife of Dallas Bache Pratt. Mr. Landon died in New York City in 1893.

Mr. Francis G. Landon was born in New York, in 1859, and after completing his preparatory education at schools in this city, became an undergraduate at Princeton College, receiving his degree in the class of 1881. He has not engaged in active business, and has devoted himself, so far as cares of that nature are concerned, to the management of his property. He is a member of a number of the leading athletic and social organizations of the city, including the Racquet, New York Athletic and University clubs, as well as of the Calumet Club, the Country Club of Westchester County, the Princeton Club, and others of similar character and objects, and has been active in furthering their interests

It is, however, with the staff of the famous Seventh Regiment, New York National Guard, that Mr. Landon has been most intimately identified. He joined the organization as a private in 1882, and was successively promoted to the various minor grades of military rank, in this notable regiment, up to that of First Sergeant of his company, the duties of which he assumed in 1887. He was distinguished from the beginning of his military service with the Seventh as a keen and enthusiastic soldier, and when, in 1891, a vacancy occurred in the position of Adjutant of the regiment, he was selected for that very responsible and exacting post. The honor was the more signal because the custom had invariably been to appoint a commissioned officer as Adjutant. Since April, 1895, he has been Captain of Company I of the Seventh.

Mr. Landon is to a rational extent a devotee of athletic and outdoor sport. He is also noted as an amateur actor of considerable versatility and talent, and has taken part, with great success, in a number of entertainments of that character. In May, 1897, Mr. Landon married Mary Hornor Toel, daughter of William Toel, of this city.

WOODBURY LANGDON

NEW HAMPSHIRE, the establishment of which as a Colony followed that of Massachusetts by only a few years, attracted some of the best elements of the original Puritan emigration Among the families of this class which made it their home none have had a more notable position from the earliest times down to the present day than the Langdons The first representative of that name in America crossed the ocean with the early Puritan emigration, since which time his descendants have held an honorable and distinguished place in New England's annals, while several of them have attained to national distinction by the prominent part that they have taken in public affairs Tobias Langdon, who settled at Portsmouth, N H, in 1662, became a selectman of the town two years later, and was otherwise locally prominent He was the ancestor of Mr. Woodbury Langdon, who is the ninth in descent from the original Puritan immigrant of his name

Mr. Langdon's progenitors were long identified with the town of Portsmouth, N H, where several generations of the family were leading merchants His great-grandfather, Woodbury Langdon, was an ardent patriot during the Revolution, and was one of the leading men who brought New Hampshire into line in the struggle for independence. He was also, after the peace, a Judge of the Supreme Court of New Hampshire, serving from 1786 to 1789 The patriot's brother, John Langdon, was also a strong figure in the Revolutionary annals of New Hampshire, and after independence was achieved became Governor of the State for two terms, and a United States Senator. The present Mr Langdon's father was also named Woodbury, and was a prominent merchant of Portsmouth, having large shipping interests in the days when America's merchant marine was a powerful factor in international commerce. His wife was Frances Cutter, daughter of Jacob Cutter, of Portsmouth, the Cutter family being of old New Hampshire descent, and of high social prominence.

Born October 22d, 1836, in the town where his family had been eminent for so many generations, Mr. Woodbury Langdon was educated at the celebrated Portsmouth Grammar School, in which some of the most famous men of New England received their training He prepared for a college course, and only abandoned that intention because of his preference for a business career He accordingly entered a Boston mercantile house at an early age, and in 1863 came to New York in charge of its business in this city. Since that date, Mr Langdon has been most notably identified with the larger mercantile interests of New York. Among other positions of a prominent character in the financial world, he is a director of the New York Life Insurance Company, the National Bank of Commerce, the Central National Bank, and the German American Insurance Company He has been a member of the Chamber of Commerce for many years, has served on the executive committee of the organization since 1888, and has been active in conserving the interests with which that important commercial organization is chiefly concerned.

In spite of the many responsibilities his business entails, Mr Langdon has taken part in movements for the advancement of the city's interests. He has not been active in politics in the ordinary sense, and yet has recognized the duty which leading citizens of his own character and influence owe to the community at large. Tenders of public office he has often refused, but was prevailed upon to accept the position of a member of the Rapid Transit Commission He is a Republican in national affairs, and is a member and served as vice-president of the Union League Club In early life, he married Edith Eustis Pugh, daughter of David B. Pugh She died some years since, and in 1896 Mr Langdon contracted a second alliance, espousing Elizabeth Langdon Elwyn, daughter of Alfred L Elwyn, of Philadelphia

Besides the Union League, Mr Langdon belongs to the Lawyers' and New York Athletic clubs, and was one of the founders, having long been an officer also, of the Merchants' Club His town house is in West Forty-fifth Street, and he also has a country place at Fox Point, Newington, N H

CHARLES LANIER

WHEN John Washington, the great-grandfather of the first President of the United States, came to America from England, in 1655, he was accompanied by several friends, chief among whom was Thomas Lanier, a Huguenot refugee from France They settled in Westmoreland County, Va., and in due course of time Thomas Lanier married a daughter of John Washington. From this couple have descended the Laniers in this country, who can claim a Colonial lineage. Sidney Lanier, the poet, was of this family, and other members of it have been distinguished in professional and commercial life. During the Revolutionary War, James Lanier, the great-grandfather of Mr. Charles Lanier, was a Captain of cavalry, in Colonel William Washington's Regiment, and a planter of considerable means, of which he gave freely to the patriot cause. In the War of 1812, his son, Alexander Chalmers Lanier, served under Harrison, and died as a result of his military service

A son of Major Alexander Chalmers Lanier was James F. D Lanier, for thirty years one of the leading bankers of New York. He was born, in 1800, at Washington, Beaufort County, N C, and was educated in an academy at Newport, Ky., and in private schools. An appointment to the military academy at West Point was declined for family reasons, the death of his father having imbued his mother's mind with a deep seated aversion to military life. He graduated from the Transylvania Law School, in 1823, and began the practice of his profession in Madison, Ind. The same year he received the appointment of assistant clerk of the Indiana House of Representatives, and, in 1827, became the chief clerk of that body In 1833, he assisted in organizing the Madison branch of the State Bank of Indiana, and was its first president. His genius for finance showed itself in this new position, and, in 1847, he was sent to London to arrange the settlement of the State debt of Indiana, a delicate mission, which he successfully accomplished. Two years later he removed to New York City, and, with Richard H. Winslow, started the firm of Winslow, Lanier & Co., primarily for the promotion of Western railroad interests, and afterwards for a general banking business. Mr. Lanier was always a public spirited and a patriotic man, and during the Civil War gave the government and the State of Indiana much practical assistance. He died in New York, in 1881.

The mother of Mr. Charles Lanier, wife of James F. D. Lanier, was Elizabeth Gardner, a member of one of the historic families of the State of Kentucky. She had seven children, five daughters and two sons Mr Charles Lanier was born in Madison, Ind, January 19th, 1837, and educated in New Haven, Conn. At the age of twenty-three, he was admitted to member-ship in the firm of Winslow, Lanier & Co., and is now the head of that house. He has been a director in many corporations, such as the West Shore Railroad, the Central Railroad of New Jersey, the Western Union Telegraph Company, the Central Trust Company, the Central and South American Telegraph Company, the National Bank of Commerce, and others.

Mr. Lanier married Sarah Egleston, daughter of the late Thomas Egleston. He belongs to the Tuxedo, Union, Metropolitan, Union League, Knickerbocker, Players, Riding, Lawyers', Aldine, New York Yacht, and Mendelssohn clubs, the Century Association, and the New England Society , is a trustee of the American Museum of Natural History, and a supporter of the Metropolitan Museum of Art, and the American Geographical Society. His city home is in East Thirty-seventh Street, and his country seat is Allen Winden, Lenox, Mass. He has a family of one son and three daughters. His eldest daughter, Sarah Egleston, married Francis C. Lawrance, Jr., and died April 20th, 1893 ; Fannie L. is the wife of Francis R. Appleton ; Elizabeth G. is the wife of George E. Turnure. The son of Mr. Lanier is James F. D Lanier, who was born in New York, in 1858, and was educated at Princeton University, graduating in 1880. He is engaged in the banking business, being a member of the firm of Winslow, Lanier & Co. His wife was Harriet A. Bishop. He belongs to the Tuxedo, Metropolitan, Union, Knickerbocker, Meadowbrook Hunt, Princeton, Calumet and Racquet clubs.

CHARLES PERCY LATTING

IN the fifteenth century, Pierre Lettin, who was the earliest known ancestor of the Lettin or Latting, family, lived at Malines, Flanders   His son, grandson and great-grandson, who in three successive generations bore the name of Jean Lettin, were secretaries and registrars of the Supreme Tribunal of Malines   John Lettin, in 1567, driven from his native land by the persecutions instigated by the Duke of Alva, settled in Norwich, England, where he died in 1640   From this John Lettin was descended Richard Lettin, Lattin or Latting, who in 1638 came from England to this country   First, he went to Concord, Mass , removed in 1646 to Fairfield, Conn , in 1653 came to Hempstead, Long Island, in 1661 settled in Huntington, and two years after removed to Oyster Bay   At Oyster Bay, he purchased from the Matinnecock Indians a large tract of land, where he established his family upon an estate that was named Lattingtown

Josias Latting, son of Richard Latting and Joana Ireland, the head of the family in the next generation, was born in Concord, Mass , in 1641, and married, in 1667, Sarah Wright, daughter of Nicholas Wright   He resided at Oyster Bay, Huntington and Matinnecock, Long Island, was the owner of extensive landed property and held many public offices   William Latting, son of Joseph and Mary (Butler) Latting, 1739–1812, married Sarah Carpenter, daughter of Zeno Carpenter   He was a great-grandson of Richard Latting, the pioneer   Charles Latting, the grandfather of Mr Charles Percy Latting, was the fifth in descent from Richard Latting   Most of his life was passed in mercantile pursuits, in association with his brothers in the firm of Latting & Deall, shipping merchants   His wife was Elizabeth Frost, daughter of Stephen Frost

John J Latting, the father of Mr. Charles Percy Latting, was a well-known lawyer, genealogist and litterateur of the generation that is just passing away   He was born in Lattingtown, Long Island, in 1819, prepared for college in the Oyster Bay Academy, and entered Middlebury College, Vermont, in 1835, graduating in 1837   Studying law in the office of Francis B Cutting, he was admitted to the bar in 1842   He began practice with Charles B Moore, afterwards entered the firm of Cutting, Moore & Latting, then was successively associated with Lathrop S Eddy and Caleb S Woodhull, and a member of the firm of Wakeman, Latting & Phelps   In 1885, he retired and went to Europe, where he spent some time in travel. He died in New York in 1890.

The mother of Mr Charles Percy Latting was Harriet A Emerson, daughter of the Reverend Brown Emerson, of Salem, Mass   The father of Mrs Latting was born in Ashley, Mass , in 1778, and died in Salem in 1872   Graduated from Dartmouth College, in 1802, he was ordained in 1805 as the colleague of the Reverend Daniel Hopkins, in the old South Church of Salem, remaining there until his death, a period of sixty-seven years, being sole pastor from 1816 to 1849   The mother of Mrs. Latting was Mary Hopkins, daughter of the Reverend Daniel Hopkins, the immediate predecessor of her husband in the pastorate of the old South Church   Daniel Hopkins was graduated from Yale College, in 1758, was a member of the Provincial Congress in 1775, and one of the leading Congregational ministers of Eastern Massachusetts in his generation   He was the great-grandson of Edward Hopkins, of Shrewsbury, England, an eminent merchant of London, who came to Boston in 1637

Mr. Charles Percy Latting is the eldest child of his father's family. He was born in New York, May 28th, 1850   His brothers are Walter S and Arthur D Latting, and his sister is Harriet Emerson van Benthuysen, widow of Clarence R van Benthuysen, of Albany   Two sisters, Grace Vernon and Alice Maud Latting, died in infancy   Mr Latting is a graduate of Yale College, in the class of 1873, is a lawyer, and has held the office of United States Loan Commissioner for many years   His clubs are the University and Seawanhaka-Corinthian Yacht, and he also belongs to the Sons of the Revolution and the Bar Association of New York   He married Isabella W Carter, daughter of James Carter, of Aberdeen, Scotland, and has three children, Helen Leslie, Emerson and Charles Percy Latting, Jr.   He lives in West Thirty-eighth Street and has a country residence, Werah House, on the old family property in Lattingtown, Long Island.

EDWARD LAUTERBACH

NEAR the historic city of Nuremburg, in the hill country of Bavaria, is the town of Burgkundstadt, the acknowledged centre for many years of the Liberal party of Germany Mr Lauterbach's family were for more than four centuries among the leading professional men and merchants of this community.   One of the most prominent of the number was Aaron Wolfgang Lauterbach, 1752–1826, a graduate of the University of Prague, and noted for his erudition, as well as for a remarkable share of wit and humor   Solon Lauterbach, the father of the subject of this article, was the youngest of his six children, and was born in 1806.   Of an adventurous spirit, and chafing under the political tyranny which oppressed Germany at that era, and which finally led to the Revolution of 1848, he left his ancestral home for this country in 1840, dying in New York in 1860   His wife, Mina Rosenbaum, was a member of a family noted for their intellectual gifts, a quality which she inherited to a remarkable degree.   Her memory for poetry was particularly retentive, and she was noted as a Shakespearian scholar   She died in 1890, leaving three children, of whom Mr Edward Lauterbach is the eldest

Mr. Edward Lauterbach was born in New York in 1844, and was educated at the College of the City of New York, graduating in the class of 1864 with high honors   He has been for some time vice-president of the alumni of his alma mater and takes an active interest in its welfare, and is also a member of Φ B K.   In 1870, Mr. Lauterbach married Amanda Friedman, daughter of Arnold Friedman, a retired merchant of this city.   The Friedman family was also of prominence in the same portion of Bavaria from which Mr. Lauterbach's ancestors came.   They were for generations respected and wealthy merchants, Aaron Friedman, 1740–1824, her great-great-grand-father, having been the owner of the baronial castle of Kunds, at Burgkundstadt, from which fortress the place took its name.   Mrs. Lauterbach's grandparents, Samuel Friedman, 1796–1880, and Sarah (Greis) Friedman, 1800–1872, were noted for their philanthropy and benevolence, having endowed the school of the district in which they lived, while Madame Friedman, at her death, bequeathed all her personal fortune to the poor of her city   Mrs I auterbach's mother, Wilhemina Straubel Friedman, was the daughter of Frederick Straubel, of Green Bay, Wis , whose wife belonged to a titled Saxon family.   Mr and Mrs Lauterbach have four children a son, Alfred, now an Assistant District Attorney of the County of New York, who took the degree of B A at Columbia in 1890, and LL B at the New York Law School in 1892, and three daughters, Edith, Florence and Alice   Florence is a graduate of the law school of the University of the City of New York, in 1897   Possessing a well trained voice, Mrs Lauterbach has utilized it for the advantage of the many charities with which she is connected, and others   She also has been instrumental, after years of effort, in securing the passage of philanthropic measures, such as the laws known as the Mercantile Bill and the Anti-Sweaters' Bill, regulating beneficially the employment of certain industrial classes

Admitted to the bar of this city soon after his graduation from college, Mr Lauterbach has been distinguished not only in its practice and for the possession of forensic and political oratorical powers, but as a law maker, having drafted and secured the adoption of many important public measures   While not an active politician, he takes a deep interest in public affairs, and was honored in 1894 by election as a delegate at large to the New York Constitutional Convention   He is also a leader in the Republican party in the city and State of New York, and for two years, 1895–1897, was the Chairman of the County Committee of the party in this city, and in 1896 was a delegate at large for New York to the National Convention at St Louis, which nominated Mr. McKinley   He has been professionally and personally associated with the largest financial and commercial enterprises of the country and with the leaders of contemporary business and finance in New York.   Though closely occupied with his profession and with the care of vast interests, Mr Lauterbach finds rest and relaxation in society, and is noted for his devotion to music and the drama.

ABRAHAM RIKER LAWRENCE

IT has been said of the Lawrences that "they were related to all that was most illustrious in England, to the ambitious Robert Dudley, Earl of Leicester, the favorite courtier of Queen Elizabeth, and to Sir Philip Sidney, who refused a throne." The earliest ancestor of this family, of whom there is an authentic record, was Sir Robert Lawrence, of Ashton Hall, Lancashire, who accompanied King Richard Cœur de Lion to Palestine, and was the first to plant his standard on the walls of Acre in 1191. His grandson, Sir James Lawrence, in the time of Henry III., married Matilda Washington Among the descendants of this marriage were Sir John Lawrence, who, in the reign of Henry VII., was the owner of thirty-four manors, Henry Lawrence, a member of the Long Parliament, and William Lawrence, the friend of Milton.

The family was one of the first of distinction to send its representatives from England to the New World. Three sons of William Lawrence came to the American Colonies John and William arrived in the ship Planter, and Thomas Lawrence, the youngest brother, afterwards joined them. They went first to New England, where their kinsman, Henry Lawrence, had received with Lord Say and Seal, Lord Brooke, Saltonstall and others a large grant of land in Connecticut, from which the settlement of Saybrook originated. Later they came to New Netherland and became landowners, men of wealth and influence in the Province. John Lawrence was Mayor of New York from 1673 to 1675, and again in 1691, and was a Justice of the Supreme Court and a member of the Governor's Council from 1672 to 1679. He left no male descendants.

Captain William Lawrence was the head of the patentees of Flushing, Long Island, in 1645, a magistrate under the Dutch administration, and a military officer under the English Government. He was the ancestor of Captain James Lawrence, U S. N., commander of the frigate Chesapeake in its memorable action with the British ship Shannon in 1813, whose dying words, "Don't give up the ship," have become immortal, and whose tomb is now a conspicuous feature of the graveyard of Trinity Church, New York

Major Thomas Lawrence, the youngest of the three brothers, was the chief patentee of Newtown, Long Island, and commander of the Queens County forces in 1689 His son William was a member of Jacob Leisler's Committee of Safety in 1689, and a Councillor of the Province in 1690, and from 1702 to 1706 Another son of Thomas, Captain John Lawrence, was the sheriff of Queens County He married Deborah Woodhull, daughter of the patentee of Brookhaven, and died in 1729 One of his sons, John Lawrence, was a Judge of the Province, and married Patience Sackett and had a large family, the descendants of which have been prominent in New York. The eldest son, John Lawrence, alderman of the Dock Ward, married Catherine, daughter of the Honorable Philip Livingston, and died without issue William Lawrence, the fifth son of John and Patience, was for many years a magistrate of Queens County. His grandson, the Honorable William Beach Lawrence, was prominent in political life, being Chargé d'Affaires in London in 1827-28, and later was Governor of Rhode Island. His son is the Honorable Isaac Lawrence. Captain Thomas Lawrence, the sixth son of John and Patience Lawrence, commanded the ship Tartar during the French War, and was a Judge in Queens County. His son, Lieutenant Nathaniel Lawrence, distinguished himself in the Revolution He was a member of the convention which ratified the Constitution of the United States, was four times a member of Assembly, and Attorney-General of the State of New York He also left no male descendants

Jonathan Lawrence, the eighth son of John and Patience, was a conspicuous patriot He was so successful as a merchant that he had accumulated a large fortune at thirty-four years of age. He lost all his possessions during the Revolution, but became a wealthy man again before his death in 1812 He was a Major in the Continental Army, a member of the Provincial Congresses of 1775, 1776 and 1777, a member of the convention which formulated the Constitution of this State in 1776-77, and a member of the State Senate from 1777 to 1783 Three sons of Jonathan Lawrence became conspicuous in State and national affairs Samuel was a county Judge and member of

Congress. William was a soldier in the War of 1812, a county Judge and Member of Congress. Another son was the Honorable John L Lawrence, who was born in 1785 and was one of the leaders of the New York bar. He also entered the diplomatic service of the United States, and was Secretary of Legation at Stockholm in 1814, and later Chargé d'Affaires He was a member of Assembly, the State Senate, and of the Constitutional Convention of 1821, president of the Croton Aqueduct Board in 1842, and Comptroller of New York City at the time of his death in 1849. He was also, for many years, treasurer of Columbia College.

The Honorable Abraham R. Lawrence, Justice of the Supreme Court of New York, is a son of the Honorable John L. Lawrence. On his mother's side he comes of an ancestry fully as renowned as that of his father. His mother was Sarah Augusta Smith, only daughter of General John Smith, of St. George's Manor, Long Island, and a granddaughter of General Nathaniel Woodhull General John Smith, whose wife was the only child of General Woodhull, was a descendant of Colonel William Smith, who was Governor of Tangier, Justice of the Supreme Court, and Chief Justice of the Province of New York, Judge of the Court of Admiralty for New York, New Jersey and Connecticut, member of the Governor's Council from 1691 to 1704, received the grant of St. George's Manor 1693, and was Governor of New York, *pro tempore*, 1701, after the death of Lord Bellomont. Born in 1756, General John Smith served in the Revolution and was a member of the Assembly from 1784 to 1800. In 1788 he was a member of the Convention which framed the Constitution of the United States. He was a member of the Fifth, Sixth, Seventh and Eighth Congresses In 1804, he succeeded General John Armstrong in the United States Senate, was elected for another term in 1807, and died in 1816.

General Woodhull was the great-grandson of Richard Woodhull, the patentee of Brookhaven, Long Island. He was a Major under General Abercrombie at Ticonderoga in the French and Indian War, and a Colonel in the army which invaded Canada in 1760. Later he was a member of Assembly. In 1775, he was commissioned Brigadier-General of the Suffolk and Queens County troops After the battle of Long Island he was captured by the British forces, by whom he was killed when a prisoner. He was three times President of the Provincial Congress, and presided over the meeting which ratified the Declaration of Independence. His wife was Ruth, daughter of Nicoll Floyd, and sister of General William Floyd, signer of the Declaration of Independence.

Justice Abraham R. Lawrence was a member of the Constitutional Convention of 1867. He has been a member of the New York bar for more than half a century, was elected a Justice of the Supreme Court in 1873, was reëlected in 1888, and is considered one of the ablest members of the judiciary. He is a member of the Union, Metropolitan, Century, Bar Association, Manhattan and other clubs. In 1860, Judge Lawrence married Eliza Miner, only daughter of Dr. William Miner, and granddaughter of Dr. William Westcott Miner, a leading New York physician. The Miner family is descended from Lieutenant Thomas Miner, one of the founders of New London, whose son, Clement Miner, was born at New London, and whose grandson, also, William Miner, of Lyme, Conn., a well-known patriot of the American Revolution, was the father of Dr. William Westcott Miner. Mrs. Lawrence's mother was Julia Caroline Williams, a daughter of Cornelius T. Williams, of Rosemount, an estate that at the beginning of the century extended from the present Fourteenth Street to Twentieth Street, and from what is now Fifth Avenue to the limits of the Stuyvesant Farm, or about the line of Third Avenue.

Judge and Mrs Lawrence have two children, William Miner Lawrence and Ruth Lawrence. William M. Lawrence at one time represented the Eleventh Assembly District of this city in the Legislature. He married Lavinia Oliver, of this city, and has two children, Oliver Lawrence and Clement Miner Lawrence Judge Lawrence's residence is at 285 Lexington Avenue. The arms of the Lawrence family, taken from the seal of Thomas Lawrence, its first American ancestor, are described as follows : Argent, a cross raguly gules. Crest, a demi-turbot in pale argent, the tail upwards Motto *Quaero Invenio*.

JOHN L LAWRENCE

THAT branch of the famous Lawrence family, of which Mr. John L. Lawrence is a representative in the present generation, is directly descended from John Lawrence, who was the chief burgess of St. Albans, England, in 1553, and Mayor of that city, 1567-75. It is now generally agreed by genealogists that this John Lawrence was the father of William Lawrence, who in 1559 married Katerin Beaumont, the grandfather of John Lawrence, who married, in 1586, Margaret Robertes, and the great-grandfather of Thomas Lawrence, who married, in 1609, Joane Anterbus, daughter of Walter and Jane (Arnolde) Anterbus or Antrobus.

Captain William Lawrence, the first American ancestor of Mr. John L. Lawrence, was the son of Thomas and Joane (Anterbus) Lawrence. Born in St. Albans, Hertfordshire, England, in 1622, he came to New England in 1635, was one of the eighteen original incorporators of Flushing, Long Island, in 1655, afterwards a magistrate, in 1657 a deputy to the council, in 1665 Captain of the Queens County militia and in 1673 schout or sheriff of Flushing. He died in 1679. His wife was Elizabeth Smith, daughter of Richard Smith. Joseph Lawrence, his son, born 1666, was an ensign of the New York provincial troops. Tradition says that he married Mary Townley, daughter of Colonel Richard Townley, of New Jersey.

Richard Lawrence, 1691-1781, son of Joseph Lawrence, married, in 1717, Hannah Bowne, daughter of Samuel and Mary Bowne. Their son, John Lawrence, 1732-94, married, in 1755, Ann Burling, daughter of John and Ann Burling. John Burling Lawrence, grandfather of Mr. John L. Lawrence, was the son of John and Ann (Burling) Lawrence. Born in 1774, he became a leading merchant at the head of the house of Lawrence, Keese & Co. His death occurred in 1844. His wife was Hannah Newbold, daughter of Caleb Newbold, of Philadelphia, by his wife, Sarah Haines, of New Jersey. Alfred Newbold Lawrence, 1813-1884, father of Mr John L. Lawrence, had a long and successful business career, being a dry goods merchant and a wholesale druggist.

The mother of Mr. John L Lawrence was Elizabeth Lawrence, daughter of the Honorable John L. Lawrence. She was descended in the sixth generation from Thomas Lawrence, a brother of William Lawrence, the ancestor of her husband, and himself a pioneer to this country in the early part of the seventeenth century. Thomas Lawrence was born in England in 1619, and was a patentee of Middleburgh, now Newtown, Long Island, in 1655. His son, John Lawrence, who married a daughter of Richard Woodhull, was a Captain in the Queens County Regiment and sheriff of the county in 1698. His grandson, John Lawrence, who married Patience Sackett, daughter of Joseph Sackett, was for many years a county magistrate. His great-grandson, Jonathan Lawrence, born in 1737, was a merchant of New York, a Captain of the militia, a Revolutionary patriot, a member of the Provincial Congress in 1775-6-7, a member of the Constitutional Convention, Major of the Queens and Suffolk County militia, and a member of the New York State Senate, 1777-83. The Honorable John L. Lawrence, maternal grandfather of the subject of this sketch, was the son of Jonathan Lawrence, by his wife, Ruth Riker. He was born in 1785 and became one of the distinguished public men of the last generation, being engaged in the diplomatic service of the United States, a member of the New York Assembly, member of the State Constitutional Convention in 1821, Presidential elector in 1840, State Senator 1847-49, Comptroller of New York City in 1850 and treasurer of Columbia College. His wife was Sarah Augusta Tangier, daughter of General John Smith, of St. George's Manor, Suffolk County.

Mr. John L. Lawrence was born June 22d, 1857. His residence is upon the ancestral estate in Lawrence, Long Island. He belongs to the Calumet, Rockaway Hunt and Seawanhaka-Corinthian Yacht clubs He married, in 1895, Alice Warner Work, daughter of I Henry Work and Marie P Warner. On her mother's side, Mrs. Lawrence is directly descended from William Bradford, who came on the Mayflower in 1620, and was the first Governor of the Plymouth Colony. He has one sister, Hannah Newbold Lawrence. The coat of arms of the Lawrence family is a fish's tail, with the motto, *Quæro Invenio.*

LEONIDAS MOREAU LAWSON

ENGLISH and Dutch families are both conspicuous in the Lawson genealogy, and among them occur several names of distinction in our national history General Robert Lawson, of Virginia, was a prominent patriot and an eminent Revolutionary officer. He entered the Continental service as Major, in 1775, and in 1777 became Colonel in command of a brigade of Virginia troops, which served under General Nathaniel Greene at the battle of Guilford. He also rendered important service to Patrick Henry and to Thomas Jefferson, when the latter was Governor of Virginia, in 1778–79, the fact being prominently mentioned by Jefferson's biographers. His son, the Reverend Jeremiah Lawson, went early in life from Virginia to Kentucky, settling in Mason County. After Missouri had been annexed to the United States, through the Louisiana purchase, he removed thither with his family, in 1804, being one of the earliest American pioneers of the State He was a noted clergyman of the Methodist Episcopal Church in the Mississippi Valley, and died at Cincinnati, in 1862, aged ninety. William Lawson, eldest son of the Reverend Mr Lawson, was the father of Colonel Leonidas M Lawson. He settled in the Boone's Lick country, now Howard County, Mo., and married Phœbe Kanslor. Her family was founded in America by Philip Kanslor, who emigrated from Holland in 1750, settled at Albany, N. Y., and served in the French and Indian War, and the Revolution. His son, John Kanslor, moved to Kentucky, in 1798, and was the father of Phœbe (Kanslor) Lawson.

Mr. Leonidas Moreau Lawson was born of this parentage, in Howard County, Mo He was named for his father's brother, Leonidas Moreau Lawson, M. D , 1812–1864 Dr. Lawson was a graduate of the medical department of Transylvania University, in which he became a professor, and was sent by his alma mater to Germany, France and England, in 1846, to investigate the progress of medical science He was also a professor in the Ohio Medical College, of Cincinnati, the Kentucky School of Medicine, at Louisville, and the University of Louisiana, and was a voluminous writer on medical topics. His daughter, Louise Lawson, is the distinguished sculptor.

His namesake, Colonel L M. Lawson, graduated at seventeen years of age from the University of Missouri, and for two years was professor of Greek and Latin at the William Jewell College, Liberty, Mo. He then studied law, was admitted to the bar, and removed to Western Missouri, where he became interested in railroad construction In 1860, he was elected to the Missouri Legislature on the Bell and Everett ticket, and, being a strong Union man, defeated a plan of the majority of the members to carry the State out of the Union by means of a militia bill. In 1861, he was offered by Governor Gamble the command of the Twelfth Missouri Cavalry. He refused this and served throughout the war on the staff of General James Craig.

After the war, Colonel Lawson again resumed the practice of the law, but became interested in railroad and business enterprises. He was a founder and first president of the State National Bank, in St. Joseph, and participated in organizing the German Savings Bank, Merchants Insurance Company, and other corporations He founded the St. Joseph Law Library Association, and was its president for several years. He was also one of the chief promoters of the St Joseph & Denver City Railroad, afterwards the St. Joseph & Western, and of the St. Louis & St Joseph Railroad, of which latter he was president. In 1868, with his brother-in-law, Robert W. Donnell, he established the banking house of Donnell, Lawson & Co., in New York, and in 1874–1878 was the firm's resident partner in London. In 1873, he organized the Kansas City Water-Works Company.

Colonel Lawson married Theodosia Thornton, youngest daughter of Colonel John Thornton, of Missouri, and has two sons : William Thornton Lawson, the elder, graduated from Columbia University, in 1882, studied at the University of Berlin, and then graduated from the law department of Columbia. Leonidas M Lawson, Jr , is a student in the medical department of Columbia. The family residence is in East Sixty-seventh Street. Colonel Lawson is a member of the Union, University, Union League, Manhattan, New York Yacht, Reform, and United Service clubs, and of the Downtown Association, the Southern Society, and other prominent bodies.

JOHN BROOKS LEAVITT

B EARERS of the Leavitt name were among the Puritans of Massachusetts   John Leavitt, from Norfolk, England, settled at Hingham in 1628, and his son, John Leavitt, established himself in the town of Suffield, Hartford County, Conn. It was there that Mr. John Brooks Leavitt's grandfather, the Honorable Humphrey Howe Leavitt, was born in 1796. The family removed to Ohio in 1800, and Humphrey Howe Leavitt, having received a classical education, was admitted to the bar in 1815 He first practiced at Cadiz, Harrison County, O , but removed to Steubenville, where he was elected prosecuting attorney and served in the Ohio Legislature and Senate. In 1830, he became a Representative in Congress, serving for two terms. He was an admirer and prominent supporter of President Andrew Jackson, by whom he was appointed Judge of the United States Court for Ohio in 1834 In a short memoir written for his children he refers to a seat in Congress as "positively irksome and repulsive," adding "In times of party division, it is impossible for anyone in Congress to preserve a conscience void of offense toward God and at the same time to bear true allegiance to the party by which he has been elected   The member must vote with his party irrespective of the public good or expect to be visited with the fiercest denunciation."   For thirty-seven years this upright and accomplished lawyer graced the Federal bench and decided cases of vital importance to the country, one of his noteworthy opinions being in the famous habeas corpus case of Clement L. Valandingham. Judge Leavitt was also an eminent member of the Presbyterian communion and served as delegate to eleven sessions of its general assembly   The degree of LL. D. was conferred upon him by Jefferson College. He married Marie Antoinette McDowell, daughter of Dr John McDowell, provost of the University of Pennsylvania and Governor of that State. Judge Leavitt died at Springfield, O , in 1872

His son, the Reverend John McDowell Leavitt, D. D , LL. D , was born at Steubenville, O., in 1824, graduated at Jefferson College in 1841 and studied law   After a few years of practice, his inclinations turned to the church and he was ordained to the ministry of the Episcopal Church in 1862. His educational talent was promply recognized, and he became a professor in Kenyon College, O , and was afterwards one of the faculty of the University of Ohio, which institution in 1874 conferred on him the degree of LL. D. He was subsequently the second president of Lehigh University, Bethlehem, Pa , and has filled the same office at St. John's College, Annapolis, Md. Doctor Leavitt's contributions to literature have been numerous, though only a few of his works can be mentioned, among them being. Hymns to Our King, Faith and other Poems, Reasons for Faith in the Nineteenth Century. He also edited The Church Review, and founded and edited The International Review. Doctor Leavitt married Bithia Brooks, of Cincinnati, daughter of Moses Brooks, born near Huntington, N. J , and his wife, Lydia (Ransom) Brooks, who was a granddaughter of Captain Samuel Ransom, slain at the Wyoming massacre in 1778.

Mr John Brooks Leavitt is the offspring of this marriage, and was born at Cincinnati, O., in 1849 He graduated from Kenyon College, O., in 1868, and from the law department of Columbia College, of this city, in 1871. Mr. Leavitt has pursued his profession with success, taking at the same time a warm interest in politics and literature. He is the author of a legal work, Law of Negligence, and a frequent contributor to the periodicals In 1896, the degree of LL. D was conferred upon him by Kenyon College His wife was Mary Keith, born at Churchtown, Lancaster County, Pa , a lady who also springs from a family of unmixed American descent. Among Mrs Leavitt's ancestors on her mother's side was Elisha Boudinot, Judge of the Supreme Court of New Jersey, brother of Elias Boudinot, president of Congress and the first lawyer admitted to the bar of the United States Supreme Court. Mrs. Leavitt and her family possess portraits of their ancestors of great interest.

Mr Leavitt is a member of the University, City, Lawyers' and Church clubs and the New England Society. He resides at 44 Stuyvesant Street, and belongs to the Onteora Club, in the Catskill Mountains

LEWIS CASS LEDYARD

ORIGINALLY the name of Ledyard was Welsh and the family is a branch of the Llwyds or Lloyds, who trace their ancestry to the early Britons who fought with Arthur against the Saxon Kings. John Ledyard, the first of the name in America, was a gentleman of considerable means and of good family, a native of Bristol, England, and in middle life a resident of London. He came to Southold, Long Island, in 1717, and there was engaged first as a teacher and then as a trader. He prospered in business and married Deborah, a daughter of Judge Benjamin Youngs, of Southold, and a granddaughter of the Reverend John Youngs, a devoted minister, who led a company of Colonists, in 1638, from Norfolkshire, England, to settle the place that they called Southold.

John Ledyard moved to Groton, Conn., in 1727 and became one of the influential men of the Colony. He was a justice of the peace, 1731-49, auditor of the Superior Court in 1741, a deputy to the General Assembly, 1742-49, one of the Committee of War in 1754 and otherwise active in the administration of Colonial affairs. The second generation of Ledyards figured prominently in the Revolution and the name is indissolubly connected with one of the most tragic events of the war, the massacre at Fort Griswold, on the banks of the Thames River in Groton, September, 1781. Colonel William Ledyard, the fourth son of John Ledyard, with his nephew, Captain Youngs Ledyard, and others of the family were killed by a British foray that was organized and conducted by Benedict Arnold. More than twenty Ledyards participated in the engagement.

The New York Ledyards are descended from the original John Ledyard through his second son, Youngs Ledyard, 1731-1762, who was a shipmaster and died mysteriously on one of his voyages to the West Indies. Benedict Arnold sailed with him as clerk on that last voyage, and there has always remained a suspicion that he knew more about the disappearance of his superior than ever was revealed. Youngs Ledyard, in 1748, married Aurelia Avery, of Groton, and their third child and second son was Benjamin Ledyard, born in Groton, March 6th, 1753. He was brought up in the family of his grandfather in Hartford and then engaged in business in New York. He served in the army during the War of the Revolution, and attained to the rank of Major. After the war he renewed his commercial pursuits, was one of the founders of the Order of the Cincinnati in 1783 and was specially active in opening up and developing the unoccupied lands in the interior of New York State.

Benjamin Ledyard, Jr., 1779-1812, the eldest son of Major Ledyard, married Susan French Livingston, daughter of Brockholst Livingston, an aide to General Alexander Hamilton in the Revolution, and later Justice of the Superior Court of New York State and Judge of the Supreme Court of the United States. His only son was Henry Ledyard, father of Mr. Lewis Cass Ledyard. Born in New York, March 5th, 1812, Henry Ledyard was a man of high culture. He entered the diplomatic service of the United States and was attached to the American Embassy in Paris when the Honorable Lewis Cass was Minister to France. In 1839, he was made Secretary of Legation and in 1842 was Chargé d'Affaires. After 1844, he withdrew entirely from public affairs.

Mr Lewis Cass Ledyard is the second son of Henry Ledyard. His mother was a daughter of the Honorable Lewis Cass, the Michigan statesman, and thus, on both sides of his house, he descends through a notable line of American ancestors. He was born in Detroit, April 4th, 1851, graduated from Harvard in 1872 and entered the legal profession. In 1878, he married Gertrude Prince, daughter of Colonel William E Prince. He is an enthusiastic yachtsman, owner of the schooner Montauk and Vice-Commodore of the New York Yacht Club By virtue of his ancestry he is a member of the New England Society and the Sons of the Revolution His clubs include the Metropolitan, Union, Tuxedo, Knickerbocker, Manhattan, Harvard, University and Seawanhaka-Corinthian Yacht, and he is a member of the Century Association, the Downtown Association and the Bar Association. His city residence is in Lexington Avenue and he has a summer home in Gibbs Avenue, Newport. He has one son, Lewis Cass Ledyard, Jr.

FREDERICK HOWARD LEE

THE Lees, as a family, have been known as devoted churchmen and supporters of the reigning families of England from time immemorial. They were adherents of the Plantagnets, and then of the Tudors and Stewarts, and so on down to the dynasty of the present day. They have had bestowed upon them lands and titles and have occupied influential positions in church and State. In 1674, King Charles II. created Sir Edward Henry Lee, Earl of Litchfield, and the title and estates descended through many generations of male heirs, but are now in possession of descendants of the female line, Lord Arthur Lee Dillon, in the last generation, whose grandfather, an Irish peer, married a daughter of the second Earl of Litchfield and who assumed the name of Lee, being the head of the family in Ditchley, Oxfordshire.

John Lee, who was a native of Colchester, Essex County, England, where he was born in 1620, came to America in 1634, went to Connecticut and subsequently was a member of the second company that went from Hartford to settle in Farmington in 1641. In 1658, he married Mary Hart, daughter of Stephen Hart, and died in 1690, having had a family of six children, from whom have sprung most of the Lees of New England and New York. John Lee, Jr., the eldest son of the pioneer, lived and died at Farmington and from him have come the Lees of Harwinton, Granby, and Kent. Mary Lee, the eldest daughter of the family, married Stephen Upson, of Waterbury, and from that alliance have come the Upsons and their descendants of Connecticut. Thomas Lee, the third son of the family, lived and died at Farmington; his descendants are among the Lees of Massachusetts and Vermont. One of his sons removed to Canada, near Niagara.

Stephen Lee, the ancestor of the subject of this sketch, was the the third child and second son of John Lee, the pioneer. From him have come the Lees of New Britain, Berlin and Kensington, Conn. Captain Stephen Lee, as he was called, had two sons, Isaac and Josiah. The eldest son was a doctor of much celebrity in Middletown, Conn., and vicinity, his sons were Isaac Lee, Jr., Stephen, Jacob and Josiah Lee. Stephen Lee went to Lenox and established a branch of the family there. Josiah Lee, who commanded a privateer in the War of the Revolution, was captured and carried to England and kept in prison several years.

William Henry Lee, the New York merchant, father of Mr. Frederick H. Lee, was descended from Colonel Isaac Lee, of the Stephen Lee branch of this family. He was born in New Britain in 1818. Early in life he went to Troy, N. Y., and engaged in business. A few years later he came to New York and entered the firm of J. R. Jaffray & Co., and in 1845 established the importing and jobbing firm of Lee & Case, a firm subsequently known as William H. Lee & Co., Lee, Bliss & Co., and Lee, Tweedy & Co. Mr Lee was one of the enterprising merchants of the last generation and a very public spirited man. He was one of the charter members of the Union League Club, an active member of the Chamber of Commerce, for many years a warden of St. Thomas' Church, a member of the Sons of the American Revolution, the New England Society and the American Geographical Society, and a patron of the American Museum of Natural History. In 1893, he removed to Hartford, Conn., where he had long maintained his summer home, and died there in 1895.

Mr. Frederick Howard Lee, son of William Henry Lee, was born in New York, November 10th, 1859, and educated at St. Paul's School, Concord, N. H., and in Columbia College, graduating from Columbia in 1882. He has been in business life as a partner in the house that his father established. He is a member of the Racquet and New York clubs, the Larchmont Yacht Club, and the Columbia College Alumni Association, and became a member of Troop A, N. G., S N. Y, in 1889. His country residence is at the Lee homestead, in Hartford, Conn. Another member of the family is Charles Northam Lee, a brother of Mr. Frederick H. Lee, who lives in West Seventy-eighth Street, and is a member of the Seventh Regiment Veteran Club and the New England Society. The mother of Frederick H. and Charles Northam Lee, was Miss Northam, of an old and respected Connecticut family. She is still living in Hartford.

JAMES PARRISH LEE

D URING the reign of Charles I, Richard Lee, of Shropshire, England, came to Virginia as Secretary of the Colony and one of the Privy Council. Descended from the Coton branch of the family, his ancestor in the fourteenth century was Roger Lee, who married Margaret Astley. In 1646, he was a magistrate of York County, and frequently represented York and Northumberland Counties in the House of Burgesses. In the second generation came Richard Lee, 1647–1714, member of the Governor's Council, in 1676–80–83–88–92–98, and member of the House of Burgesses in 1677. His wife was Letitia Corbin, daughter of Henry Corbin and Alice Eltonhead.

The last named Richard Lee had, among other children, Philip, Thomas and Henry. The eldest of these, Philip Lee, of Westmoreland County, 1681-1744, moved to Maryland in 1700, became a member of the Governor's Council and a justice of the peace and was the ancestor of the Maryland line of the family. The second son, Thomas Lee, was the father of Richard Henry Lee and Francis Lightfoot Lee, signers of the Declaration of Independence. To Richard Henry Lee belongs the honor of being the mover in Congress of the Declaration of Independence. Upon June 7th, 1776, he proposed the following resolution, the original of which is preserved in the archives of State at Washington: "Resolved, That these United Colonies are, and of right ought to be, free and independent States: that they are absolved from all allegiance to the British Crown and that all political connection between them and the State of Great Britain is, and ought to be, totally dissolved." In pursuance of this resolution, the Declaration of Independence was afterwards drafted. The third of the three sons of Richard Lee was the grandfather of Major "Light Horse Harry" Lee, of Revolutionary fame, and the great-grandfather of General Robert E. Lee, who is too well known to need special mention. Among the writings of "Light Horse Harry" Lee occurs the well-known eulogium "First in war, first in peace and first in the hearts of his countrymen."

Thomas Lee, son of Philip Lee, of Westmoreland, died in 1749, having married Christiana Sim, daughter of Dr. Patrick Sim and Mary Brooke, of Maryland. His son, Governor Thomas Sim Lee, 1745-1819, was a member of the Provincial Council of Maryland in 1777, Governor in 1779 and 1792 and a member of the Continental Congress, 1763-64. His wife was Mary Digges, daughter of Ignatius Digges and Elizabeth Parkham. John Lee, of Needwood, 1788-1871, grandfather of Mr. James Parrish Lee, was educated in Harvard and, in 1823-25, was a Member of Congress. His wife was Harriet Carroll, daughter of Charles Carroll and Harriet Chew. His son, Dr. Charles Carroll Lee, 1839-1893, was graduated from the medical department of the University of Pennsylvania in 1859, served on the medical staff of the Union Army during the Civil War, and after the war had a large private practice and was a professor in the New York Post-Graduate Hospital. He was president of the Medical Society of the County of New York at the time of his death in 1893. His wife was Helen Parrish, of Philadelphia, their children being Sarah Redwood, Richard Henry, Thomas Sim, James Parrish, Charles Carroll, Mary Helen, Helen and Mary Digges Lee. Mrs. Lee survived her husband and is now living in Tuxedo Park.

On the female side, Mr. Lee goes back to other illustrious ancestors. Henry Corbin, father of Letitia Corbin, who married the second Richard Lee, came to Virginia in 1654, and was a burgess in 1659, a justice of the peace and a member of the Governor's Council. He was a son of Thomas Corbin, of Hall End, England, and descended from Robert Corbin, who gave lands to the Abbey of Ealesworth in the twelfth century. The great-grandmother of Mr Lee was Mary Digges, descended from Edward Digges, proprietor of the Bellfield estate, Auditor-General of the Colony and Governor, 1656-58. Harriet Carroll, grandmother of Mr. Lee, was a descendant of the Carroll and Chew families. Her father was Charles Carroll, of Carrollton, signer of the Declaration of Independence.

Mr James Parrish Lee was born in New York, June 6th, 1870. Both he and his brother, Dr. Thomas Sim Lee, were educated in Harvard University, graduating in the class of 1891. He is a lawyer by profession. In 1896, he married Clara Lothrop Lincoln, only daughter of Lowell and Clara A. (Lothrop) Lincoln.

MARSHALL CLIFFORD LEFFERTS

SOME short distance north of Hoorn, in the Province of North Holland, is the village of Haughwout. There the American ancestor of the Lefferts family, Leffert Pietersen Van Haughwout, was born. Coming to this country in 1660, he settled in Midwout (Flatbush), Long Island, served on the grand jury in 1688, was a constable in 1692 and an assessor in 1703 He died in 1704. His wife was Abigail, daughter of Auke Janse Van Nuyse

Jacobus Leffert, 1686–1768, head of the family in the second generation, in 1715 was on the roll of the militia company of Flatbush, and in 1727 was one of the three freeholders of Brooklyn to defend their patent His wife was Janetje, daughter of Nicholas, or Claes, Barrentse Blom. Leffert Lefferts, 1727–1804, son of Jacobus Leffert, was a farmer in Bedford, one of the freeholders of Brooklyn, 1756–76, town clerk 1761–76, and assistant justice 1761–77. He married Dorothy, daughter of John Cowenhoven. John Lefferts, 1763–1812, great-grandfather of Mr. Marshall C. Lefferts, was a farmer of Bedford and in 1790 married Sarah, daughter of Rem and Ida Cowenhoven. His son, Leffert Lefferts, 1791–1868, married Amelia Ann Cozine, daughter of Judge John Cozine, of New York, and became the father of Colonel Marshall Lefferts.

Colonel Lefferts, 1821–1876, educated in the public schools, was first a civil engineer, but after a few years became a partner in an importing house. For eleven years following 1849, he was president of the New York, New England & New York State Telegraph Company. After that, he owned several telegraph patents, was connected with the Western Union Telegraph Company as electrical engineer, organized the Commercial News Department of the Western Union Company in 1867, and was president of the Gold and Stock Telegraph Company from 1869 to the time of his death. Joining the famous New York Seventh Regiment in 1851 as a private, he became its Lieutenant-Colonel the next year and Colonel in 1859 When the Civil War broke out, he led his regiment to the front in 1861 and again saw service with it in 1862 and 1863, when he was Military Governor at Frederick, Md. After the war, he resigned his command, but was for several years commander of the veteran corps of the regiment. Colonel Lefferts left seven children: George M. Lefferts, a practicing physician of New York; William H. Lefferts, of the firm of Morewood & Co ; Marshall C. Lefferts, the subject of this sketch; Frederick R. Lefferts, treasurer of the Celluloid Company; Grace Lefferts, who married Frederick R. Hutton, Professor of Mechanical Engineering in Columbia University; Mary E. Lefferts, who married Dwight A. Jones, of Englewood, N. J., a practicing lawyer in New York; and Louis E. Lefferts, president of the Penrhyn Slate Company.

Mr. Marshall Clifford Lefferts was born in New York in 1848, and was educated in the local schools, from which he went to the New York Free Academy, now the College of the City of New York. Leaving the academy before graduating, he was early engaged in the supply department of the American Telegraph Company, which was afterwards merged into the Western Union Telegraph Company, and later he became connected with the Gold and Stock Telegraph Company with his father, leaving it in 1872 to take a position in the Celluloid Manufacturing Company. Since 1890, he has been president of the Celluloid Company. Mr. Lefferts has never taken any active part in public life, although in 1892 he was invited and accepted a place upon the famous Committee of Seventy.

The chief relaxation of Mr. Lefferts from the cares of business is in his library of early printed books of English literature and Americana, which ranks high among the private libraries of this country. In 1878, Mr. Lefferts married Carrie Ella Baker, daughter of Peter C. Baker, of New York, and Malvina L Carpenter. He has three children Franklin B Lefferts, a student in the School of Mines of Columbia University; Mary C. Lefferts, and Marshall C Lefferts, Jr. He lives in East Sixty-fifth Street, and spends the summer in Cedarhurst, L. I , where he has a country seat. He is a member of the Union League, Grolier and Rockaway Hunt clubs, the St. Nicholas Society, the Chamber of Commerce and other social and commercial organizations

FRANCIS H. LEGGETT

IN Westchester County, New York, the name of Leggett's Point, which projects into the Sound, recalls a family that has been resident for about two hundred and fifty years in that place. The Leggetts were formerly seated in Gloucestershire, England, and were of ancient descent, the tradition being that their family name was derived from an ancestor who was a papal legate This is indicated by their arms, which are described as : ermine, a lion rampant gules; crest, a pope's mitre upheld by the claws of a lion, gules.

As early as 1661, Gabriel Leggett came to this country, having previously emigrated from England to Barbadoes He settled at Westchester, N Y , and bought a place which has remained in the hands of his descendants to our days. He married Elizabeth Richardson, daughter of John Richardson, one of the joint patentees of the Planting Neck, as it was called, by which alliance a large amount of property came into his possession. He was for years an official of Westchester, and his descendants have always been prominent in that section and in New York. Among the notable ones were Thomas Leggett, who was driven from his estate by the Tories in the Revolution, but after the war had ended, made a fortune in New York City. His sons were among the noted New York merchants of the early portion of the century. One of them, Samuel Leggett, was president of the old Franklin Bank, and president of the first gas company of the city, in 1823. Major Abraham Leggett, of another branch of the family, served as an officer of the Revolutionary Army, and was an original member of the Cincinnati. His son, William Leggett, was associated with William Cullen Bryant, in the management of The Evening Post. A son of Samuel Leggett married a daughter of Wager Hull, a descendant of Admiral Sir Wager Hull, of the English Navy, and one of his granddaughters was the philanthropic Sarah H. Leggett, who established the Home for Working Women, and the Fifth Avenue Reading Room.

Mr. Francis H Leggett descends from Gabriel Leggett, through William, one of the latter's sons, who resided at Mt. Pleasant, N. Y., in the early part of the eighteenth century His son, Ezekiel, was the father of Abraham Leggett, and grandfather of a second Abraham Leggett, born in 1805, who was the father of Mr. Francis H. Leggett. Abraham Leggett was long one of the leading merchants of New York City. For half a century he carried on a large wholesale business on Front Street, and was one of the founders of the Old Market Bank, now the Market and Fulton National Bank.

Mr. Francis H. Leggett was born in New York, March 27th, 1840, and after a substantial academic education, entered a business house. After five years of experience, he embarked in business on his own account, in 1862, in partnership with an older brother, as wholesale merchants. This relationship continued for eight years, and then, in 1870, Mr. Leggett joined with another and younger brother in organizing the firm of Francis H Leggett & Company. Although his brother, Theodore Leggett, died in 1883, the firm's name has remained unchanged to this day, and it has grown into an extremely large establishment, occupying the large building on West Broadway and Franklin Street, which is a landmark in the downtown section of the city.

Mr. Leggett still remains in active business life at the head of the concern he started twenty-seven years ago. He, however, has other business interests, being a director of the Home Insurance Company and a trustee of the Greenwich Savings Bank. For twelve years he was a director of the National Park Bank, and is a member of the Chamber of Commerce, Produce Exchange, Mercantile Exchange and Cotton Exchange. He belongs to the Union League, Metropolitan, Tuxedo, Merchants, Riding and Grolier clubs, and other artistic, literary and scientific institutions, and is a working member and one of the vice-presidents of the council of the Charity Organization Society In 1895, Mr. Leggett was married at Paris, France, to Besse (MacLeod) Sturges, a lady descended from the distinguished Scotch family of MacLeod, which has also been prominent in the United States. Besides his city residence at 21 West Thirty-fourth Street, Mr. Leggett has a country seat, Ridgely, at Stone Ridge, Ulster County, N. Y.

EUGÈNE LENTILHON

OF mingled French and English ancestry, the Lentilhons of New York trace their lineage to the Lentilhon and de Tours families of France, and to the Leaycrafts and Smiths of England. The Lentilhon ancestor, who was born about 1700, married a Mademoiselle Repon, from Bulla, in Switzerland, and had several children. His son, Antoine Lentilhon, 1732-1805, married Popon des Tours Their son, Jean Marie Joseph Lentilhon, 1773-1839, married, in Virieux, Catherine Barthelemie Pauline, daughter of Claude Antoine Gerbes de Tours. The Gerbes de Tours family was of Spanish origin, but was established before the eighteenth century in the village of Tours, near St. Didier, Rochefort Antoine Gerbes de Tours held that fief and married Jeanne du Poyet, heiress of the fief of Le Poyet. Jean Marie Gerbes de Tours, son of Antoine Gerbès de Tours, was notary royal and judge chatelaine of St. Didier, and died before 1772, having married Jeanne de Cossu Their son, Claude Antoine Gerbes de Tours, father of Catherine Barthelemie Pauline de Tours, born in 1739, was guillotined by the Revolutionists in 1793. His wife was Laurence de Flon, daughter of François de Flon and his wife, Catherine Soviche

Two sons were born to Jean Marie Joseph Lentilhon and his wife, Catherine Barthelemie Pauline de Tours. From these two sons the Lentilhon family of New York is descended The eldest son, Antoine Lentilhon, married Eliza Leaycraft Smith. They had no son, but their four daughters married, respectively, Herman Ten Eyck Foster, Peter Vandervoort King, Henry Oothout and John Garven Dale. The second son, Eugène Lentilhon, was the ancestor of that branch of the family under consideration here. He was born in Lyons, France, in December, 1810, and became a merchant in New York, where he died in 1879 In 1836, he married Emily Louisa Smith, who was born in 1819 and died in 1869 She was the daughter of Gamaliel and Mary Riker (Leaycraft) Smith Her father, Gamaliel Smith, was born in Suffield, Conn , in 1774, and died on the Island of Santa Cruz in 1823 He was a descendant of the Reverend Henry Smith, a Puritan clergyman, who, in 1638, became the first minister of the church in Wethersfield, Conn , and died in 1648. Mary Riker Leaycraft, the mother of Emily Louisa (Smith) Lentilhon, was the daughter of John and Elizabeth (Haldane) Leaycraft. Her paternal ancestor was Christopher Leaycraft, who, in 1647, was a member of the Governor's Council in the Bermudas John Leaycraft was the son of Viner Leaycraft and his wife, Elizabeth Codwise Eugène Lentilhon and his wife, Emily Louisa Smith, had seven children: Antonia Eliza, Joseph, Eugène Louis, Pauline de Tours, Jean de Tours, Edward Smith and William Augustus Lentilhon. Joseph Lentilhon, the eldest son, 1839-1895, was a Captain in the Seventh Regiment. He married Zella Trelawny Detmold, and had nine children.

Eugène Lentilhon is the eldest son of the late Joseph Lentilhon, and the representative in lineal descent of the family A graduate of the Sheffield Scientific School of Yale University, he married Rose Paret Buchanan, daughter of James A Buchanan, and has a son, Eugène Lentilhon, the third of the name The other children of Joseph Lentilhon are Zella, who married Charles Brewster Wheeler, U S A ; Emily Louisa, who married John Parkin Gilford, and has two daughters, Emily L. and Almy Gilford; Marie de Tours, who married Chester Clark Boynton, and also has two daughters; Joseph, who married Louise Everett, Pauline Leonie; Edward Detmold; Antoinette de Tours, deceased, and Minna Lentilhon

Eugene Louis Lentilhon, the second son of Eugene Lentilhon, 1810-1879, married Ida M Ward and has two children, Ida Ward and Herbert D Ward Lentilhon. His residence is Virieux sur Mer, Far Rockaway, Long Island Jean de Tours Lentilhon, the third son, died in 1850. Edward Smith Lentilhon, the fourth son, married Emily Swan, daughter of Edward H Swan, of Oyster Bay, Long Island. She died in 1890. William Augustus Lentilhon, the youngest son, married, in 1884, Julia Catherine Rodewald, and has one daughter, Julia Mac Neill Lentilhon He resides in New Brighton, Staten Island. Antonia Eliza, the eldest daughter of Eugene and Emily Louisa (Smith) Lentilhon, married Edward Fesser, of Cuba. The second daughter, Pauline de Tours Lentilhon, is unmarried.

JEFFERSON M. LEVY

IT was in early Colonial days, during the seventeenth century, that the ancestors of Mr Jefferson M Levy came to America Some of them settled in New York and others in Pennsylvania and Rhode Island, but both branches of the family maintained intimate relations from that time to the present Representatives of the name acquired land in New York as early as 1665. When the Revolution came, the men of the family were active patriots The great-grandfather of Mr Jefferson M Levy was one of the signers of the non-importation agreement, the original of which is in Independence Hall, Philadelphia, and he was one of the five commissioners appointed by the Colonial Congress to sign the money notes issued by its authority. Jonas Philips, his great-grandfather on the maternal side, served with distinction during the Revolutionary War. The grandmother of Mr Levy, who is buried at Monticello, Va., was a woman of remarkable beauty and went abroad shortly after the Revolution. Being presented at the court of St James, she created a sensation and was called the American beauty.

Several generations of Mr Levy's relatives have distinguished themselves in the service of their country His uncle, Commodore Uriah P Levy, was at the time of his death, in 1862, the ranking officer in the United States Navy. He had a brilliant career in the navy and distinguished himself in the War of 1812 He was finally captured by the British in the battle of the Argus and Pelican and held a prisoner for eighteen months, until the close of the war In 1822, at Dubardeau Inlet, he performed a notable act of bravery, saving many lives during a furious gale. The Emperor of Brazil urged him to enter the navy of that country, but he declined the honor. He was instrumental in abolishing flogging in the United States Navy, and in fact was called the Father of the Seamen of the Navy The bronze statue of Jefferson, by David D'Angiers, that stands n the old Hall of Representatives in the Capitol at Washington, was presented by Commodore Levy to the United States in 1834.

After the death of Thomas Jefferson, Commodore Levy purchased the historic house and estate of Monticello, the home of the great Democrat. The mansion, which was begun by Jefferson in 1764 and finished in 1771, is one of the finest of its date, modeled somewhat after the Petit Trianon of Versailles It stands in a commanding position on a small plateau, elevated some three hundred feet above the surrounding country and five hundred feet above the level of the sea. The estate embraces five hundred acres of park land, gardens and lawns. It is now the property of Mr Jefferson M Levy, who inherited it from his uncle, Commodore Levy.

The father of Mr Jefferson M Levy was Captain J. P. Levy, a brilliant naval officer. During the Mexican War, he commanded the United States ship America, and did noteworthy service in the siege of Vera Cruz. When that city surrendered to the United States forces, General Scott appointed him Captain of the Port. Captain Levy died in 1883

Mr Jefferson M. Levy was born in New York. His early education was under the direction of private tutors, after which he entered the University of the City of New York, and was graduated with honors. For more than twenty years he has been a prominent member of the New York bar, and also has large interests in real estate. Mr Levy is a pronounced Democrat in politics In 1891, the Democratic nomination for Congress from a New York City district was offered to him, but he declined the honor During the presidential campaign of 1892, he was an active worker in the Virginia League of Democratic Club, and as chairman of that organization contributed much towards the election of President Cleveland He was the first vice-president of the Young Men's Democratic Club of New York. Mr Levy is a member of the Manhattan, Reform, Commonwealth, New York Yacht and Democratic clubs, the Southern Society, the Sons of the Revolution, the New York Historical Society, the Westmoreland Club of Virginia and the Sandowne Park Club of England His city residence is at 66 East Thirty-fourth Street, and he also occupies the historic house at Monticello He is a generous patron of music, and in 1897 was one of the largest subscribers to the fund for the support of opera in the Metropolitan Opera House.

WILLIAM LIBBEY

JOHN LIBBEY, who was born in England about 1602, came to America about 1630 and settled near what is now Scarborough, Me. During King Philip's War, he and his family were compelled to flee to Portsmouth, N H , and then to Boston for safety Subsequently they returned to Maine, and there he accumulated a competency before he died, at the age of eighty Anthony Libbey, son of the pioneer John Libbey, was born in Scarborough about 1649, and lived in his native town and in Falmouth, N H , where he died in 1718 His son, Isaac, who was born about 1690, in Hampton, N H , spent most of his life in Rye and took an active part in the settlement of the town of Epsom His grandson, Reuben Libbey, who was born in Rye in 1734, served a year in the Continental Army, in 1776, and died in Albany in 1820

In the next generation Samuel Libbey, born in Rye in 1757, during the Revolution, was a soldier in a New Hampshire Regiment and was present at the surrender of General Burgoyne He also went on several privateering cruises, in which he was generally successful, but on two occasions was made a prisoner William Seavey Libbey, the son of Samuel Libbey and the father of the subject of this sketch, was born in Rye, N H , in 1787 His mother was Mehitable Seavey, daughter of William and Ruth (Moses) Seavey, of Rye During the early years of his life he lived in Salem, Mass , but subsequently removed to Newburgh, N Y , and then to New Brighton, Staten Island, where he died in 1869 His first wife was Sarah Farrington, daughter of Deacon Daniel and Sarah Farrington, of Windsor, Vt. She died in 1826, and he afterwards married Elizabeth Winfield, daughter of Dr Richard Winfield, of New York

William Libbey, son of the foregoing, was born in Newburgh, N Y , March 7th, 1820 Prepared for college, circumstances compelled him to forego a college career and to engage in business When he was fifteen years of age he entered a jobbing dry goods house in New York and remained about seven years Continuing in this line of trade, in 1850 he became a member of the firm of Hastings, Libbey & Forbey, and subsequently was a member of the firm of William Libbey & Graef, which had branches in Philadelphia, and in Dresden and Aix-la-Chapelle, Germany In 1859, he became associated as partner and general manager with Alexander T Stewart, and was at the time of Mr Stewart's death his sole surviving partner After that event, in 1876, he was associated with ex-Judge Henry Hilton in the great dry goods house for a few years, when he retired from active business He was an executor of Mr. Stewart's will, was for many years a director of the National Bank of Commerce, the New York, Lake Erie & Western Railroad and the American Pig Iron Storage Warrant Company, a member of the executive committee of the New York Historical Society, a trustee of the Sun Insurance Company and the United States Trust Company, and of Princeton University and Theological Seminary, a life member of the New England Society and American Geographical Society and connected with many charitable institutions His contributions to charity and education were munificent, and he was especially a generous benefactor of Princeton University His residence on Washington Heights still remains one of the finest estates upon that part of Manhattan Island

In 1850, Mr Libbey married Elizabeth Marsh, of Louisiana, daughter of Jonas Marsh and Elizabeth Morse His eldest son, William, married Mary Elizabeth Green, daughter of Professor William Henry Green, of Princeton, N J , and is a professor in Princeton University. Jonas Marsh Libbey, the second son of William Libbey, was born in Ridgewood, N. J., in 1857. He was graduated from Princeton, in 1877, and from 1877 to 1884 was editor and proprietor of The Princeton Review. He is a member of the Union League, Larchmont Yacht, Authors' and Press clubs and of the New England Society, and is a patron of the Metropolitan Museum of Art Frederick A. Libbey, the youngest son of William Libbey, was born in Jersey City, in 1860, graduated from Princeton in 1883, and married Helen Irving Dennis, of Wilkes Barre, Pa , in 1890 He lives at Montclair N J , and is engaged in business in New York

JOHNSTON LIVINGSTON

A MONG the families in the United States descended from the ancient nobility of England and Scotland, none have a more distinct title, or a lineage more clearly traced, than that of Livingston. The immediate ancestor of the American family was the Reverend John Livingston, of Ancram-in-Teviotdale, who was born in 1603, and who, from religious persecution, went or was exiled to Holland. He married Janet Fleming, daughter of Bartholomew Fleming, of Edinburgh, and died in 1672. He was the son of the Reverend William Livingston, minister at Lanark, and Agnes Livingston, and a maternal grandson of the Reverend Alexander Livingston, minister at Monyabrook, and his wife, Barbara Livingston, daughter of William Livingston, of Kilsyth. William Livingston was descended in the seventh generation through the Livingstons and Erskines, from James I. of Scotland and Lady Jane Beaufort, by their daughter, Princess Janette Stuart and her second husband, James Douglas.

According to the authority of Burke, in his Vicissitudes of Families, the house of Livingston was founded in Scotland by Levingus, who is said to have been of noble Hungarian descent and settled in West Lothian toward the end of the eleventh century. Burke says: "Amongst the chief historical families of Scotland few have risen at various periods to greater power or higher honors, or have possessed more extensive estates than the Livingstons." The representation of the main line eventually merged in the younger branch of Callender, which had risen to great power by its acquisition of the ancient Thanedom of Callender, or Calynter. The Livingstons and the Callenders married with the most illustrious houses of Scotland, even the cadet branches following this aristocratic rule. To Robert Livingston, son of the Reverend John Livingston, Queen Anne granted a tract of land in the Province of New York, which became the Manor of Livingston. He was born in 1651, came to America in 1673 and died in 1728. His wife was Alida (Schuyler) Van Rensselaer, daughter of Philip Pieterse Schuyler.

Mr. Johnston Livingston is descended in direct male line from the first Robert Livingston through the eldest son, Philip Livingston, 1686-1749, second Lord of the Manor, and his wife, Catharine Van Brugh, daughter of Peter Van Brugh, Mayor of Albany, and Robert Livingston, 1708-1790, the third Lord of the Manor, and his first wife, Mary Tong, daughter of Walter Tong and great-granddaughter of Rip Van Dam. The grandfather of Mr. Johnston Livingston was Robert Cambridge Livingston, 1741-1794, who married Alice Swift, daughter of John Swift, of Philadelphia. His parents were John Swift Livingston, 1785-1867, and Anna M. N. Thompson, daughter of Adjutant William T. Thompson, of the Pennsylvania Line in the Revolution.

Mr. Johnston Livingston, the eldest surviving son of John Swift Livingston, was born in 1817. He was educated in Union College and has been identified with important railroad interests. In 1851, he married Sylvia Livingston, daughter of Henry W. Livingston and Caroline De Grasse De Pau. Mrs. Livingston's father was a son of Henry W. Livingston and Mary M. Allen, granddaughter of Chief Justice William Allen, of Pennsylvania. The parents of the first Henry W. Livingston were Walter Livingston and Cornelia Schuyler, and his grandparents were Robert Livingston, third Lord of the Manor, and Mrs Gertrude Schuyler, his second wife. The town residence of Mr Johnston Livingston is in Fifth Avenue, and his country home is the ancient Livingston Manor House in Tivoli-on-Hudson. He is a member of the Tuxedo, Knickerbocker, Union, Union League and other clubs, the St. Nicholas Society and the Union College Alumni Association. His eldest daughter, Carola Livingston, is the wife of the Count de Laugier-Villars. Another daughter, Estelle Livingston, is the wife of Geraldyn Redmond

Another branch of this historic family is that represented at the present time by John Henry Livingston, the son of Clermont Livingston, who died in 1895. The descent of John Henry Livingston represents a union of the lines of the three Lords of the Livingston Manors, namely, of Robert, the first proprietor of Clermont, of Robert, nephew of Robert, the first Lord, who married Margaretta, daughter of Colonel Schuyler; and further through her mother, of Gilbert

Livingston, third son of the first Lord, who married Cornelia Beekman, daughter of Colonel Henry Beekman, and aunt of Margaret, wife of Judge Robert R Livingston, of Clermont. Philip Livingston, the younger son of the second Lord of the Manor, was the signer of the Declaration of Independence, and married Christiana Ten Broeck, daughter of Richard Ten Broeck

Their son, Philip P Livingston, who married Sarah Johnston, had a family of ten children, among whom was Edward P. Livingston, who was born on the Island of Jamaica, was Lieutenant-Governor of the State in 1831, and was the father of Clermont Livingston The wife of Edward P. Livingston was Elizabeth Stevens-Livingston, a daughter of Chancellor Robert R Livingston and his wife, Mary Stevens Chancellor Robert R Livingston was a son of Judge Robert R Livingston, and grandson of Robert Livingston, the first proprietor of Clermont Manor He was a delegate to the Continental Congress in 1776, was one of the committee that drew up the Declaration of Independence, was Secretary of New York State during the Revolution, and afterwards became its Chancellor Clermont Livingston was born at Clermont, Columbia County, in 1817, and made that his home throughout his life He married Cornelia Livingston, daughter of Herman Livingston, of Oak Hill. The grandfather of Cornelia Livingston was John Livingston, of Oak Hill, a son of Robert Livingston, the third and last Lord of the Manor. The only son of Clermont and Cornelia Livingston is John Henry Livingston, who is a graduate from Columbia College in the class of 1869, and who, with his daughter, Katharine L Livingston, is now the lineal representative of this branch of the family

The eldest son of John Swift Livingston and Anna M N Thompson, already referred to in this article, was the second Robert Cambridge Livingston, who was born in 1812, and married Maria B. Murray, daughter of James B Murray, 1790-1860, and Maria Bronson, daughter of Isaac Bronson, a surgeon in the Revolutionary War, and a distinguished banker of New York James B Murray was the son of John B Murray, a soldier of the Revolution, and a grandson of John Murray, a surgeon of the British Navy, and a descendant from the Archduke de Moravia. Maria B Murray traced her descent to the Bronsons and other pioneer New England families

Robert Cambridge Livingston, son of Robert Cambridge Livingston and Maria B Murray, died in 1895 His widow, who was Maria Whitney, survived him, and lives in Islip, Long Island. Mrs Livingston is a daughter of Henry Whitney and granddaughter of Stephen Whitney, the great New York merchant of the last generation. Her mother was Maria Lucy Fitch, a member of the famous Connecticut family of that name. Her grandmother was Phœbe Suydam, of the New York Suydam family Through her father, Mrs Livingston is directly descended from Henry Whitney, who founded the family in Huntington, Long Island, soon after 1620 Mrs Livingston has seven children, Robert Cambridge Livingston, who is a member of the Knickerbocker Club; John Griswold, Henry Whitney, Maud Maria, Johnston, Louis and Caroline Livingston

Maturin Livingston, who died in New York in 1888, at the age of seventy-three years, was at the time of his death the head of another branch of this family He was the youngest son of Maturin Livingston, who was at one time Recorder of the city The senior Maturin Livingston was the son of Robert James Livingston and his wife, Susan Smith, sister of Judge William Smith, the historian of New York Robert James Livingston was the son of James Livingston and Elizabeth Kierstede, and grandson of Robert Livingston and Margaretta Schuyler The wife of the senior Maturin Livingston was Margaret Lewis, daughter of General Morgan Lewis, soldier, Attorney-General, Chief Justice and Governor, and his wife, Gertrude Livingston, daughter of Judge Robert Livingston

The widow of the second Maturin Livingston was Ruth Baylies, of Taunton, Mass , a descendant of Nicholas Baylies, of England, who came to Massachusetts early in the eighteenth century She now lives in East Sixty-ninth Street, and has two daughters, her only children One of her daughters is Mrs Ogden Mills The other married in 1880 William George Cavendish-Bentinck, the son of George Augustus Cavendish-Bentinck, Judge-Advocate General, and the grandson of General Frederick Cavendish-Bentinck and his wife, Lady Mary Lowther, daughter of the first Earl of Lonsdale Mrs Cavendish-Bentinck lives in London.

PHILIP LIVINGSTON

R EPRESENTING one of the important branches of the great Livingston family of New York, which has borne such a conspicuous part in the social and political affairs of New York City and State for more than two centuries, Mr. Philip Livingston is directly descended in the fifth generation from Philip Livingston, the signer of the Declaration of Independence, 1716-1778, whose name he bears, and from that Philip Livingston's wife, Christina Ten Broeck. In generations further back, his lineage goes to Philip Livingston, the second Lord of the Manor, and his wife, Catharine Van Brugh, and Robert Livingston, the first Lord of Livingston Manor, to whom full reference will be found on other pages of this volume

Philip Philip Livingston, of Livingston Manor, son of Philip Livingston, the signer of the Declaration of Independence, was the great-grandfather of Mr. Philip Livingston of this generation He was born in Albany, and died in New York in 1787 His wife was Sarah Johnston, of the Island of Jamaica, in the West Indies. His son, Philip Henry Livingston, of Livingston Manor, married Maria Livingston, granddaughter of Robert Livingston, third Lord of the Manor. He was the father of a large family of children, among whom was Livingston Livingston, who was born at Livingston Manor, Tivoli, N. Y.; he was a well-known lawyer and referee, and died in Rome, Italy, in 1872. He was the father of the Mr. Philip Livingston who is the subject of this sketch

The wife of Livingston Livingston, whom he married in 1859, was Mary C Williamson, daughter of the Honorable William D Williamson, of Bangor, Me., 1779-1846, historian, statesman and man of public affairs Graduated from Brown University in 1804, he began to practice law in 1807 For eight years after 1808, he served as attorney for Hancock County and was a member of the Massachusetts Senate, 1816-20, the territory of Maine being at that time part of the State of Massachusetts When Maine became a separate State, William D Williamson was president of the first State Senate in 1820, and after the resignation of Governor William King was acting Governor. In 1821-23, he was a Member of Congress, in 1824-40, a probate judge for his county, and in 1838-41, bank commissioner for the State He wrote much upon historical subjects, and was a member of several historical and literary societies in New York and elsewhere.

Mr. Philip Livingston was born in New York, November 9th, 1861. When his father gave up the practice of law and went abroad to travel, he took his young son with him, who thus enjoyed the advantages of foreign life at an early age. After his father's death, the son was prepared for college at the Cutler School in New York and, matriculating at Harvard, grad-uated from that institution in the class of 1884. Pursuing his studies further in the Law School of Columbia University, he was graduated in 1887 and admitted to the bar in the same year. After spending several years in the offices of Anderson & Man, Davies & Rapallo and Turner, McClure & Rolston, he entered into partnership with Guy Van Amringe, son of Dean Van Amringe of Columbia University, and has since been engaged in the practice of his profession

In 1890, Mr. Livingston married Juliet B Morris, youngest daughter of the late William H. Morris, of Morrisania. The father of Mrs. Livingston was a grandson of Brigadier-General Lewis Morris, signer of the Declaration of Independence, and great-great-grandson of Lewis Morris, the first Governor of the Province of New Jersey. Mr. and Mrs. Livingston have a country home in Morristown, N. J. While a student at Harvard College, Mr. Livingston was a member of the Hasty Pudding Club and vice-commodore of the Harvard Canoe Club, and is now commodore of the Mt Desert Canoe Club, treasurer of the Upper East Side Association, one of the board of governors of the Sons of the Revolution and also of the Society of Colonial Wars, a trustee of the Δ Chapter of the Δ Φ Fraternity, a former vice-president of the Δ Φ Club, an honorary member of Company K, Seventh Regiment, National Guard State New York, and a life member of the Seventh Regiment Veteran Association. He is a member of the Metropolitan, Union, Δ Φ, Morris County Golf and Morristown clubs, the St. Nicholas Society, the St. Andrews Society and the Order of Descendants of Colonial Governors.

WILLISTON BENEDICT LOCKWOOD

A S his name indicates, Mr. Williston Benedict Lockwood is descended from two families which have been prominent in Connecticut ever since the first settlement of that part of the country. The Lockwoods and the Benedicts were both intimately associated with the foundation of Fairfield, Norwalk and other towns of the Colony The remote American paternal ancestor of the gentleman named above, Robert Lockwood, a native of England, came to this country as a member of one of the earliest bands of Colonists, about 1630. Landing in Massachusetts, he settled first in Watertown, of which place he was made freeman in 1636 Ten years thereafter, he moved to Fairfield, Conn , being a freeman of that town in 1652, a Sergeant in 1657, and died there in 1658 His son, Ephraim Lockwood, who was born in Watertown, Mass., in 1641, became a resident of Norwalk, Conn., where he married, in 1665, Mercy Sention, or, as the name is now written, St John, and was made a freeman in 1667

In the succeeding generations, the paternal ancestors of Mr Williston Benedict Lockwood were Deacon Joseph Lockwood and his wife, Mary Wood, daughter of John Wood, of Stamford, Joseph Lockwood and his wife, Rebecca Rogers, of Huntington, Long Island, and Ebenezer Lockwood and his wife, Mary Godfrey The son of Ebenezer and Mary Godfrey Lockwood, and the grandfather of the present Mr Lockwood, was Benjamin Lockwood, who was born in Norwalk, Conn., in 1777, and died in Brooklyn, N Y , in 1852. During the last twenty years of his life, he was a resident of Brooklyn, and engaged in business in New York His wife. Elizabeth Kellogg, whom he married in 1803, was a native of Norwalk, Conn , where she was born in 1785, and was a daughter of Jarvis and Hannah (Meeker) Kellogg

Le Grand Lockwood, the father of Mr W. B Lockwood, was born in Norwalk, Conn., in 1820 His life was spent in New York City, where he became one of the leading bankers of the last generation, a man of wealth and influential in the highest financial circles He died in 1872. His wife, the mother of the subject of this article, was Anna Louise Benedict, who was born in Norwalk, Conn , in 1823, the daughter of Seth Williston Benedict and his wife, Fanny Roe Benedict On both her father's and her mother's side, Mrs Le Grand Lockwood was descended from Thomas Benedict, the pioneer of the Benedict family in America Her father, who was a son of Nathaniel Benedict, was in the seventh generation of descent from Thomas Benedict, who came from England to America in 1638, and settled in Norwalk, Conn , in 1663 Her mother, Fanny Roe Benedict, was a daughter of William Benedict, son of Nathaniel Benedict, who was the grandfather of her husband, Seth Williston Benedict, she and her husband thus being cousins

Mr Williston Benedict Lockwood was born in New York, March 19th, 1846 He was educated in schools in New York and abroad, and afterwards at Yale College. When he was nineteen years of age, he, however, commenced the business career with which he has since been closely identified His first experiences were in the office of his father's banking house, Lockwood & Co , in 1865 He remained there for eight years From 1873 until 1879, he was in the stock brokerage business by himself. In 1879, he became connected with the house of R P Flower & Co , and is now with that firm, being a member of the New York Stock Exchange

In 1869, Mr Lockwood married Janet Isabel Dominick, of New York, who was born in 1851. The father of Mrs. Lockwood was James W Dominick, a descendant of one of the oldest New York families, whose ancestor, George Dominique, was a Huguenot emigrant early in the eighteenth century He was an early vestryman of Trinity Church, and Dominick Street was named for him. Mrs Lockwood's mother was Mary Wells, of a well-known Hartford family Mr. and Mrs Lockwood reside at 125 West Fifty-eighth Street Their children are Louise, the wife of Aldred K Warren, son of the Reverend E Walpole Warren and grandson of Samuel Warren, the author of Ten Thousand A Year, Bertha Day Lockwood and Isabel Dominick Lockwood. Mr. Lockwood is a member of the Union League, Lotos and New York Athletic clubs, of the New England Society and the Sons of the Revolution

WALTER SETH LOGAN

THE valley of the Shepaug River, in Western Connecticut, is a region of picturesque beauty, inhabited by a population of pure New England blood. Among its old towns is Washington, Litchfield County, founded by Connecticut soldiers in the Revolutionary War, who gave to the settlement the name of their illustrious commander. Mr. Logan comes of a family whose members were among the original settlers of the place, and have resided in Washington and its vicinity for several generations. Mr. Logan was born there in the year 1847. Seth S. Logan, his father, and his mother, Serene (Hollister) Logan, were both natives of the same town, as were also his paternal grandparents, Matthew Logan and Laura (Sanford) Logan, and those on the maternal side, who were Sherman Hollister and Patty (Nettleton) Hollister. The family names, Logan, Hollister, Sanford, Nettleton and Sherman, have throughout Connecticut's history been borne by many distinguished men. The famous Sherman family was closely connected with the Hollisters by numerous intermarriages.

After graduating at Yale College, in the class of 1870, Mr. Walter S. Logan chose the law as his vocation, studying his profession at the Law School of Harvard College, and in the law department of Columbia College, New York, and has the unusual honor of holding degrees from Yale, Harvard and Columbia; that of A. M. having been conferred by Yale, and LL. B. by both of the other two institutions. He made this city his permanent home, and, entering on the active practice of his profession, rapidly acquired and retains a distinguished position at the bar. He is first vice-president of the New York State Bar Association and chairman of the local council of the American Bar Association, and was on the committee of the former body which memorialized the President in regard to a permanent International Tribunal. An address which he delivered before the Arbitration Conference in 1896 was widely quoted and commended, being noted with great approval by the British Ambassador, Sir Julian Pauncefote.

In 1875, Mr Logan was married to Eliza Preston Kenyon, daughter of Pardon Whitman Kenyon and Jeannette (Kelsey) Kenyon, of Brooklyn. Their children are three in number, and are named respectively, Hollister Logan, Janette Logan and Walter Seth Logan, Jr. The family reside at 260 West Seventy-second Street, and Mr. Logan owns a country residence, The Homestead, at his native place, Washington, Conn.

A public-spirited citizen, and convinced as to the duties which citizenship implies, Mr. Logan has taken an active part in politics, and has unselfishly devoted time and attention to movements designed to further the cause of good government. He is an active member of the Civil Service Reform Association, serving on important committees of that organization, and being an effective speaker, he is often called on to address political meetings in municipal and national campaigns. Public office, however, has never had attraction for him, and his usefulness has thus far been confined to the practical advocacy of clean politics. His club connections are largely of a political character, including the Manhattan, Democratic, Patria and Reform clubs. He was one of the originators of the latter, and contributed greatly to its success.

Mr. Logan has, of course, traveled extensively, both abroad and in the United States. He is a member of the St. Stephen's Club, in London, and of the Cosmos, of Washington, D. C. The social organizations with which he is connected are numerous, and embrace the Lawyers' Club, as well as the Colonial, Lotos, Nineteenth Century, Adirondack League, New York Athletic, and Hamilton, of Brooklyn. His tastes for sport are in the direction of yachting, and he is a member of the New York Yacht Club, while membership in the Sons of the Revolution, the Society of Colonial Wars and the Order of Patriots and Founders of America, attests his descent from patriotic ancestors He is a member of the Historical Society, the Geographical Society and many other bodies devoted to science, art and literature. He is much interested in Mexico, has delivered several notable addresses on the history and law of that country, and is now engaged in the preparation of a History of Mexico Since the War of Independence.

G. WEAVER LOPER.

THE rocky coast of New England gave to the country the naval heroes who made the United States flag respected on the ocean and the navigators who carried our commerce into all quarters. Mr Loper's ancestry is of this race, his family name being one of the oldest in New London County, Conn. Through a maternal ancestor, he descends from Edmund Fanning, who came in 1662 from Ireland to New London, and a little later to Stonington, where he became a landowner and the progenitor of a family distinguished in American naval annals. Among his descendants were Edmund Fanning, a famous early American navigator, and Nathaniel Fanning, who served as midshipman on the Bonhomme Richard and commanded the main top in the famous action with the British frigate Serapis. His gallantry is commemorated in an autographic letter of John Paul Jones. Becoming a Lieutenant in the United States Navy, he died in 1805.

The grandfather of the subject of this sketch was Captain Richard Fanning Loper, a nephew of Lieutenant Fanning He was born at Stonington, in the first year of this century. He chose the sea as a profession, and before his majority was a Captain. In 1831, he left the ocean, became a resident of Philadelphia and founded a shipbuilding establishment, which grew into one of the largest in the country, over 400 vessels having been built at the works from Captain Loper's designs. He was also an inventor and a prominent and respected citizen of Philadelphia, occupying many positions of trust, including the presidency of the Philadelphia & Trenton Railroad. In 1870, Captain Loper retired from business and removed to his native town, dying in New York City in 1880.

Captain Loper's services to the Government of his country deserve detailed record. In 1846, he was consulted by the War Department in regard to building boats for the landing of General Scott's army on the Mexican coast. Other experts had declared that it would be impossible to build the desired craft, in less than three months. Captain Loper, however, declared his readiness to complete the work within the requisite time and furnished the vessels in about thirty days, their prompt arrival at the scene of operations ensuring the capture of Vera Cruz. For his services he received the thanks of the Secretary of War, General Maury. In 1861, he was again called upon to help the Government in the transportation service, and lent efficient aid, for which he was thanked by Generals Burnside and Ingalls and by President Lincoln. In both cases his knowledge and skill were given to his country gratuitously and from motives of patriotism

The wife of Captain Loper was Margaret Mercer, a native of Philadelphia, and among their children was William H. Loper, who married Annie Weaver, daughter of George J. Weaver and his wife, Emily (Fitler) Weaver, both of whom were members of Philadelphia families of wealth and influence

Mr. G Weaver Loper is the son of William H. and Annie (Weaver) Loper. He was born in New York, in 1858, and received his education at private academies in this city and Philadelphia He entered business, became a manufacturer, and has been prominent in many industrial and financial undertakings of the largest scope in Philadelphia, Cincinnati and New York. Mr Loper was married, in 1879, to Fannie Gordon, the children of this union being two minor sons, G. Gordon Loper and G Weaver Loper, Jr. Mr. Loper's tastes for sport naturally take the direction of yachting, in which he is an expert His grandfather, Captain Loper, was a famous yachtsman, joining the New York Yacht Club in 1855 and owning such famous old-time prize-winners as the schooner America, the Magic, Josephine and Palmer. Mr. Loper was recently the owner of the steam yacht Avenel, and has served as Rear Commodore of the American Yacht Club. He is also a member of the New York Yacht Club and of the Seawanhaka-Corinthian, Larchmont and Eastern Yacht clubs His family residence is 36 West Fifty-eighth Street Mr. Loper is a member of many of the prominent clubs, including the Metropolitan, Union League, Country, Calumet, Racquet and the Downtown Association, the Pendennis, of Louisville, the Queen City and Country, of Cincinnati, and the Union League, of Philadelphia.

DANIEL LORD

THOMAS LORD, who was born in England about 1585, was the American founder of the Lord family, the records of which, in the mother country, are traceable upon the Hundred Rolls, and other documents back to the thirteenth century. The family was probably of Norman origin, as indicated by the use, in the ancient records and muniments in which they figure, of the words, de Laward *alias* Lord, as the name was at times found written in various places where mention is made of its possessors during the middle ages

Thomas Lord, the founder of the American branch of the family to which attention is called in this article, sailed from London in 1635, accompanied by his wife Dorothy and his children, Thomas, Ann, William, John, Robert, Aymie and Dorothy. He first established himself at Newtown, as it was then called, but which afterwards became known as Cambridge, Mass , where his eldest son, Richard Lord, born in 1611, who preceded his father, had already settled as early as 1632. In 1635, Thomas Lord and his family formed part of the large company which was led by the Reverend Thomas Hooker, pastor of the town of Newtown, to form a new settlement on the Connecticut River, and thus he became an original proprietor and one of the first settlers of the town of Hartford, the part of the modern city still called Lord's Hill taking its name from his family. He died there prior to the decease of his wife, which, as stated in the records of the place, occurred in 1675. William Lord, the fourth child of Thomas Lord, was born in England in 1623, and was a lad of about twelve years of age when he came to this country with his parents. He settled at Saybrook, Conn., and became a large landowner both there and at Lyme, in the same Colony. He was a man of remarkably strong character and possessed unusual scholarly attainments for the generation in which he lived His relations with the Indians were most friendly, and his influence over them was marked. He was referred to by Chapeto, the famous Indian chief, as his "very loving friend," and similar relations continued with the celebrated Uncas, Chapeto's son On many occasions he was instrumental in saving the Colonists from attacks by the aborigines. William Lord's elder sister, Ann, married Thomas Stanton, who, in the early history of New England, was Interpreter-General of the United Colonies.

Thomas Lord, the second son of William, was born in December, 1645, at Lyme, married Mary Lee in 1693 and died in 1730. Their third son, Joseph, born in 1697, married Abigail Comstock in 1724, and their son, Captain Daniel Lord, born in 1736, married Elizabeth Lord, granddaughter of Thomas and Mary (Lee) Lord and daughter of Thomas and Esther (Marvin) Lord Captain Daniel Lord and his wife, Elizabeth Lord, were, therefore, first cousins. Dr Daniel Lord, the second of that name and the son of Captain Daniel, was the great-grandfather of the present Mr Daniel Lord, of New York He studied medicine with Dr Samuel Mather, of Lyme, one of a noted family of physicians, and had more than a local reputation as an excellent physician and admirable instructor He married Phœbe Crary, of Stonington, two of whose brothers, Peter and Edward Crary, afterwards became influential merchants in New York. Their only child was Daniel Lord, the third bearer of that name, who was born at Stonington, Conn., and was the grandfather of the present head of the family.

Daniel Lord, the third of the name, was graduated from Yale College in 1814, and in 1846 received from the same institution the degree of LL D He studied law with George Griffin, a distinguished advocate at the New York bar at that period. Admitted to the bar in 1817, he rapidly rose to be one of its leaders and acquired the reputation of being the first commercial lawyer of the country. On the sixteenth of May, 1818, he married Susan, second daughter of Lockwood De Forest, of the old New York family of that name, which is often referred to in these pages, its members being related to many persons of prominence in the city's history. He died in New York, March 4th, 1868, leaving a reputation of great ability, absolute integrity and striking devotion to his profession

Daniel De Forest Lord, his eldest son, was born April 17th, 1819. He also followed the profession of his father and became a prominent member of the bar in this city. He married October 15th, 1845, Mary Howard Butler, daughter of the Honorable Benjamin F Butler, who during the first half of the present century was a distinguished lawyer of New York and was at one time Attorney-General of the United States in the Cabinet of President Van Buren. The brothers and sisters of Daniel De Forest Lord were Phœbe Lucretia, who married Henry Day, both of whom are now dead; John Crary Lord, who married Margaret Hawley, daughter of Gideon Hawley, of Albany, and died some years ago, his widow still surviving; James Couper Lord, who died in 1869, having married Margaret Hunter Brown, daughter of James Brown, then the head of the well-known firm of New York bankers, Brown Bros. & Co ; Sarah, who married Henry C. Howells and is the only child of Daniel Lord now living; Edward Crary Lord, who married Cornelia Livingston, both of whom are now dead; and George De Forest Lord, who married Frances T. Shelton.

George De Forest Lord was also a lawyer of prominence and a member of the law firm of Lord, Day & Lord, established by his father and continued by the members of the family. He was born in New York in 1833, and was graduated with high honors from Yale College, in the class of 1854, and also from the Harvard College Law School, and was admitted to the bar in 1859. At the outbreak of the Civil War, he became a member of the Twenty-Second Regiment, and as First Lieutenant of Company G, was in service at the front. He died in 1892. Daniel De Forest Lord died at his country home, Sosiego, in Lawrence, Long Island, November 10th, 1894.

Mr. Daniel Lord, whose name is at the head of this article, is the elder son of the late Daniel De Forest Lord. He was born in this city in 1846, was graduated from Columbia College in the class of 1866, was admitted to the bar in 1868 and became a member of the firm of Lord, Day & Lord, and in the same year married Silvie Livingston Bolton. He has had two children, Fanny Bolton and Daniel Lord. His son graduated from Yale University in the class of 1892, and was preparing for admission to the bar in the office of Lord, Day & Lord at the time of his sudden death in 1893, which terminated a career of great promise and put an end to the name of Daniel Lord, which had been conspicuously borne by some member of this distinguished family for six generations and during a period of over one hundred and fifty years. Mr. Lord's daughter, Fanny Bolton Lord, is still living.

Mr. Daniel Lord is now the senior member of the firm of Lord, Day & Lord. The business conducted by the firm was begun by the grandfather of the present members in 1817, and is still continued by them, thus making it one of the oldest firms in the city, either in the law or other vocations, as it has had a continuous existence of over eighty years, during which time it has been under the guidance of the members of one family, and has represented interests intimately associated with the development of the city's prosperity. Mr. Lord's town residence is in Ninth Street, just east of Fifth Avenue, while his country home is at Lawrence, where he has erected a new house on the site formerly occupied by his father, which he calls by the same name, Sosiego Mr Lord belongs to the Metropolitan, Union, University, Union League, New York, Athletic, Lawyers', Downtown, Rockaway Hunt, Lawrence and Seawanhaka-Corinthian Yacht clubs, the Bar Association, the Columbia College Alumni Association, and the Sons of the Revolution and is a fellow of the National Academy of Design. He has never taken a prominent part in politics or held any public elective office, though at all times he has been deeply interested in public matters and has lent his influence to the support of proper measures for the public good

Franklin Butler Lord, brother of Daniel Lord and his partner in the law firm of Lord, Day & Lord, was born in New York, September 18th, 1850, and is a graduate of Columbia College. He was admitted to the bar in 1873, and since that time has been in active practice. In 1875, he married Josephine Gillet, daughter of Joseph Gillet, and has had four children, Franklin Butler, Jr., Howard, who died young, Edward Crary and George De Forest Lord. His residence is at Lawrence, Long Island, and he is a member of the University, Century, Lawyers', Rockaway Hunt and Lawrence clubs, and of the Columbia College Alumni Association, the Bar Association, the Downtown Association and the Sons of the Revolution.

PIERRE LORILLARD

ABOUT the beginning of the American Revolution, the Lorillard family was established in this country. It is of French origin, and its representatives came from Montpelier, in the department of the Herault, France Being Huguenots, the Lorillards were obliged to leave their native land to escape persecution, and migrated to Holland and afterwards to the New World Peter Lorillard, the founder of the New York branch of the family, settled in Hackensack, N. J , and was killed by the Hessians during the Revolution. His wife was Catharine Moore, sister of Blazius Moore, and they had a large family, among them the brothers, Peter A , George and Jacob. Peter A Lorillard, 1763-1843, married in 1789 Maria Dorothea Schultz, daughter of Major Schultz, of the Continental Army. Their children were Maria Dorothea, born in 1790, married Thomas A. Ronalds, Catherine, born 1792, married Captain W A Spencer, U S N. , Peter, born in 1796, Dorothea Ann, born 1797, married John David Wolfe; and Eleanor Eliza, born 1801, who became the second wife of Captain Spencer, after the decease of her sister

George Lorillard, brother of Peter A Lorillard, joined the latter in establishing the great tobacco manufactory now carried on by the P Lorillard Company He became the owner of considerable real estate in New York, much of which is still held by the family.

Peter Lorillard, son of Peter A. Lorillard, was born in 1796, and married Catherine Griswold, daughter of Nathaniel L Griswold, who was in the fifth generation of direct descent from Nathaniel Griswold, the first magistrate of the Saybrook, Conn., Colony, and his wife, Anna Wolcott, daughter of Henry Wolcott, the first of the Wolcott family, of Connecticut. Thus the Lorillards of this branch in the present generation trace their lineage to several famous Colonial families of New England and to noble ancestors in the old country. Peter Lorillard was a man of great public spirit He died in Saratoga in 1867 Of his children, Catherine Lorillard married James P. Kernochan, who died in 1897; Mary Lorillard married Henry L Barbey; Eva Lorillard became the wife of Colonel Lawrence Kip; Jacob Lorillard married Frances A Uhlhorn; Louis L Lorillard married Katharine, daughter of Gilbert L Beekman; and George L Lorillard married late in life and left no children.

Mr. Pierre Lorillard, son of Peter Lorillard, the third, born October 13th, 1833, was the eldest of his father's family. One of Mr. Lorillard's most notable social achievements was the founding of Tuxedo Park. He also fitted out, in connection with the French Government, the two Charnay Franco-American archæological expeditions to explore the ancient cities of Central America and Yucatan, for which France made him Chevalier of the Legion of Honor, and in 1883 an officer of that order. He has gained an international reputation as a breeder and owner of thoroughbred horses. His stables at Rancocas, N. J., were among the most important in the United States, and the winning of the Derby by his American-bred horse, Iroquois, is still remembered. His clubs include the Union, Knickerbocker and Racquet Mr Lorillard now makes his home principally in England, his interests in connection with the English turf absorbing most of his time, but he still maintains a residence in Tuxedo Park.

In 1858, Mr. Lorillard married Emily Taylor, daughter of Dr. Isaac E. Taylor, a celebrated New York physician, and one of the founders of the Bellevue Hospital Medical College His children are. Emily, who married William Kent, great-grandson of Chancellor James Kent; Pierre, Jr., and Maude Louise, who married Thomas Suffern Tailer, son of Edwin N Tailer. His second son, Griswold N. Lorillard, died at the age of twenty-five without issue. Pierre Lorillard, Jr , eldest son of Mr Pierre Lorillard, was born in New York, January 28th, 1860 He married, in 1881, Caroline J. Hamilton, daughter of George Hamilton, of Scotland, her mother being a daughter of the Reverend Dr. Phillips, of New York. They have two sons, Pierre and Griswold Lorillard. The residence of Pierre Lorillard, Jr , is Keewaydin, in Tuxedo Park He belongs to the Union, Knickerbocker, Fencers', Riding and Westminster Kennel clubs, and is also a member of the Metropolitan Club, of Washington.

SETH LOW

HOLDING a place among the foremost New Yorkers of the present day, and one of a family that has been identified with the metropolis for three-quarters of a century, President Seth Low of Columbia University is of New England blood His ancestors were among the early English settlers of Massachusetts, the representative of the family who established its New York branch being his grandfather, Seth Low, who was born in Gloucester, Mass , in 1782 For two years he was a member of the class of 1808 in Harvard College, and subsequently was a clerk in the store of a druggist in Salem, Mass. In 1828, he removed to New York, where he engaged in business on his own account, making his residence in Brooklyn, of which city, at his death in 1853, he was an honored citizen. His wife was Mary Porter, of Topsfield, Mass , whom he married in 1807.

His eldest son was Abiel Abbot Low, born in Salem in 1811. Educated in business from his youth, at first in Salem and from 1833 to 1840 in the noted American firm of Russell & Co , of China, in Canton, he became a leader of New York's commercial interests On his return from China, he organized the House of A. A. Low & Co., which was long a principal factor in the country's Eastern trade. Mr Low was prominent in advancing the material interests of New York and was president of the Chamber of Commerce from 1863 to 1866 He resided in Brooklyn, and though consistently refusing public office, was active and conspicuous in the educational, charitable and religious organizations of that city. He died in January, 1893. His wife was Ellen Almira Dow, descended from Richard Dow, an emigrant of 1646, who settled in Salisbury, N. H Her father, Josiah Dow, was an officer in the War of 1812, founded Dow's Academy in Wakefield, Mass , and was a merchant of prominence in Salem, Boston and finally in New York, being for many years a resident of Brooklyn.

The Honorable Seth Low, the youngest son of A A. Low, was born in Brooklyn, January 18th, 1850. He received his early education at the Polytechnic Institute of that city, entered Columbia College and was graduated in the class of 1870. He then entered his father's business house, and in 1875 was admitted to partnership. On the retirement of the senior partners, in 1879, Mr Low and his brothers succeeded to the control of the time-honored concern, which was finally wound up in 1888

Although he displayed an hereditary talent for business, it was not to be the occupation of his life He had taken a laudable interest in politics, and in 1880 was president of the Young Men's Republican Club of Brooklyn In 1881, he was elected Mayor of Brooklyn as a candidate of the Republican and Reform parties and was reëlected for a second term. Mr. Low's administration marked a new era in municipal affairs, and gave an example that has been fruitful of results throughout the country as the first thorough test of the benefits of the divorce of city interests from party politics. On retiring from the mayoralty, in 1886, he traveled in Europe for some time and then returned to his business duties Since he has resided in New York, he has served as a member of the Rapid Transit Commission, and was one of the commissioners to draft the charter of the Greater New York In 1897, he was the Citizens' Union candidate for Mayor.

In 1889, Mr. Low was tendered, by the unanimous vote of the trustees of Columbia College, the presidency of that venerable institution. Under his administration, Columbia has been elevated to the position of a University, its medical and other departments being consolidated with the parent body, while its educational scope has been greatly widened and strengthened. It is through Mr Low's efforts, also, that the removal of the University itself to Morningside Heights has been provided for, his own munificent gift of the new Low library, as a memorial of his father, being only one of the benefits he has conferred upon it In 1880, Mr. Low married Annie Wrae Scollay Curtis, daughter of Justice Benjamin Robbins Curtis, of the Supreme Court of the United States. Mr. Low s residence is 30 East Sixty-fourth Street, and he is a member of the Metropolitan, Century, University, City and other clubs and of many societies, literary and scientific.

CHARLES HENRY LUDINGTON

A MONG the early settlers of Charlestown, Mass, was William Ludington, who removed to Branford, Conn, and died in 1662 His son, William, married Martha Rose, and their eldest son, Henry, and his wife, Sarah Collins, had a son, William, born in 1702, who married Mary Knowles, and whose eldest son was Colonel Henry Ludington, who was born at Branford, in 1738, and was the grandfather of Mr Charles Henry Ludington.

Henry Ludington removed to Putnam County, N Y, about 1760, with his parents and his uncle, Elisha Ludington. As soon as the Revolution began, he cast his fortunes with the patriot cause He was a Captain of militia in 1773, his commission, signed by Governor Tryon, the last Royal Governor of New York, being in the possession of Mr Charles Henry Ludington, as is also his commission as Colonel from the Provincial Congress of New York, which was followed by one conferring similar rank from the State of New York, signed by Governor George Clinton. He succeeded to the command of the regiment of which Beverly Robinson had been Colonel in Dutchess County. Being posted in the northern border of the neutral ground, he was so successful in thwarting the British plans that a large reward was offered for his capture alive or dead When the British, in April, 1777, burned Danbury, Conn, Colonel Ludington led a portion of the Continental forces which attacked the enemy. At the battle of White Plains he was an aide-de-camp to General Washington. In civil life he was a member of the Legislature for several terms His death occurred in 1817. In 1760, he married his cousin, Abigail Ludington, daughter of Elisha Ludington, son of the third William Ludington

Lewis Ludington, the youngest child of Colonel Henry Ludington, was born in 1786, in Fredericksburg, Putnam County, N. Y., and died in Kenosha, Wis., in 1857. He removed to Carmel, N Y, in 1816, and was engaged in business there, but in 1839 established the firm of Ludington, Burchard & Co., afterwards Ludington & Co, at Milwaukee, Wis. He married Polly Townsend, daughter of Samuel Townsend, their children being Laura, wife of John Hustis, Delia, William Edgar, Robert, Charles H., James, Lavinia E, Emily, wife of Victor E. Tull, and Amelia, wife of John C Angell His son, James Ludington, founded the city of Ludington, Mich.

Mr Charles H Ludington was the third son of Lewis Ludington. He was born in Carmel, N Y, February 1, 1825, and was educated at Carmel Academy, and at the Polytechnic School in Owenville, now Croton Falls, Ridgefield, Conn He came to New York, when seventeen years old, and was connected with the firm of Woodward, Otis & Terbell and Johnes, Otis & Co, for some years, and ultimately became a partner of the dry goods house of Lathrop & Ludington, afterwards Lathrop, Ludington & Co, remaining a member of that latter house until his retirement in 1868. During the Civil War he assisted in the raising of regiments, and otherwise rendered patriotic service to the Union cause He has been a director in many corporations, and active in the management of important public institutions Mr Ludington married Josephine L. Noyes, daughter of Daniel Rogers Noyes, of Lyme, Conn. Her mother, whose maiden name was Phœbe Griffin Lord, was a maternal granddaughter of George and Eve (Dorr) Griffin Through the latter she was a descendant of the Griswold and Wolcott families of Connecticut, and was also a niece of the Reverend Edward Dorr Griffin, D D, President of Williams College, and of George Griffin, the eminent New York lawyer In memory of his wife's mother, Phœbe Griffin (Lord) Noyes, Mr. Ludington is now erecting a free library at Lyme, Conn, to be under the control of the Ladies' Association of that place

Mr. and Mrs. Ludington have three sons and three daughters. The eldest son, Charles H Ludington, Jr, graduated from Yale College in 1887, and married Ethel M. Saltus The second son, William Howard Ludington, graduated from Yale in 1887. The youngest son, Arthur Crosby Ludington, is now at St. Paul's School, Concord, N. H The city residence of the family has been for thirty-six years at 276 Madison Avenue, their country home being in Lyme, Conn. Mr. Ludington is a member of the Union League Club and the Century Association

EDWARD PHILIP LIVINGSTON LUDLOW

IT has been remarked by one of the historians of early New York, that few families in the United States, certainly none in this State, can trace their descent back to noble and even royal ancestors, with more certainty than the Ludlows. The genealogy descending from King Edward I. of England is clear and exact, and the American representatives of the name of Ludlow enjoy a distinct relationship with the older feudal baronage of the parent country, as well as with some of the most distinguished families of the landed aristocracy which arose after the establishment of the Tudor and Stuart dynasties on the throne. It is therefore fitting that the New York branch of the Ludlows should have occupied almost from the time of the English occupation of New Netherland, a position of the highest importance, and that the marriages of its numerous offshoots should have connected it with nearly all the Colonial families of prominence.

Edward I of England, 1272, by his second wife, Margaret, daughter of Philip III of France, became the father of Thomas Plantagenet, Earl of Norfolk. Margaret Plantagenet, daughter of Thomas Plantagenet, married John, the third Lord Segrave. Elizabeth Segrave, daughter of Lord and Lady Segrave, married the fourth Lord Mowbray, whose eldest daughter married the third Lord De le Warr. The eldest daughter of the latter married the third Lord West, whose son was the seventh Lord De la Warr; his great-granddaughter married Lord Windsor, whose daughter Edith married George Ludlow, of Hill Deverill, in Wiltshire. One of his descendants was Edmund Ludlow, the famous General of the Parliament in the Civil War, and a favorite Lieutenant of the Lord Protector, Oliver Cromwell. His most conspicuous service was the completion of the Conquest of Ireland, begun by Cromwell and Ireton. Notwithstanding his inheritance of Plantagenet blood, Edmund Ludlow, a zealous Puritan, did not hesitate to sit as one of the judges at the trial, in 1649, of King Charles I., and joined in condemning that unfortunate monarch to death He escaped the fate which overtook the other surviving regicides at the Restoration by withdrawing to the Continent and lived almost until the beginning of the eighteenth century, at Vevey, in Switzerland, where his dwelling and tomb are still shown.

Gabriel Ludlow, descended from one of the junior branches of the Ludlow, of Hill Deverill, was a soldier in the service of King William III., and commanded the forces of that monarch in the Province of New Brunswick during the war with France. He came to New York in 1694, and was one of the foremost citizens of the Province. He was the father of a numerous family, his thirteen children contracting marriages with other distinguished Colonial families, so that a list of these alliances recalls many names of prominence in the past or present social history of New York, such as Ver Planck, Livingston, Brockholst, Bogert, Morris and Goelet. One of the most famous of his grandsons was Carey Ludlow, a leading merchant of old New York, who built the celebrated Ludlow mansion in State Street, facing the Battery, which in his own time and that of his daughter, Mrs. Jacob Morton, wife of the eminent merchant of that name, was the centre of the exclusive social life of the city. It was there that Lafayette was entertained, in 1824, by a ball, which was long regarded as the most magnificent social function New York had witnessed up to that time.

Mr. Edward Philip Livingston Ludlow is the grandson of Gabriel Ludlow, who was Governor-General and Commander-in-Chief of the forces in the British Province of New Brunswick. His father, Edward H. Ludlow, married Elizabeth Livingston, daughter of Edward P. Livingston, a prominent member of the powerful Livingston connection, and at one time Lieutenant-Governor of the State of New York Mr. Ludlow's maternal grandmother was a daughter of Chancellor Livingston. He was born in Sing Sing, N. Y, in 1835, was graduated from Columbia College, and married Margaret Tonnéle Hall, daughter of Valentine Gill Hall, one of the most eminent merchants of the metropolis Their two children are Mrs. Henry Parish, Jr , and Edward Hunter Ludlow. Mr. Ludlow has not engaged in business or professional life, and resides at 6 East Seventy-sixth Street. He has a country seat in Newport, and another in Tivoli-on-Hudson. He was one of the founders of the St. Nicholas Society.

WARD McALLISTER

ONE of the conspicuous figures in the social circles of New York in the present generation was Mr. Ward McAllister, who came of an old aristocratic family, first of Pennsylvania and then of the South. His direct ancestors were of Scottish origin, belonging to the Allaster clan that flourished early in the seventeenth century and of which Allaster McDonald, maternally descended from Isabella, sister of King Robert the Bruce, was the progenitor. In 1732, Archibald McAllister and his brother Richard, of this family, came from Scotland to Big Spring, Cumberland County, Pa. Archibald married Jane McClure, of an old and noble Scottish family, and had several children, his son Richard, who founded the town of Hanover, Pa., being one of the distinguished men of York County, a Colonel in the Revolutionary War, one of the Committee of Safety in 1775, a member of the Provincial Conference of 1775 and 1776, a member of the Supreme Executive Council of the State of Pennsylvania, 1783-84-85-86, a justice of the peace and Justice of the Court of Common Pleas. He married Mary Dill, of Dillsburg, and their son, Matthew, grandfather of Mr. Ward McAllister, was appointed, by President Washington, United States District Attorney of Georgia, and was also a Judge of the Superior Court of that State. He married a sister of Thomas Gibbons, of South Carolina, brother of William Gibbons, member of the First Continental Congress and member of the Continental Congresses in 1784 and 1786.

Matthew Hall McAllister, the father of Mr. Ward McAllister, was a famous lawyer and Judge of the United States Circuit Court of California, to which State he went from Georgia in 1850. His wife was Louisa Charlotte Cutler, daughter of Benjamin C. and Sarah (Mitchell) Cutler, of Boston. The father of Sarah Mitchell was Thomas Mitchell, a Scotch Laird, who married Esther Marion, sister of General Francis Marion, the "Swamp Fox" The Marions were French Huguenots, who came to this country and settled in the Carolinas. Mr. Ward McAllister was born in Savannah, Ga., and lived there until he was sixteen years of age, but was educated in the North. From 1850 until 1852, he was a resident of San Francisco, where he practiced law with his father. In the latter year he came to New York and lived here during the remainder of his life. He died in 1895.

On her father's side Mrs. McAllister, who became the wife of Mr. Ward McAllister in 1853, is of English origin Born Sarah Tainter Gibbons, her father was William Gibbons, of Savannah, Ga , son of Thomas Gibbons. He was descended from Sir William Gibbons, who came to Barbadoes before 1700, his descendants removing to South Carolina and Georgia, where they took rank among the leading families. The paternal grandmother of Mrs. McAllister was a Heyward, sister of Thomas Heyward, of South Carolina, who signed the Declaration of Independence. To this family was granted, by the King of England, the Barony of Heyward. The mother of Mrs. McAllister was of Massachusetts Puritan descent. Among her lineal ancestors were Governor William Pynchon, of Springfield, Mass. ; Captain Richard Lord, of Connecticut, the Reverend Peter Bulkeley, of Concord, Mass ; and Sir Richard Chitwood and Lord Woodhull, of England Through the Chaunceys, Mrs. McAllister traces her descent to the Earls and Dukes of Northumberland and the Dukes of Norfolk, and thence to Louis Le Debonaire and Charlemagne, of France, and other kings in that royal line.

The city residence of Mrs. McAllister is in West Fifty-third Street, and her country place, Bayside Farm, is one of the celebrated establishments of Newport She has three children, Heyward Hall McAllister, of New York, and Ward McAllister, who is a lawyer of San Francisco, and was at one time United States Judge in Alaska. Her daughter, Louise Ward McAllister, is a member of the Society of Colonial Dames and is the Honorary State Regent of the Daughters of the American Revolution for New York State. Heyward Hall McAllister is a member of the Union Club and the Society of Colonial Wars. The arms of the McAllister family are those of the McDonalds: Quarterly first, argent, a lion rampant, gules; second, or., a hand in armor, holding a cross-crosslet, fitchée, gules; third, a row-galley, the sails furled, sable; fourth, ayent, a salmon, naiant, in fess, proper. The crest is a hand in armor, holding a cross-crosslet, fitchée, gules. The motto is. *Per mare per terras*

DAVID HUNTER McALPIN

THE McAlpins who have been prominent in New York for more than half a century are of Scotch-Irish descent, from the clan Alpin, famous in the history of Scotland. Before the time of Cromwell their ancestors settled in Ireland In common with other families of their religious faith they were subjected to persecution at that time, and leaving Ireland removed to Scotland and established themselves there. For several generations their descendants remained in Scotland, marrying into families of that country. But the grandfather of the subject of this sketch turned back towards the ancestral home of his family and, returning to Ireland, settled near the City of Belfast. His son, James McAlpin, father of Mr. David Hunter McAlpin, married Jane Hunter and came to the United States, establishing himself in business in Dutchess County, N. Y.

Mr. David Hunter McAlpin was born in Pleasant Valley, Dutchess County, N. Y., November 8th, 1816, the fourth in his father's family of eight children. Until 1836, when he was twenty years of age, he was engaged in various occupations in and about his native place. Coming then to New York, he soon went into business for himself and was so successful that in a few years he was able to embark in the tobacco trade. The career of Mr. McAlpin since that time has been one of steady progress. In 1857, he became a partner in the firm of John Cornish & Co , manufacturers of tobacco, and four years later, buying out his partners, established the firm at the head of which he has remained to this day, a period of thirty years, the concern being now for convenience incorporated under the title of the D. H. McAlpin Company.

Mr. McAlpin has for many years held large investments in real estate in New York City and elsewhere. He owns the McAlpin factory building in Avenue D, the Alpine, at Broadway and Thirty-third Street, and valuable properties in West Twenty-third Street. In 1866, ill health compelled him to move into the country for a time and he bought an estate in Morristown, N. J., to which property he has been constantly adding, until now it includes about fifteen hundred acres of valuable land. His country seat is one of the finest in New Jersey. Mr. McAlpin is a director in many corporations, including the Home Insurance Company, Manhattan Life Insurance Company, Standard Gas Light Company, Rutgers Fire Insurance Company, Union Trust Company and Eleventh Ward Bank of New York and the First National Bank of Morristown, N J. He is a member of the American Geographical Society, a patron of the Metropolitan Museum of Art and the American Museum of Natural History, and a director of the Union Theological Seminary. He has been generous in support of religious and charitable works. Olivet Chapel, in Second Street, was erected by him in memory of his son, Joseph R. McAlpin.

In 1845, he married Adelaide Rose, daughter of Joseph Rose, a member of the old Market Street Church, now Church of the Sea and Land. The Rose family has been long established in New York and gave its name to Rose Street Mr. McAlpin has had ten children, of whom two died in infancy. The eldest son, Edwin A. McAlpin, has been prominent in public life and in military affairs. At first a member of the famous Seventh Regiment, he afterwards became a member of the Seventy-First and rose to be Colonel of that regiment. Three times he has been a Presidential elector. Active in the Republican club movement, he was president of the League of Republican Clubs in New York for four years and was elected president of the National League in 1895. He was Adjutant-General of the State during the administration of Governor Levi P Morton. He married Anne Brandreth, daughter of Dr Benjamin Brandreth

The other children of Mr. David H. McAlpin were Joseph Rose McAlpin, who died in 1888; George L. McAlpin, who graduated from Yale College in 1879; Frances Adelaide McAlpin, who married James Tolman Pyle; Dr. David Hunter McAlpin, Jr , who was graduated from Princeton College in 1885, is now in active practice as a physician, and married Emma Rockefeller, daughter of William Rockefeller, of this city, William Willet McAlpin, and Charles W. McAlpin, who graduated from Princeton in 1888 The youngest son of Mr. McAlpin, John Randolph McAlpin, also graduated from Princeton in 1893 and died in the same year.

JOHN AUGUSTINE McCALL

IN Albany, the senior John A. McCall was a prominent citizen for fifty years previous to his death in 1887. Held in high esteem by his neighbors, he was frequently honored by public office. Mr. John A. McCall, the younger, now president of the New York Life Insurance Company, was born in Albany in 1849 He attended the Albany public schools, and was graduated from the Albany Commercial College in 1868. Starting at once into commercial life, he became connected with an Albany business house, and soon after secured a position as bookkeeper in the general agency for New York and Albany of the Connecticut Mutual Life Insurance Company. This was the beginning of his connection with the life insurance business, and the experience he gained in that position practically determined his career.

Giving up his position as bookkeeper, Mr McCall engaged for a time in the real estate and insurance business, and then became a clerk in the State Insurance Department under Superintendent George W Miller. From March, 1870, to May, 1872, when Mr. Miller resigned his position, Mr. McCall was employed in the actuarial branch of the department. For more than twenty years his connection with the department remained unbroken and was a record of steady advancement. In the spring of 1872, he was put in charge of the statistical work of the department's reports, and a few months later became examiner of companies by appointment of the new Superintendent, the Honorable O. W. Chapman. In 1876, when the Deputy Superintendent of Insurance, William Smythe, became the Acting Superintendent, Mr. McCall was advanced to be the Deputy Superintendent, and held that position for seven years under several superintendents.

Mr. McCall's long service made him thoroughly familiar with many evils that had crept into the Insurance Department under previous lax administrations. He also had perfect knowledge of the conditions of the different insurance companies doing business in the State, some of which were of a dishonest character. To expose fraudulent practices and to reform existing evils in the supervision of the insurance business of the State, was a Herculean task, but to this work Mr. McCall addressed himself with energy and uncompromising fidelity. Political and other influences were brought to bear to stop his investigations, but in spite of all the difficulties that were placed in his way, he pushed his work to the end, with the result that many fire insurance companies and eighteen life insurance companies of New York State, and fifteen companies outside of the State, were forced to go out of business, while three previously prominent officials of insurance companies were brought to the bar of justice, charged with fraud, and were convicted and punished by severe sentences of imprisonment.

This valuable service to the State won further promotion for Mr. McCall, and when the office of Superintendent of Insurance became vacant, in 1883, Governor Grover Cleveland elevated him to that position As was easy to foresee, his administration of the department was a distinguished success. During his term of office, many reforms were instituted and a healthful condition of insurance business maintained throughout the State. No insurance company in the Commonwealth failed in that time, and the department not only paid the expenses of its maintenance, but was able to turn over a handsome sum to the State Treasury. Upon the expiration of his term of office, Governor David B. Hill tendered a reappointment to Mr. McCall, but he declined the proffer and accepted instead the office of comptroller of the Equitable Life Assurance Society. In 1892, upon a change in the management of the New York Life Insurance Company, Mr. McCall was invited to take the presidency of that institution, and has held the position ever since with credit to himself and advantage to the interests of the company. Under his administration, the rebuilding and extension of the company's building, at Broadway and Leonard Street, making it a conspicuous object in the city's great thoroughfare, has been undertaken and completed.

Mr McCall married Mary I Haran. He lives on the West Side, near Central Park, and although the cares of his official position leave him scant time for club life, he belongs to the Metropolitan, City, Manhattan, Colonial, Merchants' and Lawyers' clubs.

JOHN JAMES McCOOK

IT is rare that any American family has achieved such notable distinction in its representatives in a single generation as has come to the McCooks. The first McCook in the United States was George McCook, of Irish blood, and also descended from an old Scottish family. Active in an Irish Revolutionary movement, he was forced to take refuge in America.

The two sons of George McCook were soldiers in the Civil War, and each of them the head of a family that furnished some of the most brilliant soldiers to the Union cause. The eldest son, Daniel McCook, was born in Canonsburg, Pa., in 1798. He was educated at Jefferson College, Pennsylvania, and went to live in Ohio. When the Civil War broke out he was sixty-three years of age, but was commissioned a Major, and was killed at Buffington's Island, Ohio, in 1863, when opposing a raid of Morgan's guerillas His wife was Martha Latimer, and nine of his sons were in the military or naval service of the United States. Dr. John McCook, the second son of George McCook, the pioneer, was born in Canonsburg, Pa., in 1806, and was a volunteer surgeon in the Civil War. His wife was Catharine Julia Sheldon, of Hartford, Conn. Five sons of this family served in the army or navy.

"The Fighting McCooks," as they have been called, are further designated as the "tribe of Dan" and the "tribe of John." In "the tribe of John" were Major-General Edward M. McCook, who served in the Tennessee and Georgia campaigns, was United States Minister to the Hawaiian Islands, and afterwards Governor of Colorado Territory; General Anson G McCook, who served in the Army of the Cumberland and in the Atlanta campaign, was a Member of Congress from New York, 1877-83, Secretary of the United States Senate, 1888-92, and City Chamberlain of New York City in 1897, Reverend Henry C McCook, a chaplain in the army, and a well-known scientist; Roderick S McCook, naval officer, and Lieutenant John James McCook, afterwards a professor in Trinity College

"The tribe of Dan" furnished the larger number of "fighting McCooks." Latimer A McCook was surgeon of an Illinois regiment. George W. McCook served in the Mexican War, organized several Ohio regiments in the Civil War, and was Attorney-General of the State of Ohio. Robert L. McCook attained the rank of Brigadier-General, and was killed during the war. Alexander McDowell McCook was a West Point graduate in 1852, and in the Civil War became a Major-General. Daniel McCook, Colonel of an Ohio regiment, commanded a brigade in the Army of the Cumberland, and was killed at Kenesaw Mountain in 1864 Edwin S McCook became Brevet Brigadier-General and Major-General, and served in the Vicksburg and Atlanta campaigns. Charles M McCook, a private in an Ohio regiment, was killed at the first battle of Bull Run

Colonel John James McCook is the youngest son of "the tribe of Dan" He was born May 25th, 1845 When the war broke out he was a student at Kenyon College, and left his books to go to the defense of his country. Enlisting in an Ohio regiment, he was promoted to a Lieutenancy in the Sixth Ohio Cavalry in 1862, and became a Captain and aide-de-camp in 1863. He was brevetted Major for gallant conduct at the battle of Shady Grove, Va , in 1864, and was afterwards advanced to the brevet rank of Lieutenant-Colonel, and Colonel for gallant services. After the war he completed his college course, and studied law at Harvard University, and then came to New York, where he has become one of the leading lawyers of the country, having devoted himself especially to corporation practice. He is an active and influential Republican, and was offered, but declined, the position of Secretary of the Interior in the Cabinet of President McKinley, a place for which his legal attainments eminently qualified him Colonel McCook lives in West Fifty-fourth Street. He is a trustee of Princeton University, and a director of many railroad, insurance and financial institutions He is a member of the Metropolitan, City, Union, Union League, Δ K E, University, Riding, Lawyers', Princeton, Harvard, New York Athletic and other clubs, the Bar Association of the City of New York, the Downtown Association, the Military Order of the Loyal Legion, and the American Museum of Natural History.

HENRY D. McCORD

IT is to Scotland that we naturally turn for the ancestry of the McCord family, which is a branch of and closely allied to the great Clan of MacDonald, the Lords of the Isles. The New York family of the present day, of which the gentleman named above is a prominent representative, traces its descent to James McCord, a personage of note in the Highlands of Argyleshire, who was born in the early portion of the seventeenth century, about 1620. His son, John, married Sarah MacDougall, and their son, James McCord, was born in 1688, and married a kinswoman, Sarah McCord. Several of their sons came to New York before the Revolution and settled upon the Hudson River, not far above New York City, in which portion of Westchester County their descendants have been numerous.

The great-grandfather of Mr Henry D McCord was Benjamin McCord, one of the sons of James and Sarah, who was born in Scotland in 1742 and who, coming to the New World, settled at Scarsdale, Westchester County, where he died in 1807 He was twice married, his second wife being Catharine Devoe, of the New York family of that name, and among their children was Jordan D. McCord, 1775-1830 He, like his father, was twice married; his first wife being Eunice H. Dusenbury, while the second one was Rachel Tompkins, a highly connected lady, also of an old Westchester County family, her uncle being the Honorable Daniel D Tompkins. The latter, who was a native of Scarsdale, was born in 1774 and became Governor of the State, and was elected Vice-President of the United States for the two successive terms of President Monroe, from 1817 to 1825. Lewis McCord, father of Mr. Henry D. McCord, who was the eldest child of Jordan D. and Rachel (Tompkins) McCord, was born in 1810, married Nancy Mangam, and died in 1855.

Their son, Mr Henry D. McCord, was born at the Village of Sing Sing, New York, September 15th, 1836. He was educated in the common schools of his native village and had no advantages beyond this Owing to the death of his parents, he was forced at an early age to begin life for himself and to depend upon his own exertions He, however, had displayed, even as a boy, a strong inclination for a business life, and consequently, while still very young, began his career with a mercantile establishment in his native place When twenty-one years old, he came to New York and formed a connection with a relative, William D. Mangam, whose place of business was in lower Broad Street. He remained with Mr. Mangam till the latter's death, in 1870, and then succeeded to the business, which, conducted under his name, has grown to be one of the largest concerns in the grain trade of the city or the country; and it is also worthy of note that Mr McCord's place of business is the same in which he started in mercantile life in the metropolis over forty years ago. Mr. McCord owes his success in life entirely to his own exertions and to his untiring industry. His strength of character asserted itself in his youth, when he voluntarily formed the exemplary habits which have since distinguished him in social and business life. While not actively connected with temperance work, Mr. McCord is a consistent opponent of the use of intoxicants. For several years he was president of the Produce Exchange, of New York, and has been active and efficient in all measures to promote or to protect the commercial interests of the metropolis. Mr. McCord has never taken an active part in politics, although it has been often suggested that nominations equivalent to election, were subject to his acceptance. His devotion to the care of his business has, however, caused him, up to the present time, to firmly decline all such offers.

In 1860, Mr. McCord married Esther E. Noé, daughter of Richard Q. Noé, of this city. They have a family of three children: William M McCord, who in 1887 married Helen Washburn; Minnie E., now the wife of Charles L. Schwartzwaelder; and Clara Belle, who married, in November, 1897, Robert Sherrard Elliot. Mr McCord's residence is on the west side, at 118 West Seventy-third Street, and since 1892 he has owned a large estate at Scarborough, N. Y, near his native place, on which he has a country house. He is a member of the Colonial Club and many social, benevolent and business societies and organizations,

HENRY MITCHELL MaCCRACKEN

BORN in Oxford, O., in 1840, the Reverend Henry Mitchell MacCracken, Chancellor of New York University, formerly the University of the City of New York, inherited from his parents a predilection for religious and educational work that has made him one of the distinguished men of his generation His father, the Reverend John MacCracken, who came of an old Scottish family, was a Presbyterian clergyman His mother, before her marriage, was an accomplished teacher and for many years presided over a private school for young ladies in Oxford Two of his great-grandfathers fought for the Colonies in the Revolution, one, Henry MacCracken, falling, in 1778, a victim of the Indians and Tories on the Susquehanna, the other, Major Samuel Wilson, living after the war in his home near Cincinnati

The education of Dr MacCracken was directed by his father and mother and at an early age he became a student in Miami University, being graduated from that institution with the degree of B A., when he was only seventeen years old Taking up the profession of teaching, he was engaged as a classical teacher and as school superintendent for four years. Entering upon the study of theology in the Theological Seminary in Xenia, O , and Princeton, N J , he subsequently applied himself to the study of philosophy and history in Tubingen and Berlin, Germany, remaining abroad for several years Before going abroad, he had been pastor of a church in Columbus, O , and there and in Toledo, O , spent fifteen years of active work in the ministry, taking an interested part in the affairs of the Presbyterian denomination.

When he was about forty years of age, Dr MacCracken was called to be Chancellor of the Western University of Pennsylvania His brilliant success in administering the affairs of this University gained him wide repute, and in 1884, during the Chancellorship of the Reverend Dr John Hall, he was called to the chair of philosophy in the University of the City of New York Shortly he was advanced to be vice-Chancellor, and in 1891, upon the resignation of Dr Hall, he was made Chancellor, a position that he now holds During his years of service to the University, he has proved himself a worthy successor to his predecessors in the office of Chancellor, James Matthews, Theodore Frelinghuysen, Gardiner Spring, Isaac Ferris, Howard Crosby and John Hall His energy and persistence, his scholarly attainments and his skill as an educator have wrought great changes in the old University, which has displayed a rapid development along all lines during the last few years A graduate seminary and a school of pedagogy have been established, the Undergraduate College and the School of Engineering have been removed from their old quarters in Washington Square to a new site on University Heights and the University, as a whole, is taking its place as one of the most important and most useful collegiate institutions in the United States

The wife of Dr. MacCracken was Catharine Hubbard, daughter of the Reverend Thomas Swan Hubbard, of Vermont, and granddaughter of Dr. Fay, of Vermont He has two sons, John Henry and George Geer MacCracken, and one daughter, Fay N MacCracken. His eldest son is a graduate from the New York University in the class of 1894, and has since been a teacher of philosophy in the University College The residence of the family is on University Heights, and in summer time at Overbrook, Pine Hill-in-Catskills Dr MacCracken is connected with several religious, educational and other societies, being an officer of the Association of Colleges in the Middle States, the American Society of Church History, the Society for the Prevention of Crime, and the American Tract Society He has been a prolific writer on philosophical, sociological, educational, historical and religious questions, and has published The Lives of the Church Leaders and other important works In 1867, as a delegate from the United States, he delivered an important address to the General Assembly of the Free Church of Scotland, in Edinburgh, and in 1884 delivered an historical address at the first meeting of the congress of the Scotch-Irish race in Belfast, Ireland He received the degree of D. D from Wittenburg College, Ohio, and the degree of LL D from Miami University.

NATHANIEL L'HOMMEDIEU McCREADY

THE ancestors of Mr Nathaniel L'Hommedieu McCready have been prominent in New York City for several generations In 1772, Thomas McCready, the first of the family in this country, came from Scotland and settled in Philadelphia, leaving that place to make his home in Westchester, just before the War of the Revolution The father of Mr. McCready, who bore the same name that he gave to his son, was born in New York City, September 4th, 1820, and went, while still a young man, to Mobile, Ala , where he was engaged as a clerk in a shipping commission house and acquired his first knowledge of business matters In 1840, he returned to his home in New York, ready to go into business for himself and established the shipping and commission firm of N L. McCready & Co , which became one of the leading concerns of its line in New York, and at the head of which he remained for a quarter of a century

When he retired from this house, in 1865, Mr. McCready continued in an allied business, associating himself with Mr Livingston and Mr Fox, forming the firm of Livingston, Fox & Co Two years later, he joined with other business associates in establishing the Old Dominion Steamship Company, of which he became the president, holding that position for twenty years, until the time of his death, in 1887 He was also a director of the Farmers' Loan & Trust Company, the Empire City Fire Insurance Company, the Washington Life Insurance Company, and the Missouri, Kansas & Texas Railway Company, of which he was at one time president He belonged to the Union and St Nicholas clubs, was an honorary member of the Marine Society from 1847, a member of the Reformed Church and a generous contributor to its charities

During the war, Mr McCready rendered great and valuable services to the Government in transporting troops and supplies to the front, and after the war, by the foundation of the Old Dominion Steamship Company, was among the first to establish friendly commercial relations with the South Mr McCready, as his name indicates, is connected with one of the most ancient families of New York. Benjamin L'Hommedieu was a Huguenot, who was born in La Rochelle and came to America in 1686, from Holland He settled in Greenport, Long Island, and married a daughter of Nathaniel Sylvester, of Shelter Island. His eldest son, Benjamin, married Martha, daughter of Ezra Bourne, of Sandwich, Mass., and their son, the Honorable Ezra L'Hommedieu, was one of the most prominent citizens of New York City during the Revolutionary period, several times a Member of Congress, a member of the United States Senate from 1788 until the time of his death, in 1811, and conspicuous in other official positions throughout his long life

The wife of Nathaniel L'Hommedieu McCready, Sr , was Carolina Amanda Waldron, a lineal descendant from Resolve Waldron, who came over to New Amsterdam in the suite of Governor Petrus Stuyvesant in the seventeenth century Mrs McCready's grandfather was Brigadier-General Mapes, who held the command of the troops on Long Island under Governor DeWitt Clinton during the War of 1812 Dr Benjamin McCready, for many years a professor in Bellevue Hospital Medical College, and one of the oldest and most esteemed members of the medical profession in New York City, was a brother of Nathaniel L'Hommedieu McCready, Sr

Mr. Nathaniel L'Hommedieu McCready of the present generation was the eldest of his father's family of five children Only a sister, Mrs William Ward Robins, with him survive their parent. Mr McCready is the administrator of his father's estate He married Jeanneton Borrowe, who is a member of the Colonial Dames He lives at 4 East Seventy-fifth Street and is a graduate of Columbia College, belongs to the Tuxedo Club, and is a member of the Metropolitan, Union, University and Country clubs, New York Yacht Club, St. Nicholas Society and of the American Geographical Society Mr. McCready divides his time between this country and France While here, he interests himself in the care of his estate, and in France both Mr. and Mrs McCready devote themselves to outdoor sports. Their favorite amusement is boar hunting, and they have brought home many trophies of the chase, and their pack, of which they are justly proud, took the first prize a few years ago at the Paris Bench Show.

RICHARD ALDRICH McCURDY

FROM the family of McKirdy, or MacKurerdy, that formerly belonged to the tribes who possessed the Western Islands of Scotland under the Crown of Sweden and the Lords of the Isles, came the McCurdys They were the principal possessors of the Island of Bute at a very early period. In 1489, James IV leased the Crown property of Bute, which in 1503 in one general charter was assigned to several families, the greatest portion to the MacKurerdys. John McCurdy, 1724-1785, the ancestor of the family in this country, emigrated from Ireland thirty years before the Declaration of Independence. His wife, whom he married in 1752, was Anne Lord, daughter of Judge Richard Lord, granddaughter of Judge Nathaniel Lynde, great-great-granddaughter of William Hyde, of Norwich, a descendant of Thomas Lord, of Hartford, and great-great-granddaughter of Elizabeth Digby, who was a daughter of Everard Digby, descended from Sir John Digby, of Eye-Kittleby, County Leicester, England.

Richard McCurdy, 1759-1857, son of John McCurdy, was the grandfather of the subject of this sketch. He graduated from Yale College in 1787, for some years practiced law, but later in life managed the estate inherited from his father. Several times he was a representative in the Connecticut Legislature. His wife was Ursula Griswold, daughter of Deacon John Griswold, of Lyme, Conn , and granddaughter of Governor Matthew Griswold and Ursula Wolcott. The father of Mr. Richard Aldrich McCurdy was Robert Henry McCurdy, one of the famous New York merchants of fifty years and more ago. He was born in 1800 in Lyme, Conn., and died in New York in 1880. Prepared to enter Yale College, he changed his plans and came to New York and started upon the business career in which he acquired wealth and reputation. Early in his career he made the acquaintance of Herman D. Aldrich and the friendship between the two was lifelong and devoted Messrs. McCurdy and Aldrich were sent by their employer to Petersburgh, Va., where they opened a branch store and remained for several years Returning to New York in 1820, they soon established the commission dry goods firm of McCurdy & Aldrich, which existed for nearly thirty years, before the senior partner retired in 1857. After 1840, the house was known as McCurdy, Aldrich & Spencer. During the Civil War, Mr. McCurdy acted as Commissary-General in the State of New York and rendered the Government valuable assistance in many ways. He was largely interested in all objects of public charity, was an incorporator of the Continental Fire Insurance Company and the Mutual Life Insurance Company, a director in the Merchants' Exchange Bank and American Exchange National Bank, member of the Chamber of Commerce and one of the founders of the Union League Club.

The mother of Mr. Richard A. McCurdy, whom his father married in 1826, was Gertrude Mercer Lee, daughter of Dr James and Gertrude (Mercer) Lee, of Newark, N J She was a niece of Chancellor Theodore Frelinghuysen, Mayor of Newark, chancellor of the University of New York, Attorney-General of the State of New Jersey, United States Senator, Vice-Presidential candidate with Henry Clay in 1844 and president of Rutgers College She was descended from the Reverend Theodorus Jacobus Frelinghuysen, who came to this country in the first part of the eighteenth century The children of Robert H McCurdy and his wife, Gertrude, were: Richard A. and Theodore F. McCurdy, Mrs. Gardiner G. Hubbard, Mrs. Elias J. Marsh and Mrs. Charles M. Marsh.

Mr. Richard Aldrich McCurdy was born January 29th, 1835. Most of his lifetime has been spent in connection with the Mutual Life Insurance Company, of which he now president. He belongs to the Metropolitan, Union League, Manhattan, Morristown and Lawyers' clubs the New England Society and the American Museum of Natural History. In 1856, he married Sarah Ellen Little, daughter of Charles Coffin Little, of Boston. His daughter, Gertrude Lee McCurdy, is now the wife of Louis A. Thebaud. His son, Robert Henry McCurdy, is a graduate from Harvard College in the class of 1881 and married Mary Suckley He belongs to the Metropolitan, Union League, University and other clubs. Mr. and Mrs. Richard A. McCurdy have a city residence in Fifth Avenue, and a country home in Morris Plains, N. J.

JAMES LAWRENCE McKEEVER

COMMODORE ISAAC McKEEVER, U. S. N , an officer of the War of 1812, was a native of Pennsylvania, born in 1793, and entered the navy as midshipman in 1809 He attained the rank of Lieutenant during the war with Great Britain, in which he took an active part.   While commanding a gunboat on Lake Borgne, La., in 1814, he was captured by the British forces then advancing on New Orleans   After the war, he became Commander in 1830, Captain in 1838, and in 1850 was promoted to be Commodore and commanded the Brazilian Squadron, being afterwards in charge of the Norfolk, Va., Navy Yard, and dying there in 1856. His wife was Mary Flower Gamble, daughter of Lieutenant Joseph Gamble, U. S N., also an officer in the War of 1812, and his wife, Mary Thomson, whose parents were Thomas Thomson and Mary Jane Hale.   Thomas Thomson, a native of Scotland, came to America before the Revolution and was Captain of a Pennsylvania troop

General Chauncey McKeever, United States Army, eldest son of Commodore Isaac McKeever, has been distinguished in the military service.   Born in Baltimore, Md , in 1829, he graduated from West Point in 1849 and was commissioned in the Third Artillery.   At the opening of the Civil War, he was appointed Captain and Assistant Adjutant-General, and served as chief of staff to General Heintzelman at Bull Run and in the Peninsula.   He was promoted to be Lieutenant-Colonel, Colonel and Brevet Brigadier-General, receiving the latter grade from Congress, in 1865, for gallant and meritorious service   After further service in the Adjutant-General's department, he was retired for age, in 1864   He is a member of the Union and University clubs in this city and the Metropolitan Club of Washington

Mr James Lawrence McKeever, of New York, is the second son of Commodore McKeever He was born in Baltimore, Md , October 4th, 1831, and passed some of his earlier years in Brazil He has, however, long been a resident of New York and prominent in the banking profession.   He married Mary Augusta Townsend, of a patriotic American ancestry, and also of an ancient and distinguished English family

Mrs. McKeever is the daughter of Robert Townsend and Mary A. Whittemore   Her grandfather, Peter Townsend, was the owner of the Sterling Iron Works, and during the Revolution rendered important services to the patriotic cause.   In his establishment was forged the great chain that was stretched across the Hudson below West Point to obstruct the progress of the British fleet, and he also cast cannon and anchors for vessels of the American navy, including those of the Constitution   On the maternal side, Mrs McKeever is descended from the Whittemores, of Hitchin, in Hertfordshire, near London, where the family has been established since Saxon times Whittemore Hall, at Whittemore, was the original seat of the bearers of the name.   Thomas Whittemore came to Malden, Mass., about 1640.   His grandson, Captain Samuel Whittemore, of Menotomy, now Arlington, Mass , who married Esther Prentice, was an active patriot, and though eighty years old, led a company to the Lexington fight, where he was severely wounded.   He was shot, and bayoneted by the British and left for dead on the field; recovering, he lived fifteen years longer   His grandson, Samuel Whittemore, 1774-1835, was Mrs McKeever's grandfather.   He was the son of Thomas Whittemore and Ann Cutler, married Jane Tileson and was an influential New York merchant in the earlier portion of the present century, being president of the Greenwich Bank   The residence of Mr McKeever is 164 Lexington Avenue, and his country seat is at Southampton, Long Island   He is a member of the Union Club, Downtown Association, Sons of the American Revolution and the American Geographical Society.

The children of Mr. and Mrs. McKeever are two sons and two daughters.   Their eldest son, Robert Townsend McKeever, is well known in connection with transportation matters and married Frances C Webb   The second son, Isaac Chauncey McKeever, is a member of the New York Stock Exchange and married Julia Draper   One daughter, Edith McKeever, married Hoffman Miller, and the remaining daughter of the family is Marion McKeever

CHARLES FOLLEN McKIM

O F Scotch-Irish ancestry, the father of Mr Charles Follen McKim, one of the most accomplished American architects of this generation, was the Reverend James Miller McKim, who was early enrolled as one of the leaders in the cause of anti-slavery. Born in Carlisle, Pa , November 14th, 1810, he first studied in Dickinson College, in his native town, but completed his education in Princeton College. Choosing the ministry for a profession, he was ordained pastor of the Presbyterian church in Womelsdorf, Pa., in 1835, soon after his graduation from college

Even before he had become of age he was an Abolitionist, and henceforth his devotion to that reform was unreserved and energetic. He was a member of the first convention of abolitionists, whose deliberations resulted in the formation of the American Anti-Slavery Society, and his interest in the cause led him to resign from the work of the ministry in 1836, after only a year of pastoral service, in order that he might enter the lecture field, under the auspices of the new Anti-Slavery Society which he had assisted in organizing. For the ensuing four years he was constantly engaged in promulgating anti-slavery doctrines upon the platform, throughout Pennsylvania, and was subjected to the indignities and persecution that were the lot of all abolitionists of that day

In 1840, Mr McKim settled in Philadelphia, where he became publishing agent and subsequently corresponding secretary of the Pennsylvania Anti-Slavery Society, a connection that he maintained for more than a quarter of a century, being in effect the exclusive and responsible manager of the society. When the Civil War broke out, he responded to every call of patriotism, and throughout the long struggle was particularly active in all movements for upholding the Union cause and for caring for the welfare of the liberated slaves, aiding also in the recruiting of many of the Pennsylvania regiments. In 1863, he was made corresponding secretary and general manager of the Pennsylvania Freedman's Relief Association. In that capacity he traveled extensively throughout the South, establishing schools and looking after the material interests of the freedmen, and accomplished very notable results. From 1865 to 1869 he was connected with the American Freedman's Union Commission, and soon after retired from public life, after about thirty-five years of unremitting activity In 1865, he was associated with several other gentlemen in founding The New York Nation His death occurred in West Orange, N J His wife was Sarah Allibone Speakman, of an old Pennsylvania family.

Mr Charles Follen McKim was born in Chester County, Pa., August 24th, 1847. His primary education was in the public schools, and then he was sent to Harvard College, where he studied in the Lawrence Scientific School for two years, 1866-67. He also studied in Bowdoin College His education in this country was supplemented by study and travel in Europe, including a three-years' architectural course at the School of Fine Arts in Paris. Returning to the United States, in 1870, he settled in New York and associated himself with W R. Mead and Stanford White in the firm of McKim, Mead & White, that has been foremost in the contemporaneous development of architecture in this country. During more than a quarter of a century that it has been in existence, this firm has contributed to the United States some of the most notable architectural structures erected in this country. Several examples of their work have been referred to elsewhere in this volume In addition to what is there enumerated, they have been the architects of the Columbia University buildings, the New York Life Insurance Company's building, the houses of Frederick W Vanderbilt and Charles L Tiffany and other structures in New York, and the Algonquin Club and Public Library building in Boston, and other important buildings elsewhere.

Mr. McKim married, in 1885, Julia Appleton, of Boston, and lives in West Thirty-fifth Street. He is a member of the Century Association, the Metropolitan, University, Racquet, Players, City and St Andrew's Golf clubs, and the Algonquin and Somerset clubs of Boston.

ROBERT MACLAY

AMONG the many clans of Scotland, none have a more ancient or more honorable record than the MacLaigs, who can be traced back in the annals of the Highlands many centuries. The American Maclays are descended from this clan. Charles Maclay, the head of the American branch of the house, came from Scotland to this country in 1734 and settled in Pennsylvania, where his descendants have been prominent in professional, business and public life Many of them were soldiers in the Revolutionary War. The Honorable William Maclay was one of the first United States Senators elected from Pennsylvania. He served only a short term, but made a very distinct impress upon the formative legislation of the young republic. He was a sturdy Democrat of the old school, and it has been claimed for him that he should share with Thomas Jefferson the honor of being the founder of the Democratic party.

The founder of the New York branch of the family was the Reverend Dr. Archibald Maclay, the grandson of Charles Maclay, the pioneer. He was an eminent Congregational clergyman, and came to New York City from Pennsylvania in 1805. Becoming afterwards a Baptist clergyman, he was pastor of one church for a period of thirty-two years. For several years he was the vice-president and general agent of the American and Foreign Bible Society, and during the latter part of his life was president of the American Bible Union. Two sons of Dr. Archibald Maclay attained to eminence Robert H. Maclay studied medicine, and during the greater part of his long life held rank among the leading physicians of New York City. He was also president of the New York Savings Bank. He married Mary Brown, daughter of William Brown, of Glasgow, Scotland. Another son was the Honorable William B. Maclay, who was a Member of Congress in 1842, and for three consecutive terms thereafter.

Mr. Robert Maclay, of this generation, so well known for his interest in public affairs, is the eldest son of Dr. Robert H. and his wife, Eliza L. Maclay. He was born in New York City, June 11th, 1834. Preparing for college in the public schools, he entered the University of the City of New York, but at the age of fourteen went to Illinois to complete his education in Judson College, graduating from that institution before he was twenty years of age. Returning then to New York City, he entered the real estate business. In 1865, he married Georgiana Barmore, whose father, Albert Barmore, was the founder and first president of the Knickerbocker Ice Company. As a result of this family alliance, Mr. Maclay became interested in the Knickerbocker Ice Company. He was elected a director of the corporation, and in 1868 became its vice-president and treasurer. When Mr. Barmore died, in 1875, Mr. Maclay was elected president of the company, a position that he has ever since retained. He has also been connected with several financial institutions, among them the Knickerbocker Trust Company, of which he is president, the Bowery Savings Bank, of which he is vice-president, and the People's Bank, of which he is a director.

The prominence that Mr. Maclay has attained in the business world and his reputation as a conservative business man has led to demands upon him for the public service. In 1892, the Supreme Court appointed him a member of the Rapid Transit Commission, a position in which he served the public faithfully and capably. For many years he has been one of the most influential members of the Board of Education, acting as chairman of the building committee of the board, and in 1895-96 its president He is a member of the Chamber of Commerce and the New York Historical Society, and belongs to numerous clubs, among them the Manhattan, Metropolitan, Grolier and Riding, and is a member of the Downtown Association. He has been officially connected with several of the clubs to which he belongs, and has served as treasurer of the Manhattan Club. He was one of the original incorporators of the Botanical Garden and is a member of the advisory committee of the New York University, a trustee of the Madison Avenue Baptist Church and a trustee of the Northern Dispensary. He lives at 50 West Fifty-seventh Street, and also has a summer residence at Elberon, N J. His son, Alfred Barmore Maclay, belongs to the Calumet, Riding and other clubs and social organizations.

GEORGE HAMMOND McLEAN

HIGHLAND tradition has ascribed the foundation of the powerful Clan of McLean, which from immemorial times has inhabited the Island of Mull, on the west coast of Scotland, to a famous warrior, Gillian-na-Tuaighe, or Gillian of the Battle-Ax, a weapon of that kind having been his constant companion   In fact, Celtic genealogists have carried the Clan's history back to fabulous ages, discovering its ultimate ancestor in a certain sage and hero, one Dougall of Scone, who flourished in far remote times.   The word Gillian signifies servant of St. John, and the name assumed by Gillian-na-Tuaighe's family and followers was originally McGillian, and in Gaelic they are always designated as the Clan Gillian.   Under successive chieftains, their power in Mull and the adjacent islands and mainlands increased for many ages, and was not diminished by a nominal dependence upon the McDonalds, Lords of the Isles.   In fact, the McLeans were allies rather than feudal vassals, and were related to the ruling house of the McDonalds, Lachlan McLean, the first of the chiefs to establish himself at the historic family stronghold, the castle of Duart, in Mull, having married the Lady Margaret, daughter of John McDonald, the first Lord of the Isles. The brother of this Lachlan was Eachann, or Hector, McLean, who founded the subordinate division of the Clan known as the McLeans of Lochbuy

The chiefs of Duart ranked among the most noble Highland families and married daughters of the Earl of Douglas, Argyle and other renowned and noble Scottish houses, both Highland and Lowland; while their warlike Clan was a participant in all the commotions to which mediæval Scotland was subjected, following the banner of the national hero, Robert Bruce, at Bannockburn, in 1314, and joining the army of Islesmen which Donald McDonald, Lord of the Isles, led in 1411, to subjugate the Lowlands, and which was defeated at the battle of Harlow, their chief, Hector Roy McLean, being slain there.   In 1493, the McDonalds were deprived, by the Scottish King and Parliament, of their sovereignty, and the McLeans were then rendered independent   The chief of McLean was killed at Flodden Field, in 1513   Feuds with the Campbells of Argyle and the Mc-Donalds, their former overlords, followed for some generations ; Lachlan Catanach McLean, of Duart, having been assassinated by Campbell, of Calder, brother of the Earl of Argyle, in 1527.

Sir Lachlan More McLean (Lachlan the Great), who was educated at the Court of King James VI , of Scotland, and died in 1602, overcame all rivals, both in war and diplomacy, and raised the Clan Gillian to a high position of power and influence   In 1632, the then chief was created a baronet, and throughout the wars of the seventeenth century the McLeans were consistent supporters of the Stuart cause, fighting under Montrose at Inverlochy and Kilsyth, while, after the fall of King Charles' cause, their island possessions were ravaged by the Covenanters   Notwithstanding this, they took up arms for Charles II , and fought against Cromwell's veterans, while in the Jacobite risings they were conspicuous at Killiecrankie, and in the battles of the Rebellion of 1745.   Later on, many of the Clan became noted for their bravery in the Highland Regiments of the British Army, the present Chief, Sir Fitzroy Donald McLean, Baronet, being a veteran of the Crimea.

It has been remarked by the historian of the McLeans, that their devotion to the Stuarts was throughout a losing business.   Many of the Clan were driven into exile, and America received a share of this enforced emigration, the bearers of the name having in this country displayed the sterling qualities that have ever marked their race, several of the family being prominent in Colonial and Revolutionary history.   Among those who came early to this country, were representatives of the McLeans of Ardgour, a cadet branch sprung from Lachlan Bronnach, the seventh chief of McLean, and from this stock the New York family referred to herein is descended   Their arms are those of the Ardgour McLeans, on which are quartered a rampant lion, a castle, a hand grasping a cross, and a galley of the Isles with a salmon beneath   The crest is a helmet surmounted by a battle-ax between crossed branches of cypress and laurel ; the motto being . *Altera Merces.* Cypress and laurel, it should be mentioned, have ever been the distinctive badge of the Clan

Gillian, and its war cry or slogan, which was heard in so many Highland battles, was the Celtic words *Bas na Beatha*, meaning Death or Life

In the family Bible possessed by Mr George Hammond McLean, the births, deaths and alliances of the family are preserved with unusual fulness and care. The record of his ancestry in this country begins with William McLean, 1679–1749, who, in 1712, married Elizabeth Merrill ; his son being Charles, 1714–1759, who married Mary Carson, in 1743 ; and his grandson, another Charles McLean, 1757–1794, married Elizabeth Swaim, in 1778 , the son of the last named couple, Cornelius McLean, born in 1787, being grandfather of the subject of this article. Cornelius McLean married, in 1807, Hannah Hammond, whose father, James Hammond, was a prominent patriot and Lieutenant-Colonel of the First Regiment of Westchester County, New York Militia, during the American Revolution

James Monroe McLean, their third son, was born in New York, in 1818, was educated in private schools, and began his business career in the old-time Guardian Fire Insurance Company, founded by John Jacob Astor and Robert Lenox In 1847, he became connected with the Citizens Fire Insurance Company, of this city, and took a leading part, by his wise and conservative course, in raising it from adversity to a high position, so that it paid large dividends, and its stock commanded a marked premium As secretary and president, Mr McLean was the active manager of the Citizens Fire Insurance Company for almost forty years. Holding a high position in the insurance world, and recognized as one of the leading exponents of the profession of underwriter, he was elected, in 1860, president of the New York Board of Fire Underwriters, serving four years, and was a prominent factor in creating harmony among the local insurance organizations, and in the establishment of the present New York Fire Department. When the National Board of Fire Underwriters was formed, in 1866, his was the only name put forward for president, and he was reëlected for a second term On the resignation of Henry Stokes, Mr. McLean was elected president of the Manhattan Life Insurance Company, of which he had long been a director and a leading spirit in its affairs. He was an incorporator and original director of the Manhattan Savings Institution, and one of the first board of directors of the National Citizens Bank, and a director and vice-president of the Union Trust Company.

The varied public services of James Monroe McLean included the presidency of the Board of Education for four years, and a trusteeship of the New York and Brooklyn Bridge. He was also president of the Institution for the Blind, and at his death, in 1890, was a member of the leading social organizations of the metropolis, including the Union, St. Nicholas and Manhattan clubs, and vice-president of the St. Nicholas Society, of which he had previously been the president In 1840, he married Louisa Theresa Williams, who died in 1857, their two sons being Mr George Hammond McLean and Cornelius McLean, of Mount Vernon, N. Y

Mr George Hammond McLean was born in this city November 24th, 1849. He was educated at private schools in New York and Connecticut, and entered Columbia College, and was a member of the Δ Ψ fraternity He was, however, forced to abandon his studies by ill health, and spent ten years in Europe One of the unusual experiences of his travels was several months passed on a Russian man-of-war as the guest of the commander Returning to New York, in 1882, Mr. McLean entered the Citizens Insurance Company, taking charge of the agency department of its business, and, in 1886, he became the company s vice-president, an office he holds at the present time.

In November, 1879, Mr. McLean married, at Trinity Chapel, Harriet Amelia Dater, daughter of Henry Dater, of this city, and has two sons, James Clarence Hammond McLean and Alan Dater McLean. Mr. McLean's residence is 126 West Fifty-seventh Street, and he is a member of the Metropolitan, St. Nicholas, Calumet, Country, Players, New York Athletic, and Suburban Riding and Driving clubs, St Nicholas Society, the Sons of the American Revolution, and of the Metropolitan Museum of Art, and the American Museum of Natural History. He is also a member of the Old Guard, of which organization his uncle, the late George Washington McLean, was long the Major in command.

HARRY WHITNEY McVICKAR

THE McVickars are an old Scotch-Irish family, and several branches have attained to prominence in New York, One of the first of the name to come to this country was Archibald McVickar, the younger son of an Irish gentleman He was in business in New York before the Revolution, being an extensive importer Two nephews of Archibald McVickar were especially prominent in the next generation John McVickar settled in New York when he was seventeen His brother, Nathaniel McVickar, emigrated in 1798 and married Catharine Bucknor, daughter of a West India merchant, whose wife was a sister of Peter Goelet One of the sons of Nathaniel and Catharine McVickar was William H McVickar, who died in November, 1896, at the age of seventy-eight In early life he was in business in Wall Street He became one of the most prominent yachtsmen in New York, was one of the incorporators of the New York Yacht Club, and Commodore of the club in 1866. He married Julia (Phelps) Mason, daughter of Thaddeus Phelps, and widow of Governor Mason, of Michigan. His eldest daughter married Lord Grantley, of England, and his second daughter became the wife of James Andariese, of New York His only son is Henry G. McVickar, who married Janet Lansing, daughter of Colonel Arthur Lansing, U. S A

John McVickar, the brother of Nathaniel McVickar, attained even greater prominence than his brother He was an importer and shipowner Accumulating a large fortune, he gratified, to the fullest extent, his disposition to help others, giving much to the cause of religion and also to assist worthy individuals He was a director in the Bank of New York, 1793-1810, one of the founders and vice-president of the St Patrick's Society in 1797, and a vestryman of Trinity Church, 1801-12. He married Ann Moore, daughter of John Moore, a first cousin of the celebrated Bishop Benjamin Moore. His eldest son, James McVickar, married Euretta Constable, daughter of William Constable, and their son was the celebrated Dr John A McVickar, whose son, the Reverend William Neilson McVickar, D D , is rector of Holy Trinity Church, Philadelphia The second son of John McVickar was Archibald McVickar, who, after graduating from Columbia College, went to Cambridge University, England, and returning, married Catharine Augusta Livingston, daughter of Judge Henry Brockholst Livingston. John McVickar, the third son, became a clergyman, author and professor in Columbia College. He married Eliza Bard, daughter of Dr Samuel Bard, and the Reverend William A. McVickar, D D , of New York, was his son Henry McVickar, the fourth son of John McVickar, was engaged in mercantile life. Edward McVickar married Matilda Constable, daughter of William Constable Nathan McVickar died young Benjamin McVickar married Josephine C Lawrence, daughter of Isaac Lawrence, president of the United States Bank in New York Eliza McVickar married William Constable. The youngest child, Augusta McVickar, married Judge William Jay, son of Chief Justice John Jay

Mr Harry Whitney McVickar, a leading representative of this interesting family in the present generation, is the son of the Reverend William A McVickar He was born in Irvington-on-Hudson, September 2d, 1860, and though an artist by profession, has also been engaged in business, being a member of the real estate firm of S V R Cruger & Co He lives in West Thirty-ninth Street, and is a member of the Players, Lawyers', Tuxedo, and Riding clubs, and the Century Association. Mr. McVickar married Maud Robbins, daughter of Henry A Robbins and his wife, Elizabeth Pelham Bend, a sister of George H Bend. Mrs. McVickar is a great-granddaughter of Philip Thomas, of the Virginia family of that name, and Frances Mary Ludlow. Through her grandmother, she is directly descended from Gabriel Ludlow, and also from Captain George Duncan, Peter Harrison, of Newport, and Elizabeth Pelham

The McVickar arms are quarterly, first and fourth: or., an eagle, displayed, with two heads, gules. Second and third: per bend, embattled, argent and gules, over all, an escutcheon, or , charged with three stag's horns erect, gules Crest, an eagle, displayed, with two heads, per pale, embattled, argent and gules Motto, *Dominus Providebit*

WILLIAM H. MACY

EVEN the casual visitor to the Island of Nantucket, that lies out in the Atlantic Ocean off the coast of Massachusetts, soon realizes that the Macy family has long been a dominant influence in that community Everybody in Nantucket seems to be connected, directly or indirectly, by birth or by marriage, with the Macys. This condition has, in fact, prevailed there for more than two and a half centuries.

Nantucket was originally settled by Thomas Macy, who came there with nine associates and bought the island from the Indians, in 1659. Thomas Macy was of Salisbury, England, where he was born in 1608. He came from the parish of Chilmark, England, in 1635, and settled in Massachusetts, going first to Newbury, becoming a freeman in that place in 1639, and in the same year was one of the first settlers of Salisbury, where he held many positions of prominence. He was an adherent of the Baptist faith, and his general liberality and tolerance in matters of religion brought him into some disfavor with his stricter Puritan neighbors. Sympathizing with the Quakers, he sheltered many of them from the persecutions to which they were subjected and for this found himself persecuted in turn. That was chief among the influences which led him to withdraw from the Bay Colony to the seclusion and freedom of the Island of Nantucket. He was the first Recorder of that place, a Lieutenant in King Philip's War, and a representative to the Massachusetts General Court every year, from 1672 to 1686.

The Macys, who have been prominent in the New York business world for several generations, are descended from this pioneer of Nantucket. One branch of the family had for its head Josiah Macy, the old New York merchant of the earlier part of the present century The father of Josiah Macy was a shipowner in Nantucket, a man of enterprise and considerable wealth for the time and place in which he lived Josiah Macy himself was born in Nantucket in 1785. His education was secured at the schools there, and at the age of fifteen he shipped on board of one of his father's vessels. For many years he followed the sea on his father's ships and then became himself a shipowner.

In 1828, Mr Macy came to New York City and established himself in the shipping and commission business, with his son, William H. Macy, as partner, under the firm name of Josiah Macy & Son. The following year, with the admission of another son into partnership, the firm name was changed to Josiah Macy & Sons. In 1853, Mr. Macy retired from business to his country seat in Rye, Westchester County, N. Y., and lived there until his death in 1872. He was one of the original founders of the City Fire Insurance Company, and a director from 1833 onward, while for many years he was a director in the Tradesmen's Bank. His wife, whom he married in 1805, and who died in 1861, was Lydia Hussey, of an old Nantucket family He left five sons, William H., Charles A., Josiah G , Francis H. and John H. Macy, and two daughters, Lydia H. and Ann Eliza Macy. William H. Macy, Sr., was the eldest son of Josiah Macy He was born at Nantucket in 1805, and was educated there. After a short term of service in a shipping office in New York, he began business on his own account in 1826 In 1828, his father joined him in the business which he had established. He became a member of the Chamber of Commerce in 1834, and was vice-president of that institution. He was also connected with the Leather Manufacturers' Bank, of which he was at one time president, and was president of the Seaman's Bank for Savings, vice-president of the United States Trust Company and a director in other fiduciary institutions. He died in 1887.

Mr. William H. Macy, the representative of the family in this generation, is the son of William H. Macy, Sr, and was born in New York in 1836. His mother was Eliza L. Jenkins, daughter of Sylvanus T. Jenkins. One of his sisters became the wife of William M. Kingsland and another married Isaac H. Walker. In 1866, Mr Macy married Angeline S. Strange, daughter of Edwin B. and Josephine L. Strange. Mr and Mrs. Macy have one daughter, Josephine L., who is the wife of George Finch Chamberlin, of this city.

CHARLES VICTOR MAPES

IN the fourteenth century, John Mapes, of Feltham, England, married the heiress of John Blount, son of Sir Hugh Blount   In 1563, Clarenceaux, King at Arms, describes the Mapes arms as sable, four fusels in fesse, or, quartered with the Blount arms, or, two bars nebule, sable, the Mapes crest being an arm in armour embowed, or, holding in the gauntlet a spur, argent, leathered sable   Thomas Mapes, of the eighth generation from John Mapes, of Feltham, was of the company from New Haven, Conn, which, in 1640, founded Southold, Long Island.   His descendants continued to reside in that town, and two brothers, James and Phineas Mapes, were in the Continental Army

General Jonas Mapes, 1768-1824, son of James Mapes, was born at Southold, but came to New York when young   In 1796, he married Elizabeth Tylee, daughter of James Tylee, a patriot, whom the British had imprisoned   Commissioned ensign in 1794, James Mapes became Brigadier-General in 1814, and was selected by Governor Tompkins to command the force defending New York City   He retained this post till the War of 1812 ended, and in 1816 became Major-General   He was later an alderman, and in 1819 was one of the organizers and directors of the first savings bank in America   A supporter of De Witt Clinton and an advocate of the Erie Canal, his name was first among the managers of the ball by which the opening of the canal was celebrated in 1825   When Lafayette visited New York in 1824, he was on the committee of reception, and received from Lafayette a pair of pistols still in the possession of the family

John Jay Mapes, his son, 1806-1866, was distinguished as a scientist, inventor and author, particularly by introducing chemical fertilizers into America   He founded and edited The American Repertory of Arts, Sciences and Manufactures, in which he published many able scientific papers   Appointed professor of chemistry and natural philosophy to the National Academy of Design, he received a similar appointment from the American Institute   In 1844, Professor Mapes became president of the Mechanics' Institute, and later of the American Institute, a position he held for twenty years   Williams College conferred the degrees of A M and LL D on him   He was a member of many prominent scientific societies, and received signal marks of public respect   He was among the personal friends of Joseph Bonaparte, who presented to him a bust of Napoleon by Canova.   In 1827, he married Sophia Furman, daughter of Judge Garrett Furman   Their second daughter is Mary Mapes Dodge, the authoress and editor of The St Nicholas Magazine

Mr Charles Victor Mapes is the surviving son of Professor Mapes   He was born in New York, July 4th, 1836, graduated from Harvard in 1857 and, while entering business life, assisted his father in editing The Working Farmer   Mr Mapes has been distinguished by his investigations of the requirements of soils and crops, and he has written numerous papers on such subjects.   He has been for twenty years the head of the Mapes Fertilizer Company, and was the first president of the Fertilizer and Chemical Exchange   He is a member of the Harvard and other clubs and of the American Association for the Advancement of Science, and was first president of the Θ Δ X club.   In 1863, he married Martha Meeker Halsted, daughter of Oliver Spencer Halsted and grand-daughter of Chancellor Oliver S Halsted, of New Jersey   Five sons were born of this marriage   Charles Halsted Mapes, the eldest, born 1864, graduated from Columbia in 1885, and from the Columbia School of Mines in 1889   He has since devoted himself to chemistry and scientific agriculture.   Dr James Jay Mapes, the second son, born 1866, graduated at Columbia in 1888, and from the College of Physicians and Surgeons in 1891, and died in 1896   Herbert Mapes, the third son, born 1868, was an undergraduate of Columbia when he was drowned at Fire Island in August, 1891   A memorial gate at the entrance of Columbia's new grounds has been erected by his fellow students and friends.   Victor Mapes, the fourth son, Columbia 1891, studied at the Sorbonne in Paris for two years, and has devoted himself to literary pursuits   Clive Spencer Mapes, the youngest son, born in 1878, is an undergraduate at Columbia   All Mr Mapes' sons were extremely popular in college and noted athletes

PETER MARIÉ

On the paternal side the Marié family is of French origin The grandfather of Mr Peter Marié was the maitre du port at Cap Français, on the Island of San Domingo, an important civil position In 1792 he lost his life in a drowning accident The French Republic had sent to the French islands in the West Indies the Marechal Rochambeau, son of the well-known General Rochambeau, who was in command of the French troops that served in the United States during our war for independence. It was the duty of the maitre du port to receive the Maréchal, and while thus engaged, one of the hurricanes, so frequent in the West Indies, arose and capsized the vessel which was carrying him.

The maternal grandfather of Mr. Marié was a planter of San Domingo, by the name of Arnaud He owned a flourishing estate in the neigborhood of Cap Français and lost his life in one of the insurrections of the blacks, being assassinated at a banquet that was being held to celebrate the cessation of hostilities and at which the leading whites and the chiefs of the blacks assisted. Through the assistance of some friendly blacks the widow of Mr. Arnaud, with her three young children, contrived to make her escape to a French merchant ship that lay in the harbor, and came to the United States The maiden name of Mrs Arnaud was Mary Nicholson She was a native of Pennsylvania, of a family well known in the Colonial days

The youngest of the three daughters of this family was Leontine Arnaud, who, at the time of her father's death, was only four years of age In 1811, when she was sixteen years old, she married John B Marié, son of the former maitre du port of Cap Français Mr Marié, who was born in Arles, Provence, France, settled in mercantile life in New York and soon became, according to the modest standard of that period, prosperous, being the owner of ships trading chiefly with Mexico.

When Mr. Marié died, in 1835, he left a widow and nine children, three daughters and six sons. The eldest daughter, Louise Marié, married the Vicomte de Bermingham, of France The second daughter married Ferdinand Thieriot, of Leipsic, whose father had been chamberlain to the King of Saxony The third daughter married Emil Sauer, who was, at one time, president of the German-American Bank The eldest son was Camille, who, up to the time of his death, in 1886, was a distinguished and esteemed citizen of New York The other sons were Albin, John, Peter, Joseph and Francis Albin went out in early life in the expedition to survey the ruins of Central America Joseph Marié married Josephine Hubbard, has two daughters, Leontine and Josephine Marié, and lives in West Forty-third Street His daughter Josephine has published several books and magazine articles which have met with favor, especially from Roman Catholic readers All the daughters of the older generation, with their husbands, and also the three eldest sons of the family are deceased

Mr Peter Marié, the fourth son of the family, was born in New York and was engaged in business in Wall Street until 1865, when he retired He has always had a taste for social life and has also cultivated letters, owning a small, but rather choice library. He has occasionally written, but rarely published, *vers de societe*, but in 1864, during the Civil War, he published a volume of selections called Tribute to the Fair, devoting the proceeds to the fair in aid of the sick and wounded soldiers. His residence, for forty-five years, was at 48 West Nineteenth Street, but in 1890, he was driven north by the march of improvement He then removed to East Thirty-seventh Street, on Murray Hill, where he now lives. His house contains many souvenirs of the metropolis notably minatures, aquarelles and photographs of the fairest of the *beau monde*, as some one has observed, "more social New York ana, than any other house in town." Mr Marie is unmarried He is a member of the Union, Knickerbocker, Grolier, City and Tuxedo clubs, the American Geographical Society, the New York Academy of Sciences and other societies and is a patron of the Metropolitan Museum of Art, the National Academy of Design and the American Museum of Natural History He is vice-president of the New York Institute for the Blind

HENRY GURDON MARQUAND

GUERNSEY, one of the Channel Islands, was the ancestral home of the Marquand family. Its first representative in America was Henry Marquand, who was born in 1737, came in 1761 to the American colonies, and died in 1772. He made his home in Fairfield, Conn., and it was there, in 1766, that his son, Isaac Marquand, was born The latter married Mehitable Perry, of the same town, a member of a Connecticut family of long standing, and moved to New York, where he was engaged successfully in business for many years He resided in Brooklyn, and died in 1838.

Mr Henry Gurdon Marquand, his son, who is distinguished not only for his many works of public beneficence, but for the leading part he has taken in promoting artistic education in this country, was born in New York, April 11th, 1819. He was educated in schools in his native city, and in Pittsfield, Mass., where he was fitted for college At an early age, however, he entered upon a life of business. He was agent for his brother, the late Frederick Marquand, in the care of his large landed and other property interests, and devoted many years to the improvement of the estate and the augmentation of its value. He also became engaged in the banking business, and interested in the development of railroad enterprises in the Southwestern States of the Union The building of the St. Louis & Iron Mountain Railroad was largely due to his efforts

In 1851, Mr. Marquand married Elizabeth Love Allen, of Pittsfield, Mass., daughter of Jonathan and Eunice W. Allen, the family being one of prominence in Berkshire County, of that State. Mrs. Marquand's grandfather was the Reverend Thomas Allen, who was born in Northampton, Mass., in 1743, and died in Pittsfield in 1810. Graduated from Harvard College in 1762, he became the first minister of Pittsfield, being ordained in 1764. He was an ardent Revolutionary patriot, and commanded a company at the battle of Bennington, thereby gaining the title of "the fighting parson " He was minister of the church in Pittsfield for forty-six years.

For more than a quarter of a century, Mr Marquand has devoted much of his attention to charitable and religious objects, as well as to the cause of art. He has been prominent in the practical administration of the city's best charities, while among his many gifts for such objects is the new wing added to Bellevue Hospital. He presented the Marquand Chapel to Princeton University and has been a liberal friend to that institution of learning His benefactions, however, have not been confined to any part of the country, and he founded and endowed the Free Library in the city of Little Rock, Ark Mr Marquand has long been one of the foremost of American collectors of painting and objects of art. His handsome private residence in East Sixty-eighth Street, notable for its architectural features, contains one of the most remarkable private art collections in the world. He has devoted unceasing labor to advancing public artistic education, and took the lead in the foundation of the Metropolitan Museum of Art, of which institution he is the honored president, and to which he has been a constant benefactor. He is a member of the Century Association, the Metropolitan, Grolier and Princeton clubs, and of many artistic, literary and charitable institutions, and in recognition of his services to art, is the first honorary member of the American Institute of Architects. His country residence is in Newport

Mr. and Mrs Marquand had six children; Linda, wife of the Reverend Roderick Terry, Allan, Frederick Alexander, Henry, Mabel, who married Henry Galbraith Ward, and Elizabeth Love Marquand, now Mrs. Harold Godwin Professor Allan Marquand, the eldest son, is a graduate of Princeton University, and took the degree of Ph D., at Johns Hopkins University. Devoting himself to art studies, after some years passed in Europe, he accepted the Professorship of Art in Princeton. He has presented the college with valuable artistic collections, and has written much upon art and cognate subjects. He married Eleanor Cross. Henry Marquand, the third son, has taken the place in the banking business vacated by his father's retirement. He married Katharine (Cowdin) Griswold. The second son of the family, Frederick Alexander Marquand, died in 1885.

WILLIAM HENRY MARSTON

MARSTON MOOR, in Yorkshire, the scene of one of the great battles of the English Civil War in the seventeenth century, took its name from an ancient family in that part of England The origin of the surname Marston is Continental rather than Saxon. It is apparently derived from the Latin Martius, signifying one devoted to the service of Mars. When William the Conqueror invaded England, one of his officers of rank bore the name, received estates in the northern part of the kingdom, and founded a family which extended its branches throughout England. Representatives of it were found as far back as five hundred years ago in Worcestershire, Staffordshire and Leicestershire, though the main stock of the race remained in Yorkshire, and it is from it that the American family of Marston traces its descent. The arms which they are entitled to bear are· a blue shield bearing a gold chevron embrasured as battlements between three gold lions' heads crowned and broken off. The crest is also a golden lion's head crowned and with open jaws.

William Marston, the ancestor of Mr William H Marston, and first of his race in America, was born in 1592. He was one of the Puritan emigrants to New England, and arrived at Salem, Mass., in 1634, a widower, bringing four children with him   In 1638, he was one of the original proprietors of Hampton, N. H., and was a Quaker in his belief. His son, Thomas, born in England, in 1617, died at Hampton in 1690, having been a town official in that place. He married Mary Estow in 1647. In the next generation came Ephraim Marston, 1654–1742, followed by Simon Marston, 1683–1735. The latter's son, Daniel Marston, 1708–1757, was an officer of the Colonial forces in the French War, and served in Nova Scotia and at the second siege of Louisburg under Amherst and Wolfe, commanded a company, being killed and buried there. He left a large fortune for those times His sister Sarah was the mother of General Henry Dearborn, of Revolutionary fame, and Commander-in-Chief of the Army of the United States in the War of 1812.

Simon Marston, son of Daniel Marston, became a Captain in the Revolutionary Army and afterwards Major of the State forces. In 1762, he settled on an estate at Deerfield, N. H. His son was Asa Marston, 1758–1834, and his grandson, Captain Eben Marston, born in 1793, also held a military command in Deerfield, represented the town in the New Hampshire Legislature, filled every office in the gift of the community where he lived, and was one of its foremost and most respected citizens. He was the father of the subject of this sketch.

Mr. William Henry Marston was born on the old family homestead at Deerfield in 1832. Educated in academies at his native place, he came in 1851 to New York, when nineteen years old, and engaged in the banking business with the house of Belknap & James. In 1853, he went West to establish banks in Illinois and Wisconsin, and remained there off and on for eight years. He became a partner in the banking house of F. P James & Co., in 1854, and in 1862 founded the firm of William H. Marston & Co , of which he was senior partner, being immediately recognized as the leader in the stock market and as one of the boldest and most successful operators that Wall Street had known at that period. During Mr. Marston's residence in the West, his headquarters were at Springfield, Ill., and Abraham Lincoln was his lawyer and friend. He was also intimate with General John A Logan, while his personal and business associations in New York have included all the prominent men of the times. At present, Mr. Marston is president of the Hopkins Alaska Gold Mining Company, an enterprise which he regards as the most important of the many he has undertaken.

In 1859, Mr Marston married Lila Irwin, daughter of Robert Irwin, a prominent banker of Springfield, Ill., and the most intimate friend of Lincoln in this latter city. Their children are Robert Irwin Marston, born in 1860, who is a graduate of Dartmouth College, and two daughters, Laura Marie and Ella Chase Marston Mr. Marston resides at 112 West Forty-fourth Street, and is a member of the Union Club and other social organizations.

BRADLEY MARTIN

THE family of Mr. Bradley Martin, who has borne so important a part in the social affairs of the metropolis in the present generation, has long been distinguished in the annals of Northern and Central New York, coming originally from old Colonial stock in Connecticut. The name of Martin was adopted as a surname by the English family at an early date, and many of its representatives were prominent in the history of England after the Norman Conquest. John Martin accompanied Sir Francis Drake in that famous seaman's voyage around the world, 1577-80. William Martin, or William Seaborn Martin, the American ancestor of the family, was first of Stratford and then of Woodbury, Conn. Tradition says that his father emigrated from England, and that the son was born on shipboard during the voyage of the family to the New World. His wife was Abigail Curtiss, daughter of Jonathan Curtiss, of Stratford, where she was born, in 1671. She was married in 1685, and died in 1735. His death occurred in 1715. He and his wife were members of the first church in Woodbury from 1685.

Samuel Martin, son of William Martin, was born in 1693, married Annis Hinman in 1716, and had a family of seventeen children. Their son, Nathan Martin, who was born in 1734, married Ellen Bradley, and died in 1794. Bradley Martin, of the next generation, was born in 1782, in Woodbury, and died in Avon, N. Y., in 1825. His wife was Harriet B. Hull, who was born in Salisbury, Conn., in 1785. Their son, Henry Hull Martin, who was born in 1809, studied law and was a prominent citizen of Albany, where he was cashier of the Albany City Bank and president of the Albany Savings Bank. In October, 1835, he married Anna Townsend, daughter of Isaiah Townsend, of the distinguished Townsend family, of Albany. One of the brothers of Anna Townsend was Frederick Townsend, who was born in Albany in 1825, and graduated from Union College in 1844. He was Adjutant-General of the State of New York in 1856, assistant provost marshal in Albany in 1863, Brigadier-General of the National Guard of the State of New York in 1878, and Adjutant-General of the State in the administration of Governor Alonzo B. Cornell. Another brother was Dr. Howard Townsend, of Albany, 1823-1867, a graduate of Union College in 1844, and from the medical department of the University of Pennsylvania in 1847, Surgeon-General of the State, 1851-52, and a professor in the Albany Medical College. Still another brother was Franklin Townsend, at one time Adjutant-General of the State of New York, and otherwise identified with the militia of the State.

Mr. Bradley Martin, son of Henry Hull Martin and Anna Townsend, was born in Albany, December 18th, 1841, and was educated in Union College. He early married Cornelia Sherman, daughter of Isaac Sherman. Isaac Sherman was a wealthy merchant of New York, and a frequent contributor to the daily press and other publications upon the subject of taxation. Three children were born to Mr. and Mrs. Martin. Sherman and Bradley Martin, Jr., and Cornelia Martin, now the Countess of Craven, who was married in Grace Church, New York, April 18th, 1893. The Earl of Craven is the present head of an old and wealthy family of England. The first to bear the name was John Craven, of Appletreewick, Craven, Yorkshire, who lived during the reign of Henry VII. His descendant, William Craven, was knighted in 1626, and later created Baron Craven, of Hampstead, Marshall, County Berks. In 1801, the seventh Baron was made Earl of Craven and Viscount Affington. The present Earl of Craven is the fourth Earl.

Since their marriage, Mr. and Mrs. Martin have given many notable entertainments and have been the hosts of distinguished guests, at their town residence, in West Twentieth Street. They have been present, when in New York, at the balls of the Patriarchs, and guests at the other important functions of society. They have been much abroad, however, and Mr. Martin rents a deer forest at Balmacaun, Scotland. Mr. Martin holds membership in nearly all of the leading clubs of New York, including the Union, Knickerbocker, Racquet, Century, Tuxedo, Metropolitan, Downtown, Σ Φ and Fencers. The arms of the family are: Gules on a chevron, or, three talbots, passant, sable. The crest is, on a globe, or, a falcon rising, argent, gored, with a ducal coronet.

ALBERT MATHEWS

IN the early annals of Westchester County, the name of Mathews is of frequent occurrence, and its possessors in different generations were prominent and influential in the affairs of the county. Mr Albert Mathews, who was born in this city in 1820, descends from the Westchester family, his father being Oliver Mathews, of New York, and his mother, Mary (Field) Mathews, granddaughter of Uriah Field, of Long Island. His paternal grandfather, Daniel Mathews, of Westchester, married Charity Smith, belonging to a family which had also been long identified with that portion of the State, having intermarried with nearly all of other older families of the section in question.

Educated at schools in this city, Mr. Mathews entered Yale, and graduated in 1842, with a high position in his class, having been editor of The Yale Literary Magazine, and a member of the Skull and Bones, and Ψ Τ His devotion to his alma mater and its interests has since been unceasing. He was identified with the organization of the Yale Alumni Association, of New York, and has served as its vice-president, as well as a member of its executive committee, taking always a warm interest in its success. Mr. Mathews' graduation from Yale was followed by a year spent in the law school of the sister university, Harvard, after which he returned to New York, was admitted to the bar, and began his professional career in 1845. He soon became prominent as a lawyer, at a time, too, when the New York bar boasted of such intellectual and forensic talent as that of Ogden Hoffman and Charles O'Connor. The knowledge of the law of equity possessed by Mr. Mathews, the ability with which he managed cases before juries, his skill in cross examination, rather than a declamatory manner of speaking, were leading elements in his success. He quickly acquired a large and lucrative clientage, and, until his virtual retirement from active practice, was retained in many civil actions in the courts. He was a founder of the New York Bar Association, and its vice-president in 1886. In 1849, Mr. Mathews married Louise Mott Strong, daughter of N W. Strong, of this city. His wife dying in 1857, he was married a second time, in 1861, to Cettie Moore Gwynne, daughter of Henry C. Flagg, of New Haven, who died in 1884.

Mr. Mathews' literary activity dates back to his college days, and even when a lawyer in active practice, his love of letters asserted itself Adopting the nom de guerre of "Paul Siegvolk," which he has always retained, he was a frequent contributor to The Knickerbocker Magazine and has contributed to The Home Journal, of this city, almost from its beginning, and for the last eight years continuously. In 1860, he published Walter Ashwood, a novel which exhibited originality and power, and attracted great attention on its appearance He neglected, however, to pursue the field of novel writing, but has continued to produce essays on literary and miscellaneous subjects. In 1879, appeared his first important book, A Bundle of Papers, of which several editions have been published. In 1877, he also published a volume of essays, Ruminations, now in its second edition.

Mr. Mathews is also a graceful poet, having published a brief poem, Nil Desperandum, while A Retrospect, delivered in 1887 at the forty-fifth anniversary of his class, was printed at the request of his classmates. A recent short poem, Lines to an Autumn Leaf, has attracted much attention; while in 1896, a small volume, entitled A Few Verses, from his pen, was printed in a limited edition only, for circulation among friends. In addition, he has written much on legal, economic and political topics, including Incidental Protection a Solecism, Thoughts on the Codification of the Common Law, and many single articles upon a variety of subjects, which have appeared from time to time in the leading periodicals.

Mr. Mathews takes an active interest in the Authors' Club. He joined the Century in 1889, and served as a member of its committees, and is, in addition, a member of the University and Reform clubs, and of the St Nicholas Society. He has spent considerable time in travel, and has visited Europe on several occasions, taking great pleasure in the literary, artistic and scientific worlds of the older countries, in all of which he possesses numerous friends.

CHARLES THOMPSON MATHEWS

ON his father's side, Mr Mathews traces his lineage to one of the oldest Dutch families of New York State His ancestor was Major Dirk Wesselse Ten Broeck, who was born in Holland in 1642 and came to Beverwyck, now Albany, in 1662 In 1686, he was the first Recorder of the city, and Mayor in 1696-8 His wife was Christian Cornelise Van Buren. He was a member of the first Assembly of New York, in 1691. It was this Dutch pioneer whom Washington Irving parodied in Knickerbocker's History. The great-great-grandmother of Mr Mathews was Gertrude Schuyler, and it is through her that he is descended from Mayor Ten Broeck His great-grandmother was Katharine Van Vorhees, of New Brunswick, N J, and his grandmother was Anna Loree, of New York City His grandfather was William Edmund Mathews, nephew and heir of Sir William Saunders, Bart

On his mother's side, Mr Mathews is descended from Francis Newman, Governor of Connecticut in 1660, and from other distinguished families His mother was Rebecca Bacon Thompson, the wife of Charles Drellincourt Mathews, of New York. Her mother was Lydia Bacon, granddaughter of J Bacon, who married Lydia Hungerford, of Farley Castle, England Her father was Charles Chauncey Thompson, of Woodbury, Conn

Through his maternal grandfather, Mr Mathews goes back to Anthony Thompson, who came over in 1637 with Governor Eaton and Dr Davenport and settled at New Haven The grandson of Anthony Thompson, Samuel Thompson, married the daughter of Lieutenant-Governor James Bishop, of Connecticut His great-great-grandson, Hezekiah Thompson, the great-great-grandfather of Mr. Mathews, was a lawyer, paymaster in the French War, and a member of the General Assembly of Connecticut. His son, Charles Thompson, 1780-1817, was a lawyer in New York City, and his grandson, Charles Chauncey Thompson, was one of the merchants of New York in the middle of this century. Through his maternal grandmother, who was second in descent from Lydia Hungerford, Mr. Mathews goes back to the Hungerfords of Farley Castle, England The founder of this family was Walter de Hungerford, of the thirteenth century. His great-grandson, Sir Thomas Hungerford, in the reign of Edward III. was the first Speaker of the House of Commons, and in the next generation Sir Walter Hungerford, in the reign of Henry VI., was Lord High Treasurer At the battle of Agincourt, he made Charles of Orleans prisoner The great-grandson of Sir Walter Hungerford was a member of the Privy Council of Henry VIII Two generations later the head of the family, Sir Edward Hungerford, surnamed "The Spendthrift," squandered his estate, which passed out of the possession of the family. The Hungerford arms were· Sable, two bars argent, in chief, three plates.

Mr Charles T. Mathews was born in Paris, March 31st, 1865 He was educated at St. Paul's School and in Paris and Nice. Graduating from Yale College in 1886, he also studied at the Columbia School of Mines, and was graduated Ph B in 1889 He studied architecture in Paris, exhibited drawings at Chicago at the World's Fair, and is a fellow of the American Institute of Architects He has written extensively upon the subject of art and architecture, his principal works being, The Renaissance under the Valois, a book that is now used at Harvard, Columbia and other universities, and The Story of Architecture, published in 1896.

Mr. Mathews resides at 30 West Fifty-seventh Street, and has a country residence at Norwalk, Conn ; built originally at great expense, it passed into the hands of W. H. Vanderbilt, from whom Mr. Mathews' father purchased it in 1876. The house is laid out upon a large scale and superbly finished. It contains a ball room, theatre, state apartments, picture gallery, and so forth. The porphyry and marbles of the peristyle were brought from Egypt, and the woodwork of the interior is considered the best of its kind in this country. Mr Mathews is a member of the Tuxedo, University, Racquet, Δ Φ and Calumet clubs He has traveled all through Europe, and has also visited China and Japan He has a valuable collection of paintings, including examples of Diaz, Moreau, Tambourini and others, and is also owner of the Latour tapestries.

TITUS BENJAMIN MEIGS

V INCENT MEIGS came from Devonshire, or Dorsetshire, England, about 1640, with his wife and several children. Soon after his arrival, he settled at New Haven, Conn Afterwards he removed to Guilford, Conn , then to East Guilford, and finally to Hammonassett, where he died in 1658 John Meigs, his son, was a resident of East Guilford, being a freeman of that place in 1657, and dying there in 1671 His wife was Tamzin Fry Next in order of descent was John Meigs, 1650-1713, and his wife, Sarah Wilcox Janna Meigs, 1672-1739, son of the second John Meigs, was the first magistrate of East Guilford, Conn , and a deputy to the General Court, 1716-26. His wife was Hannah Willard, of Wethersfield. Captain Jehial Meigs, of East Guilford, 1703-1780, son of Janna Meigs, married Lucy Bartlett, of Lynn, Mass In the next three generations came Elihu Meigs, 1749-1827, and his wife, Elizabeth Rich; Elihu Meigs, 1780-1806, and his wife, Jerusha C. Pratt, and Jabez Pratt Meigs, of Delhi, N. Y., 1805-1881, and his wife, Une Kelsey, of Madison, Conn , whom he married in 1824.

Among the many descendants of Vincent Meigs, the pioneer, who have attained to special renown in the history of the country, none stands more prominent than Return Jonathan Meigs, of Connecticut, who is a collateral ancestor of Mr. Titus Benjamin Meigs. Born in Middletown, Conn , in 1734, he marched to Boston, immediately after the battle of Lexington First assigned to duty with the rank of Major, he was engaged in the assault upon Quebec, being captured there and held a prisoner until the following year In 1777, he was promoted to be Colonel, and led in an attack upon the British at Sag Harbor, Long Island, afterwards commanding a regiment under General Anthony Wayne, at Stony Point.

The son of Colonel Return Jonathan Meigs, also named Return Jonathan Meigs, was another distinguished public man. Born in Middletown, Conn , in 1765, he died in Ohio in 1825 He was a graduate from Yale College in 1785, and studied law, and in 1803 was Chief Justice of the Ohio Supreme Court. Afterwards he was commissioned Lieutenant-Colonel in the United States Army, and placed in charge of the Louisiana District. At the same time, he was Judge of the Supreme Court in 1807, became a Judge of the United States Court of Michigan, was United States Senator from Ohio in 1809, Governor of Ohio in 1810-14, and Postmaster-General of the United States from 1814 to 1823.

Mr. Titus Benjamin Meigs was born in Hobart, N. Y., in 1831. During the greater part of his life he has been engaged in business in New York His wife, whom he married in 1860, was Lucia Jacobs, of Delhi Mrs Meigs is a lineal descendant of William Bradford and Elder Brewster, of the Mayflower Her father, who was a distinguished physician, served in the Civil War as Brigade-Surgeon under Major-General N P Banks Her brother, Ferris Jacobs, Jr , served with distinction during the entire five years of the Civil War, rising from the rank of Captain to that of Brigadier-General. Subsequently he was a Member of Congress

Mr and Mrs Meigs have had five children. Lucia Lasell Meigs married the Reverend Douglas Birnie, of Boston, Mass Titus Benjamin Meigs died in infancy Ferris Jacobs Meigs was graduated from Yale University in the class of 1889, is in business with his father, and is a member of the University, City and other clubs Walter Meigs is a member of the class of 1898, Yale University. Frances Lyman Meigs married, in 1896, Oliver Smith Lyford, Jr , of Pittsburg The home of the family is in East Sixty-fifth Street, near Fifth Avenue, and they have a summer residence, Stag-Head-on-Follensbee, near Axton, N. Y. Mr. Meigs is a member of the City, Barnard and Patria clubs

The ancestral home of the founder of the family is still standing in Dorsetshire. Over its front door the arms of the family are engraved on stone, as follows Or , a chevron, azure, between three mascles, gules, on a chief sable, a greyhound, courant argent. Crest, a talbot's head erased, argent, eared sable, collared, or , below the collar, two pellets fessways, three acorns, erect issuing from the top of head, proper

GEORGE MACCULLOCH MILLER

THE family of Mr. George Macculloch Miller was originally of Scotland. His great-grandfather on his mother's side was an officer in the English Army, who served in India and was killed at Bombay. The maternal grandfather, George P. Macculloch, was brought from India to Scotland when he was only four years of age and was educated in Edinburgh, coming to America nearly a century ago. Mr. Miller's father, the Honorable Jacob W Miller, of New Jersey, was a prominent lawyer and public man during the first half of the present century. He was born at German Valley, Morris County, N J., in 1800, and died in 1862. He became a lawyer and had a very large and remunerative practice. In 1832, he was a member of the State Legislature, in 1839 a State Senator, and from 1841 to 1853 a United States Senator, from his native State Originally a Whig, he became a Republican in 1855 on the slavery question.

Mr. George Macculloch Miller was born in Morristown, N. J., in 1832. Graduated from Burlington College when he was eighteen years of age, he studied law in his father's office and in the Harvard Law School, and in 1853 was admitted to the bar in the States of New York and New Jersey. He became a very successful practitioner and was employed as counsel for many railroad companies and other large corporate and business interests. Out of this grew ultimately his connection with transportation enterprises, and of late years much of his law practice has been for such interests. He is now at the head of the law firm of Miller, Peckham & Dixon, which was established by him, and is one of the oldest and most successful law firms in New York

In 1871, Mr Miller became president of the Newport & Wickford Railroad and Steamship Company, and two years later was elected a director of the New York, Providence & Boston Railroad Company. For ten years, 1879-89, he was president of the Providence & Stonington Steamship Company, his brother succeeding him in that position. For a period of six years, 1881-7, he was also president of the Denver, Utah & Pacific Railroad Company Other extensive and important corporations have also enlisted his services. He was vice-president of the New York, Providence & Boston Railroad Company until its merger with the New York, New Haven & Hartford Railroad Company, and is now president of the Housatonic Railroad Company and a director and one of the executive committee of the New York, New Haven & Hartford Railroad. He is a trustee of the Central Trust Company, of the Bank for Savings and of Greenwood Cemetery.

The activity of Mr. Miller in the cause of religion, education and benevolence has scarcely been less notable than in his professional labors. He has given much of his time and contributed largely of his means to many worthy institutions of the city. A member of the Protestant Episcopal Church, he has for many years been on the standing committee of the diocese of New York When the corporation of the Cathedral of St. John the Divine was chartered, in 1873, Mr. Miller became one of the original trustees and secretary of the corporation, and has done considerable work in connection with the enterprise of building the new cathedral on Cathedral Heights. Mr. Miller was one of the first to suggest this locality as a proper one for the cathedral, and he has also accomplished the locating of St Luke's Hospital there, circumstances which have tended to make that section of the city the centre of religious, scholastic and eleemosynary institutions, and creating and fostering a civic pride therewith, that is highly creditable and advantageous to the city and its progress. He was a trustee and secretary of the corporation of St. Luke's Hospital for over twenty years, 1869-90, and since 1892 has been annually elected its president. He has also been a warden of St Thomas' Episcopal Church for many years. In politics he is a Republican and has been an energetic worker in the cause of honest municipal government.

In 1857, Mr Miller married Elizabeth Hoffman, daughter of Lindley Murray Hoffman, a member of the Hoffman family, distinguished in the public service of New York City and State. His children are Hoffman Miller, who is a lawyer in his father's office, Mary Louisa, wife of William B. McVickar, and Leverett S., Elizabeth and Edith Miller His clubs include the Union League. Century, Union, City and Riding and he is a patron of the Metropolitan Museum of Art.

JOHN BLEECKER MILLER

B Y several lines of descent, Mr. John Bleecker Miller comes from old Knickerbocker and English ancestors In the sixth generation back, Eleazer Miller was a leading citizen in Easthampton, Long Island. Born in 1697, he died in 1788. From 1746 to 1769, he was a member of the New York State Assembly, in 1777 was a member of the General Convention of the State, and was one of the one hundred members of the famous Committee of Safety. Burnet Miller, also of Easthampton, son of Eleazer, 1719-1783, was a member of the Assembly, 1777-83, a member of the Constitutional Convention that met at Kingston in 1777, a Justice of the Peace in 1763, town clerk of Easthampton 1747-76, and Supervisor 1746-77. A son of Burnet Miller was Dr Matthias B Miller, an accomplished and devoted physician, who was born in 1749 and died in 1792, from yellow fever in Savannah, Ga., whither he had gone as a volunteer to help the plague-stricken people Dr Miller was a member of the Constitutional Convention with his father in 1777, belonged to the New York Medical Society and served as a surgeon in the Revolutionary Army throughout the war for independence.

The son of Dr. Burnet Miller and the grandfather of the subject of this sketch was Morris Smith Miller, of Utica, N. Y., who was prominent in the public life of the period in which he lived, 1779-1824. He was graduated from Union College in 1810, became private secretary to Governor John Jay, was a county Judge from 1810 to 1824, and a Member of Congress for one term, 1813-15. John Bleecker Miller, of the next generation, was born in Utica, N. Y., in 1820 and died in France in 1861. Graduated from the Harvard Law School, he became a member of the New York bar and practiced law for many years. For a time he was in the consular service, being the United States Consul to Hamburg, Germany, 1858-61.

Members of this historic family have connected themselves in marriage with other leading and influential families of the State for several generations. Eleazer Miller married Mary Burnet, daughter of Captain Matthias Burnet, niece of the Reverend Abraham Pierson, who was one of the founders and the first president of Yale College, and granddaughter of the Reverend Dr. Pierson, of Yorkshire, England. The wife of Dr. Matthias B. Miller was Phœbe Smith, daughter of Judge Isaac Smith, of Dutchess County, N. Y., and of Margaret Platt, descended from Captain Epenetus Platt, a patentee of Huntington, Long Island, in 1665, from Major Platt, a member of the New York State Assembly, 1723-39, and from Major Thomas Jones, Ranger-General of the Island of Nassau, 1710-13. The mother of John Bleecker Miller, Sr., was Marie Bleecker, daughter of John Rutgers Bleecker, of Albany, and a descendant from James Bleecker, Mayor of Albany in 1700; from Rutgers Bleecker, Mayor of Albany in 1726 and Judge, 1726-33; and as the names indicate, from the Rutgers family also. The wife of the same Mr. Miller, whom he married in 1850, was Cornelia Jones, daughter of Judge Samuel W. Jones, a descendant from the Honorable Samuel Jones, first Comptroller of the State of New York. Miss Jones' mother was Maria Bowers Duane, a descendant from James Duane, who was born in 1733, son of Anthony Duane and Altea Ketteltas. He was a Member of Congress, 1774-83, and Mayor of New York, 1784-87. His wife was a daughter of Robert Livingston, the third Lord of Livingston Manor.

Mr. John Bleecker Miller, the representative of this family in the present generation, was born in Utica, N Y, June 28th, 1856, and was educated in Germany, where he was graduated from the University of Berlin Returning home, he studied law in the Columbia Law School and was admitted to the New York bar. He was one of the founders of the Church Club of New York and is the author of several interesting and valuable sociological treatises, including Trade Organizations in Politics, Trade Organizations in Religion, and Leo XIII. and Modern Civilization. He resides in the old-time fashionable quarter of the city, at 56 West Ninth Street. He is a member of the Reform, Lawyers' and City clubs, the Bar Association, the St. Nicholas Society, the Sons of the Revolution and the American Geographical Society. Mr Miller's wife was Berthenia Stansbury Dunn, daughter of the Reverend Ballard Dunn, of Virginia.

SETH MELLEN MILLIKEN

IN the person of Mr Seth M Milliken, we have another example of that sturdy New England stock that has contributed so much to the growth of New York as the business and financial centre of the United States. Hugh Milliken, his ancestor and the progenitor of a family that has been prominent for two centuries and a half in Maine and Massachusetts, was a Scotchman who emigrated to this country with his family in 1650 and settled in Massachusetts. His sons and grandsons were active business men in the town of Boston, and took part in all the municipal life of the period to which they belonged One of the grandsons of the pioneer, John Milliken, who was born in 1691, married Sarah Burnett, of Boston, and this couple were the founders of the Maine branch of the family. John Milliken purchased a farm in the town of Scarborough, Me., and died there in 1779. The line of descent from John Milliken to the subject of this sketch is through John Milliken, farmer, 1723-1766, and his wife Mrs. Eleanor Sallis, Benjamin Milliken, farmer and tanner, 1764-1818, and his wife, Elizabeth Babbridge; and Josiah Milliken, 1803-1866, who married Elizabeth Freeman. Josiah Milliken, the father of Mr. Seth M. Milliken, was a farmer, tanner and lumber dealer, of Minot and Poland, Me He had a large family, and several of his sons have distinguished themselves by successful business careers. Weston E. Milliken, lumber merchant, banker, president of a steamship company and member of the Maine Legislature; Charles R. Milliken, president of the Portland Rolling Mill and the Poland Paper Company, and Seth M. Milliken, have been most conspicuous. Mrs. Josiah Milliken died in 1890.

Mr. Seth M. Milliken was born in Poland, Me., January 7th, 1836. He was educated in the public schools of Poland and spent three years in the Academy in Hebron, and two years in the Academy in Yarmouth. All this he had accomplished before he had attained to the age of seventeen Then he worked in a flour mill in Minot, Me., for a couple of years, taught school in Portland one winter, and in 1856 started a general country store in the village of Minot When, at the end of five years, he was ready to give up the little store, he had accumulated some capital and a good business experience. With that to start upon, he moved to Portland and went into the wholesale grocery business with his brother-in-law, Daniel W. True Four years later, he entered the firm of Deering, Milliken & Co., wholesale jobbers of dry goods, of Portland, and has kept his connection with that house unbroken for more than thirty years.

In 1867, Mr. Milliken established a branch of the Portland house in New York, and began the commission dry goods business in a small way. In 1873, he moved to the metropolis to take personal charge of that end of the business. He has since become largely interested in the manufacture of cotton and woolen goods, and is the guiding hand in several large manufacturing establishments, being leading owner of the Farnsworth Company, makers of flannels in Lisbon, Me.; president of the Pondicherry Company, woolen manufacturers in Bridgeton, Me.; the Cowan Woolen Manufacturing Company, of Lewiston, Me.; and the Dallas Cotton Manufacturing Company, of Huntsville, Ala.; and a director of the Forest Mills Company, of Bridgeton, Me.; the Lockwood Company, of Waterville, Me.; the Spartan Mills, of Spartanburg, S. C., and the Lockhart Mills, of South Carolina.

In New York Mr. Milliken is connected with important financial enterprises, being a director of the Mercantile National Bank and the Mutual Fire Insurance Company, and interested in other institutions. In 1892, he was a Presidential elector on the Republican ticket, but although an unswerving Republican, he has not generally taken an active interest in public affairs. He belongs to the Union League, Republican, Riding, Merchants', Driving and Suburban clubs, in New York, the Algonquin Club, of Boston, and the Cumberland Club, of Portland, Me. He is a member of the New England Society, and a supporter of the Metropolitan Museum of Art His city residence is in Madison Avenue. In 1874, he married Margaret L. Hill, daughter of Dr L G. Hill, of Dover, N. H. Mrs. Milliken died in 1880, leaving a family of three children, Seth M., Jr., Gerrish H., and Margaret L. Milliken.

DARIUS OGDEN MILLS

FAMILIES bearing the name of Mills came from the north of England, near the Scottish border, at an early date prior to the Revolution. Several of them settled on Long Island, and others in Connecticut. Before long they spread into New York State, and one branch was established in Westchester County a century ago. James Mills, the father of Mr Darius Ogden Mills, was early settled in Dutchess County. He married Hannah Ogden, who came of a Dutchess County family of prominence in the history of the State, and allied to the famous Ogden family of New Jersey. In the early part of the present century, James Mills removed to Westchester County, where he became a representative citizen. For many years he was a leading man in the town of North Salem, being a large landholder, supervisor of the town, postmaster and justice of the peace. His death occurred in 1841. He had six sons and one daughter.

Mr. Darius O Mills, the fifth son of James and Hannah (Ogden) Mills, was born in Westchester County, N Y., September 25th, 1825 He was carefully educated for a business career. In 1841, he commenced life as a clerk in New York, but in 1847, when he was twenty-two years of age, removed to Buffalo, and became cashier of a bank and partner in a business house. When gold was discovered in California, in 1848, he was among those who were attracted by the prospects of the new Eldorado. He left his home in December of that year, and arrived in San Francisco in June, 1849 Engaging in business as a banker and dealer in bullion, he was financially successful before the end of his first year on the Pacific coast. Returning East, he closed out his interests in Buffalo, and in 1850 settled permanently in California, and established in Sacramento the financial institution of D. O. Mills & Co. In 1864, in association with other business men of San Francisco, he organized the Bank of California, of which he became president, and which under his management was the largest institution of the State, and one of the best known in the country. He resigned that position in 1873, but in 1875 was called again to the presidency to rescue the bank from the ruin which had been brought upon it by his successors in the management. He retired permanently from active business on the Pacific coast in 1878.

In 1880, Mr. Mills was able to carry out his long cherished plan of returning to the East and making New York his residence. He transferred many of his interests to this city, and since that time has been financially and socially identified with New York. He still, however, retains an interest in many business enterprises in California. In this city one of his large investments is the splendid Mills Building in Broad Street, which is the headquarters of many of the most important corporations in the East. He is also the owner of a similar building in San Francisco.

While in California he manifested a deep and practical interest in matters concerning the higher education and literary advancement of the community, and was regent and treasurer of the University of California. He gave seventy-five thousand dollars to endow a professorship in the University, and has also been a generous contributor to the cause of public education in other directions. He was one of the trustees of the Lick estate, and aided materially in starting the great Lick Observatory on Mount Hamilton. In New York his benefactions have been generous, including among others the founding of the Training School for Male Nurses near Bellevue Hospital, and he has also given generously to the support of other philanthropic undertakings.

In 1854, Mr Mills married Jane T. Cunningham, daughter of James Cunningham, of New York. His son, Ogden Mills, is a graduate from Harvard College, in the class of 1878, and is active in the management of the Mergenthaler Linotype Company. He married Miss Livingston, daughter of Maturin Livingston, and lives in East Sixty-ninth Street. He is a member of the Metropolitan, Union League and other clubs. Elizabeth Mills, daughter of Mr. D. O. Mills, married the Honorable Whitelaw Reid The Mills residence is in upper Fifth Avenue, and they also have a large country place in California. Mr. Mills is a member of the Metropolitan, Union League, Union and Knickerbocker clubs, and is a trustee of the Metropolitan Museum of Art and the American Museum of Natural History.

ROBERT SHAW MINTURN

IDENTIFIED as it has been for five generations with what is best, both socially and intellectually in the community, the Minturn family holds a leading position in the City of New York. William Minturn, the elder, was during the Colonial days a shipping merchant of Newport, R. I., whence he removed to New York and became one of those who gave to this city the commercial eminence it first began to enjoy in the period directly following the Revolutionary War. His wife was Penelope Greene, a cousin of the famous General Nathaniel Greene, of the Continental Army. Their son, William Minturn, Jr., also became a leading ship-owner, married a daughter of Robert Bowne, one of the most prominent and respected New York merchants of that day, and was the father of Robert Bowne Minturn, an honored philanthropist and the founder of some of the noblest works of charity the metropolitan city possesses.

Robert Bowne Minturn became associated in business with the old-time New York merchant Preserved Fish, who was for many years one of the financial powers of the growing metropolis. In 1829, the firm name was changed to Grinnell, Minturn & Co., the famous brothers, Moses H. and Henry Grinnell, and Robert B. Minturn being equal partners in the establishment. The Grinnells came from New Bedford, Mass., being the sons of Cornelius Grinnell, a prominent merchant of that place. The firm of Grinnell, Minturn & Co., it can safely be said, held for a long period the unquestioned reputation of being the foremost shipping house in America, and up to 1861 sent by far more ships upon the ocean under the American flag than any firm in the country. Apart, however, from its enormous and successful commercial transactions with all parts of the world, it gained additional fame from the wide charities of Mr. Minturn and the liberality of his partner and brother-in-law, Henry Grinnell, who despatched to the Arctic regions the two expeditions in search of Sir John Franklin with which the name of Dr Elisha Kent Kane, the American explorer, is imperishably connected.

Robert B. Minturn was, as already stated, deeply interested in all charitable works. Among other instances of his philanthropy, he was one of the originators and the first treasurer of the New York Association for Improving the Condition of the Poor, and the establishment of St. Luke's Hospital, of which he was the first president, was largely due to his efforts and the financial aid which he gave it. He was also one of the founders of the Hospital for the Relief of the Ruptured and Crippled and served as its vice-president, being, in addition, closely identified with a great variety of other philanthropic and charitable works. His residence, at Fifth Avenue and Twelfth Street, was in that day the scene of a cordial and refined hospitality, and his wife, a daughter of Judge John Lansing Wendell, of Albany, was noted for her high intelligence and personal charm. The agitation for the establishing of Central Park was initiated by her, and carried to success by her husband and the friends whose interest in the plan she had aroused and inspired.

Their eldest son, Robert Bowne Minturn, Jr., graduated at Columbia College and was a man of high character and wide cultivation. He inherited both his father's philanthropic interest and business capacity and was a figure in the social, political, scholarly and financial life of the city. He married Susanna, daughter of the late Francis George Shaw, of Boston. One of Mrs. Minturn's sisters became the wife of George William Curtis, the renowned orator and man of letters, and her only brother was Colonel Robert Gould Shaw, the gallant young soldier, killed while leading the assault on Fort Wagner, and whose death is commemorated by the Shaw monument at Boston. Robert B. Minturn, Jr., died suddenly during the winter of 1889, while still in the prime of life.

Mr. Robert Shaw Minturn, the eldest son of Robert B. Minturn, Jr., is a graduate of Harvard University and of the Law School of Columbia College. He is a member of the bar of this city and is unmarried, residing with his mother and sisters in Gramercy Park.

EDWARD MITCHELL

THROUGH his paternal grandmother, the Honorable Edward Mitchell is descended from one of the first settlers upon the Island of Manhattan. An ancestor, Peter Anderson, received a grant of land in the city of New Amsterdam, in 1645. His son, Peter Anderson, was born here, in 1669, and the granddaughter of Peter Anderson, Cornelia Anderson, was the mother of Judge William Mitchell, Justice of the Supreme Court, and was the grandmother of the Honorable Edward Mitchell. The latter's paternal grandfather was the Reverend Edward Mitchell, who was a native of Coleraine, Ireland. He emigrated to this country, in 1791, and went to Philadelphia. After a few years, he removed to New York, where he remained until his death, in 1834. He was earnest in the cause of religion, and for many years was pastor of the Society of United Christians. The church of which he was rector is still standing, on Duane Street, east of Broadway.

The Honorable William Mitchell, son of the Reverend Edward Mitchell, was a leading lawyer of his time He was born in New York, February 24th, 1801, and died in 1886. He was prepared for college under the instruction of Joseph Nelson, and, entering Columbia, was graduated from that institution, in the class of 1820, taking the first honor. In 1823, his alma mater conferred upon him the degree of M. A., and in 1863, the degree of LL. D. After completing his college course, he entered upon the study of law, devoting himself especially to equity jurisprudence. He was admitted to practice in 1823, became solicitor in Chancery in 1824, counselor at law in 1826, and counselor in Chancery in 1827. An appointment as Master in Chancery came to him in 1840, and in 1849 he became a Justice of the Supreme Court, for the First Judicial District of the State. During the year 1856, he was a Judge of the Court of Appeals, and in 1857, was made the presiding Judge of the Supreme Court Judge Mitchell edited an edition of Blackstone's Commentaries with reference to American cases, a work of much learning.

The mother of the Honorable Edward Mitchell, who was married to Judge William Mitchell, in 1841, was Mary P. Berrian, of New York. Her father was of the old Berrian family, of Long Island. Cornelius Jansen Berrian, who was the American ancestor of the family, was a Huguenot, a native of the village of Berrien, in Finistere. Driven from his native land by religious persecution, he came to this country and settled on Long Island, in 1670.

When Judge Mitchell died he left six children Several of the sons have become well-known lawyers in this generation. The Honorable Edward Mitchell, the eldest son of the family, was born in New York City, in 1842. He graduated from Columbia College and the Columbia Law School, and had not completed his studies when the Civil War broke out. Leaving his books, he went into the service of the Sanitary Commission, his work taking him over the principal battle fields of Virginia and the West. After the war he returned to his studies and was admitted to the bar, forming a law partnership with his father and several of his brothers, and since that time has been in active practice

A prominent member of the Bar Association of the City of New York, he was for eleven years treasurer of that organization, until pressure of business compelled him to decline further reëlection. In 1879, he was elected a member of the Assembly, from the Twenty-first District in the City of New York. In 1883, and again in 1886, he was the candidate of the Republican party for a Supreme Court Judgeship. Since 1880, he has been a trustee of Columbia College, and of the College of Physicians and Surgeons. In 1889, President Harrison appointed him District Attorney of the Southern District of New York, and he held that position until 1893. He was appointed a Park Commissioner by Mayor Strong in 1897.

Mr. Mitchell holds a prominent social and professional position. He was one of the incorporators of the University Club, and is a member of the Century, Metropolitan, Union League, Riding, Tuxedo, and other clubs, and of the American Geographical Society. He married Caroline C. Woolsey, and has one daughter, Elsie Mitchell. His city home is at 31 East Fiftieth Street

CLEMENT CLARKE MOORE

FEW American men or letters hold a more honorable position than the Right Reverend Benjamin Moore, who was president of Columbia College from 1801 until 1811. Bishop Moore, who was the great grandfather of Captain Clement Clarke Moore, was distinguished both as a clergyman and an educator. He was born in Newtown, L. I., in 1748, and received his education at King's, afterwards Columbia, College. Having studied theology for several years, he went to England to be ordained to the Episcopal ministry Returning to this country, he became assistant minister of Trinity Church, and succeeded the Reverend Dr. David Provoost, as rector, in 1800. The following year, he was elected Bishop of New York. He died in Greenwich Village, then a suburb of New York City, in 1816. He was a man of high scholarship, and possessed both dignity and gentleness of character. He held at one time the offices of rector of Trinity Church, bishop of New York, and president of Columbia College, performing the duties of all these positions in a wholly satisfactory manner. He was also the first vice-president of the New York Historical Society, from the organization of that body in 1805. In 1778, he married Charity Clark, daughter of Captain Clement Clark.

Bishop Moore belonged to an old Colonial family of Long Island. He was the great-grandson of Samuel Moore, who, in 1662, was a grantee of land in Newtown, Long Island, and held various public offices, being a magistrate for many years up to his death, in 1717 His wife was Mary Reed, who died in 1738. The great-great-grandfather of Bishop Moore was the Reverend John Moore, one of the settlers of Newtown, in 1652. He was the first minister of Newtown, and was ordained in New England.

William Moore, of New York, 1754–1824, a brother of the Right Reverend Benjamin Moore, graduated in medicine from Edinburgh University, in 1780. Returning to the United States, he practiced his profession for over forty years. He was president of the New York Medical Society, trustee of the College of Physicians and Surgeons, and a vestryman of Trinity Church. He married Jane Fish, daughter of Nathaniel Fish, and among his children were Nathaniel F. Moore, who became president of Columbia College, Maria Theresa Moore, who married Henry C. de Rham; Dr. Samuel W. Moore; Jane Moore, who married Henry Major; Sarah Moore, who married Edward Hodges, and William Moore, of the firm of de Rham & Moore.

Clement Clarke Moore, the grandfather of Captain Clement C. Moore, was the son of Bishop Moore, born in New York, in 1779, and graduated from Columbia College in 1798. Although he was educated for the ministry, he never took orders, but devoted himself to the study of Oriental and classical literature The ground upon which the General Theological Seminary stands, in Ninth Avenue, was given by him to the trustees of that institution, in which he became professor of Biblical learning, and afterwards of Oriental and Greek literature, holding the chair for nearly thirty years, and becoming professor emeritus in 1851. He was the author of a Hebrew and Greek Lexicon, edited a volume of his father's sermons, and wrote much in lighter vein. He died in Newport, R. I., in 1863.

Benjamin Moore, the eldest son of Clement C. Moore, was the father of the subject of this article. He was born in 1815, married Mary Elizabeth Sing, in 1842, and died in 1886. He was devoted to a country life, being a keen sportsman, a lover of floriculture, and a student of natural history. He lived on an estate a little above Sing Sing, on the Hudson, given to him by his father.

Captain Clement Clarke Moore was born at his father's country home in 1843. He was educated at Churchill's school, in Sing Sing. During the Civil War he was Captain in a Massachusetts regiment, and was present at the operations against Richmond, and the surrender of Lee. In 1879, Captain Moore married Laura M. Williams, daughter of William S Williams. The three living sons of this marriage are William Scoville, Barrington and Benjamin Moore. Captain Moore resides in East Fifty-fourth Street, and has a house in Newport. He is a member of the United Service club, and of the Loyal Legion.

WILLIAM HENRY HELME MOORE

COMING from a family that had long been settled in Suffolk, on the western shore of England, bordering upon the North Sea, Thomas Moore, who was born about 1615, was the earliest ancestor of the family to which Mr. William Henry Helme Moore belongs. Before he was twenty years of age, he married Martha Youngs, daughter of the Reverend Christopher Youngs, Vicar of Reydon, Suffolk County, England. Landing in New England about 1636, he first resided in Salem, Mass, but shortly removed with others of his countrymen to Long Island, in that district which they named Suffolk County, after the ancient home of their ancestors across the sea.

Thomas Moore became one of the most prominent citizens of Southold, the largest tax payer there, and frequently a representative to the General Court. In 1662, he became the owner of a large tract of land, bordering on the Sound, just northwest of the present village of Greenport, and there has been the homestead of his descendants for the last two hundred and thirty-five years. When the Dutch reobtained possession of New York in 1673 by expelling the English, they offered Thomas Moore the magistracy of Southold as part of their plan to unite the territory of Long Island to the new government. But, loyal to the English rule, he declined to hold the position. In 1683, being a chief officer of the town, he was one of the committee appointed to select a representative to the first legislative assembly of the Province. He died in 1691.

The father of Mr. William Henry Helme Moore was Colonel Jeremiah Moore, a direct descendant from Thomas Moore, the pioneer. His mother was Julia Brush, of Smithtown, L. I. She was descended from the Reverend George Phillips, of Brookhaven, L. I., son of the Reverend Samuel Phillips, a graduate from Harvard College in 1650, and pastor of the Church in Rowley, Mass., until 1695 The father of the Reverend Samuel Phillips was the Reverend George Phillips, who, born in Rainham, England, in 1593, and graduated from Cambridge University, was one of the company that was brought from England by Sir Richard Saltonstall, and founded the town of Watertown, Mass., in 1630. Colonel Jeremiah Moore and his wife, Julia Brush, had three sons and three daughters. The eldest son was Charles B. Moore, who was born in 1808, was an eminent lawyer, associated at one time with Francis B. Cutting, and was also a master in chancery. He also had high standing as a genealogist, and was a vice-president of the New York Genealogical and Biographical Society. His wife was Frances Maria Jones, daughter of John H. Jones, of Cold Spring Harbor, Long Island. The second son was Jeremiah Moore, and the third was William H. H. Moore. The eldest daughter of the family, Frances Maria Moore, married the Reverend William Hunting. The other two daughters were Mary Adaline and Julia Moore.

Mr. William Henry Helme Moore was born in Sterling, Suffolk County, Long Island, in 1824. He was prepared for college at the Miller's Place Academy in his native town, and matriculated at Union College in 1840, graduating four years later. He began the study of law with his brother, Charles B. Moore. Admitted to the bar in 1847, he soon found himself most interested in that branch of his profession relating to the adjustment of marine losses. His devotion to that speciality led to his engagement with the Atlantic Mutual Insurance Company, of which he became the third executive officer, and was for thirty years its second vice-president, in 1886 becoming the first vice-president, and in 1895 president He was also president of the Life Saving Benevolent Association, the Workingmen's Protective Union, and the New York Port Society, a trustee of the Seamen's Bank, a director of the Atlantic Trust Company, and the Phœnix National Bank, and one of the vice-presidents of the American Geographical Society. Since 1882, he has been a trustee of Union College, and in 1890 was president of the Union College Alumni Association of New York. For more than twenty-five years a member of the Union League Club, he is also a member of the Reform Club and the Bar Association. Mr Moore married Adelaide L. Lewis. His residence is in West Seventy-second Street, and he has a country home at the ancestral seat of the family in Greenport, Long Island.

EDWIN DENISON MORGAN

FEW families have borne a more honorable part in public and business life in New England and elsewhere in the country than the Morgans They are descended from two brothers, who came from Wales in the early years of the seventeenth century and settled in Massachusetts, James Morgan and Captain Miles Morgan. The ancestor of that branch of the family, which has been conspicuously represented in the present generation by New York's great war Governor, Edwin D Morgan, the grandfather of Mr. Edwin Denison Morgan, was James Morgan, 1607-1685 He arrived in this country in 1636, lived in Roxbury, Mass., for several years, was one of the early settlers of Groton, Conn , a selectman of New London and one of the first deputies to the Connecticut General Court. His wife was Margery Hill, of Roxbury, Mass The line of descent to Governor Morgan, from James Morgan, was through John Morgan, 1644-1712, and his second wife, the widow Elizabeth Williams, daughter of Lieutenant-Governor William Jones; William Morgan, 1693-1729, and his wife, Mary Avery, daughter of Captain James Avery, of Groton, Conn ; Captain William Morgan, 1723-1777, and his wife, Temperance Avery, daughter of Colonel Christopher Avery and great-granddaughter of Captain James Avery; Captain William Avery, 1754-1842, who fought at Bunker Hill, and Jasper Morgan, who, born in 1783, was the father of Governor Morgan The wife of Jasper Morgan was Catharine (Copp) Avery, 1775-1822, widow of Jasper Avery, of Groton.

Governor Edwin Denison Morgan was born in Washington, Mass , in 1811, and died in New York in 1883 He engaged in mercantile life, at the age of seventeen, in Hartford. In 1836, he removed to New York, where he was soon established in business on his own account In 1843, he founded the firm of E D. Morgan & Co He became one of the great merchants of New York, and in the latter part of his life confined himself almost entirely to the banking business

Even more prominent in public life than in the business world, Mr. Morgan began his public career as a member of the City Council of Hartford, when he was only twenty-one years of age. He was an assistant alderman in New York in 1849, and a member of the New York Senate, 1850-53 In 1856, he was vice-president of the National Convention of his party, in Philadelphia, and chairman of the Republican National Committee for the ensuing eight years. He was Commissioner of Immigration, 1855-58, and United States Senator from New York, 1863-69. Governor of the State of New York, 1859-62, he rendered signal service to the Union cause. He was confirmed as Secretary of the Treasury in the Cabinet of President Arthur, but declined the appointment He was connected with many business enterprises, was governor and president of the Woman's Hospital, and for eight years vice-president of the American Tract Society. He built a dormitory for Williams College, contributed generously to the Union Theological Seminary, the Presbyterian Hospital and other institutions, and by his will bequeathed about seven hundred and fifty thousand dollars to public purposes The wife of Governor Morgan, whom he married in 1833, was Eliza Matilda Waterman, daughter of Captain Henry Waterman, of Hartford. He had several children, but only one of them survived, his son, Dr Edwin D Morgan, who was born in 1834 and died in 1881.

Mr Edwin Denison Morgan is the only surviving son of Dr. Edwin D Morgan. His mother was Sarah Elizabeth Archer, daughter of Thomas and Lucy Archer, of Suffield, Conn. He was born in New York, and graduated from Harvard College in the class of 1877 and is engaged in the banking business. He married Elizabeth Moran Devoting much time to gentlemanly sports, he is a member of the New York Yacht, Eastern Yacht, Atlantic Yacht, Coaching, Rockaway Hunt, Meadow Brook Hunt and Westminster Kennel clubs. His literary and social clubs and organizations include the Metropolitan, Tuxedo, Union League, Knickerbocker and Union clubs, the Sons of the Revolution, the National Academy of Design and the American Geographical Society He has a country estate, Wheatly, at Westbury Station, Long Island, and a cottage in Newport

JOHN PIERPONT MORGAN

POSSESSING an international reputation as a financier, Mr. Morgan is also to be considered as one of the best types of citizenship of our Republic. A New Englander by birth, he retains all the moral fibre which distinguished the Puritans. His family is one which from the first settlement of Western Massachusetts took a place of prominence in the Colony. Its founder, Miles Morgan, 1615-1699, arrived in Boston in 1636 and was one of the company, under the leadership of William Pynchon, which founded Springfield, Mass. In the allotment of lands, Miles Morgan received a plot on which he built a homestead that remained in the possession of his descendants until 1845. About 1643, he married Prudence Gilbert, of Beverly. Mass., and after her death he espoused Elizabeth, daughter of Thomas Bliss, of Springfield. The only son of this marriage, Nathaniel Morgan, 1671-1752, married Hannah Bird, their son being Joseph Morgan, born in 1702, whose wife was Mary Stebbins. The next in the line of Mr. J. Pierpont Morgan's descent was Captain Joseph Morgan, born in 1736, who married Experience Smith in 1765. His son, Joseph Morgan, 1780-1847, was for many years engaged in business in Hartford, Conn., and married Sarah Spencer, of Middletown, Conn.

Junius Spencer Morgan, their son and Mr. J. Pierpont Morgan's father, was born at Holyoke, Mass., in 1813. He began his eminently successful business career at an early age, becoming a merchant in Hartford and later in Boston. In 1854, he removed to London and was a partner of George Peabody, the famous Anglo-American philanthropist, founding in 1864, when Mr. Peabody retired, the banking house of J S Morgan & Co. His death occurred in Nice, France, in 1890, as the result of an accident, ending a life which had been wholly useful and patriotic. His activity as a layman in the affairs of the Protestant Episcopal Church was noteworthy and, among other institutions, Trinity College, Hartford, Conn., owes much to his munificence.

His wife, Juliet Pierpont, whom he married in 1836, was also of the best New England stock, while her English ancestry was a notable one. The progenitor of the Pierpont family was Sir Robert de Pierrepont, a commander in the army of William the Conqueror, who became the first Lord of the Manor of Hurst Pierrepont, in Yorkshire, his lineal representatives in successive generations holding a distinguished place in the landed aristocracy of England. Robert Pierrepont, the grandson of Sir George Pierrepont, in the seventeenth century, became the first Earl of Kingston-upon-Hull, the title being subsequently merged in that of the Dukes of Kingston, which was extinguished on the death without issue of Evelyn Pierrepont, the second duke, in 1773. William Pierrepont, a younger son of Sir George Pierrepont, was the father of James Pierepont, who died in Ipswich, Mass., in 1648, and grandfather of the Honorable John Pierepont, 1617-1682, of Roxbury, Mass. The latter's son was the Reverend James Pierpont, 1659-1714, a famous divine, who became pastor of the church at New Haven in 1685 and was one of the three ministers to whom the foundation of Yale College was due, and who, indeed, suggested it, thus reviving a plan of the Reverend John Davenport, the founder of New Haven. His third wife was Mary Hooker, granddaughter of the Reverend Thomas Hooker, the famous Puritan minister who led the migration of his flock from Newtown, now Cambridge, Mass., to Hartford, in 1636, and their son, James Pierpont, 1694-1776, graduated at Saybrook (afterwards Yale) College in 1718 and married Anna Sherman. Their son, another James Pierpont, 1761-1840, married Elizabeth Collins.

The Reverend John Pierpont, the poet, clergyman and patriot, who was Mr. Morgan's grandfather, was the son of James and Elizabeth (Collins) Pierpont and was born at Litchfield, Conn., in 1785, dying in 1866. He graduated at Yale College in 1804 and became a lawyer, but in 1819 was ordained a clergyman. Among his first charges was the pastorate of the Hollis Street Unitarian Congregation of Boston, but the earnestness of his views on slavery and temperance led to his relinquishing this post. He subsequently occupied pulpits in Troy, N. Y., and other cities, and at the beginning of the Civil War felt impelled, despite his advanced age, to enter the army as chaplain of a Massachusetts regiment, though he was soon compelled to retire. Shining as an orator, he also took a high rank among American poets of the past generation, many of his works, among them Airs of Palestine, obtaining a wide circulation He married his cousin, Mary Sheldon Lord, in 1810, their daughter, Juliet Pierpont, being born at Baltimore, Md , in 1816.

Mr. John Pierpont Morgan is the only son of Junius Spencer and Juliet (Pierpont) Morgan and was born in Hartford, Conn , April 17th, 1837 Educated at Boston and Gottingen, Germany, he returned to the United States in 1857 and entered the banking business with Duncan, Sherman & Co , of New York In 1860, he became attorney in America for George Peabody & Co , of London, and in 1864 was partner in Dabney, Morgan & Co In 1871, the famous banking house of Drexel, Morgan & Co was formed, which in 1895 was changed to the style of J P. Morgan & Co On the death of his father, Mr Morgan also became the head of the firm of J S. Morgan & Co , of London, and usually spends a portion of each year in that city

It is scarcely germane to our purpose to dwell upon Mr Morgan's eminence as a banker and financier. Indeed, the facts in this connection are too well known to require detailed mention Acknowledgment must, however, be made of his services to the country in 1894 and 1895, when, largely by his efforts, the credit of the United States Treasury was protected, while the many great corporations he has restored to solvency have made his labors a matter of national importance

In early life, Mr Morgan married Amelia Sturges, daughter of Jonathan and Mary (Cady) Sturges, of New York, who died soon after In 1865, he contracted a second matrimonial alliance, with Frances Louisa Tracy, daughter of Charles Tracy, 1810-1885, who graduated from Yale College in 1832 and was a leading member of the New York bar, and whose wife, Louisa Kirkland, was the daughter of General Joseph Kirkland, of Utica, N Y. The Tracy family possesses a notable ancestry Mrs Morgan's grandfather was William Gedney Tracy, born at Norwich, Conn , in 1768, who settled at Whitesbough, N Y , and married Rachael Huntington, of Norwich. His grandfather, Joseph Tracy, 1706-1787, for many years a town official of Norwich, was the son of Captain Joseph Tracy, 1682-1765, of Norwich, which town he frequently represented in the Connecticut Legislature He was the son of Captain John Tracy, 1642-1702, one of the original proprietors of Norwich, who in 1670 married Mary Winslow, daughter of Josiah Winslow and niece of Governor Edward Winslow, one of the Mayflower emigrants. Lieutenant Thomas Tracy, his father, who came to Salem, Mass , about 1636 and was also an original proprietor of Norwich, Conn., was the son of Nathaniel Tracy, of Tewksbury, England, and grandson of Richard Tracy, of Stanway, and his wife, Barbary Lucy, daughter of Thomas Lucy, of Charlecote, near Stratford-on-Avon, Warwickshire Richard Tracy was High Sheriff of Gloucestershire, and a cadet of the Tracy, or de Traci, family of Todington, whose representatives in the middle ages were repeatedly sheriffs of Gloucestershire and held other high office.

Mr and Mrs. Morgan have four children. Their only son, John Pierpont Morgan, Jr., born in 1867, graduated from Harvard University in the class of 1889 and is engaged in the banking business with his father In 1891, he married Jane Norton Grew, of Boston, and has a son, Junius Spencer Morgan, born in 1892. The three daughters of Mr. and Mrs Morgan are Louisa Pierpont, Juliet Pierpont, the wife of W Pierson Hamilton, and Anne Tracy Morgan The burdens of business do not prevent Mr. Morgan from enjoying the social side of life He is a member of the leading clubs, was one of the founders and president of the Metropolitan Club and is commodore of the New York Yacht Club. He also takes an active interest in many charitable organizations, is a warden of St George's Church and has several times been a lay delegate from this diocese to the general conventions of the Protestant Episcopal Church. The family residence is in Madison Avenue, and his country seat is Cragston, at Highland Falls, N. Y. The three sisters of Mr J P Morgan were Sarah Spencer, Mary Lyman and Juliet Pierpont Morgan The first named, born in 1839, married George Hale Morgan, in 1866, and died in 1896 Their children are Junius Spencer Morgan, who married Josephine Adams Perry, George D. Morgan and Caroline L Morgan Mary Lyman Morgan, born in 1844, married, in 1867, Walter H. Burns, who was a member of the firm of J S Morgan & Co , of London, until his death in November, 1897 Juliet Pierpont Morgan, born in 1847, married the Reverend John B Morgan, rector of the American Episcopal Church in Paris, France

AUGUSTUS NEWBOLD MORRIS

AMONG the great landowners of New Netherland, in the seventeenth century, were members of the Morris family. Originally of Welsh blood, the family was descended from the great chieftain Rhys, or Rice, Fitzgerald, brother to Rhys, Prince of Geventland In 1171, in company with Richard de Clare, known as Strongbow, he took part in the Anglo-Norman conquest of Ireland, and for his valiant deeds was called Maur Rhys, that is, the great Rys In the course of time, his descendants proudly held to this title, which eventually became transformed into Morris. The arms of the family are: Gules, a lion, rampant, reguardant or , quarterly with three torteauxes, argent, the crest is a castle in flames

William Morris, of Tintern, Monmouthshire, England, was the father of the two sons who became identified with this country. The elder son, Colonel Lewis Morris, inherited an estate in England, but emigrated to the West Indies in 1662, and came to New York in 1674 His brother, Richard, who had been a Captain in Cromwell's army and later a merchant in Barbadoes, preceded him to this country and bought a large plantation north of the Bronx River, part of the property of Joseph Bronck, or Bronx, a Hollander who had settled there and acquired possession from the Indians The property was in part confiscated by the Dutch when they temporarily repossessed the Colony in 1673, but Colonel Morris, coming from Barbadoes, regained possession of it for himself and for his young nephew, Lewis Morris, the only son of his brother Richard, who had in the meantime died Colonel Morris was a member of Governor Dongan's council, 1683-86, and when he died, in 1691, his nephew, Lewis Morris, succeeded to the entire estate

In 1697, Governor Fletcher confirmed to the younger Lewis Morris the grant made by Governor Andros to his uncle, and erected the lands into a lordship or manor under the name of Morrisania. This tract of land included some nineteen hundred acres Lewis Morris was born in 1672, and was in many ways a remarkable man. He was the first native born Chief Justice of the Supreme Court of New York, a Judge of East New Jersey in 1692, Governor of New Jersey, 1738-46, and was prominent in all the difficulties attending the administrations of the early Colonial Governors, Cornbury, Hamilton, Lovelace, Ingoldsby, Hunter, Cosby, Montgomerie and Burnet He died in 1746 and was succeeded by Lewis Morris, second of the name, his son by his wife, Isabella Graham, daughter of Sir James Graham, Attorney-General of the Province of New York. The second Lewis Morris, 1698-1762, was several times a member of the Colonial Assembly, and was also Judge of the Court of Admiralty and of the Court of Oyer and Terminer. Among his children were several of the most famous men of the Revolutionary period, including, as they did, General Lewis Morris, a signer of the Declaration of Independence, the Honorable Richard Morris, Judge of the High Court of Admiralty, and the Honorable Gouverneur Morris, Minister to France in 1792. Among his grandchildren were Colonel Lewis Morris, aide to General Nathaniel Greene, General Jacob Morris and Commodore R V Morris, of the United States Navy

Mr. Augustus Newbold Morris is descended from General Lewis Morris His grandfather, James Morris, was the fourth son of the General, while his grandmother was a member of the Van Cortlandt family, of Yonkers His father, William H. Morris, who was born in 1810, was the tenth child of the family His first wife was Hannah Newbold, daughter of Thomas Newbold, of New York, and the subject of this sketch is the only surviving son of their family of five children. Mr. Morris was born June 3d, 1838, and was graduated from Columbia College in 1860. He has traveled extensively in Europe and the East. His attention has been largely taken up with caring for his estates, but he has devoted much time to charitable undertakings, being on the board of management of many benevolent institutions. His former home in Pelham, now part of New York's park system, was one of the most beautiful country places in the vicinity of the city He has a city residence in East Sixty-fourth Street, and belongs to the Metropolitan and Union clubs He married Eleanor C. Jones, daughter of General James I Jones. His son, Newbold Morris, married Helen S. Kingsland.

HENRY LEWIS MORRIS

CONSPICUOUS above most families in the number of eminent sons that it has contributed to the public service of their country, has been the Morris family of Mornsania. The origin and the early American history of the family have been given on the preceding page of this volume. That branch of which Mr. Henry Lewis Morris is the prominent representative in the present generation, is derived from Lewis Morris, signer of the Declaration of Independence. The second Lewis Morris, 1698–1762, was twice married, first to Catharine Staats, daughter of Dr Samuel Staats, and again to Sarah Gouverneur, daughter of Nicholas Gouverneur. By both wives, he was the father of sons who became preëminently distinguished. His elder son, by his wife, Catherine Staats, was Lewis Morris, signer of the Declaration of Independence, and a Major-General in the Revolution. His second son, Staats Long Morris, adhered to the cause of the crown in the Revolution, and returning to England, married Lady Catherine Gordon, daughter of the Earl of Aberdeen, and widow of the Duke of Gordon, and became a General in the British Army. His third son, the Honorable Richard Morris, was Chief Justice of New York, 1779–90.

General Lewis Morris married Mary Walton, daughter of Jacob Walton and Maria Beekman, who died in 1794. Their sixth son was Commodore Richard Valentine Morris, who was a Captain in the navy in 1798, commanded the Mediterranean Squadron in 1802, and died in New York in 1815. Commodore Morris was the grandfather of Mr. Henry Lewis Morris. His first wife was Anne Walton, daughter of Jacob Walton and Mary Cruger, who was a daughter of Henry Cruger, Sr. By her he had three sons, Gerard W., Richard V., and Henry Morris. Henry Morris, the third son, married Mary N. Spencer, daughter of the Honorable John C. Spencer, Secretary of War and of the Treasury, under President John Tyler. Mr. Henry Lewis Morris, who was born August 8th, 1845, is the eldest son of Henry Morris and his wife, Mary N. Spencer. He married, in 1868, Anna R Russell, daughter of Archibald Russell and Helen Rutherfurd Watts, and granddaughter of Dr John Watts and Anna Rutherfurd. Through both her grandfather and her grandmother, who were cousins, Mrs. Morris is descended from the Rutherfurd and Watts families, who have been conspicuous in the annals of New York. Her grandfather was the son of Robert Watts and Mary Alexander, and a grandson of John Watts, member of the King's Council of New York, and also of Major-General William Alexander, Lord Stirling, of the American Army, by his wife, Sarah Livingston, daughter of Philip Livingston, second Lord of the Manor. The grandmother of Mrs. Morris was a daughter of John Rutherfurd, of New York

Mr. and Mrs. Morris reside in Morrisania, upon a portion of the old Manor property which Mr. Morris inherited from his father and grandfather. They have a city residence in West Fifty-third Street, and a country home, Mount Airy Cottage, Ridgefield, Conn. They have had two children, Eleanor Rutherfurd and Lewis Spencer Morris. Mr Morris was educated as a lawyer, and is engaged in the practice of his profession in New York. He is a member of the Bar Association, the Metropolitan, Lawyers', Church, City and Riding clubs, the St Nicholas Society, and the American Geographical Society, and a patron of the Metropolitan Museum of Art, and the American Museum of Natural History.

By his second wife, Sarah Gouverneur, the most distinguished son of Colonel Lewis Morris was Gouverneur Morris, the eminent statesman and diplomat, 1752–1816. His wife was Ann Cary Randolph, of Virginia, daughter of Thomas Mann Randolph, and a member of the Randolph, Cary, Page, Wormley, Fleming and Isham families, of Virginia. The second Gouverneur Morris, who was born in 1813, took an active part in the development of the internal resources of the United States in the first half of the present century. He was twice married, first to his cousin, Martha Jefferson Cary, of Virginia, and second, to his cousin, Anna Morris. He left two sons, Gouverneur Morris and Randolph Morris The former was a journalist and died in 1897, leaving a widow, who was Henrietta Baldwin, a daughter, Henrietta Fairfax Morris, and a son, Gouverneur Morris, who is a student in Yale University.

RICHARD MORTIMER

FOR three generations the Mortimer family has been conspicuously identified with all that is conservative and substantial in New York City. They came originally from good English stock, their ancestors being substantial residents of Yorkshire. William Mortimer, a man of prominence of Cleckheaton, Yorkshire, was the immediate ancestor of the American branch of the family. He was the possessor of independent means, and figured conspicuously in the local affairs of the community in which he lived.

Richard Mortimer, the son of William Mortimer, was born in Cleckheaton in 1791. He was brought up to follow a commercial career, and had some experience in business before he left England. His brother-in-law was William Yates, a manufacturer of woolen goods, who was then at the head of a firm that could trace back its history for more than one hundred years; and in 1816 Richard Mortimer, who was then twenty-five years of age, came to New York to represent his relative in the United States. He was eminently successful in his conduct of the interests with which he was entrusted, and at the same time took a high rank in the New York commercial community, while he also became the possessor of large personal means. In 1834, after eighteen years of successful business experience in New York, he was obliged to retire on account of ill health and paid a long visit to Europe. Returning to this country, he invested largely in New York real estate, and displayed a far-sighted appreciation of the future growth of the city.

Among his many important possessions were the Mortimer Building in Wall Street, as well as other properties in the principal up-town streets. For many years he resided in a house in Broadway near Twelfth Street. Mr. Mortimer was a director of the Standard Fire Insurance Company and of the Sixth Avenue Railroad, and was connected with many other corporations. In 1821, he married Harriette Thompson, of New Haven, Conn., a daughter of William Thompson, and a descendant from Anthony Thompson, who was one of the company that originally settled New Haven under Theophilus Eaton and John Davenport, in 1637.

William Yates Mortimer, the son of Richard Mortimer and his wife, Harriette, was born in New York City and educated principally in Europe. He married Elizabeth Thorpe, daughter of Aaron Thorpe, of Albany. Inheriting a large part of his father's fortune, his life was spent in caring for this property and in real estate investments of his own, by which he greatly increased his wealth. He was also deeply interested in the welfare of the community and was a liberal benefactor of its charitable institutions. He died in 1891, and by the terms of his will, left considerable sums of money to such objects. Two sons of William Yates Mortimer represent the family in this generation, Richard Mortimer and Stanley Mortimer. Mr. Richard Mortimer is executor and trustee of the family estate, and while not engaged actually in business has displayed the possession of hereditary talent for the management of large interests.

Mr. Mortimer resides at 382 Fifth Avenue, but spends a considerable portion of his time in Europe. He belongs to the Metropolitan, Knickerbocker, Union, City, Racquet, Coaching, Riding and Westminster Kennel clubs, has a country residence at Tuxedo Park, is a member of the Country Club of Westchester County, of the Downtown Association and of the Meadow Brook Hunt, and is a patron of the American Museum of Natural History and the Metropolitan Museum of Art. He married Eleanor Jay Chapman, the daughter of Henry Grafton Chapman. Mrs. Mortimer is the granddaughter of the Honorable John Jay, United States Minister to Austria, and his wife Eleanor Kingsland Field, daughter of the famous New York merchant, Hickson W. Field. Through her grandfather, who was the third and only surviving son of Judge William Jay, jurist, philanthropist and author, she is descended from the great Chief Justice John Jay. Her great-grandmother was the daughter of John McVickar, one of New York's eminent merchants. Going further back, Mrs. Mortimer traces her descent from Augustus Jay, the Huguenot, who came to New York in 1686, married a daughter of Balthazar Bayard and became the ancestor of one of the most distinguished families in American annals.

LEVI PARSONS MORTON

A MONG the influential Puritans of New England was George Morton, or Mourt, who was born in Yorkshire in 1585, and married, in 1612, Juliana Carpenter, daughter of Alexander Carpenter. He managed the Mayflower expedition in 1620, and coming to New England on the Anne, the last of the three Pilgrim ships, in 1623, settled in Middleboro, Mass. His book, Mourt's Relation, published in London in 1622, is the earliest account of the planting of the Plymouth Colony. His son, John Morton, 1616-1673, was a freeman of Plymouth in 1648, deputy to the General Court in 1662, and one of the twenty-six original proprietors of Middleboro. John Morton, Jr., of Plymouth, 1650-1717, kept the first public school ever opened in America. His wife was Mary Ring, daughter of Andrew Ring, and his son, Captain Ebenezer Morton, 1696-1750, married Mercy Foster, daughter of John and Hannah (Stetson) Foster Ebenezer Morton, Jr, born in Middleboro in 1726, married Sarah Cobb, their son, Livy Morton, 1760-1838, being a soldier in the Revolution and marrying Hannah Dailey, daughter of Daniel and Hannah Dailey, of Easton, Me. Their eldest son was the Reverend Daniel O. Morton, 1788-1852, who was graduated from Middlebury College, Vermont, in 1812, and ordained to the ministry in 1814. He was the father of the Honorable Levi P. Morton.

The mother of Mr Levi P. Morton was Lucretia Parsons, daughter of the Reverend Justin and Electa (Frairy) Parsons. Her father, who was born in 1759, in Northampton, Mass., served in the Continental Army in the Revolutionary War. He was a son of Benjamin Parsons and Rebecca Sheldon, grandson of Captain Ebenezer Parsons and great-grandson of Joseph Parsons, who was for twenty-three years a Judge in Hampshire County, Mass. Joseph Parsons was a son of Cornet Joseph Parsons, and was one of the founders of Springfield, Mass Other Colonial ancestors of Mr Morton are, Robert Stetson, of the Plymouth Colony, Elder John Strong, of Plymouth and Northampton; Rowland Stebbins, of Roxbury and Northampton; John Frairy, of Dedham, and Stephen Hopkins, who came on the Mayflower in 1620.

Mr. Levi Parsons Morton was born in Shoreham, Vt., May 16th, 1824, was graduated from the local academy, went into business in Hanover, N. H., and in 1849 engaged in mercantile life in Boston In 1863, he founded the banking house of Morton, Bliss & Co., and at the same time established the branch London house of Morton, Rose & Co In 1878, he was appointed honorary commissioner from the United States to the Paris Exhibition and the same year was elected a Member of Congress from a New York City district, being reëlected in 1880. President James A. Garfield appointed him Envoy Extraordinary and Minister Plenipotentiary to France in 1881, and he made a distinguished success in that diplomatic position. He was elected Vice-President of the United States in 1888, and was Governor of the State of New York, 1895-96

Mr. Morton has been twice married His first wife was Lucy Kimball, daughter of Elijah H. and Sarah W. Kimball, of Flatlands, Long Island. She died in 1871 His present wife was Anna L. Street, daughter of William L. Street and Susan Kearny. She is descended from several of the old Manhattan families. Her grandfather was General Randall S. Street, and her grandmother Cornelia Billings, daughter of Major Andrew Billings, a Revolutionary soldier, by his wife, Cornelia Livingston, who was the granddaughter of Gilbert Livingston and Cornelia Beekman and great-granddaughter of Robert Livingston and Alida (Schuyler) Van Rensselaer Mr. and Mrs. Morton have five daughters, Edith L., Lena K., Helen S., Alice and Mary Morton The city residence of the family is in upper Fifth Avenue, and they have a large country estate, Ellerslie, at Rhinecliff-on-Hudson. Mr. Morton is a member of the Metropolitan, Union, Union League, Lawyers', Republican and Tuxedo clubs, the Century Association, the Downtown Association, the New England Society, the Sons of the American Revolution and the American Geographical Society, and is a supporter of the Metropolitan Museum of Art, the American Museum of Natural History and the National Academy of Design Dartmouth College, in 1881, and Middlebury College, in 1883, bestowed upon him the degree of LL. D.

WILLIAM JAMES MORTON, M. D.

DR. MORTON'S paternal line begins with Robert Morton, one of an old Scotch family who, early in the eighteenth century, settled at Mendon, Mass., and then moved to New Jersey, purchasing a tract which is now Elizabethtown. James Morton, his son, was a member of the Friends' colony at Smithfield, R I, but with his son Thomas fought throughout the Revolution James Morton, son of Thomas, married Rebecca Needham, of Charlton, Mass, and established himself in that town, where his son, William Thomas Green Morton, was born August 9th, 1819 The discovery of surgical anæsthesia remains to this day the brightest page in our country's medical annals. Its discoverer, Dr William T. G Morton, manifested scientific tendencies in early life, and entered, in 1844, the medical department of Harvard His great discovery, the use of sulphuric ether to suppress pain, to which his friend, Dr. Oliver Wendell Holmes, first applied the term "Anæsthesia," was the result of prolonged investigation He first demonstrated that a patient could be made unconscious under the severest operation at the Massachusetts General Hospital on October 16th, 1846. In October, 1896, the semi-centennial of this event was fittingly commemorated at the hospital

Professional honors were showered upon Dr. Morton; he received decorations from the Emperor of Russia and the King of Sweden and Norway, the Montyon prize of the French Academy, and many honorary degrees, while the Massachusetts General Hospital presented him with a silver box containing one thousand dollars in gold. But despite six congressional reports in his favor, he received neither substantial reward nor honor from his own country After his death, the public erected a monument over his grave in Mount Auburn Cemetery, and one commemorating his discovery stands in the Public Garden at Boston, while his name is inscribed on the Massachusetts State House and the Boston Public Library During the Civil War, Dr. Morton volunteered his services in relation to the use of anæsthesia in the army, and was present at Fredericksburg and with Grant in the Wilderness, the latter according him special facilities. He died suddenly at New York City in 1868.

His wife, the present Dr. Morton's mother, was Elizabeth Whitman, daughter of Edward Whitman, of Farmington, Conn, who still lives, a central figure in her son's home. She is descended from Ensign John Whitman, of Weymouth, Mass, two of her ancestors, Zachariah and Samuel Whitman, having graduated at Harvard in 1668 and 1696 respectively. Of the three sons of this marriage, two, William James and N. B Morton, adopted the medical profession. The second son, Edward W., served in Africa in the Cape Mounted Rifles and won the Victoria medal.

Dr. William James Morton, the eldest son, was born in Boston, in 1845, attended the Boston Latin School, was graduated from Harvard in 1867, and from its medical department in 1872. He studied in Vienna and Paris, spent two years in South Africa, and in 1878 made his permanent home in New York, where he has since practiced his profession, making frequent and prolonged visits to Europe, Mexico and other countries. Dr. Morton not only defended the claims of his father to his great discovery, but has followed his footsteps by original research, particularly in neurology and electricity. He is an expert upon the X-ray and has written much upon medical and general topics, and is a member of the leading medical societies, as well as of the University Club, Harvard Alumni and New York Electrical Society, and is a fellow of the American Geographical Society. He has held professorships in the medical colleges, and is an authority upon diseases of the mind and nervous system.

In 1880, Dr Morton married Elizabeth Campbell Lee, daughter of Colonel Washington Lee, of Wilkesbarre, Pa Three of Mrs Morton's great-grandfathers, Colonel Lazarus Stewart, Lieutenant John Jameson and Captain Andrew Lee, fought in the Revolution, and Abigail Alden, the wife of John Jameson, was descended from John Alden Besides his residence in the city, the Doctor has a beautiful summer home, Island Redwood, of one hundred acres, in the Bay of Sag Harbor. He is a talented amateur landscape painter and is fond of outdoor sports.

HOPPER STRIKER MOTT

IN his name and person Mr. Hopper Striker Mott unites three important families of New York. The Mott family was originally French—de la Motte by name—but moved to England centuries ago. It is an old Essex family, dating as far back as 1375. The crest and arms, which are used by the Motts in America, were granted in 1615, and are: Arms, a crescent argent; crest, an estoile of eight points argent. Motto, *Spectemur agendo* The present seat of the family is Barningham Hall, Hanworth, Norfolk.

From this Essex house came Adam Mott, the founder of the family in America, who has been thought by many to have been the Adam Mott who arrived in Boston in 1635, and settled in Hingham in 1636 and in Portsmouth, R I., in 1638, and was supposed to have removed to Long Island about 1646. This opinion has been accepted by Thomson in his History of Long Island, but Austin's Genealogical Dictionary of Rhode Island and Savage's Dictionary of New England make no mention of the removal to Long Island

Little is authentically known concerning the founder of the New York Mott family. According to the records of the Dutch Church of New Amsterdam, Adam Mott, of Essex, England, was married, July 28th, 1647, to Jane Hulet, of Buckingham, England In 1646 (New York Historical Documents, Volume XIV , page 66), the Dutch Government granted him land on Mespath Kill (Newtown Creek). According to the Albany records (IV , page 187-9-190), he was a witness in court in 1644 and in 1645. On the other hand, the New England Adam Mott was from Cambridge, England; the names of his two wives, the dates of the marriages and the names of his children are different from those of Adam Mott of New Amsterdam. The will of the latter, dated March 12th, 1681-2, is in the Surrogate's office of New York. That the New York Adam Mott was not the one who came to Boston in 1635 and later to Hingham, Mass , appears from these facts.

About 1655, Adam Mott of Essex became the first Adam Mott of Hempstead, Long Island. In Book A, the oldest annals of its founders, he appears as one of the five townsmen, chosen March 17th, 1657. One of his descendants now occupies the homestead built by a son in 1715 at Mott's Point, Hempstead Harbor On February 24th, 1663, as a deputy from Hempstead on behalf of the English, he signed the agreement between Captain John Scott and Governor Petrus Stuyvesant, looking to friendly intercourse between Dutch and English. In 1684, he was one of the delegation which procured a new patent from Governor Dongan. For a second wife he married, in 1667, Elizabeth Richbell, daughter of John Richbell, original patentee of Mamaroneck. He died in 1689, aged about sixty-eight years

By his first wife, Adam Mott had eight children: Adam, Jacobus, Grace, Elizabeth, Henry, John, Joseph and Gershom. One of the sons of Joseph Mott was Jacob Mott, 1715-1805. He married Abigail Jackson, and was the father of fourteen children. His fourth child, Isaac Mott, born in 1743, married Anne Coles, of Glen Cove, Long Island She was the Anne Mott who ministered to the American prisoners confined in the military prisons in New York. The family is still in possession of the table cloth given to her in gratitude by those she cared for. She died July 16th, 1840, at the age of ninety-two, and was buried from the Mott homestead in Bloomingdale

There were four children born to Isaac and Anne (Coles) Mott· Samuel, Jordan, Jacob and Joshua. Jordan Mott, born at Hempstead Harbor in 1768, died in 1840 He married Lavinia Striker (known thereafter as Winifred Mott), daughter of James and Mary Hopper Striker, of Striker's Bay, September 24th, 1801. The youngest son of this union was M. Hopper Mott, 1815-1864, who was the father of Mr. Hopper Striker Mott Other marriages have been made with old Knickerbocker stock by members of this family, so that, besides direct descent from their Quaker forbears, the Motts of the present generation are allied to the Hoppers, Strikers, Schuylers, Van Rensselears, Van Dorens, Dykmans and Milderbergers.

Andries Hoppe, or Hoppen, with his wife, Geertje Hendricks, came from Holland in 1652. In 1653, he was a burgher of New Amsterdam, and died in 1659. His widow became the owner of Bronk's Land (Riker's History of Harlem). Records of the Dutch Church show her marriage in 1660 to Dirck Gerritsen Van Tricht. Mathew Adolphus Hopper, the youngest child and third son of the pioneer, was born in 1658 and married Anna Paulus, daughter of Jurck Paulus. Part of this family settled in Bloomingdale, and to this branch Mr. Hopper Striker Mott belongs. John Hopper, the elder, Mr. Mott's great-great-great-grandfather, owned the famous Hopper farm on the upper west side of the island, which extended from near Sixth Avenue to the Hudson River. It was acquired by a Dutch grant in 1642, confirmed by the English in 1667. Upon the death of John Hopper, in 1779, the farm was divided by his will among his children, for each of whom he had erected a house The mansion which he built for his son John was constructed in 1752, on the banks of the Hudson, at Fifty-third Street, and became the home of General Garret Hopper Striker and his descendants, and was only demolished in December, 1895. The Mott homestead, built in the middle of the last century, stood at Mott's Point, at the foot of West Fifty-fourth Street, a landmark of old New York until November, 1895, when it was razed to allow of the extension of that street. The house of Yellis Hopper was erected on Fifty-first Street, between Broadway and Eighth Avenue, and has long since disappeared. The homestead built for Andrew Hopper was located on the present site of the American Horse Exchange, at Broadway and Fiftieth Street The burial plot of the family occupied a part of this farm near Fiftieth Street and Ninth Avenue. Mrs. Greatorex in her Old New York and Valentine's Manuals for 1851, 1861 and 1870 enter fully into details regarding this property. That portion of the old farm willed to John Hopper the younger, as well as the portions deeded to him by his brother Matthew, February 17th, 1782, and by Yellis, April 4th, 1787, and the Wessell-Hopper inheritance, was set apart in an action of partition in the courts by a decree dated January 10th, 1865, to the Strikers and Motts (Tuttle's Abstracts)

In January, 1643, Jan and Jacobus Gerritsen Van Strycker received from the States General of Holland a grant of land in New Amsterdam Jacobus Gerritsen Van Strycker came over in 1651, from the village of Ruinen, in the United Provinces, and was the founder of the family in America His brother Jan, who came in 1654, was a leader of the Dutch colony on Long Island. He was a great burgher in 1653, 1655, 1657, 1658, 1660, and a schepen for many years. He moved to Flatlands about 1660, and in 1673 became schout of the Dutch towns on Long Island.

The descendants of these brothers have been numerous on Long Island and in New Jersey In Volume HH , page 10, of O'Callaghan's Calendar of Historical Documents, is found the record of the original deed of Stricker's Bay, at Bloomingdale, dated February 11th, 1653. James Striker, one of the founders of the Reformed Dutch Church, at Harsenville, and a great-grandfather of Mr. Hopper Striker Mott, inherited this property. A portion of the mansion, which succeeded that built by Jacobus Gerritsen Strycker in 1654, is still standing at Ninety-sixth Street and Riverside Drive. The only son of James Striker was Major-General Garret Hopper Striker, a Captain in the Fifth New York Regiment in the War of 1812. The camp of his command was within the northern limits of Central Park. After the war, he married a daughter of Captain Alexander MacDougall, of the British Navy, whose mother was a Miss Ellsworth, of New York City. He died in 1868

Mr Hopper Striker Mott was born in New York City, April 19th, 1854, and educated in the Military Academy at Peekskill, Charlier's French School, Columbia College and Columbia Law School. Upon the death of his uncle, Jordan Mott, he succeeded to a large inheritance, and, with his brother, became a tenant in common of a portion of the Hopper farm. The care of that property has been his chief business occupation.

In 1875, Mr. Mott married May Lenox, only child of Dr Edwin S Lenox, of New York City, and has one son, Hopper Lenox Mott, eighth in descent from Adam Mott His ancestry gives him membership in the Holland Society, and he also belongs to the Metropolitan, Union League, St Nicholas, Country and Ψ Υ clubs. His city residence is at 188 West End Avenue.

JORDAN L. MOTT

AMONG the descendants of Adam Mott, the pioneer, who settled upon Long Island in the middle of the seventeenth century, is that branch of the family to which Mr Jordan L Mott belongs, many of its representatives having been prominent in New York business and social circles in every generation.   Adam Mott, who came from Essex and settled in New Amsterdam before 1647, married his first wife, Jane Hulet, of Buckingham, in England. His son Joseph, 1651 1735, the youngest child in a family of eight, was the direct ancestor of Mr Jordan L. Mott.

Jacob Mott, the son of Joseph Mott, was born August 9th, 1715, and died October 6th, 1805   He was the father of Jacob Mott, who was born in 1756 and died in 1823, and became father of the first Jordan L. Mott.   The brothers of the second Jacob Mott became the ancestors of the various branches of the family

Jacob Mott, the great-grandson of Adam Mott, became a merchant in New York   During his early life, he lived on Long Island, and there married Deborah, daughter of Dr. William Lawrence, whose ancestor, John Lawrence, was one of the commissioners appointed to arrange the boundaries between New Amsterdam and Connecticut in 1664.   John Lawrence was a lineal descendant of Sir Robert Lawrence, and was an extensive landholder on Long Island   He became an alderman, and was Mayor of New York City in 1673.   The Honorable John W Lawrence, the Congressman; Captain James Lawrence, the naval hero of the War of 1812, and Mayor Cornelius Van W Lawrence were eminent members of the same family.   Jacob Mott became prominent in politics and was an alderman, 1804-10, president of the Board when De Witt Clinton was Mayor, and at one time acted as Deputy Mayor.   Mott Street perpetuates his name upon the map of the city

Jordan L. Mott, the first of his name, was the youngest son of Jacob Mott, and was born at Manhasset, Long Island, October 21st, 1798.   He received a good education, but reverses in the family fortunes compelled him to go into business at the age of twenty-two   He was successful in his efforts, becoming eventually an iron manufacturer.   Among other inventions, he devised the first stove for burning anthracite coal, and developed a great industrial establishment to which his name has ever since been attached.   Mott Haven, on the Harlem River, received its name from the works he established in that locality, and he was instrumental in founding and building up the village of Morrisania.   He possessed marked public spirit and was a generous contributor to charitable and religious causes   He never held public office, although President Buchanan tendered him the position of Commissioner of Patents

The only son of the elder Jordan L. Mott succeeded to his father's name and estate   He was educated at Irving Institute, at Tarrytown, and the University of the City of New York   In 1849, when he was twenty years of age, he left college and entered upon active life in his father s establishment.   After an apprenticeship of four years, he was admitted in the business, in 1853, when the Jordan L. Mott Iron Works were incorporated, and since 1866 has had full management of the concern.   Besides being president of this company, he is president of the Stax Foundry Company, the North American Iron Works, and the North River Bridge Company, a corporation organized to build a bridge across the Hudson River, and is connected with other business enterprises.   As a Democrat, Mr. Mott has been frequently honored by his party, being a Presidential Elector in 1876 and in 1888, a member and president of the Board of Aldermen in 1879, and a member of the Rapid Transit Commission which supervised the erection of New York's elevated railroads.   He is a member of the New York, Engineers', New York Yacht and other clubs, and lives in the old Mott homestead in upper Fifth Avenue.   He married Marianna Seaman.   His son, Jordan L Mott, Jr, the third to bear that name, is a member of the Union, Manhattan, Players and other clubs, and lives at 17 East Forty-seventh Street   He married Katharine Jerome Purdy and has a son, Jordan L Mott, the fourth of the name.

VALENTINE MOTT, M. D.

SOME time before 1655, Adam Mott settled at Hempstead, Long Island, and became the ancestor of a widely spread New York family. His second wife, whom he married in 1667, was Elizabeth Richbell, daughter of John Richbell, a neighbor of Adam Mott at Hempstead, but who removed to Westchester County, and was a patentee of Mamaroneck.

It is from William Mott, the fourth child of Adam and Elizabeth, that Dr Valentine Mott traces his descent. His great-grandfather, who was sixth in descent from Adam Mott, was Dr. Henry Mott, an able physician and a resident of Newtown, Long Island The latter's wife was a daughter of Samuel Way, of North Hempstead, whose family were among the original settlers of Long Island. In his later years, Dr. Henry Mott removed to New York, where he died in 1840

His son, Dr Valentine Mott, the famous surgeon, was born at Glen Cove, Long Island, in 1785 Graduating from the medical department of Columbia College in 1806, he also studied under his distinguished relative, Dr. Valentine Seaman, and in 1807 went to London, becoming a pupil of Sir Astley Cooper and other great physicians. He walked the hospitals and attended lectures both in London and Edinburgh, and returned to America in 1808 Entering upon practice in New York, his success was immediate and brilliant. He originated a great number of operations deemed impossible before his day, and which revolutionized medicine and surgery, while his life was one of constant professional activity. In 1809, he became professor of surgery in Columbia College, and then held a like appointment in the College of Physicians and Surgeons until 1832, when he was among the founders of the Rutgers School of Medicine. He was again professor in the College of Physicians and Surgeons from 1836 to 1850, and acted as surgeon to the New York, Bellevue, St. Vincent's, St Luke's, Woman's and Hebrew hospitals. Professional honors were showered on him, including the degree of M. D. of the University of Edinburgh, and fellowships of the Academy of Medicine of Paris and other European medical societies. His wife was Louise Dunmore Munn

Alexander Brown Mott, father of the present Dr. Mott, was their fourth son, and was born in New York in 1826. He was educated at Columbia Grammar School under Dr Anthon, and going abroad, led an adventurous and exciting life for some years, his experiences including service as secretary to Commodore Morris, U. S N., in the Mediterranean, and participation in a Spanish revolution, in command of a battery at the siege of Barcelona. Returning to the United States, he took his degree at the Vermont Academy of Medicine in 1850. He helped to organize St. Vincent's Hospital, and was a founder of Bellevue Medical College, in which he was a professor. He was also surgeon at St. Vincent's, Mt. Sinai and Bellevue hospitals. His patriotic service to his country in the Civil War was also a feature of his career. In April, 1861, when Surgeon to the Second New York Brigade, and about to accompany his command to the front, he was appointed Medical Director of the Department of the East He organized the United States Army General Hospital, in New York, and became its Chief Surgeon, with rank of Major. In 1864, he was appointed Medical Inspector of the Department of Virginia, served in connection with General Ord's staff, and was present at the final scene of the war when General Lee surrendered at Appomattox. He left the army with the rank of Brevet Lieutenant-Colonel. Dr. Mott was actively connected with the order of the Loyal Legion, the membership of which passed by inheritance to his son. He married, in 1851, Arabella, daughter of Thaddeus Phelps, who died in 1874, Dr. Mott's death being in 1889.

Dr Valentine Mott is his only child, and was born in New York in 1852. He was graduated from Columbia College in 1872, and also took the degree of B A at Cambridge University, England, in 1876. Following a course in medicine, he took the degree of M. D. at Bellevue Medical College in 1879, and has succeeded to the practice of his grandfather and father. He married Emily Langdon Irving, and resides at 62 Madison Avenue. He is a member of the Union, Calumet, St Anthony, Players and Seawanhaka-Corinthian Yacht clubs.

F. ADOLPHUS MULLER-URY

SWITZERLAND, which, under its liberal institutions, is the one country of Europe free from the burdens of militarism, and where peaceful pursuits or the cultivation of intellectual tendencies are uninterrupted by the hope of national aggrandisement or the fear of encroachment, has taken a leading part in the development of modern science and art and in the progress of the industries which make civilization possible   Preëminent as its people are in all peaceful pursuits, it is sometimes forgotten that, until the beginning of the present century, the Swiss were justly regarded as a race of warriors and ranked as the best soldiers in the world   Their long contest with the House of Austria and the neighboring princes, in which the freedom of the Cantons was established, roused a warlike spirit which made them the best soldiers in Europe, history being by no means silent as to their prowess or their fidelity   Their own land being free from attack, Swiss officers sought service in the armies of the other powers, and attained distinction under the banners of distant monarchs, and not a few of the patrician families of the present republic can point to ancestors ennobled by the powers which they served, or famous for their exploits on foreign fields of battle.

Mr F Adolphus Muller-Ury, the distinguished artist, represents in himself and through his ancestors these facts in connection with the history of the Swiss people.   His father, Louis Muller-Ury, was an eminent Swiss jurist, president of a Cantonal Supreme Court, and renowned as one of its foremost lawyers and statesmen.   His mother was a lady of the Lombardi family, whose members were also distinguished in the annals of their country, especially in connection with their labors for the Hospice of St. Gothard   On both sides, however, Mr. Muller-Ury's ancestors were soldiers, his grandfathers having been officers in the French Army, while two of his ancestors were Generals in the service of Spain, and were in each instance ennobled by the monarchs of the countries in question.

Born at Airolo, Switzerland, in 1862, Mr Muller-Ury exhibited artistic talent at an early age and was trained for the profession to which his inclinations and taste pointed, at the leading ateliers and schools of art in France, Germany and Italy.   Among other instructors who aided his progress, he was a pupil of the great portrait painter Cabanel, of the sculptor Vela and of the Swiss painter von Deschwanden   Since 1885, he has made America the principal scene of his labors, and in the field of portrait painting, which has been his chief specialty, has few rivals   Many of the most prominent New Yorkers of the present day, as well as leading individuals in social or political life all over the country, have been his sitters.   Among them are Mr and Mrs Theodore Havemeyer, Mr and Mrs Chauncey M. Depew, Mrs. Hobart C. Chatfield-Taylor, Cardinal Satolli, Cardinal Gibbons, Mr. Constable, Mrs. Charles Oelrichs, Mrs. Charles T. Yerkes, Mme Calvé, Mr. and Mrs. James J. Hill, Governor and Mrs. Merriam, Archbishop Ireland, of St. Paul, and others in the principal cities both East and West, while it should be mentioned that his works are justly admired when exhibited in public.

Mr. Muller-Ury's studio at 58 West Fifty-seventh Street, in this city, where he also has his bachelor apartments, is a veritable exhibition of artistic taste and luxury   He is an indefatigable collector of antique furniture, tapestry and other objects of art, his visits to Europe, which are made every year, enabling him to add constantly to his collections.   He resides a portion of each year in Paris, and in addition has a country place in Switzerland at Hospenthal.   While not a club man, Mr. Muller-Ury is prominent in society, and is an habitué of the highest artistic and social circles.   He is devoted to outdoor exercises, is a noted rider, and is fond of golfing, bicycling and other sports of that character.

The family arms are · Half a silver wheel on a blue ground, surmounted by two golden lilies on a red ground, separated by a naked sword   The wheel represents the ancient arms of the race, the lilies having been granted as an addition by the King of France, and the sword by the King of Spain

ORSON DESAIX MUNN

THE origin of the name of Munn is not definitely known, but it is doubtless of great antiquity, as shown in the armorial bearings of the English branch, which are Arms, per chevron sable and or, in chief three bezants and in base a castle triple-towered of the first Crest, a dexter arm in armor, holding a lion's paw erased proper. Motto, *Omnia vincit veritas*—Truth conquers all things. The American ancestor of the family was Benjamin Mun, who was, in 1637, living in Hartford, Conn He served in the war with the Pequot Indians in 1637, removed to Springfield, Mass, but died in Hartford in 1675 His wife was Abigail Burt, daughter of Henry Burt and widow of Francis Ball, whom he married in 1649 His children were Abigail, 1650; John, 1652; Benjamin, 1655, James, 1656; and Nathaniel, 1661. His eldest son, John Munn, was in the fight with the Indians at Turner's Falls. His grandson, James Munn, also took part in the same engagement and settled at Colchester, Conn That branch of the family to which Mr. Orson D. Munn belongs was among the first settlers of Hampden County, Mass. The town of Monson was named after them

Mr. Munn was born June 11th, 1824, in the town that bears his ancestral name. His father was Rice Munn, a prosperous farmer, and his mother was Levina Shaw. His grandparents were Reuben and Hannah Munn He was educated at Monson Academy, formerly a celebrated educational institution. Before he was out of his teens, he found employment in a book store at Springfield, Mass, where he remained two years, and afterwards in a store in Monson Soon after he came of age, he removed to New York, where, in association with Alfred E. Beach, he purchased The Scientific American, which had been founded a year before by Rufus Porter, and up to that time had had a precarious existence. Alfred E. Beach was a son of Moses Y. Beach, proprietor of The New York Sun, and had been a schoolmate of Mr. Munn in the Monson Academy, and the association there begun continued uninterruptedly for over fifty years, down to the death of Mr. Beach, in January, 1896. The business of Munn & Co. is still continued under the same firm name, but from necessity was incorporated after Mr. Beach's death. Organized in 1846, the firm of Munn & Co. soon attained phenomenal success For more than half a century The Scientific American has been recognized as the standard publication of the world in its field The development of the paper led, after a time, to the establishment of an agency for procuring letters patent for new inventions, a business then in its infancy, and which owes much to the intelligent and energetic work of this firm. To the original publication there have been added in recent years The Scientific American Supplement, an illustrated weekly, established in 1874'; The Monthly Architects' and Builders' Edition, a magazine devoted to architecture; a Spanish edition of The Scientific American, and the publication of many important scientific books

Mr. Munn is a member of the Union, Union League, Merchants' and Essex County Country clubs, the New England Society, a fellow of the National Academy of Design, and belongs to the Sons of the Revolution. He owns a notable collection of paintings by modern artists, and is a recognized connoisseur of art His city residence is in East Twenty-second Street, where he has lived for over forty years. He has a country home in Llewellyn Park, Orange, N J, and owns a large farm in West Orange, near his park residence, which is stocked with a large herd of Dutch belted cattle, in the raising and exhibiting of which at State and county fairs, he takes much satisfaction.

In 1849, Mr. Munn married Julia Augusta Allen, daughter of Mrs. Elvira Allen, of his native town. She died October 26th, 1894, leaving two sons. The elder son, Henry Norcross Munn, married Anne E. Elder, and lives in Lexington Avenue. He is a member of the Union, City and Essex County Country clubs. The younger son, Charles Allen Munn, graduated from Princeton University in the class of 1881, belongs to the Merchants', Union, City, University, Racquet, Essex County Country and Princeton clubs, and to the New England Society. Both sons are associated with their father in the house of Munn & Co

CHARLES H. MURRAY

ON both the paternal and maternal side, the Honorable Charles H Murray traces his lineage to New England ancestors who figured in Colonial and Revolutionary times   The family was planted in America by William Murray, who was born in 1690, the son of a Scotch nobleman   He joined the famous McGregor expedition to New England in 1718, and settled first in Londonderry, N H, and afterwards in Amherst, Mass   Many of his descendants attained to distinction   One of them, Captain Elihu Murray, 1753–1835, the great-grandfather of the subject of this sketch, bore an active part in the war of the Revolution   He was a resident of Deerfield, Mass , and when the news of the battle of Lexington was received there, joined the Hatfield Company and marched to Boston, taking part in the battles of Bunker Hill, Long Island, Throgg's Neck and Bennington, and being present at the surrender of General Burgoyne   After that, he was commissioned a Captain in the Continental Line and transferred to the Quartermaster-General s Department, where he served under General Wadsworth until the end of the war   An uncle of Captain Elihu Murray was General Seth Murray, also of Revolutionary fame

Through the women of the family, Mr Murray includes among his ancestors more than twenty of the early settlers of New England   The first William Murray married a descendant of Nathaniel Dickinson, who was one of the founders of Hadley, Mass , his son, William, married a descendant of Deacon Samuel Chapin, of Springfield, and Lieutenant John Hitchcock and the wife of his grandson, Elihu, was connected with the Strong, Ingersoll and other leading New England families   Dauphin Murray, 1793–1855, grandfather of Mr Charles H Murray, was Sheriff of Steuben County, N Y, and a Colonel of militia in 1812   His wife was descended from General Robert Sedgwick, who came to America in 1635, was one of the founders of the Ancient and Honorable Artillery Company of Boston, and Governor of Jamaica in 1656.   Mr Murray's mother was Abbie Shelden Billings, a granddaughter of Lieutenant Daniel Billings of the Revolution   She was also descended from William Billings, who came to America in 1650, a descendant in direct line from John Billings, of England, father of Sir Thomas Billings, Lord Chief Justice of the Queen's Bench in 1543   Among other ancestors of Mr. Murray were Elder William Brewster, of Plymouth, Samuel Starr, one of the first settlers in New London, Conn , and Captain John Dennison, of King Philip's War

Mr Murray was born in San Francisco, January 2d, 1855, but was brought to New York when he was a boy   His early education was in private schools, and he was graduated from the Mount Pleasant Military Academy with honors as valedictorian.   Studying law first in Dunkirk, and then in New York, he entered upon his profession, devoting himself specially to corporation, insurance, surrogate and mercantile law, in which he has been very successful   In the field of politics and public life, Mr Murray has become best known   He has been prominent in the local organization of the Republican party since 1884 as a district leader and delegate to conventions, and in 1892 he was a delegate to the National Republican Convention.   President Harrison appointed him United States Supervisor of the Census for the First District of New York in 1890, and the following year he was appointed special Assistant United States District Attorney and counsel to the Commissioner of Immigration of the Port of New York   In May, 1894, he was a Police Commissioner of the City of New York   In 1896, he was a delegate to the Republican National Convention

Mr Murray has taken special interest in the patriotic societies that have sprung up in recent years   He was one of the founders of the Society of Colonial Wars, and Deputy-General for New York State, and is a member of the Cincinnati and vice-president for the State of Connecticut.   He belongs also to the Sons of the Revolution, the Sons of the American Revolution and the Loyal Legion, and is one of the board of directors of the Society of the War of 1812   He married Grace Peckham, daughter of Dr. Fenner Peckham, of Providence, R I, a descendant of the Peckham, Torrey and Davis families of Rhode Island.   His residence is in West Fifty-second Street

STEPHEN PAYNE NASH

W HEN the Reverend John Davenport landed in Boston, in July, 1637, he brought with him a company of Colonists, who were people of unusually good standing, socially and financially Among his followers was Thomas Nash, who brought with him his wife and five children Thomas Nash was of a family that is supposed to have come originally from Lancaster, or Lancashire In the spring of 1638, he was one of the little company that sailed from Boston to settle Qunnipiac, or New Haven, and in November of that year, was one of the Colonists who entered into an agreement with Nomanguin, and other Indian chiefs, for the purchase of lands. In 1639, he was one of the signers to the fundamental agreement for the regulation of the civil and religious affairs of the Colony, and the same year signed the agreement of those who wished to remove to settle the town of Guilford His wife was Margery Baker, probably a daughter of Nicholas Baker, of Hertfordshire, England, one of the first emigrants to the Connecticut Colony

Thomas Nash, who died in 1658, was advanced in years when he came to this country, and his children early became prominent in the several communities in which they lived. His eldest son, John, took the oath of freeman in 1642, was a Sergeant in 1644, a Lieutenant in 1652, town treasurer and deputy in 1654, Captain of the train band in 1655, and chief of the military forces during the trouble with the Narragansett Indians He settled in New Haven, where he was a magistrate and held other offices almost constantly throughout his life Repeatedly, he was a delegate to the General Assembly, and was an assistant from 1672 until the time of his death, in 1687 Timothy Nash, another son of the pioneer, was the ancestor of that branch of the family to which Mr Stephen Payne Nash belongs. He was born in 1626, and became a freeman of New Haven in 1654 He was in Hartford in 1660, and in Hadley, Mass,, in 1663, being a Lieutenant in the militia and a representative from the town of Hadley to the General Court of Massachusetts in 1690, 1691 and 1695. He went to Hadley with the Reverend John Russell, who, in the controversies in Hartford and Wethersfield, regarding the government of the church, led away a company of decedents to settle the rich and beautiful Connecticut River Valley. Timothy Nash married, about 1657, Rebekah Stone, daughter of Samuel Stone, of Hartford, and they had twelve children He died in 1699, and his wife in 1709

Lieutenant John Nash, the grandson of the pioneer, 1667–1743, was a representative to the General Court from Hadley seven times. His second wife, the ancestress of Mr Stephen P. Nash, was Elizabeth Kellogg, daughter of Joseph Kellogg, of Farmington, Conn In subsequent generations, the line of descent was through Deacon John Nash, Jr, born 1694, and his wife, Hannah Ingram, Deacon David Nash, 1719–1803, and his wife, Elizabeth Smith, David Nash, 1755–1832, and his wife, Lois Alvord, and David Nash, 1792–1832, and his wife, Hannah Payne David Nash, 1755, removed from Connecticut to Granby, Mass , about the close of the last century, and afterwards to Watervliet, N Y , where his descendants have since lived.

Mr Stephen Payne Nash, son of David Nash and Hannah Payne, was born in 1821 He was educated for the law, studying in the public schools in Albany and the French College at Chamblay, Canada He began to practice in Saratoga, then went to Albany and afterwards came to New York, where he has spent most of his life He was one of the founders of the New York Bar Association, in 1863, being its president in 1880, and has been a trustee of Columbia College and a member of the vestry of Trinity Church His wife, Catherine McLean, was a daughter of the Honorable John McLean, of Salem, N Y He belongs to the Century Association and lives in West Nineteenth Street His eldest son, John McLean Nash, was born in Albany in 1848, was graduated from Columbia College, is a lawyer and belongs to the Metropolitan, University, Players and other clubs and the Bar Association. Another son is Stephen Edward Nash, born in 1850 who married Isabel Coggill. A third son, Thomas Nash, was graduated from Columbia University in 1882

GEORGE LIVINGSTON NICHOLS

IN the time of Edward the Confessor, Nicholas de Albine, who was also called Nigell and Nicholl, came from Normandy to England. He was the ancestor of all who bear the name of Nicholl, or Nichols The ancestor of the American branch of the family was settled in Glamorganshire Francis Nichols, the American pioneer, was born in England in 1595, and coming to this country was an original proprietor of Stratford, Conn , in 1639, and Captain of the train band His second wife was Annie Wynes, or Wines, daughter of Barnabas Wynes, one of the original proprietors of Southold, Long Island, in 1640 John Nichols, born in England, came with his father, Francis Nichols, to this country and his son, Samuel Nichols, born in 1655, married Mary Bowers, daughter of the Reverend John Bowers, of Derby, Conn , in 1682, and afterwards settled in New Jersey. He was the father of Humphry Nichols, who settled in Newark in 1738, where he died in 1765

Isaac Nichols, son of Humphry, born in Newark in 1748, was a patriot of the Revolution in 1775, was in the expedition against Quebec, was at the siege of Fort Schuyler, and the capture of Burgoyne's army, was Lieutenant in Colonel James Livingston's regiment, and was twice wounded at the battle of Rhode Island When peace came, he removed to Brooklyn, was Justice of the Peace for eighteen years, and died there in 1835. His first wife, the great-grandmother of Mr. George Livingston Nichols, was Cornelia Van Duzen, daughter of William Van Duzen and Lucretia Bogardus, who was a granddaughter of the celebrated Annetje Jans Bogardus. Lewis Nichols, 1790-1859, the grandfather of Mr Nichols, was born in Brooklyn and was a soldier in the War of 1812 He was engaged in the publishing business and brought out the first directory of the City of Brooklyn. His wife was Jane Anne Little, daughter of George Little

George L Nichols, Sr , son of Lewis Nichols, was born in Brooklyn in 1830 and died in 1892 His early business experience was secured in the house of T. B. Coddington & Co , metal importers, and he became a member of that firm in 1854 He was a member of the Chamber of Commerce, vice-president of the Phenix National Bank, a director of the Brooklyn Academy of Music and a trustee of the Atlantic Mutual Insurance Company. He was a councilor of the Long Island Historical Society, president of the Mercantile Library Association and one of the first trustees of the Brooklyn Bridge President Arthur offered him a position on the Tariff Revision Commission, which he declined, as he did other tenders of office In 1852, he married Christina Marie Cole, daughter of Jan Kool, or John Cole, and Rebecka Fransiena van Santen Her father was born in Amsterdam, Holland, in 1784, son of Andries Kool and Elsie Vander Linden Her mother, born in Amsterdam, in 1804, was the daughter of Adrian van Santen and Christina Barkmeyer

Mr George L Nichols, Jr , son of the preceding, was born in Brooklyn, May 9th, 1860 He was graduated from Williams College in 1881, and from the Columbia College Law School in 1883 In 1884, he received the degree of M A from Williams College In 1883, he was admitted to the bar He has a large practice, principally in connection with corporations. An active Republican, he was a delegate to the Republican State Convention in 1888, and in 1891 was appointed a member of the Civil Service Commission of Brooklyn, and reappointed in 1892. He married, in 1893, Mary (Chickering) Ruxton, daughter of George H Chickering, of Boston, and lives at 66 East Fifty-sixth Street He has one daughter, Christina Mary Nichols. He is a member of the Metropolitan, University, Grolier and Hamilton clubs, the Downtown Association, the Bar Association, the American Bar Association, the New York State Bar Association, the Williams College Alumni, the St. Nicholas Society, the Society of the War of 1812, the Sons of the Revolution, the Military Order of Foreign Wars, the Metropolitan Museum of Art, the Brooklyn Historical Society, and also belongs to the New York Historical, Botanical, Zoological and American Natural History societies. The other surviving children of George L. Nichols. Sr., are Kate N. Nichols, the authoress, wife of Spencer Trask; Acosta Nichols, a partner in the firm of Spencer Trask & Co , and Marie Christina Nichols.

De LANCEY NICOLL

W HEN General Sir Richard Nicolls, Governor of New York, came to this country in 1664, he was accompanied by his nephew, Matthias Nicoll, a lawyer of Lincoln's Inn, London. The Nicolls came of an ancient English family. Their coat of arms was issued to John Nicoll, of Buckingham, near Islip, Northampton County, in 1601, and the records refer to a former John Nicoll, who lived in the middle of the fifteenth century When Governor Nicolls had successfully overcome the Dutch in New Amsterdam and made the Colony an English possession, he appointed his nephew, Matthias, to be the first English Colonial secretary. After the Governor returned to England, Matthias Nicoll was a councilor of Governor Lovelace, was Mayor of the city in 1671, Speaker of the first Colonial Assembly in 1683 and one of the first Judges of the New York Court of Oyer and Terminer, appointed by Governor Dongan in 1683.

William Nicoll, son of Matthias Nicoll, married Anna, daughter of the patroon Jeremias Van Rensselaer, of Albany, and his wife, Maria Van Cortlandt, and received from the King of England a tract of land in Suffolk County, ten miles square in extent, which he settled and called Islip Grange, after the old family home in England. Upon his death, this estate descended to his eldest son, Benjamin. His younger son, William Nicoll, devoted himself to public affairs and was elected Speaker of the Colonial Legislature for eighteen consecutive years. He owned an estate of four thousand acres at Shelter Island, which he left by will to his nephew, William, the son of his brother, Benjamin This nephew, William, was one of the great lawyers of his period His descendants, through his eldest son, inherited the Islip estate, while the descendants of his second son, Samuel Benjamin Nicoll, became proprietors of the Shelter Island property. In the present generation by intermarriage the Nicolls of Bayside, Long Island, represent both branches of the family.

Benjamin Nicoll, the youngest son of the first Benjamin Nicoll, was educated in Columbia College and married Mary M Holland, daughter of Edward Holland. His son was Henry Nicoll, a wealthy New York merchant, and his grandson, Edward Holland Nicoll, married Mary Townsend, of Albany. The eldest son of Edward Holland Nicoll was Henry Nicoll, a lawyer of prominence in New York City, and a Member of Congress. His youngest son, Solomon Townsend Nicoll, became a successful merchant of New York, and married his cousin, Charlotte Ann Nicoll, of Shelter Island, the second child of Samuel Benjamin Nicoll, who died in 1866 and who was the son of Samuel Benjamin Nicoll, the head of that branch of the family in the fourth generation. In 1855, Solomon Townsend Nicoll purchased the present Nicoll estate at Bayside. His children are: Anne Nicoll, who married William M. Hoes; De Lancey Nicoll; Benjamin Nicoll, who married Grace Davison Lord, daughter of James Couper Lord, and granddaughter of the famous Daniel Lord; Edward Holland Nicoll, who married Edith M Travers ; Mary Townsend Nicoll, who married James Brown Lord, and Charlotte Nicoll, the wife of Willoughby Weston. Benjamin Nicoll and Edward Holland Nicoll both graduated from Princeton College and are merchants in New York.

Mr. De Lancey Nicoll was born in Bayside, Long Island, in 1854. He was educated in St. Paul's School, Concord, N H., and then graduated from Princeton College with high honors in 1874. Two years later he graduated from the Columbia College Law School, and was admitted to the bar. He soon became successful in his profession, and his family connections gave him high social standing. In 1885, he was appointed assistant district attorney by Randolph B Martine, and in that office preeminently distinguished himself. When District Attorney Martine's term of service expired, Mr. Nicoll, in 1887, was a candidate for the vacant position, nominated by the Independents and Republicans, but was defeated by John R. Fellows. In 1890, he was nominated by the Tammany organization for the same office and was elected, serving a term of three years In 1894, he was a member of the Constitutional Convention.

Mr. Nicoll married Maud Churchill and lives in East Thirty-eighth Street He belongs to the Tuxedo Club, and is also a member of the Metropolitan, Manhattan, Union, Law, University, Democratic, Racquet and other clubs and the Downtown Association

WILLIAM WHITE NILES

CENTURIES ago ancestors of the Niles family, which was of Norse origin, established themselves in England During the conflict between the King and Parliament, the members of the family were generally adherents of Cromwell, and after the restoration, several of them came to America Among these emigrants was John Niles, the ancestor of Mr William White Niles He was a resident of Dorchester, Mass , in 1634, and a freeman of Braintree, in 1647 His son, Captain Nathaniel Niles, 1642-1727 married Sarah Sands, daughter of James Sands. Their son, the Reverend Samuel Niles, born in 1673, graduated from Harvard College in 1699, and preached in Kingston, R I, and Braintree, Mass His wife was Elizabeth Thacher, daughter of the Reverend Peter Thacher, of Milton, Mass Samuel Niles, Jr , 1711-1804, their son, graduated from Harvard in 1731 He was a leading lawyer in Boston and a Judge for nearly forty years During the War of the Revolution, he was a patriot and a friend of John Adams He married, in 1739, his cousin, Sarah Niles, daughter of Nathaniel Niles

In the next generation came Nathaniel Niles, 1740-1828 Graduated from Princeton College, in 1766, he lived in Boston, but moved to Norwich, Conn , and was a member of the Connecticut Legislature Afterwards he went to Vermont and became an influential man in that State, being a member and Speaker of the Vermont House of Representatives, the first Member of Congress elected from that State, and Lieutenant-Governor He was for many years Judge of the Supreme Court, a trustee of Dartmouth College and six times a Presidential elector The grandfather of William White Niles was Judge William Niles, who when young went with his father to Vermont He graduated from Dartmouth College, became a lawyer and a member of the State Constitutional Convention, and was a Judge He married Relief Barron, daughter of Colonel John Barron, a Revolutionary officer On the maternal side of the house, Mr. Niles is descended from John Milburne, a victim of the Star Chamber, and from John Rogers, the first martyr burned at Smithfield.

William Watson Niles was born in Orange County, Vt , in 1822, and graduated from Dartmouth College. He studied law in Indiana, made a tour of Europe and then established himself in New York, where he has been prominent for nearly fifty years of professional life He was active in securing the construction of the first railroad west of Lake Erie and has been connected with many corporations. During the Civil War, he actively supported the Government, was one of the eleven organizers of the Loyal League of New York, which attained a membership of 100,000, one of the life senators of that body, and a founder and secretary of the Citizens' Association As a member of the New York Legislature and one of the judiciary committee, he took a leading part in the measures for the impeachment of the judicial accomplices of the Tweed Ring and was one of the managers who secured the conviction of Judge Barnard before the Court of Impeachment He was one of the commissioners who secured and located the great parks for the city. In 1855, he married Isabel White, daughter of the Honorable Hugh White, and has six children His residence is in Bedford Park He is a member of the New England Society, the American Geographical Society, the Dartmouth Alumni Association and of other societies and clubs He was one of the founders of the American Museum of Natural History and of the Young Men's Christian Association.

Mr William White Niles, son of William Watson and Isabel (White) Niles, was born in New York, is a graduate of Dartmouth College and a member of the New York bar, being the head of the law firm of Niles & Johnson. He is active in promoting the city's interests and was a member of the State Legislature in 1895, serving on the judiciary committee He was appointed a member of the Commission for the Preservation of the Adirondack Forests, and is now a school trustee of New York City He is a member of the Republican, Ardsley and Calumet clubs and the Dartmouth Alumni Association, and an honorary member of the Zoological Society. The eldest son of William Watson Niles is Robert L Niles, who is a member of the Stock Exchange, and who married a daughter of the late Bishop Lyman, of North Carolina.

GORDON NORRIE

NEW YORK had many famous merchants in the closing years of the last and the first half of the present century. They were the men instrumental in establishing the mercantile supremacy of the city in this country, and gave it the commercial prestige which rival communities in other parts of the United States had never been able to overcome. These early New York merchants came from all parts of the world, but it is not too much to say that foremost among the most energetic and enterprising of them were those who were of the intelligent and thrifty Scottish race

Adam Norrie, the American ancestor of the subject of this sketch, was a fine representative of these old-time Scotch-American merchants He was born in Aberdeen, Scotland, in 1795 Early in life he went to Sweden, where he became interested in the manufacture of iron, in which he was very successful Coming to New York about 1820, while he was still a young man, to investigate the iron trade on this side of the Atlantic, and its possibilities for extensive business, he decided to remain here.

At that time one of the great firms in New York was Boorman & Johnston. They dealt largely in Swedish iron, and were general merchants and importers of all kinds of commodities. The firm had been in existence for some time previous to the War of 1812, and when Mr Norrie came here, was, in importance and wealth, one of the foremost establishments in this country Adam Norrie joined this firm, his advent as a partner being signalized by the addition of the words "and company" to its style He was highly capable and energetic, and soon took a position in his adopted country as one of its ablest merchants and most public-spirited citizens. A chronicler of the mercantile history of that period has said of him· "He was Scotch to the backbone—that is, filled with ideas of stern honesty, sagacity and prudence, together with rapid determination He probably was remarked for these great mercantile qualities before he left Scotland, for with them he also brought to the firm he joined in this city, a splendid connection and correspondence in the old country"

Adam Norrie accumulated a fortune in his business and became interested in many other enterprises in New York and throughout the United States. He was one of the original stockholders of the canal between Lakes Michigan and Superior, a promoter and large stockholder of the Milwaukee, Lake Shore & Western Railroad, vice-president of the Bank for Savings, and a director of the Bank of Commerce and the Royal Insurance Company. He was one of the founders of St. Luke's Hospital, for ten years president of St Andrew's Society, and for many years held the office of senior warden of Grace Church. His residence was in Chambers Street, near Broadway, opposite City Hall Park, a few doors east of where the Stewart building now stands, that locality being then a fashionable residential section of the city He died in 1882, his wife having passed away ten years previously. Four children survived him, Gordon, Margaret Van Horn, Mary Van Horn and Julia Clarkson Norrie.

Mr Gordon Norrie is the only son of Adam Norrie. He was born in New York and succeeded to the large estate that his father left He married Miss Lanfear, resides at 377 Fifth Avenue, and is a member of the Metropolitan, Church, City and Union clubs, the Century Association and the Downtown Association. Mr Norrie has two sons, who are prominent in the social life of the city at the present time. A. Lanfear Norrie married Ethel Lynde Barbey, daughter of Henry I. Barbey; he lives in East Forty-first Street, and is a member of the Tuxedo, Metropolitan, Calumet, Union and Racquet clubs, the Country Club of Westchester County, and the Downtown Association The other son, Adam Gordon Norrie, was educated in Columbia University, and was graduated from that institution in the class of 1891. He is a member of the City, St Anthony, Knickerbocker and other clubs He married, in 1897, Margaret L. Morgan, a daughter of the late William Dare Morgan. The daughters of Mr Gordon Norrie are Mary, Sara G and Emily L. Norrie. The summer home of the family is in New London, Conn.

THOMAS FLETCHER OAKES

THE ancestor of the Oakes name in this country was Edward Oakes, a member of an English family that had high connections in the old country Edward Oakes and his wife, Jane, were residents of Cambridge They came to New England in 1634, and settled in Boston With them came their two children, Urian and James Urian Oakes achieved special distinction as a clergyman and educator Born in England in 1631, he was only three years old when he was brought to this country He was graduated from Harvard College in 1649, and after a few years returned to England, and was established over a church in Tichfield, Hampshire Becoming a non-conformist, he was among those who were silenced by the authorities in 1662 When the Reverend Jonathan Mitchell, pastor of the Harvard College Church, died in 1668, the Reverend Urian Oakes was called back to this country to take the vacant pulpit He also succeeded the Reverend Dr. Leonard Hoar in the presidency of Harvard College in 1675 His death occurred in 1681

Dr. Thomas Oakes, also a son of Edward Oakes, was born in 1644 and died in 1719. He graduated from Harvard College in 1662, studied medicine in London, and became one of the leading physicians of Massachusetts He was a member and speaker of the Provincial Assembly in 1689, a member of the Provincial Council, an agent for Massachusetts, in England, in 1692, and again a member of the Assembly in 1706 His son, the Reverend Josiah Oakes, who died in 1719, was a Harvard graduate in the class of 1708, and minister at Eastham, Mass., most of his life Mr. Thomas Fletcher Oakes is descended from James Oakes, a brother of the Reverend Urian Oakes and Dr. Thomas Oakes His father, Francis Garaux Oakes, was a shipmaster of Boston, and his mother was Caroline Comfort Paige His grandfather, Daniel Oakes, served as a soldier in the War for Independence.

Born in Boston, July 15th, 1843, Mr. Oakes was educated in private schools of his native city, and then began his business career as clerk for the contractors who were engaged upon the construction of the Kansas Pacific Railroad In 1863, when he had scarcely attained the age of twenty, he was a purchasing agent in St Louis for the Kansas Pacific Railroad, and it was not long before he was advanced to the position of general superintendent For more than sixteen years he made his home in St Louis and Kansas City. In 1879, he became general superintendent of the Kansas City, Fort Scott & Gulf, and the Kansas City, Lawrence and Southern railroads A year later he was called to be vice-president of the Oregon Railway & Navigation Company, and removed to Portland, Ore Scarcely a year had elapsed when he was elected vice-president of the Northern Pacific Railroad, and in 1883 he became general manager of the same company. In 1888, he was made president, and held that position for five years, until October, 1893, when the property went into the hands of receivers, of whom he was one until the reorganization of the company in 1896 He is also one of the trustees of the Manhattan Life Insurance Company

In 1864, Mr Oakes married Abby R Haskell, daughter of Henry Haskell His children are Walter, Grace, Zillah, Georgiana and Prescott Oakes He has an estate at Mamaroneck, where he makes his home. He is a member of the Metropolitan, Union League, and New York Yacht clubs, of several clubs in the Northwest, and of the American Geographical Society, of which he is a life member.

Mrs. Oakes is descended from the Coffin and the Phelps families of Essex County, Mass. Her mother was Sarah Coffin Phelps, and her grandmother was a Coffin Walter Oakes, the eldest son of Mr and Mrs Oakes, married Mary Beekman Taylor, daughter of Cortlandt Taylor, formerly of New York, and now of St. Paul, Minn. Grace Oakes, the eldest daughter, married Frederick Brooks, grandson of Peter Brooks, of Boston Zillah Oakes is the wife of George Curtis Rand, Jr, son of George C. Rand, of New York Georgiana Oakes married, in 1896, Lawrence Greer.

HERMANN OELRICHS

MORE than a century ago, the mercantile firm of Oelrichs & Lurman was one of the leading houses of Baltimore, and its members were reckoned among the foremost citizens of that city, socially and financially. The family to which the senior members of that firm traced their ancestry was distinguished in the annals of Bremen. Its records go back to 1325, when the patrician head of the family was banished to Schleswig-Holstein on account of trouble with one of the burgher class of the town. His family followed him into exile, and thenceforth became established in that duchy. The lineage of the American Oelrichs goes back in direct line to this branch of the family.

It is nearly one hundred years since a member of this firm came from Bremen to New York, to establish the branch that has remained one of the stable mercantile houses of New York down to the present time. For many years the New York firm was connected with the well-known house of H. H. Meier & Co. in Bremen, the head of which was a distinguished member of Parliament, president of the First Bank in Bremen, president of the North German Lloyd Steamship Company, and an intimate friend of Prince Bismarck. In the early years of its history, most of the partners of the New York firm were graduates from the celebrated old house, known under the peculiar name of Widow John Lang's Son & Co. Henry Oelrichs, of that branch of the family to-day represented by his son, Mr. Hermann Oelrichs, came from Bremen to this country in 1837. He was the son of Johann Gerhard Oelrichs and Catherine Holler. He has been described as a whole-souled good business man, and made a very distinct impress upon New York life after his settlement here, being a large shipping merchant and the agent for the North German Lloyd Steamship Company. He married a daughter of Dr. Frederick May, of Washington, D. C.

Mr. Hermann Oelrichs was born in Baltimore, Md., June 8th, 1850. He was instructed in private schools in his early years, and then sent to Germany to complete his education. He returned home to go into business, entering the office of Oelrichs & Co., of which firm he became a partner in 1875. Since 1887, when Gustave Schwab, Sr., retired, Mr. Oelrichs has been at the head of the house and in charge of the American business of the North German Lloyd Steamship Line. He is a member of the Metropolitan, Union, Manhattan, Lawyers', Players, Racquet, New York Yacht, Seawanhaka-Corinthian Yacht, and other clubs. He has had for years the reputation of being one of the best all-around amateur athletes in the country.

In 1890, Mr. Oelrichs married Theresa Alice Fair, daughter of the late Senator James G. Fair, of Nevada, one of the famous men of the Pacific coast. Senator Fair, who was born in Ireland in 1831, died in San Francisco in 1894. He went to California when the first excitement about gold discoveries broke out, and in 1860 moved to Nevada, where, out of the Consolidated Virginia Silver Mines on the Comstock Ledge, which the bonanza firm of Mackey, Flood, Fair & O'Brien controlled, he made a fortune. From 1881 to 1887, he was a member of the United States Senate from Nevada. Mrs. Oelrichs is the oldest daughter and third child of Senator Fair.

Mr. and Mrs. Oelrichs live in East Fifty-seventh Street. They spend much time at their summer home in Newport, where Mr. Oelrichs owns Rosecliffe, the property that was long the home of the famous historian, George Bancroft, Virginia Fair, the sister of Mrs Oelrichs, makes her home with them. Mr. and Mrs Oelrichs have one child, Hermann Oelrichs, Jr. Mr Oelrichs has taken considerable interest in political affairs. He is a Democrat, and at one time was a member of the Democratic National Committee for the State of New York, but resigned that position for personal reasons in 1895. The Democratic nomination for Mayor of the city of New York has been frequently offered to him, and as frequently declined. Lucie Oelrichs, daughter of Henry Oelrichs, married Colonel William Jay, of New York. Another daughter, Hildegarde Oelrichs, married Richard Henderson, of Liverpool, England. Henry Oelrichs, a son of this family, is unmarried, and another son, Charles May Oelrichs, married Blanche de Loosey, and has a daughter, Lily Oelrichs. He is a member of the Metropolitan and Union clubs.

DAVID B OGDEN

AMONG the many wealthy and influential families of New Jersey in the Colonial period, the Ogdens held a foremost position. They played important parts in public affairs in East Jersey, under the proprietory Government, and their descendants have distinguished themselves to an eminent degree in public life in that State and elsewhere down to the present day. John Ogden was the first of the family name in this country and a founder of the town of Elizabeth. He was settled in Stamford, Conn., in 1641, and three years later removed to Hempstead, Long Island, with the Reverend Robert Fordham. Subsequently he removed to Southampton, of which place he was a magistrate in 1656-57-58, a representative to the General Court of Connecticut in 1655—Long Island then being an appendage to the Connecticut Colony—and a member of the Upper House in 1661. He became one of the first settlers of a new Colony on the shores of Newark Bay, in 1665 was a justice of the peace there, and the same year a member of the Governor's Council, being a member of the Legislature in 1668. Under the Dutch, in 1673, he was burgomaster of the six towns of the Jersey Colony. His children were John, Jonathan, David, Joseph and Benjamin. Of these the three elder were original associates under the Governor Nicolls grants in 1665 John Ogden was conspicuous in 1671 in maintaining the rights secured by the Nicolls Patent. Jonathan Ogden was deacon of the church in 1694, and Benjamin Ogden was a sheriff in the same year.

David Ogden, the ancestor in the second generation of that branch of the family to which Mr. David B Ogden belongs, was born in 1691, and married Elizabeth Ward, daughter of Lieutenant Samuel Swayne, who went from Branford, Conn., to Newark, N. J., in 1656. His son, the Reverend Uzal Ogden, D. D , was the rector of the first Episcopal Church of Newark, which was founded by another son, Colonel Josiah Ogden, who was the ancestor in the fourth generation of Mr. David B Ogden. He was born in 1680 and died in 1763, being a man of wealth and influence, a Colonel of the militia and a member of the Provincial Assembly of New Jersey for Essex County in 1716, 1721 and 1738. His first wife was Catharine H. Low, daughter of Hardenbush Low. She was the ancestress of the subject of this sketch.

David Ogden, son of Colonel Josiah Ogden, was one of the most distinguished public men of his day. He was born in 1707 and died in 1800. Graduated from Yale College in 1728, he became one of the great lawyers of New Jersey and New York, and from 1772 to 1776, was a Judge of the Supreme Court. During the Revolutionary War he was a loyalist and lived in New York, where he was a member of the Board of Deputies, in 1779. After peace had been declared, he went to England for a time, but afterwards returned and settled in Kings County, Long Island. His wife was Gertrude Gouverneur, daughter of Abraham Gouverneur, and granddaughter of the Honorable Jacob Leisler. His son, Samuel Ogden, married Euphemia Morris, daughter of Judge Morris, of Morrisania, and his other children were allied in marriage to leading families in New Jersey and New York.

David B. Ogden, Sr , was the son of Judge David Ogden. He was born in 1769 and died in 1849, and was a distinguished lawyer. His wife was Margaretta E. Ogden, a cousin, daughter of Abraham Ogden, another great lawyer and public man The children of David B Ogden and his wife, Margaretta, were Samuel M., who married Susan Hall, Sarah Ludlow; Gouverneur M , who married Harriet Evans, daughter of Cadwalader Evans, of Philadelphia; Thomas L., who married Jane Johnson; Euphemia, Eliza Du Luze, Frances L. and David Bayard Ogden.

Mr David B Ogden, third of the name, is the son of Gouverneur M Ogden He was born in New York and was graduated from Columbia College in the class of 1869. Following in the footsteps of his distinguished ancestors, he was educated for the legal profession. He married Mary E. Sherman and lives in East Tenth Street He also has a country residence at Bar Harbor, Me He is a member of the Tuxedo, University, Church, Century and Morristown clubs and of the Bar Association.

FREDERIC PEPOON OLCOTT

DESCENDED from notable Puritan ancestors, the Olcotts trace their lineage directly to Thomas Olcott, who was one of the founders of Hartford, Conn. He belonged to a good English family and was well educated, and before he came to America was engaged in mercantile life. Historians of the early Colonial families say that he was probably a member of one of the first companies of Colonists which came from London to Massachusetts, and was settled for a few months in Newtown, now Cambridge, Mass., in 1634 When a company was formed, under the direction of the Reverend Thomas Hooker, to move westward and establish a new Colony on the banks of the Connecticut River, Thomas Olcott was one of the party and left Newtown in 1635. He became one of the leading and most active members of the new community of Hartford, and, associated with Edward Hopkins, Richard Lord, William Whiting and others, engaged in trade in Connecticut for several years. His death occurred in 1654. His widow, Abigail, lived until 1693.

Thomas Olcott, of Hartford, son of the pioneer, lived nearly through the first quarter of the eighteenth century, dying at an advanced age, and his wife lived until 1721. In the next generation, Thomas Olcott, who bore the name of his father and his grandfather, married, in 1691, Sarah Foote, daughter of Nathaniel Foote, of Wethersfield, Conn. She died in 1756 Their son, the fourth Thomas Olcott, lived throughout his life in Stratford, Conn , where he died in 1795. The second wife of the fourth Thomas Olcott, the great-grandmother of the subject of this sketch, was Sarah (Tomlinson) Thompson, of Stratford, widow of Hezekiah Thompson and daughter of Zachariah Tomlinson, of one of the earliest Connecticut families. She was descended from Henry Tomlinson, who, with his wife and several children, came from Derbyshire, England, in 1652 and settled in Milford, Conn., afterwards removing to Stratford, where he died in 1681. The English ancestor of the family was George Tomlinson, of Derby, Derbyshire, who belonged to the landed gentry and, according to tradition, came from a noble family. In 1600, hemarried Maria Hyde in St. Peter's Church, Derby Thomas Olcott died in 1795 and his wife in 1811.

The grandfather of Mr. Frederic Pepoon Olcott was Josiah Olcott, of Hudson, N. Y.; his grandmother was Deborah Worth, daughter of Thomas Worth, of Nantucket, Mass Mr. Olcott's father was Thomas W. Olcott, of Albany, a prominent citizen of that city throughout his life. For many years he was president of the Mechanics' and Farmers' Bank. His wife, whom he married in 1818, was Caroline Pepoon, daughter of Daniel Pepoon, of Stockbridge, Mass

Mr Frederic P Olcott was born in Albany, N. Y., in 1841. His early education in the local schools was supplemented by a course of study in the Albany Academy. Deciding upon a business career, he entered his father's bank as clerk, when he was sixteen years of age. Holding that position for several years, until he had secured a thorough insight into business methods, he left the bank and started in business for himself, being for some time engaged in the lumber trade in Albany and its vicinity. Afterwards he became connected with the banking house of Blake, Brothers & Co , of New York, and with Phelps, Stokes & Co., with whom he remained for several years. He was Comptroller of the State of New York, 1877-80. In 1884, he became president of the Central Trust Company of New York, a position that he has retained to the present time. Interested in many other important commercial and financial corporations, he has been a director of the New York, Chicago & St. Louis Railroad, the Bank of America, the Sixth Avenue Street Railway and the National Union Bank.

In 1862, Mr. Olcott married Mary Esmay, and has two children, Edith and Dudley Olcott. His brother, Lieutenant-Colonel Dudley Olcott, is connected with the Mechanics' and Farmers' Bank of Albany, of which his father was for so many years president. The city residence of Mr. and Mrs. Olcott is in East Fifty-third Street and their country home is in Bernardsville, N J. Mr. Olcott is a member of the Metropolitan, Union League, Riding, Ladies', Barnard, Manhattan, Essex County Country, and New York Yacht clubs and the Downtown Association. He is also a patron of the Metropolitan Museum of Art and the American Museum of Natural History.

STEPHEN HENRY OLIN

THE family of which Mr. Stephen H. Olin is the New York representative in this generation was probably of Huguenot origin. John Olin, its American ancestor, was little more than a lad when he arrived in New England. He was not a voluntary immigrant, but had been taken on the coast of Wales in 1678 by the press gang of a British man-of-war. When the man-of-war anchored in Boston Harbor, a few months later, he sought the first opportunity to escape from his captors and cast his lot in the New World From Boston he went to Rhode Island and settled in East Greenwich. In 1708, he married Susannah Spencer, whose parents came from Wales and established themselves in Rhode Island. John and Susannah (Spencer) Olin had two sons and one daughter.

Henry Olin, the second son of John Olin, had a son, Justin, who was born in 1739 in East Greenwich, R I. Justin Olin married Sarah Dwinnell and was the father of the Honorable Henry Olin, who was born in Shaftsbury, Vt., in 1768, and settled in Leicester, Vt, about 1788. He was chosen a member of the Legislature for the first time in 1799, and was reëlected for twenty-one successive terms. In 1801, he became assistant Judge of the County Court, held that office for eight years and was Chief Justice for fifteen years. In 1820 and 1821, he was a State Councilor, a Member of Congress in 1824, and Lieutenant-Governor of the State, 1827-30. In politics he was a Jeffersonian Democrat, and afterwards a Whig. He removed to Salisbury, Vt., in 1837 and died there. His wife, whom he married in 1788, was Lois Richardson.

The Reverend Stephen Olin, D. D., LL D, eldest son of Henry and Lois (Richardson) Olin, was born at Leicester, Vt, in 1797. He graduated from Middlebury College, Vermont, in 1820, and going to the South, soon after graduation, attached himself to the South Carolina Conference of the Methodist Episcopal Church, and was stationed at Charleston, S. C. For a time he was connected with a seminary in Abbeville District, S. C., and in 1826 was a professor in Franklin College, Georgia. In 1832, he was elected professor in Randolph-Macon Union College, Virginia, and in 1842 became president of Wesleyan University, at Middletown, Conn., which position he held at the time of his death, in 1851. In 1828, he was ordained an elder of the Methodist Episcopal Church; in 1834, the degree of D. D. was conferred upon him simultaneously by Randolph-Macon College and Franklin College, Yale College giving him that of LL.D. in 1837. The Reverend Dr. Olin went abroad in 1837 and made an extensive tour of the East, describing his experience in a volume, entitled, Travels in Egypt, Petraea and the Holy Land. In 1846, he was a delegate to the first meeting of the Evangelical Alliance in London. After his death, his sermons were published, as well as his Life and Letters. He had an established rank as one of the leading educators of his generation in the United States. Dr. Olin married, in 1843, Julia M. Lynch, who was born in New York in 1814, and died in 1879. Her father was Judge James Lynch, of New York, and her mother was Janet N. Tillotson, granddaughter of Judge Robert R. Livingston, of Clermont.

Mr. Stephen Henry Olin, son of the Reverend Stephen and Julia M. (Lynch) Olin, was born in Middletown, Conn., in 1847. He was graduated from Wesleyan University in 1866, and in 1895 received from it the degree of LL D He is a lawyer, and a member of the firm of Olin & Rives. He is Assistant Adjutant-General and Chief-of-Staff of the First Brigade of the National Guard, with the rank of Lieutenant-Colonel. In 1894, he was one of the Commissioners to revise the Public School Law. He has been president of the Wesleyan Alumni Association, and is a trustee of that University and of the New York Public Library. In 1879, Mr Olin married Alice W. Barlow, daughter of S. L. M Barlow. She died in 1882, leaving two daughters, Alice Townsend and Julia Lynch Olin.

The city residence of Mr. Olin is at 136 East Nineteenth Street, and his country home is Glenburn, Rhinebeck-on-Hudson He is a member of the Century, University, Players, Lawyers' and City clubs, the Downtown Association and the Bar Association.

ALEXANDER ECTOR ORR

IN the contemporary movements for the development of New York's commercial interests and for securing a healthier tone in public affairs, and a purer administration of the government of the metropolis, the business men of the community have been unusually prominent, and have energetically concerned themselves in the practical work leading to such results. One of the active citizens in this work, and one of the most untiring and influential, has been Mr. Alexander Ector Orr. Although Mr. Orr is a resident of Brooklyn, his business and social interests, as well as his activity in public affairs, have fully identified him with the metropolis. He is of Scottish descent, of the clan McGregor. His family, in the latter part of the seventeenth century, moved from Scotland to Ireland. William Orr, his father, the head of the family in his generation, lived in Strabane, County Tyrone, Ireland; his wife was Mary Moore, daughter of David Moore, of Sheephill, County Londonderry.

Mr. Alexander E. Orr was born in Strabane, March 2d, 1831. As a boy he was intended for service with the East India Company. An accident, however, led to a change in his plans, and he went to live with the Reverend John Haven, Archdeacon of the diocese of Derry and Raphoe, at Killaloo Glebe, who superintended his education. In 1850, he made a trip by sailing vessel to the United States, visiting several Southern ports Upon his return home, he made up his mind to settle permanently in this country, and returned to New York the following year His first engagement here was with a firm of shipping and commission merchants, and in 1858, he entered the employ of David Dows & Co. Three years later, he was admitted to be a partner in the firm, and in 1859 was elected to a membership in the Produce Exchange. Always active in the affairs of the Exchange, he has been several times a director and the president of the institution, and was also secretary of the committee that had charge of the important work of erecting the Exchange building

For years, Mr Orr has been chairman of the Arbitration Committee of the Exchange, and is a director in several banks, insurance companies and other fiduciary institutions. He is a member of the Chamber of Commerce, the Downtown Association, the City Club, the Hamilton Club of Brooklyn, the Marine and Field Club, the Atlantic Yacht Club and the American Geographical Society. A member of the Protestant Episcopal Church, he is one of the incorporators and a trustee of the corporation that has charge of the cathedral and schools built by Alexander T. Stewart, at Garden City, Long Island. He is also president of the Board of Rapid Transit Commissioners of the City of New York.

In 1856, Mr. Orr married Juliet Buckingham Dows, who was the daughter of Ammi Dows, of the firm of David Dows & Company His second wife was Margaret Shippen, daughter of Nicholas Luquer, and granddaughter of Dominick Lynch, of Brooklyn. Mrs Orr is a member of the famous Shippen family, that for two hundred and fifty years has been prominently identified with the State of Pennsylvania. She is in the seventh generation from Edward Shippen, the pioneer, who, the son of William Shippen, was born in England in 1639, came to Boston in 1668, and became a wealthy merchant. He married Elizabeth Lybrand, a Quakeress, and removed to Philadelphia in 1693 He was a member of the Assembly and Speaker, a member of the Provincial Council for sixteen years, a Judge of the Supreme Court and Mayor of the City of Philadelphia. His son, Joseph Shippen, was a scientist and intimately associated with Benjamin Franklin. His grandson, Edward Shippen, was a merchant, Mayor of the City of Philadelphia in 1744, Judge of the Court of Common Pleas, a county Judge, one of the founders of the town of Shippensberg, and also of the College of New Jersey and the Pennsylvania Hospital His great-grandson, Edward Shippen, was the famous Chief Justice of the Superior Court of the State of Pennsylvania, and for more than fifty years a leading member of the judiciary of that State Mrs Orr is the great-great-grandchild of Chief Justice Shippen. The children of Mr. and Mrs. Orr are Jane Dows, Mary More, and Juliet Ector Orr, who married Albert H Munsell.

JAMES OTIS

ONE of the greatest families of New England, distinguished for the patriotism of its representatives and the valuable services that they have rendered to their country in times of national peril, is that of Otis, of which Mr. James Otis is the representative in New York in this generation. John Otis, the American ancestor of the family, came with his wife and children from Hingham, Norfolk County, England, in 1635, and was one of the first settlers of the town of Hingham, Mass. His wife was Mary Jacob In the second generation, his son, John Otis, who married Mercy Bacon, was born in Hingham in 1657, and for eighteen years was a Colonel in the Massachusetts militia, for twenty years a representative to the General Court, for twenty-one years a member of the Council, for thirteen years Chief Justice of the Court of Common Pleas, and also a Judge of Probate. He died in Barnstable in 1727

Colonel James Otis, son of the second John Otis, was born in West Barnstable in 1702, and died in 1778. He was a member of the Provincial Legislature in 1758, Speaker of the House, Judge of Probate for Barnstable County, Chief Justice of the Court of Common Pleas, 1764-75, and president of the Council Board during the first years of the Revolution He was closely associated with Adams, Quincy, Hancock, and other great leaders of the Revolutionary period His wife was Mary Alleyne, of Wethersfield, Conn , daughter of Joseph Alleyne, who belonged to the Plymouth, Mass., family of that name He had a family of thirteen children One of his most celebrated sons was James Otis, 1725-1783, the Revolutionary patriot and orator, the leader in Massachussetts against the royal government, and after the war a member of the State Legislature . Samuel Alleyne Otis, son of Colonel James Otis, and great-grandfather of the subject of this sketch, was born in Barnstable, Mass., in 1740, and died in Washington in 1814 He was graduated from Harvard College in 1759, studied law, but afterwards entered upon mercantile pursuits In 1776, he was a member of the Massachusetts House of Representatives, and in 1784 was Speaker of the House In 1780, he was a member of the Board of War and also a member of the convention that framed a constitution for the State, and in 1788 a delegate to the Continental Congress In 1787, he was a commissioner to negotiate with the insurgents in Shay's Rebellion After the adoption of the Federal Constitution, he was secretary of the United States Senate His wife was Elizabeth Gray, who belonged to one of Boston's noted families, the daughter of Harrison Gray, at one time Receiver-General of the State of Massachusetts.

The grandfather of the present Mr James Otis was Harrison Gray Otis, son of Samuel Alleyne Otis and Elizabeth Gray, and one of the great orators of Boston in the first part of this century. Harrison Gray Otis was born in Boston in 1765, was graduated from Harvard College at the age of eighteen and was admitted to the bar when he had just attained his majority. Two years later, he began his career as an orator and a public man by delivering the Fourth of July oration in Boston. In 1787, he was Captain in the militia and aide-de-camp to General Brooks, in 1796 a member of the State Legislature, from 1797 to 1801 a Member of Congress, then United States District Attorney for four years, Speaker of the House of Representatives 1803-05, president of the State Senate 1805-11, and Justice of the Court of Common Pleas 1814-18. He took a prominent part in the Hartford Convention in 1814, was United States Senator 1817-22 and was elected Mayor of Boston in 1829 He married Sally Foster and his death occurred in 1848 His son, James W. Otis, married Martha C Church, and they were the parents of Mr. James Otis, of this generation

Mr. James Otis was born in New York, October 12th, 1836, and has been engaged in mercantile pursuits in this city during his entire lifetime He has taken an active interest in politics and in 1884-85 was a member of the State Senate from one of the New York City districts During the Civil War, he was a member of the Twenty-Second New York Regiment, being Captain of Company A, and saw active service at the front. On the field, in 1863, he was elected Major of the regiment He belongs to the Union League, Players and Seawanhaka-Corinthian Yacht clubs, and is also, by virtue of his ancestry, a member of the Sons of the American Revolution.

OSWALD OTTENDORFER

NO one among the adopted citizens of the Republic who have come hither during the last half century has achieved a more substantial success, or has more fully merited the approbation of his fellow citizens by disinterested public services, than Mr Oswald Ottendorfer, editor of The New York Staats Zeitung, the leading German newspaper of the United States. Mr. Ottendorfer is a native of Austria, having been born in Zwittau, in the Province of Moravia, February 28th, 1826. He studied law in the Universities of Vienna and Prague, and like other students of the Universities, embraced the revolutionary tenets that were secretly promulgated at that time. When the Revolution of 1848 broke out he identified himself with the movement and was a leader in all the proceedings against the Austrian Government. He was an active participant in the insurrection at Vienna, which led to the abdication of the Emperor Ferdinand, and when the uprising was suppresssed, in October, 1848, he was among those who escaped, going to Germany, where he took up his residence in Leipsic. In 1849, he participated in the revolutionary movements in Dresden, and later in the same year in Baden. When the liberal cause in Germany seemed totally lost, he became a political refugee, living for a time in Switzerland In 1850, finding that the active part he had taken in these insurrections made it unsafe for him to remain in Europe, he decided to emigrate to the United States When he arrived here, he was only twenty-four years of age and was without capital or influential friends. At first he took a position in a factory, but acquiring a knowledge of the English language, secured a clerkship in the office of The Staats Zeitung His ability quickly asserted itself and he was advanced from one position to another until he held important and confidential relations with the management of the paper. In 1859, he married the widow of the original proprietor of The Staats Zeitung and assumed the duties of editor and publisher of the paper, a position which he has maintained uninterruptedly to the present time.

Through the influential position which Mr. Ottendorfer has occupied he has been an important factor in the public affairs of the metropolis for a generation In the municipal uprising against the Tweed Ring, he was a hearty supporter of Samuel J Tilden and other reformers, and was a member of the famous Committee of Seventy He was also a member of the Board of Aldermen in 1873-74. For many years he was a director in the German-American Bank, the German Savings Bank, the German Hospital and the Deutcher Leiderkranz Society During the last fifteen years, he has, to a large extent, retired from active participation in general business affairs on account of ill health, confining his attention to his editorial work on The Staats Zeitung and to labor in the cause of municipal reform and wholesome politics, in which he is as deeply interested as when he stood shoulder to shoulder with the leading reformers in the days of the Tweed Ring

Mrs Ottendorfer, whose maiden name was Anna Behl, was devoted to charity, dispensing her wealth in a most generous manner In 1875, she established a Home for Old Ladies in Astoria, Long Island, and set apart a fund for its support This institution, which is now known as the Isabella Heimath, was removed in 1889 to Washington Heights, where it occupies one of the finest buildings devoted to such purposes in the city of New York. Several years before her death, which occurred in 1884, she made a donation for the assistance of schools in the city, and in 1881, she erected a woman's pavilion to the German Hospital. In 1883, she presented a handsome building to the German Dispensary in Second Avenue, together with a valuable medical library. In 1884, Mr. Ottendorfer founded the Second Avenue branch of the Free Circulating Library, located in the centre of the German district on the East Side, and called the Ottendorfer Library.

For many years, Mr. and Mrs Ottendorfer resided on an estate on Washington Heights, overlooking the Hudson River. Mr Ottendorfer now lives in Fifty-ninth Street, opposite Central Park. He is a member of the Manhattan, City, Century, Reform and Commonwealth clubs, the Leiderkranz and the American Geographical Society.

RICHARD CHANNING MANN PAGE, M. D

ONE of the most distinguished families in the history of Virginia is that of Page The American pioneer was John Page, son of Francis Page, of Bedfont, Middlesex County, England, who belonged to a branch of the family that had for its arms or , a fesse dancette between three martlets azure, a bordure of the last Crest, a demi-horse forcene, per pale dancette, or and azure. Motto· *Spe labor levis.* John Page was born in Bedfont in 1627, was a prosperous merchant in the mother country, and in Virginia became one of the most influential members of that Colony, being a member of the Royal Colonial Council He died in 1692

Matthew Page, 1659-1703, son of John Page, was a wealthy planter, married Mary Mann, was an original member of the board of trustees of William and Mary College, and a member of the Royal Council under Queen Anne. In the third generation, Mann Page, 1691-1730, was, next to Lord Fairfax, the largest landowner in Virginia, holding at one time over seventy thousand acres in several counties. John Page, 1720-1780, second son of Mann Page, was a member of the Colonial Council in 1776 After his father's death, he was the head of the North End branch of the family. His mother was Judith Carter, daughter of Robert Carter, president of the Virginia Colony His wife was Jane Byrd, daughter of Colonel William E Byrd, of Westover

Eleven children of John Page survived their parents Major Carter Page, the fourth son, 1758-1825, left William and Mary College in 1776 to join the Continental Army, and became Major and aide-de-camp to General Lafayette He married Mary Carey, daughter of Colonel Archibald Carey, a descendant of Colonel Miles Carey of the Royal Navy, and in the sixth generation from Pocahontas and John Rolfe Dr Mann Page, 1791-1850, third surviving son of Major Carter Page, was educated at Hampden—Sidney College, and graduated from the Philadelphia Medical College in 1813. He married Jane Frances Walker, descended from the Nelsons of Yorktown, Va , and from Colonel John Washington, the ancestor of General George Washington.

Dr Richard Channing Mann Page was the twelfth child and eighth son in his father's family He was born in Keswick, Albermarle County, Va , January 2d, 1841 A student in the University of Virginia, when the Civil War broke out, he followed the example of his grand-father and other ancestors of the Revolutionary period, and, abandoning his books, enlisted in Pendleton's Rockbridge Battery, attached to Stonewall Jackson's Brigade in the army of General Joseph E Johnston Engaged in the first battle of Bull Run in 1861, he was transferred to the Morris Artillery Company, and promoted to be Second Gun Sergeant After the battle of Williams-burg he was brevetted Captain of Artillery He was present at Fredericksburg, Chancellorsville and Gettysburg, served in the campaign of the Wilderness, and was promoted to be Major and Chief of Artillery on the staff of Major-General John C. Breckinridge. In the Chancellorsville campaign in 1863, Page's Battery accompanied Stonewall Jackson's corps on that famous march to General Hooker's rear It had the honor of firing the gun at sunrise on that historic third of May, as a signal for the commencement of the battle. It occupied and held Hazel Grove, the possession of which was an important factor in compassing the defeat of the Union forces

After the war, Dr Page completed his studies, and graduated from the New York University Serving as house physician to Bellevue Hospital, he was afterward district physician and then house surgeon to the Woman's Hospital, and since 1871 has been engaged in private practice In 1880, he was appointed professor in the New York Polyclinic, was honorary vice-president of the Paris Congress for the study of tuberculosis, and is the author of many works on medicine, including several important text books He is a member of the New York His-torical Society, the New York Southern Society, the Confederate Veteran Camp of New York, the Society of Medical Jurisprudence and the Sons of the Revolution. In 1874, he married Mary Elizabeth (Fitch) Winslow, of Westport, Conn , widow of Richard Henry Winslow, a founder of the banking house of Winslow, Lanier & Co Mrs Winslow is descended on her mother's side from Sarah Wilson, of Boston, and Edward Cornell, of England

EDWARD WINSLOW PAIGE

ABOUT the middle of the seventeenth century, Nathaniel Paige came to Massachusetts, was one of the proprietors of Hardwick, Leicester, and Spencer, and marshal of Suffolk County, 1686 His son, Deacon Christopher Paige, of Hardwick, married Elizabeth Reed Their son, John Paige, served in two campaigns of the French War, and was at the battle of the Plains of Abraham, where he was wounded.   He married Hannah Winslow, 1740-1812, daughter of Captain Edward Winslow, 1703-1780, of Rochester, Mass., the son of Major Edward Winslow, 1681-1760, and grandson of Colonel Kenelm Winslow, 1635-1715.   Colonel Winslow's father was Kenelm Winslow, 1599-1672, brother of Edward Winslow; he came to Plymouth in 1869.

The Reverend Winslow Paige, 1767-1838, son of John, was born at Hardwick, Mass , and became a Dutch minister. His first charge was at Stephentown, N. Y., in 1790, whither his father then removed. In 1793, he was pastor of the Dutch Reformed Church at Schaghticoke, and remained there fourteen years, after which he had successively the Dutch churches of Florida, N. Y., and Gilboa, N. Y., where he died In 1787, he married Clarissa Keyes, of Ashford, Conn , daughter of General John and Mary (Wales) Keyes.   John Keyes was a Captain under Knowlton, behind the rail fence at Bunker Hill.   He was at Harlem Heights, Trenton and Princeton, and was the first Adjutant-General of Connecticut, continuing until the end of the war.

Alonzo Christopher Paige, father of Edward Winslow Paige, was the son of Winslow Paige He was born at Schaghticoke, N. Y., in 1798, and died at Schenectady in 1868.   Graduated from Williams College in 1812, he was, from 1828 to 1846, reporter of the Court of Chancery.   During the four years, from 1826 on, he was a member of the New York Assembly, and a State Senator, 1837-1842.   In 1848 he became a Justice of the Supreme Court, and in 1867 was a member of the Constitutional Convention.   He was a trustee of Union College and with other positions of trust, was a director of the Utica & Schenectady and New York Central Railroads, 1832-1867.

Harriet Bowers Mumford, wife of Alonzo Christopher Paige, and mother of the present Mr Paige, was born in New York in 1807.   She was the daughter of Benjamin Maverick Mumford, born on Groton Bank, Conn , in 1772 The first American ancestor of the family was Thomas Mumford, one of the "gentlemen" who accompanied Captain John Smith in his exploring expeditions from Jamestown, Va , in 1608 He returned to England, and was a member of the Virginia Company.   Thomas Mumford, second of the name, came to Rhode Island, and in 1657 made the Pettaquamscutt purchase, which included Narragansett Pier and the adjacent region He married Sarah Sherman, daughter of Philip Sherman, one of the founders of Rhode Island. Thomas Mumford, third of the name, born 1656, was a deputy of Rhode Island, and his son, Thomas Mumford, fourth of the name, born at Kingstown, R. I , 1687, married Hannah Remington, and moved to Groton Bank, Conn. He founded St. James' Church, New London. Its rector, Dr Seabury, who married his daughter, was the father of Bishop Seabury.   The fifth Thomas Mumford, born 1707, was a Captain in 1736, and married Abigail Chesebrough.   His son, Thomas Mumford, born on Groton Bank, 1728, was one of the seven who furnished the means for the expedition which captured Ticonderoga He was State Commissary and a member of the Assembly or Council throughout the Revolution.   When Arnold took New London in 1781, Mr. Mumford's house was particularly singled out for destruction.   He married a granddaughter of William Nicoll and Annetje Van Rensselaer.   Benjamin Maverick Mumford was their son.

Mr. Edward Winslow Paige was born July 11th, 1844, at Schenectady.   He was graduated from Union College in 1864, and from the Harvard Law School in 1866, and was LL. D , Hobart, in 1887.   For nearly thirty years he has been in the active practice of his profession.   His residence is Schenectady His place, which overlooks the "Groot Vlacht," is the site of the former residence of Hiawat-ha, the founder of the Iroquois Indian Confederacy. In New York, he lives at 29 Washington Square He is a [member of the Bar Association, the Metropolitan, University and other clubs, the Union Alumni Association and the Society of Colonial wars.

RICHARD SUYDAM PALMER

ONE of the stirring incidents of the War of 1812 was the bombardment of the town of Stonington, Conn , by a British fleet in August, 1814. Sir Thomas M Hardy, who commanded three British ships of war, the Ramilies, the Pactolus and the Dispatch, sailed into the harbor one day and announced his purpose of destroying the town The little company of militia, reinforced by the citizens of the place, valiantly defended their homes, although they had only two eighteen-pound cannon and one four-pounder, but a good supply of ammunition, and after four days of unequal combat, drove off the British vessels in a half sinking condition Philip Freneau, the balladist of that time, celebrated this victory in one of the most popular war songs of the early part of this century.

Captain Amos Palmer, the great-grandfather of Mr Richard Suydam Palmer, was the senior warden of the borough of Stonington at the time of that famous fight, and took prominent part in the defense of the town He was Chairman of the Committee of Citizens that had been intrusted with preparations for the defense of the town many months previously, the attack upon it having been long anticipated, and his report of the affair to the Secretary of War in Washington is one of the interesting war documents of that period He was born in 1747, and his death occurred in 1816. He came of an old and respected Colonial family, being lineally descended from Walter Palmer, the American emigrant, who was a member of an ancient English family, and arrived from England in 1629 Locating first in Charlestown, Mass , Walter Palmer was made a freeman of that place in 1631 Removing to Rehoboth in the Plymouth Colony in 1642, he was a deputy to the General Court in 1643-47, and was frequently elected by his townsmen to important town offices In 1653, he removed to Connecticut, and purchased land from Governor Haynes Subsequently receiving other grants from the town of Pequot, he became one of the original proprietors of Stonington. He died in 1662 His wife, whom he married in Charlestown, was Rebecca Short

Courtlandt Palmer, the grandfather of Mr Richard Suydam Palmer, was a son of Captain Amos Palmer He was born in Stonington, in 1800, became a prominent merchant of New York, and died in 1874 At the age of eighteen, he engaged with an older brother who was in business in Maiden Lane, but started in business for himself when he was twenty-one years of age, and was at once successful Soon after the panic of 1837, he began to invest in real estate in New York and in the West, and became very wealthy. He was the first president of the Stonington & Providence Railroad, 1844-48, one of the founders and a director of the Safe Deposit Company, and a director of the Mutual Bank and Trust Company

The first wife of Courtlandt Palmer was Eliza Thurston, daughter of Governor Thurston, of Connecticut His second wife, whom he married in 1832, and who became the mother of all his children, was a daughter of Richard Suydam. He had four children, Courtlandt, Charles Phelps, Mary Anna, and Richard Suydam Palmer, who married Fannie Arnot, and was the father of the subject of this sketch Courtlandt Palmer, 1843-1888, was the distinguished lawyer and author Graduated from Williams College and the Law School of Columbia College, he devoted himself principally to the management of his father's estate, and to literary pursuits He was an advanced and radical thinker, and established the famous Nineteenth Century Club, of which he was president during his life Mary Anna Palmer married Henry Draper, who died several years ago. She lives in Madison Avenue, and has a country place, Wykaska, at Dobbs' Ferry

Mr. Richard Suydam Palmer was born in New York, September 12th, 1868, and educated in Columbia University, being graduated in the class of 1891 His residence is in East Thirty-ninth Street, near Fifth Avenue. He is a member of the Metropolitan, Union, Knickerbocker, Calumet, Riding, St Anthony, University and Meadow Brook Hunt clubs, the Country Club of Westchester County, the Columbia College Alumni Association, and the New York, Seawanhaka-Corinthian and Larchmont Yacht clubs He is especially devoted to yachting, and has three times crossed the Atlantic in his yacht, Yampa, one of the finest cruising schooner yachts in the world.

TRENOR LUTHER PARK

ONE of the oldest New England families is that founded by Richard Park, of Hadleigh, Suffolk, England, who came to this country as early as 1630. Among the distinguished descendants of this pioneer, was Trenor W Park, the eminent lawyer, railroad manager and financier, of the last generation, who was the father of Mr. Trenor Luther Park. Trenor W Park was born in Woodford, Vt, in 1823. His parents removed to Bennington when he was a child, and he received his education there, after which he studied law for five years and was admitted to practice at the Vermont bar, in 1844, the same year he attained his majority. For the next ten years he pursued his profession in his native State with considerable success. In 1852, he left Vermont and went to California, where he became a junior member of the law firm of Halleck, Peachy, Billings & Park, of which General Henry W. Halleck was the senior member. He soon became one of the most eminent lawyers on the Pacific coast, his specialty being land titles. Incidentally, he became interested in lands and mines, and accumulated wealth through business operations.

After spending eleven years in California, he returned to his native State with a competence and settled in Bennington to a life of retirement. It was not long, however, before he turned his attention to railroad and financial affairs, in which he achieved a success quite equal to that which he had won in the law. He obtained control of the Western Vermont Railroad, and reorganized the company as the Bennington & Rutland Railroad, and was also interested in the development of several large Western mining properties. He was a director in the Pacific Mail Steamship Company, and president of the Panama Railroad, for the eight years following 1874. He was generous in his benefactions, and founded an art gallery at the University of Vermont, and presented a free library and a home for veterans of the late war to the town of Bennington, Vt.

The first wife of Trenor W Park was Laura V Hall, daughter of the Honorable Hiland Hall, of Vermont. She died in 1875, and in 1882 Mr Park married Ella Nichols, daughter of A C Nichols, of San Francisco. His children, who were by his first wife, are: Trenor Luther Park, Eliza Park, who became the wife of General John G McCullough, and Laura Hall Park, who married Frederick B Jennings. The maternal grandfather of the present Mr Park, the Honorable Hiland Hall, was one of Vermont's most distinguished citizens. He was born in Bennington in 1795, being the son of Nathaniel and Abigail (Hubbard) Hall. John Hall, his Puritan ancestor, was in the early emigration, and after living in Boston and Hartford, was one of the first settlers of Middletown, Conn, in 1650. George Hubbard, his maternal ancestor, was also one of the first settlers of Middletown. Hiland Hall was admitted to the bar in 1819, was elected a member of the Vermont Legislature in 1827, and was State Attorney from 1828 to 1831, and a Whig Member of Congress for ten years, from 1833 to 1843. Afterwards, he was bank commissioner of the State for four years, Judge of the Supreme Court in 1846, and in 1850 became second comptroller of the United States Treasury, and commissioner to settle disputed titles of land in California between the citizens of the United States and the Mexicans. One of the earliest Republicans, he was a delegate to the first National Republican Convention in 1856. In 1858, and again in 1859, he was elected Governor of Vermont, and was a delegate to the Peace Congress in Washington, in 1861. Governor Hall was president of the Vermont Historical Society, vice-president of the New England Historic-Genealogical Society, and the author of a History of Vermont. He died at Springfield, Mass, in 1885.

Mr Trenor Luther Park was born in San Francisco, in 1861, and was graduated from Harvard in 1883. He has been for a number of years engaged in business in this city. He married Julia H Catlin, the residence of the family being at White Plains, Westchester County. Mr Park is a member of the Metropolitan, Union League, Lotos, New York Yacht, Seawanhaka-Corinthian Yacht, Harvard, Racquet, St. Nicholas, New York Athletic, St Andrew's Golf and Δ K E clubs, the Country Club of Westchester County, and the New England Society.

SCHUYLER LIVINGSTON PARSONS

A DOUBLE wedding interested New York in the summer of 1775 John Watts, a son of Councilor John Watts, who had been recently graduated from King's College, was married to his cousin Jane, daughter of Peter de Lancey, of Westchester The other bride was her sister, Susan de Lancey, who married Colonel Thomas Barclay The guests drove from the city to the de Lancey mansion in Westchester, and the assemblage was extremely brilliant

Colonel Thomas Barclay and his wife Susan were ancestors of the Parsons family, which has been conspicuous in New York society for several generations Colonel Barclay, 1753-1830, was the eldest son of the Reverend Dr Henry Barclay, the rector of Trinity Church. John Barclay, his ancestor and great-grandfather, was Governor of East Jersey, married Cornelia Van Schaick, and died in 1731 Governor John Barclay was the son of Colonel David Barclay, of Ury, 1610-86, and of Lady Catherine Gordon, 1621-63, who was in the thirteenth generation from Robert Bruce, King of Scotland, and his second wife, Elizabeth, daughter of Henry de Brugh, Earl of Ulster The line of descent was through a daughter of Robert Bruce, the Princess Margaret Bruce, who married William, the Sixth Earl of Sutherland, and thence through the Sutherlands and Gordons to Lady Catherine Gordon Through the Honorable Adam Gordon, in the eighth generation from Robert Bruce, who married Elizabeth, Countess of Sutherland, the Barclays could trace their descent from King James of Scotland, whose daughter Princess Janette was the mother of Adam Gordon. Colonel Thomas Barclay was for a long time British Consul General In the United States Through his wife, Susan de Lancey, the subject of this sketch is related to the ancient families of de Lancey, Van Cortlandt and Colden, famous in the early history of Manhattan The grandfather of Susan de Lancey was Etienne de Lancey, Viscount of Lavalle, her grandmother was Ann Van Cortland, and her mother was Elizabeth Colden, daughter of Cadwalader Colden.

The sons and daughters of Colonel Thomas Barclay and his wife, and their descendants, have figured notably in the history of New York. Thomas E Barclay was a Post Captain in the Royal Navy, Anthony Barclay, 1792-1877, was British Consul in New York, Elizabeth Barclay, 1776-1817, married Schuyler Livingston; Susan Barclay married Peter G Stuyvesant; Henry Barclay married Catherine Watts; de Lancey Barclay, 1780-1826, was a Captain in the English Army and married Mrs. Gurney Barclay, nee Freshfield, of Norfolk. Ann Barclay, 1788-1869, married in 1815, William Burrington Parsons, an officer in the British Navy, who was saved from the wreck of H M S. Sylph, on the coast of Long Island, January 17th, 1815. Their son, William Barclay Parsons, 1828-1887, married in 1851 Eliza Glass Livingston, daughter of Schuyler Livingston by his first marriage with Ann Hosie, a descendant from the Munroe family of Scotland, who were identified with the founding of the University at Edinburgh.

Schuyler Livingston was the great-grandson of Robert Livingston, the third and last Lord of the Manor, and of Mary Thong, his wife, the granddaughter of Governor Rip Van Dam This Robert Livingston was the grandson of Robert, first Lord of the Manor of Livingston, who emigrated to America between 1674 and 1676. He married Alida Schuyler, widow of Nicolaus Van Rensselaer and daughter of Philipse Pieterse Van Schuyler There are few families more intimately connected with the early development of this country than the Livingstons By intermarriage, the family is linked with many well known names, such as Schuyler, Barclay, de Lancey, Rutgers, Van Brugh, Van Cortlandt, Van Rensselaer, as well as that of the historic Anneke Jans. William Barclay Parsons' children, Schuyler Livingston, William Barclay, Harry De Berkeley and George Burrington Parsons, are among those of the name most prominent in this generation

Mr Schuyler Livingston Parsons, the eldest son, was born in New York, October 12th, 1852, and married in 1877, Helena Johnson, daughter of Bradish Johnson, and has three children, Helena Johnson, Evelyn Knapp and Schuyler Livingston, Jr Mrs Parsons died August 26th, 1897 Mr. Parsons has a country residence at Islip, Long Island He is a merchant, and member of the Chamber of Commerce, and of the Union, Metropolitan, Players and other clubs

WILLIAM HENRY PARSONS

ON the paternal side the subject of this article comes of an old family that has been substantially planted in Warwickshire, England, for many generations back   His father, Edward Lamb Parsons, came to this country when he was a young man of twenty-one years of age, and became a respected merchant in New York.   His wife, the mother of Mr William Henry Parsons, was Maltilda Clark, a New England woman of Colonial lineage on the paternal side, and descended from a New York Dutch family on her mother's side.

Mr William Henry Parsons was born on Staten Island, July 7th, 1831.   He was educated in a private school at Rye, N Y., where he was prepared for college.   Ill health prevented him from pursuing a collegiate course, and he eventually turned his attention toward business, going into the office of an English shipping house when he was twenty-four years old.   Two years later, as clerk, he entered the employ of a firm of paper manufacturers and dealers, and after a single year of experience in that business, was admitted to a partnership in the establishment, which continued for about two years, when the firm dissolved.   He then embarked in business for himself, and was successful, even although, with limited experience, he had to face the commercial depression of 1857.   For more than twenty-five years he sold paper on commission, but since that time has been largely interested in paper manufacturing.   His firm has been one of the most substantial and prominent houses in its line.   In 1891, after more than thirty years of existence, it was incorporated under the name of W. H. Parsons & Co., which title it had borne from the time Mr. Parsons established it.

The business interests of Mr. Parsons are numerous, and for the most part connected with the industry with which he has been identified throughout his life.   He is president of the Lisbon Falls Fibre Company, Lisbon Falls, Me.; of the Bowdoin Paper Manufacturing Company, Brunswick, Me.; of the corporation of W. H. Parsons & Co., Maine and New York, and is also a director of the Pejepscot Paper Company, Pejepscot, Me   His activities in enterprises incidental to his business calling have given him prominence in general business circles and organizations designed to benefit commercial interests.   He is president of the National League for the Protection of American Institutions, first vice-president of the Board of Trade and Transportation, a member of the Chamber of Commerce of the State of New York, a trustee of the Bowery Savings Bank, of New York City, and one of the vice-presidents of the Advisory Board of the Philadelphia Museums.   A member of the Presbyterian Church, he is a generous supporter of the institutions of that denomination, and gives much of his time to the direction of their affairs.   He is president of the Westchester County Bible Society, and one of the managers of the Presbyterian Board of Publication and Sabbath School Work, of Philadelphia.   He is also a manager of the Westchester Temporary Home for Destitute Children, one of the executive committee of the Society for the Prevention of Cruelty to Animals, and a fellow of the American Geographical Society.

Mr. Parsons has his country residence at Rye, N. Y., in the old family home, and is a member of the Apawamis Club of that place.   He is also a member of the Metropolitan, Union League and City clubs, and of the Atlantic Yacht Club, and a trustee and chairman of the house committee of the American Yacht Club.

In October, 1857, Mr. Parsons married Laura C. Palmer, daughter of John Palmer, whose father was Judge Palmer, of the Supreme Court of Pennsylvania.   Mrs Parsons, who died in 1893, was a lineal descendant from Miles Standish, the Puritan Captain of Plymouth, and from William Bradford, the second Governor of the Plymouth Colony and author of the Mayflower log. They had five children, three of whom are now living.   The sons are William H Parsons, Jr , and Marselis Clarke Parsons, who, with David S. Cowles, who married Mr. Parsons' daughter, Matilda, are connected with him in business as paper manufacturers   One son, John Palmer Parsons, a graduate of Yale, died in 1892, and a daughter, Margaret Rainsford Parsons, in 1882

EDWARD LASELL PARTRIDGE, M. D.

WHEN William Partridge, who was a native of Berwick-upon-Tweed, England, emigrated to this country, about 1640, he landed in Massachusetts, and subsequently was one of the first settlers of Hartford, and was one of the company which planted Hadley, Mass. He died in 1688 In the records, his name was often spelled Partrigg

Samuel Partridge, the son of William Partridge and of his wife, Mary Smith, was born in Hartford, in 1645 Taken to Hadley by his parents, he became one of the most distinguished citizens of Western Massachusetts, living until 1740 Educated as a lawyer, he was a Judge of the Court of Common Pleas, and Chief Justice and a Probate Judge Other responsible positions held by him were, Colonel of the militia, one of his majesty's council, and one of three leaders who controlled the affairs of Western Massachusetts, through its first century of existence.

The wife of Colonel Samuel Partridge was married to him in 1668 She was Mehitable Crow, daughter of John Crow, one of the founders of Hartford, Conn , and of his wife, Elizabeth Goodwin, the only child of Elder William Goodwin, one of the first settlers of Hartford, from Essex, England Samuel Partridge, the son of Colonel Samuel Partridge, was born in Hatfield, in 1672, and died in the same place, in 1736 His wife was Maria Atwater, daughter of the Reverend Seaborn Cotton, granddaughter of the Reverend John Cotton, and great-granddaughter of Governor Thomas Dudley, who came over as Deputy-Governor with Winthrop, in 1630, and was the second Governor of the Massachusetts Bay Colony, succeeding Governor Winthrop

Cotton Partridge, of Hatfield, Mass , son of Samuel Partridge, was born in 1705, and died in Hatfield, his native place, in 1753 His son was Lieutenant Samuel Partridge, of Hatfield, 1730–1809, who was a Lieutenant in the French War, and who married Abigail Dwight, a descendant of Captain Henry Dwight and of Elder John Strong, of Northampton, Mass. The next in descent was Cotton Partridge, of Hatfield, 1765–1846, whose wife was Hannah Huntington Lyman, daughter of the Reverend Joseph Lyman, D D , of Hatfield, who was an important man during the Revolutionary period, and trustee of Williams College

The next in descent, and father of Dr Edward Lasell Partridge, was Joseph Lyman Partridge, who was born in Hatfield, Mass , in 1804, and who graduated from Williams College, in 1828, and is now (1897) its oldest living graduate He entered the profession of teaching, being principal of the Leicester Academy, of Leicester, Mass For many years he was United States Collector of Internal Revenue, at Lawrence, Mass His wife was Zibiah N Willson, daughter of the Reverend Luther Willson, of Petersham, Mass , and sister of the Reverend Edmund B Willson, a distinguished Unitarian minister He was president of the Essex Institute of Salem, Mass His later years have been spent in Brooklyn

Born in Newton, Mass , September 27th, 1853, Dr. Edward L. Partridge early turned his attention to the study of medicine He entered the College of Physicians and Surgeons, New York, and was graduated therefrom, in 1875 Williams College bestowed the honorary degree of A M. upon him in 1880 He has been engaged in general practice in New York for more than twenty years, and has also been a professor in the College of Physicians and Surgeons, medical department of Columbia College, and visiting physician, later consulting physician, in the New York Hospital, visiting physician to the Nursery and Child's Hospital, the Sloane Maternity Hospital, and consulting physician to the New York Infant Asylum

In 1884, Dr Partridge married Gertrude Edwards Dwight, daughter of Professor Theodore W Dwight, LL D , of the Columbia College Law School Mrs Partridge numbers among her ancestors President Timothy Dwight, of Yale College , the Reverend Jonathan Edwards, the Reverend John Eliot, and Governor Thomas Dudley Dr and Mrs Partridge live at 19 Fifth Avenue, and their summer residence is Storm King, at Cornwall-on-the-Hudson Dr Partridge is a member of the University, Century and Storm King clubs, and the Society of Colonial Wars He has one child, Theodore Dwight Partridge, born in New York, December 26th, 1890.

CHARLES A PEABODY

ORN in Sandwich, N H, July 10th, 1814, the Honorable Charles A Peabody is the son of Samuel Peabody and Abigail Wood, who were natives of Boxford, Essex County, Mass. His grandfather, Richard Peabody, of Boxford, was an officer in the Revolution, and had a command at Ticonderoga. His mother was the daughter of Jonathan Wood, of Boxford, and his wife, Abigail Hale, whose family claims a descent from the younger branch of that to which Sir Matthew Hale belonged. On the paternal side, Mr. Peabody is a descendant of Francis Peabody, of St. Albans, England, who came to Massachusetts in 1635, and settled in Hampton, and finally in Boxford He was of Welch ancestry, the name Peabody signifying in that tongue, "man of the mountains." Samuel Peabody, father of the subject of this article, was a lawyer of distinction. He was graduated from Dartmouth College in 1803, being a college mate of Daniel Webster and Ezekial, his brother An intimacy between him and Ezekial Webster, contracted at college, continued throughout their lives.

In 1834, Mr. Charles A. Peabody began the study of law in Baltimore, in the office of Nathaniel Williams, then United States District Attorney of Maryland. After two years, he returned to Massachusetts and pursued his studies in the Law School of Harvard College. In 1839, he removed to New York, where he entered upon the practice of his profession, and became identified socially, through domestic ties, with the most eminent families of the metropolis. He took part in the politics of the day, aiding the formation of the Republican party in New York, in 1855, and in 1856 was appointed a Justice of the Supreme Court by the Governor of New York. In 1858, he was appointed a quarantine commissioner to succeed ex-Governor Horatio Seymour.

In 1862, President Lincoln appointed Judge Peabody a Judge of the United States Provisional Court of the State of Louisiana This court was called into existence by the necessities of the Federal Government in connection with its foreign relations. After the conquest of that part of the country during the Civil War, and while it was under military occupation, Judge Peabody's court had unlimited jurisdiction over every possible subject. His appointment empowered him to appoint court officials, make rules for the court and to hear all causes of every nature, his judgment to be final and conclusive. A large part of the business of New Orleans had been conducted on foreign capital, or by subjects of other nations, and losses sustained through the operations of war were made the basis of claims by foreign governments against the United States. It was therefore determined that these cases arising in that part of Louisiana and the adjacent country, held by the Federal forces, should be heard and decided in this court, the authority of which was made unlimited, and its judgments conclusive of the rights of all parties. William M. Seward, at that time Secretary of State, once said that all the powers of the Supreme Court of the United States were not a circumstance to those exercised by Judge Peabody in Louisiana. Judge Peabody supported this responsibility to the satisfaction of all who came under his jurisdiction In 1863, he was also made Chief Justice of Louisiana, but in 1865, he laid down his judicial office and returned to New York, where he has since resided and practiced. For many years, he has been a member and vice-president of the Association for the Reform of the Law of Nations, in which body he has taken an active part and has frequently visited Europe to attend its annual meetings.

Judge Peabody has been married three times. His first wife, the mother of his children, was Julia Caroline Livingston, daughter of James Duane Livingston, a grandson of Robert Livingston, the last Lord of Livingston Manor. His second wife was Mariah E. Hamilton, daughter of John C. Hamilton and granddaughter of Alexander Hamilton. His third, and present wife, is Athenia Livingston, daughter of Anthony Rutgers Livingston, also a grandson of the last Lord of Livingston Manor Judge Peabody has three sons and one daughter now living Charles A Peabody, Jr., is a member of the New York bar, George I. Peabody, M. D , is an eminent physician and professor; Philip Glendower Peabody is a lawyer in Boston, Mass , and Julia Livingston Peabody, the only daughter, is the wife of Charles J Nourse, Jr., of New York.

WHEELER HAZARD PECKHAM

FOR two generations the Peckhams have occupied a distinguished position in the legal profession and the judiciary of the State of New York. The father of Mr Wheeler H Peckham was Judge Rufus W Peckham, who was born in Rensselaerville, Albany County, N Y , December 30th, 1809 His father was a substantial business man, and, soon after the son was born, moved to Otsego County, on the eastern branch of the Susquehanna River, not far from Cooperstown There the boy spent his youth. He was sent to Hartwyck Seminary in Otsego County, then conducted by the Reverend Dr. Hazelius, and he remained there until 1825, when he entered Union College, being graduated with advanced standing from that institution in 1827 At the age of eighteen, Mr. Peckham settled in Utica and commenced the study of law Three years later he was admitted to the bar and moved to Albany After nine years of successful practice, Governor William L Marcy, in 1839, appointed him District Attorney for the County of Albany, and this position he filled satisfactorily for two years. In 1845, he was a candidate before the State Legislature for election to the office of Attorney-General, but John Van Buren, the son of President Martin Van Buren, defeated him in the election

In 1852, he was elected a member of the House of Representatives in the Thirty-third Congress During his term of service, he was one of the strongest opponents of the Nebraska Bill Before the expiration of his term in Congress, he returned to the practice of law in Albany, associating himself in partnership with Lyman Tremain In 1859, he was elected a Justice of the Supreme Court of the State of New York, and at the close of his first term of service of eight years was reelected, and was then elected to a seat on the bench of the Court of Appeals In November, 1873, in company with his wife he was a passenger on the Ville du Havre, which was run down in mid-ocean by the British iron ship Lock Earn. Both Judge Peckham and his wife were among those who were lost in this accident.

Mr Wheeler H. Peckham was born in 1833. After leaving Union College, he attended the Albany Law School, and was admitted to the bar in 1854 He commenced the practice of his profession in Albany, but was obliged to relinquish it on account of ill health and traveled for some time in Europe. On his return, he went to St Paul, Minn , but in 1864 settled permanently in New York, becoming a member of the law firm of Miller, Stoutenburgh & Peckham He first came prominently before the public by his work in connection with the prosecution of the members of the Tweed ring, in which he was intimately associated with Charles O'Connor and Samuel J Tilden

By birth and convictions an earnest Democrat, Mr. Peckham has always been conspicuous in the reform element of his party. He was appointed by Governor Cleveland, in 1882, to be District Attorney of New York County, to fill the vacancy caused by the death of John McKeon Finding his health inadequate for the work, he resigned after a few days service Recently he has been prominent in the movement for municipal reform. He was a leader in the Bar Association's action against Judge Isaac Maynard in 1891, and in the efforts to impeach that magistrate for his action in the election cases of 1890. An earnest advocate of the candidacy of Grover Cleveland for the Presidency in each of the three national campaigns, in 1894, he was nominated by President Cleveland to be Justice of the Supreme Court of the United States, but the opposition that was developed against him on account of the position that he had taken in the Maynard case, caused his rejection by the Senate. His brother, Rufus W. Peckham, became an Associate Judge of the Court of Appeals of New York State in 1886, and in 1895 was appointed to a seat on the bench of the Supreme Court of the United States

Mr. Peckham is a member of the Bar Association of the City of New York, of which he has several times been president He also belongs to the Metropolitan, Manhattan and Reform clubs and the Century Association, and is a patron of the Metropolitan Museum of Art. He lives at 685 Madison Avenue

446

ALFRED DUANE PELL

THE immediate ancestors of the Westchester Pells were the Reverend John Pell, Rector of Southwick, Sussex, England, who died in 1616, and his wife, Mary Holland. The Reverend John Pell was the son of another John Pell, descended from the Pells of Lincolnshire. Thomas Pell was the eldest son of the Reverend John Pell, of Southwick. Born about 1608, he was one of the first settlers of New England and among those who removed to Connecticut in 1635. He was a surgeon in the Pequot War and a deputy from Fairfield, Conn, to the General Court, and afterwards obtained the grant of land in Westchester County, that became the historic Pell Manor. He died in 1669, leaving no issue, and bequeathed his possessions to John Pell, son of his brother, the Reverend John Pell, D.D, of London, domestic chaplain to the Archbishop of Canterbury. Sir John Pell, the second Lord of the Manor, came to this country in 1670. He was first Judge of the Court of Common Pleas from 1688 until his death in 1702. He married Rachael Pinckney, daughter of Philip Pinckney, of East Chester. His eldest son, Thomas Pell, born about 1685, succeeded him. The fourth and last Lord of the Manor was Joseph Pell, son of Thomas Pell, but that male line is now extinct, the Pells of to-day being descended from Joshua, Thomas and Philip Pell, brothers of Joseph.

From Joshua Pell is descended Mr. Alfred Duane Pell, whose great-grandparents were Benjamin Pell, son of Joshua Pell, and Mary Ann Ferris, daughter of Elijah Ferris. Benjamin and Mary Ann Pell had Alfred S., William F, Maria and Ferris Pell. The eldest son, Alfred S Pell, was the grandfather of Mr. Alfred Duane Pell. He married Adelia Duane, daughter of Colonel James Duane, 1733-1797, who was Mayor of New York. The mother of Adelia Duane was a daughter of Colonel Robert Livingston, third Lord of the Livingston Manor. The parents of Mr. Pell were George W. Pell and Mary Bruen, whose family goes back in England to 1284.

Mr. Alfred Duane Pell was born in New York and graduated from Columbia College in 1887. He is a member of the New York Athletic Club. In June, 1897, he married Cornelia Livingston Crosby, daughter of Robert Ralston and Jane Murray (Livingston) Crosby. Mr. and Mrs. Pell reside in the famous Pickhardt house in Fifth Avenue.

From William Ferris Pell, the second son of Benjamin and Mary Ann Pell, comes another important branch of this family now represented by Herbert Claiborne Pell. Clarence Pell, son of William Ferris Pell, married Anne Claiborne, daughter of John Francis Hamtrank Claiborne, the famous Mississippi journalist, lawyer and publicist and Member of Congress, who was the son of Ferdinand Leigh Claiborne, of Virginia, and Magdalene Hutchins, and descended from Captain William Claiborne, of Virginia, 1587-1676. The Claibornes traced their lineage to the Kings of England and of Scotland, the line being clearly marked back to Malcolm II, King of Scotland in 1034. Herbert Claiborne Pell, second son of Clarence and Anne (Claiborne) Pell, married Catharine Lorillard Kernochan, daughter of James P. and Catharine (Lorillard) Kernochan, and has two children, Herbert Claiborne and Clarence Cecil Pell. He is a member of the Metropolitan and other clubs, and a governor of the Coney Island Jockey Club. His residence is in Tuxedo Park. The eldest daughter of Clarence Pell, Clara, married Captain Thomas Gerry Townsend, U. S. A., and has several children. The second daughter, Emily Pell, became the wife of Charles H Coster. The eldest son, James Kent Pell, died unmarried in 1885. The youngest son, Ferdinand Osmun Pell, died in 1864. Mrs. Pell resides in East Thirty-sixth Street with her youngest daughter, Charlotte Latrobe Pell.

Howland Pell is also a great-grandson of William Ferris Pell, being a grandson of Morris Pell and a son of William H. Pell. His grandmother was Mary R. Howland and his mother Adelaide Ferris, daughter of Benjamin and Anna M Schieffelin. Benjamin Ferris was a soldier of 1812 and sheriff of New York. Mr. Pell was born in New York in 1856. He married Amy Goelet Gallatin, a descendant of Albert Gallatin and Elbridge Gerry, and lives in Madison Avenue. He has served in the Seventh and Twelfth regiments, attaining to the rank of Captain

HARRISON ARCHIBALD PELL

THE Pells, whose name has been closely connected with New York and Westchester County for nearly three hundred years, are descended from an ancient English family. Their history constitutes a prominent part of the history of the settlement and development of Connecticut and New York. They come in direct line from a younger branch of the English family of Pelham, settled at Walter Willingsley and Dymbleshyer, Lincolnshire. The arms of the family, which were granted in 1594, are: Ermine on a chevron, azure, a pelican, vulned, gules. The crest shows on a chaplet vert, flowered, or a pelican of the last, vulned, gules. In the sixth generation from Walter de Pelham, 1294, was William Pelham, of Walter Willingsley, who was the direct ancestor of Thomas Pell, the founder of the family line in this country.

Thomas Pell came to Boston before 1630. He was engaged in trading in Delaware and Virginia, and afterwards went to Connecticut, where he died at Fairfield in 1669. He received a large grant of land in Westchester County, and John Pell, his nephew, succeeded to the estate in 1687. The territory, which was one of the large properties of the early days of the Province, was erected into a manor by Governor Dongan, and its proprietors, under the terms of the grant, paid a yearly rental to the City of New York of twenty shillings. John Pell married Rachel Pinckney, a daughter of Philip Pinckney, lineal representative of the Pinckneys of Pinckney Manor, Norfolk, England, and one of the ten original proprietors of the town of East Chester, N. Y. Thomas Pell, the third Lord of the Manor, married the daughter of an Indian chieftain, and their son, Joseph Pell, was the fourth and last Lord of the Manor.

The great-grandfather of Mr. Harrison Archibald Pell was William Ferris Pell, son of Benjamin Pell, grandson of Joshua Pell and great-grandson of Joseph Pell, the last Lord of the Manor. He married Mary M. Shipley, and left four sons, who were preëminently distinguished in the business and social world of New York, Clarence, Walden, Duncan C. and Morris Pell. The Honorable Duncan C. Pell, who was the grandfather of Mr. Harrison Archibald Pell, succeeded, with his brothers, to the business that his father had established. He was of splendid physique and was said to be one of the finest looking men in Wall Street. He had great commercial skill and was a lover of learning, being a founder of one of the prizes in the Free College, now the College of the City of New York. In the latter years of his life, he was a resident of Newport, and was elected Lieutenant-Governor of the State of Rhode Island in 1865. He died suddenly in January, 1874, at the age of sixty-eight. The wife of the Honorable Duncan C. Pell was Anne Clarke, of Hyde Hall, Otsego County, N. Y. She was the daughter of George Clarke, 1768–1835, and Eliza Rockford, daughter of General George Rockford, of Westmeath, Ireland, of the Royal Artillery. Through her father, who was a grandson of George Clarke, Lieutenant-Governor of the Colony of New York in the early part of the eighteenth century, she was descended through the Hydes, Nevilles, Beauchamps and Despencers from Edward I, King of England, and his wife, Eleanor, daughter of Ferdinand III, King of Castile.

Duncan Archibald Pell, the father of Mr. Harrison A. Pell, was born in 1842. During the Civil War, he served on the staff of Major-General Ambrose E. Burnside. After the war, he was a resident of Staten Island until the time of his death, in 1874, and took an active interest in public affairs there, being at one time a supervisor of Castleton and a trustee of the village of New Brighton. He married Caroline Cheever and left three sons, Duncan C. Pell, who married Anna Ogden Pemberton, Harrison A. Pell and Alexander M. Pell.

Mr. Harrison Archibald Pell was born at Newport, R. I., September 22d, 1868. Educated at the celebrated Bishops College School in Canada, he then entered upon business life in New York. He has figured prominently in the social life of the metropolis and of Newport. He is a member of the Calumet Club, the Baltusrol Golf Club and of other social organizations. His wife, to whom he was married in 1893, was Sadie D. Price, a granddaughter of Chief Justice Price, of Maryland, a representative of an old and respected family in that State.

CHARLES LAWRENCE PERKINS

S EVERAL distinct families of the Perkins name were among the early emigrants to America. John Perkins and Isaac Perkins, of Ipswich, and Abraham Perkins, of Hampton, who came to Massachusetts in the first days of the settlement, were near relatives, descended from Peter Perkins, an officer in the household of Sir Hugh Despenser about 1300.

John Perkins, of Ipswich, the ancestor of that branch of the family now under consideration, was born in Newent, Gloucestershire, England, in 1590. Sailing from Bristol, in 1630, he settled in Boston, becoming a freeman of that place in the following year In 1633, he removed to Ipswich, was a deputy to the General Court in 1636, was frequently a member of the Grand Jury, and died in 1654 John Perkins, his son, was born in England in 1614 and came to this country with his father When he grew to manhood, he became a prominent man of the town of Ipswich, was quartermaster of the military organization of that place, and died in 1686. Isaac Perkins, 1650-1725, the son of the second John Perkins, married Hannah Knight, daughter of Alexander Knight For four successive generations the descendants of Isaac Perkins lived in Ipswich. Jacob Perkins, 1678-1754, and his wife, Mrs. Susanna Butler, daughter of William and Susanna Cogswell, were the ancestors of the subject of this sketch

Francis Perkins, the son of the last-mentioned couple, was born in Ipswich in 1732. His first wife was Hannah Cogswell, and his second wife was Martha Low, daughter of Captain David and Susanna Low He was an ensign of the militia of Ipswich in 1774, became a Captain in 1776, and served in the Revolution Removing to Lunenburg, Mass, he died in 1812. David Perkins, his son, was born in Ipswich in 1770 He was prominent in the community, and, removing to Salem, died there in 1859 He was engaged in manufacturing, was a member of the Salem Mechanics' Association and a director of the Salem Laboratory Company. The wife of David Perkins was Hannah Fabens, of Salem, Mass., whom he married in 1793. She was a daughter of Peard and Hannah (Lang) Fabens, was born in Salem in 1771, and died in 1851 Their son, Benjamin Perkins, was born in Salem in 1797, and died in Roxbury, Mass, in 1870 His early life was passed in Hanover, N H, but in 1828 he removed to Boston He was treasurer of the Massachusetts Home Missionary Society, and actively interested in religious and philanthropic undertakings In 1823, he married Jane Lawrence, daughter of Abel and Abigail Lawrence, of Salem. Charles Lawrence Perkins, Sr, the offspring of this marriage, was born in Hanover, N H, in 1824 Educated in Boston, he was in early life associated with his father in business, but afterwards came to New York, where he became prominent in the iron business He married, in 1856, Elizabeth West Nevins, who survives her husband, and resides at Glen Cove, Long Island.

Mr. Charles Lawrence Perkins is the eldest son of Charles Lawrence Perkins, Sr, and Elizabeth West Nevins He was born in 1857 in Walton-on-Thames, England, and graduated from Harvard in the class of 1879. He entered business life in this city, and has been identified with large corporations, principally railroad, coal and iron interests He is a trustee of the Bowery Savings Bank and a director of the Knickerbocker Trust Company. In 1882, Mr Perkins married Margaret Gandy, and has one son, John Lawrence Perkins He has taken great interest in military affairs, and holds the rank of Major and Commissary of the First Brigade of the National Guard on the staff of General Louis Fitzgerald During the Brooklyn surface railroad strike of January, 1895, he was Chief Commissary for the united First and Second Brigades Mr Perkins' residence is in West Eleventh Street, and he has a summer home at Lawrence, Long Island He is a member of the Union, Racquet, Players, Whist and Harvard clubs, the Downtown Association, the New England Society and the National Academy of Design

The other children of Charles Lawrence Perkins, Sr, are two sons, George Endicott and Robert Paterson Perkins, and three daughters, Elsie Nevins, Frances de Forest and Mary Lawrence Perkins

PHILLIPS PHŒNIX

NORTHUMBERLAND, England, was the seat of a great landed family, the Fenwicks, whose name is pronounced in accordance with the spelling adopted by its American representatives The family here was founded by Alexander Phœnix, who often wrote his name Fenwick, and who arrived at New Amsterdam in 1640 He was a younger son of Sir John Fenwick, then head of the English family. Removing to Rhode Island, in 1652, he married for his second wife Abigail Sewall, ancestress of the Phœnix family, of New York. Jacob Phœnix, son of Alexander Phœnix, was born near New Orange (Albany), in 1651, was a freeman in 1698, and married Anna Van Vleeck. In the next generation was Alexander Phœnix, 1690–1770, a freeman in 1732, and a member of the Blue Artillery Company. His second wife was Elizabeth Burger, 1692–1757, daughter of George and Elizabeth (Thomas) Burger, and their son was Alexander Phœnix, who was born in 1726.

Daniel Phœnix (nephew of Daniel Phœnix, first treasurer of the City of New York), who was born in 1761, in New York, was the grandfather of Mr Phillips Phœnix He was a Major of the New Jersey troops in 1798. His wife was Anna Lewis Phillips, whom he married in 1784, and who died in 1854 His son, the Honorable Jonas Phillips Phœnix, was born in 1788, in Morristown, N J , and became one of New York's most distinguished merchants. He was an alderman, 1838-9, and a Presidential Elector, in 1840. A prominent Whig, he was a candidate for Mayor and in 1842 was one of the commissioners of the Croton aqueduct Elected a member of Congress, in 1843 and 1849, he was a member of the Assembly, in 1848

On the female side of the house, Mr. Phillips Phœnix includes in his ancestry several of the great families of New England and New York. His mother was Mary Whitney, a daughter of Stephen and Harriet (Suydam) Whitney Stephen Whitney was one of the leading merchants of New York in the last generation, and was descended from Henry Whitney, who came from England and settled on Long Island , his wife belonged to the Suydam family, of Hallett's Cove, Long Island The mother of Jonas Phillips Phœnix, Anna Lewis Phillips, was a daughter of Jonas Phillips and Anna Lewis, and descended on her father's side from the Reverend George Phillips, who came over on the ship Arabella, with Governor John Winthrop, in 1630 Her mother was the daughter of the Reverend Thomas Lewis, 1716–1777, of Yale College, 1741, a Presbyterian clergyman. Through the wife of her paternal great-grandfather, the Reverend George Phillips, she was descended from William Hallett, of Hallett's Cove, Long Island, and also from George Woolsey, one of the first settlers on Long Island.

The Honorable Jonas Phillips Phœnix had a large family of children Stephen Whitney Phœnix, the second son, was born in 1839, graduated from Columbia College in 1859, and Columbia Law School in 1863, and devoted most of his life to antiquarian and genealogical research. When he died, in 1881, he left his herbarium to the American Museum of Natural History, his genealogical works and fifteen thousand dollars to the New York Historical Society, his works of art to the Metropolitan Museum of Art, and his library and fortune to Columbia College. Anna Lewis Phœnix, the youngest daughter, died in 1858, unmarried ; the second daughter, Harriet Whitney Phœnix, married Isaac Bronson, son of Dr. Oliver Bronson, and died in 1864 Mary Caroline Phœnix married George Henry Warren The oldest child, Whitney Phœnix, died in 1833 Lloyd Phœnix, another son, was born in New York, in 1844, graduated from Annapolis, in 1861, and served in the Civil War, attaining to the rank of Lieutenant.

Mr Phillips Phœnix, the eldest son and the representative of the family in the present generation, was born in New York, in 1834 Graduating from the Law School of Harvard University, in 1854, he is a practicing lawyer in New York, and lives in East Sixty-sixth Street He is a member of the Metropolitan, City, Union League, Union, Knickerbocker, and New York Yacht clubs, the Downtown Association, the American Geographical Society, and New York Historical Society, and is a patron of the American Museum of Natural History.

HENRY EVELYN PIERREPONT

T WO sons of James Pierrepont, of the family of Holm Pierrepont, England, John and Robert Pierrepont, came to Roxbury, Mass , about 1636   John Pierrepont, 1619-1682, married Thankful Stowe   His eldest son died young   His second son, James Pierrepont, 1659-1714, graduated from Harvard in 1681, and settled, in the ministry, at New Haven in 1684 In 1689, he was one of three ministers who laid plans for the foundation of Yale College, and was one of the original trustees of Yale   In 1708, he was a member of the synod, at Saybrook, to formulate a plan to better enforce discipline in the churches of the Colony   The Reverend Mr. Pierrepont was married three times   His third wife was Mary Hooker, daughter of the Reverend Samuel Hooker, of Farmington   They had seven children   One of his daughters by this marriage became the wife of the celebrated Jonathan Edwards   Hezekiah Pierrepont, youngest son of the Reverend James and Mary (Hooker) Pierrepont, was born in 1712 and died in 1741, having married, in 1736, Lydia Hemenway, daughter of the Reverend Jacob Hemenway   He left a son, John Pierrepont, who was born in 1740, and died in 1805, and who married Sarah Beers, daughter of Nathan Beers, who came of an old family of Connecticut, his ancestors being numbered among the first settlers of that Colony   John Pierrepont and Sarah Beers were the great-grandparents of Mr Henry Evelyn Pierrepont

Hezekiah Beers Pierrepont, the grandfather of Mr Henry E Pierrepont, was born in New Haven in 1768, and died in Brooklyn, N Y , in 1838   He was carefully educated for commercial pursuits, and for several years was an official in the New York Custom House   Afterwards he became engaged in financial affairs, and in 1793 established the house of Leffingwell & Pierrepont.   His wife, whom he married in 1802, was Anna M Constable   She was the daughter of William Constable, who bought a large tract of wild land in Northern New York, the territory including more than one million acres, and was one of the founders of the town of Constableville, that was named after him   Hezekiah B Pierrepont left two sons, William C and Henry E Pierrepont, and several daughters

Henry Evelyn Pierrepont, Sr , was born in Brooklyn, in 1808, and died there in 1888 Receiving an academic education, he was engaged in the real estate business, and in 1833, while absent in Europe, was appointed one of the Board of Commissioners to prepare plans for laying out the public grounds and streets of the new City of Brooklyn   He was one of the founders of Greenwood Cemetery, and was instrumental in planning and carrying out the water-front improvements of Brooklyn, at the foot of Brooklyn Heights   He was the first president of the Brooklyn Academy of Music, was active in the organization of the Protestant Episcopal Church in that city, and altogether was one of Brooklyn's most prominent and most useful citizens.   The wife of Mr Pierrepont, whom he married in 1841, was Anna M Jay   She was a daughter of Peter Augustus Jay and Mary Rutherfurd Clarkson, her mother being a daughter of General Matthew Clarkson and his wife, Mary Rutherfurd   The lineages and the history of the Jay, Rutherfurd and Clarkson families are among the most brilliant in the annals of New York, and are fully treated upon several pages of this volume   The children of Henry and Anna M (Jay) Pierrepont were Mary Rutherfurd, Henry E , Jr., John Jay, Dr William Augustus, Julia Jay and Anna Jay Pierrepont. Mary Rutherfurd Pierrepont, who died in 1879, was the wife of Rutherfurd Stuyvesant.   John Jay Pierrepont married Elise de Rham, daughter of Charles de Rham

Mr Henry E Pierrepont, the eldest son of this family, was born in Brooklyn, in 1845, and educated in Columbia College, graduating in the class of 1867, and holds the degree of M A He married, in 1869, Ellen A Low, daughter of Abiel Abbot Low, and has six children Anne Low Pierrepont, who married Lea McIlvaine Luquer, Ellen Low Pierrepont, who married R Burnham Moffat, and Henry Evelyn, Jr., Robert Low, Rutherfurd Stuyvesant and Seth Low Pierrepont   The residence of the Pierrepont family is on Columbia Heights, Brooklyn   Mr Pierrepont is a member of the Hamilton Club of Brooklyn and the Sons of the Revolution

JOHN FRED PIERSON

MEMBERS of the Pierson family have been distinguished as merchants, clergymen and soldiers for more than two centuries of American history. Abraham Pierson, born in Yorkshire, England, in 1608, graduated from Trinity College, Cambridge, in 1632. Becoming a non-conformist, he emigrated to America in 1639, living for a time in Boston, where he was the friend of Governor John Winthrop. In 1640, he led a party from Boston to Long Island, where they purchased land and founded the town of Southampton He was pastor of the church there for seven years, and in 1647 moved to the New Haven Colony and founded the town of Branford, where he remained as pastor and engaged in evangelizing the Indians for twenty-five years. He was chaplain of the forces raised against the Dutch of the New Netherland in 1662-5, and when the difficulty was finally settled in a manner not agreeable to him, moved again and founded Newark, N J., which he called after the town in England where he was first ordained. He took with him nearly the entire population of Branford to the new settlement on the banks of the Passaic, and died in Newark in 1678

Abraham Pierson, Jr , graduated from Harvard College in 1668. He was ordained to the ministry the following year, and was successively pastor of the Congregational churches at Southampton, Long Island; Branford, Conn ; Newark, N J, and Killingworth, now Clinton, Conn. While at Clinton, in 1700, he was chosen as one of a committee to erect a college, and when the institution that in after years became Yale College was chartered, in 1701, he became its first rector and remained its head till his death, in 1707 The descendants of the Reverend Abraham Pierson, Jr , were active in public life. Josiah G. Pierson founded the Ramapo Iron Works, at Ramapo, N Y., in 1795, and a younger brother, the Honorable Jeremiah Halsey Pierson, born in 1766, became interested in the same enterprise and maintained his connection therewith up to his death, in 1855. He was preëminently a man of affairs, an inventor, one of the prime movers in the opening of the Erie Railroad and a Member of Congress in 1821

Henry L. Pierson, son of the Honorable Jeremiah H. Pierson and the father of Mr. John F Pierson, was born in Ramapo in 1807. He assisted on the survey that led to the building of the Erie Railroad, and in 1828 entered the firm of J G Pierson & Brothers, taking charge of its New York office. In 1830, he suggested the Erie Railroad from Lake Erie to the Hudson, was a director of the Erie Company, and for a time its treasurer, carrying through many of the early financial plans of the road in conjunction with his brother-in-law, Eleazar Lord Upon the death of his father, in 1869, he became the sole proprietor of the Ramapo Iron Works.

General John Fred Pierson, his son, soldier and merchant, was born in New York City, February 25th, 1839 Before he was twenty-one years of age, he joined the engineer corps of the Seventh Regiment, and was placed on detached service as aide-de-camp on the staff of General William Hall When the Civil War began, he recruited a company, and in May, 1861, was commissioned a Captain in the First Regiment, New York Volunteers. Promotion came rapidly, and in July, 1861, he was Major; in September, 1861, he was a Lieutenant-Colonel; in October, 1862, a Colonel, and in March, 1865, a brevet Brigadier-General He served under General Hooker in the Army of the Potomac, participated in the battles of Big Bethel, Fair Oaks, Glendale, Malvern Hill, Fredericksburg and other engagements, was wounded at Chancellorsville and Glendale, and captured at Chantilly, and confined in Libby Prison in 1862. He was the youngest officer of his rank in the army, and at times commanded a brigade at the age of twenty-three in a way that called out the heartiest appreciation of his superiors, leaving the service with a brilliant military record

General Pierson married, on December 9th, 1869, S Augusta Rhodes, and since the war he has been at the head of the New York house of Pierson & Co He lives at 20 West Fifty-second Street, and has a residence, Rose Lawn, at Newport, and also one at Ramapo, N Y He belongs to the Tuxedo, Union, New York Yacht, United Service and other clubs.

HENRY BRADLEY PLANT

JOHN PLANT, the progenitor of the Plant family, came to Connecticut, from England, in 1636 Mr. Henry B. Plant is descended in direct line from this ancestor. His paternal great-grandfather was a patriot in the War of the Revolution and served in the Continental Army, being attached to a regiment which was stationed at Washington's headquarters, in Newburgh, and he was one of the guards at the execution of Major Andre. The maternal great-grandfather of Mr Plant was a Major in the Continental Army

Mr Plant was born in Branford, Conn , October 27th, 1819 He was instructed by the Reverend Timothy O. Gillette, and then studied at the Lancastarian School, in New Haven. When eighteen years of age, he entered the employ of the New Haven Steamboat Company, and soon after was placed in charge of the express business upon the steamboat and railroad lines between New York and New Haven. When the Adams Express Company was organized, he went to the South in its interest, and in 1854 was made superintendent of the Southern Division of the company, with his office at Augusta, Ga. Mr. Plant remained in this position until 1861, when he organized the Southern Express Company, which succeeded to the business of the Adams Express Company in that section, and of which its founder has been continually president down to the present time. During the progress of the Civil War, his health failed, and he went to Bermuda and thence to Europe, remaining abroad until after peace was declared, when he returned and resumed charge of his express interests. Soon after the war, Mr. Plant became interested in developing the transportation facilities of the South, and started upon a career which has gained him a high rank among the great railway managers and financiers of the present period in the United States.

In 1879, he was the leading member of a syndicate which purchased the Atlantic & Gulf Railroad, of Georgia, and reorganized it under the title of the Savannah, Florida & Western Railroad Company. He developed and improved this line, rebuilt the Savannah & Charleston Railroad and has been active in the prosecution of other large Southern railroad enterprises.

In 1882, the charter of the Plant Investment Company was secured by Mr. Plant, in association with several prominent gentlemen of New York and other cities, including W. T. Walters, Henry M. Flagler, Morris K Jesup, Henry Sanford, Lynde Harrison and H P. Hoadley, the object being the purchase and development on a large scale of railway, steamship and other enterprises in the South. This work included the improvement of Florida railroads, the extension of several railways from Florida to connections with Northern and Western systems, the establishment of lines of fast mail steamships between Tampa, Fla., and Havana, Cuba, between various Southern ports, between New York City and Florida and between Boston and Halifax, and the creation of large modern hotels of the highest type, notably those at Tampa and Winter Park, Fla It is not too much to say that the development of Florida, since the Civil War ended, has been very largely due to the Plant Investment Company That State has been brought into close connection with the North, and the attention of investors, as well as of pleasure-seekers, has been drawn thither by improved means of communication. Mr. Plant has been the head of this remarkable development, which has not been rivaled in either magnitude or success by any enterprise of similar character ever undertaken in the United States.

Mr. Plant has a city residence at 586 Fifth Avenue and his country home is at Branford, Conn. He belongs to the Union League Club and the New England Society, and is a patron of the American Museum of Natural History. In 1842, he married Ellen Elizabeth Blackstone, daughter of the Honorable James Blackstone, of Connecticut. She died in 1861, and in 1873 Mr Plant married Margaret Josephine Loughman, only daughter of Martin Loughman, of New York. His one living son, Morton Plant, is vice-president of the railroads of the Plant system, vice-president of the Southern Express Company and vice-president and manager of the Canada, Atlantic and Plant Steamship Company.

GILBERT MOTIER PLYMPTON

THIS gentleman is the son of Colonel Joseph Plympton, and was born January 15th, 1835, at Fort Wood, Bedloe's Island, New York Harbor, then a military post under the command of his father, who at that time was a Captain in the United States Army. His education began at Fort Snelling, Minn, when he was five years old, with the Chaplain for an instructor, and was continued in a private school at Sackett's Harbor, N Y On the commencement of the war with Mexico, his father was ordered, with his regiment, to join General Scott's Army, whereupon the lad went to the home of his uncle, Gerard W. Livingston, in Hackensack, N. J , and continued his studies in that place. When his father, then Lieutenant-Colonel Plympton, returned from the Mexican War, he took his family to Jefferson Barracks, Mo., which post he commanded. The subject of this sketch then entered Shurtleff College, Alton, Ill , and remained there until he was promised a West Point cadet's warrant, when he accompanied his parents to this city and entered John Sedgwick's school to prepare for the Military Academy Not receiving the appointment, he read law and entered a law office at his father's request, and was admitted to practice in November, 1860. Shortly after, in order to perfect his professional knowledge, he entered the law department of the University of the City of New York and graduated from that institution with the degree of LL B in 1863

While he was still a law student, in 1860, his father, Colonel Plympton, died. At the beginning of the Civil War, his two brothers and the husbands of two of his sisters were in the army As a student, he was exempt from the operation of the draft, but being familiar with military duties, he offered his services gratuitously to the Government to instruct recruits and newly appointed officers His services were not required, however, and he subsequently applied for a commission in the regular army, but as all the other men of his family were already in the army, he was prevailed on not to press the application, as his mother and sisters were left in his charge.

For some years after his admission to the bar, Mr. Plympton had a general practice, but later it was confined almost entirely to the Federal courts His clients continued to grow in numbers, until they gave him an extensive practice. In his own cases, and as counsel for other lawyers, he was engaged in much of the important litigation of the time Mr. Plympton, however, never had a fondness for his profession, which he entered mainly to please his father. Having earned an independence and his health having suffered from overwork, he decided in 1889 to retire from the practice of the law. In 1892, he organized, with his present partners, the well-known banking house of Redmond, Kerr & Co., of this city, which has since occupied his entire attention.

In 1863, Mr Plympton married Mary S Stevens, daughter of Linus W. Stevens, a well-known merchant of this city, whose family was identified with the State of Connecticut from an early period in its history, and who was one of the organizers and first Colonel of the Seventh Regiment. Mr. and Mrs. Plympton have one daughter, Mary Livingston Plympton. Their son, Gilbert Livingston Plympton, died an infant Mr. Plympton has never held any public position, although asked to do so. He has, however, been a director in various corporations, and was one of the founders and vice-president of the St Nicholas Club He is a member of the Union, Metropolitan, St Nicholas, Riding, Westchester Country and New York Yacht clubs, of the Downtown Association, Sons of the Revolution, Society of Colonial Wars, Society of the War of 1812, Colonial Order of the Acorn, St Nicholas Society, New York Historical Society, American Historical Society, Metropolitan Museum of Art, Botanical Society, Zoölogical Society and the Chamber of Commerce His city residence is 30 West Fifty-second Street, where he has an exceptionally fine library, and the country home of the family is at East Gloucester, Mass Mr Plympton has been a frequent contributor to the papers and periodicals of the day, and is the author of several pamphlets, among them a monograph of the life and services of his father, Colonel Joseph Plympton, and a sketch of the Plympton family, extracts from which are freely used in this article.

The Plympton family is of English stock and originally came from the village of Plumpton, near Knaresborough, in the West Riding of Yorkshire Eldred de Plumpton was a landholder there at the time of the Domesday Survey in 1086, and from him the family is descended Its first representative in America was Thomas Plympton, born in England about 1620, who married Abigail Noyes. He was one of the founders of Sudbury, Mass , and was slain by the Indians in 1676 His son, Peter Plympton, 1666-1743, married Abigail Thomas, and their son, Thomas Plympton, 1723-1789, was a soldier in the Revolutionary Army. In the fourth American generation, Ebenezer Plympton, 1756-1834, was also a soldier in the Continental Army, and after peace had been restored was prominent in civil life, becoming a magistrate His first wife, grandmother of the subject of this article, was Susanna Ruggles, 1764-1807, of Roxbury, Mass.

Colonel Joseph Plympton, the son of Ebenezer and Susanna (Ruggles) Plympton, was born in Sudbury, Mass , in 1787 Entering the United States Army as Second Lieutenant, at the beginning of the War of 1812, he saw active service in the campaigns on the Canadian frontier during that contest. In 1821, he was promoted to be First Lieutenant, and in 1831 became Captain of the First Infantry From 1824 to 1834, he was on duty in the Northwest and took part in the Black Hawk War. He also served with signal distinction in the Florida War under General Worth, and in 1840 was raised to the rank of Major of the United States Second Infantry. At the beginning of the Mexican War, he was made Lieutenant-Colonel of the Seventh Infantry, and served under General Scott throughout the war. He was engaged in the battles of Cerro Gordo and Contreras and in the capture of the City of Mexico, and was brevetted for gallantry and coolness in action In 1854, he was made Colonel of the First United States Infantry, and died in 1860 at Staten Island, after forty-eight years of highly distinguished service in the army Many officers who afterwards became conspicuous in the Civil War saw service under Colonel Plympton, among whom were Generals Ulysses S. Grant, Philip Sheridan and others. He protected the handful of settlers in what is now the City of St Paul, Minn , from the Indians, and was the commandant of the last fort, Fort Dearborn, within the limits of the present City of Chicago In 1824, Colonel Plympton married Eliza Matilda Livingston, who was born in 1801 and died in 1873 In her youth she was famed for her beauty and her wit, and through her the present Mr Plympton, her son, is descended from some of the oldest New York Colonial families, as well as from noble ancestors in Europe She was a daughter of Peter W. Livingston and his wife, Eliza Beekman, one of the well-known New York families of that name. The famous Robert Livingston, first Lord of Livingston Manor, was her great-great-great-great-grandfather The mother of Mr Gilbert M. Plympton also traced her ancestry in a direct line to the Earl of Linlithgow of Scotland, the father of Lady Mary Livingston, who was one of the four Marys who in 1548 accompanied Mary Stuart to France to meet the Dauphin. When the Marquis de Lafayette made his second visit to America, in 1824, he displayed much interest in Lieutenant Joseph Plympton and his beautiful wife, and became their personal friend. The names by which their son, Mr Gilbert Motier Plympton, was christened, were given in remembrance of his parents' friendship for the illustrious French patriot and Revolutionary hero

Several other children of Colonel Joseph and Eliza Matilda (Livingston) Plympton were notable in their lives. Peter W. L Plympton graduated from West Point in 1847 He served in the Mexican War and greatly distinguished himself in the Civil War in New Mexico under General Canby He was twice brevetted for conspicuous bravery, attained the rank of Lieutenant-Colonel, and died in 1866 Joseph Ruggles Plympton, another son, was severely wounded in the Civil War He died in 1895 The eldest daughter, Emily Maria Plympton, married Captain Mansfield Lovell, Cornelia de Peyster Plympton married Colonel Henry M Black, and the third daughter, Louisa Edmonia Plympton, married Lieutenant John Pitman, all officers of the United States Army

The arms of the Plympton family, described in terms of heraldry, are: Azure, a fesse engrele d'or , each fusil of the engrailed fesse charged with an escallop, gules Crest, a phœnix or , surrounded by flames proper.

CHARLES COOLIDGE POMEROY

THE Reverend Benjamin Pomeroy, paternal ancestor in the fifth generation of Mr C. C. Pomeroy, was a prominent clergyman of Connecticut in the first part of the eighteenth century. He was pastor of a church in Hartford, and by his wife, Abigail, had a son, Eleazer Pomeroy, who died in 1783. Eleazer Pomeroy married, in 1764, Mary Wyllys, who was born in 1742. Samuel Wyllys Pomeroy, the eldest son of this union, born in 1764, resided for many years in Boston, whence he removed to Cincinnati, and thence to Pomeroy, O., where he died in 1841. His wife, whom he married in 1793, was Clarissa Alsop, daughter of Richard and Mary (Wright) Alsop, of Middletown, Conn., a member of an old Colonial family. His son, Samuel Wyllys Pomeroy, the father of the subject of this sketch, was born and brought up in Boston, removing later to Cincinnati, and in 1868 to Pomeroy, O., where he died in 1882. He married Catharine Boyer Coolidge, of Boston.

Through Mary Wyllys, who married Eleazer Pomeroy in 1764, Mr. Pomeroy is descended from a family famous in the annals of Connecticut. Mary Wyllys was the daughter of Colonel George Wyllys, 1710-1796. He was graduated from Yale College in 1729, was town clerk of Hartford in 1730 until his death, a Captain of the militia, and Lieutenant in the French War, 1757. In 1734, he succeeded his father as Secretary of State, and held that position for sixty-two years. The brother of Mary Wyllys was General Samuel Wyllys, 1738-1823. He was graduated from Yale College in 1758, and was a Captain and Lieutenant-Colonel in Colonel Joseph Spencer's regiment in 1775. Serving at the siege of Boston, and at the battles of Long Island and White Plains, he was from 1776 a Colonel in the Connecticut line. After the War, he succeeded his father as Secretary of State of Connecticut in 1796, holding that position until 1809, and was Brigadier-General and Major-General of the militia. His wife was Ruth Belden, a cousin. The father of George Wyllys, Hezekiah Wyllys, 1672-1741, held many offices in Hartford, and was Secretary of the Colony, 1712-34. Hezekiah Wyllys was the son of Samuel Wyllys and Ruth Haynes, and a grandson of Governor John Haynes, of Massachusetts and Connecticut. The wife of Governor John Haynes was Mabel Harlekenden, daughter of Richard Harlekenden, of England, and descended in the twelfth generation from Ralph de Neville, Earl of Westmoreland. Samuel Wyllys, the father of Hezekiah Wyllys, was for more than thirty years a magistrate of Connecticut, and was one of the earliest graduates from Harvard College. He came to this country in 1638 with his father, George Wyllys, who was Colonial Governor of Connecticut in 1642. On the family estate, in Hartford, Wyllys Hill, stood the famous "Charter Oak."

Mr. Charles Coolidge Pomeroy was born in March, 1833, at Philadelphia, and was graduated from Harvard College. During and after the war, he served in the army as Captain in the Eleventh and Twentieth United States Infantry, and was brevetted Major and Lieutenant-Colonel. The greater part of his business life has been spent in New York.

In 1863, Mr. Pomeroy married Edith Burnet, of Cincinnati, O., daughter of Robert Wallace Burnet and Margaret A Groesbeck, and granddaughter of Judge Jacob Burnet and Rebecca Wallace. Judge Jacob Burnet was born in Newark in 1770. He was the son of William Burnet, of New Jersey, 1730-1791, and grandson of Ichabod Burnet, a physician, who came from Scotland and settled in New Jersey. William Burnet was a physician, a member of the Continental Congress, Surgeon-General of the army, during the Revolution, and an original member of the Society of Cincinnati. Judge Burnet removed to Ohio in 1796 and became prominent in public affairs, being a member of the State Legislature, Judge of the Supreme Court, and United States Senator, the first president of the Colonization Society of Cincinnati, O., and otherwise a distinguished citizen. Rebecca Wallace, his wife, was the great-great-granddaughter of James Claypoole, the pioneer of Philadelphia, 1634-1686. Mr Pomeroy lives in West End Avenue. He belongs to the Metropolitan, Union and Riding clubs, the Downtown Association, and the Harvard Alumni Association. He has two daughters, Margaret B and Mary S Pomeroy.

EDWARD ERIE POOR

ONE of the first settlers of the town of Newbury, Mass., in 1635, was John Poore, or Poor, who was born in Wiltshire, England, about 1615. Some thirty acres of land in the town of Rowley, Mass , was granted to him, on which he built a house, still standing, and died in 1684. Henry Poore, his son, was born in 1650, and was a large land owner in Newbury. He served in King Philip's War, in 1675, was made a freeman in 1680, and held various public offices. His wife, Abigail Hale, daughter of Thomas Hale, Jr., was descended from old English families through both her father and her mother. In the third generation, Benjamin Poore, who was born in Rowley, in 1695, was a Captain and one of the leading men of the neighborhood. In the sixth generation, Benjamin Poor, who was born in 1794, became an eminent merchant in Boston. His wife, whom he married in 1824, was Aroline Emily Peabody, born in Salem, Mass., in 1807, daughter of Jeremiah and Catherine (Kimball) Peabody

The father of Mrs. Poor and the grandfather of the subject of this sketch was a native of Boxford, Mass., born in 1776. His father, Deacon Moses Peabody, born in 1744, belonged to one of the old families of Massachusetts. The pioneer of the Peabody family was Lieutenant Francis Peabody, of St. Albans, Hertfordshire, England. Born in 1614, he came to New England in 1635. He first resided at Ipswich, and in the summer of 1638 was one of the original settlers of Hampden, Norfolk County, Mass. There he resided for many years. In 1642, he was made a freeman, and in 1649 was chosen by the town of Hampden to administer some of its affairs. About 1650, he removed to Topsfield, Mass , and became one of the most prominent men of that town, and a large landowner in Topsfield, Boxford and Rowley His wife was Mary Foster, or Forster, whose family, so prominent in the history of the Scottish border, is mentioned in The Lay of the Last Minstrel, and in Marmion.

Captain John Peabody, son of Lieutenant Francis Peabody, was the great-grandfather of Deacon Moses Peabody, the maternal grandfather of the subject of this sketch. Captain Peabody was born in 1642, lived in Boxford, where he was made a freeman of the town in 1674 and a representative, 1689-91, The descent to the wife of Benjamin Poor was through Ensign David Peabody, of Boxford, and his son, John Peabody, also of Boxford, the father of Deacon Moses Peabody. Jeremiah Peabody, the father of Mrs. Poor, was a cousin of George Peabody, the banker and philanthropist, while there are many other distinguished names on the roll of this eminent New England family.

Mr. Edward Erie Poor, the son of Benjamin Poor and his wife, Aroline (Peabody) Poor, was born in 1837 in Boston. He was educated at schools in Boston, and in 1851 entered the dry goods commission house of Read, Chadwick & Dexter, and in 1864 removed to New York City. He became a dry goods commission merchant, being partner in the firm of Denny, Jones & Poor. In 1879, the style was changed to Denny, Poor & Co , with Daniel Denny and James E. Dean as partners. Besides the New York establishment, the firm has branches in Boston, Philadelphia, Baltimore and Chicago. Mr. Poor is vice-president of the Passaic Print Works, of Passaic. N J., was one of the incorporators of the Dry Goods Bank, and in 1888 became a director of the National Park Bank. Elected vice-president of the latter institution in 1893, he became its president in 1895, which position he now holds. Mr. Poor is also a trustee of the State Trust Company, and has been a member of the Chamber of Commerce since 1872.

In 1860, Mr. Poor married Mary Wellington Lane, daughter of Washington J. and Cynthia (Clark) Lane, of Cambridge, Mass. They have seven children: Edward Erie, Jr , and James Harper Poor, partners in business with their father; Dr. Charles Lane Poor, a professor in Johns Hopkins University; Frank Ballou Poor; Horace F Poor; Helen, wife of W. C. Thomas, of Hackensack, and Emily C. Poor Mr Poor's residence is at 16 East Tenth Street, and his home during the summer is at Hackensack, N. J. He is a member of the Union League, Manhattan, Military and Merchants' clubs of this city.

HORACE PORTER

A BRILLIANT record in both civil and military life is combined in the career of General Horace Porter with personal qualities that have made him one of New York's representative men His family has for three generations taken a distinguished part in the affairs of the country His grandfather was General Andrew Porter, 1743-1813, of Montgomery County, Pa, who, in 1776, entered the Army of the Revolution as Captain, served in the battles of Trenton, Princeton, Brandywine and Germantown, and was engaged in the expeditions against the Northwestern Indians After the Revolution, he held various offices in Pennsylvania, including those of General of the State militia and Surveyor-General He was also a commissioner to establish the boundary between Pennsylvania and New York General Horace Porter's father, the eldest son of the Revolutionary General, was the Honorable David R Porter, 1788-1867, who was for two successive terms, 1839-45, Governor of Pennsylvania An uncle, Judge James Madison Porter, 1793-1862, was prominent in State and National politics, and is remembered as a founder of Lafayette College, while General Andrew Porter, second of the name, 1819-1872, a first cousin of the present General Porter's father, was graduated from West Point, distinguished himself in the Mexican War, and in the Civil War became a Colonel in the regular army and Brigadier-General of Volunteers

General Horace Porter was born in Huntington, Pa, April 15, 1837, and was educated in the Lawrenceville Academy and in the Scientific School of Harvard, entering West Point in 1855, from which he was graduated in 1860, third in his class His first army service was in the ordnance and artillery, and on the outbreak of the Civil War he took part in the expeditions against Port Royal and Savannah, receiving promotion to the rank of Captain for gallantry at the reduction of Fort Pulaski In 1862, he became Chief of Ordnance in the Army of the Potomac, under General McClellan, and participated in the battle of Antietam, being afterwards transferred to the West and assigned to staff duty in the Army of the Cumberland He distinguished himself in the battle of Chickamauga, being on General Rosecran's staff At this point of his career, he attracted the attention of General Grant, who, when appointed Lieutenant-General of the Union Armies, made him one of his aides, with the rank of Lieutenant-Colonel Sharing in the battles of the Wilderness, the operations around Spottsylvania and Petersburg, he received successive promotions as Major, Lieutenant-Colonel, Colonel and Brigadier-General in the regular army, and in 1865 was on the staff of General Grant when the latter received the surrender of the Confederate Army from General Robert E Lee at Appomattox

After the termination of the war, General Porter continued closely connected, officially and personally, with General Grant, and was Assistant Secretary of War under the latter On the elevation of Grant to the Presidency, General Porter became his private secretary, but in 1872 he resigned that position and also relinquished his rank in the army to engage in the railway business, which engaged his attention for the next twenty-five years Since 1872, General Porter has been a resident of New York, and his record is one of business and social success He has achieved a high place in the business world, and at the same time has rendered a full share of public service as vice-chairman of the committee in charge of the Columbian Celebration in 1892 and on other notable occasions He has also won reputation as a graceful and effective public speaker His devotion to the memory of General Grant is a marked feature of General Porter's character and through his efforts the erection of the monument in Riverside Park to his dead chief was made possible

Union College, in 1893, conferred upon General Porter the degree of LL D In 1897, President McKinley appointed him United States Ambassador to France He married Sophie K McHarg Until he went abroad, his city home was in Madison Avenue and he had a country residence in Elberon, N J He has been president of the Union League Club and of the Society of the Army of the Potomac, and president-general of the Sons of the American Revolution, and is a member of New York's most prominent social organizations.

GEORGE B POST

D URING the life of the present generation, a transformation has occurred in the appearance of New York. Time-honored landmarks have disappeared, but loss in this respect is more than compensated for by the increased beauty of the city Not only has New York's architectural progress kept pace in an artistic sense with its material wealth and importance, but it is here that a national school of the art has developed, and that American architects have found examples in which beauty and utility have been united with daring and original conceptions Among the architects not only of the United States, but of the world, Mr. George B Post occupies a position of preeminence This is recognized by the public, as well as by his own profession, and it may be said that no one individual has done more to adorn the metropolis. Besides this, it is Mr Post's distinction, that he has been instrumental by his work in maintaining high standards, and in uniting utility and art

This eminent architect comes from an old New York family He is descended from Lieutenant Richard Post, who went to Southampton, Long Island, about the year 1640. The Post family is of Dutch origin, and the founder of the American branch came from Holland to this country with a party of Pilgrims and settled in Massachusetts The fourth in descent from Lieutenant Richard Post was Jotham Post, who was born in 1740 and left Westbury, Long Island, to come to New York City. He married Winifred Wright and had four sons, Wright, Joel, Jotham and Alison Post The eldest son was the celebrated Dr. Wright Post, whose picture appears in the famous group representing the Court of Washington. The second son, Joel Post, owned an estate on the upper part of Manhattan Island, where he resided throughout his life This property embraced the Claremont estate, and part of it, including the mansion and the site of General Grant's tomb, was acquired by the city from his descendants, when the Riverside Park was created The father of Mr George B. Post was Joel B. Post, the son of the above Joel Post, who married Abbey M Church, of Providence, R I, a direct descendant of Captain Benjamin Church, celebrated in the early Colonial wars

Mr George B. Post was born in New York City in 1837. His inclinations from his youth were scientific and artistic, and in 1858 he graduated in the class of civil engineering at the University of the City of New York He then began the study of architecture under the late Richard M Hunt At the beginning of the Civil War, Mr Post had just begun the practice of his profession He temporarily laid aside his chosen career, however, entered the army as Captain in the Twenty-Second Regiment, New York National Guard, participated in many engagements, including that of Fredericksburg, where he served as aide on the staff of General Burnside, and was promoted to the rank of Colonel

Returning to his profession at the close of the war, Mr. Post was not long in acquiring recognition A record of his achievements in architecture includes many of the most famous residences in the city, together with such notable structures as the Equitable, the Mills, the Times, the St Paul and the Havemeyer buildings, the New York Hospital, the Produce and Cotton Exchanges and Chickering Hall

In 1863, Mr Post married Alice M. Stone, daughter of William W. Stone, of New York. His residence is at 11 West Twenty-first Street He is a member of the Union, Metropolitan, Knickerbocker, Century and other clubs, and president of the Architectural League of New York City and the American Institute of Architects His only brother, Charles A Post, is a lawyer, who now devotes his time to real estate management He is well known as an amateur astronomer, possessing a private observatory at his place, Bayside, Long Island, and is a fellow of the Royal and other astronomical societies The arms of the Post family, as recorded at the College of Heraldry, are. Argent on a fess gules, a lion passant between two roundels of the first between three arches with columns of the second Crest, a demi-lion proper, tongued gules, resting his sinister paw on an arch with columns gules. Motto, *In me mea spes omnis.*

BROOKE POSTLEY

SEVERAL of the historic old families of Virginia are included among the antecedents of General Brooke Postley The family whose name he bears was distinguished in the earliest Colonial days, and several of its members took an active and influential part in public affairs, in the Old Dominion in the pre-Revolutionary period When the war broke out they were found upon the patriot side and rendered efficient service to the Continental cause The grandfather of Mr. Postley was an officer in the Revolutionary Army Charles Postley, his father, was an officer in the War of 1812, and in civil life was a successful business man, being the owner of extensive and valuable iron works, situated in Virginia, Maryland and Pennsylvania, and active in the developement of the industrial interests of those States.

General Brooke Postley was born in New York. His mother was Margaret Fairfax, who came of the old Virginia family of that name Receiving a thorough classical and military education, he entered upon the practice of law in New York in 1850, and since that time has been prominently identified with many important professional and business enterprises, having been a special partner in several large mercantile houses Before the Civil War, he was interested in the State militia and in the great conflict served in the Union Army, first as Colonel of the Third Cavalry Regiment of New York, and in 1866 as Brigadier-General of the Hussar Brigade of Cavalry that he organized He married Agnes Kain, daughter of James Kain, of Westchester County He is a member of the New York and the Larchmont Yacht clubs The city home of General and Mrs Postley is in upper Fifth Avenue

Colonel Clarence Ashley Postley, the son of General Brooke Postley, was born in New York, February 9th, 1849 His early education was secured in private schools, where he was prepared for admission to the United States Military Academy, at West Point Pursuing the regular course of study at West Point, he was graduated from that institution in 1870, and was assigned to the artillery branch of the army, as an officer of the Third Artillery In 1870-72, he saw service in Florida, and then was entered as a student in the artillery school at Fortress Monroe, and graduated therefrom in 1873 From 1873 to 1878, he was at West Point, as assistant professor of mathematics In 1883, he resigned from the service, having attained to the rank of Lieutenant of artillery in the regular army He also served on the staff of his father, with the rank of Colonel of engineers

Colonel Postley married Margaret Sterling, daughter of Alexander F Sterling, of Bridgeport, Conn The Sterlings date back to the earliest Colonial days of Connecticut, and the family has always been one of the most substantial in that Colony and State David Sterling came from Hertfordshire, England, in 1651. Landing in Massachusetts, he settled in Charlestown, and became one of the prominent citizens of that place His son, William Sterling, removed to Haverhill, Mass., in 1677, and came to Lyme, Conn., in 1703, being the founder of the Connecticut branch of the family. Jacob Sterling, son of William Sterling, was born in Lyme, Conn , and, later in life, was a resident of the towns of Fairfield and Stratford. His descendants have been prominent in business and public life in the Southwestern part of the State.

Colonel and Mrs Postley have two children, Elise and Sterling Postley Since 1886, the Postley family residence has been at the corner of East Sixty-third Street and Fifth Avenue, where Colonel Postley has one of the finest private libraries in the United States, bearing largely on the military history of this country. He is a member of the Union League, University, Manhattan, Racquet, Riding, Players, United Service and New York Athletic clubs, and the Country Club of Westchester County He is one of the enthusiastic yachtsmen of the metropolis, having been identified with that sport for many years, and is the owner of the yacht, Colonia, that was built as an America cup defender He is a member of nearly all the leading yacht clubs, including the American, New York, Corinthian, Larchmont and Seawanhaka-Corinthian. He is also a patron of the Metropolitan Museum of Art

HENRY CODMAN POTTER, D. D.

R EPRESENTATIVES of the Potter family in this country have for generations been pre-eminently distinguished in affairs of church and State. The first of the name came from England and settled in Rhode Island, where his descendants have remained to this day and have ranked among the leading men of the State. Israel R. Potter, the Revolutionary patriot who fought at Bunker Hill; the Honorable Samuel J Potter, Governor and United States Senator from Rhode Island; Judge Platt Potter, of New York; General Joseph H Potter, the Honorable Elisha R. Potter, Member of Congress from Rhode Island; and Captain Edward E. Potter, U. S. N., have helped, with others, to make the name illustrious in American history.

The branch of the family to which the Right Reverend Henry C. Potter, D. D., LL. D., Bishop of the Protestant Episcopal Diocese of New York, belongs, goes back to Joseph Potter, a member of the Society of Friends, who left his Rhode Island home in the latter part of the last century and came to New York State. He lived in Beekman, now La Grange, Dutchess County, and was highly esteemed as a public-spirited citizen and an influential member of the State Legislature. His sons and grandsons have added renown to the family name. Among the former were Bishop Alonzo Potter and Bishop Horatio Potter, both eminent in the Protestant Episcopal Church. The list of grandsons includes such names as the Honorable Clarkson N Potter, Member of Congress; the Reverend Dr. Eliphalet N. Potter, president of Union College, Howard Potter, financier, and General Robert B Potter.

Bishop Alonzo Potter, the first of the name to attain to high distinction in the church, was born in Beekman, July 6th, 1800, and died in San Francisco, July 4th, 1865 He was graduated from Union College in 1818, and became a professor there in 1821 With the exception of five years spent as rector of St. Paul's Church, in Boston, he remained with Union College until 1845, when he was elected to the Bishopric of Pennsylvania He had a genius for administration, and during the twenty years of his episcopate both the material and the spiritual interests of his diocese were advanced in a way that commanded general attention. As a direct result of his labors, an Episcopal hospital was founded and richly endowed, an Episcopal academy was revived, an Episcopal divinity school was established, and thirty-five new churches were built in the City of Philadelphia alone.

Bishop Henry C. Potter, the fifth son of Bishop Alonzo Potter, was born in Schenectady, N Y., May 25th, 1835 His mother was the daughter of President Eliphalet Nott, of Union College, and thus, on this side also, he comes of famous Colonial and Revolutionary ancestry. President Eliphalet Nott was a son of Deborah Selden, who married Stephen Nott about 1752, and who could trace her lineage to the two Governor Dudleys of Massachusetts, whose granddaughter and great-granddaughter she was President Nott's maternal grandfather was Samuel Selden, of Connecticut, and his uncle on the same side was the famous Colonel Samuel Selden, one of the substantial and accomplished men of his generation, and a valiant Revolutionary officer who died a prisoner in New York in 1776.

After graduating from the Theological Seminary in 1857, Bishop Potter was rector in Greensburgh, Pa., and Troy, N. Y., assistant minister of Trinity Church in Boston, and rector of Grace Church in New York from 1868 to 1883. In the latter year, he became assistant to his venerable uncle, Bishop Horatio Potter, of the New York diocese, and on the death of that prelate, in 1887, he succeeded to the bishopric. His ecclesiastical work is of the most devoted, practical character, and has been productive of substantial results in building up and developing the churches and church institutions of the diocese. He has written much on religious subjects, has received the honorary degrees of A M , D D , and LL D , from several American colleges, those of D D. and LL. D from the Universities of Oxford and Cambridge, and is a member of the Century, City, Players and Aldine clubs. He married Eliza R. Jacob. His town house is in Washington Square and he has a summer home, The Gables, in Newport.

DALLAS BACHE PRATT

FEW American families have a more ancient or more honorable history than the Pratts. In the olden time the name was variously spelled, Pratt, Prat, Pradt, Praed, Prate and otherwise. It was a surname derived from a locality, coming originally from the Latin *pratum*, a meadow, and the French *prairie*. Originally of Normandy, the family was large and powerful in that section in the early centuries of the Christian era. The Seigneurs of Preux were among the most distinguished nobles in the tenth and eleventh centuries and thereafter Representatives of the family came from Normandy with William the Conqueror, and the English records since that time abound in the name. They settled in the eastern and southern parts of England, where, until this day, their descendants are numerous. At all periods of English history they have borne a prominent part and were among the leaders in the Crusades and in the early wars, civil and foreign, that engaged the attention of the English people in the middle ages. The lineage of that branch of the family, from which came the ancestor of the American Pratts, can be traced back before 1400.

Two brothers, William Pratt and John Pratt, were the first of their name to come to this country. They were natives of Stevenage, Hertfordshire, England. Their father was the Reverend William Pratt, rector of Stevenage, who was born in 1562 and died in 1629, and their great-grandfather was Thomas Pratt, of Baldock, who died in 1539. The brothers came together to New England and settled in Cambridge, some time before 1632. Lieutenant William Pratt, the elder of the two, became engaged in the early religious controversies that disturbed the New England settlers, and in company with the Reverend Thomas Hooker, removed to Hartford, Conn., in 1636. In 1645, he was one of the pioneers who settled the town of Saybrook. He was a representative to the General Court from the town of Saybrook for twenty-three successive sessions from 1666 to 1678, the time of his death. He was a Lieutenant of the militia in 1661, and often a commissioner. His wife was Elizabeth Clark, daughter of John Clark, of Saybrook. Ensign John Pratt, the eldest son of Lieutenant William Pratt, was born in 1644, married Sarah Jones, daughter of Thomas Jones, of Guilford, Conn., and had eight children. He was a large landowner and a man of distinction, serving as a delegate from his town to the General Assembly several times and as a deputy in 1684, 1689 and 1691. His son, John Pratt, Jr., born in 1671, was the father of Lieutenant John Pratt, of the Revolutionary period.

The great-grandson of Lieutenant John Pratt was Linus Pratt, son of John and Abigail Pratt, who was born in 1792 and married Temperance Pratt, daughter of Ezra and Temperance Pratt, in 1813. He came to New York from Essex, Conn., soon after 1840, and spent the latter part of his life here. The Reverend Horace L. E. Pratt, son of Linus and Temperance Pratt, was the father of the subject of this sketch. He was born August 24th, 1823, and was a prominent member of the Protestant Episcopal priesthood. For several years, he was rector of St. Peter's Church, in Perth Amboy, N. J., and afterwards was located in Sacramento, Cal., and at St Mary's Church, Staten Island. He married, in 1847, Sarah Kate Martin and had eight children, of whom Mr Dallas Bache Pratt is the eldest. He died in March, 1897, and his widow survives him.

Mr. Dallas Bache Pratt was born February 4th, 1849, in New York. He was educated in Trinity School, and when sixteen years of age, entered the employ of the banking house of Brown Brothers & Co. There he remained for sixteen years, and then became cashier of the Bank of America After ten years he resigned his position in the bank and became a member of the firm of Maitland, Phelps & Co., now Maitland, Coppell & Co., bankers and merchants. He has been prominent in financial and banking affairs and connected with several corporations, among them the Ohio Falls Car Manufacturing Company, of Jeffersonville, Ind. In 1881, Mr Pratt married Minnie G. Landon, daughter of Charles G Landon His four children are Katherine Griswold, Alexander Dallas, Constance and Beatrice Gordon Pratt His city residence is in West Forty-eighth Street, and he is a member of the Metropolitan, Union League, Riding and other clubs.

EDWARD PRIME

IN his day Nathaniel Prime, the great banker and merchant of New York City, during the early years of the present century, was rated as one of the five richest men in America. He was probably not worth over a million dollars, but the great fortunes of this generation were not then dreamed of. He was in the fifth generation from his American ancestor, Mark Prime, who, born in England and coming to this country, was one of the first settlers of Rowley, Mass., where he died in 1683. He was an influential citizen, owned considerable property, was an overseer in 1654, and held other town offices. Samuel Prime, the only son of Mark Prime, was born in Rowley in 1649, and died in 1683, having married in 1673, Sarah Plats, a daughter of Samuel Plats, of Rowley, who was a representative to the General Court in 1681.

Samuel Prime, who was born in Rowley, in 1675, and died in 1717, was the grandfather of Nathaniel Prime. His wife, Sarah Jewett, was descended from J. J. Jewett, who came from Bradford, York County, England. Nathaniel Prime's father was Joshua Prime, 1712-1770, whose wife was Bridget Hammond, descended from Thomas Hammond, who came from Cavenham, Suffolk County, England. In 1757, Joshua Prime was Corporal in the troop of horse of Rowley. Born in 1768, Nathaniel Prime was the fourteenth child in his father's family of fifteen. He was settled in New York before the close of the eighteenth century, and became one of the greatest merchants and bankers of that period. The firm of which he was at the head, variously known as Prime, Ward & Sands, Prime, Ward, Sands & King, Prime, Ward & King, Prime, Ward & Co., and Prime & Co., was the first great banking house ever established in this country. The wife of Nathaniel Prime was Cornelia Sands, daughter of Comfort Sands, the first president of the Chamber of Commerce, and his first wife, Mary Dodge. Comfort Sands was descended from James Sands, who came to Plymouth, Mass., in 1658, and subsequently removed to Long Island.

The eldest son of Nathaniel Prime and his third child was Edward Prime, who was born in 1801. He was educated in a private school in Morristown, N. J., and entering his father's banking house early in life, soon became a member of the firm. When his father died in 1840, he succeeded to the banking business as the head of the firm of Prime, Ward & Co., which consisted of himself and John and Samuel Ward in 1847, and of Edward Prime and his two sons, Nathaniel and Edward Prime, Jr, from that time until it went out of existence in 1867. Mr. Prime died in 1883. He was one of the founders of the New York Eye and Ear Infirmary.

When Edward Prime died he left six children, three sons and three daughters. His wife was Anne Bard, daughter of William Bard and Catharine Cruger. His daughter, Cornelia, became the wife of August Ahrens; his son, Nathaniel, was an officer in the United States Army and died in 1885, his son, William Hoffman, died in San Antonio, Texas, in 1881, his daughter, Charlotte, married Leonard J. Wyeth, Jr, and his daughter, Mary Catharine, became the wife of James A. Scrymser. The second wife of Mr. Prime, who survived her husband and is still living, was Charlotte Hoffman, daughter of Dr. William Hoffman.

Mr. Edward Prime was the second son and third child of Edward Prime, Sr., and his wife, Anne Bard. He was born in New York, October 19th, 1833. Educated in private schools in White Plains and Poughkeepsie, he succeeded to his father's business in the banking house of Prime & Company. He is a member of the Country Club of Westchester County, the Good Government Club, and the Sons of the Revolution. He spends much time traveling in Europe. Mr. Prime has served in the Seventy-first Regiment, N. G. S. N. Y. During the Civil War he was six months at the front, being stationed near Washington. In December, 1889, he married Anne Rhodes Gilbert, daughter of Edward Francis Gilbert and Elizabeth Hall. Edward F. Gilbert was a lineal descendant of Sir Humphrey Gilbert, who was half brother of Sir Walter Raleigh. Mr. and Mrs. Prime have one daughter, Charlotte Hoffman Prime. The arms of this branch of the Prime family are a black human leg torn off at the thigh, on a silver shield, with the motto, *Virtute et Opere*. The crest is an eagle's claw.

DAVID PROVOST

FRENCH in origin and adherents of the Huguenot cause, the ancestors of this gentleman escaped from their native country to Holland, and thence migrated to the Colony the Dutch had founded on the Hudson. The first of the name was Guillaume Provost, a Huguenot, who resided in Paris at the time of the massacre of St Bartholomew, in 1572. His gentle birth is attested by the possession of coat armor, the heraldic devices being similar to those since borne by the successive generations of his progeny. It was Guillaume Provost's grandsons, David and Jonathan Provoost, who came to this country.

David Provoost was in the New Netherland prior to 1639, probably coming with Governor Kieft in 1638. He was an officer of the Dutch West India Company, and among other posts, held command for a time of Fort Good Hope, at Hartford, Conn., established to check the encroachments of the English, and the records show him to have been an able Lieutenant of Governor Peter Stuyvesant. In 1652, his name heads the list of the nine men who ruled New Amsterdam. In 1654, he was made the first schout or sheriff of Breucklyn, and died in 1656. His wife was Margaret Gillis. Their son, Jonathan Provoost, born here in 1651, married Catharine Van der Veen, daughter of Pieter Cornelisen Van der Veen and Eloje Tymens. Becoming a widow in 1663, the latter married the famous Captain Jacob Leisler. Johannes Provoost, the elder brother of Jonathan, was born in Holland and held the post of Secretary at Fort Orange (Albany), subsequently becoming a merchant in New York. He was a leading supporter of Leisler, in 1689, being associated with Jacob Milbourne in the commission to take charge of Fort Orange, and was among those punished by imprisonment and confiscation, when Leisler was executed by the English governor, Colonel Sloughter. David Provoost, second of the name, the great-great-grandfather of the present Mr. Provost, the son of Jonathan and Catharine Provoost, was born in New York in 1689, and married Christina Praa, daughter of Captain Peter Praa, of Bushwick. Their son, Jonathan Provoost, was born in New York in 1722, and in 1743 married Adriana Spring, and died about 1805, in Middlesex County, N. J. John Provoost, their son and the present Mr. Provost's grandfather, was long a resident of Brooklyn and married Eve Edmonton.

In tracing the genealogy of this family, it is necessary to refer to a famous representative in a collateral line, the Reverend Samuel Provoost, D. D., the first Protestant Episcopal Bishop of New York. He was fourth in descent from the first David Provoost, his father being a merchant and his mother a daughter of Hermann Bleecker. He was one of the first seven graduates from Kings, now Columbia College, in 1758. He also studied at Cambridge, England, was ordained to the ministry there in 1766, and returning, became in 1774 an assistant minister of Trinity Church. During the Revolution he espoused the patriotic cause, became rector of Trinity in 1784, and in 1786 was elected Bishop, being ordained, in company with Bishop White, of Pennsylvania, by the Archbishops of Canterbury and York at Lambeth. He resigned his bishopric, which he had adorned by his piety and learning, in 1801, and died in 1815.

David Provoost, third of the name, the father of the present Mr. David Provost, was the son of John and Eve (Edmonton) Provoost. About 1840, in common with many of the name, he changed the spelling from the old Dutch form of Provoost to Provost. He married Harriet Byron Dane, of Boston, a lady of an old New England family.

Their son, Mr. David Provost, was born at Great Neck, Long Island, in 1859; was educated at Rutgers College and the Law School of Columbia College, and is in active practice at the New York bar. In 1887, Mr. Provost married Edith Wise, born at Goshen, N. Y., daughter of James L. Wise and his wife, Isabella McDougall. Mrs. Provost's family is of English extraction and her paternal ancestors were among the earliest settlers in Portsmouth, N. H. The issue of this marriage are three children, Edith Madeleine Provost, David Lawrence Provost, and Ralph Drake Provost. Mr. Provost is a member of the Sons of the Revolution. His residence is 58 West Fifty-first Street, and his country home is at Great Neck, Long Island, on a cliff commanding a view of the Sound.

ROGER ATKINSON PRYOR

THE ancient family of Bland has for many generations been celebrated in the annals of Virginia, numbering among its members many of the most famous sons of the Old Dominion In the Revolutionary period, Colonel Theodorik Bland was a distinguished patriot, and after the war was a Member of Congress and a delegate to the Constitutional Convention He was intimately associated with all the great leaders of the period, and was a friend and counselor of Washington and Jefferson.

Judge Roger Atkinson Pryor inherits the blood not only of the Bland, but of the Randolph, Isham, Yates, Cary and Poythress families of Virginia He was born in Dinwiddie County, in that State, July 19th, 1828, his parents being the Reverend Theodorik Bland Pryor and his wife, Lucy Atkinson. His paternal grandparents were Roger Pryor and Annie Bland, and on the maternal side, Roger Atkinson and Agnes Poythress. He was graduated from Hampden-Sydney College in 1845, and after that from the University of Virginia After studying law, he entered upon the practice of his profession in Charlottesville, Va , but temporarily took an editorial position in 1854. In the following year President Franklin Pierce appointed him on a special mission to Greece. After his return from Europe, in 1857, he was offered the place of Minister to Persia, declining which, he was elected a Member of Congress from the district formerly represented by John Randolph, of Roanoke. Reëlected to Congress in 1859, he cast his lot with his State in the Southern Confederacy. Twice he was elected a member of the Confederate Congress, and entering the military service of the Confederacy as Colonel of a Virginia regiment, was promoted Brigadier-General for bravery at the battle of Williamsburg He served in the engagements around Richmond and proved himself a brave soldier and a skilful commander. A misunderstanding with President Jefferson Davis led him to resign his commission, but immediataly after he reënlisted as a private soldier, serving for two years in the ranks in the great battles of the Confederate Army of Virginia. At Petersburg he was captured, imprisoned for eight months in Fort Lafayette and released on parole only twenty days before the fall of the Confederacy.

After the war he removed to New York and engaged in legal practice. He at once took a position at the head of his profession and was engaged in many notable cases, being one of the counsel in the Beecher-Tilton trial and in important elevated railroad litigation. He was counsel for Governor William Sprague of Rhode Island in the litigation relating to the Sprague estate.

Outside of his profession, he has been prominent in the counsels of the Democratic Party and in 1876 was a delegate to the Democratic National Convention at St. Louis. He has been often called upon as an orator upon public occasions. In 1877, delivered an address at Hampden-Sydney College on The Relation of Science to Religion On Decoration Day of the same year he was the orator before the Grand Army of the Republic in Brooklyn, and among his other celebrated addresses was one before the Albany Law School. His latest published address was one made before the Virginia Bar Associaton, at White Sulphur Springs, in 1895. In 1890, he was elected to a seat on the bench of the Court of Common Pleas in the City of New York, and by the Constitution of 1894 was transferred to the Supreme Court. His term of service expires in 1905.

In 1848, Judge Pryor married Sara Agnes Rice, a lady also descended from a distinguished line of Virginia ancestors. One of her forefathers was the famous Nathaniel Bacon, the leader of what was termed Bacon's Rebellion, in 1676, against the tyranny of Governor Sir William Berkeley. Among her other ancestors were such Virginia worthies as David Rice and Samuel Blair. Mrs. Pryor's rare intellectual and social qualities have made her a helpful companion in the public career of her husband, while she has taken a leading part in philanthropic organizations and those of a social or patriotic character which interest her sex. Their son, Roger A Pryor, Jr , is a member of the New York bar Judge Pryor lives at 3 West Sixty-ninth Street He is a member of the Manhattan Club, the Colonial Club, the Southern Society and the Society of the Sons of the American Revolution

JOSIAH COLLINS PUMPELLY

A ROMAN origin is evident in the case of the Pompelly family. There was a tribune Pompilius in Rome *circa* 420 B C, and other notices of the surname occur. In its Italian form of Pompili, it appears in the mediæval records of Spoletto, and one of the family went with Pope Clement V to Avignon, and through him a branch became established in France. The arms of the race are in the records of the Italian nobility.

The founder of the American branch of the family was Jean Pompilie, a Huguenot, who early in the eighteenth century came from France to Canada, and thence to New England, where he married an heiress, Miss Monroe. His son, John Pumpelly (as the name was Anglicized), was born in 1727. In his twelfth year he ran away, became a drummer in the English Army and finally joined Roger's Rangers and served throughout the French War, was promoted for bravery and stood near Wolfe when he fell at Quebec. During the Revolution, he was commissary to General Putnam. His eldest son, Bennett, who was also an officer of the Continental Army, was honored with Lafayette's friendship. Another son, Barnard, was killed at St Clair's defeat. John Pumpelly was married first to Eppen Meijer and second to Hannah Bushnell, of Salisbury, Conn., and resided there until 1802, when he moved to Danby, N Y., where he died in 1819

Two sons of his second marriage, James and Harmon, were early settlers in Tioga County, New York State, where they became extensive land owners and agents for the Livingston and other estates. The Honorable James Pumpelly, the grandfather of Mr. Josiah C. Pumpelly, was born at Salisbury in 1775, and married Mary Pixley, daughter of David Pixley, of Stockbridge, Mass., a Colonel in the Continental Army, who came to Owego, N. Y., in 1790, and, like Mr. Pumpelly, was one of the proprietors in the large body of land between Owego Creek and the Chenango River awarded to Massachusetts, and known as the Boston Purchase or Ten Townships. James Pumpelly represented Broome County in the Legislature. His son, George James Pumpelly, born at Owego in 1805, graduated at Yale in 1826, and at Litchfield Law School in 1828. He took an active part in creating the Erie Railway, and rendered great service in advancing the agricultural interests of the southern tier of counties. He was a Christian gentleman of the old school, a true lover of books, and possessed a most generous and hospitable nature. He married his cousin, Susan Isabella Pumpelly, born in 1809, the daughter of Charles Pumpelly, who was an officer in the War of 1812, her mother being an Avery. Through her great-great-grandmother she traced her ancestry back ten centuries through a notable array of British sovereigns, statesmen and soldiers. Samuel Avery, the great-great-grandfather of Mr. Pumpelly, was a soldier of the Revolution.

Mr. Josiah Collins Pumpelly was born at Owego, in 1839, graduated at Rutgers College in 1860, and from the Columbia College Law School in 1863 Literary pursuits and social problems interested him more than professional life, and after some years of travel in Europe, the East, and the United States, he settled at Poughkeepsie, N Y, and later at Morristown, N. J. In 1876, he married Mrs Margaret (Lanier) Winslow, a descendant of the Huguenot, Louis Lanier. After the death of his wife, Mr. Pumpelly established himself in New York City, where he has become identified with public movements and particularly with the City Improvement Society, of which he was a founder, and is now the honored secretary. Its object is to secure the enforcement of laws for the improvement of the city, and the proper discharge of their duties by municipal authorities, a cause in which he has accomplished much practical good. In 1896, Mr Pumpelly married for his second wife Mary Amelia Harmer, a descendant of the Revolutionary General Josiah Harmer, and of the old Huguenot family of Sandoz. In literary and antiquarian research Mr Pumpelly has covered a wide field. He has published much on these subjects, and is an officer of the New York Genealogical and Biographical Society. He was one of the founders of the Huguenot Society, of the New Jersey State Charities Aid Association, and of the Society of the Sons of the American Revolution, and has taken a warm interest in church work as well as in philanthropic organizations. He is a veteran member of the Union League Club, and one of the Executive Board of the Civil Service Association.

GEORGE HAVEN PUTNAM

I N Buckinghamshire, England, the Putnam family was of high standing, as far back as the fifteenth century. Their arms were : Argent, crusily fitchee, sable, a stork of the last , crest, a wolf's head, gules. John Putnam, the first of the name in America, was the ancestor of all the Putnams who trace their lineage to Colonial days. With John Putnam, in 1634, came his wife Priscilla, and their three sons, Thomas, Nathaniel and John. They settled in Salem, Mass , acquired large estates, and the sons became men of prominence and influence. In 1681, one-seventh of all the tax levied upon the ninety-four tax payers of Salem was paid by the three Putnams. Thomas Putnam also acquired by marriage great wealth in Jamaica and Barbadoes.

The Putnam family has always been prominent in Eastern Massachusetts. In 1867, of the eight hundred voters in Danvers, fifty were Putnams, and in the parish of that town up to a few years ago, twenty-four of the seventy-four recording clerks, fifteen of the twenty-three deacons, twelve of the twenty-six treasurers, and seven of the eighteen Sabbath School superintendents had been Putnams. General Israel Putnam, the famous Revolutionary soldier, was the most conspicuous member of the family in his day. Other members of the family have achieved distinction, among them being General Rufus Putnam, cousin of General Israel Putnam, also a Revolutionary soldier, and one of the explorers of the Ohio region; Judge John P Putnam, of Connecticut ; Judge Samuel Putnam, of Massachusetts ; Judge William L. Putnam, of Maine ; Judge James Putnam, of New Brunswick ; General A S Putnam, of the Civil War, and Professor Frederick W. Putnam, the noted anthropologist and scientist A great-grandson of Thomas Putnam, eldest son of the founder of the family in America, was Henry Putnam, 1788-1822, a lawyer of Boston. His wife was Catherine Hunt Palmer, a daughter of General Joseph Palmer, 1718-1788, who was a member of the Provincial Congress of Massachusetts in 1774, a member of the Committee of Safety, appointed by that body, and in command of the Massachusetts militia for the defense of Rhode Island in 1777.

George Palmer Putnam, the son of Henry and Catherine (Hunt) Putnam, was the first publisher of the name Born in 1814, he became a clerk in the New York book store of Leavitt Brothers at the age of fourteen, and was in business for himself as a member of the firm of Wiley & Putnam, in 1840, and independently eight years later In 1852, he established Putnam's Magazine. In 1862, he was appointed by President Lincoln United States Collector of Internal Revenue In 1866, the publishing house that he founded in 1848 took the name of G P. Putnam & Sons Mr. Putnam was one of the earliest advocates of international copyright, organized in 1837 the first copyright association, was a founder of the Metropolitan Museum of Art and the author of several books. He died in 1872 He married, in 1840, Victorine Haven, daughter of Joseph Haven, a merchant of Boston Mrs Putnam's maternal grandfather was Colonel Francis Mason, who had command of the ordnance in the army of Washington, in 1776

Mr George Haven Putnam, born in London, England, April 2, 1844, succeeded his father at the head of the publishing house of G. P. Putnam's Sons He was educated in Columbia College and in the University of Göttingen, Germany He left the University in 1862 to enlist in the One Hundred and Seventy-sixth Regiment, New York Volunteers, in which he served until the close of the war, retiring with the rank of Major. He was a Deputy Collector of Internal Revenue in 1866, and has been a publisher for thirty years As an author he has won distinction by magazine and cyclopædia articles on literary subjects, and by several books upon copyright, publishing and kindred topics. He was one of the founders of the Reform and City clubs, and is a member of the Century and the Authors' clubs, the Savile Club of London, and the Loyal Legion, and is secretary of the Publishers' Copyright League. His services for the cause of free trade, civil service reform, sound money and international copyright, have given him a national reputation At the request of the Société des Gens de Lettres, of Paris, he received in 1891 the cross of the Legion of Honor.

EDWARD S. RAPALLO

UPON a country estate in Italy, not far from the town of Rapallo, the family of which Mr. Edward S. Rapallo is the leading American representative, has resided for many generations. There, Anthony Rapallo, who established the family in this country, was born Owing to his republican tendencies, he came into disfavor with his family and the Vatican, in consequence of which he emigrated to this country in early life and settled in New York In this city, he first supported himself by teaching, and afterwards studied law, beginning the practice of that profession in 1818. For a long time, his home was a rendezvous for Garibaldi and the other Italian patriots Later, however, he was counsel to one of the Italian Governments

Anthony Rapallo married, in 1819, Elizabeth, daughter of Benjamin Gould, of Newburyport, Mass. Benjamin Gould was a Revolutionary patriot, born in Topsfield, Mass , in 1751. When hostilities broke out, in 1775, he headed a company of minute men that marched from Topsfield to take part in the battle of Lexington. In that engagement, he received a bullet wound, but was Captain of his company at Bunker Hill, and was the last patriot to leave the Heights on Charlestown Neck after that engagement. Later in the war, he fought at White Plains, Bennington and Stillwater, and commanded the main guards at West Point when Benedict Arnold fled and Major Andre was captured. He was at one time a delegate from Massachusetts to the General Assembly A son of Benjamin Gould was Benjamin A Gould, 1787-1859, a Harvard College graduate, principal of the Boston Latin School, an East India merchant in Boston, an author and public official. A daughter of Benjamin A Gould was Hannah Flagg Gould, the poetess, 1789-1865. A son of Benjamin A Gould was Benjamin Apthorpe Gould, an astronomer of this generation, who was connected with the United States Coast Survey in 1851, was director of the Dudley Observatory in Albany, in 1856, founder and editor of The Astronomical Journal, and from 1868 to 1885, in charge of the National Observatory and the Astronomical Service of the Argentine Republic.

The Honorable Charles A. Rapallo, for many years an Associate Judge of the Court of Appeals of the State of New York, was a son of Anthony Rapallo and the father of Mr. Edward S. Rapallo He was born in New York City, in 1823. At that time, Anthony Rapallo was associated with the celebrated John Anthon. The son was brought up under the personal direction of his father, who supervised his education in his early years and personally taught him the classics and the modern languages In his boyhood, he spent many days in his father's office, where he had the advantages of contact with some of the leading lawyers of that time When he was twenty-one years of age, he was admitted to practice, and in 1848 formed a law partnership with Horace F. Clark, the firm acting for many years as principal attorneys for Cornelius Vanderbilt.

In 1867, when Mr. Clark retired, Mr. Rapallo formed a partnership with James C Spencer Three years later, in 1870, he was elected Associate Justice of the Court of Appeals of the State of New York, at the same time that Sanford E Church was elected Chief Judge of the same court In 1880, when Mr. Church died, Mr Rapallo received the unanimous nomination of the Democratic party for the position of Chief Justice, but was defeated by Chief Judge Charles Andrews. He held his seat as Associate Judge during the remainder of his life. The wife of Judge Rapallo was a daughter of Bradford Sumner, one of the most celebrated lawyers of Boston in his generation. Mr. and Mrs Rapallo were married in 1852, and Mrs Rapallo survived her husband. With her daughters, she lives in West Thirty-first Street and has a country residence at Green Farms, Conn

Mr Edward S Rapallo is the eldest son of Judge Charles A Rapallo. Born in New York, he was graduated from Columbia College in 1874, and from the Columbia Law School, and is a practicing lawyer He married Emma Van Volkenburgh and lives in Fifth Avenue. He is a member of the Manhattan, University, Democratic and University Athletic clubs, and belongs to the Century Association, the Bar Association and the Columbia College Alumni Association.

AMASA ANGELL REDFIELD

W ILLIAM REDFIN, or Redfield, came from England before 1630, with one of the first companies of Colonists. He took up land on the Charles River, near Boston, and was one of the first settlers of Newtown, which afterwards became Cambridge Later in life, he removed to Pequot, now New London, Conn, where he died, in 1662. He was the ancestor of a family that has had many distinguished representatives. The name appears in the original records variously, as Redfin, Redfen, Redfyn, Redfyne. After the family came to Connecticut, the name was gradually changed to its present form.

James Redfield, 1646-1723, son of William Redfield, married first Elizabeth How, daughter of Jeremy How, of New Haven , and second, Deborah Sturgis, daughter of John Sturgis, of Fairfield, Conn. Peleg Redfield, grandson of James Redfield, and son of Theophilus Redfield and Priscilla (Grinnell) Redfield, was born in Killingworth, Conn, in 1723, and died in 1760 In the French War, he took part as a Captain in the Second Regiment of Connecticut troops under command of Colonel Nathan Whiting. His wife was Sarah Dudley, of Guilford, Conn

The father of Mr Amasa Angell Redfield was Luther Redfield, of Tarrytown, N Y. He was the son of Luther Redfield, who was born in Richmond, Mass, in 1780, and died in Monroe, Mich, in 1867, a grandson of Beriah Redfield, 1744-1819, of Richmond, Mass, and a great-grandson of Captain Peleg Redfield. Luther Redfield was born in Junius, N Y, in 1815, and died in Bloomfield, in 1878 He was a merchant and banker of high reputation in New York His wife, whom he married in 1836, was Eliza Angell, daughter of Amasa and Mary (Ward) Angell. Miss Angell belonged to the Angell family of Providence, who were among the earliest settlers of that place Her maternal ancestry included one of the patentees of Dutchess County, N Y

Several of the Redfield family have been prominent in literature and journalism. The Honorable Lewis H Redfield, son of Peleg Redfield, a son of Theophilus Redfield, father of the first Peleg Redfield, was a well-known newspaper publisher and editor in the Onondaga Valley and Syracuse, N Y His wife, Anna Maria (Treadwell) Redfield, was a well-known authoress Of the same family was the Honorable Timothy Redfield, Chief Justice of the Supreme Court of Vermont, and professor in Dartmouth College, and his brother, Isaac F. Redfield, who acted as special counsel of the United States Government in Europe, in connection with the recovery of property of the Southern Confederacy Among the other members of the family who have attained distinction, were J S Redfield, editor and United States Consul at one time ; William C Redfield, the scientist ; and John H. Redfield, known for his researches in natural history.

Mr. Amasa Angell Redfield was born in Clyde, N Y., May 19th, 1837 Educated at the University of New York, he entered the legal profession in New York, and attained an extensive practice and high distinction. Afterwards he became official reporter of the Surrogate's Court and Court of Common Pleas, a position he held from 1877 to 1882. Early in life he devoted himself to literary work and was for many years a contributor to The Knickerbocker Magazine. He also wrote upon legal subjects, and compiled several legal works, among them A Hand-Book of United States Tax Laws, Reports of the Surrogate Courts of the State of New York, Law and Practice of Surrogate Courts, and in collaboration with Thomas G Shearman, The Law of Negligence In 1863, Mr Redfield married Sarah Louise Cooke, daughter of Robert Latimer Cooke and his wife, Caroline Eliza Van Deventer Mrs Redfield was descended from the Cookes of Vermont and the Latimers of New London, and also on the maternal side from the Talmages and the Van Deventers, who came from Holland in 1634 They have two children. Robert Latimer Redfield, their son, is a practicing lawyer, in association with his father, and married, in 1894, Emma J. Balen, a descendant of the Stickney family The daughter of Mr Amasa A. Redfield, Edith Redfield Cooper, is the wife of Frederic T Cooper, professor in the University of New York. Mr Redfield has a country residence, The Hemlocks, at Farmington, Conn., and is a member of the Lawyers' Club and the Bar Association

WHITELAW REID

THE family of which Mr, Whitelaw Reid is a representative, was originally of Scotland. His grandfather, a Scotch Covenanter, was one of the founders of the town of Xenia, O., and his mother, Marion Whitelaw Ronalds, descended from a Highland family. The parents of Mr. Whitelaw Reid gave him the advantage of a thorough education. He studied in the Academy of Xenia, his native town, and was graduated with the scientific honors from Miami University in 1856, when he was not yet nineteen. After a year he became editor and proprietor of The Xenia News, and during the first Lincoln campaign achieved reputation by his political writings and speeches. He next went to Columbus, O., as a legislative newspaper correspondent, and soon after became connected with The Cincinnati Gazette. During the Civil War, he did remarkably brilliant work as a correspondent, being at the front in the two West Virginia campaigns, and with Grant at Shiloh and elsewhere After the war he was Librarian of the House of Representatives in Washington, correspondent of The Cincinnati Gazette, and finally one of that journal's proprieters and editors. He also traveled in the South and wrote a book, After the War, and in 1868 published a two-volume history, Ohio in the War, one of the most important early works treating of the Civil War.

In 1868, Mr. Reid became connected with The New York Tribune by invitation of Horace Greeley. His first position was that of editorial writer, but he soon became managing editor, and in 1872, when Mr Greeley accepted the Liberal Republican and Democratic nomination for the Presidency, Mr. Reid was placed in full charge of the paper. Upon the death of Greeley, immediately after that campaign, Mr. Reid became the principal owner of The Tribune. The paper was not in a flourishing condition when he took charge of it, as many of its old-time readers had been alienated in the latter years of Mr. Greeley's life. Under Mr. Reid, however, The Tribune was successfully developed and put in the forefront of success and influence among Republican newspapers. The Tribune Building, which has been erected during his administration, and largely on his ideas, is a monument to his large and eminently practical views.

Public honors have naturally come to Mr. Reid. In 1876, he was chosen a Regent of the New York State University. The position of United States Minister to Germany was tendered to him by President Hayes, and again by President Garfield, but was declined in both instances. President Harrison appointed him United States Minister to France in 1889, and he made a brilliant diplomatic and social success in Paris during the four years that he occupied that post. In 1892, he was Chairman of the New York Republican State Convention to choose delegates to the National Convention, and subsequently at the National Convention of that year was nominated for the Vice-Presidency on the ticket with President Harrison. In 1897, Mr Reid was appointed by President McKinley, special Envoy of the United States, to the Diamond Jubilee of Queen Victoria, a mission which he fulfilled with great satisfaction to both Great Britain and his own country.

In 1881, Mr. Reid married Elizabeth, daughter of Darius O Mills, and has one son and one daughter. His city residence is in Madison Avenue, and his country home, Ophir Farm, in Westchester County, near White Plains, is an extensive estate.

Mr. Reid is a member of the leading literary clubs of the city, including the Century, University, Grolier, the Δ K E and Lotos. His presidency of the latter for fourteen years was one of the most notable in the history of that brilliant society of letters. Besides the books on the South and Ohio already referred to, Mr. Reid is the author of a biographical and memorial sketch of Horace Greeley, Schools in Journalism, The Scholar in Politics, and Some Newspaper Tendencies, and has also been a frequent contributor to the reviews and periodicals. His social and political club connections include the Metropolitan, Union League, Republican, Tuxedo and Riding clubs, and he belongs to the Ohio, New England, St. Andrew's and American Geographical societies. He is also an honorary member of the Chamber of Commerce, a distinction that has been conferred upon only fifteen persons during the history of that organization.

CHARLES REMSEN

A LL the Remsens are descended from Rem Jansen Vanderbeeck, who emigrated from Westphalia in the early days of the Dutch settlement of Manhattan Island. In the old country, the family was of gentle origin, the Emperor Frederick Barbarossa having granted, in 1168, to one of the house, a coat of arms displaying the waving lines which suggested the waters of a brook, and gave the family its European cognomen, Vanderbeek. Rem Jansen Vanderbeek settled in Albany and married, in 1652, Annetje, daughter of Joris Jansen de Rapelye. When his father-in-law removed to the Wallabout, on Long Island, he accompanied him and settled upon a farm. Some of the original landed possessions of this pioneer have remained in the hands of his descendants even down to this day. He was a leader in the Colony, being a magistrate during the second occupancy of New Netherland by the Dutch, and died in 1681. He left fifteen children, and the sons, in accordance with a custom of the times, adopted as their surnames their father's Christian name, with a suffix to indicate their sonship, which is the origin of the name of Remsen, by which the descendants of Rem Jansen Vanderbeeck have been known.

Many of the family were prominent in the early history of the city and of the Province. Hendrick, born in 1708, was a wealthy merchant, and his son, Henry, born in 1736, became one of the largest importers of his day, and was also prominent in public affairs in the Revolutionary period. He was a member of the famous committee of one hundred citizens, chosen in May, 1775, to control the affairs of the city, and uphold the Provincial Congress. Jeremiah Remsen was a member for Brooklyn to the first Provincial Congress of 1775. Henry Remsen, 1762-1843, the son of the first Henry, was in early life private secretary to John Jay, Secretary of Foreign Affairs, and later on, Secretary to Thomas Jefferson, when the latter was President of the United States Afterwards, in 1790, he engaged in the banking business as a partner of the firm of Henry Remsen & Son, of this city, was a teller of the Branch of the United States Bank in New York in 1793, cashier of the Manhattan Company's Bank in 1799, and in 1808 president of the Manhattan Company, which position he retained until 1826. In 1808, he married Elizabeth, daughter of Abraham R. de Peyster, who belonged to the historic New York family of that name They had nine children.

William Remsen, son of Henry Remsen and Elizabeth de Peyster, was born in New York, January 13th, 1815. His early instruction was received in the schools of the city, and he was graduated from Princeton College in 1835. After studying law for three years, he was admitted to the New York bar, but gave up a professional career in order to take charge of the estate left by his father. He became one of the leading business men of the city, being particularly interested in real estate, and was a director in several banks and other corporations. By his marriage with Jane Suydam, daughter of John Suydam, of the old New York Dutch family of that name, he became the father of eight children, five of whom, Robert G., Jr., Charles, Jane, who married Joseph T. Thompson; Elizabeth, and Sarah, who married William Manice, survived him. He was one of the founders of the St. Nicholas Society, and of the American Geographical Society. Robert G. Remsen, brother of William Remsen, and uncle to Mr. Charles Remsen, was long a conspicuous figure in New York society, and died in 1896. A full reference to him will be found in another part of this volume.

Mr. Charles Remsen, the fifth son of William Remsen, was born in New York. Through his paternal grandmother, he is not only descended from the de Peysters and from Joris Jansen de Rapelye, as has already been shown, but he can also trace his lineage to the pioneers of the Roosevelt, Rutger and Bancker families. He is a physician, and is one of the executors of the estate of his father He married Lilian Livingston Jones, and has two sons, one of whom, William Remsen, is named after his grandfather His city residence is in East Eleventh Street, in that old residence locality bordering on Washington Square. He also has a country home in Remsenburg, Long Island, where he spends most of the year.

EDWARD S. RENWICK

JAMES Renwick, the first of the family name in this country, came to New York with his son and daughter in 1785 He was a merchant, and in connection with his son, William Renwick, established the first line of packet ships sailing from New York to Liverpool at fixed regular dates William Renwick went to Liverpool to take charge of the business there, and married Jennie Jeffrey, daughter of a Scotch clergyman, a famous beauty, and the theme of Burns' poem to blue-eyed Jennie Their son, James Renwick, the second of the name, was born in Liverpool, England, in 1790, and was brought to this country by his parents when he was a child. He was graduated from Columbia College in 1807, was instructor in natural and experimental philosophy and chemistry in Columbia in 1813, was a professor in the same branches from 1820 to 1853, and was made Professor emeritus upon his retirement from active labor in his profession. In 1814, he was engaged in the United States service as topographical engineer with the rank of Major From 1817 to 1820, he was a trustee of Columbia College, and in 1829 received the degree of LL D. In 1838, he was one of the commissioners for the exploration and establishment of the northeast boundary line between the United States and New Brunswick

On his mother's side, Mr. Edward S. Renwick is descended from Henry Brevoort, and from Captain Adam Todd, whose children and grandchildren have been the ancestors of many distinguished New York families. Margaret Todd, daughter of the second Adam Todd, married, in 1756, Captain William Whetten, of Devonshire, England, who, when a boy, before the French war, emigrated from England, and after commanding vessels in trade with the West Indies, settled in New York as a merchant Sarah Whetten, daughter of this marriage, married, in 1778, Henry Brevoort, and their daughter, Margaret Ann Brevoort, became the wife of James Renwick, second of the name, in 1816

Mr. Edward S Renwick, son of Professor James Renwick, second of the name, and his wife, Margaret Ann Brevoort, was born in New York in 1823. He was graduated from Columbia College in 1839, and began his professional career as superintendent of an iron works In 1849, owing to the depression of the iron manufacture, he became a patent solicitor in Washington. He has been one of the leading experts in this branch of business for a generation, the greater part of his work having been in cases before the United States Courts. In 1855, Mr Renwick removed to New York, which he has since made the headquarters of his business He is a skilful inventor and practical civil engineer of high attainments, besides being an original scientific investigator. Among his notable engineering achievements was the repair of the steamship Great Eastern, while afloat, in association with his brother Henry Brevoort Renwick He was also one of the joint inventors of the first self-binding reaping machines, and has made other important and useful inventions Mr. Renwick is a member of the Adirondack League, Union, Engineers and New York and Larchmont Yacht clubs, the Columbia College Alumni Association, and the American Geographical Society, and a patron of the Metropolitan Museum of Art and the American Museum of Natural History.

In 1862, Mr Renwick married Alice Brevoort, daughter of Henry Brevoort of the same family as that from which his mother was descended He has a family of two sons and one daughter The elder son, Edward Brevoort Renwick, was born in 1863 He lives in West Twenty-seventh Street and is a member of the Union, Seawanhaka-Corinthian Yacht and Engineers' clubs, and of the St Nicholas Society. He is an accomplished mechanical engineer and stands in the front rank of his profession The younger son, William Whetten Renwick, who was born in 1864, is an architect and partner in the firm of Renwick, Aspinwall & Owen, which was established by his uncle, James Renwick, third of the name, and the architect of St Patrick's Cathedral The youngest child of Mr Edward S. Renwick is Mrs. W. C. Whittingham, who was born in 1867

FREDERICK WILLIAM RHINELANDER

INHERITING a name conspicuously identified with the past two hundred years of New York's history, this gentleman, in the maternal line, is also a representative of a family of New England origin and Revolutionary record, which has been firmly established in New York since the independence of the United States was secured A full account of the first American generations of the Rhinelanders will be found upon the succeeding page of this volume The first of the name, as there set forth, was Philip Jacob Rhinelander, who came to New York and settled at New Rochelle, Westchester County, in 1696 His son was William Rhinelander, 1718-1777, of New York, who instituted the policy of investing their wealth in city real estate, which has since been pursued by his descendants. William Rhinelander, 1753-1825, second of the name, was his son, and the grandfather of the gentleman whose name heads this article He married Mary Robert and was the father of five sons and two daughters Philip Rhinelander, the eldest, married Mary Colden Hoffman, and their daughter, 'Mary C Rhinelander, married John A King, the three daughters of this marriage being Mary R , Alice, who married Gerardi Davis, and Ellen King Eliza Lucile married Horatio Gates Stevens, and their daughter, Mary Lucille, married Albert R. Gallatin, their children being Albert Horatio Gallatin, who married Louisa B Ewing, Frederic Gallatin, who married Almy Goelet Gerry, and James Gallatin, who married Elizabeth Hill Dawson William Christopher Rhinelander married Mary Rogers and was the father of William Rhinelander, whose sons are J T Oakley Rhinelander and Philip Rhinelander John Robert Rhinelander married Julia Stockton, and has no descendants Mary Robert Rhinelander married Robert J Renwick Frederick William Rhinelander, father of Mr. Frederick William Rhinelander, married Mary L A Stevens, and Bernard Rhinelander married Nancy Post.

Mary (Robert) Rhinelander, 1755-1837, the wife of William Rhinelander, second of the name, was of a Huguenot family, whose ancestor, Daniel Robert and his wife, Susanne Nicholas du Gaillean, came to America in 1686 Their son, Daniel Robert, second of the name, was the father of Christopher Robert, who, in 1743, married Mary Dyer, daughter of John Dyer and Christina Marcier, of Long Island, Mary Robert being their daughter The brother of Mary (Robert) Rhinelander was Colonel Robert, of the Continental Army

Frederick William Rhinelander, the elder, was the fourth son of William Rhinelander. He was born in 1796 and died in 1836 He married Mary Lucy Ann Stevens, daughter of General Ebenezer Stevens and his wife, Lucretia (Ledyard) Sands General Stevens was a son of Ebenezer Stevens and Elizabeth Weld, of Roxbury, Mass His grandfather, Erasmus Stevens, was one of the founders of the North Church, in Boston, and his mother was descended from the Reverend Thomas Weld, minister of the church at Roxbury in 1632 He was an active patriot and, in the Revolutionary War, became the most famous Artillery Commander of the Continental Army After the Revolution, he became a merchant in New York, and was Major-General of the State Militia and commanded the defenses of New York in 1812 The children of Frederick William Rhinelander were: Lucretia Stevens, who married George F Jones; Mary E , who married Thomas H. Newbold, Frederick W and Eliza L , who married William Edgar.

Mr Frederick William Rhinelander was born in New York, in 1828, and was graduated from Columbia College in the class of 1847. In 1851, he married Frances D Skinner, daughter of the Reverend Thomas H. Skinner They have a family of eight children Mary F , who married William C Rives, Frances L , Ethel L , who married the late Le Roy King, Frederick William Rhinelander, Jr , who was graduated from Harvard in 1882; Alice K , Helen L , who married the Reverend Lewis Cameron, Thomas Newbold, Harvard, 1887, who married Katharine Blake, of Toronto, Canada, and Philip M Rhinelander, who was graduated from Harvard in 1891. Mr Rhinelander belongs to the Knickerbocker, City and Southside Sportmen's clubs, the Downtown Association, the Mendelssohn Glee Club, and the American Geographical Society He is vice-president of the Metropolitan Museum of Art

WILLIAM RHINELANDER

PHILIP JACOB RHINELANDER was the first of the Huguenot family of that name who sought refuge in America from the persecutions caused by the revocation of the Edict of Nantes. He was born near the town of Oberwesel, on the Rhine, the district being then subject to France, and, arriving in New York in 1686, settled in the town of New Rochelle. He was living in 1737, in hale old age, and acquired considerable property in Westchester County.

The son of the first settler, William Rhinelander, first of the name, was born in New Rochelle, in 1718. He purchased and long resided in a house in Spruce Street, which is now the oldest Rhinelander property in New York, died in 1777, and was buried in Trinity churchyard. He married Magdalen Renaud, daughter of Stephen Renaud, of New Rochelle.

William Rhinelander, second of the name, his son, was born in New York, in 1753, and lived until 1825. He was trustee of the family estate, and, like his ancestors and descendants, was an extensive landowner. In 1785, he married Mary Robert, 1755–1837, a sister of Colonel Robert, a line officer in the Army of the Revolution, and a descendant of Daniel Robert, a Huguenot, who arrived in America in 1686. She was the aunt of Christopher Rhinelander Robert, who founded Robert College, in Constantinople.

William Christopher Rhinelander, 1790–1878, was the third of the seven children of William and Mary Rhinelander. During the war of 1812, he served as quartermaster in Colonel Stevens' regiment, and was afterwards Lieutenant. He resided at 14 North Washington Square. In 1816, he married Mary Rogers, daughter of John Rogers and Mary Pixton, and granddaughter of John Rogers, who married Mary Davenport, niece of Dr. Benjamin Franklin. The children of William Christopher and Mary (Rogers) Rhinelander were Mary Rogers, who married Lispenard Stewart, Julia and Serena Rhinelander, and William Rhinelander, third of that name.

Mr. William Rhinelander was born September 19th, 1825. In 1853, he married Matilda Cruger Oakley, daughter of the famous jurist, Thomas Jackson Oakley. The latter, a graduate of Yale, was Chief Justice of the Superior Court of New York, from 1850 to 1858, was a Member of Congress in 1813-15, and again in 1827-29, and Attorney-General of the State in 1819. He was also requested to be a candidate for the Presidency of the United States, but declined. Judge Oakley's wife, the mother of Mrs. William Rhinelander, was Matilda Cruger, daughter of Henry Cruger, who was born in New York in 1739 and died in 1827. Removing from New York to England, he became Mayor of the City of Bristol in 1781, and was twice a member of the British Parliament for that constituency, 1774-1784, having for his colleague, Edmund Burke. Returning to New York in 1790, he became a State Senator in 1792. Henry Cruger was the grandson of John Cruger, who came to New York prior to 1700, and was Mayor of the city, 1739-44, and married Maria Cuyler, daughter of Major Hendrick Cuyler, of Albany, who served in the French and Indian War. Mr. and Mrs. Rhinelander have two sons, T. J. Oakley and Philip Rhinelander.

Thomas Jackson Oakley Rhinelander, the elder son, was born January 15th, 1858, was graduated from Columbia College in 1878, and from Columbia's Law School in 1880. He served in the Seventh Regiment, and has mainly devoted himself to the care of the family property. In 1894, he married Edith Cruger Sands, daughter of Charles Edwin and Letitia I. (Campbell) Sands, and has a son, Philip Rhinelander. Philip Rhinelander, the younger son, was born October 8th, 1865, and was graduated from Columbia College in 1882. In 1882, he married Adelaide Kip, daughter of Isaac Leonard Kip and his wife, Cornelia Brady. In 1884, the two brothers, T. J. Oakley and Philip Rhinelander, purchased the ancient castle of Schönberg, on the Rhine, near Oberwesel, overlooking the old town and in close vicinity to the lands owned by their ancestors. The castle is on the site of a Roman fortress, built by Cæsar, the building, which has suffered much from the lapse of time and the wars of many centuries, having been commenced as far back as A. D. 951.

JOHN LAWRENCE RIKER

THE Rikers were originally a German family of lower Saxony, as the district surrounding the mouth of the Elbe was known. There they possessed the manor of Rycken, from which their name takes its derivation. Hans Von Rycken, the Lord of the Manor in the eleventh century, and his cousin Melchoir took part in the first crusade to the Holy Land in 1096, leading eight hundred Crusaders in the army of Walter the Penniless, who organized the first expedition for the recovery of Jerusalem from the infidels. The Von Rycken family in the course of time, became numerous in lower Saxony, Holstein and Hamburg, and its branches also spread to Holland, and even into Switzerland.

During the fourteenth and fifteenth centuries, the ancestors of the American Rikers established themselves in the Netherlands, their home being the City of Amsterdam, Holland, where they were prominent and influential in the affairs of the municipality and of the Province of Holland for two centuries They took part in the struggle which the people of the Low Countries instituted against the tyranny of Philip II. of Spain, and were zealous supporters of William the Silent, Prince of Orange, in the movement which established the United Provinces as a free and independent power. Through the vicissitudes incident to the struggle for liberty, the Riker family encountered reverses in their fortunes, and when the establishment of the New Netherland Colony invited the venturesome to a home across the ocean, representatives of the name came hither to found the family in this country.

Among them were Abraham Rycken, or de Rycke, as his name was indifferently written in the old records of the Dutch Colony. Governor Kieft in 1638 allotted to him a large tract at the Wallabout, for which a patent was issued in 1640. He also engaged in business in New Amsterdam, his premises being on the Heeren Gracht, now Broad Street, at the corner of Beaver Street. He married Grietie, daughter of Hendrick Harmensen. They appear as members of the first Dutch Church in the list of 1649, and their children were baptized at the church which was built in the early days of the Colony by the inhabitants and the Government within the walls of Fort Amsterdam, on the site of the present Battery.

In 1654, Abraham Rycken received a grant of the farm at Bowery Bay, to which he subsequently removed. One of the last official acts of Governor Stuyvesant was to execute a patent to him on August 19th, 1664, for Hewlett's Island, in the East River. It appears that this grant was disputed by the English, as Governor Nicoll, the first English Governor, on December 24th, 1667, confirmed the Dutch Governor's grant to Rycken, and the island has ever since been called Riker's Island and continued in the possession of the family till 1845. It is now the property of the City of New York. Abraham Rycken died at his Bowery Bay residence in 1689, his will, which left his patent to his son, having been recorded with the Clerk of Queens County in that year, in Book A of the County Records. He had nine children, and to him the subject of this article traces his descent, as also do most of the Rikers of this State as well as those in other parts of the country.

Abraham, son of the pioneer, was born at New Amsterdam in 1655 and married Grietie, daughter of Jan Gerrits Van Buytenhuysen and Tryntie Van Luyt, who was born in Holland. The second Abraham added one-third of the Tudor patent to the paternal property, and died in 1746 at the age of ninety-one years. He left the homestead and estate to his son Andrew, 1699–1763, having married Jane Berrien, daughter of John Berrien and widow of Captain Dennis Lawrence. His children were prominent in the stirring affairs of the Revolutionary period, taking an active part on behalf of the patriotic cause One of his sons, John B. Riker, was educated at Princeton College and became eminent as a physician in later years. During the war he was a staunch patriot and, joining the army of Washington, served as Surgeon of the Fourth Battalion of New Jersey troops, in the Continental Army, from 1777 to the surrender of Cornwallis at York-town. The second son, Andrew, born in 1740, was commissioned a Captain in the American

Army and was in the Canadian campaign of 1775, being present at the death of General Montgomery in the assault on Quebec in the winter of that year. At the head of a company in the Second New York Continental Regiment, he afterwards participated in the campaign against Burgoyne's army, and was engaged at the battle of Saratoga and in other contests, and died from spotted fever at Valley Forge, May 7th, 1778. Ruth, daughter of Andrew and Jane (Berrien) Riker, married the famous patriot, Major Jonathan Lawrence, who was very active in the service of his country during the whole Revolutionary War, sacrificing what was considered in those times a very large fortune to meet the exigencies of the patriotic cause to which he was so earnestly devoted

The third son, Samuel Riker, was also a patriot but was a prisoner in the hands of the enemy during most of the war. When the troubles were over, he became very prominent in public life on Long Island and for several years held the supervisorship of the town of Newtown In 1784, he was a member of the State Assembly of New York, and twice represented his district in the National Congress, the last time in 1807-9. He married Anna, daughter of Joseph Lawrence, one of the Long Island Lawrence family, in 1769, and had a family of nine children, dying in 1823. Several of the sons of Samuel Riker also became prominent in public life in this city and State The one best remembered in the annals of New York City is probably the third son, the Honorable Richard Riker, who was born in 1773 and educated under the tuition of the Reverend Dr Witherspoon, the famous patriot and head of Nassau Hall, Princeton College, New Jersey. In 1795, Richard Riker was admitted to the bar and several years later received the appointment of District Attorney for New York City. That position he held for several years, and in 1815 was made Recorder. With occasional short intermissions, he retained his seat on the bench until 1838. He left a record as one of the most learned and upright judges that the city ever possessed His wife was the daughter of Daniel Phœnix, Treasurer of New York City, and one of a family of great business and civic prominence in the early part of the present century, references to them occurring throughout this work.

Another son of Samuel Riker was Andrew, a shipowner, who was Captain of the privateers Saratoga and Yorktown during the War of 1812. The youngest of the brothers was John L. Riker, who was born in 1787, educated at Erasmus Hall, Long Island, and at the age of sixteen taken into the law office of his brother, the Recorder. He remained there five years, and then entered upon the practice of his profession, continuing in it for more than a half a century. He resided throughout his long lifetime upon the paternal estate at Newtown, and married successively two daughters of Sylvanus Smith, of North Hempstead, Long Island, who for many years was Supervisor of Queens County. He was the lineal descendant of James Smith, a follower of the Reverend Richard Denton, who came to Massachusetts from England with Governor John Winthrop, settling at first at Watertown, Mass. Thence he removed successively to Wethersfield and Stamford, Conn., taking many of his congregation with him, James Smith being included among the number, the Colony finally locating at Hempstead Long Island, the site of which was purchased by them from the Indians and title to it confirmed by a patent of Governor Kieft, dated November 16th, 1644.

Mr. John L. Riker, who represents this distinguished New York family in the present generation, is the child of John L. Riker, Sr.'s, second marriage, his mother being Lavinia Smith. He was born at Bowery Bay, Long Island, in 1830, was educated at the Astoria Academy under Dr. Haskins and by private tutors, and entering upon a business career, has been a leading merchant in New York City for many years. In 1857, Mr. Riker married Mary Anne Jackson, their surviving children being John Jackson Henry Laurens, Margaret M Lavinia, Samuel, Mattina, Charles Lawrence and May J Riker. Mr Riker resides at 19 West Fifty-seventh Street and has a summer home at Seabright N J, where he passes a large part of the year. He is a member of the St Nicholas and Holland societies, St. Nicholas Club and the Sons of the Revolution, as well as of the Metropolitan, Union League, City, Riding New York Yacht, Seawanhaka-Corinthian Yacht and New York Athletic clubs

SIDNEY DILLON RIPLEY

O N the paternal side, Mr Sidney Dillon Ripley comes from several Colonial families of Massachusetts and Connecticut. His American ancestor was William Ripley, who, with his wife, two sons and two daughters, came in one of the earliest companies of Colonists from Hingham, Norfolk County, England, and settled in Hingham, Mass., in 1638. He was a native of England, and was probably born in the vicinity of Hingham He was a freeman of Hingham, Mass., in 1642, and his son, John Ripley, who lived until 1684, married Elizabeth Hobart, daughter of the Reverend Peter Hobart, first pastor of the Church of Hingham Joshua Ripley, son of John Ripley and grandson of William Ripley, the pioneer, was born in 1658 and died in 1739 His wife was Hannah Bradford, daughter of William Bradford, Jr., Deputy Governor of the Plymouth Colony, and granddaughter or Governor William Bradford of Plymouth Joshua Ripley and his wife settled first at Hingham, Mass., but moved to Norwich, Conn., in 1688, and in 1691 to Windham, Conn., of which place he was the first town clerk and treasurer, and also a justice of the peace.

Joshua Ripley was the ancestor in the seventh generation of Mr. Sidney Dillon Ripley. The line of descent is through Joshua Ripley, 1688-1773, and his wife, Mary Backus, Ebenezer Ripley, 1729-1811, and his wife, Mehitable Berbank, Abraham Ripley, 1761-1835, and his wife, Mary Leonard, Harry Ripley, 1798-1820, and his wife, Azuba Snow Josiah Dwight Ripley, the father of Mr. Sidney Dillon Ripley, was born in 1841 He married Julie Dillon, eldest daughter of Sidney Dillon, in 1862 The parents and grandparents of Josiah Dwight Ripley were long-time residents of Springfield, Mass The maternal grandfather of Mr Sidney Dillon Ripley, after whom he is named, had an international reputation as one of the greatest railroad managers and capitalists of his day. Sidney Dillon, who was born in Northampton, Montgomery County, N. Y., in 1812, lived until 1892 He came of Revolutionary stock, his maternal grandfather having been a soldier in the Continental Army of 1776 His father was a prosperous farmer of Central New York, and gave his son a good education When young in years, he made his first connection with the railroad business, which was destined to be his life employment, and in which he rose to success surpassed by very few in his generation He was employed upon the Mohawk & Hudson Railroad, and afterwards on the Rensselaer & Saratoga Railroad. In the course of time, he came to hold responsible positions in connection with the construction of the Boston & Providence, the Stonington, and other railroads in New England Afterwards becoming a contractor on his own account, he executed much of the heavy contract work on the Troy & Schenectady, the Cheshire, the Vermont & Massachusetts, the Philadelphia & Erie and other roads

The great work of Mr Dillon's life was, however, the building of the Union Pacific Railroad With that enterprise he was conspicuously identified from its beginning, in 1865, until the work was completed, in 1869 Twice he was elected president of the Union Pacific Railway, and he was also a director of the Canada Southern, Rock Island & Pacific, Delaware, Lackawanna & Western, Manhattan Elevated, Wabash and other railroads, the Pacific Mail Steamship Company, the Western Union Telegraph Company, the Mercantile Trust Company and many financial corporations Mr. Ripley's maternal grandmother, whom Sidney Dillon married in 1841, was Hannah Smith. She died in 1884 Her mother was Betsy Otis, a relative of the distinguished Massachusetts statesman, Harrison Gray Otis

Mr Sidney Dillon Ripley was born January 11th, 1863, and is the treasurer of the Equitable Life Assurance Society He married, October 14th, 1885, Mary Baldwin Hyde, daughter of Henry B Hyde Mr. and Mrs Ripley live in West Fifty-third Street, and have a country residence at Hempstead, Long Island Their children are Annah D., Henry B H., Sidney Dillon, Jr., and James H Ripley Mr Ripley belongs to the Union, Metropolitan, Meadow Brook Hunt, Westminster Kennel, Lawyers', South Side Sportsmen's and Racquet clubs and the Country Club of Westchester County.

GEORGE LOCKHART RIVES

FOR two centuries the Rives family has been conspicuous in the State of Virginia as well as in other parts of the country, and has given many useful and distinguished men to the public service. The Honorable William Cabell Rives, grandfather of Mr George L. Rives, was born in 1793 and died in 1868. He was educated in Hampden-Sidney, and William and Mary colleges, and studied law under Thomas Jefferson. In 1814, he was an aide-de-camp on the staff of General J H Cocke, of Virginia. He had a long and interesting public career, being one of the leading men of his time in Virginia He was a member of the House of Delegates, 1817-19, and again, 1822-23, a Presidential elector in 1821, a member of the National House of Representatives, 1823-29, United States Senator from Virginia, 1832-45, and United States Minister to France, 1829-32, and again, 1849-53 The mother of William Cabell Rives was descended from Dr. William Cabell, a surgeon in the British Navy, who came to Virginia and settled in 1725.

The grandmother of Mr George Lockhart Rives, whom his grandfather married in 1819, was Judith Page Walker, who was born in 1802 and died in 1882 She was the daughter of the Honorable Francis Walker, of Albermarle County, Va , who was a member of the National House of Representatives in 1793 Her mother was Jane Byrd Nelson, daughter of Colonel Hugh Nelson, of Yorktown, Va , and his wife, Judith Page. Hugh Nelson was a son of William Nelson and Judith Page was a daughter of John Page and of Jane Byrd, whose father was Colonel William Byrd, of Westover. William Cabell Rives, Jr , 1825-1890, the second son of the Honorable William Cabell Rives, married Grace Winthrop Sears, of Boston, and their sons are Dr William C. Rives and Arthur L Rives, of New York. Alfred Landon Rives, the third son of this family, was a distinguished civil engineer in Virginia, and the father of Amélie Louise Rives, the authoress. Amélie Louise Rives, the only daughter of the Honorable William Cabell Rives, married Henry Sigourney, of Boston. She, with her husband and three children, were lost on the ship, Ville du Havre, in 1873, leaving one surviving son, Henry Sigourney, Jr.

Francis Robert Rives, the father of Mr. George Lockhart Rives, and the eldest son of the Honorable William Cabell Rives, was born in 1822. Graduated from the University of Virginia, in 1841, he was secretary of the United States Legation in London, 1842-45. Afterwards he removed to New York, and practiced law, and was prominent in the professional and social activities of this city. He was the first president of the Southern Society, and a member of many of the leading clubs. In 1845 he married Matilda Antonia Barclay, daughter of George Barclay, of the celebrated New York family of that name On his mother's side, Mr. George L Rives is descended in the seventeenth generation from King James, of Scotland, through his daughter, the Princess Jane Stuart, and her second husband, James Douglas, Earl of Morton The pedigree includes the Lords Livingston and the Earls of Eglington, down to Alexander, the ninth Earl of Eglington, whose daughter, Lady Euphemia Montgomery, married George Lockhart, son of Sir George Lockhart Their grandson, General Sir James Lockhart-Wishart, married Annabella Crawford, of Glasgow, and his granddaughter, Louise Ann Matilda Aufrere, became the wife of George Barclay, 1790-1869, and the mother of Matilda Antonia Barclay, who married Francis R. Rives The Barclay family, to which George Barclay belonged, has been fully treated on other pages of this volume

Mr George Lockhart Rives, the eldest son of Francis R. Rives, was born in 1849, was graduated from Columbia College, and holds a foremost place at the New York bar, being a member of the law firm of Olin & Rives Taking a deep interest in public affairs, although not active in politics, he was the First Assistant Secretary of State under Thomas F. Bayard during the first Cleveland administration, is a member of the Rapid Transit Commission, and has also been active in movements for the promotion of municipal good government. His first wife was Clara Morris Kean, daughter of Colonel John Kean, of Elizabeth, N. J. She died in 1887, and he afterwards married Sarah Whiting. He belongs to the Tuxedo, Knickerbocker, Century, Fencers, Players and other clubs An enthusiastic yachtsman, he is a member of the New York and other yacht clubs.

FRANK TRACY ROBINSON

FULLY seven centuries the pedigree of the Robinson family goes back in unbroken line. The head of the family then was John Robinson, of Donnington, Lincolnshire, England, who married a daughter of Thomas Paule In a later generation Nicholas Robinson, a direct descendant from the original John Robinson, was the first Mayor of Boston, Lincolnshire, in 1545 The Reverend John Robinson, who was born in 1575, a grandson of Nicholas Robinson, was one of the leaders of the Puritan movement that culminated in the settlement of the Plymouth Colony in New England. He led one of the companies of Puritans to Amsterdam, Holland, in 1608, afterwards removed to Leyden, and was active in promoting emigration across the Atlantic in the Mayflower. He did not come to this country, but died in Leyden in 1625.

Isaac Robinson, son of the Reverend John Robinson, came to Plymouth in 1630 and lived in Falmouth, Tisbury, Barnstable and Duxbury In successive generations the line of descent from this John Robinson to Mr Frank Tracy Robinson was through Peter Robinson, 1665-1740, and his wife, Experience Manton; Peter Robinson, 1697-1785, and his wife, Ruth Fuller, daughter of Samuel and Elizabeth (Thatcher) Fuller, Jacob Robinson, born in 1734, and his wife, Anna Tracy, Vine Robinson, born in 1767, and his wife, Dorcas Chapman, daughter of Elijah and Sarah (Steele) Chapman, and Francis Robinson, 1814-1885, and his wife, Anna La Tourette De Groot

The mother of Mr Frank Tracy Robinson, Anna La Tourette De Groot, was a daughter of Henry La Tourette De Groot, 1789-1835, and Mary Nesbitt, daughter of Thomas and Mary (Stanbury) Nesbitt, and granddaughter of John and Mary Nesbitt, of Ireland On the paternal side Anna La Tourette De Groot was descended from Jacob De Groot, who was one of the early Dutch settlers of Bound Brook, N. J. William De Groot, 1751-1840, was the grandfather of Anna La Tourette De Groot. His wife was Anna La Tourette, daughter of Henry and Sarah La Tourette, and granddaughter of Jean and Marie (Mersereau) La Tourette. The De Groots were an ancient Norman family, long settled at Goudere, on the River Yessel, in South Holland William De Groot, the great-grandfather of Mr. Robinson, was born in New Jersey in 1751 and died in 1840 He was Sergeant, Ensign and Lieutenant in the First Middlesex County Regiment of New Jersey

Other notable Colonial families unite in the ancestry of Mr Robinson His paternal grandmother, Dorcas Chapman, was descended from Edward Chapman, who settled in Windsor, Conn , where he was a freeman in 1667 The grandfather of Dorcas Chapman was Lieutenant Samuel Chapman, justice of the peace, Captain of the First militia company in Tolland, Conn , and a participant in the siege of Louisburg. Her father, Elijah Chapman, of Tolland, was several times a representative to the General Assembly Ruth Fuller, who married Peter Robinson, was descended from Edward and Ann Fuller, who came on the Mayflower in 1620. She was the great-granddaughter of Matthew Fuller, 1610-1678, one of the leading men of the Plymouth Colony, a physician, Captain and surgeon in the militia and representative to the General Court. Anna Tracy, who married Jacob Robinson, was the great-great-granddaughter of Thomas Tracy, a prominent citizen of the Connecticut Colony, a resident of Saybrook, Wethersfield and Norwich, a delegate to the General Assembly and an officer in the militia forces. Her grandfather, Jonathan Tracy, was one of the original settlers of Preston, Conn , a Lieutenant, selectman and deputy to the Legislature

Mr. Frank Tracy Robinson was born in Brooklyn in 1847, and has been engaged in mercantile life in New York for nearly thirty years He married Ida May Frost in 1873. His city residence is in Madison Avenue. Mr. and Mrs Robinson have had three sons, Charles L F Blanchard, who died young, and Henry La Tourette Robinson. Mr. Robinson belongs to the Manhattan, Racquet, Players, New York Yacht, New York, Larchmont Yacht and other clubs, and is a member of the New England Society and the Sons of the American Revolution. His son, Charles L. F. Robinson, graduated from Yale University in 1894, and married Elizabeth H J. Beach He is a member of the Riding, Δ Φ and New York Yacht clubs.

WILLIAM ROCKEFELLER

P ROMINENT in this generation's industrial progress, the Messrs Rockefeller are the children of William A and Eliza (Davison) Rockefeller, of Tioga County, N Y. There Mr William Rockefeller, second son of his father's family, was born in 1841 He received his early education in the Academy at Owego, N Y, and finished his studies in the local schools of Cleveland, O, whither his father moved when he was about ten years of age In the year 1858, Mr Rockefeller began his business career by taking a position as a bookkeeper in an office in Cleveland, where he remained about two years He then entered the firm of Hughes & Lester in the same capacity, and, when its senior member retired from business in 1862, he became a junior partner in the firm of Hughes & Rockefeller in the produce commission business It was in this partnership that Mr Rockefeller gained the first substantial success of his business life, and prepared the way for his subsequent achievements in that field

John D Rockefeller, the elder brother of Mr William Rockefeller, born in 1839, was the first to enter the oil business, with which the Rockefeller name has been identified for more than a third of a century Educated in the public schools of Cleveland, O, he became a clerk in a business house at the age of sixteen, then was cashier and bookkeeper, and at the age of nineteen became the junior partner of the firm of Clark & Rockefeller In 1860, his firm engaged in the oil refining business under the name of Andrews, Clark & Co, and in 1865 he and Samuel Andrews became the sole proprietors of the enterprise. In 1865, Mr William Rockefeller became associated with his brother's establishment, and the new firm, known as William Rockefeller & Co, built the Standard Oil Works in Cleveland In the same year, Mr William Rockefeller came to New York and established the firm of Rockefeller & Co, which was to represent their growing interests in the metropolitan and foreign markets This arrangement continued for two years when, in 1867, the further expansion of their business compelled a dissolution of the three firms, which up to that time had conducted it, and a consolidation of the interests of the partners in the single concern of Rockefeller, Andrews & Flagler, Henry M Flagler coming in as a new partner In 1870, the Standard Oil Company, of Ohio, was incorporated with John D Rockefeller as president, and Mr William Rockefeller as vice-president

Other refineries were added to the control of the company, and in 1881 the business had reached such enormous proportions that the Standard Oil Trust was organized, and at the same time the Standard Oil Company, of New York Mr William Rockefeller was elected vice-president of the Trust and president of the New York company In 1892, the Trust was dissolved, and since that time the Messrs. Rockefeller and their associates have managed the business through the independent action of the corporations in which they have large interests as stockholders Companies with which they are connected control the larger portion of the trade in petroleum and its products in the United States, and, through a large export trade, exercise a very great influence upon the business in all parts of the world

Mr William Rockefeller has been a resident of New York for more than thirty years He was married in 1864, at Fairfield, Conn, to Almira Geraldine Goodsell, and has four children living Emma, who married Dr. D Hunter McAlpin, Jr, William G, who married Elsie Stillman, Percy Avery, and Ethel Geraldine Rockefeller. In 1875, he built and has since occupied the house at the corner of Fifth Avenue and Fifty-fourth Street His country seat is an estate on the banks of the Hudson, near Tarrytown, which he purchased a few years ago and which he has improved by laying out extensive grounds Mr Rockefeller is a director in the Consolidated Gas Company, the United States Trust Company, the National City Bank, the Hanover National Bank, the Leather Manufacturers' National Bank, the New York, New Haven & Hartford Railroad, the Delaware, Lackawanna & Western Railroad, and the Chicago, Milwaukee & St. Paul Railway, and is connected with many other corporations He is a member of the Union League, Metropolitan, and Riding clubs

HENRY PENDLETON ROGERS

A LTHOUGH the Rogers families of Connecticut and of New York existed independently in the early Colonial days, they came from one parent stock The American ancestor was settled originally in Connecticut. James Rogers came over on the ship Increase, in 1635, when he was twenty years of age He married Elizabeth Rowland, daughter of Samuel Rowland, of Stratford, Conn , and lived in Stratford, Milford and New London For twenty years, he was a near neighbor and a personal friend of Governor John Winthrop, and was one of the mainstays of the Colony He died in 1687, at the age of seventy-two, leaving a family of five sons and two daughters. James Rogers, son of James Rogers, the pioneer, was born in 1652 He was a ship-master, and on one of his voyages from Europe, brought over a company of Redemptionists, among whom was Mary Jordan, daughter of Jeffery Jordan, who afterwards became his wife James Rogers, of the third generation, who was born in 1675 and died in 1733, was the father of three sons, who are particularly interesting in this connection. The eldest son, James, was the head of that branch of the family which has been conspicuous upon Long Island for one hundred and fifty years The other sons, Dr Uriah Rogers and Samuel Rogers, were prominent in the Connecticut Colony.

Samuel Rogers, the ancestor of Mr. Henry Pendleton Rogers, was born in Norwalk, Conn., in 1712 Early in life, he was the secretary of Governor Thomas Fitch, of the Connecticut Colony. His wife, whom he married about 1748, was Elizabeth Fitch, a near relative of Governor Thomas Fitch and of illustrious ancestry Governor Fitch was a graduate of Yale College, in 1721, and for forty-six years consecutively was Judge, Chief Justice, Lieutenant-Governor, or Governor of the Colony. He was in the third generation from Thomas Fitch, who settled in Norwalk in 1639, and who was descended from Sir Thomas Fitch, Baronet, of England. Moses Rogers, son of Samuel Rogers and Elizabeth Fitch, was born about 1750 His wife was Sarah Woolsey, daughter of Benjamin Woolsey, Jr , of Dosoris, Long Island, and Esther Isaacs, of Norwalk, Conn. He was a merchant of New York City, a director of the United States Bank, an active member of the Society for the Manumission of Slaves, a director of the Mutual Insurance Company, treasurer of the City Dispensary, a vestryman of Trinity Church, one of the founders of Grace Church and a governor of New York Hospital, 1792–99.

Archibald Rogers, 1793–1850, son of Moses and Sarah (Woolsey) Rogers, was the grand-father of the subject of this sketch. His wife was Anna Pierce Pendleton, daughter of Judge Nathaniel Pendleton and his wife, Susan Bard Judge Pendleton lived at Placentia, Hyde Park, N. Y., and was an intimate friend of Alexander Hamilton, being Hamilton's second in the duel with Aaron Burr His wife was a daughter of the famous Dr John Bard, of New York, of Huguenot descent.

The children of Archibald Rogers were: Nathaniel Pendleton, Julia Ann, Archibald, who died in 1831, Edmund Pendleton, Philip Clayton, Archibald, who died in 1836, and Susan Bard Rogers, who became the wife of Herman Thorne Livingston. Nathaniel Pendleton Rogers, the eldest son of this family, was born in 1822. He was a lawyer, and resided many years in New York, but afterwards had his residence at Placentia, Hyde Park His wife, whom he married in 1849, was Emily Moulton

Mr Henry Pendleton Rogers is the eldest son of Nathaniel Pendleton Rogers and the head of the family in the fifth generation from its American founder. He was born in 1850, and is a lawyer He married Mary Shillito, of Cincinnati, O. His sisters are. Anna Pendleton Rogers, who married Charles B. Fuller, of New York, and Elizabeth M Rogers His brother, Nathaniel P. Rogers, married Catharine Wotherspoon, of New York, and he has one other brother, J. Bard Rogers Mr. and Mrs. Rogers live in West Forty-ninth Street They have two sons, John Shillito and Henry Pendleton Rogers, Jr , and one daughter. Mr Rogers belongs to the Metropolitan, Knickerbocker, Church, Seawanhaka-Corinthian Yacht and Hudson River Ice Yacht clubs

JAMES ALFRED ROOSEVELT

FEW families have borne a more conspicuous part in business, social and public affairs in New York, than the Roosevelts They are sprung from Claes Martinsen Van Roosevelt, who, with his wife, Jannetje Thomas, came from Holland to New Amsterdam From him, the line comes down to contemporaneous times through Nicholas Van Roosevelt and his wife, Hillotje Jans ; Johannes Van Roosevelt and his wife, Hyltie Syverts ; Jacobus Roosevelt and his wife, Annatje Bogaert , Jacobus I or James Roosevelt and his wife, Mary Van Schaick, and Cornelius Van Schaick Roosevelt and his wife, Margaret Barnhill

Jacobus I. Roosevelt was a commissary to the Continental Army during the war of the Revolution. Cornelius Van Schaick Roosevelt was a successful business man, and one of the founders of the Chemical Bank His wife, Margaret Barnhill, was the daughter of Robert Barnhill and Elizabeth Potts. Their children were. Silas Weir Roosevelt, the eminent lawyer , James A Roosevelt, Cornelius Van Schaick Roosevelt, Jr , who died in 1887 at the age of 60, Robert B Roosevelt, Theodore Roosevelt and William W. Roosevelt, who died young.

Mr. James Alfred Roosevelt, the second child in his father's family, was born in New York, June 13th, 1825. When he was twenty years of age, he became a member of his father's firm. In 1878, he established the banking house of Roosevelt & Sons. He is also connected with many financial institutions, being a vice-president of the Chemical National Bank, a director of the New York Life Insurance & Trust Company, and other corporations, president of the Roosevelt Hospital, and a trustee of the Society for the Prevention of Cruelty to Children. During the first year of the administration of Mayor William L. Strong, he was a member of the Board of Park Commissioners The wife of Mr Roosevelt, whom he married in 1847, was Elizabeth N. Emlen, daughter of William F Emlen, of Philadelphia. The children of this union were : May Roosevelt, Leila Roosevelt, who married Edward Reeve Merritt; Alfred, who married Catherine Lowell, of Boston, and died in 1892, and William Emlen Roosevelt Mr. and Mrs Roosevelt have a city residence in West Fifty-seventh Street, near Fifth Avenue, and a summer home in Oyster Bay, Long Island Mr. Roosevelt is a member of the Metropolitan, Riding, City and Seawanhaka-Corinthian Yacht clubs, the Century Association, the Downtown Association and the St Nicholas Society. Emlen Roosevelt married Christine Kean, daughter of John Kean, and lives in Fifth Avenue.

Robert Barnhill Roosevelt, the fourth son of Cornelius Van Schaick Roosevelt, was born in 1829 He was a commissioner of the Brooklyn Bridge, a Member of Congress, 1873-74, treasurer of the National Democratic Committee in 1892, United States minister to the Netherlands in 1893, and was the first president of the Holland Society. He married, in 1850, Elizabeth Ellis, daughter of John S Ellis, and had four children, Margaret, John Ellis, Helen L , who died young, and Robert B. Roosevelt, Jr. After the death of his first wife, he married Marion T Fortescue, widow of R. Francis Fortescue, and daughter of John O'Shea, of Nenagh, Ireland

Theodore Roosevelt, the youngest surviving son of Cornelius Van Schaick Roosevelt, was born in New York in 1831, and died in 1878 He was prominently identified with public charities, being especially interested in the Newsboys' Lodging House, which he founded, and the Young Men's Christian Association, and was one of the founders of the Union League Club, the Orthopædic Hospital, and the Children's Aid Society. The Honorable Theodore Roosevelt, his eldest and only surviving son, is a graduate from Harvard College, and has devoted himself to literature and public life He is known as the author of several books, including The Winning of the West, and is a frequent contributor to the magazines upon the political topics He was a member of the Assembly of New York State, and for several years a member of the United States Civil Service Commission. In 1895, he became president of the Board of Police Commissioners, of New York, and became Assistant Secretary of the Navy in 1897 He belongs to the Century Association, and to the Union League and other clubs He married Edith K. Carow, and has a New York residence in Madison Avenue.

SAMUEL MONTGOMERY ROOSEVELT

A MONG the first Colonists who came to New Amsterdam was Claas Martensen Van Roosevelt, who, with his wife, Jannetje, arrived in 1651. Mr. Samuel Montgomery Roosevelt is descended from him in the seventh generation through Nicholas Roosevelt, of Esopus, Johannes Roosevelt, of New York, Jacobus Roosevelt, of New York, Nicholas J. Roosevelt, of New York, and Samuel Roosevelt, of New York and Staten Island Nicholas J Roosevelt, 1767-1854, grandfather of Mr. Samuel M. Roosevelt, was a son of Jacobus Roosevelt. He was closely related to Nicholas Roosevelt, who was a member of the Provincial Congress in 1775, a member of the State Senate in 1786 and president of the Bank of New York in 1786. Interested in the problem of steam navigation, he took out a patent for a steamboat before the date of Robert Fulton's and in subsequent litigation with Fulton, established his claim to priority, as the inventor of the sidewheel steamer. He was the inventor of the vertical paddle-wheel and was associated with Colonel Stevens and Chancellor Livingston in all the steps that led to steam navigation upon the Hudson Subsequently he introduced steam vessels on Western waters, establishing a shipyard in Pittsburg, and building, in 1811, the steamship New Orleans, the pioneer steamboat on the Mississippi River. He took it from Pittsburg to New Orleans in person, making the voyage in fourteen days, with his family. He also surveyed the Ohio and Mississippi Rivers. His country house was Claremont, which is now in Riverside Park, near the Grant Monument.

The grandmother of Mr. Samuel Montgomery Roosevelt was Lydia M. Latrobe, who married Nicholas J Roosevelt in 1808. She was descended from Henry Boneval de la Trobe, a Huguenot refugee in the service of William, Prince of Orange, who was wounded at the battle of the Boyne. The father of Mrs. Roosevelt was Benjamin Henry Latrobe, who was born in England in 1764, studied in Germany in 1785, and was an officer in the Prussian Army, and died in New Orleans in 1820. Coming to this country in the latter years of the century, he attained reputation as an engineer and architect, being the architect of the Capitol in Washington. He planned the Philadelphia water system in 1800, was the architect of the Cathedral in Baltimore and designed many buildings and public works, among them the James River and Appomattox Canal.

Samuel Roosevelt, the son of Nicholas J. and Lydia M. (Latrobe) Roosevelt, and father of the subject of this sketch, was born in New York in 1813 and died in New Brighton, Staten Island, in 1878. He was a prominent business man and had large interests in the South previous to the Civil War. He married Mary Jane Horton, daughter of Stephen Horton, of Skaneateles, N. Y., who was related to the Bellamy, Beach, Van Dycke, Grosvenor and other New York families.

Mr. Samuel Montgomery Roosevelt was born in New York, February 20th, 1858. He was educated in New York and Paris, and studied painting under Benjamin Constant and Jean Paul Laurant. He is an accomplished artist, his work having been frequently exhibited, and he is a member of the Art Students' League. In recent years, however, he has engaged in business pursuits. In 1885, he married Augusta E. Shoemaker, of Baltimore, who, on her father's side, is descended from Edward Shoemaker, twice Mayor of Philadelphia, and on her mother's from J. B. Eccleston, Judge of the Court of Appeals of Maryland. They reside in Fifth Avenue and have a summer home at Skaneateles Lake. Mr. Roosevelt is a member of the Chamber of Commerce and belongs to the Tuxedo, City, Knickerbocker, Manhattan, Fencers' and Larchmont Yacht clubs, the New York Historical Society and the Holland Society. A brother of Mr Roosevelt was Nicholas Latrobe Roosevelt, who graduated from the United States Naval Academy in 1868 and saw naval service in Corea, being mentioned in dispatches to Congress for gallantry in action He attained to the rank of Lieutenant in 1873, resigned in 1874, and died in 1892, He married Eleanor Dean, daughter of Joseph A. Dean and granddaughter of Judge Francis S. Lathrop, of New Jersey; she survived him with two sons and a daughter. The elder of his two sons, Henry Latrobe Roosevelt, is a cadet at Annapolis His daughter, Louisa Dean Roosevelt, married, in 1897, Ensign Arthur Bainbridge Hoff, U. S. N., grandson of Commodore Bainbridge.

WILLIAM HAMILTON RUSSELL

ON both sides, the ancestry of this gentleman is of Scotch nationality, though in the maternal line the families represented are among the oldest and most distinguished in the records of New York's Colonial days. Mr Russell's grandfather was James Russell, of Edinburgh, Scotland, a noted scientist, president of the Royal Society of Edinburgh, and cousin of the metaphysician Sir William Hamilton, and of Lord Sinclair. He was a member of the branch of the family whose estates are Kings Seat and Slipperfield (see Burke's Peerage), and which is related to many noble and prominent houses in Scotland

The late Archibald Russell, Mr. William H Russell's father, was born in Edinburgh, in 1811 Through his mother, he was descended from the Rutherfurds, of Edgarston, and one of his maternal ancestors was Eleanor Elliott, of the family of the Earls of Minto, whose descent from James II , of Scotland, is unbroken, and who are connected with the Dukes of Buccleugh and the Earls of Angus Archibald Russell was graduated from Edinburgh University, completed his education at the University of Bonn, Germany, and studied law under the celebrated advocate, Fraser-Tytler. In 1836, he came to New York and thenceforth made it his residence, marrying a lady of one of the foremost New York families, and devoting his energies and no small part of his wealth to the cause of education and philanthropy He was identified with many institutions and societies, but was especially prominent in a most useful educational and reformatory undertaking, the Five Points House of Industry, which was mainly his creation and of which he was the president for seventeen years An inscription upon the tablet erected to his memory by the trustees of the charity with which he had been so long connected rightly says, " This institution is his monument " During the Civil War, he was one of the active members of the Christian Commission, and afterwards was chairman of the Famine Relief Committee, which effected much good in the desolated South He was one of the organizers of the American Geographical Society, and was an active member and an officer of the New York Historical Society. His country seat was in Ulster County, and he founded and was long the president of the Ulster County Savings Institution. He died in New York City in 1871.

His wife, mother of the present Mr. Russell, was Helen Rutherfurd Watts, daughter of Dr John Watts and his wife, Anna Rutherfurd. Dr. John Watts, though he died at forty, was very prominent in his profession, having been the first president of the College of Physicians and Surgeons of New York, and a founder of the New York Hospital He was the son of Robert Watts and Lady Mary Alexander, daughter of Major-General Lord Stirling His grandfather was the Honorable John Watts, of Rose Hill, and of the Kings Council in New York, who married Ann DeLancey One of their daughters married the twelfth Earl of Cassilis and Marquis of Ailsa, and another married Sir John Johnson, of Johnson's Hall, who was distinguished in this country during the Revolution Anna Rutherfurd, the grandmother of Mr William Hamilton Russell, was the daughter of John Rutherfurd and Helena, daughter of Lewis Morris, the signer of the Declaration of Independence. John Rutherfurd was a United States Senator from New Jersey, a lawyer of eminence and one of the first regents of Columbia College His father, Walter Rutherfurd, an officer of the British Army, was a son of Sir John Rutherfurd, of Edgarston, Roxburghshire, Scotland

Mr William Hamilton Russell was born in New York City in 1856 and was graduated from Columbia College in 1878 He adopted architecture as his profession and is a member of the firm of Clinton & Russell, who have designed many important buildings in this city, among the number being the Exchange Court, Hudson, Franklin and Woodbridge buildings, as well as the one at Thirty-ninth Street and Fifth Avenue

Mr. Russell is a member of many societies and clubs, including the American Institute of Architects and the Architectural League, the University, Knickerbocker, Players, and Metropolitan clubs. In 1893, Mr Russell married Florence Lucretia Sands, of the English family of that name Mr. and Mrs. Russell have one son, William Hamilton Russell, Jr

JOHN ALEXANDER RUTHERFURD

HISTORY records that the Rutherfurds were once powerful on the Scottish border. The name first appears when Robertus de Ruddyefurde witnessed a charter from David I to Gervasius de Rydel, in 1140. Edgerstone was the seat of the family from which the American branch is descended. In 1492, lands were granted to James Rutherfurd, by King James IV The Rutherfurd arms are . Argent, an orle gules and in chief three martlets sable The orle was assumed in remembrance of the family having defended the Scottish border, while the martlets commemorate the fact that some of its representatives had served in military expeditions to the Holy Land. In the eleventh generation from James Rutherfurd, Walter Rutherfurd, the sixth son of Sir John Rutherfurd, entered the navy at the age of fifteen. At one time his father had eighteen sons and grandsons in the army and navy. Walter Rutherfurd served in the navy until 1746, and then became an officer in the Royal Scots, and was paymaster in the campaigns in Flanders and Germany. In 1756, the French and Indian War brought him to this country He was Judge Advocate and Major, and retired from the army in 1760. Walter Rutherfurd became a large land proprietor, receiving in 1775 a patent for five thousand acres, in consideration of his military services He also acquired large landed property through his wife, Catharine Alexander, great-granddaughter of the Earl of Sterling During the Revolution, he retired to his estate in New Jersey, but after peace had been declared returned to New York. He was interested in many public movements of his time, being president of the Agricultural Society, a founder of the Society Library, and president of the St Andrews Society.

The Honorable John Rutherfurd, his son, 1760–1840, graduated from Princeton College, in 1779 Soon after he settled at Allamuchy, Warren County, N J , and engaged in the care of his father's landed estates in Northern New Jersey. He became a member of the New Jersey Legislature, in 1788, and in 1790 he was elected to the United States Senate, and reelected to the same position in 1796 Two years later he resigned his office and moved to near Trenton, and afterwards to an estate on the Passaic. In 1807, he was, with Gouverneur Morris and Simeon De Witt, a member of the commission to lay out the City of New York above Fourteenth Street

The grandfather of Mr. John Alexander Rutherfurd was Robert Walter Rutherfurd, the eldest son of John Rutherfurd. He was born at the family homestead, Tranquility, in New Jersey, in 1788, and graduated at Princeton College, in 1806 He was a member of the New Jersey Assembly, 1812-13-15, a member of the State Council, 1819-20, and was one of the prominent men in his section. His wife was his cousin, Sabinia Morris, daughter of Colonel Lewis Morris

Mr John A Rutherfurd's father was Walter Rutherfurd, the second son of Robert Walter Rutherfurd. He was born in 1812, and was a prominent lawyer in New York, having graduated from Rutgers College, in 1831, and studied law with Peter A Jay.· His wife, whom he married in 1846, was Isabella Brooks Her father, David Brooks, served in the Revolutionary War, and was an original member of the Society of the Cincinnati, while her grandfather, Daniel Niel, was killed at the Battle of Princeton, where he was serving as aide to General Hugh Mercer Her mother, Frances Morris, was the daughter of William Walton Morris, who served in the Revolution as aide to General Wayne, and was third son of Lewis Morris, the signer of the Declaration of Independence.

Mr John Alexander Rutherfurd is the eldest son of Walter Rutherfurd, and was born in Edgerston, N J , March 2d, 1848 He graduated at Rutgers College, and is a stock broker and member of the New York Stock Exchange. He is interested in Southern railway and industrial development, and has been vice-president of the Richmond & Danville Railroad, and of the Richmond & West Point Terminal Company. He is now a director of the Sloss Iron & Steel Company, of Birmingham, Ala Mr Rutherfurd resides at 46 East Sixty-fourth Street, and is a member of the Metropolitan, Players, Manhattan, and other clubs, the Society of the Cincinnati, and the Sons of the Revolution.

AUGUSTUS SAINT-GAUDENS

B Y common consent Mr. Augustus Saint-Gaudens stands at the head of American sculptors. His achievements have not only won him reputation at home and abroad, but they have made him a compeer with the greatest sculptors of the world in the present generation and have established in the United States a new school of sculpture far in advance of, and differentiated from anything that has preceded it.

Mr. Saint-Gaudens is a native of Ireland. He was born in Dublin in 1848. His father, Barney Saint-Gaudens, was a Frenchman, who settled in Dublin, in the early part of the present century. His mother, Mary McGuinness, came from an old Irish family. When the son was but six month old, his parents emigrated to this country, and he may therefore fairly claim to be a thorough American, even though his birth occurred in Ireland. He early manifested the artistic talent which has developed him into the great master of sculpture of his generation, and when he was thirteen years of age, was sent to the Cooper Union, to study drawing. Four years after he was a student in the Art School of the National Academy of Design. While he was pursuing his studies he learned the trade of cameo cutting, and was a remarkably skilful workman. When he was nineteen years of age, he went abroad to study, primarily, with the intention of perfecting himself in cameo cutting, but once in Europe, he made up his mind to undertake the study of sculpture, and with that end in view, entered the atelier of Jouffroy, at the Ecole des Beaux Arts. He still continued to work at cameo cutting, but made rapid progress in sculpture until 1870, when the breaking out of the Franco-Prussian war sent him to Rome, where he opened a studio, and in 1871 produced his first figure, Hiawatha. This work was the turning point in his career, for it attracted the attention of connoisseurs, and gained him several commissions, including a bust of the Honorable William M. Evarts.

In 1872, Mr. Saint-Gaudens returned to New York. His bust of Mr. Evarts secured him patronage, on the strength of which he again returned to Rome, remaining there several years. Coming back to New York, he was selected to model a statue of Admiral David Farragut, and soon after received a commission for a statue of Captain Robert R. Randall, founder of the Sailors' Snug Harbor, on Staten Island. His cast of the Farragut statue was exhibited in Paris in 1880, and was received with enthusiasm by the greatest artists and critics of the French capital. When it was set up in Madison Square, it gained him additional fame and established him at the head of a school of American sculptors, that he has held unchallenged ever since.

Other great works of Mr. Saint-Gaudens, are the statues of Lincoln, an heroic bronze, that stands in Jackson Park, Chicago; the Puritan, a statue of Deacon Samuel Chapin, that stands in a public square in Springfield, Mass ; the John A Logan statue in Chicago, one of the masterpieces of sculpture of this generation; and the bas-relief memorial to Colonel Robert G Shaw, of Boston, that was erected upon Boston Common, opposite the State House, in 1897. He modeled the reredos for St Thomas' Church, New York, the caryatids for the Cornelius Vanderbilt house, assisted in the sculpture work for the decoration of Trinity Church, Boston, made the Peter Cooper statue, that stands in the triangle in front of the Cooper Union, New York, and has modeled busts and bas-reliefs of Robert Louis Stevenson, President Theodore D Woolsey, of Yale College, General William T. Sherman, and other prominent persons. His bas-relief of the Reverend Dr. Henry W. Bellows is regarded as the most important work of its kind ever produced in this country.

In 1876, Mr Saint-Gaudens married Augusta Homer, of Boston, who comes of an old New England family He has one son, Homer Saint-Gaudens His studio is in West Thirty-sixth Street He is a member of the Metropolitan, City, Players and Riding clubs, the Century Association, the National Sculpture Society, and the Architectural League, and is numbered among the supporters of the Metropolitan Museum of Art and the National Academy of Design He has also been president of the Society of American Artists, which he was instrumental in founding.

HENRY WOODWARD SACKETT

ONE of the youngest officers in the Revolutionary Army of 1776 was Major Buel Sackett, of an old Rhode Island family He performed notable service during the war and was in command of a detachment on duty at the execution of Major Andre He was a native of Litchfield, Conn, born in 1763, his immediate ancestors having removed from Rhode Island to the former State After the close of the Revolutionary War he settled in Lebanon, N Y Twice married, his first wife was Sally C Beach, his second being Lydia Buel He was the paternal great-grandfather of Mr Henry Woodward Sackett. The founder of the Sackett family in America was John Sackett, who, in 1631, came from the Isle of Ely, England, to Massachusetts and settled in Cambridge He was of Norman ancestry, his progenitors having come to England with William the Conqueror The descendants of John Sackett went from Cambridge to Worcester, Mass, among its early settlers and thence to Rhode Island and Connecticut

The father of Mr Sackett, Dr Solon P Sackett, was born in Nassau, Rensselaer County, N Y, and died in Ithaca in 1893 He was educated for the medical profession, being graduated from the Geneva Medical College in 1843. For many years he was a prominent physician of Ithaca, and secretary of the County Medical Society His father was a Captain in the War of 1812 and married Lovedy K. Woodward, daughter of Charles Woodward, an English gentleman, who purchased a large tract of land between Cayuga and Seneca Lakes in Central New York, in the early part of the century, and settled there He was devoted to the study of natural history, and at the time of his death owned one of the finest private ornithological and conchological collections in the country. His grandfather was Benjamin Woodward, who resided in the west of England and was a famous naturalist

Mr Henry Woodward Sackett was born in Enfield, N Y, August 31st, 1853, and was prepared for college in the Ithaca Academy, then under the direction of Professor Samuel G Williams Admitted to Cornell University, when fifteen years of age, he spent one year in teaching before entering upon his college course He was graduated from Cornell in the classical course in 1875, with the degree of A B. He attained the highest rank in mathematics, was a Φ B K man, class essayist at graduation and for two terms president of the leading literary society in the college After graduation, he taught Latin and Greek for a year in the Monticello Military Academy, and then came to New York and entered the Law School of Columbia University Shortly afterwards he began to report law cases for The New York Tribune, thus supplementing his legal studies with the observation of procedure in court, until he was admitted to the bar in 1879 and entered upon practice in the office of Cornelius A Runkle He finally became associated in practice with Mr Runkle, and upon the death of the latter, in 1888, succeeded him as counsel for The Tribune He then formed a partnership with Charles Gibson Bennett, under the name of Sackett & Bennett, which continued for six years, when Mr Bennett was succeeded by William A McQuaid, the firm name becoming Sackett & McQuaid In October, 1897, Selden Bacon became a member of the firm, which has since continued under the name of Sackett, Bacon & McQuaid. For many years Mr Sackett wrote the editorials upon legal subjects in The Tribune, and in 1884 prepared a work on the law of libel, especially in relation to newspapers

In 1886, Mr. Sackett married Elizabeth Titus, daughter of Edmund Titus, of Brooklyn, one of the incorporators of the New York Produce Exchange. The family residence is in West Fifty-seventh street and their summer home is at Mamaroneck Mr. Sackett was president of the Cornell University Club in 1896 and 1897, is a member of the Φ B K Alumni Association and belongs also to the University, City and Hardware clubs, the Bar Association, the American Geographical Society, the Society of Medical Jurisprudence, of which he was one of the organizers, and many other social and scientific organizations. For several years he was a non-commissioned officer in Squadron A, of the National Guard In 1896, Governor Black appointed him aide-de-camp on his staff, with the rank of Colonel

RUSSELL SAGE

THE ancestors of Mr Russell Sage were of Connecticut extraction. The family on both sides had been well established in that State from the earliest pre-Revolutionary period, but when the West began to attract the people of New England, among those who started for the new region were Elisha Sage and his wife, Prudence Risley They proceeded, however, no further than Central New York, and settled in the township of Verona, Oneida County, in 1816, and afterwards in Durhamville, where Elisha Sage died in 1854, having become one of the substantial citizens in that section.

Mr. Russell Sage, his son, was born in Verona in 1816. He was educated in the schools of his native place. At an early age, he began life in the store of his brother in Troy, N. Y. When he had reached the age of twenty-one, he had accumulated capital of his own and went into business as a partner with another brother. After a few years, he became sole proprietor of the concern and in 1839, with a partner, established a wholesale store in Troy. From this it was a natural step to become a commission merchant with business connections with New York, and in the course of time the firm controlled the markets of Troy and Albany in several branches Before 1850, the subject of transportation began to interest Mr. Sage, and in 1852, as a member of the Common Council of Troy, he took a leading part in the sale of the Troy & Schenectady Railroad, then owned by the city, but which is now part of the New York Central system. After the panic of 1857, Mr. Sage concentrated his attention upon matters of finance. He became a large owner in the La Crosse Railroad, now the Chicago, Milwaukee & St. Paul, and was a director and vice-president of the company.

About the beginning of the war, in 1861, he began to operate in Wall Street, and since 1863 has been a resident of New York, a member of the Stock Exchange and one of the most conspicuous figures in the metropolitan financial world Closely associated with the late Jay Gould, he has been active in the management of many of the Gould properties, having a large personal interest in them. Probably no other living man in the country has taken a larger part in the development of American railroads than Mr Sage, and he has been president of more than twenty-five railroad corporations. He has also been connected with telegraph enterprises and is a director and large owner in the Western Union Telegraph Company. At the present time he is connected with many corporations, as a large shareholder and as filling important official positions in some of the largest organizations of this character.

In early life, Mr. Sage was deeply interested in public affairs and was prominent in New York State politics While residing in Troy, in 1845, he was an alderman and afterwards treasurer of Rensselaer County, for seven years. In 1848, he was a delegate to the National Convention of the Whig party and took an active part in bringing about the nomination of General Zachary Taylor for the presidency He was nominated for Congress in 1850, but he was not elected Two years later, however, he was successful at the polls and in 1854 was re-elected by the overwhelming majority of 7,000 votes. He was active in the organization of the Republican party, but since 1857 has taken no direct part in public affairs.

Mr. Sage has been twice married. His first wife, whom he married in 1841, and who died in 1867, was Maria Winne, daughter of Moses I Winne, of Troy. In 1869, Mr. Sage married Margaret Olivia Slocum, daughter of the Honorable Joseph Slocum, of Syracuse, N. Y. Mrs. Sage is descended on the paternal side from Captain Miles Standish, of Plymouth, and on the maternal from Colonel Henry Pierson, of Sag Harbor, N Y, whose name is identified with the first measures, about 1787, for the establishment of the public school system. Mrs Sage is a graduate from the Troy Female Seminary, founded by Emma Hart Willard. One of the finest buildings connected with any educational institution in this country is the dormitory of the Seminary, presented by Mr and Mrs. Sage in 1895, and known as Russell Sage Hall. Mr. and Mrs. Sage live in Fifth Avenue, near Central Park.

BENJAMIN AYMAR SANDS

ANDS POINT, Long Island, was thus called from the settlement there during the seventeenth century of the progenitors of what has become one of the leading New York families. The name, however, is one which first appears in American records on the roll of New England's early emigrants. James Sands, a native of Reading, Berkshire, England, came to Plymouth, Mass., in 1658, and two years later was one of the associates who bought Block Island from the Indians. In 1661, he moved there with his family. John Sands, his son, whose wife was Sibyl Ray, came, however, to Long Island, and from the establishment of his residence at that place, Sands Point received its name. Various members of the family have ever since been prominent in Long Island, and, naturally, soon became connected with New York both commercially and through marriages with the older families of this city. Their names have been identified with the leading interests of the metropolis, social and otherwise.

John Sands, of Sands Point, had a son and a grandson, both called John, the latter of whom married Elizabeth Cornwell, and was the father of the Revolutionary patriot and merchant, Comfort Sands and of Richardson Sands, who was the great-grandfather of the gentleman whose ancestry is traced in this article. Comfort Sands was a notable figure at a stirring period in New York's history, for he was one of those men of wealth and influence who, at the beginning of the Revolution, did not hesitate to risk their lives and fortunes in the cause of their country. He was a member of the Committee of One Hundred chosen in May, 1775, to administer the affairs of the Province when the royal authority had broken down, and also sat in the various Provincial Congresses. After the peace of Versailles, he was president of the Chamber of Commerce. His son, Joseph, became a member of the firm of Prime, Ward & Sands, the first of New York's great banking houses, his sister, Cornelia, being the wife of the famous Nathaniel Prime, the head of that establishment.

Richardson Sands, the brother of Comfort Sands, was born in 1754, and was also prominent in his generation. He married Lucretia Ledyard, daughter of John Ledyard, of Hartford, Conn., their only son being Austin Ledyard Sands, one of the foremost men in the commercial affairs of the city during the first half of the century. After the death of Richardson Sands, his widow, Lucretia (Ledyard) Sands, married General Ebenezer Stevens. Joshua Sands, the youngest brother of Comfort and Richardson Sands, was a State Senator from 1792 to 1799, a Member of Congress from New York in 1803 and again in 1825, and Collector of the Port of New York under the administration of President John Adams. Austin Ledyard Sands died in 1859. His eldest son was Samuel Stevens Sands, who was long prominent in the mercantile and financial world, as well as in social circles. He married Mary E. Aymar, who also came of a family which represented the mercantile interests of the city. Her father was Benjamin Aymar, one of the greatest shipping merchants of the preceding generation. He was classed among the most enterprising men of his time; his ships carried the American flag to all parts of the world, and his financial standing was of the highest.

Mr. Benjamin Aymar Sands, representative of the family in this generation, is the son of Samuel Stevens Sands. He was born in New York, July 27th, 1853, and was graduated from Columbia College and also from the Law School of that institution, was admitted to the bar and has practiced his profession for over twenty years in this city. He is a member of the executive committee of the Bar Association, vice-president of the Colorado Midland Railroad Company, and a director of the New York Security and Trust Company, the National Safe Deposit Company, Greenwich Savings Bank, Hudson River Bank and Commonwealth Insurance Company. In January, 1878, Mr. Sands married Amy Akin, daughter of William H. Akin, and has one daughter, Mary Emily Sands. The residence of the family is in West Forty-eighth Street, and their country home is at Southampton, Long Island. Mr. Sands is a member of the Union, University and City clubs and of the Downtown Association.

GEORGE HENRY SARGENT

HUGH SARGENT, or Sariant, as the name was most commonly used in the fifteenth and sixteenth centuries, was the earliest known ancestor of the Sargent family, many members of which have borne a conspicuous and influential part in business and public life in the United States for two hundred years. He lived in Courteenhall, Northamptonshire, England, of which place he was a native Courteenhall was an ancient inheritance of the Wake family, which traces its descent back to Hereward the Wake, in times previous to the Norman Conquest. The Sargent family was in Courteenhall early in the sixteenth century, and was of gentle blood, and it is quite possible that it had been established there even before the Wakes had entered into possession. The wife of Hugh Sargent was Margaret Gifford, daughter of Nicholas and Agnes (Masters) Gifford, of the Abbey of St. James, a suburb of the town of Northampton. Hugh Sargent was born about 1530, and had a family of fifteen children. He died in 1595.

William Sargent, the ancestor of the American family, was a son of Roger Sargent and grandson of Hugh Sargent. He came from Northampton, England, to Charlestown, Mass , in 1638, accompanied by his third wife, Sarah, and two daughters by his first wife. He first settled in Charlestown, but when a settlement was made on the banks of the Mystic River, he removed there with his family In 1638, he was made a freeman and became one of the important men in the Colony. In 1648-50, he was a lay preacher in Malden, and was at one time a selectman. Removing to Barnstable, about 1656, he was a preacher there, and a freeman of Plymouth Colony in 1657 His death occurred in 1682, and his wife died in 1688

John Sargent, son of William Sargent, was born in Charlestown. He made his home in Malden for the greater part of his lifetime, and was a selectman for six years. His son, John Sargent, born in 1639, was married three times. His first and third wives were born in Plymouth Colony, so that the mingled blood of Pilgrim and Puritan flows in the veins of his descendants The mother of his son, Joseph, was Deborah Hillier, of Barnstable, 1643-1669, daughter of Hugh Hillier. Joseph Sargent, his son, was born in 1663, and died in 1717. He married Mary Green, 1668-1759, daughter of John Green, and was a resident of Malden and Charlestown, Mass. For four successive generations thereafter, sons of the family, the ancestors in direct line of the subject of this sketch, were named Joseph The grandfather of Mr. George H Sargent, Joseph Sargent, of Leicester, Mass., 1757-1787, was a great-grandson of Joseph and Mary (Green) Sargent He married Mary Denny, daughter of Thomas Denny. His father, Colonel Joseph Denny Sargent, of Leicester, 1787-1849, married Mindwell Jones, daughter of Phineas Jones. The Denny and Jones families were among the most ancient in the history of New England. The lineage of Mr. George H Sargent also goes back to the Baldwin family, another famous New England stock.

Mr. George Henry Sargent was born in Leicester, Worcester County, Mass , October 29th, 1828. Educated at the academy in his native town, he then went to Harvard College, from which institution he was graduated in 1853. The same year that he graduated, he removed to New York and engaged in the hardware business An elder brother, Joseph Bradford Sargent, who was already settled in that business, became associated with him, under the firm name of Sargent & Company, in 1853, and since then he has been continuously connected with the establishment of which he is now the head. His father established, in the town of Leicester, a manufactory of cards used for carding cotton and wool by hand, and upon his death, the business passed into the hands of the sons, Joseph B., Edward and George H Sargent. The firm also has extensive factories in New Haven

In 1855, Mr. Sargent married Sarah Shaw, daughter of the Honorable John H. Shaw, of Nantucket, Mass. His daughter, Emily Shaw Sargent, married, in 1895, Wilfred Lewis, of Philadelphia. Mr Sargent belongs to the Union League, Harvard and Hardware clubs, and the New England Society, and is a patron of the National Academy of Design. Politically, he is a Republican. He is a member of the Unitarian Church, and a director of the Mercantile National Bank.

LEWIS A. SAYRE, M. D.

EPHRAIM SAYRE, of New Jersey, was a soldier in the War of the Revolution, holding the office of quartermaster General Washington occupied his house as headquarters before the battle of Springfield. The descendants of Ephraim Sayre have continued to live in New Jersey down to the present time. Archibald Sayre, son of Ephraim Sayre, was a resident of Morris County, and a man of wealth, and was active and influential in public affairs.

Dr. Lewis Albert Sayre was the son of Archibald Sayre, and was born at Battle Hill, now Madison, Morris County, N. J., February 29th, 1820. His education was begun in his native place, and continued at the Wantage Seminary, at Deckertown, N. J. He took a collegiate course at Transylvania University, Kentucky, where he was graduated in 1839. At that time he was living with his uncle, in Lexington, Ky., and was intended for the church. His uncle was David Austin Sayre, a wealthy merchant and banker who, during his lifetime, gave more than half a million dollars to benevolent institutions, and founded the Sayre Female Institute. The inclination of the young man was toward the study of medicine, and when his college career was completed he returned to the East and entered the office of Dr. David Green, of New York. Taking a course in the College of Physicians and Surgeons, he graduated in 1842. When he took his degree, he read a thesis upon Spinal Irritation that attracted considerable attention, and is now of special interest as indicative of the early leaning of his thoughts toward that branch of medical practice wherein he has since become famous.

In the year that he graduated, Dr. Sayre was appointed prosector to the Professor in Surgery of the College of Physicians and Surgeons, Dr. Willard Parker, a position that he held until the pressure of private practice compelled him to resign it in 1852, when he was honored by the appointment of emeritus prosector In 1855, he was made surgeon to Bellevue Hospital, and two years later became surgeon to the Charity Hospital and its consulting surgeon in 1873.

Dr. Sayre was one of the founders of the New York Pathological Society, the New York Academy of Medicine and was one of the first members of the American Medical Association; being its vice-president in 1866 and president in 1880. He was one of the first to advocate the Bellevue Hospital Medical College, in which he became the first Professor of Orthopœdic Surgery, Fractures and Luxations. In 1866, he was resident physician of the City of New York. From 1871 to 1881 he went abroad several times, and his fame in surgery had spread so widely that he was received with great distinction. In his specialties he stands at the head of his profession. He was the first in America to successfully perform excision of the joint for hip disease, and his study and treatment of spinal complaints has revolutionized medical science. He has devised new methods of treatment and invented numerous appliances and instruments Certain methods of treatment, now universally adopted, are known the world over by his name The contributions of Dr Sayre to medical literature have been abundant. He has written many papers for medical and other periodicals, and has published important medical and surgical treatises. His services to the afflicted have brought him recognition from all parts of the world Many honors have been bestowed upon him. King Charles IV of Sweden and Norway decorated him with the order of Wasa, and he was elected an Honorary Member of the Medical Society of Norway, and also of those of St. Petersburg and Edinburgh, and of the British Medical Association At home he is an honored member of all the leading medical societies, belongs to the club of the Σ Φ and other social organizations, and is a patron of the Metropolitan Museum of Art, the American Museum of Natural History and the American Geographical Society.

Dr. Sayre married in 1849 Eliza A Hall, daughter of Charles Henry Hall, of New York His surviving son, Dr Reginald Hall Sayre, is a graduate from Columbia College and the Bellevue Hospital Medical College. He is engaged in practice with his father, and is a lecturer on orthopœdic surgery in the Bellevue Hospital Medical College. The only daughter of Dr Sayre, Mary Hall Sayre, assists her father in his literary work. Dr. Sayre lives at 285 Fifth Avenue.

EDWARD HEARTT SCHELL

RICHARD SCHELL, of Germany, who left the Old World about the middle of the eighteenth century, was the American ancestor of the Schells, who have been preëminently distinguished in the political and business life of the metropolis in the last generation. He went to Dutchess County, N Y, and settled upon the Rhinebeck patent, and marrying there, had a large family of children. Christian Schell, son of Richard Schell, married Elizabeth Hughes, of Staatsburg, whose parents were of Welsh origin. He was a prominent business man in Rhinebeck and of high standing in the community. During the War of 1812, he commanded a company of troops that were enlisted from that section of the State. He died in 1825, at the age of forty-six, and his widow survived him forty-one years, dying in 1866 at the age of eighty-three

Several of the children of Christian and Elizabeth Schell attained to distinction in public affairs. There were two daughters and six sons in the family. Of the sons, Julius Schell died in boyhood, and Francis Schell died at the age of twenty-two. The eldest brother, Richard Schell, who was born in 1810, died in 1879. He was several times elected a member of the State Senate, and was also a member of the United States House of Representatives Robert Schell, who was born in 1815, was president of the Bank of the Metropolis, of New York, for many years. The brother who was most conspicuous in political life was Augustus Schell, the third child and second son of the family. He served for several years as Collector of the Port, was a Democratic Presidential elector in 1876, and chairman of the Democratic National Committee the same year.

Edward Schell, the youngest male member of this interesting family, was born in Rhinebeck, Dutchess County, N Y, November 5th, 1819. He was educated in Rhinebeck, under the instruction of Professor Holbrook, until he was seventeen years of age. Then he became junior clerk in the house of Littlefield & Shaw, of New York, importers of Irish linens When he was about twenty-six years of age, he joined his elder brother, Robert, in business as the junior member of the firm of Lewis S. Fellows & Schell. After remaining in this business for seventeen years, he entered the banking business, principally engaged with the Manhattan Savings Institution, of which, eight years previous, he had been elected a trustee. He became treasurer of that institution, and in a few years was its president, a position that he held for over thirty years.

Besides his connection with the Manhattan Savings Institution, Edward Schell was identified with many other corporations, being a trustee of the Union Trust Company, and a director in the National Citizens' Bank, the Manhattan Life Insurance Company, the Citizens' Insurance Company and the Park Fire Insurance Company. He was also interested in the literary, art and philanthropic institutions that are the pride of New York. He was a life member of the New York Historical Society and the St Nicholas Society, and for many years a trustee of the New York Society Library, the New York Institution for the Blind and St. Luke's Hospital, a member of the Century Association and a governor of the Manhattan Club, a member and vestryman of the Protestant Episcopal Church of the Ascension and warden of Christ Church, Rye, N. Y. He died December 24th, 1893 The wife of Mr. Schell was Jane L. Heartt, daughter of the Honorable Jonas C. Heartt, of Troy, N. Y., Mayor of that city for several successive terms. Mrs. Schell died in 1880.

Mr. Edward Heartt Schell, son of Edward Schell, was born in Troy, N. Y., September 30th, 1848. He was graduated from Yale College, studied law under Professor Dwight, of Columbia Law College, and is now a practicing lawyer of New York. In 1886, he married Cornelia E. Barnes, daughter of William Evarts and Mary (Spies) Barnes His town house is at 19 East Twenty-fourth Street and he has a country residence in Rye His clubs are the Manhattan and St Nicholas, and he also belongs to the Bar Association and the Yale Alumni Association.

CHARLES STEWART SCHENCK

PETER H. SCHENCK, grandfather of this gentleman, was one of the prominent merchants of New York City in the period after the Revolution. He was especially distinguished as being the first to begin the manufacture of domestic fabrics in this State. He established a cotton factory at Fishkill Landing, on the Hudson River, now Mattewan, called the Mattewan Company ; his associates being John Jacob Astor, William B Astor, Philip Hone, Robert Hone, Gardiner and Samuel Howland and Joseph Kernochan. In 1812, when war was declared, the factory was fully under way. A British fleet blockaded New York and other Atlantic ports, but while the war lasted he had cotton for the factory hauled by wagons, from Charleston to Fishkill Landing, a distance of over nine hundred miles. Peter H. Schenck gave the Government earnest support in the war, contributing at one time ten thousand dollars. He had a residence at Fishkill, N. Y., and a city home in Bowling Green. His wife was Harriet Courtney, elder daughter of Sarah Henderson Courtney. The eldest daughter of their family, Margaret Matilda, married Russell Dart. Sarah Ann, another daughter, married for her first husband John A Manning, and for her second husband, Lewis Timberlake, while Ellen Courtney married Peter Van Der Vort, and Harriet Eliza married Charles Wells. The father of Mr. Charles Stewart Schenck was Courtney Schenck, who was born in 1816, the oldest surviving son of his father's family. In 1837, he married Eliza Stewart, of Philadelphia

The Schenck family is of ancient origin, the first of the name of whom mention is made being Edgar de Schecken, who, in 798, was Imperial Seneschal to Charlemagne. In America, the different branches of the family have sprung from two sources, both of them coming from the Schencks van Nydeck, of Holland One comes from the brothers, Jan Martense Schenck and Roelof Martense Schenck, who settled in Flatlands, about 1650. The second branch is derived from Johannes Schenck, of Bushwick, Long Island, also of the Van Nydeck family.

Johannes Schenck, the progenitor of the Bushwick Schencks, was born in Holland, and emigrated to America in 1683 His father, Martin, was a Lieutenant and Judge in the Province of Overyssel, an office that had been held in the family for several generations. Before coming to this country, he married Maria Magdalena Haes. After living in Bushwick some time, he removed to Esopus, but, in 1691, was town clerk of Flatbush, and in 1698, was a freeman of New York and again town clerk of Flatbush in 1700, Supervisor of Kings County in 1719, and died in 1748. His grandson, Judge Abraham Schenck, 1720-1790, son of Johannes Schenck and Maria Lock, married Elsie Vandervooert. He represented Kings County in the Colonial Legislature for several successive terms. He was the grandfather of Peter H. Schenck. The parents of Peter H Schenck were Major Henry Schenck, 1743-1799, of Fishkill, and Hannah Brett. There have been many distinguished representatives of this ancient family, among them Admiral James Findley Schenck, U. S. N ; Robert C. Schenck, Major-General and Minister to Great Britain ; and the Reverend Noah Hunt Schenck. Mrs Hicks Lord was a cousin of the subject of this sketch Her great-great-grandfather was Sir Francis Rumbout, who settled at Fishkill nearly two centuries ago A daughter of Sir Francis married a Schenck, and their great-granddaughter was Wilhelmina Wilkens, afterwards Mrs. Hicks Lord.

Mr Charles Stewart Schenck was the eldest son of Courtney Schenck and his wife, Eliza Stewart. Born in Philadelphia, he was educated at College Hill, Poughkeepsie, N. Y., and has been engaged in mercantile life in New York City, being at the present time president of the Elevator Barge Company During the Civil War, he was a Lieutenant of cavalry and a member of the Seventh Regiment of New York Volunteers In 1865, Mr. Schenck married Harriet Chesebrough Kearny, of New York, a daughter of Philip R Kearny, who was for many years president of the New York Life Insurance & Trust Company, of this city, a cousin of Major-General Philip Kearny Mr. and Mrs. Schenck live at Rye, Westchester County. They have two daughters, Lulu L. and Helen Elise, and one son, Stewart Courtney Schenck.

FREDERICK AUGUSTUS SCHERMERHORN

ONE of the first settlers in New Netherland was Jacob Janse Schermerhorn, and his descendants have been conspicuous and influential in the city and State ever since that time. Jacob Janse Schermerhorn was a native of Holland, born in 1620, and came to this country in 1636, in the ship Van Rensselaerwyck. He was an enterprising man with considerable means, and settled in Beverwyck or Albany, then on the frontier, becoming an Indian trader. His business prospered, and he became one of the wealthiest men of his time In 1648, he had trouble with Governor Petrus Stuyvesant, who accused him of selling guns and powder to the Indians, and he lost much of his property. He married Jannetje Van Voorhandt, daughter of Cornelius Sergense Van Voorhandt, and his family of nine children and their descendants married with the Beekmans, Van der Bogarts, Ten Eycks and other prominent Dutch families.

The Schermerhorns were long active in the affairs of the Manor of Rensselaerwyck, that great feudal estate of Kiliaen Van Rensselaer, which included the entire territory comprised in the present counties of Albany, Columbia and Rensselaer. A son of Jacob Janse Schermerhorn, named after his father, Jacob, born in 1662 and died in 1740, married Gerritje Hendrickse Van Buren, daughter of Hendrick Van Buren and granddaughter of Cornelius Maas and Catalyntje (Martense) Van Buren. Several of the Schermerhorns were among the original settlers of Schenectady. When that village was destroyed and its inhabitants massacred by the Indians in 1690, it was Simon Schermerhorn who carried the news of the disaster through the wilderness to Albany.

In more recent times Abraham Schermerhorn was a well-known New Yorker, the son of Peter and Elizabeth Bussing Schermerhorn, and great-grandson of Maria Beekman, who was a granddaughter of the famous William Beekman, founder of the Beekman family in New York. Abraham Schermerhorn married Helen White, a descendant of the Yonkers branch of the Van Cortlandt family One of his sons married a daughter of James A. Bayard, of Delaware; one of his daughters married Charles Suydam, and another daughter is Mrs. Caroline Astor, who, the widow of William Astor, has long been at the head of the celebrated Astor family, and a recognized leader of New York society. John P. Schermerhorn, brother of Abraham, married Rebecca, daughter of General Ebenezer Stevens, and his sister married the Reverend William Creighton

Captain Frederick Augustus Schermerhorn, representative of this old family in the present generation, was born in New York, November 1st, 1844. He was educated in private schools, and entered Columbia College in the class of 1865. Desiring to prepare for the United States Military Academy at West Point, he did not continue his course at Columbia, but the breaking out of the Civil War changed all his plans, and he enlisted in 1864, being commissioned as Second Lieutenant in the One Hundred and Eighty-Fifth Regiment, New York Infantry In January, 1865, he was mustered in as First Lieutenant of Company C in the same regiment. He went to the front with the Army of the Potomac, and was aide-de-camp to Major-General Charles Griffin. He served until peace was declared, and was brevetted Captain for gallant conduct at the battle of Five Forks in 1865.

After the war, Captain Schermerhorn returned to his studies, entering the School of Mines of Columbia College, in 1865, and graduating in 1868 with the degree of Mining Engineer. He served seven years in the National Guard of the State of New York, as private, Corporal, Sergeant and First Lieutenant of Company K, Seventh Regiment. A prominent society and club man, he belongs to the Tuxedo, Metropolitan, Coaching, Riding, Country, Rockaway Hunt, Union, City, and Knickerbocker clubs. His interest in yachting is indicated by his membership in the New York and Sewanhaka-Corinthian Yacht clubs Since 1877, he has been a trustee of Columbia College, is manager and recording secretary of the New York Institution for the Blind, is a supporter of the Metropolitan Museum of Art, a member of the Loyal Legion, and a member of the American Geographical Society.

GEORGE RICHARD SCHIEFFELIN

JACOB SCHIEFFELIN, of Weilheim, Germany, came to America early in the last century. His family has been traced in that country back to the thirteenth century, but his own ancestor was Conrad Schieffelin, son of Franz Schieffelin, of Nuremberg, who had migrated to Switzerland. The first Jacob Schieffelin died in 1746, in which year his son, also named Jacob, 1732-1769, came to Philadelphia. The wife of the second Jacob Schieffelin was Regina Margaretta Kraften Ritschaurin and their son, Jacob Schieffelin, third of the name and founder of the New York Schieffelin family, was born in Philadelphia in 1757.

Early in life, Jacob Schieffelin, the third, was secretary at the then frontier post of Detroit and acquired property there. In the Revolution he was a loyalist, served as aide to the English General, Henry Hamilton, and, coming to New York in 1780, held a commission in the British Army. After the war he removed to Montreal, and spent some time in London. His wife, Hannah Lawrence, was a member of the notable Long Island family of that name, being the daughter of John and Ann (Burling) Lawrence, and in 1794 Jacob Schieffelin returned to New York and became the partner of his brother-in-law, John Burling Lawrence, in the wholesale drug business. In 1799, he became the sole proprietor of the establishment which has remained in the name of his descendants to this day, its centenary anniversary having been celebrated in 1894. He retired from business in 1814 and died in 1835, his sons being Henry Hamilton, Effingham, Jacob and Richard Lawrence Schieffelin.

Richard Lawrence Schieffelin was the father of the gentleman referred to in this article. He was born in 1801, graduated from Columbia College, studied law with his brother-in-law, Benjamin Ferris, and practiced until 1843. For the rest of his life he devoted himself to the care of his real estate and corporate interests. Elected a member of the Common Council of New York City in 1843, he was president of the board and afterwards declined a nomination for Congress. He was prominent in the Protestant Episcopal Church, was one of the earliest members of the Church of St. Mary, which his father founded at Mahattanville, and at the time of his death, in 1889, was its senior warden. For more than sixty years he represented that church in the Diocesan conventions and was also prominently identified with Grace parish. In early life, he was interested in military matters and held the commission of Brigadier-General. In 1833, he married Margaret Helen McKay, daughter of Captain George Knox McKay, of the United States Artillery. His children were Sarah Sophia Schieffelin, who married the Reverend Cuthbert Collingwood Barclay; Helen Margaret Schieffelin, who married, first, William Irving Graham, and after his death, Alexander Robert Chisolm; and George Richard Schieffelin.

Mr. George Richard Schieffelin was born July 27th, 1836. Graduated from Columbia College in the class of 1855, he has been engaged in the practice of law in this city. In 1866, he married Julia Matilda Delaplaine. The grandfather of Mrs. Schieffelin was John F. Delaplaine, an old New York shipping merchant. Her father, the Honorable Isaac C. Delaplaine, was born in New York in 1817 and died in 1866. Graduated from Columbia College in 1834, he became a prominent lawyer. In 1861, he was elected a member of the National House of Representatives.

Mr. and Mrs. Schieffelin have had five children. Their eldest daughter, Julia Florence Schieffelin, married Joseph Bruce Ismay, of Liverpool, England, one of the owners of the White Star Steamship Company. She has two children, Margaret Bruce and Thomas Bruce Ismay. The second daughter, Margaret Helen Schieffelin, married Henry G. Trevor. There are two unmarried daughters of the family, Matilda Constance and Sarah Dorothy Schieffelin, and one son, George Richard Delaplaine Schieffelin. The city residence of Mr. and Mrs. Schieffelin is in East Forty-fifth Street, near Fifth Avenue, and their country place is The Anchorage, at Southampton, Long Island. Mr. Schieffelin is a member of the Tuxedo, Union, Knickerbocker, New York Yacht, Riding and Shinnecock Golf clubs, the St. Nicholas Society, the Century Association, the Downtown Association and the Society of Colonial Wars. In 1895, he was deputy governor of the latter organization.

SAMUEL BRADHURST SCHIEFFELIN

IN the present generation, the Schieffelin family, which has held such an important place in New York, has a number of branches   The preceding page of this volume affords a detailed account of the founder of the family, Jacob Schieffelin, 1757–1835, and his wife, Hannah Lawrence   Henry Hamilton Schieffelin, their second son, was born in 1783   He was named after General Henry Hamilton, who commanded the English forces in the Northwest during the Revolution, and under whom Jacob Schieffelin served   Graduating from Columbia College in 1801, Henry Hamilton Schieffelin studied law under Cadwalader Colden, but in 1805 entered into partnership with his father, as Jacob Schieffelin & Son, and when Jacob Schieffelin retired, in 1814, the firm became H H Schieffelin & Co   Henry Hamilton Schieffelin was the first vice-president of the New York College of Pharmacy, in 1829, and became its president on the incorporation of the college in 1831.   He retired in 1849 and died in 1865.   He married Maria Theresa Bradhurst, daughter of Dr. Samuel Bradhurst, 1749-1826, and his wife, Mary Smith, daughter of Lieutenant Richard Smith   The sons of Henry Hamilton Schieffelin were Henry Maunsell, Samuel Bradhurst, James Lawrence, Philip, Sidney Augustus, Bradhurst and Eugene Schieffelin   After their father's retirement in 1849, the brothers carried on the business under the style of Schieffelin Brothers & Co.   Samuel B., James Lawrence and Sidney A Schieffelin were the leading members

Mr. Samuel Bradhurst Schieffelin was born February 24th, 1811, and continued at the head of the firm until his retirement, in 1865   He has since devoted much of his attention to literature and has written The Foundations of History and a number of other works chiefly of a religious character   He married Lucretia Hazard and resides at 958 Madison Avenue. William Henry Schieffelin, son of Mr Samuel B Schieffelin, was born August 20th, 1836, and early in life entered the firm of Schieffelin Brothers & Co , of which, in 1865, he became the head, the style being changed to W. H. Schieffelin & Co   In 1862, he entered the Union Army, was Major of the First New York Mounted Rifles, and saw active service in Virginia He married Mary Jay, daughter of the Honorable John Jay   He held positions of trust, and was identified with many scientific and philanthropic organizations   He died in 1895

William Jay Schieffelin, his son, was born in New York in 1866 and was graduated from Columbia College in 1887.   Making chemistry his profession, he pursued postgraduate studies at the University of Munich, Bavaria, graduating there in 1889 with the degree of Doctor of Philosophy   Entering the firm of William H Schieffelin & Co , he is now active in its successor, Schieffelin & Co   He has been interested in the reform of the municipal administration, and in 1896 was appointed a member of the Civil Service Commission.   In 1891, he married Marie Louisa, daughter of Colonel Elliott Fitch Shepard and a granddaughter of William H. Vanderbilt   They have four children, two sons and two daughters, the eldest being William Jay Schieffelin, Jr   Their residence is in West Fifty-seventh Street.   Mr Schieffelin is a member of the City, Century and Church clubs, the Military Order of the Loyal Legion, the St Nicholas Society and the Society of Colonial Wars

Sidney Augustus Schieffelin, the fifth son of Henry Hamilton Schieffelin, born in 1818, was long a member of the house of Schieffelin Brothers & Co , from which he retired in 1865 He died in 1894   He married Harriet A Schuyler, 1836–1882, daughter of Arent Henry Schuyler and his wife, Mary C Kingsland   Their sons are Henry Hamilton Schieffelin, born in 1863, and Schuyler Schieffelin, born in 1866   The latter, in 1889, left the Massachusetts Institute of Technology in his junior year and entered the firm of Schieffelin & Co   His residence is 173 Fifth Avenue.   He is a Captain in the Twelfth Regiment, National Guard.   His clubs are the Union, Fencers', City, Ardsley Country, Badminton, Knickerbocker and Riding, and he is a member of the St Nicholas Society, Society of Colonial Wars, Colonial Order, Metropolitan Museum of Art and the New York Historical Society, of which he is a life member.

PHILIP SCHUYLER

IN the seventh generation from Philip Schuyler and Margaretta Van Slichtenhorst, the American ancestors of a family that has been one of the most distinguished in the history of the United States, General Philip Schuyler is descended, through Johannes Schuyler and his wife, Elizabeth Staats, Johannes Schuyler and his wife, Cornelia Van Cortlandt, and General Philip Schuyler, the eminent Revolutionary patriot and soldier, and his wife, Catharine Van Rensselaer. General Philip Schuyler, the great-grandfather of the subject of this sketch, was the son of Philip Jeremiah Schuyler, born in 1768. The first wife of Philip Jeremiah Schuyler was Sarah Rutsen, daughter of Colonel Jacob Rutsen, of an old Kingston, N. Y., family that had married with the Van Rensselaers and other great families of that day. The second wife of Philip Jeremiah Schuyler and the grandmother of General Philip Schuyler of the present generation, was Mary A Sawyer, of Newburyport, Mass , a member of one of the old families of the Massachusetts Bay Colony.

The father of General Philip Schuyler was George Lee Schuyler, who is especially remembered by this generation from his connection with the America Cup, the famous yachting prize, the struggle for its possession having resulted in the most brilliant international yachting events in this century. George Lee Schuyler was born in Rhinebeck in 1811, but lived the greater part of his lifetime in New York, with whose interests he was thoroughly identified. He was deeply interested in yachting matters and was one of the donors of the America Yachting Cup trophy, and in 1882 was the sole surviving member of the syndicate which prepared that prize. He also gave considerable attention to historical research, particularly in relation to the family whose name he bore. Among his principal literary works were Correspondence and Remarks upon Bancroft's History of the Northern Campaign, and The Character of Major-General Philip Schuyler. The first wife of George Lee Schuyler and the mother of General Philip Schuyler, was Eliza Hamilton His second wife was Mary Morris Hamilton, a sister of his first wife The maternal grandfather of General Schuyler was James Alexander Hamilton, son of Alexander Hamilton and his wife, who was a daughter of the General Philip Schuyler of Revolutionary renown. General Schuyler is therefore descended from his illustrious ancestor and namesake through both his paternal and maternal lines, his father being a grandson and his mother a great-granddaughter of the General.

James Alexander Hamilton, the maternal grandfather of General Schuyler, was born in New York in 1788, and died in Irvington in 1878. He was graduated from Columbia College in 1805. During the war of 1812, he was Brigade-Major and Inspector in the New York State militia. Afterwards he studied law and became a prominent member of the bar. In the first administration of President Andrew Jackson, he was for a few days, in 1829, acting Secretary of State previous to the accession of Martin Van Buren to that place in the Cabinet Later he was United States District Attorney for the Southern District of New York He was the author of Reminiscences of Hamilton, or, Men and Events at Home and Abroad during Three-quarters of a Century.

General Philip Schuyler was born in New York and has made his home in this city and at his ancestral estate in Irvington. His Irvington home is Nevis, the old-fashioned Colonial house that was the home of Alexander Hamilton and that abounds in historical and social memories of a century ago. General Schuyler is an ardent yachtsman as well as a general sportsman. He is a member of the New York Yacht Club and has closely identified himself with the interests of the social life in and about Irvington and Ardsley. During the entire Civil War period, he served with distinction in the regular army, resigning his commission at the close of the war. He married Harriet (Lowndes) Langdon. He was a prominent member of the Patriarchs during the brilliant life of that social organization. His clubs include the Union and Knickerbocker, the Century Association, the Hudson River Ice Yacht Club, and he also belongs to the Seventh Regiment Veterans, the Sons of the Revolution, the Society of the Cincinnati, the Military Order of the Loyal Legion, and the American Geographical Society, and is a patron of the Metropolitan Museum of Art and the American Museum of Natural History

GUSTAV H. SCHWAB

W HEN Frederick the Great, of Prussia, determined to establish the Berlin Royal Academy of Science, he called upon John Christopher Schwab to be a member of that body, and to assist in its establishment and direction Professor Schwab at that time occupied the chair of philosophy and mathematics in the University of Stuttgart and declined the offer of King Frederick, preferring to remain in the position with which he had been long associated. Piofessor Schwab was the great-grandfather of the subject of this sketch His son, the grandfather of Mr. Gustav H. Schwab, was a well-known German author.

Gustav Schwab, the father of Mr. Gustav H. Schwab, was born in 1822, in Stuttgart, Germany, where his ancestors had lived for many generations. When he was seventeen years of age, he entered the counting house of H. H. Meier & Co., a large firm in Bremen. There he remained for five years, but in 1844, when twenty-two years of age, he came to New York, to enter the house of Oelrichs & Kruger. In less than five years after his arrival in New York, he had sufficiently familiarized himself with commercial methods in this country to go into business for himself as the junior partner in the firm of Wichelhausen, Recknagel & Schwab. Ten years after, in 1859, he returned to the concern with which he had been first associated in New York, becoming a partner in the firm of Oelrichs & Company, which succeeded Oelrichs & Kruger. Soon after, the firm became agents for the North German Lloyd Steamship Line, a connection that has been maintained ever since.

Outside of the shipping business, with which Mr. Schwab was principally identified, he had numerous other interests He was among the directors of the Central Trust Company, the Washington Life Insurance Company, and the Orient Mutual Insurance Company, and at the time of his death was the oldest director and vice-president of the Merchants' National Bank. He was a member of the Protestant Episcopal Church, and warden of St. James' Church, Fordham. Deeply interested in charitable matters, he was a patron and for many years treasurer of the German Hospital, and a generous benefactor of other philanthropic organizations. He was also a member of the Chamber of Commerce, and at one time a commissioner of the Board of Education In 1850, Mr. Schwab married Catharine Elizabeth Von Post, daughter of L. H Von Post, of New York City. When he died, in 1888, his widow and a large family of children survived him

Mr. Gustav H. Schwab is the eldest of the children of Gustav Schwab, and was born in New York, May 30th, 1851. He was educated here and at Stuttgart, Germany. In 1876, he married Caroline Wheeler, niece of William B. Ogden, of New York and formerly of Chicago, of which city he was the first Mayor, and also president of the Chicago & Northwestern Railway. Mr. and Mrs. Schwab have two children, Emily Elizabeth and Gustav.

Entering his father's firm of Oelrichs & Company, in 1876, Mr. Schwab had charge of the steamship business. He has, however, taken an active and useful part in all measures to advance the commerce of New York, or to create better municipal government. He has frequently been interested in committees of the Chamber of Commerce, appointed to advance the cause of honest money and of political reform, and is now chairman of the Chamber's Committee on foreign commerce and the revenue laws. He also succeeded his father as director of the Merchants' National Bank, and is also a director in the United States Trust Company. He lives at 4 East Forty-eighth Street, his country residence being at Irvington-on-Hudson. He is a member of the Tuxedo colony, and the principal New York clubs of which he is a member are the Metropolitan, Century, City, Reform, Commonwealth, Liederkranz, and Mendelssohn Glee A brother of Mr. Schwab, Herman C. Schwab, who is associated with him in business, is a member of the Reform, Commonwealth, and other clubs, and resides on the old family place at Morris Heights. Another brother is the Reverend Lawrence H. Schwab, a graduate of Yale College and rector of St. Mary's Protestant Episcopal Church, in New York City. A third brother, John C. Schwab, Ph. D., is professor of political economy in Yale University.

GEORGE SLESMAN SCOTT

T HE family to which Mr George Slesman Scott belongs is of ancient Scottish origin, and was seated several centuries ago at Dipple Parish, Morayshire From that place came the member of the family who established the American branch in Virginia nearly two hundred and fifty years ago The arms of the family as they appear on the tomb of one of the Scottish ancestors are on a bend, a star between two crescents, in a bordure, eight stars The crest is a dove, and the motto, *Gaudia nuncio magna* Similar to this are the arms generally used by the family, which are, or on a bend azure, a bezant between two crescents of the field, in a bordure argent, eight bezants The crest is a dove proper, holding in its beak an olive branch, and the motto is as already given above

The Reverend John Scott, of Dipple Parish, Morayshire, Scotland, was born about 1650 He was a college bred man, and rector of Dipple Parish, Moray, in 1699, dying there in 1726 By his wife Helen Grant, he had a son, the Reverend James Scott, who was born in Dipple Parish, and was the first American ancestor of the family that bears his name He came to Virginia before 1739, and in 1745 was rector of Dettingen Parish Educated at Aberdeen University, he was ordained by the Lord Bishop of London, in 1735 His wife was Sarah Brown, 1715-1784, daughter of Dr Gustavus and Frances (Fowke) Brown

In the second American generation, came the Honorable Gustavus Scott, who was born at Westwood, Prince William County, Va, in 1753, and died in Washington, D C, in 1801 His education was secured at Kings' College, Aberdeen, Scotland, and from 1767 to 1771, he studied law in the Middle Temple, London Returning to this country, he located in Maryland, became a prominent member of the bar and active in Revolutionary affairs In 1774-75, he was a deputy from Somerset County to the Maryland Convention, a member of the Maryland Association in 1775, and in 1776 a delegate to the Constitutional Convention. After the adoption of the State Government, he removed to Dorchester County and represented that county in the Assembly, 1780-84, being a delegate from Maryland to the Continental Congress in 1784-85. His wife, whom he married in 1777, was Margaret Hall Caile, daughter of Hall Caile of Annapolis, Md.

John Caile Scott, son of the Honorable Gustavus Scott, grandson of the Reverend James Scott, the American pioneer, and grandfather of the gentleman whose name appears at the head of this sketch, was born in 1782 He lived at his country seat, Western View, Culpepper County, Va, until 1828, when he removed to Ross County, Ohio He died at Muhlenberg Farm, Pickaway County, O, in 1840. His wife, whom he married in 1802, was Ann Love, 1780-1832, daughter of Samuel Love and Ann Jones of Fairfax County, Va. Samuel Love, grandfather of Ann Love, was a member of the Committee of Safety in Maryland in the Revolutionary period, an associate freeman and a delegate to the Maryland Convention Charles Jones, the maternal grandfather of Ann Love, was a citizen of Frederick County, Md, and active in measures for equipping the Continental troops and providing them with ammunition The father of Mr George Slesman Scott was John Caile Scott, who was born in Strawberry Vale, Fairfax County, Va,, in 1809 Removing to Philadelphia, he married Louisiana Eleanor Slesman, who was born in Philadelphia in 1807, the daughter of George and Elizabeth (Scull) Slesman. He died in Philadelphia in 1875

Mr. George Slesman Scott was born in Chillicothe, O, in 1837 He has been for many years engaged in the banking business in New York He married Augusta Isham, and the family residence is in West Fifty-seventh Street, near Fifth Avenue Mr Scott belongs to the Metropolitan, Tuxedo, City, Riding, New York Yacht, Seawanhaka-Corinthian Yacht and American Yacht clubs, and the Sons of the American Revolution, and is a patron of the Metropolitan Museum of Art, and the American Museum of Natural History He was at one time vice-president and director of the Pacific Mail Steamship Company, a director of the Union Pacific Railway Company, and the Chicago & Northwestern Railroad Company, and president of the Richmond & Danville Railroad Company

CHARLES SCRIBNER

ORIGINALLY Scrivener, meaning a professional writer, there seems to be special fitness in the name Scribner, borne by a family that for three generations has been foremost in the publishing business in the United States. The first in America was Matthew Scrivener, a member of the Council of the Virginia Colony, in 1607 Benjamin Scrivener was in Norwalk, Conn., in 1680, and married Hannah Crampton. From his youngest son, Matthew, the Scribners of the United States are mostly descended The name was changed to Scribner, in the case of the grandchildren of Benjamin Scrivener, after 1742, as appears by the records of the town clerk of Norwalk Little is known of Matthew Scribner, save that he married Martha Smith, of Long Island, in 1742, and had nine children His second son, Matthew, who was born in 1746 and died in 1813, was graduated from Yale College, in 1775, and was a Congregational minister, occupying pulpits in Westford and Tyngsboro, Mass. He married Abigail Rogers, daughter of Dr. Uriah Rogers. The father of Abigail Rogers, who was born about 1710 and died in 1773, was a prominent phyiscian of Norwalk, Conn. His wife was Hannah Lockwood, daughter of James Lockwood, of Norwalk, and Lydia Smith. Dr. Rogers was the father of a large family and many of his descendants have been distinguished in the history of Connecticut and New York. One of his daughters married Moss Kent and became the mother of the celebrated Chancellor James Kent.

The grandfather of the present generation of the Scribner family was Uriah Rogers Scribner, 1776-1853, eldest son of the Reverend Matthew Scribner and Abigail Rogers. He engaged in business in New York, and was one of the successful merchants of his time. His first wife was Martha Scribner, daughter of Nathaniel Scribner, of Norwalk. In 1812, he married Betsey Hawley, daughter of Thomas and Keziah (Scribner) Hawley, of Ridgefield, Conn. Thomas Hawley was the son of the Reverend Thomas Hawley, who was born in Northampton, Mass., in 1690, and graduated from Harvard College, in 1709 The father of the Reverend Thomas Hawley was Captain Joseph Hawley, a graduate from Harvard College, in 1674, whose wife was Lydia Marshall, daughter of Captain Samuel Marshall, of Windsor, Conn.

Nine children of Uriah R. Scribner and his wife survived their father. Charles Scribner, publisher and bookseller and founder of the house now known as Charles Scribner's Sons, was the third son. He was born in New York, in 1821, and died in Luzerne, Switzerland, in 1871. Graduated from Princeton College in 1840, he studied law for three years, but did not enter upon the practice of that profession. In 1846, with Isaac D Baker, he organized the firm of Baker & Scribner, for the publishing of books, and for many years was in business on the site of the Old Brick Church, at the corner of Nassau Street and Park Row. From 1850 to 1857, he was alone in business, his partner having died, and in the latter year he bought the importing business of Banks, Merwin & Co , and took Charles Welford as a partner. Then the firms of Charles Scribner & Co., American publishers, and Scribner, Welford & Co., importers of foreign books, were established In 1865, Mr. Scribner began the publication of The Hours at Home Magazine, which was merged in The Scribners Magazine, established in 1870. Subsequently the firm sold The Scribner's Magazine to its present owners, and it became The Century Magazine. A few years later the second Scribner's Magazine, that is now in successful publication, was started. In 1848, Mr. Scribner married Emma E. Blair, daughter of John I. Blair, of New Jersey

Mr. Charles Scribner, second of the name, and now at the head of the publishing house which his father established, was born in New York, and graduated from Princeton College, in 1875 He married Louise Flagg, lives in East Thirty-eighth Street, and has a country home, The Gables, in Morristown, N J. He is a member of the Century, Aldine and other literary clubs, belongs also to the Union, University and Morristown clubs, and is a patron of the Metropolitan Museum of Art, and the American Geographical Society. His brother, Arthur H Scribner, who is also a member of the publishing firm, is a graduate from Princeton College, in the Class of 1881, and is a member of the Century, Aldine, Grolier and other clubs.

LOUIS LIVINGSTON SEAMAN, M. D

A MONG the eminent physicians in New York City, in the last century, was Dr. Valentine Seaman, who was born in 1770   He had the distinction of introducing the practice of vaccination into New York City in 1799, when he was less than thirty years of age.   Dr Seaman was graduated from the University of Pennsylvania in 1792, having studied under Dr Benjamin Rush, and was a surgeon in the New York Hospital from 1796 until his death, in 1817   He was a voluminous writer upon medical subjects, and was the author of treatises on Vaccination and other subjects.

Dr Louis Livingston Seaman is a grandson of Dr Valentine Seaman   His great-grandfather was Willett Seaman, a merchant in New York in 1760, one of the founders and original governors of the New York Hospital.   His paternal ancestor, Captain John Seaman, received a Colonial grant in 1637 at Hempstead Plains, Long Island, from King Charles I   Members of the Seaman family were prominent in the early Dutch, French and Indian wars, and it is recorded that twenty-two of them served in one company in the Revolution.   The mother of Dr Seaman was Anna Amelia Ferris, descended from Robert Livingston, first Lord of the Manor, and from Philip L Livingston, signer of the Declaration of Independence.   Also on his mother's side, Dr. Seaman is the eighth in descent from Abraham de Peyster, Mayor of New York in 1692, and ninth in descent from Philip Pieterse Schuyler and Margaritta Van Schlichtenhorst.   Major Hendrick Cuyler, who commanded the Albany troops in the French and Indian War, 1685-89, nine generations back Johannes de Peyster, Brant Arents Van Schlichtenhorst and Captain Peter Van Brugh are among his other Knickerbocker ancestors

Born in Newburgh, N Y , October 17th, 1851, Dr Louis Livingston Seaman was a member of the first class that entered Cornell University in 1868.   He studied medicine at the Jefferson Medical College in Philadelphia, being an office student of the celebrated Dr. Samuel D Gross. He won the gold medal on graduating in 1876   Subsequently he attended the University Medical College, New York City, for a post-graduate course, and received his degree in 1877   In 1884, he graduated from the law department of the University of New York

In 1876, he was appointed house physician of the Charity Hospital in New York.   One year later he became resident surgeon to the Ward's Island State Emigrant Hospital, a position he held for two years   In 1879-81, he was superintendent of the Emigrant Insane Asylum on Ward's Island and chief resident surgeon to the emigration institutions   In 1881, he was appointed Chief of Staff of the hospitals on Blackwell's Island.   In 1886, while making a tour of the world, he investigated especially the contagious and epidemic diseases of the East   Since his return from abroad, Dr Seaman has engaged in regular practice.   He is visiting physician of the Old Marion Street Maternity Hospital and consulting physician to the Colored Orphan Asylum.   He has visited Europe several times, and made a special study of cholera in the hospitals of Paris and Hamburg in 1892.   He is a member of the American Medical Association, the Medical Society of the State of New York, the Medical Society of the County of New York, the New York County Medical Association, the New York Medical Union, the New York Pathological Society, the American Association for the Advancement of Science, the Society of Medical Jurisprudence of New York, and the American Academy of Political and Social Science, and is a fellow of the New York Academy of Medicine   He is also a member of the Society of Colonial Wars, and his social clubs include the Reform, Lotos, Calumet, Players, Quaint and the Cornell University Club, of which he is the vice-president

In 1881, Dr Seaman was a delegate to the London International Medical Congress, and again in 1890 a delegate to the Congress in Berlin.   He has devised various apparatus for medical and surgical use, and is the author of many papers on medical and social subjects.   Dr Seaman was married in 1889 to Fannie Blackstone Freeman, a great-great-granddaughter of Sir William Blackstone, the eminent English jurist.   Mrs Seaman died in 1895.

ROBERT SEDGWICK

G ENERAL ROBERT SEDGWICK was born in England, in 1611, and was one of the ablest leaders of the Massachusetts Colony Coming to America in 1636, he settled in Charlestown, Mass , and thenceforward was conspicuous in the young community In 1637, he was a representative of the town of Charlestown in the General Court. He commanded the Ancient and Honorable Artillery Company and was chosen Major-General of the Colony in 1652. Soon after that time, he went to England and was in the service of the Protector, Cromwell Upon his return, in 1654, he was appointed to head an expedition against the Dutch "on Hudson's River and at the Manhatoes"; but peace being declared, he led his forces against the French of Nova Scotia and captured St. John, Port Royal and other forts Afterwards he was despatched to the Island of Jamaica with a fleet, and there succeeded General Venables in command of the English forces A supreme executive council was established, with Sedgwick at the head, and Cromwell sent him a commission giving him supreme command While upon this service in the West Indies, he died in 1656

Five children of General Sedgwick survived him William Sedgwick was the second son; his elder brother dying childless He married Elizabeth Stone, daughter of the Reverend Samuel Stone, the second minister of Hartford, and had one son, Samuel, 1667–1735 His wife was Mary Hopkins, granddaughter of John Hopkins, one of the founders of Hartford The great-great-grandfather of the present Mr. Sedgwick was Benjamin Sedgwick, 1716-1757, son of Samuel Sedgwick. One of his sons was General John Sedgwick, a distinguished Revolutionary soldier.

Theodore Sedgwick, 1746-1813, another son, was born in Hartford and studied in Yale College, and in 1766 was admitted to the bar and practiced in Massachusetts, frequently representing the town of Sheffield in the Legislature, and was a delegate to Congress in 1785. In the expedition to Canada in 1776, he was an aide to General Thomas. In 1788, he was a member of the Massachusetts Convention that ratified the Federal Constitution, and a Member of Congress from 1789 to 1796, when he was elected to the United States Senate, of which he became president pro tem In 1799, he was again elected to the House of Representatives and became Speaker. From 1802 until his death, he was a Judge of the Supreme Court of Massachusetts Princeton College gave him the degree of LL D in 1799, and he was one of the few with whom Washington shared his confidences.

His son was Robert Sedgwick, 1787-1841, who married Elizabeth Dana Ellery, daughter of William Ellery, of Rhode Island. She was the great-granddaughter of Lieutenant-Governor Ellery, the Rhode Island signer of the Declaration of Independence. William Ellery Sedgwick, the father of the present Mr. Sedgwick, was the eldest son of Robert Sedgwick and his wife, Elizabeth Dana Ellery He married Constance Irving Brevoort, daughter of Henry Brevoort and his wife, Laura Carson Henry Brevoort's mother, Sarah Whetten, was a descendant of Adam Todd, one of the ancestors of the Astor, Kane and other New York families. Mr. Robert Sedgwick, the eldest son of William Ellery Sedgwick, was born in New York in 1852. He married, in 1878, Meta Brevoort Renwick, granddaughter of the late Professor James Renwick, of Columbia College. They have two sons, Robert Sedgwick, Jr , born in 1880, and Henry Renwick Sedgwick, born in 1881. Mr. Sedgwick did not enter Harvard University, as almost all his male relatives have done, preferring to travel He went to China from London, around the Cape of Good Hope, in a sailing vessel, and for upwards of five years traveled in the East and in Europe He is a member of the Century, Union, Tuxedo, New York Yacht and Downtown clubs, as well as the New York Genealogical and Biographical Society, the Ex-Libris Society of England, the American Book Plate Society and similar bodies. His city home is 129 East Thirty-sixth Street. Mr Sedgwick resided for many years in Berkshire County, Mass , and spends a portion of every summer there

The Sedgwick arms are Argent on a cross gules five bells or. Crest, a lion proper passant through sedge on cap of maintenance. Motto, *Confido in Domino*

MRS. CLARENCE ARMSTRONG SEWARD

THE lady whose name appears at the head of this sketch, and who has been prominent in the social world of New York throughout the present generation, comes from a noble Prussian family. The first of the name in America was Baron Frederick Augustus de Zeng. He was born in Dresden, in 1756, the second son in his father's family His father was Baron de Zeng, of Ruckerswalde, Wolkenstein, near Marienberg, Saxony. He was Lord Chamberlain to the Duchess of Saxe-Weissenfels and High Forest Officer to the King of Saxony. The mother of Baron de Zeng was Lady Johanna Phillipina Von Ponickau, of Altenberg.

Baron de Zeng was educated for the military service of his native country, and in 1774 received his commission as Lieutenant of the Guard in the service of the landgrave of Hesse-Cassel. Coming to this country, in 1780, he settled here, and in 1792 was Major of a battalion of militia in Ulster County, N. Y He became an intimate friend of Governor Clinton and General Schuyler, and was associated with General Schuyler in the work of organizing the Western Inland Lock Navigation Company, and in 1796 was one of the three proprietors who established a manufactory of window glass near Albany. The construction of the Chemung Canal was begun by him in 1814. For many years he resided in Kingston, Ulster County, but in his later years, lived at Bainbridge, Chenango County

Baron de Zeng was the grandfather of Mrs. Clarence A. Seward. The grandmother of Mrs. Seward was Mary Lawrence, daughter of Caleb Lawrence and Sarah Burling, of Flushing, Long Island. She was married to the Baron de Zeng, in 1784, in Trinity Church, New York. Her father was the grandson of Joseph Lawrence, of Flushing, Long Island, the eldest son of the first William Lawrence, of Great St. Albans, Hertfordshire, England, who came to America in 1635, and married Elizabeth, daughter of Richard Smith, of Long Island. The father of Mrs. Seward was William Steuben de Zeng, the fourth child of Baron de Zeng. He was born at Little Falls, N. Y, in 1793. He was named after Baron Von Steuben, who was an intimate friend of his parents and who was visiting them at the time of the child's birth. His wife was Caroline Cutbush Rees, daughter of Major James Rees, of Geneva, N. Y. She was born in 1796, in Philadelphia, and married Mr. de Zeng in 1817.

By her marriage, in 1851, to the Honorable Clarence Armstrong Seward, Caroline de Zeng became allied to a family that has been preëminently distinguished in public affairs in the State of New York. Her husband was born October 7th, 1828. His father was a son of Dr. Samuel Seward, a prominent physician of Orange County and the first vice-president of the County Medical Society. He died in 1849. The family was of New Jersey origin. His great-great-grandfather, John Seward, served in the War of the Revolution as a Captain, was promoted to be Colonel of the First Sussex Regiment and married a Miss Jennings, who belonged to an Orange County family. The parents of the Honorable Clarence A. Seward dying when he was a mere child, he was brought up in the family of his uncle, the Honorable William H. Seward, the great New York statesman. Graduating from Hobart College, in 1848, he began the practice of law in Auburn, N Y., and in 1854 established himself in New York City. In 1856–60, he was Judge Advocate-General of the New York State militia. For a time after the attempted assassination of Secretary of State William H. Seward, in 1864, he was acting Assistant Secretary of State of the United States. In 1876, he was a delegate to the National Republican Convention and a Presidential elector in 1880.

For many years previous to his death, in July, 1897, Mr. Seward was president of the Union Club of New York He was also a member of the Century Association, the University, Manhattan, New York Yacht, Players, A Δ Φ and Mendelssohn Glee clubs and the Bar Association. Mrs. Seward resides at 33 Madison Avenue and passes the summer months at her ancestral home in Geneva. There are two daughters in the family, Alice de Zeng and Caroline Rees Seward, who married Robert Endicott

MRS. ELLIOTT FITCH SHEPARD

MARGARET LOUISA (VANDERBILT) SHEPARD, widow of Colonel Elliott Fitch Shepard, was born on Staten Island, and is a daughter of the late William H Vanderbilt and grand-daughter of Commodore Cornelius Vanderbilt Colonel Shepard, who married Miss Vanderbilt on the 18th of February, 1868, at the Church of the Incarnation, New York, was prominent by birth and ancestry, as well as for his personal qualities On the paternal side, he was descended from the Reverend Thomas Shepard, a graduate of Cambridge, who came to this country to be minister at Cambridge, Mass , and died in 1649 The father of Colonel Shepard was Fitch Shepard, of Jamestown, N Y., the son of Noah Shepard, his grandmother being Irene Fitch, a descendant of the Reverend James Fitch, who came to New England in 1638 Another ancestor was Major James Fitch, who commanded the Connecticut forces against the Indians, and was a contributor to the founding of Yale College Major Fitch's wife was Alice, daughter of Major William Bradford, who commanded the Plymouth troops in King Philip's War, and a grand-daughter of Governor William Bradford, of Plymouth

Fitch Shepard, of Jamestown, N Y., Colonel Shepard's father, was born in Connecticut, in 1802, and was the founder of the Chautauqua County Bank. In 1828, he married Delia Maria Dennis, whose ancestor, Robert Dennis, emigrated from England in 1635 Her father, Paul Dennis, represented Washington County in the New York Legislature. His wife was Elizabeth May, the daughter of Surgeon Theodore May, of the Revolution, and descended from the Ellis and Bedlow families, of New York

Fitch Shepard's only brother was Burritt Shepard, who entered the United States Navy in 1826 He was First Lieutenant of the frigate Raritan, in the Mexican War. He married Mary Joan Norsworthy, daughter of Samuel Norsworthy, one of the old merchants of New York Fitch Shepard removed from Jamestown to New York, where he established the National Bank Note Company, of which he was long president. He had three sons, of whom one, Burritt Hamilton Shepard, was lost at sea, in 1848, when nineteen years of age. He was then a member of the senior class of the University of the City of New York He was intended for the ministry, and was a young man of great promise. Another son is Augustus Dennis Shepard, of New York.

Colonel Elliott Fitch Shepard was born in Jamestown, N. Y., July 25th, 1833, being the second son He was graduated from the University of the City of New York, was called to the New York bar, and became one of its leading members. During the Civil War, his services to the Government were of the most arduous character Governor E D Morgan appointed him on his staff, with the rank of Lieutenant-Colonel, and he was especially commissioned to equip regiments of volunteers He organized and sent to the field from the State of New York, more than forty-seven thousand troops, the Shepard Rifles, Fifty-First Regiment, New York Volunteers, being named in his honor After the war, Colonel Shepard was counsel for the New York Central Rail-road He was the founder of the New York State Bar Association, in 1876, and its first president

From 1884 to 1887, he traveled in Europe with his family, and returning, in 1888, purchased The Mail and Express, and devoted himself largely to that newspaper property, assuming the duties of editor. He was throughout his career warmly interested in religious work, being a member of the Fifth Avenue Presbyterian Church, president of the American Sabbath Union, and founder of St Paul's Institute in Asia Minor, an educational institution that was largely supported by him At the same time, Colonel and Mrs. Shepard were prominent in social circles and he was a member of the leading clubs of New York and a generous supporter of literary, art, scientific and philanthropic institutions. He died suddenly, in 1893. Mrs Shepard's children are four in number, the three married daughters being Mrs William Jay Schieffelin, Mrs Ernesto Fabbri and Mrs David Morris Mrs Shepard's home is in West Fifty-second Street and her summer residence is Woodlea, at Scarborough-on-Hudson, where a handsome memorial chapel has been erected by Mrs Shepard in memory of her late husband

GARDINER SHERMAN

IN Dedham, Essex County, England, a town on the river Stour, in one of the most beautiful rural districts of England, between London and Ipswich, the Shermans were settled, more than three centuries ago. They were prominent and influential citizens of the place, several of them at different times being members of the House of Commons. In business life they were woolen manufacturers, and generally prosperous. From this family sprang the Shermans, who have been prominent in the history of the United States. Henry Sherman, of Dedham, the earliest English ancestor of whom there is historical record, was born in 1520, and died in 1589. His wife was Agnes Butler. Edmond Sherman, son of Henry Sherman, was a wealthy merchant, and the founder of the English school at Dedham, which is still in existence with quarters in his old home, known as Sherman Hall. The wife of Edmond Sherman was Anna Cleave, granddaughter of John Cleave, of Colchester, manufacturer, alderman and member of the House of Commons.

John Sherman, who was born in Dedham in 1613, a son of Edmond Sherman and Anna Cleave, came to New England in 1634, and was the ancestor of that branch of the family which is here under consideration. A resident of Watertown, Mass., he was a Captain, surveyor, town clerk and representative to the General Court. In 1660, and after, he was the steward of Harvard College. Captain Sherman died in 1690. His wife, who died in 1701, was Martha Palmer, daughter of Roger and Grace Palmer, of Long Sutton, Southampton County, England.

Joseph Sherman, who was born in Watertown in 1650, son of Captain John Sherman, was the grandfather of the Honorable Roger Sherman, who in turn was the great-great-grandfather of Mr. Gardiner Sherman. Joseph Sherman was a representative to the General Court of Massachusetts, 1702-05, and frequently a selectman and assessor. He married Elizabeth Winship, daughter of Lieutenant Edward Winship, of Cambridge, and had a family of eleven children. William Sherman, the ninth child and seventh son, who was born in 1792, was a farmer of Stoughton, Mass. By his second wife, Mehetabel Wellington, daughter of Benjamin Wellington, he had seven children, among whom was Roger Sherman, signer of the Declaration of Independence.

Roger Sherman was born at Newton, Mass., in 1721, and became one of the most active and most devoted public men of the Revolutionary period. Most of his life was spent in Connecticut, where he was a Judge, member of the General Assembly, and otherwise prominent. He was a member of the committee that drafted the Declaration of Independence, being a member of the Continental Congress in 1774, was Mayor of New Haven, and member of the United States Senate. His wife was Elizabeth Hartwell, daughter of Deacon Joseph Hartwell, of Stoughton, Mass. His son, Colonel John Sherman, the great-grandfather of Mr. Gardiner Sherman, was born in 1750, married Rebecca Austin, and died in 1802. During the War of the Revolution he was a paymaster in the Fourth Regiment of the Connecticut Line, and served in other capacities during the rest of the war. His son was the Reverend John Sherman, who was one of the original owners and first settlers of Trenton Falls, N. Y. The Reverend John Sherman and his wife, Abigail Perkins, were the parents of John Sherman, who married Mary A. Evans, and was the father of the subject of this sketch.

Mr. Gardiner Sherman was born in New York, December 29th, 1840. He was graduated from the College of the City of New York in 1859. For fifteen years he was a member of the New York Stock Exchange, but sold his seat and retired in 1879. Subsequently, he became president of the Seventh National Bank, but retired permanently from business in 1890. He has been twice married. His first wife was Jessie Gordon, daughter of Dr. Charles and Mary (Upham) Gordon, of Boston, and by her he had one daughter, Jessie Gordon Sherman. His second wife is Mary Moore Ogden, daughter of John D. and Mary C. (Moore) Ogden, of New York. The city residence of Mr. and Mrs. Sherman is in West Seventy-second Street, and they have a country home at Bar Harbor, Me. He is a member of the Metropolitan, Union and City clubs, the Society of the Cincinnati, and the Sons of the American Revolution.

WILLIAM WATTS SHERMAN

IN the great Anglo-Saxon emigration of the eleventh century, members of the Sherman or Shurman family moved from Germany to England and established themselves in the vicinity of London. There their descendants have been numerous and influential, and have borne a distinguished part in English public affairs. In this country, several branches trace their lineage to Colonial days. The progenitor of one branch came from Dedham, Essex County, England. The arms of this family are: On a shield or, a lion rampant, sable, between three oak leaves vert. Crest, a demi-lion, rampant, sable. It is to this branch that Mr. William Watts Sherman belongs. Henry Sherman, of Dedham, was the oldest member of the family of whom there is accurate historical record. He was the son of Thomas Sherman, and was born about 1520. His son, Henry Sherman, who married Susan Hill; his grandson, Samuel Sherman, 1573-1615, who married Phyllis Ward, and his great-grandson, Philip Sherman, 1610-1686, who married Sarah Odding, were the ancestors in successive generations of the founder of the family in this country. Philip Sherman, 1610-1686, was the father of Eber Sherman, of Roxbury, Mass., who was born in 1634 and died in 1706, and his grandson was also Eber Sherman, of North Kingston, who married Martha Remington. Henry Sherman, the great-grandson of the American founder of the family, was born in 1724 and married, in 1747, Ann Higginbottom, daughter of Dr. Charles Higginbottom.

Watts Sherman, born in 1775, was the maternal grandfather of the subject of this sketch. He was a son of Captain Nathaniel Sherman and Lucy Tisdale, and in 1794 married Olivia Gillson, daughter of James Gillson and Amy Whipple, of Attleboro, Mass. Removing to Utica, N. Y., he was engaged in business there for many years. In 1813, he became associated in business with Henry B. Gibson, his son-in-law, and Alexander Seymour, and removed to New York, becoming a leading merchant of this city.

Watts Sherman, of New York, son of Henry Sherman and Sarah Mitchell, and grandson of Captain Nathaniel Sherman and Lucy Tisdale, was the father of Mr. William Watts Sherman. Born in 1809, he married first Lois Sarah Weld, daughter of Thomas Weld. She died in 1838, and he afterwards married his cousin, Sarah Maria Gibson, daughter of Henry B. Gibson and Sarah Sherman, who was a granddaughter of Captain Nathaniel Sherman. Henry B. Gibson was born in Reading, Pa., in 1783. He moved to Ballston, N. Y., with his father, John Gibson, when only nine years old, becoming one of the first settlers of that place. He was cashier of the Ontario Bank in Canandaigua, and subsequently in business in New York, was a partner of Watts Sherman, the elder.

Watts Sherman, second, began his career as a teller of the Ontario County Bank, and was afterwards cashier of the Lexington County Bank, at Geneseo. For many years he was cashier of the Albany City Bank. In 1851, he removed to New York, and became the manager of the banking house of Duncan, Sherman & Co. He died in 1865, on the Island of Madeira, and his wife died in New York, in 1878. The children of Mr. Sherman, by his first wife, were Erastus Corning, and Henry Gibson Sherman. By his second wife, he had William Watts, Duncan, Harry Gibson, Frederick, Charles A., and Alexander Sherman.

Mr. William Watts Sherman was born in Albany, in 1842. In 1871, he married in Newport, Annie Derby Rogers Wetmore, daughter of William Shepard Wetmore and Anstiss Rogers. Mrs. Sherman died in 1884, leaving two daughters, Georgette Wetmore Sherman, who married Harold Brown, son of John Carter Brown, of Providence, R. I., and Sybil Katherine Sherman, who married John Ellis Hoffman. In 1885, Mr. Sherman married Sophia Augusta Brown, daughter of John Carter Brown. The two children of this marriage are Irene Muriel Augusta, and Mildred Constance Sherman. The city home of Mr. and Mrs. Sherman is 838 Fifth Avenue, and their summer residence is in Newport. Mr. Sherman belongs to the Metropolitan, City, Coaching, Century, Knickerbocker and other clubs, the St. Nicholas Society and the American Geographical Society.

HENRY F. SHOEMAKER

ONE of the leaders among the founders of Germantown, Pa., which historic village, associated as it is with a battle of the Revolutionary War, is now included in the limits of the City of Philadelphia, was the ancestor of the Shoemaker family, who was also numbered among the trusted friends of William Penn and was a coworker with Francis Daniel Pastorious The latter, who was a man of high education and gentle birth in Germany, being the son of a judge, became imbued with the religious principles of the sect of Pietists and first conceived the idea of founding a religious colony in what is now Pennsylvania. Becoming acquainted with Penn, whose religious ideas accorded with his own and those of his associates, he acquired a large tract in the transatlantic domain which had been granted by Charles II to Penn, and in 1683 led there, from Holland, a body of his coreligionists, who settled at Germantown. Among their men of prominence, was the first of the family line from which the subject of this article descends, the name having ever since been noted in Pennsylvania and in the City of Philadelphia, while its bearers are now found occupying various distinguished stations in many different portions of the country

Members of the Shoemaker family have always been numbered among the patriotic citizens of the Republic. Notwithstanding their original Quaker belief, Peter Shoemaker, the great-great-grandfather of this sketch, served in the Indian Wars of the Colonial period, and John Shoemaker, his son, was a soldier in the War for Independence Both grandfathers of Mr. Henry F. Shoemaker, Henry Shoemaker and William Brock, were soldiers in the War of 1812, while he himself was an officer in the Union Army during the Civil War.

Other representatives of the family were among the first Pennsylvanians to engage in the work of developing the anthracite coal mines of that State. Colonel George Shoemaker, of Pottsville, Pa, a great-uncle of Mr Henry F Shoemaker, made the earliest attempt to introduce anthracite coal in Philadelphia, loading nine wagons from his coal mines at Centerville, and carrying it by teams to Philadelphia, a distance of one hundred miles. But the people of that day regarded him and his fuel askance, and he was actually denounced for trying to foist upon them what appeared to be simply black stones Colonel Shoemaker persisted, however, in his efforts to dispose of the coal, and succeeded in selling two loads at the cost of transportation. The remainder he either gave away or marketed for a trifle to blacksmiths and others who promised to try it. But his troubles did not end with his disposal of the coal; and though he lost money and time in his efforts to introduce a fuel which has since aided so materially in making Pennsylvania one of the greatest manufacturing States of the Union, in raising Philadelphia to the position of one of the most prosperous cities in the world, and which, moreover, has been an inestimable boon to the country at large, the very people to whom he had given his coal asked the authorities of the city to arrest him for imposing on their credulity Colonel Shoemaker was compelled to leave in haste, and only saved himself from arrest by taking a circuitous route around the Quaker City on his way home

Meanwhile, Mr White, one of the owners of the Fairmount Nail and Wire Works, who had bought a load of coal from Colonel Shoemaker, was anxious to succeed in burning it, and with his men spent a whole morning in trying to ignite it for the purpose of heating one of his furnaces. Every expedient which the experimenters' knowledge of other fuels could suggest was tried, but to no purpose Colonel Shoemaker's rocks apparently would not burn. Dinner time arriving, the men shut the furnace doors in disgust and abandoned the attempt. Returning from dinner they were astonished at the sight they beheld. The doors were red and the furnace was in danger of being melted down with a heat never before experienced On opening it, a glowing fire was discovered, hotter than had ever before been seen in the furnace The purchasers of the other loads also succeeded in using it successfully, and from that time on anthracite stone coal found friends and advocates, and the results of this success being published in the papers, added to its reputation and led within a few years to its general adoption as fuel   To the Shoemaker family, therefore, belongs the credit of initiating the anthracite coal industry of the country, which has become such a factor in its development, from a commercial and industrial standpoint, and from that time down to the present day their interests are largely and closely identified with the industry which representatives of their name and blood did so much to create.

John W. Shoemaker, Mr. Henry F. Shoemaker's father, was a noted operator in the anthracite coal region, possessing and working large mines at Tamaqua.   The mother of Mr. Henry F. Shoemaker was Mary A. Brock, daughter of William Brock, also an extensive owner of anthracite coal lands   The Wyoming Valley branch of the family has been notably able and successful; and in the various localities in which the members of the different branches have made their homes, especially in Baltimore, Philadelphia and Cincinnati, they became people of prominence, leaving their impress on the social and business communities where they reside.

Mr Henry F. Shoemaker was born in Schuylkill County, Pa., March 28th, 1845.   He was educated in schools at Tamaqua, his native place, and in Genesee Seminary, New York.   When General Lee, with the Confederate Army, invaded the State of Pennsylvania in 1863, Mr. Shoemaker, who was then only eighteen years of age, promptly responded to the call of the Government for troops to defend the State.   Enlisting a company of sixty volunteers from the workmen in his father's mines, he was elected Captain and took his command to Harrisburg, where it was mustered into the Federal service as part of the Twenty-Seventh Pennsylvania Volunteer Militia and was attached to the Sixth Army Corps   After this military experience, Mr. Shoemaker went to Philadelphia, in 1864, made that city his residence, and entered the wholesale coal shipping trade with one of the leading establishments of that city, and in 1866 began business on his own account as the senior member of the firm of Shoemaker & McIntyre.   In 1870, he formed the firm of Fry, Shoemaker & Co , and engaged in the business of mining anthracite coal at Tamaqua, Pa.

After a few years, he found that the transportation business afforded him wider opportunities than mining, and having disposed of his coal interests, he became in 1876 secretary and treasurer of the Central Railroad of Minnesota   In 1878, he took an active part in the construction of the Rochester & State Line Railroad, which afterwards became known as the Buffalo, Rochester & Pittsburg Railroad   In 1881, he added to his business ventures the banking house of Shoemaker, Dillon & Co., in Wall Street, New York   His transactions in the negotiation of railroad securities and properties since that time have been on an exceedingly extensive scale.   He became interested in the Wheeling & Lake Erie Railroad in 1886, was president of the Mineral Range Railroad in 1887, chairman of the executive committee of the Cincinnati, Hamilton & Dayton Railroad in 1888, president of the Dayton & Union and the Cincinnati, Dayton & Ironton Railroad, vice-president of the Indiana, Decatur & Western Railway, and a director in the Cincinnati, Hamilton & Indianapolis, the Cincinnati, New Orleans & Texas Pacific, the Cleveland, Loraine & Wheeling, the Alabama Great Southern Railroad, and also of the English corporation controlling the latter in London, England, and of other railroads.   Other large industries and enterprises have engaged Mr. Shoemaker's attention and have had the benefit of his wide and successful business experience.   He was at one time among the principal owners and a director in the New Jersey Rubber Shoe Company, which now forms part of the industrial combination formed under the title of the United States Rubber Company

Since 1877, Mr Shoemaker has been a resident of New York City.   In 1874, he married Blanche Quiggle, of Philadelphia, daughter of the late Honorable James W. Quiggle, at one time United States Consul at Antwerp and afterwards United States Minister to Belgium.   Their family consists of two sons and one daughter.   Mr. Shoemaker is a member of the Union League, Lotos, Riverside Yacht and American Yacht clubs, and belongs to the Sons of the Revolution and the Grand Army of the Republic.   His city residence is at 22 East Forty-sixth Street, his country residence being Cedar Cliff, on the shore of Long Island Sound, near Riverside, Conn.

EDWARD LYMAN SHORT

ONE of the passengers on the Mary and John, which arrived at Boston in 1634, was Henry Short, the ancestor of Mr. Edward Lyman Short. He settled in Ipswich, Mass., moved to Newbury, and was a delegate to the General Court in 1664, dying in 1673 His son was Henry Short, Jr., who, in 1692, married Ann (Sewall) Longfellow, widow of William Longfellow. Her father, Henry Sewall, was Mayor of Coventry, England, and five of his descendants were Judges in the Colony, three attaining the Chief Justiceship

Charles Short, LL D., 1821-1886, father of the subject of this article, was born in Haverhill, Mass., and graduated from Harvard College in 1846, was an eminent classical scholar and man of letters In 1863, he became president of Kenyon College and professor of moral and intellectual philosophy. In 1868, he was appointed professor of Latin in Columbia College, and held that position till his death. In 1871, he was a member and secretary of the American Committee for the Revision of the New Testament He published a number of works on classical philology and collected one of the largest private classical libraries in the country In 1849, he married Ann Jean Lyman, daughter of the Honorable Elihu Lyman, 1782-1826, of Greenfield, Mass., and his wife, Mary Field, daughter of Robert Field Elihu Lyman was graduated from Dartmouth College in 1803, became an eminent lawyer and influential citizen of Franklin County, Mass., being high sheriff, 1811-15, and was afterwards State Senator. The ancestor of the Lyman family, Thomas Lyman, of Navistoke, Essex, who died in 1509, married a great-grand-daughter of Sir William Lambert, whose marriage with Johanna de Umfreville, it has been said, united the two ancient and honorable lines of Lambert and Umfreville. It was their descendant, Richard Lyman, who came from High Ongar, England, in 1631, to Hartford, Conn. His great-great-grandson was Major Elihu Lyman, 1741-1823, a native of Belchertown, Mass., and a Captain in the expedition against Quebec under Montgomery and Arnold in 1775. He was the father of Elihu Lyman, the maternal grandfather of Mr Edward Lyman Short

Mr Short was born in Philadelphia, September 30th, 1854 He was educated at schools in New York and at Phillips Academy, Andover, Mass., and was graduated from Columbia College in 1875 and from the Columbia Law School in 1878. He read law in the office of Foster & Thomson, was admitted to the bar in 1878, and since 1884 has been a member of the firm now known as Davies, Stone & Auerbach. His specialties are railway, corporation and insurance law, and he is general solicitor of the Mutual Life Insurance Company He is a strong and logical speaker at the bar, and has appeared in many important railroad and other litigations, and has recently published an exhaustive work on the Law of Railway Bonds and Mortgages

In 1887, Mr Short married Anna Livingston Petit, whose family has been identified for generations with the social life of New York. Among her ancestors are Robert Livingston, the first Lord of Livingston Manor, Johannes de Peyster, John Roosevelt and Colonel Gerardus Beekman Mrs Short and her sister, Emily Petit, own a Dutch portrait of one of the first de Peysters who came to this country. On the paternal side, her family came from Bordeaux, where the ancient street of Nauté is named after them Mr and Mrs Short have two children, Anna Livingston and Livingston Lyman Short Their residence is in West Thirty-seventh Street, and their country home has been recently in Islip, Long Island Mr Short is a member of the Metropolitan, University, Calumet, Lawyers' and Church clubs, the Bar Association, the Columbia College Alumni Association, the Downtown Association, the Sons of the Revolution and the Society of Colonial Wars

The eldest son of Dr Charles Short, and brother of Mr Edward Lyman Short, is the Reverend Charles Lancaster Short, of Worcester, Mass., and the youngest son is Henry Alford Short, Ph. D., a graduate of Columbia in the class of 1880. The Short coat of arms, a copy of which has been in the possession of the family since the emigration, bears this inscription . " He beareth sable a griffon passant argent and a chief ermine, by the name of Short."

JOSEPH EDWARD SIMMONS

BORN in Troy, N. Y., a little over fifty years ago, Mr. Joseph Edward Simmons is another instance of the important part which the mingling of the Holland Dutch and New England blood has played in the State and City of New York, and of the position which representatives of the union of ₜthe two races hold in the present, as in the past, history of the metropolis He is descended from Revolutionary ancestry, one of his great-grandfathers on the maternal side having been a soldier of the Continental Army He was educated in the Troy Academy and in a private school and was graduated from Williams College in 1862. He studied also in the Albany Law School, receiving the degree of LL B in 1863, was called to the bar the same year and successfully practiced his profession in his native city until 1867.

Mr. Simmons' eminent success was, however, destined to be gained in other lines of activity than the law, while to a man of his capacity and energy New York City presented the true field for the exercise of his talents and ambition In the year last mentioned, he removed hither and entered the banking business. Becoming a member of the New York Stock Exchange, he was in 1884 called to its presidency at a time when public confidence was disturbed, and even that institution—the most important business body of the country—felt the shock. His administration was eminently successful and his reëlection for a second term, in 1885, confirmed his title to the approval and gratitude of the financial public. In 1888, he became president of the Fourth National Bank of New York. In this position his success has given him a national reputation He has taken a leading and influential part in the deliberations of the New York Clearing House Association, and in 1896 received the highest compliment which can be paid by the members of his own profession in his election as president of the Clearing House. He is vice-president of the Chamber of Commerce, president of the Panama Railroad Company, and of the Columbian Line of Steamships. He is also interested in the philanthropic institutions of the city, being the treasurer and one of the board of governors of the New York Hospital

Nor has Mr. Simmons failed to win distinction in public life, though political ambition has found no place in his character. He has repeatedly refused to become a candidate for offices of distinction, even declining a nomination to the Mayoralty of New York when such nomination could have been considered equivalent to an election. On the other hand, he is one of the limited class of men of affairs who take an intelligent and useful interest in politics, and in 1881 he accepted the honorable and laborious position of a member of the Board of Education, becoming president of the Board in 1886 During a connection of nine years in this capacity with the city's educational system he labored unceasingly and successfully to extend and improve its scope, and was instrumental in creating many beneficial changes, notably the conferring of collegiate powers on the Normal College for Women, the act of the Legislature to that effect having been passed by his personal influence. He also gave much attention to the College of the City of New York, a part of the city's fine educational facilities which owes much to his intelligent interest in its welfare. In short, the executive ability which has won him high place in the business and financial world has been unstintingly given to further the cause of popular education, and in a position which involved no small amount of personal sacrifice. When he relinquished his connection with the Board of Education, owing to exacting business engagements, he had gained the reputation of being the most efficient president that the Board had ever had.

Mr Simmons is also distinguished in the Masonic Order, having served as grand master of the Grand Lodge of this State He has traveled abroad extensively and, in addition to his residence in West Fifty-second Street, has a summer home at Monmouth Beach, N. J. He is a member, among other organizations, of the Metropolitan, University and Manhattan clubs, and of both the New England and St Nicholas societies. He married Julia Greer, daughter of George Greer, of New York, and he has two children, Joseph Ferris and Mabel Simmons. In 1888, he received' the degree of LL D., from the University of Norwich, Vermont.

HENRY WARNER SLOCUM

ONE of the purchasers, in 1637, of Cohannet, afterwards incorporated in the town of Taunton, Mass., was Anthony Slocombe. In 1650, he was a juryman of the town; in 1654 a surveyor of the highways, and in 1657 a freeman. In 1662, he removed to Dartmouth, of which he was one of the first settlers, and in 1675 was killed in King Philip's War He married a sister of William Harvey, of Taunton Giles Slocombe, their son, was born in Somersetshire, England, and settled in Portsmouth, R. I., in 1638, becoming a freeman in 1655. Eliezer Slocombe, 1664-1727, in the third American generation, married Elephel Fitzgerald.

Benjamin Slocum, 1699-1726, son of Eliezer Slocum, was born in Dartmouth, Mass., and married Meribah, daughter of Ralph Earl. He was the father of John Slocum, who was born in Dartmouth, and settled in Newport, R. I., in 1746, where he became a merchant. His wife was Martha Tillinghast, daughter of Pardon Tillinghast and Avis Norton, a daughter of Benjamin Norton. The grandfather of Martha Tillinghast was Philip Tillinghast, of Providence. Her grandmother was Martha Holmes, who was a granddaughter of Obadiah Holmes. Philip Tillinghast was a son of Pardon Tillinghast, a Baptist minister, of Beechy Head, Sussex, England, who came to Providence in 1645. The mother of Philip Tillinghast was Lydia Tabor, daughter of Philip Tabor, of Tiverton, R. I.

The next in line of descent was Benjamin Slocum, 1761-1805, who married Elizabeth Coggeshall Born in Newport, he became a resident of Marietta, O. His son, Matthew Barnard Slocum, born in Newport in 1788, settled in Delphi, Onondaga County, N. Y., engaged in business, and married Mary Ostander in 1814.

Major-General Henry Warner Slocum, son of Matthew B. Slocum, and father of the subject of this sketch, was a distinguished officer in the Civil War, and also had a notable career in political life. He was born in Delphi, N. Y., in 1826, entered the United States Military Academy in 1846, and upon graduation became Second Lieutenant of the First Artillery. After serving in the Florida War he resigned from the army in 1856, and was soon after admitted to the New York State bar. In 1858, he was a member of the Assembly. At the beginning of the Civil War he was appointed Colonel of the Twenty-Seventh New York Volunteers, and was wounded at the first battle of Bull Run. He was promoted to be Brigadier-General in 1861, and served in the Peninsular campaign with the Army of the Potomac, being present at Yorktown and at Gaines' Mill, Malvern Hill and other battles. He was engaged throughout the Northern Virginia campaign, and at Gettysburg commanded the right wing of the army In 1864, General Slocum succeeded Hooker in command of the Twentieth Army Corps, and the same year was transferred with his command to the Army of the West He was engaged in Sherman's march to the sea, and, in 1865, was placed in command of the Department of the Mississippi. At the close of the war, General Slocum returned to civil life, and in 1865 was nominated for Secretary of State of New York by the Democratic party, but was defeated in the election Removing to Brooklyn in 1866, he was elected a member of the National House of Representatives in 1868, and again in 1870, and was president of the Brooklyn Board of Public Works in 1876. He died in Brooklyn in April, 1894. In 1854, he married Clara Rice, daughter of Israel and Dorcas (Jenkins) Rice, of Woodstock, N. Y. They had four children, Caroline, Florence Elizabeth, Henry Warner and Clarence Rice Slocum.

Mr Henry Warner Slocum, the eldest son of General Slocum, was born in Syracuse, N. Y., May 28th, 1862. He was educated at Yale University, graduating from that institution in 1883 He studied law, and has been for many years engaged in practice. In October, 1888, he married Grace Edsall, daughter of Henry and Emma (Jerome) Edsall Mrs. Slocum's mother was the daughter of Thomas Jerome, the eldest brother of Leonard Jerome. Mr. and Mrs. Slocum have two daughters, Gertrude and Nathalie Slocum. The family resides in East Fortieth Street. Mr Slocum is a member of the Racquet and University Athletic clubs, and of the Military Order of the Loyal Legion.

CHARLES STEWART SMITH

IN every period of New York's history its merchants have been the real mainstay of the community, and from among them have come its natural leaders. A century ago, when the storms of the Revolution broke, New York merchants like Philip Livingston and Francis Lewis were foremost in adopting the patriotic cause. To-day, when the chief dangers to republican institutions are of a domestic character, the leaders of the business world in New York have been no less ready to come forward in the public interest.

In the revolt of intelligence and material interests against corruption and misgovernment, and in the movement for municipal reform, the city's merchants have taken a conspicuous part. No name is more likely to occur in this connection than that of Mr. Charles Stewart Smith, who in recent years has been an important factor in public affairs, and a spokesman at a juncture of great importance for the New York mercantile world as the head of a body which, for more than a century, has represented the financial, commercial and industrial interests of the city.

A New Englander by birth, Mr. Smith is descended from families that were among the earliest settlers of Massachusetts, Connecticut and New Jersey. Samuel Smith, his first American paternal ancestor, came, in 1634, with his wife, Elizabeth, from Ipswich, Suffolk, England, and settled at Watertown, Mass. In the following year, he moved to the valley of the Connecticut and was a founder of the town of Wethersfield, Conn., and represented that place in the General Court from 1641 to 1653. In 1659, he moved to Hadley, Mass., where he was also a representative from 1661-73, also a magistrate and Lieutenant of militia. His fourth son, John Smith, married Mary Partridge in 1663, and in 1676 was killed by the Indians in the Falls fight, while leading his command with conspicuous valor. Benjamin Smith, his youngest son, born in 1673, and who was three years old at his father's death, was the great-great-grandfather of the subject of this article. He moved to Wethersfield, married Ruth Buck in 1700, and Josiah, his second son, born 1707, married in 1740 Mary Treat, daughter of Joseph Treat, a descendant of Richard Treat, one of the founders of Connecticut. James, the youngest son of this marriage, born in 1756, was the grandfather, and his fourth son, John, born in Wethersfield in 1796, the father, of Mr. Charles Stewart Smith. John Smith became a clergyman of the Congregational Church and married, in 1826, Esther Mary Woodruff and had seven children, of whom Mr. Charles Stewart Smith was the third.

The Treat family has already been referred to in mentioning the marriage of Mary Treat to Mr. Smith's great-grandfather, Josiah Smith. The family is of English origin, its American ancestor, Richard Treat, having been born in 1584 at Pitminster, Somersetshire, England. In 1615, he married Alice Gaylord, daughter of Hugh Gaylord, and it is presumed that he was one of the company which came to Massachusetts with Saltonstall in 1630. His name occurs first in 1641 in the records of Wethersfield, Conn. He was elected by the town of Wethersfield to offices of trust, and was in 1663 a member of Governor Winthrop's council. He was also a patentee and charter member of the Colony of Connecticut. Many of his descendants served in the French and Indian Wars and in the Revolution, being distinguished for their sturdy patriotism at the latter period.

Robert Treat, the second son of the pioneer, began his public career at the age of eighteen and thenceforward his life was spent in constant public service. As a Major, he was Commander-in-Chief of Connecticut's forces in King Philip's War. He was a deputy to the General Court, a magistrate for eight years, seventeen years Deputy Governor and fifteen years Governor. His great-grandson was Robert Treat Paine, signer of the Declaration of Independence. James Treat, the youngest brother of Governor Robert Treat, was a Lieutenant of the Wethersfield train band in the Indian Wars and held many public local offices at a time when to hold office was a patent of a good name and a title of honor. He was deputy from Wethersfield, 1672-1707, a member of the Council of Safety in 1689, commissioner in 1693-97, Justice of the Peace for Hartford County, 1698-1708, and a member of the Governor's Council, 1696-98. From him descended Mary Treat, who was the great-grandmother of the subject of this sketch.

Through his mother, who was Esther Mary Woodruff, Mr Smith is descended from Elias Woodruff, who was his great-grandfather and was Commissary-General of the Revolutionary forces of New Jersey. Elias Woodruff's wife was Mary Joline, a direct descendant of a Huguenot merchant of New York, André Joline. Their son, Aaron Dickinson Woodruff, a resident of Trenton, and Mr. Smith's grandfather, graduated from Princeton College as valedictorian of the class of 1779 He was admitted to the bar in 1784 and was Attorney-General of New Jersey for seventeen years. Both father and son were ardent patriots and were personal friends of Washington Some thirty members of the Woodruff family took part in the Revolutionary War, of whom nine were commissioned officers The history of Princeton College records the names of the various members of the Woodruff family among its founders and benefactors.

Born in 1832, at Exeter, N H, where his father, the Reverend John Smith, had a parish, Mr Charles Stewart Smith was educated in his native place, came to New York a mere youth in 1846, and entered the wholesale dry goods trade His business career throughout was attended by a success corresponding with his ability and the broad-minded energy which is one of his characteristics. Soon after attaining his majority, he became associated with the well-known firm of S. B. Chittenden & Co, and was for a number of years their representative in Europe Afterwards he became the senior of the firm of Smith, Hogg & Gardner His prominence and success as a merchant only ended in 1887, when he permanently retired from active business Possessing, however, extensive interests, Mr Smith is associated in the direction of some of the foremost financial, insurance and other similar institutions of the city, including the United States Trust Company, the Merchants, Fourth National and Fifth Avenue banks, the Equitable Life Assurance Society and the German-American Insurance Company

Although consistently declining public office, his interest in politics was always keen, and, an active member of the Union League Club, he has served as vice-president of that institution His great service to New York was, however, rendered in 1894 As president of the Chamber of Commerce, he impressed upon the members of that venerable body the fact that the prevalent mal-administration of the affairs of the city was a menace to its material prosperity Largely through Mr Smith's efforts, the celebrated Committee of Seventy, of which he was a leading member and chairman of the executive committee, was formed and his effective and disinterested share in bringing about the civic revolution of that year was warmly acknowledged by all classes of his fellow citizens. The value of the work which he performed at this crisis in New York's municipal affairs in fact becomes more apparent with the lapse of time The overthrow of a corrupt adminis-tration of the city's affairs is but one feature of the matter It was of even more importance that the citizens should be aroused to a sense of their power and of the real weakness of the mercenary and often corrupt class of politicians The demonstration of these facts, it is generally admitted, have had a most salutary effect and will for many years to come exercise an influence on the action of political parties in selecting candidates for municipal honors as well as on the conduct of the duly elected officials It is due to Mr Smith to say that he was one of the few who realized that New Yorkers of all ranks and stations possessed a civic pride and an attachment for their city, and it was on his initiative that this feeling was so successfully appealed to in the instance referred to

Mr Smith is a member of the Union League, Metropolitan, Century, Players, Lawyers' and other clubs, a trustee of the Metropolitan Museum of Art, a patron of the American Museum of Natural History and the National Academy of Design, and a member of the New England Society, and the Sons of the American Revolution He has a city residence, 25 West Forty-seventh Street, and a country seat, Fairlawn, at Stamford, Conn. He has two sons, Stewart Woodruff Smith and Howard Caswell Smith, who are engaged in business in New York City

James Dickinson Smith, the brother of Mr Charles Stewart Smith, is the head of the bank-ing firm of James D Smith & Co, of this city He has long been a leading member of the New York Stock Exchange and is an ex-president of that institution Some years since he was commo-dore of the New York Yacht Club His son is Archibald H Smith and his daughter, Helen Woodruff, is the wife of Homer S Cummings

GOUVERNEUR MATHER SMITH, M. D.

ON both sides, Dr Smith's descent is from families famous in the early Colonial history of New England and New York as well as in the Revolutionary struggle He is a native of the metropolis, his father being the distinguished Dr. Joseph Mather Smith, who was born in New Rochelle, and was for many years one of the foremost physicians in America, and professor for forty years in the New York College of Physicians and Surgeons, where an annual prize now bears his name. His grandfather was Dr. Matson Smith, who came of an old New England family, having been born at Lyme, Conn , but who established himself at New Rochelle, where he became a leading physician and was also known for his activity in religious matters. He was president of the Westchester County Medical Society, founded in 1797. His wife, the grandmother of the subject of this sketch, was a daughter of Dr Samuel Mather, of Lyme

The position of the Mather family in New England Colonial history is well known, and a branch of it settled in Connecticut at an early day Dr Smith's great-grandfather, Dr. Samuel Mather, 1741-1834, was a Captain in Colonel Saltonstall's regiment of Connecticut militia, 1775-79, but exchanged it for the equally honorable and useful rank of Surgeon in Colonel Parson's regiment, 1779-80. His father, Dr. Eleazer Mather, of Lyme, 1716-1798, also served the patriotic cause, having been appointed by the General Assembly of Connecticut to examine candidates for the post of surgeon in the Continental army and navy. Joseph Mather, another direct ancestor, one generation further removed, was Lieutenant during the French and Indian War.

In the maternal line, Dr. Smith is related to a number of the older New York families, such as the Lispenards, Marstons and Rutgers. He is a descendant of Antoine or Anthony Lispenard, 1643-1696, the founder of the family of that name, which now exists only through its female descendants. It was this Anthony Lispenard, a Huguenot refugee, who, among other public services, bore despatches from Governor Dongan to the French Governor of Canada. Another ancestor was the famous Colonel Leonard Lispenard, 1715-1790, who was a member of the Provincial Assembly of New York in 1759–68, and a delegate to the first Colonial Congress held in 1765 at Philadelphia. Another worthy who appears in Dr. Smith's family tree is Anthony Rutgers, member of the New York Assembly, 1726–37, while, going further back, we find among his ancestors on the paternal side Major-General Humphrey Atherton, Commander of the Ancient and Honorable Artillery Company in 1650, Major-General in 1661, Speaker of the Massachusetts House of Deputies in 1653, and Governor's Assistant of Massachusetts, 1654-61

Dr. Gouverneur Mather Smith was graduated from the New York University in 1852. He studied at the College of Physicians and Surgeons and received the degrees of M A. and of M. D. in 1855, entering at once upon active practice. The beginning of the Civil War aroused his patriotic instincts, and he offered his services gratuitously as medical officer of the United States Sanitary Commission transport Daniel Webster. In 1862, he was appointed Acting Assistant Surgeon in the army and served until the end of the war In 1864, he was appointed executive officer in charge of the United States Army General Hospital, at which he was stationed. On the death of his father, in 1866, he succeeded him as an attending physician at the New York Hospital, where he is now one of the consulting physicians. Dr. Smith's professional honors cannot, however, be traced in full, though it should be mentioned that he was vice-president of the New York Academy of Medicine, 1875-78, and since then has been one of its trustees. In 1887–88, he was president of the New York Society for the Relief of Widows and Orphans of Medical Men Dr. Smith has been a writer not only on medical topics, but is a contributor to periodical literature in a lighter vein of both verse and prose He is a member of the Metropolitan Club and the Century Association, was a manager of the Sons of the Revolution and is a member of the Society of Colonial Wars He is surgeon of the Society of the War of 1812, consulting physician of the St. Nicholas Society, and one of the managers of the New York Association for Improving the Condition of the Poor, and of the New York Institution for the Blind.

WILLIAM ALEXANDER SMITH

ANCESTORS of Mr William Alexander Smith, who were of Scotch origin, were early settled in Colonial New York. His great-grandparents were William and Elizabeth C Smith His grandfather, Robert Smith, 1752-1838, served as a Major during the War of the Revolution, being wounded at the battle of White Plains After the war, he was in business in Philadelphia. Upon the establishment of the United States Bank, he was elected a director and then a trustee, serving in that capacity for forty-eight years

The wife of Robert Smith was Rebecca (Hobart) Potts, daughter of Enoch Hobart and great-granddaughter of Thomas Hobart, son of Enoch Hobart, of Hingham, Mass , by his wife, Hannah Harris, daughter of Thomas Harris. The father of Enoch Hobart was Joshua Hobart, 1614-1682, who came to this country with his parents in 1633, and went to Hingham, Mass , in 1635, being a freeman in 1634, a selectman in 1662, a deputy to the General Court for twenty-four years after 1643, Speaker of the House of Deputies in 1674 and Captain of a military company in King Philip's War. His wife was Ellen Ibrook, daughter of Richard Ibrook. His father was Edmund Hobart, of Hingham, 1570-1646, who arrived in Massachusetts in 1633 from Hingham, England, was a freeman in 1634, and a deputy to the General Court in 1642, he married Margaret Dewey

Robert Hobart Smith, father of Mr William Alexander Smith, was a native of Philadelphia. Graduated from the University of Pennsylvania, he studied law and then entered the Theological Seminary at Princeton. He was licensed to preach in 1829, and for many years was ruling elder in the Second Presbyterian Church of Philadelphia and treasurer of the General Assembly. His death occurred in 1858 The wife of Robert Hobart Smith was Mary Potts, of Pottsgrove, Pa , daughter of Joseph Potts, 1766-1824, and Sarah Potts, daughter of David and Mary (Aris) Potts The grandfather of Mary Potts was Samuel Potts, 1736-1793, who during the Revolution was engaged in casting heavy cannon for the Continental Army, was a member of the Assembly from Philadelphia County in 1767-69, associate judge and member of the First Constitutional Convention in Pennsylvania. His wife was Joanna Holland, daughter of Thomas Holland, of Philadelphia Samuel Potts was a son of John Potts, 1710-1768, the founder of Pottstown, Pa , whose wife was Ruth Savage, daughter of Samuel and Anna (Rutter) Savage and granddaughter of Thomas and Rebecca (Staples) Rutter The father of John Potts was Thomas Potts, a native of Wales. He was sheriff in Germantown in 1702. His first wife, the mother of John Potts, was Martha Keurlis, a member of one of the twelve families that accompanied Pastorius to America.

Mr. William Alexander Smith, the eldest surviving son of Robert Hobart Smith and his wife, Mary Potts, was born in Pottstown, Pa., September 9th, 1820 Soon after coming of age, he settled in New York, and in 1845 entered Wall Street, being now senior partner of the banking house of William Alexander Smith & Co He has been much interested in religious and philanthropic work In 1848, he was treasurer of the New York Bible Society, has been president of the Sheltering Arms since 1893, treasurer of the General Clergy Relief Fund since 1868, trustee of the permanent fund of the Orphans' Home and Asylum since 1863, trustee of the parochial fund of the Protestant Episcopal Church since 1864, manager of St. Luke's Hospital since 1868, and vice-chairman of the executive committee of the same institution since 1896, vice-president of the Protestant Episcopal City Mission, and manager of the Home of Incurables and of the Society for Promoting Religion and Learning. He has been president and treasurer of the New York Stock Exchange, and is a vice-president of the Continental Trust Company

In 1847, Mr Smith married Clara Mary Bull, daughter of the Reverend Dr Levi Bull She died in 1857 His second wife, whom he married in 1863, was Margaret Jones, daughter of George and Serena (Mason) Jones His children are Robert Hobart Smith, who married Dinah Watson Dunn, Clara H Smith, who married the Reverend L C. Stewardson, and William Alexander Smith, Jr., who married Emily Louisa Gurnee The city residence of the family is in Madison Avenue and their country home is West Hill, Nyack-on-Hudson.

LORILLARD SPENCER

WILLIAM Spencer came from England to America in 1631, and settled in Cambridge, Mass. He returned to England the following year, but came again to this country in 1633, bringing with him his brothers, Thomas and Jared. These three brothers were the ancestors of the various branches of the Spencer family which trace their lineage to Colonial times. William Spencer and his brother, Thomas, were among the first settlers of Hartford, Conn, where William was a land proprietor, a selectman of the town, and a deputy to the General Court of Connecticut, in 1639. He died in Hartford, in 1640.

Ambrose Spencer, great-grandfather of Mr Lorillard Spencer, was lineally descended in the fifth generation from William Spencer, the Hartford settler. He was born in Salisbury, Conn., in 1765, and died in Lyons, N Y, in 1848. Educated at both Yale College and Harvard College, and graduated from the latter in 1783, he made his home in Hudson, N Y, and entered upon a career in which he became highly distinguished as a lawyer, Judge and public man. He was elected a member of the assembly of New York State, in 1793, and was a member of the State Senate for seven years after 1795. In 1796, he was Assistant Attorney-General of New York, in 1802 Attorney-General of the State, and in 1804 became Justice of the Supreme Court, being its Chief Justice, 1819-23. In 1809, he was Presidential elector, a member of the Constitutional Convention in 1821, Mayor of Albany 1824-26, a member of the National House of Representatives 1829-31, and president of the National Convention in Baltimore, in 1844.

The grandfather of Mr. Lorillard Spencer was Captain William Ambrose Spencer, U. S N. He was born in New York in 1793, and died in 1854. Educated in the United States Naval Academy at Annapolis, Md, he entered the navy as a midshipman in 1809, was promoted to be a Lieutenant in 1814, attained to the rank of Captain in 1841, and resigned from the service in 1843. When Commodore Thomas McDonough achieved his famous victory over the British naval forces on Lake Champlain in 1814, Captain Spencer, who was then Acting Lieutenant, took part in that engagement, and for his bravery was presented with a sword by act of Congress. Captain Spencer was twice married. His first wife was Catherine Lorillard, born 1792, daughter of Peter A. Lorillard, 1763-1843, and his wife, Maria Dorothea Schultz. After her death, Captain Spencer married her younger sister, Eleanor Eliza Lorillard, born in 1801.

Lorillard Spencer, Sr, the son of Captain William A. Spencer, was born in New York in 1826, and died in Paris, France, in 1888. Inheriting considerable wealth, he did not enter professional or business life, devoting himself, in a large degree, to scholarly pursuits. During the greater part of the last twenty years of his life, he resided in Europe. He married Sarah J Griswold, daughter of Charles C Griswold, a famous New York merchant, who, with his brother, John Griswold, owned the London line of packet ships. Mrs Spencer was the granddaughter of Governor Matthew Griswold and Ursula Wolcott. The children of Lorillard Spencer, Sr., can thus trace, in both the paternal and maternal line, a descent from the most eminent families of Colonial Connecticut.

Mr Lorillard Spencer, of the present generation, was born in New York, February 14th, 1860. He has spent much time in foreign travel, but resides in the city of his birth, where he possesses important interests. He has been particularly known as the owner of The Illustrated American. He married Caroline S Berryman, a granddaughter of Stephen Whitney, one of old New York's most prominent merchants. The family has been conspicuous in the social life of the period in New York and in Newport, where Mr Spencer's residence, Chastellux, is one of the most beautiful places in that city. Mr Spencer is a member of the Metropolitan, Union, Whist and Aldine clubs, the Society of Colonial Wars, the Sons of the Revolution, and the Military Society of the War of 1812. The only sister of Mr Lorillard Spencer is Eleanor Spencer, who married Virginio Cenci, Prince of Vicovaro, Grand Chamberlain to the King of Italy. The Princess Cenci was the first American to be appointed *Dame du Palais* by Queen Marguerita.

JAMES SPEYER

A LTHOUGH the name of Spire, or Spira, appears in the chronicles of Frankfort-on-Main as early as the middle of the fourteenth century, the first member of the Speyer family of whom accurate records have been kept, and from whom Mr James Speyer is a direct descendant, was Michael Speyer, who died in 1586. The family has long been known for the broad spirit of philanthropy it has manifested and for its well-directed efforts in aiding those in need and in bettering the condition of the poor. In the commercial world, moreover, it has also, through the business enterprise and integrity of its members, long occupied a distinguished and prominent position. An interesting comment on the important standing of the family, even in 1792, is found in the fact that when, in that year, the French general, Custine, brought three leading citizens of Frankfort to Mayence as hostages to guarantee the payment of a war tax, one of them was the Imperial Court Banker, Isaac Michael Speyer.

In 1691, Michael Isaac Speyer was chosen head of the Hebrew community in Frankfort, in which position his two sons, Joseph Michael and Moses Michael, succeeded him. A third son, Isaac Michael Speyer, was the special representative of the entire Jewish community at the Imperial Court of Vienna, as well as before all other civil and judicial authorities of the country. Another member of the family was Imperial Court-factor at Michelstadt, and Wilhelm Speyer, who died in 1878, was a well-known musical composer of his day. The practical philanthropy of the family is shown by the establishment of various funds for the help of the poor and needy in different ways by Joseph Speyer in 1729, Isaac Speyer in 1807, and Moses Michael Speyer in 1801, all of which funds are still in existence and are the means of alleviating much distress.

Mr. James Speyer was born in New York in 1861. His father, Gustavus Speyer, who married Sophie Rubino in 1860, followed his brother, Phillip Speyer, to New York in 1845. Together, they founded the New York house of Phillip Speyer & Co., which, in 1878, became the firm of Speyer & Co. His grandfather, Joseph Speyer, died in 1846, and his grandmother, Jeanette Ellissen, in 1828. After receiving his education at Frankfort-on-Main, Mr. Speyer began his business career in his father's banking house in Frankfort when twenty-two years of age. He then went to Paris and London, and in 1885 returned to New York, where he is now a partner in the well-known banking house of Speyer & Co., as well as in the Frankfort house and its European branches.

Mr. Speyer has taken a prominent part in every kind of intelligent and well-directed philanthropic work in this community. He was one of the founders of the Provident Loan Society, of New York, of which he is now the president, and is also treasurer of the University Settlement Society and a trustee of the German Savings Bank. In politics, he is a Democrat, but is independent and non-partisan, especially in municipal affairs. He was an active member of the executive committee of the Committee of Seventy, vice-president and treasurer of the German-American Reform Union in the Cleveland campaign of 1892, and is also an original member of the Citizens' Union. In 1896, he was appointed a member of the Board of Education by Mayor William L. Strong.

In November, 1897, Mr Speyer married Ellin L. Prince (Mrs John A. Lowery), daughter of the late John Dyneley Prince and Mary Travers, who was the daughter of John Travers and Susan Moale, both descendants of the oldest families of Baltimore, Md. Mrs. Speyer has long been prominent in efforts to brighten the lives and better the condition of the less fortunate, especially in connection with the working girls' clubs. She is treasurer of the Woman's Auxiliary of the Hospital Saturday and Sunday Association, vice-president of the Woman's Auxiliary of the University Settlement Society and a member also of the board of managers of the Loomis Sanitarium for Consumptives. Mr Speyer is a member of the City, Manhattan, Players, Racquet, Reform, Lawyers', Whist and New York Yacht clubs, and the Deutscher Verein. Mr. and Mrs Speyer reside at 257 Madison Avenue.

PAUL NELSON SPOFFORD

HALF a century ago, Paul Spofford was one of the great New York merchants He was born in 1792, his family being of old Massachusetts stock. When he was a boy of sixteen, he entered business in Haverhill, Mass., and was soon a junior partner, remaining there until 1818. He then formed a partnership with Thomas Tileston and came to New York, where he established an agency for the Boston Packet Line, and gradually engaged in trade with the West Indies and South America. Ultimately his firm came to have one of the largest shipping establishments in New York, and among their many notable achievements was the first successful inauguration of steam navigation on the ocean in this country. During the Civil War, the members of the firm gave substantial assistance to the Government. Outside of the shipping business, Paul Spofford had many important interests. He was also a member of the Council of the University of the City of New York and treasurer of the corporation.

Paul Spofford was a descendant from John Spofford, 1612-1678, who in 1638 settled in the town of Rowley, Mass. The ancestors of the family in successive generations down to Paul Spofford were John Spofford, 1648-1696, and his wife, Sarah Wheeler; Jonathan Spofford, 1684-1772, and his wife, Jemima Freethe ; Abel Spofford, 1718-1785, and his wife, Eleanor Poore; and Joseph Spofford, who died in 1825, and his wife, Mary Chaplin.

Not many families in this country can trace their lineage to European ancestry more surely and more accurately than the Spoffords. The name appears in the Domesday Book. Gamel, son of Orm, was Lord of Thorp-Arch on the river Wharf, Yorkshire, and had other domains in the eleventh century. From Gamelbar, Lord of Spofford, son of Gamel, Lord of Thorp-Arch, sprang the Spoffords of Yorkshire. Walter de Spofford was among those who were killed during the invasion of England by Malcolm II., King of Scotland Thomas de Spofford became Bishop of Hereford in 1420 In 1642, John Spofford was appointed by Parliament vicar of Silkeston, in Yorkshire, and it was his son, John Spofford, who came to Massachusetts.

In 1822, Paul Spofford married Sarah Spofford, also descended from John Spofford, of Rowley, the ancestor of her husband. Her father was Daniel Spofford, 1770-1805; her mother being Mary Nelson, of Georgetown, Mass. Her grandfather was Moody Spofford, 1744-1828, a justice in Georgetown, Mass., a representative to the General Court of Massachusetts for several successive terms, and a Lieutenant in the Revolutionary War. The great-grandfather of Mrs. Spofford was Colonel Daniel Spofford, who married Judith Follansbee, daughter of Francis and Judith (Moody) Follansbee, of Newbury, Mass. He was Colonel of the Seventh Regiment, Essex County, and led his regiment to Lexington and to Cambridge at the time of the battle of Bunker Hill He was a representative of the General Court in 1776 and a member of the Constitutional Convention, in 1780. The great-great-grandfather of Mrs Spofford was Captain John Spofford, who was born in 1678, a brother of Jonathan Spofford, the great-grand-father of Paul Spofford. By his wife Sarah, Paul Spofford had two children The youngest child, a daughter, Mary Louisa, died in infancy. By his second wife, Susan B Spring, daughter of the Reverend Gardiner Spring, he had five children, four sons and a daughter.

Mr Paul Nelson Spofford is the only son of Paul Spofford and his first wife. He is a member of the Union and Union League clubs, the American Geographical, Botanical, and New York Historical societies, the Society of Colonial Wars, and other organizations. When the engineer department in the militia of this State was established, he was appointed by Governor Young Engineer-in-Chief, with the rank of Brigadier-General. He organized the department and continued at its head, on the staff of Governor Hamilton Fish Since then, Mr. Spofford has been much occupied with his own affairs and those of his father's estate He is a bachelor, and resides at Hunt s Point, New York City, with his brother, Joseph L. Spofford, who married Cecilia, daughter of Lieutenant-Colonel Haws, and who has one son, Paul Cecil Spofford The other surviving brother, Edward Clarence Spofford, resides on his estate at Tarrytown, N. Y.

MYLES STANDISH

ONE of the most picturesque figures in New England's early Colonial history was Miles, or Myles, Standish, the Pilgrim soldier. His fame has 'not been excelled by any of his associates in the Plymouth Colony, and Longfellow has preserved his memory in that famous poem, "The Courtship of Miles Standish" He was the ancestor in the ninth generation of the gentleman whose name is at the head of this article He came of an ancient English family of knightly rank, dating back before 1200, the records being legible to Thurston de Standish, in 1221. Myles Standish was born in 1584, in Lancashire, England, and was the rightful heir of the Standish Hall estates in that county One of his ancestors, "the Squier of Kynges, called John Standysshhe," as Froisart has it, slew Watt Tyler in the time of Richard II.

Inheriting the profession of arms, Myles Standish accepted a commission from Queen Elizabeth in aid of the Dutch and passed much time in the Low Countries He joined the Pilgrims, in Leyden, and came to this country in the Mayflower, in 1620. With him, came his wife, Rose, who died the same year He later married his cousin, Barbara Standish, from whom the family in this country is descended His military skill and bravery made him a leading man of the Plymouth Colony. He was one of the first signers of the "Compact," the "Germ of the American Constitution" He was the champion of the settlement, defending it against the Indians.

In 1625, he revisited England as a representative of the Colony, returning the next year with supplies. After that, he settled in Duxbury, to which place he gave the name of the English home of his race, and for the remainder of his life was one of the Governor's Council and a magistrate. In 1649, he was chosen General-in-Chief of all the companies in the Colony, and in 1653, at the breaking out of the hostilities between England and Holland, he was again honored with the chief command. He died in 1656, "and the Pilgrims mourned for him as one who had ever been their stay in the time of peril, their support in more peaceful and prosperous times and their reliable counselor under any and all circumstances." A granite monument, surmounted by his statue, is erected to his memory, on Captain's Hill, Duxbury, dedicated to "The First Commissioned Military Officer of New England." His grave has been recently identified and appropriately marked.

Alexander Standish, the oldest son of Myles Standish, was a freeman of Duxbury, in 1648, the third clerk of the town, 1695-1700. He died in 1702. There is a special romantic interest attached to his first marriage, for his wife, Sarah Alden, was the daughter of John Alden, who was his father's friend and who, according to tradition, was commissioned to negotiate a marriage by Captain Standish with Priscilla Mullins, a transaction that ended in Alden marrying her himself In the ensuing generations, the ancestors of Mr Myles Standish were Ebenezer Standish, of Plympton, Mass, 1672-1759, son of Alexander and his wife, Hannah Sturtevant; Zachariah Standish, of Plympton, 1698-1770, and his wife, Abigail Whitman; Ebenezer Standish, 1721-1747, and wife, Averick Churchill; Shadrack Standish, of Plympton, 1745-1837, and his wife, Mary Churchill, Levi Standish, of Westport, Mass., 1779-1843, and his wife, Lucy Randall; John Avery Standish, of New Bedford, Mass, 1806-1865, and his wife, Emmeline, daughter of Joseph Bourne. Shadrack Standish was a soldier in the War of the Revolution. He was a member of Captain Thomas Sampson's company that formed part of Colonel Lothrop's regiment, and saw service in 1777 and 1781, when the British threatened a descent on Rhode Island.

Mr Myles Standish was born in 1847, being the youngest and only surviving son of the late John Avery Standish, of New Bedford, Mass. He was educated at the Friends Academy, in New Bedford, and the Massachusetts Institute of Technology. He has been a resident of this city for a number of years, and married the youngest daughter of the late James F D. Lanier, of New York. He is a member of the Century, Metropolitan, City and Lawyers' clubs, the Society of Colonial Wars, and the New England and American Geographical Societies. His residence is in Fifth Avenue, near Washington Square.

JOHN STANTON

HISTORY will record how much the development of the material prosperity of the United States during the present century should be credited to those of our citizens who, born in foreign lands, have come to this country and taken an energetic part in opening up new fields of enterprise, and in increasing the wealth of the country Prominent among those who have been thus engaged will stand Mr John Stanton and his father, who preceded him in the line of business in which he has now been engaged for nearly half a century The father of Mr Stanton was a native of England. He belonged to an old family and had been prosperous in business before he came to this country Educated as a mining engineer, he was a considerable owner of coal properties in his native 'and and had accumulated a substantial capital In 1835, looking to the New World for better opportunities for investment and enterprise, he came to this country For a short time he lived in New York, but soon after removed to Pottsville, Pa , where he invested largely in coal mines Afterwards he disposed of his interests in Pennsylvania and became interested in the iron mines near Dover, N J

Mr. John Stanton was born in Bristol, England, February 25th, 1830, and as a lad accompanied his father when the latter removed to this country He received his education in Pennsylvania, principally under the direction of his father, its tendency being chiefly of a scientific character. When, in 1846, his father engaged in iron mining in New Jersey, the son, although only sixteen years of age, was fully qualified to take an active part in the direction of mining operations About 1852, he engaged in copper mining and for the next nine or ten years most of his time was devoted to the development of the copper deposits in Maryland, Virginia and Tennessee. The breaking out of the Civil War put an end to his business operations in that section of the country, and he lost heavily in the troubles incident to the time through the confiscation of his properties by the Confederate Government.

Thereupon Mr. Stanton turned his attention to the copper mines of the Lake Superior district In a short time, he established business relations with several of the leading mining companies of that region, and became one of the most successful copper mine operators in the United States He owns large interests in several important mines and is active, not alone in the material development of the property, but as well in the management of the financial affairs of the corporations by which they are owned. He is president of the Atlantic Mining Company, the Central Mining Company, the Allouez Mining Company and the Wolverine Copper Mining Company In addition to his large mining interests in the Lake Superior region, he is also connected with mining affairs in Colorado and Arizona. Believing also in the ultimate value of the mineral deposits of the South, he has been one of the pioneers in the development of mining in that section of the country, and has done much to promote its industrial progress

One of the founders and most enthusiastic supporters of the New York Mining Stock Exchange, Mr Stanton was the first president of the Exchange in 1876, and upon the expiration of his term of service was elected to the treasurership. He is a member of the American Institute of Mining Engineers, the American Society of Mechanical Engineers and the North of England Institute of Mining and Mechanical Engineers His wife was Elizabeth Romaine McMillan His residence is in West Twenty-third Street, in old Chelsea Village He is a member of the Lawyers', Union League, Engineers' and Lotos clubs, the Downtown Association and the American Geographical Society, and of the Metropolitan Museum of Art and the American Museum of Natural History His family consists of three children John R Stanton, the elder son, is engaged in business with his father, being treasurer of the Wolverine Copper Mining Company He has been a member of the Seventh Regiment and belongs to the Engineers' and Seventh Regiment Veteran clubs, and the Sons of the Revolution The younger son, Frank McMillan Stanton, is a mining and mechanical engineer and a graduate of Columbia College School of Mines. The only daughter of the family is Helen Louise Stanton

FREDERICK AUGUSTUS STARRING

ESCENDED in the fifth generation from Nicholas Starring, or Starin, General Frederick Augustus Starring represents one of the most important branches of this interesting family, of which no less than forty-three representatives are found on the muster rolls of the Ulster and Tryon County regiments in the Revolutionary War, while members of it also served in the French and Indian wars. Nicholas Staring came to this country from Holland in 1696, and settled in Albany, and afterwards in German Flats, on the Mohawk River. Philip Frederick Adam Staring was the youngest son of the pioneer. He was born at German Flats, N. Y., in 1715, and married first, in 1743, Elizabeth Evertson, and second, Elizabeth Simmons, of German Flats.

Frederick Adam Starring, 1762-1854, was the youngest son of his father's first marriage. He lived in the counties of Montgomery and Herkimer, and in early life was a teacher, becoming in later years a merchant. He was a prominent member of the Dutch Reformed Church at Stone Arabia, N. Y., one of the oldest in the Mohawk Valley. Sylvanus Seaman Starring, the third son of Frederick Adam Starring, was the father of the gentleman whose name heads this sketch. He was born in Herkimer County in 1807, and died at St. Charles, Ill., in 1862. Receiving a good education, he became a civil engineer. He removed to Buffalo in 1830, and became successful in his profession and a prosperous man of affairs. He took a prominent part in the Papineau Rebellion in Canada in 1836, and in that connection obtained the title of Captain, being one of the party which boarded the steamboat Caroline, when that vessel was set on fire and sent adrift over Niagara Falls. The first wife of Sylvanus Seaman Starring was Adaline Morton Williams, who was born at Fredonia, N. Y., in 1810. Her father, William Williams, was one of the founders of Fredonia, N. Y. Two of her brothers were killed in the battle on Lake Erie.

General Frederick Augustus Starring is the eldest son of Sylvanus Seaman Starring. He was born at Buffalo, May 24th, 1834. Graduated from the High School of Buffalo in 1851, he afterwards studied at Harvard College and also in Paris. He became a civil engineer on the Illinois Central Railroad, and in 1856 located the boundary line between Arkansas, Texas and the Indian Territory. When the Civil War began, he at once volunteered, and was in the first battle of Bull Run, and was made Major of the Forty-Sixth Illinois Infantry in the summer of 1861, and in the autumn Major of artillery. In 1862, he was selected as Colonel of the First Chicago Board of Trade Regiment, Seventy-Second Illinois Infantry, was Provost Marshal, General of the Department of the Gulf, 1864-66, and made Brigadier-General for gallant and meritorious services in 1865. He was in all the campaigns in the Mississippi Valley, and took part in the actions of Fort Donaldson, Fort Henry and Island Number Ten, Fort Pillow, the Yazoo Pass Expedition and the siege and campaign of Vicksburg, Grand Gulf, Raymond, Jackson, Champion Hills, Big Black, etc, and that against Mobile, as well as other operations, and was assigned by General Grant to the surrender of arms from the Confederates at the fall of Vicksburg. He received the Vicksburg medal of honor, the MacPherson badge and other decorations.

After the war, General Starring traveled extensively in Europe, and, returning home, assisted in organizing the Grand Army of the Republic, of which he was the first Inspector-General, in 1869. He designed the Badge and Ritual and has Badge No. 1. From 1869 to 1883, he was engaged in the public service, one of his most conspicuous duties being that of agent to examine consular and diplomatic affairs in Europe, to which position he was appointed in July, 1869. He has traveled extensively in all parts of the world. He married, in 1889, Louise Perle (Whitehouse) Evans. General Starring's residence is in Fifth Avenue. He belongs to the Union League, Manhattan, United Service and New York Yacht clubs, the Military Order of the Loyal Legion and the Army and Navy Club, of Washington. The Starring arms, borne by their ancestors in Guilderland, Holland, are: Azure, an eight-pointed star, or., in an annulet of the same. Crest, an eight-pointed star, or

EDWIN AUGUSTUS STEVENS

FOR three generations Castle Point, Hoboken, has been the home of a family foremost in all that has made New York preeminent John Stevens, the first of the name to come to this country, was a native of Middlesex County, England He arrived in New York in 1699, and was a law officer of the Crown His wife was Ann Campbell, daughter of John Campbell, one of the original proprietors of New Jersey, and related to the Duke of Argyle

John Stevens, second of the name, was the eldest son of his father's family He was born in Perth Amboy, N J , and early in life was in mercantile business, afterwards having interests in the Rocky Hill copper mine, and being engaged in foreign trade He was paymaster of the Old Blues Regiment, of New Jersey, an Indian commissioner in 1758, a member of the King's Council in 1762, vice-president and afterwards president of the Board of Proprietors of East New Jersey, and president of the Convention of New Jersey in 1787. He died in 1792 His wife was Elizabeth Alexander, a daughter of James Alexander, whose wife was a granddaughter of Johannes de Peyster, and whose son was the Revolutionary hero, General William Alexander, Lord Stirling.

John Stevens, third of the name, 1749-1838, was graduated, in 1768, from Kings College, and developed a genius for mechanical invention. One of his chief titles to fame is his labors for the introduction of steam navigation, in which work he was intimately associated with Robert Fulton and Chancellor Livingston. His wife, whom he married in 1738, was Rachel Cox, daughter of John Cox, of Bloomsburg, N J , one of the founders of Hoboken He left a family of thirteen children, five of whom were sons. During the latter part of his life he lived on the Castle Point estate, which he acquired in 1784.

Three of the sons of John Stevens were famous as engineers, or in the transportation business, Robert L , James H , and Edwin A. Stevens Another son, John C. Stevens, was a prominent yachtsman The other son, Richard Stevens, died young Edwin Augustus Stevens, who was born in 1795, through inheritance and by purchase from his brothers, acquired the entire Castle Point property He was distinguished for his benefactions, and established and endowed the Stevens Institute of Technology in Hoboken He died in 1868, leaving a widow and eight children.

Mr Edwin Augustus Stevens, the present head of this family, was born in Philadelphia, March 14th, 1858, and graduated from Princeton College in 1879. He is president of the Hoboken Land and Improvement Company, and is actively interested in many other business enterprises and in public affairs He has been park commissioner, tax commissioner, president of the Hoboken Ferry Company, and of the Hackensack Water Company, a director in several banks, and a trustee of the Stevens Institute Prominent in State and national politics, he has been a member of the Democratic State Committee of New Jersey, and was Democratic Presidential elector in 1888 and in 1892. In military affairs he has been Adjutant of the Ninth Regiment, N G N J , an aide on the Governor's staff, and Colonel of the Second Regiment He is a member of the Society of Mechanical Engineers, an associate of the Association of Naval Architects and Marine Engineers, and a member of many other societies and clubs, including the University and Lawyers' clubs, of New York, and the German and Columbia clubs, of Hoboken. He married Emily C. Lewis, and lives at Castle Point

The elder son of this family, John Stevens, born in 1856, married Mary McGuire, and died a few years ago. The third son, Robert Livingston Stevens, was born in 1862, graduated from Columbia College in 1887, and married Mary Whitney The fourth son, Charles Albert Stevens, was born in 1863, graduated from Columbia College in 1887, and married Mary M. Brady The youngest son, Richard Stevens, born in 1865, graduated from Columbia College in 1890, and married Elizabeth Stevens The eldest daughter, Caroline Bayard Stevens, who was born in 1859, married Archibald Alexander, who is not now living. The other daughter is Julia Augusta Stevens The widowed mother of the family, Mrs. Edwin A. Stevens, Sr , is still living at Castle Point

GEORGE THOMAS STEVENS, M. D

IN the first records of Connecticut, John Stevens's name appears as one of the Colonists who, under the lead of the Reverend John Davenport, came to New Haven in 1639. John Stevens, who was of a Devonshire family, joined, soon after his arrival in America, in the settlement of the town of Guilford, Conn, where he gained prominence and influence His son, William Stevens, lineal ancestor of the subject of this article, was the first settler of Killingworth, Conn One of his descendants, at the period of the American Revolution, was Elnathan Stevens, Dr. Stevens's paternal grandfather, who served in the Continental Army throughout the struggle A son of this patriot was the Reverend Chauncey Coe Stevens, who became a noted minister in the Congregational Church, and who, leaving his native Connecticut after his ordination, passed fifty years in Essex County, of this State, during forty of which he was pastor of the Second Church at Crown Point.

Dr. George Thomas Stevens was born in Essex County, N Y, in 1832, and was the son of the Reverend Chauncey Coe Stevens and his wife, Lucinda Hoadley Stevens Dr Stevens's first maternal ancestor in America was John Hoadley, also of the New Haven Colony, and one of those who went to Guilford, where he was one of "the seven pillars" in the church. Returning to England, he became Chaplain to Oliver Cromwell. One of his sons was Benjamin Hoadley, the famous liberal Bishop of Winchester William Hoadley, a son of John, who remained in this country, was an original settler at Saybrook, and is the direct ancestor of Dr. Stevens The maternal grandfather of Dr. Stevens, Samuel Hoadley, was, like Elnathan Stevens, a soldier in the Army of the Revolution Dr Stevens received the degree of Doctor of Philosophy from Union College. He graduated in medicine in 1857 at the Castleton Medical College, Vt., and has been active in professional practice since that time. At the outbreak of the Civil War, he was commissioned Surgeon of the Seventy-seventh New York Volunteers, and took part in all the campaigns of the Army of the Potomac, becoming operating Surgeon to his brigade and for a time Medical Inspector of the Sixth Corps At the conclusion of the war, he was elected Professor of Physiology and of Diseases of the Eye and Ear in the Medical College of Albany, N. Y. In 1880, Dr Stevens removed to New York, where he has since continued in practice. He is the author of many medical works, more particularly of several upon subjects relating to the eye, which are well known in his profession, and he has devised a number of important optical, surgical and scientific instruments, which are in use both in America and in Europe Among other works from his pen are Three Years in the Sixth Corps, The Flora of the Adirondacks, and Through North Wales by Train and Coach.

In 1861, Dr. Stevens married Harriet W., daughter of William L Wadhams, of Wadhams Mills, N Y, and his wife, Emeline Cole Wadhams Mrs Stevens's family is of Somersetshire extraction, the founder of Wadham College, Oxford, having been of it John Wadhams, who was an original settler of Weathersfield, Conn, in 1650, was the American ancestor. Luman Wadhams, a Major in the United States Army, was Mrs Stevens's grandfather He served at the battle of Plattsburg, in the War of 1812, and was officially complimented for his conduct He subsequently became a Brigadier General of State troops and was a man of much prominence. The late Reverend Dr. Edgar P. Wadhams, Bishop of Ogdensburg, was Mrs. Stevens's uncle, while among her ancestors was Governor Leete, of Connecticut.

The two children of Dr and Mrs. Stevens are, Frances Virginia, now the wife of Dr. George Trumbull Ladd, Professor of Philosophy in Yale University, and Dr Charles Wadhams Stevens, a graduate of Princeton and of the College of Physicians and Surgeons, who is a practicing physician in the city. In their frequent visits abroad, Dr. and Mrs Stevens have met and enjoyed social relations with many of the most distinguished persons in social and scientific circles, and have entertained many European visitors in the United States Dr. Stevens is a member of a number of clubs and societies in New York, and of scientific bodies.

JOHN AIKMAN STEWART

A S the name would indicate, the subject of this sketch comes of Scottish stock. His father, John Stewart, was a native of the Hebrides, and emigrated from Stornoway to this country in 1815, and although a man of moderate circumstances, soon established himself successfully in business and became a citizen of prominence. For many years he was one of the assessors for the old Twelfth and Sixteenth Wards, and subsequently became Receiver of Taxes of the City of New York. In 1817, he married Mary Aikman, who was also a member of a Scottish family. He died in 1849 at the age of fifty-eight, leaving a large family of children.

The first son of John Stewart was Mr. John Aikman Stewart, who was born in Fulton Street, New York, August 22d, 1822. His father had attained comfortable circumstances while he was growing up, and he, in consequence, secured a liberal education. After his preparatory schooling was over, he entered Columbia College, from which institution he was graduated in the literary and scientific course in 1840. Two years after graduation, when he was only twenty years of age, the clerkship of the Board of Education of this city was offered to him, and he held that position until 1850, when he resigned his place in the Board of Education to become the actuary of the United States Life Insurance Company.

In 1853, Mr. Stewart, with other business men, undertook the organization of the United States Trust Company, and secured its charter from the Legislature. He became the first secretary of the corporation, with which he has been connected ever since, succeeding to the presidency in 1865, when its president, Joseph Lawrence, resigned on account of ill health and advancing years. As president of the United States Trust Company, Mr Stewart occupies an extremely influential position. The institution is the largest, as well as one of the oldest, trust companies in the country, and under his management has become an important factor in the New York financial world. Mr. Stewart has other weighty financial responsibilities in addition to the presidency of the United States Trust Company. He is a director in the Equitable Life Assurance Society, the Merchants' National Bank, the Greenwich Savings Bank, the Liverpool and London and Globe Insurance Company and the Bank of New Amsterdam.

For about a year, Mr. Stewart held public office, when, in 1864, at the urgent invitation of President Lincoln and the Honorable William Pitt Fessenden, Secretary of the Treasury, he became Assistant Treasurer of the United States at New York. The office had been tendered to him before, but was declined, and he finally accepted it only from a sense of patriotic duty to his country, then distracted by Civil War. In his early life, Mr. Stewart was a Democrat, but on the issues of 1861 he supported President Lincoln, and has been a Republican in his political views from that time forward.

Feeling a deep interest in religious and charitable work, Mr. Stewart gives considerable time to organizations for such objects, being a director of the New York Eye and Ear Infirmary, a trustee of the John F. Slater fund for the industrial education of the negroes of the South, a trustee of the Brick Presbyterian Church, of which the Reverend Henry van Dyke is pastor, and one of the trustees of Princeton University. Mr Stewart married, in 1845, Sarah Youle Johnson, of New York. His second wife, whom he married in 1894, was Mary O. Capron, daughter of Francis B. Capron, of Baltimore. He has had four children, the two now living being a son, John A Stewart, Jr., who is engaged in the real estate business in this city, and married Anne Thomas, and a daughter, Emily Stewart, who is the wife of Robert Waller, Jr., a member of the New York Stock Exchange. Mr Stewart's elder son, now deceased, was William A Walker Stewart, a prominent member of the New York bar, and who married a daughter of William Gray, of Boston. At his death, he left four children, Mary, Frances V, Francis G, and William A. Walker Stewart. The deceased daughter of Mr. John A Stewart was Mary, who married George St John Sheffield. Mr. Stewart is a member of the Metropolitan, Union League and Riding clubs.

WILLIAM RHINELANDER STEWART

SCOTCH and Huguenot families of distinction are the paternal ancestors of this gentleman His father, the late Lispenard Stewart, was a descendant of Robert Stewart, who came to New York before the Revolution, and whose grandson, Alexander L. Stewart, married Sarah Lispenard, daughter of Captain Anthony Lispenard and his wife, Sarah Barclay The Huguenot family of Lispenard came to America after the revocation of the Edict of Nantes In the charter of Trinity Church, granted by William III , in 1693, is the name of David Lispenard Other bearers of the name held important positions in the early history of the city, among them Leonard Lispenard, born in 1716, who was a delegate to the Stamp Act Congress in 1765. By his marriage with Alice Rutgers, daughter of Anthony Rutgers, he acquired an extensive property on the west side of the city, long known as the Lispenard estate Captain Anthony Lispenard, father of Sarah (Lispenard) Stewart, was the younger son of Leonard Lispenard.

Lispenard Stewart, the elder, was the son of Alexander L Stewart. He was born in New York, and died in 1867 He was twice married, his first wife being Louisa Stephania Salles. After her death, he espoused Mary Rogers Rhinelander, who survived until 1893 She was a daughter of William Christopher Rhinelander. The three children of this marriage are William Rhinelander and Lispenard Stewart and Mary R. Stewart, the wife of Frank S. Witherbee By his first marriage, Lispenard Stewart had two daughters, Louisa Stephania, who married John B. Trevor, and Sarah Lispenard, who married Frederick Graham Lee.

Mr. William Rhinelander Stewart, the head of the family, was born in New York, December 3d, 1852. Educated by tutors, and at the Charlier's and Anthon's schools, he graduated from the Law School of Columbia College in 1873 Admitted to the bar, he was with a leading law firm for some years, and now gives attention to the management of the family estates In 1879, he married Annie M , daughter of the late John A Armstrong, of Baltimore, the surviving children of this marriage being a daughter, Anita, and a son, William Rhinelander Stewart, Jr.

Representing families with extensive interests in New York, Mr Stewart takes an active part in all public movements to advance the municipal interests He joined Company K of the Seventh Regiment in 1871, and served eight years in that command In 1882, Governor Cornell appointed him a member of the State Board of Charities, to which office he was reappointed by Governors Flower and Black, and on the death of the Honorable Oscar Craig, in 1894, was unanimously elected to succeed him as president of the board During most of his long service on the board, Mr Stewart has been chairman of the Committee on Reformatories, and on Schools for the Deaf, and has annually visited all parts of the State to inspect institutions Many of the reports of the different committees of this board are from his pen His duties as president of the board require the gratuitous devotion of fully one-half his time Mr. Stewart was also president of the Twenty-fifth National Conference of Charities and Corrections For the Centennial of Washington's Inauguration, in 1889, he originated the idea of spanning Fifth Avenue, at Washington Square, with a triumphal arch, and carried it to completion He was treasurer of the committee which erected the present permanent arch. Mr Stewart is a vestryman of Grace Church and its treasurer since 1893 He is a trustee of the Greenwich Savings Bank, and a member of the Chamber of Commerce, and belongs to the Union, Metropolitan, Century and many other clubs, and the Downtown Association, being secretary of the latter.

Lispenard Stewart, the second son of Lispenard Stewart, Sr., was born in Westchester County in 1855 He was graduated from Yale College in 1876, and from the Columbia College Law School in 1878 He has been active in politics, and in 1889–90 was a member of the State Senate, a Presidential elector in 1888, and a delegate to the Republican National Convention in 1896. Since 1895, he has been president of the State Prison Commission, and is identified with several philanthropic organizations He is a member of the Union, Metropolitan. University and Union League clubs, and resides at 6 Fifth Avenue, having a summer home in Newport

JAMES STILLMAN

GEORGE STILLMAN, the first American ancestor of Mr James Stillman, was born in London, England, in 1654, and came to Hadley, Mass, afterwards removing to Wethersfield, Conn While living in Hadley, he was a selectman in 1696, and a deputy to the General Court of Massachusetts in 1698 In Wethersfield he was a selectman in 1708, and left an estate valued at nearly three thousand pounds, a large sum at that time. His wife, whom he married in 1685, was Rebecca Smith, daughter of Deacon Philip Smith, one of the first settlers of Hadley, in the company led by Governor Webster. Nathaniel Stillman, the son of George Stillman, was born in 1691, and married Anna Southmayd, daughter of William Southmayd, and had for his second wife Sarah Allyn, daughter of Captain Joseph Allyn His son, Nathaniel Stillman, 1791-1811, married Mehitable Deming, daughter of David Deming, of Wethersfield In the next generation, Nathaniel Stillman, born in 1752, married Martha Hanmer. Their son, Francis Stillman, 1785-1838, married Harriet Robbins, and their son, Charles Stillman, was the father of Mr James Stillman All the ancestors of Mr Stillman were public-spirited men His four great-grandfathers served in the Continental Army, two of them as officers. Charles Stillman was a successful shipping merchant, being one of the first financiers of New York interested in developing the Southern section of the country. He married Elizabeth Pamela Goodrich, daughter of Joshua Goodrich and Clarissa Francis.

The American ancestor of the Goodrich family was William Goodrich, who, born in England, near Bury St. Edmunds, came to New England with his brother, John Goodrich He was a freeman of Connecticut in 1656, and a deputy from Wethersfield to the General Court in 1662 In 1663, he was an ensign of the militia, and died in 1676. In 1648, he married Sarah Marvin, daughter of Matthew Marvin, of Hartford, and his wife, Elizabeth William Goodrich, his son, married Grace Riley, and their son, Lieutenant Joseph Goodrich, who married Mehitable Goodwin, daughter of Nathaniel Goodwin, was the great-great-grandfather of Elizabeth Pamela Goodrich Their son was Nathaniel Goodrich He married Martha Deming, his son, Isaac Goodrich, who married Elizabeth Raymond, was Mr James Stillman's great-grandfather.

Mr James Stillman was born in Brownsville, Tex, June 9th, 1850 His parents temporarily resided there at the time, while his father was engaged in the management of important business interests Returning from the South to Hartford, Conn, Mr Stillman was brought up in that city, and was educated principally at Churchill's school, in Sing Sing, N. Y. When he had attained his majority, in 1871, he entered the firm of Smith, Woodward & Stillman, cotton merchants of New York, and has maintained an unbroken connection with the house down to the present time, becoming a partner in 1873 of the firm of Woodward & Stillman, which succeeded the earlier establishment, and having been its head for many years. Aside from his connection with mercantile affairs, he has been identified with large financial interests, and is connected with several banks and railroad companies He is president of the National City Bank, and a director of the United States Trust Company, the Farmers' Loan & Trust Company, the New York Security & Trust Company, the Hanover National Bank, the Delaware, Lackawanna & Western Railroad, the Chicago & Northwestern Railroad, the Northern Pacific Railway, the Consolidated Gas Company, and the Queen Insurance Company

Mr. Stillman married Sarah Elizabeth Rumrill, their five children being Elsie, who married William G Rockefeller, son of William Rockefeller, James A, Isabel Goodrich, Charles Chauncey, and Ernest Goodrich Stillman The city residence of Mr. and Mrs Stillman is in East Fortieth Street, and they also have a summer home, Oaklawn, in Newport Mr Stillman is a member of the Chamber of Commerce and the Cotton Exchange His clubs include the Century, Metropolitan, Union, Union League, Reform, New York Yacht, Seawanhaka-Corinthian Yacht, Eastern Yacht, St Augustine Yacht, Jekyl Island, Storm King, Tuxedo, Riding and Lawyers, while he also belongs to the New York Historical Society and the Metropolitan Club, of Washington

ANSON PHELPS STOKES

HE family of which Mr. Anson Phelps Stokes is the prominent representative in the present generation was of Norman origin, a branch of the ancient and illustrious house of Montespedon. Several of its members went to England from Normandy soon after the Conquest, and there obtained large landed possessions, and were people of high standing. Thomas Stokes, the American emigrant, was a son of William Stokes, of London, and was born in that city in 1765. His wife was Elizabeth Ann Boulter, daughter of James Boulter, of Lowestoff, Wales. He came to New York in 1798, and was one of the most distinguished men of that generation in philanthropic and religious work. Before coming to this country he was a merchant of considerable wealth, and one of the founders of the London Missionary Society. In this country he was one of the founders of the American Bible Society, the New York Peace Society and the American Tract Society.

James Stokes, 1804-1881, father of Mr Anson Phelps Stokes, was the son of Thomas Stokes. Early in life he was engaged in business with his father, but later became a member of the metal importing firm of Phelps, Dodge & Co. After remaining in this business connection for about forty years, he assisted in establishing the banking house of Phelps, Stokes & Co. Interested in charitable and religious institutions, he contributed generously to their support, and was associated with Peter Cooper and others in the development of the public school system.

James Stokes married Caroline Phelps, daughter of Anson G. Phelps, in 1837. Anson G. Phelps, 1781-1853, was directly descended in the sixth generation from George Phelps, the pioneer, who was one of the first settlers of Windsor, Conn. Mr. Phelps also had descent from the Watson, Griswold, Woodbridge, Wyllys, Haynes, Dudley Egleston and other great Colonial families. Among his most distinguished ancestors were three Colonial Governors, John Haynes, Thomas Dudley and George Wyllys. His father was Lieutenant Thomas Phelps, who served in the Continental Army under Generals Washington, Putnam, Greene and others   Seven children of James Stokes and his wife, Caroline Phelps, survived their parents: Anson Phelps, James, Jr., Thomas, William E. Dodge, Olivia Egleston Phelps, Dora, wife of Henry Dale, and Caroline Phelps Stokes.

Mr. Anson Phelps Stokes, the eldest son of this family, was born in New York, was a partner in Phelps, Dodge & Co., and afterwards in the banking business of Phelps, Stokes & Co., with his father. In late years, he has been principally occupied in looking after his real estate and other investments. He married Helen L. Phelps, daughter of Isaac Newton Phelps, who was descended in the sixth generation from George Phelps, of Windsor, the ancestor of her husband's mother. Her father, who was born in 1802, was a leading banker of New York. His parents were Joseph Phelps and Elizabeth Sadd, and his great-grandparents, Captain Joseph Phelps and Abigail Bissel, daughter of Thomas Bissel, of Connecticut. The mother of Mrs. Stokes was Sarah Maria, daughter of Sylvester and Sarah (King) Lusk, both the Lusk and King families being among the earliest settlers of Connecticut.

The city residence of the family is in Madison Avenue, and their country place is Shadow Brook, near Lenox. They have four sons and five daughters, I N. Phelps, J. G. Phelps, of Yale, 1892; Anson Phelps, Jr., of Yale, 1896; Harold M. Phelps, Sarah Phelps, wife of Baron Halkett; Helen Olivia Phelps, Ethel V. Phelps, wife of John Sherman Hoyt; Caroline M. Phelps, and Mildred Phelps. Mr. Stokes is a member of the Tuxedo, Metropolitan, Knickerbocker, Union League, City, Lawyers', Reform, New York Yacht, Seawanhaka-Corinthian Yacht, Riding, City and Church clubs, the Century Association, the National Academy of Design and the Society of Colonial Wars, and is a patron of the Metropolitan Museum of Art, and the American Museum of Natural History. He was twice vice-president of the New York Yacht Club and the first president of the Reform Club. He is the author of Joint-Metallism, of which many editions have been published.

ANDROS BOYDEN STONE

EARLY in the seventeenth century, the name of Stone appears in Massachusetts Its representative, Simon Stone, settled in Cambridge in 1635. The late Andros Boyden Stone was born in 1824 at Charlton, Mass , being the youngest son of Amasa Stone and seventh in descent from his Puritan ancestor   Successful energy applied to the concerns of life is a common possession of New Englanders The career of Andros B Stone presents, however, features of higher interest, from the predominance of intellectual qualities which made him a leader in the applications of science to industry and in the personal qualities which found expression in a wide and practical sympathy.

Being one of a large family, his educational advantages were slight, and at the age of sixteen he was apprenticed to an elder brother to learn carpentering. An opportunity for advancement, however, soon presented itself His eldest sister married William Howe, the patentee of the Howe truss, which revolutionized bridge building. Of the five Stone brothers, three had already become bridge builders, when, at the early age of eighteen years, Andros was made superintendent for his brother-in-law, Mr Howe, and his brother, Amasa Stone; and, notwithstanding his exacting duties, used every spare moment to supplement his education Soon after his majority, Mr Stone formed a partnership and built bridges in the New England States

Then, attracted by the great West, he formed another partnership with his brother-in-law, the late Lucius B Boomer, and in 1852 removed to Chicago In the then undeveloped country, these young men attained a position which could justly be called phenomenal. Mr. Stone was at the head of the firm which secured the Howe patent rights for the States of Illinois, Iowa, Wisconsin and Missouri, where railroad building had assumed great activity. Results proved them equal to their opportunity, as they built the first bridge across the Mississippi River at Rock Island, the longest span of a wooden bridge up to that time, as well as the first bridge across the Illinois River, with the largest revolving draw then known, besides completing other important contracts In addition to this business the firm manufactured cars in Chicago

In 1858, Mr Stone removed to Cleveland, O , and gave his attention to iron manufacturing He identified himself with a small mill at Newburg, near Cleveland, and giving his entire energy to the scientific features of this industry, he soon became master of the profession. The growth of the business necessitated the formation, in 1863, of the Cleveland Rolling Mill Company, with Mr Stone as president, which office he filled for fifteen years, and then became vice-president. Constantly creating new departments and introducing new processes, the industry grew under his administration to be the largest enterprise in Cleveland

The crowning achievement of Mr Stone's business life was the introduction of the Bessemer steel process in America. He was greatly interested in the new methods of Sir Henry Bessemer, and visited Europe twice to thoroughly investigate the subject. This resulted in the construction of a new steel plant by his company, skilled workmen being also imported, and in 1869 steel rails were first produced in this country from American ore at Cleveland, and sold at one hundred and sixty dollars a ton This was the foundation of one of the leading industries in the United States, and the entire credit for this epoch-making step is due to Mr Stone

It was during these busy years in Cleveland that our country was going through its struggle to preserve the Union, which no one more earnestly supported than Mr Stone His modest use of large opportunities was conspicuous in all relations of life. A prominent member of St Paul's Church, Cleveland, he gave his time to mission work, to the support of which he was also a generous contributor His rare business capacity naturally brought him prominent positions in various enterprises He was first president of the American Iron and Steel Association, and throughout his life was an earnest advocate of the protective policy, and wrote able articles upon the subject Another notable characteristic of Mr Stone was the friendship he inspired in all who came in contact with him, whether in business or socially. Not only was his career marked by lofty integrity, but by scrupulous consideration of the rights of others and an extreme modesty where his own ability was concerned   Among the many tributes by prominent men to him, none was more just than that of his friend, President Garfield, soon after the Bessemer steel experiment had succeeded.   President Garfield said, that the foremost citizens were the scientific men of industrial life "like my friend, Mr A B Stone, who," he added, "have nothing to start with but a clear inheritance, the power of self-denial, industry, capacity, in short all New England in their veins   He saw the significance of the great Bessemer idea, made an earnest study of it in Europe and has, through this great industry, helped more than any man I know to determine the prosperity of whole communities   Mr Stone is what I call a first-rate type of American citizen, the kind we must multiply if we do not want this tremendous experiment to go to pieces "

In 1871, Mr. Stone removed to New York, making his home on Murray Hill   He was married early in life to the daughter of the Reverend J. B. Boomer, of Worcester, Mass., a lady whose family on both sides occupied prominent positions, having in three generations produced several distinguished clergymen of Worcester County, and who by birth and training was fitted to fill the responsible place she has always held in ministries for the good of others.   From early life, Mrs. Stone has used her pen with ability, publishing books as well as essays, but she has always disclaimed ambition as a writer except for benevolent work, asserting that woman's noblest opportunity in life was to help others through the influences of home life, her success in such directions being one which will endure in many grateful memories   In the thirteen years of their residence in Cleveland, Mr. and Mrs Stone's home in Euclid Avenue was the centre around which the literary, musical and artistic circles of that city gathered

The time of Mr and Mrs. Stone's early residence in New York was an epoch of brilliant luminaries in the literary world of our city.   Besides William Cullen Bryant, E. C. Stedman, Professor Youmans, and R H Stoddard, able writers like Dr. Holland, Bayard Taylor, John Hay, Noah Brooks, Whitelaw Reid, Bret Harte, W D Howells, Thomas W. Knox and others became residents here   Mr Hay married a niece of Mr Stone and was their intimate acquaintance in Paris   Naturally, the doors of their home were open wide to him and his talented coworkers, so that it was not long before the Stone house, 13 East Thirty-sixth, Street, became a centre for cultivated people.   Informal gatherings there, with so responsive a host and hostess, as well as brilliant receptions for men of the highest positions, made a unique chapter in the social life of New York, which has never been repeated.   Mrs Stone was a founder and the first president, 1889-1891, of the Wednesday Afternoon Club

Mr. and Mrs. Stone were hearty coworkers in religious and benevolent causes   About five years after coming to New York, Mr. Stone became interested in what was being accomplished for poor children, which thrilled his generous heart, and from that time he gave his untiring energy to the work of the Children's Aid Society.   He became a trustee, and proved one of its greatest benefactors, giving regular hours of his time to its affairs as long as he lived   In a letter to Charles L Brace, Mr Stone said, with characteristic feeling, "I have not been up and down the streets of New York without having my heart touched with pity for the poor children, and often ask myself what can I do to make their hard lives more comfortable and happy "   Mr Stone made his own answer by a gift, which is his lasting monument   The summer home at Bath Beach, Long Island, where so many little ones are made happy, given to the society in 1881, represents a value of one hundred thousand dollars, and over eighty thousand children have enjoyed the benefits of his generous humanity.

His earnest, sincere life peacefully ended December 15th, 1896   A devoted member of Grace Church, the founder of one of the great industries of our country, the donor of a permanent home for helpless children, he left an honorable record in all phases of life   Mr and Mrs Stone's family consists of twin daughters ; one of them resides in New York and is the widow of Francis F Marbury; the other is the wife of Dr. Arthur Little, an English physician, of the Island of Jersey   Twelve years ago Mr. and Mrs. Stone changed their residence from Murray Hill to 150 Central Park South, where Mrs Stone still resides

JOSEPH SUYDAM STOUT

AN old-time merchant and banker of New York City, Andrew Varick Stout, father of Mr Joseph Suydam Stout, was descended from several of the pioneer families of Manhattan Island He was born in New York early in the present century, and died at his country home in Bernardsville, N J, in 1883, at the age of seventy-one He received a substantial education, and at the age of eighteen became a teacher in the public schools After a few years of teaching, he became manager of the New York Orphan Asylum and later on went into business, establishing the firm of Stout & Ward He was eminently successful in his business ventures and accumulated a fortune His prominence as a business man led to his identification with financial enterprises. He became vice-president of the Shoe and Leather Bank, and in 1855 was advanced to the presidency, holding the latter position for twenty-eight years He was a director of the New York Mutual Gas Light Company, the Loan and Improvement Company, the New York and Brooklyn Ferry Company, the Phœnix Fire Insurance Company, the Broadway Fire Insurance Company and the American Bank Note Company

Maintaining an interest in municipal affairs, Mr Stout was at one time a member of the Board of Education He was originally a Democrat and a supporter of Fernando Wood, and when Mr. Wood was Mayor of the city he appointed Mr. Stout City Chamberlain When the disturbances occurred over the metropolitan police force, during Mayor Wood's administration, Mr. Stout advanced the money necessary for the payment of the police from his own private funds When the Civil War broke out, he was numbered among the war Democrats, who became Republicans upon the issues of that period. He was a devoted member of the Methodist Episcopal denomination, being a trustee of St Paul's Methodist Episcopal Church. Before his death he gave forty thousand dollars each to Wesleyan University and Drew Theological Seminary, the leading educational institutions of the Methodist Church The wife of Mr. Stout, Almira H Stout, survived him by seven years, dying in 1890 There were two daughters in the family, Jane K Stout, who married John N. Ewell, banker, of New York, and Almira H. Stout, who married A. Francis Southerland.

Mr Joseph Suydam Stout, the only son of Andrew V Stout, was born at the family homestead in Ridge Street, New York, December 27th, 1846, and was educated in the public schools and in the College of the City of New York. At the age of seventeen, he entered upon business life, taking a clerkship in the Shoe and Leather Bank, of which his father was then president. Two years later he was made assistant cashier of the bank In 1865, he went into business for himself in Wall Street His first connection was with the firm of Wiley & Co. Subsequently he was the senior partner of Stout & Dickinson, and afterwards was associated with his brother-in-law, John N Ewell, under the firm name of Ewell, Stout & Co For over twenty years he has been at the head of the firm of Stout & Co

Mr Stout is vice-president of the New York Mutual Gas Light Company, a director of the National Shoe and Leather Bank, the American Bank Note Company, the Broadway Insurance Company and the Holland Trust Company He has been for many years a member of the Stock Exchange, the Produce Exchange and the Chamber of Commerce, belongs to the Union League and Metropolitan clubs, and is a member of the New England Society. Inheriting the religious predilections of his parents, he belongs to the Methodist Episcopal Church, being a member of the Madison Avenue Society Deeply interested in the educational and benevolent undertakings of the denomination, he is a member of the board of directors of the Methodist Episcopal Hospital of Brooklyn, a trustee of Wesleyan University and of Drew Theological Seminary, and for ten years has been treasurer of the Board of Education of the Methodist Episcopal Church He married, in 1868, Julia Frances Purdy, and his children are, Newton E , Andrew V., Joseph S and Arthur P. Stout He lives in East Sixty-seventh Street.

JAMES SAMUEL THOMAS STRANAHAN

IT is only four generations from Mr. James Samuel Thomas Stranahan, who has been distinguished in the closing years of the nineteenth century as one of the most public-spirited citizens of New York and Brooklyn, to his ancestor, who came to this country in the first part of the eighteenth century James Stranahan, who was born in 1699, came from the Old World to Scituate, R. I, in 1725 Later he removed to Plainfield, Conn., and there he died in 1792, at the age of ninety-three years. His son, James, had a large family, of which Samuel Stranahan, who removed to Peterboro, Madison County, N Y, and died in 1816, was the fifth son.

Mr James Samuel Thomas Stranahan, son of Samuel Stranahan, was born in Peterboro, April 25, 1808 He was sent to the local academies and before he was of age, he engaged in teaching and then fitted himself as a civil engineer Mercantile life allured him, however, and in 1827 he became a trader along the Great Lakes. In 1832, Gerrit Smith, the philanthropist, who had made his acquaintance, engaged him to assist in the work of founding a manufacturing village in Oneida County, an enterprise represented to-day by the flourishing village of Florence He was a member of the Whig party in those days, and in 1838 was a representative in the Assembly

In 1840, Mr Stranahan removed from Florence to Newark, N J, and went into the business of railroad construction, in which he was engaged for some four years, when he took up his residence in Brooklyn, and began a career of public usefulness that has lasted for half a century In 1848, he was elected to the Board of Aldermen, and three years later he was nominated for Mayor, but was not elected In 1854, he was elected a Member of Congress

When the Metropolitan Police Commission was organized, in 1857, Mr Stranahan became a member of the board In 1860, he was a member of the Republican National Convention, which nominated Lincoln, was a member of the National Convention of 1864, and the same year a presidential elector for Lincoln and Johnson, and also an elector in 1888 for Harrison and Morton. During the Civil War period, he was president of the War Fund Committee of Brooklyn As the head of the Brooklyn Park Commission for twenty-two years, and made president of the commission by act of the Legislature in 1882, the crowning triumph of Mr. Stranahan's public labors was Prospect Park and the other parks and boulevards which are the pride of the city A recognition of his unselfish public service by his fellow-citizens is seen in the bronze statue of him unveiled at the entrance to Prospect Park in 1891. For many years Mr Stranahan was president of the Union Ferry Company, and was one of the originators of the plan for the Atlantic Docks, becoming their largest owner He was a member of the first board of directors and a trustee of the Brooklyn Bridge, and was president of the board at the time of the dedication of that structure.

In 1837, Mr Stranahan married Marianne Fitch, daughter of Ebenezer R Fitch, of Westmoreland, Oneida County, N Y, and by her he had two children, a daughter, Mary, and a son, Fitch James, who died December 3d, 1896 Mrs Stranahan was distinguished for her valuable work in the charities of Brooklyn She was first directress of the Old Ladies' Home for many years up to the time of her death She was at the head of the Sanitary Fair held for the benefit of the soldiers of the Civil War, and through her conduct of its affairs four hundred thousand dollars were collected She died in 1866 The second wife of Mr Stranahan was Clara C Harrison, of Massachusetts, of the noted Baldwin ancestry. She was for many years a principal of one of the large private seminaries for young ladies in Brooklyn, and is still actively interested in educational work, being a founder and trustee of Barnard College, and vice-president of the alumnæ association of Troy Female Seminary, from which she was graduated She is also president of the State Charities Aid Association for Kings County, vice-president general for New York State of the Daughters of the American Revolution, and was vice-president of the New York State Board of Women Managers for the Columbian World's Fair at Chicago in 1893 She has also won reputation as an authoress, her work entitled A History of French Painting, being recognized as a valuable contribution to the history of art

WILLIAM A STREET

A MONG the pioneers who came to New England in the exodus from the Old Country for the settlement of the Massachusetts Bay Colony, in the first twenty-five years of the seventeenth century, was the Reverend Nicholas Street, a clergyman of the Church of England, who immigrated in 1630 He was born in 1603, in Bridgewater, Somersetshire, where his family were prosperous merchants He was graduated from Oxford in 1624, was living in Taunton, Mass, in 1638, and in New Haven, Conn, in 1659 His son, the Reverend Samuel Street, graduated from Harvard College in 1661 These divines were the first ancestors in this country of Mr William A. Street

On his mother's side, Mr. Street's great-grandfather was Joseph Reade, of New York, a member of the Governor's council during the administration of Governor Robert Monckton, in 1761. Reade Street, in this city, was named for him He was also a warden of Trinity Church from 1721 to 1770. The Reades came from a line of British landed gentry of the name, who for centuries exercised great influence in public affairs. Lawrence Reade, the father of Joseph Reade, was born and married in England, removing to New York in the early part of the eighteenth century. His immediate ancestors were Sir William Reade and Sir Richard Reade A son of Joseph Reade was John Reade, for whom Reade Hoeck (Red Hook) was named By his descent from Joseph Reade, Mr. Street is connected with the Stuyvesant, Watts, Livingston, Kearny, de Peyster, and other great families of New York. Another of Mr Street s ancestors—namely, his great-grandfather—Major Andrew Billings, was a member of General Washington's staff during the Revolutionary War. Mr Street now has in his possession an autograph letter from Washington to Major Billings, dated June 7th, 1783 Attached to it is a lock of the hair of General and Mrs. Washington, which the letter refers to as having been sent General Philip Kearny was Mr Street's second cousin, and the latter bears the same relationship to Frederick de Peyster, long the president of the New York Historical Society

The great-grandfather of Mr Street was Caleb Street, a prosperous New York merchant of the early part of the present century. His grandfather, General Randall S Street, was a lawyer of Poughkeepsie He was of excellent rank in his profession and highly respected by his townsmen Mr Street's father, William I Street, was also a lawyer by profession, and married Susan Watts Kearny, daughter of Robert Kearny and his wife, Anna Reade His brother, Alfred B Street, the poet and author, was well known as a man of letters in the period of this country's intellectual and literary history which was dominated by Washington Irving and his associates, who were known as the Knickerbocker authors.

Mr William A. Street was born in Poughkeepsie, N Y., in 1843, but in 1850 his family removed to New York. His education was received in the city, but at an early age he entered upon a business career, entering the house of Sir Roderick W. Cameron, the shipping merchant In 1862, he went to Australia, and during the next three years traveled extensively in that part of the world, gaining an invaluable knowledge of business and trade conditions in the countries through which he journeyed In that time, he visited and studied the peoples of China, New Zealand, Java, Australia, the west coast of South America and islands of the Pacific In 1870, Mr Street became a partner of Sir R. W Cameron, with whom he had long been associated, and the firm took the name of R W. Cameron & Co For nearly half a century this house has been one of the most active and most important in trade between the United States, Australasia and the far East

In 1874, Mr Street married Lucy Morgan, the children of this alliance being Arthur F Street, Rosamond Kearny Street, Susan Watts Street and Anna Livingston Street Mr Street has a city residence at 43 Park Avenue. His country home is The Hermitage, at Seabright, N J He belongs to the Union and other clubs, and is a supporter of the prominent institutions of public interest, such as the Metropolitan Museum of Art and others of a similar character

JOSEPH MONTGOMERY STRONG

NORTHAMPTON, Mass, ranks among the oldest of New England towns, and was founded by John Strong, who was born at Taunton, Somersetshire, England, in 1605, and emigrated to the New World in 1630. Elder John Strong, as he was called, played a leading part in all the affairs of Church and State in early Massachusetts history, but, in addition, he became the progenitor of a large family whose branches now extend throughout the entire country. Many of its members have inherited not only the name but the energy and force of character of their Puritan ancestors, and among them are a number who have occupied positions of high distinction in public and private life. The Strong crest is an eagle rising from a mural crown, and its motto, *Tentanda via est*, and has been borne with honor by many men of eminence in the most distinguished stations of American professional and business life.

The New York branch of this typically American race was established by a great-grandson of Elder John Strong, Selah Strong, Jr., born in 1713 His son was Major Samuel Strong, born 1744, whose son, Joseph Strong, born 1766, married, 1792, his second cousin, Margaret, daughter of Judge Selah Strong, of Setauket, Long Island This couple were the grandparents of Mr. Joseph Montgomery Strong, whose father, the Reverend Paschal Neilson Strong, was born in this city, in 1793, graduated from Columbia College in 1810, and adopted the profession of the ministry. The Reverend Paschal Neilson Strong became an eminent New York clergyman, and was for a long time the pastor of the old Collegiate Dutch Reformed Church, whose edifice then stood at the corner of Cedar and Nassau Streets, and is now located at the corner of Twenty-ninth Street and Fifth Avenue. His wife was Cornelia Adelaide Kane, a daughter of John Kane, Jr., a leading New York merchant in the early portion of the present century, and was a near relative of Dr. Elisha Kent Kane, the famous Arctic explorer, the Kane family being related to many of the most prominent names in the early history of the city and State.

The birth of Mr Joseph Montgomery Strong occurred February 6th, 1822, and his marriage, October 15th, 1856, allied him to one of the foremost Colonial and Revolutionary families of the State—the Livingstons. Mrs. Strong, by birth Elizabeth Ludlow Livingston, was born at the Livingston Manor, at Dobbs Ferry, on the Hudson, and was the daughter of Van Brugh Livingston and granddaughter of Philip Livingston, secretary to Sir Henry Moore, the last English Governor of the Province of New York. Her great-grandfather, Peter Van Brugh Livingston, married Mary Alexander, sister of William Alexander, the Lord Stirling of the Army of the Revolution, and was president of the New York Provincial Congress in 1775, while his brother, Philip Livingston, was a signer of the Declaration of Independence, and another brother, William, was Governor of New Jersey. The descent of the family from Robert Livingston, the first Lord of Livingston Manor, and the public services which so many of its members rendered both in the days of the Province and in the modern State of New York are well known, the history of the family for many generations back being virtually that of the Colony and afterwards that of the State, to which it has ever supplied distinguished citizens.

The children of the Strong-Livingston alliance are Joseph Montgomery Strong, Jr., Peter Van Brugh Livingston Strong, Mary Livingston Strong, Philip Alexander Strong, Charles Livingston Strong and Josephine Gebhard Strong, the two latter being deceased.

The residence of the family is 41 West Fifty-fourth Street, while Mr. Strong's country seat is Cliffwood, an estate at Esopus, on the Hudson. Engaged in active business as a merchant for many years, he has, however, traveled in almost every part of Europe, and has been intimately connected with all that is best in the artistic or social development of New York. He was a stockholder of the Academy of Music, and joined the New York Club in 1846, while his membership in the Union Club dates from 1854. Mr. Strong was also some years ago a member of all the leading yacht clubs and other organizations devoted to the interests of sport, but with the approach of years relinquished active interest in that connection.

THERON G. STRONG

THE families of Strong, in England, Scotland and of Ireland, have been closely associated, although the lines of connection have long been lost sight of The English family, from which was descended John Strong, who came to this county in 1630, was originally of Shropshire, the name appearing on the old records as McStrachan, Strachan, Strahan and Strong One of its members married into a family of County Caernarvon, Wales, and went thither to live in 1545 Richard Strong, who was born in the County Caernarvon, in 1561, was of this branch of the family. He removed to Taunton, Somersetshire, England, in 1590, and died in 1613 John Strong, son of Richard Strong, was born in Taunton, England, in 1605 Being a Puritan, he sailed for the New World, in 1630, and settled in Dorchester, Mass In 1635, he removed to Hingham, being a freeman there the following year, and a freeman of Plymouth, in 1638 In 1641-3-4, he was a deputy to the General Court of the Plymouth Colony Removing to Windsor, Conn, he had charge, with four others, of the settlement of that place, and in 1659, removing to Northampton, Mass., became a leading man in that community also. The second wife of Elder John Strong was Abigail Ford, of Dorchester, Mass, daughter of Thomas Ford, who came over in 1630

Jedediah Strong, son of Elder John Strong, was born in 1637, and was one of the early settlers of Coventry, Conn His first wife was Freedham Woodward, daughter of Henry Woodward, of Dorchester, Mass. Preserved Strong, son of Jedediah Strong, was one of the prominent men of Coventry, Conn., and a member of its board of selectmen, in 1730 His great-grandson, Colonel Adonijah Strong, 1743-1824, was a Revolutionary patriot, a Colonel of a Connecticut regiment, and afterwards Commissary-General. In civil life he was a lawyer, and subsequently a Judge Judge Martin Strong, of Salisbury, Conn, 1778-1838, was the eldest son of Colonel Adonijah Strong He was a leading man in the community, a justice of the peace, and a member of the Legislature, and of the State Senate, and County Judge of Litchfield County.

The father of Mr. Theron G. Strong was the Honorable Theron R. Strong, second son of Judge Martin Strong, and was born in Salisbury, in 1802 He studied law in his father's office and afterwards in the law school of Judge Gould, at Litchfield. Removing to the western part of the State of New York, he settled first in Salem, and then in 1826 in Palmyra, where he practiced for the next twenty-six years For many years he was a master and examiner-in-chancery, in 1834-39, was district attorney for Wayne County from 1839 to 1841, was a member of the United States Congress, and in 1842 a member of the Assembly of the State of New York. In the autumn of 1851, he was elected a Justice of the Supreme Court of the State of New York, in which capacity he served for eight years, the last year of his term as an Associate Justice of the Court of Appeals In 1856, he removed to Rochester, and practiced there with great success for the next ten years, after which he came to New York City, where he continued the practice of law for the remainder of his life, which terminated in 1873 The mother of Mr. Theron G Strong was Cornelia Wheeler Barnes, daughter of Wheeler Barnes, of Rome, N. Y.

Mr Strong was born in Palmyra, N Y, August 14th, 1846. In 1868, he was graduated from the University of Rochester, and then attended the Columbia Law School, graduating in 1870 In 1878, he married Martha Howard Prentice, daughter of the late John H. Prentice, a leading resident of Brooklyn He is now the senior member of the firm of Strong, Harmon & Mathewson. In 1884, he was nominated to be a Judge of the Court of Common Pleas, and was renominated in 1885 He has been identified for many years with the public and religious life of the city, having been a deacon and elder in the Church of the Covenant, an elder in the Brick Church, one of the trustees of the Presbytery, a delegate to the General Assembly, a director of the New York Juvenile Asylum, the New York Bible Society, and other similar organizations. He is a member of the Society of the Cincinnati, of the State of Connecticut, the Society of Colonial Wars, the Sons of the Revolution, the New England Society, the Century Association, the Union League Club, the Downtown Association, and the Bar Association He resides in East Sixty-fifth Street

WILLIAM EVERARD STRONG

THE family to which Mr. William Everard Strong belongs is one of the largest in New England, where it has existed for more than two centuries and a half. Its ancestor, Elder John Strong, of Northampton, Mass., came to this country in 1630, his career and that of his son, Thomas, being frequently referred to in this volume. In the third generation, Joseph Strong, 1672-1763, removed in 1716 from Northampton to Coventry, Conn., and was town treasurer there. In 1721, and for fifty-two times thereafter, he represented the town in the Legislature, being a member in 1762, when he was over eighty-nine years old. His wife was Sarah Allen, daughter of Nehemiah Allen and Sarah Woodford, of Northampton.

In the next generation, Captain Joseph Strong was born in 1701, in Northampton. He was for thirteen years a selectman of Coventry, Conn., a justice of the peace and for thirty-four years, 1739-73, a deacon of the First Congregational Church and a member of the Assembly at nine sessions. In 1724, he married Elizabeth Strong, a second cousin, daughter of Preserved Strong and Tabitha Lee. The son of Captain Joseph Strong was Deacon Benajah Strong, 1740-1809. He was a resident of Coventry, frequently a selectman, a justice of the peace, deacon of the First Congregational Church, 1782-1809, and a member of the General Assembly in 1781. His wife was Lucy Bishop, daughter of Caleb Bishop and Keziah Hebbard, of Lisbon, Conn. Elizabeth Hale, the mother of Captain Nathan Hale, the Revolutionary martyr, was his sister.

Dr. Joseph Strong, the son of Benajah and Lucy (Bishop) Strong, was born in 1770 and graduated from Yale College in 1788. During the frontier troubles in the Northwest Territory, in the latter part of the last century, he was, from 1793 to 1795, surgeon under General Wayne. He settled in Philadelphia in 1795, practicing his profession there for several years, and died in 1812. His wife was Rebecca Young, of Philadelphia. The father of Mr. William E. Strong was William Young Strong, who was born in Philadelphia in 1806, while his father, Dr. Strong, was residing there in the practice of his profession. His youth was spent in Ohio, whither he went when a child of six years and he became identified with the development of that portion of the country. He afterwards removed to Terre Haute, Ind., where he died in 1866.

The wife of William Young Strong and the present Mr. Strong's mother, was Ann Massie, 1809-1860, a member of a notable family. Her father was General Massie, of Chillicothe, O., and her mother was Susan Everard Meade, a member of the well-known Meade family of Virginia. General Nathaniel Massie was born in Goochland County, Va., in 1793, and died at Paint Creek Falls, O., in 1813. When only seventeen years of age, he enlisted in the Continental Army and served during the closing years of the struggle for independence. Afterwards he became a surveyor, and among the important professional tasks in which he was employed was the survey, in 1791, of the first settlements upon the lands in Ohio, granted to Virginia's soldiers of the Revolution, between the Scioto and Little Miami rivers. In 1793-6, he was engaged in laying out the town of Chillicothe, and became, at the beginning of the present century, one of the largest land owners in Ohio. He took an intrepid and energetic part in the Indian Wars, was several times a member of the Ohio State Senate, served for one term as president of the Senate, was Major-General of the militia and a member of the Ohio Constitutional Convention in 1802. In 1807, he declined a nomination for Governor of the State.

Mr. William Everard Strong was born in Chillicothe, O., August 11th, 1836. He was educated in the public schools of his native place and came to New York to enter business at an early age. For many years past he has been one of the leading stock brokers of the metropolis. He married Alice Corbin Smith of Alexandria, Va. Mr. Strong's city residence is 176 Madison Avenue, and he has a summer home, The Point, Seabright, N. J. He is a member of the Metropolitan, City, Union, Knickerbocker, Riding, Lawyers', Racquet, Players and South Side Sportsmen's clubs and other organizations. Mr. and Mrs. Strong have two daughters, Anne Massie and Alice Everard Strong.

WILLIAM L. STRONG

A CONSPICUOUS exemplar of the American merchant, the Honorable William L. Strong, Mayor of the City of New York, has won approval as a successful business man and a capable chief magistrate. His parentage was of New England stock, his father, Abel Strong, being a native of Hartford, Conn , born in 1792. When eighteen years of age, he emigrated to Ohio, became a farmer in Richland County, and soon after his arrival there married Hannah Burdine, who was born in Pennsylvania in 1798

The family of Abel Strong and his wife consisted of five children, of whom Mr. William L Strong, born in 1827, was the eldest   Upon his father's death, when he was only thirteen years old, it devolved upon him to assume the responsibilities of caring for his mother and younger brothers and sisters   He accordingly commenced life as an employee in country stores of Londonville and Mansfield, O , where he remained until he was twenty-six years of age   Then, in 1853, he came to New York and started on a career that was to bring him fortune At first he was connected with the wholesale dry goods house of L G Wilson & Co , and then held a position with Farnham, Dale & Co and its successors for eleven years ending in 1869   The following year, with thirty years of commercial experience behind him, he founded the house of William L Strong & Co   The firm commanded success from the start, and it now ranks as one of the leading houses in the wholesale dry goods trade

Nevertheless, the business interests of Colonel Strong have not been limited to the dry goods trade. To the public at large he is known as a banker, having been, until he was elected Mayor, president of the Central National Bank of New York, an institution in which he had long been a director   He is also vice-president of the New York Security and Trust Company, and a director in the New York Life Insurance Company, the Hanover Fire Insurance Company, the Plaza Bank, and a director or officer of many railroads and corporations.

Maintaining a deep interest in public affairs, Colonel Strong has actually come into political prominence in later years   He has always been earnestly attached to the principles of the Republican party, but held himself aloof from the party machinery   A supporter of General Fremont for the presidency in 1856, he has since favored the Republican candidates in every subsequent national campaign   For many years his services to his party, in moulding the sentiment of the business community, was earnest and efficient   As an organizer of business men's campaign clubs in several presidential campaigns, he was conspicuously successful   Once, however, he ran for office, when, in 1882, at the earnest solicitation of friends, party associates and representatives of the business community, he made a campaign for Congress in the Eleventh New York District, which was, however, largely Democratic, and though he made a notable canvass, he naturally failed of election.   His greatest distinction as a public man came to him in 1894, when the combined opposition to Tammany Hall in municipal affairs, headed by the Chamber of Commerce Committee of One Hundred, agreed upon him as its candidate for Mayor He was elected by the large majority of forty-five thousand over his Tammany opponent, ex-Mayor Hugh J Grant   His administration has been conspicuous for its business-like, non-partisan character.   Mayor Strong has since been often mentioned as a candidate for Mayor of the Greater New York and for Governor of the State.

Mayor Strong was for some years a vestryman of the Church of the Incarnation on Madison Avenue, and is an attendant of St. Thomas' Church.   His club connections include the presidency of the Wool Club and membership in the Metropolitan, Union League, Merchants', Republican, Colonial and Riding, and he belongs to the Ohio Society, the New England Society, the American Museum of Natural History, the Metropolitan Museum of Art and the American Geographical Society   He married, in 1866, Mary Aborn, daughter of Robert W. Aborn, of Orange, N J , and has two children, P Bradlee Strong and Mary, who married Albert R. Shattuck   Mr. Strong's city residence is 12 West Fifty-seventh Street

MALCOLM STUART

A T all times in its history New York City has owed more to its mercantile class, probably, than to any other of its citizens The world at large has contributed very much to the membership of this class and it has included in its ranks many of foreign birth, who have found in their adopted country opportunities for the exercise of a wholesome public interest in the affairs of the community.

The United Kingdom of Great Britain and Ireland has sent us, in every period, many individuals who have in time become our most substantial merchants and most honored and useful citizens. Among these, Joseph Stuart, who was the grandfather of the subject of this sketch, must be accorded an exceedingly high position He was one of a family of six brothers, who became distinguished in the banking business, and in commercial affairs generally, both in Europe and in this country. The six brothers were associated in business, and had branch houses in Liverpool and Manchester, and afterwards in Philadelphia and New York, when they had established themselves in this country. Joseph Stuart came to the United States after attaining mature years, settled in New York and became the senior member of the firm of J. & J. Stuart & Co., which for a full half century, from 1840 to 1890, was one of the leading and most influential banking houses in the metropolis, transacting a large business here and having also important connections abroad in Great Britain and on the Continent.

During his long business career in New York, Joseph Stuart held many offices of trust and honor in connection with financial institutions and other corporations. For many years he was president of the Emigrant Industrial Savings Bank and of the Friendly Sons of St. Patrick. He was vice-president of the Fourth National Bank of this city and of the Irish Emigrant Society, and a director in the Mercantile National Bank, the Mercantile Fire Insurance Company, the Standard Fire Insurance Company, the Queen Insurance Company and other large and important corporations A consistent and devoted member of the Presbyterian Church, he was a generous supporter of the institutions of that denomination, giving freely of time and money to religious and philanthropic causes. He was for many years trustee and treasurer of the Fourth Presbyterian Church of New York City. Joseph Stuart, the second, his son, and father of Mr. Malcolm Stuart, succeeded to the business of J & J Stuart & Co, and also held important official positions in the management of large corporations. The mother of Mr. Malcolm Stuart was Marieanne Malcolm, his maternal grandmother was Anna Pentland, and his paternal grandmother was Anna Watson, all of the town of Lurgan, in County Armagh, Ireland.

James Malcolm, the maternal grandfather of Mr. Malcolm Stuart, whose family name he bears, was a prominent linen manufacturer of Lurgan, Ireland, a man of considerable wealth, of high social standing and influential in the local affairs of the community in which he lived, serving as justice of the peace, and holding other offices of honor at the hands of his fellow townsmen and of the central authorities of Ireland. A son of James Malcolm, also named James Malcolm, and an uncle of Mr. Malcolm Stuart followed his father in his large business interests as a linen manufacturer in Lurgan. He, also, was a justice of the peace and deputy lord lieutenant for the County of Armagh, under appointment by Queen Victoria.

Mr. Malcolm Stuart was born of this notable ancestry in New York City, August 16th, 1869. His early education was secured in the school of Miss Du Vernet, and after that he attended the private school of Dr. Holbrook at Sing Sing. When his school days were completed, he went into mercantile life and is now a merchant in the foreign and domestic trade. He has traveled extensively abroad and has become thoroughly acquainted with nearly all the countries of Europe.

Mr. Stuart lives at 120 East Thirty-sixth Street, and for the summer occupies a handsome cottage with other members of his family at Quogue, Long Island. Interested in military matters, he is a private in the famous Seventh Regiment and belongs to the Seventh Regiment Veteran Club and the Quogue Field Club.

FREDERICK STURGES

THE grandfather of Mr Frederick Sturges was the Honorable Jonathan Sturges, of Fairfield, Conn , in which place he was born in 1740, and died in 1819. Graduating from Yale College in 1759, he became a leading member of the Connecticut bar He took an active part in the pre-Revolutionary movements, and was a representative from Connecticut in the First and Second Federal Congresses, in 1789-93 After completing his Congressional terms, he was a Judge of the State Supreme Court from 1793 to 1805

Jonathan Sturges, Jr., son of Jonathan Sturges of Connecticut, and the father of the subject of this sketch, was one of the great merchants of New York in the last generation He was born in Southport, Conn , in 1802, and died in New York in 1874. After receiving a good education, he came to New York as a young man and entered upon mercantile life, being first connected with the firm of R & L Reed Beginning in 1821, when he was nineteen years of age, he was rapidly advanced in business, until in 1828 he was a partner in the concern, which after fifteen years became Sturges, Bennett & Co , a name that was retained until 1865, when it was changed to Sturges, Arnold & Co Mr Sturges continued at the head of the house for three years longer, but in 1868 he retired Outside of the mercantile business which principally engaged his attention, he had many other important commercial and financial interests He was one of the founders of the Bank of Commerce, of which he was a director, and was also a director of the Illinois Central Railroad, and the New York, New Haven & Hartford Railroad.

In social affairs Jonathan Sturges was no less prominent than in the business world Devoted to the cause of the Union in the dark days of the war, he was one of the founders of the Union League Club, and most energetic in all the work undertaken by that organization in support of the nation In 1863, he was president of the club A member of the Chamber of Commerce from early in his business career, he was twice vice-president of the organization. He was also one of the founders of the Century Association, often known as the Century Club. The wife of Mr. Sturges, whom he married in 1829, was Mary Cady, daughter of John Cady. His sons were Frederick, Edward, Arthur P., and Henry C. Sturges His eldest daughter was Virginia R Sturges, who became the wife of William H Osborne, and has a city residence at 32 Park avenue, and a country house, Castle Rock, at Garrison-on-the-Hudson. Another daughter, Amelia Sturges, married John Pierpont Morgan, in 1861, and died the following year

Mr Frederick Sturges was born in 1833 In 1849, when he was sixteen years of age, he entered upon business life by taking a place in his father's office. Continuing in the establishment for nearly twenty years, he retired when his father gave up business, in 1868 Since that time he has devoted himself to the corporate and other interests of the estate which his father left He is a director of the National Bank of Commerce, the Atlantic Trust Company, the Seaman's Bank for Savings, and has been a director of the Illinois Central Railroad Deeply interested in religious and philanthropic work, he has devoted considerable time to such causes. The Presbyterian Hospital, the Hospital for the Ruptured and Crippled, the American Bible Society and the Seamen's Fund Society have been special objects of his attention, and have received from him generous financial support, besides having the benefit of his capable business management in the administration of their affairs. Mr. Sturges married, in 1863, Mary Reed Fuller, daughter of Dudley B. Fuller His children are Jonathan, Arthur Pemberton, Frederick, Jr , and Mary Fuller Sturges He is a member of the Century and Grolier Clubs, the Downtown Association and the American Geographical Society, and is a supporter of the Metropolitan Museum of Art The city residence of the family is at 36 Park avenue, and their country home is at Fairfield, Conn Jonathan Sturges, the eldest son of Mr Frederick Sturges, is a graduate of Princeton College, and has devoted himself to literary pursuits He is a member of the Metropolitan, University, Fencers, Players and other clubs Arthur Pemberton Sturges, the younger son, is also a graduate of Princeton, and a member of the Metropolitan, Calumet, Players and University clubs.

FRANK KNIGHT STURGIS

N ATIVE of the metropolis, Mr. Frank K. Sturgis is a thorough New Yorker in education, in spirit and in devotion to those institutions that have made this the foremost city of the New World. He is now fifty years of age, having been born September 19th, 1847. His father was William Sturgis and his mother Elizabeth K. Hinckley. He traces his ancestry to early pioneer families of New England The years of his maturity have been passed in Wall Street, and he long ago took rank as one of the able financiers of his time After an excellent education, he entered the banking house of Capron, Strong & Co There he served a brief apprenticeship of one year, devoting himself assiduously to the theoretical and practical study of the general subject of finance. The ability he displayed, his aptitude in financial affairs and his close application to business soon brought him into partnership connection with the house in which he had commenced his career. The firm of Capron, Strong & Co. was succeeded, in 1871, by that of Work, Strong & Co., and Mr. Sturgis has maintained his partnership relationship with the house unbroken from the day that he entered the original firm in January, 1869, when he was only twenty-one years of age, down to the present time, the firm name now being Strong, Sturgis & Co.

Mr. Sturgis has the highest standing as a banker and broker, and has been honored in many ways by those who recognize his strength of character and his ability. One of the highest honors that can be conferred upon a man in financial circles in New York was awarded to him in 1892, when he was elected to the presidency of the New York Stock Exchange, of which he has been a member since 1869. He was reelected in 1893. Before his elevation to that position, there had been forty-two presidents of the Stock Exchange from 1817, the date of the formal organization and adoption of a constitution under the name of the New York Stock and Exchange Board. Mr. Sturgis during his incumbency achieved a brilliant reputation, second to none of his able predecessors. It was largely at his suggestion and through his labors, in association with other leading financiers, that the Clearing House was established, and he has been instrumental in introducing many reforms in the administration of the business of the Stock Exchange that have redounded to the benefit of its members and to the general advantage of the business community.

Notwithstanding close application to his profession, Mr. Sturgis has found time to culti-vate the social side of life and has been engaged in other enterprises of a distinctly different character. He has been an important factor in the social, benevolent and political life of the city, and has been active in the general direction of important social organizations. Particularly inter-ested in gentlemanly sports, he has devoted much time to the turf. When the Jockey Club was organized by August Belmont and others, Mr. Sturgis was urged to become a member of the board of stewards and treasurer and secretary of the club, and in that position has exercised a strong and wholesome influence upon those turf matters with which the Jockey Club has especially concerned itself In the organization of the Madi on Square Garden Company he also took a prominent and influential part, being president of the company and one of the hardest working members of its board of directors. He has also been an officer of the National Horse Show Association and is credited with much of the success that has attended the annual exhibitions that have been held under the auspices of that organization. He has been a governor of the Metropolitan and Knicker-bocker clubs, of the Westchester Racing Association and of the Turf and Field Club, and otherwise a prominent representative of the best social element of the city in club life

Mr Sturgis married, October 16th, 1872, Florence Lydig, daughter of Philip Mesier Lydig, and a member of the famous old New York family whose name she bears. The city residence of the family is in Thirty-sixth Street, at the corner of Fifth Avenue and their summer home is Clipston Grange, at Lenox, Mass. Mr. Sturgis is a member of the Metropolitan, Union, Knick-erbocker, City, Union League, Coaching, Players, Whist, Rockaway Hunt, Larchmont Yacht and New York Yacht clubs, the Century Association, the Country Club of Westchester County, the American Geographical Society and the National Academy of Design.

RUTHERFURD STUYVESANT

LINEALLY descended from several great Colonial ancestors of New York and New England, Mr Rutherfurd Stuyvesant comes from Governor Stuyvesant of New Amsterdam, Governor John Winthrop of Massachusetts, Governor Dudley of Connecticut, Lewis Morris, Chief Justice of New York and first Governor of New Jersey, and also traces his descent to Robert Livingston, Balthazar Bayard, Walter Rutherfurd, Lewis Morris, the signer of the Declaration of Independence, and others who were numbered among the great men of their day. The father of Mr Stuyvesant was Lewis Morris Rutherfurd, who was born in Morrisania in 1816. Graduated from Williams College in 1834, he studied law with the Honorable William Henry Seward, in Auburn, N Y., and was admitted to the bar in 1837. In 1849, he gave up the practice of law, devoting himself to scientific pursuits. His special work was astronomical photography and spectral analysis In 1863, he began the publication of a series of papers on Astronomical Observations with the Spectroscope, in The American Journal of Science. In 1863, he was appointed by Congress one of the fifty original members of the Academy of Science In 1885, he was an American delegate to the International Meridian Conference in Washington For more than twenty-five years he was a trustee of Columbia College, was an associate of the Royal Astronomical Society, and received many medals. He died in 1892, at Tranquillity, the New Jersey home of the Rutherfurd family.

The mother of Mr. Rutherfurd Stuyvesant was Margaret Stuyvesant Chanler She was the daughter of the Reverend John White Chanler and Elizabeth Winthrop, and through her mother was descended from Governor Petrus Stuyvesant and Governor John Winthrop. Her maternal grandmother was Judith Stuyvesant, daughter of Petrus Stuyvesant, and great-great-granddaughter of the famous Dutch Governor of the West India Company on Manhattan Island. Her maternal grandfather was Benjamin Winthrop, great-great-great-grandson of Governor John Winthrop. Her maternal great-grandmother, the wife of Petrus Stuyvesant, was Margaret Livingston, daughter of Gilbert Livingston, son of Robert Livingston, first lord of the Livingston Manor. Gilbert Livingston inherited a large estate near Saratoga, and married Cornelia Beekman.

On the paternal side Mr Stuyvesant is descended from the Rutherfurd and Morris families, that have played such an important part in social, business and public affairs in New Jersey and New York. The Rutherfurds are descended from Sir John Rutherfurd, of Scotland, whose grandfather, John Rutherfurd, married Barbara Abernethy, daughter of the Bishop of Caithness, and who was the sixteenth in descent from Hugo De Rutherfurd, a Scottish Baron of 1225. Walter Rutherfurd, the head of the family in this country, was the great-grandfather of Lewis M. Rutherfurd. His wife was Catharine Alexander, sister of the Earl of Stirling Their son John, who married Helen Morris, daughter of Lewis Morris, represented New Jersey in the United States Senate from 1791 to 1798. He was the great-grandfather of Mr. Rutherfurd Stuyvesant, and in the next generation, Robert Walter Rutherfurd, who was the grandfather of the subject of this sketch, married Sabina, daughter of Colonel Lewis Morris Helena Sarah Rutherfurd, aunt of Lewis Morris Rutherfurd, was born in 1789 and died in 1873 She was the second wife of Peter Gerard Stuyvesant.

Mr. Rutherfurd Stuyvesant was named Stuyvesant Rutherfurd, and was graduated from Columbia College in the class of 1863. By the will of his mother's great-uncle, Peter Gerard Stuyvesant, property was left him upon the condition of changing his family name, and consequently, by act of the Legislature, he took the name that he now bears. In 1863, he married Mary Rutherfurd Pierrepont, daughter of Henry Evelyn Pierrepont and Anna Maria Jay. Mrs Stuyvesant died in 1879. Mr. Stuyvesant lives at Tranquillity, N. J , and his city residence is in East Fifteenth Street. He is a member of the Union, Century, City, Racquet, New York Yacht, Atlantic Yacht and Sewanhaka-Corinthian Yacht clubs, the Downtown Association, the Columbia College Alumni Association and the American Geographical Society, and is a patron of the American Museum of Natural History and the National Academy of Design, and a patron and trustee of the Metropolitan Museum of Art.

THEODORE SUTRO

DISTINGUISHED at the New York bar, as well as in public and social life, the subject of this article belongs to a family which has given to Germany many eminent scholars and professional men. Mr. Sutro was born at Aix-la-Chapelle, Prussia, March 14th, 1845, and is a son of Emanuel Sutro, a native of Bavaria, and his wife, Rosa Warendorff, a highly educated and accomplished lady, who was born at Dueren, near Aix-la-Chapelle. On both the paternal and maternal sides, his relatives were nearly all lawyers or doctors, one of the most distinguished among them being his mother's uncle, the famous jurist Edward Gans, *professor extraordinarius* at the University of Berlin, who died in 1839.

Mr. Sutro is the youngest of twelve children and of seven sons, each of whom have achieved high positions, two of his brothers having national reputations. The Honorable Adolph Sutro, of San Francisco, the owner of Sutro Heights, donor of Sutro Park to the city, and one of its most prominent citizens, has been Mayor of that city, while Otto Sutro, of Baltimore, who died in 1896, was widely known as one of the foremost patrons of music in the United States. Mr. Sutro's father, who was a manufacturer at Aix-la-Chapelle, died in 1847, and his son Theodore, brought to the United States at an early age, received his education here. This included preparatory studies in Baltimore and at Phillips Academy, Exeter, N. H , after which he entered Harvard University, graduating with distinction in the class of 1871. Adopting the profession of law, he attended lectures at the Boston University Law School and at the law department of Columbia College, in this city. Called to the bar in 1874, Mr. Sutro has continued in successful practice, and represents large corporate and business interests. He possesses a striking personality, with oratorical gifts of a high order, and is singularly effective before a jury

In 1895, Mr. Sutro, although a Democrat, was appointed by Mayor Strong to fill an important office in the municipal administration, that of Commissioner of Taxes and Assessments Mr. Sutro has distinguished himself in this post no less than in the other positions which he has occupied in life, and he has proved a credit to the Reform Government. He has made many important decisions on novel points in the matter of taxation of corporations and estates which have, almost without exception, been sustained by the courts when subjected to judicial review.

In 1884, Mr. Sutro married Florence Edith Clinton, a lady of literary and artistic tastes similar to his own, and whose beauty and personal and intellectual qualities render her a favorite in society. Both Mr. and Mrs. Sutro are musical in their tastes, the latter being known to a wide circle as a talented amateur pianist They are also among the most regular patrons of the opera, and are frequent guests at the important social functions of fashionable life. Mr. Sutro is distinguished as a speaker and writer, and has published numerous articles on legal and general subjects in periodicals and in the newspaper press, while Mrs. Sutro also possesses marked literary ability, and frequently appears as an author of similar articles. She has also been the patroness and promoter of many large charities and philanthropic works. In 1897, she founded and acted as president of the woman's department in the Music Teachers' National Association, and achieved a national reputation in bringing forward woman's compositions in music. She has also been elected president of the National Federation of Woman's Musical Clubs throughout the United States Mr. and Mrs Sutro are enthusiastic book collectors and possess a large library, which includes many rare editions and examples of the bookbinders' art. They are noted for their hospitality, and have entertained many distinguished foreigners

Mr. Sutro's residence is at West One Hundred and Second Street and Riverside Drive The interior decorations of the house indicate the refined taste of the owner, and represent in their details his individual artistic sense He has there, among other art treasures, a collection of some of the choicest productions of American painters. He is a member of numerous clubs and societies, a few among them being the Harvard, Reform, German, and National Civic clubs, as well as the Patria, Φ B K and the Bar Association.

JOHN RICHARD SUYDAM

FEW families have a greater antiquity than the Suydams, who are of Dutch origin and have been identified with Long Island since the first settlement of that part of the State. Back in the tenth and eleventh centuries, those who bore the name owned large estates in Holland and the Netherlands. Hendrick Rycken, the ancestor of the family in this country, was a member of the Riker family. Some authorities have held that he belonged also to the Suydam family in Holland and his sons adopted that name. He arrived in the New World in 1663, and located in Smith's Vly, in the suburbs of New Amsterdam Afterwards, he removed to Flatbush, Long Island, where he died in 1701

Ryck Suydam, son of Hendrick Rycken, was born in 1675. His mother was Ida Jacobs From 1711 until the time of his death, in 1741, he served as supervisor of the town of Flatbush and was sometimes a Judge His son, John Suydam, died in Brooklyn about the close of the Revolutionary War. John Suydam's son, Hendrick Suydam, was born in 1736, and before the date of the Revolution, removed to Hallett's Cove, where he owned a mill on Sunswick Creek. For many years, he was an elder in the church in Newtown His death occurred in 1818 He was married three times. His first wife, whom he married in 1762, was Letitia Sebring. She died in 1765, and he afterwards married Harmtie Lefferts, and in 1770, Phœbe Skidmore, daughter of Samuel Skidmore. His son, John Suydam, by his wife Letitia Sebring, was born in 1763, and was the grandfather of Mr. John R. Suydam. John Suydam was one of the prominent merchants of New York in the early years of the present century, being a member of the firm of Suydam & Wyckoff. One of his brothers, Samuel Suydam, was also a well-known merchant of the firm of Suydam & Heyer. John Suydam continued in business until 1821. He lived at 4 Broadway for many years, but late in life moved to Waverley Place. His wife was Jane Mesier, and he had a large family of children His eldest daughter, Katherine Suydam, married Philip M Lydig, and his youngest daughter, Jane Suydam, married William Remsen. He had several sons, who were also prominent in business and professional circles. His third son, John R. Suydam, father of Mr. John R. Suydam, of the present day, was born in the family mansion at 4 Broadway

The mother of Mr John R. Suydam was Ann Middleton Lawrence, who was born in 1823 and died in 1870, having married John R. Suydam, Sr., in 1854. She was the daughter of John L. Lawrence, 1785-1849, the eminent diplomat and man of public affairs, Secretary of the United States Legation to Sweden, a member of the New York State Assembly, State Senator, 1847-49, and Comptroller of the City of New York in 1849 The mother of Ann Middleton Lawrence was Sarah Augusta Smith, daughter of General John Smith, of Long Island, Revolutionary patriot and United States Senator, by his wife Elizabeth Woodhull, who was a daughter of General Nathaniel Woodhull of Revolutionary fame The ancestry of John L Lawrence, who was of the famous Lawrence family of Long Island and New York, has been reviewed on other pages of this volume.

Mr. John R Suydam was born in Sayville, Long Island, and was educated in Columbia College, being graduated in the class of 1879 with the degree of M E, and has since been engaged in the practice of his profession in New York. In 1883, he married Harriet Cochran, of Philadelphia, and has two children, John R Jr, and Lisa Cochran Suydam. Mrs Suydam is a daughter of William Cochran, of Philadelphia, who was born in 1832, and his wife, Eliza Penrose, daughter of John Penrose William Cochran was a son of William G. Cochran and Elizabeth Travis, who was the daughter of John Travis, of Philadelphia, and Elizabeth Bond. The maternal grandfather of Elizabeth Travis was Dr. Phineas Bond, of Philadelphia, 1717-1773, who married Williamena Moore, daughter of Judge William Moore, 1699-1783, and Lady Williamena Wemyss, 1704-1784, sister of David Wemyss, third Earl of Wemyss, and descended through the Wemyss and Leslie families from Robert III, of Scotland. The residence of the family is in East Forty-first Street, and their country home is Edgewater, in Sayville, Long Island, on the great South Bay. Mr Suydam belongs to the Union and the Southside Sportsmen's clubs.

WALTER LISPENARD SUYDAM

I N the eleventh century the Suydams held large possessions in Holland, their arms being argent, a chevron azure, of the chief two crescents gules, and a star of the same. Crest, a swan swimming among rushes, on a bar azure and argent. Motto, *De Tyd Vliegt* Hendrick Rycken Van Suyt-dam, of this family, came in the seventeenth century from Suydam, Holland, to New Amsterdam, and settled at Flatbush, Long Island His sons adopted the name of Suydam, and for many generations have been prominent in Long Island, especially in Kings County. Mr. Walter L. Suydam is a direct descendant of Judge Ryck Suydam, 1675-1743, the youngest son of the original Hendrick Rycken Van Suyt-dam.

Among his ancestors Mr. Suydam also embraces the names of Van Cortlandt, Van Rensselaer, Schuyler, Schermerhorn and others of similar note in New York history. On the maternal side he comes, in several unbroken lines of descent, from royalty His grandmother, Helen White, who married Abraham Schermerhorn, was the granddaughter of Augustus Van Cortlandt, of Yonkers, and his wife, Catharine Barclay, granddaughter of the eminent Colonial divine, the Reverend Thomas Barclay. The latter was the son of John Barclay, who was deputy governor of New Jersey, and a son of Colonel Davis Barclay, of Ury, and his wife, Catherine Gordon, granddaughter of Dr. Gordon, dean of Salisbury, in 1603 The Gordon ancestry is traced to Henry III., of England, through his successors the three Edwards. Joan, daughter of Sir John de Bellfort, in the seventh generation from Henry, married James I., of Scotland, their descendants being the Earls of Huntly and Lords Gordon Mr. Suydam is in the twenty-second generation from Henry III

In 1875, Mr. Suydam married his distant cousin, Jane Mesier Suydam, daughter of John R. Suydam. Mrs. Suydam's ancestry is fully as distinguished as her husband's. Her grandfather was the famous John L. Lawrence, 1785-1849, Comptroller of New York 1849, and the incumbent of many State and national offices, including that of Secretary of Legation and Chargé d'Affaires of the United States at Stockholm, State Senator and Presidential elector. His wife was the daughter of United States Senator, General John Smith, of Long Island. The Lawrence ancestry leads back to John Lawrence, progenitor of the Lawrences of Seahouse, St Ives and St. Albans, who married a daughter of Eudo de Welles and Lady Maude Greystock A descent from Henry III. is traced through his son, Edmund, Earl of Leicester, and the Lords of Mowbray and Welles to Eudo de Welles, in the seventh generation. From Ethelred, the Unready, it comes through his daughter, the Princess Goda, and the Earls of Hereford, Barons de Sudeley and Barons de Clifford, to which family Lady Maude de Greystock belonged. Through them, respectively, Mrs Suydam descends in the twenty-second generation from Henry III. and in the twenty-seventh from Ethelred, the Unready. Mrs. Suydam is a member of the Colonial Dames of America, through descent from fifteen different ancestors distinguished in Colonial times

Mr Walter Lispenard Suydam was born in New York, May 20th, 1854. He was educated in Paris and this city, engaged in business in his youth, and was one of the original subscribing members of the New York Produce Exchange. After five years he retired from active business, but remained a member of the Exchange. He was long one of the managers of the Society for Improving the Condition of the Poor, but resigned in 1896. He is active in the Republican party organization in Suffolk County, has been long chairman of the Republican Committee of Brookhaven and was a delegate to the Republican National Convention, in 1896 He has, however, declined several nominations, believing that he can accomplish more good in a private station. Mr. Suydam resides at 43 East Twenty-second Street, and has a country house and estate of eighty acres called Manowtasquott, at Blue Point, on Great South Bay, Long Island He belongs to the Metropolitan club, the Society of Colonial Wars, and the Westbrook Golf and the Great South Bay Yacht clubs, being an enthusiastic yachtsman. He is also interested in canoeing and belongs to the Canoe Club of Mount Desert, where he is a summer visitor Mr. and Mrs. Suydam have a son, Walter L. Suydam, Jr., born in 1884.

FREDERICK GEORGE SWAN

AMONG the freemen of Medford, Mass, in 1639, was Richard Swan, 1600–1658, who presumably arrived in America at least five years before. He and his wife, Ann, were members of the first church in Boston in 1638, and were dismissed from the church at Rowley in 1639. He was a settler of Rowley, Mass, in 1640, a representative to the General Court for thirteen years, served in King Philip's War, and was one of the proprietors of the Narragansett grant of land. His son, Robert Swan, of Haverhill, Mass, 1629–1697, was a soldier in King Philip's War. His son, Samuel Swan, of Haverhill, 1672–1751, had a son Timothy, 1694–1746, who removed to Charlestown, Mass., and served in the Indian wars.

Samuel Swan, Sr., of Charlestown, 1720–1808, son of Timothy Swan, was born in Charlestown, in 1720 The battle of Bunker Hill was fought on his farm. He was town treasurer of Charlestown, 1777–80, and died in 1808. In 1746, he married Joanna Richardson, of Woburn His eldest surviving son, Samuel Swan, Jr, 1750–1825, grandfather of Mr Frederick G Swan, served under General Benjamin Lincoln during the Revolutionary War, being purchasing agent and quartermaster with the rank of Major. He married Hannah Lamson.

Benjamin Lincoln Swan, 1787–1866, father of Mr. Frederick George Swan, was the fifth child and fourth son of Major Samuel Swan. Removing to New York in 1810, he established himself in business and was very successful, retiring in 1821. He was a director in the Bank of America, and the Bank for Savings, a member of the University Place Presbyterian Church (the old Duane Street Church), vice-president of the New York Bible Society, and a governor of the New York Hospital and the Bloomingdale Asylum for the Insane. He married Mary C Saidler, 1800–1857, and had a family of six children The eldest son was Benjamin L Swan, Jr, who died in 1892, he resided in West Twentieth Street, and his country place was Woodside Farm, Oyster Bay, Long Island. He was educated at Amherst College, was a member of the Union, New York and Century clubs, and the National Academy of Design. His first wife was Caroline Post, by whom he had two children, William L., and Caroline E. Swan, who married Thomas J. Young, his second wife was Mary Renwick

Edward H Swan, the second son, graduated from Columbia and Harvard, and married Julia S Post. He lives in Oyster Bay, Long Island, and has four sons and four daughters. His daughter Elizabeth married Commodore McKay, of the Cunard Steamship Line His daughter Julia married the Reverend William Irvin, son of the late Richard Irvin. Otis Dwight Swan, another son, was educated at Columbia and Harvard. He married, first, Charlotte Anthon, daughter of the Reverend Dr. Henry Anthon, his second wife being Sarah M Weed, by whom he had four children, Benjamin Lincoln, Mary C., Eliphalet W, and Sarah L Swan. A fourth son was Robert J Swan, president of the New York State Agricultural Society, who owned a model farm in Geneva, N Y He married Margaret Johnston, and two daughters survived him, Margaret Johnston and Agnes Swan, who married Waldo Hutchins, Jr. Mary C. Swan, the only daughter of Benjamin L Swan, Sr., married Charles N. Fearing.

Mr. Frederick George Swan, the youngest son of Benjamin Lincoln Swan, Sr, was born in New York, February 22d, 1831. He was educated in private schools, and engaged in the dry goods commission business. In 1861, he joined the Open Board of Stock brokers, and afterwards the New York Stock Exchange, remaining in Wall Street until 1890 In 1861, Mr Swan married Emily Wyeth, daughter of Leonard Jarvis Wyeth, a merchant of New York, who came of an old Massachusetts Colonial family, three of his uncles having been in the Lexington alarm in 1775 Mr and Mrs Swan have one daughter, Frances Wyeth Swan, who married Benjamin Welles Mr. Swan was one of the first twenty members of the Union League Club He also belongs to the Metropolitan Club, the Sons of the Revolution, the Society of Colonial Wars, the Order of Patriots and Founders of America, and the Metropolitan Museum of Art He is a life director of the New York Bible Society, and belongs to the New York Genealogical and Biographical Society.

HENRY COTHEAL SWORDS

THOMAS SWORDS, the progenitor in this country of the family that bears his name, was born in Maryborough, near Dublin, Ireland, in 1738. He was of a family of importance in that country and secured a commission as ensign in the Fifty-Fifth Regiment of Foot in the British Army He came to America in 1756, with the expedition under General Abercrombie, was wounded in the attack on Ticonderoga and promoted to be Lieutenant Afterwards he was in command of military stations in the northern part of New York, notably that of Fort George In 1776, he resigned from the army and made a home on land granted him by the Government in Saratoga County. During the Revolution, his sympathies were with the mother country, although he took little active part. At one time his house was the headquarters of the Royal Army, and the battles of Freeman's Farm and Green's Heights were fought not far away from his home. After the defeat of Burgoyne, he took his family to New York and remained there until his death, in 1780. The wife of Captain Thomas Swords, whom he married in Albany in 1762, was Mary Morrell, who died in 1798, in New York. Captain Swords and his wife are buried in the churchyard of St. Paul's Chapel. Three sons and two daughters were born to this couple. The eldest daughter married for her first husband Allan Jackson, her second husband being Douglass Anderson, a Scotch gentleman, and their daughter became the wife of Thomas B. Cummings, of New York The youngest daughter married Henry Brewerton, and the son of this union was Brevet Major-General Henry Brewerton, U. S. A.

Richard Swords, the eldest son of Captain Thomas Swords, held a commission in the British Army and distinguished himself for bravery. While on service in Virginia in 1781, he was killed at the age of eighteen The two youngest sons, Thomas and James Swords, learned the art of printing, and in 1786 established themselves in Pearl Street, New York, as booksellers and printers, soon taking the foremost position in that line of trade. Being members of the Episcopal Church, they became in effect the official publishing house of that denomination. Among their publications were the authorized versions of the Common Prayer Book and standard editions of the Bible and a Church Almanac, which was one of the most important church publications brought out in this country up to that time.

After remaining in the publishing business nearly fifty years, James Swords retired and became president of the Washington Fire Insurance Company, a position which he held until his death. He left one daughter and two sons. The eldest son was Charles R. Swords, a well-known New York merchant of the last generation. Robert S Swords, the youngest son, was Lieutenant-Colonel of the Second New Jersey Cavalry during the Civil War. Thomas Swords was for thirty years an active member of the vestry of Trinity Church. He continued in the publishing business until his death, in 1843 He married Mary White, of Philadelphia, who died in 1868. One of his sons, Andrew Jackson Swords, was killed in the Mexican War, and another son was Brevet Major-General Thomas Swords, U. S. A , who was distinguished in the Florida, Mexican and Civil Wars Two other sons, Edward J. Swords and James R Swords, succeeded their father in the management of the publishing business. James R. Swords, the youngest, married Ann M. Cotheal, who survives him, and with her daughter, resides in West Thirty-sixth Street

Mr. Henry Cotheal Swords, the representative of this interesting family in the present generation, is the son of James R. and Ann M (Cotheal) Swords. He has been a member of the New York Stock Exchange since 1877, is president of the Real Estate Trust Company and a member of the Chamber of Commerce. His city residence is in West Thirty-eighth Street. He married Elizabeth Clarkson, daughter of the late Samuel Clarkson, of Philadelphia. Mr Swords is a member of the Union League, Union, Calumet, Church and Riding clubs, the Downtown Association, the Seventh Regiment Veterans, the Sons of the Revolution, the Society of Colonial Wars, the St. Nicholas Society and the Metropolitan Museum of Art

EDWARD NEUFVILLE TAILER

A WEALTHY and enterprising merchant of Boston in the seventeenth century was William Tailer, 1611-1682. He married Rebecca Stoughton, daughter of Israel and Elizabeth Stoughton. Stoughton, a man of property and good family, came to America in 1632 and received a grant of land in Dorchester, near Boston, Mass. He was a representative to the General Court, commanded the Massachusetts forces in the Pequot War, and was one of the original incorporators of Harvard College. His death occurred in England in 1644. His most distinguished son was Governor William Stoughton, 1631-1701, Chief Justice of the Colony from 1692 to 1701.

William Tailer, 1675-1731, son of the first William Tailer and Rebecca Stoughton, became a prominent public man in the Colonial annals of Massachusetts. In the expedition sent by Governor Dudley against the French at Port Royal, now Annapolis, Nova Scotia, commanded by Sir William Phipps, William Tailer was an officer under Colonel Nicholson. He was a soldier of great valor and his services gained for him the approval of his commanding officers, as well as promotion. When he went to England, soon after, he carried letters of recommendation from his brother-in-law, Governor Stoughton, to the authorities there and brought back a commission as Lieutenant-Governor of the Province. He succeeded Povey in the office in question in 1704, and held it under Governors Dudley and Burgess, at one time acting as Governor in the interval between the departure of Dudley and the arrival of Burgess. He died while Lieutenant-Governor, in 1731.

The gentleman whose name heads this article is a descendant of William Tailer and Israel Stoughton. His father, Edward N. Tailer, was the senior partner of the firm of Tailer & White, which was one of the best known financial houses in New York City three-quarters of a century ago, and retired from business in 1837. On his mother's side, Mr. Tailer traces his ancestry to the Bogerts, who came from Holland at the time of the first colonization of New Netherland. They settled in the upper part of Manhattan Island and were prominent on Long Island.

Mr. Tailer was born in New York City, July 20th, 1830, and was educated at the Penquest French Academy, a famous school at that date. In 1848, he became a clerk of the firm of Little, Alden & Co. He was subsequently connected with several other firms, and finally became a founder and partner in the importing and commission house of Winzer & Tailer, afterwards known as E. N. & W. H. Tailer & Co., one of the most prominent establishments of its class in the country. After a business life of thirty-six years, Mr. Tailer retired, and since that time has been principally occupied as the executor of important trusts and estates. He has traveled considerably, having crossed the Atlantic more than forty times since he made his initial voyage in the old steamship Arago in 1857. In the New York social world, Mr. Tailer and his immediate family have been more than ordinarily conspicuous for many years. His marriage to Agnes Suffern in 1855 united him with another prominent New York family. Miss Suffern was the daughter of Thomas Suffern, a merchant whose name was associated with all the affairs of the city, social, commercial and philanthropic, in the early part of the century. He was one of the first prominent men of his day to build a residence in Washington Square, and there he lived for fifty years. The children of Edward N. and Agnes (Suffern) Tailer are Mrs. Henry L. Burnett, Mrs. Robert L. Livingston, Mrs Sidney J. Smith and T. Suffern Tailer, who married Maud Louise Lorillard, daughter of Pierre and Emily (Taylor) Lorillard.

Mr. Edward N Tailer is a member of the vestry of the Church of the Ascension, takes part in the management of several religious and benevolent institutions, and is a director of the Northern Dispensary, the Greenwich Savings Bank and German-American Bank. His clubs include the Union, Union League, Merchants', Reform and Country. He is numbered among the prominent New Yorkers who have country residences at Tuxedo, is a patron of the Metropolitan Museum of Art and American Museum of Natural History, and a member of the New England and St. Nicholas societies and the American Geographical Society. His city residence is the old Suffern mansion, Washington Square North.

EDWARD BAKER TALCOTT

W ARWICKSHIRE was the original home of the Talcott family, though the first ancestor of whom there is a record was John Talcott, of Colchester, Essex. His son resided in Braintree, England, where he was a Justice of the Peace, and from him the American branch of the family sprung, through his son, John Talcott, who came to Boston in 1632. John Talcott removed to Hartford in 1636, where he was a magistrate

Lieutenant-Colonel John Talcott, his son, was born in England, and came to America with his father. In 1650, he was Ensign, a Captain in 1660, a Deputy in 1654, and Treasurer of the Colony, 1660-76. In King Philip's War, he commanded the troops with the rank of Major and Lieutenant-Colonel. He was one of the patentees named in the Connecticut charter, and in 1650 married Helena Wakeman, daughter of John Wakeman, Treasurer of Connecticut, dying in 1688 His son, Hezekiah, was born in 1685, married Jemima Parsons, was one of the original proprietors of the town of Durham, and died in 1764 In the next two generations, the ancestors of Mr Edward Baker Talcott were John Talcott, 1712-1765, and his wife, Sarah Parsons, and David Talcott, 1744-1786, and his wife, Anne Lyman Noah Talcott, the son of the latter pair, who was born in Durham, Conn., 1768, and died in New York in 1840, became a merchant of New York in the early years of the present century. From 1798 to 1809, he was a partner of one of the famous Ellis brothers, and after continuing alone in business for the next six years, took his brother David into partnership, under the firm name of N. & D Talcott. The firm was dissolved after eight years, but he continued in business, either alone, with other partners, or with his sons, until the end of his life. His wife, to whom he was married by Bishop Moore in Trinity Church, in 1803, was Eliza Woods, of Oxford, England, 1787-1866. Noah Talcott was one of the original members of the New England Society.

Frederick Lyman Talcott, his son, was born in 1813. Graduating from Columbia College in 1832, he and his brother, Daniel W. Talcott, were taken into partnership by their father, the firm becoming Noah Talcott & Son, and continued under that style until 1858, when Frederick L. Talcott retired and, with his two sons, Frederick L , Jr., and August B Talcott, established the banking house of Talcott & Sons Frederick L Talcott was known as the "Cotton King," from his successful operations in the cotton market, and was president of the organization of merchants which afterwards became the Cotton Exchange. In 1842, he married Harriett Newell Burnham. Their children were Frederick L Talcott, who married Mary Picard ; August Belmont Talcott, who married Therese Polhemus; James Carleton Talcott, who married Laura Belknap, Mary Alice, who married Charles F Palmeter, Harriett Elliott, wife of James R Harrison; Edward Baker Talcott and Florence Louise Talcott.

Mr Edward Baker Talcott, the fourth son of Frederick L. Talcott, was born in New York, January 21st, 1858, and was educated at the Fort Washington Institute He began business in 1874, with Talcott & Sons, then passed four years with the house of Charles F Hardy & Co., for whom he made successful business trips abroad and was offered a partnership. This he refused, and returning to Wall Street, he became a partner in Talcott & Sons in 1880, and joined the Stock Exchange. He remained with the firm for three years, and then became a most successful trader in the market In January, 1897, he entered the firm of Bell & Co. Mr. Talcott represents the house, which is one of the leaders of the street, on the Exchange. From 1890 to 1894, he was identified with baseball affairs, and on returning from Europe in 1892, found the New York Baseball Club in a bankrupt condition. He was made managing director, with complete control, and at the end of the season of 1894 had discharged its debt and placed the club on a dividend-paying basis He then sold his interest to the present owners.

In 1879, Mr. Talcott married Sara T. Roberson, daughter of W. H. Roberson In 1880, a son was born to them, who died in 1886 Mr Talcott resides at 147 West Seventy-second Street, and is a member of the Colonial, Manhattan, New York Athletic and Atlantic Yacht clubs

JAMES TALCOTT

SAMUEL TALCOTT, a younger son of John Talcott, 1600-1660, who came to Boston in 1632, was the founder of a notable branch of the ancient Connecticut Talcott family Born in Newtown, Mass, about 1634, Samuel Talcott, as an infant, accompanied his parents in the migration to Hartford, in 1636, and graduated from Harvard in 1658. He was a deputy to the General Court of Connecticut, 1670-84, and a Lieutenant and Captain of the militia during the Indian wars His wife was a daughter of Elizur Holyoke and Mary Pyncheon, who were of historic Massachusetts families

The subject of this article is a descendant in a maternal line of the Reverend Thomas Hooker, the first settled clergyman of Hartford, Conn., and of Thomas Hart Hooker, member of the Second Connecticut Regiment, which took part in the battle of Bunker Hill, and in Arnold's Quebec Expedition This branch of the Talcott family has given to the State of Connecticut some of its most distinguished citizens. Joseph Talcott, grandson of John Talcott, the pioneer, was born in 1669, was an assistant in 1711, and Governor of Connecticut from 1724 until his death in 1741 Brigadier-General George Talcott, 1786-1862, was a distinguished officer of the United States Army from 1813 to 1851. Captain Andrew Talcott, 1797-1883, served in the Engineer Corps of the United States Army, in 1834-36 had charge of the improvement of the Hudson River, and afterwards in civil life was connected with railroad and other important enterprises. Lieutenant-Colonel George Henry Talcott was a graduate from West Point, and served in the Mexican War. Brigadier-General S. V Talcott was at one time Quartermaster-General of the State of New York on the staff of Governor Horatio Seymour.

Mr. James Talcott is a representative in the metropolis in this generation of this Colonial and Revolutionary family, and is a native of West Hartford, Conn, in which place he was born in 1835. His father was a manufacturer and landowner, and the son received a good education in the schools of his native place, at Easthampton, Mass, and elsewhere When he had reached the age of nineteen, he left his native place, and, coming to New York, established himself in business here. An elder brother had for a time been proprietor of an extensive knitting mill in New Britain, Conn, and Mr. Talcott's first engagement in New York was as agent for his brother's establishment. The New York agency proved successful from the outset, and Mr. Talcott has been connected with that and business of allied nature ever since, a period of over forty years He is now one of the prominent wholesale merchants of the dry goods district of the city, conducting a business of great magnitude, consisting of many departments of varied characters, domestic and foreign. He is agent for several of the largest mills in New York and New England Mr Talcott is a member of the Chamber of Commerce, and of the Board of Trade and Transportation. He is also a director of the Manhattan Company, and has been a member on the board of directorate of the Broadway National Bank, the Broadway Savings Bank and other financial institutions. He is a life member of the American Geographical Society and the New England Society, and is a member of the American Museum of Natural History, and of several clubs

Mr. Talcott has not allowed his business interests to interfere with the discharge of the higher duties devolving upon the citizen His name has been identified with almost every movement during the past twenty-five years, looking to the improvement of the city government To charitable and educational objects in this city and elsewhere, irrespective of creed, he has freely contributed in time and money.

In 1860, Mr. Talcott married Henrietta E Francis, daughter of the Reverend Amzi Francis, of Bridgehampton, Long Island They have five children. The Reverend J Frederick Talcott is a graduate of Princeton University, and lives at 60 West Eighty-seventh Street Francis Edgar Talcott lives at Westfield, N J, and Arthur Whiting Talcott is in business with his father, and resides at 39 West Seventy-sixth Street The two daughters are Grace and Edith Charlotte Talcott Mr and Mrs Talcott reside at 7 West Fifty-seventh Street.

548

FREDERICK D. TAPPEN

DURING the Spanish persecutions in the Netherlands, the Tappen family fled from Holland to England, whence its American ancestor came to New York in 1630, settling in Fort Orange and at Kingston in 1637. Descendants are now found throughout the State of New York and other Middle States. One of the most picturesque figures of New York during the last half of the nineteenth century was Colonel Charles Barclay Tappen, who belonged to this respected family. His grandfather settled in Morris County, N. J, before the Revolution, and his father was John Tappen, editor of The Plebian, now The Ulster Gazette. Born before the century began, Colonel Tappen almost lived to see its end, dying April 20th, 1893, having passed his ninety-seventh birthday.

Colonel Tappen was an architect and builder, and many of the buildings in New York City of the last generation were designed by him. An intensely patriotic man, he served in the War of 1812, and in 1833, Governor Marcy commissioned him Colonel of the Two Hundred and Thirty-Sixth Regiment, National Guard, State of New York. He maintained a deep interest in military affairs through life. Among other offices, he filled, from 1835 to 1838, that of Superintendent of Repairs of the City of New York, a post equivalent to the present Public Works Department. He was a man of striking personality and vigorous to the time of his last illness. Living in East Sixty-eighth Street, it was his regular practice, on every pleasant day, to walk down Fifth Avenue and Broadway to Wall Street. He had a family of eleven children and saw thirty grandchildren and great-grandchildren grow up around him. His wife, Elizabeth Tappen, was a woman of much force of character and natural vigor, and also lived to a ripe old age, passing away only a few years before her husband died

Mr. Frederick D. Tappen is a son of the late Colonel Charles B. Tappen. Born in New York City, January 29th, 1829, he was prepared for college in the Columbia College Grammar School, and then entered the New York University, from which institution he was graduated in 1849 The following year he entered the service of the National Bank of New York, now the Gallatin National Bank, and has maintained that connection for nearly half a century. In 1857, he became cashier, and in 1868 was elected president, a position that he has retained to the present time.

For more than forty years, Mr. Tappen has been one of the most prominent factors in the banking business of New York Problems of finance have been the occupation of his life, and he is one of the leading authorities upon the subject, and his opinions and advice have often been asked by the State and National officials. One of the most striking features in Mr. Tappen's career has been his service to the banking interests of the metropolis in times of panics In 1873, 1884, 1890 and 1893, he took a leading part in devising and executing measures that carried the allied banks of the city through the storms. During these critical times, he was chairman of the loan committee of the Clearing House Association. In 1893, his work was particularly successful and won for him the approval of the business community generally As a token of appreciation, Mr. Tappen's banking associates presented him with an antique silver tankard that had a peculiarly interesting and pertinent significance The tankard was originally presented to Sir John Houblon, Lord Mayor of London and first governor of the Bank of England, for his efforts in tiding over a financial crisis, in 1693, as shown by an inscription on the tankard It finally came into possession of a New York gentleman, and it was particularly fitting that just two centuries from the time of its first presentation it should again be used for a like purpose in the financial centre of the New World. Mr Tappen has been president of the Clearing House Association twice, is vice-president of the Metropolitan Trust Company, and a director in the Bank of New Amsterdam, the Sixth National Bank and Queen Insurance Company, and a trustee of the Royal Insurance Company, of Liverpool Mr. Tappen married Sarah A. B Littell His clubs include the Metropolitan, Union League, Union, Grolier and Players, and he is a member of the Holland Society, St. Nicholas Society and the Downtown Association. His residence is at 49 East Sixty-eighth Street.

ALEXANDER TAYLOR

OF Scottish origin, the grandparents of Mr. Alexander Taylor, Jr., were residents of Leith until 1822, when they emigrated to the United States, bringing with them their eldest, and at that time only, son, Alexander. The father engaged in mercantile business in New York, and died in 1840. The son, Alexander, father of the subject of this sketch, was educated in New York, and engaged in business early in life. First he was connected with a Wall Street firm of brokers, but soon established himself independently. Subsequently, with two brothers as partners, he founded the firm of Taylor Brothers, at the head of which he continued until 1870, when, with his son, Alexander Taylor, Jr., he organized the firm of Alexander Taylor & Son. Soon after, he removed to London as the resident partner there of the banking house of Clews, Habicht & Co. His firm was the fiscal agent of the United States in England, and had part in some of the most important financial enterprises of that time.

After the panic of 1873, Mr. Taylor returned to New York to take charge of the affairs of the house with which he was connected, and at the same time represented the British bondholders of the Burlington, Cedar Rapids & Northern Railroad Company. Eminently successful in reviving the fortunes of the banking house, and in protecting the interests of the bondholders, for whom he was attorney, he afterwards became connected with other financial undertakings. He assisted in establishing the Gramme Electric Company, of which he was director and treasurer, was an early promoter of the plan for a canal across Nicaragua, being a director and chairman of the executive committee of the company, and maintained an active connection with the New York, West Shore & Buffalo Railroad, of which he,was treasurer and a director, and with the Ontario & Western Railroad and the Walkill Railroad, in each of which he was a director. He was for many years a member of the New York Stock Exchange, frequently being called upon to occupy official position in that body, was a member of the St. Andrew's Society, the Burns and Union League clubs, a vice-president of the National Academy of Design, and also connected with the Scottish Union and National Insurance Company, of Scotland, of which he was one of the three American trustees.

Mr. Alexander Taylor, Jr., the oldest son in his father's family, was born in New York, June 22d, 1848. His primary education was secured in the famous Charlier Institute, and he afterwards attended Churchill's Military Academy in Sing Sing. Before he had become of age, he entered his father's office as a clerk, subsequently becoming a member of the firm of Alexander Taylor & Son. Ultimately he became the sole proprietor of the firm. While in no sense a politician, Mr Taylor has given much attention to the cause of political reform and the honest administration of municipal government. He has never held political office, but was at one time persuaded to be a candidate for Congress from the Twelfth Congressional District, and although defeated, made a strong campaign. He has been particularly distinguished by his interest in gentlemanly sports and by his activity in promoting organizations devoted to those pursuits. The Gentlemen's Driving Association of New York owed its origin solely to his efforts, and he was one of the organizers and a director of the National Horse Show Association of America, and one of the originators and governors of the Country Club of Westchester County. He is a member of the Megantic Fish and Game Club, of Maine, the Adirondack Club, the oldest organization in the Adirondack Mountains, the Caribou Club, of Maine, and other similar organizations, and belongs to the Union League and New York Yacht and Larchmont Yacht clubs, and some twenty other clubs.

In 1868, Mr. Taylor married Fannie Taylor, daughter of the Honorable Henry J. Taylor, of Jersey City. Mr. and Mrs. Taylor have had seven children, of whom only three are living. Laura Taylor married C. T. W. Hollister, lives in Cleveland, O., and has one son, Alexander Taylor Hollister. Frances Taylor, the youngest daughter, married J. C. Baldwin, Jr., of New York, where they are now living. They have one son, J. C. Baldwin, third. Alexandrina Taylor, the only unmarried daughter, lives with her parents. The Taylor residence is Chrismere, Mamaroneck, N. Y., one of the handsomest estates on Long Island Sound.

HENRY AUGUSTUS COIT TAYLOR

O NE of the leading merchants of New York City, in the first half of the eighteenth century, was Moses Taylor, whose business was advertised in the New York Gazette of 1750, as "at the corner house opposite the Fly Market." This Moses Taylor, the first of his name in the New World, was a London merchant and settled in New York about 1736. His younger son was born in 1739, soon after the arrival of the family in this country, became a man of considerable wealth and had a large family. During the British occupation of New York, he removed to the interior of New Jersey, where his son, Jacob B. Taylor, was born.

After the war and when he had attained to manhood, Jacob B Taylor came to New York and followed in the footsteps of his father and his grandfather in business. He rapidly advanced to prominence in social and political, as well as in business walks of life He was a member of the board of aldermen with such men as Philip Hone, John Ireland, and others, at a time when the solid business men of the city considered it a duty and an honor to engage in public affairs, and to devote part of their time to advancing and conserving the welfare of the municipality For many years he lived in Broadway, at the corner of Morris Street, and there entertained generously, surrounding himself with the most interesting people of the city, He was associated in business with John Jacob Astor for many years.

Moses Taylor, son of Jacob B. Taylor, was born in 1806, and died in 1882. He was educated with the end in view of fitting himself for the business life that had been mapped out for him, and at the age of fifteen, began his career. Gradually undertaking small business ventures, he found himself, at twenty-six years of age, with a capital of $15,000, a fortune for a young man in those days. Thereupon he went into business for himself and prospered for a time, but in the great fire of 1835, lost all that he possessed. He quickly recovered from this disaster, however, and became one of the wealthiest and most prominent business men of his day In 1855, he was elected president of the City Bank, a position that he retained until his death, in 1882 His ability in the direction of financial affairs was generally recognized, and President Lincoln offered him the position of Secretary of the Treasury after the resignation of Secretary Chase. He became largely interested in railroad properties, and at one time practically owned the Delaware, Lackawanna & Western Railroad. He also made profitable investments in the Lackawanna Coal & Iron Company, and the Manhattan Gas Company, and, with Peter Cooper, Marshall O Roberts and Chandler White, he was a supporter of Cyrus Field in the Atlantic cable undertaking

The wife of Moses Taylor, whom he married in 1832, was Catharine A Wilson, daughter of a New York merchant She died in 1892 Mr. and Mrs. Taylor were survived by five children Their daughter, Alberta S Taylor, married Percy R. Pyne, the banker, and has two sons, Percy Rivington Pyne, who married Maud Howland, and Moses Taylor Pyne, who married Margaretta Stockton. Another daughter, Katherine Winthrop Taylor, married Robert Winthrop, and is the mother of Albertina T , Robert Dudley, Frederic and Beekman Winthrop. George C. Taylor, the eldest son, lives in Islip, Long Island, and is a member of the Metropolitan, Union League, Union and Knickerbocker clubs.

Mr. Henry A. C. Taylor, the youngest son, was born in New York, January 19th, 1841, and was graduated from Columbia College in the class of 1861. He is a partner in the firm of Moses Taylor & Co. He married, in 1868, Miss Fearing, daughter of Daniel B Fearing, lives in East Seventy-first Street, has a summer home in Newport, and is a member of the Metropolitan, Union, Knickerbocker, and New York Yacht clubs, and the Downtown Association. He has two sons and one daughter. His eldest son, Henry Richmond Taylor, graduated from Columbia University in the class of 1891, is a member of the Metropolitan, Knickerbocker and other clubs, and is engaged in the practice of law. His younger son, Moses Taylor, was graduated from Yale University in 1893, is a member of the Metropolitan and Knickerbocker clubs, and married Edith Bishop, daughter of Heber R. Bishop.

JOHN TAYLOR TERRY

A MONG the most notable Puritan pioneers in the settlement of the Connecticut Colony were John Haynes and George Wyllys John Haynes was Governor of Massachusetts in 1635 He removed to Hartford, and in 1639 became the first Governor of Connecticut, and thereafter was seven times elected in alternate years to the same office, being also Deputy Governor five times George Wyllys was a wealthy English gentleman of Warwickshire and had a farm prepared for him in Hartford before he came over with his family in 1638 He took a leading position; was a magistrate in 1639, Deputy Governor in 1641, and Governor in 1642. He died in 1644, but his descendants became prominent and three of them held in succession the office of Secretary of State of the Colony. Upon the land of Governor Wyllys stood the famous Charter Oak, in whose hollow trunk the charter of Connecticut was hidden Samuel Terry was the original patentee of the town of Enfield, Conn, about 1657, and was the first Colonist married at Springfield, Mass

Mr. John T Terry can trace his lineage to all three of these famous Puritans. His ancestral lines also go back on both sides to Governor William Bradford, who led the Mayflower Pilgrims His maternal ancestress, Mabel Harlakenden, the wife of Governor John Haynes, was a member of a family whose descent is traced to King Edward III. One of Mr Terry's maternal forefathers was the Reverend Edward Taylor, who married a granddaughter of Governor Wyllys. The direct line of descent is from Samuel Terry, of Enfield, Conn, who was born in 1661, was Selectman, Ensign and Captain, and died in 1730. His son Ephraim, of Enfield, 1701-1783, married Governor Bradford's great-granddaughter, Ann Adams, and his grandson, Eliphalet, 1741-1812, was a justice of the quorum in 1778, a representative in the Connecticut Assembly for thirty-three consecutive years, most of that time being Speaker of the House, and a judge of the County Court from 1798 until his death Another member of the family was Colonel Nathaniel Terry, who led a company of soldiers from Enfield to Boston as soon as the news of Concord and Lexington reached there Major General Alfred H Terry, a distinguished officer of the Civil War, is of the same family

The father of the subject of this sketch was Roderick Terry, 1788-1849, a merchant of Hartford, Conn, for forty years, and president of the Exchange Bank there for fifteen years. His mother was a daughter of the Reverend John Taylor, of Deerfield, Mass, whose wife was a daughter of Colonel Nathaniel Terry, and who could trace his descent to the Days, the Smiths and other leading families of Western Massachusetts The grandfather of the Reverend John Taylor was Edward Taylor, of Westfield, Mass, who graduated from Harvard College in 1671.

Mr. John Taylor Terry has been one of New York's foremost merchants in the generation that is fast passing away. He was born in Hartford in 1822, and, coming to New York in 1841, went into business with Edwin D Morgan, first as a merchant and then as a banker. After the death of Governor Morgan, in 1883, Mr Terry continued the business under the original firm name He has been one of the leading bankers and financiers of the metropolis, interested in large undertakings, and a director in various railroad, insurance and telegraph corporations, among them the Mercantile Trust Company, of which he is vice-president, the Western Union Telegraph Company, the Metropolitan Trust Company, the American Exchange Bank and a number of railroad companies He has a country residence at Irvington-on-the-Hudson, and belongs to the Union League Club, the American Geographical Society, the New England Society, the Sons of the Revolution, the Society of Mayflower Descendants, and is a patron of the American Museum of Natural History and the Metropolitan Museum of Art

In 1846, Mr Terry married, in Brooklyn, Elizabeth Roe Peet. Their elder son, the Reverend Roderick Terry, D. D., is pastor of the South Reformed Church, of New York He married Linda Marquand, their two children being Eunice and Roderick Terry, Jr John T. Terry, Jr, the younger son, a graduate of Yale and a member of the bar, married Bertha Halsted and has two children, a son and a daughter

PAUL LOUIS THEBAUD

FRANCE and Holland gave to America the ancestor of the Thebaud family, of New York, which for more than a century has taken a notable and honored part in the commercial activity of the metropolitan city, and has, at the same time, held a distinguished position in its social relations. The first of the name to come to this country was Joseph Thebaud, who landed at Boston, Mass., arriving from China, in 1771, as the accredited representative in America of the French East India Company and of other large mercantile interests in his native land, to which the growth of business between the two countries made an agent here necessary. Joseph Thebaud was a man of high education, and had enjoyed a long training in commercial affairs, and had, also, in the course of his business career, traveled extensively and become familiar with all parts of the world. He took at once a leading place in American business life of that day, his talents and experience, as well as the influential connections he possessed in Europe, placing him, ere many years after his first arrival in this country had passed, among the foremost merchants that his adopted land possessed in those days. Living for a time in Boston, he removed to New Haven, Conn., which at that date, and for some decades after, was a considerable shipping port, and enjoyed more or less foreign trade, which, however, gradually shifted to New York about the beginning of the present century, owing to the superior natural advantages the latter port possessed as an entrepôt of commerce. Perceiving this tendency, Joseph Thebaud accordingly established himself in the growing metropolis, where he and his descendants have ever since been citizens. He was one of the substantial men of his time, and in his business relations was noted for an inflexible integrity, his motto being that his word was as good as his bond, which principle he observed in all his extensive affairs. The commercial house which he established, and which three generations of his descendants have now conducted with success and honor through the vicissitudes of a century, has ever been governed according to the principles of its founder, and presents an instance of permanency rare in the history of such establishments in this country, where business changes are frequently of so marked a character.

Joseph Thebaud acquired social distinction as well as wealth in New York. He resided in Beekman Street, then a neighborhood of dwellings occupied by the most substantial citizens, his near neighbors being the Stuyvesant family, and his country seat was on a large tract of land extending from Orchard and Rivington Streets to the East River. One of his favorite personal tastes was for flowers, and his greenhouses, in which he took great pride, were the admiration of the town and a decided novelty. Among his most intimate friends in New York was the elder Dr. Hosack. He was active in the various charities of the city, being the founder of the French Benevolent Society. In 1795, he married a daughter of Philip Le Breton, a wealthy merchant of the French island of Martinique, in the West Indies, and at his death, in 1811, left a large estate to his wife and sons, John J. and Edward Thebaud.

The latter received his education at Moravian College, Bethlehem, Pa., and then entered the office of the famous New York shipping merchant, Gardiner G. Howland, where he obtained a sound commercial training. His father's business manager, Joseph Bouchaud, was the executor of the estate, and continued the elder Mr. Thebaud's business, subsequently marrying his widow. In 1820, Edward Thebaud joined his stepfather, the firm being very successful, but he retired in 1824 and visited relatives in France.

During his stepson's absence, Mr. Bouchaud became involved in his affairs through the failure of one of his foreign correspondents and suspended payment. He, however, in due time, paid his debts in full, and resuming business with the confidence of all, retrieved his fortune and became once more a rich man. In 1835, Edward Thebaud returned to the firm, which was increased in importance and in the volume of its business, by further French connections, as well as an extensive Mexican trade, and owned a line of fast sailing ships. During the War of 1812, Edward Thebaud was an officer of the New York State forces engaged in that struggle for the defense of the city, while his stepfather fitted out some of their vessels, as privateers, and with them rendered considerable aid to the American cause The wife of Edward Thebaud, whom he married in 1823, was a young lady belonging to a noble French family, Emma, daughter of Vincent Classe van Schalkwyck de Boisaubin Her father had been a playmate of Charles X , and an officer of the body guard of Louis XVI. He lost his estates in the French Revolution, and fleeing with his family to America, became a prominent member of the Colony of *émigrés* which was such a feature of New York's social life in the early years of this century The sons of Edward Thebaud and his wife, Emma de Boisaubin, were Edward Vincent, Paul Louis and Francis F Thebaud, all of whom have been active in the commercial life of the city

Edward V Thebaud, the eldest brother, was born in New York in 1824, and was educated at St Mary's College, in Baltimore On the completion of his education, he entered the counting house of his father's firm, and continued in active business until 1892, when he retired and made his residence at Madison, N J , at which place his father had also lived on his country estate for some years.

Paul L Thebaud, who is now the head of the time-honored family business establishment, was born in Morristown, N J , and graduated from St John's College, Fordham, N. Y He also entered his father's business office in 1845, and now counts more than half a century of honorable and successful mercantile life He is a member of the Chamber of Commerce of the State of New York, and is a director of a number of the city's important financial institutions Mr Thebaud has also devoted no small portion of a busy life to the cause of charity, and is a trustee and officer of many institutions or societies for that object, while he is also a member of the most prominent social clubs of the metropolis His wife was Caroline E. Gibert, a member of the well-known Gibert family of New York, which is also of French origin, and has been long prominent in business and society On her mother's side, Mrs Thebaud is descended from General Ebenezer Stevens, the Revolutionary hero, afterwards a notable figure in the New York business world, and whose descendants have been for several generations prominent in the professions, in financial affairs and in the social life of the metropolis

Francis F Thebaud, the youngest brother, was graduated from Seton Hall College, New Jersey, and then received a special training for business He entered the establishment of his father and brothers at an early age, and supplemented his experience by a course of extensive travel in the countries with which the firm has business relations, thus acquiring a knowledge of physical conditions, of individuals and of languages which has been invaluable in his subsequent career His whole attention has been devoted to the serious occupation of his life, and he is esteemed in a wide circle for the uprightness and generosity of his character, and holds high rank in the metropolitan mercantile and financial world.

Paul Gibert Thebaud, the representative of the next generation of this family, is the son of Paul L Thebaud and his wife, Caroline (Gibert) Thebaud He was educated at the Columbia Grammar School in this city, with a view to taking the place he now fills in the venerable firm of which his father is the senior. Going into business under the care of his parent and uncles, he gradually passed through the various grades which fitted him for a partnership in the house He married early in life, his bride being Mathilde Reynal, only daughter of Jules Reynal de St Michel, and granddaughter of the late Nathaniel Higgins, of this city Their family consists of two sons, Paul Gibert Thebaud, Jr , and Reynal de St Michel Thebaud, both of whom it is their parents' desire shall maintain the social and business prestige of their ancestors By right of descent, Mr Thebaud is entitled to membership in the Sons of the Revolution, the St Nicholas Society, the Society of Colonial Wars and the Society of the War of 1812 His name is found upon the rolls of a number of the most prominent clubs, and he holds the office of vice-president of the Knollwood Country Club, a leading social and athletic organization of Westchester County Paul Gibert Thebaud's town residence is 158 Madison Avenue, and his country home is Rocky Dell Farm, near White Plains He is one of the best known and most deservedly popular of the younger married men of the city

ADDISON THOMAS

GENERAL JOHN ADDISON THOMAS, the father of the above gentleman, was born in Cabarrus County, N. C, May 28th, 1810, but resided in Columbia, Tenn. He graduated from West Point in 1833 He was made Brevet Second Lieutenant of the Third Artillery, the same year, and performed garrison duty at Fort Wolcott, R I. In 1835, he became Second Lieutenant, and First Lieutenant in 1837 For seven years after 1834, he was assistant instructor of infantry tactics at West Point, and assistant professor of geography, history and ethics In 1841-42 he was aide-de-camp to Brigadier-General John E Wool, and for three years following 1842 was commandant of cadets and instructor of infantry tactics Advanced to be Captain of the Third Artillery in 1843, he resigned in 1846.

Upon returning to civil life, General Thomas practiced law in New York, for seven years In 1846, he was Colonel of the Fourth New York Regiment, raised for service in the Mexican War He was also engineer-in-chief on the staff of the Governor, with rank of Brigadier-General in 1852 In 1853, he was sent to London to represent the United States in the Convention with Great Britian for the adjustment of American claims, and upon his return in 1855, served as Assistant United States Secretary of State for two years He established an international reputation by his report of the proceedings of the Convention of 1853 and other State papers He died in Paris, France, March 20th, 1858 The parents of General Thomas were Isaac Jetton Thomas, of Cabarrus County, N C, and Asenath Houston The old plantation is still in the family and is now owned by John Addison Thomas, a grandson of Isaac Jetton Thomas and a son of James Houston Thomas

General Thomas married Catharine L Ronalds, the daughter of Thomas A Ronalds and Maria D Lorillard. The father of Catharine Ronalds was a leading merchant of New York in the first quarter of the century. He also was a director in the Mechanics' Bank, and took an active part in military affairs during the War of 1812. His death occurred in 1835 He was the son of James Ronalds, a Revolutionary patriot of Scottish origin.

Colonel Addison Thomas, the oldest son of General John A. and Catharine L. (Ronalds) Thomas, was born at West Point. Prepared for college in Europe, he entered the Law School of Harvard University, graduating in the class of 1867, and was admitted to the New York bar Much of his time in recent years has been spent in travel abroad He has a residence at Newport. His clubs are the Harvard, Military, and New York Yacht, and the Metropolitan of Washington, D. C. For more than twenty-one years he has served in the National Guard of the States of New York, New Jersey and Rhode Island His last command was the Newport Artillery, the oldest active military organization in the United States, having received its charter from King George II, in February, 1741. Colonel Thomas married Alice Gridley Abbott, of Boston, who died at Paris in 1874 In 1878, he married Susan Cox, daughter of the late Reverend Samuel Hanson Cox, D D, of Brooklyn. His only son, Houston A Thomas, who married Daisy Bonnet, of Geneva, Switzerland, lives in Boston, Mass

John Addison Thomas had three other children, Ronald, Catherine Lorillard, and George L. Thomas Ronald Thomas, who was born in New York, November 3d, 1848, was educated in Europe, and was engaged in business in New York as a broker He has retired and lives at Santa Barbara, Cal, but is still a member of the Union League, New York Athletic and New York Yacht clubs and a life member of the Country club of Westchester County In Santa Barbara, he is a member of the Santa Barbara and Santa Barbara Country clubs In 1881, he married Daisy Richards, of Chambersburgh, Pa Catherine Lorillard Thomas, born in Paris in 1850, married, in 1869, Ernest Christian de la Haye, Viscount d'Auglemont, and has since resided in Paris The Viscountess d'Auglemont was widowed in 1885, and has two children, Henri and Blanche. The youngest of the family is George L Thomas, of Columbia, Tenn, who married his cousin, Nora Clayton Thomas, daughter of James Houston Thomas, a prominent member of the Confederate Congress

EBEN BRIGGS THOMAS

FOR twelve centuries back the pedigree of the Thomas family can be historically traced. Sir Rhysap Thomas, in the reign of Henry VIII, was the ancestor of numerous branches bearing his name, in both England and America, at the present time. He was descended from Urien Rheged, a British Prince, who lived in the early part of the sixth century, and tradition in regard to the family goes further back than that, writers on Welsh history and genealogy holding that its records are distinguishable in the early centuries of the Christian era. There are many branches of the Thomas family in the United States. Several pioneers came from the Old World to the New during the early years of the migration in the seventeenth century. They established themselves in different parts of the country, and their representatives have since become distinguished in every walk of life. Several of the name settled at an early date in New England, where their descendants have been numerous and influential.

The special branch of the family now under consideration, and of which Mr. Eben Briggs Thomas is a representative in New York in the present generation, was founded by William Thomas, who settled in Eastern Massachusetts soon after the beginning of the eighteenth century. Benjamin Thomas, son of William Thomas, was a prominent resident of Middleboro, Mass., where he was a deacon in the First Congregational Church, and otherwise active in the affairs of the church and the community in which he lived. His wife was Elizabeth Churchill, who was a member of an old Massachusetts family. Ezra Thomas, son of Benjamin and Elizabeth (Churchill) Thomas, married Lucy Sturtevant, of Carver, Mass., and lived in the old family homestead in Middleboro. Ezra Thomas of the third generation, was born in 1786, and lived in Middleboro throughout his entire life, his death occurring in 1825. He was married in 1812, at Carver, Mass., by the Reverend John Shaw, to Hannah Cole, who was born in 1786. Ezra Thomas and Hannah Cole were the grandparents of Mr. Eben Briggs Thomas. The father of Mr. Thomas was the third Ezra Thomas, of Middleboro. He was born in 1814 and died in Cleveland, O., in 1891. His wife, whom he married in 1837, was Mary Nelson Briggs, daughter of the Reverend Ebenezer Briggs and Hannah Nelson. The father of Mary Nelson Briggs was a son of Ebenezer Briggs, who was born in 1731, and his wife, Elizabeth Smith, and a grandson of Nathaniel Briggs and Sarah Whittaker, of Rehoboth, Mass., who were married in 1719.

Mr. Eben Briggs Thomas was born in Chatham, Canada, December 22d, 1838. Early in life he entered upon a business career with the American Telegraph Company. In the course of time he made his first connection with railroad management, with which he has now been identified for nearly forty years. In 1870, he was made a receiver of the railway property which is now the Cleveland, Lorain & Wheeling Railway Company, and subsequently became general manager of the Bee Line, at present included in the Cleveland, Cincinnati, Chicago & St. Louis Railroad. Remaining with that corporation for several years, he then became connected with the Richmond & Danville system. In 1888, he was elected second vice-president of the New York, Lake Erie & Western Railroad, and took charge of the Western division of that system. In 1890, he was advanced to be first vice-president of that road, and 1894, upon the retirement of John King from the presidency, was elected to fill the vacancy, and holds that office in the Erie Railroad as the reorganized company is known. He ranks among the foremost railroad officials in the country, being a master of details in all departments of the business.

In 1868, Mr. Thomas married, in Cleveland, O., Helen Gertrude Streator, daughter of Dr. Worthy Stevens Streator and his wife, Sarah Wakeley Sterling. Mrs. Thomas, on the paternal side, is descended from Dr. John Streator, through Isaac H. Streator, who was born in 1758, and Isaac H. Streator, Jr., who was born in 1786 and was her grandfather. The children of Mr. and Mrs. Thomas are: Gertrude Streator and Helen Sterling Thomas. The city residence of the family is in West Fifty-eighth Street. Mr. Thomas belongs to the Tuxedo, Manhattan, Lawyers', Union League, Engineers and Riding clubs, the Century Association and the Ohio Society.

THEODORE GAILLARD THOMAS, M. D.

FOR many generations, the Thomas and Gaillard families, from both which this gentleman is descended, have been prominent in South Carolina; the Reverend Samuel Thomas having been sent by the Church of England in 1700, to establish a church in that Colony, while Joachim Gaillard emigrated from France in 1689, soon after the revocation of the Edict of Nantes. The Reverend Edward Thomas, father of Dr. Theodore Gaillard Thomas, was a native of South Carolina and was one of the ablest ministers of the Episcopal Church in that State. His wife, Jane Gaillard, was a daughter of Judge Gaillard, of the Supreme Court of South Carolina. The Honorable John Gaillard, her uncle, was born in St Stephen's District, S. C , in 1765, and died in Washington in 1826. Active in public affairs, he was elected to the United States Senate in 1805, succeeding the Honorable Pierce Butler, and served until his death, a period of twenty-one years. From the Eleventh to the Eighteenth Congress, inclusive, he presided over the deliberations of the Senate as president *pro tempore*, being elected to that chair on account of the death of two successive vice-presidents, George Clinton and Elbridge Gerry. Thomas H. Benton, in his Thirty Years' View, says of him, "There was probably not an instance of disorder or a disagreeable scene in the Chamber during his long continued presidency."

Dr. Theodore Gaillard Thomas was born in Edisto Island, S. C , in 1831. His early education was secured in the Charleston, S. C., Literary College, from which he was graduated. He then pursued the study of medicine in the Medical College of Charleston, from which institution he received the degree of M. D. in 1852. Fixing upon New York for his future home, he came to this city immediately after completing his medical education, and attached himself to Bellevue Hospital and the Ward's Island Hospital, as house physician. Shortly after he went abroad for further study, and for a year and a half walked the hospitals of London, Dublin and Paris He then returned to New York and established himself in general practice, and has now for more than forty years been a resident of this city, where he is recognized as a leading physician.

Dr. Thomas, aside from his private practice, has been professionally connected with the leading hospitals and medical colleges of the metropolis. In 1855, he received the appointment of lecturer in the medical department of the New York University, retaining that position until 1863, when he was made professor of obstetrics and diseases of women and children in the College of Physicians and Surgeons of New York. For more than fifteen years he was attached to Bellevue Hospital as visiting physician. In 1872, he was appointed one of the attending surgeons of the Woman's Hospital, and for some time was consulting surgeon of St. Mary's Hospital for Women in Brooklyn. He has also been connected with the Stranger's, St. Luke's and Roosevelt hospitals, and in 1875 was president of the medical board of the Nursery and Child's Hospital, with which he had previously been connected for several years. Despite his busy professional life, Dr Thomas has found time to write much upon medical topics. He assisted in the preparation of A Century of Practical Medicine, wrote and published a valuable work, A Practical Treatise on Diseases of Women, and has also written several books and papers for medical journals treating of the specialty in medical practice to which he has devoted himself

The first wife of Dr. Thomas was Mary Gaillard, of South Carolina, who died in 1855. For his second wife, he married, in 1862, Mary Willard, granddaughter of the celebrated Emma Willard, of Troy, N. Y. Dr. and Mrs. Thomas live in upper Madison Avenue and have a summer home, The Dunes, Southampton, Long Island. John Metcalfe Thomas, eldest son of Dr. Thomas, married Louisa Carroll Jackson, the daughter of Oswald Jackson, of New York, a direct descendant of Charles Carroll, of Carrolton, one of the signers of the Declaration of Independence. Howard Lapsley Thomas, a younger son, married Adele B Larocque, daughter of Joseph Larocque He was a prominent figure in New York social circles until his death, in June, 1896 Dr. Thomas is a member of the Metropolitan, Riding, and Shinnecock Golf clubs, the Century Association and the Metropolitan Museum of Art.

FREDERICK DIODATI THOMPSON

REPRESENTING in a direct line two of the oldest manorial families of Long Island, the Thompsons and the Gardiners, Mr. Frederick Diodati Thompson also includes in his ancestry famous names in Colonial New York and New England, as well as that of the Diodati, Counts of the Holy Roman Empire, a family of great distinction in Italy and other European countries The ancestor of the Thompsons of Suffolk County, N Y., was the Reverend William Thompson, of Winwicke, Lancashire, 1597–1666, who graduated at Brazenose College, Oxford, in 1619, and emigrated to America in 1634. His son, John Thompson, came to Ashford, Long Island, in 1656, and was one of the proprietors of the town of Brookhaven The family seat, Sagtikos Manor, or Apple Tree Wicke, Islip, Long Island, of which Mr Frederick Diodati Thompson is the owner, has been in the possession of his race for many generations. His great-grandfather, the Honorable Isaac Thompson, 1743–1816, a Judge of the Court of Common Pleas, member of the Colonial Assembly, and a magistrate for more than forty years, was born there. His grandfather, the Honorable Jonathan Thompson, also born at the Manor, in 1773, became a prominent citizen of New York, holding a high social position. He was president of the Bank of the Manhattan Company, Collector of the Port of New York under Presidents Madison, Monroe and the younger Adams, and chairman of the Democratic-Republican National Committee, being also the personal friend of five presidents of the United States.

David Thompson, of Sagtikos, son of the Honorable Jonathan Thompson, was the father of Mr. Frederick Diodati Thompson. He was well known to New Yorkers of his day, and was noted for his distinguished appearance. He was one of the earliest members of the Union Club. He married Sarah Diodati, daughter of John Lyon Gardiner, seventh Lord of the Manor, of Gardiner's Island, and of his wife, Sarah (Griswold) Gardiner. The children of this marriage were: Sarah Gardiner Thompson, who married Colonel David Lyon Gardiner, her children being David, Sarah Diodati and Robert Alexander Gardiner; Gardiner Thompson and David Gardiner Thompson, who both died unmarried; Charles Griswold Thompson, Frederick Diodati Thompson, Elizabeth Thompson, and Mary Gardiner Thompson. The present Mr Thompson is thus descended on the maternal side from one of the foremost Colonial families. Its founder was Captain Lion Gardiner, full reference to whom and his descendants will be found in the article devoted to the present representative of the family, Colonel John Lyon Gardiner. Mr. Thompson also traces his descent to Governor Matthew Griswold, of Connecticut; Governor Roger Wolcott, who commanded the Colonial forces at the siege of Louisburg; and Roger Ludlow, Deputy-Governor of Massachusetts Bay and of Connecticut, a descendant of the Ludlows, of Ludlow Castle.

Mr Frederick Diodati Thompson was born in this city in 1849, and was graduated from Columbia College Law School. He was admitted to the bar, but has found active occupation in travel, society and literature. In the latter field his work includes many contributions to periodicals and a book of travel, In the Track of the Sun. His travels have been varied and extensive, and he has attended the state ceremonies and presentations of nearly all the courts of Europe, and has been received by most of the Sovereigns. By descent from the noble family of Diodati, he is entitled to the title of Count Among his friends in Europe he numbers many people of distinction, noblemen and officers of high rank in various countries. The Sultan conferred on him the orders of the Osmanlieh and Medjidieh.

Mr. Frederick Diodati Thompson's permanent home is the Long Island seat of his ancestors. In this city he is a member of the Metropolitan, Union, Knickerbocker and Riding Clubs, and of the Lenox Club, at Lenox, Mass. He is also a member of the Society of Colonial Wars, the Sons of the Revolution, the St. George's Society, Δ Ψ Fraternity, New York Historical Society, Long Island Historical Society, and New York Genealogical and Biographical Society, and he is a fellow of the National Academy of Design.

ROBERT MEANS THOMPSON

S COTCH and Scotch-Irish families were, on both sides, the ancestors of this gentleman. His father, John J. Y. Thompson, was for many years a lay Judge of Jefferson County, Pa. His forefathers came to this country from the Parish of Ellerslie, Scotland, the home of the Wallace, and it is a tradition in the Thompson family that they are descended from the race that produced the Scottish national hero. Judge John J. Y. Thompson married Agnes Kennedy, daughter of the Reverend William Kennedy, who came to Corsica, Jefferson County, Pa, as pastor of the Scotch-Irish colony in that place, and ministered to three other congregations in the county. He married Mary McClure, whose great-grandfather, John McClure, came to America about 1740, settled in North Carolina, but removed to Chester County, Pa, and obtained a grant of land in Uwchland Township, from Thomas and Richard Penn, proprietors of Pennsylvania. These lands are still in possession of his descendants. One of the present Mr Thompson's great-grandfathers was the Reverend John Jameson, who was a missionary to the Indians and to the Presbyterian congregations of the mountain regions from Pennsylvania to North Carolina.

Mr. Robert Means Thompson is the son of Judge John J. Y and Agnes (Kennedy) Thompson and was born March 2d, 1849, in Corsica, Jefferson County, Pa. Educated in the local schools and at Elder's Ridge Academy, in Indiana County, he received an appointment to the Naval Academy in 1864, and graduated with distinction in 1868, being the tenth in a class of eighty. He served in the West Indian and Mediterranean squadrons and was commissioned ensign in 1869 and master in 1870. During 1871, he served on the Wachusett in the Mediterranean squadron and in October of that year resigned from the navy. He studied law and was admitted to the Pennsylvania bar in 1872, afterwards entered the Dane Law School of Harvard University, and graduated in 1874, with the degree of LL. B. He served for a time as assistant reporter of the Supreme Judicial Court of Massachusetts, and practiced his profession in Boston. In 1876, and again in 1877 and 1878, he was a member of the Common Council of that city.

In 1879, Mr Thompson turned his attention to business and assumed the active management of the Orford Nickel & Copper Company. His success in this important field has been pronounced, and he now holds a position in the front rank of American metallurgists. One of his notable achievements has been the economical smelting of copper ore in large quantities. The Orford Copper Company, of which he is president, is one of the largest producers of nickel in the world, and in this connection has rendered the United States Government invaluable service by furnishing the nickel necessary for use in the manufacture of armor plate. It was entirely through Mr Thompson's efforts, working to meet the requirements of the Government, that the nickel industry was established in this country on its present basis, so that the metal is produced at the lowest cost ever known in the world, and of superior quality.

In 1873, Mr Thompson married Sarah Gibbs, daughter of Governor William C. Gibbs, of Newport, and a granddaughter of Mary Channing, aunt of the famous Reverend William Ellery Channing, and great-granddaughter of John Kane, of Albany, and seventh in descent from the Reverend Jonathan Russell, of South Hadley, Mass., in whose home the regicides, Whalley and Goff, were protected for many years. Mr and Mrs Thompson have one daughter, Sarah Gibbs Thompson. The city residence of the family is at 5 East Fifty-third Street, their summer home being in Southampton, Long Island. Mr. Thompson is a member of the University, Players, Racquet, New York, Engineers', United Service and New York Athletic clubs, the Century Association, the Downtown Association, and the Metropolitan Club, of Washington.

Three brothers of Mr Thompson, John Jameson Thompson, Albert C. Thompson and Clarence Russell Thompson, were in the military service of their country during the Civil War. The latter was killed at the battle of Malvern Hill. Albert C Thompson was wounded at the second battle of Bull Run. Since the war he has been a resident of Ohio, where he was elected a Judge and for three terms was a Member of Congress.

LEONARD MORTIMER THORN

A N original patentee of Flushing, Long Island, in 1645, was William Thorne, the American ancestor of several branches of a family that has been distinguished in New York for two hundred and fifty years. Notwithstanding some differences of opinion among genealogists, it is now generally agreed that William Thorne, of Flushing, was the William Thorne who came from England to the Massachusetts Bay Colony in the early part of the seventeenth century and settled in Lynn, Mass., where he was a freeman in 1638 and had land apportioned to him. He came to Long Island in 1642, and after living several years in Flushing, was one of the proprietors of the town of Jamaica, in 1657. In the same year, he was a signer of the remonstrance to Governor Petrus Stuyvesant, protesting against the treatment of the Quakers. Some of his descendants dropped the final letter e from their name and adopted the surname Thorn.

John Thorn, of the second generation, in 1664, was a freeman of Connecticut, to which Colony the Long Island settlement then pertained. His son, Joseph, who died in 1753, married, in 1695, Martha Johanna Bowne, daughter of John Bowne, of Flushing. In 1704, with several others, Joseph Thorn was a purchaser of three hundred and sixty acres of land in Nottingham township, Burlington County, N. J., but it is not known that he ever lived there. Thomas Thorn, 1704-1764, son of Joseph Thorn, lived in Flushing and Cortlandt Manor. His first wife, the ancestress of that branch of the family to which the subject of this sketch belongs, was Penelope Coles, daughter of Joseph and Elizabeth (Wright) Coles, of Oyster Bay, one of the oldest and most important families of Long Island. The great-grandfather of Mr. Leonard Mortimer Thorn was Daniel Thorn, 1726-1765, son of Thomas and Penelope Thorn. His wife was Mary Frost, daughter of William and Susannah (Coles) Frost. The grandparents of Mr. Thorn were Charles Thorn, 1755-1818, and Anne Kirby, 1752-1845, daughter of Daniel and Hannah (Latting) Kirby.

William Thorn, 1777-1861, father of Mr. Leonard Mortimer Thorn, married Anne Knapp, of Greenwich, Conn., and had a family of twelve children, Charles Edgar, Anne Augusta, Julius Oscar, William Knapp, Frances Mathilda, Mary Elizabeth, Alfred Ferdinand, Ferdinand Alfred, Leonard Mortimer, George Frederick, Samuel and Caroline Mathilda Thorn. Of his daughters, Anna Augusta married G. N. Allen. Frances Mathilda married Thomas Garner, of England, who died in 1867. She died in 1862. Their children were: Frances, who married Francis C Lawrance, of New York; Josephine, who married James L. Graham, of New York; Thomas, who married Harriet Amory, of Boston; William T., who married Marcellite Thorn; Caroline, who married Samuel Johnson, of Bridgeport, Conn., and Anna T., who married George H. Watson, of New York. Frances Garner Lawrance, daughter of Francis C. Lawrance and Frances Garner, became the wife of George William Venables Vernon, the seventh Lord Vernon, of Sudbury Park, Derbyshire, England, whose mother was a daughter of the Earl of Litchfield. Francis C. Lawrence, Jr., married Sarah Egleston Lanier. William Thorn Garner and his wife, Marcellite Thorn, had three daughters, Marcellite, Florence and Adele. The parents were drowned in the Mohawk yachting accident in New York harbor, in 1876, the recollection of which, as one of the saddest affairs in New York yachting annals, has not been obscured by the passing years. William Knapp Thorn, of the same family, married for his first wife, Harriet Cooke, of Bridgeport, Conn., and after her death, married, in 1839, Emily A. Vanderbilt, daughter of Commodore Cornelius Vanderbilt.

Mr Leonard Mortimer Thorn was born in 1816. In early life, he spent many years in Texas and acquired a thorough knowledge of Indian life and customs, being at one time proficient in thirteen Indian tongues. During his active business career, he was a member of the firm of Garner & Co. In 1858, he married Augusta Amelia Raguet and has had a family of four children, L. Mortimer, Jr., Conde R, Marcia, who died in 1885, and Emily Augusta Thorn Leonard Mortimer Thorn, Jr, graduated from 'Columbia College. He married Lillian Gwynn and lives in West Fifty-fifth Street Condé R. Thorn is also a Columbia graduate. He married Louise Akerly Floyd-Jones, lives in East Tenth Street and is a member of the Δ Φ and Calumet clubs.

SAMUEL THORNE

WILLIAM THORNE was made a freeman of Lynn, Mass., in May, 1638. After remaining in Massachusetts for a few years, he moved to Long Island, and in 1645 was one of the patentees of Flushing. In 1646, a plantation in Gravesend was granted to him, and in 1657 he became a proprietor of Jamaica. The Long Island pioneers of the Thorne family were Quakers, and prominent in the early history of that society in their section. Joseph, son of William Thorne, married Mary Bowne, daughter of John Bowne, one of the most noted Quakers of his time, who for his religion was sent to Holland, to be tried, but was acquitted, the authorities of New Amsterdam being censured for their intolerance. The mother of Mary Bowne was Hannah Feake, daughter of Robert Feake, who settled in Watertown, Mass. Martha Johanna Bowne, sister of Mary Bowne, afterwards became the wife of Joseph, son of John Thorne, the two sisters thus marrying uncle and nephew. Joseph Thorne, son of Joseph Thorne and Mary Bowne, was born in 1682 and lived for the greater part of his life at Hempstead. His wife was Catharine Smith, and his son, William, born in 1745, married Jemima Titus, while his grandson, Samuel, married Phœbe Dean, daughter of Jonathan and Margaret Dean.

Jonathan Thorne, son of Samuel Thorne and Phœbe Dean, and descendant in the fifth generation from William Thorne, was born at Washington, Dutchess County, N. Y., in 1801. His father was living at Thornedale at the time of the son's birth, and the latter was educated in the local schools. At an early age, he came to New York and was a clerk in the dry goods business. When he was twenty-three years of age, he married Lydia Ann Corse, daughter of Israel Corse, of New York, formerly of Maryland, who was largely interested in the leather business, in which thenceforward his son-in-law was engaged. He learned the art of tanning, and in time became the manager of tanneries in New York and Pennsylvania, and the proprietor of one of the largest establishments of the trade in New York. He was also connected with other commercial and financial enterprises, such as the Central Trust Company and the Leather Manufacturers' National Bank, of which he was a director for forty years. He died in 1884.

Mr. Samuel Thorne, son of Jonathan Thorne, was born in Dutchess County, N. Y. September 6th, 1835. He was educated in this city and, entering the counting house of his father's firm, acquired a knowledge of the business, in which he was engaged for a short time. Since his father's death, Mr. Thorne has been principally occupied with the care of the estate. He is president of the Pennsylvania Coal Company, and a director of the Central Trust Company, the Sixth Avenue Railroad, and the Bank of America. For some fourteen years he resided upon the family homestead, Thornedale, in Millbrook, Dutchess County, N. Y. Becoming interested in the importation and breeding of short horned cattle, he had one of the finest herds of these animals in the country.

In 1860, Mr. Thorne married Phebe Van Schoonhoven, daughter of William Van Schoonhoven, of Troy, N. Y. They have five children, the eldest son, Edwin Thorne, being a graduate of Yale, and president of the Polar Construction Company. He married Phebe Ketchum, daughter of Landon Ketchum, of Saugatuck, Conn., and granddaughter of Morris Ketchum, the well-known New York banker. The second son, William Van S. Thorne, is a graduate of Yale and vice-president of the Pennsylvania Coal Company. The two other sons of Mr. Thorne are Joel W. and Samuel Thorne, Jr., and the only daughter of the family is Margaret B. Thorne. Mr. Thorne's residence is 8 East Fifty-fifth Street, and he has a country residence in Dutchess County, adjoining the old family seat. He is a member of the Metropolitan, Union League, Century, Downtown and Riding clubs, the American Geographical Society, and the Metropolitan Museum of Art.

Mr. Samuel Thorne's younger brother, Jonathan Thorne, a graduate from Haverford College, is engaged in the leather business, and is a member of the Metropolitan, Union League and other clubs. Another brother, William Thorne, was also in the leather trade, but retired some time since. He is a member of the Union League Club.

CHARLES LEWIS TIFFANY

THREE brothers of the Tiffany name came to this country from England at a very early period, and for five succeeding generations their descendants resided in the town of Attleborough, Mass. James Tiffany, the ancestor of Mr. Charles Lewis Tiffany, lived on what is still known as the Tiffany Farm in that town. He was born there in 1697, and died in 1776 His son, Ebenezer, who died in 1807, had a son, Comfort Tiffany, who was born in 1777, and moved from Massachusetts to Connecticut, where he was for the greater part of his life engaged in the manufacture of cotton goods. He died in Brooklyn, N.Y., in 1844. He was the father of Charles Lewis Tiffany.

The mother of Mr. Tiffany was Chloe Draper, daughter of Isaac Draper, of Attleborough. Her father was born near Dedham, Mass., in 1736, and was a successful tanner of Attleborough. He was the son of Ebenezer Draper, 1698–1784, by his wife, Dorothy Child, daughter of Joshua and Elizabeth (Morris) Child, of Brookline, Mass. The grandparents of Isaac Draper were James Draper of Roxbury, 1654–1698, and his wife, Abigail Whiting, daughter of Nathaniel Whiting, and great-granddaughter of John Dwight. James Draper was a soldier in King Philip's War. He was a son of James Draper, who was born in England in 1618, and died in Roxbury, Mass., in 1694, being a freeman of Roxbury in 1690 The mother of James Draper, Jr., was Miriam Stansfield, daughter of Gideon and Grace (Eastwood) Stansfield, of Wadsworth, Yorkshire, England. The first James Draper was the American ancestor of the family, and was a son of Thomas Draper, of Heptonstall Parish, England. The Drapers were people of good standing and substantial merchants, Thomas Draper being a clothier.

Mr. Charles L. Tiffany, the eldest son of Comfort Tiffany, was born in Killingly, Conn., February 15th, 1812. He was educated in the public schools and the Plainfield Academy. Moving to New York in 1837, he started in business under the firm name of Tiffany & Young, and in 1857 began the special business career as manufacturer of and dealer in jewelry, silverware and bronzes, that has made his name famous throughout the world. A review of the history of this notable business house is not called for here, for its name has become a household word on two continents. Mr. Tiffany has received many honors from foreign governments In 1878, he was made Chevalier of the National Legion of Honor, of France, and the Czar of Russia gave him a gold medal, *Praemio Digno*. He has also received letters of appointment from the Queen of England, the Czar and Czarina of Russia, the Emperors of Austria, Germany and Brazil, the Prince and Princess of Wales, the Kings of Belgium, Greece, Spain, Italy, Denmark and Portugal, the Shah of Persia, the Khedive of Egypt and other crowned heads. He was one of the founders of the New York Society of Fine Arts, is a patron of the Metropolitan Museum of Art, and a trustee of the American Museum of Natural History. He is also a life member of the New England Society, the National Academy of Design, the American Geographical Society, and the New York Historical Society His club membership includes the Union League, New York, Union, City and New York Yacht clubs.

In 1841, Mr. Tiffany married Harriet C. Young, of Killingly, Conn. Mrs. Tiffany's father was Ebenezer Young, who was born in 1784 and died in 1851 He was one of the notable public men of the State of Connecticut in the early part of the present century. He was graduated from Yale College in 1806, was elected a State Senator in 1823, and twice thereafter, was for two years president of the Connecticut Senate, and was a member of the National House of Representatives, 1829-35. Mr. and Mrs. Tiffany had two sons and two daughters. Their eldest son, Louis C Tiffany, is the well-known artist. He married Louise W. Knox, lives in East Seventy-second Street, and has three children, Mary Woodbridge, Hilda G., and Charles L. Tiffany, second He is a member of the Metropolitan, Union League, Grolier, Century and other clubs and social organizations Charles L Tiffany's residence is at the corner of Madison Avenue and Seventy-second Street, one of the most artistic houses in the city, and architecturally one of the most notable private residences in the country Mrs Tiffany died in November, 1897

FRANK TILFORD

THE origin of the Tilford family, that has been prominent in New York City, can be traced back for almost a thousand years. The name, as it is in modern use, is a contraction from one of the various spellings of the old Norman surname Taillefer. The family is frequently referred to in works upon Norman-French genealogy. The general opinion of Perigourd and of the L'Augoumois, which is justified by the testimony of many distinguished scholars and critics, is to the effect that the house of Taillefer was descended from the ancient Counts d'Augouleme, and this idea has been confirmed in the fact that the surname is illustrated by heraldic devices in the coat of arms borne by the various branches of the race for so many centuries. Wlguin, chief of this race, was invested with great possessions in the year 866 by King Charles Le Chauve. Guillaume de Taillefer, first of the name and the son and successor of Wlguin, as Count de L'Augoulesme, transmitted the name, de Taillefer, to his descendants by an act of valor and extraordinary strength, during a battle for the Normans, in the year 916. From this notable ancestor, the line of lineage has been clearly traced down through the successive generations of the family to the subject of this sketch.

The immediate ancestors of Mr Tilford came from Scotland. The first of the name in this country emigrated during the reign of George II, and settled in Argyle, a village north of Albany. James Tilford, the grandfather of Mr Frank Tilford, was a Captain during the War of 1812 and his great-grandfather served throughout the War of the Revolution. John M Tilford, the father of Mr Frank Tilford, came to New York when he was only twenty years old, having been born in 1815. Finding employment in the store of Benjamin Albro, he remained there five years. In 1840, with Joseph Park, a fellow clerk, he organized the firm of Park & Tilford, which has become the leading house in its line in the world.

Mr Frank Tilford, the youngest son, and the successor of his father in the firm of Park & Tilford, was born in New York City, July 22d, 1852. He was educated in private schools and completed his studies in the Mount Washington Collegiate School, and entered the paternal business house at Sixth Avenue and Ninth Street early in life. When the business became a joint stock corporation, in 1890, the senior Mr Tilford was made vice-president of the company, and upon his death, in January, 1891, Mr Frank Tilford succeeded him. Mr. Tilford is also associated with other financial undertakings. He has been a member of the Real Estate Exchange since 1873, and has made investments in property on the upper west side of the city. In 1874, he became a director of the Sixth National Bank, and in 1885, a trustee of the North River Savings Bank. In company with George G Haven and other gentlemen, in 1889, he organized the Bank of New Amsterdam, of which he is now the president. He has also been conspicuous in the management of many philanthropic institutions and in other public enterprises, being a member of the Chamber of Commerce since 1887, a school trustee, president of the New Amsterdam Eye and Ear Hospital, a trustee of the Babies' Hospital, treasurer of the Hancock Memorial Association, and one of the most active members of the executive committee of the Grant Monument Association, which accomplished the work of completing General Grant's tomb in Riverside Drive.

In 1881, Mr. Tilford married Julia Greer, daughter of the late James A Greer, and a granddaughter of George Greer, one of the great sugar refiners of the last generation. Mr. and Mrs Tilford have two daughters, Julia and Elsie Tilford. Mr. Tilford has been a member of the Union League Club since he attained his majority, and belongs also to the New York Athletic, Lotos, Press, Colonial, Republican, Rockaway Hunt and several other clubs. By virtue of his ancestry, he is a member of the Society of the Sons of the Revolution. His country residence, Mar-a-Vista, is at Cedarhurst, Long Island. His city home, at 245 West Seventy-second Street, is one of the handsomest residences of that section of the new west side of New York. It was built by Mr Tilford himself in 1895, and, largely embodying his own ideas, is architecturally one of the most notable buildings in its neighborhood.

HENRY ALFRED TODD

JOHN TODD, of Rowley, born in England about 1617, was the founder of the American family of Todds, of Rowley, Mass. He is recorded as of Boston in 1637, of Rowley, Mass., in 1649; and was a member of the Great and General Court of Massachusetts in 1664 and later. The first two generations of the family in America spelled the name Tod. The son of the pioneer, John Todd, himself bearing the same name, was born in 1655, and married Elizabeth Brocklebank, a daughter of Captain Samuel Brocklebank, of Rowley, Mass., under whom he served in the campaigns of King Philip's War, 1675-76. A son of the second John Todd, also John Todd, was born in 1688, and was married to Ruth Lunt. In the fourth generation, Benjamin Todd was born in 1744, and married Elizabeth Saunders. He was a staunch supporter of the American cause in the War of the Revolution. In the next generation, Wallingford Todd, born in 1778, was the grandfather of the subject of this sketch. He was an officer in the United States merchant marine, and he married Hannah Todd, his cousin german, and daughter of Moses Todd and Elizabeth Carleton. His son, Richard Kimball Todd, was born in 1814, and became the father of Mr. Henry Alfred Todd. He was graduated from Princeton College in 1842 and entered the ministry. For many years he was the principal of Todd Seminary for boys, an institution that he founded. In 1847, he was married, at the Broadway Tabernacle, to Martha Clover, daughter of Lewis P. Clover, of New York City, officer of the United States Customs. She was a sister of the late Reverend Lewis P. Clover, D. D., of New Hackensack, N. Y., and of Judge Henry Alfred Clover, LL. D., of St. Louis, Mo.

Mr. Henry Alfred Todd is in the seventh generation from the founder of the family in this country. He was born at Woodstock, Ill., March 13th, 1854, prepared for college at his father's seminary, and graduated from Princeton with the degree of A. B. in 1876. Following his graduation, he was a fellow and tutor in Princeton College, 1876-80. Then he went abroad and remained three years, studying in the universities of Paris, Berlin, Rome and Madrid. Returning to the United States, he became instructor and associate in Johns Hopkins University, Baltimore, 1883-91, was made Doctor of Philosophy by the same institution in 1885, was a professor in Leland Stanford University, California, 1891-93, and in 1893 became a member of Columbia University as professor of Romance Philology. He is the author of various works in philology and literature.

Mr. Todd was married, in 1891, to Miriam Gilman, of Baltimore, Md., the second daughter of the late John S. Gilman, of the Gilmans of Gilmanton, N. H., who was president of the Second National Bank of Baltimore. A sister of Mrs. Todd is Mrs. D'Arcy Paul, of Baltimore. Mr. and Mrs. Todd have three children, Lisa Gilman, Martha Clover, and Richard Henry Wallingford Todd, born August 2d, 1897. The town house of Mr. Todd is at 824 West End Avenue, at the corner of One Hundredth Street, an attractive residence, a modern adaptation in light brick and stone of the domestic Renaissance architecture, with American basement and broadly lighted and balconied foyer on the southern exposure. It contains valuable paintings, inherited from Lewis P. Clover, the elder. Woodlands, at Baltimore, the country house of the family, is noteworthy among the beautiful and stately homes of Maryland, and is enriched by numerous portraits and works of art of early and recent periods.

Mr. Todd is a member of various clubs and literary and scientific societies. He belongs to the Century Association and the Princeton Club of New York City, the New York Academy of Sciences, the American Oriental Society, the American Philological Association, the Modern Language Association, the Dante Society, the American Dialect Society, the Phi Beta Kappa Society, and is a member of the Société des Anciens Textes Français. The arms of the family, as engraved on silver plate, brought by the founder of the family from England, are: Vert, a fox grimpant, argent, crest, a dove with wings displayed. Motto "By cunning, not by craft."

HENRY PENNINGTON TOLER

WHETHER in social life, in business, or in sport, the name this gentleman now bears has been eminent in New York for several generations. It is of Irish origin, directly descended from the Norbury family (Lord Norbury—Judge Toler), which bears relationship to the aristocracy of that country. Its first representative to come to America was Mr Toler's great-grandfather, who first settled in Providence, R. I., in the early portion of the century, but finally came to New York, where he was prominent in business life for many years.

His son, Hugh K. Toler, was also an eminent and respected New York merchant throughout the period preceding the Civil War, and was a founder and partner of the firm which afterwards became E. S. Jaffray & Co. He was also a figure in metropolitan social life, but by his residence in Newark, was identified with the State of New Jersey and took a prominent part in many local institutions there. It was his custom for a long period to drive daily from Newark to Jersey City, cross the Hudson to his place of business in New York, and to return in the same way each evening, it being recorded that he was never known to miss a trip of this kind irrespective of the weather. The present Mr. Toler's father is Hugh A. Toler, who is still active in business pursuits in New York. The latter's brother, Henry K. Toler, Mr. H. P. Toler's uncle, was, however, one of the most renowned of the early champions of sport in America, and is mentioned in Frank Forresters' Warwick Woodlands as the greatest shot in the State. He was also foremost in the turf of his time, and was instrumental in arranging the great race between Fashion and Boston in 1842. The mare, which was bred at Madison, N. J, by Mr. Gibbons, represented the North, and Boston the South, so that the race was a test between the sections, and when it was run at the old Union Course, on Long Island, was regarded as a national event, attracting 40,000 people to the track. The race, as was then the custom, was run in four-mile heats and Boston, who held the record at that distance, 7 37, was beaten by Fashion, who made the time 7.32. Mr. H. P. Toler now has, in his home at Short Hills, N. J., original paintings of the horses, showing Mr. Gibbons' stables.

On his mother's side, Mr. Toler descends from one of the foremost Revolutionary families of New Jersey, his mother having been a daughter of the Honorable William Pennington, 1796-1862, who was Chancellor of the State and its Governor from 1837 to 1843 and who, in 1860, became Speaker of the National House of Representatives. Her grandfather, Judge William S. Pennington, 1757-1826, was a Major of Artillery in the army of the Revolution, became in 1804 a Judge of the Supreme Court of New Jersey, was Governor of the State in 1813, and afterwards United States District Judge.

Mr. Henry Pennington Toler was born at Newark, N J., April 28th, 1864, and graduated from Princeton College in the class of 1886. While a student of that institution, he was distinguished as an athlete, being a member of the baseball nine and playing half-back on the football team with Lamar, when the latter made his celebrated run against Yale, winning the game and championship for the year. He was also very active in track athletics, holding the best college record for pole vaulting throughout his college course. He has fully retained his taste for athletics, having turned his attention recently to golf, in which pastime he ranks as one of the foremost amateurs in America, and has been a participant in some of the most famous matches that have been played here, having also won several of the open tournaments. He engaged in the business of a stock broker and is now a member of the New York Stock Exchange. In 1888, Mr. Toler married Virginia Wheeler, of Scarsdale, N. Y., daughter of the late George Minor Wheeler. The issue of this marriage is two children, Dorothy and Henry Pennington Toler, Jr. He is a member of the Union Club, in this city, and of many organizations devoted to golf and other sports. Mr. Toler's two brothers are William P. Toler, who married Miss Foote of Elizabeth, N J., and Hugh K. Toler, a widower, who married the daughter of the late Dr. Thebaud, of New York. Mr. Toler lives at Short Hills, N. J., where he built a residence during the first year of his marriage.

JOHN CANFIELD TOMLINSON

IN England, in the early centuries after the Conquest, the Tomlinsons belonged to the landed gentry. They were descended from a member of the nobility, who had received a coat of arms which is still handed down in the family. These arms are. Fess between three ravens volant; Crest, out of a ducal coronet a griffin's head, argent. George Tomlinson, the English ancestor of the American family, was a native of Yorkshire, and married Maria Hyde. His son, Henry Tomlinson, was the American pioneer With his wife, Alice, and several children he arrived in 1652 and settled in Milford, Conn After four years, he removed to Stratford and engaged in business there, dying in 1681. Jonas Tomlinson, son of Henry Tomlinson, married, and about 1675 settled in Derby, Conn , where he died in 1692 In the next generation, Abraham Tomlinson, who lived in Stratford in 1728, removed to Derby

Augur Tomlinson, the great-great-grandfather of Mr. John Canfield Tomlinson, was a son of Abraham Tomlinson He was born in Derby in 1713, married, in 1734, Sarah Bowers, daughter of the Reverend Nathaniel Bowers, and died in 1800. In the next succeeding generation came Joseph Tomlinson, of Derby, a man of wealth and position He married for his first wife Nethiah Glover, and for his second wife, Jedida Wakelee.

David Tomlinson, son of Joseph Tomlinson, was one of the noted physicians of New York. Born in Derby, in 1772, he graduated from Williams College in 1798, studied medicine and surgery under the celebrated Dr. Wheeler, of Dutchess County, and began to practice in Rhinebeck, N Y , in 1802. At one time he was president of the Dutchess County Medical Society, in 1812 was surgeon of the Second Regiment of New York Militia, and in 1819 was a member of the New York Assembly. The grandmother of Mr John Canfield Tomlinson was Cornelia Adams, granddaughter of Chief Justice Andrew Adams, of Connecticut, and of the Honorable John Canfield, a member of the Continental Congress. She married David Tomlinson in 1810 Chief Justice Adams was born at Stratford, Conn , in 1736, and died at Litchfield, Conn., in 1797. Graduated from Yale College in 1760, he was admitted to the bar in Fairfield County, and practiced law in Stamford and Litchfield. He was a member of the Connecticut Legislature, 1776-81, a delegate to Congress for two terms prior to the adoption of the Constitution, a member of the Governor's Council, a Judge of the Supreme Court in 1789, and Chief Justice in 1793

The father of Mr Tomlinson was the Honorable Theodore E. Tomlinson, who was born in Rhinebeck, N Y , in 1817. Graduated from the University of the City of New York in 1836, he studied in the Law School of Yale College, and being admitted to the bar in 1839, began practice in New York. In 1850, he was attorney to the Corporation of the city, and was intimately associated with Charles O'Connor, James T Brady, William C Noyes and David Graham. He was an influential representative of the old Whig party, and was chairman of the Whig State Committee, 1850-55. In 1859, he was a member of the Assembly of New York State. His wife, whom he married in 1844, was Abbey Esther Walden

Mr John Canfield Tomlinson was born in New York in 1856, and graduated from New York University with the degree of A. B. in 1875, and from the Law School of the same institution with the degree of LL B in 1877. He received the degree of A M in 1882, and throughout his professional life has been in practice at the bar of the City of New York. In 1879, he married Frances French Adams, daughter of Charles W Adams, of Boston, and Frances (Barker) French, of Bangor, Me. She died in 1886. For his second wife, he married, in 1888, Dora Morrell Grant, daughter of Daniel J. and Elizabeth (Crane) Grant, of Boston. Mr. Tomlinson has two children by his first wife, John C. Tomlinson, Jr , and Esther Walden Tomlinson. By his second wife, he has one son, Daniel G Tomlinson Mr and Mrs Tomlinson live in West Eighty-eighth Street, and have a country home at Goshen, Mass Mr Tomlinson is a member of the Bar Association, the Sons of the Revolution and the Society of Colonial Wars, and his clubs are the Manhattan, Lawyers', Colonial and Democratic.

AUGUSTUS CLIFFORD TOWER

IN most cases throughout the United Kingdom, the name of the Tower family is spelled Towers, though in Scotland it is sometimes found as Towars. Many in America who bear the name, trace their descent to John Tower, who came to this country early in the seventeenth century. Among the parishes in England that were in sympathy with the Puritian movement of that period, that of Hingham was prominent. There the Reverend Robert Peck had been installed as rector some years before John Tower was born, and it was under his ministry that the American pioneer passed his early life. The clergyman became an open dissenter, and, under the administration of Archbishop Laud, was reduced to the alternatives of submitting to the authorities or abandoning his parish. Choosing freedom of conscience to compliance, he decided to emigrate to this country, and in 1637 led hither a company drawn mainly from the members of his flock, among whom was John Tower.

John Tower, the founder of the family in America, was the son of Robert and Dorothy (Raymond) Tower and was born in 1609. After coming to this country, he was made a freeman of Massachusetts in 1638 and had land granted to him in Hingham, Mass., named after his home in the old country. In 1657, he was one of the way wardens and two years after was a constable of the town. His wife, whom he married in Charlestown, Mass., in 1638, was Margaret Ibrook, daughter of Richard Ibrook, who was among the early settlers of Hingham, Mass., coming thither with his wife and three unmarried daughters, Ellen, Margaret and Rebecca. In 1639, Rebecca Ibrook married the Reverend Peter Hobart, the minister of Hingham. Being thus by his marriage related to the clergyman of his town, John Tower became a leader in the community. In the second American generation came Benjamin Tower, 1654–1721, who had for his wife Deborah Garnet, daughter of John and Mary Garnet. Ambrose Tower, the son of Benjamin and Deborah Tower, was born in Hingham, in 1699, and through his wife, Elizabeth, became the ancestor of most of the Tower name, who were settled in Middlesex County, Ambrose Tower having removed from Hingham to Concord, Mass.

The great-great-grandfather of the gentleman whose name heads this article was Joseph Tower, born in 1723, who resided successively in Weston, Sudbury, Princeton, Shrewsbury and Rutland, Mass., dying in the latter place in 1779. His wife was Hepzibah Gibbs, whom he married in Sudbury in 1748. She was born in Sudbury, in 1730, the daughter of Isaac and Thankful (Wheeler) Gibbs, and died in Waterville, N. Y., in 1816. The great-grandfather of Mr. Augustus Clifford Tower was Jonas Tower, who was born in 1768. His wife was Fanny Parmenter, of Petersham, Mass., daughter of John Parmenter. She was the mother of Oren Tower, who was the grandfather of the subject of this sketch. Oren Tower was born in Petersham, Mass., in 1794. His first wife, whom he married in 1823, was Harriet Gleason, a daughter of Joseph Gleason. The parents of Mr. Augustus Clifford Tower were William A. Tower, who was born in Petersham in 1824, and his wife, Julia Davis, of Lancaster, Mass., who was born in Princeton in 1824, and whom he married in 1847. The children of William A. and Julia (Davis) Tower were Ellen May, Charlotte Gray, Augustus Clifford and Richard Gleason Tower.

Mr. Augustus Clifford Tower was born in Cambridge, Mass., in 1853. He was graduated from Harvard in 1877, and during his collegiate course took a prominent part in athletics. For three years he was a member of the First Corps of Cadets of Boston, and participated in the various Centennial celebrations of that period. He removed to New York early in life, entered business in Wall Street, served on the board of governors of the New York Stock Exchange, and has been identified with conservative banking and brokerage houses. In 1883, Mr. Tower married Louise G. Dreer, of Philadelphia. His home is at Lawrence, Long Island, and he was for a number of years president of the Rockaway Hunt Club, of Long Island, which is considered one of the foremost organizations of its character in the country. He is also a member of the Union, University and Westminster Kennel clubs.

HENRY ROBINSON TOWNE

WHEN William Towne, the first American ancestor of this distinguished family, came to this country early in the seventeenth century, he brought with him his wife, Joanna Blessing, whom he had married in 1620. He was a native of Yarmouth, Norfolk County, England, and upon his arrival in New England, went to Salem, Mass., afterwards becoming the proprietor of an estate in Topsfield. Edmund Towne, the son of William Towne, was born in England, in 1628, and was brought to this county by his father. When he grew to manhood he became a prominent member of the community in Topsfield, and, in 1675, was interested in the organization of the first military company to protect the inhabitants from the Indians. His wife was Mary Browning, daughter of Thomas Browning, and he died in 1678. The four successive generations of the family leading to the grandfather of the gentleman whose name appears at the head of this sketch were: Joseph Towne, 1661-1717, of Topsfield, and his wife, Amy Smith, daughter of Robert Smith, Nathan Towne, 1693-1762, of Topsfield, Boxford and Andover, and his wife, Phœbe, Nathan Towne, of Andover, and his wife, Mary Poole; Benjamin Towne, of Andover, who was born in 1747, and his wife, Mehitable Chandler

John Towne, the grandfather of Mr. Henry Robinson Towne, was born in Andover, in 1787, and was, in many ways, a remarkable man. Early in life he was a teacher, but afterwards went to Baltimore, where for several years he was associated in business with Henry Robinson, of England. Then, in 1817, Mr. Towne, who had accumulated considerable means, went West and purchased a large tract of land near Pittsburg, where he made his home, and where he was also engaged in the steamboat business. In 1833, he removed to Boston and again became associated with Mr. Robinson in the ownership and management of gas works. Finally, he purchased a country seat in Huntington Valley, near Philadelphia, and spent the rest of his life there, dying in 1851. His wife, who died in 1833, was a sister of Henry Robinson.

John Henry Towne, the father of Mr. Henry Robinson Towne, was born near Pittsburg, in 1818. He was first educated at the Chauncey Hall private school, of Boston, and then studied engineering in Philadelphia with the firm of Merrick & Agnew. He then entered into a partnership with S V. Merrick, under the firm name of Merrick & Towne, a relation that was continued until 1848, their works being known as the Southwark Foundry. Then he was engaged in the erection of gas works in various cities of the country, and before the Civil War, became a junior partner in the engineering concern of I. P. Morris, Towne & Co. He was actively interested in scientific pursuits of all kinds, and particularly in those connected with his profession. He was a member of the Franklin Institute, the American Philosophical Society, and of other institutions of similar character. Much of his time and means were given to the advancement of the University of Pennsylvania, and when he died, in 1875, he left one million dollars to its scientific department, which is named the Towne Scientific School, in his honor. The wife of John Henry Towne was Maria R Tevis, of Philadelphia

Mr Henry Robinson Towne is a native of Philadelphia, where he was born August 28th, 1844 Educated in a private school and the University of Pennsylvania, he entered the Port Richmond Iron Works, with which his father was connected, and gained practical experience in manufacturing, being particularly engaged in building engines for the United States monitors. In 1868, he joined in organizing the Yale & Towne Manufacturing Company, for the manufacture of the celebrated Yale locks, and has ever since been the president of the company. He is interested in other large corporations, and is a member of the American Society of Civil Engineers, and the American Society of Mechanical Engineers. He married Cora E. White, daughter of John P. White, of Philadelphia, and the children of this union are: John Henry and Frederick Tallmadge Towne. The city residence of Mr Towne is in lower Madison Avenue, and he has a country seat in Stamford, Conn He is a member of the Century Association and the Engineers', University, Lawyers', Reform, St Anthony and Hardware clubs.

HOWARD TOWNSEND

ON his mother's side, Mr Howard Townsend is a descendant from no less than six of the greatest New York families of the Colonial period, the Van Rensselaers, Van Cortlandts, Livingstons, Schuylers, Bayards and Loockermans. He is in the ninth generation from Kiliaen Van Rensselaer, the director of the West India Company, who established the family name and fortunes in this country. By his second wife, Anna Van Wely, Kiliaen Van Rensselaer had four sons and four daughters. His second son, Jeremias, who married Maria Van Cortlandt, daughter of Olaf Stevensen Van Cortlandt, was the head of the extensive family to which Mr. Howard Townsend belongs. Jeremias and Maria (Van Cortlandt) Van Rensselaer had three sons. Johannes Van Rensselaer died unmarried, and from Kiliaen Van Rensselaer and his younger brother, Hendrick, have come all the members of the family in later generations who have borne the paternal name. Kiliaen Van Rensselaer, the grandson of the director of the West India Company, was the first lord of the Rensselaerwyck Manor, and married Maria Van Cortlandt in 1701 His second son, Stephen, was the sixth patroon, born in 1707, and dying in 1747 He married Eliza Grosbeck in 1729. In the next generation, Stephen Van Rensselaer married Catharine Livingston, daughter of Philip Livingston, signer of the Declaration of Independence.

Stephen Van Rensselaer, who was born in 1742, died in 1769, and his eldest son, Stephen, who was born in 1764, and was the great-grandfather of the subject of this sketch, was one of the most notable figures in social and public life in New York during the post-Revolutionary period. He attended Princeton College, and was graduated from Harvard in 1782, was Major-General of the militia in 1801, a member of either the State Assembly or the State Senate from 1788 to 1795, Lieutenant-Governor in 1795 and again in 1798, president of the Erie Canal Commission, 1824-39, a Major-General in the War of 1812, when he led the United States troops in the storming of Queenstown, a Regent of the State University in 1809, and Chancellor at the time of his death, and a Member of Congress, 1823-29. In 1824, he established in Troy a school for instruction in mechanical and industrial art, now known as the Rensselaer Institute, and for fourteen years supported it himself. General Van Rensselaer died at the Rensselaer Manor House, in Troy, in 1839 His first wife was Margaret Schuyler, daughter of General Philip Schuyler. His second wife, whom he married in 1802, was Cornelia Paterson, daughter of William Paterson, Judge of the Supreme Court of the United States, and second Governor of the State of New Jersey. His widow, with ten children, survived him.

Stephen Van Rensselaer, son of Major-General Stephen Van Rensselaer, was the grandfather of Mr Townsend. He was born in 1789, and died in 1868. His wife was Harriet Elizabeth Bayard, daughter of William Bayard, and a descendant from Balthazar Bayard and his wife, Maria Loockermans, daughter of Govert Loockermans The father of Mr. Townsend was Dr. Howard Townsend, for many years one of the leading physicians in Albany, brother of Adjutant-General Frederick Townsend. Dr. Townsend was born in Albany in 1823, and died there in 1867. He was a graduate from Union College, and from the Medical Department of the University of Pennsylvania. In 1851-52, he was Surgeon-General of the State of New York, and afterwards professor in the Albany Medical College. Mrs. Townsend, who was Justine Van Rensselaer, daughter of Stephen Van Rensselaer and Harriet Elizabeth Bayard, is still living. She has been president of the National Society of Colonial Dames and of the Colonial Dames of the State of New York, regent of the Mount Vernon Association, and vice-president of the Society of the Daughters of the Cincinnati.

Mr. Howard Townsend was born in New York and educated at Harvard College, graduating in the class of 1880. Admitted to the bar, he has since been active in the practice of his profession. He lives in West Thirty-ninth Street His wife was Anne Langdon. He belongs to the Tuxedo colony, and is a member of the Century Association, the Union, University, City and Harvard clubs, the Bar Association, the Downtown Association, the American Geographical Society and the Metropolitan Museum of Art.

JOHN POMEROY TOWNSEND

ARRIVING at Lynn, in the Massachusetts Bay Colony, in 1637, Thomas Townsend was the first American ancestor of the subject of this article. The descendants of this Puritan pioneer lived for five generations in the City of Boston, and vicinity. Ebenezer Townsend, one of the representatives of the family in the latter generation, removed, however, to New Hampshire and settled in Chester, in that Colony, in 1775. John Townsend, the son of Ebenezer Townsend, was a prominent citizen of Merrimack County, N H , in the early portion of the present century. He held a portion of local offices, and was a member of the State Legislature for several terms. He married Anne Baker, daughter of Benjamin Baker, of Salisbury, N. H , and their son, the father of Mr. John Pomeroy Townsend, was John Baker Townsend, who was born in Salisbury. He married Eliza C. Alvord, a member of a notable Vermont family, and removed to Middlebury, in that State. In 1835, he, however, established himself at Troy, N. Y., and became a prosperous and influential resident of that city.

Mr. John Pomeroy Townsend is the eldest son of John Baker and Eliza (Alvord) Townsend. He was born at Middlebury, Addison County, Vt , October 10th, 1832, and received his early education in the schools of Troy, N. Y. In 1850, he came to New York and entered business life. He has long been an active and prominent member of the Chamber of Commerce, and among other positions held the office of president of the Maritime Exchange from 1885 to 1888, and treasurer of the New York Produce Exchange in 1885 and 1886. In 1875, he became vice-president of the Bowery Savings Bank and was elected president of the Knickerbocker Trust Company in 1889, holding that office until 1894, when he became president of the Bowery Savings Bank, an office he still holds. He is also a director of the Knickerbocker Trust Company and of the Farmers' Loan & Trust Company, as well as of several railroad corporations.

Taking an interest in public affairs, especially in connection with the municipality of New York, Mr. Townsend was a member of the famous Committee of Seventy, in 1894. He is a director and trustee of several benevolent and charitable organizations, being secretary of the Hospital for the Ruptured and Crippled in this city. He has also been, for a number of years, a member of the board of trustees of the University of Rochester, which institution conferred upon him the degree of LL. D Mr. Townsend is an authority upon savings banks, and has made valuable contributions to the literature of that subject, having written numerous essays on savings banks and postal savings banks, as well as on the silver question and other financial and economic topics. He is a foreign associate and honorary president of the Society of the Universal Scientific Congress of Provident Institutions of Paris, France, and contributed and read papers upon American savings banks at the meetings of that body in Paris, in 1878, 1883 and 1889 He is also the author of the section descriptive of savings banks in The Cyclopedia of Political History and Political Economy of the United States, as well as of A History of Savings Banks in the United States, which was published in 1896, and of A History of the Bowery Savings Bank of New York from 1834 to 1888, and other works of a similar character.

In 1853, Mr Townsend married Elizabeth A. Baldwin, daughter of Nehemiah Baldwin, of New York. Mrs. Townsend s ancestry is traced to Joseph Baldwin, one of the founders of Milford, Conn , who came from England in 1635. Mr. and Mrs. Townsend have three children. Their daughter, Mary Eliza Townsend, married Alfred L. White. Their second child and eldest son, Charles John Townsend, married Louisa C Wright, and their younger son, John Henry Townsend, married Caroline S Van Dusen. Mr. Townsend has resided, since 1870, in East Fifty-fourth Street, near Madison Avenue, and owns a country place at Chester, N. H , on which is the house built by his great-grandfather, Ebenezer Townsend, in 1775 He is a member of the Union League, Reform and Grolier clubs, the Downtown Association, the National Academy of Design and the New England Society.

BENJAMIN FRANKLIN TRACY

ENTRAL and southern New York was largely settled in the years immediately following the Revolution, by families from New England. Among these pioneers was Thomas Tracy, who, in 1790, with his wife and infant son Benjamin, settled on Tracy Creek, Broome County, the creek receiving its name from him. Two years after he removed to Caroline, in Tompkins County, and then to the Holland Purchase near Buffalo. His son, Benjamin Tracy, returned to Tioga County and settled on Appalachin Creek, near Oswego, and died in 1883.

The Honorable Benjamin Franklin Tracy, son of Benjamin Tracy, was born in Oswego, Tioga County, April 26th, 1830. He was educated in the Oswego Academy and in the law office of N. W. Davis and was admitted to the bar in 1851. Politics engaged his attention early in life. In 1853, he became the Whig nominee for district attorney in Tioga County, and was elected, although Tioga was at that time a Democratic stronghold, and three years later was reelected. In 1859, he declined another nomination for district attorney and two years later was elected a member of the State Assembly on a union Republican and Democratic ticket. In the Assembly he was chairman of several committees, including that of railroads.

In 1862, Governor Edwin D. Morgan appointed Mr. Tracy on the committee to oversee and promote volunteering in Tioga and the adjoining counties, and he recruited two regiments, the One Hundred and Ninth, and the One Hundred and Thirty-Seventh New York Infantry, becoming Colonel of the One Hundred and Ninth. For two years this regiment saw active service in and around Baltimore and Washington and then became part of the Ninth Army Corps of the Army of the Potomac. Colonel Tracy led his regiment at the battle of the Wilderness and at Spottsylvania, and as a result of his service was prostrated and obliged to retire on sick leave. Returning home, he was appointed Colonel of the One Hundred and Twenty-Seventh United States Colored Infantry and put in command of the military post, with prison post and draft rendezvous at Elmira, N. Y. In March, 1865, he was brevetted Brigadier-General of Volunteers.

After the war, General Tracy resumed the practice of law and became a member of the firm of Benedict, Burr & Benedict, in New York City. In 1866, he was appointed United States District Attorney for the Eastern District of New York. He was also the author of an internal revenue bill regulating the collection of taxes on distilled spirits, which, when put into effect, increased, annually, the national revenues from that source from thirteen million to fifty million dollars. In 1873, he resigned his official position to devote himself more to the general practice of law, but in 1881 was appointed Associate Justice of the New York Court of Appeals, a position which he held for one year, retiring to become a partner of Honorable W. C. DeWitt and his son, F. B. Tracy, in Brooklyn.

In 1889, he was called into the public service again, when he became a member of the Cabinet of President Harrison, as Secretary of the Navy. In that position he proved himself a zealous, hard working official. He took a large and creditable part in the development of the new navy, along the lines that had been laid down by his predecessors and left a record as one of the ablest Secretaries of the Navy in the present generation. His Washington life was marred by the sad death of his wife and youngest daughter, in a fire that destroyed their home in February 1890. Since his retirement from the Navy Department, General Tracy has been counsel in many celebrated cases in both the State and Federal courts. His most conspicuous recent service to the public has been rendered as president of the commission appointed by Governor Morton to draft a charter for the Greater New York. In 1897, he was the Republican candidate for Mayor of the City of New York. He is now a member of the law firm of Tracy, Boardman & Platt. He has one son, Frank B. Tracy, and one daughter, the widow of Ferdinand Wilmerding. His granddaughter, Alice T. Wilmerding, married Frederick R. Coudert, Jr. The residence of the family is in West Twentieth Street. General Tracy is a member of the Union League, Lawyers', Brooklyn and Hamilton clubs.

SPENCER TRASK

THE ancestor of the gentleman whom we are now considering was Captain William Trask, who came to this country in 1628 with Endicott and the other adventurous spirits forming the Massachusetts Bay Colony. He sailed with the others in the ship Abigail from Weymouth, England, June 20th, 1628, to prepare the Colony for those upon whom the hand of oppression had been too heavily laid in their old home. Upon his arrival, he settled at Salem, Mass., and at once became prominent in the affairs of the town. He was an intimate friend of Governor Endicott, a deputy to the General Court, and he was a commander in the wars in which the Colonists became engaged with the Pequot Indians. It was in 1636 that he was appointed Captain and he so distinguished himself in the troubles of the Colony that it was written of him in the annals of Salem that "he was one of the first military commanders in Massachusetts, and we can safely say of him that what Captain Standish was to Plymouth, Captain Trask was to the Massachusetts Bay Colony." He died in 1666, and was given a public burial with military honors, the town records saying "It is ordered that Shouldyers that atend Capt. Trask to his Grave shall have some alowance to make them drink at Mr. Gidney * * * price not exceeding the som of twenty shillings and cloth to cover ye drum." He gave the first land ever given to an educational institution in this country, and from his donation sprang what is now Harvard College. The family name is mentioned many times in the annals of Salem, and the children of Captain Trask and their children were prominent throughout the Colonial period; several of the family held commissions in the Revolutionary Army, and served during the war with distinction.

The father of Mr. Spencer Trask, Alanson Trask, was born in Salem on the 22d of May, 1808. Coming early to New York, he married, on October 2d, 1833, Sarah E. Marquand, who had been born in New York on March 29th, 1811, and who died on September 21st, 1881.

Mr. Spencer Trask was born in Brooklyn, in September, 1844, and was graduated from Princeton College. On the 12th of November, 1874, he married Kate Nichols, of Brooklyn. The mother of Mrs. Trask was Christina Marie Cole before her marriage. She was a daughter of Rebecca Van Santen and Jan Van Kool, of Holland, who came to this country at the beginning of this century, and changed his name to John Cole. Upon the side of her father, George L. Nichols, Mrs. Trask is directly descended from Anneke Jans. She has written many articles for the various magazines, and has published Under King Constantine, Poems and Lyrics, White Satin and Homespun, and other works.

Mr. Trask is a banker in New York and the senior member of the firm of Spencer Trask & Co., which was established by Mr. Trask in 1869. As bankers the firm has been largely identified with railroads, having reorganized and successfully managed several important lines. Mr. Trask has also been prominently identified with the electric light industry from its inception, having developed the Edison Electric Light Companies in New York, Brooklyn and other cities from small beginnings to concerns of great financial and commercial importance. Mr. Trask's energies have not, however, been confined strictly to business. He is president and largest owner of The New York Times, and is president of the Teachers' College, a unique institution among those devoted to higher education; he is interested in various philanthropic and civic associations, taking an active part in movements for municipal reforms and for the preservation of the country's credit, being prominent in the councils of the National (Gold) Democracy. Notwithstanding his many and far-reaching business interests, Mr. Trask has traveled extensively abroad, and has taken a prominent part in social life. He is a member of the Union League, the Metropolitan, the City, the Reform and the Lawyers' clubs.

Besides his house in town, Mr. Trask has a beautiful summer residence, Yaddo, at Saratoga. The house, a large gray stone structure, is finely situated on the drive to the lake, and with its surroundings embracing some five hundred acres, diversified with woods, lakes and some miles of drives, is one of the great attractions of the famous resort.

WILLIAM RIGGIN TRAVERS

FEW names on the roll of its society are more thoroughly identified with the metropolitan city than that which heads this page The late William R. Travers, of whom the gentleman now referred to is the son and namesake, acquired a popularity without parallel in the history of New York. A Virginian by descent, and a Baltimorean by birth as well as by his marriage, he became, however, an accepted type of social New York, and has left an enduring memory of his personality among all classes of his adopted fellow townsmen

Colonel Travers, a prominent citizen of Baltimore, and the grandfather of the present Mr W. R Travers, descended from a Virginia family of ancient lineage, the name occurring frequently in the early history of the Old Dominion His son, William R Travers (the elder), was born in Baltimore, in 1819 About 1834, his father removed to New York, and purchased a country seat in Monmouth County, N J. The house itself, after the lapse of more than half a century, is still known throughout the country side as the Travers place. Military instincts ran in the veins of the son, who secured an appointment from New Jersey as a cadet at West Point, but after two years he was prevailed on to forego this ambition and prepare himself for a business career. He accordingly entered Columbia College, graduating from that institution in the class of 1838 In the same year the family returned to Baltimore, where W R Travers engaged in active business, and became a shipping merchant. In 1843, he married Maria Louisa, daughter of the Honorable Reverdy Johnson, 1796-1876, of Baltimore. The national reputation of the latter makes it almost needless to mention the facts that he twice represented Maryland in the United States Senate, held the position of Attorney-General in President Taylor's cabinet, and was Minister to the Court of St James in 1868, as well as being the leader of the Maryland bar for half a century, and one of the most prominent lawyers of the country

In 1853, W R. Travers again removed to New York, which continued to be his home until his death, that event occurring at Hamilton, in the Island of Bermuda, in 1887. He became a member of the New York Stock Exchange in 1856, and achieved both reputation and success as a financier His social relations with the most prominent men of New York were peculiarly intimate He was a member of all the leading clubs, and, though not actively identified with the sport, he was one of the group of gentlemen who established the Jerome Park course, and gave to racing in New York a prestige which it had not previously enjoyed. He was also the first president of the New York Athletic Club, and had a large share in establishing its standing This was duly acknowledged by the club in naming its country property on Long Island Sound, Travers Island Mr Travers was also a vestryman of Grace Episcopal Church

The elder Mr Travers' reputation as a wit can only be compared with that of Selwin, or other famous *beaux esprits* of the last century He possessed the highest sense of humor, with keen powers of repartee, and a most effective manner Such of his *bon mots* as have not been lost, retain a vitality in spite of time, and reveal a character fundamentally sincere, simple and incapable of malice

Mr William Riggin Travers, son of William R and Maria Louisa (Johnson) Travers, was born, in 1861, near this city. He was educated at St Mark's School, Southboro, Mass., and graduated from Columbia College. In 1890, he married Lillie Harriman, daughter of Oliver Harriman, of New York. He has not followed any profession or active business, devoting his attention to the care of his family property. Mr. Travers has, in the main, made Newport his residence, his winter home being in Aiken, S C. He is identified with fashionable sport, is a distinguished whip, and a member of the Coaching and Four-in-Hand clubs. He is vice-president of the Newport Golf Club and secretary of the Newport Casino His clubs in New York are the Knickerbocker and Racquet Of Mr Travers' sisters the eldest, Mary, is the wife of John G Heckscher; Elise married William Alexander Duer, Matilda married Walter Gay, and Susan is unmarried His brothers John and Reverdy Johnson Travers, are both dead

HENRY GRAFF TREVOR

JOHN B TREVOR, grandfather of Mr. Henry Graff Trevor, was a member of an old family of the Keystone State. His father was Samuel Trevor, of Cornellsville, Pa. Engaged in business in Philadelphia throughout his life, he occupied a high business and social position, and was several times a member of the Legislature His son, John B. Trevor, the father of Mr. Henry Graff Trevor, was one of the leading bankers of New York in the last generation. He was born in Philadelphia, in 1822, and died in New York in 1890 He entered business life in a wholesale dry goods house of Philadelphia, and coming to New York, in 1849, was elected, in the following year, a member of the Stock Exchange. From that time forth he was successful in the highest degree, and soon attained to a distinguished rank in financial circles. During his business career after 1852, he was associated with James B. Colgate, under the firm name of Trevor & Colgate, bankers.

A devoted member of the Baptist Church, he was untiring in his zeal for religious, educational and charitable works, and gave liberally of his means for benevolent causes Indeed, it has been estimated that during his lifetime he bestowed fully one million dollars on such objects. The Rochester University and the Theological Seminary of that institution were special recipients of his favor. At one time, when those institutions of learning were in financial straits, and their very existence was threatened, Mr. Trevor was their main support. Trevor Hall, of Rochester University, was built by him, and also the gymnasium of the same institution. He was president of the board of trustees of Rochester Seminary and a member of the board of trustees of Rochester University. Colgate University, formerly Hamilton College, was also generously supported by him. With Mr. Colgate he was associated in the building of the Warburton Avenue Baptist Church, of Yonkers, the entire cost of which was met by the two partners, and he was also a liberal contributor to missionary societies. In 1880, he was a Republican Presidential elector. The first wife of Mr Trevor was Louisa Stephania Stewart, a daughter of Lispenard Stewart and Louisa Stephania Salles, whose other daughter, Sarah Lispenard Stewart, married Frederick Graham Lee. By his second wife, Mary R. Rhinelander, Lispenard Stewart was the father of William Rhinelander Stewart, Lispenard Stewart and other children, who have been conspicuous in New York in the present generation Lispenard Stewart, the elder, was the son of Alexander L. Stewart and Sarah Lispenard. His paternal grandfather was Robert Stewart, brother of Charles Stewart, who was a commissary during the Revolution and a friend of General Washington. Robert Stewart was a grandson of Robert Stewart, of Londonderry, an officer of dragoons The Lispenard family, also, was one of the most distinguished in the annals of New York. Sarah Lispenard, the great-grandmother of Mr. Henry G. Trevor, was a daughter of Captain Anthony Lispenard, a younger son of Leonard Lispenard and Alice Rutgers. His wife was his cousin, Sarah Barclay, daughter of Andrew Barclay and Helen Roosevelt, and a niece of the Reverend Henry Barclay The second wife of John B Trevor, whom he married in 1871, was Emily Norwood

Mr. Henry Graff Trevor is the son of John B. Trevor and his first wife, Louisa Stephania Stewart. Mr. Trevor was born in New York, April 25, 1865, and has been engaged in business as a banker. In 1890, he married Margaret Helen Schieffelin, daughter of George R. Schieffelin. Their children are: George Schieffelin and Margaret Estelle Trevor. His city residence is 20 East Forty-Ninth Street, and his summer home Meadowmere, Southampton, Long Island Mr. Trevor belongs to the Metropolitan, Union, Seventh Regiment Veterans, St. Andrew's and Shinnecock Golf clubs, the Country Club of Westchester County, the Downtown Association, the Sons of the Revolution, the Society of Colonial Wars and the St Nicholas Society. He was a member of Company K of the Seventh Regiment, from 1883 to 1888. In 1892-93, he built and presented to the Warburton Avenue Baptist Church, of Yonkers, a handsome parsonage adjoining the church

The younger brother of Mr. Trevor, by his father's second marriage, is John B. Trevor, Jr, and the daughters of that marriage are· Emily H. Trevor and Mary T Trevor, wife of Grenville L. Winthrop

CHARLES HENRY TRUAX

THE progenitor of the Truax family in this country was one of the first settlers in the New Netherland. Originally the family name was du Trieux Philip du Trieux, a Walloon, born in 1585, was in New Amsterdam during the administration of Governor Peter Minuit, 1624-29 He was appointed a court messenger in 1638, and two years later received a patent for land in Smits Valley His wife was Susanna De Chiney, and three of his daughters married, respectively, Isaac de Foreest, Evert Janse Wendell and Dirk Janse De Groot Descendants of Philip du Trieux moved to Albany, and were among the first settlers of that part of the State They were especially prominent in the foundation of Schenectady, and became connected by marriage with many of the great families of that day—the Van Slycks, the De Groots, the de la Granges, the Vroomans, the Van Santvoords, the Vedders and others The family has always been one of prominence and dignity in that section

Judge Charles H Truax, descended in direct line from Philip du Trieux, was born in Durhamville, Oneida County, N Y., October 31st, 1846 His father was Henry P Truax, and his mother Sarah A Shaffer His grandfathers were Henry D Truax and Gilbert Shaffer He studied at Vernon Academy and at Oneida Seminary, and then entered Hamilton College, but was obliged to abandon his college career in his junior year, and engaged in teaching school and studying law In 1868, he came to New York and continued the study of law in the office of his uncle, Chauncey Shaffer, a well-known practitioner of that period. The same year he passed the examination for admission to the bar

So rapidly did he advance in his profession, that in less than ten years from the time he was admitted to the bar he began to be spoken of for judicial honors. In 1880, he was elected a Judge of the Superior Court, and held that position for a term of fourteen years At the present time, he is a Justice of the Supreme Court for a term expiring in 1910. The career of Judge Truax on the bench has been distinguished by many important decisions One of these was the case against the Western Union Telegraph Company, in which he affirmed the right of companies to consolidate and issue new stock, a decision that was reversed by the General Term, but finally sustained by the Court of Appeals. Another important decision was delivered by him in 1887, when he held that private real estate owners were entitled to relief by injunction against the New York Elevated Railroad Company where their property rights were infringed.

In social life and in literary circles, Judge Truax is not less distinguished than in his legal career. He has traveled extensively in all parts of Europe, and is one of the most cultured and most discriminating bibliophiles in this country. His private library contains over ten thousand volumes, including many old and rare editions and priceless manuscripts; being one of the most valuable private libraries in New York City. The gem of the collection is the celebrated fifteenth century missal known as the Trivulzio Breviary, probably as fine an example of illuminated manuscript as there is in existence

Judge Truax received the degree of M A from Hamilton College, in 1876, and the degree of LL D from the same institution in 1890, and he gave to that college one thousand two hundred and fifty volumes, known as the Truax Classical Library He is vice-president of the Manhattan Club, president, in 1896, of the Holland Society, a trustee of the Mott Memorial Library, many years a trustee of the Church of the Puritans, and a member of the Democratic, New York Athletic and Harlem clubs, and of the St Nicholas Society In 1871, Judge Truax married Nancy C. Stone, who was descended on her mother's side from Anthony Demilt, Sheriff of New York, in 1673 Her father's ancestor, Simon Stone, came over to this country from England in 1635 in the ship Increase, landing in Massachusetts Mrs Truax died, March 30th, 1886, leaving four children —Arthur D , Elizabeth, Nancy and Charles H , Jr , who died July 6th, 1886 Judge Truax married again in 1896, his second wife being Caroline Sanders, who was born at Cincinnati, O The city residence of the family is at 12 East Sixty-fifth Street

EDWARD TUCK

A LL the Tuck or Tucke families that have lived in New Hampshire, of whom the gentleman whose name appears at the head of this sketch is a representative, are descended from Robert Tuck, of Gorlston, Suffolk County, England. The pioneer came to New England in 1636, and lived first in Watertown, Mass., afterwards in Salem, and then in Hampton, Rockingham County, N. H., where he was a freeman in 1639. In 1648-49-52-57, he was a selectman of the town, and in 1647 was the town clerk. He died in 1664. Edward Tuck, son of Robert Tuck, married Mary Philbrick, a daughter of Thomas Philbrick, and their son, John Tuck, who was born in 1652, married Bethia Hobbs, daughter of Maurice and Sarah Estow Hobbs. From 1680 to 1717, John Tuck was ten times elected a selectman. Jonathan Tuck, in the next generation, was born in 1697 and died in 1781. He was eight times a selectman and twice elected a member of the General Assembly. His wife was Tabitha Towle, daughter of Benjamin and Sarah (Borden) Towle, of Hampton.

The great-grandfather of Mr. Edward Tuck was Jonathan Tuck, 1736-1780. His first wife was Betsey Batchelder, daughter of John and Elizabeth (Moulton) Batchelder. She died in 1772, and he then married Huldah Moulton, daughter of John and Mary (Marston) Moulton. John Tuck, son of Jonathan and Huldah Tuck, was born in 1780 and died in 1847. He married Betsey Towle, daughter of Amos and Sarah Towle, of Hampton, and removed from Hampton, the ancestral home of the family, to Parsonsfield, Me., where the Honorable Amos Tuck, father of the subject of this sketch, was born in 1810. Amos Tuck studied at Effingham, N. H., where he prepared for college, and in 1831 went to Dartmouth, from which institution he was graduated four years later. He taught in the Academy in Pembroke, N H., and was a preceptor in Hampton Academy, at the same time applying himself to the study of law. In 1838, having completed his legal education, he abandoned teaching and entered upon professional life, opening a law office in Exeter, where he became the partner of the Honorable James Bell, United States Senator from New Hampshire.

Mr. Tuck began his political career in 1842, when he was elected a member of the New Hampshire Legislature. At that time he was a Democrat, but two years later, upon the slavery issue, changed his party affiliations, and in 1846 received an independent nomination for Congress, being elected by a combination of Independent Democrats and Whigs. Assisting at the birth of the Republican party, he was a member of the committee which selected the name Republican for the new party organization at the Philadelphia Convention, and in 1860 was a delegate to the Chicago Republican Convention that nominated Abraham Lincoln. He served three terms in Congress, until 1853. President Abraham Lincoln appointed him naval officer of the port of Boston in 1861, and reappointed him again in 1865. He was a trustee of Dartmouth College, of Phillips Academy of Exeter, and of Robinson's Female Seminary. His wife, the mother of Mr. Edward Tuck, was Sarah Ann Nudd, daughter of David and Abigail (Emery) Nudd, of Hampton. She died in Exeter, N. H., in 1847.

Mr. Edward Tuck was born August 25th, 1842. Educated at Dartmouth College, he was graduated from that institution in 1862. For a short time he studied law, but afterwards went to Europe, where he became connected with the American Consulate in Paris. In 1865, he was vice-consul and acting consul. In 1866, he resigned from the consular service and returned home, soon after settling in New York and entering upon the banking business in the firm of John Munroe & Co., in which house he became a partner in 1871. He retired from active business in 1881. In 1872, Mr. Tuck married, in Paris, Julia Stell, daughter of William Shorter Stell, of Philadelphia, who, during the greater part of his life, was at the head of a business house in Manchester, England. Mr. and Mrs. Tuck live in East Sixty-first street, in the vicinity of Central Park, and spend considerable time in Paris. The club membership of Mr. Tuck includes the Metropolitan, Union, Union League, Grolier and Reform, and he is also a member of the New England Society and a patron of the American Museum of Natural History.

PAUL TUCKERMAN

THE American family of Tuckerman is descended from an old English family of Devon
County. Their English ancestor was Thomas Tuckerman, whose son, John Tuckerman,
the first of the name to appear in America, came to Boston about 1651. John Tuckerman,
of Boston, in the second American generation, was born in 1655, and died, it is supposed, about
1735. He was a merchant, but in King Philip's War was a soldier in defense of the Colonies.
His wife, who was the ancestress of the Tuckermans of this generation in Boston and New York,
was Susanna Chamberline, daughter of John Chamberline, of Boston. Edward Tuckerman, 1701-
1751, son of the second John Tuckerman, was also a merchant, and married Dorothy Kidder. He
was the father of Edward Tuckerman, 1740-1818, one of the prosperous merchants and distinguished men of his day in Boston, a Lieutenant in the militia and a member of the artillery company
in 1771. He was a member of the Legislature, 1805-07. His wife was Elizabeth Harris, and they
were the great grandparents of Mr. Paul Tuckerman.

One of the sons of the second Edward Tuckerman was also Edward Tuckerman, of Boston,
1785-1843. He was a merchant, deacon and vestryman of St. Paul's Church, director of the Massachusetts Bank, justice of the peace, and trustee of the Massachusetts General Hospital   Another
son of this family, the grandfather of Mr Paul Tuckerman, was the Reverend Joseph
Tuckerman, the distinguished philanthropist, who was born in 1778, and died in 1840.
Graduated from Harvard College in 1798, he received the degree of D. D. from the same
institution in 1824. He became a Unitarian minister in 1801, and was first settled over a
church in Chelsea, Mass. In 1826, he was appointed by the American Unitarian Association
minister-at-large in Boston, and thenceforth devoted his life principally to the scientific study of
pauperism and the practical administration of charity

Among other distinguished members of this family was Henry Theodore Tuckerman,
1813-1871, one of the most prolific and most popular writers upon art and literary subjects in the
present generation. He was a nephew of the Reverend Joseph Tuckerman, and another nephew
was Edward Tuckerman, 1817-1886, the scientist and professor in Amherst College. Arthur
Lyman Tuckerman, the architect who was superintendent of the Metropolitan Museum of Art
Schools, in 1888, was of this family, and so are Bayard Tuckerman, of New York, the accomplished
historian, author of A History of English Prose Fiction, A Life of General Lafayette, Life of Peter
Stuyvesant, and editor of the Diary of Philip Hone, Stephen Salisbury Tuckerman, the artist,
Leverett Saltonstall Tuckerman and Charles S. Tuckerman, of Boston.

The father of Mr. Paul Tuckerman was Lucius Tuckerman, a merchant of New York in the
last generation, who was actively identified with the leading art, educational and philanthropic
institutions of the metropolis. He was a patron of the Metropolitan Museum of Art, a director of
the Children's Aid Society, and gave his generous support to other enterprises of like character.
On his mother's side, Mr. Tuckerman is descended from the Gibbs family, of Newport, R I., and
the Wolcotts of Connecticut. His maternal grandfather was Colonel George Gibbs, of Sunswick,
Long Island, the distinguished scientist. His maternal grandmother was Laura Wolcott, daughter of
Oliver Wolcott, Secretary of the Treasury in the first Cabinet of President George Washington, and
granddaughter of Governor Oliver Wolcott, signer of the Declaration of Independence.

Mr. Paul Tuckerman, who was born in New York in 1856, and graduated from Harvard
College, is a trustee of his father's and other estates. He married Susan Minturn, daughter of John
W. Minturn, and granddaughter of Robert B. Minturn, and has one daughter, Dorothy Tuckerman.
Mr. and Mrs. Tuckerman's residence is in Tuxedo Park. Mr Tuckerman is a member of the
Knickerbocker, Tuxedo and Racquet clubs, and the Downtown Association   The other children of
Lucius Tuckerman are: Alfred Tuckerman, Walter Cary Tuckerman, who died in 1894; Laura
Wolcott, wife of James Lowndes, of Washington; Emily Tuckerman, of Washington; Bayard
Tuckerman, the author referred to above, and Lucy, the wife of Arthur George Sedgwick.

HERBERT BEACH TURNER

THE Reverend Joseph Turner, known for years as Parson Turner, of the old Swedes Church of Gloria Dei, Southwark, Philadelphia, came over from England not long after the middle of the last century   He appears to have descended from Nicholas Turner, who lived at Halberton, near Exeter, in 1620   Assisted by a wealthy uncle, Philip Hulbeart, who had urged him to settle in America, he opened a large warehouse and went into business in Philadelphia. Not long after he returned to England and married Elizabeth, daughter of Dr. Mason, a physician of Exeter.   He then came back and remained permanently in his new home.   He was a thorough Englishman, and was at one time sent to jail by the patriot party during the Revolutionary War for his Tory sentiments.   He was a great admirer of the famous Dr White, the first Bishop of Pennsylvania, and was induced by him to enter the ministry of the Protestant Episcopal Church, which he did when somewhat advanced in life.   He became associate rector of the Gloria Dei Church, originally built by the Swedes, who had endeavored to found a Colony on the banks of the Delaware long prior to the coming of William Penn, for which reason it is still commonly known as the old Swedes Church, and is to this day one of the most venerable landmarks of Philadelphia   He was at another time rector of St. Mark's Church, at Marcus Hook, below Philadelphia

Samuel Hulbeart Turner, D. D., was the youngest of the Reverend Joseph Turner's eight children.   He was born in the family mansion in South Second Street, Philadelphia, in 1790.   He entered the ministry, was ordained by Bishop White and became rector of the church at Chestertown, Md.   Here he established the first Protestant Episcopal Sunday School in America.   He left this parish to become Professor of Biblical Learning and Interpretation of the Scripture in the Protestant Episcopal Theological Seminary in New York, which post he held, with conspicuous success, for nearly forty-three years.   Many of the most prominent and learned clergymen for some two generations were instructed by him, and he exercised, during the long period in question, a wide influence in the affairs of the church.

His wife, the mother of Mr Herbert Beach Turner, came from New England families.   She was Mary Esther Beach, daughter of Burrage Beach, of Cheshire, Conn., and his wife, Julia (Bowden) Beach, whose father was Professor John Bowden, one of the clergy of Trinity Church, New York, and subsequently a professor in Columbia College   The Beach family is one of the oldest in Connecticut, its ancestor being John Beach, the Pilgrim, who in 1643 was among the first settlers of New Haven, where his descendants rose to great and deserved prominence in the affairs of the Colony and the succeeding State.   On the side of his maternal grandmother, Mr. Turner descends from Major Thomas Bowden, an officer of the British Army, who served in America in the French and Indian War.

Mr. Herbert Beach Turner was born at Cheshire, Conn., in 1835.   He was graduated from Columbia College in 1855 and adopted the profession of the law after taking a course at the Albany Law School.   In 1863, he married Sarah Kirkland Floyd, daughter of John Gelston Floyd, of Mastic, Long Island.   The name of Floyd is prominent in the history of Long Island and of New York.   Richard Floyd, who migrated from Wales in 1654, was the ancestor of the family. General William Floyd, Mrs Turner's great-grandfather, served in the Revolutionary Army, and was a member of the New York Committee of Safety and of the Continental Congress, and was one of the signers of the Declaration of Independence.   Mr. and Mrs. Turner have three children, Thornton Floyd, Mary Esther Beach and Anna Tracy Turner.   Mr. Turner's home is at Englewood, N. J., where the family resides more than half of the year.   During the winter months, they reside at 125 East Thirtieth Street.

Mr Turner belongs to the Century, University, Reform, Church and Δ Φ clubs, and the Downtown Association.   He is an active Protestant Episcopalian, is greatly interested in economics, and is concerned in all movements for the reform of national and municipal politics.

LAWRENCE TURNURE

L EAVING his ancestral home in Picardy, to escape religious persecution, Daniel De Tourneur, a member of an ancient family of France, settled in Leyden, Holland, in the early part of the seventeenth century His wife, whom he married in 1650, was Jacqueline Parisis, of a family whose members were refugees from Hesdin, in Artois. Her brother was the Reverend Eustachius Parisis, a minister in Harlem, Holland.

Two years after his marriage, Daniel de Tourneur with his wife and infant child sailed for New Netherland. He was one of the earliest settlers in the village of Harlem on Manhattan Island. In 1661, he was an associate schepen, and a schepen in 1662, being also chosen *brandt meester* or fire warden. In 1663, he was a magistrate, and in 1665 an under sheriff and president of the court, and held other offices. Later he lived in Flatbush, where he died in 1672 Daniel Tourneur, his son, was a freeman of Flatbush in 1672, and afterwards a magistrate and Lieutenant His son, the third Daniel Tourneur, was an overseer, 1676–81, and commissioner in 1686. Jacques Tourneur, son of the first Daniel Tourneur, married, in 1683, Aefie Kortright, daughter of Michael Kortright, and their son, Michael, married Maria Oblenis, a descendant of Joost Oblenis, a magistrate of Harlem in 1666, succeeding his father, Joost Oblenis, who was named in the patents of Governors Nicolls and Dongan

Mr. Lawrence Turnure is the prominent representative of this ancient Huguenot family. He is a native of New York, and has been identified with mercantile and financial affairs, having been associated with the late Moses Taylor, and being now the head of Lawrence Turnure & Co He married Jane Redfield, daughter of Heman Judd Redfield. Mrs Turnure is descended from William Hyde, of Norwich, Conn., one of the first settlers of that place. Elizabeth Hyde, granddaughter of William Hyde, married, in 1682, Lieutenant Richard Lord, of Saybrook, grandson of Thomas Lord, who came to Newtown, Mass , in 1635, and to Hartford, Conn., in 1636, being afterwards among the first settlers of Saybrook In the next generation, Phœbe Lord, who was born in Lyme, Conn., about 1686, married Joseph Sill, son of Captain Joseph Sill, who was born in England about 1636, came to Cambridge, Mass., with his father, John Sill, previous to 1638, and in 1676 removed to Lyme, Conn. Jabez Sill, son of Captain Joseph Sill, moved from Lyme, Conn., to Wilkesbarre, Pa , in 1770, and died there in 1790. His wife was Elizabeth Noyes, daughter of Moses Noyes and Mary Ely, of Lyme, and granddaughter of the Reverend Moses Noyes Mary Sill, daughter of Jabez and Elizabeth (Noyes) Sill, married James Gould, of Wilkesbarre, Pa. The mother of Mrs. Turnure, Abigail Noyes Gould, was born at Lyme in 1795. She married, in 1817, Heman Judd Redfield, who was born in 1788 in Suffield, Conn , the son of Peleg Redfield and Mary Judd, and in the seventh generation from William Redfield, who settled in New London. Heman Judd Redfield was a master in chancery, and collector of customs at New York.

The Turnure residence is in Fifth Avenue. Mr. Turnure is a member of the Tuxedo, Manhattan and Democratic clubs, the Downtown Association, the American Geographical Society, and many of the leading artistic and benevolent organizations of the city. He has four sons and two daughters Lawrence Turnure, Jr , who was at one time in the banking business with his father, is a member of the Union, Rockaway Hunt and Country clubs, and married Romaine Stone. The third son, George Evans Turnure, was graduated from Harvard in 1889, married Elizabeth G. Lanier, is in business with his father and belongs to the Calumet, Racquet and other clubs The eldest daughter, Jeannie Turnure, married Major John C. Mallery, U. S. A. The other children, Redfield, Mary G and Percy R. Turnure, who was graduated from Harvard in 1894, are unmarried

The late David M Turnure, a brother of Mr. Lawrence Turnure, also a banker and merchant in New York, died several years ago, leaving a widow. Mrs. Turnure, whose maiden name was Mary E. Baldwin, is a daughter of the Honorable Harvey Baldwin. She has two children. Her son, Arthur B. Turnure, Princeton, 1876, married Elizabeth Harrison Her daughter, Mary S. Turnure, is unmarried

JULIEN STEVENS ULMAN

D URING the present century, Germany has contributed a very large and important element of population to the United States, and especially to New York City These newcomers, from all parts of the kingdom, have been representatives of many of the best families of their native land As adopted citizens or as native-born Americans in the second and third generations, they have been among the most useful and most successful contributors to the preeminence of New York, as the business, professional and social metropolis of the New World

Prominent among these citizens of the metropolis who are of German descent, is Mr. Julien Stevens Ulman On both the paternal and maternal side of the family he descends from ancestors who, from time immemorial, have been among the substantial people of Bavaria and have held high rank in the communities in which they lived The Ulmans, for more than four centuries, have been residents of Augsberg, that celebrated city which is one of the principal seats of commerce of South Germany Augsberg has always been famed for its important manufacturing interests and for the high intellectual position maintained by its inhabitants Few of its families have stood better in professional life than the Ulmans. The paternal great-grandfather and great-great-grandfather of the gentleman whose family is here under consideration were especially distinguished in their time for high professional attainments On the maternal side, the ancestors of Mr Ulman were among the oldest families of Furth, in Bavaria

Mr. Julien Stevens Ulman is a native New Yorker, having been born in this city October 1st, 1865. His father was Solomon B Ulman and his mother was Johanna Bach His paternal grandparents were Bernhard and Sophie Ulman On his mother's side, his grandparents were Joseph Bach and Cecelia Englander. Mr Ulman received his preparatory education in the Charlier Institute He was prepared for college when he was seventeen years of age and passed the examinations for Harvard in 1882 Being moved by a desire to travel, however, he gave up his plans for a collegiate education and went to Europe, where he spent considerable time in study and in visiting all parts of the Continent Returning to his native city, he engaged in business pursuits In 1884, he was connected with a banking house, where he remained for six years In 1890, he went into the leather business, and is now at the head of one of the largest and most successful houses engaged in that line of trade, having valuable connections with all foreign countries and doing an extensive exporting business

Mr Ulman is unmarried and lives at 66 West Thirty-ninth Street, in a house that has been occupied by his family for thirty-three years, they being now the oldest residents in that street During the summer he lives in Newport, where he is well known and popular Interested in gentlemanly sports, he is a member of several clubs and similar organizations devoted to those interests, among them the New York Yacht Club, the Richmond County Hunt and the Polo Association He is a patron of the opera and is a member of the Opera Club. His other clubs are the Lawyers', Reform and Michaux

Many members of the family to which Mr Ulman belongs have been distinguished in the public service. One of his uncles, who is now retired from active service, was a Surgeon-General in the Bavarian Army, his period of service extending over half a century The grandfather of Mr Ulman on the maternal side served under Napoleon as Quartermaster-General during the Crimean War In every generation members of the family have been prominent in the military service of their native land Mr Ulman's great-grandmother, Englander, nee Cann, founded a home for impoverished families of title in Frankfort-on-the-Main ; her people came from Holland, where also she founded an institution for homeless women His brother, Morris S Ulman, has been a member of the Senate of Rhode Island and was a Judge of the Probate Court He still maintains his connection with New York, being a member of several of the clubs of this city and of Providence, R I.

EDWARD CARLTON UNDERHILL

AMONG the companions of Winthrop at the settlement of Boston was Captain John Underhill, a veteran soldier, who had served in the Low Countries under Maurice, of Nassau. He came of the old landed family of the Underhills, of Hunningham, in Warwickshire, the coat of arms which he bore, and which has been inherited by his descendants in this country, being three trefoils between a red chevron on a silver shield with the crest of a tripping buck, being that of their English ancestors. The family still possesses representatives in the old country.

Captain Underhill's extensive military knowledge was of the greatest service to the New England Colonists in the Pequot War of 1637. He was a leader of the band of whites who overcame and nearly exterminated the only formidable savage tribe in that region. He was one of the first officers of the famous Ancient and Honorable Artillery Company, of Boston, and, in 1638, published in London a narrative of the Pequot War, under the title of News from America, which ranks among the most curious and interesting literary productions which have come to us from the early Colonial period of New England.

Being involved in what was termed the Antinomian dispute, Captain Underhill was exiled from Massachusetts to New Hampshire, being chosen Governor of the latter Colony at Dover, in 1638. Even in this station, the enmity of some of the leading Puritans and the religious intolerance of the times pursued him, and he again withdrew, going to the Dutch settlements on the North River, where other victims of the unhappy, intolerant spirit which animated the early history of Massachusetts found a refuge and complete religious security, among the number being counted the famous Ann Hutchinson.

His military experience was at once recognized by the masters of the New Netherland. In 1644, he commanded the Dutch forces in a successful attack upon the hostile Indians near Stamford, which, for the time, ended all opposition by the redskins to the whites. He settled at Oyster Bay, Long Island, in 1655. He warmly espoused the occupation of the New Netherland by the English, and died in 1672. During his lifetime, he was commonly called "Lord Underhill," the designation having reference to his gentle birth and the superiority of his descent to that of many of the New England Colonists.

The youngest son of the renowned soldier and Colonist was Nathaniel Underhill, born in 1663, who, in 1685, purchased a large tract two miles from Westchester, N. Y., and became the ancestor of the Westchester branch of the Underhill family. He married Mary Ferris, and was followed by three successive Abraham Underhills, the last of them, who died toward the close of the eighteenth century, having been Mr. Edward C. Underhill's great-grandfather. The branch of the family continued for almost two hundred years to reside in Westchester, where they had numerous offshoots and connections, and ranked among the most influential people of the county. The land originally purchased by Nathaniel Underhill, in 1685, was also, until the present century, still in the hands of his descendants. The published History of Westchester County is full of references to the bearers of the name, and to their intermarriages with other families of the greatest prominence in the same and other portions of the State.

It is to this ancient race that Mr. Edward Carlton Underhill belongs. His grandfather, James Underhill, born at Westchester in 1784, married Lydia Carpenter, and was father of Abraham Underhill, born in 1804, also in his ancestral town, but who became a resident and prominent citizen of New York. The wife of Abraham Underhill and the mother of the present Mr. Underhill was Eliza Ostrander, born 1814, in Columbia County, N. Y., also a member of an old Colonial family. Mr. Underhill was born in this city in 1858, was educated here, and adopted the profession of the law. In 1882, he married Esther Reynolds, the issue of this marriage being two daughters, Caroline Elizabeth and Dorothy Underhill. Mr. Underhill resides at 166 West Ninety-fifth Street, and is a member of the Republican Club.

THEODORE NEWTON VAIL

IN 1710, John Vail, a Quaker preacher, settled in Morris County, N J He was a descendant of John Vail, who came from Wales, and whose children and grand children were, in later generations, the heads of families prominent and influential in New York, New Jersey and elsewhere. One of the most distinguished members of the family was the Reverend Stephen M. Vail, of the Methodist Episcopal Church, author and professor of Hebrew and the Oriental languages. The grandfather of Mr. Theodore N. Vail was Lewis Vail, civil engineer, who was one of the first to engage in building canals and railroads in the State of Ohio Another relative, Samuel Vail, was the owner of the Speedwell Iron Works in Morristown, N J , and with his brother, George, and his son, Alfred, was the financial supporter of Professor S F B Morse in perfecting and bringing to public attention the magnetic telegraph Alfred Vail invented many of the appliances that helped to perfect the telegraph, and in the estimation of scientists who are familiar with the subject, is entitled to a large share of credit for all the important and practical features of the telegraph of to-day. George Vail was a Member of Congress, 1853–57, United States Consul to Glasgow in 1858, and a member of the Court of Pardons of the State of New Jersey.

Davis Vail, the father of the subject of this sketch, was born in Ohio, but became connected with the Speedwell Iron Works of his brother He married Phœbe Quinby, daughter of Judge Isaac Quinby, of Morris County, N. J , and returned to Ohio, where he lived several years, and where his son, Theodore N Vail, was born, July 16th, 1845 Through his mother, Mr. Vail is connected with one of the most eminent families of New Jersey. One of his uncles was General Quinby, a graduate of West Point and a hero of the Civil War

Mr. Theodore N. Vail was educated in the Morristown, N J , Academy, and then studied medicine in the office of his uncle, Dr William Quinby. But telegraphy soon attracted him, and acquiring knowledge of the system, he took a position in New York on the staff of the general superintendent of the metropolitan and Eastern divisions of the United States Telegraph Company He then went West, and in 1868 was an operator and agent at Pine Bluffs, Wyo., on the Union Pacific Railroad. In 1869, he was appointed clerk in the railway mail service between Omaha and Ogden, and his efficient work in that position led to repeated promotions, until upon the establishing of the railroad post office on the Union Pacific lines he was made chief clerk.

In 1873, he was summoned to Washington and appointed general superintendent of the railway mail service, a position where he had special charge of the distribution of the mails, an onerous duty that he performed in a remarkably satisfactory manner. Promotions came fast to him after that In 1874, he was made assistant superintendent of the railway mail service, in 1876, assistant general superintendent, and in 1876, general superintendent. Thus he had attained to the highest grade in the service at the age of thirty-one years, the youngest officer in that branch of the post office department. His administration was thoroughly efficient. He expanded and improved the civil service system of the department, reduced the rates for transporting the mails, and introduced other reforms.

In 1878, Mr. Vail resigned from the postal service to become the general manager of the Bell Telephone Company, a position that he retained for ten years, during which time he built up the business of the company in a remarkable degree, establishing long distance telephones, introducing copper wires and making other improvements that practically revolutionized the business Since his retirement from active business in 1888, he has traveled extensively, chiefly in the telephone interests His country home, Speedwell Farms, is an estate of fifteen hundred acres, in Lyndon Center, Vt , where he raises French coach horses, Jersey cattle, sheep and ponies. He belongs to the Union League, New York, and New York Athletic clubs, and is also a member of the Algonquin and the Union clubs, of Boston. He married, in 1869, Emma Louise Righter, of Newark, N J , and has one son, David Righter Vail, a graduate from Harvard University in the class of 1893, and now engaged in the practice of law

AUGUSTUS VAN CORTLANDT

THE Van Cortlandts of Yonkers trace their descent from the first Van Cortlandt in this country, Oloff Stevense Van Cortlandt, of Wyk bif Diernstede, Netherland, a soldier in the service of the West India Company, who came to America in the ship Haring, with Governor William Kieft, in 1638. He was a schepen in 1654, one of the commissioners to treat with the Colony of Connecticut in 1663, a member of the council of Governor Andros and otherwise of prominence, influence and usefulness in the Colony, during the period of the Dutch occupation. A man of noble ancestry, he was lineally descended from the Dukes of Courland in Russia. The family name was Stevens or Stevenson, from Courland, and the latter was adopted as a surname, in Dutch being Kortelandt. His wife was Annetje Loockermans, sister of Govert Loockermans.

Descendants of Oloff Stevense Van Cortlandt have been among the most noted citizens of New York, prominent in business, social and political circles. They have married into all the leading families of the metropolis for three centuries, and so are connected with the Van Rensselaers, Schuylers, Philipses, Ver Plancks, de Peysters, Jays, Livingstones, Barclays, de Lanceys and others. Jacobus Van Cortlandt, the youngest member of the first Van Cortlandt's family, Mayor of New York for nine years and the ancestor of the Van Cortlandts of Yonkers, married Eve Philipse, daughter of Frederick Philipse, the first lord of the Philipse manor. His son Frederick married Frances Jay, daughter of Augustus Jay and his wife, Anna Maria Bayard. Augustus Jay was the son of Pierre Jay, the head of the family in this country, and his wife was the daughter of Balthazar Bayard. The elder sons of Frederick Van Cortlandt died without issue, and the entail fell to Augustus Van Cortlandt, who married Catherine Barclay.

With the death of Augustus Van Cortlandt, in default of male heirs, the family property and name passed to the grandsons, children of Anne Van Cortlandt, who had married Henry White, her cousin, son of her father's youngest sister Eve. Henry White was of Welsh descent. His grandfather was a Colonel in the English Army, came to Maryland in 1712, was a merchant in New York, and president of the Chamber of Commerce in 1772. Augustus White, the eldest son of Henry and Anne White, inherited the property by will from his grandfather and took the name of Van Cortlandt. When he died without issue, in 1839, his brother succeeded him and upon the death of the latter, also without issue, only a few months after Augustus had died, the entail fell to his nephew, the son of his sister, who was the wife of Dr. Edward N Bibby. The father of Dr. Bibby was Captain Thomas Bibby, of Revolutionary fame.

Mr. Augustus Van Cortlandt Bibby, who thus succeeded to the estate by the terms of his uncle's will, changed his name to Van Cortlandt, and is still living. The City of New York acquired by the right of eminent domain, in 1884, seven hundred acres of this land, with the Van Cortlandt mansion built by Frederic Van Cortlandt, in 1748, and it is now included in Van Cortlandt Park. The present Augustus Van Cortlandt lived on this property until it was taken by the city, and still owns one hundred acres of it. From 1847 to 1853, he was engaged in the banking business, and in 1859 was a member of the New York State Assembly. He was an early president of the St Nicholas club, is a member of the New York Historical Society, the Metropolitan and City clubs, and the St Nicholas Society, and otherwise identified with the social institutions of the city. The wife of Mr Van Cortlandt was Charlotte Amelia Bunch, daughter of Robert Bunch, of Nassau, Island of New Providence, and granddaughter of Dr. Richard Bayley, the first health officer of the port of New York and a close friend of Sir Guy Carleton. The children of this marriage are: Augustus, Jr., Henry W., Robert B., who is a member of the Metropolitan, Knickerbocker and other clubs and a Columbia College graduate; Oloff de Lancey and Mary B Van Cortlandt.

The Van Cortlandt arms are: argent, four wings of niell, sable and gules (forming St. Andrew's cross), five estoiles gules. Crest, over an esquire's helmet a wreath argent and gules, surmounted by an estoile gules. Motto, *Virtus sibi manus.*

CORNELIUS VANDERBILT

B ILT, or Bild, a manor in the Province of Friesland, in the Netherlands, a few miles from
Zeyst, gave its name to one of the foremost American families of the present day. Jan
Aertsen Vanderbilt emigrated from that manor to New Netherland in 1650, and established
himself in Flatbush. He was married three times; to Anneken Hendricks, a native of Bergen,
Norway; to Dierber Cornellis, and to Magdalentje Hansz. Aris, his eldest son, married, in
1677, Hildegonde, or Hilletje, daughter of Rem Janse Venderbeeck. He died after 1711

In the third American generation came Jacob Vanderbilt, 1692–1759, who was the first of
the family living on Staten Island. By his wife, Neiltje, he had a son, Jacob Vanderbilt, who
was born in 1723 and married Mary Sprague Jacob and Mary (Sprague) Vanderbilt were the
parents of Cornelius Vanderbilt, their youngest child, who, born in 1764, married Phebe Hand
and became the father of the celebrated Commodore Cornelius Vanderbilt. The Vanderbilt
family was settled on Staten Island, near New Dorp, and owned considerable valuable farming
property there. The senior Cornelius Vanderbilt removed to Stapleton, Staten Island, and
managed an extensive farm. He also regularly ran boats between Staten Island and New York
for the transportation of produce to the New York markets and to accommodate occasional
travelers.

Cornelius Vanderbilt, who made the family name famous in the last generation, was
born on Staten Island, near Stapleton, May 27th, 1794. A moderate education was given to
him, and this was supplemented by exceptional mental vigor and business genius that led him
to success. In 1810, when he was only sixteen years of age, he instituted a ferry service
between Staten Island and the City of New York, thus commencing his career as a master of
transportation. His career from this point onward is part of the familiar commercial history of
the country. In the course of time, he became the greatest shipowner of his generation. At
the outbreak of the Civil War, he presented to the Government the steamship Vanderbilt, representing a value of one million dollars. For this generous gift, Congress bestowed upon him a
vote of thanks and a gold medal, inscribed, "A grateful country to her generous son." His
success in the railroad business was even more pronounced, and the series of consolidations that
resulted in the creation of the New York Central system stamped him as one of the master minds
of his generation in business and finance. When he died, in 1877, he ranked among the richest
men of the world, and left to his family a fortune almost without parallel. Commodore Vanderbilt was a generous benefactor to religious and educational institutions, among his large
gifts being one million dollars to Vanderbilt University, in Nashville, Tenn., and the building
occupied by the Church of the Strangers, on Mercer Street, a memorial to the Reverend Charles
F. Deems.

At the age of nineteen, Commodore Vanderbilt married Sophia Johnson, who died in
1867. He married again in 1868, his wife being Frances A. Crawford, of Mobile, Ala By his
first wife, he was the father of thirteen children; Phœbe Jane, wife of James N. Cross, Ethelinda,
wife of Daniel B. Allen; Eliza, wife of George A. Osgood; William H ; Emily, wife of William
K Thorn; Sophia J , wife of Daniel Torrance; Maria Louise, wife of Horace F Clark; Francis;
Cornelius Johnson; Mary Alicia, wife of Nicholas La Bau; George W , Catharine Johnson, wife
of Smith Barker, Jr., and George W., second. The second George W. Vanderbilt died in 1866,
as a result of service in the Union Army.

William H. Vanderbilt, the eldest son of Commodore Vanderbilt, was born in New Brunswick, N. J., May 8th, 1821, and died December 8th, 1885 He was educated in the Columbia
Grammar School, and at the age of eighteen, went into mercantile life. In 1864, he was elected
vice-president of the New York & Harlem Railroad, and upon his father's death, in 1877,
succeeded to the presidency of the New York Central & Hudson River and other railroad properties, and became the head of the Vanderbilt family. He was one of the great railroad magnates

of this generation, but in the latter years of his life devoted much time to travel and art collecting. He was a lover of fine horses, and owned Maud S , Aldine, Small Hopes, Lady Mac and other famous roadsters and trotters   He gave large sums of money to Vanderbilt University, the College of Physicians and Surgeons, the Metropolitan Museum of Art, St Luke's Hospital, and other institutions

The wife of William H. Vanderbilt was Maria Louisa Kissam Mrs Vanderbilt was a daughter of the Reverend Samuel Kissam, who was born in 1796, and was pastor of the Reformed Dutch Church, at Cedar Hill, near Albany. Her mother was Margaret H. Adams The grandparents of Mrs. Vanderbilt were Peter Rutgers Kissam, a Columbia College graduate and a merchant of New York, and his wife, Deborah Townsend, daughter of Penn Townsend The parents of Peter Rutgers Kissam were Benjamin Kissam, of Long Island, and his wife, Catherine Rutgers, daughter of Petrus Rutgers Benjamin Kissam was a celebrated lawyer, member of the Committee of Safety in 1776, and member of the First and Second Provincial Congresses. His father was Joseph Kissam, who was a justice of the peace of Manhasset, Long Island, and married Deborah Whitehead, daughter of the Honorable Jonathan and Sarah (Field) Whitehead The parents of Joseph Kissam were Daniel Kissam, of Long Island, 1669-1752, and his wife, Elizabeth Coombs. Daniel Kissam was the son of John Kissam, of Flushing, who was born in 1644, of English origin, and married Susannah Thorne, daughter of William Thorne. His father emigrated from England, and was one of the first settlers of Flushing The children of William H. Vanderbilt were Cornelius, William K , Frederick W , George W., Margaret Louisa, Emily Thorn, Florence Adele and Eliza O Vanderbilt

Mr. Cornelius Vanderbilt, the eldest son of William H. Vanderbilt, was born on Staten Island, November 27th, 1843 In 1865, he entered the office of the New York & Harlem Railroad, and successively held various important official positions in connection with the Vanderbilt system of railroads, becoming, upon the death of his father, the head of the house, and actively in control of the Vanderbilt properties, being now chairman and controlling director in the various companies that make up that magnificent transportation system He is a trustee of Columbia University, the General Theological Seminary, the Metropolitan Museum of Art, the American Museum of Natural History, St Luke's Hospital, and other institutions, and is noted for his interest in charitable work He erected the building on Madison Avenue occupied by the railroad branch of the Young Men's Christian Association, and gave a dormitory to Yale University He is a member of the Union, Metropolitan, Union League, Knickerbocker, Tuxedo, Grolier, Players, Century and Lawyers' clubs, and of many other social organizations. He married Alice Gwynne, daughter of Abraham Gwynne Their children are: Cornelius, Gertrude, Alfred G , Reginald C and Gladys M Vanderbilt. Their eldest son, William H Vanderbilt, died while a student in Yale University Cornelius Vanderbilt, Jr., is a graduate from Yale, and married, in 1896, Grace Wilson, daughter of Richard T Wilson. Gertrude Vanderbilt married Henry Payne Whitney, son of the Honorable William C. Whitney.

William K. Vanderbilt, the second son of William H. Vanderbilt, married Alva Murray Smith. He has two sons and one daughter, William K , Jr , Harold S , and Consuelo. His daughter married, in 1895, the Duke of Marlborough. She has one son, born in 1897, to whom the Prince of Wales is the godfather, and who is the heir to the historic name of Marlborough Mr. Vanderbilt owns the Valiant, one of the finest steam yachts in the world. He is a member of the Metropolitan, Knickerbocker, Union, Manhattan, New York Yacht, and Players clubs. Frederick W. Vanderbilt graduated from Yale College in the class of 1876, and married Miss Anthony He belongs to the Tuxedo, Metropolitan, University, New York Yacht and other clubs George W Vanderbilt is unmarried He belongs to the Metropolitan, Century, Players, Grolier, New York Yacht and other clubs His country estate, Biltmore, near Asheville, N C , is one of the handsomest establishments of its kind in the world. Margaret Louisa Vanderbilt married Colonel Elliott F. Shepard, whose family is treated more extensively elsewhere in this volume Emily T Vanderbilt is the wife of William D Sloane. Florence Adele Vanderbilt is the wife of Hamilton McK Twombly, Eliza O Vanderbilt is the wife of William Seward Webb

CHARLES HENRY VAN DEVENTER

NOT only on the paternal, but also upon his mother's side, this gentleman's ancestry is carried back with unusual exactitude through a line of Dutch progenitors, extending to the early foundation of New Netherland.   The Old World ancestor of his family, to whom the record extends, was Peiter Pieters, of Deventer, Holland, whose wife was Janneken Jansen, and it was their son, Jan Pietersen, born in 1628 at Deventer, whence the surname of his descendants was derived, who came out, in 1662, to the Colony established on the Hudson River by the Dutch West India Company.   He brought with him his wife, Engel Teunis, and was a resident of Brooklyn and New Utrecht, being a man of prominence and schepen of the latter place in 1673   Peter Jans Van Deventer, who was born about 1653 and died in 1747, resided at Martins' Neck, Long Island, and was a deacon of the Reformed Church at New Utrecht while he was on Long Island   In 1698, he lived in New York, but removed to New Jersey, and in 1709, was an elder of the Reformed Church of Freehold, Monmouth County, and about 1720, it is recorded, lived in Bound Brook, N. J   In 1686, he married Maria Christiaan, who came from the town of Doorn, Holland, members of her family being among the early emigrants to New Netherland who settled in the New Jersey Colony.

Their son, Jacob Van Deventer, was an inhabitant of Freehold, and was born in 1709, dying in 1756   He married for his first wife Margaretta Field, and after her death, Elizabeth Van Clief. His son, Jeremiah Van Deventer, of Bound Brook, 1741-1806, a patriot and a soldier in the Army of the Revolution, married Elizabeth Conover, while his grandson, Peter Van Deventer, a resident of Rahway, who was born in 1789 and died in 1817, married Elizabeth Vail. Peter Van Deventer was the grandfather of Mr. Charles Henry Van Deventer, whose father, Henry Bergen Van Deventer, of Bound Brook, N. J., and St Louis, Mo , was born in 1809 and died in 1879, his wife being a lady who, like him, was of direct Holland descent

As already stated, Mr Van Deventer comes of another old Dutch family. His mother, Elizabeth Degroot Voorhees, who married Henry Bergen Van Deventer in 1846, was a descendant of Coert Alberts van Voor Hees, who lived, prior to 1600, in the village of Hees, near Ruiken, in the Province of Drenthe in the Netherlands.   His son, Steven Coerte van Voor Hees, born in 1600, who came to New Netherland in 1660, was the first of the family in the New World   He purchased a tract of thirty-one morgens of land at Flatbush, Long Island, for three thousand guilders, being evidently a man of substance.   His name appears in the records of that town, where he was a magistrate in 1664, and where he died in 1684.   He was married in Holland and brought his children with him   In the next generation, his son, Jan Stevens van Voorhees, born in 1652, appears on the assessment roll of Flatlands in 1675 and 1683, and afterwards took the oath of allegiance in 1687.

Jan Janse Van Voorhees, the next in line of descent, who was baptized in 1686 at Brooklyn and moved to Staten Island, was the father of Jacobus Van Voorhees, 1720-1771, who married Sarah Culver, and resided first at Hackensack and afterwards in Somerset County, N. J   James Voorhees, 1748-1810, his son, was born in Hackensack and married Anna Harris, by whom he had John Harris Voorhees, 1783-1856, who married Eleanor Tunison, after whose death he married, in 1811, Susan P Degroot, who was the mother of Mrs. Henry Bergen Van Deventer.

Mr. Charles Henry Van Deventer was born in New Jersey, January 7th, 1847, and was educated in the academy at Lawrenceville, N J   He entered the brokerage business in early life, and since 1869 has been a member of the New York Stock Exchange.   In 1876, Mr Van Deventer married Christine Miller, daughter of James and Mary A (Roe) Miller   The two children of this union are Lloyd M and R Craig Van Deventer   The family residence is 60 West Fifty-third Street, near Fifth Avenue   Mr. Van Deventer is a member of the Union League and New York Athletic clubs, and by right of his Dutch origin through several lines of descent, has been a member of the Holland Society since 1885

HENRY van DYKE, D. D.

IN the ninth generation of an old Dutch family, the ancestors of whom came to New Amsterdam in 1652, the Reverend Dr. Henry van Dyke is the second of his name who has achieved distinction in the pulpit. He is the eldest son of the late Reverend Dr. Henry Jackson van Dyke, who was a noted Presbyterian clergyman. The elder Dr. van Dyke was born in Abingdon, Montgomery County, Pa., in 1822, being the fourth son of Dr. Frederick A. van Dyke. Graduated from the University of Pennsylvania in 1843, he studied at Princeton Theological Seminary, and in 1845 was ordained to the ministry. He married, in the same year, Henrietta Ashmead, of Philadelphia. His first charge was the Presbyterian Church at Bridgeton, N J, from 1845 to 1852. The following year he preached in Germantown, Pa., and in 1853 went to Brooklyn, where he was pastor of the First Presbyterian Church, remaining in that pulpit for fifteen years.

In 1872, Dr. van Dyke resigned from his Brooklyn pastorate to accept a call to the Presbyterian Church at Nashville, Tenn. Making a trip to Europe before entering upon this new field of labor, upon his return home he changed his plans and returned again to Brooklyn, where he remained until his death, in 1891. During his lifetime, he made several visits to Europe and wrote interesting and valuable sketches of his experiences abroad. He was an effective pulpit orator, and had a wide influence upon the questions of his day. In 1876, he was elected moderator of the Presbyterian General Assembly.

Three names are inseparably connected with the Brick Presbyterian Church of New York, organized in 1767. The united pastorates of the Reverend Dr. John Rodgers and the Reverend Gardiner Spring, the first two occupants of that pulpit, covered more than the first century of its existence. During the last part of its first century, however, a decline set in and the congregation became depleted. It remained for the Reverend Dr. Henry van Dyke, the present pastor, to restore the church to its former high position as one of the most prominent religious societies of New York City.

The Reverend Dr. Henry van Dyke was born in Germantown, Pa., in 1852, and graduated from Princeton College in 1873, and from the Princeton Theological Seminary in 1877. He studied at the University of Berlin for two years, and then returned home to become, in 1878, pastor of the United Congregational Church at Newport, R. I. He remained in Newport for four years, and in 1882 was installed as the fifth pastor of the Brick Presbyterian Church, and occupies that pulpit at the present time. In 1884, he received the degree of D D. from Princeton College and was made a director of the Princeton Theological Seminary. The degree of Doctor of Divinity was also conferred on Dr. van Dyke by Harvard in 1893, and by Yale University in 1896. Princeton gave him the degree of Doctor of Literature in 1897. In 1896, he was appointed to deliver the Ode at the Sesqui-Centennial of Princeton. He was university preacher at Harvard for two years, delivered the Lyman Beecher lectures on preaching at Yale in 1896, and was appointed to the Levering lectureship at Johns Hopkins University for 1898. Dr. van Dyke's literary work is well known in England and America. Among his books are The Reality of Religion, The Story of the Psalms, The Poetry of Tennyson, The Christ Child in Art, The Story of the Other Wise Man, Little Rivers, The Gospel for an Age of Doubt, The Builders and other Poems, and The First Christmas Tree. He is also a frequent contributor to the leading American reviews and magazines, and a number of his works have been reprinted in the mother country.

The wife of the Reverend Dr. van Dyke, whom he married in 1881, was Ellen Reid, a great-great-grandniece of George Washington. He lives in East Thirty-seventh Street. He is a member of the Century Association, the City, Princeton, University and Authors' clubs, the Holland Society, of which he is a trustee, the St. Nicholas Society, of which he is chaplain, and the Sons of the Revolution.

GEORGE WILLETT VAN NEST

PETER PIETERSE VAN NEST, who came to New Netherland in 1647, settling in Brooklyn, was the founder of the American Van Nest family In 1663, he was in the convention of delegates from the Dutch towns of Long Island. His wife was Judith Rapelje, whose father, Joris Janse Rapelje, immigrated in 1623 Joris Rapelje was a grandson of Colet Rapelje, an officer in the army of Henry of Navarre.

The ancestors in the ensuing generations of the gentleman now referred to have been George Van Nest, 1660-1747, of Raritan, N. J , Peter Van Nest, 1700-1795 ; George Van Nest, 1736-1821, and his wife, Catalyna Williamson. Next in line came Rynier Van Nest, 1771-1859, and George Van Nest, 1795-1824, whose wife was Phœbe Van Nest, daughter of Abraham Van Nest, another son of George Van Nest and Catalyna Williamson. Abraham Van Nest, born in 1777, was a prominent citizen of New York during the first half of this century, being president of the Greenwich Savings Bank and an officer of other financial institutions. He was an alderman of the city, and Van Nest Hall, at Rutgers College, was named after him on account of his liberality to the institution He died in 1864, at what was originally his country place, but from 1840 on had been his permanent residence—the old mansion and property of Sir Peter Warren, on Bleecker Street This historic house and its grounds remained substantially as they were in Sir Peter's day until Abraham Van Nest's death. The latter's wife was Margaret Field, of the old New York family of that name.

The Reverend Abraham Rynier Van Nest, father of Mr. G. Willett Van Nest, was the son of George and Phœbe Van Nest and was born in New York in 1823. He graduated at Rutgers College, and received from that college the degree of D. D He was the author of a life of the Reverend Dr. George Bethune. On his mother's side, Mr. Van Nest is connected with the Willett and Bronson families of New York She was the daughter of Dr. Marinus Willett and his wife, Caroline Bronson. Her grandfather was Colonel Marinus Willett, 1740-1830, the Revolutionary patriot He was an officer in De Lancey's Regiment in 1758, was in Bradstreet's successful expedition against Fort Frontenac, and from the beginning of the Revolution to its close was Lieutenant-Colonel and Colonel in the Continental Army. He was one of the earliest Sons of Liberty in New York, and for his rescue of Fort Stanwix in 1777 received a sword from Congress. After the war he was tendered an appointment as Brigadier-General by Washington, but declined it, was in the Assembly, became Sheriff of New York in 1785, serving for several terms, and was Mayor of the city in 1807. In the War of 1812, he planned the defenses of New York.

The great-grandfather of Colonel Willett was Colonel Thomas Willett, 1645-1722, a member of the Governor's Council, Commander of the Queens County Militia and an opponent of Jacob Leisler He lived in great state for those times at Flushing. From his father, Thomas Willett, he acquired the plot granted in 1645, which comprises most of the block bounded by Hanover Square, Pearl and Stone Streets and Coenties Alley. Colonel Thomas Willett's mother was Sarah Cornell, daughter of Thomas Cornell, of Cornell's Neck. The wife of Colonel Marinus Willett was Margaret Bancker, a descendant of Evert Bancker, Mayor of Albany, 1695-6 and 1707-9, and of Johannes de Peyster, Mayor of New York, 1696. Mrs. Abraham R. Van Nest's mother, Caroline Bronson, was a daughter of Dr. Isaac Bronson, 1760-1839, a prominent banker and financier and a descendant of John Bronson, who came to Connecticut in 1636.

Mr. G. Willett Van Nest was born in New York, and is a graduate of Harvard, where he also took the degree of LL B. Since 1882, he has been a practicing lawyer in New York, and has argued several cases of great importance in the highest courts. He was an editor of the Seventh Edition of Sedgwick on the Measure of Damages, and is the author of a number of articles on legal and political subjects which have appeared in the leading periodicals. Mr Van Nest's city residence is at 345 Fifth Avenue He is a member of the Metropolitan, Harvard, and University clubs, the Downtown Association, the Bar Association and the Holland Society.

WARNER VAN NORDEN

IT was in 1623 that the name of which this gentleman is the distinguished representative in the present generation first appears in the records of the early Dutch settlement in the New Netherland. Since that date, however, the family has been identified with New York, both in the city and the State, and is now connected by blood or marriage with many of the more prominent Knickerbocker families, such as the Kips, Vermilyeas, Van Cortlandts, De La Noys, Waldrons, Van Dams and Van Nests. In fact, Mr Warner Van Norden boasts of a descent of the most distinguished kind from the Dutch and Huguenot founders of New York on both the paternal and maternal sides of his family line. Among his maternal ancestors is numbered the famous Reverend Everardus Bogardus, the first Dutch domine or minister of the Reformed Church of Holland, who came to the Colony in 1633, in the same ship which brought over the second Dutch Governor of the New Nethlerland, Wouter Van Twiller. The wife of Domine Bogardus, whom he married in 1638, was the famous Annetje Jans. He is also descended from Adrian Hoghland, who at one time owned the greater part of the property on the upper west side of Manhattan Island, now included in Riverside Park, which was long known in the city's early history as the De Kay farm. At the same time he inherits, through the maternal side of his ancestry, the blood of two distinguished Huguenot refugees, who, as their names indicate, were of noble rank, and who, driven from France previous to the issue of the Edict of Nantes, 1598, and during the persecution directed against their Protestant subjects by Charles IX. and Henry III , in which period occurred the massacre of St. Bartholomew, sought refuge first in Holland, and then later, they or their children, found religious freedom, and opportunity to better their condition in that country's transatlantic possessions. They were Abraham de lay Noy and Jean Mousnier de la Montagnie, the latter of whom, under the administration of Stuyvesant, was vice-director and ruler of Fort Orange—or, as we know it, the City of Albany—and was in many ways prominent in the affairs of the New Netherland in its formative period

Mr Warner Van Norden was born in New York City in 1841, and after completing his education, and while still a mere youth, was sent to New Orleans as the representative of a large New York mercantile house At a very early age, he developed great force of character as well as marked executive ability, and embarking in business for himself became a successful man of affairs in the Crescent City, and president of one of its banks. In 1876, he, however, returned to New York and engaged in business as a private banker, and also took part, successfully, in the management of railroad and other undertakings. In 1891, he became president of the National Bank of North America, of this city. He is a director of the Home Insurance Company and other financial and business institutions, and is a member of the Chamber of Commerce.

Mr. Van Norden is a man of active habits, both in mind and body, and has traveled extensively, both in European countries and in America His residence, at 16 West Forty-eighth Street, contains a fine collection of paintings and statuary and a large library, to the gathering of which he has devoted much attention, and in which he finds relaxation. He is a member of the Metropolitan, Union League and Lawyers' clubs. His Dutch ancestry is shown in his active participation in the Holland Society, of which he is a leading member and its ex-president.

In philanthropy and church work, Mr Van Norden takes an earnest and practical share. He is a director of the Association for Improving the Condition of the Poor, a trustee of the Presbyterian Synod and was for many years president of the Presbyterian Union of New York City, while he has served as a member of the Church Extension Committee and as a member of the Board of Foreign Missions and a director of the American Tract Society.

In 1867, Mr Van Norden married Martha Philips, of this city, and has two sons and two daughters. The older son, the Reverend Theodore L. Van Norden, is pastor of the Presbyterian Church at South Salem, N. Y. The younger, Warner M. Van Norden, is connected with his father in the banking business.

CORTLANDT SCHUYLER VAN RENSSELAER

THREE great New York families are recalled by the names borne by the subject of this sketch, the Van Rensselaers, the Van Cortlandts and the Schuylers, whose beginning in this country was coincident with the founding of New Netherland Kiliaen Van Rensselaer, the paternal ancestor of Mr. Cortlandt Schuyler Van Rensselaer, was one of the wealthiest directors of the Dutch West India Company. He was descended from a long line of honorable ancestors, and married Anna Van Wely. His eldest son by this marriage, Jeremias Van Rensselaer, the founder of the American family to which the present Mr. Van Rensselaer belongs, married Maria Van Cortlandt, daughter of Oloff Stevense Van Cortlandt.

A great-grandson of Jeremias Van Rensselaer and his wife, Maria, was James Van Rensselaer, who married Elsie Schuyler, and was the great-grandfather of Mr Cortlandt Schuyler Van Rensselaer His son, Philip Schuyler Van Rensselaer, who was born in 1797, married Henrietta Ann Schuyler, and his grandson, Gratz Van Rensselaer, who was born in 1834, married Catharine Van Cortlandt Van Rensselaer. He was therefore in the sixth generation of descent from the first patroon of Rensselaerwyck, whose great estates comprised the larger part of what is now the counties of Albany, Rensselaer, Delaware, Greene and Columbia. James Van Rensselaer, the grandfather of Gratz Van Rensselaer, was an officer during the Revolutionary War, with rank of Major, serving without pay, part of the time on the staff of General Montgomery.

On the female side of this house. Mr. Van Rensselaer is descended through several lines of ancestry from the Schuyler family. His grandmother, Henrietta Ann Schuyler, who married Philip Schuyler Van Rensselaer, belonged to that famous race. Her father was John H. Schuyler, and her mother, her father's first wife, was the youngest daughter of Hendrick and Henrietta Ann Fort. Her paternal grandparents were Harmanus Schuyler and Christiana Ten Broeck. Harmanus Schuyler was the son of Nicholas Schuyler and Elsie Wendell, the grandson of Philip Schuyler and Elizabeth De Meyer, and the great-grandson of Philip Piertersen Schuyler and Margeritta Van Slichtenhorst, the remote ancestors of the American Schuyler family.

Harmanus Schuyler was the father of Elsie Schuyler, who became the wife of Major James Van Rensselaer. He belonged to the Schenectady branch of the family, and settled in Albany before the middle of the eighteenth century. He was an assistant alderman there in 1759, and sheriff, 1761-70 In 1776, he was assistant deputy commissary-general of the Northern Department, stationed at Lake George. His wife, Christiana Ten Broeck, was the daughter of Samuel Ten Broeck, and granddaughter of Dirck Wesselse Ten Broeck, who came to America with Governor Peter Minuet. The mother of Christiana Ten Broeck was Maria Van Rensselaer, daughter of Hendrick Van Rensselaer and his wife, Catharine Van Brugh, and a granddaughter of Annetje Jans.

Mr. Cortlandt Schuyler Van Rensselaer, son of Gratz Van Rensselaer, was born in Albany, but was brought up in New York, whither his parents came soon after his birth. He was graduated from Hobart College, and afterwards pursued a course of study in the Law School of Columbia College. Subsequently removing to Eau Claire, Wis., he was admitted to the bar Returning to New York in 1884, he became an assistant United States District Attorney under Elihu Root, retaining that position under William Dorsheimer, Stephen A. Walker and Edward Mitchell He has taken an interest in political matters, has been frequently a delegate to Republican conventions, and was once a candidate for Congress. Since 1891, he has been counsel for the American Surety Company, and is also a large real estate owner. In 1891, Mr. Van Rensselaer married Horace Macaulay, daughter of William Macaulay, of a well-known family distinguished for literary ability. She is also descended on the maternal side from Captain John Underhill. They reside at 40 East Sixty-first Street Mr. Van Rensselaer is a member of the Metropolitan, St. Nicholas, Church, University and Country clubs, the Bar Association, Sons of the Revolution, Huguenot Society, St. Nicholas Society, Society of Colonial Wars, of which he is a governor, and the Colonial Order, of which he is vice-president.

KILIAEN VAN RENSSELAER

THE Colony of Rensselaerwyck was the most successful attempt to plant feudal customs in the New World. In 1630, Kiliaen Van Rensselaer, a rich merchant of Amsterdam, obtained from the Dutch West India Company and their High Mightiness, the States General of the United Provinces, an enormous grant of land in the New Netherland. The tract included nearly all the present counties of Albany and Rensselaer, and in it the patroon ruled as a lord over his subjects Settlers were sent out from Holland, who, in all respects, were bound by a feudal tenure to the lord of the Colony The grant of the manor was confirmed after the English occupation of the New Netherland, and by the Legislature of the State of New York, and its possession continued uninterruptedly in a line of patroons, descendants from the first grantee The original patroon never visited his transatlantic possession, and died, in 1647, in Holland His sons, however, came to this country, and one of them, Jeremias, married Maria Van Courtlandt, and had a son, Kiliaen, who wedded a maternal cousin, also named Maria Van Courtlandt The son of the latter couple, Stephen, succeeded his elder brother, Jeremias, as a lord of the manor Stephen Van Rensselaer, first of the name, died in 1747, and was succeeded as patroon by a son, Stephen, died 1769, whose wife was Catherine Livingston The last of the number was General Stephen Van Rensselaer, third of the name, the "Old Patroon," as he was known, who died in 1830, whereupon the manor was for the first time divided among the heirs, and ceased to exist as an almost independent division of the State.

The father of the present Mr Kiliaen Van Rensselaer was William P Van Rensselaer. His mother was Sarah Rogers, of a well-known New York family, allied with the Bayards and other prominent names in the Colonial and Revolutionary history of the State His paternal grandfather was General Stephen Van Rensselaer, the fifth and last patroon, whose mother was Catherine Livingston, above referred to, a daughter of Philip Livingston, signer of the Declaration of Independence, whose wife was Margaret, daughter of General Philip Schuyler

The patroon at the time of the Revolution, despite his large possessions, was an ardent patriot, and his son, Stephen Van Rensselaer, inherited the same quality, served as Major-General of the United States Army in the War of 1812, and commanded the forces on the Niagara frontier during a part of the war. He was later Lieutenant-Governor of the State and Member of Congress, while the foundation of the Rensselaer Polytechnic Institute, at Troy, is a testimonial of his far-sighted philanthropy, few institutions in the country having been productive of so much real benefit to the people of the United States

Mr Kiliaen Van Rensselaer was born at Albany, in 1845, and was educated in this city. A youth at the outbreak of the war between the States, he, nevertheless, entered the army before the close of the conflict, and, becoming a Captain in the Thirty-Ninth New York Volunteers, served under Generals Grant and Hancock, and took part in some fourteen different engagements. After the close of the war, he traveled abroad extensively, engaged in business in New York, and, in 1870, married Olivia Atterbury, of New York. Mrs Van Rensselaer is a granddaughter of Anson G Phelps, the merchant and philanthropist Her great-great-uncle was Elias Boudinot, the first president of the Congress of the United States The Atterbury family descends from the celebrated Bishop Atterbury, of England The issue of this marriage is five children, Olive Atterbury, Sarah Elizabeth, Katharine Boudinot, Kiliaen, Jr, and William Stephen Van Rensselaer.

Besides membership in the Loyal Legion and the G A R., as well as of the Holland, St Nicholas and Huguenot societies, Mr. Van Rensselaer is an active and prominent figure in many organizations of a religious and philanthropic character He is, among others, a director of the American Tract Society, of the City Missions, president of the Grand Army Mission, and of the Sanitary Aid Society, and an elder of the New York Presbyterian Church, in which he takes great interest, in addition to which he gives much of his time and active labors in the cause of other organizations of the same type

ABRAHAM VAN WYCK VAN VECHTEN

TEUNIS DIRCKSEN VAN VECHTEN was a native of Vechten, near Utrecht, Holland. With his wife, child and servants, he came to Beaverwyck, or Fort Orange, in the ship Arms of Norway, in 1638. In 1648, he was the owner of land near Greenbush, N. Y., which remains in the possession of his descendants. The eldest son of Teunis Dircksen Van Vechten was Dirk Teunisse Van Vechten, who was born at Vechten, in 1634, and died in 1702 at the place in Catskill purchased in 1681 and confirmed to him by Governor Dongan in 1686, part of which is still in the family, together with the old house built in 1690. He married Jannetje Vreelant, daughter of Michiel Jansen and Fytje (Hartman) Vreelant, of Communipaw His son, Teunis Van Vechten, 1668–1707, married Cathlyntje Van Petten, daughter of Claas Frederickse Van Petten, of Schenectady.

In the next generation, Teunis Van Vechten, 1707–1785, married Judiky Ten Broeck, daughter of Jacob Ten Broeck He was an officer in the Colonial militia, and was present at Braddock's defeat. Samuel Van Vechten, the son of Teunis Van Vechten, 1742–1813, was born in Catskill, was an officer in the Revolution, a county judge and a large land owner. His wife was Sarah Van Orden, sister of Jacob Van Orden, of Catskill. One of his sons was the Reverend Dr. Jacob Van Vechten, long pastor at Schenectady.

Samuel Van Vechten, the father of the subject of this sketch, was born in 1796, the son of Samuel Van Vechten. He was graduated from Union College in 1818, and from Rutgers Theological Seminary in 1822. He was the second pastor of the Bloomingburgh Reformed Dutch Church, 1824–41, and was afterwards at Fort Plain; dying at Fishkill, November 3d, 1882. Other distinguished members of the family were Teunis Van Vechten, Mayor of Albany in 1837; Abraham Van Vechten, Attorney-General in 1810; Abraham Van Vechten, City Attorney of Albany in 1843, and Acting Adjutant-General in 1852; and Colonel Cornelius Van Vechten, who in 1757 married Annetje Knickerbocker, of Albany. Anthony Van Vechten was prominent in Revolutionary times and married Margaret Fonda, daughter of Jelles Fonda, who founded the town of Fonda. Michiel Van Vechten, oldest son of Dirck Teunis Van Vechten, removed in 1685 to Raritan, N. J., and established an important family. His Dutch family Bible, dated 1603, inherited from his father and grandfather, is in the collection of the American Bible Society, and is an interesting relic of the eighty years war of the Netherlands for religious freedom. In Brooklyn Claes Arentse Van Vechten built at Gowanus, in 1699, a large house, which has but recently disappeared.

The mother of Mr. Abraham Van Wyck Van Vechten was Louisa, second daughter of General Abraham Van Wyck, of Fishkill. She was the granddaughter of Theodorus Van Wyck, a member of the second and third Provincial Congresses, a great-granddaughter of Theodorus Van Wyck, one of the first settlers of Fishkill, and in the fifth generation of descent from Cornelius Barentse Van Wyck, who came to Flatbush, Long Island, in 1659. The American Van Wycks are descended from Jacob Van Asch Van Wyck, one of the first presidents of the University of Utrecht.

Mr. Abraham Van Wyck Van Vechten was born in Bloomingburgh, New York, March 24th, 1828. He was educated in the Poughkeepsie Collegiate School, and graduated from Williams College in 1847 He then came to New York, studied law with Horace Holden, was admitted to the bar and has been in practice for nearly half a century. In 1853, Mr Van Vechten married Mary Van Zandt Lane, great-granddaughter of Peter Praa Van Zandt, a merchant who came to New Amsterdam in the seventeenth century He had a substantial city house, at the corner of Water Street and Burling Slip, and his country place was near Beekman Hill. Mrs. Van Vechten died in 1864. Mr. Van Vechten has a country home at the family homestead in Catskill. He is a member of the University Club, Bar Association, St. Nicholas Society, Sons of the Revolution, Society of Colonial Wars, Holland Society, Genealogical and Biographical Society, Historical Society, Clinton Hall Association and Society of the War of 1812. He has two daughters, Effe, wife of Charles H Knox, and Marie, wife of Samuel Van Vechten Huntington.

ROBERT ANDERSON VAN WYCK

CORNELIUS BARENTS VAN WYCK, who came from the town of Wyck, in Holland, in 1650, was the ancestor of all the American Van Wycks who boast of a Colonial descent His wife, whom he married at Flatbush, in Kings County, soon after his arrival in the Colony, was Ann Polhemus, daughter of the Reverend Johannes Theodorus Polhemus, the first Dutch Reformed minister in that portion of the Colony, and the ancestor of many families of note in New York

The Van Wyck family was of aristocratic origin in their parent country Its members in Holland use, to the present day, exactly the same coat-of-arms that was brought to this country by the representatives of their name two centuries ago. While not a numerous family—less so, indeed, than the average race of the Holland descent—the American branch of the Van Wycks has furnished to the State and to the country many individual members prominent in the professions and the public service, while intermarriages have connected it by ties of relationship with almost all the old representative family names of New York, such as Van Rensselaer, Van Cortlandt, Beekman, Gardiner, Van Vechten, Livingston and Hamilton, to designate only a few of the many with which it is related

Judge Van Wyck, who was born in New York, in 1849, is a son of William Van Wyck and his wife, Lydia Anderson Maverick His descent on the paternal side is from Samuel Van Wyck, grandson of the original Colonist of the name Samuel Van Wyck married Hannah Hewlett, and had two sons, Captain Abraham Van Wyck and Samuel Van Wyck The latter married Mary Thorn, and was the father of an Abraham Van Wyck and Samuel Van Wyck, born at Huntington, Long Island, in 1767 His uncle, Abraham Van Wyck, was an officer of the Revolutionary Army, married Elizabeth Wright, and had a daughter, Zernah Van Wyck, who married her cousin Abraham, and thus united the two branches of the family The offspring of this marriage was William Van Wyck, born in 1803, at Huntington, Long Island, who, as already mentioned, was the Honorable Robert A. Van Wyck's father

On his mother's side, Judge Van Wyck's ancestors were descended from prominent families of the State of South Carolina His own Christian names were given for his maternal great-grandfather, General Robert Anderson, a distinguished soldier in the war of the Revolution, and a public officer of the State for over thirty years The County of Anderson, in South Carolina, was named in his honor by the Legislature. Elizabeth Anderson, his daughter, born at Pendleton, Anderson County, married Samuel Maverick, born at Charleston, S C, in 1772, their daughter, Lydia Anderson Maverick, born in 1814, at Charleston, becoming the wife of William Van Wyck. Her son is a descendant in the seventh generation from John Maverick, who was among the earliest settlers of Charleston, and whose brother, Samuel Maverick, came to Boston in 1630, members of the family having also been very prominent in the affairs of New York when it passed into the possession of the Duke of York, the Southern branch of the same family having been extremely prominent in several States

In 1872, Judge Van Wyck graduated from Columbia College and was valedictorian of his class He studied law, was admitted to the bar and practiced his profession until 1889. In that year he was elected a Judge of the City Court, and became presiding Judge of the court In November, 1897, he was elected Mayor of the enlarged city at the first election held under the charter creating the Greater New York It is certainly a notable fact that this honor should fall to the direct descendant of one of the New Netherland's founders The Honorable Robert Anderson Van Wyck is unmarried. His clubs are the Manhattan and St Nicholas, and he was one of the founders of the Holland Society. His brother, the Honorable Augustus Van Wyck, of Brooklyn, also has had a distinguished career at the bar, and some years ago was elected a Justice of the Supreme Court of New York in the Second, or Kings County, Judicial District. He is a member of the Holland Society.

JAMES M. VARNUM

FIRST of the Varnum name recorded in the annals of American history, was George Varnum, who was born about 1593 in the hamlet of Draycot, England. He came to this country about 1634 and settled in Ipswich, Mass. With him came his married son, Samuel, born in Draycot in 1619. The elder Varnum died in Ipswich in 1649, and Samuel was one of the founders of the town of Dracut, now part of the city of Lowell, and named it after his old home in England, there two of his sons were killed by the Indians, and there he died about 1673. His fifth son, Joseph Varnum, 1672–1749, was a Colonel in the Massachusetts militia and a member of the Massachusetts Colonial Legislature. Samuel Varnum, the third son of Joseph, was a Major in the Massachusetts militia, and his sons were conspicuous figures of the Revolutionary period, particularly Major-General James M Varnum and Major-General Joseph B. Varnum. The elder brother, James M. Varnum, born in Dracut, December 17th, 1748, was graduated from Brown University in 1769, admitted to the bar in 1771, and settled in Greenwich, R. I. When the war began, he was commissioned as a Colonel of a Rhode Island regiment of infantry, and in 1777 became a Brigadier-General in the Continental Army. He was at Valley Forge and in many engagements in New Jersey and Rhode Island, and retired from the service in 1779. But he was again on duty from 1779 to 1788, as a Major-General of the Rhode Island militia, and was a Member of the Continental Congress from Rhode Island, 1780–82 and 1786–87 He was later appointed a United States Judge for the Northwestern Territory. He was one of the original members of the Society of the Cincinnati, and was only forty years of age when he died.

Joseph B. Varnum, 1750–1821, had a career longer and even more brilliant than that of his brother. During the Revolution he served as a Captain in the Massachusetts militia, was a State Senator, 1785–95, and in 1817–18, and 1820–21, Sheriff of Middlesex County, Justice of the Court of Common Pleas and Chief Justice of the Court of General Sessions of the same county, and a member of the Massachusetts State Convention that ratified the Federal Constitution In 1787, he was Colonel of the Seventh Regiment of Massachusetts militia, in 1802 was promoted to be Brigadier-General, and in 1805 was made a Major-General From 1795 to 1811, he was a representative from Massachusetts to the National Congress and Speaker of the House during the tenth and eleventh Congresses He was United States Senator, 1811–17, and during that time was President *pro tempore* of the Senate and Acting Vice-President of the United States from December 6th, 1813, to April 17th, 1814

The third son of the Honorable Joseph B Varnum, James M. Varnum, 1786–1821, was a Captain in the War of 1812, and married a niece of Postmaster-General Gideon Granger; their son, Joseph B. Varnum, born in 1818, was graduated from Yale in 1838 and studied law in Baltimore. He settled in New York and became a well-known lawyer He was a member of the Assembly of New York State, 1849–51, being Speaker the latter year In 1852, he was a Whig candidate for Congress, and in 1857 was returned to the Assembly again. He wrote much for publication, being a contributor to newspapers and magazines and the author of several works

General James M Varnum is the son of the Honorable Joseph B Varnum, last named. He was born in New York City, June 29th, 1848, and educated in Yale College, taking the degree of B A. in 1868 and the degree of LL B. from Columbia College in 1871 He has since been engaged in the active practice of the law in New York City. He was a member of the Assembly of New York State, 1879–80, Republican candidate for Attorney-General of the State in 1889, permanent chairman of the Republican State Convention in 1891 and candidate of the Republican and anti-Tammany Democrats for Judge of the Superior Court in 1890 Taking an active interest in the affairs of the National Guard, he was senior aide-de-camp to Governor Cornell from 1880 to 1883, with the rank of Colonel, and was subsequently appointed by Governor Morton, in 1895, as Paymaster-General of the State, with the rank of Brigadier-General He is a member of the Tuxedo, Metropolitan, Union and other clubs.

JOHN DAVIS VERMEULE

AMONG the ancestors of Mr. John Davis Vermeule were members of several of the first Dutch families that settled in New York and New Jersey, in the early years of the seventeenth century. The American branch of the Vermeule family sprang from John Cornelissen Vermeule, who was a prominent citizen of Vlissengen, in Zeeland, being a town officer and church elder. His son, Adrian Vermeule, was the American ancestor of the family, coming to this country in 1699. He had no intention of settling here, but came out to visit friends, who were among the residents of the town of Harlem. It happened at that time that the Reformed Church of Harlem had fallen into difficulties, principally through disagreements between its members, and Adrian Vermeule, who was an educated man, was engaged temporarily to fill the position of town clerk and *voorleser*, or lecturer, that had just been vacated by John Tiebout. This opening led him to a decision to remain permanently in the Colony, and for eight years he served the town of Harlem and the Reformed Church acceptably. At the end of that time the people of Bergen, N. J., invited him to that village to become *voorleser* of their church.

After he had settled in Bergen, Adrian Vermeule married Christina Cadmus, descended from Thomas Fredericksen Cadmus and Andries Hopper, who were among the earliest Dutch settlers of New Amsterdam Andries Hopper came to America in 1652, and acquired large real estate possessions, principally upon Manhattan Island. His descendants of one branch of the family moved to New Jersey and became prominent in the early development of that Colony. Descendants of Thomas Fredericksen Cadmus also moved from New Amsterdam to New Jersey in the early part of the eighteenth century, and members of the family married with the Vermeules, Vreelands, Runyons, Van Buskirks and others who were prominent in that Province.

Cornelius Vermeule, who died in 1735, a son of Adrian Vermeule, became a large landowner, his estate covering over twelve hundred acres. He was a man of prominence, and was several times a member of the Provincial Congress of New Jersey. He and his four sons were devoted patriots in the War for Independence, and the latter were valiant soldiers One of these sons, Frederick Vermeule, became distinguished in public life after the war was ended, being for many years presiding Judge of the Court of Common Pleas of Somerset County, N. J. Judge Vermeule lived for a long time in Bergen County, but in 1756 he moved to Plainfield, and there his family remained.

Mr. John Davis Vermeule, grandson of Judge Frederick Vermeule, was born in Plainfield, September 21st, 1822, was instructed in private schools until he was eighteen years of age, and then entered mercantile life. Having fully prepared himself for business, he became a manufacturer, interesting himself in the production of rubber boots, shoes and clothing, as far back as 1844, when that industry was in its inception. For nearly forty years he has been the president, treasurer and manager of the Goodyear India Rubber Glove Manufacturing Company. He is also interested in banking, and has an active connection with important financial institutions, being president of the Holland Trust Company, vice-president of the American Savings and Loan Association, and in the directorate of other fiduciary institutions of New York. Industrial corporations have also enlisted his services, and he is president of the York Cliffs Improvement Company and the York Water Company.

Public life has had no attractions for Mr. Vermeule. At one time, when a resident of Castleton, Staten Island, he served as supervisor of the town, but has never held other public office. He married, in 1846, Mary C. Kelly, daughter of John W. Kelly, a merchant of Philadelphia. He has been one of the active members of the Holland Society from the birth of that organization, and is a supporter of the Metropolitan Museum of Art In his town residence, in West Forty-sixth street, adjoining Fifth Avenue, he has a valuable library and a choice collection of pictures. He also has a country place at York Cliff, Me. His clubs include the Manhattan, Reform, Riding, Commonwealth and Merchants.

WILLIAM EDWARD VER PLANCK

HISTORIC mansions still in the possession of descendants of their original owners are unhappily rare in the neighborhood of New York, where improvement has played such havoc with the monuments of the past The Ver Planck house, in Fishkill-on-Hudson, is one of the exceptions to this rule. The land on which it stands was bought from the Indians, in 1683, by Gulian or Geleyn Ver Planck, and, before 1750, his grandson, another Gulian, built the house which he called Mount Gulian, and in which inheritors of the name have dwelt ever since, its present owner being Mr. William Edward Ver Planck. In Revolutionary times the mansion was the headquarters of Baron Steuben, and in it, in 1783, the officers of the patriot army instituted the Order of the Cincinnati In the present century it was the home of the Honorable Gulian Crommelin Ver Planck, whose reputation was not merely national, but extended to foreign lands. Mount Gulian contains an important collection of family heirlooms and relics of the past, including many interesting and valuable paintings of the members of the Ver Planck family and their numerous connections.

The Ver Planck family is one of the most ancient in New York. Its ancestor was Abraham Isaacse Ver Planck, who came from Holland before 1638, and married Maria Vinge. His son, Gulian, born in 1637, died in 1684, and, as mentioned above, became the owner of the lands in Fishkill, part of which are still held by his descendants. Samuel Ver Planck, who came next in succession, married Arriantje Bayard, and died in 1698. His son, Gulian, 1698-1751, was the builder of the mansion, and married Mary Crommelin, a member of an old Huguenot family in France and the Low Countries.

The Honorable Gulian Crommelin Ver Planck was the grandson of the last named Gulian, and the grandfather of Mr. W E. Ver Planck. He was born in New York in 1786, and his long life, which terminated in 1870, was devoted throughout to the public service and to literary activity, which made him one of the most famous Americans of his time. A member at various times of both branches of the State Legislature and of Congress, he also occupied a seat in the Court of Errors, of New York, and for many years acted as president of the Board of Emigration. His fame as an orator and man of letters was of the highest, his works being voluminous, extending through many fields of literature, and included an edition of Shakespeare, of whom he was the first American commentator. His wife, born Eliza Fenno, belonged to a family of prominence in Boston, and was connected with many other notable names in New England's history. She died in early life.

His son, William Samuel Ver Planck, born in New York in 1812, married Anna Biddle Newlin, and was the father of Mr. William Edward Ver Planck, who was born in Fishkill in 1856, educated at Phillips (Exeter) Academy, and graduated from Columbia College, in the class of 1876. Mr. Ver Planck adopted the bar as his profession and is in active practice in this city. He has inherited the literary tastes of his grandfather, and has published a monograph history of the Ver Planck family. In 1880, he married Virginia Eliza Darby Everett, born in Brownville, N. Y., daughter of the Reverend Henry Darby, and adopted daughter of William E. Everett. Mrs. Ver Planck is the granddaughter of Colonel Edmund Kirby, U. S A., a distinguished officer of the Mexican War, and great-granddaughter of Major-General Jacob Brown, the "fighting Quaker" of the War of 1812, under whom the regular army of the United States at Chippewa, Lundy's Lane, and Fort Erie gained its first laurels. Her uncle, and father by adoption, William E. Everett, U. S. N., was an engineer officer associated with the late Cyrus Field in laying the Atlantic cable. Mr. and Mrs. Ver Planck have three children, William Everett, Virginia Darby and Edward Ver Planck. They have a city residence in West Ninety-Eighth Street Mr Ver Planck has traveled abroad and is a member of the University and New York clubs.

The arms of the Ver Planck family are. Ermine, on a chief engrailed sable; three mullets argent. Crest, a demi-wolf proper. Motto, *Ut vita sic mors.*

WILLIAM H. VIBBERT, S. T. D.

D R VIBBERT'S paternal ancestors were, as the name clearly indicates, French Huguenots, coming of that stock, the loss of which was so full of evil consequence to France itself, while their high mental qualities, energy of character and moral fibre supplied an element in the life of the American people which is constantly making itself felt. The Vibbert family was among those which escaped from France at the revocation of the Edict of Nantes, and found religious and political freedom in the American Colonies of England and Holland New York and South Carolina absorbed the largest number of these desirable emigrants, but New England also claimed its share. The settlement of members of the Vibbert family, at Windsor, Hartford County, Conn., dates from the latter part of the seventeenth century, some of its branches having from an early date become identified with the State and City of New York The subject of this sketch traces his descent through one of these offshoots, his grandfather, Elisha Vibbert, having been an American sea-captain and master of New York ships in the East India trade at the beginning of the present century He married Priscilla Moore, of Salisbury, Conn , but at the early age of twenty-one was lost at sea, within sight of Sandy Hook, while returning from a voyage to China

His son, the father of Dr William H Vibbert, was the Reverend William E. Vibbert, D D , a clergyman and theologian of distinguished reputation in the American branch of the Church of England, who died in December, 1895, at the venerable age of eighty-three. Dr. Vibbert, Sr , was born in New York, and married Mary E Cooke, of the well-known Cooke family, of New Haven, Conn. Her father was John H Cooke, of that city, and her mother, born Maria Mix Judd, of New Britain, Conn , came of a race of prominence in the Colonial and Revolutionary annals of the State. Dr. Vibbert's great-great-grandfather in this line, William Judd, was an officer in the Revolutionary Army, who fought throughout the war, and after the close of the struggle for independence became a conspicuous figure in the politics of Connecticut and of the country, and a leader of the Democratic, or, as it was then called, the Republican party, holding many public offices in the State and in the national service His son, Dr. Vibbert's great-grandfather, William S Judd, was a Major of the United States Army in the War of 1812 with Great Britain, in which struggle he served with distinction.

Born at New Haven, in 1839, Dr. William H. Vibbert was educated at the Connecticut Episcopal Academy, graduated from Trinity College, Hartford, in 1858, and pursued his studies for the ministry at Berkley Divinity School, where he was professor of Hebrew for over ten years. He was ordained to the priesthood in 1863, and received the degree of Doctor of Sacred Theology from Racine College, Wisconsin, in 1883. He traveled abroad several times, held charges in Philadelphia and Chicago, but devoted himself more especially to Oriental studies in connection with theology, his work, published in 1868, on the Hebrew text of the Old Testament, being an authority on a subject of the greatest importance to the clergy, and to students of Oriental philology.

Dr Vibbert's marriage, in 1866, with Julia Newbold Welsh, connected him with a Philadelphia family of the highest social prominence. Mrs Vibbert's father, the late William Welsh, was an eminent merchant and financier in Philadelphia, a distinguished philanthropist, interested especially in the humane treatment of the Indians By his disinterested efforts, a new era was inaugurated in the government's policy towards the aborigines. He also, for a long time, held the position of president of the Board of City Trusts, of Philadelphia. Her uncle, the Honorable John Welsh, was also an eminent citizen of Philadelphia, was United States Minister to the Court of St James, and was regarded as one of the most eminent laymen in the Protestant Episcopal Church Dr Vibbert has three children, William Welsh Vibbert, Mary Howard Vibbert and Aubrey Darrell Vibbert. The family residence is 11 East Twenty-fourth Street Dr. Vibbert is Vicar of Trinity Chapel, the most important chapel of Trinity Parish, and his life is one of scholarship, coupled with an active interest in church affairs, though both he and his family are well known in metropolitan social circles.

EGBERT L. VIELE

A N ancestry that embraces founders of the New Netherland is in General Viele's case supplemented by his own services in both war and peace The first of the name in America was Cornelius Cornelison Viele, who settled at Fort Orange in 1630 His son, Arnaud Cornelius, 1620-1700, was a leading personage in the Colony on account of his influence over the Iroquois Indians, was the envoy of the Duke of York to the tribes, and was appointed their Governor by Leisler Ludovicus Viele was General Viele's ancestor, his grandson, Judge John L Viele, being the father of the subject of this article The Honorable John Ludovicus Viele was born at Valley Falls, N Y, in 1788, graduating from Union College in 1808. He served in the army during the War of 1812, was admitted to the bar in 1814, and became a Judge of the Court of Errors, and was State Senator in 1822. He died in 1832, being then a Regent of the University, and Inspector General

From his mother General Viele inherits the blood of leading Colonial families She was Cathalina Knickerbocker, daughter of Colonel Johannes Knickerbocker, of Schaghticoke, and married to Judge Viele in 1810 Her father commanded a regiment at Saratoga, and her direct ancestor was John Van Berghen Knickerbocker, who came to the New Netherland early in the seventeenth century, and who was a son of Godfrey Van Berghen, Count Van Grimberghen, Captain in the Dutch Navy. General Viele possesses the old Knickerbocker family Bible and other relics of a race which, apart from the unique celebrity due to Washington Irving, has ever filled a worthy part in New York. Born at Waterford, N. Y., June 17th, 1825, Egbert Ludovicus Viele entered West Point and graduated in 1847, and was assigned to the First Infantry as Lieutenant He served throughout the Mexican War under Generals Taylor and Scott, and was distinguished for gallantry, serving also with the First Dragoons. He was then stationed in Texas and in the far West, engaging in Indian campaigns, and became Military Governor of Laredo, Tex, but resigned from the army in 1853 to take up the profession of engineer When the Civil War came, he tendered his services to the Government, became engineer officer of the Seventh Regiment, was commissioned Brigadier General of Volunteers August 17th, 1861, and to the end of the war was in constant service. Among his exploits was the forcing of the Potomac River to Washington, commanding the first troops to reach the capital by that route. He was second in command at the capture of Port Royal, led the victorious attack on Fort Pulaski, and participated in the capture of Norfolk, of which city he was Military Governor for three years

His civil and professional career has been equally notable He is one of the earliest American sanitarians and started the agitation which resulted in the establishment in 1866 of the New York City Board of Health, the first organization in America empowered to enforce sanitary regulations From this movement arose the Boards of Health throughout the country. Another of his titles to public gratitude is his service as Chief Engineer and designer of Central Park and Prospect Park, Brooklyn, while as member and President of the New York City Park Commission he added to his benefits to the metropolis. In 1885 General Viele was elected Member of Congress and labored successfully for the Harlem ship canal As State Engineer of New Jersey, 1854-56, he directed its geodetic survey, and he has been consulting engineer for many railroads, among them the elevated and cable systems of this city.

General Viele wrote a Handbook of Active Service, and a life of General Robert Anderson, and is the author of the well-known Topographical Atlas of New York, besides many articles on military and scientific subjects He is vice-president of the American Geographical Society, and a member of many clubs and literary organizations While visiting England in 1895, he was examined by a committee of the House of Lords as an authority on municipal administration and received flattering social attentions. The General's home in New York overlooks Riverside Park, the establishment of which was largely due to his efforts.

SALEM HOWE WALES

NATHANIEL WALES, the founder of the Wales family in this country, was a Puritan, who came over with Richard Mather, in 1635. He was the ancestor of the subject of this sketch, and his descendants have been among the substantial men of affairs of New England. The father of Mr. Salem H. Wales was Captain Oliver Wales, a woolen manufacturer in Massachusetts and a Captain of the militia in the War of 1812.

Mr. Salem Howe Wales was born in the town of Wales, Massachusetts, October 4th, 1825. After preparatory education in the schools of his native town, he attended an academy in Attica, N. Y. In 1846, when he came of age, he removed to New York and entered the office of a prominent importing house. After two years of business experience, he became associated with Orson D. Munn and Alfred E. Beach, publishers of The Scientific American, being engaged as managing editor, a position that he held uninterruptedly for nearly twenty-four years. In 1855, Governor Horatio Seymour appointed him a commissioner for the State of New York to the Paris Exposition of that year, and he remained abroad several months in the discharge of the duties of that position. Again, in 1867, Mr. Wales went abroad, was absent for over a year, visiting all the principal countries of Europe and contributed an account of his travels and observations to The Scientific American. During the Civil War, he was a patriotic supporter of the National Government and active in all enterprises that were the special need of the hour. He was particularly prominent as a member of the executive committee of the United States Christian Commission.

Always an earnest Republican, in 1872, he was a delegate to the Republican National Convention, at Philadelphia, that nominated General Grant the second time for the Presidency, and in that campaign was a Presidential elector for New York. In 1876, he was again a delegate to the Republican National Convention, at Cincinnati. His interest in public affairs led to his appointment as a member of the Board of Park Commissioners by Mayor William F. Havemeyer, in 1873, and he became president of the board. In 1874, the Republicans nominated him for Mayor of the city Acting Mayor S. B. H. Vance appointed him to a vacancy in the Department of Docks in 1874, and he served for two years as president of the board. From 1880 to 1885, he was again a member of the Board of Park Commissioners, serving part of the time as president.

He was one of the early members of the Union League Club, being for a long time chairman of its executive and finance committee and for several years its vice-president. He had charge of the construction of the present Union League Club building. Interested in many public institutions, he was a founder of the Metropolitan Museum of Art, and for many years treasurer, and is now a member of its executive committee.

Governor John A. Dix appointed him one of the trustees of the Insane Asylum at Middletown, N. Y. He was one of the founders of the Hahnemann Hospital and the New York Homœopathic Medical College, and has been president of both those institutions. He was a director in the Bank of North America and in the Hanover Insurance Company, and has been connected with other corporations. Under appointment by the Supreme Court, he was one of the commissioners to determine the amount of damage caused to private property by the construction of the elevated railroads, and in 1895, was appointed by Mayor Strong one of the commissioners to oversee the construction of the new suspension bridge between New York and Brooklyn, being elected president of the commission.

Mr. Wales lives at 25 East Fifty-fifth Street. He is a member of the Union League, Century, Church, Press, City and other clubs, and the Golf and Meadow Brook Hunt clubs, of Southampton, belongs to the New England Society and is a patron of the American Museum of Natural History and the National Academy of Design. In 1851, he married Frances E. Johnson, only daughter of James D. Johnson, of Bridgeport, Conn. They have two children, Clara, who married Elihu Root, and Edward Howe Wales, a member of the New York Stock Exchange and of the Union League, Players, New York Yacht and Larchmont Yacht clubs.

JOHN BRISBEN WALKER

BORN in Pennsylvania in 1847, John Brisben Walker is a grandson of General S G Krepps, who was a prominent figure in Pennsylvania political life about 1820, and of Major John Walker, one of the first commissioners appointed for the improvement of western rivers. Major Walker, who was a great-grandson of Carl Christopher Springer, prominent in the founding of the Swedish Colony on the Delaware, was among the first to establish shipyards west of the Alleghany Mountains. General Krepps was chairman of the committee in the Pennsylvania Senate, which, in 1827, reported the resolution asking the abolition of slavery in the District of Columbia

At the age of ten, Mr. John Brisben Walker was sent to a classical school in Washington, D C. Later he entered Georgetown College, and in 1865 was appointed to West Point. In 1868, when Minister Burlingame arrived from China, Mr Walker was aided by him in his desire to enter the Chinese military service and, resigning from the Military Academy, he accompanied the Honorable J Ross Brown, United States Minister to Peking. In 1870, he returned to the United States, engaging in manufacturing and other enterprises connected with the development of the Kanawha Valley, in West Virginia. Two years later, he was nominated for Congress by the Republicans in a strong Democratic district, and was defeated. In 1873, he represented West Virginia in the Immigration Convention held at Indianapolis, and in 1874, as a State delegate, was chairman of the committee on resolutions of the first Ohio River Improvement Convention. In the panic of 1873 his entire fortune was swept away. He was then engaged by Murat Halstead to prepare a series of articles upon the mineral and manufacturing interests of the United States for The Cincinnati Commercial, a few months later was offered the managing editorship of The Pittsburgh Daily Telegraph, and at the beginning of 1876 became managing editor of The Washington Chronicle, then one of the two leading dailies at the National Capital. In 1879, at the request of the Commissioner of Agriculture, he visited the arid lands of the West with reference to their redemption by irrigation. Later he purchased, on the outskirts of Denver, a portion of what became known as Berkeley Farm, the most extensive alfalfa farm in Colorado.

For nine years thereafter, Mr. Walker was engaged in the development of alfalfa interests, in which he was a pioneer. At the same time, by a series of careful engineering operations, he was recovering a large plot of river bottom from overflow, thus adding more than five hundred lots to the area of the most valuable part of Denver. In 1889, he removed to New York and purchased The Cosmopolitan Magazine, which he still edits. Mr Walker is an author as well as a publisher and editor, having written much upon social and industrial topics. He is one of the original thinkers of the day, a man of radical ideas on social and economic questions and in earnest sympathy with every project that looks to the improvement of the status of the masses

In 1870, Mr Walker married Emily Strother, daughter of General David Hunter Strother. The father of Mrs Walker was born in Berkeley Springs, Virginia, in 1816, and died in 1878 He studied drawing in Philadelphia and New York, traveled throughout the West and in Europe, and then, returning to New York, made himself famous in the decade preceding the Civil War, by the inimitable Porte Crayon sketches in Harper's Magazine, illustrated by himself. During the Civil War, he served in the Union Army successively on the staffs of General McClellan, General Banks, General Pope and afterwards as Chief of Staff to his cousin, General David Hunter, while in command of the Army of the Valley of Virginia. From 1879 to 1885, he was United States Consul General to the City of Mexico. As poet, painter, a charming descriptive writer, and soldier he was much admired by his generation.

Mr and Mrs Walker reside in Irvington-on-Hudson. They have a family of seven sons John Brisben, Jr, David Strother, James Randolph, Justin, Harold, Wilfred and Gerald, and one daughter Mr Walker belongs to the Century Association, the University Club of Chicago and the Ardsley Country Club.

JOHN QUINCY ADAMS WARD

J OHN WARD, of Norfolk, England, came to America in the ship Elizabeth in 1621, landing at Jamestown, Va. He was living in "Elizabeth Cittie" in 1623. His son, Charles Ward, settled in Boutetort County, and was the progenitor of James Ward, born in 1724, who lived in Greenbriar County Ensign James Ward was with the Virginia forces sent in 1754 to resist French encroachments on the frontier He began the fort at the forks of the Ohio, but was compelled to retire by the French under Contrecoeur, who completed the works, calling them Fort Duquesne. As a Colonel he was killed in 1774, at the battle of Point Pleasant, by the Indians under the lead of Puckeshinwa, father of Tecumseh Colonel William Ward, 1752-1820, the son of James Ward, was born in Greenbriar County, and saw much service against the Indians. In 1789, he moved to Mason County, Ky., but in 1798 settled in the valley of the Mad River, being one of the earliest settlers of Ohio He owned large tracts in what are now Champaign and Clark Counties, and in 1805 laid out and named the town of Urbana, O

John A Ward, 1783-1854, his son, was born in Greenbriar County, Va , and died at Urbana. He married Eleanor, daughter of Alexander and Rachel (Whitehill) Macbeth The latter's father, Robert Whitehill, 1735-1813, was a member of the Pennsylvania Council of Safety, was elected to the first Congress that sat in Philadelphia, and was a Member of Congress when he died Eleanor (Macbeth) Ward possessed marked ability and artistic tastes which foreshadowed her son's talent.

Mr John Quincy Adams Ward is the son of John A and Eleanor Ward, and was born in Urbana, O , June 29th, 1830 He displayed a talent for modeling when a lad, and when nineteen years of age, while visiting his sister, Mrs J W Thomas, in Brooklyn, began the study of sculpture in the studio of Henry K Brown, where he remained until 1857, assisting in many of his instructor's works, including the Washington statue in Union Square He then spent two winters in Washington and modeled busts of Alexander H Stephens, Joshua R. Giddings, and other statesmen He also made the sketch for the Indian Hunter, the first statue erected in Central Park To complete this he visited the Northwest and made original studies of Indians. In 1861, Mr Ward opened his studio in New York and has since practiced his profession here He became an associate of the National Academy of Design, in 1863, vice-president in 1870 and president in 1874

At present, Mr Ward is regarded as one of the foremost American sculptors His Americanism has always been one of his characteristics He has visited Europe several times, but has never been tempted to attain foreign artistic development and bias His work records features of American character and he has set an example that an American can attain national reputation without leaving his own country His first serious study was the statuette of The Freedman A partial list of his important works approximately in order of production would include the Good Samaritan, at Boston, Indian Hunter, Citizen Soldier (Seventh Regiment Memorial), The Pilgrim, and Shakespeare, in Central Park; Commodore Perry's statue at Newport, Lafayette, at Burlington, Vt ; General Daniel Morgan, at Spartanburg, S. C ; Washington, before the Sub-Treasury in New York, the equestrian statue of General G. H Thomas, in Washington, the Garfield monument, in the same city, the Beecher monument, in Brooklyn, William E. Dodge, in Herald Square; Horace Greeley, in Printing House Square, Roscoe Conkling, in Madison Square; and the Holly monument, Washington Square; besides many monumental and portrait busts of distinguished men Mr Ward has been twice married His first wife, Anna Bamman, died in 1870, and in 1877 he married Julia Devens Valentine, who died in 1879 Mr Ward's first residence and studio was on West Forty-ninth Street, but he now occupies a more commodious studio in West Fifty-second Street, which he built in 1880 He is vice-president of the Fine Arts Federation, president of the National Sculpture Society, a trustee of the Metropolitan Museum of Art and of the American Academy in Rome, an honorary member of the National Institute of Architects, a member of the Architectural League, vice-president of the Century Association, and a member of the Union League Club and the Ohio Society.

REGINALD HENSHAW WARD

AMONG the Normans who accompanied William the Conqueror to the conquest of England in 1066 was Ward, one of the noble Captains. Subsequently the name appears as William de la Ward, residing in Chester in 1175. The arms anciently belonging to the family were: Azure, a cross baton, or.; crest, wolf's head erased; and these were retained by the Durham branch of the family, to which belonged William Ward, who came to America.

William Ward was a resident in Sudbury, Mass., in 1639, a representative to the General Court in 1644, and one of the founders of the adjoining town of Marlborough in 1660 He had a family of fourteen children, and his grandson, Nahum Ward, 1684-1755, was a sea captain and shipmaster, one of the first settlers and proprietors of Shrewsbury, a magistrate, a justice of the Court of Common Pleas, representative to the General Court for seven years, a Colonel of the militia, and altogether a substantial man, and the most prominent member of his father's family.

In the following generation, a son of Colonel Nahum Ward distinguished himself as one of the most notable public men of the Revolutionary period. Artemas Ward, who was born in Shrewsbury, Mass., in 1727, was a justice of the peace when he was twenty-five years of age, a Major of the militia in 1755, a Major in the expedition under General Abercrombie against Canada, returning as Lieutenant-Colonel, and a representative to the General Court In 1774, the Provincial Congress elected him a Brigadier-General, and in May of the following year he became Commander-in-Chief of the Massachusetts forces. When Washington was elected to command the Continental Army, in 1775, Artemas Ward was chosen first Major-General. He was sixteen years a representative in the Massachusetts Legislature, serving as Speaker in 1785, a Member of Congress 1791-95, president of the Massachusetts Executive Council, and Chief Justice of the Court of Common Pleas in his native county One of the sons of General Ward, Captain Nahum Ward, was a Revolutionary soldier, and another, the Honorable Artemas Ward, was a graduate from Harvard, a Member of Congress and Chief Justice of the Court of Common Pleas for the State of Massachusetts. Another son, Thomas W. Ward, 1758-1835, was seventeen years a magistrate and a sheriff eighteen years.

Mr. Reginald Henshaw Ward is a great-grandson of Thomas W. Ward. Through his grandmother, he is also of ancient lineage She was Sarah Henshaw, a direct descendant of Joshua Henshaw, who came from Liverpool, England, in 1653, and settled in Massachusetts. Mr. Ward's grandfather, Andrew Henshaw Ward, was a graduate from Harvard in 1808, a lawyer, a custom house officer in Boston, United States Commissioner of Insolvency, justice of the peace, antiquary and author. He was born in 1784, and married Sarah Henshaw, of the Henshaw family, which was ably represented in the Parliamentary Army and otherwise prominent in public life in England. He died in 1864. Andrew Henshaw Ward, the father of Mr. R. H. Ward, was born in 1824 and was for many years in the wholesale drug business in Boston, in the firms of Henshaw, Ward & Co., and Ward & Boot. His wife was Anna Harriet Walcott Field, of Providence, R. I., and this marriage allied him to the Field and Walcott families, both of English origin and among the earliest settlers of the United States. The Field family was one of the largest owners of real estate in and about Providence, R. I., and the Walcott family which settled in Connecticut has given to the country some of its most brilliant public men.

Mr. Reginald Henshaw Ward was born in Newtonville, Mass., April 22d, 1862. After a thorough public school education, he entered upon a business career as a clerk in a banking house in Boston, and in 1885, with J. F. A Clark, established the banking and brokerage house of Clark, Ward & Co., of Boston and New York. In 1889, he married Edith Ward Newcomb, daughter of H Victor Newcomb, and also a descendant of the Ward family. Mr. Ward is a member of the Metropolitan, Union, Country, Turf and Field and Suburban clubs, and belongs to the Sons of the Revolution, the New England Society, the Society of Mayflower Descendants, and the Military Order of Foreign Wars.

LUCIEN CALVIN WARNER, M. D.

WARNER MOUNTAIN, which rises from the Housatonic Valley, in Berkshire County, Mass, takes the name of a family descended from the earlier settlers of the old Plymouth Colony, which furnished some of the most prominent pioneers of the hill country of Western Massachusetts. Dr. Lucien Calvin Warner belongs to this Colonial family, being a descendant of Abel Warner, who was born about 1755 and resided in Hardwich, Worcester County, Mass. The wife of Abel Warner was Sarah Cook, a direct descendant of Francis Cook, who was one of the famous company which came over in the Mayflower, and was a relative of Captain John Cook, the celebrated navigator. Among the children of Abel Warner were Justus Warner, the father of Charles Dudley Warner, and Ira Warner, the grandfather of the subject of this sketch. Ira Warner married Asenath Hitchcock, of Hadley, and moved to Windsor, Berkshire County, where his son, Alonzo F Warner, was born.

The first half of the present century witnessed a further movement of the energetic population of Western New England. Dr. Warner's father, Alonzo F Warner, was among the number who joined the exodus and became a citizen of Cortland County, N Y He married Lydia Anne Converse, who also came of New England parentage. Their son, Dr. Lucien Calvin Warner, was born at Cuyler, N. Y., in 1841.

Dr Warner entered Oberlin College, but left his studies during the progress of the Civil War to enter the army, serving in the One Hundred and Fiftieth Ohio Volunteers, and after completing the term of his enlistment, returned to college and was graduated in 1865 He then was graduated from the medical department of the New York University in 1867, and spent six years in the practice of medicine. In 1873, he gave up the practice of his profession, came to New York and engaged in business. He is now connected with a large number of financial and business institutions as president, director, or partner, and has large mill interests

Dr Warner is widely known for the interest he takes in public affairs, and especially in benevolent and philanthropic work. Besides being active in church affairs, he was for ten years president of the Harlem branch of the Young Men's Christian Association, chairman of the State Committee of that organization, and has been for several years chairman of the International Committee, a trustee of Oberlin College, a trustee of the local, State and International Young Women's Christian Association, a member of the executive committee of the American Missionary Association, and president of the Congregational Church Building Society. Dr Warner's gifts to educational and charitable institutions have been generous He gave a building costing over one hundred thousand dollars to Oberlin College for a conservatory of music, was largely instrumental in the erection of a one hundred and fifty thousand dollar building for the Harlem branch of the Young Men's Christian Association, and in connection with his brother built a club house at Bridgeport, Conn, for the use of the girls in their employ

Dr. Warner married, in 1868, Keren S Osborne, daughter of Judge Noah Humphrey Osborne, and a descendant of Michael Humphrey, who came from England and settled in Windsor, Conn, in 1643. Their children are Agnes Eliza, Franklin Humphrey, Lucien Thompson and Elizabeth Converse Warner Their eldest daughter, who is a graduate of Oberlin, married, in 1896, Seabury C. Mastick, a member of the New York bar. Dr. Warner's remaining three children, it should be mentioned, have also entered Oberlin College, the two sons being members of the senior class, and the daughter a member of the sophomore class. Dr. Warner is a member of the Merchants' Club, Harlem Club, Congregational Club, of which he was for some years the president, Ardsley Casino and the Chamber of Commerce. His residence is at Irvington-on-Hudson, and is regarded as one of the finest country mansions overlooking the historic Hudson It is built of granite and Carlisle sandstone in early English style His art treasures have been collected in the course of extensive tours in Europe, and comprise a valuable example of Andrea del Sarto, together with pictures by Zeim, Rico, Schenck, Detti, Henry, Rehn, Guy and other modern masters.

GEORGE HENRY WARREN

THE father of the subject of this sketch was George Henry Warren, Sr., a noted lawyer of New York. He was born in Troy, N. Y., in 1823, graduated from Union College in 1843, and was engaged in the practice of law and in financial operations in New York throughout his life. On the maternal side, George H. Warren, Sr., was descended from John Bouton, a Huguenot who came to Boston in 1635. He joined in the migration to Hartford in 1636 and, assisting in the settlement of Norwalk in 1661, was a selectman of that place in the year 1671, and died in 1703 or 1704.

John Bouton's wife was Abigail Marvin, daughter of Matthew Marvin, who came to New England in 1635 from London with his wife, Elizabeth, and was one of the original proprietors of Hartford in 1638 and a representative from Norwalk in 1654. Sergeant John Bouton, 1659–1749, son of John Bouton, married Sarah Gregory, daughter of John Gregory, of Norwalk, and granddaughter of John Gregory, of New Haven. His daughter, Elizabeth Bouton, married Edmund Warren, the great-great-grandfather of George H Warren, Sr. Edmund Warren was a resident of Oyster Bay, Long Island, and of Norwalk, Conn., and died in 1749. He was the son of Richard Warren, or Warring, who was one of the original proprietors of Brookhaven, Long Island, settled in 1655. In the records of Brookhaven appears the signature of Richard Warring in his own handwriting, and the name is written "Waring." Eliakim Warren, son of Edmund Warren, was born at Norwalk, Conn., in 1717, married Anna Reed in 1738, and their son, Eliakim Warren, who was born in Norwalk in 1747, removed in 1798 to Troy, N. Y., where he was senior warden of St. Paul's Church from 1804 until his death, in 1824. His wife was Phœbe Bouton, 1754–1835, who came of the same family as the wife of his grandfather.

Nathan Warren, the father of George H. Warren, Sr., was born in 1777 in Norwalk, and died in 1834 in Troy. He was a prominent business man of Troy and a vestryman of St. Paul's Church. His wife, Mary Bouton, was born in Norwalk in 1789, and died in Troy in 1859. She was the daughter of Nathan Bouton, 1756–1838, and his wife, Abigail Burlock, 1736–1827. She was the great-granddaughter of Jachin Bouton, the brother of Elizabeth Bouton, who was the granddaughter of John Bouton, the pioneer, and the wife of Edmund Warren, of Oyster Bay, Sergeant John Bouton being the great-great-grandfather of both Nathan Warren and his wife. Mrs. Warren was devoted to charity and religious work. In 1844, she built and endowed the Church of the Holy Cross in Troy, supported the Mary Warren Free Institute, and contributed generously to other educational and religious undertakings.

The mother of Mr. George Henry Warren was Mary Caroline Phœnix, a daughter of the Honorable Jonas Phillips Phœnix. She was born in 1832 in New York, was married in 1851 and descends from families that have been distinguished in the history of New York and Connecticut. She is a sister of Lloyd Phœnix, Phillips Phœnix, and also of Stephen Whitney Phœnix, the antiquarian and genealogist, who died in 1881. A full account of her ancestry on both her father's and her mother's side is given in the article relating to Phillips Phœnix.

Mr. George Henry Warren was born in Troy, N. Y., October 17th, 1856, and is a stock broker, having been also educated as a lawyer, and is a graduate from the Columbia College Law School. He is a member of the Bar Association. He married in 1885 Georgia Williams, of Stonington, Conn. Mr. and Mrs. Warren live in East Sixty-fourth Street and at Seafield, Newport, R. I. Mr. Warren is a member of the New York Stock Exchange and the Metropolitan and Union clubs. His children are George Henry Warren, Jr., and Constance Whitney Warren. The mother of Mr. Warren, Mrs. George Henry Warren, Sr., lives at 520 Fifth Avenue, and also has a residence at Newport, R. I. Younger sons of the family are Whitney Warren and Lloyd Warren, members of the Union, Racquet and Calumet clubs. The sisters of Mr. George Henry Warren are Mrs. R. Percy Alden, Mrs. Robert Goelet, Mrs. William Starr Miller and Emeline W. D. Warren, who is unmarried.

JAMES MONTAUDEVERT WATERBURY

ONE of the most prominent figures in society, club life and sport, Mr. James M. Waterbury is a Puritan by race, the family of which he is the head descending from a founder of Connecticut John Waterbury, his ancestor, was born in England, in 1615, came to America in the early years of the struggling Colonies, and settled, in 1646, at Stamford, Conn., which then formed part of the debatable ground between the Dutch, of Manhattan, and the English, of New Haven. From this pioneer, who died in 1658, sprang a family of eminence during Connecticut's Colonial era, and which furnished a member of Washington's staff, in the person of General Waterbury, while in later times its members have gained distinction in many and varied spheres of activity.

The present Mr. Waterbury's father, Lawrence Waterbury, a descendant of the Revolutionary hero, was not only one of the most successful and influential of New York's merchants in the period prior to and immediately succeeding the Civil War, but is remembered as originator of an institution in which all Americans take a legitimate pride With his brother, James M. Waterbury, he founded the New York Yacht Club, in 1844, and was one of the nine yacht owners who incorporated the club, and constituted the nucleus of that famous body, probably the foremost of its kind in the world.

His interest in yachting ceased only with his death, and he also took an extremely active part in establishing and promoting those yachting events which are classical to the present generation of sportsmen The late Lawrence Waterbury married Caroline A. Cleveland, daughter of Palmer Cleveland, one of the most eminent lawyers of Connecticut, who, in his lifetime, held various positions of note in that State. His wife, Mr. Waterbury's grandmother, was Catherine Livingston, one of the prominent New York family of that name, whose history is interwoven with that of the State in the Colonial and Revolutionary period.

Born at New York, in 1851, Mr James M Waterbury was an only son His three sisters are now Mrs. John S Ellis, Mrs. Frank C Winthrop and Mrs. Pierrepont Edwards He graduated at Columbia College, in the class of 1873, and immediately entered business under his father's guidance, becoming, in a short time, a member of the latter's firm, and ultimately its head Inheriting commercial talent of a high order, as well as wealth, Mr. Waterbury has been instrumental in carrying out many great enterprises, and has been intimately associated with the leading financiers and men of affairs of the country

In 1874, Mr. James M. Waterbury married Kate Anthony Furman, their children being eight in number. It may also be noted that the younger generation of the family inherit their father's tastes for sport, his sons being distinguished in the polo field. Mr Waterbury's home, Pleasance, at Westchester, N Y., is renowned for its hospitality, and, in making their permanent home in that district, Mr and Mrs. Waterbury have done much to attract other residents of social position to Westchester. The Country Club, at Westchester, one of the most popular institutions of fashionable New York in the present generation, of which Mr. Waterbury became president, owes its success and vogue, in a large degree, to his efforts on its behalf to promote its interests and influence

Mr Waterbury has long been prominent in the club life of the metropolis, and is a member of the Union, Knickerbocker, Metropolitan, Riding, Racquet and Tuxedo clubs, and the Downtown Association He has held the position of director or officer in a number of the most prominent organizations of this kind, and has served in an official capacity in various semi-public and benevolent bodies In the realm of outdoor sports, his inherited devotion to yachting is shown by active membership in the New York and Seawanhaka–Corinthian Yacht clubs, while among the many other organizations of a similar character, of which he is a conspicuous supporter, are the Coney Island Jockey Club, the American Hackney Association, the Rockaway and Meadow Brook Hunts and the Newport Golf Club.

GEORGE GOODHUE HEPBURN WATSON

NEW YORK in no other way manifests its position as the cosmopolis, or world city of the Western hemisphere, better than by the manner in which it attracts within the sphere of its social and commercial life representatives of leading families from all portions of the continent. The great Canadian Dominion comes under this influence as readily as any American State, and furnishes an important and valuable constituent element in the great city's upper classes. It is particularly strong in the banking profession, the financial interests of Montreal and other seats of the wealth, culture and refinement of the Dominion, being closely interwoven with those of New York. Mr. Watson exemplifies these circumstances, having been born at Montreal, Province of Quebec, in 1857, and represents families of the highest social and political standing in Canadian annals.

His father, Walter Watson, is of Scotch birth, and has been long a prominent and respected banker in this city, representing in the financial centre of the West some of the largest British and Canadian banking interests. His wife, the mother of Mr. George G. H. Watson, came of a family of the highest personal and political importance in Canada. She was the daughter of the late Honorable George Jervis Goodhue, 1800–1873, long a member of the Canadian Parliament and a prominent figure in the politics of the separate Provinces prior to their federation, and later in those of the Dominion after the passage of the British North America Act in 1867 by the Imperial Parliament.

His marriage illustrated the tendency toward alliances between members of the Canadian aristocracy of wealth and talent and the families of the military and civilian representatives of the English rule stationed in Canada. Mrs. Goodhue, the grandmother of Mr. Watson, was Louisa Mathews, a daughter of Major Mathews, aide-de-camp to the Duke of Richmond and an officer of distinction in the British service, who came to Canada with the forces which, until within recent years, were maintained in garrisons throughout the Provinces. The Goodhue family is one of antiquity in American history, having branches in both the United States and Canada, and furnishes many names of distinction. The genealogy of the family was compiled by E R Andrews, and published in book form at Rochester, N. Y, in 1891. The family has been conspicuous in American annals on both sides of the international boundary, many of its members having occupied high stations in professional and business life, and has not been without some notable representatives in the metropolis.

Mr George G. H. Watson is a graduate of Hellmuth College, London, Province of Ontario, and, after the completion of his education, engaged in the banking profession in this city, having been connected with the New York Stock Exchange for some years. He has traveled abroad extensively, and took much interest in military matters, having held commissions as First and Second Lieutenant in the Twenty-Second Regiment, National Guard, State of New York, giving efficient service to his command. In 1883, Mr. Watson married Annie Townsend Barber, born 1857, at Davenport, Ia., a lady whose descent is given in full in the genealogy of the Barber family, published in 1890, and in that of the Atlee family, published in 1884 Mr. and Mrs. Watson have two children, Walter Malcolm and George Atlee Watson.

Though taking considerable part in metropolitan society, a patron of the opera, and possessed of a keen enjoyment for sport, Mr. Watson prefers a permanent rural residence, and lives in Elizabeth, N. J., where he has a handsome home adorned by a well-chosen collection of paintings and engravings, mainly antiques. Among his art treasures, an original painting of Washington, by Rembrandt Peale, holds the place of honor. He is also an eager collector of postal cards, and ranks as the leading expert on that subject in the United States, if not in the world, having published a catalogue of the leading postal cards of all countries. At present he conducts and issues a monthly, The Postal Card, for collectors, which has a wide circulation among those interested in such pursuits both here and abroad.

EDWIN HENRY WEATHERBEE

ON both the paternal and maternal side, the subject of this article descends from New England ancestry. The family line which he represents is an ancient English one, being traced back to the Norwegian and Danish conquest of the Northern counties of the present kingdom. This is shown by the name itself, which is a territorial one, indicating the establishment of the family, and the calling after it of Wetherby, a well-known and picturesque market town in the county of Yorkshire, situated between the cities of York and Leeds, and possessing an interesting history and many local antiquities of a notable character. It was called by the Saxons Wedderbi, the final syllable being the Danish equivalent of the English town or the Norman-French *ville*, and would thus denote that it was originally the seat of a race of large landed possessions and decided importance. References to the Weatherbee family are, indeed, not lacking in the earlier records of the landed aristocracy of England, and its branches, it would seem, extended throughout the Northern and Eastern counties. As far back as 1461, mention is made in an ancient record of the daughters and coheiresses of Thomas Wetherby, a landed proprietor of Intwood, Norfolk, and similar references to the family occur in wills and deeds in subsequent generations

It was from Norfolk and the Eastern counties that the principal stream of the Puritan immigration to America flowed, and in its roll of fame is found the name of John Witherby, who, in 1630-32, came to Sudbury and Marlboro, Mass., and became the ancestor of the American branch of the family. The spelling of the patronymic has, however, assumed in the course of time various forms and its bearers, while tracing their descent to the same original source, are to-day found in all parts of the United States under such slight transformations as Weatherbee, Witherby, Wetherby, Witherbye, Witherbee and Witherbe. In whatever form it has assumed, its possessors have ever borne a distinguished part in the creation and upbuilding of America, descendants of the family having figured, in the country's earliest days, as members of the Colonial councils and legislative bodies of Massachusetts, Vermont and other New England States, or earned distinction in the clerical and learned professions, while the name had other representatives who fought gallantly in the early wars on this continent; and in the later history of our country they have in many instances been prominent in every walk of life.

Mr. Weatherbee's father, Henry Micajah Weatherbee, was a worthy representative of the sterling, energetic New England blood which he inherited. As a lawyer, he won reputation, and was also prominent in business life and politics, in which he attained distinction and held many important offices, while he took a successful and useful part in the creation of a number of the earlier railroad enterprises in the West. His wife, the mother of the present Mr. Weatherbee, was Mary Angell, a member of one of the most ancient families of Providence, R. I., in which city their standing is locally commemorated in many ways. Her father, John Angell, of Chatham, N. Y., was a direct descendant of Dr. Thomas Angell, who accompanied Roger Williams from England on the ship Lion, and took part with him in the establishment of Rhode Island. Representatives of the family from that time forward were distinguished in the history of the Colony, and that of New England in general, during the Colonial and Revolutionary epoch, the great-grandfather of the subject of this article having been Colonel Joshua Angell, who commanded a regiment of the Continental troops under General Sullivan on Long Island. John Angell, Mr. Weatherbee's maternal grandfather, was one of a large family, the other members of which were noted in professional life or as eminent merchants. He, however, became a large landowner in the neighborhood of Chatham, N. Y., as he preferred a quiet country life. The Methodist Episcopal Church at Chatham, one of the handsomest in the country, was mainly erected by the Angell family, its beautiful chancel and windows having been contributed by Mr. and Mrs. Weatherbee as memorials. Through the intermarriage of his ancestors, Mr. Weatherbee is also related to many old and prominent New England families, among whom may be mentioned the names of Drake,

Gillett, Manton, Marsh, Olney, Butler, Sprague, Tuttle, Whipple and Williams Born at Chatham, N Y, Mr. Weatherbee received his earlier education at the Hudson River Institute, Clavarack, N. Y.; Amenia Seminary, and the Hopkins Grammar School, New Haven, class of 1871, being an honor man at the latter place. He entered Yale College, graduating in the class of 1875. After pursuing post-graduate studies for a time, he entered, in 1877, upon the study of law at Boston, in the University School of Law, and afterwards in the law department of Columbia College, in this city, graduating from the latter in 1879. He was for some years associated in the practice of his profession with General Stewart L. Woodford, then United States District Attorney, but abandoned the law to engage in the business career which now engrosses his energies.

In 1881, Mr. Weatherbee married Amy Henrietta Constable, daughter of James M. Constable, of New York. Mrs Weatherbee's maternal grandfather, Aaron Arnold, came from the Isle of Wight, England, where his family had lived on one property for over two hundred years—Waytes Court, Brixton, at which place many generations of his ancestors were interred. He established the famous New York business house of Arnold & Constable, which was started early in this century in Canal Street. Her father, James M. Constable, a native of Storington, Surrey, England, married Henrietta, daughter of Aaron Arnold. Mrs. Weatherbee, with her father, her brother, Frederick A Constable, and her sister, Mrs. Hicks Arnold, built, in 1887, the beautiful Episcopal Church at Mamaroneck, N. Y., as a memorial to her late mother. Mr. and Mrs. Weatherbee have three children, Henrietta Constable Weatherbee, Hicks Arnold Weatherbee and Mary Angell Weatherbee.

The Weatherbee arms are Vert, a chevron ermine between rams, or. Those of the Angell family were granted to Roger Angell, a Captain under Henry VII, in 1485, who distinguished himself at Bosworth Field. They are described as : Or. three fusils azure. Crest, a demi-Pegasus argent, crined gules. Motto, Fortitude and Courage.

While residing at 240 Madison Avenue, in the Murray Hill district of New York, the Weatherbees own a country place, Waytes Court, at Orienta Point, Mamaroneck, N. Y., comprising some thirty acres, which was originally the property of the DeLancey family and was part of a grant to them made by Queen Anne. The estate has a decided historic interest, having been the residence of Bishop DeLancey, while Fenimore Cooper made it the scene of some of his most celebrated novels. The house, which was built by its present occupants, is of stone in old English style, while the interior is remarkable for the rich woodwork, nearly every room being finished, in appropriate style, with material from some foreign land. One room is thus entirely decorated with woods from Japan, others represent the productions of natural wood and carvings from Spain, Holland and India, while in other cases they are the reproductions of Old English work, following in their details photographic reproductions of leading manorial residences and castles of England and Spain, which were made especially for the purpose. The furniture and decorations bear the same marks of selection and are the fruit of many years' experience in travel, Mr. and Mrs. Weatherbee having visited all parts of the world, while almost every year they make a European trip. Mr. Weatherbee has a decided inclination for sport of all kinds, as well as for athletics. He is devoted to yachting, to riding and driving, and has been a successful exhibitor of horses at various horse shows At the same time, his taste for literature is a discriminating one, and he is an art amateur and a collector of antiques. Mr. Weatherbee is a member of the Chamber of Commerce, and, among other clubs, belongs to the Metropolitan, Union League, University, Reform, City, Riding, Michaux Bicycle, Westchester County, Knollwood, Suburban Riding and Driving, Jockey, New York Yacht, American Yacht and Larchmont Yacht clubs. He is also a member of the Sons of the Revolution, the Yale Alumni, the New England Society, the Metropolitan Museum of Art, the American Museum of Natural History, the Historical Society and the Westchester Horse Show Association, as well as of many other bodies of a social, literary or artistic character. He devotes no little interest and attention to religious work, being a director of the Young Men's Christian Association, besides being a liberal supporter of various religious and charitable bodies.

WILLIAM HENRY WEBB

MANY distinguished and useful men have been given to the country by the family of which Mr. William Henry Webb, the renowned shipbuilder and founder of Webb's Academy and Home for Shipbuilders, is a representative. Richard Webb, the first of the name in America, came to Massachusetts and was a freeman in Cambridge in 1622. When Governor Haynes and the Reverend Thomas Hooker led the great emigration from Massachusetts to Connecticut, Richard Webb was one of the company and settled in Hartford, Conn., where he was a member of the grand jury in 1643. He moved afterwards to Norwalk, Conn., of which place he was one of the first settlers, owning the first mill ever built in Norwalk. When he died, in 1665, his estate was one of the largest owned by any of the inhabitants of the town.

Richard Webb had five sons, Joseph, Richard, Joshua, Caleb and Samuel. One or more of these brothers were among the first settlers of Stamford, Conn. There Joseph died in 1684, and from him Mr. William H. Webb is descended. Richard Webb, the second son of the pioneer, was a man of large estate and represented Stamford in the Connecticut General Court as early as 1667. Members of the Webb family bore a conspicuous part in the military annals of the Colony during the Indian, French and Revolutionary Wars. Benjamin Webb, the great-grandson of Richard Webb, and the ancestor in the fifth generation of the subject of this sketch, was an officer in a Colonial regiment, in the war with the French, and took part under Wolfe in the capture of Quebec in 1759,

Colonel Charles Webb, a son of Charles and May Smith Webb, was born at Stamford in 1724. He was elected a selectman nineteen times, and represented the town in the State Legislature twenty-three times. In 1760, he was Captain in the Militia and in 1775 was sent by the Continental Congress on a tour of military investigations to Ticonderoga In the same year, he was put in command of the Seventh Regiment of the State Militia. At the battle of Long Island in 1776, he commanded the Nineteenth Connecticut Regiment, and afterwards distinguished himself at the battle of White Plains and at the battle of White Marsh, in December, 1777. His son Charles served in the same regiment with his father, being a Lieutenant in 1775, and Adjutant in 1776. He was a prisoner in New York during the British occupation, and was finally killed on a gunboat in Long Island Sound. Colonel Webb, besides being an able and energetic officer, also gave liberally of his means to the patriotic cause.

Isaac Webb, the youngest son of Colonel Charles Webb, was born in 1766, and his grandson, Isaac Webb, son of Wilsey Webb, who was born in 1794, was the father of Mr William Henry Webb. The parents of Isaac Webb removed from Stamford, Conn., to New York City. He was apprenticed to the famous Henry Eckford, who had made a national reputation as a shipbuilder during the War of 1812. Isaac Webb worked on the vessels built on the lakes for the Government of that time. Afterwards, with two fellow apprentices, he organized the firm of Webb, Smith & Dimon. This firm built, under contract with Henry Eckford, the Chancellor Livingston, the Robert Fulton, in 1819, and the steamship Robert Fulton, the second ocean steamship ever built. Mr. Webb designed and built, in association with Henry Eckford, the famous line-of-battleship, Ohio, and also constructed several of the famous packets whose performances still remain one of the glories of the American merchant marine. In 1825, he joined Eckford, under the firm name of Henry Eckford & Co, and built four frigates for South American Republics. After Mr. Eckford retired from business, the firm became Isaac Webb & Co., and Webb & Allen, in which form it remained until the death of the senior partner.

Mr. William Henry Webb was born in New York City, June 19th, 1816. His mother was a member of a Huguenot family It was not intended that he should become a shipbuilder, but his education under private tutors and in the Columbia College Grammar School revealed the bent of his mind. He was a born mathematician, and at an early age was proficient in algebra and geometry. At the age of twelve he built a skiff row boat, and before he was fifteen he had built several other small craft. Soon after he began the study of marine architecture, and before he was twenty-three built three packet ships under sub-contract in his father's shipyard. His health becoming impaired by a too close application to his labors, he made a voyage to Europe for rest and recreation He sailed on the packet ship New York, one of his own creations, in 1839, and while abroad, the news of his father's death reached him and caused his immediate return to the United States. For the ensuing three years he remained in partnership, which he conducted under a new firm name, in association with his father's former partner, but in 1843 succeeded to the entire business.

From that time, and for nearly thirty years, Mr. Webb was one of the most prominent shipbuilders in this country. When he retired, in 1872, he had to his credit more than one hundred and fifty vessels of all sizes, of an aggregate tonnage much greater than that of any other shipbuilder in this or any other country. He was then one of the largest owners of tonnage in the United States, his interests covering in part or in whole about fifty vessels, most of them of his own construction.

A record of Mr. Webb's achievements would include much of the best part of the history of American shipping Some of the most famous American clipper sailing ships of the first half of the present century came from his yard. He built the steamship Cherokee, in 1848, the first steamship to run between New York and Savannah, the first steamship for the New Orleans trade in 1847, as well as the first steamship for the Pacific Mail Steamship Company. He also designed and constructed the General Admiral of the Russian Navy, in 1858, a ship that revolutionized the construction of war vessels Subsequently he built ironclads for the United States, Italy and France The steam ram Dunderberg, which he built during our Civil War, and which was purchased by the French Government and renamed Rochambeau, was the fastest vessel of war up to that time and the most formidable war ship afloat. The ironclad men-of-war which Mr. Webb constructed were the first vessels of that kind that crossed the Atlantic. The Long Island Sound steamships, Bristol and Providence, the largest and finest vessels built up to that time for such service, were the product of his genius.

Other business enterprises also engaged the attention of Mr. Webb. He was an original shareholder of the Pacific Mail Steamship Company and one of its first directors. He was one of the original subscribers to the building of the Panama Railroad and contributed as much money as any other person to that enterprise. From 1868–70, he was largely interested in the line of steamships engaged in the European trade, sent the first American passenger steamship into the Baltic, and established the first line of mail steamships between San Francisco and various ports of Australia.

From his work Mr. Webb won both fame and fortune. The Russian Grand Duke Constantine sent him a letter of commendation and valuable presents. King Victor Emmanuel conferred decorations upon him, and the French Government promised him the Order of the Legion of Honor. Three times he was offered the nomination of Mayor of the city, but politics never attracted him, although for fourteen years he was president of the Council of Political Reform and was instrumental in defeating the Aqueduct Commissioners in their plans for a dam at the mouth of the Croton River The crowning act of Mr. Webb's long and useful career has been the establishment of the Webb Academy and Home for Shipbuilders, a free educational institution for instruction in shipbuilding and marine architecture, and a home for old and decrepit shipbuilders. The Academy and Home on Fordham Heights overlooking the Harlem River, is a handsome building, finely appointed, and a splendid monument to the generous public spirit of its projector. Mr. Webb has a city residence at 415 Fifth Avenue He owns a country place on the Heights of Tarrytown, called Waldheim, an estate of about one hundred acres, in one of the most sightly and picturesque situations on the Hudson River. He married, in 1843, Henrietta A. Hidden, daughter of Enoch Hidden His children are William E. and Marshall Webb. He belongs to the Union, Union League, Republican, Century and City clubs, and has been connected with many prominent bodies of a business or social character.

WILLIAM SEWARD WEBB

A MONG the earliest settlers in New England was Richard Webb, of Gloucestershire, England, who was made a freeman of the city of Boston in 1632 He accompanied the Reverend Thomas Hooker in the settlement of Hartford, Conn , in 1635, when the Dutch, who were then living on the spot subsequently known, locally, as Webb's Point, were driven away The sixth in direct descent from Richard Webb was Samuel Blatchley Webb, who was born in Wethersfield, Conn , December 15th, 1753 His mother married Silas Deane for her second husband, and Samuel B Webb became the private secretary of his stepfather. At an early age, he took an active part in the movements that led up to the Revolution, and when the war broke out he led a company of light infantry from Wethersfield to participation in the battle of Bunker Hill He was appointed aide to General Israel Putnam, became private secretary and aide-de-camp to Washington, was wounded at White Plains and Trenton, was captured on the expedition to Long Island in 1777, became a Brigadier-General of infantry on his release, and after the war was one of the founders of the Society of the Cincinnati.

James Watson Webb, journalist, diplomat and soldier, a son of Samuel B. Webb, was not less distinguished than his father. He served in the army from 1819 to 1827, and from that time until 1861 owned and edited the famous Courier and Enquirer, of New York. At the beginning of the Civil War he was offered a Brigadier-Generalship, which he declined. He refused appointment as Minister to Turkey in 1861, but accepted a similar appointment to Brazil, and held that position until 1869 General Webb's first wife was Helen L. Stewart, granddaughter of Lispenard Stewart. His second wife was Laura Virginia Cram, daughter of Jacob L. Cram, a leading New York merchant before the Civil War

Dr William Seward Webb, son of General James Watson Webb and Laura V Cram, was born in New York, January 31st, 1851, and when only nine years old went to Brazil with his father He was sent back to the United States in 1864, and for five years attended Colonel Churchill's Military School at Sing Sing, N Y He spent two years in Columbia College, and then went abroad to study medicine in Vienna, Paris and London Returning home, he entered the College of Physicians and Surgeons of New York City, and graduated therefrom in 1875. For several years he engaged in practice, but attention to financial interests gradually interfered with his professional work, and finally compelled him to relinquish it altogether.

In 1881, he married Lila Osgood Vanderbilt, daughter of William H Vanderbilt, and soon after became connected with the Vanderbilt railroad system He was made president of the Wagner Palace Car Company, and became connected with the Adirondack & St Lawrence Railroad, a line that runs through the Adirondack region from Herkimer, N Y , to the St Lawrence River, a distance of two hundred and thirty-three miles. He is the president of this company, and is also a director in other business corporations.

Socially, Dr. Webb is a notable figure in New York. He is a member of nearly all the leading clubs, including the Metropolitan, Union League, Republican, University, Manhattan, Players, Church, Country, Jockey, Racquet, New York Yacht, Coaching, Riding, Tuxedo, Westminster Kennel and Downtown. He is a member of the Sons of the American Revolution, for three years was president-general of the National Society He is vice-president of the Vermont branch of that society, and is also a member of the Society of Colonial Wars His interest in sporting matters is shown in the large preserve that he has established in the Adirondacks and has called Ne-ha-sa-ne Park. He is also a prominent member, and secretary and treasurer of the American Hackney Horse Society. He owns a large farm at Shelburne, Vt., and there gives much attention to horse breeding, his stud having an international reputation. Through his farm and summer country seat at Shelburne, Dr. Webb holds citizenship in the State of Vermont. In 1896, he was elected a member of the Vermont Legislature, and since 1891, he has held a commission, as inspector of rifle practice, on the staff of the Governor of Vermont.

JOHN A. WEEKES

COMING originally from Devonshire, England, one branch of the Weekes family has been settled on Long Island for more than two hundred and fifty years The name and the family are alike of ancient origin. In the old records the name appears in various forms such as Weekes, Wykes, Wicks, Wickes, Wick, Wicke, Wycke, Weik, de Weik and de Wyke It was derived originally from the Saxon, Wic, Wyc, Wich or Wiche, akin to the Latin Wicus, or the Greek Oikos, having the general signification of a dwelling place, and would seem to indicate that those who adopted it were especially home lovers Those families known as the Wykes, of North Wyke, England, the Wykes, of Cocktree, and the Weekeses, of Honey Church, are closely allied and belong to the same stock from which the Weekeses of Long Island and New England are derived.

Francis Weekes and George Weekes, who were respectively the heads of the Long Island and New England families of their name, came from England together to this country in 1635. They belonged to a branch of the family that had been seated at North Wyke, in Tawton Hundred, about twenty miles west from Exeter, long before the latter part of the fourteenth century. On one side their ancestors were of the Wrey family and of Huguenot descent, it is said by some authorities; others assert that they were among those refugees who had fled from Holland to England to escape the persecutions of the infamous Duke of Alva

According to Playfair's British Antiquities, the first member of the Wrey family of whom there is definite historical account, was Robert le Wrey, who was living in 1135. In the sixth generation from Robert le Wrey, a daughter of the family, Jane le Wrey, married John Wykes, of Cocktree, and their son, Roger, held a quarter part of a knight's fee, Charleigh in Broney, in Oak-hampton, in 1346. In the fourteenth century, Roger le Wrey, the head of the family, held a quarter part of a knight's fee in North Wyke. His son, William le Wrey, married Catharine, daughter and coheiress of John Burnell, of Cocktree, who, in the time of Richard III., 1377-99, assumed the name of Wykes. It is from this ancient family that Francis and George Weekes, the American pioneers, were descended.

Francis Weekes, of Oyster Bay, Long Island, and his brother, George, came to the Massachusetts Bay Colony in 1635 George located in Dorchester and became the ancestor of a family well known in Eastern Massachusetts, but Francis went to Salem. The following year he removed to the Providence plantations, where he was secretary of the Colony, and where he married Elizabeth Luther. In 1641, he was among those who came to Long Island and settled. In 1648, he was residing at Gravesend, and in 1650, was one of the joint proprietors of Oyster Bay His descendants have been numerous on Long Island and in New York.

Mr John A Weekes, the leading representative of this historic family at the present time, is lineally descended from Francis Weekes, the pioneer. For a generation he was one of the foremost lawyers of the bar of New York City He married Miss Delano, and lives in East Twentieth Street, having a summer residence in Oyster Bay, the ancestral home of the family. He belongs to the Century Association, the Union League Club and the St Nicholas Society. His four sons are also lawyers. Arthur D. Weekes is a graduate from Columbia College in the class of 1872. He lives in West Twenty-first Street, and is a member of the Metropolitan, Union and other clubs. Henry De Forest Weekes is known as a man of public affairs. He is a member of the Metropolitan, Union, Racquet, Seawanhaka-Corinthian Yacht, and New York Yacht clubs, is a patron of the Metropolitan Museum of Art, and is also a member of the Portland Club, of London, the Travelers' Club, of Paris, and the Chicago Club, of Chicago. He has been treasurer of the Union Club since 1889. Frederick D. Weekes was graduated from Columbia in 1877, and is a member of the Union and the Fencers clubs. John A. Weekes, Jr., married, in December, 1897, Estelle (Durant) Bowers, widow of the late Henry C. Bowers, of Cooperstown, N. Y. He is a member of the Union, Racquet, Seawanhaka-Corinthian Yacht and other clubs.

BENJAMIN SUMNER WELLES

OF ancient origin and high rank in Normandy and England is the Welles family. For more than seven centuries it was one of the most powerful families in those countries and frequently intermarried with royal houses and the nobility. From this English source sprang Thomas Welles, who came to this country in 1636. He was one of the most influential members of the Connecticut Colony in its early period, serving as a magistrate throughout his life, being annually reëlected to that honorable position. In 1639, he was treasurer of the Colony; in 1643, Secretary of State, and in 1649, one of two commissioners to represent Connecticut in the attempted confederation of the New England Colonies. In 1654, he was Deputy-Governor, and in 1655 and several times thereafter was Governor. His death occurred in 1660.

Samuel Welles, son of Thomas Welles, was born in Essex, England, in 1630. He was a freeman of Hartford in 1657 and deputy magistrate, 1657-61. After 1649, he was a resident of Wethersfield. His first wife, the ancestress of the subject of this sketch, was Elizabeth Hollister, daughter of John Hollister. She was married in 1659 and died in 1683. Captain Samuel Welles, grandson of Thomas Welles, the pioneer, was born in Wethersfield in 1660, removed to Glastonbury in 1685, and died there in 1731. He was a selectman of Glastonbury, and for many years a member of the Connecticut Legislature. His wife was Ruth Rice.

Samuel Welles, son of Captain Samuel Welles, was born in Glastonbury in 1689 Graduated from Yale College in 1707, he studied theology, and took charge of a parish in the town of Lebanon, where he remained until 1719. In that year he married Abigail Arnold, and removed to Boston, where he was a Judge, for several years a member of the Colonial Council and held other positions of trust. He died in 1770. The grandfather of Mr. Benjamin Sumner Welles was Samuel Welles, a prominent merchant of Boston, who was born there in 1725, graduated from Harvard College in 1744, and died in 1799, having married, in 1772, Isabella Pratt, daughter of Chief Justice Pratt, of New York. His son was Benjamin Welles, a merchant of Boston, who was born there in 1781, and died in 1860. Graduated from Harvard College in 1800, he traveled several years in Europe, and then, returning to Boston, engaged with his brother, Samuel Welles, in establishing the first American banking house in Paris, France. The wife of Benjamin Welles, whom he married in 1815, was Mehitable Sumner, daughter of Increase Sumner, who was the Governor of Massaceusetts, in 1799. By her he had three children, Elizabeth, Georgiana and Benjamin Sumner Welles By his second wife, Susan Codman, he had one daughter, who married Russell Sturgis, of Boston.

Mr. Benjamin Sumner Welles was born in Boston, and moved to New York in 1859. He married, in New York, in 1850, Catharine Schermerhorn, daughter of Abraham Schermerhorn, who was connected with several of the great families of New York Abraham Schermerhorn was the third son of Peter and Elizabeth (Bussing) Schermerhorn, and descended from Jacob Janse Schermerhorn, who settled in New York in 1636. His great-grandmother was Maria Beekman, granddaughter of the famous William Beekman, founder of the Beekman family in New York. His wife was Helen White, daughter of Henry and Anne (Van Cortlandt) White, and his daughters married General James I. Jones, Charles Suydam, John Treat Irving, Benjamin Sumner Welles and William Astor.

Mr. Welles has had five children ; Benjamin, Helen Schermerhorn, Katharine, Elizabeth and Harriet Welles. His eldest daughter, Helen Schermerhorn, married George L. Kingsland, son of former Mayor Ambrose C Kingsland. His son, Benjamin Welles, was born in Boston, in 1857, and graduated from Harvard University in 1878. He is a member of the Union and Harvard clubs, and a patron of the American Museum of Natural History. He married Frances W. Swan, daughter of Frederic G. Swan, of New York, and has two children, Emily Frances and Benjamin Sumner Welles, Jr. The senior Mr Welles is a member of the Union Club, lives in West Thirty-ninth Street and has a country seat at Islip, Long Island.

JULIA CHESTER WELLS

THE Reverend William Wells came of a family of position in the eastern countries of England, a grant of arms having been made to his forefathers by James I., in 1614. Imitating the early Puritan settlers of New England, he came to the United States from Biggleswade, Bedfordshire, England, in 1793, for the sake of liberty of conscience. He became minister at Brattleboro, Vt., where he remained for forty years, being distinguished by his refusal to accept pecuniary reward for his services, and by insisting upon an annual reëlection by his congregation

By his wife, Jane Hancock, the Reverend William Wells was the father of Ebenezer Custerson Wells, 1777-1850, who married Mary, daughter of the famous Revolutionary officer, Colonel John Chester. The Chester family came from London and Barnet, Hertfordshire, England Leonard Chester settled at Wethersfield, Conn., in 1633, and was the founder of a race which furnished the leading men of that district for generations. John Chester, born 1703, was a graduate of Yale, a judge, a member of the Connecticut Assembly, and married Sarah, daughter of the Reverend Joseph Noyes and his wife, Abigail Pierrepont, a lady descended from John Haynes, one of the Puritan gentlemen who came to Massachusetts in the earliest days of its settlement, accompanying the famous ministers, Cotton and Hooker. He was Governor of the Massachusetts Bay Colony in 1635, and in the succeeding year was the principal layman in the company which founded Hartford, being chosen in 1637 the first Governor of Connecticut. Among Governor Haynes' wife's ancestors were the Nevilles, Earls of Westmoreland and the royal house of Plantagenet.

Colonel John Chester, 1749-1809, son of John Chester, graduated from Yale in 1766 and married Elizabeth Huntington, daughter of General Jabez Huntington, who descended from Simon Huntington, one of the founders of Connecticut. John Chester, though a man of considerable property, risked fortune and life by espousing the patriotic cause in the Revolution. He was present at the battle of Bunker's Hill and is represented in Trumbull's picture assisting the dying General Warren. He was Captain of a company which he recruited, one of the first commands for the war, serving in the Continental Army. He received particular commendation from Washington for the discipline and military efficiency of his command, which was one of the few uniformed companies in the army and was frequently employed on particular service as escort to the French officers visiting the American headquarters. After the war, he attained great prominence in civil life, holding a number of important offices in Connecticut. His children and descendants intermarried with distinguished families of both New England and New York.

William Henry Wells, of New York, was the third son of Ebenezer C. and Mary (Chester) Wells, and was born at Brattleboro, Vt., in 1811. He removed permanently to New York in 1858, and was a man of influence and public spirit, and became distinguished in national affairs and philanthropic work of many practical kinds, to which he contributed his unsparing labor. During the war between the States, he took an active interest in the work of the Sanitary Commission and was an intimate friend and associate of the leading public men of the past generation, though never a holder or seeker of public office. His relations with President Lincoln were particularly close. His charities were numerous and unostentatious. He died in 1891, having married in 1852, Frances Tracey, daughter of William Gedney Tracey, of Whitesboro, N.Y., the lady whose name heads this article being the daughter and only child of the marriage.

The Tracey family, to which Miss Wells' mother belonged, is of ancient English descent, its lineage being traced back to Anglo-Saxon royalty. The progenitor of the American branch of the family was Lieutenant Thomas Tracey, who came to Salem, Mass, in 1636, and was afterwards one of the first proprietors of Norwich, Conn., being frequently mentioned in the early history of that Colony. Miss Wells inherited and has in her possession a number of old portraits of members of the distinguished Colonial and Revolutionary families from which she is descended, painted by contemporary artists, which form one of the most authentic as well as most interesting private collections of that nature.

BURR WENDELL

REPRESENTING one of the oldest families of New York State, the subject of this article, which refers not only to the gentleman whose name is given above, but to his brothers, B. Rush Wendell and Ten Eyck Wendell, is a direct descendant of Evert Jansen Wendell, who came to this country from Embden in 1640, and is mentioned in the early records of New Netherland, where he established himself and founded a family which has since held a distinguished place in both Colonial and later times. Jacob H Wendell, the present Mr. Wendell's great-grandfather, was an officer in the Continental Army during the American Revolution, and participated, in 1783, in the organization of the Society of the Cincinnati. According to the rules of this order, its honors are inherited by the first born male in each generation, and Mr. Burr Wendell, being the eldest of the three brothers, accordingly succeeded his father as a member of the New York Society of that distinguished organization.

Mr. Wendell's parents were B. Rush Wendell, of Albany, and Margaret Ten Eyck Burr, of Cazenovia, N. Y., his paternal grandfather and grandmother being Dr. Peter Wendell and Elizabeth Van Kleeck. On the side of his mother, his grandparents were William M. Burr and Catharine Ten Eyck.

In addition to these names, which at once recall the foremost families of the Hudson River counties and the central portions of the State, the numerous alliances of their ancestors make the Messrs Wendell direct descendants of such old Dutch and Colonial families as those of Du Trieux, Van Witbeck, Van Vechten, Lansing, Van Schaick, Schuyler, Van Dyck, Staats, Coeymans, Bleecker, Glen, Van Buren, Coster, Ten Broeck, Cuyler, Van Dusen, De Vos, Beck and Van Eslant. The family connection to which they belong is consequently a wide one, and it would be difficult to name any family of the old New York stock to which they are not in some degree related or affiliated through marriages at different times in the past. Several of their remote ancestors fought in the Colonial French wars, among whom may be prominently mentioned Colonel Peter P. Schuyler, of the New York Provincial forces. The membership of the Messrs. Wendell in the Colonial Order fittingly commemorates the part which so many of their progenitors took in the affairs of the Province from which the present State is derived.

Mr. Burr Wendell was born at Cazenovia, in 1853, and was graduated from the Albany Law School in 1878 In 1881, he married Emily Lentilhon Smith, of New York, daughter of Gamaliel Gates Smith and Margaret Ten Eyck Foster, the issue of this marriage being a daughter, Margaret Ten Eyck Wendell. In addition to the inherited membership of the Cincinnati, Mr. Wendell is a member of the Union Club, the St. Nicholas Society, the Colonial Order and the St. Nicholas Club. His country home is The Farms, at Cazenovia.

B. Rush Wendell, the second of the three brothers, was born at Cazenovia, in 1855, and was educated at Yale, from which institution he was graduated B. A, in 1878, and received the degree of M. A, in 1882. He prepared for the legal profession at the Columbia College Law School, in New York, which conferred on him the degree of LL. B, in 1882 Mr. Wendell's country residence is at Cazenovia. He has traveled extensively in all parts of the world. He is a member of the Union Club and St. Nicholas Society, and the Colonial Order. In 1895, he married Sarah Delano Swift, daughter of Dr. Foster Swift and his wife, Alida Carroll Fitzhugh. The paternal grandfather of Mrs. Wendell was General Joseph Gardner Swift, LL. D., the first graduate of the United States Military Academy at West Point, and a distinguished soldier. Her grandfather on the maternal side, was Dr. Daniel H. Fitzhugh, of Geneseo, N. Y. The youngest brother, Ten Eyck Wendell, was born at Cazenovia, in 1857, was graduated B. A. from Yale University in 1880, and received the degree of LL B, in 1882, from Columbia College Law School, where he prepared for the practice of law. He has traveled extensively at home and abroad, has a country home in Cazenovia, is unmarried, and is a member of the Union and St. Nicholas clubs.

JACOB WENDELL

EVERT JANSEN WENDELL, the ancestor of all who bear the name in this country, was born in Embden, East Friesland, in 1615. Emigrating to the New Netherland, in 1640, he lived for a time in New Amsterdam, and then went to Fort Orange, now Albany, where he died, in 1709. He was a magistrate and held other positions. His wife, whom he married in 1644, was Susanna Du Trieux, daughter of Philip Du Trieux, whose wife was Susanna de Scheene. The second wife of Evert Jansen Wendell was Maritje Abramhamse Vosburg, daughter of Abraham Pieterse Vosburg. The gentleman whose name appears at the head of this sketch is descended in the seventh generation from Evert Jansen Wendell and his first wife.

In the second American generation came Johannes Wendell, a merchant of Albany, magistrate in 1684, and a commissioner to treat with the Five Nations, in 1690. His first wife was Maritje Jellisse, and his second wife was Elizabeth Staats, daughter of Major Abraham Staats, of Rensselaerwyck. Abraham Wendell, son of Johannes Wendell, was born in Albany in 1678, and became an importer in New York, and afterwards in Boston, dying in 1734. He married Katarina, daughter of Tunis and Helena (Van Brugh) De Key, descended from the Honorable Johannes Pieterse Van Brugh, burgomaster of New Amsterdam, in 1656 and 1673. John Wendell, son of Abraham Wendell, born in New York, in 1703, became a well-known merchant of Boston. He was connected with the Ancient and Honorable Artillery, being its commander in 1740. He married in 1724, Elizabeth Quincy, daughter of the Honorable Edmund Quincy, the grandson of Edmund Quincy, who came to Boston in 1633. The younger Edmund Quincy graduated from Harvard in 1699, was Colonel of the Suffolk Regiment and Justice of the Supreme Court.

John Wendell, 1731–1808, the son of John Wendell and his wife, Elizabeth Quincy, was the grandfather of Mr. Jacob Wendell. He graduated from Harvard College in 1750, and, removing to Portsmouth, N. H., became a well-known lawyer. His first wife was a descendant of Lieutenant-Governor John Wentworth, of Portsmouth. His second wife, the grandmother of Mr. Jacob Wendell, was Dorothy Sherburne, daughter of Judge Henry and Sarah (Warner) Sherburne, of Portsmouth. Judge Sherburne was a Harvard graduate in 1728, a delegate to the Colonial Congress of Albany, in 1754, and Justice of the Superior Court of New Hampshire.

Jacob Wendell, Sr., was born in Portsmouth, N. H., in 1788, and became a successful merchant. His wife was Mehetabel Rindge, daughter of Mark and Susanna Rogers, of Portsmouth, N. H., and descended on both sides from early pioneers to New England.

Mr. Jacob Wendell was born in Portsmouth, N. H., July 24th, 1826. After completing his education in his native place, he entered upon mercantile life in Portsmouth, and then went to Boston, where he became a partner in the commission house of J. C. Howe & Co. Removing to New York in 1863, he has since then been engaged in business in this city, first as partner in J. C. Howe & Co., then in the firm of Wendell, Hutchinson & Co., and finally at the head of the firm of Jacob Wendell & Co. He is also a director in several banks, insurance and real estate associations, and a member of the Chamber of Commerce. In 1854, Mr. Wendell married Mary Bertodi Barrett, daughter of N. A. Barrett, of Boston. He has four sons : Barrett Wendell, Harvard, 1877, who married Edith, daughter of W. W. Greenough, of Boston, and who is one of the professors of Harvard University ; Gordon Wendell, Harvard, 1882, who is in business with his father and who married Frances, eldest daughter of the Reverend Alfred Langdon Elwyn, of Philadelphia ; Evert Jansen Wendell, who graduated from Harvard in 1882, and who is identified with many philanthropic enterprises in New York ; and Jacob Wendell, Jr., who graduated from Harvard, in 1891, and in 1895 married Marian, daughter of the late Major Philip R. Fendall, of Virginia. The city residence of Mr Wendell is in East Thirty-eighth Street, and his country home is Frost Fields, New Castle, N. H. He is a member of the New York Historical Society, the New York Biographical and Genealogical Society, the Holland Society, the New England Society, the American Geographical Society, the Metropolitan and Union League clubs, and the Century Association.

GEORGE PEABODY WETMORE

BORN in England in 1615, Thomas Whitmore, the ancestor of the Wetmore family, came to America in 1635, landing in Boston. He was in Wethersfield, Conn., in 1639, and afterwards in Hartford. His first wife, Sarah Hall, daughter of John Hall, was the mother of his son, Izrahiah, one of the first settlers of Middletown, a freeman in 1652, and a representative to the General Court in 1654-1655. Izrahiah Whitmore, or Wetmore, 1656-1742, was a magistrate, and in 1721-28 a deputy to the General Court His wife was Rachel Stow, daughter of the Reverend Samuel and Hope (Fletcher) Stow, of Middletown. The Reverend Izrahiah Wetmore, their son, 1693-1728, was pastor of the First Presbyterian Church of Stratford. His wife was Sarah Booth, of Stratford. The most famous Wetmore in the early generations of the family, was Judge Seth Wetmore, 1700-1778, son of the Reverend Izrahiah Wetmore. For forty-eight successive times, between 1738 and 1771, he was a deputy to the General Court of the Connecticut Colony. He was also a magistrate of Middletown, and a Judge of the county court. By his second wife, Hannah Whitmore, daughter of Joseph Whitmore, of Middletown, he had a son, Seth Wetmore, the great-grandfather of the Honorable George Peabody Wetmore.

The second Seth Wetmore, 1744-1810, was a Captain in the Revolutionary War. His wife was Mary Wright, daughter of William and Lucy (Downing) Wright, the eighth in descent from John Rogers, the martyr, and in the fifth generation from George Wyllys, Deputy-Lieutenant-Governor, and Governor of Connecticut, 1640-43. Seth Wetmore, third, 1769-1830, was a lawyer in St. Albans, Vt., sheriff, a member of the Governor's Council, and a judge of probate. He was married three times; first to Nancy Shepard, daughter of General William and Nancy (Dewey) Shepard, of Westfield, Mass., second to Salome Smith, of St. Albans, Vt., and third to Mrs Anne Goodrich. William Shepard Wetmore, son of the third Seth Wetmore, was the father of the Honorable George Peabody Wetmore. Born in 1801, he engaged in business in Middletown, Conn., and afterward in Providence, R. I. For several years he was settled in Valparaiso, and afterwards went to China as the head of the house of Wetmore & Co. He was twice married; first to Esther Phillips Wetmore, daughter of Samuel Wetmore, of New York; and second to Anstice Rogers, of Salem, Mass. He had three children, William Shepard, George Peabody and Anne Derby Rogers Wetmore.

The Honorable George Peabody Wetmore was born in London, England, and was graduated from Yale College in the class of 1867. He has made his home principally in Newport, but in business and social affairs, has been closely identified with New York. He has served as Governor of the State of Rhode Island, and at the present time is a member of the United States Senate. He married Miss Keteltas, and has two daughters, Edith and Maud Wetmore. He is a member of the Metropolitan, Tuxedo, Knickerbocker, Union League, Union, Riding and other clubs, the Metropolitan Club of Washington, and the Somerset Club of Boston.

Another branch of this family is represented in New York by Edmund Wetmore, great-great-grandson of Judge Seth Wetmore, by his third wife, Hannah Edwards, daughter of the Reverend Timothy and Esther (Stoddard) Edwards. The great-grandparents of Mr. Wetmore were Oliver Wetmore and Sarah Brewster, a descendant in the fifth generation from Elder William Brewster, of Plymouth. His grandparents were the Reverend Oliver Wetmore, 1774-1852, and Esther Arnold Southmaid, daughter of Captain Jonathan Southmaid. His father was Edmund Arnold Wetmore, a distinguished lawyer of Western New York, and for two terms, after 1845, Mayor of the City of Utica. The mother of Mr Wetmore was Mary Ann Lothrop, daughter of John H. and Jerusha (Kirkland) Lothrop. Mr Wetmore was born in Utica in 1838, and graduated from Harvard College in 1860. He is engaged in the practice of law. He married Helen Howland, lives in Lexington Avenue, and is a member of the Metropolitan and other clubs Major William Boerum Wetmore, U. S. A., is another great-grandson of Judge Seth Wetmore. His mother, who lives in Newport, was Sarah T. Boerum, daughter of Captain William Boerum, U. S. N.

WILLIAM FISHBOURNE WHARTON

THOMAS WHARTON, ancestor of the Pennsylvania family of that name, came to this country in the latter part of the seventeenth century. He was a son of Richard Wharton, of Kellorth, Parish of Orton, or Overton, Westmoreland, England. Thomas Wharton became a man of prominence in Philadelphia, and was an influential member of the Society of Friends In 1713, he was a member of the Council of the city, and died in Philadelphia in 1718. John Wharton, his son, and his wife, Mary Dobbins, daughter of James Dobbins, were the parents of Thomas Wharton, 1735-1778, one of the most celebrated men in the early history of Pennsylvania Thomas Wharton was born in Chester County, Pa., and became highly esteemed for his integrity and patriotism. During the agitation that preceded the Revolution, he took a decided stand on the side of the Colonies, and in 1774 was a member of the Committee of Correspondence. In the following year, he was on the Committee of Safety, being its president in 1776. In 1777, he was chosen Governor of Pennsylvania, and when the British occupied Philadelphia, removed with the Executive Council to Lancaster, where he died. The famed entertainment known as the Meschianza, given by the British officers during Howe's occupation of Philadelphia in 1778, was held at Walnut Grove, the Wharton mansion and grounds.

Thomas Wharton's first wife was Susannah Lloyd, daughter of Thomas Lloyd and great-granddaughter of Thomas Lloyd, president of the Pennsylvania Council in 1684-88 and 1690-93. His second wife was Elizabeth Fishbourne, daughter of William Fishbourne and Mary Tallman. William Fishbourne was the son of William Fishbourne, a member of the Provincial Council 1723-31, and grandson of Ralph Fishbourne, of Talbot County, Md. The elder William Fishbourne moved to Philadelphia, and in 1702 married Hannah, daughter of Samuel Carpenter.

Fishbourne Wharton, 1778-1846, son of Governor Thomas Wharton, and grandfather of Mr. William Fishbourne Wharton, married Susan Shoemaker in 1804. She died in 1821, and he married, in 1832, her sister, Mary Ann Shoemaker. George Mifflin Wharton, 1806-1870, the son of Fishbourne Wharton and Susan Shoemaker, was one of the leaders of the Philadelphia bar. He was also interested in public education, and gave much time to its promotion. Active in public affairs in Philadelphia, he was for many years a director and president of the Board of Control of the city. He was also a member of the Select Council, and at one time president of that body, and for one term held the office of United States District Attorney A graduate from the University of Pennsylvania in 1823, he was for many years a trustee of the institution. His wife, whom he married in 1835, was Maria Markoe, daughter of John Markoe and Hitty Coxe. The present Mr. Wharton is related to the Wadsworth family, of Geneseo, prominent in the history of New York State. Mary Craig Wharton, a descendant of the original Thomas Wharton through his son Joseph, married, in 1834, James Samuel Wadsworth, afterwards General in the Civil War, who commanded the First Army Corps at Gettysburg, and was mortally wounded at the Wilderness.

Mr. William Fishbourne Wharton, the son of George Mifflin Wharton, was born in Philadelphia in 1846. Graduated from the University of Pennsylvania in 1865, he has since lived in New York, where he has been engaged in business, and is a member of the Stock Exchange and connected with important financial enterprises His wife, whom he married in 1871, was Frances Turner Fisher, daughter of William Fisher and Sarah Julia Palmer, of Philadelphia. Mrs. Wharton is the niece of Admiral Palmer and Admiral Turner, and a great-granddaughter of Sarah Livingston and Major John Ricketts, while she is the great-great-granddaughter of Mary Alexander and Peter Van Burgh Livingston, and is a descendant in the sixth generation from James Alexander and his wife, Mary Provoost, the parents of General William Alexander, Lord Sterling. The children of Mr. and Mrs. Wharton are George Mifflin, Richard and Percival Charles Wharton. The residence of the family is in West Thirty-sixth Street, and their summer home is at East Islip, Long Island. Mr. Wharton is a member of the Metropolitan and Union clubs, and he was one of the originators of the Riding Club.

EVERETT PEPPERRELL WHEELER

ONE of the most picturesque figures in the early Colonial days of New England was Sir William Pepperrell, the hero of Louisburg. The story of his life reads like a romance His father was born in Tavistock, Cornwall, of parents in the humblest circumstances He took up his residence upon the Isles of Shoals, off the coast of New Hampshire, and became a fisherman   Prospering in business, he removed to Kittery Point, Me, and engaged in trade with the West Indies, accumulating a considerable fortune before he died.

Sir William Pepperrell, who was born in 1696, received a good education, and then went into business with his father, in conjunction with whom he achieved a handsome fortune in mercantile business and in real estate transactions   They owned over one hundred vessels.   He was Chief Justice of the Common Pleas in York County, and was also a Colonel in command of the Maine Militia.   Several times he was representative to the General Court at Boston, and was a member of the Council of Massachusetts in 1727, and afterwards its president   Placed in command of the expedition against Louisburg in 1745, he achieved so signal a success that he was made a baronet, the first native-born American to be thus honored by the mother country   In 1755, he was Major-General of the British Army in Maine, he afterwards became General in that army, and was acting Governor of Massachusetts, 1756–8.

Mr. Everett P Wheeler is descended through his mother from Sir William Pepperrell, whose name he bears.   His mother was Elizabeth Jarvis, daughter of Consul William Jarvis, of Boston, Mass., who, during the administrations of Presidents Jefferson and Madison, was the United States Chargé D'Affaires at Lisbon, Portugal, and introduced the merino sheep into the country.   The paternal grandfather of Mr Wheeler was John B. Wheeler, of Oxford, N. H.   His father was David Everett Wheeler, who was born in Vermont, educated at Dartmouth College, and was a practicing lawyer in New York City from 1830 until the time of his death, in 1870

Mr. Everett P. Wheeler was born in New York, March 10th, 1840.   He was educated in the public schools and in the New York Free Academy, now the College of the City of New York, from which he graduated in 1856.   He graduated from the law school of Harvard College in 1859 ; and was admitted to the bar in 1861, and since then has been one of the most prominent members of the legal profession in New York, having been associated with many of the most important cases before the New York and Federal courts during the last thirty years. He is the author of a work on the Modern Law of Carriers.

He has taken a very active interest in public affairs, municipal, State and National, and has been an influential adviser of public men, and foremost in the advocacy of reform principles in governmental administration.   For many years he was president of the New York Free Trade Club, being a pronounced advocate of tariff reform, a cause to which he has contributed much by public addresses and otherwise   He was one of the earliest advocates of civil service reform, for sixteen years was chairman of the executive committee of the New York Civil Service Reform Association, and has represented the association in numerous litigated cases.   Mayor Edson, in 1882, appointed him chairman of the supervisory board of the Civil Service for New York City, and in 1895 Mayor Strong appointed him chairman of the Board of Civil Service Commissioners. In 1894 he was a member of the Committee of Seventy.

In 1866, Mr Wheeler married Lydia Lorraine Hodges, daughter of the Honorable Silas H. Hodges, of Washington, D C., and a descendant of Elder William Brewster, who came over on the Mayflower.   He has four children, Annie Lorraine Wheeler, David Everett Wheeler, Ethel Jarvis Wheeler, and Constance Fay Wheeler.   He is a member of the Bar Association of New York City, of which he was one of the founders, and of which he has been vice-president; belongs to the City, Reform, Century, Church, and A Φ Δ clubs, is a member of the Downtown Association, the Historical Society, and the Society of Colonial Wars, and is president of the New York College of Music.   His city residence is at 731 Park Avenue.

OBED WHEELER

MANY of the most distinguished families of our city and State possess an ancestry, the American originators of which were among the early settlers of Long Island. This is the case with the Wheelers Nathan Wheeler established himself on Long Island in 1705, though his immediate descendants removed in 1740 to South Dover, Dutchess County, N Y., where the family homestead has since remained. Captain Thomas Wheeler, one of the ancestors of Mr Obed Wheeler, was an officer in the Colonial forces during the French and Indian War and took a distinguished part in the conflicts of that epoch, dying at Hudson, N. Y., in 1755. The removal of the branch of the Wheeler family to which the subject of this article belongs from Long Island to Dutchess County was due to the marriage of Henry Wheeler to Catherine Wing, they being the grandparents of Mr. Obed Wheeler. The family of Wing was first established in this country by one of the New England Pilgrims. John Wing and his wife, Deborah Batchelder, daughter of the Reverend Stephen Batchelder, were among the incorporators of the town of Sandwich in 1639. They arrived in this country several years earlier, and first lived in Saugus, Mass. The present generation of Wheelers consequently trace their ancestry to some of the founders of both the Province of New York and the New England Colonies. Thomas Wheeler, father of the present Mr. Wheeler, was the son of Henry and Catherine (Wing) Wheeler, and married Rhoda Ann Olney

Mr. Obed Wheeler was born at the old seat of the family, in South Dover, Dutchess County, in 1841. He entered Yale College in 1862, but gave up his studies to serve his country in the great Civil War. Joining the army as First Lieutenant of the One Hundred and Fiftieth Regiment, New York Volunteers, he saw arduous and continued service till the close of the conflict, taking part in the battle of Gettysburg and afterwards in the campaign of the West, which culminated in Sherman's March to the Sea. During the latter campaign, he received the brevet of Major of Volunteers for meritorious and gallant services.

Returning to civil life at the close of the war, Mr. Wheeler studied law and was admitted to the bar in 1867. He has, however, devoted his attention more particularly to financial affairs, and in 1868 became a member of the New York Stock Exchange. He has been connected with many large financial institutions and has engaged successfully in the banking business At the same time political life has not been without its strong attractions for him, and for three terms he represented his home district of Dutchess County in the New York Legislature. Mr. Wheeler's permanent residence is the family mansion in South Dover. He, however, passes a portion of his time in New York. Though taking an active part in society, he has not married. Interested in club life, he is a member of the Union League, United Service and New York Yacht clubs. He is also prominent in the Military Order of the Loyal Legion and in the Grand Army of the Republic, and is an earnest patron of art and literature.

William Bailey Wheeler, the younger son of Thomas and Rhoda A. (Olney) Wheeler, has been prominent both as a business man and sportsman. He was born in South Dover, N Y, June 6th, 1850, and in 1868 entered Yale College, from which he was graduated with the degree of A B in 1872. In the succeeding year, when only twenty-three years of age, he became a member of the New York Stock Exchange and has since been in active business as a banker and broker, and is widely known in financial circles. His devotion to business has not prevented his taking a decided interest in sports, especially those of an athletic character, and he has been prominent in that connection. He married Mary Toffey, daughter of George Toffey, of Jersey City, N. J., and niece of Admiral John L Worden, U S N, the hero of the fight between the Monitor and the Merrimac. Mrs. Wheeler is also a descendant of the celebrated Peter de la Noy, Mayor of New York City, 1689-1690. They have two children, a daughter, Mary, and a son, William Bailey Wheeler, Jr. William B Wheeler is a member of the Union League, Lotos and New York Athletic clubs, and has a country residence on Quaker Hill, Dutchess County, N. Y

STANFORD WHITE

JOHN WHITE, a passenger on the ship Lion in 1632, settled in Cambridge and the following year became a freeman, and in 1634–35 was a selectman of that town. He was in the migration from Massachusetts to Connecticut in 1636, and became one of the original proprietors of Hartford. Later on, he moved to Hadley, Mass., and was a representative to the General Court in 1664 and 1669, and died in 1683. Nathaniel White, 1629–1711, his son, remained in Connecticut and frequently represented Middletown in the General Court.

The great-grandfather of Mr. Stanford White, the Reverend Calvin White, was born in 1763 and died in 1853. He was an Episcopal clergyman and for many years rector of St. James Parish, Derby, Conn. In his later years, he became a convert to the Roman Catholic faith, but did not enter its priesthood. Richard Mansfield White, a shipping merchant of New York, was the grandfather of Mr Stanford White. The latter's father was Richard Grant White, one of the most accomplished men of letters of his day. He was born in New York City, May 22d, 1821, and was intended for the church, but after graduating from the University of the City of New York, studied medicine and law and in 1845 was admitted to the bar. Literature had, however, more attractions for him, and he became the critic on art of The New York Courier and Inquirer in 1845, and assisted in founding The New York World in 1860, and for twenty years, 1858 to 1878, was chief of the United States Revenue Marine Bureau for the District of New York. He was the writer of the weekly letters to The London Spectator signed "A Yankee" during the Civil War, compiled an anthology of the poetry of the war, published books on the English language, on foreign travel and on Shakespearean study, the great labor of his lifetime being an annotated edition of Shakespeare's plays.

Mr. Stanford White, his son, stands in the front rank of American architects of to-day. He was born in New York City, November 9th, 1853, and was educated in private schools and under tutors, taking the degree of A M at the University of New York. His architectural training was in the office of Charles D. Gambrill and H. H. Richardson, and he was the chief assistant of Mr. Richardson in the construction of that artist's masterly work, Trinity Church, Boston. From 1878 to 1880, he passed his time in Europe, traveling and studying, and when he returned in 1881, formed a partnership with Charles F. McKim and William R. Mead, under the firm name of McKim, Mead & White.

Some of the most notable architecture of the country during the last fifteen years has come from Mr. White, either independently or in collaboration. Most of his work is in New York. He was the architect of the Villard House on Madison Avenue, now belonging to the Honorable Whitelaw Reid; the Madison Square Garden, the Century Club, the Metropolitan Club, the University of New York, the University of Virginia, and the Washington Arch; besides many private houses in both city and country. He has also designed the architectural features for Augustus St. Gaudens' sculptures, his most conspicuous mark in this line being the pedestals of the Farragut statue in New York City, the Chapin statue in Springfield, Mass., the Lincoln and Logan statues in Chicago, and the Adams tomb in Washington. He is an accomplished interior decorator, as his work in the Players Club, the Villard houses, the Metropolitan Club and on the altars of the Church of the Paulist Fathers and the Church of the Ascension clearly shows.

In 1884, Mr. White married Bessie Smith, a member of a family descended from Colonel Richard Smith, the original patentee of Smithtown, Long Island, among her ancestors being General Nathaniel Woodhull, who was slain at the battle of Long Island. Mr. and Mrs. White have one son, Lawrence Grant White. Mr. White is a member of the Institute of Architects and of the leading clubs, including the Metropolitan, Union, University, Grolier, Players, Century, Meadowbrook and the Adirondack League He also belongs to many prominent artistic and literary organizations His New York residence is in Gramercy Park, and his country home is at St. James, Long Island.

JAMES NORMAN de RAPELJE WHITEHOUSE

FOR many generations, the members of the Whitehouse family were principally clergymen of the Church of England, though many bearers of the name also acquired distinction in the navy, the law, the diplomatic service, in architecture, or in various branches of art and science. The first of them to make America his home was James Whitehouse, who came to this country and established himself in New York City, in 1798 He was a native of Taunton, Somersetshire, England, his wife, Elizabeth Christina, who accompanied him to the United States, was the daughter of a gentleman having landed estates near that place This couple were the great-grandparents of Mr James Norman de Rapelje Whitehouse. The most famous of their children was the eldest son, the Right Reverend Henry J. Whitehouse, born in 1803, who entered the ministry, was famous as a preacher, and became rector of St. Thomas' Church in this city, and was subsequently consecrated as the first Protestant Episcopal Bishop of Illinois. He died in 1874, and his son, Frederick Cope Whitehouse, who graduated from Columbia College, in 1861, has devoted his life and fortune to archæology and exploration, being one of the most eminent Egyptologists of the age. His discoveries in regard to the situation of the classical Lake Moeris are well known, and his writings upon that and other subjects pertaining to ancient Egypt are of an authoritative nature.

Bishop Whitehouse's younger brother, Edward Whitehouse, was the grandfather of the subject of this sketch He married Julia Cammann, one of the old New York family of that name. Their son, James Henry Whitehouse, born in New York, married Mary Schenck, a daughter of John Schenck and his wife, Elizabeth Remsen, both of whom represented old and highly respected Long Island families

Mr. James Norman de Rapelje Whitehouse is the son of James Henry Whitehouse and his wife, Mary (Schenck) Whitehouse, and was born in Brooklyn, in 1858. He thus inherits the blood of a number of families of position and influence in both this country and Europe. His mother's ancestry in particular is notable as including in the number Jans Joris de Rapelje and his wife, Catelina Trico, who came to New Netherland on the ship Eendragt, or Unity, in 1623 The couple in question were famous as the parents of Sarah Rapelje, the first girl born to any of the Colonists in the new settlement. de Rapelje was a Huguenot, of La Rochelle, France, and was a leader among the persecuted Walloons of the Reformed faith, who fled to this country and established the hamlet at the Waalbought, on the Long Island shore of the East River, which now gives the name of Wallabout to that portion of the modern City of Brooklyn Sarah de Rapelje became ancestress of the Bergen and Bogaert families, and of many of the most prominent people in Kings County. The name of Rapelje occurs with great frequency in the early annals of the New Netherland and in those of the Province after the English occupation, often in positions of trust and public importance.

Mr. Whitehouse was mainly educated abroad, attending schools in Switzerland and Germany, and completed his training at Oxford University, England, being one of the few living New Yorkers who boast of such distinction. His travels have been very extensive, and include visits to nearly every part of the civilized world. He is engaged in the banking business in this city, and has his town residence at 5 East Seventeenth Street His country seat is The Larches, a large mansion and grounds at Irvington-on-the-Hudson, his time being divided between his city and country residences.

It is safe to say that there is no better known figure in New York society than Mr. Whitehouse. He has been unusually active in that connection, and has been a popular member of many of the most prominent social organizations. Some years ago he, however, resigned from all his clubs, except the Union and the Calumet. He is a constant guest at the prominent functions of the higher social world, and takes part in all the sports and amusements which are patronized by the leading element of society.

WILLIAM COLLINS WHITNEY

A MONG those who came to New England in 1635 with Sir Richard Saltonstall were John Whitney, his wife, Elinor, and his son, Richard Richard Whitney, 1660-1723, second of the name, and grandson of the pioneer, was the first of the family born in this country. He was a native of Watertown, Mass, married Elizabeth Sawtell, daughter of Jonathan Sawtell, of Groton, and had a grant of land in Stow in 1682. His son, Richard Whitney, 1694-1775, married Hannah Whitcomb, daughter of Josiah Whitcomb, of Lancaster.

General Josiah Whitney, 1731-1806, son of Richard and Hannah Whitney, was the great-great-grandfather of the Honorable William C. Whitney. His wife was Sarah Farr. In 1755, General Whitney fought against the French and Indians at Crown Point, in 1774 was in command of a militia company of Harvard, Mass, and the following year was Lieutenant-Colonel of one of the Colonial regiments He was Brigadier-General in 1783. In civil life he was a justice of the peace, delegate to the Constitutional Convention in 1788, and a member of the Legislature, 1780-89. His son, Josiah Whitney, 1753-1837, married Anna Scollay, and served in the Continental Army.

Stephen Whitney, 1784-1852, grandfather of the Honorable William C. Whitney, was a representative from Deerfield to the Massachusetts General Court, 1834-35. His son, General James Scollay Whitney, 1811-1878, was the father of Mr Whitney, whose mother, Laurinda Collins, was descended from Governor William Bradford, of the Plymouth Colony. A Democrat of the old school, James S. Whitney was Brigadier-General of the Second Brigade of the Massachusetts militia, in 1843, town clerk of Conway, Mass, a member of the Legislature in 1851 and 1854, sheriff of Franklin County in 1851, superintendent of the National Armory at Springfield in 1854, collector of the port of Boston in 1860, and a member of the Massachusetts Senate in 1872.

Born in Conway, Mass, in 1841, the Honorable William Collins Whitney was graduated from Yale College in 1863, and in 1865 from the Dane Law School of Harvard College, soon after beginning the practice of law in New York. He early interested himself in public affairs in New York. He was active in the campaign that elected Samuel J. Tilden for Governor, and in 1875 was elected Corporation Counsel, and in that office brought about the codification of the laws relating to New York City, which is still in use. In 1882, he resigned office in order to devote his attention to private business, but in 1885, he became a member of President Grover Cleveland's Cabinet, holding the portfolio of Secretary of the Navy. His record at the head of the Navy Department need not be dwelt upon in detail here, except to say that he proved to be one of the most efficient secretaries that the country has ever had, and that he laid the foundation of our present navy. Since 1889, he has been active in national politics, especially in the campaigns of 1892 and 1896, but has resolutely declined all political preferment.

In 1869, Mr. Whitney married Flora Payne, daughter of the late Honorable Henry B. Payne, United States Senator from Ohio Mrs. Whitney died in 1892, leaving four children. The eldest, Harry Payne Whitney, who is a graduate from Yale University, married, in 1896, Gertrude Vanderbilt, daughter of Cornelius Vanderbilt. The eldest daughter, Pauline Whitney, married in 1895, Almeric Hugh Paget, who is by birth an Englishman, and a member of a family represented for centuries in the peerage. The two remaining children are Payne Whitney, a student at Yale, and a daughter, Dorothy Whitney. In 1896, Mr. Whitney contracted a second matrimonial alliance, his bride being Edith S (May) Randolph, daughter of the late Dr. William May, of Baltimore, and widow of Captain Arthur Randolph, of East Court, Wiltshire, England The city residence of Mr and Mrs Whitney is in upper Fifth Avenue, opposite Central Park, and their country home October Mountain, near Lenox, Mass Mr Whitney is a member of all the leading clubs, has been a governor of the Metropolitan, Manhattan and University clubs, is a member of the Society for the Prevention of Cruelty to Children, the Society for the Prevention of Cruelty to Animals, and many other such institutions, and is one of the trustees of the Peabody Museum of Yale University and of the American Museum of Natural History.

LOUIS CLAUDE WHITON

HOTTENS' List of the early Puritan emigrants to America states that Thomas Whiton sailed in 1635 with his family on the ship Elizabeth and Ann to New England. He was originally from the County of Kent, in England, and the town records of Hingham, Mass., show that members of the Whiton family and ancestors of the subject of this sketch were residents and prominent citizens of that place as early as 1646. Mr. Louis Claude Whiton, of New York, is thus a descendant of one of those who founded the famous Massachusetts Bay Colony early in the seventeenth century. Thomas Whiton, a member of the family and a lineal ancestor of the present Mr. Whiton, fought ably and bravely in the French Wars of 1755, and in the company of which he was a Lieutenant he had many of his kinsmen as companions, for the muster rolls, now existing, contain the names of eleven brothers and cousins who served with him. Twenty years or so later, at the commencement of the War of the American Revolution, his son Thomas volunteered in the so-called Lexington Alarm, when the New England Colonists took up arms against the British Crown. He served with distinction in Rhode Island during the war, and was also a member of the Committee of Safety of the town of Hanover, of which place he was long a resident.

Mr. Louis Claude Whiton's parents were Augustus S. Whiton and his wife, Caroline Ward, and he was born in Jersey City, on the 29th of December, 1857. His preparation for college was made with the aid of a private tutor. In 1878, he was graduated from the University of the City of New York, being the first honor man and also valedictorian of his class. He then entered the Columbia College Law School, from which he graduated two years later, in 1880. After his admission to the bar, Mr. Whiton traveled extensively in various parts of Europe, remaining abroad during the years 1882 and 1883. On June 10th, 1884, he married Harriet L. Bell, daughter of Charles Bell, of New York City. Three children have been born to Mr. and Mrs. Whiton, Angelina, Augustus Sherrill and Louis Claude Whiton, Jr.

Mr. Whiton is now a practicing member of the bar of New York City, and he has become well and extensively known in professional circles, being identified with much litigation of a very important character, which he has conducted as counsel. His legal business constantly involves questions connected with the interests of the leading insurance companies of the city and country, and he is also active in the practice of the real estate branch of his profession. He has been a public-spirited citizen, greatly interested in the welfare of the community, and, although he has resolutely refused to accept any public office whatever, he has been prominent in politics and has taken a very active part in all the movements of late years designed to effect reform in the personnel and conduct of the municipal government of New York. All such efforts enlist his warm sympathy and practical assistance, and he has been prominently connected as an officer or member with a number of the most prominent and effective bodies and committees formed to promote such objects. Notwithstanding his manifold professional, political and social duties, he has found time and opportunity to write frequently on various legal subjects of interest for the leading law journals of the country, and he has contributed many poems and other articles to the prominent magazines and periodicals of the day.

Mr. Whiton was a First Lieutenant of the New York Hussars, now known as Troop A. He is a member of the New York Bar Association, belongs to the West Side Republican Club, the Φ B K Society, the Society of Colonial Wars, and to the Sons of the American Revolution, the Society of Medical Jurisprudence and the Academy of Science.

His residence in New York City is at 114 West Seventy-sixth Street; and on the Upper St. Regis Lake, in the Adirondacks, Mr. Whiton owns Camp Deerfoot, which is his summer home. The arms of the Whiton family are : A gyronny of four azure and ermine, over all a leopard's head in chief in gold, three bezants. The crest is a lion rampant beneath a helmet resting upon the shield.

CHARLES ALBERT WHITTIER

SEVERAL families bearing the name of Whittier, Witcher and Whitcher can trace their descent to the earliest Colonial period, their first American ancestor being Thomas Whittier, a native of England. Coming to this country in 1638, when he was a boy of only sixteen years of age, Thomas Whittier went first to live in Newbury, Mass., where he remained for six or seven years. In 1645 he appears on the records of the town of Salisbury as a resident of that place. Afterwards he removed to Haverhill, where he built a house, known in subsequent generations as the Whittier Homestead, and especially distinguished as the birthplace of the poet of New England, John G. Whittier, who was one of his descendants.

For many years Thomas Whittier was selectman of the town of Haverhill, and in 1669 was chosen to be constable, a position, however, that he declined on account of religious scruples, for he was among the earliest Quakers in New England. He died in 1696, and his wife, Ruth Green, whom he married in Salisbury, died in 1710. Nathaniel Whittier, son of Thomas Whittier, the pioneer, was born in Haverhill in 1668, and died in Salisbury in 1722. He changed the spelling of his family name at one period of his life from Whittier to Whicher and Whitcher, and some of his descendants, heads of families, which have become distinguished in New England, have always retained those spellings. His first wife, the ancestress of that branch of the family to which Mr. Charles A. Whittier belongs, was Mary Ellsworth Osgood, whom he married in 1685, and who was the daughter of William Osgood. She died in 1705. His second wife, whom he married in 1710, was Mary Wing Brown, daughter of Philip and Mary (Buzwell) Brown. She was born in 1676, in Salisbury, and died there in 1742.

In the third American generation came the second Nathaniel Whittier, who was born in Salisbury in 1711. He lived at the family homestead for many years, but afterwards removed to Poplin, Fremont, N. H., and then to Chester, Vt. He died in Winthrop, Me., at the residence of his son, in 1784. His wife, whom he married in 1734, was Hannah Clough. The third Nathaniel Whittier was born in Salisbury in 1743. After residing in Raymond, N. H., for many years, he removed to Maine, where he became one of the first settlers of the town of Winthrop and prominent in the early history of that place. With several other pioneers, he was one of the purchasers of the township of Vienna, Me., from the Commonwealth of Massachusetts, which then owned that territory. He died in Readfield, Me., in 1798. His wife, whom he married in 1766, was Elizabeth Prescott, daughter of Jedediah and Hannah (Batchelder) Prescott. She was born in Brentwood, N. H., in 1745, and died in Vienna, Me., in 1814.

In the following generation in the direct line of descent from Thomas Whittier was the fourth Nathaniel Whittier, grandfather of Mr. Charles Albert Whittier. He was born in Winthrop, Me., in 1783, and with his father became one of the early settlers of Vienna, attaining to high position in all the local affairs of that community. For many years he was town clerk, selectman, surveyor of the highways, and trial justice, and held other positions. During the War of 1812, he was a Captain in the militia, and after 1816 was a justice of the peace. He died in Vienna in 1869. His wife, whom he married in 1804, in Mt. Vernon, Me., was Nancy Merrill, daughter of James Merrill. She was born in Raymond, N. H., in 1785, and died in Vienna in 1843. Subsequently he married, in New Sharon, Me., Sarah (Bodwell) Jayne. She died in 1861. The parents of Mr. Whittier, of this generation, were Joseph Merrill Whittier, who was born in 1811, and Mary E. Morgan.

Mr. Charles Albert Whittier was born in 1840, was graduated from Harvard College in 1860, and has long been a resident of New York. He served in the United States Army nine years, being brevetted Brigadier-General for valuable and distinguished services. He married Lilla Chadwick, and lives in West Tenth Street. He has two daughters, Susie Whittier, who married the Prince Serge Belosselsky-Belozersky, and lives in St. Petersburg, and Pauline Whittier. He belongs to the Metropolitan and Union clubs.

REYNOLD WEBB WILCOX, M D.

O N both sides of the house, the Wilcox family of the present generation is descended from some of the oldest and most honored races of Colonial New England   Even before the time of William the Conqueror, the Wilcoxes were substantial citizens of Bury St Edmunds, Suffolk County, England   Sir John Wilcox, in the reign of Edward III , was leader of the crossbowmen of the English Army in the French Wars

In the seventeenth century, one of the direct descendants of Sir John Wilcox was William Wilcoxson, who was born at St. Albans Hertfordshire   He emigrated to America, as a member of the expedition that came on the ship Planter, and settled at Stratford, Conn , in the New Haven Colony   In 1647, he was a representative at the General Court at Hartford

The father of Dr Wilcox was Colonel Vincent Meigs Wilcox, who was born at Madison, Conn , in 1828, a descendant in the fifth generation from the pioneer William Wilcoxson   He attended Lee's Academy at Madison, became a merchant in his locality in the State of Connecticut and also served in the Connecticut State Militia with the rank of Lieutenant   Moving to Pennsylvania in 1860, he entered into business there, and, at the commencement of the Civil War enlisted a company of volunteers, and in 1862 became Brigade Judge-Advocate on the staff of General Meylert, with the rank of Major, and later was made Lieutenant-Colonel of the One Hundred and Thirty-Second Regiment of the Pennsylvania Volunteers   With this regiment he went to the front, fought at Antietam and was promoted to be Colonel, resigning his commission in 1863 on account of illness   After the war, he settled in New York City and became connected with the firm of E. & H T Anthony & Co , of which, when it became a corporation, he was successively secretary, vice-president and president. He died in 1896

Through both his grandmothers, Dr. Wilcox is descended from Vincent Meigs, an early settler of Guilford, Conn , who came from England in 1638. Among the descendants of this Vincent Meigs have been many men who have distinguished themselves in military and civil life. In another line of ancestry, through his paternal great-grandmother, Olive Doude, Dr Wilcox is descended from Henry Doude, who came from Surrey, England, in 1639, with the Colonists under the Reverend Henry Whitfield, who settled at Guilford, Conn.   His mother was Catherine Millicent Webb, daughter of Dr. Reynold Webb, an eminent Connecticut physician, descended from Richard Webb, of Stamford, Conn , in 1636, who founded the family of that name

Dr Wilcox was born in Madison, Conn , in 1856   He graduated with honors from Yale College in 1878, with the degree of B A   In 1881, Hobart College conferred the degree of M A upon him ; the same year he received the degree of M. D from Harvard University, and in 1892 Maryville College gave him the degree of LL D   While studying medicine at Harvard University, he served as house physician in several of the hospitals of Boston   His education in this country was supplemented by study in Vienna Heidelberg, Paris and Edinburgh, after which he commenced practice as a physician in New York City   In 1884, he was appointed clinical assistant at the New York Post-Graduate Medical School   In 1886, he became an instructor in the same institution, and in 1889 Professor of Medicine and Therapeutics   He has been visiting physician to several other hospitals, is a member of or an officer in nearly all the prominent scientific and medical societies, has been for many years on the editorial staff of The American Journal of the Medical Sciences, has edited White's Materia Medica and Therapeutics, which has passed through three editions, and has published about two hundred papers upon medical and scientific subjects. He has compiled the genealogical history of the Wilcox, Meigs and Webb families, and many of his historical addresses have been published   He is a member of the Societies of the Colonial Wars, Sons of the Revolution, War of 1812, Loyal Legion, War of the Union and Sons of Veterans; of the last he has been Surgeon General   He also belongs to the Metropolitan and Harvard clubs He married, in 1895, Frances Maud, daughter of Samuel Weeks, a descendant of Francis Weeks, one of the first settlers of Oyster Bay, and resides at 749 Madison Avenue.

GEORGE G. WILLIAMS

THE family of which Mr George G Williams is the representative in New York in this generation has been one of the most distinguished in the history of Wales Roger Williams, who founded Rhode Island, was one of its most famous members. Robert Williams, who came from Norwich, England, soon after the landing of the Pilgrims and settled in Roxbury, Mass , was the American progenitor of that branch which is now being considered Robert Williams was a freeman of Roxbury in 1638, and died in 1693, a centenarian Land that he acquired in Roxbury has remained in the possession of his family for nearly three centuries

Descendants of Robert Williams have been numerous, and have taken an active part in the work of developing the New World One of his grandsons, the Reverend Elisha Williams, was the third president of Yale College, and another descendant, Colonel Ephraim Williams, was a brave officer in the French and Indian War, falling in battle in 1755 and gave his name to Williams College, which institution he founded The Honorable William Williams was one of the signers of the Declaration of Independence. Captain Samuel Williams was killed in the battle of Lexington. Lieutenant John Williams was an officer at the battle of Bunker Hill General Otho H Williams distinguished himself in the battle of Eutaw, and was a confidant of Washington David Williams was one of the soldiers who captured Major John Andre, the British spy. General Jonathan Williams, a distinguished officer of the American Army, was the founder of the corps of engineers at West Point, and many other members of the family have been prominent

A grandson of Robert Williams removed to Connecticut in the early part of the eighteenth century and established a branch of the family there His great-great-grandson was Dr Datus Williams, who was born in 1793, and was the father of Mr George G Williams Dr Williams resided and practiced for nearly half a century in East Haddam, Conn , and was one of the leading men of the State, professionally and socially. He married Clarissa Maria Peck, of East Haddam, and his eldest son, who followed him in the medical profession, was an assistant surgeon of volunteers during the Civil War, and afterwards connected with the Freedman's Bureau

Mr George G Williams is the second son of Dr Datus Williams Born in East Haddam, in 1826, he was educated in the public schools and in Brainard Academy, and looked forward to a professional career But John Q Jones, the cashier of the Chemical Bank of New York City, and a friend of Dr Williams, persuaded the parents of the boy to let him be trained for business. Accordingly, at the age of fifteen, he began his connection with the Chemical Bank that has continued uninterruptedly for fifty-six years. At first an assistant to the paying teller, in 1846, when he was only twenty years old, he succeeded to the position of paying teller, being then the youngest person so employed in any bank in the city Next he became discount clerk, and in 1855, when John Q Jones was elected president of the bank, he was promoted to be cashier During the latter years of Mr Jones' life the active management of the bank was largely in the hands of Mr Williams, and when his friend and patron died, in 1878, he was made president of the institution, and has held that office since

As president of the Chemical Bank, one of the most famous institutions of its kind in the United States, Mr Williams has occupied a position of exceptional responsibility and influence, and is recognized as one of the ablest financiers in the country. He is connected with many commercial institutions, the Union Trust Company, the United States Life Insurance Company, the Eagle Fire Insurance Company, the Fidelity and Casualty Company, and the Pennsylvania Coal Company, being the principal corporations in which he is interested He has been president of the Clearing House Association, treasurer of the Bank for the Savings of Merchants' Clerks, and trustee or director in several religious and charitable organizations He is not particularly a club man, but belongs to the Metropolitan and the Riding clubs, and is a member of the New England Society and the Metropolitan Museum of Art He married, in 1867, Virginia F King, daughter of Aaron King, of Massachusetts His residence is in West Fifty-Eighth Street.

RICHARD T. WILSON

NO contemporaneous phase of metropolitan life has been more interesting or more important than that which is the outgrowth of the influx of Southern families into New York during the last quarter of a century. Since the close of the Civil War, that section of the country has contributed to this city a considerable number of those enterprising business and professional men who have helped to make the closing years of the century preëminently distinguished in the United States. Seeking in New York a broader field for activity in various walks of life than could be found in the South, which was still suffering from the effects of war, they have taken a foremost part in the business and social affairs of the metropolis and are numbered among our most patriotic and most useful citizens.

Among these Southern families, who have made New York their place of residence during the last quarter of a century, that of which Mr. Richard T. Wilson, the well-known banker, is at the head, stands foremost in the business and social world. Mr. Wilson is a native of Georgia, having been born in that State some sixty years ago, and being a member of one of the old families in that section of the country. Early in life, he engaged in business occupations and was very successful. When the Civil War broke out, he cast his lot with his native State and entered the Confederate Army. In the military service, his excellent business ability was immediately recognized and was of great value to the Confederate cause, and he rose by successive promotions until he became a Commissary-General.

When the war ended, Mr. Wilson, who was the possessor of a considerable fortune, came to New York with his wife, who was a Miss Johnston, of Macon, Ga. Fixing upon this city for his permanent residence, he entered Wall Street, and has been for many years one of the leading and influential bankers of the metropolis, having handled many important financial enterprises. His city residence is in Fifth Avenue, near Forty-third Street, and he has a country place in Newport. He is a member of the Metropolitan, Manhattan and Union clubs, the Downtown Association and the Southern Society.

The family of Mr. Wilson has been notably conspicuous in the social life of New York and Newport. His sons and daughter are connected by marriage with several of the leading New York families. His eldest son, Marshall Orme Wilson, graduated from Columbia College in the class of 1882, and is engaged in the banking business with his father. He married Caroline Astor, daughter of William and Caroline (Schermerhorn) Astor. Mrs. Astor was the daughter of Abraham Schermerhorn. He is a member of the Metropolitan, Manhattan, Union, Knickerbocker, Tuxedo, Racquet, St Anthony and New York Yacht clubs, the Downtown Association and the Columbia College Alumni Association. He lives in Fifth Avenue, near Fortieth Street, and is a summer resident of Newport. The other son of the family, Richard T. Wilson, Jr., is one of the best known of the younger society men in New York. He was educated in Columbia College, being graduated from that institution in the class of 1887. He is prominent in many social functions and was an usher at the wedding of the Duke of Marlborough and Consuelo Vanderbilt. He is engaged in the banking business with his father, and is a member of the Metropolitan, Knickerbocker, Union, St. Anthony, Racquet and New York Yacht clubs, the Downtown Association, the Columbia College Alumni Association and the Country Club of Westchester County.

Mr. and Mrs. Richard T. Wilson, Sr., have three daughters. The eldest daughter, Mary R. Wilson, married Ogden Goelet, who died in the summer of 1897. She lives in Fifth Avenue and has a summer residence at the Cliffs, in Newport, but in recent years has spent considerable time abroad. She has two children, Mary Goelet, who is a young lady in society, and Robert Goelet, who is not yet of age. The second daughter, Lelia Belle Wilson, married the Honorable Michael Henry Herbert, of Milton House, Salisbury, England, an attache of the British Embassy in Washington and a representative of one of the oldest and most aristocratic families of England. The youngest daughter is Grace Wilson, who married, in 1896, Cornelius Vanderbilt, Jr.

JOHN D. WING

FROM time immemorial families bearing the name of Winge have been settled in Wales. Early in the seventeenth century representative bearers of this patronymic are known to have removed from Wales to Lincolnshire, and had numerous descendants in that and the other Eastern countries of England.

The first emigrants to America belonging to this family were Puritans. John Wing, the pioneer representative of the name, came to New England early in the seventeenth century. Settling first in Lynn, Mass., he removed, in 1637, to the Plymouth Colony and made a home on the shores of Barnstable and Buzzard's Bays, becoming one of the incorporators of the town of Sandwich, in 1639. The leader of the company of Colonists of which he was a member was the Reverend Stephen Batchelder, whose daughter, Deborah, he married. The Reverend Stephen Batchelder, who was thus on the maternal side the first American progenitor of the Wing family in this country, was born in England in 1561. He was one of the clergy who adopted the Puritan doctrine, and, coming to this country, was first minister of the church in Saugus, now Lynn, Mass., for three years, and in 1635 was admitted a freeman. Afterwards he lived in Ipswich, Newbury and Hampton. In 1647, he was living at Portsmouth, N. H., and returning to England in 1651, died at Hackney, near London, at the age of one hundred. Deborah Batchelder, who married John Wing, was his third daughter.

Daniel Wing, of the second generation in this country, came with his father from England and was active in the public affairs of the town of Sandwich. In 1658, he became a Quaker, and died some time before 1664. His wife was Anna Swift, daughter of John Swift. Their son, Daniel Wing, second of that name, was born in 1664, and was enrolled as a townsman of Sandwich, in 1691. His wife was Deborah Dillingham, daughter of Henry Dillingham. Edward Wing, the son of Daniel Wing, second of the name, was born in 1687, in Sandwich, and removed to Dartmouth. He was married three times, first to Desire Smith, of Dartmouth, second to Sarah Tucker, daughter of Abraham and Hannah Tucker, and third to Patience Ellis. In the four succeeding generations the ancestors of the gentleman whose family is under consideration were Joseph Wing and his wife, Catharine; Daniel Wing, who removed about 1775 to Dutchess County, N. Y.; John Wing, of Dutchess County, who died in 1858, having married Miriam Thorn, and Jacob Wing, born in 1810, who married Anna M. Cornell, the last named couple being the parents of the subject of this article.

Mr. John D. Wing was born near Ellenville, Ulster County, in 1834, but while very young, came to New York, which has since been his place of residence except during two years of his early manhood which were spent in California. He received a mercantile education. In 1858, on his return from California, he began business life in New York, on his own account, as a commission merchant in chemicals, and is still engaged in that branch of commerce. His two sons, John Morgan and Louis Stuart Wing, are now associated with him in business. Mr. Wing's city home is in West Forty-Ninth Street, but he has a country seat at Millbrook, Dutchess County, where he has resided many years. The extensive stock farm which he maintains at that place is well known to those interested in high grade stock. He was president of the New York State Agricultural Society, and of the American Jersey Cattle club, and has been a large importer of thoroughbred cattle and sheep. The wife of Mr. Wing was Adelaide W. Hinman, of an old New England family. His elder son, J. Morgan Wing, married Josephine G. Ireland, and is a member of the Metropolitan, Downtown, Calumet, Knollwood and New York Yacht clubs, and resides in West Forty-Eighth Street. The younger son, L. Stuart Wing, married Bertha L. Hurlbut and is a member of the Metropolitan, Downtown, Racquet, Knollwood and New York Yacht clubs, and resides in West Fiftieth Street. The only daughter of Mr. John D. Wing, Marion Wing, is the wife of Dr. Austin Flint, Jr. Mr. Wing is a member of the Metropolitan, Downtown, New York Yacht and Riding clubs.

EDWARD WINSLOW

IN the person of Mr. Edward Winslow, the persecuted Puritan of England and the persecuted Huguenot of France unite On his father's side, Mr. Winslow is a lineal descendant of Kenelm Winslow, brother of Governor Edward Winslow, of the Plymouth Colony, while his mother was of the Huguenot Laniers, of Virginia. He is, therefore, a son of Massachusetts and of Virginia, as well as of New York. Kenelm Winslow, the first American ancestor of this branch of the family, was the third son and fourth child of Edward Winslow, of Droitwitch, Worcestershire, England. Born in 1599, he came to Plymouth in 1629. Although less prominent than his brother, the Governor, Kenelm Winslow was a man of consequence in the Colony. He was a freeman in 1632, and had a grant of valuable lands, removed to Marshfield, Mass., where he was a planter and a shipowner, was a representative to the General Court 1642-46 and 1649-53, and died in 1672 at the age of seventy-three years. His wife was the widow, Eleanor Adams. His son, Lieutenant Job Winslow, who was born in 1641 and died in 1720, was a representative to the General Court and held other offices. Joseph Winslow, son of Lieutenant Job Winslow, married Mary Tisdale, of Taunton, Mass., in 1686. She was the daughter of Joseph and Mary (Leonard) Tisdale, of Taunton, and granddaughter of John and Sarah (Walker) Tisdale, of Duxbury. Their son, Job Winslow, who was born in 1718, was the father of Captain Job Winslow, who was born in Dighton, Mass., in 1738. Captain Job Winslow carried the family name to Connecticut, where he owned a shipyard in Saybrook for many years. Later in life he removed to Canaan, N. Y., and died there in 1809. He was twice married. His first wife was Temperance Hayden, of Saybrook. She died in 1777, and he afterwards married Mary Rogers.

Richard Winslow, son of Captain Job Winslow, was born in 1771. In his younger days he was a ship captain on the Hudson River, being ranked as one of the most enterprising and most successful men engaged in that business nearly a century ago. After that he became an iron master in Albany, owning furnaces and mines. During the War of 1812, he was connected with the commissary department of the army, and was engaged at Plattsburg and elsewhere on the Northern frontier. When peace was proclaimed, he went into the shipping business again, being master of several vessels on the Hudson, and finally, as a miller, owning several large flouring establishments, accumulated a fortune and retired from business in 1834. He died in 1847. He was the great grandfather of Mr Edward Winslow. His wife was Mary Corning, daughter of Asa and Cynthia (Seymour) Corning, and sister of Jasper Corning.

Several of the sons of Richard Winslow were notably successful. John Flack Winslow was manager and owner of iron works in Troy, and connected with other enterprises of similar character. In 1863-68, with John A. Griswold, he was interested in introducing the Bessemer process in this country, and with the same partner enjoyed the distinction of building the first monitor for Ericsson. James Winslow, another son, was the eminent New York banker. Born in Hartford, Conn., in 1815, he lived to the age of fifty-nine, being one of the great financiers of his day. Starting in life as a clerk in the hardware store of Erastus Corning, in Albany, he afterwards became a partner in the banking house of Winslow, Lanier & Co., which was established by his brother, Richard H. Winslow, and his father-in-law. The firm was one of the first to be interested in the national banking system, and at the time of his death, Mr. Winslow was vice-president of the Third National Bank. He married Margaret Downing Lanier.

Mr. Edward Winslow, born January 14th, 1850, entered the banking house of Winslow, Lanier & Co. in 1873, with his father, James Winslow, his uncle, Richard H. Winslow, and his grandfather, J. F. D Lanier, and is now recognized as one of the leading financiers of New York. His clubs include the Metropolitan, Tuxedo, New York Yacht, Larchmont Yacht and others. He is a trustee of the New York Skin and Cancer Hospital, and actively interested in other philanthropic institutions. He married, in 1873, Emma Corning Sweetser, daughter of J. A. Sweetser, and has one daughter, Marguerite Lanier Winslow. He resides at 27 West Fifty-third Street.

BUCHANAN WINTHROP

THIS gentleman is the head of the Winthrop family, being the eldest son in direct descent from John Winthrop, 1587-1649, the first Governor of Massachusetts He is descended through John Still Winthrop, 1720-1776, of Boston and New London, the only son of John Winthrop, 1681-1747, fellow of the Royal Society, whose wife was Anne Dudley, daughter of Governor Joseph Dudley, of Massachusetts. The grandfather of John Still Winthrop was Major-General Wait Still Winthrop, 1643-1717, Chief Justice of Massachusetts, and his great-grandfather was John Winthrop, 1606-1676, Governor of Connecticut for many years, and the son of Governor John Winthrop, the founder of Massachusetts.

John Still Winthrop was the great-great-grandfather of the subject of this sketch, who is thus a descendant, in the eighth generation, from the founder of the family in this country. He was born in 1720, graduated from Yale College in 1737 and died in 1776. His first wife, the ancestress of Mr. Buchanan Winthrop, was Jane Borland, daughter of Francis Borland, of Boston. The sons of John Still Winthrop were the heads of two families that have been prominent in New York City during the present century. Francis Bayard Winthrop, 1754-1817, the great-grandfather of Mr. Buchanan Winthrop, was the head of one of these branches. His first wife, from whom the Winthrops of this generation are descended and whom he married in 1779, was Elsie Marston, daughter of Thomas Marston, a prominent New York merchant of the Revolutionary period, who married Cornelia Lispenard, sister of Anthony Lispenard. His father was Nathaniel Marston, merchant, one of the governors of Columbia College, named in the charter of that institution. He was descended from Nathaniel Marston, who settled on Long Island in 1639. For his second wife, Francis Bayard Winthrop married Phœbe Taylor, daughter of John Taylor. Benjamin Winthrop, the head of the other branch of the New York Winthrops, was a brother of Francis Bayard Winthrop.

John Still Winthrop, the eldest son of Francis Bayard Winthrop and grandfather of Mr. Buchanan Winthrop, was born in 1785, graduated from Yale College in the class of 1804 and died in 1855. He was one of New York's most successful merchants. The grandmother of Mr. Buchanan Winthrop, whom John Still Winthrop married in 1808, was Harriet Rogers, the fourth child of Fitch Rogers, a son of Samuel Rogers, of Norwalk, Conn., and his wife, Elizabeth Fitch, a relative of Governor Thomas Fitch. He was born about 1748, and about 1769 married Hannah Bell, daughter of Isaac Bell, of Stamford, Conn.

Henry Rogers Winthrop, the father of Mr. Buchanan Winthrop, was the eldest son of John Still Winthrop and his wife, Harriet Rogers. He was born in 1811, graduated from Yale College in 1830 and was a practicing lawyer in New York during his entire life, being a member of the Century Association, the Bar Association, the National Academy of Design and the New England Society. His first wife, whom he married in 1838 and who was the mother of Mr. Buchanan Winthrop, was Margaret Hicks, daughter of Thomas Hicks, of the Long Island family of that name. He married, in 1875, his second wife, Mary Gelston, daughter of Maltby Gelston, and died in 1896

Mr. Buchanan Winthrop, the only son of Henry Rogers Winthrop, was born in New York in 1841, and graduated A. B. from Yale College in 1862, receiving his A. M. degree in due course. He graduated from the Columbia Law School in 1864, and is a practicing lawyer. In 1891, he was elected by the alumni of Yale a fellow of that University, and was reëlected in 1895. He has been for many years the treasurer of the General Convention of the Protestant Episcopal Church in the United States He belongs to the Tuxedo, Metropolitan, University, Century, Union, Downtown, New York Yacht and Riding clubs, the Yale Alumni Association, the Bar Association, and the New England Society, and is a patron of the Metropolitan Museum of Art. He married, in 1872, Sarah Helen Townsend, daughter of Isaac Townsend. Mr Winthrop's city residence is at 279 Fifth Avenue, and he also has a country home at Lenox, Mass. He has one son, Henry Rogers Winthrop, a student at Yale University, and a daughter, Marie Winthrop.

EGERTON LEIGH WINTHROP

MASSACHUSETTS, Connecticut and New York have each owed much to the Winthrop family, which has been well described as the flower of New England Puritanism. Its numerous branches are now found occupying distinguished places in these three States, while in every generation the number of its representatives possessing marked ability has been exceptionally large   Through the marriages of members of the family the name and ancestry of the Winthrops are frequently referred to in this work.   John Winthrop, the founder of this notable family in America, was the most eminent of the leaders by whose efforts New England was colonized.   He belonged to a landed family in the County Suffolk, England, Adam Winthrop having been an influential merchant in London and Master of the Clothworkers' Company, a post of civic importance.

John Winthrop, who was a grandson of Adam Winthrop, was born at Groton, Suffolk County, in 1587, graduated from Trinity College, Cambridge, about 1605, and was bred to the bar. He became an earnest Puritan, and took a leading part in the plans for the establishment of a Colony in America under Puritan auspices and government.   In 1629, he became Governor of the Massachusetts Bay Company, and when, in the following year, it was determined to carry the company with its charter and organization to the New World, he headed the great emigration. Landing at Salem, he finally settled in Boston, the rest of his life being a history of the Massachusetts Colony.   With the exception of a few years, he was annually elected Governor until his death, in 1649

His son, the second John Winthrop, was scarcely less famous and shared all his father's fine qualities.   Born at Groton, in 1606, he graduated from Trinity College, Dublin, studied law in the Temple at London, traveled on the Continent and obtained a military and diplomatic experience. Following his father to Massachusetts in 1631, he became a magistrate in 1633, and returning to England obtained a commission as Governor of Connecticut, under which he erected the fort at Saybrook and founded New London.   From 1657, until his death in 1676, he was annually chosen Governor of Connecticut, and it was through his efforts and influence at the Court of Great Britain, that the charter of 1662 was granted to Connecticut.   His wife, Elizabeth, was a daughter of Edmund Reade, of Wichford, Sussex, and step-daughter of the famous Hugh Peters.   Their son, Wait Still Winthrop, 1643-1717, was Chief Justice of Massachusetts, and a Major-General, and his son, John Winthrop, 1681-1747, graduated from Harvard in 1700, and became famous as a scientist and was a member of the English Royal Society.

John Still Winthrop, 1720-1776, the only son of the third John Winthrop, was the ancestor of the family represented by the subject of this article.   One of his great-grandsons, Benjamin R. Winthrop, was the father of Mr. Egerton Leigh Winthrop.   Born in New York in 1804, Benjamin R Winthrop was maternally descended from the Stuyvesants and other leading New York families.   He possessed literary tastes, and was an intimate friend of Fitz-Greene Halleck. Inheriting a large property, he was in early life occupied with the care of his real estate and interested in many philanthropic undertakings.   He married Eliza A. C., daughter of William Neilson, and died in London in 1879.

Mr. Egerton Leigh Winthrop is a native of New York, and was graduated from Columbia College in 1860.   He belongs to the Union, Knickerbocker, Metropolitan, Riding and other clubs, the Century Association, and the St. Nicholas Society.   His eldest son, Egerton Leigh Winthrop, Jr., was born in Paris, France, August 14th, 1862, and graduated from Harvard University in 1885.   In 1890, he married Emeline Dora Heckscher, daughter of John G. Heckscher, of New York   He is a member of the Metropolitan, Union, Knickerbocker, Meadow Brook Hunt, Rockaway Hunt and other clubs, and lives in East Thirty-ninth Street   Another son is Frederick Bronson Winthrop, who graduated from Trinity College in 1886, and is a member of the Metropolitan, Knickerbocker, Racquet and other clubs.

FRANK SPENCER WITHERBEE

T HE family of which Mr. Frank S. Witherbee is the representative in this generation was
originally settled near Witherby in Yorkshire, England, to which place it gave the name,
and whence in the course of centuries its members were scattered throughout the
Northern and Eastern counties. John Witherbee, the pioneer of the family in this country, came
from Norfolk, England, soon after the first Pilgrims, and settled in the Massachusetts Bay Colony.
He was a freeman there before 1650. His descendants became leading men in public affairs in what
is known as the Essex County section of Massachusetts Captain Silas Witherbee, the direct
ancestor of the subject of this sketch, was one of the most important men of Salem, Mass., where
he was born in 1707 His descendants have been numerous, and active participants in public
affairs in Eastern Massachusetts and elsewhere in every generation since his time.

Jonathan Gilman Witherbee, the father of Mr. Frank S. Witherbee, was born in Crown
Point, N. Y., June 7th, 1821. In 1839, when he was eighteen years of age, he entered upon business life, at first in Port Henry, N Y, and afterwards at Saugerties, N Y, where he remained
for several years In 1849, in association with an uncle, he organized the iron manufacturing
firm of S. H. & J. G. Witherbee, in which he was the junior partner. Three years later they
purchased an iron mine near Port Henry, and ultimately Lee & Sherman, an old established
concern in the same line, joined forces with them, the new firm being Witherbee, Sherman & Co,
which became one of the largest iron manufacturers in the Eastern States.

In addition to his connection with this firm, Mr Witherbee maintained other important
business connections in Northern and Eastern New York, including railroad enterprises in that
section and transportation facilities upon Lake Champlain, aiding materially in developing the
resources of that part of the State. He promoted the Port Henry Iron Company, the Cedar
Point Iron Company, the Port Henry Towing Company, the First National Bank of Port Henry,
and other corporations

.   Mr. Frank Spencer Witherbee, the eldest son of Jonathan Gilman Witherbee, was born
in Port Henry, N Y., May 12th, 1852, prepared for college at New Haven, Conn., and
graduated from Yale College in the class of 1874. A year after he had taken his degree, his
father died, and he succeeded to the management of the estate, entering at once upon a business life, instead of upon the professional one which he had marked out for himself. He has
been one of the most successful business men of his section of New York State.

In 1893, he assisted in reorganizing the Troy Steel & Iron Company, a corporation of
which he became president, and which succeeded to the management of the famous iron works
established two generations ago in Troy by Erastus Corning, John F Winslow, John A Griswold,
and others. Soon after, the company erected a large plant on Breaker Island, near Troy, for the
manufacture of basic steel. It is one of the largest and best equipped establishments of its kind
in this country. Another enterprise which Mr. Witherbee fostered a few years ago was the
exportation of Lake Champlain iron ores to Europe.

In 1883, Mr. Witherbee married Mary Rhinelander Stewart, daughter of Lispenard Stewart,
the elder, of New York City. Mr. and Mrs Witherbee reside at 4 Fifth Avenue. Their summer
residence is at Port Henry, N. Y. Mr. Witherbee belongs to the Metropolitan, Union League,
Union, University, Riding, University Athletic, Westminster Kennel and Engineers' clubs, and
is also a member of the Downtown Association, the American Museum of Natural History,
the Metropolitan Museum of Art, the Sons of the Revolution, and the American Geographical
Society. He is a Republican in politics, has taken an active part in the party's councils, and
in 1888 was a Presidential elector on the Harrison and Morton ticket. For several years he was
a member of the Republican State and National Committees He has traveled extensively, and
belongs to the American Institute of Mining Engineers, the American Association for the Advancement of Science and other scientific organizations.

GERARDUS HILLES WYNKOOP, M. D.

T HE gentleman whose family history is considered in this sketch traces his descent in unbroken line back to the first American pioneer of the name, Peter Wynkoop, who came to the New Netherland before 1639. He was a commissary superintendent of wares and merchandise for the Patroon Van Rensselaer, and after remaining a few years in New Amsterdam settled in Rensselaerwyck, where he resided in 1644. He was commissioned by the Patroon Van Rensselaer to purchase land about Catskill from the natives and, in connection with Commissary General Arendt Van Curler, to recover land and other property that had been purchased and misapplied by a former agent, Adrian Van Derdonck. In the second generation, Cornelius Wynkoop, son of Peter Wynkoop, came from Utrecht, Holland, of which place he was a native, and settled at Fort Orange, now Albany, in 1665. After a time he removed to Hurley, Ulster County, where he was a schepen in 1673.

Gerrit Wynkoop, son of Cornelius Wynkoop, took the oath of allegiance to the English authorities in 1689. He was an ensign of the Foot Company in Ulster and Dutchess County in 1700, and a deacon of the church at Kingston in 1712. In 1717, he removed to Moreland, then Philadelphia, now Montgomery County, Pa., and was an elder of the church, 1744-45, in North and South Hampton. He married a daughter of Gerrit Fokker and Jakomyntje Slecht, and their son Gerrit was the father of Gerardus Wynkoop, who was an officer in the Revolutionary War and in time of peace was for nineteen years a member of the Lower House of the General Assembly of Pennsylvania, being several times its Speaker. His wife was Elizabeth Bennett. He died about 1812. David Wynkoop, son of Gerardus Wynkoop and grandfather of Dr. Gerardus H. Wynkoop, lived in Bucks County, Pa., and was a representative in the Legislature for six years.

The father of Dr. Wynkoop was the Reverend Stephen Rose Wynkoop, son of David Wynkoop and his wife, Mary Van Horn. He was born in 1806 and graduated from Union College in 1829 Four years later, he went on an expedition to the western coast of Africa as a commissioner on behalf of the American Board of Foreign Missions, to explore that region with the view to establishing a missionary station there Upon his return home, he entered upon the study of theology at the Theological Seminary connected with Princeton College and was licensed to preach in 1837. The following year he was installed as pastor of the First Presbyterian Church of Wilmington, Del., and filled that pulpit for twenty years, until his resignation, in 1858. He died in 1876. The wife of the Reverend Stephen Rose Wynkoop, whom he married in 1836, was Aurelia Mills, daughter of Judge Mills, of New Haven, Conn.

Dr. Gerardus Hilles Wynkoop was born in 1843 He received his preparatory education in schools and seminaries and then went to Yale College, from which institution he was graduated in the class of 1864. Coming to New York, he began the study of medicine under the direction of the celebrated Dr. Willard Parker, and has now been engaged in general medical practice in New York for more than thirty years. The wife of Dr Wynkoop, whom he married in 1866, was Ann Eliza Woodbury, daughter of General Daniel Phineas Woodbury, of the United States Engineer Corps. Dr. Wynkoop lives in Madison Avenue His clubs include the Union, City, Democratic, Riding, University and Rockaway Hunt, and he belongs to the Yale Alumni Association, the Holland Society and the American Geographical Society, and is a patron of the Metropolitan Museum of Art. He has four children: Gerardus Mills, who is a member of the Union and City clubs, Kate Childs, who married Harold Stanley Forwood, eldest son of Sir William B. Forwood, Daniel Woodbury, and Elizabeth Hilles Wynkoop A brother of Dr. Wynkoop was the Reverend Theodore Stephen Wynkoop, who was born in 1839, graduated from Yale College in 1861 and from the Presbyterian Theological Seminary of Princeton in 1864, and the same year was ordained pastor of the Second Presbyterian Church of Huntington, Long Island. Afterwards he engaged in foreign missionary work and for many years was in charge of a station at Allahabad, Northern India.

FERNANDO YZNAGA

FROM an ancient Spanish family came Antonio Yznaga del Valle, the father of the gentleman whose name appears at the head of this sketch. His immediate ancestors for several generations were residents of Cuba, where they were among the wealthiest and most aristocratic people of that island. Antonio Yznaga was born in Cuba in 1823. In common with many Cuban young men, he came to this country to be educated, when he was a mere boy, and received instruction in private schools in the vicinity of New York. When his education had been completed, he returned to his native island with the intention of complying with his parents' wishes, and settling in business there. But his residence in the United States and his education had thoroughly Americanized him, and, after two years, finding his interests and his sympathies fixed more firmly in this country than in his native island, he came back to the United States and established himself in business in New York, settling here finally in 1847. He first engaged in the commission business almost exclusively with Cuba, and for more than a quarter of a century his house was one of the leading commission establishments in New York. He also owned several large sugar plantations in Cuba, and had other real estate holdings there. During the Civil War, although his business connections were largely with the South, he was an enthusiastic supporter of the Union cause. He died in 1892.

The mother of Fernando Yznaga, whom Antonio Yznaga del Valle married in 1850, was Ellen Maria Clements. She was the daughter of J Clements, of Louisiana, and his wife, Maria Augusta Little, and the granddaughter of William Little, of Boston, and Frances Boyd, William Little being a well-known Boston merchant of the famous Little family, and Frances Boyd being the daughter of James Boyd, of Newburyport, Mass., and his wife, Susannah Coffin, also of Newburyport. James Boyd, of Newburyport, who was the maternal great-grandfather of Mrs. Yznaga, was born in 1732, and died in 1798. He was the first of his family to come to this country, being a son of Robert Boyd, of Kilmanrock, Scotland, and in the seventeenth generation through the Leslies and Earls of Sutherland from Robert Bruce, King of Scotland.

Through their wealth and high family connections, Antonio Yznaga and his wife occupied high social position in New York. They had one son, Fernando Yznaga, and three daughters, Consuelo, Natica and Emily Yznaga. One of the most brilliant social events in New York in the spring of 1876, was the marriage of Consuelo Yznaga to George Victor Drogo Montague, Viscount Mandeville, who succeeded his father as Duke of Manchester, and died several years ago. The first ancestor of the house of Manchester was Drogo de Monte Acuto, a warrior who came with Robert, Earl Morton, at the time of the Conquest. From him sprang the Montecutes and Montagues, among them Sir Edward Montague, the progenitor of the Earls and Dukes of Manchester, who was the Lord Chief Justice of England, in 1539, and appointed by the will of Henry VIII. to be regent of the kingdom. His grandson, Sir Henry Montague, was Lord Chief Justice of the King's Bench in 1616, and Lord Treasurer in 1620, and was created Earl of Manchester in 1626. The last Duke of Manchester was born in 1853, and previous to his accession to the head of the house was a Captain in the Third Battalion of the Royal Irish Fusileers. The children of the Duchess of Manchester are William Angus Drogo, Viscount Mandeville, and Jacquiline-Mary-Alva, and Alice Eleanor Louise. Natica Yznaga, the second daughter of Antonio Yznaga, married, in 1881, Sir Pepys Lister Kaye, who was born in 1853.

Mr. Fernando Yznaga, the oldest child and only son of Antonio Yznaga and his wife, Ellen Maria Clements, was born in New York in 1851. He has been engaged in the banking business, and has been a prominent figure in the social life of the city in this generation. He is a member of the Tuxedo Club, and has his permanent residence in Tuxedo Park. He also belongs to the Metropolitan, Union, Country, Manhattan, Athletic and Meadow Brook Hunt clubs. He is a graduate from the Lawrence Scientific School, of Harvard University, and has received the degree of LL. D. from the Louisiana Law School.

ANDREW CHRISTIAN ZABRISKIE

A NOBLEMAN, who belonged to an ancient Polish family, was driven from his native land by political oppression in the middle of the sixteenth century and, fleeing to Holland, joined there in the tide of emigration which at that time had begun to set in toward the new Colonies in America. Albrecht Zaborowsky was the name of this Polish refugee who came to New Netherland in the ship Fox in 1662. He had been intended for the Lutheran ministry, but the authorities had sought to force him into the army, and had also inflicted other indignities upon him which finally forced him into self-imposed exile. On his arrival here he settled on the banks of the Hackensack River at Paramus, N. J., and married a daughter of one of the Dutch families which are already established there. His five sons founded the numerous branches of the Zabriskie family in this country. The ancient records exhibit curious vagaries in the spelling of the family name, but finally usage settled upon the present form of Zabriskie, which has remained fixed for several generations past.

The fourth son of Albrecht Zaborowsky married in 1715 Lea Hendriksze Hoppe, or Hopper, a name which is identified with one of the oldest land-owning families of New York. Descendants of this couple have notably figured in the history of the States of New York and New Jersey. Abraham O. Zabriskie, 1807-1873, State Senator and Chancellor of New Jersey, was one of the most illustrious members of the family. One of Chancellor Zabriskie's sons, Augustus Zabriskie, is a prominent lawyer in New Jersey, who married Josephine Booraem and resides at South Orange.

Another descendant was Andrew C. Zabriskie, a well-known New York merchant a hundred years ago, and Adjutant of a squadron of horse in Bergen County, N. J., where he lived. He was the grandfather of Mr. Andrew Christian Zabriskie, of this generation, who was named after his ancestor. The father of Mr. Zabriskie was Christian A. Zabriskie, who lived a retired life until his death in 1879, upon an estate in Paramus, N. J., which is part of the land handed down from the original founder of the family in America.

On the maternal side, Mr. Zabriskie's grandfather was William M. Titus, a merchant of New York, and an officer of the Eleventh Artillery in the War of 1812. After the war, he became a Captain in the same regiment, which was subsequently called the Twenty-Seventh Infantry, and finally became the famous Seventh Regiment. The maternal great-grandfather of Mr. Zabriskie was Thomas Gardner, also a man of wealth and business prominence.

Mr. Andrew Christian Zabriskie was born in New York, May 30th, 1853, and was educated in private schools and in Columbia College. Inheriting large real estate properties, he has devoted himself mainly to the business connected with those interests. Military matters, however, have also engrossed his attention. He enlisted in 1873 in Company B, of the Seventh Regiment, and served for over seven years. Elected Captain of Company C, in the Seventy-First Regiment, he held that position until he was promoted to the rank of Inspector of Rifle Practice on the staff of the same regiment. He presented to the regiment the Zabriskie trophy, a handsome bronze, to be annually competed for at rifle practice.

In 1895, Mr. Zabriskie married Frances Hunter, youngest daughter of the late Charles F. Hunter, president of the People's Bank. They have one child, Julia Romeyn Zabriskie. Mr. Zabriskie has a beautiful country place, Province Island, in Lake Memphremagog, Me. The island embraces over one hundred acres of fertile land, the international boundary line passing through it. Mr. Zabriskie belongs to the Metropolitan, City, United Service, Military and Church clubs and the Seventh Regiment Veteran Association. He is a member of the Holland Society, the Society of the War of 1812, the New York Historical Society, the American Geographical Society, the National Academy of Design, the American Museum of Natural History and the American Numismatic and Archæological Society, of which he is the president. He is also active on the board of management of several charitable organizations, and has found time to write considerable upon subjects connected with the early history of New York City.

INDEX

LaVergne, TN USA
28 November 2010
206466LV00005B/8/P